HUGH JOHNSON'S
MODERN
ENCYCLOPEDIA
of
WINE
THIRD EDITION
REVISED AND UPDATED

Simon & Schuster
New York London Toronto Sydney Tokyo

Published by Simon & Schuster
A Division of Simon & Schuster Inc.
Simon & Schuster Building, Rockefeller Center,
1230 Avenue of the Americas, New York, New York 10020
SIMON & SCHUSTER and colophon are registered trademarks
of Simon & Schuster Inc.

Edited and designed by Mitchell Beazley International Limited,
Artists House, 14–15 Manette Street, London W1V 5LB

Editors Jane Eaton, Anne Ryland, Kirsty Seymour-Ure
Associate Editors Alison Franks, Rupert Joy, Alessandra Perotto
Art Editors Gaye Allen, Paul Drayson
Production Ted Timberlake
Illustrations Paul Hogarth
Grape Illustrations John Davis
Colour Maps Eugene Fleury

Managing Editor Chris Foulkes
Senior Art Editor Nigel O'Gorman

Library of Congress Cataloging-in-Publication Data

Johnson, Hugh, 1939–
[Modern encyclopedia of wine]
Hugh Johnson's modern encyclopedia of wine / Hugh Johnson.
p.   cm.
"A Mitchell Beazley book"--T.p. verso.
Includes index.
ISBN 0-671-73638-8
1. Wine and wine making.   I. Title.   II. Title: Modern
encyclopedia of wine.
TP548.J632   1991
641.2'2--dc20   90-20732   CIP

Filmset in Garamond by Servis Filmsetting Ltd., Manchester, England
Reproduction by Bridge Graphics, Hull, England
Printed in Spain by Graficas Estella, S.A., Navarra, Spain

Acknowledgments appear on page 576

CONTENTS

INTRODUCTION
6

MODERN WINE
8

In the Vineyard 12
Grape Varieties: The Vine 17   The Classic Grapes 18   France 20   Italy 23   Germany 26
Spain and Portugal 28   California 30   Southeast Europe 32   From Grapes to Wine 33   Making Wine 34

WINES, VINEYARDS
AND WINEMAKERS OF THE WORLD
42

FRANCE 43

Bordeaux 45   Bordeaux Châteaux Index 104
Burgundy 106   Jura 154   Savoie 157
Loire 158   Champagne 177   Alsace 187   Rhône 195
Provence 205   The Midi 209   Corsica 220
The Southwest 221   Vins de Pays 230

GERMANY 235

Mosel-Saar-Ruwer 242   Ahr and Mittelrhein 253
Rheingau 255   Nahe 264   Rheinhessen 269
Rheinpfalz 274   Hessische Bergstrasse 279
Franken 280   Württemberg 283   Baden 286

ITALY 292

Piedmont 294   Valle d'Aosta 306   Liguria 307
Lombardy 308   Trentino-Alto Adige 313
Veneto 318   Friuli-Venezia Giulia 323
Emilia-Romagna 327   Tuscany 331   Umbria 344
The Marches 347   Latium 349   Abruzzi 352
Campania 353   Molise 354   Apulia 355
Calabria 359   Basilicata 361   Sicily 361   Sardinia 365

SPAIN 368

Northern Spain 370   Rioja 374   Catalonia 380
Central Spain 384   Southern Spain 386   Sherry 388

PORTUGAL 395

Portuguese Table Wines 396   Port 401   Madeira 407

SWITZERLAND 409

AUSTRIA 417

SOUTHEAST EUROPE 424

Hungary 424   Czechoslovakia 426   Yugoslavia 427
Romania 429   Bulgaria 430   Greece 431   Cyprus 433
Turkey 434

THE LEVANT AND NORTH AFRICA 435

Lebanon 435   Israel 435   Tunisia 435
Algeria 436   Morocco 436

USA 437

California 438   The Pacific Northwest 478
Other Regions of the USA 482

AUSTRALIA 489

NEW ZEALAND 508

SOUTH AFRICA 513

CENTRAL AND SOUTH AMERICA 520

Chile 520   Argentina 522   Brazil 523   Mexico 523

ENGLAND 524

ENJOYING WINE
527

Buying 528   Choosing 530   Storing 536   Glasses 542   Serving 544   Corks and Corkscrews 549   Tasting 551

INDEX 556   ACKNOWLEDGMENTS 576

INTRODUCTION

To live in the Golden Age of one of life's great pleasures is something we all do, but few of us seem to realize. There never was a time when more good wine, and more different kinds of wine, were being made.

It was 157 years ago that Cyrus Redding, a London wine merchant, wrote his great *History and Description of Modern Wines*. To him the word 'Modern' distinguished the wines of his time from those of the Ancients, still then reverentially supposed to have been, like their architecture, of a quality that could be only humbly imitated.

Redding asserted the new world of nineteenth-century wine, based on the technology of the Industrial Revolution. If the great mass of wine in his day was still made by medieval methods, the leaders were setting the styles and standards and devising the techniques that today we accept as classic.

These methods are now old. Our understanding of wine and our techniques for making it have moved into a new phase, led by sciences that were not dreamed of in the last century. It is time to use the word modern again with a new meaning to describe the brilliant new age of wine that has opened in the past generation.

The nineteenth century closed, and the twentieth opened, with crisis and calamity in the vineyards of the world. Phylloxera, mildew, war, Prohibition and slump followed in a succession that prevented the majority of wine growers from making more than a meagre living. For the privileged there were wonderful wines to be had – and cheap, too. But little that was new or exciting developed into commercial reality until the 1960s. Then suddenly the product and the market rediscovered one another.

There were stirrings everywhere, but it was California that led the way. The coincidence of ideal wine-growing conditions and a fast-growing, educated and thriving population were the necessary elements. A generation of inspired university researchers and teachers in California and Europe (and also in Australia) were the catalysts. In the 1970s sudden intense interest in every aspect of wine caught on in country after country. In the 1980s it even caught on (though this sounds strange) in France and Italy, countries where wine was so familiar and so essential that it was only professionals who gave it a second thought. Throughout the decade the knowledge of wine among both producers and consumers grew very much broader, and in places deeper, too. This very success, though, provoked first the national hypochondria that bedevils the United States, then a vocal minority in some other countries, into reaction. Wine has never been so much in the news as it is today. From that moment in the 1960s to this the process has continued to gather momentum.

This book is a portrait of this new world of wine: its methods, its plant of vineyards and cellars, and above all its practitioners. It is designed to be a practical companion in choices that become more varied and challenging all the time. Like any portrait, it tries to capture the reality of a single moment. The moment is past as soon as the shutter has clicked. The closer the focus and the greater the detail the more there is to change and grow out of date. Yet the detailed record of a single season in wine's long history is as close to reality as it is possible to get. This edition has been revised and updated to reflect the reality of 1990.

To be a practical companion I have tried to give the essential information about each wine country and wine region you are likely to encounter or which is worth making an effort to know. I have shunned a great catalogue of the legislation that surrounds the wine business increasingly each year. It casts little light and does nothing to add to the pleasure of our subject – which is, after all, either a pleasure or a failure.

The essentials, it seems to me, are the names and as far as possible (which is not very far) descriptions of the world's worthwhile wines, who makes them, how much there is of them, an idea of their price, how well they keep, and where they fit into our lives – which are too short, alas, to do justice to anything like all of them. You will also find answers to the recurring questions about grape varieties, production methods and the ways of the wine trade. You will not find a historical survey or a technical treatise; just enough technical information, I hope, to indicate essential differences and the trends of change in wine-making today.

The heart of the book is arranged by countries on the same system as my *Pocket Encyclopaedia of Wine*, with the Index as the alphabetical alternative to find a name you cannot immediately place in a national or regional context. This is updated far less frequently than its annual pocket-sized stablemate, leaving to its more ephemeral editions the questions of current vintages, their quality and maturity. Both will be much clearer if you possess the current (third) edition of *The World Atlas of Wine*, in which the regions are graphically displayed.

Each national or regional section gives the essential background information about the wines in question, then lists with succinct details the principal producers. In a few well-trodden areas the lists make themselves. In most others a complete catalogue would be as unhelpful as it would be unmanageable. My method then has been to consult first my own experience, then the advice of friends, local brokers and officials whom I have reason to respect. I have corresponded with as many producers as possible, asking them specific questions about their properties or firms, their methods, products and philosophies. Often, unfortunately, the exigencies of space have forced me to leave out good producers I would have liked to include. In most countries I have also employed intermediaries to research, interview and pass me their findings. I have tasted as many of the wines described as I could (which is why specific tasting notes go back ten years or more).

The enjoyment of wine is a very personal thing. Yet if you love it, and spend your life among other wine lovers, you will find a remarkable consensus about which wines have the power to really thrill and satisfy us. Prejudice and narrow-mindedness have no place; preferences are what it is all about. I have not tried to hide mine among the fabulous variety described in this book.

Stainless steel is one of the trademarks of modern wine-making. It is increasingly replacing wood as the material for vats and storage tanks.

Modern Wine

At its simplest, wine is made by crushing grapes and allowing the yeast naturally present on the skins to convert the sugar in their juice to alcohol. This is the process of fermentation. No more human intervention is needed than to separate the juice from the skins by pressing. Crushed and fermented like this, white grapes make white wine and red grapes red.

The art of the wine maker can be equally simply expressed. It is to choose good grapes, to carry out the crushing, fermenting and pressing with scrupulous care and hygiene, and to prepare the wine for drinking by cleaning it of yeasts and all foreign bodies. For some sorts of wine this entails ageing it as well; for others the quicker it gets to market the better.

These are the eternal verities of wine and wine-making, well understood for hundreds of years. They can be carried to perfection with no modern scientific knowledge or equipment whatever – with luck. Great wines came to be made in the places where nature, on balance, was kindest. Given a ripe crop of grapes in a healthy state, the element that determined success more than any other was the temperature of the cellar during and after the fermentation. France (but not the south), Germany, the Alps, Hungary, had these conditions. The Mediterranean and places with a similar climate did not.

If there is one innovation that has made the most difference between old and modern wine-making it is refrigeration. Refrigeration and air conditioning have added the whole zone of Mediterranean climate to the world of potentially fine wine.

But technology has advanced on a broad front. Every aspect of grape-growing and wine-making is now under a degree of control undreamed of before. These controls are now common practice in almost all the bigger and newer plants where wine is made. Its scientific basis is widely understood even in traditional areas and among small properties.

One California professor confesses that wine makers now have more controls than they know how to use. In California white-wine making is so clinically perfected that one of the main problems is deciding what sort of wine you want to make.

On the other hand, as Professor Peynaud, the leading consultant wine maker in Bordeaux, says, 'The goal of modern oenology is to avoid having to treat the wine at all.'

SPARKLING WINE

HOW WINE IS MADE

Wine is simply fermented grape juice. The basic techniques are explained above, variations on the theme are listed on the right.

White wine

1) Red or white grapes are put through a crusher-stemmer that crushes the grapes and tears off the stalks.

2) The broken grapes are pumped into a horizontal press.

3) The juice falls into a trough from which it is pumped into a fermenting vat.

4) Fermentation may be arrested to produce sweet or sparkling wine, or allowed to continue until all the sugar is consumed to make dry wine.

Red wine

5) Red grapes are fed through a crusher or crusher-stemmer and pumped into a vat.

6) The grapes ferment (usually with skins) until all the sugar is consumed.

7) The free-run wine runs off.

8) The skins are pressed in a hydraulic basket press. Some press wine is usually mixed with free-run wine.

Rosé

9) Red grapes are crushed, pumped into a fermentation vat, and almost immediately the juice is run off into another vat, having taken a pink colour from the skins.

Port

(The process is similar for other fortified wines.)

10) Red grapes are trodden in a stone trough.
11) The juice ferments in a vat until half the sugar is converted to alcohol.
12) Brandy, from a still, is added to stop fermentation.

Brandy

13) White wine is made in the normal way and distilled to produce brandy.

VARIATIONS

DRY WHITE WINES

Plain dry or semi-dry wine of no special character, fully fermented, not intended to be aged. Usually made with non-aromatic grapes, especially in Italy, southern France, Spain, California. Outstanding examples are Muscadet and Soave. Wine-making is standard, with increasing emphasis on freshness by excluding oxygen and fermenting cool.

Fresh, fruity, dry to semi-sweet wines for drinking young, made from aromatic grape varieties: Riesling, Sauvignon Blanc, Gewürztraminer, Muscat Blanc, for example. Extreme emphasis on picking at the right moment, clean juice, cool fermentation and early bottling.

Dry but full-bodied and smooth whites usually made with a degree of 'skin contact', fermentation at a higher temperature, sometimes in barrels. Bottled after a minimum of 9 months and intended for further ageing. Chardonnay from Burgundy is the classic example. Sauvignon Blanc can be used in this way.

SWEET WHITE WINES

Fresh, fruity, light in alcohol, semi-sweet to sweet in the German style. Now made by fermenting to dryness and 'back-blending' with unfermented juice.

The same style but made by stopping fermentation while some sugar remains. Usually has higher alcohol and more winey, less obviously grapey flavour. Most French, Spanish, Italian and many New World medium-sweet wines are in this category.

Botrytis (noble rot) wines with balance of either low alcohol with very high sugar (German style) or very high alcohol and fairly high sugar (Sauternes style).

Very sweet wines made from extremely ripe or partially raisined grapes. Italian vino santo is the classic example.

ROSE WINES

Pale rosé from red grapes pressed immediately to extract juice with very little colour, sometimes called Vin Gris ('grey wine') or Blanc de Noirs.

Rosé with more colour made from red grapes crushed and 'saigné' or 'blooded' by a short red-wine type maceration or vatting, then pressed and fermented like white wine. The more common method used for Tavel rosé, Anjou rosé, Italian Chiaretto and vin d'une nuit.

Champagne rosé is the only rosé traditionally made by blending red and white wines.

RED WINES

Light, fruity wines made with minimum tannin by short vatting on the skins. Should be drunk early as the extract, pigments and tannin necessary for maturation are absent. Can be made with aromatic grapes but are more commonly made of simple fruity or neutral grapes.

Softer, richer, more savoury and deep-coloured wines (but still low in tannin) made by macération carbonique or interior fermentation of the grapes before pressing. Heating the must is another method of producing colour and smoothness.

Full-blooded reds for maturing (vins de garde) made by long vatting of the skins in the juice to extract pigments, tannins, phenols, etc. All great red wines are made this way.

FORTIFIED WINES

Vin doux naturel is naturally very sweet wine fermented to about 15% alcohol, when further fermentation is stopped (muté) by adding spirits.

Port follows the vin doux naturel procedure, but fermentation is stopped earlier, at 4–6°, by a larger dose of spirits: a quarter of the volume.

Sherry is naturally strong white wine fully fermented to dryness. Then a small quantity of spirits is added to stabilize it while it matures in contact with air.

Madeira is white wine with naturally high acidity stopped with alcohol before fermentation has stopped. Then it is baked in 'stoves' before ageing in barrels or big glass jars.

SPARKLING WINES

White (or sometimes red) wines made to ferment a second time by adding yeast and sugar. The gas from the second fermentation dissolves in the wine. In the classic champagne method the second fermentation takes place in the bottle in which the wine is sold, involving complicated and laborious processing (see page 180). Cheaper methods are:

The transfer process. The wine is transferred, via a filter, under pressure to another bottle.

Cuve close. The second fermentation takes place in a tank; the wine is then filtered under pressure and bottled.

Carbonization. Carbon dioxide is pumped into still wine.

The following pages summarize some of the more important modern techniques and currently held views on the many factors that affect the qualities of wine. They follow the processes of grape-growing and wine-making more or less sequentially so that they can be read as an account or referred to as a glossary. Some processes apply to white wine only, some to red, some to both.

IN THE VINEYARD

Grape Varieties

The choice of grape varieties is the most fundamental decision of all. The subject is covered, in colour and with a number of detailed distribution maps, on pages 17–32.

Source of Grapes

There are arguments both for and against growing your own grapes. Those in favour are that you have total control over the management of the vineyard and thus decide the quality of the grapes. The argument against is that an independent wine maker can pick and choose among the best grapes of specialist growers in different areas.

In France and throughout most of Europe almost all quality wine (except for most champagne) is 'home-grown'. In California and Australia the debate is more open. Wine makers who buy their grapes (almost always from the same suppliers) include some of the very best.

Virus-free Vines

Certain authorities (notably at the University of California) are convinced that the only way to achieve a healthy vineyard is to 'clean' the vine stocks in it of all virus infections. It was not appreciated until recently that the beautiful red colouring of vine leaves in autumn is generally a symptom of a virus-infected plant.

Plants can now be propagated free of virus infection by growing them very fast in a hot greenhouse, then cutting off the growing tips and using them as mini-cuttings (or micro-cuttings, growing minute pieces of the plant tissue in a nutrient jelly). The virus is always one pace behind the new growth, which is thus 'clean' and will have all its natural vigour.

It must be said on the other hand that virus elimination is not a substitute for selection of the best vines for propagation. The Office International du Vin officially declared in 1980 that 'it is a fantasy to try to establish a vineyard free of all virus diseases' and recommended its members to 'select clones resistant to dangerous virus diseases and which will still be capable, after infection, of producing a satisfactory crop both as to quality and quantity' (see Cloning).

Cloning

Close observation in a vineyard will tend to show that some vine branches are inherently more vigorous, bear more fruit, ripen earlier or have other desirable characteristics. These branches (and their buds) are 'mutations', genetically slightly different from the parent plant. The longer a variety has been in cultivation the more 'degenerate' and thus genetically unstable it will be, and the more mutations it will have. The Pinot family is extremely ancient and notoriously mutable.

A recent technique is to select such a branch and propagate exclusively from its cuttings. A whole vineyard can then be planted with what is in effect one identical individual plant – known as a clone. There is thus not one single Pinot Noir variety in Burgundy but scores of clones selected for different attributes. Growers who plant highly productive clones will never achieve the best-quality wine. Those who choose a shy-bearing, small-berried clone for colour and flavour must reckon on smaller crops.

One advantage of a single-clone vineyard is that all its grapes will ripen together. A disadvantage is that one problem, pest or disease will affect them all equally. Common sense seems to indicate that the traditional method of selecting cuttings from as many different healthy vines as possible (known as 'mass selection') rather than one individual, carries a better chance of long-term success.

The Choice of Rootstocks

The great majority of modern vineyards are of a selected variety of European vine grafted on to a selected American rootstock which has inbuilt resistance to the vine-killing pest phylloxera. Compatible rootstocks have been chosen and/or bred and virus-freed to be ideal for specific types of vineyard soil. Some are recommended for acid to neutral soils (such as most in California) while others flourish on the limey or alkaline soils common to most of Europe's best vineyards.

Grafting

The grafting of a 'scion' of the chosen vine variety on to an appropriate rootstock is either done at the nursery before planting ('bench grafting') or on to an already-planted rootstock in the vineyard ('field grafting'). In California recently it has become common practice for a grower to change his mind after a vine has been in production for several years, deciding that he wants (say) less Zinfandel and more Chardonnay. In this case he simply saws off the Zinfandel vine at rootstock level, just above the ground, and 'T-bud' grafts a Chardonnay scion in its place. Within two years he will have white wine instead of red.

Hybrid Vines
After the phylloxera epidemic in Europe a century ago a number of France's leading biologists started breeding hybrid vines by marrying the European classics to phylloxera-resistant American species. Once the technique of grafting the French originals on to American roots was well established the French establishment rejected these '*producteurs directes*', or 'PDs' (so-called because they produced 'directly' via their own roots). Good, hardy and productive as many of them are they are banned from all French appellation areas for fear of altering their precious identity. Their American parenthood, however, has made them highly suitable for use in the eastern United States, where hardiness is a perpetual problem (*see* page 486). They are also very popular in the new vineyards of England and New Zealand.

New Crossings of European Vines
Germany is the centre of a breeding programme quite distinct from 'hybrid' vines. Its object is to find within the genetic pool of varieties of *Vitis vinifera* a combination of desirable qualities which could supplant, in particular, the Riesling, Germany's finest vine but one that ripens relatively late, thus carrying a high risk element at vintage time. So far no cross has even remotely challenged the Riesling for flavour or hardiness – though many have for productivity, strongly aromatic juice and early ripening. The Müller-Thurgau was the first and is still the best-known example.

The University of California also has a *vinifera* breeding programme which has produced some useful additions, particularly among high-yielding grapes for hot areas which retain good aromas and acidity. The best-known examples are Ruby Cabernet (Cabernet Sauvignon × Carignan), Carnelian and Centurion (Cabernet Sauvignon × Grenache), Carmine (Cabernet Sauvignon × Merlot), Emerald Riesling (Riesling × Muscadelle) and Flora (Gewürztraminer × Semillon), all produced by Dr. Harold Olmo at Davis.

South Africa has produced the Pinotage, said to be a cross between Pinot Noir and Cinsaut (though unfortunately with none of the qualities of the former). With more than 3,000 named varieties already in circulation to choose from there seems to be a limited point in breeding for the sake of breeding.

Soil
Soil is always given pride of place in French discussions of wine quality. It is considered from two aspects: its chemical and its physical properties. Current thinking is that the latter is much the more important. Most soils contain all the chemical elements the vine needs. The physical factors that affect quality are texture, porosity, drainage, depth and even colour. In cool climates anything that tends to make the soil warm (i.e. absorb and store heat from the sun) is good. Stones on the surface store heat and radiate it at night. Darker soil absorbs more radiation. In Germany vine rows are oriented to expose the soil to maximum sunlight.

Dry soil warms up faster. Another important advantage of good deep drainage (e.g. on Médoc gravel) is the fact that it makes the vine root deep to find moisture. Deep roots are in a stable environment: a sudden downpour just before harvest will not instantly inflate the grapes with water. On the other hand experiments at Davis, California, recently have shown that where the soil is cooler than the above-ground parts of the vine the effect can be good for the grape pigments and give deep-coloured red wine. (Château Petrus on the iron-rich clay of Pomerol would seem to bear this out. St-Estèphe also has more clay and its wines often more colour than the rest of the Médoc.)

In California clay also seems to produce stable white wines that resist oxidation and therefore have a greater ability to mature. But in California over-rapid ripening often leads to wines that are low in acid and easily oxidized. The cool of clay may simply be slowing the ripening process: the very opposite of the effect required in, say, Germany.

A reasonable conclusion would be that the best soil is the soil that results in the grapes coming steadily to maturity: warm in cool areas, reasonably cool in hot areas. It should be deep enough for the roots to have constant access to moisture, since a vine under acute stress of drought closes the pores of its leaves. Photosynthesis stops and the grapes cannot develop or ripen.

Expert opinion seems to be that if the soils of the great vineyards (e.g. Bordeaux first-growths) have more available nutrients and minerals (especially potassium) it is because their owners have invested more in them. The closest scrutiny of the Côte d'Or has not revealed chemical differences between the soils of the different crus which would account for their acknowledged differences of flavour.

Sites, Slopes and Microclimates

It is conventional wisdom that wine from slopes is better. The words *côtes* and *coteaux*, meaning slopes, constantly recur in France. The obvious reasons are the increased solar radiation on a surface tipped towards the sun, meaning warmer soil, and the improved cold-air drainage, reducing the risk of frost.

A south slope is almost always the ideal, but local conditions can modify this. In areas with autumn morning fog a westerly slope is preferable, since the sun does not normally burn through the fog until the afternoon. The best slopes of the Rheingau are examples. But in Burgundy and Alsace easterly slopes have the advantage of sun all morning to warm the ground, which stores the heat while the angle of the sun decreases during the afternoon. Alsace also benefits from a particularly sunny local climate caused by the 'rain shadow' of the Vosges mountains to its west.

Many of the best Old World vineyards (e.g. in Germany, the Rhône valley, the Douro valley for port) were terraced on steep slopes to combine the advantages of the slope with some depth of soil. Being inaccessible to machinery, terraces are largely being abolished. In Germany huge earth-moving projects (known as *Flurbereinigung*) have rebuilt whole hills to allow tractors to operate. The Douro valley is being remodelled with wide sloping terraces instead of the old narrow flat ones. Experiments with 'vertical' planting on the steep Douro slopes – doing away with terraces altogether – have been inconclusive. Heavy rains can wash soil nutrients to the bottom of the slope.

A flat valley floor (as in the Napa Valley) is the riskiest place to plant vines because cold air drains to it on spring nights when the vines have tender shoots (*see* Frost Protection).

It is noteworthy that in Burgundy the Grands Crus vineyards have a lower incidence of frost damage than the Premiers Crus – presumably because growers have observed the cold spots and lavished their attentions on the safer ones. The same is even true of the incidence of hail.

The term microclimate refers to the immediate surroundings of the vine. The slightest difference can become important in the long period between bud break and harvest. In the Rheingau wind is considered a principal enemy since it can blow out

accumulated warmth from the rows – which are therefore planted across the prevailing summer southwest wind.

Another microclimatic factor is the shade and possible build-up of humidity under a dense canopy of leaves (*see* Training and Trellising). Yet another is the greater incidence of frost over soil covered with herbage than over bare earth, which makes it worth cultivating the vine rows in spring.

Irrigation

Another piece of conventional wisdom considers that any irrigation of the vines can only lower wine quality (by diluting the juice). It is hard to discern any logical distinction between rainfall and water applied by hoses or sprinklers, provided it is done within reason and at the right time (i.e. not shortly before the harvest). Irrigation is still strictly forbidden in all French appellation areas, but is standard practice in many warm countries. Australia has whole vineyard regions which would be desert without irrigation. Chile's vineyards depend on flood irrigation devised by the Incas. In California drip irrigation (by perforated hoses laid along the rows) is widely used for establishing new vine plants. The sprinkler systems installed for frost protection (q.v.) also usefully double as artificial rain in times of drought or for cooling the air in times of excessive heat. Irrigation should only take place during the period of active growth of the vine with the object of maintaining a proper balance between moisture supply to the roots and evaporation from the leaves.

Frost Protection

A dormant *vinifera* vine in winter can survive temperatures down to $-28°C$ ($-18°F$). In regions where lower temperatures regularly occur it is

Mechanical harvesting in California

common practice to bury the lower half of the vines by earthing-up in late autumn. A vine is most vulnerable to frost in spring when its new growth is green and sappy. The only old means of protection (still practised in many places) was to light stoves (or 'smudge pots') in the vineyards on clear spring nights. It was often a forlorn hope. An improvement introduced in frost-prone areas of California, for example, was a giant fan to keep the air in the vineyard moving and prevent cold air accumulating, but it has proved ineffectual without heaters as well. The latest and much the most effective protective device is the sprinkler, which simply rains heavily on the almost-freezing vine. The water freezes on contact with the young shoots and forms a protective layer of ice, which looks dangerous but acts as insulation and prevents the shoot being damaged by temperatures below freezing. Such sprinklers can be an excellent investment, doubling as a method of irrigation during dry, hot summers.

Training and Trellising

Most vineyards used to consist of innumerable individual bushes, 'head' or *Gobelet*'-pruned back to a few buds from the short trunk after each harvest. With a few famous exceptions (among them the Moselle, parts of the Rhône, Beaujolais) most modern vineyards are 'cordoned' – that is, with the vines trained on to one or more wires parallel to the ground, supported at intervals by stakes.

Recent developments, encouraged by the need to use mechanical harvesters, have been to use higher trellising systems, often designed to spread the foliage at the top by means of a crossbar supporting two parallel wires four feet apart. The first such trellis was developed in Austria in the 1930s by Lenz Moser.

High trellises are not suitable for cool areas such as Germany, where heat radiation from the ground is essential for ripening. On the other hand they have been used immemorially in northern Portugal to produce deliberately acidic wine. Widespread 'curtains' of foliage, or 'double curtains' where the vine is made to branch on to two high supporting wires, have several advantages in warm areas. They expose a larger leaf surface for photosynthesis, at the same time shading the bunches of grapes from direct sunlight. In fertile soils which can support vigorous growth the so-called 'lyre' system, spreading the vine top into two mounds of foliage, is experimentally very successful, if not for top-quality wine, at least for good quantities of ripe grapes.

Pruning Methods

Pruning methods have been adapted to new methods of vine training where necessary. By far the most significant new development is mechanical pruning, which dispenses with skilled but laborious hand work in the depths of winter by simply treating the vine row as a hedge. Aesthetically appalling as it is, results (initially in Australia) show that a system of small circular saws straddling the vine and cutting all wood extending beyond a certain narrow compass is just as satisfactory as the practised eye and hand. Some follow-up hand pruning may be necessary, but the same method has been used in commercial apple orchards for some years with no harmful effects, and is certain to become more common in vineyards. Experience in California has shown that mechanical pruning costs as little as 15 per cent of the cost of hand pruning.

Growth Regulators

For many years it has been customary to trim excessively long leafy shoots from the tops and sides of vines in summer. A new development is the growth-regulating spray. Ethephon, a chemical which slowly releases ethylene gas, can be sprayed on the foliage when it has reached an ideal point of development. It inhibits further leaf growth, preventing the canopy from becoming too dense and making the plant's reserves of carbohydrates available to the fruit, instead of allowing it to waste them on useless long shoots. It apparently also encourages ripening and makes it easier for a mechanical harvester to detach the grapes from their stems.

Systematic Sprays

The traditional protection against fungus diseases such as mildew in the vineyard is 'Bordeaux mixture', a bright blue copper-sulphate solution sprayed on from a long-legged tractor (but washed off again by the next rain). New 'systematic' sprays are chemicals that are absorbed into the sap-stream of the plants and destroy their fungus (or insect) victim from inside the leaf or grape when the parasite attacks. Unfortunately fungus diseases and such pests as red-spider mites can rapidly develop resistance to specific chemicals, making it necessary for manufacturers to vary the formula (at great expense). The best-known systemic fungicide, benomyl, is now of limited use for this reason.

Organic Cultivation

Wine can be grown by organic methods, just as can any other crop. This cuts out artificial fertilizers and insecticides and other sprays. Three years must pass since the vineyard was last artificially fertilized before the wine can be called 'organic'. Some sprays can be used – old-fashioned copper sulphate is one. And of course the organic logic must be followed through into the winery.

Continued on page 33

THE VINE

A wine grower in the Clos de Vougeot has no choice about what grapes to plant. It has been a sea of Pinot Noir for centuries. Nothing else is permitted.

A wine grower in the Médoc has an important choice to make. Half a dozen varieties within the family of the Cabernets are allowed. The emphasis he places on the harsher or the smoother varieties is the basis of his house style.

A wine grower in the New World is free as air. His own taste and his view of the market are his only guide. This choice, and the debates it has started, has made all wine lovers far more grape-conscious than ever before. Not only are more and more wines named by their grape varieties, but this very fact has made the clear ascendancy of some varieties over others public knowledge.

What is a variety? It is a selection from among the infinity of forms a plant takes by natural mutation. In the basic economy of viticulture a wine grower looks first for fruitfulness, hardiness and resistance to disease in his plants. Then he looks for the ability to ripen its fruit before the end of the warm autumn weather. Lastly he looks for flavour and character.

There has been plenty of time since the discovery of wine to try out and develop different varieties. In the botanical genus *Vitis*, the vine, there are more than 20 species. The wine vine is only one, a wild woodland plant of Europe and eastern Asia, *Vitis vinifera*. It was scrambling through the treetops of France long before the idea of crushing and fermenting its grapes was imported, via Greece, from the Near East.

Nobody knows the precise origins of any of the varieties of vine that were developed locally in France, Italy, Spain, along the Danube and in the rest of wine-growing Europe. But the assumption is that they started as selections by trial from local vine varieties, possibly interbreeding with imported ones of special quality. In Germany, for instance, the Romans made the brilliant discovery of a variety with habits perfectly adapted to the cool northern climate: the Riesling, or its ancestor. Selections, adaptations or descendants from it have become all the other grapes in the German style.

There are now 4,000 or more named varieties of wine grape on earth. Perhaps 40 have really recognizable flavour and character. Of these a bare dozen have moved into international circulation, and the dozen can be narrowed again to those that have personalities so definite (and so good) that they form the basis of a whole international category of wine. They are the principal red and white grapes of Bordeaux, the same of Burgundy, the Riesling of Germany, the Gewürztraminer of Alsace and the grandfather of them all, the Muscat.

Today there is an increasing temptation to plant the champion grapes everywhere. It is a difficult argument between quality and that most precious attribute of wine – variety.

THE CLASSIC GRAPES

Riesling (Johannisberg Riesling, Rhine Riesling, White Riesling). The classic grape of Germany disputes with Chardonnay the title of the world's best white grape. The Riesling produces wines of crisp fruity acidity and transparent clarity of flavour. Even its smell is refreshing. In Germany it ranges from pale green, fragile and sharp on the Mosel to golden, exotically luscious wines, especially in the Rheinpfalz. It is remarkably versatile in warmer climates; perhaps at its most typical in Alsace, becoming more buxom in California and Australia where it ages to its unique mature bouquet of lemons and petrol more rapidly.

Chardonnay. The white Burgundy grape makes fatter, more winey and potent-feeling wine than Riesling, less aromatic when young, maturing to a rich and broad, sometimes buttery, sometimes smoky or musky smell and flavour. The finesse of Blanc de Blancs champagne, the mineral smell of Chablis, the nuttiness of Meursault, the ripe fruit smells of Napa Valley wines show its versatility. It is adapting superbly to Australia, Oregon, New Zealand, northern Italy.

Cabernet Sauvignon. The Médoc grape. Most recognizable and most versatile of red grapes, apparently able to make first-class wine in any warm soil. Small, dark, rather late-ripening berries give intense colour, strong blackcurrant and sometimes herby aroma and much tannin, which makes it the slowest wine to mature. It needs age in oak and bottle and is best of all blended with Merlot, etc., as in Bordeaux (page 48).

Pinot Noir. The red Burgundy and Champagne grape. So far apparently less adaptable to foreign vineyards, where the fine Burgundian balance is hard to achieve. Sweeter, less tannic, richer-textured than Cabernet and therefore enjoyable far younger. Never blended except in Champagne.

Gewürztraminer. The beginner's grape for its forthright spicy smell and flavour, until recently almost unique to Alsace but now spreading rapidly.

Sauvignon Blanc. The name derives from *sauvage*, wild, which could well describe its grassy or gooseberry flavour. Widespread in Bordeaux, where it is blended with Sémillon for both sweet and dry wines, but most characteristic in Sancerre. A successful transplant to the New World. It can be light and aromatic, or heavier like Chardonnay.

Muscat (de Frontignan, Muscat Blanc, Moscato Canelli). The finest of the ancient tribe of Muscats is the small white used for the sweet brown Frontignan, Asti Spumante and dry Muscats of Alsace.

Riesling

Chardonnay

Cabernet Sauvignon

Sauvignon Blanc

Pinot Noir

Gewürztraminer

Muscat

FRANCE

All of the seven classic grapes shown on pages 18 and 19 are grown to perfection in France. The Muscat, Riesling and Gewürztraminer are long-established imports, but the remaining four, the reds and whites of Burgundy and Bordeaux, appear to be France's own natives, representing an eastern and a western tradition; that of the Alps and that of the Atlantic. (They meet on the Loire.)

The map shows a selection of the other grapes that make up this great tradition. Nobody can say with confidence how many there are all told: a single variety may have four or five different names in different areas quite close together – or indeed the grape may be a local strain and not quite the same variety. Some 95 of these local characters, ranging from such common plants as the red Carignan of the Midi (there are more than 400,000 acres) to such rare ones as the white Tressallier (limited to one tiny zone), are plotted here as close to home as possible.

Gamay
The Beaujolais grape bears the name of a village in the Côte d'Or, but it has found its perfect home in the light soils of southern Burgundy, where it makes the world's most gaily flowing mealtime wine.

RED GRAPE VARIETIES

Abouriou grown in Cahors; also known as 'Gamay du Rhône'.

Aléatico muscat var. of Corsica, makes a wine of the same name.

Alicante syn. of Grenache.

Alicante-Bouschet prolific var. of southern table-wine vineyards.

Aramon high-yielding southern table-wine var.

Aspiran an old var. of the Languedoc.

Auxerrois syn. of Malbec in Cahors.

Bouchet syn. of Cabernet Franc in St-Emilion.

Braquet main var. of Bellet, near Nice.

Brocol local Gaillac var.

CABERNET FRANC high-quality cousin of Cabernet Sauvignon used in Bordeaux (esp. St-Emilion) and on the Loire.

CABERNET SAUVIGNON *see* p18.

Cahors syn. of Malbec.

CARIGNAN the leading bulk-wine producer of the Midi; harmless but dull.

Carmenère archaic Bordeaux name for Cabernet.

César tannic traditional var. of Irancy (Yonne).

CINSAUT prominent southern Rhône var. that is used in Châteauneuf-du-Pape, etc.

Cot syn. of Malbec in the Loire.

Duras local Gaillac var.

Fer or **Ferservadou** used in VDQS Vins de Marcillac in the southwest.

Fuelle Noir Bellet var.

GRENACHE powerful but pale red used in Châteauneuf-du-Pape, for rosés (e.g. Tavel) and dessert wines in Roussillon.

Grolleau or **Groslot** common Loire red used in, for example, Anjou Rosé.

Grosse Vidure syn. of Cabernet Franc.

Jurançon Noir Gaillac (Tarn) grape – not used in Jurançon.

MALBEC important var. now fading from the best Bordeaux but basic to Cahors.

Malvoisie used for dessert wines (VDN) in Roussillon.

Mataro syn. of Mourvèdre.

MERLOT essential element in fine Bordeaux; the dominant grape of Pomerol.

MEUNIER or PINOT MEUNIER inferior 'dusty-leaved' version of Pinot Noir 'tolerated' in Champagne.

MONDEUSE chief red of Savoie.

MOURVEDRE tolerable Midi grape (also grown in northeast Spain).

Négrette var. of Malbec grown in Frontonnais.

Nielluccio Corsican var.

Noirien syn. of Pinot Noir.

PETIT VERDOT high-quality subsidiary grape of Bordeaux.

Pineau d'Aunis local to the Loire valley, esp. Anjou.

PINOT NOIR *see* p18.

Portugais Bleu widespread in the southwest, especially Gaillac.

Poulsard Jura var. blended with Trousseau.

Pressac St-Emilion syn. for Malbec.

Sciacarello Corsican var.

SYRAH widespread and the great grape of Hermitage (Rhône), blended in Châteauneuf-du-Pape.

Tannat tannic var. of the southwest, esp. Madiran.

Tempranillo Spanish (Rioja) var. grown in the Midi.

Trousseau majority grape in Jura reds but inferior to Poulsard.

Valteliner or **Velteliner** pink Savoie var., alias Malvoisie.

Vidure, Petit, syn. of Cabernet Sauvignon.

For white grape varieties, see page 22.

• Reims
Marne
Sacy
CHARDONNAY
MEUNIER
CHAMPAGNE
PINOT
Pinot NOIR
PARIS Blanc
Seine
Seine

Moselle

Pinot
Gris
Sylvaner RIESLING
MUSCAT
ALSACE • Strasbourg
CHASSELAS
GEWURZTRAMINER
Klevner Pinot
Blanc

YONNE
César
Beaunois
Chablis
CHARDONNAY

PINOT
NOIR
Pinot
Blanc
SAVAGNIN Nature
JURA
Cacaralet
CHARDONNAY Gamay Blanc
Poulsard
Trousseau

Loire
Arbois Domorgina
Poteau
d'Aunis
Angers Tours
FOLLE
BLANCHE Loire CHENIN BLANC LOIRE CHENIN BLANC
GAMAY CAB FRANC
MUSCADET Grolleau Cot GAMAY
Nantes CAB FRANC
Gros Plant Vienne

SAUV BLANC
Pouilly
PINOT CHASSELAS
NOIR Blanc
Fumé

Bébét PINOT
NOIR
ALIGOTE
BURGUNDY

Vaughine
MONDEUSE
SAVOIE
Roussette Jaquère
Isère SAMAY
Ste Marie

GAMAY
CHARDONNAY
SAUV BLANC

Cher
Allier
GAMAY
Tresallier
CHARDONNAY
PINOT
NOIR
Loire

GAMAY

Lyon
Rhône

Charente
Colombard FOLLE Cognac
BLANCHE Jurançon
St-Emilion Blanc
Frontignan MERLOT
CAB SAUV.
MERLOT
Blaye
Bouchet Fronsac
St-Emilion
Bordeaux CAB FRANC CAB SAUV.
UGNI BLANC MALBEC SAUV BLANC
FOLLE PETIT SEMILLON
BLANCHE VERDOT
MUSCADELE
SAUVIGNON SEMILLON
BLANC MERLOT
CAB SAUV.
SYRAH
Picpoul
Baroque Béarn Courbu
Arrufiac SAUV BLANC
Jurançon CAB FRANC
Gros CAB.SAUV.
Manseng
CHARDONNAY
Petit Manseng

Dordogne
Auxerrois Lot
MALBEC Cahors
Abouriou Fer
GAMAY Gaillac
Duras Port Bleu
Negrette Mauzac Brocol Tarn
Jurançon Loin de
Noir l'Oeil
CAB SAUV
Aspiran
CLAIRETTE CINSAUT
Bourboulenc
Alicante CARIGNAN
Bouschet Bourboulenc
Mauzac
CHARDONNAY
Baise
Garonne
Adour
ROUSSILLON
CHARDONNAY CAB.SAUV. CAB FRANC

Cognier
Rhône
SYRAH
MARSANNE
Roussanne

SYRAH
FLINETTE
GRENACHE Roubouloc
SYRAH CINSAUT
MUSCAT
Alicante
Bouschet GRENACHE
CINSAUT PROVENCE
MOURVEDRE Alicante
Bouschet
MUSCAT CINSAUT UGNI BLANC
MOURVEDRE Rolle GRENACHE
MERLOT
Aramon
CHARDONNAY
UGNI BLANC
MACABEU
Malvoisie
CARIGNAN
GRENACHE
LANGUEDOC
Durance
Fuelle Noir Braquet
• Nice

GAMAY
Legend:

GAMAY **MAIN RED GRAPE VARIETIES**
Tannat Other red grape varieties
ALIGOTE **MAIN WHITE GRAPE VARIETIES**
Arbois Other white grape varieties

Vineyard areas

AOC and VDQS areas

Km. 0   80   160   240
Miles 0   80   160

21

Chenin Blanc
Almost neutral in flavour, Chenin Blanc of the Loire possesses an inbuilt balance of strength and acidity that makes it capable of many styles from fresh and appley to old, brown and buttery.

Sémillon
The one grape that makes only truly great wine when it rots. Sémillon is grown and blended with Sauvignon in Bordeaux because of its proclivity to rot nobly in a misty autumn.

ALIGOTE secondary Burgundy grape of high acidity. Wines for drinking young.

ALTESSE Savoie var. Wines are sold as 'Roussette'.

Arbois main white or tinted var. of Touraine.

Arruffiac Béarnais var. (Pacherenc du Vic Bilh).

Auvergnat or **Auvernat** Loire term for the Pinot family.

Baroque used in Béarn for Pacherenc du Vic Bilh.

Beaunois syn. of Chardonnay at Chablis.

Beurot syn. in Burgundy of Pinot Gris.

Blanc Fumé syn. of Sauvignon at Pouilly-sur-Loire.

Blanquette syn. of Mauzac.

Bourboulenc Midi (Minervois, La Clape) var., also goes into (red) Châteauneuf-du-Pape.

Camaralet Jurançon var.

CHARDONNAY *see* p18.

CHASSELAS neutral var. used in Pouilly-sur-Loire and Alsace.

CLAIRETTE common neutral-flavoured Midi grape, also makes sparkling Rhône Clairette de Die.

Colombard minor Bordelais grape.

Courbu Madiran var. (alias Sarrat).

FOLLE BLANCHE formerly the chief Cognac grape, also grown in Bordeaux and Britanny.

Frontignan syn. of Ugni Blanc in Blaye, Bordeaux.

Gamay Blanc syn. of Chardonnay in the Jura.

GEWÜRZTRAMINER *see* p18.

Gros Manseng one of the main grapes of Jurançon.

Gros Plant syn. of Folle Blanche in the western Loire.

Jaquère the grape of Apremont and Chignin in Savoie.

Jurançon Blanc minor Cognac var. (not in Jurançon).

Klevner name used for Pinot Blanc in Alsace.

Loin de l'Oeil south-western var. used in Gaillac.

MACABEU or MACCABEO Catalan var. used in Roussillon for dessert 'VDN'. A sort of Malvoisie.

Malvoisie syn. of Bourboulenc in the Midi.

MARSANNE with Roussanne the white grape of Hermitage (northern Rhône).

Mauzac used in Blanquette de Limoux and Gaillac.

Morillon syn. of Chardonnay.

MUSCADELLE minor, slightly muscat-flavoured var. used in Sauternes.

MUSCADET gives its name to the wine of the western Loire.

MUSCAT *see* p18.

Nature syn. of Savagnin at Arbois.

Ondenc Gaillac var.

Petit Manseng southwestern var. used in Jurançon, etc.

Petite Sainte Marie syn. of Chardonnay in Savoie.

Picpoul syn. of Folle Blanche in Armagnac, the southern Rhône and the Midi (Picpoul de Pinet).

Pineau de la Loire syn. in the Loire of Chenin Blanc (not a Pinot).

Pinot Blanc closely related to Pinot Noir; grown in Burgundy, Champagne and Alsace.

Pinot Gris (Tokay d'Alsace) a mutation of the Pinot Noir, widespread in Alsace.

Piquepoul *see* Picpoul.

RIESLING *see* p18.

Rolle Italian Vermentino in Provence.

Romorantin grown only at Cheverny on the Loire; makes dry, often sharp wine.

Roussanne (with Marsanne) makes white Hermitage.

Roussette syn. of Altesse in Savoie.

Sacy minor var. of Champagne and the Yonne.

St-Emilion syn. of Ugni Blanc in Cognac.

SAUVIGNON BLANC *see* p18.

SAVAGNIN the 'yellow wine' grape of Château-Chalon (Jura); related to Gewürztraminer.

Sylvaner the workhorse light-wine grape of Alsace.

Traminer *see* Gewürztraminer.

Tresallier var. of the extreme upper Loire (St-Pourçain-sur-Sioule), now fading.

UGNI BLANC common Midi grape; Italy's Trebbiano; 'St-Emilion' in Cognac.

Vermentino Italian grape known in Provence as Rolle; possibly the Malvoisie of Corsica.

Viognier rare aromatic grape of Condrieu in the northern Rhône.

ITALY

Italy's grape catalogue is probably the longest of all. With wine-growing so universal a factor of Italian life, uninterrupted for millennia before the phylloxera, local selection has blurred the origins and relationships of many varieties beyond recall. Is the fish caught off Tunisia and called by an Arab name the same as a similar one caught in the Adriatic and called by a name peculiar to the Romagna? Italian grapes are scarcely less slippery a subject.

In general their selection has been on the grounds of productivity and good health, along with adaptability to the soil and reliable ripening, rather than great qualities of flavour or ability to age. The mass of Italian grapes are therefore sound rather than inspiring; their flavours muted or neutral. The only international classic to (maybe) come from Italy is the (Gewürz)traminer, from the South Tyrol.

But once you start to list the exceptions, the Italian grapes with personality and potentially excellent quality, it does seem strange that more of them have not yet made a real name for themselves in the world. The Nebbiolo, the Barbera, the Teroldego, the Brunello, the Montepulciano, the Aglianico are reds with much to offer. There are fewer first-class whites, but Cortese, Greco, Tocai, Verdicchio and Vernaccia all make original contributions, and the Moscato of Piedmont, while not exclusively Italian, is a very Italian interpretation of the most ancient of grapes.

More and more is being heard of Cabernet, Merlot, Pinot Bianco and even Chardonnay and Rhine Riesling. The northeast is now almost as international in its ampelography as any of the wine areas of the New World. The appearance of Cabernet and Chardonnay in Chianti in recent years is an important sign of changes in the wind.

The central question over the future of Italian wine is how far she will defend her traditions (which is the purpose of the DOC legislation) in sticking to her indigenous grapes, and how far she will bow to the international trend – as she is tending to do in wine-making techniques.

For the moment, while the world is still only beginning to learn what variety Italy offers, she will do well to develop her native flavours to the full. They include as wide a range as the wines of any country – France included.

As the map on the following page shows, there is little of agricultural Italy where no grapes at all are grown. On the map, areas of intensive viticulture are distinguished from areas where wine-growing may be important but wines are anonymous, and the

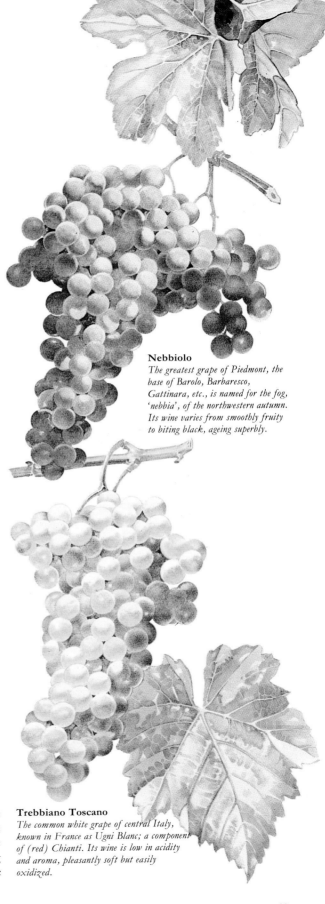

Nebbiolo
The greatest grape of Piedmont, the base of Barolo, Barbaresco, Gattinara, etc., is named for the fog, 'nebbia', of the northwestern autumn. Its wine varies from smoothly fruity to biting black, ageing superbly.

Trebbiano Toscano
The common white grape of central Italy, known in France as Ugni Blanc; a component of (red) Chianti. Its wine is low in acidity and aroma, pleasantly soft but easily oxidized.

grape varieties listed on page 25 are located in the regions where they play a dominant role – although a dozen or so varieties are found as major performers or supporting actors in many different regions. Barbera, Trebbiano, Sangiovese, for example, appear on the map in capitals where they are most prominent and in small letters elsewhere.

There is no general rule on the mention of grape varieties on labels: local custom dictates whether the wine is labelled by place, grape or a name unrelated to either. With the current increase in variety consciousness, it seems likely that producers will make more of the grape varieties in future – at least on wines destined for export.

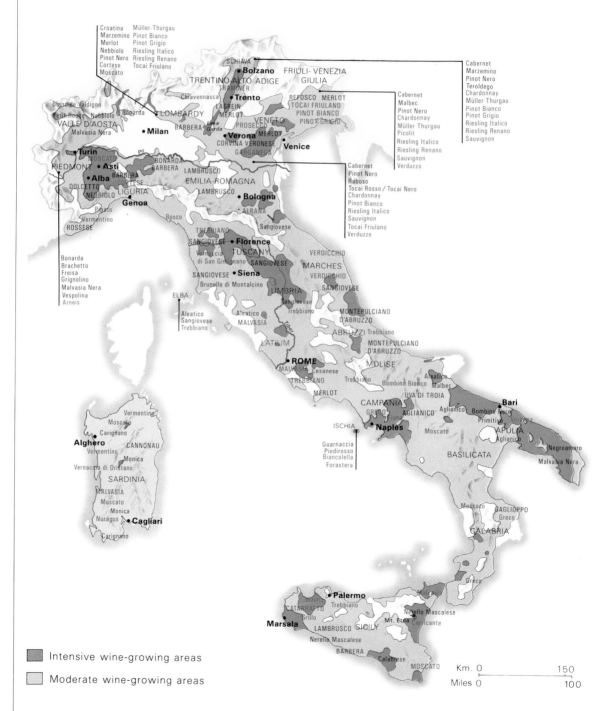

Intensive wine-growing areas

Moderate wine-growing areas

Km. 0   150

Miles 0   100

RED GRAPE VARIETIES

Aglianico source of full-bodied Taurasi in Campania and Aglianico del Vulture in Basilicata.

Aleatico muscat-flavoured grape used for dark dessert wines in Latium, Apulia and elsewhere.

Barbera dark, acidic Piedmont var. widely grown in the NW.

Bombino Nero used in Apulia's Castel del Monte *rosato*.

Bonarda minor var. widespread in Lombardy and Piedmont.

Brachetto makes pleasant, fizzy Piedmont wines.

Brunello di Montalcino a noble strain of Tuscany's Sangiovese.

Cabernet widespread in the NE; increasing elsewhere.

Calabrese source of Sicilian DOC Cerasuolo light reds.

Cannonau leading dark var. of Sardinia for DOC wines.

Carignano (French Carignan), prominent in Sardinia.

Cesanese good Latium red.

Chiavennasca Nebbiolo in Valtellina, N Lombardy.

Corvina Veronese main grape of Valpolicella, Recioto, Bardolino.

Croatina much used in Lombardy's Oltrepò Pavese.

Dolcetto low-acid Piedmont var., source of several DOCs.

Freisa Piedmont var., makes sweet, often fizzy wines.

Gaglioppo source of most Calabrian reds, inc. Cirò.

Grignolino makes light, pleasant wines around Asti in Piedmont.

Guarnaccia red var. of Campania, esp. Ischia.

Lagrein grown in Alto Adige for faintly bitter reds and dark rosés.

Lambrusco prolific source of Emilia's effervescent wines.

Malbec seen occasionally in Apulia and Venezia.

Malvasia Nera makes sweet, fragrant, sometimes sparkling DOC reds in Piedmont; also a fine dessert wine in Apulia.

Marzemino dark grape grown in Trentino and Lombardy.

Merlot Bordeaux native widely grown in Italy, esp. in the NE.

Monica makes Sardinian DOC reds.

Montepulciano dominant dark var. of Abruzzi; Molise.

Negroamaro potent Apulian var. of the Salento peninsula.

Nerello Mascalese Sicilian grape, source of Etna reds and rosés.

Petit Rouge used in some Valle d'Aosta reds.

Piedirosso or **Per'e Palummo** features in Campanian reds.

Pinot Nero Burgundy's Pinot Noir, grown in much of NE Italy.

Primitivo Apulian grape, said to be Zinfandel.

Raboso worthy Veneto native.

Refosco source of dry, full-bodied Friuli DOC reds. Known as Mondeuse in France.

Rossese fine Ligurian var., makes DOC at Dolceacqua.

Sangiovese mainstay of Chianti and one of Italy's most widely planted vines.

Schiava widespread in Alto Adige.

Spanna syn. for Nebbiolo.

Teroldego unique to Trentino, makes Teroldego Rotaliano.

Tocai Rosso or **Tocai Nero** makes DOC red in Veneto's Colli Berici.

Uva di Troia main grape of several DOC wines in N Apulia.

Vespolina often blended with Nebbiolo in E Piedmont.

Pinot Grigio
France's Pinot Gris (Ruländer in Germany) is one of the successes of northeast Italy, where it can make first-class full-bodied fruity wine.

WHITE GRAPE VARIETIES

Albana Romagna grape, makes dry and semi-sweet wines.

Arneis Piedmont var. that is enjoying a revival.

Biancolella native of Ischia.

Blanc de Valdigne source in Valle d'Aosta of Blanc de Morgex, Blanc de La Salle.

Bombino Bianco main grape of Apulia's San Severo *bianco*; in Abruzzi, known as Trebbiano d'Abruzzo.

Bosco in Liguria the main ingredient of Cinqueterre.

Carricante main Etna white.

Catarratto widely grown in W Sicily; used in Marsala, Bianco d'Alcamo, etc.

Chardonnay grown in Trentino-Alto Adige, Veneto and Friuli.

Cortese used in S Piedmont's finest whites; found also in Lombardy's Oltrepò Pavese.

Fiano in Campania makes Fiano di Avellino.

Forastera partners Biancolella in Ischia *bianco*.

Garganega main grape of Soave.

Greco Campania's best white.

Grillo figures, usually with Catarratto, in Marsala.

Inzolia used in Sicilian whites, inc. Marsala and Corvo *bianco*.

Malvasia common for both dry and sweet wines, esp. in Latium (for Frascati, etc.).

Moscato widespread in sparkling wines (e.g. Asti Spumante) and dessert wines (e.g. the Moscatos of Sicily).

Müller-Thurgau increasing in Friuli, Trentino-Alto Adige.

Nuragus ancient Sardinian grape.

Picolit Friuli source of Italy's most expensive dessert wine.

Pigato grown only in SW Liguria; makes good table wines.

Pinot Bianco Burgundy's Pinot Blanc, grown all over N Italy. Weissburgunder in Alto Adige.

Prosecco prominent in Veneto, mainly for sparkling wines.

Rheinriesling *see* Riesling Renano.

Riesling Italico not a true Riesling, probably native to NE Italy. Used in DOCs.

Riesling Renano the Rhine Riesling, superior to Riesling Italico.

Sauvignon grown in parts of NE Italy for DOC varietals.

Tocai Friulano used for DOC whites in Lombardy and Veneto as well as in its native Friuli.

Traminer native of Alto Adige.

Trebbiano d'Abruzzo *see* Bombino Bianco.

Verdeca Apulian grape used in southern DOC whites.

Verdicchio main light grape of the Marches.

Verduzzo Friulian var. used also in the Veneto for both dry and dessert wines.

Vermentino source of DOC white in Sardinia and good table wines in Liguria.

Vernaccia di Oristano in Sardinia makes a sherry-like dessert wine.

Vernaccia di San Gimignano ancient Tuscany var., wine of the same name.

GERMANY

The international reputation of German wine for a unique effect of flowery elegance is based on one grape alone: the Riesling. But the widespread use of the Riesling as we know it is probably no more than two or three hundred years old. Germany has several old varieties of local importance which continue to hold their own. More significantly, her vine breeders have been struggling for a century to produce a new vine that offers Riesling quality without its inherent disadvantage – ripening so late in the autumn that every vintage is a cliffhanger. The centenary of the first important Riesling cross (with Silvaner) was celebrated in 1982. The past 100 years have seen its fruit, the Müller-Thurgau,

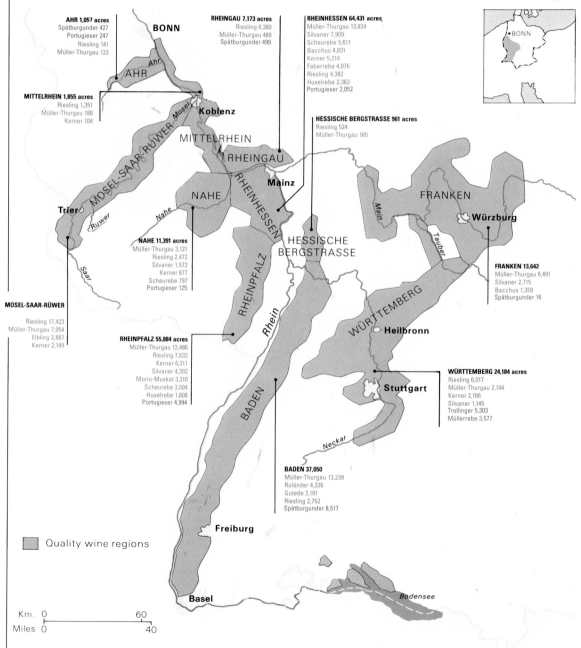

AHR 1,057 acres
Spätburgunder 427
Portugieser 247
Riesling 141
Müller-Thurgau 123

RHEINGAU 7,173 acres
Riesling 6,380
Müller-Thurgau 489
Spätburgunder 499

RHEINHESSEN 64,431 acres
Müller-Thurgau 13,834
Silvaner 7,909
Scheurebe 5,611
Bacchus 4,831
Kerner 5,214
Faberrebe 4,076
Riesling 4,382
Huxelrebe 2,363
Portugieser 2,052

MITTELRHEIN 1,855 acres
Riesling 1,351
Müller-Thurgau 188
Kerner 104

HESSISCHE BERGSTRASSE 961 acres
Riesling 524
Müller-Thurgau 165

NAHE 11,391 acres
Müller-Thurgau 3,121
Riesling 2,472
Silvaner 1,572
Kerner 877
Scheurebe 797
Portugieser 125

FRANKEN 13,642
Müller-Thurgau 6,491
Silvaner 2,715
Bacchus 1,359
Spätburgunder 16

MOSEL-SAAR-RÜWER
Riesling 17,423
Müller-Thurgau 7,054
Elbling 2,887
Kerner 2,149

RHEINPFALZ 55,884 acres
Müller-Thurgau 12,486
Riesling 7,632
Kerner 6,311
Silvaner 4,392
Morio-Muskat 3,310
Scheurebe 3,504
Huxelrebe 1,808
Portugieser 4,994

WÜRTTEMBERG 24,184 acres
Riesling 6,017
Müller-Thurgau 2,144
Kerner 2,166
Silvaner 1,145
Trollinger 5,303
Müllerrebe 3,577

BADEN 37,050
Müller-Thurgau 13,239
Ruländer 4,336
Gutede 3,191
Riesling 2,752
Spätburgunder 8,517

Quality wine regions

Km. 0 — 60
Miles 0 — 40

become Germany's most popular grape, with 62,500 acres planted. (Riesling is an easy second, with 48,500 acres.)

Yet none of the new varieties, not even the Müller-Thurgau, has supplanted Riesling in the best and warmest vineyards. None has achieved more than either a sketch or a caricature of its brilliant balance and finesse. Nor have any survived such ultimate tests of hardiness as January 1979, when the temperature dropped by 40 degrees, to $-20°F$ ($-29°C$), in 24 hours. Thousands of vines were killed. Riesling survived.

Eighty per cent of the German vineyard is white. Of the 12 per cent that is red, Spätburgunder (Pinot Noir) is marginally more widely planted than the inferior Portugieser, and twice as common as Trollinger. The map shows the acreages of the most widely planted varieties, white and red, region by region, together with the total vineyard area under cultivation for each region.

GRAPE VARIETIES

Bacchus a new early-ripening cross of (Silvaner × Riesling) × Müller-Thurgau. Spicy but rather soft wines, best as Ausleses, frequently used as *Süssreserve*.

Ehrenfelser (Riesling × Silvaner). A good new cross, between Müller-Thurgau and Riesling in quality.

Elbling once the chief grape of the Mosel, now only grown high upriver. Neutral and acidic but clean and good in sparkling wine.

Faber Weissburgunder × Müller-Thurgau, with a certain following in Rheinhessen and the Nahe.

Gewürztraminer *see* p18.

Gutedel south Baden name for the Chasselas, or Swiss Fendant. Light, refreshing but short-lived wine.

Huxelrebe (Gutedel × Courtillier musqué). A prolific new variety, very aromatic, with good sugar and acidity. Popular in Rheinhessen.

Morio-Muskat 6,500 acres. It is hard to believe that this early-ripening cross of Silvaner and Weissburgunder has no Muscat blood. The wine it makes in Rheinpfalz and Rheinhessen is good but often too blatant and best blended with something more neutral (e.g. Müller-Thurgau).

Optima (Silvaner × Riesling × Müller-Thurgau). An improvement on Bacchus, particularly in Rheinpfalz. Delicately spicy.

Ortega (Müller-Thurgau × Siegerrebe). Very early ripening, aromatic and spicy with good balance. On trial on the Mosel and in Franken.

Perle (Gewürztraminer × Müller-Thurgau). A very aromatic new cross under trial in Franken.

Reichensteiner Müller-Thurgau × (Madeleine angevine × Calabreser Fröhlich). A Euro-cross, slightly better for both sugar and acid than Müller-Thurgau.

Riesling *see* p18.

Scheurebe the second cross (Riesling × Silvaner) to become celebrated, now well established (Rheinhessen, Rheinpfalz) for highly aromatic, often unsubtle wine. At its best when sweet.

Silvaner a late ripener like the Riesling, also badly affected by drought in light or thin soils, steadily giving ground to Müller-Thurgau and others. Scarcely noble, but at its best (in Franken and Rheinhessen) the true yeoman; blunt, trustworthy, with unsuspected depths.

Weissburgunder (Pinot Blanc) makes good fresh full-bodied wine in Baden.

Kerner
The most successful of the new crosses (Riesling × Trollinger), an early-ripening understudy for Riesling, which it superficially resembles in liveliness and balance. A Muscat aroma betrays it.

Müller-Thurgau
Germany's most widely grown grape is the elder brother of many compromises between the ultimate quality of Riesling and such mundane matters as early ripening and heavy crops.

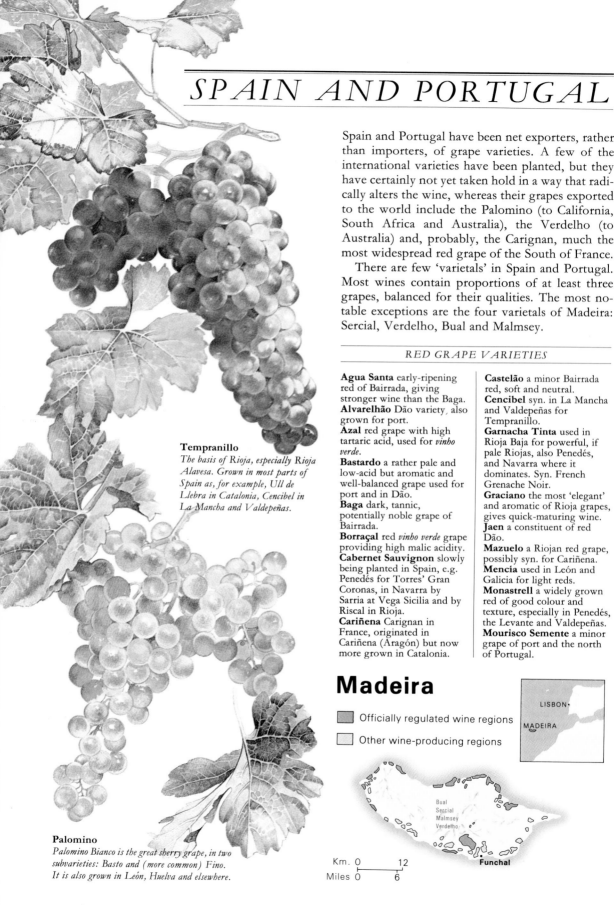

SPAIN AND PORTUGAL

Spain and Portugal have been net exporters, rather than importers, of grape varieties. A few of the international varieties have been planted, but they have certainly not yet taken hold in a way that radically alters the wine, whereas their grapes exported to the world include the Palomino (to California, South Africa and Australia), the Verdelho (to Australia) and, probably, the Carignan, much the most widespread red grape of the South of France.

There are few 'varietals' in Spain and Portugal. Most wines contain proportions of at least three grapes, balanced for their qualities. The most notable exceptions are the four varietals of Madeira: Sercial, Verdelho, Bual and Malmsey.

RED GRAPE VARIETIES

Agua Santa early-ripening red of Bairrada, giving stronger wine than the Baga.
Alvarelhão Dão variety, also grown for port.
Azal red grape with high tartaric acid, used for *vinho verde*.
Bastardo a rather pale and low-acid but aromatic and well-balanced grape used for port and in Dão.
Baga dark, tannic, potentially noble grape of Bairrada.
Borraçal red *vinho verde* grape providing high malic acidity.
Cabernet Sauvignon slowly being planted in Spain, e.g. Penedés for Torres' Gran Coronas, in Navarra by Sarria at Vega Sicilia and by Riscal in Rioja.
Cariñena Carignan in France, originated in Cariñena (Aragón) but now more grown in Catalonia.

Castelão a minor Bairrada red, soft and neutral.
Cencibel syn. in La Mancha and Valdepeñas for Tempranillo.
Garnacha Tinta used in Rioja Baja for powerful, if pale Riojas, also Penedés, and Navarra where it dominates. Syn. French Grenache Noir.
Graciano the most 'elegant' and aromatic of Rioja grapes, gives quick-maturing wine.
Jaen a constituent of red Dão.
Mazuelo a Riojan red grape, possibly syn. for Cariñena.
Mencía used in León and Galicia for light reds.
Monastrell a widely grown red of good colour and texture, especially in Penedés, the Levante and Valdepeñas.
Mourisco Semente a minor grape of port and the north of Portugal.

Tempranillo
The basis of Rioja, especially Rioja Alavesa. Grown in most parts of Spain as, for example, Ull de Llebra in Catalonia, Cencibel in La Mancha and Valdepeñas.

Palomino
Palomino Bianco is the great sherry grape, in two subvarieties: Basto and (more common) Fino. It is also grown in León, Huelva and elsewhere.

Madeira

LISBON

MADEIRA

■ Officially regulated wine regions

□ Other wine-producing regions

Bual
Sercial
Malmsey
Verdelho

Funchal

Km. 0   12
Miles 0   6

Pinot Noir Torres grows Pinot for his red Santa Digna. Also found in Navarra.
Ramisco the tannic, blue-black secret of Colares. Needs very long ageing.
Samsó Penedés variety.
Souzão deeply coloured and excellent port grape.
Tinto Aragonés a form of Garnacha Tinta; one of the grapes of Vega Sicilia.

Tinta Pinheira minor Bairrada variety; pale, low acid but alcoholic.
Tintorera one of the Valdepeñas grapes.
Touriga Nacional big-yielding port variety, also used in Dão.
Ull de Llebre Penedés synonym for Tempranillo.
Vinhão *vinho verde* red grown for its relatively high alcohol.

sharper Arinto.
Bual sweet Madeira grape with luscious flavours, also used in Carcavelos and Alentejo.
Chardonnay only experimentally grown in Spain, e.g. by Torres.
Gouveio minor white-port variety.
Lairén (alias Airén) the main white grape of Valdepeñas and La Mancha.
Listan syn. of Palomino.
Macabeo syn. in Catalonia of Viura. Used for sparkling wines.
Malvasía important white grape in port, Rioja, Navarra, Catalonia and the Canary Islands.
Maria Gomes the principal white grape of Bairrada.
Moscatel widespread sweet

wine grape.
Pansa grown in Alella. Syn. of Xarel-lo of Penedés.
Parellada used in Penedés for delicately fruity whites and sparklers.
Pedro Ximénez grown for blending in Jerez, Málaga, and the principal in Montilla: dried, it adds intense sweetness and colour.
Traminer used (with Moscatel) by Torres for Viña Esmeralda.
Verdelho white Dão variety, better known in Madeira.
Viura the principal grape of white Rioja, also Navarra. Alias Macabeo.
Xarel-lo Catalan grape, important in Penedés.
Zalema main variety in *vino generoso* of Huelva, being replaced by Palomino.

WHITE GRAPE VARIETIES

Airén *see* Lairén.
Albariño the best Galician variety for clean, dry, often *pétillant* whites, also grown in Portugal for *vinho verde*.
Albillo used, with red grapes, in Vega Sicilia.
Arinto used for white Dão

and Bairrada and to make the rare, dry Bucelas and sweet Carcavelos.
Barcelos recommended white Dão variety.
Bical fragrant and fine Bairrada white, complementary to the

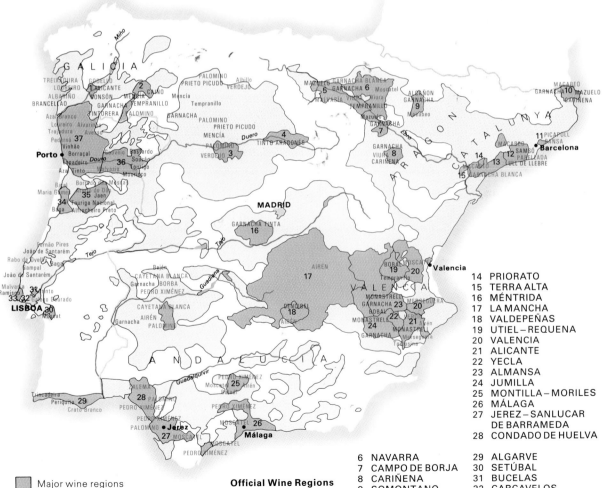

14	PRIORATO
15	TERRA ALTA
16	MÉNTRIDA
17	LA MANCHA
18	VALDEPEÑAS
19	UTIEL–REQUENA
20	VALENCIA
21	ALICANTE
22	YECLA
23	ALMANSA
24	JUMILLA
25	MONTILLA–MORILES
26	MÁLAGA
27	JEREZ–SANLUCAR DE BARRAMEDA
28	CONDADO DE HUELVA

6	NAVARRA	29	ALGARVE
7	CAMPO DE BORJA	30	SETÚBAL
8	CARIÑENA	31	BUCELAS
9	SOMONTANO	32	CARCAVELOS
10	AMPURDÁN–COSTA BRAVA	33	COLARES
11	ALELLA	34	BAIRRADA
12	PENEDES	35	DÃO
13	TARRAGONA	36	DOURO
		37	VINHO VERDE

■ Major wine regions

□ Other wine-producing regions

Km. 0 — 200
Miles 0 — 100

Official Wine Regions
1 RIBEIRO
2 VALDEORRAS
3 RUEDA
4 RIBERA DEL DUERO
5 RIOJA

Zinfandel
The one (good) grape that is California's own – a generous giver of versatile, fruity, sometimes spicy (but sometimes metallic) wine in any style from Beaujolais to port. It may be the Primitivo from the south of Italy.

Emerald Riesling
New California-bred varieties are designed to make refreshing wines in a hot climate. Emerald Riesling is one of the best known, with attractively lively flavours.

CALIFORNIA

California's vigorous and uninhibited experimentation with grape varieties in her multifarious microclimates has already proved that Cabernet Sauvignon and Chardonnay can be grown to perfection. It is now rapidly demonstrating that Riesling, Pinot Noir and Gewürztraminer can be ideally accommodated. Petite Sirah and Semillon have also made noble wine, though so far only in very small quantities.

From the 1930s on, the School of Viticulture of the University of California at Davis has insisted that varieties must be carefully matched to microclimates, and has surveyed the State thoroughly to establish its five climate regions (plotted opposite and described on page 413). The cooler climate zones where the finest varieties for table wines develop a good balance of acidity with sugar are all in the coastal counties mapped here.

The State is now in the process of matching supply and demand of the best grapes while searching for ideal vineyards, often in places where no vine has grown before. While the potential of the well-established counties of Napa, Alameda, Santa Clara and, to some extent, Santa Cruz and Sonoma is well known, recent bold plantings in Monterey, San Luis Obispo, Santa Barbara, Mendocino and elsewhere are only beginning to show their worth.

The diagrams opposite – each crate of grapes represents up to 500 acres harvested – show how dynamic this process was in the decade 1975 to 1985, for each of the four top-quality varieties. On pages 418 and 419 the State-wide increase of other varieties are given for the whole decade.

To speculate about further developments is not so easy, but it is unlikely that growers will specialize as narrowly as they do in Europe. There is an insurance policy against both market changes and untimely storms in having a portfolio of varieties. And the market changes in California can be swift. A prediliction for white wine, especially Chardonnay, was apparent in the early 1980s. This was superceded to some extent by a fashion for 'blush' wines from red grapes. Field-grafting is the growers' response. It would be desirable to see trials of some of the many varieties that California has not yet planted on any worthwhile scale. The true Syrah of the Rhône, for example, is almost unknown, and there are a dozen others that should be tried.

Ultimately perhaps California will develop away from 'varietal' wines to wholly indigenous styles arrived at with blends untried in Europe. Creative wine-making like this should be right up her street.

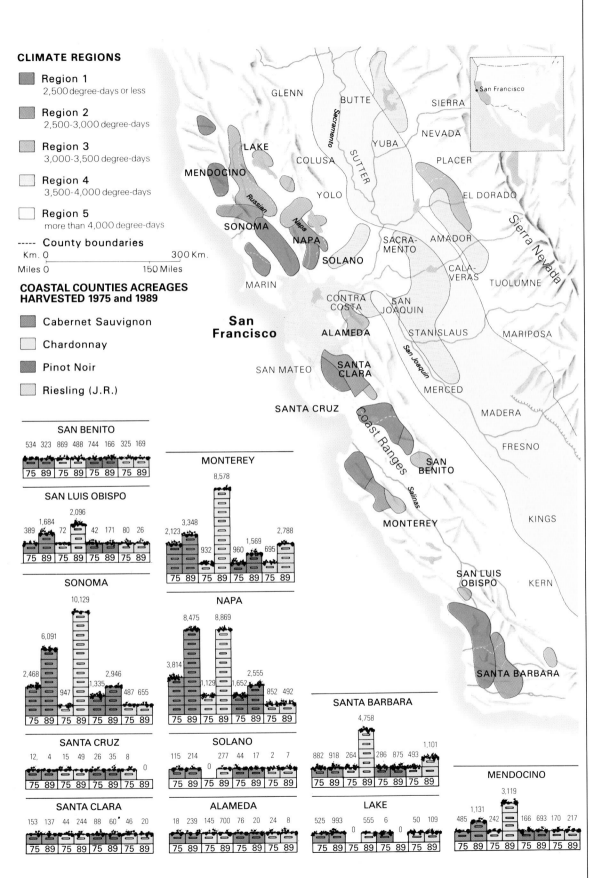

CLIMATE REGIONS

Region 1
2,500 degree-days or less

Region 2
2,500-3,000 degree-days

Region 3
3,000-3,500 degree-days

Region 4
3,500-4,000 degree-days

Region 5
more than 4,000 degree-days

----- County boundaries

Km. 0   300 Km.
Miles 0   150 Miles

COASTAL COUNTIES ACREAGES HARVESTED 1975 and 1989

Cabernet Sauvignon

Chardonnay

Pinot Noir

Riesling (J.R.)

SAN BENITO
534 323 869 488 744 166 325 169
75 89 75 89 75 89 75 89

SAN LUIS OBISPO
        2,096
   1,684
389   72   42 171 80 26
75 89 75 89 75 89 75 89

SONOMA
        10,129
   6,091
2,468   2,946
      947 1,335 487 655
75 89 75 89 75 89 75 89

SANTA CRUZ
12 4 15 49 26 35 8 0
75 89 75 89 75 89 75 89

SANTA CLARA
153 137 44 244 88 60 46 20
75 89 75 89 75 89 75 89

MONTEREY
        8,578
3,348
2,123   960 1,569 2,788
      932   695
75 89 75 89 75 89 75 89

NAPA
8,475 8,869
3,814   2,555
      1,129 1,652 852 492
75 89 75 89 75 89 75 89

SOLANO
115 214 277 44 17 2 7
      0
75 89 75 89 75 89 75 89

ALAMEDA
18 239 145 700 76 20 24 8
75 89 75 89 75 89 75 89

SANTA BARBARA
        4,758
              1,101
882 918 264 286 875 493
75 89 75 89 75 89 75 89

LAKE
525 993 555 6 50 109
      0   0
75 89 75 89 75 89 75 89

MENDOCINO
        3,119
   1,131
485   242 166 693 170 217
75 89 75 89 75 89 75 89

SOUTHEAST EUROPE

The grape varieties of southeast Europe are as old as those of the west. The Romans colonized the Danube at the same time as the Rhine. Under the Austro–Hungarian Empire the only wines to reach international fame were those of Hungary, led by Tokay. The local grapes, therefore, evolved slowly on their own course making their own sort of spicy, often sweetish whites and dry tannic reds.

The eastern fringes of the Alps in Slovenia, Austria and north into Bohemia (Czechoslovakia) are essentially white wine country, dominated by their local low-key form of the Riesling (variously known as Italian, Welsch, Olasz or Laski), and Austria by its sappy, vigorous Grüner Veltliner. Hungary is most prolific in native white grapes of strength and style, led by the Furmint of Tokay. Its red, the Kadarka, is widespread in the Balkans, more recently joined by the Pinot Noir (Nágyburgundi) and Gamay (Kékfrankos). Warmer climates near the Adriatic and Black Seas have favoured reds and sweet whites. The last 20 years, however, have seen an invasion of classics from the west.

Wine-growing areas

FROM GRAPES TO WINE

Controlling Yield

Higher quantity means lower quality. Acceptance of this golden rule is built into the appellation regulations of France, Italy and most other wine-producing nations. In France the highest-quality areas limit the *rendement*, or yield, to 35 hectolitres a hectare (about two tons an acre) or even less. *Vins de pays* are allowed to produce up to 80 hectolitres or even more. In Italy the limits are expressed in a similar way, as so many quintals (100 kg) of grapes a hectare, with a limit on the amount of juice that may be extracted from each quintal.

California as yet has no regulations in this regard – which, in view of its *laissez-faire* philosophy, is not surprising. It is surprising, however, that Germany permits such enormous crops. In 1900 the average yield there was 25 hectolitres a hectare; 100 hectolitres a hectare is now normal in Germany. Modern German wine-making deliberately concentrates on lightness and transparency of flavour. It lays all the emphasis on 'balance' between sweetness and fruity acidity. As a result most of its wines lack concentration and the ability to improve from more than a few years in bottle. Today it is more realistic to rewrite the golden rule to read 'higher quantity means lighter, more rapidly maturing wine' – the style which is most in demand.

A recent rebellion by top German growers has seen voluntary restraint on yields, bringing Germany once more into line with the other quality wine zones. Even so, 55–60 hl/ha is considered 'low' in the Mosel.

Mechanical Harvesting

A machine for picking grapes, saving the stiff backs (and high wages) of the tens of thousands who turn out to the harvest each year, only became a reality in the 1960s (in New York State, picking Concord grapes). By the 1980s, machines harvested one third of all America's wine grapes. The mechanical harvester is an inevitable advance. In France it has gained wide acceptance in big vineyards, though some quality areas still resist.

The machine works by straddling the vine row and violently shaking the trunks, while slapping at the extremities of the vine with flexible paddles or striker bars. The grapes fall on to a conveyor belt, which carries them from near ground level to a chute above the vine tops. Here they pass in front of a fan which blows away any loose leaves and are shot into a hopper towed by a tractor in the next alley between the vines. In many cases the hopper leads straight to a crusher and the crusher to a closed tank, so that the grapes leave the vineyard already crushed, sheltered from sunlight and insects and dosed with sulphur dioxide to prevent oxidation.

The harvester has many advantages. It can operate at night, when the grapes are cool. It needs only two operators. Whereas a traditional team may have to start while some grapes are still unripe, and finish when some are overripe, the machine works fast enough to pick a whole vineyard at ideal maturity. The harvesting rate in California is up to 150 tons (or up to about 40 acres) a day.

Disadvantages include the need for especially robust trellising, the loss of perhaps ten per cent of the crop and the slight risk of including leaves in the crush. The machines may not yet be fully reliable, and there is a shortage of skilled operators.

Botrytis Infection

The benevolent aspect of the fungus mould *Boyrytis cinerea* as the 'noble rot' which produces great sweet wines receives so much publicity that its malevolent appearance in the vineyard at the wrong time can be forgotten. In some regions (particularly in Germany) its prevalence has made it the most serious and widespread disease the grower has to deal with. The more fertile the vineyard and luxuriant the vine, the more likely it is to strike at the unripe or (most vulnerable) semi-ripe grapes and rot the bunch. It starts by attacking grapes punctured by insects or 'grape worm': controlling the bugs is therefore the most effective protection. Only when the sugar content in the grapes has reached about 70° Oechsle or 17° Brix (enough to make wine of about 9° natural alcohol) does evil rot become noble rot. For a description of noble rot *see* page 80 (Château d'Yquem).

The occurrence and exploitation of noble rot in the vineyards of California has been one of the most noteworthy innovations of recent years. California has coined the inelegant word 'botrytized' (with the stress on the 'bot') to mean infected with *Botrytis cinerea* – of the noble variety.

Sugar and Acid Levels

The crucial decision of when to pick the grapes depends on the measurement of their sugar and acid contents. As they ripen sugar content increases and acid decreases. For each type of wine there is an ideal moment when the ratio is just right.

Ripening starts at the moment called *véraison*, when the grape, which has been growing slowly by cell division, still hard and bright green, begins to grow rapidly by the enlargement of each cell. This is when red grapes begin to change colour.

Sugar content is usually measured with a hand-held 'refractometer'. A drop of juice is held between two prisms. Light passing through it bends at a different angle according to its sugar content: the angle is read off on a scale calibrated as degrees Brix, Oechsle or Baumé, the American, German and French systems respectively for measuring ripeness.

In warm weather sugar content may increase by up to 0.4° Brix a day, while acidity drops by as much as 0.15°. 'Ripe' grapes vary between about 18° and 26° Brix (i.e. with a potential alcohol level of 9.3 to 14 per cent by volume). Different levels of acidity are considered ideal for different styles of wine. In Germany acid levels as high as 0.9 per cent would be commendable for a wine of 11.3 per cent potential alcohol (90° Oechsle). In France or California the recommended acid level for grapes with the same sugar content would be approximately 0.7 per cent for white wine and slightly lower for red.

The third variable taken into account is the pH of the juice. This is a measure of the strength, rather than volume, of its acidity. The lower the figure, the sharper the juice. Normal pH in wine is in the range 2.8 to 3.8. Low pH readings are desirable for stability and (in red wines) good colour.

A leading California wine maker, Walter Schug, uses the pH reading as his signal to pick. 'A sharp rise in pH, usually upon reaching 3.25 or over, means that the fruit should be picked regardless of the degree Brix.'

MAKING WINE

Handling the Fruit

A good wine maker will not accept grapes that have been badly damaged on the way from the vineyard, or with a high proportion of mouldy bunches or what the Californians call MOG (matter other than grapes, e.g. leaves, stones and soil). For wine-making at the highest standard the bunches are picked over by hand – '*triage*' – and rotten grapes thrown out. Where large quantities are involved a degree of imperfection has to be accepted.

Several regions of Europe specify the size and design of container that must be used for bringing in the grapes. The object here is to prevent the weight of large quantities from crushing the grapes at the bottom before they reach the cellar. The huge 'gondolas' often used for transporting grapes in California, often under a hot sun, have the distinct drawback that many of the grapes at the bottom will be broken, and macerating in juice, long before they even reach the carefully controlled hygienic conditions of the winery.

SO_2

The first step in all wine-making procedures is the addition of a small dose of sulphur dioxide to the crushed grapes, or must. Nothing has supplanted this universal antiseptic of the wine maker in protecting the must from premature or wild fermentation, and both must and wine from oxidation, though some advanced wine makers use very little and strive to use none – putting instead physical barriers (e.g. inert gases) between the juice or wine and the oxygen in the atmosphere.

The amount of SO_2 allowed is regulated by law. Wine with too much has a sharp brimstone smell and leaves a burning feeling in the throat – a common occurrence in the past, particularly in semi-sweet wines where the sulphur was used to prevent refermentation in the bottle. Sterile filters have now eliminated the need for this and the consumer should be unaware that wine's old preservative is still used at all. Some people may suffer ill-effects from SO_2 in wine or anything else: thus the US regulation that labels should state 'contains sulfites'.

White-Wine – Immediate Pressing or 'Skin-contact'

Fashionably light, fresh and fruity white wines are made by pressing the grapes as soon as possible after picking. The object is to prevent the juice from picking up any flavours or 'extract' from the skin. The grapes are gently crushed (*foulé*) just hard enough to break their skins. This 'pomace' is then loaded directly into the press. In some wineries looking for the greatest freshness, the juice or even the grapes may be chilled.

Many bigger wineries now use a 'dejuicer' between the crusher and the press. This may consist of a mesh screen, sometimes in the form of a conveyor belt, through which the 'free' juice falls. A dejuicer reduces the number of times the press has to be laboriously filled and emptied, but it also increases the chance of oxidation of the juice. A form of dejuicer that avoids oxidation is a stainless steel tank with a central cylinder formed of a mesh screen. The crushed pomace is loaded into the space around this cylinder and carbon dioxide is pumped under pressure into the headspace. The free juice is gently forced to drain out via the central cylinder, leaving relatively little pomace to go into the press. Up to 70 per cent can be free-run juice, leaving only

30 per cent to be extracted by pressing.

Fuller and more robust wines with more flavour, and tannins to preserve them while they age, are made by holding the skins in contact with the juice in a tank for up to 24 hours after crushing. This maceration (at low temperature, before fermentation starts) extracts some of the elements that are present in the skins but not the juice. The pomace is then dejuiced and pressed as usual. Some old-fashioned wine makers might go even further and ferment white wines with their skins, like red wines – but the resulting wine would be too 'heavy' for today's taste.

White Wine: Stems or No Stems
White grapes are usually pressed complete with their stems. The reason is that unfermented grape flesh and juice is full of pectins and sugar, slippery and sticky. The stems make the operation of the press easier, particularly when it comes to breaking up the 'cake', to press a second time. The press should not be used at a high enough pressure to squeeze any bitter juice out of stems or pips.

Types of Press
There is a wide choice of types of press, ranging from the old-fashioned vertical model, in which a plate is forced down on to the pomace contained in a cylindrical cage of vertical slots, to the mass-production continuous 'Coq' press. The first is the most labour intensive but still produces the clearest juice; the second is very cheap and easy to run but cannot make better than medium-grade wine. Most good wineries choose either a Vaslin horizontal basket press, which works on a principle similar to the old vertical press, squeezing the pomace by means of plates which are brought together by a central screw, or a Willmes 'bladder' or 'membrane' press. A bladder press contains a sausage-shaped rubber balloon which when inflated squeezes the pomace against the surrounding fine grille. Both are 'batch' presses, meaning that they have to be filled and emptied anew for each batch of pomace, whereas the continuous press spews forth an unending stream of juice below and 'cake' at the far end.

White Wine – Cold Fermentation
The most revolutionary invention in modern wine-making is controlled-temperature fermentation, particularly for white wines, which in warm climates used to be flat, low in acid and lack-lustre. What used to be achieved naturally by using small barrels in the cold cellars of Europe is now practised industrially in California, Australia and elsewhere by chilling the contents of often colossal stainless steel vats. Most of such vats are double-skinned or 'jacketed' with a layer of glycol or ammonia as the cooling agent between the skins. Another cooling technique is to dribble cold water continuously down the outside surface. A second-best method is to circulate the wine through a heat exchanger (or a coil submerged in cold water) outside the vat.

Each wine maker has his own idea about the ideal temperature for fermentation. Long, cool fermentation is reputedly good for fruity flavours, though when practised to extremes on certain grapes, particularly nonaromatic sorts, it seems to leave its mark on the wine as a 'pear-drop' or acetaldehyde smell. A number of modern Italian white wines, and even occasionally red ones, are spoilt by over-enthusiastic refrigeration. In Germany, to the contrary, very cold fermentation has gone out of fashion. The normal temperatures for white-wine fermentation in California are between 8° and 15°C (46°–59°F). In France 18°C (64°F) is considered cold. If the temperature is forced down too far the fermentation will 'stick' and the yeasts cease to function. It can be difficult to start again and the wine will almost certainly suffer in the process.

A completely different approach is used to make 'big', richer, smoother and more heavy-bodied wines from Chardonnay and sometimes Sauvignon Blanc. They are fermented at between 15° and 20°C (59°–68°F), or in barrels even as high as 25°C (77°F). California Chardonnay in this style is made in exactly the same way as white burgundy (*see* page 109).

White Wine – Clarifying the Juice
Modern presses are more efficient than old models but they tend to produce juice with a higher proportion of suspended solids (pieces of grape skins, flesh, pips or dirt). Fermentation of white wine with these solids tends to produce bitterness, so the juice must be cleaned first. This can be done by holding it for a day or more in a 'settling' tank, allowing particles to sink to the bottom, by filtering through a powerful 'vacuum' filter, or (the fastest method) by use of a centrifuge pump, which uses centrifugal force to throw out all foreign bodies. Over-centrifuged wine can be stripped of desirable as well as undesirable constituents: great care is needed.

White Wine – Adjusting Acidity
Either de- or re-acidification of white-wine must may be necessary, depending on the ripeness of the crop. Overacid juice is de-acidified by adding calcium carbonate (chalk) to remove tartaric acid, or a substance called Acidex, which removes malic acid as well by 'double-salt precipitation'. In Germany

the addition of sugar and (up to 15 per cent) water to wines of Qualitätswein level and below naturally lowers the proportion of acidity. In France chaptalization with dry sugar (permitted in the centre and north) has the same effect to a lesser degree. In the south of France, on the other hand, only concentrated must, not sugar, is allowed for raising the alcoholic degree: it naturally raises the acid level at the same time.

In California and other warm countries where the usual problem is too little acid it is permitted to add one of the acids that naturally occur in grapes. Malic, citric and tartaric acid are all used. Tartaric is to be preferred since it has no detectable flavour and also helps towards tartrate stability (*see* Cold Stabilization). But it is more expensive.

Tanks and Vats

The unquestioned grandeur and nobility of traditional fermenting vats of oak (or sometimes such woods as chestnut, acacia or redwood) is accompanied by many disadvantages. Most important are the problems of disinfecting them and keeping them watertight between vintages.

Early in this century concrete began to replace them in newer and bigger wineries. It is strong, permanent and easy to clean. Moreover it can be made in any shape to fit odd corners and save space. Like wood, however, it is a bad conductor of heat. The only way to cool wine in a concrete vat is to pump it out through a cooling plant.

In modern wineries stainless steel is king. It is strong, inert, very easy to clean and simple to cool (conducting heat perfectly). A steel vat can even be moved with relative ease. Moreover it is versatile: the same tank can be used for fermentation and, later in the year, for storage, ageing or blending. Its high initial cost is thus quite quickly recouped.

To make good wine a winery must have ample capacity. It often happens that in an abundant vintage there is a shortage of space. Grapes cannot be stored so the only answer is to cut short the fermenting time of the early batches. With red wines this will mean shorter maceration on the skins and thus lighter wine. Well-designed modern wineries not only have plenty of tank space, they have tanks in a variety of sizes to avoid leaving small lots of wine in half-full containers or being obliged to mix them.

Yeasts

There are yeasts naturally present in every vineyard which will cause fermentation if they are allowed to. Some consider them part of the stamp, or personality, of their property and believe they help to give their wine its individuality. Many modern wineries, wanting to keep total control, take care to remove the natural yeast (by filtering or centrifuging), or at least to render it helpless with a strong dose of SO_2. Some even 'flash-pasteurize' the juice by heating it to 55°C (131°F) to kill off bacteria and inhibit the wild yeasts. They then proceed to inoculate the must with a cultured yeast of their choice which is known to multiply actively at the temperature they choose for fermentation. Some of the most popular yeasts in California go by the promising names of 'Montrachet', 'Champagne' and 'Steinberg'.

The secret is to start the fermentation with a generous amount of active yeast; once the whole vat is fermenting such problems as oxidation can temporarily be forgotten. The activity of yeast increases rapidly with rising temperature. For each additional degree Celsius, yeast transforms ten per cent more sugar into alcohol in a given time. The ceiling to this frantic activity occurs at about 30° to 35°C (86°–95°F) when the yeasts are overcome by heat. A 'run-away' fermentation can 'stick' at this temperature, just as most yeasts will not function below about 10°C (50°F).

Specialized use of flor yeast for producing sherry has greatly advanced in recent years. New methods have been found of producing the sherry effect much faster and more certainly than with the traditional naturally occurring layer of flor floating on the wine.

White Wines – Malolactic Fermentation

Secondary or malolactic fermentation (*see* Red Wine – Malolactic Fermentation) is less common with white wine then with red. It is sometimes encouraged, to reduce excess acidity in wines from cool climates (e.g. Chablis and other parts of Burgundy, the Loire, Switzerland, but less commonly in Germany). Its complex biological nature may help to add complexity to flavours. In regions where acidity tends to be low, such as California, malolactic fermentation in white wines is generally avoided.

White Wines – Residual Sugar

A completed natural fermentation makes a totally dry wine, all its sugar converted to alcohol. The only exceptions are wines made of grapes so sweet that either the alcohol level or the sugar, or both, prevents the yeasts from functioning.

To make light sweet wines, either the fermentation has to be artificially interrupted or sweet juice has to be blended with dry wine. The former was the old way. It needed a strong dose of SO_2 to stop the fermentation, and more in the bottle to prevent it starting again. The invention of filters fine enough to remove all yeasts, and means of bottling in conditions of complete sterility, now solve the sulphur problem. But wine makers today generally prefer the second method: blending with 'sweet reserve'. This is the standard procedure for producing the sweet and semi-sweet wines of Germany up to Auslese level and is increasingly used elsewhere.

The method used is to sterilize a portion of the juice instead of fermenting it. (It can be stored in a deepfreeze as a block of ice.) The majority of the wine is made in the normal way, fermented until no sugar is left. The 'sweet reserve' (in German *Süssreserve*) is then added to taste and the blend bottled under sterile conditions. The addition of unfermented juice naturally lowers the alcohol content of the wine.

Some of the best wine makers prefer to maintain a small degree of unfermented ('residual') sugar in certain wines (California Rieslings and Gewürztraminers, for example) by cooling the vat to stop fermentation at the appropriate moment, then using a centrifuge and/or fine filtering to remove the yeasts and sterilize the wine.

White Wine – After Fermentation
After white wine has fermented it must be clarified. The traditional method was to allow it to settle and then rack it off its lees (largely of dead yeast cells). When Muscadet is bottled *sur lie* this is exactly what is happening. Modern wineries, however, tend to use a centrifuge or a filter for this clarification, too, if necessary with the additional precaution of fining with a powdery clay (from Wyoming) called bentonite, which removes excess proteins, potential causes of later trouble in the form of cloudy wine. Bentonite fining is also sometimes used on the must before fermentation.

White wines not intended for ageing (i.e. most light commercial wines) then need only to be stabilized and filtered before they can be bottled and distributed.

White Wine – Cold Stabilization
The tartaric acid which is a vital ingredient in the balance and flavour of all wines has an unfortunate habit of forming crystals in combination with either potassium (quite big sugary grains) or calcium (finer and whiter powdery crystals). In former times wine was kept for several years in cool cellars and these crystals formed a hard deposit on the walls of their casks, known in Germany as '*Weinstein*' – 'wine stone'. With faster modern methods, most wineries consider it essential to prevent the crystals forming after the wine is bottled – which they will unless something is done about it. Although the crystals have no flavour at all and are totally natural and harmless, there are always ignorant and querulous

customers who will send back a bottle with any sign of deposit.

Unfortunately it is a costly business to remove the risk of tartrate crystals. The simplest way is to chill the wine to just above freezing point in a tank for several days. The process is accelerated by 'seeding' with added tartrate crystals to act as nuclei for more crystals to form. More efficient ways of achieving this strictly unnecessary object will keep research chemists busy for years to come.

Red Wine – Stems or No Stems
Each red-wine maker has his own view about whether the grape stems should be included, wholly or in part – and it changes with the vintage. In Beaujolais and the Rhône the stems are always included, in Burgundy usually a proportion, in Bordeaux few or none, in Chinon on the Loire the stems are left on the vine. Opinions are equally divided in other countries, but in California stems are usually excluded.

The argument for leaving the stems out is that they add astringency, lower the alcohol content, reduce the colour and take up valuable space in vat. The argument for keeping some of them in is that they help the process of fermentation by aerating the mass, they lower the acidity and they make pressing easier.

Red Wine – Pumping Over
When a vat of red wine ferments the skins float to the surface, buoyed up by bubbles of carbon dioxide, which attach themselves to solid matter. The 'cap' (French, '*chapeau*', Spanish '*sombrero*') that they form contains all the essential colouring matter – and is prone to overheat and be attacked by bacteria. It is therefore essential to keep mixing the cap back into the liquid below. There are several methods.

In Bordeaux the cap is often pushed under by men with long poles. In Burgundy, with smaller vats, it is trodden under ('*pigeage*') by men, formerly naked, who jump into the vat. Another widespread method is to fit a grille below the filling level which holds the cap immersed ('*chapeau immergé*'). Mechanical 'plungers' attached to a crankshaft are also used. But the most widespread modern method is 'pumping over', taking wine by a hose from the bottom of the vat and spraying it over the cap, usually several times a day.

Several ingenious alternatives have been invented. The 'Rototank' is a closed horizontal cylinder which slowly rotates, continually mixing the liquids and solids inside. An automatic system developed in Portugal, where the traditional way of extracting the colour was night-long stomping by all the village lads to the sound of accordions, involves an ingenious gusher device activated by the build-up of carbon dioxide pressure in a sealed tank.

Red Wine – Heating the Must

One of the modern ways of achieving the goal of deep-coloured red wine without the astringency of tannins arising from long vatting is to boil the must before fermentation. It was a method apparently used centuries ago to darken the 'black' wine of Cahors. It is only recommended, however, for wines with a limited potential life span.

Red Wine – Pressing

By the time fermentation is finished, or nearly finished and merely simmering slightly, most (up to 85 per cent) of the red wine is separated from the solid matter and will run freely from the vat. This 'free run' or *vin de goutte* is siphoned out of the vat into either barrels or another tank. The remaining 'marc' is pressed.

Red wine is pressed in the same types of presses as white, but after fermentation the pulp and skins have partly disintegrated and offer less resistance.

Relatively gentle pressure will release very good quality *vin de presse*, which is richer in desirable extracts and flavours than the *vin de goutte*. It may need such treatment as fining to reduce astringency and remove solids, but in most cases it will be a positive addition and make better wine for longer keeping. Wine from a second, more vigorous, pressing will almost always be too astringent and be sold separately, or used in a cheap blend.

The Value of Barrels

Developments in California have drawn attention to what has long been known, but taken for granted, in France and elsewhere: that new barrels have a profound effect on the flavour of wine stored in them – and even more on wine fermented in them. California Chardonnays fermented in the same French oak as white burgundy can have an uncanny resemblance to its flavour.

Barrels were invented (probably by the Romans) of necessity as the most durable and transportable of containers, supplanting the amphora and the goat-skin in regions that could afford them. They have developed to their standard sizes and shapes over centuries of experience. The 200-odd-litre barrels of Bordeaux, Burgundy and Rioja are the most that one man can easily roll or two men carry – but they also happen to present the largest surface area of wood to wine of any practicable size.

The advantages of this contact lie partly in the very slow transfer of oxygen through the planks of the barrel, but mainly through the tannin and other substances that the wine dissolves from the wood itself. The most easily identified (by taste or smell) of these is vanillin, which has the flavour of vanilla. Oak tannin is useful in augmenting, and slightly varying the tannins naturally present in wine as preservatives. Other scents and flavours are harder to define, but can be well enough expressed as the 'smell of a carpenter's shop'.

Which wines benefit from this addition of extraneous flavours? Only those with strong characters and constitutions of their own. It would be disastrous to a fragile Moselle or a Beaujolais Nouveau. The 'bigger' the wine and the longer it is to be matured, the more oak it can take.

New barrels are extremely expensive. $470 is a typical 1990 price. The full impact of their oak flavour diminishes rapidly after the first two or three years' use, but there is a lively trade in secondhand barrels, particularly those that have contained great wines. Barrels can also be renewed to full pungency by shaving the wine-leached interior down to fresh wood.

Another way of achieving the complexity of oak flavour in wine is by blending in a fraction in which oak chips or shavings have been macerated to produce an intensely oak-flavoured brew. Mention of this method is considered shocking in winemaking circles, but it is practised, is very effective and entirely harmless.

A completely different role is played by the huge permanent oak barrels, *foudres* or *demi-muids* in French, *Fuders* or *Stücks* in German, which are common in southern France, Germany, Italy, Spain and eastern Europe. Their oak flavour has been minimized or completely neutralized by constant impregnation with wine, and often by a thick layer of tartrate crystals. Their value seems to lie in offering an ideal environment, with very gradual oxidation, for the maturing and slow stabilizing of wine. Before the advent of efficient sterile bottling, a big oak vat was simply the safest place for a grower to keep his stock – sometimes for years on end, topped up with fresh wine as necessary.

In California cooperage has become something of a fetish. Comparative tastings are held between the same wine aged in oak from different French forests; even from the same forest but different barrel makers. The names of Demptos and Nadalie of Bordeaux, of Taransaud and Séguin-Moreau of Cognac and François Frères and the Tonnelleries de Bourgogne of Burgundy are more familiar in the Napa Valley than in France. Current opinion seems to be that Limousin oak, faster growing with wider growth rings, has less flavour and is better for Chardonnay and Pinot Noir (which in California are only kept in oak one year or less); Nevers and Tronçais oak, slower-grown and offering more extract, is better for Cabernet, which spends two or even three years in barrel. American white-oak uncharred Bourbon barrels are also used. They offer less flavour and tannin (but a higher tannin/flavour ratio) – good for Cabernet and Zinfandel, less so for white wines. Baltic, Balkan and other oaks are also used and much has been written about their relative merits. Since there is no visual difference and a cooper's shop contains oak from many sources, one may well be sceptical about such fine distinctions in any case. Other factors such as the thickness of the staves, whether they have split or sawn, air dried or kiln dried, steamed or 'toasted', even whether the barrel is washed in hot water or cold can all start arguments among the initiated.

Red Wine – Carbonic Maceration

The technique of fermenting uncrushed grapes known as *macération carbonique* has been developed in France since 1935 by Professor Michel Flanzy and other. The method is described on page 150. It began to make a real impact in the early 1970s in dramatically improving the quality of the better Midi wines. It is now well established in France as the best way to produce fruity, 'supple', richly coloured reds for drinking young, but its acceptance has been surprisingly slow in other countries. It is particularly surprising that California has paid so little attention to it. Low acidity tends to make pure maceration wines short lived, which is inappropriate for the finest growths. But a proportion can be a valuable element in a blend with a tannic and/or acidic red.

Fining

The ancient technique of pouring whipped egg-whites, gelatin, isinglass (fish glue), blood or other coagulants into wine is still widely used both on must and finished wine, despite modern filters and centrifuges. Its object is to clean the liquid of the finest suspended solids, which are too light to sink. The 'fining', poured on to the surface, slowly sinks like a superfine screen, carrying any solids to the bottom. Certain finings such as bentonite (*see* White Wine – After Fermentation) are specific to certain undesirable constituents. 'Blue' fining (potassium ferrocyanide) removes excess iron from the wine.

Racking

Once the gross lees, or sediment, in a barrel or vat have sunk to the bottom, the wine is 'racked' off them simply by pouring the clear liquid from a tap above the level of the solids. In wines that are kept over a length of time in barrels, racking is repeated every few months as more solids are precipitated. If the wine is judged to need more oxygen, racking is done via an open basin; if not, it is done by a hose linking one barrel directly to another.

Red Wine – Malolactic Fermentation

Wine growers have always been aware of a fresh activity in their barrels of new wine in the spring following the vintage. Folklore put it down to a 'natural sympathy' between the wine and the rising sap in the vineyards. It seemed to be a further fermentation, but it happened in wine that had no sugar left to ferment.

In the last 50 years the science of microbiology has found the answer. It is a form of fermentation carried on by bacteria, not yeasts, which are feeding on malic (apple) acid in the wine and converting it to lactic (milk) acid, giving off carbon dioxide bubbles in the process. It has several results: a lowering of the quantity and of its sharpness (lactic acid is milder to taste than malic); increase of stability, and a less quantifiable smoothing and complicating of the wine's flavour. For almost all red wines, therefore, it is highly desirable, and wine makers take steps to make sure that it takes place.

In most cases a gentle raising of the temperature in the cellar to about 20°C (68°F) is sufficient. Sometimes it is necessary to import the right bacteria. Sometimes (this is considered very desirable) the malolactic fermentation can be encouraged to happen concurrently with the first (alcoholic) fermentation.

Blending for Complexity

Champagne, red and white Bordeaux, Rhône reds, Chianti, Rioja, port, are examples of wines made of a mixture of grapes. Burgundy, Barolo, sherry, German and Alsace wines are examples of one-grape wines. American varietal-consciousness has tended to put a premium on the simplistic idea that '100 per cent is best'. But recent research has shown that even among wines of humble quality a mixture of two is always better than the lesser of the two and generally better then either. This is taken to prove that 'complexity' is in itself a desirable quality in wine; that one variety can 'season' another as butter and salt do eggs.

There is a general trend in California, therefore, towards Bordeaux-style blending of Merlot with Cabernet and Semillon with Sauvignon Blanc. On the other hand no other grape has been shown to improve Pinot Noir, Chardonnay or Riesling. Added complexity in their already delicious flavours either comes with the help of barrel-ageing, in Riesling with 'noble-rot', or simply with years in bottle.

Filtration

The Seitz Company of Bad Kreuznach, Germany, has been the pioneer in the developing of ever finer and finer filters capable of removing almost everything, even the flavour, from wine if they are not used with discretion. Most filters consist of a series of 'pads' alternating with plates, through which the wine is forced under pressure. The degree of filtration depends on the pore size of the pads. At 0.65 microns they remove yeast, at 0.45 bacteria as well. To avoid having to change them frequently, wine is nearly always clarified by such other means as fining or centrifuging before filtration.

Some wine makers make a point of labelling their wine 'unfiltered'. They believe that it is worth running the risk of slight sediment for the sake of extra flavour. So do I.

Pasteurization

Louis Pasteur, the great French chemist of the late nineteenth century who discovered the relationship of oxygen to wine, and hence the cause of vinegar, gave his name to the process of sterilization by heating to kill off harmful organisms. In wine this means any yeast and bacteria that might start it refermenting.

A temperature of 60°C (140°F) for about 30 minutes is needed – although an alternative preferred today (for bulk wine only) is 'flash' pasteurization at a much higher temperature, 85°C (185°F), for a much shorter time (up to one minute). Normally pasteurization is only used on cheap wines not intended to mature further, although there is evidence that it does not permanently inhibit further development. Modern sterile handling and filtration is steadily phasing out pasteurization from modern wineries.

Ageing

There are two separate and distinct ways in which wine can age: 'oxidative' ageing in contact with oxygen and 'reductive' ageing when the oxygen supply is cut off. Barrel-ageing is oxidative; it encourages numerous complex reactions between the acids, sugars, tannins, pigments and multifarious polysyllabic constituents of wine.

Bottle-ageing is reductive. Once the wine is bottled the only oxygen available is the limited amount dissolved in the liquid or trapped between the liquid and the cork. (No oxygen enters through a cork.) In wines with a high carbon dioxide content (e.g. champagne) there is not even this much oxygen. Life-forms depending on oxygen are therefore very limited in their scope for activity. 'Reductive' means that the oxygen is reduced – eventually to zero. In these conditions different complex reactions between the same constituents occur at a much slower rate. The ultimate quality and complexity in most wines is only arrived at by a combination of these two forms of ageing, though the proportions of each can vary widely. Many white wines are bottled very young but improve enormously in bottle. Champagne and vintage port are matured almost entirely in bottle. Fine red wines may spend up to three years in barrel and then perhaps two or three times as long in bottle. Tawny port and sherry are matured entirely in barrel and are not normally intended for any further bottle-age.

Bottling

The question of where and by whom wine should be bottled has been much debated, but since the introduction in France of the mobile bottling unit in the 1960s it has become the rule, rather than the exception, for producers even on a small scale to bottle their own wine. The unit is simply a lorry equipped as a modern semi-automatic bottling plant. Its arrival meant that the evocative words *mis en bouteille au château* or *au domaine*, widely supposed (especially in America) to be a guarantee of authenticity and even quality, could be used by all the little properties that used to rely on merchants to bottle for them. The change rubbed both ways: some merchants' names were a guarantee of well-chosen, well-handled wine; others were not.

Modern automatic bottling lines, particularly for fragile semi-sweet wines such as Germany makes, can be like a cross between an operating theatre and a space shuttle, with airlock doors to maintain total antiseptic sterility. The wine is often 'sparged', or flushed out with carbon dioxide or an inert gas such as nitrogen, to remove any oxygen. The bottle is first filled with nitrogen and the wine filled into it through a long nozzle (a 'Mosel cock') to the bottom, pushing out the gas as the level rises. Another common precaution with standard wines is 'hot-bottling': heating the wine to about 54°C (130°F) at the moment of filling the bottle. All this is to avoid any chance of refermentation. For naturally stabilized wines that have spent a long time in barrel, such precautions should not be needed.

Carbon Dioxide for 'Spritz'

Many light white, rosé and occasionally red wines benefit from being bottled with a degree of carbon dioxide dissolved in them – just enough for a few faint bubbles to appear at the brim or the bottom of the glass. In many wines this is a natural occurrence. In others it is an easy and effective way of giving a slight prickle of refreshing sharpness to wines that would otherwise be dull, soft and/or neutral.

Cooperatives

It is arguable that the most important development for the majority of wine makers in Europe has been the rise of the cooperative movement. By pooling resources and qualifying for generous government grants and loans, the peasant wine-farmers of the past are now nearly all grape growers who deliver their whole harvest to a well-equipped central winery. Some are still fly-ridden and unpainted, 'viticultural dust-bins' as they have been called, but most are now extremely up-to-date with vats and presses far better than the district would otherwise have, and a qualified oenologist to make the wine. A few are outright leaders in their regions: nobody else can afford such heavy investment in modern plant. Nearly all use premiums to encourage farmers to produce riper, healthier, cleaner grapes and charge fines for rot, leaves and soil in the crop. Recent years have seen Australian and Californian consultant wine makers hired by coops to further improve the quality, and enhance the marketability, of the wine.

Sparkling Wines

The *méthode champenoise* is not susceptible to many short cuts or labour-saving devices, although machines have been devised for most of the laborious hand work involved. The latest and most notable is an automatic 'riddling rack' to replace the unremitting chore of shaking and turning each bottle regularly (*see* page 181). The massive framework, which vibrates and tips automatically at intervals, is known in France as a Gyropalette, in America simply as a VLM – 'Very Large Machine'.

Other methods of making sparkling wine, none of which achieves the same degree of dissolved gas as the champagne method, include refermenting the wine in a bottle, then decanting it into a tank under pressure, filtering out the sediment (still under CO_2 pressure) and rebottling it. These wines may be labelled 'fermented in the bottle', but not 'fermented in *this* bottle' – or '*méthode champenoise*'. The *cuve close* or Charmat process avoids the first bottling by inducing the secondary fermentation in a tank, then filtering and bottling. This is the most common method for cheaper sparkling wines. Very cheap ones are sometimes simply 'carbonated' by pumping CO_2 into still wine. It does not stay there long.

Chemical Analysis

Whoever coined the phrase 'a chemical symphony' described wine perfectly. (There are, of course, string quartets too.) Good wine gets its infinitely intriguing flavour from the interweaving of innumerable organic and inorganic substances in amounts so small that they have hitherto been untraceable. But this is no longer the case.

A gas chromatograph is an instrument capable of identifying and measuring up to 250 different substances in wine so far. It (and similar instruments) can produce a graphic 'chemical profile.' Researchers at the University of California are playing the fascinating computer game of trying to match the sensory (e.g. smell and taste) perception of teams of tasters with the drawings of the chromatograph to discover which substance is responsible for which taste – the idea presumably being that once we know, vineyards and grapes will become obsolete.

At a more humdrum level it is normal to do simple laboratory checks on about 20 constituents, from alcohol and acidity to sugar and sulphur, before giving any wine a clean bill of health.

The Critical Audience

A catalogue of the influences and advances in modern wine would be one-sided without a mention of the consumer. At least as striking as the technological changes of the past 25 years has been the snowballing interest in wine as a topic as well as a drink. It began in England, spread rapidly to America, Holland, Germany, Scandinavia, and in the past few years has even stirred the great bastions of conservatism and complacency: France, Italy and Spain, the major wine-producing nations.

Books and articles about wine, comparative tastings, newsletters and reviews have turned the spotlight on the individual wine maker. The motivation is there not just to sell, but to excel. The spirit of rivalry and the friendly confrontation between producer and consumer may be the most important driving force of all. We are all the beneficiaries.

Wines Vineyards and Winemakers of the World

FRANCE

Nobody will argue with the primacy of France as the country that set the international standards by which wine is judged. Germany's Rieslings, Spain's sherry and Portugal's port are the only non-French wines to be accepted as universal models to be imitated and emulated. This is not to invalidate Chianti or Barolo or Rioja; but they remain vernacular styles, while Bordeaux, burgundy, champagne and certain wines of the Loire, the Rhône and Alsace are targets that wine makers all over the world aim at – in the first instance by planting their grapes.

It was a form of natural selection that gave France these ideas of what wine can be. Her first vineyards were planted in the Midi in the sixth or seventh centuries BC. The Romans established what are now all the highest-quality vineyard areas – Burgundy, Bordeaux, Champagne, the

Loire – with the exception of Alsace. They chose them because they were promising-looking slopes near centres of population and with reasonable transport facilities; ideally by water, but failing water by a main trade route with good going for heavy wagons. They planted them, after trying Italian vines, with selections of the native woodland vines of Gaul and her neigbours Spain, the Rhineland and the Alps. We can be fairly certain that their descendants are the vines grown today, selected and reselected every time a vineyard was replanted.

The soils are the same; the climate and the conditions of cellarage have not changed very much. With allowances for different techniques and tastes, we can speculate that French wines have gradually defined their identities over almost 2,000 years.

Identity and fame once established, there comes the inevitable problem of fraud. For every person who actually knows what a given wine ought to taste like there are a hundred who are ready to pay for something they will not be able to identify.

The problem is age-old. Many laws have been passed (and taxes raised) to regulate how wine is made, how much, when, where, by whom, of what grapes, and under what name and at what price it can be sold. At the turn of this century the problem became acute. The devastation of phylloxera had left Europe with a serious shortage. Such long-term customers of the best producers as the British were largely protected from the crisis, but in France it was clear that a national system of control was needed.

In 1932 the Institut National des Appellations d'Origine was founded in Paris, with offices and *ingénieurs* all over France, to regulate the whole of the quality wine industry. Another central institute, the Office National Interprofessional des Vins de Table, was founded to keep order among the peasantry producing *vins ordinaires* without the dignity of an *appellation d'origine*.

These distinctions are now central to the whole European wine system. In EEC terms every wine is either a Vin de Qualité Produit dans Une Région Determinée (VQPRD) or a *vin de table* – an absurd choice of category, incidentally: Château Lafite is surely a table wine. In France the system has become more elaborate. There are now four categories of wine representing a basic classification of all the wines of France:

Appellation (d'Origine) Contrôlée (AC or AOC) A strict control of origin, grape varieties and methods used, alcoholic strength and quantity produced. Most AOC wines are limited to a basic production in the region of 40 hectolitres a hectare (445 cases of wine an acre) but a complicated system of annual reassessment usually allows more, and sometimes very considerably more.

The nature of the AC control varies region by region. In Bordeaux the most specific and restricted appellation is a whole village, within which the individual properties ('châteaux') are given wide liberties to plant where and what (within the regional tradition) they like. By contrast, in the best sites of Burgundy each field has its own appellation. The appellation Champagne covers a whole region and its method of working. Each region is a particular case with its own logic.

The ceiling on production, or *Plafond Limite de Classement* (PLC), is always lower for Grands Crus (in regions that have them) than for humbler appellations. The differences used to provide

manoeuvring space for notorious fiddles. But now stricter controls try to ensure that each appellation is treated entirely separately in the grower's cellar – an enormous task.

The AOC system was not instituted originally to provide quality control – only guarantees of origin and authenticity. Quality control by compulsory tasting has now been introduced in theory. In practice there are not enough qualified and impartial tasters, nor the organization nor the time to check on every wine.

Vin Délimité de Qualité Supérieure (VDQS) The second rank of appellations was instituted in 1945 for regions with worthwhile identities and traditions producing 'minor' wines. It has similar systems of control, allowing rather larger crops and (sometimes) lower strengths. In practice it has become the training ground for future AOCs. Promotion from VDQS has happened to several regions – Corbières being the best known. Others are under active survey for further promotion. To be realistic, there is no sudden jump between the two. VDQS may fade away as *vins de pays* get promoted straight to AOC.

Vins de Pays 'Country wine' is a free translation of the latest category, which came into use in 1973. *Vins de pays* are *vins de table* from specified origins, which may be as limited as a village or as wide as the whole Loire valley. Very large crops and a wide latitude of grape varieties are usually allowed. Standards vary enormously.

Many *vin de pays* labels are in practice a new way of marketing *vin ordinaire*. But an individualist who decided to grow, for example, Pinot Noir in Bordeaux, and therefore buck the appellation system, would have to call his wine *vin de pays* however good it might be (*see* page 230).

Vin de Consommation Courante Wine for current consumption. The official name for *vin ordinaire*, the daily drink of the man in the street. Its origin is not specified. Its price depends on its alcoholic degree.

Prices
The prices that are quoted for some of the appellations and *crus* are intended as an indication of relative values – at least as they are perceived by the market. They are *not* the prices the consumer will pay but in the case of 'generic' wines (i.e. those sold under simple appellation names) they are the prices applicable from a Bordeaux wholesale merchant in late 1989. The prices in French francs per bottle given per individual château are the 'opening' prices for the '89 vintage in July 1990. Therefore they are not to be taken as representing more than the state of the market at a particular time.

BORDEAUX

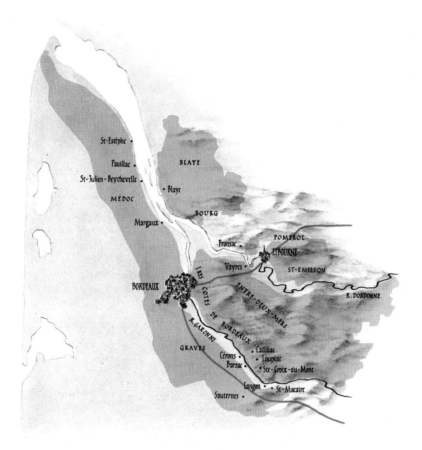

Four factors make Bordeaux the most important vineyard region of all: its quality, size, variety and unity. The last two are not contradictory but complementary. They are the reason we keep coming back for more: the range of styles and types of Bordeaux is wide enough for everybody; no two are ever identical, and yet there is an unmistakable identity among them, a clean-cut, appetizing, stimulating quality that only Bordeaux offers.

The Bordeaux character comes from the strains of grapes and the maritime climate rather than the soil (which varies from gravel to limestone to clay). And of course it comes from traditions of making, handling and enjoying wine in a certain way, an amalgam of the tastes of the French and their northern neighbours, the British, Belgians, Dutch, Germans and Scandinavians, who have paid the piper since the Middle Ages.

Today half Bordeaux's white wine and two-thirds of its red are exported. But the proportion among the best growths (Pauillac, Graves and Margaux, for example) rises to two-thirds or even three quarters.

Bordeaux supplies four basic styles of wine: light, everyday red, fine red, dry white and sweet, sticky, 'liquorous' white. There is not a great deal to be said about the first except that there is a vast supply, up to 2,400,000 hectolitres (320 million bottles) a year, varying from the excitingly tasty to the merely passable or occasionally poor and watery. It may be offered under a brand name or as the production of a Petit Château.

There is a degree of overlap between this everyday red and 'fine' red, where the former excels itself or the latter lets the side down, but the fine red is really a distinct product, a more concentrated wine made for keeping and matured in oak. This is where the distinctions between different soils and situations produce remarkable differences of flavour and keeping qualities, more or less accurately reflected in the system of appellations and of classifications within the appellations. The total quantity available in this category is even more impressive for this class of wine: approaching one bottle for every two of the everyday red.

The dry white wines belong, in the main, alongside the light reds. A very few rise to the level of fine white burgundy but this is an area where Bordeaux is making rapid progress. Modern techniques are finding great character in Bordeaux's traditional white grapes, and ageing in oak is adding to their stature. There is half as much made as there is of comparable red. The sweet whites are a drop in the ocean, only about one bottle in 40, but a precious speciality capable of superlative quality, and much

appreciated in Bordeaux even at a humble level as an aperitif.

Every Bordeaux vintage is subject to the most fickle of climates. Overriding all other considerations is the unpredictable seaside weather. A great vintage will give even the commonest wines an uncommon vitality, but conversely the category of fine wines can be sadly depleted by a really bad one, and the sweet whites can be eliminated altogether.

This shifting pattern of vintages against the already complicated background of appellations and properties, and the long life span of the good wines, makes the appreciation of Bordeaux a mesmerically fascinating pursuit which never ends.

BORDEAUX IN ROUND FIGURES

Over the 35 years 1955 to 1990 the total areas of appellation contrôlée vineyards in Bordeaux dwindled for a while, then recently began rapidly to increase. In 1989 for the first time ever it reached 247,000 acres. Only 5% of the entire Gironde vineyard is now non-AOC. Of this total, red-wine vineyards occupy 181,000 acres and white 48,000 acres – a marked increase in the proportion of red to white even over the previous five years.

Meanwhile the number of individual properties continues steadily to decrease. In 1955 it was 56,000, in 1980 24,000 and in 1989 17,800. The average size

of holding edges up; from three and half acres in 1955 to nearly fifteen acres today.

With this concentration of ownership, efficiency has improved. The five years at the beginning of the period (admittedly including a disastrous frost in 1956) produced an average crop of 26 hectolitres a hectare. The first six harvests of the 1980s produced an average crop of 47hl/ha. 1982 was particularly bountiful at 60.

The figures below are for 1989, an above-average vintage at 59hl/ha, with a comparison with 1988 figures, where production was notably lower.

PRODUCTION: RED WINES

	1989	1988
Bordeaux (basic red appellation; the wine need only attain 10% alcohol)	1,881,000 hl	1,337,000 hl
Bordeaux Supérieur (as above with an alcoholic degree of 10.5% or more)	595,000 hl	490,000 hl
The 'Côtes' (Blaye, Bourg, Castillon, Francs and the Premières Côtes de Bordeaux; outlying areas of slightly higher quality and individuality)	740,000 hl	530,000 hl
St-Emilion	298,000 hl	231,000 hl
Pomerol	48,000 hl	30,000 hl
St-Emilion area – total	678,000 hl	517,000 hl
Lower Médoc	244,000 hl	194,000 hl
Haut-Médoc	213,000 hl	168,000 hl
Graves	99,000 hl	76,000 hl
St-Estèphe	61,000 hl	61,000 hl
Margaux	69,000 hl	57,000 hl
Pauillac	65,000 hl	55,000 hl
St-Julien	50,000 hl	47,000 hl
Moulis & Listrac	68,000 hl	42,000 hl
Pessac-Léognan	45,000 hl	34,000 hl
Médoc and Graves areas – total	924,000 hl	735,000 hl

PRODUCTION: WHITE WINES

Bordeaux (basic)	648,000 hl	565,000 hl
Entre-Deux-Mers	137,000 hl	134,000 hl
Graves	46,000 hl	39,000 hl
Total dry whites	804,000 hl	712,000 hl
Sauternes	32,000 hl	32,000 hl
Barsac	14,000 hl	13,000 hl
Total sweet whites	134,000 hl	133,000 hl

BORDEAUX SALES IN FRANCE AND ABROAD (1987–88)

Total Bordeaux Reds	France	72%	export	28%
Pauillac	,,	36%	,,	64%
Margaux	,,	36%	,,	64%
St-Emilion	,,	63%	,,	37%
Pomerol	,,	66%	,,	44%
Total Bordeaux Whites	France	46%	export	54%
Graves	,,	59%	,,	61%
Sauternes	,,	58%	,,	42%

Over the years 1987–89, Bordeaux accounted for 31% of French AOC wine exports by volume, and 37.3% by value.

Export figures fluctuate from year to year but in 1988–89 the main customers were:

UK	284,000 hl.	3.1m.	cases	(67% red)	USA	162,000 hl.	1.8m.	,,	(60% red)
W. Germany	251,000 hl.	2.8m.	,,	(72% red)	Canada	87,000 hl.	970,000	,,	(35% red)
Belgium	219,000 hl.	2.4m.	,,	(87% red)	Denmark	87,000 hl.	960,000	,,	(88% red)
Holland	201,000 hl.	2.2m.	,,	(58% red)	Switzerland	69,000 hl.	760,000	,,	(92% red)

In terms of average price paid for a bottle the order was: Japan, Switzerland, USA, Belgium, Canada, UK, W. Germany, Denmark.

CLASSIFICATIONS

The appellations of Bordeaux are themselves a sort of preliminary classification of its wines by quality, on the basis that the more narrowly they are defined the higher the general level of the district.

This is as far as overall grading has ever (officially) gone. More precise classifications are all local to one area without cross-referencing.

The most effective way of comparing the standing of châteaux within different areas is by price – the method used for the first and most famous of all classifications, that done for the Médoc for the Paris Exhibition of 1855.

In 1855 the criterion was the price each wine fetched, averaged over a long period, up to 100 years, but taking into account its recent standing and the current condition of the property. The list is still so widely used that it is essential for reference even 136 years later. A few châteaux have fallen by the wayside; the majority have profited by their notoriety to expand their vineyards, swallowing lesser neighbours. It is certain that the original classification located most of the best land in the Médoc and gave credit to the proprietors who had planted it. What they subsequently did with it has proved to be less important than the innate superiority of the gravel banks they chose to plant.

THE CONCEPT OF A CHATEAU

The unit of classification in Bordeaux is not precisely the land itself (as it is in Burgundy) but the property on the land – the estate or 'château'. It is the château that is either a first- or a fourth-growth or a Cru Bourgeois. A proprietor can buy land from a neighbour of greater or lesser standing and add it to his own and (given that it is suitable land) it will take his rank. Vineyards can therefore go up or down the scale according to who owns them.

An example. Château Gloria is an estate of great quality in St-Julien, formed since World War II by buying parcels of land from neighbouring Crus Classés. When the land changed hands it was 'classed', but because the buyer had no classed château the vines were demoted to Cru Bourgeois.

Conversely, many classed growths have added to their holdings by buying neighbouring Cru Bourgeois vines. When the Rothschilds of Château Lafite bought the adjacent Château Duhart-Milion they could theoretically have made all its wine as Lafite.

The justification for this apparent injustice is that a château is considered more as a 'marque' than a plot of ground. Its identity and continuity depend so much on the repeated choices the owner has to make, of precisely when and how to perform every operation from planting to bottling, that he has to be trusted with the final decision of what the château wine consists of. A recent sign of how seriously owners take their responsibilities is the proliferation of 'second labels' for batches of wine that fail to meet self-imposed standards.

This is the Médoc method. St-Emilion is different. Some of its châteaux, the Premiers Grands Crus, have a semi-permanent classification renewable (in theory) after ten years – and last reviewed in 1985. Others, the Grands Crus, have to submit each vintage for tasting.

Only the Médoc and the single Château Haut-Brion in Graves were classified in 1855. The list divides them into five classes, but stresses that the order within each class is not to be considered significant. Only one official change has been made since: the promotion in 1973 of Château Mouton-Rothschild from second- to first-growth.

CRUS BOURGEOIS AND PETITS CHATEAUX

Whether an unclassed château has any official rank or not is not simple either. It depends partly on whether the owner is a loner or a joiner, since membership of the Syndicate of Crus Bourgeois, the next ranking authority, is purely voluntary. A dozen estates that have been semi-officially considered 'exceptional' (but unclassed) ever since 1855 have never joined and have no official rank – which does not necessarily prevent them from calling themselves 'exceptionnel'. EEC regulations forbid the use of the terms 'exceptionnel' and 'grand bourgeois' on labels.

On its latest (1978) list the Syndicate has 127 members divided into three categories described in the following paragraphs. Its members are given their official rank in the entries that follow.

Meanwhile the unofficial Crus Exceptionnels are: Ch'x Angludet (Cantenac, Margaux); Bel-Air-Marquis-d'Aligre (Soussans, Margaux); La Couronne (Pauillac); Fonbadet (Pauillac); Gloria (St-Julien); Labégorce (Margaux); Labégorce-Zédé (Margaux); Lanessan (Cussac); Maucaillou (Moulis); de Pez (St-Estèphe); Siran (Labarde, Margaux); La Tour de Mons (Soussans, Margaux); Villegeorge (Avensan, Haut-Médoc).

A **Cru Bourgeois** is a property of seven hectares (17 acres) upwards where the owner makes his own wine and meets Syndicate standards. There are 68.
A **Cru Grand Bourgeois** satisfies the requirements of Cru Bourgeois and ages its wine in oak *barriques*. There are 41.
A **Cru Grand Bourgeois Exceptionnel** must be in one of the communes between Ludon and St-Estèphe, the area of the Crus Classés. It must also bottle its own wine. There are 18. A number of châteaux have joined the Syndicate since 1978, bringing the 1989 membership to 235, but are not classified due to EEC regulations. There are thus over 100 châteaux which are, or are not, Cru Bourgeois depending upon which list you use.

The terms Cru Artisan and Cru Paysan are sometimes used for properties below Cru Bourgeois in size and/or quality. In 1989 the Syndicat des Crus Artisans was formed for properties of under seven hectares (17 acres). It has 236 members. The wine trade tends to lump them all together as Petits Châteaux – a relative term, since no doubt Rothschilds consider Crus Grands Bourgeois in these terms.

A great number of the thousands that used to exist are now allied to the *caves coopératives*, but more and more are sought out by wine merchants and given the dignity of their own labels. Many, indeed, lose their identity in the anonymity of the cooperative and then miraculously find it again later. There is no object in listing their endless names, however evocative, but to the claret lover with an open mind they are always worth exploring, offering some of the best bargains in France. In good vintages, drunk at no more than three or four years old, they can be both delicious and reasonable in price.

THE BORDEAUX CLASSIFICATION OF 1855

First-Growths (Premiers Crus)

Château Lafite-Rothschild, Pauillac
Château Latour, Pauillac
Château Margaux, Margaux
Château Haut-Brion, Pessac, Graves

Second-Growths (Deuxièmes Crus)

Château Mouton-Rothschild, Pauillac
Château Rausan-Ségla, Margaux
Château Rauzan-Gassies, Margaux
Château Léoville-Las-Cases, St-Julien
Château Léoville-Poyferré, St-Julien
Château Léoville-Barton, St-Julien
Château Durfort-Vivens, Margaux
Château Lascombes, Margaux
Château Gruaud-Larose, St-Julien
Château Brane-Cantenac, Centenac-Margaux
Château Pichon-Longueville-Baron, Pauillac
Château Pichon-Lalande, Pauillac
Château Ducru-Beaucaillou, St-Julien
Château Cos d'Estournel, St-Estèphe
Château Montrose, St-Estèphe

Third-Growths (Troisièmes Crus)

Château Giscouirs, Labarde-Margaux
Château Kirwan, Cantenac-Margaux
Château d'Issan, Cantenac-Margaux
Château Lagrange, St-Julien
Château Langoa-Barton, St-Julien
Château Malescot-St-Exupéry, Margaux
Château Cantenac-Brown, Cantenac-Margaux
Château Palmer, Cantenac-Margaux
Château La Lagune, Ludon
Château Desmirail, Margaux
Château Calon-Ségur, St-Estèphe
Château Ferrière, Margaux
Château Marquis d'Alesme-Becker, Margaux
Château Boyd-Cantenac, Cantenac-Margaux

Fourth-Growths (Quatrièmes Crus)

Château St-Pierre (Bontemps et Sevaistre) St-Julien
Château Branaire-Ducru, St-Julien
Château Talbot, St-Julien
Château Duhart-Milon-Rothschild, Pauillac
Château Pouget, Cantenac-Margaux
Château La Tour-Carnet, St-Laurent
Château Lafon-Rochet, St-Estèphe
Château Beychevelle, St-Julien

Château Prieuré-Lichine, Cantenac-Margaux
Château Marquis-de-Terme, Margaux

Fifth-Growths (Cinquièmes Crus)

Château Pontet-Canet, Pauillac
Château Batailley, Pauillac
Château Grand-Puy-Lacoste, Pauillac
Château Grand-Puy-Ducasse, Pauillac
Château Haut-Batailley, Pauillac
Château Lynch-Bages, Pauillac
Château Lynch-Moussas, Pauillac
Château Dauzac, Labarde-Margaux
Château Mouton-Baronne-Philippe, Pauillac (formerly known as Mouton d'Armailhacq)
Château du Tertre, Arsac-Margaux
Château Haut-Bages-Libéral, Pauillac
Château Pédesclaux, Pauillac
Château Belgrave, St-Laurent
Château de Camensac, St-Laurent
Château Cos Labory, St-Estèphe
Château Clerc-Milon-Rothschild, Pauillac
Château Croizet-Bages, Pauillac
Château Cantemerle, Macau

THE LICHINE CLASSIFICATION

In 1959, the late Alexis Lichine proposed a totally new classification for the whole of Bordeaux to unify the system. His ranking is in five steps up from Bon Cru to Cru Hors Classe. It is a thoroughly well-worked-out idea, even if the placings would cause arguments. Although over 30 years have passed, it may still bear fruit. Certainly Bordeaux is always rumbling with discussion about new classifications. However much the knowledgeable affect to despise them, they still have a powerful hypnotic effect.

Outstanding growths

(*Crus Hors Classe*)

Haut-Médoc
Château Lafite-Rothschild, Pauillac
Château Latour, Pauillac
Château Margaux, Margaux
Château Mouton-Rothschild, Pauillac

Graves
Château Haut-Brion, Pessac, Graves

Saint-Emilion
Château Ausone
Château Cheval-Blanc

Pomerol
Château Pétrus

Exceptional growths

(*Crus Exceptionnels*)

Haut-Médoc
Château Brane-Cantenac, Cantenac-Margaux
*Château Cos d'Estournel, St-Estèphe
Château Ducru-Beaucaillou, St-Julien
Château Gruaud-Larose, St-Julien
Château Lascombes, Margaux
Château Léoville-Barton, St-Julien
*Château Léoville-Las-Cases, St-Julien
Château Léoville-Poyferré, St-Julien
Château Montrose, St-Estèphe
Château Palmer, Cantenac-Margaux
*Château Pichon-Lalande, Pauillac
Château Pichon-Longueville (Baron), Pauillac

Graves
*Domaine de Chevalier, Léognan
*Château La Mission-Haut-Brion, Talence
Château Pape-Clément, Pessac

Saint-Emilion
Château Figeac
Château Magdelaine

Pomerol
Château La Conseillante
Château l'Évangile
Château Lafleur
Château La Fleur-Pétrus
Château Trotanoy

Great growths

(*Grands Crus*)

Haut-Médoc
Château Beychevelle, St-Julien
Château Branaire-Ducru, St-Julien
Château Cantemerle, Haut-Médoc
Château Duhart-Milon-Rothschild, Pauillac
*Château Giscours, Labarde-Margaux
Château Grand-Puy-Lacoste, Pauillac
Château d'Issan, Cantenac-Margaux
*Château La Lagune, Haut-Médoc
*Château Lynch-Bages, Pauillac
Château Malescot-St-Exupéry, Margaux
Château Mouton-Baronne-Philippe, Pauillac
*Château Prieuré-Lichine, Cantenac-Margaux
Château Rausan-Ségla, Margaux
Château Rauzan-Gassies, Margaux
Château Talbot, St-Julien

Graves
*Château Haut-Bailly, Léognan

St-Emilion
*Château Belair
*Château Canon
Clos Fourtet
Château la Gaffelière
Château Pavie
Château Trottevieille

Pomerol
Château Gazin
Château Latour à Pomerol
*Château Petit-Village
*Vieux Château Certan
Château Nénin

Superior growths

(*Crus Supérieurs*)

Haut-Médoc
Château Batailley, Pauillac
*Château Boyd-Cantenac, Cantenac-Margaux
Château Cantenac-Brown, Cantenac-Margaux
Château Chasse-Spleen, Moulis
Château Clerc-Milon-Rothschild, Pauillac
Château Durfort-Vivens, Margaux
Château Gloria, St-Julien
*Château Haut-Batailley, Pauillac
*Château Kirwan, Cantenac-Margaux

Château Lagrange, St-Julien
Château Langoa, St-Julien
Château Marquis d'Alesme-Becker, Margaux
Château Marquis de Terme, Margaux
Château Pontet-Canet, Pauillac
Château La Tour-Carnet, Haut-Médoc

Graves
Château Carbonnieux, Léognan
Château de Fieuzal, Léognan
Château La Louvière, Léognan
*Château Malartic-Lagravière, Léognan
Château Smith-Haut-Lafitte, Martillac

St-Emilion
Château l'Angélus
*Château Balestard-la-Tonnelle
Château Beau-Séjour Bécot
Château Beauséjour-Duffau-Lagarrosse
Château Berliquet
Château Cadet-Piola
Château Canon-la-Gaffelière
Château La Clotte
Château Croque-Michotte
Château Curé-Bon-la-Madeleine
Château La Dominique
*Château Larcis-Ducasse
Château Larmande
Château Soutard
Château Troplong-Mondot
Château Villemaurine

Pomerol
Château Beauregard
Château Certan-Giraud
*Château Certan-de-May
Clos l'Eglise
Château l'Eglise-Clinet
Château Le Gay
Château Lagrange
Château La Grave
Château La Pointe

Good growths

(*Bons Crus*)

Haut-Médoc
Château d'Agassac, Haut-Médoc
*Château Angludet, Cantenac-Margaux
Château Beau-Site, St-Estèphe
Château Beau-Site Haut-Vignoble, St-Estèphe
Château Bel-Air-Marquis d'Aligre, Soussans-Margaux
Château Belgrave, St-Laurent
*Château de Camensac, Haut-Médoc ·

Château Citran, Haut-Médoc
Château Clarke, Listrac
Château Cos Labory, St-Estèphe
*Château Croizet-Bages, Pauillac
Château Dauzac, Labarde-Margaux
Château Ferrière, Margaux
Château Fourcas-Dupré, Listrac
Château Fourcas-Hosten, Listrac
Château Grand-Puy-Ducasse, Pauillac
Château Gressier-Grand-Poujeaux, Moulis
Château Hanteillan, Haut-Médoc
Château Haut-Bages-Libéral, Pauillac
Château Haut-Marbuzet, St-Estèphe
Château Labégorce, Margaux
Château Labégorce-Zédé, Margaux
Château Lafon-Rochet, St-Estèphe
Château Lamarque, Haut-Médoc
Château Lanessan, Haut-Médoc
Château Lynch-Moussas, Pauillac
Château Marbuzet, St-Estèphe
Château Maucaillou, Moulis
*Château Les-Ormes-de-Pez, St-Estèphe
Château Pédesclaux, Pauillac
*Château de Pez, St-Estèphe
Château Phélan-Ségur, St-Estèphe
Château Pouget, Cantenac-Margaux
Château Poujeaux, Moulis
*Château St-Pierre, St-Julien
Château Siran, Labarde-Margaux
Château du Tertre, Arsac-Margaux

Château La Tour-de-Mons, Soussans-Margaux
Château Villegeorge, Haut-Médoc

Graves
Château Bouscaut, Cadaujac
Château Larrivet-Haut-Brion, Léognan
Château La Tour-Haut-Brion, Talence
Château La Tour-Martillac, Martillac

St-Emilion
Château l'Arrosée
Château Bellevue
*Château Cap-de-Mourlin
Domaine du Châtelet
Clos des Jacobins
Château Corbin, Giraud
Château Corbin, Manuel
Château Corbin-Michotte
Château Coutet
Château Dassault
Couvent-des-Jacobins
Château La Fleur-Pourret
Château Franc-Mayne
Château Grâce-Dieu
Château Grand-Barrail-Lamarzelle-Figeac
Château Grand-Corbin
Château Grand-Corbin-Despagne
Château Grand-Mayne
Château Grand Pontet
Château Guadet-St-Julien

Château Laroque
Château Moulin-du-Cadet
Château Pavie-Decesse
Château Pavie-Macquin
Château St-Georges-Côte-Pavie
Château Tertre-Daugay
Château La Tour-Figeac
Château La Tour-du-Pin-Figeac
Château Trimoulet
Château Yon-Figeac

Pomerol
Château Bourgneuf-Vayron
Château La Cabanne
Château Le Caillou
*Château Clinet
Clos du Clocher
Château La Croix
Château La Croix-de-Gay
Clos de l'Eglise
Château l'Enclos
Château Gombaude-Guillot
Château La Grave-Trignant-de-Boisset
Château Guillot
Château Moulinet
Château Rouget
*Clos René
Château de Sales
Château du Tailhas
Château Taillefer
Château Vraye-Croix-de-Gay

These wines are considered better than their peers in this classification.

THE WINE TRADE IN BORDEAUX

Since Roman times, when a *negotiator britannicus* was reported buying wine in Burdigala, Bordeaux's overseas trade has been one of the mainstays of the life of the city. In the Middle Ages the chief customer was England. From the seventeenth century it became the Dutch, and later the Germans, then the English again and latterly the Americans. In the 1980s the Japanese joined in. The north of France, and above all Belgium, now absorb the biggest share, much of it by direct sales.

For two centuries up to the 1960s the trade was largely in the hands of a group of négociants, nearly all of foreign origin, with their offices and cellars on the Quai des Chartrons, on the river just north of the centre of the city. The oldest firm still in business is the Dutch Beyermann, founded in 1620. The

---

The red grapes of Bordeaux
The particulars given in the following pages of each of the principal Bordeaux châteaux include the proportions of the different grape varieties in their vineyards, as far as they are known.

The classic Bordeaux varieties are all related, probably descended from the ancient *biturica*, whose name is still preserved as Vidure (a synonym for Cabernet in the Graves). Over the centuries, four main varieties have been selected for a combination of fertility, disease resistance, flavour and adaptability to the Bordeaux soils.

Cabernet Sauvignon is dominant in the Médoc. It is the most highly

flavoured, with small berries making dark, tannic wine that demands ageing, but then has both depth and 'cut' of flavour. It flowers well and evenly and ripens a modest crop relatively late, resisting rot better than softer and thinner-skinned varieties. Being a late ripener it needs warm soil. Gravel suits it well, but the colder clay of Pomerol makes it unsatisfactory.

Its close cousin, the **Cabernet Franc**, is a bigger, juicier grape. Before the introduction of Cabernet Sauvignon in the eighteenth century, it was the mainstay of Bordeaux and is still widely planted, particularly in Pomerol and St-Emilion, where it is called the Bouchet.

Its wine has delicious soft-fruit flavours (which are vividly seen in Chinon and Bourgueil, wines made from it on the Loire) but less tannin and 'depth'. Less regular flowering and a thinner skin are also drawbacks, at least in the Médoc.

More important today is the **Merlot**, a precocious grape that buds, flowers and ripens early, making it more vulnerable in spring but ready to pick sooner, with an extra degree of alcohol in its higher sugar. Unfortunately, at harvest time its tight bunches need only a little rain to start them rotting.

Merlot wine has good colour and an equally spicy but softer flavour than Cabernet Sauvignon, making wine that

'Chartronnais' families, including Cruse, Calvet, Barton & Guestier, Johnston and Eschenauer, were household names and their power was considerable.

Their role has changed and their importance diminished with the modern growth of direct sales from the châteaux, of bottling at the châteaux and above all of the value of stock. A serious slump in the mid-1970s crippled several of the best-known firms. A number have been taken over by foreign interests. New ways of selling new kinds of brand-name wines have created a new class of trader. The following are the 28 top Bordeaux merchants.

André Quancard André
Principal: Joel Quancard. A house with a good reputation for bourgeois growths. 27% is export.

Barton & Guestier
Principal: Myron Roeder. Offices in Blanquefort, near Bordeaux. 77% of the business is export, mostly of appellation wines in bottle. The original firm, founded in 1725 by an Irishman whose descendants still own Ch. Langoa-Barton, is now reduced to a name belonging to Chemineau Frères, part of Seagram's.

Borie-Manoux
Principal: Emile Castéja. 57% export, mainly appellation wines, with a growing share of the French restaurant business. Properties include Ch'x Batailley and Trotte-vieille. M. Castéja's brother Pierre owns Joanne & Co., specialists in fine wines (about 70% export).

Calvet & Compagnie
Owned by Allied Lyons. Founded in Bordeaux in 1870 but originally from the Rhône, and still with connections there and in Burgundy. 43% is export of many appellations. 'Caldor' is the main table wine brand. Includes the well-known firm of Hanappier.

Castel Frères
Principal: Pierre Castel. Offices in Bordeaux. 6% of the business is export, the great bulk of it Castelvin, 'V.C.C.' (*Vin de consommation courante*). Castel have huge properties in Arcins, Haut-Médoc, where they bought the grower's cooperative and two big châteaux, in the lower Médoc and the Côtes de Bourg.

Cheval Quancard
Principal: M. Quancard. Family firm based in La Grave d'Ambarès (Entre-Deux-Mers). 42% export, largely to UK, Holland and Belgium. Own several châteaux including Terrefort and several brands, including Bordeaux Rouge 'Le Chai des Bordes' and white 'Canter'.

C.V.B.G. (Consortium Vinicole de Bordeaux et de Gironde)
Includes Dourthe, Krewssmann and several other old firms now owned by a Dutch firm. Principal: Jean-Paul Jauffret, who as head of the C.I.V.B. introduced a successful price stabilizing system. Offices in Bordeaux, cellars at Ch. Maucaillou, Moulis. 70% is export, all of appellation wines.

Etablissement Cordier
The Cordier family sold to a big financial group in 1984. 59% of the business is export. The firm owns 10 well-known châteaux including Gruaud-Larose, Talbot, Meyney, Lafaurie-Peyraguey, Clos des Jacobins.

Cruse & Fils Frères
The arch-Chartron family firm, founded in 1819, was sold in 1980 to the Société des Vins de France, specialists in branded table wines. Laurent Cruse is the buyer. 47% export, mainly of bottled appellation wines.

Mme Jean Descaves
One of the characters of Bordeaux with the biggest stock of rare old top wines at ever-increasing prices.

Dubos
Principals: 'Wum' Kaï-Nielsen and Philippe Dubos. Specialists in selling top wines to the jet set.

Duclot
Principal: Jean-François Moueix. A subsidiary of J-P Moueix of Libourne, based in Bordeaux, specializing in top-quality wines, largely to private customers.

Dulong Frères & Fils
Principal: J.M. Dulong. 55% of business is export, mainly of AC wines in bottle and bulk to UK and the USA.

Louis Eschenauer
Bought out from the Brent Walker group by a manage-

---

matures sooner. In the Médoc a judicious proportion – rarely above 40 per cent – is used; rather more in the Graves; more again in St-Emilion, and in Pomerol up to 95 per cent. This is the grape that gives Château Pétrus its opulent texture and flavour.

A fourth red grape that is still used in small amounts in the Médoc is the **Petit Verdot**, another Cabernet cousin that ripens late with good flavour and ageing qualities, but flowers irregularly and has other quirks. A little in the vineyard is nonetheless a source of added complexity and 'backbone' in the wine.

A fifth, found more in St-Emilion and largely in the minor areas, is the **Malbec**

(alias Pressac), a big, juicy, early-ripening grape which has serious flowering problems (*coulure*). It is grown in the Gironde more for quantity than quality. Paradoxically, under its synonym Auxerrois (or Cot) it is the grape of the 'black wines' of Cahors.

In the long run, a château proprietor 'designs' his wine by the choice and proportions of varieties he plants.

The white grapes
The classic white wine vineyard in Bordeaux is a mixture of two principal varieties and one or two subsidiary ones as variable in proportions as the red. **Sauvignon Blanc** and **Sémillon** make

up at least 90 per cent of the best vineyards, Sauvignon for its distinct flavour and good acidity, Sémillon for its susceptibility to 'noble rot'. Thus the sweet wine vineyards of Sauternes tend to have more Sémillon, and often a small plot of the more highly flavoured **Muscadelle**. Unfortunately Sauvignon Blanc has flowering problems in Bordeaux which makes it an irregular producer; to keep a constant proportion of its grapes means having a disproportionate number of vines. Recently some excellent fresh dry white has been made entirely of Sémillon. Other white grapes include Ugni Blanc, Folle Blanche, Colombard and Riesling.

ment team in 1990. The properties, which include Ch'x Rausan-Ségla, Smith-Haut-Lafitte and La Garde, are now independent, with Eschenaur retaining a special selling link.

Maison Ginestet
Principal: Jean Merlaut. A complicated company with a great history. 99% of the business is Bordeaux wine (in bottle and bulk). 28% is export.

Nathaniel Johnston
Principal: Nathaniel Johnston. A Bordeaux family firm founded in 1734. 50% export, mostly fine wines. Exclusives include Bahans, the second wine of Haut-Brion.

Lebègue & Compagnie
Principal: J. de Coninck. Largely a bulk business, AC and table wines. 35% is export.

Alexis Lichine & Co
The company was sold in the late '80s to Société des Vin Francais who intend to group their wine interests in Bordeaux with the possible consequence that Lichine may lose its identity. 70% export business.

Gilbey de Loudenne
Based at Ch. Loudenne in the Médoc and owned by Grand Metropolitan Ltd. 65% is exported, mainly to UK, all Bordeaux wines including brands (La Cour Pavillon, La Bordelaise) and Ch'x Faurie-de-Souchard, de Pez, Loudenne, etc.

De Luze
Principal: Yves Trangosi. 83% export business specializing in Bordeaux wine in bottle and bulk. This traditional négociant house was bought by Rémy Martin Cognac in 1981. A large part of the business is in fine wines. Exclusive rights include Ch'x Cantenac-Brown.

Mähler-Besse
Principals: Henry and Franck Mähler-Besse. Family firm in Bordeaux, also in Holland, Belgium, Spain and Portugal, with the majority shareholding in Château Palmer, specializing in old vintages and branded AC Bordeaux, e.g. Le Vieux Moulin.

Yvon Mau
Principal: Jean-François Mau. Based near La Réole. 48% export, largely bulk AC and table.

Mestrezat SA
Principal: Jean-Pierre Angliviel de la Beaumelle. Office in Bordeaux. Merchants in Bordeaux wines from Petits Châteaux to first-growths, all in bottle. Owners and managers of 750 acres of vineyards, including Ch'x Grand-Puy-Ducasse, Rayne Vigneau, La Motte Bergeron, etc.

De Rivoyre & Diprovin
Principal: Bertrand de Rivoyre. Owned by Rémy Martin. Offices at St-Loubès (Entre-Deux-Mers) for fine wines and Ambarès for Diprovin, the bulk wine division. 30% is export.

Schröder & Schÿler
Founded in Bordeaux in 1739 and still in their original premises with medieval cellars on the Quai des Chartrons. Principal: Jean-Henri Schÿler. Owners of Ch. Kirwan. There are links with A. Moueix of Pomerol. 87% is export.

Maison Sichel
Principal: Peter Sichel. Office in Bordeaux. 97% export business, selling Bordeaux and Midi wines in bottle and bulk, mainly to the Anglo-Saxon world. Part-owners of Palmer, and Peter Sichel owns Ch. Angludet. Also own a winery at Verdelais in the Premières Côtes which produces fruity modern claret, and interests in the Corbières. 'Sirius' is the Sichel brand of excellent white Bordeaux.

S.D.V.F. (Société de Distribution des Vins Fins)
Principal: A. Hernandez. Founded in 1973 in difficult times to market fine wines bought at slump prices. 50% is export; all château wines.

William Pitters
Principal: Bernard Magrez. An enterprising merchandising house in Bordeaux. 8% is export.

MEDOC

The Médoc is the whole of the wedge of land north of Bordeaux between the Atlantic and the wide estuary of the Gironde, the united rivers Garonne and Dordogne. Its vineyards all lie within a mile or two of its eastern estuarine shore on a series of low hills, or rather plateaux, of more or less stony soil separated by creeks, their bottom land filled with alluvial silt.

Dutch engineers in the seventeenth century cut these *jalles* to drain the new vineyards. Their role is vital in keeping the water table down in land which, despite its gravel content, can be very heavy clay two or three metres down where the vine roots go.

The proportion of *graves* (big gravel or small shingle) in the soil is highest in the Graves region, upstream of Bordeaux, and gradually declines as you go downstream along the Médoc. But such deposits are always uneven, and the soil and subsoil both have varying proportions of sand, gravel and clay. The downstream limit of the Haut-Médoc is where the clay content really begins to dominate the gravel, north of St-Estèphe.

The planting of the *croupes*, the gravel plateaux, took place in a century of great prosperity for Bordeaux under its *Parlement*, whose noble members' names are remembered in many of the estates they planted between 1650 and 1750. The Médoc was the Napa Valley of the time and the

Pichons, Rauzans, Ségurs and Léovilles the peri-wigged Krugs, Martinis, de la Tours and Beringers.

The style and weight of wine these grandees developed have no precise parallel anywhere else. In some marvellous way the leanness of the soil, the vigour of the vines, the softness of the air and even the pearly seaside light seem to be implicated. Of course, it is a coincidence (besides being a terrible pun) that 'clarity' is so close to 'claret' – but it does sound right for the colour, smell, texture, weight and savour of the Médoc.

The centuries have only confirmed what the original investors apparently instinctively knew: that the riverside gravel banks produce the finest wine. The names that started first have always stayed ahead. The notion of 'first-growths' is as old as the estates themselves.

Today the Médoc is divided into eight appellations: five of them limited to one commune (St-Estèphe, Pauillac, Moulis, Listrac and St-Julien), one (Margaux) to a group of five small communes, one (Haut-Médoc) a portmanteau for parts of equal merit outside the first six, and the last, Médoc, for the northern tip of the promontory.

MARGAUX

The Margaux appellation covers a much wider area than the village: vineyards in the commune of Margaux (963 acres), plus the neighbouring communes of Cantenac (988 acres), Labarde (321 acres), Arsac (235 acres) and Soussans (370 acres) – a total of 2,877 acres, or a little more than Pauillac or St-Estèphe, with more Crus Classés than any other, and far more high-ranking ones.

Margaux is a big sleepy village, with a little *Maison du Vin* to give directions to tourists. Wine from Margaux itself comes from the lightest, most gravelly land in the Médoc and is considered potentially the finest and most fragrant of all. That of Cantenac in theory has slightly more body and that of Soussans, on marginally heavier, lower-lying land going north, less class. The châteaux of Margaux tend to huddle together in the village, with their land much divided into parcels scattered around the parish. Postcode: 33460 Margaux. Price (1988) 32 francs a bottle.

PREMIER CRU

Château Margaux

1er Cru Classé 1855. Owners: Mentzelopoulos family.
AOC: Margaux. 193 acres red, 30 acres white; 32,000 cases.
Grape var. red: Cab.Sauv. 75%, Merlot 20%, Petit Verdot and Cab.Franc 5%; White: Sauvignon Blanc 100%

With Ch. Lafite, the most stylish and obviously aristocratic of the first-growths both in its wine and its lordly premises. The wine is never blunt or beefy, even in great years; at its best it is as fluidly muscular as a racehorse and as sweetly perfumed as any claret – the very taste and smell of elegance.

Like Lafite, Margaux emerged in the late 1970s from 15-odd years of unworthy vintages. The late M. André Mentzelopoulos, whose daughter Corinne directs the estate today, bought the property (for 72 million francs) in 1977, invested huge sums in a total overhaul of château, vineyards and plant. His ambition for perfection showed immediately with the excellent 1978. Professor Peynaud advised sweeping changes that put Ch. Margaux back at the very top.

The château is a porticoed mansion of the First Empire, unique in the Médoc; the *chais* and cellars, pillared and lofty, are in keeping. Magnificent avenues of plane trees lead through the estate. Some of the lowest riverside land is planted with white (Sauvignon) grapes to make a light, fittingly polished dry wine, Pavillon Blanc. The second label for red is Pavillon Rouge.

MARGAUX CRUS CLASSES

Châteaux Boyd-Cantenac

3eme Cru Classé 1855. Owner: P. Guillemet.
AOC: Margaux, 44 acres; 8,000 cases. Grape var: Cab.Sauv. 67%, Cab.Franc 7%, Merlot 20%, Petit Verdot 6%.

The strange name, like that of Cantenac-Brown, came from a 19th-century English owner. A small property not widely seen nor much acclaimed but full of stalwart old-fashioned virtues, long lasting and highly flavoured in such excellent years as 1970, '75, '78, '83, '88 and '89.

Château Brane-Cantenac

2eme Cru Classé 1855. Owner: Lucien Lurton.
AOC: Margaux. 210 acres; 12,500 cases.
Grape var: Cab.Sauv. 70%, Cab.Franc 15%, Merlot 13%, Petit Verdot 2%.

The most respected name of the Margaux second-growths; a very big and well-run property on a distinct pale gravel plateau. The wine is generally enjoyable and 'supple' at a fairly early stage but lasts well, although some critics faulted it during the '70s for coarseness and for developing too fast. Good vintages of the '80s hold their own among the good second-growths. The second label is Ch. Notton.

Château Cantenac-Brown

3eme Cru Classé 1855. Owners: AXA Millésimes.
Administrator: Jean-Michel Cazes.
AOC: Margaux. 100 acres; 16,000 cases. Grape var: Cab.Sauv. 67%, Cab.Franc 7%, Merlot 26%.

A great prim pile of a building like an English public school on the road south from Margaux. Conservative wines capable of terrific flavour (1970 is a monster), greatly improved since the mid-'80s. But most Cantenac is finally a coarser wine than classic Margaux.

Château Dauzac
5eme Cru Classé 1855. Owners: MAIF.
AOC: Margaux. 123 acres; 15,000 cases. Grape var: Cab.Sauv.
60%, Cab.Franc 5%, Merlot 30%. Petit Verdot 5%.
A property taken in hand by new owners since 1978.
Great efforts have resulted in reliable, if not inspiring,
wines.

Château Desmirail
3eme Cru Classé 1855. Owner: Lucien Lurton.
AOC: Margaux, 61 acres; 2,500 cases. Grape var: Cab.Sauv.
80%, Cab.Franc 9%, Merlot 10%. Petit Verdot 1%.
A third-growth that disappeared for many years into the
vineyards and vats of Ch'x Palmer and Brane-Cantenac.
M. Lurton owns the name and has relaunched it, with a
second label, Ch. Baudry.

Château Durfort-Vivens
2eme Cru Classé 1855. Owner: Lucien Lurton.
AOC: Margaux. 62 acres plus; 3,000 cases. Grape var:
Cab.Sauv. 82%, Cab.Franc 10%, Merlot 8%.
The name of Durfort, suggesting hardness and
strength, sums up the character of this almost all-
Cabernet wine – which seems to want keeping for ever.
The same owner makes the much more agreeable
second-growth Brane-Cantenac. Since 1985 new efforts
have been mending matters – although second-growth
quality is still far off. The second label is Domaine de
Curebourse!

Château Ferrière
3eme Cru Classé 1855. Owner: Mme Villard.
AOC: Margaux. 12 acres; 1,000 cases. Grape var: Cab.Sauv.
47%, Cab.Franc 8%, Merlot 33%, Petit Verdot 12%.
A small plot without a château. The wine is made at Ch.
Lascombes and could perhaps be a selection of that
growth made primarily for the restaurant trade.

Château Giscours
3eme Cru Classé 1855. Owner: G.F.A. du Château Giscours.
AOC: Margaux (at Labarde). 200 acres; 29,500 cases. Grape
var: Cab.Sauv. 75%, Cab.Franc 3%, Merlot 20%,
Petit Verdot 2%.
Price (1989): 137 francs a bottle.
One of the great success stories of modern Bordeaux and a
popular candidate for promotion; though more outstanding in the '70s than the '80s. The vast Victorian property
has been virtually remade since the 1950s by the Tari

family, including making a 20-acre lake to alter the
microclimate: by creating turbulence between the vines
and the neighbouring woodland it helps to ward off
spring frosts. The wines are tannic, robustly fruity, often
dry but full of the pent-up energy that marks first-class
claret – not the suavely delicate style of Margaux.

Château d'Issan
3eme Cru Classé 1855. Owners: The Cruse family.
AOC: Margaux. 79 acres; 10–15,000 cases. Grape var:
Cab.Sauv. 75%, Merlot 25%.
One of the (few) magic spots of the Médoc: a moated 17th-
century mansion down among the poplars where the
slope of the vineyard meets the riverside meadows. Issan
is never a 'big' wine, but old vintages have been
wonderfully, smoothly persistent. Recent ones appear
rather too light to last as well, though '82 and '83 were
excellent.

Château Kirwan
3eme Cru Classé 1855. Owners: Schröder & Schÿler.
AOC: Margaux. 86 acres; 15,000 cases. Grape var: Cab.Sauv.
40%, Cab.Franc 20%, Merlot 30%, Petit Verdot 10%.
The third-growth neighbour to Brane-Cantenac. It seems
to have few friends among the critics, although it is
carefully and lovingly family run and at its best (1961, '70,
'75, '79) is as long-lived and classic as any of the Margaux
second-growths, making elegant, feminine claret. Much
money has been invested; '85, '86, '88 show the results.

Château Lascombes
2eme Cru Classé 1855. Owners: Bass Charrington.
AOC: Margaux. 232 acres; 35,000–40,000 cases. Grape var:
Cab.Sauv. 65%, Cab.Franc 3%, Merlot 30%,
Petit Verdot 2%.
A superb great property (one of the biggest in the Médoc)
restored by the energy of Alexis Lichine in the 1950s to
making delectable, smooth and flavoury claret. Since his
days it has rarely made great wine, though the top
vintages of the '80s are very good. The second label is Ch.
La Gombaude.

Château Malescot-St-Exupéry
3eme Cru Classé 1855. Owner: Roger Zuger.
AOC: Margaux. 71 acres; 17,000 cases. Grape var: Cab.Sauv.
50%, Cab.Franc 10%, Merlot 35%, Petit Verdot 5%.
A handsome house in the main street of Margaux with
vineyards scattered north of the town. For many years it

Enjoying claret
There are four important variables
among the red wines of Bordeaux. The
most important is the vintage, the next
the class or quality of the wine, the third
its age and the fourth the region.
Ripe vintages upgrade all qualities
and districts, intensify their characters,
make them slower to mature and give
them a longer life span.
The Bordeaux habit is to drink young
wines rather cooler than mature ones,
and Médocs cooler than St-Emilions
and Pomerols. Wines still in the
firmness of their youth are served with
such strongly flavoured or rich dishes as
game or duck (and especially young St-

Emilion with Dordogne lampreys
cooked in red wine). Mature wines are
served with plain roasts of lamb or beef
and very old wines with all kinds of
white meat or fowl.
It is worth noting that lamb is the
almost inevitable choice at banquets in
the Médoc.

Enjoying Sauternes
Sauternes and the other sweet white
wines of Bordeaux (Barsac, Ste-Croix du
Mont) are served locally with such rich
first courses as foie gras or smooth
pâtés, melon, fish or sweetbreads in
creamy sauces, or to bring out the
sweetness in lobster. They are popular

as apéritifs and also survive the
onslaught of a salty Roquefort much
better than red wines. They go
excellently with simple fruit tarts, or
fruit, or alone after a meal. 'Very cool,
but not iced,' is the regular formula for
describing the right temperature.

Enjoying dry white Bordeaux
Dry white Bordeaux is served in the
region with almost any fish dish,
especially with oysters (which are often
served iced, accompanied by hot and
peppery little sausages – an exciting
combination). It cuts the richness of
pâtés and terrines, but is generally not
served as an apéritif without food.

was run in tandem with Marquis d'Alesme-Becker, but since 1979 has taken flight on its own, showing signs of becoming even finer – with fruity flavour hidden by the tanic hardness of youth.

Château Marquis d'Alesme-Becker
3eme Cru Classé 1855. Owner: Jean-Claude Zuger.
AOC: Margaux. 25 acres; 5,000 cases.
Grape var: Cab.Sauv. and Cab.Franc 60%,
Merlot 30%, Petit Verdot 10%.

A small vineyard in Soussans, run by the brother of the owner of Ch. Malescot. Its wines are known for old-fashioned toughness, the flavour of the heavier soil of Soussans, giving them long life. The wine-making is modern, but the Zuger zeal is perennial.

Château Marquis de Terme
4eme Cru Classé 1855. Owner: M Ph. Sénéclauze.
AOC: Margaux. 94 acres; 14,000 cases.
Grape var: Cab.Sauv. 60%, Cab.Franc 3%,
Merlot 30%, Petit Verdot 7%.

A respected old name not enough seen in commerce; the greater part is sold direct to French consumers. It is made notably tannic for very long life, although since 1985 a more delicate touch has given it more immediate charm.

Château Palmer
3eme Cru Classé 1855. Owners: Société Civile du Château Palmer.
AOC: Margaux. 111 acres; 12,500 cases. Grape var: Cab.Sauv.
55%, Cab.Franc 3%, Merlot 40%, Petit Verdot 2%.

A candidate for promotion to first-growth, whose best vintages (1961, '66, '70, '75, '78, '79, '83, '86, '88) set the running for the whole Médoc. They combine finesse with most voluptuous ripeness, the result of a superb situation on the gravel rise just above Ch. Margaux and old-fashioned long fermentation with not too many new barrels, but, probably most of all, the very skilful selection by the three owners, French, Dutch and English, whose flags fly along the romantic roof-line of the château.

Château Pouget
4eme Cru Classé 1855. Owner: Pierre Guillemet.
AOC: Margaux. 25 acres; 4,500 cases. Grape var: Cab.Sauv.
66%, Merlot 30%, Cab.Franc 4%.

The same property as, and in practice an alternative label for, Boyd-Cantenac.

Château Prieuré-Lichine
4eme Cru Classé 1855. Owner: Sacha Lichine.
AOC: Margaux. 153 acres; 25,000 cases. Grape var: Cab.Sauv.
58%, Cab.Franc 4%, Merlot 34%, Petit Verdot 4%.
Price (1989): 65 francs a bottle.

The personal achievement of the late Alexis Lichine, now upheld by his son, who assembled a wide scattering of little plots around Margaux in the 1950s and created one of the most reliable and satisfying modern Margaux, harmonious and even rich at times, needing 10 years to show its real class. The second label is Ch. de Clairefont.

Château Rausan-Ségla
2eme Cru Classé 1855. Owners: Holt Frères & Fils. Dir:
Jacques Théo.
AOC: Margaux. 116 acres; 13,000 cases. Grape var: Cab.Sauv.
67%, Cab.Franc 3%, Merlot 30%.

The larger of the two parts of the estate that used to be second only to Ch. Margaux, but has fallen far behind in recent times. At its best ('61, '75, '83) exceedingly fragrant in the Margaux manner, but not the echoing symphony a second-growth should be. 1983 seems to have been the beginning of a major revival: '85, '86 and '88 are setting a new standard. The former Cru Bourgeois Lamouroux has been absorbed into the vineyard.

Château Rauzan-Gassies
2eme Cru Classé 1855. Owners: Mme Paul Quié & J.-M.
Quié.
AOC: Margaux. 74 acres; 10,000 cases. Grape var: Cab.Sauv.
40%, Cab.Franc 23%, Merlot 35%, Petit Verdot 2%.
Price (1989): 67 francs a bottle.

No more remarkable than its twin over the last 2 decades. Its 1970 was fading at only 10 years old. A new generation took over in the late 1970s; wines of the '80s are full of flavour, if not finesse. 2nd label Enclos de Moncabon.

Château du Tertre
5eme Cru Classé 1855. Owner: Philippe Capbern-Gasqueton.
AOC: Margaux. 124 acres; 15,000 cases. Grape var: Cab.Sauv.
85%, Cab.Franc 5%, Merlot 10%.

Over the last decade there has been better and better wine (starting with a superb 1970) from this formerly obscure vineyard in the backwoods at Arsac. The owner of Calon-Ségur has taken it in hand and given it a strong, robustly fruity character. Both 1982 and '83 were very fine, and the 1986 a resounding success.

OTHER CHATEAUX

Château L'Abbé-Gorsse-de-Gorsse
Margaux. 25 acres; 4,000 cases. One of a group playing with the name Labégorce north of Margaux. Has not made the reputation of its bigger neighbours.

Château d'Angludet
Cantenac. Owners: M & Mme Peter Sichel. 75 acres; 12,000 cases. Home of the English partner of Ch. Palmer and, like it, badly undervalued in the official classification. Firm, foursquare wines which take time to show their unquestionable class.

Château Bel-Air-Marquis d'Aligre
Margaux. Owner: Pierre Boyer. 42 acres; 3,500 cases plus. Despite its grand name, one of the more basic and backward Margaux. It usually rewards patience.

Château Canuet
Margaux. 20 acres; 4,000 cases. Little-known property with a house in Margaux and scattered vineyards reconstituted since 1967 by the former owner of Ch. Labégorce. Changed hands in 1987 and may lose its identity.

Château Deyrem-Valentin
Soussans. Owner: Jean Soye. 24 acres; 3,000 cases.

Château La Gurgue
Margaux. Owners: Société Civile du Château La Gurgue. 29 acres; 5,000 cases. A formerly run-down château in the centre of Margaux. Since 1978 under the same energetic direction as Ch. Chasse-Spleen and now re-emerging. Price (1985): 30 francs a bottle.

Château Haut Breton Larigaudière
Soussans. Owners: The De Schepper-de Moor family. 20 acres; 3,300 cases. A tiny property better known as one of the few good restaurants in the Médoc.

Domaine de l'Ile Margaux
Margaux. Owner: Mme L. D. Sichère. 33 acres; 3,000 cases. On an island on the river and therefore outside the Margaux appellation, but a fascinating place and rather good wine.

Château Labégorce
Margaux. Owner: M. Perrodo. 69 acres; 10,000 cases. A potential frontrunner, grand mansion and all, considered unofficially a Cru Exceptionnel. At present making wine with less than real Margaux elegance.

Château Labégorce-Zédé
Soussans. Owner: Luc Thienpont. 66

acres; 10,000 cases plus. Among the best minor Margaux, in the same Flemish family as the famous Vieux-Château-Certan. One of nature's Crus Exceptionnels. Second label: Domaine Zédé.

Château Marsac-Séguineau
Soussans. Owners: Société Civile du Château. 25 acres; 4,400 cases. Part of the same group as Ch. Grand-Puy-Ducasse (Pauillac).

Château Martinens
Grand Bourgeois, Cantenac-Margaux. Owners: Mme Dulos and J. P. Seynat-Dulos. 74 acres; 8,000 cases. A good property which is getting better, re-equipped in 1989. The 18th-century château was built, I am told, by three English sisters, the Whites (of Limerick fame).

Château Montbrun
Cantenac. Owner: Lebègue. 20 acres;

3,400 cases. 75% Merlot.

Château Paveil de Luze
Grand Bourgeois, Soussans. Owner: Baron Geoffrey de Luze. 59 acres plus; 7,000 cases. A gentlemanly estate with smooth, well-mannered wine to match. The small vineyard is being enlarged.

Château Pontac-Lynch
Cantenac. Owner: Marie-Christine Boudon 25 acres; 4,000 cases. A little place between Ch. Palmer and the river, chiefly remarkable for bearing two of Bordeaux's most illustrious names.

Château Siran
Labarde. Owner: William-Alain Miailhe. 74 acres; 12,500 cases. A fine estate run by a fanatic, regularly making most attractive wine and determined to win classed-growth status (which 40% of his vineyard formerly had, before changes of ownership). Miailhe has commissioned a historical map to put

Château Margaux: the avenue

the cat among the pigeons by proving that many classed-growths have a lower proportion of '1855' land than Siran. Heliport and antinuclear cellar seem to point to a man who means business.

Château Tayac
Cru Bourgeois, Soussans-Margaux. Owner: André Favin. 84 acres; 15,000 cases. Estate with modern ideas, supplies the 'Savour-Club de France'.

Château La Tour-de-Mons
Soussans. Owner: Bertrand Clauzel. 74 acres; 14,000 cases. A romantic, old-fashioned property owned for many years by the family who sold Ch. Cantemerle in 1981. Generally considered a natural Cru Exceptionnel with round, well-structured wines (40% Merlot).

MOULIS AND LISTRAC

Moulis and Listrac are two communes of the central Haut-Médoc whose appellations (each has its own) are considered more stalwart than glamorous. Between Margaux and St-Julien the main gravel banks lie farther back from the river with heavier soil. No château here was classified in 1855 but a dozen Crus Bourgeois make admirable wine of the more austere kind. The best soil is on a great dune of gravel stretching from Grand Poujeaux in Moulis (where Châteaux Chasse-Spleen and Maucaillou are

both regularly among the best value in the Haut-Médoc) inland through Listrac.

The total area of vines is 1,240 acres in Moulis (which has seen some of the biggest expansion in the last few years), 1,422 in Listrac. Closer to the river the villages of Arcins, Lamarque and Cussac have only the appellation Haut-Médoc (q.v.). Postcode: 33480 Castelnau de Médoc.
Price (1988): Moulis 31, Listrac 23 francs a bottle.

MOULIS AND LISTRAC CHATEAUX

Château La Bécade
Cru Bourgeois, Listrac. Owner: J.-P.
Théron. 56 acres; 13,000 cases.
Château Bel-Air Lagrave
Cru Bourgeois. Moulis. Owner: Jeanne
Bacquey. 17 acres. 3,500 cases.
Château Biston-Brillette
Moulis. Owner: Michel Barbarin.
44 acres; 7,500 cases.
Château Brillette
Cru Bourgeois, Moulis. Owner: the
Berthault family. 70 acres; 4,000 cases.
A rising reputation among the good
bourgeois wines of Moulis, on the next
plateau to the various Poujeaux.
Château Cap Léon Veyrin
Cru Bourgeois, Listrac. Owner: Alain
Meyre. 44 acres; 7,500 cases.
Château Chasse-Spleen
Grand Bourgeois Exceptionnel, Moulis.
Dir: Mme B. Villars. 180 acres; 25,000
cases. Regularly compared with Crus
Classés for style and durability. Expertly
made with classic methods.
Château Clarke
Cru Bourgeois, Listrac. Owner: Baron
Edmond de Rothschild. 350 acres;
45,000 cases. A new (since 1973)
Rothschild project with every
advantage. Second labels: Ch.
Malmaison and Ch. Peyrelebade. Very
good wines in '85 and '86.
**Château La Closerie du
Grand-Poujeaux**
Cru Bourgeois, Moulis. Owner: Mme
Bacquey. 12 acres; 2,500 cases. Small but
one of the best.
Château Duplessis-Fabre
Cru Bourgeois, Moulis. Owner: Ch.
Maucaillou. 42 acres; 6,500 cases. Until
1989 run jointly with Ch. Fourcas-
Dupré in neighbouring Listrac.
Château Duplessis
Grand Bourgeois, Moulis. Owner:
Lucien Lurton. 44 acres; 4,000 cases.
Lighter, more easy-going wine than
most in this parish. Part of the same
group as Ch. Grand-Puy-Ducasse

(Pauillac).
Château Dutruch Grand Poujeaux
Cru Bourgeois Exceptionnel, Moulis.
Owner: François Cordonnier. 62 acres
plus; 10,000 cases. Old family property,
now one of the leaders of the parish.
Tannic wine for long maturing.
Château Fonréaud
Cru Bourgeois, Listrac. Owner: Jean
Chanfreau. 94 acres; 18,500 cases. Well
known with its sister-château Lestage
for pleasant, rather light wines.
Château Fourcas-Dupré
Grand Bourgeois Exceptionnel, Listrac.
Dir: Patrice Pagès. 100 acres; 20,000
cases. (Part of the vineyard is in
Moulis.) One of the best in an area of
excellent Crus Bourgeois. Second label
is Ch. Bellevue-Laffout.
Château Fourcas-Hosten
Grand Bourgeois Exceptionnel, Listrac.
Dirs: Bertrand de Rivoyre and Patrice
Pagès. 98 acres; 18,000 cases. The
outstanding property of Listrac today;
perfectionist wine-making. 40% Merlot
suits the relatively heavy soil, making
stylish, concentrated wine to lay down.
Château Gressier Grand-Poujeaux
Cru Bourgeois Supérieur, Moulis.
Owners: The Ste-Affrique family. 44
acres; 9,000 cases. Formerly owners of
Fourcas-Hosten, hence the confusingly
similar label.
Château Lafon
Grand Bourgeois, Listrac. Owner: J.-P.
Théron. 28 acres; 6,500 cases.
Château Lestage
Cru Bourgeois, Listrac. Owners: The
Chanfreau family. 128 acres; 25,000
cases. See Ch. Fonréaud.
**Château Lestage-Darquier-Grand
Poujeaux**
Moulis. Owner: François Bernard.
10 acres; 1,800 cases.
Château Maucaillou
Moulis. Owners: The Dourthe family.
135 acres; 20,000 cases. Important
property of at least Grand Bourgeois

standing, with vineyards partly in
Listrac and Lamarque. Good deep wine,
tannic but fruity.
Château Mauvesin
Moulis. Owners: Société Viticole de
France. 148 acres; 30,000 cases. A big
new estate and, like nearby Ch. Clarke, a
sign of the growing importance of the
Moulis-Listrac area.
Château Moulin à Vent
Grand Bourgeois, Moulis. Owner:
Dominique Hessel. 59 acres; 10,000
cases. Run with energy and competence
by a young owner since 1978.
Château Moulis
Moulis. Owner: Jacques Darricarrère.
30 acres; 6,500 cases.
Château Pomeys
Moulis. Owner: Xavier Barennes.
20 acres; 2,500 cases.
Château Poujeaux
Grand Bourgeois Exceptionnel, Moulis.
Owner: François and Philippe Theil.
123 acres; 20,000 cases. Sometimes
known as Poujeaux-Theil. The principal
property of the Poujeaux plateau,
known for wines of firm underlying
structure, fine but daunting when
young. Second label: La Salle de
Poujeaux.
Château Haut Franquet
Moulis. Owner: Jeanne Bacquey.
23 acres; 1,000 cases.
Château Ruat-Petit-Poujeaux
Moulis. Owner: Pierre Goffre-Viaud.
37 acres; 5,000 cases.
Château Saransot-Dupré
Listrac. Owner: Yves Raymond.
25 acres; 5,000 cases. Also 5 acres of
Bordeaux Blanc.
Château Séméillan Mazeau
Cru Bourgeois, Listrac. Owner: H.
Mazeau. 33 acres; 3,500 cases.

Cave Coopérative Grand Listrac
Listrac. 395 acres; 66,650 cases plus.
One of the biggest Médoc cooperatives
with a good reputation.

ST-JULIEN

St-Julien, with a high proportion of Crus Classés, is the smallest of the top-level appellations of the Médoc. It has only 2,025 acres, but most of this is classed second-, third-, or fourth-growth (no first and no fifth, and very little Cru Bourgeois). Its prominent gravel plateau by the river announces itself as obviously one of the prime sites of Bordeaux.

St-Julien harmonizes force and fragrance with singular suavity to make the benchmark for all red Bordeaux, if not the pinnacle. Farther inland, towards the next village, St-Laurent, the wine is less finely tuned.

The two villages of St-Julien and Beychevelle are scarcely enough to make you slow your car.

Postcode: 39320 St-Julien.

Price (1988): 32 francs a bottle.

ST-JULIEN CRUS CLASSES

Château Beychevelle

4eme Cru Classé 1855. Owners: a French pension fund.
President: Jean Louis Petriat.
AOC: St-Julien 173 acres; 25,000 cases. Grapes var: Cab.Sauv.
70%, Merlot 30%.

A regal 17th-century château with riverside vineyards and dazzling roadside flowerbeds on the hill up to St-Julien from the south. Its silky, supple, aristocratic wine is the one I most associate with the better class of English country house. Blandings must have bulged with it. It can be difficult when young but finds a blue-blooded elegance after 10 years or so. 1964, '66, '67, '70, '71 and '75 are all good examples. Recent ownership changes and investment herald a return to consistency: both 1982 and '83 were good wines; '85 is sensational. The curious boat on the label commemorates its admiral founder, to whose rank passing boats on the Gironde used to *baisse les voiles* — hence, they say, the name. Second label is Amiral de Beychevelle.

Château Branaire-Ducru

4eme Cru Classé 1855. Owners: Groupe privé.
AOC: St-Julien. 118 acres; 20,000 cases. Grape var: Cab.Sauv.
73%, Cab.Franc 5%, Merlot 20%, Petit Verdot 2%.
Price (1989): 67 francs a bottle.

One of the most reliable Bordeaux estates. Vineyards in several parts of the commune; the château opposite Beychevelle. Model St-Julien, relying more on flavour than force; notably fragrant and attractive wine with a track-record of reliability. The second label is Ch. Dulac.

Château Ducru-Beaucaillou

2eme Cru Classé 1855. Owner: Jean-Eugène Borie.
AOC: St-Julien. 123 acres; 18,000 cases. Grape var: Cab.Sauv.
65%, Cab.Franc 5%, Merlot 25%, Petit Verdot 5%.
Price (1989): 125 francs a bottle.

Riverside neighbour of Ch. Beychevelle with a château almost rivalling it in grandeur, if not in beauty, built over its barrel cellars. One of the few great châteaux permanently lived in by the owner, who also owns Ch'x Grand-Puy-Lacoste and Haut-Batailley in Pauillac. Always among the top Médocs with the firm but seductive flavour of the best St-Juliens. The Cru Bourgeois Lalande-Borie (q.v.) is also made here.

Château Gruaud-Larose

2eme Cru Classé 1855. Owners: Etab. Cordier.
AOC: St-Julien 207 acres; 37,500 cases. Grape var: Cab.Sauv.
64%, Cab.Franc 9%, Merlot 24%, Petit Verdot 3%.

Second-growth with a magnificent vineyard on the south slope of St-Julien, the pride of the powerful merchant house of Cordier (*see also* Talbot, Meyney, Cantemerle, Lafaurie-Peyraguey, etc). Consistently one of the fruitiest, smoothest, easiest to enjoy of the great Bordeaux, although as long-lived as most. A good bet in an off vintage. Cordier wines come in long-necked bottles. Second wine: Sarget de Gruaud-Larose.

Château Lagrange

3eme Cru Classé 1855. Owners: Suntory.
AOC: St-Julien 279 acres 20,000 cases. Grape var: Cab.Sauv.
66%, Merlot 27%, Petit Verdot 7%.

A magnificent wooded estate inland from St-Julien. The Japanese owners took over in 1983 and started to expand and re-equip. The results are extremely promising. The second label is Les Fiefs-de-Lagrange.

Château Langoa-Barton

3eme Cru Classé 1855. Owners: The Barton family.
AOC: St-Julien. 37 acres; 7,000 cases. Grape var: Cab.Sauv.
70%, Cab.Franc 8%, Merlot 20%, Petit Verdot 2%.

The noble sister château of Léoville-Barton and home of the Bartons. Similar excellent wine, although by repute always a short head behind the Léoville.

Château Léoville-Barton

2eme Cru Classé 1855. Owners; The Barton family.
AOC. St-Julien 111 acres; 20,000 cases. Grape var: Cab.Sauv.
70%, Cab.Franc 8%, Merlot 20%, Petit Verdot 2%.
Price (1989): 68 francs a bottle.

The southern and smallest third of the Léoville estate, the property of the Irish Barton family since 1821. One of the finest and most typical St-Juliens, often richer than Léoville Las Cases, made with very conservative methods in old oak vats at the splendid 18th-century Ch. Langoa, built over its barrel cellars. Major investments recently are raising standards even higher — while prices remain remarkably steady.

Château Léoville Las Cases

2eme Cru Classé 1855. Owners: Société Civile du Château Léoville Las Cases. Dir: Michel Delon.
AOC: St-Julien. 235 acres; 32,000 cases. Grape var: Cab.Sauv.
65%, Cab.Franc 12%, Merlot 20%, Petit Verdot 3%.
Price (1989): 135 francs a bottle.

The largest third of the ancient Léoville estate on the boundary of Pauillac, adjacent to Ch. Latour. Still owned by descendants of the Léoville family; now run by Michel Delon, son of Paul Delon, one of the Médoc's best wine makers. A top-flight second-growth and a favourite of the critics, consistently producing connoisseur's claret, extremely high-flavoured and dry for a St-Julien, needing long maturing and leaning towards austerity. The stone gateway of the vineyard is a landmark but the *chais* are in

The sculpted lion at Château Léoville Las Cases

the centre of St-Julien beside the château, which belongs to Léoville-Poyferré. The second wine is Clos du Marquis. *See also* Château Potensac (Médoc).

Château Léoville-Poyferré
2eme Cru Classé 1855. Owners: The Cuvelier family.
AOC: St-Julien 190 acres; 33,000 cases. Grape var: Cab.Sauv.
65%, Merlot 25%, Petit Verdot 8%, Cab.Franc 2%.
Price (1989): 80 francs a bottle.
The central portion of the Léoville estate, including the château. Potentially as great a wine as Léoville Las Cases, although not the same critical success in the last 20 years. A new director, one of the Cuvelier family, is set on rivalling his neighbour. The second wine takes the name of a Cru Bourgeois, Ch. Moulin-Riche.

Château St-Pierre (-Sevaistre)
4eme Cru Classé 1855. Owner: Henri Martin.
AOC: St-Julien. 42 acres; 6,700 cases. Grape var: Cab.Sauv.

70%, Cab.Franc 10%, Merlot 20%.
Price (1989): 75 francs a bottle.
The smallest and least-known St-Julien classed growth but superbly situated and excellently managed by M. Martin of Ch. Gloria. No glamour, but fruity, deep-coloured wine from old vines at a reasonable price.

Château Talbot
4eme Cru Classé 1855. Owners: Etab. Cordier.
AOC: St-Julien. 242 acres; 40,000 cases. Grape var: Cab.Sauv.
70%, Cab.Franc 5%, Merlot 20%, Petit Verdot 5%.
One of the biggest and most productive Bordeaux vineyards, just inland from the Léovilles, sister château to Gruaud-Larose and home of its owner. Marshal Talbot was the last English commander of Aquitaine. Like Gruaud-Larose, a rich, fruity, smooth wine but without quite the same plumpness of structure. A small quantity of dry white 'Caillou Blanc' is produced on 15 acres. The second label is Connétable Talbot.

OTHER CHATEAUX

Château Beauregard
St-Julien. Owner: H. Palomo. 5 acres. 2,000 cases.

Château La Bridane
Cru Bourgeois, St-Julien. Owner: P. Saintout. 38 acres; 8,000 cases.

Château du Glana
Grand Bourgeois Exceptionnel, St-Julien. Owner: Gabriel Meffre. 111 acres; 20,000 cases. Oddly unrenowned as one of St-Julien's only two big unclassed growths. The owner is a wine merchant with several properties who has built a giant *chai* more like a warehouse just north of St-Julien. His splendidly sited vineyards produce respectable wine.

Château Gloria
St-Julien. Owner: Henri Martin. 110 acres; 20,000 cases: The classic example of the unranked château of exceptional quality, the creation of the illustrious mayor of St-Julien (and Grand Maître of the Commanderie du Bontemps, the ceremonial order of the Médoc). He assembled the vineyard in the 1940s with parcels of land from neighbouring Crus Classés, particularly Ch. St Pierre. The wine is rich and long-lasting with less oak flavour than most fine Médocs, being matured in 7,000-litre casks instead of 225-litre *barriques*. Ch. Haut-Beychevelle-Gloria and Ch. Peymartin are names for selections made for certain markets.

Château Lalande Borie
St-Julien. Owner: J. E. Borie. 45 acres; 8,000 cases. A vineyard bought in 1970 by the owner of Ch. Ducru-Beaucaillou, where the wine is made. In effect, a baby brother of Ducru.

Château Moulin de la Rose
St-Julien. Owner; G. Delon. 10 acres; 2,000 cases.

Château Terrey-Gros-Caillou and Château Hortevie
St-Julien. Owners: MM. Fort and Pradère. 46 acres; 8,500 cases. A union of two small properties producing very creditable St-Julien.

Château Teynac
St-Julien. Owner: P. Gauthier. 14 acres; 2,500 cases.

PAUILLAC

Pauillac is the only town in the vineyard area of the Médoc, and a pretty quiet one at that. Within the last generation it has been enlivened (if that is the word) by a huge Shell oil refinery (now half-derelict) on the river immediately north and a marina (although the word sounds more animated than the fact) along its tree-lined quay. Disappointingly there is no old hotel, no restaurant haunted by wine growers. Only the *Maison du Vin* (worth a visit) on the quay gives a hint of its world renown. That, and the famous names on signs everywhere you look in the open steppe of the vineyards.

The wine of Pauillac epitomizes the qualities of all red Bordeaux. It is the virile aesthete; a hypnotizing concurrence of force and finesse. It can lean to an extreme either way (Latour and Lafite representing the poles) but at its best strikes such a perfect balance that no evening is long enough to do it justice. There are 2,590 acres of vineyards with more Crus Classés than any other commune except Margaux, surprisingly weighted towards fifth-growths – some of which are worth better than that.
Postcode: 33250 Pauillac.
Price (1988): 32 francs a bottle.

PAUILLAC PREMIERS CRUS

Château Lafite-Rothschild
1er Cru Classic 1855. Owners: The Rothschild family.
AOC: Pauillac. 250 acres; 30,000–40,000 cases. Grape var:
Cab.Sauv. 70%, Cab.Franc 10%, Merlot 20%.
See The Making of a Great Claret, page 62.

Château Latour
1er Cru Classé 1855. Owners: Allied-Lyons.
AOC: Pauillac. 150 acres; 17,000 cases. Grape var: Cab.Sauv
80%, Cab.Franc 4%, Merlot 15%, Petit Verdot 1%.
Price (1989): 230 francs a bottle.

Ch. Latour is in every way complementary to Ch. Lafite. They make their wines on different soils in different ways; the quality of each is set in relief by the very different qualities of the other. Lafite is a tenor; Latour a bass. Lafite is a lyric; Latour an epic. Lafite is a dance; Latour a parade.

Lafite lies on Pauillac's northern boundary with St-Estèphe, Latour on the southern, St-Julien, limit of the commune four miles away on the last low hill of river-deposited gravel before the flood plain and the stream that divides the two parishes. The ancient vineyard, taking its name from a riverside fortress of the Middle Ages, surrounds the modest mansion, its famous domed stone tower and the big square stable-like block of its *chais*. Two other small patches of vineyard lie half a mile inland near Ch. Batailley.

For nearly three centuries the estate was in the same family (and up to 1760 connected with Lafite). Its modern history began in 1963, when the de Beaumonts sold the majority share to an English group headed by the banker Lord Cowdray and including the wine merchants Harveys of Bristol. They set in hand a total modernization, starting with temperature-controlled stainless steel fermenting vats in place of the ancient oak. Combined English and French talent has since rationalized and perfected every inch of the property, setting such standards that Latour has, rather unfairly, become almost more famous for the quality of its lesser vintages than for the splendour of such years as 1961, '66, '70, '75, '78, '82, '83, '86, '88 and '89. Its consistency and deep, resonant style extends into its second label, Les Forts de Latour, which fetches a price comparable to a second-growth château and is unusual in not being offered until it is at least halfway to bottle maturity (e.g. 1981 released 1986). Les Forts comes partly from vats of less than the Grand Vin standard, but mainly from two small vineyards (35 acres) formerly Latour, farther inland towards Batailley. These were replanted in 1966 and their wine first used in the blend in the early 1970s. There is also a third wine, modestly labelled Pauillac, which by no means disgraces its big brothers.

In 1989 Allied-Lyons Ltd (owners of Harveys of Bristol) bought the Cowdray-Pearson share, valuing the property at around $100 million and making it the world's most expensive vineyard.

Château Mouton-Rothschild

1er Cru Classé 1973. Owner: Baron Philippe de Rothschild S.A.

AOC: Pauillac. 17 acres; 25,000 cases. Grape var: Cab.Sauv. 85%, Cab.Franc 7%, Merlot 8%.

Price (1989); 230 francs a bottle.

Mouton is geographically neighbour to Lafite, but gastronomically closer to Latour. Its hallmark is a deep

The late Baron Philippe de Rothschild, proprietor of Mouton, achieved a lifetime's ambition in 1973 when the property joined the first-growths

concentration of the flavour of Cabernet Sauvignon, often described as resembling blackcurrants, held as though between the poles of a magnet in the tension of its tannin – a balancing act that can go on for decades, increasing in fascination and grace all the time. In 1976 I noted of the 1949 Mouton: 'Deep unfaded red; huge, almost California-style nose; resin and spice; still taut with tannin, but overwhelming in its succulence and sweetness. In every way magnificent.'

More than any other château, Mouton-Rothschild is identified with one man, the late Baron Philippe de Rothschild, who came to take it over as a neglected property of his (the English) branch of the Rothschild family in 1922 and died in 1989. This remarkable man of many talents (poet, dramatist, racing-driver among them) determined to raise Mouton from being first in the 1855 list of second-growths to parity with Lafite. It took him 51 years of effort, argument, publicity, and above all perfectionist wine-making. He gained official promotion in 1973, the only change ever made to the 1855 classification.

Baron Philippe and his American wife Pauline created a completely new house in the stone stable block and

Commanderie du Bontemps de Médoc et des Graves

The Médoc unites with the Graves in its ceremonial and promotional body, the Commanderie du Bontemps de Médoc et des Graves. In its modern manifestation it dates from 1950, when a group of energetic château proprietors, on the initiative of the regional deputy, M. Emile Liquard, donned splendid red velvet robes and started to 'enthronize' dignitaries and celebrities, wine merchants and journalists at a series of protracted and very jolly banquets held in the *chais* of the bigger châteaux.

The Commanderie claims descent from an organization of the Knights-Templar of the Order of Malta at St-Laurent in the Médoc in 1154 – a somewhat tenuous link. Its three annual banquets are the festivals of Saint Vincent (the patron saint of wine) in January, the Fête de la Fleur (when the vines flower) in June and the Ban des Vendanges, the official proclamation of the opening of the vintage, in September. Male recruits to the Commanderie are usually entitled Commandeur d'Honneur, and female Gourmettes – a pun meaning both a woman gourmet and the little silver chain used for hanging a cork around the neck of a decanter.

A selection of wine blended for its use is marketed as Cuvée de la Commanderie.

collected in the same building the world's greatest museum of works of art relating to wine, displayed with unique flair (and open to the public by appointment). He was succeeded in 1989 by his daughter Philippine.

The baron's love of the arts (and knack for publicity) led him to commission a different famous artist to design the top panel of the Mouton label every year from 1945 on. Of these vintages the most famous are the 1949 (the owner's favourite), '53, '59, '61, '66, '70, '75, '82, '85, '86, '88, and '89.

The baron's empire expanded over the years to include Châteaux Mouton-Baronne-Philippe and Clerc-Milon, and La Baronnie, his company that produces and markets Mouton-Cadet, the best-selling branded Bordeaux. Mouton itself has no second label; wine not up to Grand Vin standard is blended (along with much else) into Mouton-Cadet, which maintains a consistently high level of value for money.

PAUILLAC CRUS CLASSES

Château Batailley
5eme Cru Classé 1855. Owners: Emile Castéja.
AOC: Pauillac. 123 acres; 22,000 cases. Grape var: Cab.Sauv. 70%, Cab.Franc 5%, Merlot 22%, Petit Verdot 3%.

The name of the estate, another of those divided into easily confusable parts, comes from an Anglo-French disagreement in the 15th century. Charles II's favourite wine merchant was called Joseph Batailhé – I like to think he was a son of this soil, the wooded inland part of Pauillac. Batailley is the larger property and retains the lovely little mid-nineteenth-century château in its 'English' park. Its wine is tannic, muscle-bound for years, never exactly graceful but eventually balancing its austerity with sweetness: old (20-year) bottles keep great nerve and vigour. These are the Pauillacs that approach St-Estèphe in style.

Château Clerc-Milon
5eme Cru Classé 1855. Owner: Baron Philippe de Rothschild S.A.
AOC: Pauillac. 74 acres; 15,000 cases. Grape var: Cab.Sauv. 75%, Cab.Franc 5%, Merlot 20%.

An obscure little estate known as Clerc-Milon-Mondon until 1970, when it was bought by Baron Philippe de Rothschild. The vineyard (there is no château) is promisingly positioned between Château Lafite, Château Mouton-Rothschild and Pauillac's notorious riverside oil refinery. Typical Rothschild perfectionism, energy and money have made a series of good vintages, starting with a remarkably fine 1970.

Château Croizet-Bages
5eme Cru Classé 1855. Owners: Mme L. Quié and J. M. Quié.
AOC: Pauillac. 60 acres; 8,000 cases. Grape var: Cab.Sauv. 37%, Cab.Franc 30%, Merlot 30%, Petit Verdot and Malbec 3%.

A property respected for round and sound, not exactly glamorous Pauillac, belonging to the owners of Ch. Rauzan-Gassies, Margaux. No château, but vineyards on the Bages plateau between Lynch-Bages and Grand-Puy-Lacoste. Compared with the firmness and vigour of the Lynch-Bages of the same year, the 1961 at 20 years old was rather old-ladyish, sweet but fragile. Recent vintages have a name for consistency, not excitement.

Château Duhart-Milon-Rothschild
4eme Cru Classé 1855. Owners: The Rothschild family.
AOC: Pauillac. 150 acres; 25,000 cases. Grape var: Cab.Sauv. 70%, Cab.Franc 5%, Merlot 20%, Petit Verdot 5%.

The little sister (or baby brother) of Ch. Lafite, on the next hillock inland, known as Carruades, bought by the Rothschilds in 1964 and since then completely replanted and enlarged. Its track record was for hard wine of no great subtlety, but the resolve (seen at Lafite recently) to make the best possible extends to Duhart-Milon. As the young vines age this is becoming a great château again. The second label is Moulin de Duhart.

Château Grand-Puy-Ducasse
5eme Cru Classé 1855. Owners: Société Civile de Grand-Puy-Ducasse.
AOC: Pauillac. 90 acres; 11,500 cases. Grape var: Cab.Sauv. 62%, Merlot 38%.

Three widely separated plots of vineyard, one next to Grand-Puy-Lacoste, one by Pontet-Canet, the third nearer Batailley, and *chais* and château on the Pauillac waterfront. Much replanted and renovated by the same company that owns Ch. Chasse-Spleen (Moulis) since 1971 but already known for big, well-built and long-lived wine (e.g. 1961, '64, '66, '67, '70). Vintages of the '80s have been consistently good, and good value. Artiges-Arnaud is a second label.

Château Grand-Puy-Lacoste
5eme Cru Classé 1855. Owners: The Borie family.
AOC: Pauillac. 123 acres; 13,000 cases. Grape var: Cab.Sauv. 70%, Merlot 25%, Cab.Franc 5%.
Price (1989): 75 francs a bottle.

For a long time, in the words of the 'Bordeaux bible', *'très supérieur à son classement'*. Sold in 1978 by the Médoc's greatest gastronome, Raymond Dupin, to one of its most dedicated proprietors, Jean-Eugène Borie (of Ducru-Beaucaillou, Haut-Batailley, etc.), whose son Xavier runs it. A rather remote but attractive property with an extraordinary romantic garden, a thousand miles from the Médoc in spirit, on the next 'hill' inland from the Bages plateau. The wine has tremendous 'attack', colour, structure and sheer class. The second label is Lacoste-Boné.

Château Haut-Bages Libéral
5eme Cru Classé 1855. Owner: Mme B. Villars.
AOC: Pauillac. 64 acres; 10,000 cases. Grape var: Cab.Sauv. 74%, Merlot 23%, Petit Verdot 3%.
Price (1989): 75 francs a bottle.

A vineyard bordering Ch. Latour to the north. The owner, who also runs Chasse-Spleen, has invested heavily. A property making much better wine than its rather limited reputation suggests, with every sign of realizing its high ambitions.

Château Haut-Batailley
5eme Cru Classé 1855. Dirs: Jean-Eugène and François-Xavier Borie.
AOC: Pauillac. 52 acres; 10,000 cases. Grape var: Cab.Sauv. 65%, Cab.Franc 10%, Merlot 25%.
Price (1989): 57 francs a bottle.

Another property of the men whose gifts have established

continued on page 64

CHATEAU LAFITE-ROTHSCHILD

The Making of a Great Claret

This is the place to study the author's control of his superlatives. Wine for intelligent millionaires has been made by this estate for well over 200 years, and when a random selection of 36 vintages, going back to 1799, was drunk and compared in recent times the company was awed by the consistency of the performance. Underlying the differences in quality, style and maturity of the vintages, there was an uncanny resemblance between wines made even a century and a half apart.

It is easy to doubt, because it is difficult to understand the concept of a Bordeaux 'cru'. As an amalgam of soil and situation with tradition and professionalism, its stability depends heavily on the human factor. Sometimes even Homer nods. Lafite had its bad patch in the 1960s and early 1970s. Since 1976 it has once again epitomized the traditional Bordeaux château at its best.

As a mansion, Lafite is impeccably chic rather than grand; a substantial but unclassical eighteenth-century villa, elevated on a terrace above the most businesslike and best vegetable garden in Médoc, and sheltered from the north by a titanic cedar of Lebanon. There are no great rooms; the red drawing room, the pale blue dining-room and the dark green library are comfortably cluttered and personal in the style of 100 years ago. The Rothschild family of the Paris bank bought the estate in 1868. It has been the apple of their corporate eye ever since. In 1974 the 34-year-old Baron Eric de Rothschild took over responsibility from his uncle Elie, who had been in charge since 1946.

Grandeur starts in the *cuvier*, the vat house, and the vast low barns of the *chais*, where the barrels make marvellous perspectives of dwindling hoops seemingly for ever. In 1989 a unique and spectacular new circular *chai*, dug out of the vineyards and supported by columns to test Samson, was inaugurated. History is most evident in the shadowy moss-encrusted bottle cellars, where the collection stretches back to 1797 – the first Bordeaux ever to be château-bottled, still in its original bin.

Quality starts with the soil: deep gravel dunes over limestone. It depends on the age of the vines: at Lafite an average of 40 years. It depends even more on restricting their production: the figure of 40–45 hectolitres a hectare is achieved by modest manuring and stern pruning.

Vintage in the Médoc starts at any time between early September and late October, depending on the season, when the grapes reach an optimum ripeness, judged above all by the sugar content (although allowance may have to be made for the threat of rainy weather or an attack of rot). In a big vineyard (Lafite has 250 acres) it is impossible to pick every grape at precisely the ideal moment. Picking teams start on the Merlot, which ripens first, and move as quickly as they can. Lafite employs 250 people to shorten the harvest as far as possible.

The vital work of selection starts in the vineyard, with bunches that are unevenly ripe or infected with rot being left on the ground. It continues at the *cuvier*, where the grapes arriving in *douilles*, which hold enough for one barrel of wine, are inspected before being tipped in the *égrappoir-fouloir*, a simple mill that first strips the grapes off the stalks, then half crushes them. (A subtle difference here; most estates uses a *fouloir-égrappoir* that crushes and destems at the same time: perfectionists remove the stalks first. By controlling the speed of the rollers it is possible to prevent green grapes being crushed at all.)

The crushed grapes, each variety separately, are pumped into splendid upright oak vats, gleaming with varnish on the outside, each holding between 15,750 and 20,250 litres. If the natural sugar in the grapes would produce less than 11.5 per cent of alcohol in the wine, enough pure sugar is added to make up the difference. In mild weather the juice and pulp start to ferment spontaneously within a day. In cold weather the whole *cuvier* is heated.

The temperature of fermentation is controlled to rise no higher than 30°C (85°F) – enough to extract the maximum colour from the skins; not enough to inhibit the yeasts and stop a steady fermentation. If it threatens to go higher, the must wine is pumped from the bottom of the vat to the top through a serpentine cooling system. Pumping it over the floating 'cap' of skins also helps to extract their colour.

Fermentation may take anything from one week to three depending on the yeasts, the ripeness of the grapes and the weather. The wine may be left on the skins for up to a total of 21 days if necessary to leach the maximum colour and flavour from them. By this time, with luck, the malolactic fermentation will be under way or even finished. The juice is now run off into new 225-litre *barriques* made at the château of Limousin oak from the forest of Tronçais, north of the Massif Central. The remaining 'marc' of skins and pips is pressed in a hydraulic press. Some of the 'press' wine, exaggeratedly tannic, can be blended in if necessary. At Lafite the proportion varies between ten per cent and none at all.

The *barriques*, up to 1,100 of them in a plentiful year, stand in rows in the *chai*, loosely bunged at the top while the malolactic fermentation finishes. Early in the New Year the proprietor, his manager, the *maître de chai* and the consultant oenologist, Professor Boissenot, taste the inky, biting new wine to make the essential selection: which barrels are good enough for the château's Grand Vin, which are fit for the second wine, Carruades de Lafite, and which will be rejected as mere Pauillac. This is the moment for the '*assemblage*' of the wines of the four different varieties, up to now still separate. The barrels are emptied into vats to be blended, the barrels washed and slightly sulphured and the assembled wine put back.

For a further year they stand with loose bungs,

being topped up weekly to make good any 'ullage', or loss by evaporation. During this year they will be 'racked' into clean casks two or three times and 'fined' with beaten egg whites. The white froth poured on to the top coagulates and sinks, taking any floating particles with it to the bottom. When the year is up the bungs are tapped tight with a mallet and the casks turned '*bondes de côte*' – with their bungs to the side. From now on the only way to sample them is through a tiny spiggot hole plugged with wood at the end of the cask.

At Lafite the wine is kept in cask for a further 9–12 months, until the second summer or autumn after the vintage, then it is given a final racking, six casks at a time, into a vat which feeds the bottling machine. If it were bottled straight from individual casks there would be too much variation.

Complicated as it is to relate, there is no simpler or more natural way of making wine. The factors that distinguish first-growth wine-making from more modest enterprises are the time it takes, the number of manoeuvres and the rigorous selection.

In recent years Rothschild enterprise has been at work to use the technical (as well as financial) strength of Lafite in new fields both near and far. The neighbouring Château Duhart-Milon has been bought and renovated; Château Rieussec in Sauternes acquired; and joint ventures started in both Chile and California.

Baron Eric de Rothschild

Ducru-Beaucaillou among the leaders. They makes similar but rather less rustic and more gentlemanly wine than their Batailley neighbour. For reliability and sheer tastiness there are few wines you can choose with more confidence. The second label of Haut-Batailley is La Tour l'Aspic.

Château Lynch-Bages
5eme Cru Classé 1855. Owners: The Cazes family.
AOC: Pauillac. 210 acres; 35,000 cases. Grape var: Cab.Sauv. 75%, Cab.Franc 10%, Merlot 15%.
Price (1989): 115 francs a bottle.

An important estate fondly known to its many English friends as 'lunch-bags'; a perennial favourite for sweet and meaty, strongly Cabernet-flavoured wine, epitomizing Pauillac at its most hearty. The Bages plateau, south of the town, has relatively 'strong' soil over clay subsoil. The best vintages ('82, '85, '86, '88) are very long-lived; the '61 is perhaps now at its peak. The director, Jean-Michel Cazes, Pauillac's leading insurance broker and son of its very popular mayor, has rebuilt the crumbling château and the former cavernous, gloomy *chais*. His other property is Les Ormes-de-Pez in St-Estèphe. In addition he is director of Ch. Pichon-Baron. The second label is Haut-Bages-Averous. There is also a tiny supply of soft, fruity Sémillon white.

Château Lynch-Moussas
5eme Cru Classé 1855. Owner: Emile Castéja.
AOC: Pauillac. 64 acres; 12,500 cases. Grape var: Cab.Sauv. 70%, Merlot 30%.

Stablemate since 1969 of its neighbour Ch. Batailley. M. Castéja has replanted and totally renovated the château and chais. So far it has shown no serious sign of catching up with Lynch-Bages.

Château Mouton-Baronne-Philippe
5eme Cru Classé 1855. Owner: Baron Philippe de Rothschild S.A.
AOC: Pauillac. 111 acres plus; 18,000 cases. Grape var: Cab.Sauv. 70%, Cab.Franc 10%, Merlot 20%.

Originally Mouton-d'Armailacq, bought in 1933 by Baron Philippe de Rothschild and renamed in 1956, the name altered again from Baron to Baronne for the Baroness Pauline (d. 1976) in 1974. The vineyard is south of Mouton, next to Pontet-Canet, on lighter, even sandy soil which with a higher proportion of Merlot gives a rather lighter, quicker-maturing wine, but a star nonetheless, made to the customary Mouton standards.

Château Pédesclaux
5eme Cru Classé 1855. Owner: Bernard Jugla.
AOC: Pauillac. 49 acres; 8,000 cases. Grape var: Cab.Sauv. 70%, Cab.Franc 7%, Merlot 20%, Petit Verdot 3%.

The least renowned classed growth of Pauillac, scattered around the commune like Grand-Puy-Ducasse, enthusiastically making solid wines much to the taste of its principal customers, the Belgians. M. Jugla (*see also* Ch. Colombier Monpelou) uses the names of two of his Crus Bourgeois, Grand Duroc Milon and Belle Rose, as second labels.

Château Pichon-Longueville au Baron de Pichon-Longueville
2eme Cru Classé 1855. Owners: AXA Millésimes.
AOC: Pauillac. 135 acres; 20,000 cases. Grape var: Cab.Sauv. 75%, Merlot 25%.

The next entry gives the background to the unwieldy name. New owners (an insurance company) since 1987 have set lustily about competing with the Comtesse across the road, which for years had made much better wine. With J-M. Cazes (*see* Ch. Lynch-Bages) as director, and a seemingly bottomless purse, a spectacular building programme has transformed the place. The wine is now an earnest contender with its neighbour; perhaps more full-bloodedly Pauillac in style with its preponderance of Cabernet.

Château Pichon-Longueville, Comtesse de Lalande
2eme Cru Classé 1855. Dir: Mme de Léncquesaing.
AOC: Pauillac. 185 acres; 33,000 cases. Grape var: Cab.Sauv. 45%, Cab.Franc 12%, Merlot 35%, Petit Verdot 8%.
Price (1989): 125 francs a bottle.

Two châteaux share the splendid 225-acre Pauillac estate that was planted in the 17th century by the same pioneer who planted the Rauzan estate in Margaux. The châteaux were long owned by his descendants, the various sons and daughters of the Barons de Pichon-Longueville. Two thirds of the estate eventually fell to a daughter who was Comtesse de Lalande – hence the lengthy name, which is often shortened to Pichon Lalande or Pichon Comtesse. The family of the present owners bought it in 1925.

The mansion (recently restored, with splendid new underground *chais*) lies in the vineyards of Ch. Latour, but most of its vineyard is across the road, on gravelly soil with clay below, surrounded by the vines of the other Pichon château and parts of the vineyards of Ch'x Latour, Ducru-Beaucaillou and Léoville Las Cases. The southern portion of the vineyard is actually in St-Julien. With its relatively generous proportion of Merlot the wine lacks the concentrated vigour of Ch. Latour but adds a persuasive perfumed smoothness which makes it one of the most fashionable second-growths.

Big investment since the 1960s and new administration and expert advice since 1978 are now making fabulously good wine of the kind everyone wants – stylish Pauillac of the St-Julien persuasion; not so rigid with tannin and extract that it takes decades to mature. Each vintage since 1975 is among the best of their year with spectacular successes in '81, '82, '83, '84 and '86. The second label is Réserve de la Comtesse.

Château Pontet-Canet
5eme Cru Classé 1855. Owner: Guy Tesseron.
AOC: Pauillac. 173 acres; 26,000 cases. Grape var: Cab.Sauv. 70%, Cab.Franc 4%, Merlot 26%.
Price (1989): 70 francs a bottle.

Sheer size has helped Pontet-Canet to become one of Bordeaux's most familiar names. That, and over a century of ownership by the shippers Cruse & Fils Frères. This situation near Mouton promises top quality; the 1929 was considered better than the Mouton of that great year. But 1961 was the last great vintage Pontet-Canet has made, and that, like all its wines of that epoch, was very variable from bottle to bottle. The Cruse family did not believe in château bottling. In 1975 the estate was sold to M. Tesseron of Cognac (and Ch. Lafon-Rochet, St-Estèphe), son-in-law of Emmanuel Cruse. The '75 was impressive, the '76 pleasant, the '78 sternly tannic and the '79 very good, and the '80s have seen further improvement, though greatness still seems elusive. The double-decker *cuvier*, *chais* and bottle cellars are on an enormous scale even by Médoc standards. The second label, Les Hauts de Pontet (13,000 cases produced annually), was introduced in 1982.

OTHER CHATEAUX

Château Anseillan
Owners: Soc. Lafite-Rothschild. No vines at present.

Château Belle Rose
Cru Bourgeois. Second wine of Ch. Pédesclaux.

Carruades de Lafite
New name for Moulin de Carruades.

Château Colombier Monpelou
Grand Cru Bourgeois. Owner: Bernard Jugla. 40 acres; 6,000 cases. Usually attractive stablemate of the Cru Classé Ch. Pédesclaux.

Château La Fleur Milon
Grand Cru Bourgeois. Owner: André Gimenez. 30 acres; 4,600 cases.

Château Fonbadet
Owner: Pierre Peyronie. 38 acres; 5,700 cases. A good growth in the category considering itself 'exceptionnel', not officially recognized as such. Part of the vineyard is now Ch. Plantey (q.v.). M. Peyronie also owns Ch'x La Tour du Roc Milon, Haut-Pauillac, Padarnac and Montgrand Milon, all in Pauillac.

Les Forts de Latour
See Ch. Latour. The first of the 'second' wines of the Médoc, and still the best.

Château Gaudin
Owner: Pierre Bibian. 21 acres; 3,000 cases.

Château Grand Duroc Milon
Cru Bourgeois. A second label of Ch. Pédesclaux.

Château Haut-Bages Monpelou
Cru Bourgeois. Owners: Hérit. Borie-Manoux (Emile Castéja). 25 acres; 4,500 cases. Part of the former vineyard of Ch. Duhart-Milon, now in the same hands as Ch. Batailley and better than its rank.

Château Haut-Padarnac
Cru Bourgeois. Owner: Bernard Jugla. Another wine from the Ch. Pédesclaux estate.

Moulin des Carruades
The second wine of Ch. Lafite-Rothschild.

Château Pibran
Cru Bourgeois. Owners: AXA Millésimes. 25 acres; 4,000 cases.

Château Plantey
Owner: Gabriel Meffre. 74 acres. Formerly part of Ch. Fonbadet, M. Meffre, a merchant, also owns Ch. du Glana (St-Julien).

Château Roland
Owners: Soc. Lafite-Rothschild. No vines at present. The manager of Ch. Lafite lives in the house.

La Tour l'Aspic
Owner: Jean-Eugène Borie. Second label of Ch. Haut-Batailley.

Château La Tour Pibran
Owner: Jacques Gounel. 20 acres; 3,400 cases.

Château La Tour du Roc Milon
Owner: Pierre Peyronie. 12 acres; 2,000 cases. *See* Ch. Fonbadet.

Cave Coopérative La Rose Pauillac
Growers' cooperative with an average production of 52,000 cases a year of well-made Pauillac. Labels include Château La Rose.

Caves Coopératives of the Médoc
Fourteen *coopératives* make wine both under trade names and on behalf of small châteaux. These châteaux wines are from grapes grown at the estate in question, though the vinification is done at the cooperative. The wines thus keep their own identity. Among them are: Bégadan coop: Ch'x Le Barrail, Bernet, Bégadanet, Breuil-Renaissance, Haut-Cordissas, Labadie, Lassus, Meilhan, Monge, Pey-de-By, Rose-du-Pont and Vimenay. Ordonnac coop: Ch'x Belfort, de Brie, du Grand-Bois, Les Graves, Lagorce, Moulin-de-Buscateau, Moulin-de-la-Rivière, L'Oume-de-Pay, Pavillon de Bellevue, La Rose-Picot. St-Roch coop: Ch'x Laubespin, Pessange, Trois-Tétons. St Yzans coop: Talford, Tour St Vincent.

ST-ESTEPHE

St-Estèphe is more pleasantly rural than Pauillac; a scattering of six hamlets with some steepish slopes and (at Marbuzet) wooded parks. It has 2,820 acres of vineyards, mainly Crus Bourgeois, on heavier soil planted with, as a rule, a higher proportion of Merlot to Cabernet than the communes to the south. Typical St-Estèphe keeps a strong colour for a long time, is slow to show its virtues, has less perfume and a coarser, more hearty flavour than Pauillac, with less of the tingling vitality that marks the very best Médocs. With a few brilliant exceptions the St-Estèphes are the foot soldiers of this aristocratic army. Postcode: 33250 Pauillac.
Price (1989): 19 francs a bottle.

ST-ESTEPHE CRUS CLASSES

Château Calon-Ségur

3eme Cru Classé 1855. Dir: Philippe Capbern-Gasqueton.
AOC: St-Estèphe. 232 acres; 21,000 cases. Grape var: Cab.Sauv. 65%, Cab.Franc 15%, Merlot 20%.

The northernmost classed growth of the Médoc, named after the 18th-century Comte de Ségur who also owned Lafite and Latour but whose 'heart was at Calon' – and is remembered by a red one on the label. The wine sometimes has more flesh than excitement, but is impressively full of flavour as befits its class. The walled vineyard surrounds the fine château. Other Capbern-Gasqueton properties are du Tertre (Margaux) and d'Agassac (qq.v.).

Château Cos d'Estournel

2eme Cru Classé 1855. Owners: Domaines Prats.
Dir: Bruno Prats.
AOC: St-Estèphe. 173 acres; 20,000 cases. Grape var: Cab.Sauv. 60% Cab.Franc 2%, Merlot 38%.
Price (1989): 115 francs a bottle.

Superbly sited vineyard sloping south towards Ch. Lafite. No house but a bizarre chinoiserie *chai*. The most (perhaps the only) glamorous St-Estèphe, one of the top second-growths with both the flesh and the bone of great claret and a good record for consistency. The director, Bruno Prats, uses modern methods to make wine with old-fashioned virtues, including very long life. The second label is Ch. (de) Marbuzet; Ch. Petit-Village in Pomerol also belongs to him. The 's' of Cos is sounded, like most final consonants in southwest France.

Château Cos Labory

5eme Cru Classé 1855. Owner: Mme Cécile Audoy.
AOC: St-Estèphe. 37 acres; 7,000 cases. Grape var: Cab.Sauv. 40%, Cab.Franc 25%, Merlot 30%, Petit Verdot 5%.

Price (1989): 45 francs a bottle.

A business-like little classed growth next door to Cos d'Estournel, but only geographically. The rather scattered vineyards with a high proportion of Merlot vines make a blunt, honest St-Estèphe, relatively soft and fruity for drinking in 4 or 5 years.

Château Lafon-Rochet

4eme Cru Classé 1855. Owner: Guy Tesseron.
AOC: St-Estèphe. 98 acres; 15,000 cases. Grape var: Cab.Sauv. 60%, Merlot 34%, Cab.Franc 6%.
Price (1989): 47 francs a bottle.

A single block of vineyard sloping south towards the back of Ch. Lafite on the south bank of St-Estèphe. The château was rebuilt in the 1960s by the cognac merchant Guy Tesseron, who spares no expense to make good wine and has steadily improved the property making further changes recently. He makes full-bodied, warm, satisfying wine which is worth keeping for smoothness, but does not seem to find great finesse. A very good '82. Numero 2 is the second label.

Château Montrose

2eme Cru Classé 1855. Owner: Jean-Louis Charmolüe.
AOC: St-Estèphe. 168 acres; 22,500 cases. Grape var: Cab.Sauv. 65%, Cab.Franc 10%, Merlot 25%.
Price (1989): 90 francs a bottle.

Isolated, seemingly remote property overlooking the Gironde north of St-Estèphe with a style of its own; traditionally one of the 'firmest' of all Bordeaux, hard and forbidding for a long time, notably powerful in flavour even when mature. The deep colour and flavour of the wine probably come from the clay subsoil under reddish, iron-rich gravel. Being right on the river also helps the grapes to early ripeness. Wines of the period '78–'85 let the standard drop, being much softer and 'easier', and '86 promises sterner stuff again. The second label is La Dame de Montrose.

The eccentric Chinese pagoda-style architecture of Château Cos d'Estournel, restored in 1990, makes it a landmark in St-Estèphe

---

OTHER CHATEAUX

Château Andron-Blanquet
Grand Bourgeois Exceptionnel. Owner: Mme Cécile Audoy. 39 acres; 5,500 cases. Made at Cos Labory (Cru Classé see Cos Labory). Second label: Ch. St-Roch (Bourgeois).

Château Beau Site
Grand Bourgeois Exceptionnel. Owners: The Castéja-Borie family (see Ch. Batailley, Pauillac). 67 acres; 15,000 cases. A fine situation in the hamlet of St-Corbin. Distributed by Borie-Manoux.

Château Le Boscq
Cru Bourgeois. Owner: Claude Lapalu. 64 acres; 14,000 cases.

Château Capbern-Gasqueton
Grand Bourgeois Exceptionnel. Owner: same family as Calon-Ségur (Cru Classé see Calon-Ségur). 85 acres; 20,000 cases. Ch'x Grand-Village-Capbern, La Rose-Capbern, Moulin-de-Calon all refer to the same property. Distributors: Dourthe Frères.

Château Chambert-Marbuzet
see Ch. Haut-Marbuzet.

Château Coutelin-Merville
Cru Bourgeois. Owner: Bernard Estager. 42 acres; 8,000 cases.

Château Le Crock
Grand Bourgeois Supérieur. Owners: Cuvelier & Fils. 82 acres; 17,000 cases. A classical mansion in a fine park, home of the owners of Léoville-Poyferré (Cru Classé, St-Julien). Second label: Cru St-Estèphe La Croix.

Château Haut-Marbuzet
Grand Bourgeois Exceptionnel. Owners: H. Duboscq & Fils. 114 acres; 25,000 cases. Today the outstanding Cru Bourgeois of St-Estèphe, and regularly one of the best buys of the Médoc; oaky, fleshy, luxurious and instantly appealing. Ch. Chambert-Marbuzet and Ch. MacCarthy-Moula are Crus Bourgeois with the same owners. Second label: Ch. Tour de Marbuzet.

Château Houissant
Owners: Jean Ardouin & Fils. 49 acres; 10,000 cases.

Château Laffitte-Carcasset
Owner: Vicomte de Padirac. 111 acres; 29,000 cases. Ch. Brame Les Tours is on the same estate.

Château MacCarthy
Grand Bourgeois. Owner: Jean Raymond. 14 acres; 2,500 cases. Now the second label of Ch. Chambert-Marbuzet.

Château MacCarthy-Moula
Cru Bourgeois (see Ch. Haut-Marbuzet).

Château (de) Marbuzet
Grand Bourgeois Exceptionnel. The second label of Cos d'Estournel (Cru Classé; see Cos d'Estournel). A guarantee in itself.

Château Meyney
Grand Bourgeois Exceptionnel. Owners: Cordier (the négociants; see also Ch. Gruaud-Larose, St-Julien). 125 acres; 25,000 cases. One of the best of the many reliable Crus Bourgeois in St-Estèphe.

Château Morin
Cru Bourgeois. Owners: The Sidaine family. 24 acres; 4,000 cases.

Château Les-Ormes-de-Pez
Grand Bourgeois. Owner: Jean-Michel Cazes (see Ch. Lynch-Bages, Pauillac). 80 acres; 15,000 cases. Extremely popular and highly regarded property.

Château de Pez
Owners: The Bernard family. Dir: Robert Dousson. 60 acres; 14,000 cases. One of the best Cru Bourgeois in St-Estèphe, although it is not a member of the Syndicate. Noble, very long-lived wine of classed-growth standard. At 20 years the 1970 was magnificent. (Cab.Sauv. 70%, Merlot 15%, Cab.Franc 15%.) Distributors: Gilbeys of Loudenne.

Château Phélan-Ségur
Grand Bourgeois Exceptionnel. Owner: Xavier Gardinier. 125 acres; 22,000 cases. Important property including also Ch'x Fonpetite and La Croix. Recently totally rebuilt and full of ambition.

Château Tronquoy-Lalande
Grand Bourgeois. Owner: Mme Castéja. 40 acres; 7,000 cases. Well distributed by Dourthe Frères.

OTHER GROWTHS

Château Beauséjour
42 acres; 7,000 cases (also Ch. Picard).

Château Beau-Site-Haut-Vignoble
50 acres; 8,000 cases.

Château Canteloup
41 acres; 3,500 cases (also Ch. La Commanderie; property of G. Meffre, *see* Ch. Glana, St-Julien).

Château Clauzet
9 acres; 1,750 cases.

Château Lartigue
17 acres; 3,000 cases

Château St-Estèphe
34 acres; 8,000 cases

Château La Tour de Marbuzet
18 acres; 3,000 cases.

Château La Tour-des-Termes
65 acres; 13,500 cases.

HAUT-MEDOC

Haut-Médoc is the catch-all appellation for the fringes of the area that includes the most famous communes. It varies in quality from equal to some of the best in the very south, where Château La Lagune in Ludon and Château Cantemerle are out on a limb, to a level only notionally higher than the best of the lower, northerly end of the Médoc. Some of this land lies along the river in the middle of the appellation, in the low-lying communes of Arcins, Lamarque and Cussac – which also, it must be said, have some very good gravel. Some lies back inland along the edge of the pine forest.

With a total of 8,267 acres, the Haut-Médoc appellation is only an indication, not a guarantee, of high quality.

Price (1988): 19 francs a bottle.

HAUT-MEDOC CRUS CLASSES

Château Belgrave
5eme Cru Classé 1855. Owners: CVBG – Dourthe-Kressmann. Manager: Merete Larsen.
AOC: Haut-Médoc. 136 acres; 20,000 cases. Grape var: Cab.Sauv. 40%, Cab.Franc 20%, Merlot 35%, Petit Verdot 5%.
A lost property until 1980, now ultra-modernized with the initial advice of Professor Peynaud. Hold your breath.

Château de Camensac
5eme Cru Classé 1855. Owners: The Forner family.
AOC: Haut-Médoc. 149 acres; 20,000 cases. Grape var: Cab.Sauv. 60%, Cab.Franc 20%, Merlot 20%.
Neighbour of Ch'x Belgrave, La Tour-Carnet and Lagrange in the St-Laurent group, inland from St-Julien and out of the serious running for many years. Largely replanted since 1965 by M. Forner, the former owner of the neighbouring huge Cru Bourgeois Larose-Trintaudon. The result is good, full bodied, forthright wine with plenty of vigour, needing much longer maturing than the 'easy' Cru Bourgeois.

Château Cantemerle
5eme Cru Classé 1855. Dir: Jean Cordier.
AOC: Haut-Médoc. 148 acres; 29,000 cases. Grape var: Cab.Sauv. 45%, Cab.Franc 10%, Merlot 40%, Petit Verdot 5%.
The next château north from La Lagune, hidden behind a wooded 'park' of mysterious beauty with canals reflecting graceful white bridges and immense trees. The tree beside the house on the pretty engraved label is a plane that now dominates the house completely – a monster.
The old-fashioned estate with dwindling vineyards (half their former size) and totally traditional methods was sold in 1981 to a syndicate led by Cordier, who have extended and modernized it. The old peculiarities included de-stalking the grapes by rubbing the bunches through a wooden grille, fermentation at a high tempera-ture and the use of well-aged barrels for as long as two and a half years. The result, with light soil and a good deal of Merlot, was wine of incredible charm yet formidable stability. Vintages of the '50s and '60s were marvellous; those of the '70s not quite so good, but quality was regained with '82 and '83 and now stands high, as in all Cordier properties.

Château La Lagune
3eme Cru Classé 1855. Owner: Jean-Michel Ducellier.
AOC: Haut-Médoc. 173 acres; 25,000 cases. Grape var: Cab.Sauv. 60%, Cab.Franc 15%, Merlot 20%, Petit Verdot 5%.
The nearest important Médoc château to Bordeaux and a charming 18th-century villa. The vineyard had almost disappeared in the 1950s, when it was totally replanted and equipped with the latest steel vats and pipes. In 1961 the owners of Ayala champagne bought it and have been making better and better wine as the vines have rooted deeper in the light, sandy gravel. Sweetness, spiciness, fleshiness and concentration are all qualities found in it by critics. In poor vintages it can almost caricature itself with a rather jammy effect; in great ones it is now on a par with such second-growths as Léoville Las Cases and Ducru-Beaucaillou. Like a first-growth, La Lagune uses new barrels for all the wine every year.

Château La Tour Carnet
4eme Cru Classé 1855. Owner: Guy François Pelegrin.
AOC: Haut-Médoc. 99 acres; 15,000–18,000 cases. Grape var: Cab.Sauv. 53%, Cab.Franc 10%, Merlot 33%, Petit Verdot 4%.
Price (1989): 61 francs a bottle.
A moated medieval castle in the relatively rolling, wooded back country of St-Laurent, restored in the 1960s and still perhaps suffering from the youth of its vines. The vine is light in colour and pretty in style, maturing quickly. Enjoyable, but scarcely a fourth-growth if Cantemerle is a fifth.

Visiting châteaux

Visitors to the Médoc will have no difficulty in finding châteaux willing to show them how they make their wine, and to let them taste it from the barrel. One simple way of arranging a château visit is to call at one of the little offices called *Maison du Vin*. The principal one is in the heart of Bordeaux near the Grand Théâtre. Margaux, Pauillac, St-Estèphe and several other villages have local ones. They will suggest an itinerary and if necessary make contacts.

An even simpler method, but only really practicable for those who speak some French, is to stop at any of the many châteaux that advertise *vente directe* – direct sales – on roadside signs. They include some important châteaux as well as many modest ones. At any reasonable time (i.e. not during the harvest or any period of frantic activity, and not at lunch time, from noon to two o'clock) you can expect a more or less friendly welcome from the *maître de chai*, the cellar master.

In big châteaux he is a man of considerable dignity and responsibility, whatever he is wearing. He has seen many visitors pass and will make up his own mind, rightly or wrongly, about how much to show you. He will expect moderate praise for the chilly, tannic and (to the non-expert) almost untastable sample he draws from the barrel and hands you in a glass. Unless an obviouis receptacle (often a tub of sawdust) is provided you may – indeed must – spit it out on the floor. I tend to wander off ruminating to the doorway and spit into the outside world. It gives me a chance to compose my thoughts – and recover from my grimace.

Clearly the idea of *tente directe* is that you should buy a bottle or two, but you need not feel obliged. The *maître de chai* would often just as soon accept a 10 franc tip.

Advanced students will have to judge for themselves how far into detailed discussion of techniques, weather conditions and earlier vintages the *maître de chai* is prepared to go. It is not unknown for young and even not-so-young bottles to be opened in the enthusiasm of explanation. But it is scarcely reasonable to expect such treatment.

OTHER CHÂTEAUX

Château d'Agassac
Grand Bourgeois Exceptionnel, Ludon. Dir: P. Capbern-Gasqueton. 74 acres plus; 9,000 cases. The Médoc's most romantic château, medieval, moated and deep in the woods. The owner (also of Ch'x Calon-Ségur and du Tertre) is making increasingly good wine. The Cru Classé La Lagune is nearby.

Château Aney
Cru Bourgeois, Cussac. Owners: Raimond Père & Fils. 61 acres; 12,000 cases. Cussac is the nearly flat parish south of St-Julien.

Château d'Arche
Ludon. Owner: F. Duchesne. 25 acres; 2,500 cases. A good wine.

Château d'Arcins
Arcins. Owners: Castel. 172 acres; 37,500 cases. The two biggest Arcins properties have recently been restored by the important wine-merchant family of Castel, famous for their Castelvin brand. Their huge new stone-clad warehouse seems to fill the village. Their presence here is bound to make the neglected name of Arcins familiar. Its wine should be of Cussac standard, which can be high.

Château d'Arnauld
Arcins. Owner: M. Roggy. 37 acres; 4,500 cases. (*See* Ch. Poujeaux, Moulis.) A very good wine.

Château Balac
Cru Bourgeois, St-Laurent. Owner: Luc Touchais. 34 acres; 6,500 cases. The Touchais family are better known for their Anjou wines.

Château Barreyres
Arcins. Owners: Castel. 370 acres; 32,000 cases. An imposing property near the river, now linked with Ch. d'Arcins (q.v.).

Château Beaumont
Grand Bourgeois, Cussac. Owner: GMF/MAIF. 210 acres plus; 30,000 cases plus. Grand but dormant château in the woods north of Poujeaux, awakened by a new owner in 1979. Second label: Moulin d'Arvigny.

Château Bel-Orme-Tronquoy-de-Lalande
Grand Bourgeois, St-Seurin. Owner: Mme L. Quié and J.-M. Quié. 60 acres; 10,000 cases. Well-regarded property of the family that owns Ch'x Rauzan-Gassies and Croizet-Bages. Tannic wines for keeping. Easily confused with Ch. Tronquoy-Lalande, St-Estèphe.

Château Bonneau
Cru Bourgeois, St-Seurin. Owner: Lucien Eyquem. 12 acres; 3,300 cases.

Château Le Bourdieu
Vertheuil. Owner: Mike Barbe. 134 acres; 12,000 cases plus. Vertheuil lies just inland from St-Estèphe on similar clayey gravel. This big property (which includes the château with the promising name of Victoria) can make good St-Estèphe-style wine.

Château Le (du) Breuil
Cru Bourgeois, Cissac. Owner: Gerard Germain, 57 acres; 13,000 cases. On the edge of the parish just behind the Carruades plateau of Pauillac and Ch. Duhart-Milon. Stylish wines.

Château Caronne-Ste-Gemme
Grand Bourgeois Exceptionnel, St-Laurent. Owner: J. and F. Nony-Borie. 111 acres; 20,000 cases. A substantial property whose label is a mass of medals, but all of long ago. Well made, somewhat lean wine, capable of charm with time.

Château du Cartillon
Cru Bourgeois. Owner: Gérard Maltête. 70 acres. 17,000 cases.

Château Charmail
St-Seurin. Owner: Olivier Sèze. 49 acres; 8,500 cases.

Château Cissac
Grand Bourgeois Exceptionnel, Cissac. Owner: Louis Vialard, 80 acres; 14,000 cases. A pillar of the bourgeoisie; reliable, robust, mainstream Médoc at its best after 10 years or so. M. Vialard is a man of authority and style. Second label: Ch. de Marting.

Château Citran
Grand Bourgeois Exceptionnel, Avensan. Owner: Touko-Hans. 220 acres; 32,000 cases. A pace-setting Cru Exceptionnel with a wide following and a long record of good vintages. Round, full wine (42% Merlot) with ageing potential. Sold in 1987 to the Japanese. A programme of major works is now underway.

Château Coufran
Grand Bourgeois, St-Seurin. Dir: Jean Miailhe. 158 acres; 33,600 cases. The northernmost estate of the Haut-Médoc, it is unusual in being 85% Merlot to make softer, more 'fleshy' wine than its neighbouring sister – Ch. Verdignan (q.v.). Miailhe is president and spokesman for the league of Crus Bourgeois (*see also* Ch. Citran, Avensan).

Château La Dame Blanche
Le Taillan. Owner: Henri-François Cruse. 15 acres; 2,500 cases plus. The other side of the house at Ch. du Taillan: the name given to the pleasant white of Sauv.Bl. and Colombard.

Château Dillon
Blanquefort. Owner: Ecole d'Agriculture. 86 acres; 18,500 cases. The local agricultural college. Some good wines, including dry white Ch. Linas.

Château Fonpiqueyre
Cru Bourgeois, St-Sauveur. Included in Ch. Liversan. 2,500 cases.

Château Fontesteau
Grand Bourgeois, St-Sauveur. Owner:
Jean Renaud. 27 acres; 5,000 cases.
Good conservative wine in the classic
Médoc style for maturing.

Château Fort Vauban
Cru Bourgeois, Cussac. Owner: André
Noleau. 25 acres; 4,000 cases. Vauban
was the military architect who built the
Fort-Médoc on the river at Cussac.

Château Le Fournas
St-Sauveur. Owners: Bernadotte and
Proche-Pontet. 74 acres; 13,000 cases.

Château Grandis
St-Seurin-de-Cadourne. Owner: M.
Figeron. 14 acres; 1,700 cases.

Château Grand Moulin
Grand Bourgeois, St-Seurin. Owner: R.
Gonzalvez. 92 acres; 25,000 cases. Also
appears under the name Ch. La Mothe.

Château Hanteillan
Grand Bourgeois, Cissac. Owners:
SARL du Château Hanteillan. 205 acres;
35,000 cases. Old property lavishly
restored and replanted since 1973, now
making exciting wine. Since 1979 Ch.
Larrivaux-Hanteillan has been part of
the same estate. The second wine is Ch.
La Tour du Vatican.

Château Hourtin-Ducasse
Cru Bourgeois, St-Sauveur. Owner:
Maurice Marengo. 54 acres; 10,000
cases. An elegant wine.

Château Lamarque
Grand Bourgeois, Lamarque. Dir:
Roger Gromand. 116 acres; 25,000
cases. The finest remaining medieval
fortress in the Médoc, in the village
where the ferry leaves for Blaye.
Developed by the present owners up to
Cru Exceptionnel standards, proving the
potential of the central Médoc.

Château Lamothe-de-Bergeron
Cru Bourgeois, Cussac. Owners: Les
Grands Vignobles. 123 acres; 25,000
cases. The same owners as Ch. Grand-
Puy-Ducasse.

Château Lamothe-Cissac
Grand Bourgeois, Cissac. Owner: G.
Fabre. 82 acres; 12,000 cases. Up-to-date
property related (by marriage) to Ch.
Cissac.

Château Landat
Cru Bourgeois, Cissac. Owner: G. Fabre

(*see* Lamothe-Cissac). 37 acres; 6,500
cases.

Château Lanessan
Cussac. Owners: The Bouteiller family.
106 acres; 28,000 cases. Includes Ch.
Lachesnaye and Ste-Gemme. An
extravagant Victorian mansion and park
with a popular carriage museum. The
best-known estate in Cussac with the
standards of a Cru Exceptionnel, if not a
Cru Classé. Polished rather than exciting
wine.

Château Larose-Trintaudon
Grand Bourgeois, St-Laurent. Owners:
Assurances Générales de France.
President: J. Papon. 425 acres; 83,000
cases. The biggest estate in the Médoc,
planted since 1965, built up by the
Forner family, owners of the admirable
Rioja Marques de Caceres (and the
neighbouring Cru Classé Ch. de Camensac).
Modern methods include mechanical
harvesting. Quantity does not seem to
impede steady, enjoyable quality.
The Forners sold the estate in 1986 and
continued to manage it until 1989.

Château Larrivaux
Cissac. 62 acres; 11,000 cases. Now
mostly swallowed up by Ch. Hanteillan.

Château Lartigue de Brochon
Cru Bourgeois, St-Seurin. Owner: J.
Gautreau. 30 acres; 4,000 cases. M.
Gautreau is also proprietor of the
admirable Sociando-Mallet.

Château Lestage Simon
Cru Bourgeois, St-Seurin. Owner: C.
Simon. 74 acres; 16,600 cases.
Concentrated and fruity.

Château Lieujean
St-Sauveur. Owner: André Baron. 30
acres; 6,700 cases.

Château Liversan
Cru Bourgeois, St-Sauveur. Owner:
Prince Guy de Polignac. 115 acres;
15,000 cases. Charming property
including Ch. Fonpiqueyre.
Conscientious wine-making backed by
new investment. Second labels Ch. des
Hormes.

Château Ludon-Pomiés-Agassac
Ludon. A name belonging to Ch. La
Lagune. Cru Classé.

Château Malescasse
Lamarque. Owner: Guy Tesseron. 82

acres; 13,000 cases plus. Estate replanted
in the 1970s by American owners,
bought in 1981 by the Tesserons of Ch.
Pontet-Canet. Promises good wine as
the vines mature. Very good in '82, '85,
'86.

Château de Malleret
Grand Bourgeois, Le Pian. Owner:
Comte Bertrand du Vivier. 145 acres;
25,000 cases. The handsome country
house of the head of the shipping firm
de Luze, on the doorstep of Bordeaux.

Château Le Meynieu
Grand Bourgeois, Vertheuil. Owner: J.
Pédro. 34 acres; 6,500 cases. A recent
addition to the number of serious and
competent bourgeois châteaux.

Château du Moulin Rouge
Cru Bourgeois, Cussac. Owner: Guy
Pelon. 37 acres; 8,000 cases.

Châteaux Peyrabon
Grand Bourgeois, St-Sauveur. Owner:
Jacques Babeau. 130 acres; 18,500 cases.
Well-structured, round wine from a
75% Cabernet vineyard, sold more to
appreciative private clients than through
merchants. The château had the rare
distinction of a visit by Queen Victoria.
Second labels include Ch. Pierbone.

Château Pichon
Parempuyre. Owners: C. Fayat. 56 acres;
8,000 cases.

Château Plantey de la Croix
Cru Bourgeois, St-Seurin. Second label
of Ch. Verdignan.

Château Pontoise-Cabarrus
Grand Bourgeois, St-Seurin. Owner: M.
Terreygeol. 56 acres; 13,500 cases. A
serious, well-run property.

Château La Providence
Bordeaux Supérieur, Ludon. Owners:
The Bouteiller family. 17 acres; 3,000
cases. The vineyard is just outside the
appellation Haut-Médoc. Rather good
wine.

Château Puy Castéra
Cru Bourgeois, Cissac. Owners: MM.
Marès. 62 acres; 17,000 cases. A recent
creation, apparently in good hands.

Château Ramage La Batisse
Cru Bourgeois, St-Sauveur. Owners:
Société Civile. 133 acres; 15,000 cases. A
creation of the last 25 years. Now one of
the bigger Cru Bourgeois with modern

The châteaux – how the list was compiled
'The only complete list of wine growers
in any serious part of France is the
telephone directory.' The remark was
made to me in Burgundy but it is
equally true for much of Bordeaux.
Everybody is a wine grower. So who do
you put in and who do you leave out?

The answer is a long sifting process,
starting with published lists of classified

properties at various levels of
importance, going through members of
syndicates, reviewing wine lists, books
and articles, re-reading tasting notes and
finally, most of all, relying on people on
the spot – merchants, mayors of
villages, brokers who specialize in one
corner of the country. I am acutely
aware of the subjectivity of everything
short of the telephone book – but this is
the nature of the subject matter.

Some growers have reputations
exceeding their worth; others are
worthy workers and reliable suppliers
but have never known how, or felt the
need, to build a reputation.

In some areas where vineyards are
very small I have simply had to employ
the guillotine – which has been
abolished for its original purpose.
Otherwise I would not have dared. (*See*
index pages 104–105.)

methods but traditional oak-aged style, winning medals for quality.

Château du Retout
Cussac. Owner: R. Kopp. 56 acres; 12,500 cases.

Château Reysson
Grand Bourgeois, Vertheuil. Owners: Grands Vignobles de Bordeaux. 113 acres; 15,000 cases. A member of the same group as Ch. Grand-Puy-Ducasse with the same competent management.

Château Romefort
Cru Bourgeois, Cussac. Owner: Laurent Poitou. *See* Ch. La Tour du Haut Moulin.

Château de la Rose Maréchal
Cru Bourgeois, St-Seurin. A second label of Ch. Verdignan.

Château de St-Paul
St-Seurin. Owner: M. Bouchet. 47 acres; 12,000 cases.

Château Ségur
Grand Bourgeois, Parempuyre (alias Ch. Ségur-Fillon). Owners: Société Civile. 81 acres; 15,000 cases. One of the finer Crus Bourgeois, on good, deep gravel in the extreme south of the Médoc. Popular in Holland.

Château Sénéjac
Le Pian. Owner: Charles de Guigné. 59 acres; 10,000 cases plus. Old family property with a New Zealand winemaker; immaculate and often exciting wines.

Château Senilhac
St-Seurin. Owner: M. Grassin. 28 acres; 5,700 cases.

Château Sociando-Mallet
Grand Bourgeois, St-Seurin. Owner: J. Gautreau. 99 acres; 13,000 cases. A star of the bourgeoisie. Recent vintages have outshone many *crus classés*. *See also* Ch. Lartigue.

Château Soudars
Cru Bourgeois, St-Seurin. Owner: Eric Miailhe (son of Jean, Ch. Coufran). 38 acres; 11,000 cases.

Château du Taillan
Grand Bourgeois, Le Taillan. Owner: Henri-François Cruse. 52 acres; 10,000 cases. Pleasant red, 40% Merlot, from a charming estate north of Bordeaux. La Dame Blanche is the estate's white wine.

Château du Terrey-Gros-Caillou
Cru Bourgeois, St-Julien. Owners: André Fort & Henri Pradère. 38 acres; 8,000 cases.

Château Tour du Haut Moulin
Grand Bourgeois, Cussac. Owner: Laurent Poitou. 86 acres; 17,000 cases. Full-flavoured wine (45% Merlot) with a wide following. Until his retirement in 1982, M. Poitou managed several other estates for les Grands Vignobles.

Château La Tour du Mirail
Cru Bourgeois, Cissac. Owners: Hélène and Danielle Vialard (*see* Ch. Cissac). 44 acres; 9,000 cases.

Château Tour du Roc
Cru Bourgeois, Arcins. Owner: Philippe Robert. 30 acres; 6,000 cases.

Château La Tour St-Joseph
Cru Bourgeois, Cissac. Owners: M. and C. Quancard. 32 acres; 8,000 cases.

Château Tourteran
St-Sauveur. 24 acres; 8,500 cases. Same owner as Ch. Ramage La Batisse.

Château Verdignan
Grand Bourgeois, St-Seurin. Owner: Jean Miailhe. 114 acres; 26,000 cases. In contrast to its sister-château Coufran, Verdignan has the classic Médoc proportion of Cabernet and needs keeping 2 or 3 years longer.

Château Villegeorge
Avensan. Owner: Lucien Lurton. 27 acres; 2,500 cases. A minor property of the owner of Ch. Brane-Cantenac and many others. Deep, rich-flavoured wine from a 60% Merlot vineyard.

Caves Coopératives
Château Chevalier d'Ars-Arcins – 125 acres; 12,000 cases plus.
'Cru La Paroisse St-Seurin de Cadourne' – St-Seurin de Cadourne. 325 acres; 61,000 cases. The coop of the next parish north from St-Estèphe.
Fort Médoc – Cussac 100 acres; 12,000 cases. Sound cooperative cellar at the impressive riverside fort built by Vauban to command the Gironde.

APPELLATION MEDOC

The lower Médoc (in the sense of being farther down the Gironde) was formerly called Bas-Médoc, which made it clear that it was this area and not the whole peninsula under discussion. The soil and therefore the wines are considered inferior here. The last of the big-calibre gravel has been deposited by glaciers higher up between Graves and St-Estèphe. Although the ground continues to heave gently the humps become more scattered and their soil much heavier with a high proportion of pale, cold clay, suited to Merlot rather than Cabernet (although patches of sandier soil persist here and there). The wine has distinctly less finesse and perfume, but good body and 'structure' with some of the tannic 'cut' that makes all Médocs such good wines at table. Good vintages last well in bottle without developing the sweet complexities of the Haut-Médoc at its best.

The last decade has seen a great revival of interest in this productive area. Half a dozen big properties have made the running and now offer a good deal, if not a bargain. The 1989 basic price was about 16 francs a bottle compared with 19 francs for the appellation Haut-Médoc. The best properties fetch about 150 per cent more than this, whereas in the Haut-Médoc the range runs up to about 800 per cent of a base price.

In 1972 there were 4,535 acres in production in the appellation. By 1987 this figure had grown to 8,598 acres. The legally permitted yield here is slightly higher than in the Haut-Médoc: 45 hecto-litres compared with 43 a hectare.

Much the most important commune is Bégadan, with several of the most prominent estates and a very big growers' cooperative. Nearly a third of the whole appellation comes from the one parish. Next in order of production come St-Yzans, Prignac, Ordonnac, Blaignan, St-Christoly and St-Germain.

The principal producers are given here in alpha-betical order, followed by the names of their communes. The central town for the whole area is Lesparre (postcode for all the communes mentioned is 33340 Lesparre Médoc).
Price (1988): 16 francs a bottle.

LOWER MEDOC CHATEAUX

Château Bellerive
Cru Bourgeois, Valeyrac. Owner:
G. Perrin. 27 acres; 4,700 cases.

Château Bellevue
Cru Bourgeois, Valeyrac. 49 acres;
12,500 cases.

Château Les Bertins
Cru Bourgeois, Valeyrac. Owner:
Domaine Codem (*see* Ch. Greysac). 54
acres; 10,000 cases.

Château Blaignan
Cru Bourgeois. Owners: Société Civile.
136 acres; 25,000 cases of red.

Château Le Bosq
Cru Bourgeois, St-Christoly. Owner:
C. Lapalu (*see also* Ch. Patache d'Aux).

Château Bournac
Owner: P. Secret. 30 acres; 4,500 cases
of red

Château Carcannieux
Cru Bourgeois, Queyrac. Dir: M. Paul.
52 acres; 8,000 cases.

Château La Cardonne
Grand Bourgeois, Blaignan. Owners:
Groupe Lafite-Rothschild. 210 acres;
36,000 cases. A Rothschild development
since 1973, a great boost to the lower
Médoc with its prestige and predictably
well-made wine.

Château du Castéra
Cru Bourgeois, St-Germain. 111 acres;
15,000 cases. A lovely old place with a
drawbridge, relic of more exciting times
(it was besieged by the English in the

14th century) belonging to the owners
of Ch. Lascombes, Margaux. Stainless
steel in use since 1981.

Château La Clare
Cru Bourgeois, Bégadan. Owner: Paul
de Rozières. 49 acres; 10,000 cases. Also
owns Ch. Grivière, Blaignan.

Château La France
Cru Bourgeois, Blaignan. Owner: M.
Querre. 54 acres; 13,000 cases.

Château Gallais-Bellevue
See Ch. Potensac, Ordonnac.

Château Greysac
Bégadan. Owner: Dom. Codem. Dir:
François de Gunzburg. 148 acres; 35,000
cases. Big, efficient property making
sound wine, well-known in the USA;
approachable young but can age.
Second label: Ch. Les Bertins.

Château Haut-Canteloup
Grand Bourgeois, Couquèques. Owner:
J. Sarrazy. 42 acres; 7,500 cases.

Château Hauterive
St-Germain d'Esteuil. Owner: M.
Lafage. 168 acres; 32,000 cases plus.

Château Haut Garin
Cru Bourgeois, Bégadan. Owner: M.
Hue. 16 acres; 4,900 cases.

Château Hourbanon
Cru Bourgeois, Prignac. Owner: Mme
Delayat. 30 acres; 5,000 cases.

Cru Lassalle
See Château Potensac, Ordonnac.

Château Laujac
Bégadan. Owner: Mme. H. Cruse. 74
acres; 10,000 cases. A home of the
famous family of shippers, hence well
known abroad long before most of the
other châteaux in the district.

Château Lavalière
Cru Bourgeois, St-Christoly. Owners:
Cailloux family. 38 acres; 7,500 cases.

Château Lestruelle
St-Yzans
See Cave Coop.

Château Livran
St-Germain (includes La Rose
Garomey). Owner: Robert Godfrin. 123
acres; 20,000 cases. A lovely old country
house with old vines (50% Merlot).
Says M. Godfrin: 'We have the
pleasures we deserve.'

Château Loudenne
Grand Bourgeois, St-Yzans. Owner:
Gilbeys. Dir: Charles Eve MW. 123
acres; 20,000 cases. The showplace of
the area; a low, pale pink château on a
hill of gravelly clay overlooking the
river. In English hands for over a
century. Great care in wine-making
produces well-balanced and long-lived
red and one of Bordeaux's best dry
whites. Seat of a wine *Ecole*.

*Racking the wine in the Victorian chai at
Château Loudenne*

Château Monthil
Cru Bourgeois, Bégadan. Owner: M.
Gabas. 49 acres; 9,500 cases.

Château Les Ormes Sorbet
Cru Bourgeois, Couquèques. Owner:
Jean Boivert. 52 acres; 8,500 cases. A
conscientious wine maker to be
watched. A gold-medal '82.

Château de Panigon
Cru Bourgeois, Civrac. Owner: J.K. and
J.R. Leveilley. 99 acres; 17,000 cases.

Château Patache d'Aux
Grand Bourgeois, Bégadan. Owner:
Claude Lapalu. 90 acres; 26,000 cases.
Popular full-flavoured Médoc with wide
distribution.

Château Pontet
Cru Bourgeois, Blaignan. Owner: M.
Courrian. 27 acres; 7,000 cases.

Château Potensac
Grand Bourgeois, Ordonnac (includes
Ch. Gallais-Bellevue, Cru Lasalle and
Ch. Goudy La Cardonne). Owner: Mme
Paul Delon. 98 acres; 20,000 cases. A
very successful enterprise of the owners
of Ch. Léoville Las Cases. Well-made,
fruity, enjoyable claret (by whatever
name) with a stylish flavour of oak – no
doubt barrels retired from Léoville.

Château Sestignan
Cru Bourgeois. Owner: B. de Rozières.
37 acres; 7,500 cases.

Château St-Bonnet
Cru Bourgeois, St-Christoly. Owner:
M. Solivères. 86 acres; 18,000 cases.

Château Sigognac
Grand Bourgeois, St-Christoly. Owner:
Mme Bonny-Grasset. 104 acres; 20,000
cases. A good light wine.

Château La Tour-Blanche
Cru Bourgeois, St-Christoly. Owner:
D. Hessel (*see also* Ch. Moulin à Vent,
Moulis). 62 acres; 11,000 cases.

Château La Tour de By
Grand Bourgeois, Bégadan (includes
Ch'x La Roque de By, Moulin de la
Roque, Caillou de By). Dir: Marc Pagés.
150 acres; 30,000 cases. Extremely
successful estate with a high reputation
for enjoyable and durable, if not literally
fine, wine.

Château La Tour du Haut-Caussan
Cru Bourgeois, Blaignan (alias Ch.
Pontet). Owner: M. Courrian. 26 acres;
6,000 cases.

Château des Tourelles
Cru Bourgeois, Blaignan. Owner:
F. Miquau. 50 acres; 13,000 cases.

Château La Tour Prignac
Prignac. Owner: Philippe Castel. 324
acres; 77,000 cases. Vast new enterprise
of the Castelvin family, whose Haut
Médoc headquarters is at Arcins (*see* Ch.
d'Arcins).

Château La Tour St-Bonnet
Cru Bourgeois, St-Christoly. Owner:
P. Lafon. 100 acres; 15,000 cases plus.
One of the pioneers of the lower Médoc
renaissance. Consistently good wine.

Château Vernous
Cru Bourgeois, Lesparre. Owners:
Ducourt family. 50 acres; 10,000 cases
plus. A new recruit: just planted, and
the only property at the local market
town.

Château Vieux Robin
Cru Bourgeois, Bégadan. Owner:
Maryse Roba. 42 acres; 6,500 cases.

Vieux-Château Beaujus
Pontiac. Owner: Thea Uther. 40 acres;
5,000 cases.

Vieux-Château Landon
Cru Bourgeois, Bégadan. Owner:
Philippe Gillet. 61 acres; 14,000 cases.
An energetic proprietor with ambitions.
Sound, lively wine.

Caves Coopératives
Bégadan – the largest in the area, with
grapes from about 1,400 acres. Labels
include Ch. Bégadanais.
Prignac – about 250 acres.
St-Yzans – about 500 acres. Ch.
Lestruelle is a label for their better wine.
As an example of cooperative quality,
the 1970 was excellent at 12 years old.

GRAVES

Wine was first made at Bordeaux in what is now the
city and the suburbs immediately across the river
and to the south. Graves was the name given to the
whole of the left (city) bank of the Garonne for as far
as 40 miles upstream, beyond the little town of
Langon, and back away from the river into the pine
forests of the Landes – an area not much different in
size from the wine-growing Médoc, but more cut up
with woodland and farms and containing few
extensive vineyards or big châteaux. Graves' distinguishing feature (hence its name) is its open,
gravelly soil, the relic of Pyrenean glaciers in the Ice
Ages. In fact, the soil varies within the region just as
much as that of the Médoc. Sand is common. Pale
clay and red clay are both present. But as in the
Médoc, it is pretty certain that by now most of the
potentially good vineyard land is being put to good
use. In all there are some 7,886 acres of vineyards.

But Graves is too diffuse to grasp easily. It would
be helpful (and accurate) if the authorities established an appellation Haut-Graves to distinguish the
few communes of the northern section where all the
Crus Classés are situated. Instead they have established the AC Pessac-Léognan for a rather wider
area. An enclave in the south of the region has quite

different styles – of landscape, ownership and wine.
This is Sauternes.

Although Graves is almost equally divided
between red wine and white, the great majority of
the top-quality wine is red. The words commonly
used to explain how red Graves differs from Médoc
all make it sound less fine: 'earthy', 'soft', 'maturing
sooner' sound more homely than inspiring. The late
Maurice Healey got it in one when he said that
Médoc and Graves were like glossy and matt prints
of the same photograph. The matt picture can be
equally beautiful, but less crisp and sharp-edged,
with less glittering colours.

White Graves at its best is a rare experience – and
an expensive one. Very few estates even aim for the
unique combination of fullness and drive that comes
to white Graves with time. The best is equal in
quality to the great white burgundies. Opinion is
divided even on the grapes to make it with. Some
favour all Sémillon, some all Sauvignon and some a
mixture, in various proportions. Some make it in
stainless steel and bottle it in the early spring. Others
(including the best) make it and mature it, at least
briefly, in new oak barrels. The tendency among the
lesser growths making dry wine has been to pick too

early for full ripeness. Sauvignon Blanc in any case ripens unevenly here. The best makers now concentrate on full ripeness and complete fermentation to give clean, dry wine with plenty of flavour.

The communes of what might be called 'Haut-Graves' are as follows, starting in the north on the doorstep of Bordeaux: Pessac and Talence (in the suburbs); Gradignan and Villenave-d'Ornon (with very little wine today); Léognan, the most extensive, with six classed growths; Cadaujac and Martillac. Up to 1987 all shared the single appellation Graves. In that year the new AC Pessac-Léognan was created, to include 55 châteaux and domaines in 10 communes; a total of 2,350 acres of vines. South of this district, but increasingly important for similar wine, is Portets. Cérons, on the threshold of Barsac and Sauternes, makes both sweet and dry

white wine, the dry now gaining in quality and popularity.

Price (1988): 19 francs a bottle.

The châteaux of Graves were classified in 1953 and 1959 in a blunt yes-or-no fashion which gives little guidance. Château Haut-Brion having been included in the Médoc classification 100 years earlier, 12 other châteaux were designated Crus Classés for their red wine, in alphabetical order. In 1959, six of them and two additional châteaux were designated Crus Classés for white wine. There is no other official ranking in Graves so all the rest can call themselves Crus Bourgeois (or presumably, come to that, Crus Exceptionnels) as they like. Lichine's classification usefully included Graves (and St-Emillion and Pomerol) as well as the Médoc. He recognized 14 Graves châteaux.

GRAVES PREMIER CRU

Château Haut-Brion

1er Cru Classé 1855, Pessac. Owner: Domaine Clarence Dillon.
AOC: Pessac-Léognan. 106 acres; 12,000 cases. Grape var:
Cab.Sauv. 50%, Cab.Franc 15%, Merlot 35%.

Price (1989): 225 francs a bottle.

The first wine château to be known by name, late in the 17th century, and although now surrounded by the suburbs of Bordeaux still one of the best of all, regularly earning its official place beside the four first-growths of the Médoc.

The situation of the 16th-century manor house of the Pontacs is no longer particularly impressive, but its 10 metres deep gravel soil gives deep-flavoured wine that holds a remarkable balance of fruity and earthy flavours for decades. Mouton has resonance, Margaux has coloratura; Haut-Brion just has harmony – between strength and finesse, firmness and sweetness. I shall never forget the taste of an Impériale of the 1899 – the most spellbinding claret I have ever drunk. The present owners, the

family of an American banker, Clarence Dillon, bought the estate in a near-derelict condition in 1935. In 1983 they added the next-door Ch. La. Mission-Haut-Brion (q.v.). The present president is Dillon's granddaughter. Haut-Brion was the first of the first-growths to install stainless steel vats for the quite quick and relatively warm fermentation which is its policy. Rather than select the 'best' strain of each vine, M. Delmas, the administrator, believes in diversity. He reckons to have nearly 400 different clones in the vineyard. This, and the fairly high proportion of Cabernet Franc, contribute complexity and harmony. As for age, Haut-Brion demands it. The good vintages of the 1970s – '71, '75, '78, '79 – are only now reaching their peak; the apogee of the 1980s is still some time away. A tiny quantity of very good white Graves (50–50 Sauvignon-Sémillon) is also made and sold at an extravagant price.

The second wine of Haut-Brion, Bahans-Haut-Brion, was unusual in being a non-vintage blend until 1983.

GRAVES CRUS CLASSES

Château Bouscaut

Cru Classé de Graves (red and white), Cadaujac. Owners:
Société Anonyme du Château Bouscaut. (Jean-Bernard Delmas and Lucien Lurton.)
AOC: Pessac-Léognan. 111 acres; 15,000 cases red, 6,250 cases white. Grape var: red: Merlot 50%, Cab.Sauv. 35%,
Cab.Franc 15%; white: Sém. 60%, Sauv. 40%.

The object of vast expense by American owners from 1969; a handsome 18th-century house with rather low-lying vineyards which have badly needed draining. The Merlot suits this soil better and dominates the vineyard, giving solid wine, although without overwhelming charm.

The 25 acres of white grapes are predominantly Sémillon; their wine is also more sound than thrilling. In 1980 Lucien Lurton of Ch. Brane-Cantenac bought the estate in collaboration with its former administrator, the man who runs Ch. Haut-Brion.

Château Carbonnieux

Cru Classé Graves (red and white), Léognan. Owners: Société des Grandes Graves. Dir: Antony Perrin.

AOC: Pessac-Léognan. 222 acres; 20,000 cases white, 25,000 cases red. Grape var. red: Cab.Sauv. 60%, Merlot 30%,
Cab.Franc 7%, Malbec 2%, Petit Verdot 1%; white: Sauv.
60%, Sém. 35%, Musc. 5%.

An old embattled monastery built around a courtyard, restored and run by a family who left Algeria in the 1950s. Bigger and hence better known than most Graves properties, particularly for its white wine, one of the flag-carriers for white Graves. The white is aged briefly in new oak barriques, then bottled young, thus keeping freshness while getting some of the proper oak flavour. Quality took a marked step forward in the late '80s. Three or four years in bottle perfect it. The red faces more competition but is well-made typical Graves, dry and persistent.

Antony Perrin has also recently restored a small red vineyard, Ch. Le Sartre, and a white one, Ch. La Tour-Léognan, in the same commune.

Domaine de Chevalier

Cru Classé de Graves (red and white), Léognan. Owners:
Société Civile. Dirs: Claude Riccard & Oliver Bernard.
AOC: Pessac-Léognan. 49 acres; 7,800 cases. Grape var:

Cab.Sauv. 65%, Cab.Franc 10%, Merlot 25%, white: Sauv. 70%, Sém. 30%

Price (1989): 160 francs a bottle.

A strange place to find a vineyard, in the middle of a wood and accompanied by no memorable château; just a plain house. Tree lover that I am, I always wonder why M. Riccard does not chop down a few to add to one of the best but smallest Graves vineyards. The soil and the style of the red wine are similar to the nearby Haut-Bailly; starting stern, maturing dense and savoury. 1961, '64 and '66 were all magnificent and '80s have been very fine.

The white wine is second only to Laville Haut-Brion in quality, designed for astonishingly long life. It is made with the care of a great Sauternes, fermented and matured in barrels. To drink it before 5 years is a waste, and the flavours of a 15-year-old bottle can be breathtaking.

Château Couhins Inra

Cru Classé de Graves (white), Villenave-d'Ornon. Owners: Institut National de la Recherche Agronomique.

AOC: Pessac-Léognan. 6 acres; 1,250 cases. Grape var: Sauv. 80%, Sém 20%.

The property of the National Institute for Agricultural Research and a Cru Classé without either château or identity at present. It was managed throughout the 1970s by André Lurton, who made both the Grand Vin and a rosé at his Ch. La Louvière, down the road at Léognan. Another part of the property had been run separately at Cantebau-Couhins. Now apparently they are reunited and run by I.N.R.A. The white, when last sighted, was a very high-quality modern, vibrant, grapey wine, good for cutting rich food; not intended for laying down.

Château Couhins-Lurton

Cru Classé de Graves. A 14-acre fraction of Ch. Couhins run by André Lurton, making 2,000 cases of 100% Sauvignon white.

AOC: Pessac-Léognan.

Château de Fieuzal

Cru Classé de Graves (red), Léognan. Owner: SA Château de Fieuzal. Dir: Gérard Gribelin.

AOC: Pessac-Léognan. 99 acres; 17,000 cases. Grape var. red: Cab.Sauv. 60%, Merlot 30%, Petit Verdot and Cab.Franc 10%; white: Sauv. 50%, Sém. 50%.

One of the smallest classed Graves châteaux, capable of tuning the masculine, tannic, earthy style of the region to fine harmony and in recent years a regular top performer. The production (2,000 cases) of white is not technically 'classé' although it is better than some that are.

Château Haut-Bailly

Cru Classé de Graves (red), Léognan. Owner: SCI Sanders. Dir: Jean Sanders.

AOC: Pessac-Léognan. 70 acres; 10,000 cases. Grape var: Cab.Sauv. 65%, Cab.Franc 10%, Merlot 25%.

Price (1989): 70 francs a bottle.

A modest-looking place with a farmyard air, the property of a Belgian family, generally considered one of the top five châteaux of (red) Graves. It makes no white wine. One quarter of the vineyard is a mixed plantation of very old vines. Relatively shallow stony soil over hard clay is an unusual site for a great vineyard and the result can be problems during drought.

The great years (1966, '70, '78, '79, '81, '86) I can best describe as nourishing, like long-simmered stock, deep, earthy and round. I love them.

Château Laville-Haut-Brion

Cru Classé de Graves (white), Talence. Owner: Domaine Clarence Dillon.

AOC: Pessac-Léognan. 10 acres; 1,000 cases. Grape var: Sém 60% Sauv. 40%.

The white wine of La Mission-Haut-Brion, first made in 1928 on a patch where former owner M. Woltner decided the soil was too heavy for his red. Bordeaux's best dry white wine. Drunk young its quality may go unnoticed – and its price will certainly seem excessive. The wine is fermented in oak *barriques* and bottled from them the following spring. Its qualities – apart from an increasingly haunting flavour as the years go by – are concentration and the same sort of rich-yet-dry character as Ygrec, the dry wine of Ch. d'Yquem, but with more grace.

Château Malartic-Lagravière

Cru Classé Graves (red and white), Léognan. Owner: Jacques Marly.

AOC: Pessac-Léognan. 42 acres; 7,500 cases red, 850 cases white. Grape var. red: Cab.Sauv. 50%, Cab.Franc 25%, Merlot 25%, white: Sauv. Blanc 100%.

Bordeaux glossary

Barrique the standard Bordeaux barrel for ageing and sometimes shipping the wine; holds 225 litres.

Cépage, encépagement grape variety; choice of grape varieties in a vineyard.

Chai, maître de chai the storage place for wine in barrels, in the Médoc usually a barn above ground or slightly sunk in the earth for coolness; in St-Emilion frequently a cellar. The cellar master in charge of all wine-making operations.

Chef de culture in larger properties, the outdoors equivalent of the *maître de chai*; the foreman of the vineyard.

Collage fining; clarification of the wine, usually with beaten egg white.

Cru 'growth' – any wine-making property, as in Cru Classé, Cru Bourgeois, etc.

Cuve, cuvier, cuvaison vat, vat-house, vatting (i.e. time the wine spends fermenting in the vat).

Engrais (chimique, organique) fertilizer (chemical, organic).

Fouloir-égrappoir (foulage, éraflage) rotary machine for tearing the grapes off their stalks and crushing them. *Foulage* is crushing, *éraflage* removing the stalks.

Gérant general manager of a property, the man in charge.

Grand Vin not a recognized or regulated term, but generally used to mean the first or selected wines of a property, in contrast to the second or other wines.

Millésime the vintage year (e.g. 1982).

Monopole a contract between a grower and shipper for the monopoly in handling his wine.

Négociant a merchant or 'shipper'.

Oenologue oenologist or technical wine-making consultant.

Porte-greffe root-stock of phylloxera-resistant vine on to which the desired variety is grafted.

Propriétaire owner.

Récolte harvest.

Régisseur manager or bailiff of an estate.

Rendement (à l'hectare) crop (measured in hectolitres per hectare).

Taille pruning.

Tonneau the measure in which Bordeaux is still bought and sold from the château (900 litres, or from *barriques*) although such big barrels are no longer in use.

Viticulteur a wine-grower.

PROFESSOR EMILE PEYNAUD

No single man has had such a direct influence over the style and standards of wine-making in Bordeaux over the last 40 years as Emile Peynaud. A former director of the Station Oenologique of the University of Bordeaux, he is France's most celebrated consultant oenologist, with an astonishing list of clients among the châteaux and the growers' cooperatives of Bordeaux. His great book *Le Goût du Vin* is an exposition of his philosophy of wine. To his clients his preliminary advice has sometimes been brutal: he has declined to advise a château unless the owner is prepared to be more selective in choosing his 'Grand Vin', and to sell substandard vats under a second label – or in bulk.

Peynaud has looked for better balance and keeping qualities with less harshness in claret by encouraging harvesting of the grapes as ripe as possible, then adding to the 'free-run' wine at least some of the more tannic pressed wine to give a firm tannic structure. But above all he emphasizes selection at every stage. His clients include, or have included: Châteaux Lafite, Margaux, Cheval Blanc, Rauzan-Gassies, Brane-Cantenac, Giscours, Boyd-Cantenac, Malescot, Prieuré-Lichine, Léoville Las Cases, Léoville-Poyferré, Ducru-Beaucaillou, Lagrange, Beychevelle, Branaire-Ducru, Pichon-Lalande, Duhart-Milon, Batailley, Haut-Batailley, Grand-Puy-Lacoste, La Lagune, Pape-Clément, La Mission-Haut-Brion, Malarctic-Lagravière, Haut-Bailly, Pavie . . .

A generally underrated château of notable quality for both red and white wine. A square stone house in a typical Graves landscape, patched with woods and gently tilted vineyards. M. Marly (with Professor Peynaud's advice) succeeds in making traditional wine by modern methods (and with unusually high yields for such quality). The red is a firm, austere, dark-coloured *vin de garde*, finishing fine rather than fleshy. The white (unusual in being all Sauvignon) is dazzling when young but becomes even better – and more typical of Graves – with 5 or 10 years in bottle.

Château La Mission-Haut-Brion
Cru Classé de Graves (red). Talence. Owner: Domaine Clarence Dillon.
AOC: Pessac-Léognan. 49 acres; 8,000 cases. Grape var: Cab.Sauv. 50%, Cab.Franc 10%, Merlot 40%.
Price (1989): 200 francs a bottle.

The immediate neighbour and former rival to Haut-Brion, equally in the Bordeaux suburbs of Pessac and Talence with the Paris–Madrid railway running in a cutting (good for the drainage) through the vineyard. Owned since 1983 by the proprietors of Haut-Brion. The claim is that the urban surroundings give the advantage of one degree centigrade (1.8°F) higher temperature than the open country, and also a large harvesting force at short notice.

The wines show the effect of warm and dry conditions: concentration and force. Beside Haut-Brion, which is no weakling, they can appear almost butch. Michael Broadbent makes use of the words iron, earth, beef and pepper in his notes on various vintages. After due time (often 20 years) they combine warmth with sweetness in organ-like tones. Laville-Haut-Brion, is discussed separately.

Château Olivier
Cru Classé de Graves (red and white), Léognan. Owner: P. de Bethmann.
AOC: Pessac-Léognan. 99 acres; 12,000 cases red, 10,000 white. Grape var. red: Cab.Sauv. 65%, Merlot 35%, white: Sém. 65%, Sauv. 30%, Muscadelle 5%.

A moated fortress with vineyards operated for the owner until 1981 by the shippers Eschenauer & Co, but now under the control of the family again. Its red wine has never enjoyed the fame of its white, which is of the modern school of easy-come, easy-go Graves; a good, light meal-opener. The red vineyards were replaced not long ago and promise serious wine.

Château Pape-Clément
Cru Classé de Graves (red and white), Pessac. Owners: The Montagne family.
AOC: Pessac-Léognan. 146 acres; 11,000 cases. Grape var. red: Cab.Sauv. 60%, Merlot 40%; white: Sém. 33⅓%, Sauv. 33⅓%; Muscadelle 33⅓%.

One-time property of Bertrand de Goth, the 14th-century Bishop of Bordeaux who, as Clement V, brought the papacy to Avignon, in fact the Pape du Châteauneuf. The vineyard is in scattered plots and one large block at the extreme edge of Pessac, where it is quasi-rural and the gravel soil finer but no less deep. There is no Cabernet Franc in the vineyard but a high proportion of Merlot. New barrels are used for the whole crop and M. Mussyt, the manager, works closely with Professor Peynaud. The result is a sort of St-Julien among the Graves: wine with plenty of punch but no exaggerated tannin; easier, more 'supple', ready to drink sooner than the Haut-Brions. The '70 was superb at 12 years old; the '75 and the '78 were ready at 10.

Château Smith-Haut-Lafitte

Cru Classé de Graves (red), Martillac. Owner: Holt Frères et Fils.

AOC: Pessac-Léognan. 135 acres; 18,000 cases red, 2,800 white. Grape var. red: Merlot 26%, Cab.Sauv. 63%, Cab.Franc 11%; white: Sauv. 100%.

A famous old estate now separated from its original château (which reminded me of an English country rectory) to be reborn and rebuilt, with an almost Californian air of good times ahead. It has had a good reputation for many years and looks set to increase and improve on it under new British ownership. The red is round, satisfying Graves; the white (14 acres, not a classed growth) a modern-style grapey Sauvignon.

Château La Tour-Haut-Brion

Cru Classé de Graves (red), Talence. Owner: Domaine Clarence Dillon.

AOC: Pessac-Léognan. 12 acres; 2,000 cases. Grape var: Cab.Sauv. 65%, Cab.Franc 10%, Merlot 25%.

Formerly the second label of Ch. La Mission Haut-Brion, but now run as a separate vineyard. A greater character than Haut-Brion's 'Bahans', distinctly tannic up to '83, but easier wines emerging.

Château La Tour Martillac

Cru Classé de Graves (red and white), Martillac. Owner: Jean Kressman.

AOC: Pessac-Léognan. 50 acres red, 15 acres white; 10,000 cases red, 2,000 white. Grape var. red: Cab.Sauv. 60%, Merlot 30%, Malbec and Cab.Franc 5%; white: Sém 55%, Sauv. 40%, Muscadelle 5%.

The home of the retired shipper Jean Kressman, a remote little property once in the Montesquieu family (who owned the magnificent moated La Brède nearby). The owner is an enthusiast who patiently cultivates old vines for quality. The white wine, now made in small quantities, is classic Graves, best with bottle-age; the red is a good example of the robust, savoury style of the region.

OTHER CHATEAUX

Château Arricaud

Landiras. Owner: A. J. Bouyx. 70 acres; 8,000 cases white: Sém. 70%, Sauv. 25%, Muscadelle 5%; 3,000 cases red: Cab.Sauv. 65%, Merlot 30%, Malbec 5%. Substantial property overlooking the Garonne valley from the south of Barsac, recently making medal-winning wines.

Château Baret

Villenave-d'Ornon. Owners: The Ballande family. 33 acres; 2,000 cases white, 4,000 cases red. Property in the heart of 'Haut-Graves', formerly high among Graves' second growths.

Château Les Carmes Haut-Brion

Pessac. Owners: H. Chantecaille. 9 acres; 1,500 cases red: Cab.Sauv. 10%, Cab.Franc 40%, Merlot 50%. A miniature neighbour of Haut-Brion with good Cru Bourgeois standards.

Château Cazebonne

St-Pierre-de-Mons. Owner: Marc Bridet. 15 acres red; 2,700 cases. 20 acres white; 2,300 cases.

Château de Chantegrive

Podensac. Owners: Henri and Françoise Lévèque. 99 acres; 35,000 cases red: Cab.Sauv. 60%, Merlot 40%. 111 acres; 12,000 cases white: Sém. 50%, Sauv. 30%, Muscadelle 20%. A substantial property, using modern methods. The wines are sold under several names including Ch. Bon Dieu des Vignes, Mayne-Lévêque and Mayne d'Anice.

Château Cheret-Pitres

Portets. Owner: J. Boulanger. 30 acres; 5,300 cases red: Merlot 50%, Cab. 50%.

Château Chicane

Toulenne. Dir: Pierre Coste. 15 acres; 3,000 cases red: nearly two thirds Cab.Sauv. M. Coste, the leading wine merchant of Langon, makes some of the best wines of the district: ripe, vigorous reds and fresh but ripe, grapey whites.

Château de Courbon

Toulenne. Owner: Philippe Sanders (see Ch. Haut-Bailly). 20 acres; 2,500 cases white: Sauv. 50%, Sém. 50%.

Château Crabitey

Portets. Owners: a convent. Minor property making some 11,000 cases of useful red wine and 1,700 cases of white.

Château de Cruzeau

St-Médard-d'Eyrans. Owner: André Lurton, 101 acres; 17,000 cases red. 22 acres; 3,500 cases white: Sauv. 85%, Sém. 15%. A Lurton property bought and replanted in 1973. St-Médard, on the southern fringe of 'Haut-Graves', has deep, pebbly soil which should mean good wine.

Château de Doms

Portets. Dir: M. Duvigneau and L. Parage. 55 acres; 3,500 cases white, 3,000 cases red. Second label: Clos du Monastère.

Château Ferrande

Castres. Dir: Marc Teisseire. 83 acres; 15,000 cases red: Cab.Sauv. 40%, Merlot 40%, Cab.Franc 20%. 22 acres; 5,000 cases white: Sauv. 35%, Sém. 60%. Musc. 5%. The principal property of Castres, just north of Portets, with a good reputation. Ch. Lognac is the second label.

Clos Floridène

Bequey. Owners: M. et Mme. Dubourdieu. 7.5 acres; 1,700 cases: Sém. 70%, Musc. 30%.

Château de France

Léognan. Owner: Bernard Thomassin. 66 acres; 12,000 cases red: Merlot 50%, Cab.Sauv. 25%, Cab.Franc 25%. 500 cases white. A minor property among some of the best of the district recently modernized and enlarged. The second wine is Ch. Coquilles (Bordeaux Supérieur).

Domaine de Gaillat

Langon. Dir: Pierre Coste (see Ch. Chicane). 27 acres; 5,500 cases red.

Château La Garde

Martillac. Owners: Louis Eschenauer & Co. 100 acres; 20,000 cases red: Cab.Sauv. 70%, Merlot 30%. 15 acres; 3,000 cases white: Sauv. 100%. One of the biggest and best Graves bourgeois estates. The red in good vintages is robust and meaty. I have never encountered the white.

Château Gazin

Léognan. Owner: P. Michotte. 32 acres; 5,000 cases red: Cab.Sauv. 80%, Merlot 10%, Cab.Franc 10%.

Château du Grand Abord

Portets. Owner: M. Dugoua. 44 acres; 4,200 cases red, 2,000 cases white. Recently a well-made red.

Domaine La Grave

Portets. Owner: Peter Vinding-Diers. 17 acres; 2,000 cases red: Merlot 60%, Cab.Sauv. 40%; 600 cases white: Sém. 100%. Very promising new property run by the Danish wine maker of Ch. de Landiras.

Château des Jaubertes

St-Pardon de Conquer. Owner: Marquis de Pontac. 57 acres red, 12 acres white.

Château Jean-Gervais

Portets. Owners: M. F. Counilh & Fils. 74 acres; 10,000 cases white.

Château de Landiras

Landiras. A new enterprise in the south of the region managed by the innovative Peter Vinding-Diers. Very stylish whites.

Château Larrivet-Haut-Brion

Léognan. Owner: Mme Jacques Guillemaud. 40 acres; 7,600 cases red: Cab.Sauv. 60%, Merlot 35%, Mal. and Petit Verdot 5%. 400 cases white. One of the better second-rank Graves, although a long way from Haut-Brion in every sense.

Price (1989): 49 francs a bottle.

Château La Louvière

Léognan. Owner: André Lurton. 106 acres; 19,000 cases red: Cab.Sauv. 70%,

Merlot 20%, Cab.Franc 10%. 44 acres; 5,500 cases white: Sauv. 85%, Sém. 15%. The show place of M. Lurton's considerable estates, a noble 18th-century house where he makes avant-garde dry white of Loire-like freshness and typically masculine, earthy red of Cru Classé standard.

Château Magence
St-Pierre-de-Mons. Owner: Dominique Guillot de Suduiraut. 74 acres; 10,000 cases white: Sém. 36%, Sauv. 64%. 22 acres; 5,800 cases red: Cab.Sauv. 40%, Cab.Franc 32%, Merlot 27%. Prominent over the last two decades as one of the most modern properties; a leader in fresh, dry white wine and fruity red for drinking young. The owner is president of a group of like-minded proprietors.

Château Millet
Portets. Owners: Henri & Thierry Mette. 138 acres; 25,000 cases. The biggest property in Portets, with the most imposing château. The vineyard was formerly half red and half white, but the emphasis is increasingly on red wine. Second label: Ch. du Clos Renon.

Château Montalivet
Pujols-sur-Ciron. Dir: Pierre Coste (*see* Ch. Chicane). 26 acres; 7,500 cases red. 9 acres; 2,500 cases white.

Château Pique-Caillou
Owner: Alphonse Denis. 37 acres; 10,000 cases: 45% Cab.Sauv., 20% Cab.Franc, 35% Merlot. A very good '73.

Château St-Pierre
See Ch. Les Queyrats.

Château Piron
St-Morillon. Owner: P. Boyreau. 49

acres; 7,500 cases white; 2,000 cases red. An old family property in the hinterland of Graves on gravel slopes with a chalk content that favours white wine.

Château de Portets
Portets. Owner: Jean-Pierre Théron. 36 acres; 6,000 cases red: one third Cab.Sauv. two-thirds Merlot; 2,000 cases white: Sém. 64%, Sauv. 36%. The reputation of Portets is growing, particularly for red wine. A good workmanlike example.

Château Les Queyrats
St-Pierre-de-Mons. Owners: The Dulac family. 64 acres white; 32 acres red. A traditional Graves estate with mixed farming and mixed wines: whites both dry and sweet and a sturdy red. Clos d'Uza (once a Lur Saluces farm) is attached. Some of the wine is sold abroad as Ch. St-Pierre; good, tasty, conservative Graves.

Château Rahoul
Portets. Owner: Alain Thienot. 34 acres; 5,000 cases red: Merlot 60%, Cab.Sauv. 40%; 1,000 cases white: Sém. 100%. Estate with a reputation for stylish wood-aged reds and crisp whites. The leader in the commune.

Château Respide
St-Pierre-de-Mons and Langon. Owner: Pierre Bonnet & Fils. 98 acres in St-Pierre; 5,000 cases white and 70 acres of red, on the sandy soil of Langon, have been known longer than most in this up-and-coming area. A 20-year-old bottle of white Respide at the old Café de Bordeaux was nearly great, soft but sappy Graves.

Château de Rochemorin
Martillac. Owner: André Lurton. 165

acres; 21,000 cases red. 15 acres; 3,500 cases white: Sauv.Bl. 90%, Sém. 10%. A major old estate abandoned in the 1930s, replanted since 1973 by M. Lurton. A name to look out for.

Château Le Sartre
Léognan. Owners: GFA. Manager: Antony Perrin. Cab.Sauv. 60%, Merlot 40%. (*See* Ch. Carbonnieux.)

Château Toumilon
St-Pierre-de-Mons. Owner: Jean Sévenet. 30 acres. A Graves producing some 2,500 cases of pleasant red and the same of dry white. Second label: Ch. Cabanes.

Château La Tour Léognan
Léognan. Owners: Soc. Civile. Manager: Antony Perrin. Second label of Ch. Carbonnieux.

Château La Tour-Bicheau
Portets. Owners: Y. Daubas & Fils. 50-acre property among the good red producers of Portets. About 7,000 cases.

Château Tourteau-Chollet
Arbannats. Owners: Société Civile. 74-acre property owned by the Mestrezat-Preller group. Red and white wines.

Château Le Tuquet
Beautiran. Owner: Paul Ragon. 54 acres; 8,000 cases white: Sauv. and Sém. 54 acres; 8,000 cases red: Cab., Merlot, Malbec. Beautiran's principal property on main Bordeaux to Langon road.

Château La Vieille France
Portets. Owner: Michel Dugoua. 12 acres; 1,500 cases red. 12 acres; 2,500 cases white. 17 acres; 4,000 cases Bordeaux Supérieur Rouge. A sound and enterprising proprietor who also owns Ch. Grand-Abord.

SAUTERNES

Towards the south of the Bordeaux region, red wine-making dwindles to insignificance compared with white. A slightly warmer and drier climate and very limey soil are ideal for white grapes; the wine naturally has what the French call great '*sève*' – sap – a combination of body and vitality.

The best of the region is the relatively hilly enclave of Sauternes, an appellation that applies to five villages just south of a little tributary of the Gironde call the Ciron. On the other side of the Ciron (on flatter land) lies Barsac, which also has the right to the appellation. The Ciron is said to be responsible for misty autumn conditions that give rise to the famous 'noble rot', and the possibility of *vin liquoreux*. For the last 150 years Sauternes has specialized in this extraordinarily concentrated golden dessert wine. For the last ten the tide of fortune has turned strongly in its favour.

Unlike most of the Graves region, Sauternes has big estates in the manner of the Médoc. Historically its position on the inland route up the Garonne gave it military importance. Later, its fine climate and its good wine made it a desirable spot to replace castles with mansions. A score of these were already famous for their 'sappy' white wine when the 1855 classification was made for the Paris Exhibition. They were classified in three ranks, with Château d'Yquem alone in the first, nine classed as Premiers Crus and another nine as Deuxièmes Crus – which is, broadly speaking, still a fair classification, except that divisions of property have increased the Premiers Crus to 11 and the Deuxièmes to 12. They are surrounded by a host of unofficial Crus Bourgeois, some of a comparable quality. The combined vineyard area of the six communes is 5,434 acres. There is no *cave coopérative*.

The laborious procedure for making great Sauternes is described on pages 80 and 81. With sweet wines out of fashion in the '60s and '70s, it became unrealistic for most proprietors, who could not afford the labour needed to pick single grapes at a time, or the new barrels, or the years of waiting. But fashion, and apparently climate, have both changed so radically recently that Sauternes is entering a new golden age.

The ultimate short cut, used by many of the humbler growers, is simply to wait for fully ripe grapes (hoping that at least a few are 'nobly rotten'), pick them all together, add sugar to bring the potential alcohol up to about 18 per cent, then stop the fermentation with sulphur dioxide when the fermentation has produced 13 or 14 degrees, leaving the wine sweet. It is a bastard approach to wine-making, with predictably mediocre results. The wine has none of the classic Sauternes flavour and should, in fairness, be called something else.

What is the classic flavour? It depends on the vintage. In some it is forceful, hot and treacly. In others it is rich and stiff with flavour, but almost literally sappy and not very sweet. In the best, with all the grapes 'nobly rotten', it is thick with sugar yet gentle, creamy, nutty, honeyed. Barsacs tend to be a little less rich than Sauternes, but can produce their own spellbinding equilibrium of the rich and the brisk. Bottles can be better than ever after as much as 40 or 50 years.

The postal address for the whole of Sauternes is 33210 Langon.

Price (1988): 50 francs a bottle.

PREMIER GRAND CRU

Château d'Yquem

1er Cru Supérieur 1855. Owner: Comte Alexandre de Lur Saluces.

AOC: Sauternes. 250 acres; 6,500 cases (plus up to 2,000 dry white Bordeaux). Grape var: Sém. 80%, Sauv. 20%.

Indisputably the greatest sweet wine of France, but recognized as the best white wine of Bordeaux long before the fashion for sweet wine was initiated in the 19th century. The same family has controlled its destiny throughout. The extreme pains that go into its making are described in detail on pages 80 and 81. Yquem also makes 'Y' (pronounced Ygrec), a dry wine, made from half Sauvignon, half Sémillon. It has some of the concentration of Yquem, and the same alcohol content, but only a trace of sweetness for balance.

SAUTERNES PREMIERS CRUS

Château Climens

1er Cru Classé 1855. Owner: Lucien Lurton.

AOC: Barsac. 62 acres; 6,500 cases. Grape var: Sém. 98%, Sauv. 2%.

Barsac's sweetest and richest wine, made by the old methods with a crop nearly as derisory as that at Yquem, giving it almost caramel concentration as it ages, yet with a touch of elegance that is typical of Barsac. The property was bought in 1971 (a superb vintage) by the owner of Ch. Brane-Cantenac (Margaux). Since then it has only enhanced its reputation with such wines as the '83 and '86. The locals pronounce the final 'ns' emphatically, with a sort of honking effect.

Château Coutet

1er Cru Classé 1855. Owner: Marcel Baly.

AOC: Barsac. 95 acres; 5,500 cases. Grape var: Sém. 75%, Sauv. 23%, Muscadelle 2%.

With Ch. Climens, the leading growth of Barsac, using traditional methods of barrel fermentation to make exceptionally fine and stylish wine (although strangely failing in the great '67 vintage). The old manor house dates back to the English rule of Aquitaine. In the best years (1971, '75, '81, '83, '86) a selection of the richest wine is labelled 'Cuvée Madame'.

Château Guiraud

1er Cru Classé 1855. Owners: Société Civile Agricole. Dir: Frank Narby.

AOC: Sauternes. 134 acres, plus 37 acres of red grapes (Bordeaux Supérieur); 7,000 cases plus 8,000 cases red plus 1,000 cases dry white.

Grape var: white: Sém. 54%, Sauv. 42%, Muscadelle 4%; red: Cab.Sauv. 55%, Merlot 45%.

The southern neighbour of Yquem which was coasting, looking for a buyer, until a Canadian company took up the challenge in 1981. The new owners employ Yquem-like methods, picking individual grapes and fermenting in new barrels. Existing vintages scarcely showed the potential, but the '83 and '86 are as splendid as they should be. The quantity of red wine, Le Dauphin Château Guiraud, is surprising. A dry white, 'G' is another innovation.

Château Clos Haut-Peyraguey

1er Cru Classé 1855, Bommes. Owner: Jacques Pauly.

AOC: Sauternes, 37 acres; 3,000 cases. Grape var: Sém. 83%, Sauv. 15%, Musc. 2%.

Price (1989): 150 francs a bottle.

Formerly the upper part of the same estate as Ch. Laufaurie-Peyraguey, separated in 1879 and in the Pauly family since 1914. A modest estate making relatively light wine with care. The Cru Bourgeois Ch. Haut-Bommes has the same owners.

Château Lafaurie-Peyraguey

1er Cru Classé 1855, Bommes. Owner: Cordier family.

AOC: Sauternes. 93 acres; 4,500 cases. Grape var: Sém. 90%, Sauv. 8%, Musc. 2%.

A fortress to challenge Yquem – militarily, that is – with a fine reputation for beautifully, structured, long-lived Sauternes, particularly since 1979.

Château Rabaud-Promis

1er Cru Classé 1855, Bommes. Owner: GFA Rabaud-Promis. Administrator: Mme Michèle Dejean.

AOC: Sauternes. 79 acres; 3,750 cases. Grape var: Sém. 80%, Sauv. 18%, Muscadelle 2%.

The larger part of the formerly important Rabaud estate, now no longer in the front rank, but showing marked improvement in the '80s. To watch.

Château Rayne-Vigneau

1er Cru Classé 1855, Bommes. Owners: Société Civile. Dir: Jean-Pierre Angliviel de la Beaumelle.

AOC: Sauternes. 167 acres; 16,500 cases. Grape var: Sém. 50%, Sauv. 50%.

A big estate now detached from its château but celebrated in history for its soil being – literally – full of precious stones. The fortunate Vicomte de Roton (a Pontac, whose descendants still have the château) found himself picking up sapphires, topaz, amethysts and opals by the thousand. (The rest of the soil is gravel.) Modern methods produce rich and good, but not the most ambitious, Sauternes and a little Rayne-Vigneau Sec.

Château Rieussec

1er Cru Classé 1855, Fargues. Owners: Domaines Rothschild. Dir: Albert Vuillier.

AOC: Sauternes. 163 acres; 6,000 cases plus. Grape var: Sém. 80%, Sauv. 19%, Muscadelle 1%.

The eastern neighbour of Yquem, perched even higher on the same line of hills, with a strange gazebo a little too like a gun emplacement to be considered an ornament. Particularly arid gravel soil contributes to a very low yield of relatively light, less-sweet wine sometimes compared with Barsac. The wine is fermented in stainless steel and kept in cellars in mature barrels, which seem to keep it particularly fresh and lively. The '62 has been a favourite of mine for years. 1971, '75, '79 and '88 are all first class. A dry white, inspired by Yquem's 'Y', is called 'R'. The (Lafite) Rothschilds bought the property in 1985, with the highest ambitions for it.

Château Sigalas Rabaud

1er Cru Classé 1855, Bommes. Owner: Marquis de Lambert des Granges.

AOC: Sauternes. 34 acres; 2,000 cases. Grape var: Sém. 90%, Sauv. 10%.

One third of the former Rabaud estate, descended for over a century in the Sigalas family. The wine is mainly made and aged in tanks to avoid oak flavours and concentrate on richness and finesse, which it has in abundance.

Château Suduiraut

1er Cru Classé 1855, Preignac. Owners: L. Fonquernie and Mme. Fronin.

AOC: Sauternes. 210 acres; 1,000 cases. Grape var: Sém. 80%, Sauv. 20%.

A château of great splendour with a park of great, if neglected, beauty and the next vineyard to Yquem, going north. One of the most respected names, despite a period of relative neglect in the early 1970s. The new manager, Pierre Pascaud, is forthright and determined. Suduiraut at its best ('67, '76 and '82) is plump and unctuous, truly *liquoreux*; the poor man's Yquem. Other vintages (eg '83) can be oddly disappointing.

Château La Tour Blanche

1er Cru Classé 1855, Bommes. Owners: Ministère d'Agriculture, Dir: Jean Pierre Jausserand.

AOC: Sauternes. 74 acres; 4,000 cases. Grape var: Sém. 75%, Sauv. 20%, Musc. 5%.

Probably the first estate on which sweet Sauternes was made (*see* Ch. d'Yquem, The Making of a Great Sauternes) and placed first after Yquem in the 1855 classification. Bequeathed to the French state in 1912 by M. Osiris, whose name still appears on the label. The vineyard slopes steeply westwards towards the river Ciron, the Bommes–Barsac boundary. It is now a college of viticulture, and students help in the nursery and bottling. Fermentation is temperature controlled in steel tanks, stopped by chilling and filtration at about 14% alcohol, then 2 years in barrels. Not great wine, but businesslike. 1985 and '86 are signs of new emphasis on quality. The second label is Cru St-Marc. A little red wine is also made.

SAUTERNES DEUXIEMES CRUS

Château d'Arche

2eme Cru Classé. Owners: The Basit-St-Martin family.

AOC: Sauternes. 70 acres; 3,350 cases. Grape var: Sém. 75%, Sauv. 23%, Muscadelle 2%.

Respectable rather than inspired Sauternes, at its best typically luscious. *See also* Ch. d'Arche-Lafaurie. A part of Ch. Lamothe also belongs to the Bastit-St-Martins.

Château d'Arche-Lafaurie

2eme Cru Classé 1855. Owners The Bastit-St-Martin family.

AOC: Sauternes. 30 acres; 2,000 cases.

The junior partner of Ch. d'Arche.

Château Broustet

2eme Cru Classé 1855. Owner: Fournier family.

AOC: Barsac. 39 acres; 3,000 cases. Grape var: Sém. 63%, Sauv. 25%, Muscadelle 12%.

Remembered as the property of the cooper who standardized the now-universal Bordeaux *barrique*. His descendants who also run the great Ch. Canon, St-Emilion) make an adequate but scarcely distinguished wine, rich but not *liquoreux*. Also a dry white, Camperos. Their second label is Ch. de Ségur.

Château Caillou

2eme Cru Classé 1855. Owners: J.B. and M.J. Bravo.

AOC: Barsac. 37 acres; 3,000–4,000 cases. Grape var: Sém. 90%, Sauv. 10%.

Price (1989): 100 francs a bottle.

A businesslike property on the higher ground of 'Haut' Barsac, near Ch. Climens. With the owner's other Barsac property, Ch. Haut Mayne, it also produces a dry white, Domaine Sarraute, which I have found rather clumsy.

Château Doisy-Daëne

2eme Cru Classé 1855. Owner: Pierre Dubourdieu.

AOC: Barsac. 37 acres; 5,000 cases. Grape var: Sém. 70%, Cab.Sauv. 20%, Muscadelle 10%.

In the forefront of modern wine-making with sophisticated use of steel and new oak to make fresh, lively sweet wines of real class and a trend-setting dry one, a model for growers who want to restore the old prestige of Graves. The same estate contains Ch. Cantegril (49 acres), making both sweet white and a good red. Two dry whites are also produced under the labels Grand Vin Sec de Doisy-Daëne and Ch. Doisy-Daëne-St-Martin.

Wine has few legends more imposing than the hilltop fortress of Yquem and its golden nectar. Only France could produce such a monument to aristocratic craftsmanship. The Lur Saluces family of Yquem has made quality its dynastic vocation for 200 years.

In 1785 Josephine Sauvage d'Yquem, whose family has already held the estate for 200 years, married the Comte de Lur Saluces. Two years later Thomas Jefferson paid a famous visit to the château and rated the wines so highly that he ordered a consignment for America. But if you want to taste the wine that impressed him you must seek out the rare 'Y', the dry wine of the château, because the modern concept of Sauternes as a *vin liquoreux*, an intensely sweet, concentrated and unctuous dessert wine, was only gradually introduced from the late 18th century onwards. Legend says that the German proprietor of Château La Tour-Blanche, Monsieur Focke, experimented with the method used to make the great sweet wines of the Rhine. 1847 is the first Yquem vintage recorded as being entirely *liquoreux*.

Today, the painstaking care at Yquem is hard to exaggerate. A description of its methods is a description of the ideal – to which other châteaux only approximate to a greater or lesser degree.

The principle must first be understood. Under certain autumnal conditions of misty mornings and sunny afternoons, one of the forms of mould common in vineyards reverses its role; instead of ruining the grapes, it is entirely beneficial. Given a healthy, ripe and undamaged crop without other fungus infections, it begins to feed on the sugar and

the tartaric acid in each grape, probing with roots so fine that they penetrate the microscopic pores of the grape-skin. The grapes rapidly shrivel, turning first grey with fungus spores, then warm violet-brown, their skins mere pulp. By this time they have lost more than half their weight, but less than half their sugar. Their juice is concentrated, extremely sweet and rich in glycerine. If conditions are perfect (as they were in 1967 and 1989) the process is sudden and complete; not a grape in the bunch is recognizable. They are a repulsive sight.

Unfortunately in most years the process is gradual; the berries rot patchily – even one by one. At Yquem the pickers, in four gangs 40 strong, move through the vines at a snail's pace gathering the grapes, if necessary, one at a time, then going back over the same vines again and again, up to ten, once up to eleven, times. The final crop amounts to about one glass of wine per vine.

In the *cuvier* the grapes are slightly sulphured, put through a gentle wooden *fouloir* (crusher), then immediately pressed in old-fashioned vertical presses three times, the 'cake' being cut up with shovels and thrown into a strange mill to remove the stalks between pressings. The whole day's picking – up to 40 barrels – is assembled together in one vat, then poured straight into new oak *barriques*, filling them three quarters full, to ferment. The day's crop, the '*journée*', is the critical unit to be tasted again and again to see whether it has the qualities of the Grand Vin. If it does not have those qualities it will be sold to the trade as anonymous Sauternes. There is no

Château Doisy-Dubroca
2eme Cru Classé 1855. Owner: Lucien Lurton.
AOC: Barsac. 11 acres; 700 cases. Grape var: Sém. 100%.
A small property linked for a century to the neighbouring Ch. Climens and now made with the same traditional techniques of intense care (and Professor Peynaud's advice).

Château Doisy-Védrines
2eme Cru Classé 1855. Owner: Pierre Castéja.
AOC: Sauternes. 62 acres; 3,000 cases. Grape var: Sém 80%, Sauv. 20%.
I always assumed from its quality that this was a first rather than a second-classed growth. It is one of the rich Barsacs, fermented in barrels and built for long life. It is much liked in the UK.

Château Filhot
2eme Cru Classé 1855. Owner: Comte Henri de Vaucelles.
AOC: Sauternes. 148 acres; 9,500 cases. Grape var: Sém. 50%, Sauv. 45%, Muscadelle 5%.
A palace, or nearly, built by the Lur Saluces family in the early 19th century on the edge of the woods south of Sauternes. The big vineyard on sandy soil produces distinctively light wines by classical Sauternes standards. They are all the more appetizing and savoury for it; excellent for rich fish dishes and such shellfish as lobster, crawfish and crab cooked with cream. The 1975 had a slightly salty tang that I found delicious.

Château Lamothe
2eme Cru Classé 1855. Owner: Jean Despujols.
AOC: Sauternes. 20 acres; 2,000 cases. Grape var: Sém. 70%, Sauv. 15%, Muscadelle 15%.
Minor Sauternes bottled within a year for early drinking.

Château de Malle
2eme Cru Classé 1855, Preignac. Owner: Comtesse Pierre de Bournazel.
AOC: Sauternes (and Graves). 67 acres Sauternes, 57 acres Graves; 4,000 cases Sauternes. Grape var. white: Sém. 70%, Sauv. 28%, Muscadelle 2%; red: Cab.Sauv. 80%, Merlot 20%.
The most beautiful house and garden in Sauternes – possibly in Bordeaux – and much appreciated by tourists. Built for the owner's family (related to the Lur Saluces) about 1600. 'Italian' gardens were added 100 years later. The vineyard is in Sauternes and Graves and produces roughly equal quantities of sweet white and red. The two Graves reds (made by carbonic maceration) are Ch'x de Cardaillan and Tours de Malle: the dry whites are Chevalier de Malle (Graves) and M. de Malle (Bordeaux). The vineyard, on light sandy soil, was entirely replanted in 1956. The late owner was a trained oenologist who 'designed' his wine, using both stainless steel and new oak to produce fruitiness with undertones – excellent Sauternes.

Château de Myrat
2eme Cru Classé 1855, Barsac. Owner: M. Pontac.
Aoc Barsac. 54 acres. Grape var: Sém. 85%, Sauv. 10%, Musc. 5%.
The father of the present owner uprooted the vines in 1976. 22 acres were replanted in time to produce the first vintage in '89 but the appellation was not allowed until 1990.

court of appeal, no second wine, at Yquem.

The *chai* is heated to 20°C (68°F) to encourage a steady fermentation, which lasts between two and six weeks. When it reaches between 13 and 14 degrees of alcohol a miraculous natural control, an antibiotic produced by the botrytis, stops the yeasts working, leaving up to 120 grammes of sugar to a litre (12 per cent of the wine). Without this antibiotic the alcohol would reach 17 degrees, throwing the wine right out of balance. The sums are critical here. Twenty per cent total sugar ('potential alcohol') in the juice is ideal. With 25 per cent, the fermentation would stop at nine or ten degrees – as in Trockenbeerenauslese. (The extreme example is Tokay Essence, with so much sugar that the potential alcohol content is 35 degrees but fermentation never starts at all.)

Château d'Yquem is kept for no less than three and a half years in cask, racked every three months and never bunged tight – which means twice-weekly topping up over the whole period, and a loss by evaporation of 20 per cent. The wine is so thick that it never 'falls bright', or clears itself fully by gravity. The sediment, at the same density as the liquid, remains in suspension. So it must be '*fined*' – but never with egg whites, says Alexandre de Lur Saluces; one of the eggs might be bad.

The Comte Alexandre de Lur Saluces, the present proprietor, is nephew of the famous Marquis Bertrand, whose last vintage before his death was the great 1967. He also owns the exceptional Cru Bourgeois Château de Fargues.

Château Nairac

2eme Cru Classé 1855, Barsac. Owner: Thomas Heeter.
AOC: Sauternes. 37 acres; 1,400 cases. Grape var: Sém. 90%.
Sauv. 6%, Muscadelle 4%.

One of the most positive signs of a renaissance in Sauternes. A young American, Tom Heeter, made this formerly run-down estate one of the leaders of the district, with wines of the racy, less sticky Barsac style that bear keeping 10 years or more. Professor Peynaud was called in for his invaluable advice. The dignified mansion lies on the low ground near the village of Barsac and the Garonne. The new owner renovated the house, which was not lived in for many years. Sadly, floods did terrible damage to the property in 1982.

Château Romer du Hayot

2eme Cru Classé 1855. Owner: André du Hayot.
AOC: Sauternes. 37 acres; 4,000 cases. Grape var: Sém. 70%,
Sauv. 25%, Musc. 5%.

The château was demolished for the new autoroute and the wine is made at the owner's Cru Bourgeois Ch. Guiteronde in Barsac. A modern Sauternes, aged 2 years in tanks.

Château Suau

2eme Cru Classé 1855. Owner: M. Roger Biarnès.
AOC: Barsac. 20 acres; 1,500 cases. Grape var: Sém. 80%,
Sauv. 10%, Muscadelle 10%.

The relic of a more important property, near the Garonne on heavier soil than the best growths. The wine, made at the owner's home, is Château de Navarro, Illats, Graves, together with Sauternes Cru Bourgeois and Domaine du Coy.

OTHER CHATEAUX

Château Bastor-Lamontagne
Cru Bourgeois, Preignac. Owners: Crédit Foncier de France. 99 acres; 9,000 cases. A substantial and well-kept property with a history of good vintages to substantiate its claim to be 'as good as a second-growth'.

Château Cantegril
Cru Bourgeois, Barsac. Owner: A. Masencal. 50 acres; 4,500 cases. Part of the former Ch. Myrat vineyard, beautifully kept but rather unambitious in its wine: clean, fresh, sweet – not much more.

Château Gilette
Owner: Christian Médeville. 8.6 acres; 400–900 cases. A unique producer of long-aged Sauternes of great splendour: e.g. '49, '55, '59, '61, '62, not bottled until its idealistic owner considers it ready to drink – at 25 years or so.

Château de Fargues
Cru Bourgeois, Fargues. Owner: Comte Alexandre de Lur Saluces. 25 acres; 1,000 cases. Grape var: Sém. 80%, Sauv. 20%.
A proud castle in ruins, with a diminutive vineyard but the perfectionist standards of Yquem. Lighter wine, but impeccable and sometimes brilliant (e.g. '67, '75).

Château Haut-Bommes
Cru Bourgeois, Bommes. Owner: Jacques Pauly (see Ch. Clos Haut-Peyraguey). Well-sited, potentially excellent little property. The 1929 was perfection of cream and toffee in 1981.

Château Liot
Cru Bourgeois, Barsac. Owner: J. David. 49 acres; 5,500 cases. Grape var: Sém. 60%, Musc. 35%, Sauv. 15%.
Large property on the best slopes in Barsac. The unusual proportion of Muscadelle makes certain years very flavoury; the general level is 'good commercial', sometimes over-sulphured.

Château du Mayne
Cru Bourgeois, Barsac. Owner: Jean Sanders. 20 acres; 1,500 cases. Grape var: Sauv. 30%, Sém. 70%. A pretty cream house among ancient vines (many 80 years old) cultivated for small amounts of very good wine. The same owner as Ch. Haut-Bailly (Graves).

Château de Ménota
Cru Bourgeois, Barsac. Owner: N. Labat. 40 acres; 4,500 cases. A very good wine.

Château Pernaud
Cru Bourgeois, Barsac. Owner: P. Pascand. 50 acres; 5,500 cases. An old property down by the Ciron, replanted and now run by the dynamic manager of Ch. Suduiraut. Worth watching.

Château Piada
Cru Bourgeois, Barsac. Owner: Jean Lalande. 32 acres; 3,800 cases. Grape var: Sauv. 70%, Ries. 30%. One of the better-known lesser Barsacs, unconventional in methods but successful with both its sweet wine and dry 'Clos du Roy'.

Château Raymond-Lafon
Cru Bourgeois, Sauternes. Owner: Pierre Meslier. 49 acres; 2,000 cases. Grape var: Sém. 80%, Sauv. 20%. Owned by the ex-manager of Ch. d'Yquem, neighbour to the great château, made with similar care and regularly first-class (e.g. '75, '78, '83, '85, '86).

Château de Rolland
Cru Bourgeois, Barsac. Owners: Jean and Pierre Guignard. 50 acres; 4,000 cases. An attractive little hotel and restaurant (the only one in Barsac) with worthwhile wine of its own.

Château Roumieu
Cru Bourgeois, Barsac. Owner: R. Bernadet. 2,000 cases. A 50-acre vineyard next to Ch. Climens, divided between the Goyaud and Bernadet families. The wines I have tasted have been respectable.

Ch. Roumieu-Lacoste
Cru Bourgeois, Barsac. Owner: Mme S. Dubourdieu-Bouchet. 30 acres; 2,500 cases. The sister-in-law of the owner of the excellent Doisy-Daëne makes good wine here.

Château Simon
Cru Bourgeois, Barsac. Owner: J. Dufour. 40 acres; 2,000 cases. A well-run property, in the same hands as the little Ch. Grand-Mayne (Barsac).

ST-EMILION

As a town, every wine lover's idea of heaven; as an appellation, much the biggest for high-quality wine in France, producing not much less than the whole of the Côte d'Or of Burgundy. Nowhere is the civic and even the spiritual life of a little city so deeply imbued with the passion for making good wine.

St-Emilion, curled into its sheltered corner of the hill, cannot expand. Where other such towns have spread nondescript streets over the countryside, around St-Emilion there are priceless vineyards, most of its very best, lapping up to its walls. It burrows into its yielding limestone to find building blocks and store its wine – even to solemnize its rites. Its old church is a vast vaulted cave, now used for the meeting of the Jurade (see below).

The vineyards envelop several distinct soils and aspects while maintaining a certain common character. St-Emilion wines are a degree stronger than Médocs, with less tannin. Accessible, solid tastiness is their stamp, maturing to warm, gratifying sweetness. They are less of a puzzle than Médocs when young and mature faster, but are no less capable of asking unsolvable questions as they age.

The best come from the relatively steep côtes, the hillside vineyards and the cap of the escarpment around the town, and from an isolated patch of gravel soil on the plateau two miles northwest, almost in Pomerol. The côtes wines are the more smiling, in degrees from enigmatic to beaming; the wines of the graves more earnest and searching. Michael Broadbent defines the difference as 'open' (côtes) and 'firm' (graves). But they can easily be confused with each other, with Médocs, with Graves and even with burgundy. And some of the same qualities are found in vineyards on substantially different soils, both down in the sandy sables region in the Dordogne valley below the town and in the five 'satellite' villages to the north and east.

The classification of St-Emilion follows a pattern of its own. It was settled in 1954 and is the only one planned to be regularly revised; even, for the third category, to be revised every year. There are now, since the 1985 vintage, two appellations, simple AOC St-Emilion and AOC St-Emilion Grand Cru. The Grands Crus come in three classes: Premier Grand Cru Classé, Grand Cru Classé, and Grand Cru. The top class is divided into two: 'A' and 'B'. The current classification names two châteaux (Cheval Blanc and Ausone) as Premiers Grands Crus Classés 'A' and nine as 'B'. The Bs are the approximate equivalent in value to Médoc second- and third-growths. Then come 63 Grands Crus Classés, elected for (about) ten years. They were revised in 1969 and again in 1986; the next revision is in 1994.

The third category is simply Grand Cru, for which proprietors have to reapply every year by submitting their wines for tasting.

Obviously St-Emilion is not an area of big estates. The average size of holding is about 20 acres, the biggest not much more than 100 and many as small as five or six, making a mere few hundred cases. Of the 172 Grands Crus applicants 94 were over seven hectares (17 acres), the qualifying size for a Médoc Cru Bourgeois. In fact 'Grand Cru' in St-Emilion, unqualified, is the same broad category as the three levels of the bourgeoisie in the Médoc.

Postcode: 33330 St-Emilion.

Price (1988): 23 francs a bottle.

ST-EMILION PREMIERS GRANDS CRUS

Château Ausone

1er Grand Cru Classé 1985. Owners: Mme J. Dubois-Challon & Héritiers Vauthier.

AOC: St-Emilion. 17 acres; 2,250 cases. Grape var: Merlot 50%, Cab.Franc 50%.

Price (1989): 270 francs a bottle.

If you were looking for the most obviously promising vineyard site in the whole Bordeaux area this would be first choice. No wonder its name is associated with the Roman poet Ausonius (connoisseur also of the Moselle). It slopes south and east from the rim of the St-Emilion escarpment, whose limestone cap has been quarried for

---

The Jurade de St-Emilion

The ceremonial and promotional organization of St-Emilion is probably the oldest in France. The Jurade de St-Emilion was formally instituted by King John of England and France in 1199 as the body of elders to govern the little city and its district – a dignity granted to few regions at the time. Nobody seriously pretends that the modern institution is a linear descendant, but its impressive processions to Mass in the great parish church and to its own candle-lit solemnities in the monolithic former church, cut out of the solid limestone in the centre of the town, are full of dignity as well as good humour.

The Jurade also plays an increasing role in the control of quality and administration of the various categories of châteaux. Its newly initiated annual tastings are likely to give a boost to St-Emilion quality in a similar way to the tastevinage undertaken by the Chevaliers de Tastevin in Burgundy.

On a memorable autumn weekend in 1981 the Jurade visited the great medieval city of York, arriving by river in a state barge, to process to the Minster for a service conducted by the Archbishop, and to dine in the splendour of Castle Howard. They do these things with style.

building and provides perfect cool, commodious cellars. The soil is pale alkaline clay, in a shallow layer over permeable limestone (which vine roots love). The château (where the owner lives) is a dainty building perched above and among the vines, where an old white mare shambles around doing the cultivating, hull-down in the green leaves.

Ausone went through a long eclipse when its wine was good, but not good enough. Its neighbours seemed to dim their lamps at the same time. Matters were put right from 1975 by a new manager, Pascal Delbeck, and each good vintage now takes its proper place among the first-growths. 1976, '78 and '79 were all confirmed excellent and the vintages of the '80s will (as they mature) continue the high standards.

Winemaking here is exactly the same in principle as in the Médoc. New barrels are used for the whole, pathetically small crop. (I was present by chance at a cellar tasting of Ausone from barrels washed before filling with steam, hot water and cold water. The differences were astonishing. Hot water won.) The wine is bottled slightly sooner than Médoc first-growths and its whole evolution to drinkability is slightly quicker, yet its potential life span, judging by very rare old bottles, is no shorter. The final result is the pure magic of claret, sweet lively harmony with unfathomable depths.

A horse still works the steep vineyards set close to the town of St-Emilion

Château Cheval Blanc

1er Grand Cru Classé 1985. Owners: Société Civile du Cheval Blanc. Administrator: Bernard Grandchamp.
AOC: St-Emilion. 89 acres; 12,500
cases. Grape var: Cab.Franc 66%,
Merlot 33%, Malbec 1%.

Although it shares the first place in St-Emilion with Ausone, the soil and situation (and tradition) of Cheval Blanc are totally different. It lies back on the plateau near the boundary of Pomerol on much deeper soil, an irregular mixture of gravel, sand and clay with clay subsoil. The main grape is Cabernet Franc (known in these parts as Bouchet).

There is no white horse here, and the château is an unfanciful cream-painted residence that for some reason always reminds me of Virginia. The new *chais* are a more imposing building. The same family have owned the property since its 19th-century beginning.

Cheval Blanc is the Mouton of St-Emilion: the block-buster. The 1947 is a legend, a wine of heroic style and proportions, with the combined qualities of claret, port, sculpture and Hermès or Gucci – or is this lèse-majesté? The '61 is still not really ready; a tough piece of beef that seems to need to marinate for years. Not all vintages are so awe-inspiring: but 1975, '82 and '89 are for the 21st century.

Château Beau Séjour Bécot
1er Grand Cru Classé 1969. Owners: Michel Bécot & Fils.
AOC: St-Emilion. 41 acres; 6,500 cases. Grape var: Cab.Sauv.
6%, Cab.Franc 24%, Merlot 70%.

Two thirds of an estate that was divided in 1869 (the smaller part got the house). The vineyard slopes west from the crest behind Ch. Ausone. Michel Bécot, helped by his two sons, Gérard and Dominique, since 1969 has modernized the property with a complete new *cuvier* and restored its dimmed reputation to that of a leader in the tight circle of the St-Emilion *côtes*, making the sort of rich wine for the medium term (say 10 years) that makes St-Emilion so popular. Demoted in the 1985 classification because M. Bécot had extended the property by buying two other vineyards. Second label is La Tournelle des Moines.

Château Beauséjour
1er Grand Cru Classé 1985. Owners: Duffau-Lagarosse heirs.
Dir: Jean-Michel Fernandez.
AOC: St-Emilion. 17 acres; 3,000 cases. Grape var: Cab.Sauv.
15%, Cab.Franc 25%, Merlot 60%.

The smaller part of Beauséjour but with the charming house and garden. Run in the traditional small family château style but without the technical wizardry that makes St-Émilion a faster track every year.

Château Belair
1er Grand Cru Classé 1985. Owner: Mme J. Dubois-Challon.
AOC: St-Emilion. 21 acres; 4,500 cases. Grape var: Merlot
60%, Cab.Franc 40%.
Price (1989): 100 francs a bottle.

The bigger but junior brother of Ch. Ausone with the same owner and manager. Part of the same sloping vineyard, plus a patch on the flat top of the hill behind. It has its own quarry caves and, like many St-Emilion châteaux, its own chapel (full of lumber). The wine is now excellent (e.g. the 1989), close to Ch. Ausone but perhaps, to split hairs, a shade clumsier (or less deft).

Château Canon
1er Grand Cru Classé 1985. Owner: Eric Fournier.
AOC: St-Emilion. 44 acres; 6,500 cases. Grape var: Merlot
55%, Cab.Franc 40%, Cab.Sauv. 3%, Malbec 2%.

My instinct is to spell the name with two 'n's: a great bronze gun-barrel (rather than a genteel cleric) expresses the style of Canon nicely. If it were only bigger this would be one of the most famous Bordeaux; generous, masculine, not too aggressive young, but magnificent with 20 years in bottle. Recent vintages put it among the very top St-Emilions.

Château Figeac
1er Grand Cru Classé 1985. Owner: Thierry de Manoncourt.
AOC: St-Emilion. 85 acres; 21,000 cases. Grape var: Cab.Sauv.
35%, Cab.Franc 35%, Merlot 30%.

Ch. Figeac has the aristocratic air of a Médoc Cru Classé and once had an estate on the grand Médoc scale, including what is now Ch. Cheval Blanc, and two others which still bear the name of Figeac. The house could be called a mansion and the park has a seigneurial feeling absent in most of the Libournais. The owner even has the features of an old-school aristocrat. The present vineyard, still among the biggest in St-Emilion, has stonier ground and a higher proportion of Cabernet Sauvignon than the others – which may account for its different style from Cheval Blanc. Figeac is more welcoming, less dense and compact; closer to a Médoc (again) in its structure of sweet flesh around a firm spine. It is big but not strapping, maturing relatively early and beautifully sweet in maturity. The 1970 was deceptively easy drinking even at 5 years old. Recent vintages ('82, '85, '86, '88, '89) have been notably successful.

The second wine is La Grange Neuve de Figeac, which was launched in 1983. It was formerly a wine drunk only by the de Manoncourt family, production having started in 1954.

Clos Fourtet
1er Grand Cru Classé 1985. Owners: Lurton Brothers.
AOC: St-Emilion. 45 acres; 4,160 cases. Grape var: Merlot
70%, Cab.Franc 20%, Cab.Sauv. 10%.

The first Cru Classé that visitors stumble on as they walk out of the lovely old walled town into the vineyards. A modest-looking place, but with a warren of limestone cellars. (The old quarry-cellars are said to run for miles under the plateau, one château's cellars connecting with another. Paradise for an oenospelaeologist-burglar.) Old vintages of Clos Fourtet were tough going for many years. The 1966 was still immature in 1982. More recently (with Professor Peynaud's advice) the wine has been made a bit kindlier, but without reaching the peaks. Lucien Lurton is the proprietor of Ch. Climens (Sauternes), who also owns Ch. Brane-Cantenac (Margaux).

Château La Gaffelière

1er Grand Cru Classé 1985. Owner: Comte Léo de
Malet-Roquefort.
AOC: St-Emilion. 54 acres; 8,000 cases. Grape var: Cab.Sauv.
10%, Cab.Franc 25%, Merlot 65%.

The tall Gothic building at the foot of the hill up to St-
Emilion, with vineyards at the foot of Ausone and Pavie.
Three centuries in the de Malet-Roquefort family, a
history of noble vintages ('55 was a favourite), although
recent experience has been less consistent. The '79 is rich
and well balanced, both '82 and '83 are fine wines and
newer vintages are looking good.

Château Magdelaine

1er Grand Cru Classé 1985. Owners: Etablissements Jean-
Pierre Moueix.
AOC: St-Emilion. 26 acres; 9,000 cases. Grape var: Cab.Franc
10%, Merlot 90%.

Impeccably conducted little property next to Ch. Belair,
with a vineyard on the plateau and another on the south
slope. The wine is made like a first-growth by Christian
Moueix and Jean-Claude Berrouet, the brilliant resident
oenologist of the house of J.P. Moueix at Libourne. Its
high proportion of Merlot makes it almost a Pomerol, but
less plummy, with the 'meat' of St-Emilion and great
finesse. There can scarcely be a more reliable or fascinating St-Emilion to watch vintage by vintage.

Château Pavie

1er Grand Cru Classé 1985. Owners: Consorts Valette.
Administrator: Jean-Paul Valette.
AOC: St-Emilion. 89 acres plus; 15,000 cases. Grape var:
Cab.Sauv. 20%, Cab.Franc 25%, Merlot 55%.
Price (1989): 125 francs a bottle.

A priceless site, the whole south-by-west slope of the
central St-Emilion *côtes*; the biggest vineyard on the hill
with the advantage of both top and bottom as well; some
good should come out of almost every vintage. The
spacious cellars are dug under the top part of the vineyard,
whose vine roots can be seen rejoicing in their fragrant
humidity. The house lies in the middle of the vines. Pavie
was formerly known for warm, round claret of medium
weight, more delicious than deeply serious: 'supple' is the
technical term. Recent vintages have displayed a firmer
hand, making them one of St-Emilion's most consistent
top growths. The Valettes also own Ch. Pavie-Décesse on
the not-quite-so-good slopes next door.

Château Trottevieille

1er Grand Cru Classé 1985. Owner: Philippe Castéja.
AOC: St-Emilion. 24 acres; 4,000 cases. Grape var: Cab.Sauv.
5%, Cab.Franc 45%, Merlot 50%.

Detached from the solid block of Crus Classés along the
côtes, on the plateau east of the town, on richer-looking
but still shallow clay with pebbles over limestone. The
owners are the Médocain Castéja family of Ch. Batailley
(Pauillac). Full-flavoured wine with plenty of character,
particularly good since the '80s and even better since '85.

ST-EMILION GRANDS CRUS CLASSES

Château L'Angélus

Owners: The Boüard de Laforest family. 61 acres; 12,500
cases. Grape var: Cab.Franc 45%, Merlot 50%, Cab.Sauv. 5%.
On the slope below Ch. Beauséjour where the soil is
heavy. Very up-to-date techniques are producing better
and better wine. L'Angélus is now undoubtedly a best
buy.

Château L'Arrosée

Owner: François Rodhain. 24 acres; 4,100 cases. Grape var:
Merlot 50%, Cab.Sauv. 35%, Cab.Franc 15%.
Price (1989): 90 francs a bottle.
At the bottom of the *côtes* near the town. The name means
'watered' (by springs). The wine, on the contrary, is
extremely concentrated and serious; regularly one of the
stars of St-Emilion.

Château Balestard La Tonnelle

Owner: Jacques Capdemourlin. 26 acres; 5,000 cases. Grape
var: Merlot 65%, Cab.Franc 20%, Cab.Sauv. 10%, Malbec
5%.
Price (1989): 62 francs a bottle.
The same family has held this property since the 15th-
century poet Villon described its wine as '*ce divin nectar*'. I
have been more prosaically satisfied with this full-bodied,
meaty wine.

Château Bellevue

Owners: The daughters of Louis Horeau.
15 acres; 3,500 cases. Merlot 67%,
Cab.Sauv. and Franc 33%.
Price (1989): 60 francs a bottle.
Well named for its situation high on the west slope of the
côtes. I have not tasted the wine.

Château Bergat

Owner: Castéja family. Adm.: Emile Castéja (*see* Ch. Batailley,
Pauillac). 9 acres; 1,100 cases. Grape var: Merlot 50%,
Cab.Sauv. 25%, Cab.Franc 25%.
Tiny vineyard in the sheltered gully east of the town
linked by ownership with Ch. Trottevieille.

Château Berliquet

Owners: Vicomte & Vicomtesse de Lesquen. 20 acres; 3,200
cases. Grape var: Merlot 70%, Cab.Sauv. and Cab.Franc 30%.
Price (1989): 65 francs a bottle.
Old estate modernized in the 1970s, promoted in 1985,
and being closely followed for serious quality.

Château Cadet-Piola

Owners: Jabiol family. 17 acres; 3,000 cases. Grape var:
Merlot 51%, Cab.Sauv. 28%, Cab.Franc 18%, Malbec 3%.
Memorable for the only Bordeaux label to portray (and
very prettily) the female bosom. But a sturdy, even
masculine, wine.

Château Canon-La-Gaffelière

Owners: Comtes de Neipperg. 48 acres; 8,000 cases. Grape
var: Merlot 55%, Cab.Franc 40%, Cab.Sauv. 5%.
German-owned property on sandy soil by the railway
under the *côtes*. All aspects of the winemaking have been
under review since 1984, with excellent results in '85 and
'86.

Château Cap-de-Mourlin

Owner: Jacques Capdemourlin (*see* Ch. Balestard). 35 acres;
6,000 cases. Grape var: Merlot 60%, Cab.Franc 25%,
Cab.Sauv. 12%, Malbec 3%.
Price (1989): 56 francs a bottle.

Situated one mile north of St-Emilion on clay soil. For several years until 1982 this estate was divided, but is now one again, and is making strikingly high-flavoured wine.

Château Le Chatelet

Owner: Pierre Berjal. 14 acres; 2,500 cases. Grape var: Merlot 50%, Cab.Franc and Cab.Sauv. 50%.
Price (1989): 53 francs a bottle.
Immediate neighbour of the best *côtes* vineyards, jointly owned by M. Bécot of Ch. Beau-Séjour and M. Berjal, and now linked to Beau-Séjour.

Château Chauvin

Owners: Marie-France Février and Béatrice Ondet-Raynaud. 32 acres; 5,500 cases. Grape var: Merlot 60%, Cab.Franc 30%, Cab.Sauv. 10%.
An unexceptional *graves* vineyard which celebrates its centenary in 1991.

Château La Clotte

Owners: Héritiers Chaileau. 8 acres; 1,550 cases. Grape var: Merlot 85%, Cab.Franc 15%.
Beautifully situated in the fold of the hill east of the town.

Château La Clusière

Owners: Consorts Valette. 7 acres; 1,000 cases. Grape var: Merlot 70%, Cab.Franc 30%.
Price (1989): 55 francs a bottle.
Part of the vineyard of Ch. Pavie (q.v.) not quite up to Premier Grand Cru standard.

Château Corbin

Owners: Domaines Giraud. 32 acres; 6,000 cases. Grape var: Merlot 65%, Cab.Franc 35%.
Corbin is the northern hamlet of *graves* St-Emilion, near the Pomerol boundary and sloping gently northeast. Some flesh, some tannin but, on balance, not very distinctive wine.

Château Corbin-Michotte

Owner: Jean Noël Boidron. 15 acres; 3,000 cases. Grape var: Merlot 65%, Cab.Franc 30%, Cab.Sauv. 5%.
See the previous entry; but this seems to me more delicate and 'supple'.

Château Couvent-des-Jacobins

Owner: Mme Joinand-Borde. 22 acres; 3,500 cases. Grape var: Merlot 65%, Cab.Franc 25%, Cab.Sauv. 9%, Malbec 1%.
Excellent *côtes* vineyard right under the town walls to the east, with venerable cellars in the town centre. Well-structured, ripe and juicy wine.

Château Croque-Michotte

Owner: Mme Rigal. 33 acres; 6,700 cases. Grape var: Merlot 90%, Cab. 10%.
Graves property on the Pomerol border near Corbin; wine with the plumpness of a Pomerol and the intensity of a fine St-Emilion.

Château Curé-Bon-La-Madeleine

Owner: Maurice Landé. 12 acres; 2,000 cases. Grape var: Merlot 80%, Cab.Franc 20%.
Bon was the curé who owned this little patch among the great *côtes* vineyards of Canon, Belair, etc. This is concentrated and powerful wine, jammy but tannic – most impressive.

Château Dassault

Owners: SARL Château Dassault. 56 acres; 9,000 cases. Grape var: Merlot 65%, Cab.Franc 28%, Cab.Sauv. 8%.
One of the biggest *graves* vineyards, northeast of the town. Steady rather than distinguished; mainstream St-Emilion.

Château La Dominique

Owner: Clément Fayat. Administrator: Étienne Prion. 47 acres; 6,500 cases. Grape var: Cab.Sauv. 5%, Cab.Franc 15%, Merlot 75%, Malbec 5%.
Neighbour to Cheval Blanc reflecting its privileged position in an almost unbroken sequence of concentrated, fleshy, very fine wines.

Château Faurie-de-Souchard

Owners: The Jabiol family. 26 acres; 5,000 cases. Grape var: Merlot 60%, Cab.Franc 30%, Cab.Sauv. 10%.
Confusingly the neighbour of Petit-Faurie-de-Soutard. Same owners as of Ch. Cadet-Piola and Ch. Cadet-Peychez; not quite as good.

Château Fonplégade

Owner: Armand Moueix. 44 acres; 7,500 cases. Grape var: Merlot 60%, Cab.Sauv. 5%, Cab.Franc 35%.
One of the grander châteaux, on the *côtes* among the very best, yet never one of the great names. Delicious meaty wine that seems persistently underrated.

Château Fonroque

Owners: Ets J-P. Moueix. 48 acres; 8,000 cases. Grape var: Merlot 85%, Cab.Franc 15%.
A relatively modest member of the impeccable Moueix stable. Dark, firm wine of definite character.

Château Franc-Mayne

Grand Cru Classé 1969. Owners: AXA Millésimes. 18 acres; 3,000 cases. Grape var: Merlot 70%, Cab.Franc 15%, Cab.Sauv. 15%.
A serious little property on the western *côtes*, acquired in 1984 by the insurance group AXA, and to be run by Jean-Michel Cazes of Château Lynch-Bages. To watch.

Château Grand Barrail Lamarzelle Figeac

Grand Cru Classé 1969. Owners: Association E. Carrère. 47 acres. Grape var: Merlot 80%, Cab.Sauv. 20%.
Price (1989): 65 francs a bottle.
Widely seen: not otherwise outstanding. *see* also Ch. La Marzelle.

Château Grand Corbin

Owner: Alain Giraud. 31 acres; 6,500 cases. Grape var: Merlot 65%, Cab.Franc 35%.
Property with old vines, very near to Pomerol. Produces standard-quality wine.

Château Grand-Corbin-Despagne

Grand Cru Classé 1969. Owners: The Despagne family. 62 acres; 11,000 cases. Grape var: Merlot 65%, Cab.Franc 30%, Cab.Sauv. and Malbec 5%.
One of the northernmost St-Emilions in the Pomerol corner of the *graves* plateau. Produces dark, well-made, manly wine.

Château Grand Mayne

Owner: Jean-Pierre Nony. 47 acres; 10,000 cases. Grape var: Merlot 50%, Cab.Sauv. 10%, Cab.Franc 40%.
Smooth, 'supple' wine from the western *côtes*. becoming increasingly serious in the late '80s.

Château Grand-Pontet
Owners: The Bécot and Pourouquet families. 35 acres; 6,000 cases. Grape var: Merlot 75%, Cab.Franc 15%, Cab.Sauv. 10%.
Owned by the shippers Barton & Guestier from 1965 to 1980 and made smooth, attractive and easy drinking wine. Michel Bécot (of Beau Séjour, its sister château) calls it 'Gironde Burgundy' – surely a two-edged compliment.

Château Guadet-St-Julien
Owner: Robert Lignac. 15 acres; 2,000 cases. Grape var: Merlot 75%, Cab.Franc and Cab.Sauv. 25%.
Vineyard just out of town to the north; cellars in the rue Guadet. A property to follow.

Château Haut-Corbin
Owner: Edward Guinaudie. 16 acres; 2,500 cases. Grape var: Merlot 70%, Cab.Sauv. 20%, Cab.Franc 10%.
The least of the Corbins up near the Pomerol border.

Château Haut-Sarpe
Owner: Joseph Janoueix. 28 acres; 6,000 cases. Grape var: Merlot 70%, Cab.Franc 30%.
Price (1990): 87 francs a bottle.
The Janoueix family are merchants in Libourne with 6 small properties in Pomerol. Haut-Sarpe straddles the border of St-Christophe des Bardes, east of St-Emilion, among good properties making firm, earthy wine.

Château Clos des Jacobins
Owners: Ets. Cordier. 18 acres; 3,500 cases. Grape var: Merlot 85%, Cab.Franc 10%, Cab.Sauv. 5%.
The house of Cordier makes characteristically attractive wine here; in the centre of the commune where côtes begins to shade to graves. This is an excellent example of the 'open' côtes style.

Château Laniote
Owners: Freymond-Schneider family. 12 acres; 2,700 cases. Grape var: Merlot 70%, Cab.Sauv. 20%, Cab.Franc 10%.
One of the many little properties so appreciated in Belgium that they are unknown elsewhere. The cave in the hillside where Saint Emilion himself lived in the 7th century is on the property.

Château Larcis-Ducasse
Owner: Mme H. Gratiot Alphandery. 24 acres; 5,000 cases. Grape var: Merlot 65%, Cab.Franc and Cab.Sauv. 35%.
Price (1989): 58 francs a bottle.
The best vineyard of St-Laurent-des-Combes, splendidly sited on the côtes just east of Ch. Pavie (q.v.). A good bet, but much less elegant than its Premier Grand Cru neighbour.

Château Larmande
Owners: The Meneret-Capdemourlin family. 54 acres; 8,000 cases. Grape var. Merlot 60%, Cab.Franc 30%, Cab.Sauv.10%.
Next door to Ch. Cap de Mourlin. The '80s have seen this property come to the fore, with generous, fleshy, well-structured wines.

Château Laroze
Owner: Georges Meslin. 62 acres; 10,000 cases. Grape var: Merlot 50%, Cab.Franc 47%, Cab.Sauv. 3%.
Low on the western côtes on sandy soil. Not one of the outstanding vineyards, but modern and well managed, capable of very good wine for 4–5 years' maturing.

Clos La Madeleine
Owner: Hubert Pistouley. 5 acres; 1,000 cases. Grape var: Merlot 50%, Cab.Franc 50%.
Tiny côtes plot belonging to the owner of Ch. Magnan-La-Gaffelière (Grand Cru). Apparently all sold in Belgium.

Château Matras
Owner: Jean Bernard-Lebèbvre. 43 acres; 5,500 cases. Grape var: Cab.Franc 50%, Merlot 40%, Cab.Sauv. 10%.
Beautifully sited château at the foot of the western côtes next to Ch. L'Angélus. Recent replanting suggests much-needed new ideas.

Château Mauvezin
Owner: Pierre Cassat. 9 acres; 3,000 cases. Grape var: Merlot 55%, Cab.Franc 40%, Cab.Sauv. 5%.
A côtes property I have never been able to find; not to be confused with the Moulis (Médoc) château. Its reputation is high.

Château Moulin du Cadet
Owners: Ets. J-P. Moueix. 12 acres; 1,800 cases. Grape var: Merlot 85%, Cab.Franc 15%.
Impeccably made wine typical of the Moueix establishment. A combination of clay soil and a côtes situation gives solidity and sweetness.

Château La Marzelle
Owner: Edmond Carrère. 32 acres. Grape var: Merlot 75%, Cab.Franc 15%, Cab.Sauv. 10%.
Promoted in 1985, a property in the same ownership as Ch. Grand Barrail Lamarzelle Figeac.

Clos de L'Oratoire
Owners: Soc. Civile Peyreau. 25 acres; 5,000 cases. Grape var: Merlot 75%, Cab.Franc 25%.
A côtes property that has grown recently, it is now making solid, unassuming wines in mainstream St-Emilion style.

Château Pavie-Decesse
Owners: The Valette family. 22 acres; 4,500 cases. Grape var: Cab.Franc 30%, Merlot 70%.
Price (1989): 66 francs a bottle.
The junior partner of Ch. Pavie, from the flatter land at the top of the côtes. The wine is considered a shade harder, less supple and 'giving' than Pavie but can (eg in '85) be as fine.

Château Pavie-Macquin
Owner: Antoine Corre. 37 acres; 4,000 cases. Grape var: Merlot 70%, Cab.Franc 30%.
A worthy neighbour of Ch. Pavie with less ambitious but worthy wines.

Château Pavillon-Cadet
Owner: Anne Llammas. 7 acres; 750 cases. Grape var: Cab.Franc 50%, Merlot 50%.
A little côtes property with Breton connections.

Château Petit-Faurie-de-Soutard
Owner: Mme Françoise Capdemourlin. 20 acres; 3,500 cases. Grape var: Merlot 60%, Cab.Franc 30%, Cab.Sauv. 10%.
Price (1989): 45 francs a bottle.
Neighbour of the Cap-de-Mourlin, now managed by Jacques C. Readily confused with next-door Faurie-de-Souchard. Technically côtes wines, but like Ch. Soutard (of which it was once a part) harder to penetrate.

Château Le Prieuré

Owner: SCE Baronne Guichard. 12 acres; 1,500 cases. Grape var: Merlot 70%, Cab.Franc 30%.

On the eastern *côtes* in an ideal situation but apparently ticking over at present.

Château Ripeau

Owner: Mme Françoise de Wilde. 38 acres; 7,000 cases. Grape var: Merlot 60%, Cab.Franc 20%, Cab.Sauv. 20%.
Price (1989): 49 francs a bottle.

A well-known *graves* château in the past, considered on a par with La Dominique. Less prominent recently, but heading for a revival.

Château St-Georges (Côte-Pavie)

Owner: Jacques Masson. 13 acres; 2,500 cases. Grape var: Merlot 80%, Cab.Sauv. and Franc 20%.

An enviable spot between Pavie and Ch. La Gaffelière. Worth seeking out.

Château Sansonnet

Owner: Francis Robin. 20 acres; 3,500 cases. Grape var: Merlot 60%, Cab.Franc 20%, Cab.Sauv. 20%.

Potentially fine neighbour to Ch. Trottevieille on the eastern *côtes*. On 'hold' recently.

Château La Serre

Owner: Bernard d'Arfeuille. 17 acres; 3,000 cases. Grape var: Merlot 80%, Cab.Franc 20%.

Just outside the town on the *côtes* to the east. Despite its surprising proportion of Merlot, this seems a tougher wine than its neighbour La Clotte although the '85 and '86 vintages were well received.

Château Soutard

Owners: François, Isabelle and Hélène des Ligneris. 55 acres; 8,000 cases. Grape var: Merlot 60%, Cab.Franc 40%.

An important property on a rocky outcrop north-by-east of the town. Well-made, warm and powerful wine. The great vintages are long-keeping classics.

Château Tertre-Daugay

Owner: Léo de Malet-Roquefort. 39 acres; 5,000 cases. Grape var: Merlot 60%, Cab.Franc 40%.

A spectacularly well-sited château on the final promontory of the *côtes* west of Ch. Ausone, in disarray for some years, but since 1978 in the same hands as La Gaffelière and replanting. Recent vintages have shown the true class of the property. 15 acres of young vines produce Roquefort, a St-Emilion Grand Cru.

Château La Tour Figeac

Owners: Soc. Civile. 34 acres; 6,000 cases. Grape var: Merlot 60%, Cab.Franc 40%.

Formerly part of Ch. Figeac, now owned by Franco-German interests. This is a very worthy wine.

Château La Tour-du-Pin-Figeac (Giraud Belivier)

Owner: GFA Giraud Belivier. 24 acres; 4,000 cases.

A predominantly Merlot vineyard north of Figeac, beside Cheval Blanc, but not above average in quality.

Château La Tour-du-Pin-Figeac

Owner: Héritiers Marcel Moueix. 21 acres; 4,000 cases. Grape var: Merlot 60%, Cab.Franc 30%, Malbec, Cab.Sauv. 10%.

Powerful, pungent wines from a privileged situation among the great plateau vineyards.

Château Trimoulet

Owner: Michel Jean. 39 acres; 7,500 cases. Grape var: Merlot 60%, Cab.Sauv. 10%, Cab.Franc 30%.

A *côtes* vineyard in name, but on deep soil on the slope northwards down to the boundary of St-Georges.

Château Troplong-Mondot

Owner: Claude Valette. 72 acres; 11,000 cases. Grape var: Merlot 70%, Cab.Sauv., Cab.Franc and Malbec 30%.
Price (1989): 55 francs a bottle.

A famous vineyard on the crest of the *côtes* east of the town, above Ch. Pavie. Reliably good wine in the '80s, deserving much better in the classification than many of its 'peers'.

Château Villemaurine

Owner: Robert Giraud. 20 acres; 4,000 cases. Grape var: Cab.Sauv. 20%, Merlot 80%.
Price (1989): 65 francs a bottle.

At the gates of the town, a *côtes* vineyard with more Cabernet Sauvignon than most, consequently less easy wine but worth wating for. There are splendid cellars.

Château Yon-Figeac

58 acres; 7,500 cases. Grape var: Merlot 33⅓%, Cab.Sauv. 33⅓%, Cab.Franc 33⅓%.

A former part of the Figeac domaine in the *graves*; one of the better reputed of its class.

Caves Coopératives of St-Emilion

Les Producteurs Réunis de Puisseguin St-Emilion & Lussac St-Emilion
Puisseguin, 33570 Lussac. 150 members, 1,480 acres, 300,000 cases. Flourishing modern cooperative using the brand names Roc de Puisseguin and Roc de Lussac and making wine for several small estates including: AOC Puisseguin St-Emilion: Châteaux Bayens, Champ de Hayet, Côtes de Mouchet, Côtes de St-Clair, du Roy, St-Jacques: AOC Lussac St-Emilion: Châteaux Les Adams, Le Bourdil, Les Bruges, La Chevalière,

Haut Drouillard, Girard Tiffray, Lagrange, Pichon, La Rose, Taureau, Terrien, Verdu, Les Vieux Chenes.

University research
The standard of wine-making and the understanding of problems that beset both grapes and wine have been immeasurably enhanced over the last century, but especially the last 40 years, by the Station Oenologique of the University of Bordeaux. A succession of famous directors has included Professor Ulysse Gayon, a pupil of Louis Pasteur, who introduced the science of microbiology to wine-making. His

grandson, Jean Ribereau-Gayon, succeeded him and was in turn succeeded in guiding the wine makers of Bordeaux along scientific lines by his pupil, Emile Peynaud, and his own son, Pascal Ribereau-Gayon.

GRANDS CRUS

*The quality of such a number of châteaux obviously varies very widely. Those marked with an asterisk are known to me to have particularly high and consistent standards.

Château Badette
St-Emilion. Owner: Daniel Arraud. 11 acres; 4,000 cases.

Château Barde-Haut
St-Christophe des Bardes. Owner: Jean-Claude Gasparoux. 36 acres; 6,500 cases.

Château Beau-Mayne
St-Emilion. Owners: Soc. Joinaud-Borde. Second label of Couvent des Jacobins.

Château Bellefont-Belcier*
St-Laurent des Combes. Owner: Jean Labusquière. 32 acres; 6,000 cases.

Château Bellefont-Belcier-Guillier
St-Laurent des Combes. Owner: Philippe Guillier. 21 acres; 2,750 cases.

Château Bellegrave
Vignonet. Owner: Pierre Dangin. 26 acres; 6,250 cases.

Château Bellisle-Mondotte
St-Laurent des Combes. Owners: Escure. 69 acres; 8,650 cases.

Château Bigaroux
St-Sulpice de Faleyrens. Owner: Didier Dizier. 34 acres; 7,000 cases.

Château Bonnet
St-Pey d'Armens. Owner: M. Bonnet. 61 acres; 8,500 cases.

Château Cadet-Bon
St-Emilion. Owner: Bernard Gans. 10 acres; 2,500 cases.

Château Cadet-Pontet
St-Emilion. Owner: Michel Merias. 25 acres; 2,250 cases.

Château Calvaire
St-Etienne de Lisse. Owner: J-P. Cisterne. 24 acres; 4,800 cases.

Château Cantenac
St-Emilion. Owners: The Brunot family. 37 acres; 6,000 cases.

Château Canteranne
St-Etienne de Lisse. Owner: Trabut-Cussac. 24 acres; 4,150 cases.

Château Capet-Guillier
St-Hippolyte. Owners: Soc. du Château. 37 acres; 5,500 cases.

Château Carboneyre
Vignonet. Owner: Raby-Saugeon. 52 acres; 11,000 cases.

Château Cardinal Villemaurine*
St-Emilion. Owner: J-F. Carrille. 20 acres; 4,000 cases.

Château Carteau-Côtes-Daugay*
St-Emilion. Owner: J. Bertrand. 29 acres; 6,000 cases.

Château Carteau Matras
St-Emilion. Owner: Claude Bion. 31 acres; 5,700 cases.

Château du Cauze

St-Christophe des Bardes. Owner: Bruno Laporte. 49 acres; 12,000 cases.

Château La Chapelle-Lescours
St-Sulpice de Faleyrens. Owner: Pierre Quentin. 17 acres; 4,500 cases.

Château Chapelle-Madelaine
Owner: Mme Dubois-Challow. 0.5 acres.

Château Cormeil-Figeac*
St-Emilion. Owners: Héritiers R. & L. Moreaud. 62 acres; 4,000 cases.

Château Côtes Bernateau
St-Etienne de Lisse. Owner: Régis Lavau. 26 acres; 6,300 cases.

Château Côtes de la Mouleyre
St-Etienne de Lisse. Owner: Pierre Roques. 22 acres; 4,150 cases.

Château Côte Puyblanquet
St-Etienne de Lisse. Owner: Daniel Bertoni. 89 acres; 5,800 cases.

Château Couvent des Templiers
St-Emilion. Owners: Hérit. Meneret. 41 acres; 6,750 cases.

Château Croix de Bertinat
St-Sulpice de Faleyrens. Owner: Christian Lafaye. 19 acres; 4,570 cases.

Château La Fagnouse
St-Etienne de Lisse. Owner: Mme Coutant. 18 acres; 3,500 cases.

Château de Faleyrens
St-Sulpice de Faleyrens. Owner: Jacques Brisson. 26 acres; 3,650 cases.

Château Ferrand*
St-Hippolyte. Owner: Baron Bich. 74 acres; 13,500 cases.

Château La Fleur*
St-Emilion. Owner: Lily Lacoste. 16 acres; 2,000 cases.

Château La Fleur Pipeau
St-Laurent des Combes. Owner: Pierre Mestreguilhem. 55 acres; 13,150 cases.

Château Fombrauge*
St-Christophe des Bardes. Owners: The Bygodt family. 123 acres; 25,000 cases.

Château Fonrazade
St-Emilion. Owner: Guy Balotte. 22 acres; 4,500 cases.

Château Fourney
St-Pey d'Armens. Owners: Vignobles Rollet. 44 acres; 7,000 cases.

Château Franc Bigaroux
St-Sulpice de Faleyrens. Owner: Yves Blanc. 25 acres; 5,000 cases.

Château Franc-Grâce-Dieu
St-Emilion. Owner: Germain Siloret. 20 acres; 3,000 cases.

Château Gaillard
St-Hippolyte. Owner: Jean-Jacques Nouvel. 49 acres; 9,000 cases.

Château Gaubert
St-Christophe des Bardes. Owner: Honoré Menager. 38 acres; 1,250 cases.

Château La Grâce Dieu
St-Emilion. Owner: Maurice Pauty. 27 acres; 7,000 cases.

Château La Grâce-Dieu-Les-Menuts
St-Emilion. Owner: Max Pilotte. 32 acres; 5,800 cases.

Château Gravet
St-Sulpice de Faleyrens. Owner: Jean Faure. 25 acres; 3,750 cases.

Château Gueyrot
St-Emilion. Owners: Tour de Fayet Frères. 21 acres; 4,000 cases.

Château Guillemin La Gaffelière
St-Emilion. Owner: Yves Fomperier. 21 acres; 8,500 cases.

Château Guinot
St-Etienne de Lisse. Owner: Simone Tauziac. 18 acres; 4,000 cases.

Château Haut Brisson*
Bignonet. Owner: Yves Blanc. 27 acres; 5,500 cases.

Château Haut-Lavallade
St-Christophe des Bardes. Owner: Jean Pierre Chagneau. 25 acres; 5,500 cases.

Château Haut-Plantey
St-Emilion. Owner: Michel Boutet. 23 acres; 5,000 cases.

Château Haut Pontet*
St-Emilion. Owners: Limouzin Frères. 13 acres; 2,500 cases.

Château Haut Ségottes
St-Emilion. Owner: Danielle André. 17 acres; 2,650 cases.

Château L'Hermitage
St-Emilion. Owner: Brunot. 35 acres.

Château Jacques Blanc
St-Etienne de Lisse. Owner: Pierre Chouet. 47 acres; 6,500 cases.

Château Jean-Voisin
St-Emilion. Owners: Soc. Chassagnoux. 29 acres; 3,700 cases.

Château Le Jurat
St-Emilion. Owner: Edward Guinaudie. 17 acres; 3,500 cases.

Château Lapelletrie
St-Christophe des Bardes. Owners: Jean family. 30 acres; 6,000 cases.

Château Lapeyre
St-Etienne de Lisse. Owner: Simone Tauziac. 18 acres; 4,000 cases.

Château Laroque*
St-Christophe des Bardes. Owners: Société Civile. 111 acres; 20,000 cases.

Château Lassèque
St-Hippolyte. Owner: J. P. Freylon. 57 acres; 13,000 cases.

Château Legrange de Lescure
St-Sulpice de Faleyrens. Owner: J. Pesquier, 42 acres; 9,700 cases.

Château Lescours
St-Sulpice de Faleyrens. Owners: Soc. du Château. 74 acres; 11,200 cases.

Château Marquis de Mons
St-Hippolyte. Owner: Micheau-Maillou and Palatin. 32 acres; 7,000 cases.

Château Mazerat
St-Emilion. Owners: Gouteyron & Fils. 28 acres; 5,800 cases.

Clos des Menuts
St-Emilion. Owner: Pierre Rivière. 60 acres; 11,500 cases.

Château Milon
St-Christophe des Bardes. Owner: Christian Bouyer. 49 acres: 8,500 cases.

Château Monbousquet*
St-Sulpice de Faleyrens. Owners:
The Querre family. 74 acres; 12,000
cases.

Château Montlabert
St-Emilion. Owners: Société Civile. 27
acres; 6,000 cases.

Château Moulin Bellegrave
Vignonet. Owner: Max Perier. 20 acres;
4,000 cases.

Château Palais Cardinal La Fuie
St-Sulpice de Faleyrens. Owner: Gérard
Frétier. 34 acres; 7,300 cases.

Château Panet
St-Christophe des Bardes. Owner: Jean-
Claude Carles. 60 acres; 10,350 cases.

Château Patris
St-Emilion. Owner: Michel Querre. 30
acres; 6,000 cases.

Château Peyreau
St-Emilion. Owner: Michel Boutet. 32
acres; 6,000 cases.

Château de Peyrelongue
St-Emilion. Owner: Pierre Cassat. 29
acres; 6,000 cases.

Château Pindefleurs*
St-Emilion. Owner: Micheline Dior. 19
acres; 2,300 cases.

Château Pipeau
St-Laurent des Combes. Owner: Richard
Mestreguilhem & Fils. 62 acres; 13,500
cases.

Château Pontet-Clauzure
St-Emilion. Owners: Société Civile. 25
acres; 4,000 cases.

Château Pourret
St-Emilion. Owner: François Ouzoulias.
42 acres; 3,900 cases.

Château de Pressac
St-Etienne de Lisse. Owner: Jacques
Pouey. 69 acres; 16,000 cases.

Château Puy-Blanquet*
St-Etienne de Lisse. Owner: R. Jacquet.
57 acres; 10,000 cases.

Château Puyblanquet Carille
St-Christophe des Bardes. Owner: Jean-
François Carrille. 37 acres; 7,500 cases.

Château Quentin
St-Christopher des Bardes. Owners:
Société Civile. 74 acres; 18,000 cases.

Château du Rocher
St-Etienne de Lisse. Owners: GFA du
Château. 32 acres; 4,500 cases.

Château de Rol
St-Emilion. Owner: Jean Sautereau. 17
acres; 3,000 cases.

Château La-Rose-Côtes Rol
St-Emilion. Owner: Yves Mirande. 21
acres; 3,500 cases.

Château La Rose Pourret
St-Emilion. Owner: Bernard Warion. 17
acres; 2,500 cases.

Château Rozier
St-Laurent des Combes. Owner: Jean-
Bernard Saby. 43 acres; 8,500 cases.

Château La Sablière
St-Emilion. Owner: Robert Avezou. 22
acres; 5,300 cases.

Château St-Christophe
St-Christophe des Bardes. Owner:
Gilbert Richard. 21 acres; 4,000 cases.

Château de St-Pey
St-Pey d'Armens. Owner: Maurice
Musset. 40 acres; 7,500 cases.

Château Tour des Combes
St-Laurent des Combes. Owner: Jean
Darribéhaude. 30 acres; 5,000 cases.

Château Tour-St-Pierre
St-Emilion. Owner: Jacques Coudineau.
28 acres; 4,500 cases.

Château Touzinat
St-Pey d'Armens. Owner: Yves Nérac.
19 acres.

Château Trapaud
St-Etienne de Lisse. Owner: André
Larribière. 30 acres; 6,000 cases.

Château Trimoulet
St-Emilion. Owner: Michel Jean. 42
acres; 8,000–10,000 cases.

Château Val d'Or
Vignonet. Owner: Roger Bardet. 24
acres; 6,000 cases.

Vieux Château Chauvin
St-Emilion. Owner: Pierre Manuel. 28
acres; 4,800 cases.

Château Vieux Rivallon
St-Emilion. Owner: Charles Bouquey.
21 acres; 2,550 cases.

Château Vieux Sarpe*
St-Christophe des Bardes. Owner: J.-F.
Janoueix. 16 acres; 4,000 cases.

MERCHANTS IN LIBOURNE

Most of the thriving trade of St-
Emilion, Pomerol and their neighbours
is handled by a group of négociants
clustered on the Quai du Priourat, by
the rustic riverside of the Dordogne. A
peculiarity of Libourne business is the
number of independent salesmen known
as *Les Corréziens* (they hail from the
Corrèze, up-country along the
Dordogne and scarcely a land of
opportunity). *Les Corréziens* spend a
winter season in the north of France and
Belgium collecting private orders, which
they pass to the Quai du Priourat. Other
houses are based in St-Emilion and the
villages around.

Principal Libourne négociants in
approximate order of importance are:

Etablissements Jean-Pierre Moueix,
Libourne.
Founder: Jean-Pierre Moueix. His son
Christian is also a celebrated figure. The
family firm that makes the runing in
Libourne, owning or managing a score
of the best châteaux (see the château
entries). Duclot in Bordeaux is related.

Maison Lebègue, Libourne.
Dealers in a wide range of wines in
bottle and bulk.

Armand Moueix, Pomerol.

Merchants and proprietors based at
Château Taillefer, Pomerol.

Etablissements Pierre Jean, St-
Christophe-des-Bardes.
Specialists in St-Emilion in bottle and
bulk.

Maison Grenouilleau, Ste-Foy-La-
Grande.

Maison Horeau-Beylot, Libourne.
A family firm of proprietors and
shippers founded in 1740.

Maison Jean Milhade, Galgon.
Merchants based in the Fronsac area.

Maison d'Arfeuille, Libourne.
Merchants and proprietors.

Maison Audy, Libourne.

Etablissements Marcel Bonneau,
Branne (Entre-Deux-Mers).

Maison Daniel Querre, St-Emilion.
Merchants and proprietors of Château
Monbousquet, St-Emilion.

Maison Pierre Rivière, St-Emilion.

Maison Joseph Janoueix, Libourne.

Maison Michel Querre, Libourne.

Etablissements Jean-René Feytit,
St-Emilion.

Maison René Vedrenne, Libourne.

Maison François-Bernard Janoueix,
Libourne.

Bordeaux trade measures

For official and statistical purposes, all
French wine production is measured in
hectolitres, but each region has its
traditional measures for maturing and
selling its wine. In Bordeaux the
measure is the *tonneau*, a notional
container since such big barrels are no
longer made. A *tonneau* consists of 4
barriques – the barrels used at the
châteaux, and still sometimes for
shipping. A *barrique bordelaise* must by
law contain 225 litres, which makes 25
cases of a dozen 75 cl. bottles each. The
tonneau is therefore a simple and
memorable measure: 100 cases of wine.

THE 'SATELLITES' OF ST-EMILION

Apart from the five saintly villages (SS Emilion, Laurent, Christophe, Etienne and Hippolyte) that are considered part of the appellation St-Emilion, five more to the north and east are granted the privilege of adding St-Emilion to their names. They are known as the satellites. They lie just north of the little river Barbanne, which forms the northern boundary of glory and renown. Their citizens argue that the formation of the valley gives two of them, St-Georges and Montagne, a better situation than some of St-Emilion. Be that as it may, those two, plus Puisseguin, Lussac and Parsac, are honoured.

Proprietors in St-Georges and Parsac may call their wine Montagne-St-Emilion if they wish. Those in Parsac do, but St-Georges has a splendid château that gives it pride in its own name. Their wine is indeed like St-Emilion and can be made almost equally meaty and long lived. More growers, however, prefer using a good deal of Merlot and making softer (still strong) wine that can be delicious in two or three years. Postcode: 33570 Lussac.
Price (1988): 18 francs a bottle.

PUISSEGUIN-ST-EMILION LEADING CHATEAUX

Château Beauséjour
Owner: Annick Dupuy. 46 acres; 7,600 cases.
Château Bel-Air
Owner: Robert Adoue. 37 acres; 8,500 cases.
Château Guibeau
Owner: Henri Bourlon. 101 acres; 20,000 cases.
Château des Laurets
Owner: GFA du Domaine des Laurets et de Malengin. 160 acres; 40,000 cases.
Château de Puisseguin
Owner: Jean Robin. 47 acres; 8,500 cases.
Château Roc de Boissac
Owner: Jean Sublett. 72 acres; 13,000 cases.
Château de Roques
Owner: Michel Sublett. 82 acres; 12,500 cases.
Château Soleil
Owner: Jean Soleil. 49 acres; 8,500 cases.
Château Teyssier
Owners: Société Civile. 35 acres; 6,500 cases.
Roc de Puisseguin
Owners: Union des Producteurs Réunis, Cave Coopérative de Puisseguin. 315 acres; 60,00 cases.

PUISSEGUIN-ST-EMILION OTHER CHATEAUX

Château Cassat 64 acres.
Château Le Chay 32 acres.
Château Chêne-Vieux 28 acres.
Château Durand Laplaigne 32 acres.
Château Gontet 29 acres.
Château Haut Bernon 24 acres.
Château Hermitage la Garenne 18 acres.
Château Le Mayne 20 acres.
Château de Mole 28 acres.
Château du Moulin 32 acres.

Château Moulin des Laurets 25 acres.
Château Moulins Listrac 23 acres.
Château La Tour Guillotin 37 acres.
Château Vaisinerie 26 acres.

LUSSAC-ST-EMILION LEADING CHATEAUX

Château de Barbe Blanche
Owner: A. Bouvier. 69 acres; 12,500 cases.
Château Bel-Air
Owner: J.-N. Roi. 50 acres; 8,500 cases
Château Lucas
Owner: M. Vauthier. 8,000 cases red, 2,000 white.
Château de Lussac
Owner: Marquis de Sercey. 7,500 cases.
Château du Lyonnat
Owner: GFA des Vignobles Jean Milhade. 123 acres; 25,000 cases.
Château Petit-Refuge
Owner: M. Brunot. 62 acres; 12,500 cases.
Château Tour de Grenet
Owner: M. Brunot. 72 acres; 15,000 cases.
Château La Tour de Ségur
Owner: Maitre Boncheau (monopoly of Dourthe Frères). 6,000 cases red, 1,000 white.
Château des Vieux Chênes
Owner: M. Debès. 10,000 cases.

MONTAGNE-ST-EMILION CHATEAUX

Château Barraud
Owner: Robert Laydis. 34 acres; 7,000 cases.
Château Bayard
Owner: Christian Bruno Laporte. 61 acres; 12,000 cases.
Château Bayard
Owner: Philippe Gouze & Fils. 34 acres; 7,000 cases.
Château Beauséjour
Owner: Lucien Laporte, 31 acres; 6,000 cases.

Château Biquette
Owner: Yvette Bertin. 23 acres; 4,500 cases.
Château Bonneau
Owner: Alain Despagne. 25 acres; 5,000 cases.
Château Calon
Owner: Jean-Noël Boidron. 86 acres; 15,000 cases.
Château Corbin
Owner: François Rambeaud. 50 acres; 10,000 cases.
Château Coucy
Owners: The Maurèze family. 46 acres; 11,000 cases.
Château Fontmuret
Owners: Simonnet Père & Fils. 25 acres; 5,000 cases.
Château Tour de Gillet
Owner: G. Cally. 42 acres; 2,500 cases.
Château Gilet Bayard
Owner: Michel Darnajou. 25 acres; 4,600 cases.
Château Haute Faucherie
Owner: Yvette Audinet. 22.5 acres; 4,500 cases.
Château des Moines
Owner: Raymond Edgard Tapon. 26 acres; 5,000 cases.
Château Montaiguillon
Owner: M. Amart. 69 acres; 17,000 cases.
Château Mouchet
Owner: Primo Grando. 29 acres; 5,500 cases.
Château Roudier
Owner: Jacques Capdemourlin. 74 acres; 15,000 cases.
Château St-André-Corbin
Owner: Robert Carré. 54 acres; 10,000 cases.
Château Teyssier
Owner: Durand Teyssier. 48 acres; 9,000 cases.
Château des Tours
Owner: GFA Louis Yerlès. 178 acres; 45,000 cases.
Vieux-Château-St-André (Corbin)
Owner: Jean-Claude Berrouet. 12 acres; 3,000 cases.

MONTAGNE-ST-EMILION OTHER CHATEAUX

Château Bertinau 22.5 acres.
Château Bonde 14.5 acres.
Château Colas Nouet 39 acres.
Château Goujon 15 acres.
Château Négrit 28.5 acres.
Château Plaisance 48.5 acres.

ST-GEORGES–ST-EMILION CHATEAUX

Château Macquin St-Georges
Owner: Denis Corre-Maquin. 74 acres;
12,000 cases.
Château Maison Neuve
Owner: Michel Coudroy. 37 acres; 7,000
cases.
Château St-Georges
Owner: M. G. Desbois. 123 acres; 2,500
cases.

PARSAC–ST-EMILION CHATEAUX

Château Parsac
27 acres.
Château Plaisance
Owner: Robert René Erésue. 26 acres;
5,00 cases.
Château du Puy
18.5 acres.

POMEROL

If there are doubters (and there are) about the differences that different soils make to wine, they should study Pomerol. In this little area, flanked by the huge spread of St-Emilion, like a market-garden to Libourne on the north bank of the Dordogne, there are wines as potent and majestic as any in France cheek by jowl with wines of wispy, fleeting fruitiness and charm – and dull ones, too.

The soil grades from shingly sand around the town of Libourne through increasingly heavy stages to a climactic plateau where the clay subsoil is very near the surface. A yard down, the clay is near-solid and packed with nuggets of iron. This, at the giddy height of 50 feet above its surroundings, is in every sense the summit of Pomerol.

Pomerol will always be an abstruse, recherché corner of the wine world. Its whole vineyard area is no larger than St-Julien, the smallest of the great communes of the Médoc. Perhaps half of this (as against two thirds of St-Julien) is of truly distinctive, classed-growth standard. The size of the properties is correspondingly small. There are 185 members of the growers' syndicate, sharing 1,850 acres: ten acres each on average. The biggest estate is 120 acres. Many growers have a mere acre or two – enough for 200 or 300 of the annual total of about 330,000 cases entitled to the appellation. There is no cooperative: small growers tend to make their wine and sell it direct to consumers all over France, and particularly to Belgium.

It is only 100 years since the name of Pomerol was first heard outside its immediate area, yet tradition has already provided it with a clear identity. Its best soil is clay; therefore cold. The early-ripening Merlot does better than the later Cabernet, and of the Cabernets the Franc (alias Bouchet) rather than the Sauvignon. The mellow, brambly Merlot and the lively, raspberryish Bouchet pick up the iron from the clay, are matured in fragrant oak – and *voilà*, you have a greatly over-simplified recipe for Pomerol. Where does it get its singular texture of velvet, its chewy flesh, its smell of ripe plums and even cream, and even honey? Wherever, it was more than an edict from the bureaucracy that fixes appellations.

Authorities put Pomerol between St-Emilion and the Médoc in style. To me it is closer to St-Emilion; broader, more savoury and with less 'nerve' than Médocs of similar value, maturing in five years as much as Médocs do in ten – hence tending to overlay them at tastings, as California wines do French. Great Pomerols, however, show no sign of being short lived.

No official classification of Pomerol has ever been made. Professor Roger published a personal one in 1960, in *The Wines of Bordeaux*, dividing 63 châteaux into four ranks, with Château Pétrus on its own, Yquem-like, at the head. I have taken the advice of the most influential voice in the district, the merchants and proprietors Etablissement Jean-Pierre Moueix of Libourne, in listing some 40 properties as the best in the district. Below these I list only others with more than the average (ten acres) of vineyard. Postcode: 33500 Libourne. Price (1988): 40 francs a bottle.

POMEROL FIRST-GROWTH

Château Pétrus
Owners: Mme Lacoste and Jean-Pierre Moueix.
AOC: Pomerol. Area: 27 acres; 3,700 cases. Grape var: Merlot 95%, Cab.Franc 5%.
See Pétrus, Pomerol's First-Growth, page 95.

POMEROL LEADING CHATEAUX

Château Beauregard
Pomerol. Owners: Héritiers Clauzel. 32 acres; 5,000 cases.
Grape var: Merlot 50%, Cab.Franc 50%.
In contrast to most of the modest 'châteaux' of Pomerol, the 17th-century Château Beauregard is so desirable that

Mrs Daniel Guggenheim had it copied stone for stone on Long Island. Relatively light gravel and lots of 'Bouchet' make this a delicate, round and 'charming' wine.

Château Le Bon-Pasteur

Pomerol. Owner: Michel Rolland. 17 acres. 3,500 cases.
Merlot 90%, Cab.Franc 10%.

The owner has emerged not only as a maker of his own richly sensuous Pomerol, but as a valuable consultant partly responsible for a new era of more luscious Pomerols.

The statue of St Peter at Pétrus; the saint appears on the label, too

Château Bourgneuf-Vayron

Pomerol. Owners: Charles and Xavier Vayron. 22 acres; 5,000 cases. Grape var: Merlot 80%, Cab.Franc 20%.

In the heart of Pomerol between Trotanoy and Latour. Potent, plummy wine; not the most stylish.

Château La Cabanne

Pomerol. Owner: Jean-Pierre Estager. 25 acres; 5,000 cases.
Grape var: Merlot 90%, Cab.Franc 10%.
Price (1990): 79 francs a bottle.

The name means 'the hut' or the 'shanty', which seems excessively modest for an estate situated in the heart of Pomerol with Trotanoy as a neighbour. The soil is middling between gravel and clay; the wine is not remarkable.

Château Certan de May

Pomerol. Owner: Mme Barreau-Badar.
12 acres; 2,000 cases. Grape var: Merlot 70%,
Cab.Franc 25%, Cab.Sauv. 5%.

Formerly called Ch. Certan. Perfectly sited next to Vieux Château Certan and Pétrus; but verging more towards Pétrus in richness and concentration. One of the top Pomerols today.

Château Certan-Giraud

Pomerol. Owners: Domaines Giraud. 17 acres; 3,750 cases.
Grape var: Merlot 65%, Cab.Franc 35%.

Includes the former Ch. Certan-Marzelle. Geographically close to the last, but much easier-going in style; soft and creamy. It is also sold under the label of Clos du Roy.

Château Clinet

Pomerol. Owner: Georges Audy. 17 acres; 3,000 cases. Grape var: Merlot 75%, Cab.Sauv. 15%, Cab.Franc 10%.

Formerly a lean, almost Médoc-style wine, but recently much fatter. The '88 is outstandingly rich.

Château du Clocher

Pomerol. Owner: Jean Audy. 14 acres; 1,500 cases.

Central vineyard next to the Certans making well-balanced, middle-weight wine with plenty of flavour.

Château La Conseillante

Pomerol. Owners: Héritiers Louis Nicolas.
31 acres; 5,000 cases.
Grape var: Merlot 45%, Cab Franc 45%, Malbec 10%.

The splendid silver-on-white label is designed around an 'N' for the family that has owned the château for more than a century. Coincidentally, London's Café Royal has the same motif for the same reason.

La Conseillante lies between Pétrus and Cheval Blanc, but makes a more delicate, as it were high-pitched wine. Sometimes as fine and fragrant as any Pomerol but less plummy and fat. Fermentation is now in stainless steel. Recent vintages are first class.

Château La Croix

Pomerol. Owners: Société Civile J. Janoueix. 35 acres; 6,100 cases. Grape var: Merlot 60%, Cab.Sauv. 20%, Cab.Franc 20%.
Price (1990): 100 francs a bottle.

Includes Ch. La Croix-St-Georges. Another 6 acres is La Croix-Toulifaut. These crosses are in the south of the commune on relatively light soil with a high iron content, not to be confused with Croix de Gay on the northern edge. Sturdy, generous wine not noted for great finesse but repaying bottle age.

Château La Croix de Gay

Pomerol. Owner: Noël Raynaud. 29 acres; 6,000 cases. Grape
var: Merlot 80%, Cab.Sauv. 10%, Cab.Franc 10%.

A well-run, second-rank vineyard on the gravelly clay
sloping north down to the river Barbanne. As in so many
Pomerol properties, its wines are being made with more
care for a more demanding market, and it shows.

Clos L'Eglise

Pomerol. Owners: Michel and François Moreau. 14.5 acres;
1,750 cases. Grape var: Merlot 55%, Cab.Franc 20%,
Cab.Sauv. 25%.

A superb little vineyard on the north rim of the plateau,
bought in the 1970s by the owners of the bigger but less
distinguished Ch. Plince on the outskirts of Libourne.
Old vintages were backward, long-lived wines. Cabernet
Sauvignon keeps the wine rather lean.

Château L'Eglise-Clinet

Pomerol. Owner: Mme G. Durantou. 11 acres; 1,700 cases.
Grape var: Merlot 60%, Cab.Franc 30%, Malbec 10%.

For long generally rated above Clinet; a stouter production with tannin and even brawn. Recently reaching far
higher: luscious deep wines of top class. Second label: La
Petite Eglise.

Château L'Enclos

Pomerol. Owner: Societé Civile du Chateau L'Enclos.
Administrator: Mme Marc and M. Weydert.
23 acres; 3,750 cases.
Grape var: Merlot 80%, Cab.Franc 19%, Malbec 1%.

With Clos René, one of the most respected châteaux of the
western half of Pomerol, with the sort of deeply fruity and
rewarding wine that impresses you young but needs at
least 7 or 8 years in bottle to do it justice.

Château L'Evangile

Pomerol. Owners: Dom. Barons de Rothschild and Héritiers
P. Ducasse. 33 acres; 4,500 cases. Grape var: Merlot 67%,
Cab.Franc 33%.

In the top 10 of Pomerol for both quality and size. At its
best (e.g. 1985) a voluptuous, concentrated wine for a
long life, but accused of being facile in lesser vintages. The
(Lafite) Rothschilds bought a majority share in 1990. Its
situation between Pétrus and Cheval Blanc is propitious,
to say the least.

Château Feytit-Clinet

Pomerol. Owners: The Domergue family. 16 acres; 3,000
cases. Grape var: Merlot 85%, Cab.Franc 15%.

I have had some wonderful old wines from this little
château, across the road from the illustrious Latour à
Pomerol. Under Moueix management since the mid-
1970s. Largely replanted in 1975 and 1976, so the new
vines are beginning to deliver the goods.

Château La Fleur Gazin

Pomerol. Owner: Maurice Borderie. 17 acres; 3,000 cases.
Grape var: Merlot 90%, Cab.Franc 10%.

Northern neighbour of Ch. Gazin, makes elegant,
smooth, well-bred wine. I found myself noting the 'noble
flavour' of the '79.

Château La Fleur-Pétrus

Pomerol. Owner: Jean-Pierre Moueix. 20 acres; 2,500 cases.
Grape var: Merlot 80%, Cab.Franc 20%.

The third best Moueix Pomerol – which is high praise.
The vineyard is more gravelly than Pétrus and Trotanoy,
the wine less fat and fleshy with more obvious tannin at
first, poised, taut, asking to be aged. The vintages of the
'80s show the consistent standards of the property.
Somehow the jaunty label with a waving flag fails to give
the right impression.

Château Le Gay (*see* Château Lafleur)

Pomerol. Owner: Mlle Marie Robin. 22 acres; 3,000 cases.
Grape var: Merlot 80%, Cab.Franc 20%.

Château Gazin

Pomerol. Owner: E. de Balliencourt dit Courcol. 45 acres;
10,000 cases. Grape var: Merlot 80%, Cab.Franc 15%,
Cab.Sauv. 5%.

One of the biggest properties, despite selling a section to
its neighbour, Ch. Pétrus, in 1970. The record is uneven;
at best a fittingly fruity, concentrated wine but usually a
shade full. 1989 seemed to mark a turning point in an
excellent long-term wine. Second label is Château
l'Hospitalet.

Château Gombaude-Guillot

Pomerol. Owners: The Laval family. 17 acres; 2,400 cases.

A well-regarded property (listed by Prof. Roger as a 'first-
growth') right in the centre near the church, but its wine
never appears on the open market.

Château la Grave (Trigant de Boisset)

Pomerol. Owner: Christian Moueix. 20 acres; 3,300 cases.
Grape var: Merlot 90%, Cab.Franc 10%.

Not the most full-bodied Pomerol, but particularly well
balanced and stylish with tannin to encourage long
development. The pretty château near the *route nationale* to
Lalande and Perigueux was restored in the 1970s by the
man who runs Ch. Pétrus. The soil here is *graves*, not clay –
hence finesse rather than flesh.

Château Lafleur

Pomerol. Owner: Mlle Marie Robin. 12 acres; 1,800 cases.
Grape var: Merlot 50%, Cab.Franc 50%.

The two adjacent properties of Mlle Robin are united in
the statistics, but distinct in quality. Lafleur (next to La
Fleur Pétrus) is a model of balance, body with finesse and
considerable style. Le Gay (40 acres, across the road to the
north) is a shade plainer and perhaps less potent. Both are
nursed by their elderly owner like children and must be
among the most consistently good Pomerols.

Château Lafleur du Roy

Pomerol. Owner: Yvon Dubost. 7 acres; 1,700 cases. Grape
var: Merlot 80%, Cab.Franc 10%, Cab.Sauv. 10%.
Price (1989): 65 francs a bottle.

Little property on the outskirts of Libourne, near Ch.
Plince. A minor wine with a good name.

Château Lagrange

Pomerol. Owner: Ets Jean-Pierre Moueix. 20 acres; 4,000
cases. Grape var: Merlot 90%, Cab.Franc 10%.

Another Moueix property in the Pétrus group on the
plateau. Less spectacularly flavoury than some of its
neighbours.

Château Latour à Pomerol

Pomerol. Owner: Mme Lacoste-Loubat. 19 acres; 2,400 cases.
Grape var: Merlot 80%, Cab.Franc 20%.

The property is run by the house of Moueix for one of the
family who own a share of Pétrus (and used to run the best
restaurant in Libourne). They regard it as their number

four Pomerol, with a fuller, fruitier style than La Fleur Pétrus: more fat, less sinew – words can be very misleading. Paradoxically, it is a *graves* wine, from westwards of the fat band of clay.

Château Moulinet

Pomerol. Owner: Société Civile. Dir: Armand Moueix. 45 acres; 7,500 cases. Grape var: Merlot 50%, Cab.Franc 40%, Cab.Sauv. 10%.

An isolated estate on the northern edge of Pomerol where both the soil and the wine are lighter; the wine is stylish notwithstanding. A very good '79.

Château Nenin

Pomerol. Owner: François Despujol. 66 acres; 10,000 cases. Grape var: Merlot 50%, Cab.Franc 30%, Cab.Sauv. 20%.

One of the biggest properties, lying between the great Trotanoy and La Pointe, but raising two cheers rather than three from most critics. On an upsurge, though, since '85.

Château Petit-Village

Pomerol. Owner: AXA Millésimes. 27 acres; 3,900 cases. Grape var: Merlot 80%, Cab.Sauv. 10%, Cab.Franc 10%.

Uppermost Pomerol from the Cheval-Blanc zone. Sold in 1989 by the owner of Cos d'Estournel to the insurance group that also bought Ch. Pichon-Baron. A long-respected property with plenty of money behind it.

Château Plince

Pomerol. Owner: The Moreau family. 20 acres; 3,500 cases. Merlot 75%, Cab.Franc 20%, Cab.Sauv. 5%.

The same owners as at Clos l'Eglise produce a more 'supple', fruity wine on sandier soil.

Château La Pointe

Pomerol. Owner: Bernard d'Arfeuille. 51 acres; 8,000 cases. Grape var: Merlot 80%, Cab.Franc 80%, Malbec 20%. Price (1989): 58 francs a bottle.

Sister château of La Serre, St-Emilion, and big enough to be widely known. The vineyard is on the doorstep of Libourne, in gravel and sand over the famous iron-bearing clay. Its full potential should be realized by the new consultant oenologist, Michel Rolland, starting in '85.

Clos René

Pomerol. Owner: Pierre Lasserre. 30 acres; 6,000 cases. Grape var: Merlot 60%, Cab.Franc 30%, Malbec 10%. Price (1989): 90 francs a bottle.

Unpretentious and on the unfashionable (western) side of the commune, yet unmistakably serious Pomerol. The style of wine has grown lusher in the '80s. Very fine wines.

Château Rouget

Pomerol. Owner: François-Jean Brochet. 32 acres; 5,000 cases. Grape var: Merlot 90%, Cab.Franc 10%.

I cast envious eyes on Ch. Rouget each time I pass; it has the prettiest situation in Pomerol in a grove of trees leading down to the river Barbanne. Ideas here are conservative: the wine tough by modern standards and needs 7–8 years. Although the recent installation of new stainless steel tanks and considerable modernisation may change this.

Château de Sales

Pomerol. Owners: GFA du Château de Sales – the Lambert family. Dir: Bruno de Lambert. 116 acres; 22,500 cases. Grape var: Merlot 70%, Cab.Franc 15%, Cab.Sauv. 15%.

The only noble château of Pomerol, remote down long avenues to the northwest, then rather disconcertingly having the railway line running right through the garden. The big vineyard is beautifully run and the wine increasingly well made, yet without the concentration and sheer personality of the great Pomerols. The second label is Château Chantalouette.

Château du Tailhas

Pomerol. Owners: Société Civile P. Nebout & Fils. 26 acres; 5,000 cases.

The southernmost Pomerol vineyard, a stone's throw from the edge of the sandy riverside area of St-Emilion. It still has Pomerol's iron-rich clay subsoil, hence its dense, if somewhat rustic, character – which is very popular in Belgium.

Château Taillefer

Pomerol. Owner: Armand Mouix. 45 acres. 7,000 cases. Grape var: Merlot 55%, Cab.Franc 30%, Cab.Sauv. 20%.

Owned by the Moueix family since 1923 and forms the centre of the Armand Moueix enterprise.

Château Trotanoy

Pomerol. Owner: Ets Jean-Pierre Moueix. 20 acres; 3,000 cases. Grape var: Merlot 85%, Cab.Franc 15%.

Generally allowed to be the runner-up to Ch. Pétrus, made by the same hands to the same Rolls-Royce standards. The little vineyard is on the western slope (such as it is) of the central plateau. The vines are old, the yield low, the darkly concentrated wine matured in new *barriques* (which lend it a near-Médoc smell in youth). For 10 years or more the best vintages have a thick, almost California-Cabernet texture in your mouth. Tannin and iron show through the velvet glove. The 1982, '79, '76 and '71 are considered the best recent vintages.

Vieux Château Certan

Pomerol. Owners: Héritiers Georges Thienpont. 33 acres; 5,000 cases. Grape var: Merlot 50%, Cab.Franc 25%, , Cab.Sauv. 20%, Malbec 5%. Price (1989): 150 francs a bottle.

The first great name of Pomerol, though overtaken at a canter by Pétrus in the last 30 or 40 years. The style is quite different; drier and less fleshy but balanced in a Médoc or Graves manner. At early tastings substance can seem to be lacking, to emerge triumphantly later. The 1945 was unforgettable in 1980. The handsome old château lies halfway between Pétrus and Cheval Blanc. Its Belgian owners take intense pride in its unique personality. '82, '85 and '86 are recent triumphs.

Château Vray-Croix-de-Gay

Pomerol. Owner: La Baronne Guichard. 9 acres; 1,100 cases. Grape var: Merlot 80%, Cab.Franc 15%, Cab.Sauv. 5%.

The name means 'the real Croix-de-Gay', implying that the neighbours pinched the name. Jockeying for position seems appropriate here on the northern rim of the precious plateau. Good Pomerol, but I have no record of very notable bottles.

Château La Violette

Pomerol. Owner: Vignobles S. Dumas. 8 acres; 2,000 cases.

A little neighbour of the big Ch. Nenin, as modest as its name, and not known for consistency.

CHÂTEAU PÉTRUS
Pomerol's First-Growth

As Château Yquem is to Sauternes, so Château Pétrus is to Pomerol; the perfect model of the region and its aspirations. Like its region, Pétrus is a miniature; there are 4,000 cases in a good year, and often less. Among first-growths it is unique in that it has never been officially classified, and that its emergence as a wine worth as much or more than any other red Bordeaux only started in 1945. The Loubat family were the promoters of its quality and status. Since 1961 it has been owned jointly by Madame Loubat's niece, Madame Lacoste, and Jean-Pierre Moueix.

The house of Moueix, directed by Jean-Pierre with his son Christian and his nephew Jean-Jacques, holds centre stage in Pomerol. Its modest offices and vast *chais* on the Libourne waterfront have a position of prestige without an exact equivalent anywhere in France. The resident oenologist, Jean-Claude Berrouet, has technical control of a score of the best properties both in St-Emilion and Pomerol.

Pétrus is the flagship. Outwardly it is a modest little place. The *cuvier* is a cramped space between batteries of narrow concrete vats. The *chais*, recently rebuilt, are more spacious, but by no means grand.

The magic lies in the soil. No golf course or wicket is more meticulously tended. When one section of ancient vines (the average age is 40 years) was being replaced I was astonished to see the shallow topsoil bulldozed aside from the whole two-acre patch and the subsoil being carefully graded to an almost imperceptible slope to give a shade more drainage. It was a remarkable opportunity to see how uninviting this famous clay is.

The principle of wine-making at Pétrus is perfect ripeness, then ruthless selection. If the October sun is kind, the Merlot is left to cook in it. It is never picked before lunch, to avoid diluting the juice with dew. The crop is small, the new wine so dark and concentrated that fresh-sawn oak, for all its powerful smell, seems to make no impression on it. At a year old the wine smells of blackcurrant. At two a note of tobacco edges in. But any such exact reference is a misleading simplification. Why Pétrus (or any great wine) commands attention is by its almost architectural sense of structure; of counterpoised

weights and matched stresses. How can there be such tannin and yet such tenderness?

Because Pétrus is fat, fleshy, not rigorous and penetrating like a Médoc but dense in texture like a Napa Cabernet, it appears to be 'ready' in ten years or less. Cigar smokers probably should (and anyway do) drink it while it is in full vigour. To my mind it takes longer to become claret. In a sense the great vintages never do.

OTHER CHATEAUX

Château Bel-Air
Owners: Sudrat & Fils. 32 acres; 6,000 cases.
Château Bellevue
Owner: R. Brieux. 12 acres; 1,300 cases.
Château de Bourgueneuf
Owners: M. Meyer. 11 acres; 2,000 cases.
Château Le Caillou
Owner: L. Giraud. 17 acres; 1,700 cases.
Château Cloquet
Owner: M. Vigier. 15 acres; 1,300 cases.
Château La Commanderie
Owners: F. & Mlle M. H. Dé. 14 acres; 2,500 cases.

Château La Croix du Casse
Owners: Soc. du Ch. La Croix du Casse. 22 acres; 4,000 cases.
Domaine de l'Eglise
Owner: P. Castéja. 17 acres; 3,500 cases.
Château Ferrand
Owners: Soc. Civ. du Ch. Ferrand. 36 acres; 4,850 cases.
Château Franc-Mallet
Owner: G. Arpin. 12 acres; 1,500 cases.
Château Grand-Moulinet
Owner: J.-M. Garde, 39 acres; 6,900 cases.
Château de Grange-Neuve
Owner: Yves Gros. 15 acres; 2,500 cases.

Château Grate-Cap
Owner: A. Janoueix. 23 acres; 4,500 cases.
Château Haut-Maillet
Owner: P. Delteil. 12 acres; 2,500 cases.
Château Maison Blanche
Owner: Gérard Despagne. 10 acres; 1,500 cases.
Château Mazeyres
Owner: S. A. Querre. 21 acres; 5,000 cases.
Clos Mazeyres
Owners: Laymarie & Fils. 23 acres; 3,500 cases.
Château La Patâche
Owner: Mme Forton. 13 acres; 2,250 cases.

LALANDE-DE-POMEROL

The northern boundary of Pomerol is the little river Barbanne. The two communes on its other bank, Lalande and Néac, share the right to the name Lalande-de-Pomerol for red wine which at its best is certainly of junior Pomerol class. Traditionally, they have grown more of the Malbec (or Pressac), a difficult grape which is now going out of fashion. But the gravel-over-clay in parts is good and two châteaux, Bel-Air and Tournefeuille, have high reputations. Altogether there are 2,500 acres of vines; 750 more than Pomerol. Some 272 growers (without a cooperative) make an average total of 350,000 cases. The price is generally a shade higher than for a plain St-Emilion, though a third less than for Pomerol. Postcode: 33500 Libourne.

LALANDE-DE-POMEROL CHATEAUX

Château des Annereaux
Lalande-de-Pomerol. Owners: MM. Hessel-Milhade. 54 acres; 10,000 cases.

Château de Bel-Air
Lalande-de-Pomerol. Owner: Jean-Pierre Musset. 25 acres; 4,500 cases.

Château La Commanderie
Lalande-de-Pomerol. Owner: H. R. Lafon. 48 acres; 8,000 cases.

Château La Croix St André
Néac. Owner: M. Carayon. 37 acres; 5,000 cases.

Château La Gravière
Lalande-de-Pomerol. Owner: Mme Cascarret. 3,000 cases.

Château Haut-Chaigneau
Lalande-de-Pomerol. Owner: M. & Mme. André Chatonnet. 49 acres; 10,000 cases.

Château Les Hauts-Conseillants
Lalande-de-Pomerol. Owner: Pierre Bourotte. 22 acres; 4,000 cases.

Château Laborde
Lalande-de-Pomerol. Owner: J-M.

Trocard. 44 acres; 6,500 cases.

Château des Moines
Owner: M. W. Darnazou. 28 acres; 2,000 cases.

Château Moncet
Néac. Owners: Baron L-G. and E. de Jerphanion. 46 acres; 8,000 cases.

Château Moulin-à-Vent
Néac. Owners: Société Civile. 14 acres; 2,250 cases.

Château Perron
Lalande-de-Pomerol. Owner: Michel Massonié. 37 acres; 6,500 cases.

Château Sergant
Lalande-de-Pomerol. Owner: Jean Milhade. 6,000 cases.

Château Siaurac
Néac. Owner: Olivier Guichard. 69 acres; 12,500 cases.

Château Teysson
Lalande-de-Pomerol. Owner: Mme Servant-Dumas. 32 acres; 6,000 cases.

Château Tournefeuille
Néac. Owners: The Sautarel family. 43 acres; 8,000 cases.

BORDEAUX'S MINOR REGIONS

The vast extent of the Gironde vineyards begins to sink in when you look at the number and size of growers' cooperative cellars dotted over the *département*. Most of the areas covered by this section are cooperative-dominated. Most communes have one or two well-established châteaux – old manor houses, whose wine has long been made in the manner of a not-very-ambitious family business.

In many cases the small grower has sold his vineyard to the bigger grower as an alternative to joining the cooperative. A number of well-run larger châteaux are thereby adding to their acreage, revising their methods and starting to specialize in either red or white instead of dabbling in both. In some cases they have switched from third-rate sweet wines to second-rate (occasionally even first-rate) dry ones. There is no question that a new understanding of wine-making techniques, coupled with a far more enterprising, diligent and demanding generation of wine-buyers and -drinkers, is transforming the outlying regions of Bordeaux, as it is the whole of south-west France and even the Midi.

They cover a wide spectrum of styles and qualities, which are discussed in the head-note to each area. In each area I list the châteaux, their proprietors and production, which I have tasted or which have been recommended to me by local brokers and friends.

FRONSAC AND CANON-FRONSAC

The town of Libourne lies on the Dordogne at the mouth of its little northern tributary, the Isle. In its enviable situation it has Pomerol as its back garden, St-Emilion as its eastern neighbour, and only one mile to the west another, surprisingly different, little wine area.

Fronsac is a village on the Dordogne at the foot of a jumble of steep bumps and hollows, a miniature range of hills (up to 300 feet) where vines and woods make pictures as pretty as any in Bordeaux. Several of the châteaux were obviously built as country villas rather than as plain farms. Under it all there is limestone. The vines are nearly all red, the usual Bordeaux varieties, traditionally with more stress on the soft and juicy Malbec than elsewhere. Having plenty of colour and alcohol, Fronsac wine has been much used in the past as *vin de médecin* for weaklings from more famous places.

Historically Fronsac took precedence over Pomerol. In the 18th century its wines were even drunk at court. But circumstances gave Pomerol the advantage it has so profitably exploited, and it is only in the past 20 years that Fronsac has begun to climb back – and in the past 10 years that real investment has changed its image. Now the Libourne house of J. P. Moueix owns three châteaux and offers excellent generic Fronsac, while the important and well-publicized estate of Ch. La Rivière offers large quantities of good wine.

There are 2,700 acres of vineyards divided into two appellations. Two thirds of the hills (the lower parts) are Fronsac; the top third, where the soil is thinner with more lime, is Canon-Fronsac. Its wines can be delectable, full of vigour and spice, hard enough to resemble Graves or St-Emilion more than Pomerol, and worth a good five years' ageing. Postcode 33126 Fronsac. Price (1988): Fronsac, 15 francs a bottle; Canon-Fronsac, 20 francs a bottle.

CANON-FRONSAC CHATEAUX

Château Bodet
Fronsac. Owner: M. Leymarie, 37 acres; 5,000 cases.
Château Canon
St-Michel-de-Fronsac. Owner: Christian Moueix. 3 acres; 700 cases.
Château Canon-de-Brem
Canon-Fronsac. Owners: Ets J.-P. Moueix. 10 acres; 2,000 cases.
Château Coustolle
Fronsac. Owner: Alain Roux. 49 acres; 10,000 cases.
Château Dalem
Saillans, Fronsac. Owner: Michel Rullier. 36 acres; 7,500 cases.
Château du Gaby
Fronsac. Owner: M. de Kermoal. 24 acres; 4,250 cases.
Château du Gazin
St-Michel-de-Fronsac. Owner: Henri Robert. 74 acres; 17,000 cases.
Château Junayme
Fronsac. Owners: Héritiers de Coninck. 38 acres; 7,000 cases.
Château Mausse
St-Michel-de-Fronsac. Owner: Guy Janoueix. 25 acres; 4,500 cases.
Château Mazeris
St-Michel-de-Fronsac. Owner: M. de Cournuaud. 46 acres; 6,000 cases.
Château Mazeris-Bellevue
St-Michel-de-Fronsac. Owner: Jacques Bussier. 27 acres; 5,000 cases.
Château Moueix (formerly Ch. Pichelèbre) Canon-Fronsac. Owner: Ets J. P. Moueix. 10 acres; 2,000 cases.
Château Moulin-Pey-Labrie
Fronsac. Owner: Yvette Seurt. 19 acres; 3,500 cases.
Château du Pavillon and Château Grand-Renouil
Fronsac and St-Michel-de-France. Owners: Michel Ponty & Fils. 23 acres; 3,500 cases.
Château Toumalin
Fronsac. Owner: M. d'Arfeuille. 19 acres; 4,000 cases.
Château Vincent
St-Aignan. Owner: Bernard Oulié. 25 acres; 3,500 cases.
Château Vray-Canon-Boyer
St-Michel-de-Fronsac. Owners: R. de Coninck (Horeau-Beylaut). 20 acres; 2,200 cases.
Château Vrai Canon Bouché
St-Michel-de-Fronsac. Owner: Françoise Roux. 31 acres; 6,000 cases.

FRONSAC CHATEAUX

Château de Carles
Saillans, Fronsac. Owner: Antoine Chastenet de Castaing. 49 acres; 10,000 cases.

Château de La Dauphine
Fronsac. Owner: Ets J.-P. Moueix. 25 acres; 5,000 cases.
Château de Fronsac
Fronsac. Owners: The Seurin family. 20 acres; 5,000 cases.
Château Lagüe
Fronsac. Owner: Françoise Roux. 18 acres; 4,000 cases.
Château Mayne-Vieil
Galgon, Fronsac. Owners: The Sèze family. 59 acres; 13,000 cases.
Château Puyguilhem
Saillans, Fronsac. Owner: Mlle Mothes. 25 acres; 5,000 cases.
Château Richelieu
Fronsac. Owners: M. Viaud Père & Fils. 50 acres; 6,000 cases.
Château La Rivière
La Rivière, Fronsac. Owner: Jacques Borie. 107 acres; 20,000 cases.
Château Villars
Saillans, Fronsac. Owner: J. C. Gaudrie. 61 acres; 11,500 cases.

COTES DE CASTILLON AND COTES DE FRANCS

Two areas adjoining the St-Emilion satellites to the east, still within the general appellation area of Bordeaux, were granted their own independent AOCs in 1989. The larger is the Côtes de Castillon in the hills to the north of the Dordogne valley overlooking Castillon-la-Bataille, where the French defeated the English forces in 1452 and ended English rule in Aquitaine. 10 communes are affected, with a total of some 5,680 acres of vines.

To its north, the Côtes de Francs is about one quarter of its size, taking in parts of the communes of Francs, Les Salles, St-Cibard and Tayac; tranquil and remote country long known as a good producer of Bordeaux Supérieur, but only now recognized on its distinctive merits.

Côtes de Castillon and Côtes de Francs wines in general are like lightweight St-Emilions. But several Chx show real ambition and are making wine to mature 5 years or more.

COTES DE CASTILLON CHATEAUX

Château Blanzac
St-Magne-de-Castillon. Owners: Michel Depons & Fils. 39 acres; 6,500 cases.
Château Cafol
St-Magne-de-Castillon. Owner: M. G. Castéra. 50 acres; 8,500 cases.
Château Chinchon-La-Bataille
Castillon-La-Bataille. Owners: The Larmazelle family. 42 acres; 8,000 cases.

Château de Clotte
St-Philippe-d'Aiguille. Owner: Mme Guerret-Deniés. 41 acres; 8,000 cases.
Château des Demoiselles
St-Magne-de-Castillon. Owner: Rémy Daut. 138 acres; 40,000 cases.
Château Faugères
Ste-Colombe. Owner: Esquissaud de Faugères. 62 acres; 10,000 cases.
Château La Fourquerie
Gardegan. Owners: Vignobles Rollet. 20 acres; 4,000 cases.
Château Gerbay
Gardegan. Owner: Alix Yerlès. 32 acres; 6,000 cases.
Château Lartigue
Belvès-de-Castillon. Owner: Veuve Larroque. 25 acres; 3,500 cases.
Clos Maison Rouge
St-Magne-de-Castillon. Owner: M. Goumaud. 37 acres; 6,500 cases.
Château Mansy
St-Magne-de-Castillon. Owner: M. de Lestang. 25 acres; 4,500 cases.
Château de Monbadon
Monbadon. Owner: Le Baron José de Montfort. 124 acres; 6,000 acres.
Château Moulin Rouge
St-Magne-de-Castillon. Owner: M. Bassilieaux. 57 acres; 14,000 cases.
Château Paret
St-Genès-de-Castillon. Owner: Jean Fauché. 34 acres; 5,000 cases.
Château la Pierrère
Tourtirac. Owner: Robert de Marcillac. 37 acres; 6,500 cases.
Château de Pitray
Gardegan. Owner: Vicomte de Pitray. 64 acres; 12,000 cases.

COTES DE FRANCS CHATEAUX

Château Puyfromage
St-Cibard. Owner: SCE Puyfromage. 99 acres; 20,000 cases.
Château Puygeraud
St-Cibard. Owner: M. François Thienpoint. 37 acres; 8,000 cases.

COTES DE BOURG

The right bank of the Gironde was a thriving vineyard long before the Médoc across the water was planted. Bourg, lying to the north of the Dordogne where it joins the Garonne (the two form the Gironde), is like another and bigger Fronsac: hills rising steeply from the water to 200 feet or more, but unlike the hills of Fronsac almost solidly vine covered. The Côtes de Bourg makes as much wine as the lower Médoc – and so does its immediate neighbour to the north, the

Côtes de Blaye. Bourg specializes in red wine of a very respectable standard, made largely of Merlot and Cabernet Franc, round and full-bodied and ready to drink at 4 or 5 years – but certainly not in a hurry. The châteaux that line the river bank have to all appearances a perfect situation. Farther back from the water is largely cooperative country with an increasing proportion of white wine of no special note. Postcode: 33710 Bourg sur Gironde.

Price (1988) 10 francs a bottle.

COTES DE BOURG CHATEAUX

Château de Barbe
Villeneuve. Owner: M. Savary de Beauregard. 137 acres; 32,000 cases.

Château La Barde
Tauriac. Owner: Alain Darricarrère. 38 acres; 6,600 cases.

Château du Bousquet
Bourg. Owners: Castel Frères. 148 acres; 44,000 cases.

Château Brûlesécaille
Tauriac. Owners: Jacques and Martine Rodet. 40 acres; 6,000 cases.

Château de Civrac
Lansac. Owner: M. and Mme A. Jaubert. 54 acres; 10,000 cases.

Château La Croix de Millorit
Bayon. Owner: M. Jaubert. 51 acres; 10,000 cases.

Château Falfas and Château La Joncarde
Bayon. Owner: Mme M. Jaubert. 44.5 acres; 8,750 cases. 38 acres; 8,000 cases.

Château Grand-Jour
Prignac-et-Marcamps. Owner: Mme Gaignerot. 62 acres; 12,500 cases red, 1,500 white.

Château de La Grave
Bourg. Owner: Robert Bassereau. 99 acres; 14,000 cases red.

Château Gros Moulin
Bourg. Owner: M. Eymas. 67 acres; 2,500 cases.

Château Guionne
Lansac. Owner: Richard Porcher. 28 acres; 6,250 cases.

Château Haut Macõ
Tauriac. Owners: Bernard and Jean Mallet. 104 acres; 15,000 cases.

Château Les Heaumes
St-Ciers-de-Canesse. Owner: Max Robin. 37 acres; 8,500 cases.

Château Lalibarde
Bourg. Owner: Roland Dumas. 84 acres; 20,000 cases red, 2,000 white.

Château Lamothe
Lansac. Owner: Pierre Pessonier. 50 acres; 7,500 cases.

Château Laurensanne
St-Seurin-de-Bourg. Owner: Jean-François Levraud. 50 acres; 10,000 cases

red, 2,000 white.

Château Mendoce
Villeneuve. Owner: Philippe Darricarrère. 36 acres; 7,700 cases.

Château Mille-Secousses
Bourg. Owner: Société Civile de Mille-Secousses. 150 acres; 33,000 cases (red and white).

Château Peychaud
Teuillac. Owners: Jacques and Bernard Germain. 83 acres; 16,600 cases.

Château Rousset
Samonac. Owners: M. et Mme Teisseire. 57 acres; 8,000 cases.

Château Tayac
Bayon. Owner: Pierre Saturny. 56 acres; 7,000 cases.

Château de Thau
Gauriac. Owner: Léopold Schweitzer. 111 acres; 15,000 cases.

PREMIERES COTES DE BLAYE

Two miles of water, the widening Gironde, separates Blaye from the heart of the Médoc. Blaye is the northernmost vineyard of the 'right bank'; the last place, going up this coast, where good red wine is made. North of this is white-wine country; the fringes of Cognac. Blaye already makes about one third white wine, a rather nondescript, full-bodied, sometimes semi-sweet style which no doubt could be improved.

Premières Côtes de Blaye is the appellation reserved for the better vineyards, nearly all red, whose wine is to all intents like that of Bourg – although generally considered not quite as good or full-bodied. Cooperatives handle about two thirds of production. Nonetheless the following châteaux are worth noting. Postcode: 33390 Blaye. Price (1988): 10 francs a bottle.

PREMIERES COTES DE BLAYE CHATEAUX

Château Barbé
Cars. Owner: Xavier Carreau. 52 acres; 11,000 cases.

Château de Beaumont
Plassac. Owner: Léopold Schweitzer. 22 acres; 4,000 cases.

Château Belair
St-Paul-de-Blaye. Owner: Pierre Mourlot. 37 acres; 4,000 cases red, 4,000 white.

Château Bellevue
Plassac. Owner: M. de la Garcie. 44 acres; 8,000 cases.

Château Bourdieu
Berson. Owner: Jean-Kléber Michaud. 82 acres; 20,000 cases (red and white).

Château Les Carrelles
St-Paul-de-Blaye. Owner: Xavier

Carreau. 66 acres; 12,000 cases.

Château Charron
St-Martin-Lacaussade. Owners: M. Doudet-Beaudry. 62 acres; 13,000 cases (red and white).

Château Les Chaumes
Fours. Owner: Robert Parmentier. 49 acres; 10,000 cases red.

Château L'Escadre
Cars. Owners: Georges Carreau & Fils. 79 acres; 17,000 cases (red and white).

Domaine de Florimond-La-Brède
Berson. Owners: Monique Martin-Marinier and Marie-Hélène Mesnard-Marinier. 124 acres; 21,000 cases (red and white).

Château Gontier
Blaye. Owner: M. F. Levraud. 74 acres; 12,500 cases.

Château Grolet
Plassac. Owner: J. B. Mallambic. 84 acres; 20,000 cases (red and white).

Château de Jussas
St-Christoly-de-Blaye. Owners: R. and B. Bourdillas. 74 acres; 1,000 cases red, 15,000 white.

Château Le Menaudat
St-Androny. Owner: Mme. Edouard Cruse. 37 acres; 7,000 cases.

Château Monconseil Gazin
Plassac. Owner: Michel Baudet. 40 acres; 9,000 cases.

Château Pardaillan
Cars. Owner: Chantal Jourdan. 32 acres; 7,000 cases.

Château Perenne
St-Genés-de-Blaye. Owner: M. & P. Oudinot. 117 acres; 20,000 cases. A good wine.

Château Peyredoulle
Berson. Owners: Jacques and Bernard Germain. 38 acres; 7,700 cases.

Château La Rivalerie
St-Paul-de-Blaye. Owner: M. Gillibert. (Reg. Mme. Bernabé .) 82 acres; 17,000 cases red, 850 white.

Château Segonzac
St-Genés. Owner: Mme Micheline Dupuy. 79 acres; 13,000 cases.

Château Les Tuileries
Berson. Owner: Christian Alins. 62 acres; 10,000 cases red.

Château Valrone
On the island of Patiras, Bordeaux Supérieur. Owners: MM. Bertolus and Poullet. 74 acres; 12,000 cases red, 8,000 white.

Château Virou
St-Girons. Owner: Mme François Monier. 10,000 cases red, 10,000 white.

PREMIERES COTES DE BORDEAUX

A long, narrow strip of the east bank of the Garonne facing Graves enjoys the doubtful prestige of this appellation. Its hinterland is Entre-Deux-Mers. The wooded and often very beautiful riverside bluffs have no such clear identity. At their northern end they were some of Bordeaux's original Roman and medieval vineyards – now buried under houses. At their southern end, at Cadillac and into Sainte-Croix-du-Mont, they are known for sweet wines, at their best up to Sauternes standards.

Along the way the mix is about two thirds red and one third white, the white recently made much drier and fresher than formerly. (Château Reynon is perhaps the best example.) Red Premières Côtes is potentially much better than plain Bordeaux Supérieur from less well-placed vineyards, but only fetches the same price or a few sous more. Lack of incentive is a real problem. Nonetheless there are those who do, and some very grand and prosperous names appear among the owners who are improving this area.

A notable example of a pioneer in the region is Peter Sichel, who has a New World-style winery at Verdelais where he vinifies the grapes he buys in the district to make very fruity and attractive claret for drinking young. Oddly, the practice of buying grapes, common elsewhere, is almost unknown in Bordeaux except in the cooperative, profit-sharing system.

Price (1988): 11 francs a bottle.

LEADING CHATEAUX OF THE PREMIERES COTES

Château Arnaud-Jouan
Cadillac. Owner: Albert Darriet. 3,000 cases red, 18,000 white.

Château Beau-Rivage
Baurech. Owner: M. Languens. 84 acres; 15,000 cases red, 1,000 white.

Château Beau-Site
Monprimblanc. Owner: M. Desmerie. 49 acres; 18,000 cases red, 6,000 white.

Château du Biac
Langoiran. Owners: Ets. Cordier. 25 acres; 1,000 cases red, 5,000 white.

Château Birot
Béguey. Owner: Jacques Boireau. 84 acres; 5,000 cases red, 15,000 white.

Château de Bouteilley
Yvrac. Owner: Jean Guillot. 50 acres; 10,000 cases red.

Château Brethous
Camblanes. Owner: François Verdier. 32 acres; 7,000 cases red.

Château de Caillavet
Capian. Owners: Soc. Civ. 16,000 cases red, 3,000 white.

Château de l'Espinglet
Rions. Owner: M. Raynaud. 74 acres; 4,000 cases red, 8,000 white.

Château Fayau

Cadillac. Owner: Jean Médeville, 10 acres; 8,500 cases.

Château du Grand Moueys
Capian. Owners: MM. N. Lacour and A. Icard. 102 acres; 9,200 cases red, 3,800 white.

Château du Grava
Haux. Owner: Jean-Luc-Duale. 247 acres; 40,000 cases red.

Château Gravelines
Semens. Owner: M. Dubourg. 74 acres; 6,000 cases red, 8,000 white.

Château Grimond
Quinsac-Camblane. Owner: Pierre Young. 197.5 acres; 33,000 cases red.

Château Haut-Brignon
Cenac. Owner: René Fourès. 148 acres; 25,000 cases red.

Château Jourdan
Rions. Owner: A. Guillot de Suduiraut. 111 acres; 4,000 cases red, 8,000 white.

Château du Juge
Cadillac. Owner: P. Dupleich. 74 acres; 8,500 cases red, 13,000 white.

Château du Juge
Haux. Owner: Jean Médeville. 58 acres; 9,000 cases red, 5,500 white.

Château Justa
Cadillac. Owner: Michel Mas. 47 acres; 8,000 cases red, 5,000 white.

Château Lafaurie
Semens. Owner: A. Croizet-Sauvestre. 62 acres; 5,000 cases red, 5,000 white.

Château Lafitte
Camblanes. Owner: SCE. 11,500 cases red.

Château Le Gardéra (red) and Château Tanesse (red + white)
Langoiran. Owners: Ets. Cordier. 185 acres; 23,500 cases red, 12,000 white.

Château Lamothe
Haux. Owner: Fabrice Néel. 123 acres; 21,000 cases red, 8,500 white.

Château Léon and Domaine de Camélon
Carignan. Owner: M. F. Mähler-Besse. 3,000 cases red, 2,000 white.

Château Maillard
Yvrac. Owner: Francis Germe. 50 acres; 4,000 cases red, 4,000 white.

Château Malagar
St-Maixant. Owner: M. Dubourg. 31 acres; 2,000 cases red, 4,500 white.

Château Mony
Rions. Owner: Marquis de Barbentane. 62 acres; 3,000 cases red, 10,000 white.

Château de Palette
Béquey. Owners: Yung brothers. 19 acres; 4,000 cases.

Château Péconnet
Quinsac. Owner: M. Amiel. 49 acres; 9,000 cases red.

Château Peyrat
Beguey. Owner: Mme David. 99 acres; 5,000 cases red, 20,000 white.

Château du Peyrat
Capian. Owner: Société Civile. 158 acres; 6,000 cases red, 15,000 white.

Château Poncet
Omet. Owner: Jean-Luc David, 91 acres; 4,500 cases red, 12,000 white.

Château de Ramondon
Capian. Owners: M. Georges Van Pé 62 acres; 10,000 cases (red, white and rosé).

Château Reynon
Béguey. Owners: Denis and Pierre Dubourdieu-David. 'Vieilles Vignes de Sauvignon'. 98 acres; 12,500 cases.

Château La Roche
Baurech. Owner: Julien Palau. 50 acres; 4,000 cases red, 4,000 white.

Château Suau
Capian. Owner: Monique Aldebert. 143 acres (not yet fully in production); 29,000 cases.

Château du Tasta
Camblanes. 5,000 cases red, 500 white.

Château Videau
Cardan. 74 acres; 5,000 cases red, 10,000 cases white.

ENTRE-DEUX-MERS

The two 'seas' in question are the rivers Dordogne and Garonne, whose converging courses more or less define the limits of this big wedge-shaped region; the most diffuse and territorially the most important (with 7,400 acres under vines in 125 communes) in Bordeaux. The appellation is now for dry white wine only. The red made here is Bordeaux or Bordeaux Supérieur (or just *vin de consommation courante*).

The south of the region is relaxed patchwork countryside with as much woodland and pasture as vineyard. The north is almost a monoculture of the vine. Its biggest cooperative, at Rauzan, makes over one million cases a year.

Entre-Deux-Mers is the one wine Bordeaux has succeeded in redesigning in modern marketing terms. The region was bogged down with cheap sweet wine nobody wanted any more. Some bright spark thought of the catch-phrase '*Entre deux huitres, Entre-Deux-Mers*' ('Between two oysters,' etc . . .) and a rosy future opened up for dry white: the Muscadet of the southwest.

I have yet to taste an Entre-Deux-Mers of the sort of quality that would win medals in California – but the world needs its staples too. It varies from the briskly appetizing to the thoroughly boring, but in ways that are hard to predict. A good cooperative is just as likely to produce a clean and bracing example as a property with a long name. La Gamage, a blend of the best wines from the union of cooperatives, sets a standard that others emulate.

Within the appellation an area limited to the southern communes with theoretically superior wine can use the

appellation 'Haut-Benauge' in addition to 'Entre-Deux-Mers' or 'Bordeaux'.
Price (1988): 9.50 francs a bottle.

ENTRE-DEUX-MERS CHATEAUX

Château Bonnet
Grézillac. Owner: André Lurton. 620 acres; 138,000 cases, red and white.
Château de Camarsac
Camarsac. Owner: Lucien Lurton. 148 acres; 20,000 cases.
Château Canet
Guillac. Owner: Jacques Large. 102 acres; 12,000 cases red, 15,000 white.
Château de Courteillac
Ruch. Owner: Baron du Foussat. 74 acres; 6,000 cases red, 8,000 white.
Château de Cugat
Blasimon. Owner: B. Meyer. 61 acres; 11,500 cases red, 4,500 white.
Château Fonchereau
Montussan. Owner: Mme Georges Vinot-Postry. 69 acres; 11,000 cases red.
Château La France
Beychac-et-Caillau. Owner: André Bleynie. 148 acres; 35,000 cases red, 7,000 white.
Château Le Gay
St-Sulpice-Cameyrac. Owner: Romain Maison. 44 acres; 12,000 cases red, 4,000 white.
Château de Goélane
St-Léon. Owner: Angel Castel. 123 acres; 20,000 cases red, 5,000 white.
Château du Grand-Puch
St-Germain-du-Puch. Owner: André Weber. 195 acres; 42,000 cases (red and white).
Château Guibon
Daignac. Owner: André Lurton. 99 acres; 11,000 cases white.
Château Launay
Soussac. Owner: M. Greffier. 259 acres; 17,000 cases red, 40,500 cases white.
Château Martinon
Gornac. Owner: M. Trolliet. 99 acres; 10,000 cases red, 13,000 white.
Château de Martouret
Nérigean. Owner: Dominique Lurton. 49 acres; 12,000 cases red, 5,500 white.
Château Peyrebon
Grézillac. 37 acres; 5,500 cases.
Château Puymiran
Montussan. Owner: The Degueil family. 111 acres; 23,000 cases red, 13,000 white.
Château de Quinsac
Quinsac. Owners: Soc. Civ. du Château. 5,000 cases red.
Château Raymond & Ch. Ramonet
Owner: Baron R. de Montesquieu. (Excl. Dourthe.) 20,000 cases red, 5,000 white.
Château Reynier
Grézillac. Owner: Dominique Lurton. 149 acres; 36,000 cases, red and white.

Château La Sablière & Dom. de Fongrave
Gornac. Owner: Pierre Perromat. 111 acres; 10,000 cases red, 15,000 white.
Château Senailhac
Tresses. Owners: The Margnat family. 133 acres; 33,000 cases red.
Château Thieuley
Owner: Francis Courselle. 10 acres; 3,000 cases.
Château La Tour-Puymiraud
Montussan. Owner: Emile Fazilleau. 148 acres; 10,000 cases red, 7,500 white.
Château de Toutigeac
Targon. Owner: René Mazeau. 370 acres; 45,000 cases red, 25,000 white.
Château de Tustal
Sadirac. Owner: Mme. d'Armaillé. 104 acres; 3,500 cases red, 850 white.

STE-CROIX-DU-MONT AND LOUPIAC

The southern end of the Premières Côtes de Bordeaux faces Barsac and Sauternes across the Garonne. From Cadillac southwards the speciality is sweet white wine, growing more 'liquorous' the nearer it gets to Sauternes. Ste-Croix-du-Mont gazes across at the hills of Sauternes from its higher river bank and often shares the same autumnal conditions that lead to noble rot and sticky wines. Without quite the same perfection of soil or pride of tradition it cannot afford the enormous investment in labour needed to make the greatest wines, but it succeeds remarkably often in producing wine at least as good as run-of-the-mill Sauternes, and often better.
To my surprise, I have been given Ste-Croix-du-Mont in the German Palatinate by a grower famous for his Beerenausleses, who told me he thought it compared well with his wines. (I must admit the Riesling said more to me.)

The only differences in the regulations between Sauternes and these right-bank wines is the quantity allowed. The same grapes and alcohol content are required but the grower is allowed 40 hectolitres per hectare as against only 25 for Sauternes. This is not to say that perfectionist growers make their full quota. They also make dry wines of potentially fine quality and a little light red. There are 1,050 acres of vineyards with some 140 proprietors and a *cave coopérative*, producing an average total of some 450,000 cases, which is rather more than Barsac. It sells for a mere half of the Sauternes price.

Loupiac is not quite so well placed and makes slightly less liquorous wines on 820 acres. Half the proprietors take their grapes to the cooperative.

Postcode: 33410 Cadillac.
Price (1988): 16 francs a bottle.

STE-CROIX-DU-MONT CHATEAUX

Château Bel-Air
Owner: Michel Méric. 4,500 cases white.
Château Bertranon
Owner: M. Remeau. 1,000 cases red, 2,500 white.
Château Bouchoc
Owner: M. Ballade. 2,000 cases white.
Château Coullac
Owner: Gérard Despujols. 3,500 cases white.
Château Lagrave
Owner: M. Trinon. 3,000 cases white.
Château Lafüe
Owner: Jean Sicres. 2,000 cases red, 2,000 white.
Château Lamarque
Owner: Roger Bernard. 4,000 cases red, 5,000 white.
Château Laurette
Owner: François Pons. 1,000 cases red, 7,000 white.
Château Loubens
Owner: M. de Sèze. ('Fleuron Blanc' is dry white.) 2,000 cases red, 1,250 white.
Domaine de Morange
Owner: M. Durr. 5,000 cases white.
Château L'Oustau-Vieil
Owner: M. Sessac. 2,000 cases white.
Château du Pavillon
Owner: M. d'Arfeuille. 5,000 cases white.
Château La Rame
Owner: F. Armand. 10,000 cases white.
Château de Tastes
Owners: Prats family. 300 cases white.

LOUPIAC CHATEAUX

Château du Cros
Owner: Michel Boyer. 20,000 cases white.
Château Dauphiné-Rondillon
Owner: J. Darriet. 10,000 cases white.
Château de Loupiac, Domaine de Gaudiet and Château Pontac (also called Ch. Loupiac-Gaudiet)
Owner: Marc Ducau. 7,500 cases white.
Château Mazarin
Owner: M. Courbin-Meyssan. 15,000 cases white.
Château de Ricaud
Owners: Soc. Civile Garreau-Ricaud. 12,000 cases white.
Château du Vieux-Moulin
Owner: Mme J. Perromat. 1,500 cases red, 3,500 white.

GRAVES DE VAYRE AND STE-FOY-BORDEAUX

Within the same block of vineyard two smaller zones have separate appellations defined with Gallic precision, one on the basis of its soil and potential for something out of the rut, the other, I suspect, for political reasons.

Graves de Vayres, across the river from Libourne, has more gravel than its surroundings. Unfortunately its name invites comparison with Graves, which it cannot sustain. The whites are made sweeter than Entre-Deux-Mers. The quickly maturing reds have been compared in a charitable moment to minor Pomerols.

The other appellation, Ste-Foy-Bordeaux, looks like a natural part of the Bergerac region cobbled on to Bordeaux. Its wines are not notably different from the Dordogne wines of Bergerac, and its history is identical. For centuries the Dutch came here for the 2 commodities most in demand in the Low Countries and the Baltic: sweet wine and wine for distilling.

COTES-DE-BORDEAUX-ST-MACAIRE

Ten villages beyond Ste-Croix-du-Mont rejoice in this appellation for their 45,000 cases of semi-sweet wine, a trickle of which finds its way to Belgium.
Postcode: 33490 St-Macaire.

CERONS

The appellation Cérons applies to the 3 Graves villages (Podensac and Illats are the other 2) that abut on to Barsac on the north and have a natural tendency to make sweet wines. Their wines are classified according to their natural degree of alcohol as either Graves or Graves Supérieures (at 11 or 12 degrees and naturally dry), or at half a degree more as Cérons, which inclines to be *moelleux*, the grey area which is sweet but not *liquoreux*. Occasionally it attains *liquoreux* stickiness. All depends on the autumn and the vinification, which used sulphur as its crutch and left much to be desired. Modern methods can mean much cleaner and better wine, as the growing reputations of some of the properties indicate.

460 acres with 140 growers produce some 70,000 cases of Cérons (and more Graves), but sweet or dry it only fetches a moderate price. France consumes nearly all of it; the only export is a trickle to Belgium and Germany.

Postcode: 33720 Podensac.

CERONS CHATEAUX

Château d'Archambeau
Illats. Owner: J.-Philippe Dubourdieu. 5,000 cases red; 8,500 white.
Château du Barrail
Mourens. Owners: Yung Brothers. 13,000 cases.
Château de Cérons and Château de Calvimont
Cérons. Owner: Jean Perromat. 6,500 cases.
Château de Chantegrive
Podensac (*see* Graves).
Château de Ferbos and Lalannette-Pardiac
Cérons. Owner: Jean Perromat. 3,000 cases white.
Château Mayne-Binet
Cérons. Owner: Jean Perromat. 2,000 cases.
Grand Enclos du Château de Cérons
Cérons. Owner: Olivier Lataste. 850 cases Cérons, 6,500 Graves white.

BORDEAUX AND BORDEAUX SUPERIEUR

The basic appellations underlying all the more specific and grander names of Bordeaux are available to anyone using the approved grape varieties, achieving a certain degree of alcohol and limiting the harvest to a statutory maximum (which varies from year to year).
The standing definitions for red wines:
Bordeaux must have 10 degrees at a maximum of 55 hectolitres a hectare.
Bordeaux Supérieur needs 10.5 degrees at a maximum of 40 hectolitres a hectare – hence more concentration and flavour.
For white wines:
Bordeaux must have 10.5 degrees at 65 hectolitres.
Bordeaux Supérieur needs 11.5 degrees at 40 hectolitres a hectare.

CUBZAC

The districts that regularly carry the simple appellation, having no other, include St-André-de-Cubzac and the nearby Cubzac-Les-Ponts, and Guitres and Coutras. Cubzac is where the great iron bridge built by Eiffel (of the tower) crosses the Dordogne on the way from Bordeaux to Paris. It lies between the hills of Fronsac and those of Bourg, on flat land which can nonetheless make respectable wine. Postcode: 33240 St-André-de-Cubzac.

CUBZAC CHATEAUX

Château Timberlay
St-André-de-Cubzac. Owner: R. Giraud. 185 acres; 50,000 cases red, 6,000 cases white.
Château du Bouilh
St-André-de-Cubzac. Owner: Patrice Comte de Feuilhade de Chauvin. 124 acres; 8,500 cases.
Château de Terrefort-Quancard
Cubzac-les-Ponts. Owners: The Quancard family. 150 acres; 33,000 cases red.

GUITRES AND COUTRAS

Guitres and Coutras are very much on the fringe, to the north of Cubzac where wine-growing used to be directed towards Cognac. One property in the area uses a typically Pomerol mix with 75% Merlot on clay soil with encouraging results. Postcode: 33230 Coutras.
Château Méaume
Maransin. Owner: Alan Johnson-Hill. 70 acres; 15,000 cases red.

Bordeaux wine prices
In the first edition of this book, individual prices were quoted for the majority of the *Crus Classés*. These were the amounts asked at the château for the 1980 vintage in the middle of 1982, when that vintage was entering the market. Since 1982, the furious ferment in the marketplace started by the success of the 1982 vintage has made sensible price comparisons very hard. The question is: what price, when, and to whom? Consumers are buying wine *en primeur* to a far greater extent than formerly, and fashionable wines become scarce. Proprietors have been competing to out-do each other. Some châteaux are releasing only enough wine to set a price – only a few *tonneaux* – and holding back much of their stock in the hope that the market will rise. Merchants have been forced to buy less fashionable vintages – such as 1984 and 1987 – before they are given an 'allocation' of more favoured wines such as 1985 or 1988. And then in 1990 the fuss about the '89s almost equalled the '82 campaign – and prices rose once again.

All this makes comparison between properties, the intended purpose of the prices in the first edition, still more difficult. Prices are given in this edition where they are available. The figures show the price per bottle ex-cellar in the summer of 1990, when the '89 vintage was being released. While these figures allow the relative market worth of properties to be compared, they should be treated with considerable caution.

BORDEAUX CHATEAUX INDEX

A

L'Abbé-Gorsse-de-
Gorsse 55
d'Agassac 68
Andron-Blanquet 66
Aney 68
L'Angélus 86
d'Angludet 55
des Annereaux 98
Anseillan 65
d'Archambeau 103
d'Arche: Haut-Médoc
68; Sauternes 79
d'Arche-Lafaurie 79
d'Arcins 68
Arnaud-Jouan 101
d'Arnauld 68
Arricaud 76
L'Arrosée 86
Ausone 83–4

B

Badette 90
Balac 90
Balestard La Tonnelle
86
Barbé 100
de Barbe 100
de Barbe-Blanche 92
La Barde 90
Barde-Haut 90
Baret 76
du Barrail 103
Barraud 92
Barreyres 68
Bastor-Lamontagne 81
Batailley 61
Bayard (Laporte) 92
Bayard (Gouze) 92
Beau-Mayne 90
Beaumont 68
de Beaumont 100
Beauregard: Pomerol
93; St-Julien 59
Beau-Rivage 101
Beau Séjour Becot 85
Beauséjour: Montagne-
St-Emilion 92;
Pouisseguin-St-
Emilion 92; St-
Emilion 85; St-
Estèphe 67
Beau-Site: Premières
Côtes de Bordeaux
101; St-Estèphe 66
Beau-Site-Haut-
Vignoble 67
La Bécade 57
de Bel-Air 98
Bel-Air: Lussac-St-
Emilion 92; Pomerol
97; Puisseguin-St-
Emilion 92; Ste-
Croix-du-Mont 102
Belair: Premières Côtes
de Blaye 100; St
Emilion 85
Bel-Air Lagrave 57
Bel-Air-Marquis
d'Aligre 55
Belgrave 67
Bellefont Belcier 90
Bellefont-Belcier-
Guillier 90
Bellegrave 90
Bellerive 71
Belle Rose 65
Bellevue: Médoc 71;
Pomerol 97;
Premières Côtes de
Blaye 100; St-
Emilion 86
Bellisle-Mondotte 90

Bel-Orme-Tronquoy-
de-Lalande 68
Bergat 86
Berliquet 86
Bertinau 93
Les Bertins 71
Bertranon 102
Beychevelle 58
du Biac 101
Bigaroux 90
Biquette 92
Birot 101
Biston-Brillette 57
Blaignan 71
Blanzac 99
Bodet 99
Le Bon-Pasteur 94
Bonde 93
Bonneau: Haut-Médoc
68; Montagne-St
Emilion 92
Bonnet: Entre-Deux-
Mers 102; St-Emilion
90
Le Bosq 66
Le Bosq 71
Bouchoc 102
du Bouilh 103
Bourdieu 100
Le Bourdieu 68
Bourgneuf-Vayron 94
de Bourgueneuf 97
Bournac 71
Bouscaut 73
du Bousquet 100
Bouteilley, de 101
Boyd-Cantenac 53
Branaire-Ducru 58
Brane-Cantenac 53
Bréthous 101
Le (du) Breuil 68
La Bridane 59
Brillette 57
Broustet 7
Brûlesécaille 100

C

La Cabanne 94
Cadet-Bon 90
Cadet-Piola 86
Cadet-Pontet 90
Cafol 91
de Caillavet 101
Caillou 79
La Caillou 97
Calon 92
Calon-Ségur 65
Calvaire 90
de Calvimont 103
de Camarsac 102
Camélon, Dom. de 101
de Camensac 68
Canet 102
Canon: Canon-Fronsac
99; St-Emilion 85
Canon-de-Brem 99
Canon-La-Gaffelière 86
Cantegril 91
Canteloup 67
Cantemerle 67
Cantenac 90
Cantenac-Brown 53
Canteranne 90
Canuet 55
Cap Léon Veyrin 57
Cap de Mourlin 86
Capbern-Gasqueton 66
Capet-Guillier 90
Caboneyre 90
Carbonnieux 73
Carcannieux 71
Cardinal Villemaurine 90

La Cardonne 71
Les Carelles 100
Des Carles 99
Les Carmes Haut-Brion
76
Caronne-Ste-Gemme 68
Carruades de Lafite
(Medoc)
La Carte et Le Châtelet
87
Carteau-Côtes-Daugay
90
Carteau Matras 90
du Cartillon 68
Cassat 92
du Castéra 71
du Cauze 90
Cazebonne 76
de Cérons 103
Certan de May 94
Certan-Giraud 94
Chambert Marbuzet 66
Chantegrive 103
de Chantegrive 76
La Chapelle-Lescours
90
Chapelle-Madelaine 90
Charmail 68
Charron 100
Chasse-Spleen 57
Le Chatelet 87
Les Chaumes 100
Chauvin 87
Le Chay 92
Chène-Vieux 92
Cheret-Pitres 76
Chevel Blanc 84
Chevalier, Dom. de 73
Chevalier d'Ars-Arcins
70
Chicane 76
Chinchon-La-Bataille 99
Cissac 68
Citran 68
de Civrac 100
La Clare 71
Clarke 57
Clauzet 67
Clerc-Milon 61
Climens 78
Clinet 94
Clocher, Clos du 94
Cloquet 97
La Closerie Grand
Poujeaux 57
de Clotte 99
La Clotte 87
La Clusière 87
Colas Nouet 93
Colombier Monpelou
65
La Commanderie:
Lalande-de-Pomerol
98; Pomerol 97
Le Conseillante 94
Corbin: Montagne-St-
Emilion 92; St-
Emilion 87
Corbin-Michotte 87
Cormeil-Figeac 90
Cos d'Estournel 65
Cos Labory 65
Côtes Bernateau 90
Côtes de la Mouleyre 90
Côtes Puyblanquet 90
Coucy 92
Coufran 68
Couhins-Inra 74
Couhins-Lurton 74
Coullac 92
de Courbon 76
de Courteillac 102
Coustolle 99

Coutelin-Merville 66
Coutet: Barsac 78
Couvent-des-Jacobins
87
Couvent des Templiers
90
Crabitey 76
Le Crock 66
La Croix 94
Croix de Bertinat 90
La Croix du Casse 97
La Croix de Gay 95
La Croix de Millorit
100
La-Croix-St-André 97
Croizet-Bages 61
Croque-Michotte 87
du Cros 102
du Cruzeau 76
de Cugat 102
Curé-Bon-La-Madeleine
87

D

Dalem 99
La Dame Blanche 68
Dassault 87
de la Dauphine 97
Dauphiné-Rondillon
102
Dauzac 54
Les Desmoiselles 99
Desmirail 54
Deyrem-Valentin 55
Dillon 68
Doisy-Daëne 79
Doisy-Dubroca 81
Doisy-Védrines 81
La Dominique 87
de Doms 76
Ducru-Beaucaillou 58
Duhart-Milon-
Rothschild 61
Duplessis 57
Duplessis-Fabre 57
Durand Laplaigne 92
Durfort-Vivens 54
Dutruch Grand
Poujeaux 57

E

L'Eglise, Clos 95
L'Eglise, Dom. de 97
L'Eglise-Clinet 95
L'Enclos 95
L'Escadre 100
de l'Espinglet 101
L'Evangile 95

F

La Fagnouse 90
Faleyrens 90
Falfas 100
de Fargues 81
Faugères 99
Faurie-de-Souchard 87
Fayau 101
de Ferbos &
Lalannette-Pardiac
103
Ferrand: Pomerol 97;
St-Emilion 90
Ferrande 76
Ferrière 54
Feytit-Clinet 95
de Fieuzal 74
Figeac 85
Filhot 81
La Fleur 90
La Fleur Gazin 95
La Fleur Milon 65
La Fleur-Pétrus 95
La Fleur Pipeau 90

Florimond-La-Brède,
Dom. de 100
Floridène 76
Fombrauge 90
Fonbadet 65
Fonchereau 102
Fongrave, Dom. de 102
Fonpiqueyre 68
Fonplégade 87
Fonrazade 90
Fonréaud 57
Fonroque 87
Fontesteau 69
Fontmuret 92
Fort Vauban 95
Les Forts de Latour 65
Fourcas-Dupré 57
Fourcas-Hosten 57
Le Fournas 69
Fourney 90
La Fourquerie 99
Fourtet, Clos 85
Franc Bigaroux 90
Franc-Grâce-Dieu 90
Franc-Mallet 97
Franc-Mayne 87
de France 76
La France: Entre-Deux-
Mers 102; Médoc 71
de Fronsac 99

G

de Gaby 99
La Gaffelière 86
Gaillard 90
Gaillat, Dom. de 76
Gallais-Bellevue 71
La Garde 76
Le Gardéra 101
Gaubert 90
Gaudiet, Dom. de 102
Gaudin 95
Le Gay: Entre-Deux-
Mers 102; Pomerol
95
Gazin: Graves 76;
Pomerol 95
du Gazin 98
Gerbay 99
Gilet Bayard 92
Gilette 82
Giscours 54
du Glana 59
Gloria 59
de Goélane 102
Gombaude-Guillot 95
Gontet 92
Gontier 100
Goujon 93
La Grace-Dieu 90
La Grâce-Dieu-Les-
Menuts 90
du Grand Abord 76
Grand Barrail
Lamarzelle Figeac 87
Grand-Corbin 87
Grand-Corbin-
Despagne 87
Grand Duroc Milon 65
Le Grand-Enclos 103
Grand-Jour 100
Grand Mayne 87
du Grand Moueys 101
Grand Moulin 69
Grand-Moulinet 97
Grand-Pontet 88
du Grand-Puch 102
Grand-Puy-Ducasse 61
Grand-Puy-Lacoste 61
Grandis 69
de Grange-Neuve 97
Grate-Cap 97
du Grava 101

de la Grave 100
La Grave, Dom. 76
La Grave (Trigant de
Boisset) 95
Gravelines 101
Gravet 92
La Gravière 98
Gressier Grand-
Poujeaux 57
Greyssac 71
Grimond 101
Grolet 100
Gros Moulin 100
Gruaud-Larose 58
Guadet-St-Julien 88
Gueyrot 90
Guibeau 92
Guibon 102
Guillemin La Gaffelière
90
Guinot 90
Guionne 100
Guiraud 78
La Gurgue 55

H

Hanteillan 69
Haut-Bages-Libéral 61
Haut Bages Monpelou 65
Haut-Bailly 74
Haut Batailley 64
Haut Bernon 92
Haut-Bommes 82
Haut Breton
Larigaudière 55
Haut-Brignon 91
Haut-Brion 73
Haut Brisson 90
Haut-Canteloup 71
Hauts Chaigneau 98
Hauts Conseillants 98
Haut-Corbin 88
Haut Franquet 57
Haut Garin 71
Haut-Lavallade 90
Haut-Macò 100
Haut-Maillet 97
Haut-Marbuzet 66
Haut-Padarnac 65
Haut-Peyraguey, Clos
78
Haut-Plantey 90
Haut-Sarpe 88
Haut Ségottes 90
Haute Faucherie 92
Hauterive 71
Les Heaumes 100
L'Hermitage 90
Hermitage La Garenne
92
Hourbanon 71
Houissant 66
Hourtin-Ducase 69

I

L'Ile Margaux, Dom.
de 55
d'Issan 54

J

Jacobins, Clos des 88
Jacques Blanc 90
des Jaubertes 76
Jean-Gervais 76
Jean-Voisin 90
La Joncarde 100
Jourdan 101
du Juge: Cadillac 101;
Haux 101
Junayme 99
Le Jurat 90
de Jussas 100
Justa 101

K
Kirwan 54

L
Labégorce 55
Labégorce-Zédé 55
Laborde 98
Lafaurie 101
Lafaurie-Peyraguey 78
Lafite-Rothschild 59,
  62–3
Lafitte 101
Laffitte-Carcasset 66
Lafleur 95
Lafleur du Roy 95
Lafon 57
Lafon Rochet 66
Lafüe 102
Lagrange: Pomerol 95;
  St-Julien 58
Largronge de Lescure
  90
Lagrave 102
Lagüe 99
La Lagune 67
Lalande Borie 59
Lalibarde 100
Lamarque: Haut-Médoc
  69; Ste-Croix-du-
  Mont 102
La Marzelle 88
Lamothe: Côtes de
  Bourg 100; Premières
  Côtes de Bordeaux
  101; Sauternes 81
Lamothe-de-Bergeron
  69
Lamothe-Cissac 69
Landat 69
De Landiras 76
Lanessan 69
Langoa-Barton 58
Laniote 88
Lapelletrie 90
Lapeyre 90
Larcis-Ducasse 88
Larmande 88
Laroque 90
Larose-Trintaudon 69
Laroze 88
Larrivaux 69
Larrivet-Haut-Brion 76
Lartigue: Côtes de
  Castillon 99; St-
  Estèphe 67
Lartigue de Brochon 69
Lascombes 54
Lassalle, Cru 71
Lassèque 90
Latour 59
Latour à Pomerol 95
Laujac 71
Launay 102
Laurensanne 100
des Laurets 92
Laurette 102
Lavalière 71
Laville-Haut-Brion 74
Legrange de Lescure 90
Léon 101
Léoville-Barton 58
Léoville-Las Cases 58
Léoville-Poyferré 59
Lescours 90
Lestage 57
Lestage-Darquier-
  Grand Poujeaux 57
Lestage Simon 68
Lestruelle 71
Lieujean 69
Liot 82
Liversan 69
Livran 71
Loubens 102
Loudenne 102
de Loupiac 102
Loupiac-Gaudiet 102

La Louvière 76
Lucas 92
Ludon-Pomiés-Agassac
  69
de Lussac 92
Lynch-Bages 64
Lynch-Moussas 64
du Lyonnat 92

M
MacCarthy 66
MacCarthy-Moula 66
Macquin 93
La Madeleine, Clos 88
Magdelaine 86
Magence 77
Maillard 101
Maison Blanche 97
Maison Neuve 93
Maison Rouge, Clos 99
Malagar 101
Malartic-Lagravière 74
Malescasse 69
Malescot St-Exupéry 54
de Malle 81
de Malleret 69
Mansy 99
(de) Marbuzet 66
Margaux 53
Marquis d'Alesme-
  Becker 54
Marquis de Mons 90
Marquis de Terme 55
Marsac-Séguineau 56
Martinens 56
Martinon 102
de Martouret 102
La Marzelle 88
Matras 88
Maucaillou 57
Mausse 99
Mauvesin: Moulis 57;
  St-Emilion 88
du Mayne 82
Le Mayne 92
Mayne-Binet 103
Mayne-Vieil 99
Mazarin 102
Mazerat 90
Mazeris 99
Mazeris-Bellevue 99
Mazeyres 97
Mazeyres, Clos 97
Méaume 103
Le Menaudat 100
Mendoce 100
de Ménota 82
Menuts, Clos des 90
Meyney 66
Le Meynieu 69
Mille-Secousses 100
Millet 76
Milon 90
La Mission-Haut-Brion
  75
des Moines: Lalande-
  de-Pomerol 98;
  Montagne-St-
  Emilion 92
de Mole 92
de Monbadon 99
Monbousquet 91
Moncet 92
Monconseil Gazin 100
Montaiguillon 92
Montalivet 99
Montbrun 56
Monthil 72
Montlabert 91
Montrose 65
Mony 101
de Morange, Dom. 102
Morin 66
Mouchet 92
Moueix 99
du Moulin 92
Moulin Bellegrave 90

Moulin-du-Cadet 88
Moulin des Carruades
  65
Moulin des Laurets 92
Moulin-Pay-Labrie 99
Moulin de la Rose 59
Moulin Rouge: Côtes
  de Castillon 99; Haut
  Médoc 69
Moulin-à-Vent: Lalande
  de Pomerol 98;
  Moulis 57
Moulinet 96
Moulins Listrac 92
Moulis 57
Mouton-Baronne-
  Philippe 64
Mouton-Rothschild
  60–1
de Myrat 81

N
Nairac 82
Négrit 93
Nenin 96

O
Olivier 75
L'Oratoire, Close de
  88
Les Ormes-de-Pez 66
Les Ormes-Sorbet 72
L'Oustau-Vieil 102

P
Palais Cardinal La Fuie
  91
Da Palette 101
Palmer 55
Panet 91
de Panigon 72
Pape-Clément 75
Pardaillan 100
Paret 99
Parsac 93
La Patache 97
Patache d'Aux 72
Patris 91
Paveil de Luze 56
Pavie 86
Pavie Decesse 88
Pavie-Macquin 88
du Pavillon: Canon-
  Fronsac 99; Ste-
  Croix-du-Mont 102
Pavillon-Cadet 88
Péconnet 101
Pédesclaux 64
Perenne 100
Pernaud 82
Perron 88
Petit-Faurie-de-Soutard
  88
Petit-Refuge 92
Petit-Village 95
Pétrus 93–7
Peychaud 100
Peyrabon 69
Peyrat 101
du Peyrat 101
Peyreau 91
Peyrebon 102
Peyredoulle 98
Peyrelongue, Dom. de
  91
de Pez 67
Phélan-Ségur 67
Piada 82
Pibran 65
Pichon 69
Pichon-Longueville au
  Baron de Pichon-
  Longueville 64
Pichon Longueville,
  Comtesse de Lalande
  64
La Pierrière 99

Pindefleurs 91
Pipeau 91
Pique-Caillou 76
Piron 76
de Pitray 99
Plaisance: Montagne-St-
  Emilion 93; Parsac-
  St-Emilion 93
Plantey 65
Plantey de la Croix 69
Plince 96
La Pointe 96
Pomeys 57
Poncet 101
Pontac 102
Pontac-Lynch 56
Pontet 72
Pontet-Canet 64
Pontet-Clauzure 91
Pontoise-Cabarrus 69
de Portets 76
Potensac 72
Pouget 55
Poujeaux 57
Pourret 91
de Pressac 91
Le Prieuré 89
Prieuré-Lichine 55
La Providence 69
de Puisseguin 92
du Puy 93
Puy-Blanquet 91
Puyblanquet-Carille 91
Puy Castéra 69
Puyfromage 99
Puygeraud 99
Puyguilhem 99
Puymiran 102

Q
Quentin 91
Les Queyrats 77
de Quinsac 102

R
Rabaud-Promis 78–9
Rahoul 77
Ramage La Batisse 69
La Rame 102
de Ramondon 101
Ramonet 102
Rausan-Ségla 55
Rauzan-Gassies 55
Raymond 102
Raymond-Lafon 82
Rayne-Vigneau 79
René 96
Respide 77
du Retout 70
Reynier 102
Reynon 101
Reysson 70
de Ricaud 102
Richelieu 99
Rieussec 79
Ripeau 89
La Rivalerie 100
La Rivière 99
Roc de Boissac 92
Roc de Puisseguin 92
La Roche 101
de Rochemorin 77
de Rocher 91
de Rol 91
Roland 65
de Rolland 82
Romefort 70
Romer du Hayot 81
de Roques 92
La-Rose-Côtes-Rol 91
de la Rose Maréchal 70
La Rose Pourret 91
Roudier 92
Rouget 96
Roumieu 82
Roumieu-Lacoste 82
Rousset 100

Rozier 91
Ruat-Petit-Poujeaux 57

S
La Sablière: Entre-
  Deux-Mers 102; St-
  Emilion 91
St-André-Corbin 92
St-Bonnet 72
St-Christophe 91
St-Estèphe 67
St-Georges 93
St-Georges (Côte-
  Pavie) 89
de St-Paul 70
de St Pey 91
St-Pierre 76
St-Pierre (Sevaistre) 59
de Sales 96
Sansonnet 89
Saransot-Dupré 57
La Sartre 77
Segonzac 100
Ségur 70
Sémeillan Mazeau 57
Senailhac 102
Sénéjac 70
Senilhac 70
Sergant 98
La Serre 89
Sestignan 72
Siaurac 98
Sigalas Rabaud 79
Sigognac 72
Simon 82
Siran 56
Smith-Haut-Lafitte 76
Sociando-Mallet 70
Soleil 92
Soudars 70
Soutard 89
Suau: Barsac 82;
  Premières Côtes de
  Bordeaux 101
Suduiraut 79

T
du Tailhas 96
du Taillan 70
Taillefer 96
Talbot 59
Tanesse 101
du Tasta 101
de Tastes 102
Tayac: Côtes de Bourg
  100; Margaux 56
de Terrefort-Quancard
  103
Terrey-Gros-Caillou 59
du Terrey-Gros-Caillou
  70
du Tertre 55
Tertre-Daugay 89
Teynac 91
Teyssier: Montagne-St-
  Emilion 92;
  Puisseguin-St-
  Emilion 92
Teysson 98
de Thau 100
Thieuley 102
Timberlay 103
Toumalin 99
Toumilon 77
La Tour l'Aspic 65
La Tour-Bicheau 77
La-Tour-Blanche:
  Médoc 72; Sauternes
  79
La Tour de By 72
La Tour-Carnet 67
Tour des Combes 92
La Tour Figeac 89
Tour de Gillet 92
Tour de Grenet 92
La Tour Guillotin 92
La Tour-Haut-Brion 76

La Tour du Haut-
  Caussan 72
Tour du Haut Moulin
  70
La Tour Léognan 77
La-Tour-de-Marbuzet
  67
La Tour Martillac 76
La Tour du Mirail 70
La Tour-de-Mons 56
La Tour Pibran 65
La Tour-du-Pin-Figeac
  89; (Giraud Belivier)
  89
La Tour Prignac 72
La Tour-Puymiraud
  102
Tour du Roc 70
La Tour du Roc Milon
  65
La Tour St-Bonnet 72
La Tour St-Joseph 70
Tour-St-Pierre 91
La Tour de Ségur 92
La Tour-des-Termes 67
des Tourelles 72
Tournefeuille 98
des Tours 92
Tourteau-Chollet 77
Tourteran 70
Toutigeac, Dom. de
  102
Touzinat 91
Trapaud 91
Trimoulet 89
Trimoulet, Clos 91
Tronquoy-Lalande 66
Troplong-Mondot 89
Trotanoy 96
Trottevieille 86
Les Tuileries 100
Le Tuquet 77
de Tustal 102

V
Vaisinerie 92
Val d'Or 91
Valrone 100
Verdignan 70
Vernous 72
Videau 101
La Vieille France 77
Vieux-Château Beaujus
  72
Vieux Château Certan
  96
Vieux Château Chauvin
  91
Vieux-Château Landon
  72
Vieux-Château-St-
  André (Corbin) 92
des Vieux Chênes 92
de Vieux Moulin 99
Vieux Rivallon 91
Vieux Robin 72
Vieux Sarpe 91
Villars 91
Villegeorge 70
Villemaurine 89
Vincent 99
La Violette 96
Virou 100
Vrai Canon Bouché 99
Vray-Canon-Boyer 99
Vray-Croix-de-Gay 96

Y
Yon-Figeac 89
d'Yquem 80–1

BURGUNDY

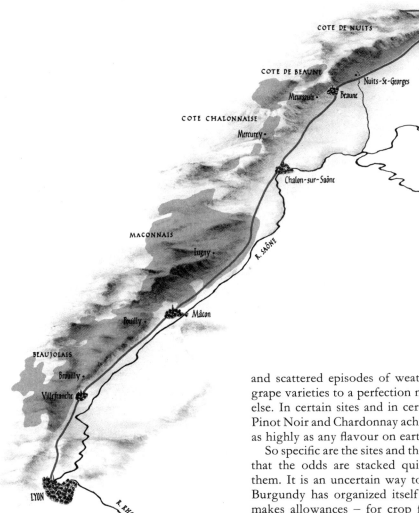

and scattered episodes of weather that bring two grape varieties to a perfection not found anywhere else. In certain sites and in certain years only, the Pinot Noir and Chardonnay achieve flavours valued as highly as any flavour on earth.

So specific are the sites and the conditions needed that the odds are stacked quite strongly against them. It is an uncertain way to make a living. So Burgundy has organized itself into a system that makes allowances – for crop failures, for human errors, for frailties of all kinds. Its legislation is a delicate structure that tries to keep the Burgundian one jump ahead of his clients without them tumbling to the fact.

The Burgundy of wine falls into five distinct parts. What is true of the Côte d'Or is equally true of Chablis, its northern outpost, but much less so of the region of Mercurey and the regions of Mâcon and Beaujolais to the south. The chapters on these areas summarize the local issues and conditions.

There is no simple or straight answer to the conundrum of Burgundy. The essential information is presented here in the form of geographical lists of the vineyards, their appellations and official ranking, and alphabetical lists of selected growers and merchants, showing who owns what and giving some idea of his standing.

Burgundy has the best-situated shop window in France, if not in Europe. The powerful, the influential, the enterprising and the curious have been filing by for two millennia along the central highway of France, from Paris to Lyon and the south, from the Rhine and the Low Countries to Italy. Every prince, merchant, soldier or scholar has seen the Côte d'Or, rested at Beaune or Dijon, tasted and been told tall tales about the fabulous wine of this narrow, scrubby hillside.

Whether any other hillside could do what the Côte d'Or can is a fascinating speculation – without an answer. What it does is to provide scraps of land

THE CLASSIFICATION OF BURGUNDY

Bordeaux has a random series of local classifications of quality. Burgundy has a central system by which every vineyard in the Côte d'Or and Chablis (although not in Beaujolais and the Mâconnais) is precisely ranked by its appellation. Starting at the top, there are some 30 Grands Crus which have their own individual appellations. They do not (except in Chablis) use the names of their communes. They are simply and grandly Le Corton, Le Musigny, Le Montrachet. In the nineteenth century the villages that were the proud possessors of this land added the Grand Cru name to their own: Aloxe became Aloxe-Corton; Chambolle, Chambolle-Musigny; Puligny and Chassagne both added Montrachet to their names. Hence the apparent anomaly that the shorter name in general means the better wine.

In parentheses it must be said that the decisions about which sites are Grands Crus are old and in some cases unfair. They were taken on observations of performance over many years. Their soil is ideal. They are generally the places that suffer least from spring frost, summer hail and autumn rot. But they can be well or badly farmed. There are certainly some of the next rank, Premier Cru, which reach or exceed the level of several Grands Crus. The rank of Premier Cru is given with much deliberation over detail to certain plots of land in the best non-Grand Cru vineyards of all the best communes. For several years a review was in progress that entails nitpicking over minute parcels of vines. It was only finally completed in 1984. The upshot is, for example, that in the Pommard vineyard (or *climat*) of Les Petits Epenots plots 2 to 8 and 13 to 29 are classed as Premier Cru, while plots 9 to 12 are not. I give this instance not to confuse the issue but to show how extremely seriously the authorities take the matter.

The biggest and best Premiers Crus have reputations of their own, particularly in the Côte de Beaune (where Le Corton is the only red Grand Cru). Such vineyards as Volnay Caillerets and Pommard Rugiens can be expected to produce fabulously good wine under good conditions. In such cases the producer proudly uses the name of the vineyard. The law allows the vineyard name to be printed on the label in characters the same size as the commune name. There are smaller Premiers Crus, however, without the means to acquire a great reputation, whose wine is often just sold as, for example Volnay Premier Cru. Often a grower's holdings in some vineyards are so small that he is obliged to mix the grapes of several holdings in order to have a vatful to ferment. This wine will have to settle for an unspecific name.

The Grands Crus and Premiers Crus form an almost unbroken band of vineyards occupying most of the Côte d'Or slope. The villages with their evocative names – Gevrey-Chambertin, Aloxe-Corton, Pommard – generally sit at the foot of the slope, encompassing in their parish boundaries both the best (upper) land and some, less good or even distinctly inferior, either on the flat at the bottom or in angles of the hills that face the 'wrong' way. This also is classed. The best of it, but not up to Premier Cru standard, is entitled to use the name of the village and the vineyard. In practice not many vineyards below Premier Cru rank are cited on labels. The law in this case demands that a vineyard name be printed in characters only half the size of the commune name. The *appellation contrôlée* here applies to the village name, not the vineyard. In the descriptions of properties that follow, I refer to these as 'Village' wines.

Inferior land within a village is not even allowed the village name. It falls under the rubric of *appellations régionales*: the most specific name it can have is Bourgogne (when it is made from the classic grapes, red and white, of the region), Bourgogne Passetout-Grains, Bourgogne Aligoté or Bourgogne Grand Ordinaire. For an explanation of these terms see pages 110/111.

GRAPES AND WINE

Burgundy is easier wine to taste, judge and understand than Bordeaux. The Pinot Noir, which gives all the good reds of the Côte d'Or, has a singular and memorable smell and taste, sometimes described as 'pepperminty', sometimes as 'floral' or 'fleshy'; certainly beyond the reach of my vocabulary.

Singular as it is, it varies in 'pitch' more than most grapes from one site to another and one vintage to another. In unripe years it smells mean, pinched and watery (German red wines give a good idea of the effect). At the other extreme it roasts to a raisiny character (many California Pinot Noirs are out of key in this way).

The ideal young red burgundy has the ripe-grape smell with neither of these defects, recognizably but lightly overlain with the smell of oak. And it tastes very much as it smells; a little too astringent for total pleasure but with none of the wither-wringing, impenetrable tannin of a great young Bordeaux. Good burgundy tastes good from birth.

The object of keeping it in barrels is to add the flavour of oak and some tannin and to allow the wine to stabilize naturally. The object of maturing it in bottle is to achieve softness of texture and a complex alliance of flavours that arise from the grape, yet seem to have little to do with it. Fine old red burgundy arrives at an intense, regal red with a note of orange (the decorator's 'burgundy' is that of young wine). It caresses the mouth with a velvet touch which loses nothing of vigour by being soft. And it smells and tastes of a moment of spring or autumn just beyond the grasp of your memory.

Strange to say, white burgundy can have a distinct resemblance to red – not exactly in smell or taste but in its texture and 'weight' and the way that it evolves.

Chardonnay wine is not markedly perfumed when it is new: just brisk and, if anything, appley. The traditional burgundy method of fermenting it in small barrels immediately adds the smell of oak. Thereafter, the way it develops in barrel and bottle depends very much on which district it comes from, and on the acid/alcohol ratio of the particular vintage. An ideally balanced vintage such as 1978, 1983 or 1986 keeps a tension between the increasingly rich flavours of maturity and a central steeliness, year after year. A sharp, barely ripe vintage such as 1977 leans too far towards the steel – and not very springy steel at that. A very ripe vintage such as 1976 produced many wines that were too fat and lacked 'cut'. All in all, however, the success rate of white burgundy vintages is very much higher than that of red.

HOW BURGUNDY IS MADE

Red burgundy is normally made in an open-topped cylindrical wooden *cuve* filled to about two thirds of its capacity with grapes crushed in a mill (*fouloir/ égrappoir*) which removes some or all of the stalks. Every grower has his own theory of how much or little of the stems should be included, depending on the ripeness of the grapes (and of their stalks), the colour and concentration of the vintage, and whether he wants to make a tannic *vin de garde* or a softer wine to mature more quickly. Ultra-conservative growers still tend to include all the stalks. Among the arguments in favour are that it makes the pressing easier – to the contrary that it robs the wine of colour and can add bitter tannin. Avant-garde growers today often use 'cold maceration' – keeping the skins in the juice at a low temperature that prevents fermentation for a few days to encourage fruity flavours.

To start the pulpy mass fermenting it is sometimes necessary to add a measure of actively fermenting wine from another vat, with a teeming yeast population – known as a *pied de cuve*. In cold weather it may also be necessary to warm the must with heating coils. The ancient way to get things moving was for all (male) hands to strip naked and jump in, lending their body heat to encourage the yeast. In an account of the Côte d'Or in 1862 by Agoston Haraszthy, reporting to the government of California, 'Five days is generally sufficient for the fermenting of wine in this part, unless it is cold weather, when the overseer sends his men in a couple of times more in their costume *à l'Adam* to create the necessary warmth.' He adds that 'This, in my eyes, rather dirty procedure could be avoided by throwing in heated stones or using pies filled with steam or hot water.' And indeed it is. Pinot Noir needs a warm fermentation to extract all the colour and flavour from the skins.

The operation of *pigeage*, or mixing the floating cap of skins with the fermenting juice, is still sometimes performed in small cellars by the vigneron or his sons, scrupulously hosed down, in bathing shorts, but more up-to-date establishments either pump the juice from the bottom of the vat over the '*chapeau*' ('*remontage*') or use a grille which prevents the cap from floating to the top ('*chapeau immergé*'). I am told by practitioners that it is the positively physical rubbing of the 'marc' by *pigeage* that is important. It liberates elements that *remontage* or *chapeau immergé* cannot possibly obtain.

Individual ideas on the right duration of this '*macération*' of the skins in the *cuve* vary from a very few days to up to almost three weeks, by those who are determined to get deep-dyed wine with maximum 'extract' – hence flavour. The 'free-run' wine is then drawn off and the *marc* pressed in presses of every shape and form. The wine of the first pressing is usually added to the free-run juice and the ensemble filled into barrels, old or new according to the means and motives of the proprietor, to settle down and undergo its quiet secondary, malolactic, fermentation as soon as may be. The malolactic fermentation is often encouraged by raising the temperature of the cellar. Once they have finished this infantile fretting they are moved ('racked bright') into clean barrels.

Fine red burgundies are usually kept in barrel for up to two years – not quite as long as the best Bordeaux. Unlike Bordeaux, they are racked from one barrel to another as little as possible to avoid contact with the air. They are simply topped up and left alone until it is time for bottling. Two months before bottling they may need to be 'fined' to remove the very faintest haze. Some cellars use filters to clarify the wine, but other producers avoid this. Others – and this is the subject of heated debate – prefer to pasteurize their red wines before bottling to eliminate micro-organisms.

MAKING WHITE BURGUNDY

The procedure for making all dry white wines, white burgundy included, is virtually standardized today. The object is maximum freshness, achieved by minimum contact with the air. Careful, clean and cool handling of the grapes is followed by a quick pressing and slow, cool fermentation.

In big modern plants in Chablis, and the best of the big cooperative cellars of the Mâconnais, this clinical procedure is carried out and the flavours of the resulting wines owe everything to grape and soil. Chablis, having more acidity and a more distinctive flavour, can benefit from maturing in a steel or concrete vat and then in bottle for a considerable time. The simpler, rounder taste of Mâcon wines has little to gain by keeping.

The ancient way of warming the must to start burgundy fermenting.

But the classic white burgundies of the Côte d'Or are another matter. They are fermented in small oak barrels, filled to allow a little airspace on top. The finest and most concentrated wines are given new barrels for at least half of the crop every year. The pungent, almost acrid smell of new oak becomes part of the personality of the wine from the start. The majority of growers, those with good but not the finest land, settle for barrels that have been used several times before, perhaps replacing a few each year. In this case the oak has less of the obvious carpenter's-shop effect on the wine; the barrel is simply the ideal size and shape of container for maintaining fermentation at an even, low temperature, cooled by the humid ambience of the cellar. A greater volume of wine would generate too much heat as fermentation progresses.

Fermentation over, the wine stays in the barrel, on its yeasty sediment, until it becomes clear, which may take a good six months. It is then racked into clean barrels and kept until the maker judges it is ripe for bottling. What he is doing is allowing a gentle and controlled oxidation of the wine to introduce nuances and breadth of flavour that would otherwise not develop. It is then ready for drinking – unless the buyer wants to continue the ageing process in the bottle. To me the possibility of this 'reductive' ageing is the whole point of buying the great white burgundies. No other white wines reward patience so well.

ADDING SUGAR

It is regular practice to add sugar to the must, the unfermented grape juice, in Burgundy, as it is in most of France. According to growers, long experience has shown that slightly more than the natural degree of sugar produces a better fermentation and a more satisfactory final wine. It is not purely the extra one or two degrees of alcohol but the evolution and final balance of the wine that is affected (they say).

All 'chaptalization' is strictly controlled by law. Until 1979 there was a statutory allowance for each Burgundy appellation. Since 1979, each year has been treated *ad hoc*, the minimum natural degree and the maximum degree after chaptalization being decided in view of the vintage as a whole. Nobody in any appellation is permitted to add more than two per cent alcohol to any wine by adding sugar. (There is a temptation to add the maximum: sugar not only increases the total volume of wine, it makes it easier to sell. The extra alcohol makes it taste more impressive and 'flattering' in its youth when buyers come to the cellar to taste.)

In 1987, a typical year, the regulations in Burgundy stipulated that to use the humblest appellation for red wine, Bourgogne, the wine must have a natural alcoholic degree of 10. The maximum degree allowable, after chaptalization, was 13 degrees. So a 10-degree wine was permitted to be raised to 12 degrees, 10.5 to 12.5, and 11 and upwards to 13.

The equivalent figures for white wine are always 0.5 degree higher: e.g. Bourgogne Blanc must be naturally 10.5 degrees and may be pushed up to 13.5 degrees.

As the dignity of the appellation increases, so does the degree. The minimum and maximum figures set for 1988 in higher appellations were as follows:

Appellation communale or 'Village'; e.g. Aloxe-Corton:

red	minimum 10.5°	maximum	13.5°
white	„ 11°	„	14°

Premier Cru, e.g. Aloxe-Corton Les Fournières:

red	minimum 11°	maximum	14°
white	„ 11.5°	„	14.5°

Grand Cru, e.g. Corton:

red	minimum 11.5°	maximum	14.5°
white	„ 12°	„	14.5°

The best producers, using their judgement, usually chaptalize between 1 and 1.5 degrees – rarely to the maximum, but rarely not at all (except for white wines, which in good vintages often reach 13° naturally).

GENERAL APPELLATIONS

There are four appellations that are available to growers in the whole of Burgundy with certain provisos:

Bourgogne
Red, white or rosé wines. The whites must be Chardonnay and/or Pinot Blanc. The reds must be Pinot Noir, Pinot Liebault or Pinot Beurot, with the exception of the Yonne, where the César and the Tressot are traditional and are admitted, and the 'crus' of Beaujolais, whose Gamay may be sold as 'Bourgogne'. No other Beaujolais wine or other Gamay is allowed.

The maximum crop is 55 hectolitres a hectare for red and rosé, 60 for white. Strength: 10 degrees for red and rosé, 10.5 degrees for white. It is worth ageing Bourgogne Rouge at least two years.

Bourgogne Passe-tout-grains
Red or rosé wines from any area made of two thirds Gamay and at least one third Pinot Noir fermented together. Maximum crop 55 hectolitres a hectare. Minimum strength 9.5 degrees. Bourgogne Passe-tout-grains can be delicious after at least one year's ageing, and is not heady as Beaujolais.

Bourgogne Aligoté

White wine of Aligoté grapes, with or without a mixture of Chardonnay, from anywhere in Burgundy. Maximum crop 60 hectolitres a hectare. Minimum strength 9.5 degrees. One commune, Bouzeron in the Côte Châlonnaise has gained its own appellation for Aligoté; the permitted maximum crop is 45 hectolitres per hectare. Aligoté often makes a sharp wine with considerable local character when young.

Bourgogne Grand Ordinaire (or Bourgogne Ordinaire)

Red, white or rosé from any of the permitted Burgundy grape varieties. Maximum crop is 55 hectolitres a hectare for red and rosé, 60 for white. Minimum strength 9 degrees for red and rosé, 9.5 degrees for white.

This appellation is now not often used.

BURGUNDY IN ROUND FIGURES

'Greater Burgundy', the region including not only the Côte d'Or but Beaujolais, the Mâconnais, Mercurey and the Yonne (Chablis), now produces 15 per cent of all *appellation contrôlée* wines.

In the past 30 years the area under vines has increased by nearly one half from 66,700 acres to 98,800 acres. The increase has been uniform in all districts except the Yonne, where the Chablis vineyards have expanded by more than 160 per cent. At the same time vineyards producing non-appellation *'vins de consommation courante'* have decreased sharply.

The trend, as in Bordeaux and elsewhere in France, has been towards more specialization and fewer but bigger holdings of vines. For example, in the Côte d'Or in 1955, 16,500 farmers had vineyards of less than 2.5 acres. The figure today is less than 2,000. In contrast the number of 'exploitations' of between 12.5 and 25 acres has more than doubled, of those between 25 and 50 almost trebled, and of those of 50 acres and upwards quadrupled. Similar trends, if anything more marked, apply to the other areas of Burgundy. Today approximately 18,000 growers own 98,800 acres and produce a total of over a million hectolitres (25 million cases).

The average production for the five years 1983–87 is given below for the principal brackets of Burgundy appellations.

White wines	hl.	cases
Côte d'Or Grand Crus	3,000	33,300
Côte d'Or other ('Village') wines	39,000	433,300
Chablis	120,000	1,333,000
Côte Chalonnaise	12,000	133,000
Mâcon 'Crus' (e.g. Pouilly Fuissé)	68,000	750,500
Mâcon Blanc (other)	135,000	1,500,000
Beaujolais	7,800	86,700
Regional appellations (simple Bourgogne, etc.)	101,000	1,122,000
Total production of white wines	485,800	5,396,800

Red wines	hl.	cases
Côte d'Or Grand Crus	11,000	122,200
Côte d'Or other ('Village') wines	151,000	1,668,000
Côte Chalonnaise	35,000	189,000
Mâcon	62,000	689,0000
Beaujolais and Beaujolais-Villages	960,000	10,670,0000
Beaujolais 'Crus' (e.g. Fleurie)	348,000	3,870,000
Regional appellations (simple Bourgogne, etc.)	247,000	2,744,000
Total production of red wines	1,814,000	20,152,200

Total 2,299,800 hl. 25,549,000 cases

In 1989 Burgundy accounted for 9.6% of French AOC wine exports by volume, and 20% by value. The principal export markets for Bugundy in 1989 were:

USA	19% by volume	20% by value	(more white than red)
Switzerland	12% ,, ,,	12% ,, ,,	(more red than white)
UK	22% ,, ,,	22% ,, ,,	(more white than red)
West Germany	12% ,, ,,	10% ,, ,,	(more white than red)
Belgium/Luxembourg	9% ,, ,,	9% ,, ,,	(mainly red)

CHABLIS

Chablis and the few other scattered vineyards of the *département* of the Yonne are a tiny remnant of what was once the biggest vineyard area in France. It was the 100,000 acres of the Yonne, centred around the city of Auxerre, that supplied the population of Paris with its daily wine before the building of the railways brought them unbeatable competition from the Midi. Whether one is to draw any conclusion from the fact that its best vineyard was called La Migraine is hard to say.

Any vineyard so far north is a high-risk enterprise. When falling sales were followed by the phylloxera disaster, Auxerre turned to other forms of agriculture. Chablis dwindled but held on, encouraged by the merchants of Beaune, who provided its chief outlet. When it was first delineated as an appellation in the 1930s there was not much more than 1,000 acres, but they included the hillside of the Seven Grands Crus. Nobody could ignore the quality of their wine. I remember a 45-year-old half-bottle of Les Clos 1923 as being one of the best white wines I ever drank.

It was the merchants of Beaune who made Chablis famous. In the simple old days when Beaune, being a nice easy name to remember, meant red burgundy, Chablis meant white. The name was picked up and echoed around the wine-growing world as a synonym for dry white wine. In California it still is.

But the real thing remained a rarity. Year after year, spring frosts devastated vineyards and discouraged replanting. Only in the 1960s did new methods of frost control turn the scales. The introduction of sprinkler systems to replace stoves among the vines on cold spring nights made Chablis profitable. Advances in chemical weed and rot control made it very attractive to invest in a name that was already world famous. Within a decade the acreage doubled, with each acre yielding far more wine more reliably than ever before. It continues to grow. Today there are over 6,500 acres, and an average crop is around one quarter to one third of all white burgundy.

There is inevitably an old guard that strongly resists the granting of the appellation to so much new land. As in the rest of Burgundy, however, the Grands Crus and Premiers Crus are more or less sacrosanct: it is in Chablis '*simple*' or 'Village', without a vineyard name, that there is room for more expansion.

Straight unqualified 'Village' Chablis, as it is generally made today, competes in the marketplace with Mâcon-Villages. In style it is lighter, sharper, drier and cleaner, with more of a 'lift' in your mouth. A good example is distinctly fruity with a quality that only Chardonnay gives. A poor one, on the other hand, is simply neutral and more or less sharp. A small amount of wine from inferior plots is only allowed the appellation Petit Chablis. Many say it should not be called Chablis at all.

Premier Cru and Grand Cru Chablis are different wines; distinct steps upward in body, flavour and individuality. Some people find the best Premiers Crus the most satisfyingly typical, with plenty of flavour and a distinctive 'cut' of acidity. The Grands Crus add a richness and strength which rounds them out; occasionally too much so. To be seen at their best they need at least three and sometimes up to ten years ageing in bottle. Those made in barrels (the minority) keep longest and best.

The scent and flavour that develop are the quintessence of an elusive character you can miss if

---

The Vineyards of Chablis

Chablis comes in 4 grades: Chablis AC (also known as '*simple*' or '*village*'), Petit Chablis, Premier Cru and Grand Cru. In 1989 the superior Premier Cru covered 1,605 acres with a further 250 authorized. Vineyard names (listed here) are sometimes used in conjunction with Premier Cru names. In the same year the Grand Crus occupied 93% of their authorized area of 247 acres. In Chablis new vines are being planted at a rate of 500 acres a year and it is estimated that by the turn of the century the total area under vine could be as great as 10,000 acres.

Premiers Crus

Premier Cru Chablis may be sold either with the names of individual vineyards or those of groups of fields. The latter is generally the case, so in practice only a relatively small number of names are in use. In alphabetical order, together with the names of the vineyards that have the right to use the name in question (since 1986): Les Beauregards (Côte de Cuissy); Beauroy (Troesmes, Côte de Savant); Berdiot; Chaume de Talvat; Fourchaume (Vaupulent, Côte de Fontenay, l'Homme Mort, Vaulorent); Les Fourneaux (Morein, Côte des Prés-Girots); Côte de Jouan; Les Landes et Verjuts; Côte de Léchet; Mont de Milieu; Montée de Tonnerre (Chapelot, Pied d'Aloup, Côte de Bréchain), Montmains (Forets, Butteaux); Vaillons (Chatains, Sécher, Beugnons, Les Lys, Mélinots, Roncières, les Epinottes); Côtes de Vaubarousse; Vaucoupin; Vau de Vey (Vaux Ragons); Vau Ligneau; and Vosgros (Vaugiraut).

Grands Crus

Blanchot (31 acres); Bougros (31 acres); Les Clos (67 acres); Grenouilles (22 acres); Preuses (28 acres); Valmur (33 acres); and Vaudésir (36 acres). La Moutonne is a vineyard of 5.75 acres in Vaudésir and Les Preuses.

you only ever drink Chablis young. I can only define it as combining the fragrances of apples and hay with a taste of boiled sweets and an underlying mineral note that seems to have been mined from the bowels of the earth.

Chablis' price has not kept pace with its value. Grand Cru Chablis is happily in much better supply than Bâtard-Montrachet, otherwise it could well fetch as high a price. Premier Cru Chablis from a good grower is the best value in white burgundy.

CHABLIS GROWERS

René and Vincent Dauvissat
8 rue Emile Zola, 89800 Chablis.

René Dauvissat's great-grandfather was a cooper, so it is no surprise that his cellars, unlike most in Chablis today, are still full of barrels. He ages the wine from his 22 acres for about 12 months in wood in the old style. His best wines are the Grands Crus Les Clos and Les Preuses – 7 acres in all. His remaining acres are all Premier Cru.

Jean-Paul Droin
Rue Montmain, 89800 Chablis.

Droin's great-grandfather presented his wines to Napoleon III when he visited Auxerre in 1866. His cellars have not changed overmuch. But he keeps the wines from his 17 acres of Premiers Crus (mainly Vaillons) in barrels for 6 months, and his Grands Crus for 12 months, whereas his great-grandfather would have kept them for several years. The Grands Crus are Vaudésir, Les Clos, Valmur and Grenouilles – 9 acres in all. They are some of the finest Chablis made today.

Maison Joseph Drouhin
7 rue d'Enfer, 21200 Beaune.

The famous Beaune négociant has since 1979 added 89 acres of Chablis to his domaine and makes immaculate, beautifully tender and aristocratic wine from the Grands Crus Vaudésir, Les Clos, Preuses and vividly typical Premier Cru from his holdings in Vaillons, Côte de Lechet, Mont de Milieu, etc.

Jean Durup
4 Grande rue, Maligny, 89800 Chablis.

The large and growing estate of Jean Durup, President of the lobby that favours expanding the appellation Chablis. He has a total of 370 acres, of which 81 are in Premiers Crus (principally Fourchaume and Van de Vey). An impeccable modern winery whose wines appear under the names Domaine de l'Eglantière and Château de Maligny. 55% is exported.

William Fèvre
Dom. de la Maladière. 14 rue Jules Ratier, 89800 Chablis.

The largest owner of Chablis Grands Crus and a traditionalist in his wine-making – one of the very few in Chablis to ferment his wine in new oak barrels. His 40 acres of Grands Crus include 10 of Les Clos, 15 of Bougros and 7 of Les Preuses, with 3 each of Valmur and Vaudésir and 1.5 of Grenouilles. He has a similar amount of Premiers Crus, split into 7 vineyards of which the biggest are 6.5 acres in Vaulorent and 6 in Montmains-Forêt. He also owns 49 acres of Chablis 'simple'. William Fèvre heads the *Syndicat de Défense de l'Appellation Chablis*, the body which is in favour of restricting the appellation to well-proven sites. He is also a négociant, using the Filippi label.

Domaine Alain Geoffrey
4 rue de l'Equerre, 89800 Chablis.

A third of the 86 acres domaine is Premier Cru, mainly Beauroy (17.2 acres), with 7.4 acres of Vau Ligneau and 3.7 acres of Fourchaume.

Lamblin & Fils
Maligny, 89800 Chablis.

A négociant and grower, whose 26 acres account for only 10% of his wine: the rest is bought as grapes or juice from others. 'Domaine' wines include small parcels of Grands Crus Valmur (2 acres) and Les Clos (2.5 acres), and 12 acres of Premiers Crus. Chablis is 70% of his business; the rest is white Bourgogne Blanc, Aligoté, white table wine and sparkling. The Lamblin style is light and fresh; the wines are for drinking young and not for ageing. Other labels include Jacques Arnouls, Jacques de la Ferté, Paul Javry, Bernard Miele.

Domaine Laroche
L'Obédiencerie, 22 rue Louis Bro, 89800 Chablis.

Michel Laroche is the fifth-generation owner of an estate of 240 acres. There are 15 acres of Chablis Grand Crus, including 11 acres of Les Blanchots, and 72 of Premier Cru. Modern equipment makes Chablis in an austere, vigorous style, though some new oak is used for the Grand and Premier Crus. Their Grand Crus should be kept for 3 to 6 years. The name Laroche also appears on a wide range of non-domaine wines, including a good brand of simple Chablis, St Martin.

Long-Depaquit
45 rue Auxerroise, 89800 Chablis.

A first-class old family company now merged with the négociants Bichot of Beaune but run autonomously. Of their 100-odd acres 47 are Chablis '*simple*', 30 Premiers Crus and 20 Grands Crus, including 6.4 of Vaudésir. Their most famous property is the 6-acre Moutonne vineyard, a part of the Grands Crus Vaudésir and Les Preuses, whose history goes back to the Abbey of Pontigny and its monks, who apparently skipped like young sheep under its inspiration. Long-Depaquit wines are very thoughtfully and professionally made with modern methods, but not for instant drinking.

Domaine des Malandes
63 rue Auxerroises, 89800 Chablis.

A 17.3-acre domaine with 2.2 acres in Grand Cru Vaudésir, and 7.3 acres of Premiers Crus including Fourchaume (3 acres) and Montmains (3 acres).

Louis Michel & Fils
11 boulevard de Ferrières, 89800 Chablis

The son and grandson of small growers who has tripled his acreage by dedicated wine-making. He now has 33 acres of Premiers Crus (some in Montmains and Montée de Tonnerre) and 6 acres of Grands Crus (Vaudésir 3; Grenouilles and Les Clos 1.3 each). Michel believes in letting the wine make itself as far as possible. He uses no barrels, but by modest yields and careful handling makes concentrated wines that repay years of bottle-age. 80% of his wine is exported.

J. Moreau & Fils
Route d'Auxerre, 89800 Chablis.

The largest proprietor in Chablis, and now a big business in non-Chablis white wines from the north of France, skilfully made and marketed. Total sales are some 375,000 cases a year. The Moreaus have been in business since 1814 and built up an estate of 175 acres. 125 acres of this is the Domaine de Biéville, appellation Chablis *'simple'*, and 25 is Premier Cru Vaillons. Of their 25 acres of Grands Crus, 17 are Les Clos and include the Clos des Hospices bought by the Moreaus from the local hospital in 1850. All the wine is made to be drunk young and fruity – very fruity in the case of Les Clos.

François Raveneau
Rue de Chichée, 89800 Chablis.

A little domaine (18 acres) in Grands Crus (Valmur, Les Clos, Blanchots) and Premiers Crus, but considered by some to be Chablis's best. Very traditional wines aged in barrels for at least 12 months and sold mainly to restaurants in France (including the Hôtel de l'Etoile in Chablis which has a fine selection of some of his earlier vintages). His wines age admirably. François' son Jean-Marie is now involved.

A. Regnard & Fils
28 boulevard du Docleaur Tacussel, 89800 Chablis.

A family firm of négociants, founded in 1860, handling wine of all qualities. Patrick de Ladoucette now has a large holding. Their specialities are Premier Cru Fourchaume and Grands Crus Vaudésir and Valmur. As well as Chablis they sell Aligoté and Sauvignon de St-Bris. Other labels used are Michel Rémon and Albert Pic. They now own 25 acres of vineyard, as well as buying in from over 370 acres.

Simonnet-Febvre & Fils
9 avenue d'Oberwesel, 89800 Chablis.

A small domaine of 9 acres but a well-known négociant going back five generations. The present head is Jean-Pierre Simonnet. The company makes wine from bought-in juice as well as its own, particularly from the Premiers Crus Mont de Milieu, Montée de Tonnerre, Fourchaume and Vaillons. Their best wine is the Grand Cru Preuses. Other wines they offer are Aligoté, Irancy, Sauvignon de St-Bris, and Crémant de Bourgogne. Other labels are Jean-Claude Simmonet, André Vannier, Georges Martin, Jean Deligny, Alexandre Goulard and Gilles Blanchard. 60% is exported.

Robert Vocoret
Rue d'Avallon, 89800 Chablis.

A century-old family domaine of 76 acres, 10 in Grands Crus (Les Clos, Valmur, Blanchots), 33 in Premiers Crus and 33 in Chablis *'simple'*. Vocoret is one of the very few Chablis growers left who ferment as well as age their wine in barrels. The result is wine with less of the immediately appealing 'fruit' but a firm grip that rewards keeping.

Cave Coopérative La Chablisienne
89800 Chablis

One quarter of the whole production of Chablis comes from this growers' cooperative, founded in 1923 and now handling the grapes from 1,225 acres, of which 827 are Chablis *'simple'*, 237 Premiers Crus, 123 Petit Chablis and 37 Grands Crus. Of the Grands Crus vineyards, 17 acres of Grenouilles and 12.5 acres of Preuses are significant holdings. Fourchaume, with 86 acres, is much their most important Premier Cru. All their methods are modern and their wine well made, clean and honest; they have recently begun experimenting with oak. Most of it is exported, under about 50 different labels, usually the names of grower-members. 'La Chablisienne' is sometimes seen.

Other Chablis producers

Other leading Chablis producers include: Jean Collet, Jean-Pierre Grossot, Bernard Legland, A. Pic, Dom de Malandes, Louis Pinson, Marcel Servin, Dom. Phillipe Testut, Dom. Gérard Tremblay, Dom. de Vauroux.

THE COTE D'OR

The heart of Burgundy is the 30-mile line of hills running south from Marsannay on the southern outskirts of Dijon, inclining westwards as it goes and presenting a broadening band of southeast-facing slopes until it stops at Santenay. The eight villages of the northern sector, ending at Prémaux, are the Côte de Nuits. The 20 villages running south from Aloxe-Corton are the Côte de Beaune.

The Côte de Nuits is almost exclusively devoted to red wine – almost all Pinot Noir. On these steep, sharp slopes the most potently flavoured, concentrated, eventually smooth and perfumed wines are made.

The villages are listed here from north to south. Each is briefly described with an appreciation of its wine and a list of its Grands Crus (if any) and Premiers Crus, their acreages and the vineyard acreage of the whole commune. The figures given are those arrived at in 1984 after a long process of official deliberation. The first edition of this book gave an average 1981 price for each of the majority of the appellations. Fluid market conditions in 1987 make this information impossible to obtain. Burgundy prices are in a state of rapid change. The growers listed under each village entry are those whose particulars will (in most cases) be found in the list of Côte d'Or growers starting on page 126. It is by no means an exhaustive list – only the telephone directory is that. The details of growers' holdings, in almost every case supplied by themselves, give a vivid picture of the infinitely complex structure of the world's most highly prized vineyards.

Marsannay-la-Côte

1983 production 13,400 cases of red, white and rosé. Famous for its superlative Pinot Noir rosé with its own appellation. In 1987 Marsannay range was given its own appellation.

Fixin

The Premiers Crus are splendidly situated and capable of wines as good as those of Gevrey-Chambertin. Even the 'village' wines are stout-hearted and long-lived. Between Fixin and Gevrey-Chambertin the village of Brochon has no appellation of its own. Its better vineyards are included in Gevrey-Chambertin. The lesser ones are plain Côte de Nuits-Villages.

PREMIERS CRUS	GROWERS
Total area 805 acres:	Bart
Premiers Crus 54 acres:	Clemencey Frères
Arvelets (8)	Pierre Gelin
Clos du Chapitre (11.8)	Philippe Joliet
Cheusots (4.5)	de la Perrière
Hervelets (9.5)	Charles Quillardet
Meix-Bas (5)	
Perrière (12)	
Queue de Hareng (Brochon)	
Appellation Communale	
246 acres.	
Appellations Régionales	
486 acres.	

Gevrey-Chambertin

There is a very wide range of quality in the production of Gevrey – the biggest of any of the townships of the Côte d'Or. Some of its flat vineyards beyond the valley road are of middling quality only. But there is no questioning the potential of its constellation of Grands Crus. Chambertin and the Clos de Bèze are acknowledged to lead them; an extra charge of fiery concentration gives them the edge. The seven others must always keep the 'Chambertin' after their names; Clos de Bèze may put it before, or indeed simply label itself Chambertin. They are all stern, essentially male (since everything in France has a gender) wines that I cannot imagine even Astérix himself tossing back in bumpers. Obélix, perhaps. French critics claim for Chambertin the delicacy of Musigny allied to the strength of a Corton, the velvet of a Romanée and the perfume of the Clos Vougeot. I have certainly tasted fabulous complexity, but delicacy is not the word I would choose. Great age is probably the key. Two of the Premiers Crus of Gevrey on the hill behind the village, Les Verroilles and Clos St-Jacques, are widely thought to be on the same level of quality as the bevy of hyphenated Chambertins.

GRANDS CRUS	
Chambertin (31.9)	Champonnets (8)
Chambertin Clos de Bèze (38)	Clos du Chapitre (2.5)
Chapelle-Chambertin (13.6)	Cherbaudes (5)
Charmes- (or Mazoyères-)	Closeau (1.3)
Chambertin (76)	Combe-au-Moines (11.78)
Griotte-Chambertin (6.7)	Combottes (11.3)
Latricières-Chambertin (18)	Corbeaux (7.5)
Mazis-Chambertin (22.4)	Craipillot (6.8)
Ruchottes-Chambertin (8.2)	Ergot (3)
	Etournelles (5)
PREMIERS CRUS	Fonteny (9)
	Gémeaux*
Total area 210 acres:	Goulots (4.5)
Bel Air (6.5)	Issarts (1.5)
La Boissière*	Lavaux (23.5)
Cazetiers (25)	Perrière (6)
Champeaux (16.5)	Poissenot (5.5)
Champitonnois (also called	Clos Prieur-Haut (5)
Petite Chapelle) (10)	La Romanée*
	Clos St-Jacques (16.5)

Les Verroilles (15)
*No acreage specified in the latest official documents.
Appellation Communale
892 acres.
Appellations Régionales in the commune: 234 acres.

GROWERS

Pierre Amiot et Fils	Maison J. Faiveley
Denis Bachelet	Pierre Gelin
Bart	Antonin Guyon
Thomas Bassot	René Leclerc
Adrien Belland	Georges Lignier & Fils
Maison Albert Bichot	Hubert Lignier
J.C. Boisset	Henri Magnien
Bouchard Père & Fils	J.P. Marchand
Alain Burquet	Maume
Camus Père & Fils	Moillard-Grivot
Bruno Clair	Georges Mugneret
Damoy	Naigeon-Chauveau
Maison Joseph Drouhin	J.M. Ponsot
Dujac	Charles Quillardet
	P.L. Rossignol
	Joseph Roty
	Armand Rousseau
	Thomas-Moillard
	Tortochot
	Louis Trapet
	des Varoilles
	Vienot

Morey St-Denis

The least known of the villages of the Côte de Nuits despite having four Grands Crus to its name and part of a fifth. Clos de la Roche is capable of making wine with the martial tread of a Chambertin; Clos St-Denis marginally less so; Clos de Tart (at least as its sole owner interprets it) is considerably lighter. All the wines of Morey are worth study, for authenticity and a chance of a bargain.

GRANDS CRUS	Meix-Rentiers
	Les Millandes
Bonnes Mares (a small part)	Monts-Luissants
(4)	Riotte
Clos des Lambrays (22)	Ruchots
Clos de la Roche (41.75)	Clos Sorbé
Clos St-Denis (16.35)	Les Sorbé
Clos de Tart (18.5)	Appellation Communale
	158 acres.
PREMIERS CRUS	Appellations Régionales
	305 acres.
Total area 106 acres:	
Bouchots	GROWERS
Maison Brûlée (2.5)	Pierre Amiot et Fils
Calouères	Bertagna
Clos de la Bussière (7.5)	Georges Bryczek
Chabiots	Bruno Clair
Chaffots (2.5)	Dujac
Charmes (2.5)	R. Groffier
Charrières (5)	Georges Lignier & Fils
Chénevery (7.5)	Hubert Lignier
Façonnières (2.5)	Mommessin
Fremières	Ponsot
Froichots	Ropiteau
Genevrières (7.5)	Armand Rousseau
Gruenchers (7.5)	

Chambolle-Musigny

The lilt of the name is perfectly appropriate for the wines of this parish – and so is the apparent evocation of the muse. It is hard to restrain oneself from competing in similes with the much-quoted sages of Burgundy, but here it seems to me Gaston Roupnel has it precisely right. Musigny, he says, 'has the scent of dewy garden ... of the rose and the violet at dawn.' Le Musigny is my favourite red burgundy, closely followed by the Premiers Crus Les Amoureuses and Les Charmes and the other Grand Cru, Les Bonnes Mares. A contributory reason is that some particularly good wine makers own this land.

GRANDS CRUS	
Bonnes Mares (also in Morey St-Denis) (33.5)	
Musigny (26)	

PREMIERS CRUS	
Total area 148 acres:	
Amoureuses	
Aux Beaux Bruns	
Borniques (2.5)	
Carrières	
Chabiots	
Charmes (12.5)	
Châtelots (5)	
Combes d'Orveaux	
Combottes (5)	
Aux Combottes (5)	
Cras (10)	
Derrière la Grange (10)	
Echanges	
Fousselottes (10)	
Fuées	
Grands Murs	
Groseilles	
Gruenchers	
Niorts	
Plantes (5)	
Sentiers (10)	

Appellation Communale
315 acres.
Appellations Régionales
83.5 acres

GROWERS

Pierre Amiot et Fils
Bart
Bouchard Père & Fils
Château de
  Chambolle-Musigny
Georges Clerget
Maison Joseph Drouhin
Drouhin-Laroze
Dufouleur Frères
Dujac
Faiveley
Jean Grivot
Antonin Guyon
Maison Leroy
Georges Lignier et Fils
Hubert Lignier
Dom. Machard de Gramont
Georges Mugneret
Maison G. Roumier
des Varoilles
Henri de Villamont
Comte de Vogüé

G. Roumier
Thomas-Mollaird
des Varoilles

Vienot

Vougeot

Historically the great vineyard of the Clos (de) Vougeot has the most resounding reputation in Burgundy. 125 acres within a single wall built by the fourteenth-century monks of Citeaux had a certain presence. Unquestionably the land at the top of the slope, next to Musigny and Grands Echézeaux, is equal to the best in Burgundy. But with its present fragmented ownership (some 80 growers have parcels) it is rare to meet a bottle that answers this description. Or perhaps I do not try often enough. Classical references to it always stress its perfume. My impression is generally of a more meaty, extremely satisfying but less exotic wine than those of its great neighbours.

GRAND CRU	
Clos de Vougeot (125)	

PREMIERS CRUS RED	
Total area 21.25 acres:	
Cras	
Petit Vougeot	

PREMIER CRU WHITE	
Total area 7.4 acres:	
Vigne Blanche or Clos Blanc de Vougeot (4.5)	
Appellation Communale 17 acres.	
Appellations Régionales 10.5 acres.	

GROWERS

Pierre André
Bertagna
Champy Père & Cie
Georges Clerget
Maison Joseph Drouhin
Dufouleur Frères
René Engel
Faiveley
Jean Grivot
Hudelot-Noëllat
Lamarche
Maison Leroy
Machard du Gramont
Georges Mugneret
Charles Noëllat
Maison Pierre Ponnelle
Jacques Prieur

Flagey-Echézeaux

Exists as a village but not as an appellation, despite the fact that it has two Grands Crus in the parish. They are effectively treated as being in Vosne-Romanée, having the right to 'declassify' their wine under the Vosne name. In reality Grands Echézeaux is at Grand Cru level – an ideal site adjacent to the best part of the Clos Vougeot. Its wines can have all the flair and the persuasive depths of the greatest burgundy. But the huge 75-acre Les Echézeaux would be more realistically classified as one or several Premiers Crus. Its lack of any readily spotted identity joined with its apparently unmanageable name means that it sells for a reasonable price. There is a lightness of touch, a gentle sweetness and airy fragrance about a good Echézeaux which make it less of a challenge than the biggest burgundies.

Vosne-Romanée

If Chambertin has the dignity, the name of Romanée has the glamour. Only the very rich and their guests have ever even tasted La Romanée-Conti. The Domaine de la Romanée-Conti, sole owner of that vineyard and the next greatest, La Tàche, casts its exotic aura equally over Richebourg, Romanée-St-Vivant and Grands Echézeaux, where it also owns or manages property. The Domaine's wines are marked with a character that seems

The walled city of Beaune is honeycombed with magnificent vaulted cellars dating back to the Middle Ages

Enjoying burgundy

White burgundy is incomparable as the white wine to accompany the first course of a formal meal and pave the way for a fine red wine – of either Burgundy or Bordeaux. Lighter and more acid wines are excellent with characuterie; mature full-bodied ones are as satisfying with poultry or veal.

Red burgundy can be so delicate that it begs to be appreciated alone, without food. In contrast, it can be so massive in flavour and vinosity that the pungency of well-hung game is not too much for it. Lighter wines benefit by being served relatively cool. Only full-scale well-matured burgundies should be served at the 'room temperature' of Bordeaux. In Burgundy red wine is seldom, if ever, decanted.

to be their own, rather than that of Vosne-Romanée as a whole. Out of the torrent of words that has poured around Vosne and its sacred ground over the centuries I would pick three: 'fire', 'velvet' and 'balance'. In the excitement of the Grands Crus, the Premiers Crus of Vosne-Romanée can be unwisely overlooked.

GRANDS CRUS

Total area 163.5 acres:
Echézeaux (93)
Grande Rue (2.5)
Grands Echézeaux (22.5)
Richebourg (21)
La Romanée (2)
Romanée-Conti (4.5)
Romanée-St-Vivant (23)
La Tâche (15)

PREMIERS CRUS

Total area 146 acres (of which 30.5 are in Flagey-Echézeaux):
Beaux Monts
Chaumes (17.5)
Croix Rameau
Cros Parentoux
Orveaux
Gaudichots (14.5)
Malconsorts (14)
Petits Monts (9)
Clos de Réas (5)
Orveaux
Raignots (4.5)
Rouges du Dessus

Suchots (33.5)
Appellation Communale
260 acres of which 33 are in Flagey-Echézeaux.
Apellations Régionales 198 acres.

GROWERS

Maison Albert Bichot
Bruno Clair
Georges Clerget
Réne Engel
Jean Grivot
Jean Gros
H. Jayer
J. Jayer
Lamarche
Machard du Gramont
Méo-Camuzet
Moillard
Mongeard-Mugneret
Mugneret-Gibourg
Mugneret-Gouachon
Charles Nöellat
Bernard Rion
Dom. de la Romanée-Conti
Thomas-Moillard
Charles Viénot

Nuits-St-Georges

As a town, Nuits does not bear comparison with the alluring city of Beaune; its walls have gone and it has no great public monuments. But it is the trading centre of the Côte de Nuits, seat of a dozen négociants, its endless silent cellars maturing countless big-bellied *pièces*. In another way, too, it echoes Beaune: its long hill of vines produces highly prized and famous wine without a single peak. If Nuits had a Grand Cru it would be Les St-Georges, and possibly Les Vaucrains, Les Cailles and Les Porrets on the slope above and beside it. But none of these vineyards has convinced the world that its wine alone rises consistently above the Premier Cru level.

Compared with the wines of Beaune, which they sometimes are, those of Nuits are tougher, less fruity and giving in their youth, and often for many years. It is hard to understand why they should be the popular favourite of Anglo-Saxon countries, as they are, since ten years is often needed to turn toughness to warmth of flavour. The best Nuits has marvellous reserves of elusive character that demand leisurely investigation.

Prémeaux, the village to the south (whose name recalls the spring waters which are its other product) is part of the appellation Nuits-St-Georges and itself has a run of Premiers Crus of equal merit, squeezed on to a steep and narrow slope between the road and the woods.

PREMIERS CRUS

Total area 353 acres:
De l'Arlot
Aux Argillats (4.5)

Les Argillères, Prémeaux (11)
Clos Arlots, Prémeaux (16.5)
Boudots (15)
Bousselots (10.5)
Cailles (8.5)

Chaboeufs (7.5)
Chaignots (14.5)
Chaînes-Carteaux (6)
Champs Perdrix (1.8)
Corvées, Prémeaux (19)
Cras (7.5)
Crots (10)
Damodés (21)
Didiers, Prémeaux (6)
Les Foréts, Prémeaux (17.5)
Les Grandes Vignes,
    Prémeaux (5)
Clos de la Maréchale,
    Prémeaux (25)
Murgers (12.5)
Aux Perdrix, Prémeaux (8.5)
Perrières (7.5)
Perrière-Noblot (0.75)
Poirets (17.5)
Poulettes (5)
Procès (5)
Pruliers (17.5)
Richemone (5.5)
Roncière (5)
Rue de Chaux (5)
Les St-Georges (18.5)
Thorey (12.5)
Vallerots (2)
Vaucrains (15)
Vignes Rondes (9.5)
Appellation Communale
42 acres. Appellations
    Régionales 735 acres.

GROWERS

J.-C. Boisset
F. Chauvenet
Robert Chevillon
Robert Dubois & Fils
Dufouleur Frères
Faiveley
Henri Gouges
Jean Grivot
Jean Gros
de la Juvinière
Chantal Lescure
Lupé-Cholet et Cie
Machard du Gramont
A. Michelot
Missery
Moillard
Mugneret-Gibourg
Mugneret Georges
Hospices de
    Nuits-st-Georges
de la Poulette
Henri et Gilles Remoriquet
Daniel Rion
Thomas-Moillard
Charles Viénot

Côte de Nuits-Villages

This appellation is a consolation prize for the parishes at either end of the main Côtes: Prissey, Comblanchien and Corgoloin next to Prémeaux on the road south, and Fixin, Brochon and Marsannay on the Dijon road beyond Gevrey-Chambertin. Fixin and Marsannay have appellations of their own. For the others this is the highest aspiration. Stone quarries are more in evidence than vineyards on the road to Beaune. The marble sawn from the hill here is some of France's best. Only one important vineyard stands out as a Premier Cru *marqué*; the Clos des Langres, property of La Reine Pédauque, the extreme southern tip of the Côte de Nuits.

Ladoix-Serrigny

The Côte de Beaune starts with its most famous landmark, the oval dome (if you can have such a thing) of the hill of Corton. The dome wears a beret of woods but its south, east and west flanks are all vines, forming parts of three different parishes: in order of approach from the north Ladoix-Serrigny, Aloxe-Corton and – tucked round the corner out of sight – Pernand-Vergelesses. The best vineyards of all three are those on the mid- and upper slopes of the hill, which share the appellation Corton Grand Cru (the only red Grand Cru of the Côte de Beaune) and in parts, for white wine, Corton-Charlemagne.

Ladoix-Serrigny has the smallest part of 'Corton', and not the best, in its vineyards of Rognet-Corton and Les Vergennes, names which are not used but subsumed in the general title of Corton, as all the Grand Cru territory can be. Similarly the 'village' wines of Ladoix, which few people have heard of, then to take advantage of the appellation Côte de Beaune-Villages.

GRANDS CRUS

Total area 55 acres:
AOC Corton-Charlemagne
white wines only
Basses Mourettes (2.5)
Hautes Mourettes (4.5)
Le Rognet-Corton (7.85)

AOC Corton red and white
wines
Les Carrières (1)
Les Grandes Lolières (7.5)
Les Moutottes (2)
Le Rognet et Corton (20.75)
La Toppe au Vert (0.25)
Les Vergennes (8.5)
Parts of Ladoix-Serrigny may
be sold under the appellation
Aloxe-Corton, the rest may
be sold as Côte de Beaune-
Villages. Total area 845
acres.

PREMIERS CRUS

Total area 56.5 acres:
Basses Mourettes (2)
Bois Roussot (4.5)
Le Clou d'Orge (4)
La Corvée (17.5)
Hautes Mourettes (1.5)
Les Joyeuses (2)
Les Lolières
La Micaude (4)
Appellation Communale
Ladoix-Serrigny: 298 acres.
Appellations Régionales
421 acres.

GROWERS

Bouchard Père & Fils
Serrigny

Aloxe-Corton

The major part of the Grands Crus Corton and Corton-Charlemagne dominates this parish, but leaves a substantial amount of lower land with the appellation Aloxe-Corton, both Premier Cru and 'Village'. It is important to remember that Corton is always a superior appellation to Aloxe-Corton.

It is almost impossible (and in any case not really essential) to grasp the legalities of the Grands Crus here. 'Corton' embraces a dozen different adjacent vineyards, the top of which is actually called Le Corton. The others may be labelled either Corton, or, for example, Corton-Clos du Roi, Corton-Bressandes. On such a big hillside there is inevitably a wide range of style and quality. Bressandes, lowest of the Grands Crus, is considered to produce richer wine (from richer soil) than Clos du Roi above it . . . and so on.

Corton-Charlemagne is a white Grand Cru from some of the same vineyards as red Corton – those on the south slope and the top ones where the soil is paler and more impregnated with lime. Perversely enough there is also a (rarely seen) appellation for white Grand Cru Corton.

True to their national inclinations, the French rate (red) Corton the best wine of the hill, comparing it for sheer force of personality with Chambertin, whereas the British speak of Corton-Charlemagne in the same breath as Le Montrachet. I have certainly been surprised to see French authors mildly liken it to Meursault. It expresses great driving vigour of a kind closer to Montrachet, though with more spice, even earth, and correspondingly less of the simple magic of ripe fruit. It is in the nature of Corton-Charlemagne to hide its qualities and show only its power, as red wines do, for as many as seven or eight years. Red Corton needs keeping as long as the Grands Crus of the Côte de Nuits. The dominant name among Corton growers, both red and white, is Louis Latour, whose press-house and cellars are cut into the foot of the hill and who gives the name of his château, Grancy, to a selection of Corton of even greater than usual power.

GRANDS CRUS

Total area 120.5 acres:
AOC Corton red wines only
Le Charlemagne (41.85)
Le Corton (28.85)
Les Languettes (17.85)
Les Pougets (24.25)
Les Renardes (7)
AOC Corton-Charlemagne
for white wines on (in same
parcels as reds above)
Le Charlemagne (41.85)
Le Corton (28.85)
Les Languettes (17.85)
Les Pougets (24.25)
AOC Corton for red and
white wines (i.e., *not* Corton-
Charlemagne) (177.5 acres):
Les Bressandes (43)
Les Maréchaudes (11)
Les Perrières (23.5)
Les Renardes (28)
Le Clos du Roi (26.5)
Parts (smaller than 10 acres)
of Les Chaumes and
Voirosses, Les Combes, Les
Fiètres, Les Grèves, Les
Meix, Les Meix Lallemand,
Les Paulands, Le Village and
La Vigne au Saint in Aloxe-
Corton.

PREMIERS CRUS

Appellation Aloxe-Corton
Premiers Crus, 72 acres:
Les Chaillots (11.5)
Les Fournières (13.75)
Les Guérets (6.5)
Les Valozières (16)
Les Vercots (10.5)
Maréchaudes, Les Meix,
Basses Moutottes, Les
Paulands, La Toppe au Vert,
Les Grandes Lolières,
Les Petites Lolières

Appellation Communale

222 acres.
Appellation Régionales
13.25 acres.

GROWERS

Pierre André
Adrien Belland
Bonneau du Martray
Bouchard Père & Fils
Maurice Chapuis
Jean-François Coche-Dury
Daudet-Corcelle
Maison Doudet-Naudin
Maison Joseph Drouhin
Dubreuil-Fontaine
Faiveley
Girard-Vollot
Goud de Beaupuis
Antonin Guyon
Maison Louis Jadot
de la Juvinière
Louis Latour
Lequin Roussot
Lucien Jacob Leroy
Machard du Gramont
Prince Florent de Mérode
Moillard
Maison Pierre Ponnelle
Rapet Père et Fils
Daniel Senard
Serrigny
Thomas-Moillard
Tollot-Beaut & Fils
Tollot-Voarick
Charles Viénot
Michel Voarick

Pernand-Vergelesses

The Grand Cru of Pernarnd-Vergelesses is Corton-Charlemagne; there is no red Corton on the western slope of the hill (the only western slope in the whole of the Côte d'Or). But its Premiers Crus are in a completely different situation, directly facing Corton-Charlemagne across the narrow valley that leads up to this hidden village. The Premiers Crus are red; they continue the best vineyards of neighbouring Savigny, and in a sense those of Beaune.

GRAND CRU

Total area 42.6 acres:
AOC Charlemagne (white
only) and AOC Corton (red
only) are both in same parcel:
En Charlemagne (42.5)

PREMIERS CRUS

Total area 138 acres:
Basses Vergelesses (45)
Caradeux (35)
Creux de la Net (7.5)
Fichots (27.5)
Ile des Hautes Vergelesses
(23)
Total area 828 acres.
Appellation Communale
Pernand-Vergelesses: 338
acres.

Appellations Régionales
350 acres

GROWERS

Bonneau du Martray
Chanson Père & Fils
Daudet-Corcelle
Maison Doudet-Naudin
Jacques Germain
Girard-Vollot
Antonin Guyon
Dom. Laleure Piot
Maison Louis Latour
Lucien Jacob Leroy
Rapet Père & Fils
Tollot-Voarick
Michel Voarick

Savigny-Les-Beaune

Savigny, like Pernand-Vergelesses, stops the head of a little valley cut back into the Côte and grows vines on both sides of it. On the Pernand side they face south, on the Beaune side northeast. The best are at the extremities of the parish, where both incline most to the east; respectively Les Vergelesses and Lavières, and La Dominode and Marconnets. The valley is drained by the little river Rhoin. Savigny has a substantial château, a great number of good growers, and best of all a tendency to more moderate prices than its neighbours. Its wines are in every way classic, apt to age, yet never ultra-chic. They need a good vintage to bring them up to their full strength – but whose do not?

PREMIERS CRUS	GROWERS
Total area approx. 530 acres:	Pierre André
Basses Vergelesses (4.5)	G.A.E.C. Simon Bize
Bataillère (also called Aux	Bouchard Père & Fils
Vergelesses) (42.5)	Chandon de Briailles
Charnières (5)	Chanson Père & Fils
Clous (38)	Bruno Clair
Fourneaux	Daudet-Corcelle
Gravains (16.5)	Doudet-Naudin
Guettes (53.5)	P. Dubreuil-Fontaine Père &
Jarrons (37.5)	Fils
Hauts Marconnets (23)	Girard-Vollot
Lavières (45)	Goud de Beaupuis
Bas Marconnets (23)	Antonin Guyon
Narbantons (25)	de la Juvinière
Petits Godeaux (19)	Lucien Jacob Leroy
Peuillets (53)	Machard du Gramont
Redrescut (2.5)	Ch. de Meursault
Serpentières	Jean-Marc Pavelot Père
Talmattes	Pierre Seguin
Appellations Regionales	Tollot-Beaut & Fils
148 acres.	Tollot-Voarick
	Henri de Villamont

Beaune

Beaune offers more temptation than any town to turn an encyclopaedia into a guide book. It begs to be visited. Walking its wobbly streets between its soothing cellars is one of the great joys. The oldest, biggest, grandest and most of the best négociants have their warrens here. They also own the greater part of its wide spread of vineyards. Do not look to Beaune for the most stately or the most flighty wines. 'Franc de goût' is the classic description, which is almost impossible to translate, 'Franc' signifies straight, candid, open, real, downright, forthright and upright. Not dull, though. Young Beaune is already good to drink; as it ages it softens and broadens its bouquet. If there is a pecking order among the Premiers Crus the following are near the top of it: Les Grèves, Fèves, Cras, Champimonts and Clos des Mouches (which also produces a rare and excellent white wine). But nobody would claim to be able to distinguish them all, and more depends on the maker than the site. For this reason the various 'monopoles' of the négociants are usually worth their premium. Their names are prefixed with the word 'Clos'. The three biggest landowners are Bouchard Père & Fils, Chanson and the Hospices de Beaune.

PREMIERS CRUS	
	Avaux (33.5)
	Bas Teurons (17.9)
Total area 795 acres:	Belissand
Aigrots (37)	Blanches Fleurs (23)

ROMANEE – CONTI
A Great Burgundy Estate

All the conundrums of wine come to a head at this extraordinary property. It has been accepted for at least three centuries that wine of inimitable style and fascination comes from one four-and-a-half-acre patch of hill, and different wine, marginally but consistently less fascinating, from the sites around it. Romanée-Conti sounds like a supersuccessful public relations exercise. In some ways it is even organized as one. But there is no trick.

On such a small scale, and with millionaires eager for every drop, it is possible to practise total perfectionism. Without the soil and the site the opportunity would not be there: without the laborious pursuit of perfection it would be lost. A great vineyard like this is largely man-made. The practice in the days of the eighteenth-century Prince de Conti, who gave it his name, was to bring fresh loam up from the pastures of the Saône valley in wagonloads to give new life to the soil. Ironically, today the authorities would forbid so much as a bucketful from outside the appellation. Does this condemn the great vineyard to a gradual decline?

The coproprietors of the Domaine today are Mme Bize-Leroy and M. Aubert de Villaine, whose home is at Bouzeron near Chagny (where he makes

particularly good Aligoté). Their policy is to delay picking until the grapes are consummately ripe, running the gauntlet of the autumn storms and the risk of rot, simply rejecting all the grapes that have succumbed. The proportion of stems put in the vat depends on the season. Fermentation is exceptionally long: from three weeks to even a full month. All the wine is matured in new barrels every year. There is a minimum of racking and filtration. It is indeed, as Mme Bize-Leroy says, the grapes that do it.

As the prices of the Domaine's wines are so spectacularly high, one expects to find them not only exceptional in character but in perfect condition. They are essentially wines for very long bottle-ageing. What is surprising is that they often show signs of instability. It is almost the hallmark of 'D.R.C.' wines that they are instantly recognizable by their exotic opulence, yet rarely identical from bottle to bottle. Too often bottles are in frankly poor condition.

The same elusive quality applies to the wine in your glass. Of a bottle of La Tâche 1962, which has been one of the very best burgundies for years (at least in my view), I noted in 1982: 'Overwhelming high-toned smell of violets to start with, changing within 20 minutes to a more deep and fruity bouquet which seemed at first like oranges, then more like blackcurrants. The flavour was best about half an hour after opening – exotically rich and warm – then seemed to become a bit too alcoholic and lose some of its softness. Very exciting wine – not least for the speed and range of its metamorphoses.'

The precise holdings of the Domaine are as follows:

La Romanée-Conti, 4.45 acres, average production 6,000 bottles.

La Tâche, 14.8 acres, 20,000 bottles.

Richebourg, 8.6 acres, 12,000 bottles.

Grands-Echézeaux, 7.4 acres, 12,000 bottles

Echézeaux, 11.5 acres, 16,000 bottles

Romanée-St-Vivant is rented 'en fermage' from the Domaine Marey-Monge, whose name appears on the label.

Le Montrachet, 1.66 acres, 3,000 bottles.

M. de Villaine conducts the distribution in the United States, which buys 50 per cent of the crop, and Britain, which buys 10 per cent. The house of Leroy takes care of the rest of the world: 5 per cent each goes to Germany, Switzerland and Japan, 5 per cent to other countries, and 20 per cent is sold in France. (See also Leroy, page 136.)

Boucherottes (22)
Bressandes (44)
Cent Vignes (58)
Champs Pimont (41)
Chouacheux (12.5)
Coucherias (57)
Cras (12.5)
A l'Ecu (7.5)
Epenottes (35)
Fèves (10.5)
En Genèt (12.5)
Grèves (79.5)
Sur les Grèves (10)
Marconnets (25.2)
Mignotte (5)
Montée Rouge (41)
Montrevenots (20)
Clos des Mouches (61.4)
Clos de la Mousse (8)
En l'Orme (5)
Perrières (8)
Pertuisots (14)
Reversées (13)
Clos du Roi (34)
Seurey (3)
Sizies (21)
Teurons (38)
Tiélandry (4)
Toussaints (15)
Tuurlains
Vignes Franches (25)
Appellation Communale 316 acres.
Appellations Régionales 370 acres.
Acreages in Beaune are not officially confirmed.

GROWERS

Robert Ampeau & Fils
Besancenot-Mathouillet
Billard-Gonnet
Jean-Marc Boillot
Bouchard Aîné & Fils
Bouchard Père & Fils
Pierre Bourré
Louis Carillon & Fils
Chanson Père & Fils
Coron Père & Fils
Daudet-Corcelle
Maison Doudet-Naudin
Maison Joseph Drouhin
Michel Gaunoux
Jacques Germain
Goud de Beaupuis
Hospices de Beaune
Maison Louis Jadot
Michel Lafarge
Maison Louis Latour
Lycée Viticole
Machard du Gramont
Mazilly Père & Fils
Ch. de Meursault
Moillard
Jean Monnier & Fils
René Monnier
Albert Morot
André Mussy
Patriarche Père & Fils
Jacques Prieur
Rapet Père & Fils
Guy Roulot & Fils
Daniel Senard
René Thévinin-Monthélie & Fils
Thomas-Moillard
Tollot-Beaut & Fils
Tollot-Voarick

Chorey-Les-Beaune
The little appellation of Chorey-Les-Beaune slips off the map down into the plain. Its wine is generally commercialized as Côte de Beaune-Villages.

Côte de Beaune
This appellation was instituted, as it seems, to discover who was dozing during the complexities of Côte de Beaune-Villages (see page 126). It applies only to wine from Beaune (which has no reason to use it) or from another 22 acres adjoining, which appear to be just as deserving. La Grande Châtelaine and the Clos de Topes are the only vineyards I know that use it, for an admirable white as well as red.

Pommard
In the war of words that continually tries to distinguish one village from another, the wines of Pommard seem to have been labelled 'layaux et marchands': 'loyal and commercial'. The suggestion is not of poetic flights. Pommard makes solid, close-grained wines of strong colour, aggressive at first, bending little even with age. Les Rugiens with its iron-red soil is the vineyard with most of these qualities, considered best of the village. Les Epenots, on the edge of Beaune, gives rather easier wine. But there are some proud and decidedly loyal growers in the parish.

PREMIERS CRUS

Total area 309 acres:
Argillières (10)
Arvelets (20)
Bertins (8.5)
Clos Blanc (11)
Boucherottes (4.5)
Chanière (25)
Chanlins Bas (17.5)
Chaponnières (8)
Les Charmots (7)
Combes Dessus (7)
Chanlins Bas (11)
Clos de la Commaraine (10)
Croix Noires (3)
Les Charmots (24)
Derrière St-Jean (0.5)
Fremiers (12.5)
Grand Epenots (25)
Les Jarolières (8)
Clos Micot (7)
Petits Epenots (51)
Pézerolles (14.5)
Platière (6)
Poutures (11)
Refène (6)
Rugines-Bas (15)
Rugiens-Hauts (14)
Saussiles (9)
Clos de Verger (6)
Appellation Communale 522 acres.
Appellations Régionales 823 acres.

GROWERS

Robert Ampeau & Fils
Marquis-d'Angerville
Billard-Gonnet
Jean-Marc Boillot
Pierre Boillot
Bouchard Père & Fils
Y. Clerget
de Courcel
Clos des Epeneaux
F. Gaunoux
Michel Gaunoux
Goud de Beaupuis
Bernard & Louis Glantenay
Lequin Roussot
Maison Leroy
Machard du Gramont
Mazilly Père & Fils
Ch. de Meursault
Michelot-Buisson
Jean Monnier & Fils
René Monnier
Monthélie-Donhairet
de Montille
André Mussy
Parent
Jean Pascal & Fils
Ch. de Pommard
Henri Potinet
Dom. de la Pousse d'Or
Ropiteau-Mignon
Serrigny
Joseph Voillot

Volnay
Corton and Volnay are the extremes of style of the Côte de Beaune. The first regal, robust, deep-coloured and destined to dominate; the second tender, 'lacy', a lighter red with a soft-fruit scent, all harmony and delight. The dictum goes that Volnay is the Chambolle-Musigny of the Côte de Beaune. Personally I find it exact: each is my favourite from its area. To shift the ground a little, Château Latour answers to Corton; Lafite lovers will want Volnay.

The lovely little village hangs higher in the hills than its neighbours, its Premiers Crus on the mid-slopes below. The long ramp of vines that leads down to Meursault contains Les Caillerets, in now-obsolete terms the *tête de cuvée*; something between a Premier Cru and a Grand Cru. Champans, beside it under the village, reaches the same class. There is no clear division between Volnay and its southern neighbours, Meursault in the valley and Monthélie on the hill. The same style of wine, even the same vineyard names continue. Meursault is allowed to use the name of Volnay for red wine grown in its part of Caillerets, Santenots, Petures and Cras (as long as it uses Pinot Noir). To taste them beside the white Premiers Crus of Meursault is to discover that red and white wine are by no means chalk and cheese.

PREMIERS CRUS

Total area 284 acres:
Angles
Bousse d'Or (5)
Brouillards (14)
En Caillerets (7)

Cailleret Dessus (28)
Carelle sous la Chapelle (9.5)
Carelle Dessous (3.5)
Champans (28)
Chanlins (7)
Clos des Chênes (38)
Chevret (15)

Clos des Ducs (6)
Frémiets (18.25)
Lurets (5)
Mitans (10)
En l'Ormeau (11)
Pitures Dessus (9)
Pointes d'Angles (3)
Robardele (7.5)
Ronceret (5)
Santenots (20)
Taille Pied (22)
En Verseuil (1.5)
Le Village (16)
Appellation Communale
 Volnay: 527 acres.

GROWERS

Robert Ampeau & Fils
Marquis-d'Angerville
Pierre Boillot
Bouchard Père & Fils

Y. Clerget
Jean-François Coche-Dury
Jacques Gagnard-
 Delagrange,
 Chassagne-Montrachet
F. Gaunoux
Bernard & Louis Glantenay
Antonin Guyon
Michel Lafarge
Joseph Matrot & Pierre
 Matrot
Ch. de Meursault
René Monnier
Monthélie-Donhairet
de Montille
André Mussy
Jean Pascal & Fils
Henri Potinet-Ampeau
Dom. de la Pousse d'Or
Jacques Prieur
Ropiteau-Mignon

Total area 305 acres:
Appellation Communale
Monthélie: 267 acres,
Appellation Régionales:
103.5 acres

GROWERS

Jean-François Coche-Dury

Monthélie-Donhairet
Ropiteau-Mignon
Robert de Suremain
René Thévenin-Monthélie &
 Fils

Monthélie

Just as Corton-Charlemagne goes on round the corner into Pernand-Vergelesses, so the best Volnay vineyard flows into the lesser-known Monthélie. It changes its name to Les Champs-Fulliots. The centre of interest in the village of Monthélie is its château, the property of its most distinguished grower, Robert de Suremain.

PREMIERS CRUS

77 acres:
Cas Rougeot (1.5)
Champs Fulliot (20)
Duresses (16.5)

Château Gaillard (1.2)
Clos Gauthey (4.5)
Sur La Velle (15)
Meix-Bataille (6.5)
Riottes (1.85)
Taupine (4)
Vignes Rondes (7)

Meursault

If Meursault has convinced itself that it is a town, it fails to convince visitors looking for amenities – still less action. Its streets are a bewildering forest of hoardings to cajole the tourist into the cellars that are its whole *raison d'être*. Levels of commercialism vary. In one property half-hidden with invitations to enter I was told, and curtly, that I could not taste unless I was going to buy. There seemed to be no answer to my mild protest that I could not tell if I was going to buy until I had tasted.

There is a mass of Meursault, and it is mixed. Its model is a drink that makes me thirsty even to think of it; a meeting of softness and succulence with thirst-quenching clarity and 'cut'. A 'Village' Meursault will be mild; the higher up the ladder you go the more authority and 'cut' the wine will have. I am thinking of a '78 Premier Cru Charmes from Joseph Matrot, which at three years old was almost painful to hold in your mouth: this is the authority and concentration of a first-class wine of a great vintage. With age comes rounding out, the onset of flavours people have described with words like oatmeal and hazelnuts and butter; things that are rich but bland.

The white wine vineyards of Meursault are those that continue unbroken into Puligny-Montrachet to the south, and the best those that are nearest to the parish line: Les Perrières, Les Charmes, Les Genevrières. The hamlet of Blagny, higher on the same hill, also contains Meursault Premiers Crus of the top quality: Sous le Dos d'Ane and

Château Meursault

La Pièce sous le Bois – names that seem to express a rustic crudity which is far from being the case. Village wines from high on the hill (Les Tillets, Les Narvaux) are excellent. Like Blagny they are slow to develop.

The red wines of Meursault go to market as Volnay.

PREMIERS CRUS	
Total area 397 acres:	Appellations Régionales 103.5 acres.
Red and white: 215 acres; white only: 272 acres; red only (Volnay): 128 acres.	*GROWERS*
Divided as follows	Robert Ampeau & Fils
Red and white:	Marquis-d'Angerville
Bouchères (10.5)	Pierre Boillot
Caillerets (2.5)	Bouchard Pére & Fils
Charmes Dessous (41.6)	Jean-François Coche-Dury
Charmes Dessus (32.25)	Darnat
Clos des Perrières (74)	F. Gaunoux Fils
Chaumes de Narvaux (0.3)	Antonin Guyon
Cras (8.75)	Jean Joliot & Fils
Genevrières Dessous and	Michel Lafarge
Genevrières Dessus (39.5)	des Comtes Lafon
Gouttes d'Or (13)	Leflaive
Jennelotte (13)	Maison Leroy
Perrières Dessous and	du Duc de Magenta
Perrières Dessus (34)	René Manuel
Petures (26)	Joseph Matrot & Pierre
La Pièce sous le Bois (28)	Matrot
Porusots (10.75)	Mazilly Père & Fils
Porusot Dessus (17.5)	Ch. de Meursault
Santenots Blancs (7.5)	Michelot-Buisson
Santenots du Milieu (20)	Jean Monnier & Fils
Sous le Dos d'Ane (7.5)	René Monnier
Red (Volnay) only:	Monthélie-Donhairet
Les Plures (26)	Henri Potinet-Ampeau
Les Santenots Blancs (7)	Jacques Prieur
Les Santenots Dessous (19)	Ropiteau Frères
Les Santenots du Milieu (20)	Guy Roulot & Fils
Total acreage: 1,257 acres.	Etienne Sauzet
Appellation Communale	René Thévenin-Monthélie &
Meursault: 735 acres.	Fils
	Joseph Voillot

Blagny

Blagny has no appellation of its own, but possesses excellent vineyards in both Meursault and Puligny-Montrachet. Total area 134 acres.

PULIGNY-MONT-RACHET PREMIERS CRUS	
51 acres:	La Jeunelotte (12.5)
La Garenne (24.5)	La Piece sous le Bois (29)
Hameau de Blagny (10.5)	Sous Blagny (5.5)
Sous le Puits (16.75)	Sous le Dos d'Ane (12.5)
Appellations Communales	Appellations Communales
Blagny: 19.5 acres.	Blagny: 4.5 acres.
	GROWERS
MEURSAULT PREMIERS CRUS	Robert Ampeau & Fils
	Leflaive
58 acres:	Joseph Matrot & Pierre
	Matrot
	Jean Pascal & Fils

Auxey-Duresses

The village above and behind Meursault where a valley at right angles to the Côte provides a south slope at the right mid-point of the hill for a limited patch of Premier Cru vineyard, mostly planted in Pinot Noir. Among other growers, the Duc de Magenta produces white wine like very crisp Meursault which I find more exciting than Auxey red. Much of the red, I gather, is sold as Côte de Beaune-Villages. The village also shelters the fabulous stocks of Leroy, the '*Gardien des Grands Millésimes*'.

PREMIERS CRUS	
78 acres:	Auxey-Duresses: 341 acres.
Bas des Duresses (20)	Appellations Régionales 815 acres.
Bréterins	
Duresses (20)	*GROWERS*
Ecusseaux (8)	Robert Ampeau & Fils
Grands Champs (10)	Jean-François Coche-Dury
Reugne (8)	Maison Leroy
Climat or Clos du Val (23)	du Duc de Magenta
Total acreage: 1,235 acres.	Henri Potinet-Ampeau
Appellation Communale	Guy Roulot & Fils
	Roland Thévenin

St-Romain

A pretty little village lurking in the second wave of hills, behind Auxey-Duresses, and only recently promoted to Côte de Beaune-Villages status. It has no Premier Cru land, being too high on the hills, and makes more and better white wine than red.

Puligny-Montrachet

Puligny and Chassagne appear at first sight like Siamese twins linked by their shared Grand Cru, Le Montrachet. But the impression is false. Puligny is a dedicated white-wine parish. Chassagne, despite the Montrachet of its name, earns most of its living from red.

There is no magic by which white wine from Meursault Charmes must taste different from the Puligny Premier Cru Les Combettes, which meets it at the boundary. I can only repeat that I would expect the Puligny-Montrachet to have a slightly more lively taste of fruit, a bit more bite and perhaps a floweriness which is not a Meursault characteristic. Sheaves of old tasting notes tend to contradict each other, so my description is pure Impressionism – all that airy metaphor in dabs of paint representing orchards does seem to have something to do with the taste I cannot describe.

What is more tangible is the superiority of the Premiers Crus. Those of Combettes and Champs Canet at the Meursault end of Puligny, and the part of Blagny that lies in this parish with the appellation Blagny Premier Cru, can be expected to be closer to Meursault in style. A slightly higher premium is normally put on the ones that border the Grands Crus: Le Cailleret and Les Pucelles.

Two of the Grands Crus that are the white-wine climax of Burgundy lie entirely in Puligny-Montrachet; Chevalier-Montrachet, the strip of hill above Montrachet, and Bienvenues-Bâtard-Montrachet, half the shallower slope below. The accepted appreciation of 'Chevalier' is that it has the fine flavour of Montrachet but in less concentrated form (concentration being the hallmark of this grandest of all white wines). The critics do not normally distinguish between Bienvenues and Bâtard (to shorten their unwieldy names). Any such generalization is inevitably overturned by the next tasting of a different vintage or a different grower's wine.

As for Puligny-Montrachet 'Village' without frills – it is still expensive. Is it worth more than Meursault? It is probably more consistent, and a shade more aggressive in flavour. In 1982 Meursault came about midway among the prices of premium California Chardonnays; Puligny-Montrachet near the top.

GRANDS CRUS

Total area 56.5 acres:
Bâtard-Montrachet (15)
Bienvenues-Bâtard-
   Montrachet (9)
Chevalier-Montrachet (18)
Montrachet (10)

PREMIERS CRUS

Total area 247 acres:
Cailleret (9.75)
Chalumeaux (14.25)
Champ Canet (8)
Clavoillon (13.5)
Combettes (16.5)
Folatières (43)
Garenne (28)
Hameau de Blagny (11)
Pucelles (16.5)
Referts (34)
Sous le Puits (16.75)
Appellation Communale
Puligny-Montrachet: 272
acres.
Appellations Régionales
606 acres.

GROWERS

Robert Ampeau & Fils
Adrien Belland
Jean-Marc Boillot
Bouchard Père & Fils
Louis Carillon & Fils
Chartron & Trebuchet
Maison Joseph Drouhin
Maison Louis Jadot
Leflaive
Maison Leroy
Lycée Viticole
du Duc de Magenta
Jean Monnier & Fils
René Monnier
Jean Pascal & Fils
Jacques Prieur
Dom. de la Romanée-Conti
Ropiteau Frères
St-Michel
Etienne Sauzet
Roland Thévenin

Chassagne-Montrachet

Almost half of the Grands Crus Le Montrachet and Bâtard-Montrachet and the whole of Criots-Bâtard-Montrachet occupy the hill corner that ends the parish to the north. Unfortunately, the steep south-facing slope that runs at right angles to them, along the road to St-Aubin in the hills, has not enough soil for vines. If this were the Douro there would be terraces. Between here and the village there is some Premier Cru land, but the famous wines begin again where the Côte picks up its momentum and its tilt in the Clos St-Jean above the little township. Caillerets, Ruchottes and Morgeot are names seen on expensive and memorable white bottles. Clos St-Jean, La Boudriotte . . . in fact all the rest stress red.

Any association of ideas that suggests that red Chassagne should be a light wine is quite wrong. Far from being a gentle fade-out from Volnay, Chassagne returns to the meat and muscle of Corton or the Côte de Nuits. The best example I know of the brilliant duality of this land is the Duc de Magenta's Clos de la Chapelle, part of the Premier Cru Abbaye de Morgeot, which is half red and half white, and (at least in the early 1970s) was brilliant on both counts. Red Chassagne, moreover, sells at the price of the lesser-known villages – much cheaper than the grand names of the Côte de Nuits and every bit as satisfying.

GRANDS CRUS

Total area 28 acres
(all white):
Bâtard-Montrachet (14)
Criots-Bâtard-Montrachet (4)
Montrachet (10)

PREMIERS CRUS

Total area 395 acres:
(both red and white, except
that En Cailleret produces
red only and Cailleret, also
known as Chassagne,

produces white only):
Abbaye de Morgeot
Boudriotte (45)
Brussonnes (45)
Cailleret (15)
En Cailleret (15)
Champs Gain (71)
Chenevottes (28)
Fernand Coffinet
Grandes Ruchottes (7.5)
Macherelles (10)
Maltroie (23)
Morgeot (9.75)
Romanée

Clos St-Jean (36)
Vergers (23)
Appellation Communale 442
   acres.

GROWERS

Bachelet-Ramonet Père &
   Fils
Adrien Belland
Louis Carillon & Fils

Jacques Gagnard-Delagrange
J.N. Gagnard Dupont
Vincent Leflaive
Lequin-Roussot
du Duc de Magenta
Ch. de la Maltroye
Albert Morey & Fils
Jacques Prieur
Ramonet-Prudhon
Etienne Sauzet

Le Montrachet

All critics agree that the best Montrachet is the best white burgundy. In it all the properties that make the mouth water in memory and anticipation are brought to a resounding climax. The first quality that proclaims it at a tasting with its neighbours is a concentration of flavour. I have wondered how much this is due to its singular site and its soil and how much to the regulations (and common sense) that keep its crop to a minimum. There is little doubt that other good vineyards could pack more punch if their keepers kept them more meanly pruned and fertilized, picked late and used only the best bunches. Such economics only work for a vineyard whose wine is as good as sold before it is made, at almost any price. The principal owners of Le Montrachet are the Marquis de Laguiche (whose wine is handled by Drouhin of Beaune), Baron Thénard of Givry, Bouchard Père & Fils, Fleurot-Larose of Santenay, Roland Thévenin and the Domaine de la Romanée-Conti.

St-Aubin

St-Aubin is a twin to St-Romain, a village tucked into the first valley behind the Côte but with a slight advantage of situation that gives it some Premiers Crus, mainly exploited for red wine. The village of Gamay (presumed source of the grape that makes Beaujolais but is a taint to the Côte d'Or) contributes about half the land in this appellation. Raoul Clerget and Hubert Lamy make a speciality of it, but the greater part is sold as Côte de Beaune-Villages.

Santenay

It is a conceit, I know, but I have always found the names of the villages of Burgundy a useful clue to the nature of their wines. Chambertin has a drum-roll sound, Chambolle-Musigny a lyrical note, Pommard sounds precisely right for its tough red wine and so does Volnay for its more silky produce. Santenay sounds like good health. (Funnily enough it has a far-from-fashionable spa that treats rheumatism and gout.) Healthiness is the right sort of image to attach to its wines. They are rather plain, even-flavoured with no great perfume or thrills but good solid drinking. At their best, in Les Gravières, La Comme and Le Clos de Tavannes, they are in the same class as Chassagne-Montrachet, weighty and long-lived. Other parts of the parish with stonier, more limey soil have paler reds and a little white wine.

PREMIERS CRUS

Total area 306 acres
(red and white):
Beauregard (82)
Beaurepaire (42.5)
Comme (80)
Clos Foubard
Gravières (72.5)

Maladière (33)
Passe Temps (31)
Clos des Tavannes (66)
Appelation Communale 628
   acres

GROWERS

Bart

Adrien Belland
Fleurot-Larose
Lequin-Roussot
Mestre Père & Fils

René Monnier
de la Pousse d'Or
St-Michel

Maranges

This new (1989) appellation covers the three rather forlorn little villages which share the vineyard Les Maranges, along the hill just west of Santenay and to their regret just over the *département* line of the Côte d'Or, in the outer darkness of Saône-et-Loire. Their names are Sampigny, Dézize and Cheilly – but Côte de Beaune-Villages is more likely to appear on their labels. The wines are well structured with deep colour, generally quite tannic. They age well and make splendid drinking when 8 years old, as the local clientele buying direct have proved time and again. In an average year some 130,000 cases make use of this appellation.

CHEILLY-LES-MARANGES

Premiers Crus (red and white):
Boutières, Maranges and Plantes de Maranges (together 108 acres)

DEZIZE-LES-MARANGES

Premier Cru (red and white):
Maranges (150)

SAMPIGNY-LES-MARANGES

Premiers Crus (red and white):
Clos des Rois (36)
Maranges (35)

Côte de Beaune-Villages

All the villages of the Côte de Beaune, with the exception of Beaune, Pommard, Volnay and Aloxe-Corton, have this as a fallback appellation in red wine (only).

GROWERS AND MERCHANTS

The almost literally priceless land of the Côte d'Or is broken up into innumerable small units of ownership, variously expressed as ares (a hundredth of a hectare) and centiares (a hundredth of an are) or as *ouvrées* (an old measure which is one twenty-fourth of a hectare, or about a tenth of an acre). These little plots come about by the French system of inheritance, by the size of the capital needed to buy more, and by the dread of local disasters, which make it inadvisable to put all your eggs in one basket.

They mean that a grower who has, say, 20 acres may well have them in 30 different places – in many cases just a few rows of vines separated from his others in the same vineyard.

Meanwhile, the precious land is also divided by ancient custom into a jigsaw of *'climats'*, or fields, sometimes with natural and obvious boundaries, sometimes apparently at random. Each *'climat'* is a known local character with a meaning and value to the farmers that is hard for an outsider to grasp.

Overlay the one pattern on the other and you have the fragmentation of ownership which bedevils buyers of burgundy. Whereas in Bordeaux a château is a consistent unit doing one (or at most two) things on a reasonably large scale, a Burgundy domaine is often a man and his family coping with a dozen or more different wines with different needs and problems. If he is a good husbandman of vines his talent does not necessarily extend to the craftsmanship of the cellar – or vice versa. For any number of reasons, inconsistency is almost inevitable.

There are important exceptions in the form of bigger vineyards with richer owners. But the concept of the little man trying to do everything is fundamental. It explains the importance of the négociants or 'shippers', whose traditional role is to

buy the grower's new wine, mature it and blend it with others of the same vineyard or village or district to make marketable quantities of something consistent.

It does not need much imagination to see that an unscrupulous merchant could get away with almost anything under these conditions. Consumers have probably always, since Roman times, had grounds for complaint. Now the old and profitable game of 'stretching' the limited supplies with imports from the south is made very much harder by the application of the strict appellation laws. But there is still plenty of room for manoeuvre in the area of quality. There are government inspectors, but nobody pretends there is comprehensive and effective inspection.

When most consumers hear that merchants are venal their reaction is to look for authenticity from the growers, direct. Bottling at the domaine has been presented as the answer. It brings us back, though, to the basic question: who is more competent and more conscientious? Ownership of a corner of a fine and famous field does not carry with it a technical degree in wine-making or *'élévage'* – the 'bringing up' of wine in the cellar – or bottling.

It can be a depressing experience to taste a set of broker's samples submitted to a négociant from good vineyards even after a good vintage. A considerable proportion of the wines are likely to be either oversugared or in poor condition, or both.

The greatest change of the past decade in Burgundy, though, has been the growing competence of a younger generation of growers, well-schooled and innovative, who are making often small lots of far better wine than Burgundy has probably ever seen.

André Gaget of Maison Louis Jadot

Domaine Pierre Amiot & Fils
21220 Gevrey-Chambertin

A traditionalist grower with small plots in Grands Crus Clos de la Roche and Clos St-Denis as well as Gevrey-Chambertin Les Cambolles and Chambolle-Musigny. 26 acres in all.

Robert Ampeau & Fils
6 rue du Cromin 21190 Meursault.

An outstanding domaine of 25 acres whose white wines are particularly respected. The best known are the whites from Meursault Perrières, Charmes and La Pièce sous le Bois (partly in Blagny), 11 acres in all, and 2 acres in Puligny Combettes; wines with a good 10-year life span. Unusually M. Ampeau only sells wines well bottle-aged in his own cellars. Reds include 1 acre of Beaune Clos du Roi, 4 of Savigny Premier Cru (Lavières and Fourneaux) and 4 of Pommard. 'Its is always difficult,' says M. Ampeau, 'to talk objectively about your own wine.'

Pierre André
Château de Corton-André, 21420 Aloxe-Corton.

Négociants and growers on the largest scale. Pierre André founded La Reine Pédauque. His 'château' at Corton is the centre for the 74-acre estate, which includes parts of Clos Vougeot (2.6 acres), Corton (including Clos du Roi, Combes and Charlemagne), and Savigny Premier Cru Clos des Guettes (7.5 acres). Products also include Bourgogne Réserve Pierre André, Mâcon-Villages and Supérieur 'Domaine du Prieuré de Jocelyn'; Fleurie 'Domaine de la Treille', Beaujolais-Villages, Coteaux du Tricastin from the Rhône, etc. Sales are largely to restaurants and private clients in France, with 35% exports.

Domaine Marquis-d'Angerville
Volnay, 21190 Meursault.

The impeccable domaine of a totally dedicated nobleman: 28 acres of Volnay Premier Cru, 1 of Pommard and 2.5 of Meursault Santenots – a rare appellation and a singularly succulent white. The Monopole Clos des Ducs is an unusual steep and chalky 5.9-acre vineyard whose wine is noticeably alcoholic, tends to be pale and to my mind misses the velvet of the best Volnay. I prefer the domaine's more sumptuous Champans (from 10 acres). All its wines are beautifully made. I believe the greater part is exported to America, Great Britain and Switzerland.

Domaine de l'Arlot
Prémeaux, 21700 Nuits-St-Georges

Formerly the property of négociants Jules Belin, the domaine is now owned by the insurance group AXA (*see* Ch. Pichon-Baron, Bordeaux, etc.). The director in Burgundy, Jean-Pierre De Smet, worked for many years at Domaine Dujac. The 32-acre domaine comprises three 'monopoles' – Nuits-St-Georges Premiers Crus 'Clos de l'Arlot' (red and white) and 'Clos des Forêts St Georges' and Côte de Nuits-Villages 'Clos du Chapeau'. 1988s are outstandingly good value.

Domaine du Comte Armand
21630 Pommard

see Clos Epeneaux.

Domaine Denis Bachelet
21220 Gevrey-Chambertin

A young man's tiny (7-acre) enterprise in Gevrey-Chambertin, Premier Cru les Corbeaux and Charmes-Chambertin. But brilliantly stylish wines.

Domaine Bachelet-Ramonet Père & Fils
Chassagne-Montrachet, 21190 Meursault.

A domaine founded in 1979 by fourth-generation growers in Chassagne with 25 acres, including parcels of Bâtard-Montrachet, Chassagne Les Caillerets, Ruchottes and La Romanée, La Grande Montagne of the highest land and Morgeot, Clos St-Jean and Clos de la Boudriotte (and last two red) at the foot of the slopes. The Bâtard is extremely fine wine.

Domaine Bart
24 rue de Mazy, 21160 Marsannay-La-Côte.

André Bart is handing his property to his children, Odile and Martin, and it is now known as Domaine Bart. The domaine has 32 acres, including 20 at Marsannay, 3.5 at Fixin, 4 at Santenay and 2 in the Grands Crus Bonnes Mares and Clos de Bèze. Rosé de Marsannay, and

Marsannay Blanc and Fixin Premier Cru Les Hervelets are the specialities.

Thomas Bassot
21220 Gevrey-Chambertin

Old-established (1850) négociants at Gevrey-Chambertin now belonging to the Swiss firm of Ziltener (q.v.).

Domaine Adrien Belland
21590 Santenay

In 1954 Adrien Belland's father divided his domaine between his four sons, and the present domaine of 27 acres includes parcels of one Chambertin Grand Cru, three Corton Grands Crus, three Santenay Premiers Crus and one Chassagne-Montrachet Premier Cru.

Domaine Bertagna
Rue du Vieux Château 21640 Vougeot.

Owners of some of the limited area of Vougeot Premier Cru outside the Clos Vougeot, including the 'monopole' Clos de la Perrière (5 acres), the hill just below Le Musigny. I have found this wine much better than many other growers' Clos Vougeot. Bertagna have a total of 27 acres, with 1 in Clos St-Denis and 5 in Chambertin.

Domaine Besancenot-Mathouillet
21200 Beaune

A small (27-acre) domaine with high standards created not long ago by a Beaune citizen of great repute and scholarship, M. Besancenot, whose advice I gratefully acknowledge. He died, alas, in 1981. 17 acres are in Beaune Premiers Crus (Bressandes, Clos du Roi, Toussaints, etc.), of which half is a parcel of Cent-Vignes with venerable vines, some 50 years old, which can give one of the best wines of Beaune. A part of the domaine which is rented includes a little Aloxe-Corton Premier Cru and 2.5 acres of Pernand-Vergelesses, where there are some vines of Pinot Blanc.

Maison Albert Bichot
6 bis, boulevard Jacques Copeau, 21200 Beaune.

The biggest exporter of burgundy, with 85% of its 100-million-franc turnover in exports. The firm was founded in Beaune in 1831 and in 1927 opened an office in Bordeaux (where it owns the firm of Chantecaille). As a négociant Bichot also trades under the names of several of the companies it has taken over: Paul Bouchard, Charles Drapier, Rémy Gauthier, Bouchot-Ludot, Léon Rigault, Maurice Dard, etc. As a grower, Bichot owns 2 domaines: Clos Frantin in the Côte d'Or and Long-Depaquit in Chablis. The Domaine du Clos Frantin, based at Vosne-Romanée, has 23 acres, scattered through Gevrey-Chambertin, Richebourg, Clos de Vougeot, Grands-Echézeaux, Echézeaux, Vosne-Romanée Les Malconsorts, Nuits-St-Georges and Corton Charlemagne. *See also* Lupé-Cholet. Their own wines are first-rate; as négociants they sell all sorts.

Domaine Billard-Gonnet
21630 Pommard

12.5 acres of the 24.7-acre domaine is scattered between seven Pommard Premiers Crus including 3.7 acres in Le Clos de Verger. There is also a small parcel of Beaune Premier Cru Clos des Mouches (blanc).

Simon Bize & Fils
21420 Savigny-Les-Beaune

A domaine of 25 acres entirely in Savigny, with 12.5 acres in the Premiers Crus Vergelesses (5.4 acres), Guettes, Talmettes, Fournaux and Marconnets. Father and son go to the length of buying new barrels for a third of their wine, which might be taken as a model of the lively, crisp style of Savigny. Vergelesses is their speciality. They also make 1,600 cases of a Bourgogne Blanc.

Domaine Henri Boillot
Volnay, 21190 Meursault.

A total of 53 acres makes this a major domaine in Volnay (10 acres), Puligny-Montrachet (10 acres, including the 'monopole' Clos de la Mouchère) and Pommard Premier Cru (5.5 acres).

Jean-Marc Boillot
21630 Pommard

Jean-Marc was given vines by his grandfather, Henri Boillot, when he divided his domaine among his grandchildren. Jean-Marc's share includes parcels in Beaune Premier Cru Les Montrevenots, Pommard Premier Cru Les Saucilles (perhaps his top wine) and Rully Premier Cru Blanc Montpalais.

Domaine Lucien Boillot & Fils
21220 Gevrey-Chambertin

Two more grandchildren of Henri Boillot, Louis and Pierre, run this flourishing domaine in Gevrey, Nuits, Pommard, Volnay and Fixin. Excellent quality.

Pierre Boillot
21190 Meursault

A 15.6-acre domaine that includes 1.3 acres of Meursault-Charmes Premier Cru, where the vines are 60 years old, and half an acre of Meursault Goutte d'Or Premier Cru as well as very tasty, powerful Pommard and Volnay Santenots.

Jean Claude Boisset
21701 Nuits-St-Georges

A recent (1961) foundation with ultramodern methods and equipment and huge stocks, including fine Côte d'Or wines as well as Côte du Rhône, Beaujolais, etc. A small domaine ('Claudine Deschamps') of 17 acres is in Nuits Premier Cru Les Damodes, Gevrey-Chambertin, Côte de Nuits-Villages and appellation Bourgogne. The house also buys grapes, and has made some important purchases of wine at the Hospices de Beaune. It also owns the Nuits négociant house of Charles Vienot (q.v.). Secondary labels include Honoré Lavigne, Blanchard de Cordambles, Georges Meurgey and Louis Deschamps.

Domaine Bonneau du Martray
Pernand-Vergelesses, 21420 Savigny-Les-Beaune.

One of the biggest producers of the inimitable Corton-Charlemagne, with a solid block of 22 acres making some 4,000 cases a year, and an adjacent 5 acres giving red Corton Grand Cru. The famous Cuvée François de Salins, the costliest wine of the Hospices de Beaune, comes from the same prime hill-corner site. The domaine's wine is made in an unpretentious cellar in Pernand by the owner, Comte Jean Le Bault de la Morinière, using a modern press but otherwise strictly traditional methods, including new barrels for fermentation. New cellars are currently being built to hold more bottles, in order to put the Grands Crus on the market at 7–10 years according to vintage. The Corton-Charlemagne behaves more like a red, ageing majestically. Three-star restaurants, alas, offer it at 3 years old when it should be 10. 90% is exported – I hope to people with cellars.

Bouchard Aîné & Fils
36 rue Ste-Marguerite, 21203 Beaune.

The smaller Bouchard, although almost as old as the giant. A domaine with 57 acres of (all red) vines in Mercurey (Le Clos la Marche and La Vigne du Chapitre) and Beaune, which also makes (in Beaune) the wines of the Domaine Marion at Fixin (Clos du Chapitre, La Mazière and a little Chambertin-Clos de Bèze). Their wines are generally considered correct rather than exciting. A second trade name is H. Audiffred.

Bouchard Père & Fils
Au Château, 21202 Beaune.

The biggest domaine in Burgundy and one of the best négociants, run by Bouchards from father to son since 1731. No less than 190 of their 247 acres (Domaines du Château de Beaune) are Grands Crus and Premiers Crus; their magnificent cellars in the old fortress of Beaune itself hold stocks of 20,000 *pièces* (barrels) or 6 million bottles.

Their biggest holdings are in Beaune, where their 43 acres of Premiers Crus include the 'monopoles' of the famous 10-acre Grèves Vigne de l'Enfant Jésus, the 8-acre Clos de la Mousse and the 5-acre Clos St-Landry. Other large plots are 10 acres of Marconnets and about 6 each of Cent Vignes and Teurons. Wine from smaller parcels is made and sold as Beaune du Château Premier Cru. Beyond Beaune their principal parcels are 17 acres in Corton (some 9 of red Corton and 8 of Corton-Charlemagne), 10 in Savigny Les Lavières, 13.5 in Volnay (of which 10 is Caillerets), a little Pommard, and important plots of 2.5 acres in Le Montrachet and 5 – the biggest part – in Chevalier-Montrachet. Among their more notable wines are Volnay Caillerets labelled as 'Ancienne Cuvée Carnot', untypically foursquare and long-lived Volnay from very old vines. They also have exclusive distribution rights over the Grand Cru La Romanée, an excellent Premier Cru Nuits-St-Georges, 'Clos St-Marc', and two thirds of the production of Bourgogne Aligoté Bouzeron (a new appellation, since 1979).

All Bouchard's domaine reds are aged in new barrels, for a relatively short period to keep them fruity while adding the scent of the oak. Their domaine wines, while sometimes more powerful than elegant, have never shown the slightest sign of quantity chasing out quality. While such important houses as this, Jadot, Latour and Drouhin maintain their standards, there is no danger of burgundy declining in its influence and appeal. 65% of Bouchard's wines are exported.

Pierre Bourée Fils
21220 Gevrey-Chambertin.

Pierre Bourée is both a négociant and a grower. The major part (5.2 acres) of the 9.8-acre domaine is in Clos de Justice. 60–90% of production is exported.

Lionel J. Bruck
6 quai Dumorey, 21700 Nuits-St-Georges.

A flourishing merchant house which has contracts with growers totalling 110 acres in the Côte d'Or, including the 15-acre Domaine of the Château de Vosne-Romanée, a parcel of Corton Clos du Roi and 17 acres of the Savigny Premier Cru Les Guettes. The same firm uses the name F. Hasenklever.

Domaine Georges Bryczek
Morey St-Denis, 21220 Gevrey-Chambertin.

A Pole, and a sculptor as well as a grower, with the 8-acre Premier Cru Clos-Sorbés and a parcel of Morey-Village where he makes strapping wines from old vines. Bryczek caused a stir by dedicating a 'Cuvée du Pape'.

Domaine Alain Burquet
21220 Gevrey-Chambertin

A small domaine of Village vines that has grown from 5 acres to 15 since beginning in 1974. The average age of the vines is 50 years. The *'cuvée vieilles vignes'* is considered better than some Premiers Crus in the village.

Domaine Camus Père & Fils
21220 Gevrey-Chambertin

A family property built up between 1860 and 1934 to a total of 42 acres, including 4 of Chambertin and 7.5 of Charmes-Chambertin, with parcels of Latricières and Mazis. M. Camus uses a long maceration of the skins under a blanket of carbon dioxide to extract maximum colour and flavour. They produce, on average, 7,500 cases a year.

Louis Carillon & Fils
Puligny-Montrachet, 21190 Meursault.

A proud little family domaine, going back 350 years, with 3 generations, Robert, Louis and Jacques, all working together on their 29 acres. They include a little patch of Bienvenues-Bâtard-Montrachet, 6 acres of Puligny Premier Cru and 12 of Puligny 'Village', with smaller parcels of Chassagne and Mercurey. Half the crop is sold in barrels to négociants, half in bottles to clients, who consider the name Carillon close behind the great domaines of Laflaive and Sauzet. Carillon's Bienvenues-Batard-Montrachet 1986 is particularly respected.

Yves Chaley
Curtil-Vergy, 21220 Gevrey-Chambertin.

A skilful grower of the lighter wines of the Hautes Côtes de Nuits with 32 acres of Pinot Noir and Chardonnay, with smaller parcels of Aligoté and Gamay. The red is vatted for 12 days in stainless steel and aged 18 months in oak barrels. Five years is a good age for it. The fruity white is bottled at 1 year for immediate drinking.

Château de Chambolle-Musigny
Chambolle-Musigny

The property of the Mugnier family, taken in hand by Fréderic Mugnier in 1984. His wines from Bonnes Mares, Le Musigny and Chambolle-Musigny Premiers Crus (Amoureuses and Les Fuées) are some of the finest of the commune, and steadily improving.

Domaine Chandon de Briailles
1 rue Soeur Goby, 21420 Savigny-Les-Beaune.

An important 32-acre property, largely in the best red-wine vineyards of Savigny (Les Lavières) and the neighbouring Ile des Vergelesses in Pernand. Also considerable owners in Corton with 7.5 acres in Bressandes, 2.5 in Clos du Roi and a little Corton Blanc.

Chanson Père & Fils
10 rue Paul Chanson, 21201 Beaune.

Négociants and growers (founded 1750) with a fine domaine of 110 acres, 60 of them in Beaune Premiers Crus, 10 in Savigny and 19 in Pernand-Vergelesses (which include 6 acres of Chardonnay). Their best wines are perhaps their Beaune Clos des Fèves (9.3 acres), Teurons (13 acres) and Bressandes (5.2 acres), but they have parts of all the best Beaune '*climats*' and make excellent Savigny Premier Cru La Dominode. The taste of the company is for wine aged in wood until it seems to lack fruit and colour, but will mature, as they assure us, '*sans surprise*'. It is an old-fashioned way of producing stable wines for long keeping.

Maurice Chapuis
21420 Aloxe-Corton

Maurice, son of Louis (who retired in 1985) farms 22 acres, of which he owns 2.5 and rents the rest. They include 9.5 acres of Corton-Charlemagne, producing 250 cases a year. Nearly 8 acres of Corton produce 700 cases of red. This, together with over 10 acres of Aloxe-Corton and 2 acres of Aloxe-Corton Premier Cru, accounts for more than half of their total production. White wine fermented in barrels; red in open vats to be *vins de garde*. His 1976 Corton was outstanding, as are the '83 and '88.

Chartron & Trebuchet
Puligny-Montrachet, 21190 Meursault

The recent marriage of the Chartron domaine and the négociant Trebuchet, much talked about for oaky wines very much to some clients' taste.

F. Chauvenet
6 rue de Chaux, 21700 Nuits-St-Georges.

One of the larger merchant houses, founded in 1853, currently connected with Margnat, the table-wine company. It owns 108 acres at the Domaine de Pérignon in the Yonne (near Chablis) making Passe-tout-grains, and large estates in the Côtes du Rhône and Corsica. Also 2 acres in Nuits-St-Georges. Its most famous product is Red Cap sparkling red burgundy, which has a big Canadian market. It has the biggest share of the Burgundy direct-sales business in France and Belgium. Other names include Chevillot (selection of the Hôtel de la Poste at Beaune) and a 50% share (with the Max family) in the brand Louis Max.

Robert Chevillon
68 rue Felix Tisserand, 21700 Nuits-St-Georges.

A typical, family-run 32-acre estate, part owned and part rented, producing splendid Premier Cru Nuits-St-Georges from (especially) Les Cailles, Les St-Georges, Les Vaucrains, etc. His cousins Georges and Michel Chevillon also make fine Nuits-St-Georges.

Domaine Clair-Daü
21160 Marsannay-la-Côte

In 1985 the Domaine, which until then was probably the largest family-owned property in the Côte d'Or, was divided between Bruno Clair (q.v.) and his aunt, who sold her share to Louis Jadot (q.v.) the same year. These wines are sold under the Domaine Louis Jadot label.

Bruno Clair
21160 Marsannay-la-Côte

When Domaine Clair Daü was divided in 1985, Bruno Clair received 43.6 acres, and he now sells his wines under his own name in conjunction with his neighbour, André Geoffroy, who contributes an unusual Fixin Blanc, Clos Moreau. He has just under an acre of Chambertin Clos de Bèze Grand Cru, and 8.5 acres of Premiers Crus in Givry, Gevrey-Chambertin and Savigny-les-Beaunes (The excellent Les Dominodes). There are also 14.5 acres of

Marsannay rouge, 7 acres of Marsannay rosé and small parcels of Marsannay blanc, Vosne-Romanée and Morey St-Denis, rouge and blanc.

Domaine Y. Clerget
Volnay, 21190 Meursault.

A domaine of 13 acres with an incredibly long history: the Clergets made wine in Volnay in 1268, the time of the Crusades. The pride of the house is their resounding Pommard Rugiens. Other parcels are in the Premier Cru Carelle sous la Chapelle and Volnay Caillerets and Meursault 'Village'. Yvan Clerget only bottles good vintages. 90% is exported to countries including Australia and Great Britain.

Georges Clerget
21640 Vougeot

Owner of 7.5 acres and farmer of another 2.5: a very small domaine divided with equal (1.25-acre) plots in Chambolle-Musigny Premier Cru Charmes, Chambolle 'Village', Vougeot Premier Cru, Morey St-Denis and Vosne-Romanée. The rented parts are 2.5 acres in Echézeaux and a bare third of an acre in Bonnes Mares. The 'Charmes' is M. Clerget's own favourite; he does not like his wines too 'hard'. He removes three quarters of the stems and ferments for 8-10 days.

Raoul Clerget
St-Aubin, 21190 Meursault.

For sheer antiquity the Clergets have no competitors. This house was apparently founded in 1268. They are now growers in a moderate (42-acre) way and négociants in quite a big one with a range of Côte d'Or wines of a high standard, and Beaujolais, table wines, and one of Burgundy's best Crèmes de Cassis. Their St-Aubin (red and white) is a house speciality. 1979 was the first vintage of their own replanted St-Aubin Domaine de Pimont (27 acres).

Jean-François Coche-Dury
21190 Meursault

Jean-François is the third generation of this 21-acre domaine that includes a small parcel of Meursault-Perrières Grand Cru. He has an almost fanatical following for his powerful and oaky, yet wonderfully balanced white wines – even his Bourgogne Blanc. His Volnay and Auxey-Duresses reds are less well-known.

Fernand Coffinet
Chassagne-Montrachet, 21190 Meursault

A family domaine that was founded about 200 years ago. Now there are just 5.5 acres (Chassagne-Montrachet white and red, and Batard Montrachet), the original holding having recently been divided up. 80% of the wine is exported.

Coron Père & Fils
B.P. 117, 21200 Beaune.

Three generations of Corons ran their house until 1970, when it was inherited by Bernard Dufouleur. It changed hands again in 1989 and is now owned by the Lanvin family, under the direction of Claude Lanvin. Principal sites are on the Côte de Beaune and Côte de Nuits. They have exclusive distribution of Château de Loché in Macon including 7 acres of Pouilly Loché.

Domaine de Courcel
21630 Pommard

The Courcels have made Pommard here for 400 years. Their 20-acre domaine includes the 12-acre 'Grand Clos des Epenots' within the Premier Cru Epenots, and 2.5 acres of Rugiens. The vats, vertical press and cellars are strictly traditional. I opened a 16-year-old bottle of 1966 Courcel Rugiens to find out where I should be pitching my enthusiasm. Pommard is not normally my favourite burgundy. This wine was astonishingly dark and pure 'burgundy' red. The smell and taste were stubborn and inaccessible on first opening. After 2 hours in a decanter it began to give off a seductive creamy smell of nuts and damsons, which developed into what Michael Broadbent describes as fish-glue – in any case the smell of very fine old burgundy. Yet curiously the flavour remained austere and straight backed. Good but not great.

Domaine Pierre Damoy
20 rue des Forges, 21190 Meursault.

The biggest single share of Chambertin and Clos de Bèze (14 acres) belongs to the Damoy family. (Their other interests include the Château du Moulin à Vent in Beaujolais and Château La Tour de By in the Médoc.) Apart from 170 cases of Chambertin and 1,800 of Clos de Bèze of high quality, they make 900 of Chapelle-Chambertin and 600 of a Gevrey-Chambertin 'Monopole' Clos du Tamisot. Their wines are fine, but seem to lack real Grand Cru authority.

Domaine Darnat
20 rue des Forges, 21190 Meursault.

The owner of the tiny 'Clos Richemont', and a small parcel of the Premier Cru Goutte D'Or. Darnat also has another acre of Meursault 'Village' and a little Bourgogne Blanc. Foreign investment and the support of wine enthusiasts have resulted in recent improvements to the estate.

Domaine Daudet-Corcelle
21420 Savigny-Les-Beaune

The 12 acres are split between 10 sites, including a Grand Cru (Corton Charlemagne) and 7 Premiers Crus.

Domaine Delagrange-Bachelet
Chassagne-Montrachet, 21190 Meursault.

One of the best-known domaines in Chassagne, of 25 acres which include 1.25 acres each of Bâtard- and Criots-Bâtard-Montrachet, 2.5 of Premier Cru Caillerets, 5 of Morgeot (red and white) and small plots of Volnay and Pommard Premiers Crus. I have had impeccable white wines, both the grand Bâtard and 'Village' Chassagne-Montrachet, from this domaine.

Maison Doudet-Naudin
1 rue Henri Cyrot, 21420 Savigny-Les-Beaune.

A house associated with 'old-fashioned', very dark-coloured, concentrated, almost 'jammy' wines which have had a great following in Britain in the past. Berry Bros. & Rudd of St. James's bottled many of them. To today's taste, looking for fresh grapey flavours, they seem 'cooked'. But they last, and 20-year-old bottles can be richly velvety and full of character. Their own domaine of 12 acres is in Savigny (Les Guettes, red, and Le Redrescut, a not-very-graceful white), in Beaune Clos du Roy, Corton Charlemagne, Corton Maréchaudes and Pernand-Vergelesses. Other names are Albert Brenot and Georges Germain.

Maison Joseph Drouhin
7 rue d'Enfer, 21000 Beaune.

A leading family-owned (founded in 1880) négociant with one of the biggest domaines in Burgundy, augmented by 89 acres in Chablis. Now a total of 151 acres comprises Chablis, Chablis Grand Cru, Chablis Premier Cru, Chorey-Les-Beaune, Beaune Premier Cru, Beaune Clos des Mouches, Corton Charlemagne, Corton Bressandes, Volnay Clos des Chenes, Clos de Vougeot, Chambolle-Musigny Premier Cru, Chambertin en Griotte, Chambertin Clos de Bèze, Chambolle Musigny Amoureuses, Echèzeaux, Grands Echézeaux, Musigny and Bonnes Mares. The head of the house is Robert Drouhin.

The whole gamut of wines is very conscientiously made, rising to the appropriate peaks and never falling below fine quality in the Grands Crus. The speciality of the house is the excellent Beaune Clos des Mouches: long-lived, full-bodied wine, both red and white. After a serious fire in 1972 things did not go well for a while, but from 1976 on standards are first class. Red wines are fermented in oak at a fairly high temperature with at least half of their stems, and macerated for up to 2 weeks. New barrels are used for half the red and a quarter of the white. The best vintages (e.g. '85 red, '88 red and white, '85 white) are designed for long maturing. Drouhin also has sole rights on the superb Montrachet of the Marquis de Laguiche. As a négociant, he handles a wide range of well-chosen wines from all over Burgundy of which 75% is exported. Drouhin is the first Burgundian to plant Pinot Noir in the USA in the Willamette Valley, Oregon.

Robert Dubois & Fils
Prémeaux-Prissey, 21700 Nuits-St-Georges.

An up-to-date family estate with 44 acres, of which 10 in Nuits include 2.5 in the Premiers Crus Les Pôrets and Clos des Argillières. They use 'thermovinification', heating the must to get plenty of colour, followed by the usual methods. 40% of their production of 8,300 cases is exported.

Domaine P. Dubreuil-Fontaine Père & Fils
Pernand-Vergelesses, 21420 Savigny-Les-Beaune.

Bernard Dubreuil, the present manager, is the grandson of the founder of this 44-acre domaine, with 6 acres of Grand Cru Corton (principally Bressandes) and 2 of Corton-Charlemagne, as well as 9 of Savigny-Vergelesses Premier Cru and 13 of Pernand (red and white). They own the whole of the 2.5-acre Clos Berthet in the village of Pernand. His father Pierre has been mayor of Pernand for years and does the honours of the village for visitors with a perfect range of the wines of this privileged corner. His Grands Crus need keeping for a good 10 years.

Dufouleur Frères
1 rue de Dijon, 21701 Nuits-St-Georges

An old family firm of négociants (4 brothers and their father) with a small domaine in Nuits-St-Georges, Clos Vougeot and Musigny and also vineyards at Mercurey in the Côte Chalonnaise. Their wines are powerful and full of flavour.

Domaine Dujac
Morey St-Denis, 21220 Gevrey-Chambertin.

Jacques Seysses is the 'Jac' of the name. He is a qualified oenologist and is widely regarded as the most serious wine maker in Morey St-Denis, with natural patient (necessarily expensive) methods: fermenting stems and all for as long as possible, using new barrels, never filtering. The result is freshness with depth, as red burgundy should be. Clos de la Roche, where he has 4.8 acres, is his own favourite of his 27-acre domaine, which includes nearly 4 acres of Clos St-Denis, 8 of Morey 'Village', 3 of Gevrey-Chambertin Premier Cru 'Combottes', and small parcels of Charmes-Chambertin, Chambolle-Musigny Premier Cru, Echézeaux and of Bonnes Mares. Domaine Dujac wines are listed by most of France's three-star restaurants and have been served as the Elysée. 80% of production is exported.

Domaine René Engel
3, Place de la Mairie, 21700 Vosne-Romanée.
A well-known name in Burgundy as raconteur as well as vigneron. *Propos sur l' Art de Bien Boire* is his philosophy in print. The domaine of 17 acres includes 3.4 acres on the upper slope of the Clos Vougeot and plots in Grands-Echézeaux, Echézeaux and Vosne-Romanée (both Premier Cru and 'Village'). The wines are fine, masculine, powerful characters.

Domaine du Clos des Epeneaux
Place de l'Eglise, 21630 Pommard.
The 13-acre section of the Pommard Premier Cru Epenots belonging to the Comte Armand has different spelling to signify its identity. Part of the plot has 60-year-old vines. It makes undramatic burgundy that demands the word 'serious' and lasts for many years. They assure me of dramatic changes since the arrival of régisseur Pascal Marchand in 1985. The '88 is excellent.

Maison J. Faiveley
21700 Nuits-St-Georges
The Faiveleys, an unbroken family succession since 1825, have the biggest domaine in Burgundy: 270 acres. 160 acres are in Mercurey, where their 13-acre 'monopoly' Clos des Myglands is their best-known wine. 12 are in the neighbouring Rully. In Nuits their 74-acre holding includes the entire Clos de la Maréchale, a 24-acre Premier Cru 'monopoly' in Prémeaux and 4 acres of the Premier Cru Les Pôrets. 21 acres in Gevrey-Chambertin includes 3 each of the Grands Crus Mazis, Latricières and Clos de Bèze and 8.5 of Premiers Crus. They own 3 acres of Clos Vougeot, 2 of Echézeaux, 1.25 of Chambolle-Musigny, including a parcel of Le Musigny, and in the Côte de Beaune they have a 7-acre 'monopole' Corton Clos des Cortons Faiveley at Ladoix and a little Corton Blanc. In addition they have 20 acres of Bourgogne Rouge scattered about, and in communes where they own no vines they buy grapes and make the wine themselves at Nuits.

As if all this were not activity enough, Guy Faiveley, father of the present president of the company, François,

has been the most active and entertaining protagonist of the Chevaliers de Tastevin for many years.

Faiveley wines are solidly structured, built-to-last burgundies at all levels. In Corton, Clos de Bèze etc they reach the summit.

Domaine Fleurot-Larose
21590 Santenay
This domaine of 42 acres also has vineyards at Pouilly-sur-Loire. Its main holding is 16 acres of Chassagne-Montrachet Premier Cru Abbaye de Morgeot (red and white) and 12.5 of Santenay Premier Cru, but it also owns three quarters of an acre of Le Montrachet and half as much Bâtard-Montrachet.

Domaine Gagnard-Delagrange
Chassagne-Montrachet, 21190 Meursault.
A seventh-generation family of growers whose 12-acre domaine includes a small parcel of Le Montrachet 5 of Chassagne Premier Cru (Morgeot and La Boudriotte), half an acre of Bâtard-Montrachet and 2 acres of red Chassagne. Also 1 acre of Volnay Champans (their top red).

Domaine F. Gaunoux
21190 Meursault
François Gaunoux is the President of the Comité de Viticulture of the Côte d'Or and brother of Michel Gaunoux of Pommard. His 28-acre domaine, started in 1955, has 11 acres in Meursault (5 in the Premiers Crus Perrières and Goutte d'Or), 3 in Volnay Clos des Chênes, 2 each in the Premiers Crus Beaune Clos des Mouches and Pommard (Rugiens and Epenots). Also 7 more of Pommard 'Village'. M. Gaunoux's own favourites are his Beaune and Volnay.

Domaine Michel Gaunoux
Rue Notre Dame, 21630 Pommard.
Brother of François of Meursault, considered by Hubrecht Duijker to contest the crown of best grower in Pommard with Jacques Parent. Gaunoux has 17 acres, about 8 of them in Pommard Premier Cru with the biggest part in Epenots and the best (nearly 2 acres) in Rugiens. There are also nearly 1.5 acres of Corton Renardes and 5 acres of Beaune including the Premier Cru Boucherottes.

The wine is made with a fairly cool, slow fermentation which seems to extract all the lasting power of Pommard, staying firm and robust for a good decade. Most of their wine is sold direct to fine French restaurants; only 20% is exported.

Crémant – a new term of quality
Three high-quality French white-wine regions are successfully establishing a new appellation for their best-quality sparkling wine. The term 'crémant', originally used in Champagne for wines produced at about half the full sparkling-wine pressure, thus gently fizzing instead of frothing in the glass, has been borrowed (with the consent of Champagne) as a controlled term for these full-sparklers of high quality. A new term was needed because the old one, 'mousseux', had acquired a

pejorative ring: any old fizz made by industrial methods could (and can) use it. Burgundy and the Loire in 1975, and Alsace in 1976, joined in agreeing that *crémant* had to be made with champagne-type controls. Specifically, they concern the grape varieties used, the size of the crop, the way it is delivered to the press-house with the bunches undamaged and the pressure that should be applied (with a limit of two thirds of the weight of the grapes being extracted as juice). Thereafter, the champagne-method rules apply, with the

minimum time in bottle with the yeast being specified as 9 months in Burgundy and Alsace and 12 in the Loire. (An influential lobby wants to increase the 9 months to 12.)

The result of these controls is a category of sparkling wine of excellent quality, though so far in very small supply. Heavy initial investment deters cellars from upgrading from *mousseux* to *crémant*. But in 1982 for the first time the overall total passed 5 million bottles and there is no doubt that appreciation for the new idea will rapidly increase once

Domaine Pierre Gelin
2 rue du Chapitre, Fixin, 21220 Gevrey-Chambertin.

Stephen Gelin and André Molin run this well-known estate at the very northern end of the Côte de Nuits. They have 7 acres in Gevrey-Chambertin (including 1 acre of Mazis and 1.5 of Clos de Bèze) and 29 in Fixin, with important parts of the best-known Premiers Crus; Clos du Chapitre (12 acres), Clos Napoléon (4.5 acres) and Les Hervelets (1.5 acres). They destem all their grapes before a long fermentation in traditional oak *cuves*; age in some old barrels and some new. Critical opinion seems to favour their Clos du Chapitre first, Napoléon second. Their Clos de Bèze is on a heroic scale.

Domaine Jacques Germain
Château de Chorey-Les-Beaune, 21200 Beaune.

Françoise Germain's turreted medieval Château de Chorey, below the *côtes* north of Beaune, has 10 acres of red in Chorey, 15 in Beaune Premier Cru and 7 (white) Pernand-Vergelesses. His Beaune includes Teurons (5 acres), Cent Vignes, Vignes Franches, Cras and Boucherottes. Total production is about 6,000 cases. Germain's philosophy is gentle and natural wine-making from old vines. The grapes are fermented with stems and aged in new barrels for some time before racking, letting fermentation finish slowly and naturally. The result is real finesse in full-bodied wines needing age.

Jean Germain
9 rue de la Barre, 21190 Meursault.

A committed cellar-craftsman who sets very high standards in the small quantities (about 1,000 cases in total) of white burgundies from his own small property in Meursault (La Barre, Meix Chavaux), Puligny-Montrachet and St-Romain. He also makes the wine of the little Domaine Darnat in Meursault, whose Clos Richemont is outstanding. 'Maison Jean Germain' is run in conjunction with Tim Marshall of Nuits-St-Georges and Joseph de Bucy.

Domaine Girard-Vollot & Fils
21420 Savigny-Les-Beaune

A domaine of 37 acres with sites in three Savigny-Les-Beaune Premiers Crus – 1.7 acres each in Rouvreret and Les Peuillets and 11 acres in Narbantons. There are also 12 acres of Pernand-Vergelesses Premier Cru.

Soc. des Domaines Bernard & Louis Glantenay
Rue de Vaut, 21190 Volnay.

The 18-acre domaine of the mayor of Volnay and his brother; largely Volnay 'Village' (5 acres) and Premier Cru (6 acres), with a little Pommard 'Village', 3 acres of Premier Cru, 1 acre of Puligny-Montrachet and just under an acre each of Bourgogne, Passe-tout-grains and Aligoté. A wholly traditional establishment selling partly in cask to the négociants but increasingly bottling at the domaine.

Domaine Elmerich Gouachon
21700 Nuits-St-Georges

Their 12-acre 'monopole' Nuits Premier Cru Clos des Corvées is held up by some as the outstanding vineyard of the commune.

Domaine Goud de Beaupuis
Château des Moutots, 21200 Chorey-Les-Beaune.

A family domaine founded in 1787 with 25 acres, principally red wines in the Premiers Crus of Pommard (Epenots), Beaune (Grèves, Vignes Franches, Theurons), Savigny (Vergelesses) and Aloxe-Corton. Also some white Aligoté. Sales are largely to restaurants in France.

Domaine Henri Gouges
7 rue du Moulin, B.P. 70, 21700 Nuits-St-Georges.

In many minds and for many years the top grower of Nuits; a complete specialist with almost all his 30 acres in the Premiers Crus, including the whole 8 acres of the Clos des Porrets. His other main plots are in Les St-Georges (2.5 acres), Les Pruliers (4.2) and Les Vaucrains (2.5). Gouges' reds reach Grand Crus class: powerful, slow to develop and long in the finish

Jean Grivot
Vosne-Romanée, 21700 Nuits-St-Georges.

Etienne Grivot (son of Jean) is a deeply dedicated grower with a number of small parcels of exceptionally good land – 31 acres in all. He has 4.5 acres of Clos Vougeot and nearly 10 of Vosne-Romanée, including 2.3 in the excellent Premier Cru Beaumonts and bits of Suchots and Brûlées, which are sandwiched between the Grands Crus Richebourg and Echézeaux. 5 acres of Nuits Premiers Crus and 1.5 of Chambolle-Musigny give a wide range of top-class wines. Grivot believes in dense planting for small crops. He likes ripe wines without acidity or 'brutality' but with bouquet.

Domaine Robert Groffier
Morey St-Denis, 21220 Gevrey-Chambertin

An excellent little domaine in the best sites of Bonnes Mares, Clos de Bèze, and above all his favourite Chambolle-Musignys, Les Amoureuses and Les Sentiers. He captures the elegance of Musigny.

---

the term *crémant*, in its new meaning, is well understood.

Among concerns producing Crémant de Bourgogne are:
Bouchard Aîné, Beaune
R. Chevillard, La Rochepot
Caves de Bailly, St-Bris-le-Vineaux
Caves Delorme-Meulien, Rully
Cave de Lugny-St-Gengoux, Lugny
Cave de Viré, Viré
Labouré-Gontard, Nuits-St-Georges
Moingeon-Gueneau Frères, Nuits-St-Georges
Henri Mugnier, Charnay-les-Mâcon

Parigot-Richard, Savigny-Les-Beaune
Picamelot, Rully
SICA du Vignoble Auxerrois, Bailly, St-Bris-le-Vineaux
Simmonet-Febvre, Chablis
Veuve Ambal, Rully
Vitteau Alberti, Rully

Marc de Bourgogne and Cassis
The pulpy residue of skins, pips and stalks left in the press after the juice has been run off is often distilled to produce a spirit known as marc. The clear spirit is matured in oak to give it colour and,

with luck, a little finesse.

Most marc is made by growers for private consumption. Some of the larger houses, such as Bouchard Père & Fils and Louis Latour, make carefully aged commercial versions.

Cassis is an alcoholic blackcurrant liqueur which serves to soften the sharpness of white wine – in Burgundy usually Aligoté – in a proportion of 1 of cassis to 3 or 4 of wine. The resulting drink is often called Kir after a brand of cassis which was developed by Canon Félix Kir, one-time mayor of Dijon.

Domaine Jean Gros
Vosne-Romanée, 21700 Nuits-St-Georges.
A grower well known for his Vosne-Romanée who has expanded with a plantation of 12.5 acres up in the Hautes Côtes at Arcenant, some 7 miles west of Vosne. In Vosne he has a little Richebourg, and the 'monopole' of the 5-acre Clos des Réas, a Premier Cru down by the road, as well as 7.5 acres of 'Village' land. Two acres are in a frost-prone gully where he has ingeniously doubled the spacing between the vines to allow free movement of air on spring nights. In 1990 the 1980 Clos des Réas was superb.

Domaine Antonin Guyon
21420 Savigny-Les-Beaune
A very substantial domaine of 116 acres, half of it at Meuilley in the Hautes Côtes de Nuits, where vineyards abandoned after the phylloxera have been replanted in the last 20 years. Otherwise the biggest holdings are 5.3 acres of Corton Grand Cru, 5.5 acres in Pernand-Vergelesses Premier Cru and 8.5 in Chambolle-Musigny; 6 each in Gevrey-Chambertin 'Village' and Aloxe-Corton Premier Cru, 5.5 in Savigny and 2 each of Meursault-Charmes and Volnay Clos des Chênes. Also a tiny parcel of Charmes-Chambertin. Altogether a remarkable spread of good sites, considering which it is strange that the name is not better known. Being a recent creation the firm uses modern methods (e.g. keeping white wines under a blanket of inert nitrogen to preserve freshness). Their Cortons are their particular pride.

Domaine Hudelot-Noëllat
Vougeot 21640
Well-reputed 25-acre estate in Clos Vougeot, Richebourg, Romanée-St-Vivant, Chambolle-Musigny and Nuits. The owner is Alain Hudelot, who believes in tenacious wines.

Jaboulet-Vercherre
1 rue Colbert, 21200 Beaune.
A family firm of négociants originally from the Rhône, with notable wines from their own 30-acre domaine. The 10-acre Premier Cru Clos de la Commaraine around the old château of the same name in Pommard is their particular pride. They also have some excellent Grand Cru Corton-Bressandes, Beaune, Clos de l'Ecu, 'monopoles' Premier Cru Volnay Caillerets, Puligny-Montrachet Les Folatières and Santenay Clos Rousseau. Their wines are made at a modern plant visible from the autoroute.

Maison Louis Jadot
5 rue Samuel Legay, 21200 Beaune.
The American concern Kobrand now own this firm based in the medieval Couvent des Jacobins since the early 19th century, when they were growers on the slopes of Beaune. The Domaine Louis Jadot now covers almost 100 acres, including their original holding, the 6-acre Clos des Ursules in Les Vignes Franches, and the part of Clair-Däu which was bought when the property was split up in 1985. In Beaune they also own part of the Premier Cru Theurons. Clos des Coucherous, Les Couacheux, Les Bressandes, and 6 acres of Boucherottes on the edge of Pommard, with Pommard-like sturdy wine. In Corton they have holdings of Pougets (Grand Cru) and Corton-Charlemagne. In Puligny-Montrachet they own parcels of Les Folatières and Chevalier-Montrachet (a plot they call Les Demoiselles, after the spinster sisters Adèle and Julie Voillot who sold it to them in 1846). Since 1985 they have purchased the grapes of Domaine du Duc de Magenta (q.v.), although the wine is sold under that label. Their brilliant white wines are probably their greatest pride: especially their Corton-Charlemagne or Chevalier-Montrachet. But Jadot reds are equally reliable: their domaine wines lead a first-class list of classic burgundies. A shining example of a grower-cum-négociant.

Maison Jaffelin
Caves du Chapitre, 2 rue Paradis, 21200 Beaune.
An old company of négociants, originally distillers, occupying the magnificent 13th-century cellar of the canons of Notre Dame in the centre of Beaune. The company was bought by Joseph Drouhin (q.v.) in 1969 but still acts as an independent négociant. Jaffelin wines are long-macerated, pungent with oak, intense and long-lived.

Henri Jayer
Vosne-Romanée, 21700 Nuits-St-Georges
A famous estate for many years. Pre-1988 wines will be found from Nuits, Vosne and Echézeaux under this label. Jayer has now retired; his vineyards have reverted to the Méo-Camuzet family or been leased to his nephew, Emmanuel Rouget.

Jacqueline Jayer
Vosne-Romanée, 21700 Nuits-St-Georges
Excellent little domaine in Vosne, Nuits and Echézeaux. The wines are made by the owner's nephew.

Domaine Jean Joliot & Fils
Nantoux, 21190 Meursault.
Nantoux is a village in the hills only 3 miles west of Pommard, the northernmost of the Hautes Côtes de Beaune. Jean Joliot has 27 acres in the Hautes Côtes, where he makes some 1,000 cases of good red wine, which is austere for burgundy but highly popular with private clients, half of them abroad. On the Côte d'Or he has a parcel of Beaune Premier Cru Boucherottes, 3 acres of Pommard, and 5 acres of Meursault and a little Aligoté. He also makes about 250 cases of Crémant de Bourgogne.

Domaine de la Juvinière
Clos de Langres, Corgoloin, 21700 Nuits-St-Georges.
The Clos de Langres is the southernmost limit of the Côte de Nuits on the way to Beaune, a walled vineyard still equipped with the ancient *pressoir* of the Bishop of Langres. The domaine centred here is the property of La Reine Pédauque, négociants in Beaune. Apart from the 8-acre Clos, the substantial 60-acre estate has 10 in Savigny, 13 in Corton and Aloxe-Corton, 2.7 of Clos Vougeot and 1.5 of Corton-Charlemagne. Their wines tend to be written off as commercial and lacking individuality, but those visiting Beaune may try them for themselves in the domaine's hospitable exhibition cellars.

Maison Labouré-Roi
21700 Nuits-St-Georges
A négociant emerging as one of the most consistent and reliable at quite modest prices. His specialities are domaine wines from René Manuel in Meursault and Chantal Lescure in Nuits. Also surprisingly good Chablis Premier Cru.

Domaine Michel Lafarge
Volnay, 21190 Meursault.
An old family estate which survived the doldrums of Burgundy in the mid-1930s by the initiative of M. Lafarge's grandfather, who bottled his wine and attacked

the Paris market with it in person. There are still bottles of 1904 in the cellar. Of the 23 acres, 10.5 are in Volnay (4.5 Premier Cru), 2.5 in Meursault, 1 in Beaune Grèves and the rest in rather good Bourgogne vineyards (including Passe-tout-grains and Aligoté). Painstaking vinification, throwing out rotten grapes, fermenting for 10-plus days and using about one third new barrels produces lovely clean and elegant wines.

Domaine des Comtes Lafon
Clos de la Barre, 21190 Meursault.

The most famous part of the 32-acre Lafon domaine is their three-quarter-acre parcel of Le Montrachet, which year by year makes one of the finest of all white wines. The biggest part (16 acres) is in Meursault and includes 2 acres of Premier Cru Perrières, more than 4 of Charmes, parts of Genevrières and Goutte d'Or and 7.4 of Meursault 'Village', the best of which is the Domaine's 'Clos de la Barre'. For red wines the Lafons have 11 acres in Volnay (Santenots 8.6, Champans 1.2, Clos des Chénes 1). René Lafon, who runs them for the family, in an innovative wine maker. To get the maximum colour in Volnay he starts the wine in an open *cuve*, then moves it to a closed one, under strictly controlled temperature, where its cap is submerged. For white wine he encourages immensely long fermentation – until the following March or April. It gives, he says, 'long' wines.

Domaine Laleure Piot
Pernand-Vergelesses, 21420 Savigny-Les-Beaune.

A 20-acre domaine producing reputable Pernand-Vergelesses, particularly 1,000 cases of white, with some Grand Cru Corton Bressandes and Premier Cru Vergelesses from Savigny and Pernand.

Domaine Henri Lamarche
Vosne-Romanée, 21700 Nuit-St-Georges.

A fourth-generation little family domaine with the good fortune to own the 'monopole' of La Grande Rue, a narrow strip of 3.5 acres running up the hill between Romanée-Conti and La Tâche, the two greatest Grands Crus. A bottle of the 1961 at 21 years old was a miracle of subtle sensuality; understated beside La Tâche, but in its quieter way among the great bottles of my experience. The rest of the 30-acre property includes 2.5 acres of Clos de Vougeot, and parcels of Grands-Echézeaux and the Vosne-Romanée Premiers Crus Malconsorts and Suchots.

Domaine Lamy
Chassagne-Montrachet, 21190 Meursault

The domaine was founded in 1968 by René Lamy, who was *régisseur* for the Duc de Magenta from 1968–73, and his brother. Their 42 acres are in St Aubin, Santenay, Blagny and Chassagne-Montrachet including 5 acres of red Premiers Crus and 2.5 of white.

Jean Lamy & Fils
St-Aubin, 21190 Meursault.

A much-respected family with 33 acres in Chassagne and Puligny-Montrachet, Santenay and St-Aubin, and a little Bâtard-Montrachet, divided between the Lamy sons Hubert and René.

Maison Louis Latour
18 rue des Tonneliers, 21204 Beaune.

One of Burgundy's names to conjure with, founded in the 18th century and since 1867 owned and directed, father-to-son, by Latours called Louis. The centre of their domaine is the 'Château' de Grancey at Aloxe-Corton, one of the first large-scale, purpose-built 'wineries' in France: 3 stories above ground and 2 below. The domaine totals 116 acres, of which some 103 are in Corton and Aloxe-Corton, including 25 of Corton-Charlemagne, 47 of red Corton Grand Cru, a 6-acre 'monopole' of Grand Cru Clos de la Vigne au Saint and 11 of Premier Cru Les Chaillots. Some 12 acres in Beaune Premier Cru include 7 of Vignes Frances. There are 2 acres of Chambertin and similar parcels of Romanée-St-Vivant and Pernand-Vergelesses Ile des Vergelesses. Latour has a famous 1.3 acres of Chevalier-Montrachet Les Demoiselles.

Latour is most celebrated for his white wines, above all Corton-Charlemagne, which he almost literally put on the map at the end of the 19th century. They are powerful and must be kept. I was surprised to learn that he pasteurizes his reds, which in theory should mean there is no point in keeping them – which is certainly not the case.

Domaine wines account for one quarter of their turnover. Their selections of other wines, particularly whites, are reliable. Montagny is a speciality to look out for, and they have introduced a Chardonnay Vin de Pays d'Ardèche which is remarkable in character and volume. 90% of the firm's business is in export.

Domaine René Leclerc
21220 Gevrey-Chambertin

The larger share of a family property concentrated in Gevrey-Chambertin Premiers Crus. René's brother Philippe has the smaller. Both are good conscientious producers.

Domaine Leflaive
Puligny-Montrachet, 21190 Meursault.

Perhaps the most highly regarded white-wine specialist of the Côte d'Or, a family property dating back to 1745, now totalling 52 acres in superb sites. They include 5 acres each in Bâtard- and Chevalier-Montrachet, 3.7 of Bienvenues-Bâtard, 7.5 of the Puligny Premier Cru Les Pucelles, 10 of Clavoillon next door and 2 of Combettes. He also has 9 acres of Puligny 'Village' and a patch of (red) Blagny. Vincent Leflaive proceeds by caution and good taste to make exceptional white burgundy. This combination of power and finesse is the benchmark of Puligny – the sublimation of Chardonnay.

Oliver Leflaive Frères
21190 Puligny-Montrachet

Nephew of Vincent Leflaive, now the most highly-regarded négociant in the area, with brilliant Pulignys and excellent St Romain, Auxey-Duresses etc: model wines from the Côte de Beaune.

Domaine Lequin-Roussot
21590 Santenay

A well-known domaine founded by the Lequin family in 1734. Each generation, say the brothers René and Louis, has contributed its stone to the edifice. They now have 33 acres, of which 23 are in Santenay (7 Premier Cru). In Chassagne they have 1.5 acres of red Premier Cru Morgeot and 14 of white Premier Cru Morgeot; also three quarters of an acre of Bâtard-Montrachet producing 600 bottles a year. The rest of the domaine is in small parcels in Corton (Les Languettes), Pommard and Nuits-St-Georges. The policy is to destem the bunches and aim for big but not hard wines, then to sell them as they mature.

Maison Leroy
Auxey-Duresses, 21190 Meursault.

A company known to the world almost as much for the personality (and reputed wealth) of its owner, Mme Lalou Bize-Leroy, as for its wines. She is both grower and négociant as well as coproprietor and distributor of the Domaine de la Romanée-Conti (of which she inherited half from her father). She is also a well-known mountaineer and a formidable wine taster. Leroy's total of 10.5 acres is small but choice, including white vines in Meursault and Auxey-Duresses and small parcels of red in Chambertin, Musigny, Clos de Vougeot, Pommard and Auxey-Duresses. In 1988 Leroy absorbed the distinguished Domaine Noellat which added 35 acres, including Clos Vougeot (4 acres), Richebourg and Romanée-St-Vincent (3.5 acres), plus Nuits and Savigny. In 1989 Mme Leroy added 6 acres in Gevrey-Chambertin, including part of Le Chambertin. The style of the house is very firmly aimed at *vins de garde*. The reds are unstemmed and stay in the vat for 3 weeks, are racked only once, fined with egg whites and never filtered. Strength comes from fully ripe grapes – never more than 1 degree of chaptalization. At 10 years the wines taste young; at 20 in full bloom. Other growers' wines passing through Leroy's hands seem to acquire (or are chosen for) the same qualities. They need patience, and they cost a fortune. The '*Gardien des Grands Millésimes*', as she styles herself, has a stock of 2.5 million bottles.

Domaine Georges Lignier & Fils
21220 Gevrey-Chambertin

The 34 acre domaine is a patchwork of 60 different sites spread over nearly 4 miles from north to south. The best parcels are in Grands Crus Clos St-Denis, Clos de la Roche and Bonnes Mares, and Premiers Crus Morey St-Denis and Gevrey Chambertin. 50% of the wine is sold to various négociants. The Lignier label goes on the best.

Hubert Lignier
21220 Gevrey-Chambertin

The great-grandfather of the present owner began working in 1860 on what is now the domaine, working his way up to become the *maître-chai*. The family took over the property in 1890. There are now 18.5 acres. The most important sites are 1.9 acres of Clos de la Roche, and small holdings in Chambolle-Musigny and Gevrey-Chambertin Premiers Crus.

Lupé-Cholet
17 ave. Général de Gaulle, 21700 Nuits-St-Georges.

Two amusingly aristocratic sisters, the Comtesses Inès and Liliane de Mayol de Lupé, run this old family business, best known for its Nuits Premier Cru 'Chateau Gris', a 6.6-acre parcel of Les Crots above the town which has produced some memorable *vins de garde*. Their elegant house in Nuits also has the 5.6-acre Clos de Lupé (appellation Bourgogne) beyond the garden. Some years ago the company merged with Bichot of Beaune.

Lycée Viticole
21207 Beaune

The young farmers' college (47 acres) of Beaune, founded in 1884, includes 4 small parcels of Beaune Premiers Crus, as well as 2.5 acres of white Puligny-Montrachet. They make some 2,500 cases of first-rate, long-lived wine, of which 20% is exported.

Domaine Machard de Gramont
6 rue Gassendi, 21700 Nuits-St-Georges.

A 47-acre domaine created over the last 25 years by 2 young brothers with amazing energy and professionalism. Much of their best land was abandoned '*friches*', the stony edges of good vineyards, until they planted it. A family problem sadly reduced their holdings from 75 acres in 1983. Their biggest plots now are in Nuits (6.5 acres of Premier Cru, especially Hauts-Pruliers, 7.5 of 'Village'), Pommard (10 acres of the excellent Clos Blanc, a 'Village' site of Premier Cru quality), and Savigny-les-Beaune (5 acres, mostly Premier Cru Les Guettes). They also have

France's most historic and beautiful
charitable hospital; the medieval Hospices de
Beaune

The Hospices de Beaune

The Hospices de Beaune has a unique
role as a symbol of the continuity, the
wealth and the general benevolence of
Burgundy. It was founded as a hospital
for the sick, poor and aged of Beaune in
1443 by the Chancellor to the Duke of
Burgundy, Nicolas Rolin, and his wife
Guigone de Salins. They endowed it
with land in the Côte de Beaune for its
income; a practice that has been
followed ever since by rich growers,
merchants and other citizens. The
Hospices now owns about 106 acres of
vineyards and much more farmland.

The wine from its scattered vineyard
plots is made in *cuvées*, not necessarily
consisting of the wine of a single *climat*
but designed to be practicable to make

and agreeable to drink. Each *cuvée* is
named after an important benefactor of
the Hospices. There are 32 *cuvées*, all but
one in the Côte de Beaune.

The wine is sold, *cuvée* by *cuvée* and
cask by cask, at a public auction on the
third Sunday of November in the
market hall across the road from the
Hospices. The profits are spent on
running the hospital, which now has
every sort of modern equipment. Its
original wards, chapel and works of art
are open to the public.

Buyers include merchants,
restaurants, individuals and syndicates
from all over the world, who are
attracted by the idea of supporting this
ancient charity, and the publicity that
accompanies it. The wine-making of the

Hospices has been much criticized
recently, and it is certainly not easy to
judge the wines so soon after the
harvest, when buyers have to make their
choice. Both excellent and second-rate
bottles are produced, but the cachet of a
Hospices label means a great deal.

The third weekend in November is
the most important date in the
Burgundy calendar, known as *Les Trois
Glorieuses* from the three feasts which
make it a stiff endurance test. On
Saturday the Chevaliers de 'Tastevin'
hold a gala dinner at the Clos de
Vougeot. On Sunday after the auction
the dinner is at the Hospices and
Monday lunch is a wine-growers' feast
known as the *Paulée* at Meursault: this
last a gigantic bottle party.

2.5 acres of Beaune Premier Cru Epenottes and small parcels in Chambolle-Musigny and Aloxe-Corton (very tasty, this). They ferment at a high temperature ($35°C/95°F$) with most of the stems, age in barrels in cellars and rack their wine as little as possible. Their policy is only to bottle selections from good vintages and old vines, and to sell the rest in bulk. The brothers are modest about their achievement, but they make some of the best red burgundy of its class today.

Domaine du Duc de Magenta
Abbaye de Morgeot, Chassagne-Montrachet, 21190 Meursault.
The descendant of the French victor of the battle of Magenta (1859, with Piedmont against the Austrians) owns 30 acres, of which 11 – half red and half white – are the Clos de la Chapelle of former Cistercians of the Abbaye de Morgeot, a dependency of Cluny. 5 acres are the Premier Cru 'Clos de la Garenne' in Puligny, 8 (red and white) in Auxey-Duresses and 2 in Meursault 'Miex Chavaux'. In the past, his wines were firm, vigorous and full of character, keeping well. His red 'Morgeot' has been outstanding. The 1969 in 1982 had a beautiful flavour of cherries and almonds. Then followed some vintages which were less impressive. Since 1985 the wines have been made by Maison Louis Jadot (q.v.).

Domaine Henri Magnien
21220 Gevrey-Chambertin
A 300-year old family domaine of 7.4 acres. It includes a parcel of Ruchottes-Chambertin Grand Cru and 4 Gevrey-Chambertin Premiers Crus, of which Estournelles is the biggest. Well-oaked, stylish wines.

Château de la Maltroye
Chassagne-Montrachet, 21190 Meursault.
The source of some outstanding bottles of white Chassagne under the 'monopole' label of the château. The 32-acre estate also has a small piece of Bâtard-Montrachet and red-wine vineyards in Chassagne Clos St-Jean and Santenay La Comme.

Domaine Jean-Philippe Marchand
21220 Gevrey-Chambertin
A family property in Gevrey (including a little Charmes-Chambertin) and Morey St-Denis. Rather tannic but sufficiently rich wines. Also a small négociant business.

Domaine Tim Marshall
47c rue Henri Challand, 21700 Nuits-St-Georges.
A small property of 4 acres in the Nuits Premiers Crus Les Perrières and Les Argillats, and Volnay, the work of a Yorkshireman who has carved out a unique place for himself as a broker, guide, philosopher and friend to Anglo-Saxons (and Burgundians too) in Burgundy.

Domaine Joseph Matrot & Pierre Matrot
21190 Meursault
A family domaine of 44 acres. 4 acres are in the Puligny Premiers Crus Combettes and Chalumeaux, 4 in Meursault Charmes and Perrières and another 4 of white in the Meursault section of Blagny. There are 3.5 acres of red Volnay-Santenots and an unusual red Blagny, the 6-acre La Pièce sous le Bois, which makes a vivid, rather harsh wine as a change from the gentler Volnay. I have found his Meursault (particularly his Charmes) beautifully made.

Prosper Maufoux
21590 Santenay
One of the most respected of family firms in the traditional business of buying, 'bringing-up' and selling burgundy from small growers. The present principal, Pierre Maufoux, is grandson of the founder. Maufoux red wines are reliably *vins de garde*; on occasions I have found even his 'Village' wines have been in pefect condition at 20 years and his Premiers and Grands Crus exceptional. For Maufoux has a share in the Domaine St-Michel (q.v.), which also supplies him with Pouilly Fumé. I have found his Chablis Mont de Milieu and Vaudésir reliable, typical and good value; his Santenay Blanc, Meursault Charmes and (particularly) Puligny-Montrachet Les Folatières first class. This house is the answer to anyone who thinks that all good burgundy is domaine bottled. Marcel Amance is another trade name.

Domaine Maume
21220 Gevrey-Chambertin
Bernard Maume is a professor of biochemistry at Dijon University as well as being proprietor of the 9.8-acre domaine. He is assisted by his son, Bertrand, who has a degree in oenology and has worked in an Australian winery. He believes in macerating the skins at low temperatures before fermentation to accentuate the fruit flavour. The largest and best parcel is 1.5 acres of Mazis-Chambertin Grand Cru. There is also a small site of Charmes-Chambertin Grand Cru and 3 Gevrey-Chambertin Premiers Crus. 80–90% of the 11,600 case production is exported.

Maizilly Père & Fils
Meloisey, 21190 Meursault.
Growers in the Côte de Beaune since 1600, largely in the Hautes Côtes (8.5 acres) with 3.4 acres of Pommard, 2 of Meursault and 1 of Beaune Premier Cru. Sound, strong wines aimed for body more than finesse.

Domaine Prince Florent de Mérode
21550 Ladoix-Serrigny
A domaine of high standing in Corton and Pommard. Of the 28 acres, some 9 are in Corton Grand Cru and the same in the 'monopole' Pommard Clos de la Platière.

Domaine Méo-Camuzet
21700 Vosne-Romanée
A long-established grower in Vosne, Nuits, Clos de Vougeot, Corton and Le Richebourg which has emerged in the '80s as one of the highest class, with rich but well-structured wines.

Mestre Père & Fils
Place du Jet d'Eau, 21590 Santenay.
One of the bigger domaines (44 acres) of Santenay, in the fifth generation, with 17.5 acres of Premiers Crus in all the best vineyards, and smaller holdings in Aloxe-Corton (including a small portion of Corton Grand Cru), Chassagne-Montrachet, and Ladoix (Appellation Côte de Beaune). Careful wine-making, but surprisingly only 20% is bottled at the domaine. The Swiss (who love Santenay) buy the greater part in cask.

Château de Meursault
21190 Meursault
An 89-acre domaine with the signature of the Comte de Moucheron, the former own, bought in 1973 by the négociants Patriarche of Beaune and turned into a

showplace for visitors, with a permanent help-yourself tasting in the spectacular medieval cellars. The vineyards include substantial parcels of the Meursault Premiers Crus Charmes and Perrières – which are sold as Ch. de Meursault – and the former gardens of the château, replanted with vines as the 'Clos du Château'. Red vineyards include part of the Premiers Crus of Volnay (Clos des Chênes), Pommard (Clos des Epenots), Beaune (Fèves, Grèves, Cent Vignes, Clos du Roi) and Savigny. The total production averages 17,000 cases. My impression is that the whole range, but particularly the Meursaults, are extremely well made – and expensive.

Domaine Alain Michelot
21700 Nuits-St-Georges

A 21-acre property, mostly in Nuits, created by the last two generations of the Michelots. His Premiers Crus (especially Richemore and Vaucrains) are Nuits-St-Georges at its best; solid and searching.

Maison P. Missery
21702 Nuits-St-Georges

The Missery family's vines are all in Nuits-St-Georges Premiers Crus: five parcels making a total of 4.4 acres. Maison Missery also has long-term contracts with domaines in the Côte de Nuits and Côte de Beaune, and vinifies more than 26 different appellations of Premier Cru and Grand Cru status. Jules Belin is now owned by Missery.

Maison Moillard and Domaine Thomas-Moillard
21700 Nuits-St-Georges

A family firm in the fifth generation (the name is now Thomas) with a 64-acre domaine, but also making wine from purchased grapes from a much larger area and playing the traditional role of négociants with stocks of no less than 8 million bottles – certainly the biggest in Nuits. They are known for the efficiency and modernity of their techniques, and still respected for their domaine wines, which are made 'supple' and round for relatively early drinking. The domaine includes little parcels of 8 different Nuits Premiers Crus (Clos de Thorey and Clos des Grandes Vignes are 'monopoles'), Chambertin and Clos de Bèze, Bonnes Mares, Clos Vougeot, Romanée St-Vivant and Vosne-Romanée Beaux Monts and Malconsorts, Corton Clos du Roi and Corton-Charlemagne.

Domaine Mommessin
La Grange St-Pierre, B.P. 504, 71009 Mâcon.

The famous Beaujolais growers have owned the whole of the 18.5-acre Grand Cru Clos de Tart in Morey St-Denis since 1932. They use the unusual technique of keeping the 'cap' of skins immersed throughout the fermentation. The wine is fine but still on the light side, surprisingly for a Grand Cru, neighbour to Bonnes Mares.

Mongeard-Mugneret
21670 Vosne-Romanée

50-acre estate making long-lived Vosne Les Suchots, Echezeaux, Grands-Echézeaux, Vougeot, etc.

Domaine Jean Monnier & Fils
20 rue du 11 Novembre, 21190 Meursault.

The Monniers have been growers in Meursault since 1720. Their 41 acres comprise 15 acres of Meursault (including Charmes and Genevrières), 2.5 acres of Puligny-Montrachet, 2.5 acres of Beaune, 10 acres of

Pommard, 10 acres of Bourgogne Rouge and 1.75 acres of Bourgogne Aligoté, including their 'monopole' Clos des Cîteaux in Les Epenots.

Domaine René Monnier
6 rue Docteur Rolland, 21190 Meursault.

The Monnier family has built up one of the biggest private domaines in the Côte de Beaune – 45 acres – over 150 years. The biggest plots are in Meursault Chevalières and the Premier Cru Charmes, Beaune Cent Vignes and Toussaints and Puligny Folatières. Other plots are in Pommard, Volnay and Santenay. The reds are fermented for as long as possible at a high temperature (for plenty of colour) and aged in one third of new barrels a year. The whites are balanced between half new oak and half stainless steel, aimed at wine with plenty of flavour not needing long ageing. Well known in three-star restaurants.

Domaine Monthélie-Douhairet
Monthélie, 21190 Meursault.

Octogenarian Mlle Armande Douhairet, the current proprietor, is a figure of living history in Burgundy. The domaine of 15 acres includes 2.5 acres of Premiers Crus Pommard, Volnay and Monthélie rouge, some juicy Meursault and just under an acre of Monthélie blanc.

Domaine Hubert de Montille
Volnay, 21190 Meursault.

The 17-acre property of a Dijon lawyer, scattered among the Premiers Crus of Volnay (Champans, Taillepieds, Mitans) and Pommard (Epenots, Rugiens, Pézerolles). Both Pommard and Volnay are richly coloured, flavoursome and durable.

Albert Morey & Fils
Chassagne-Montrachet, 21190 Meursault.

An old family domaine of some 30 acres, largely in Chassagne and almost equally divided between white and red wines. 'The French drink the red', says M. Morey. His best-known white wine is the Premier Cru Les Embrasées (2.5 acres), though his 2 acres of Caillerets, 1 each of Morgeot and Les Champs-Gains and a tiny plot in Bâtard-Montrachet are all excellent. He also owns 2 acres of Santenay for red and rents 2 of Beaune Grèves. His cousins Bernard and Jean-Marc Morey are also reputed growers in Chassagne-Montrachet, Santenay and Beaune.

Albert Morot
Château de la Creusotte, 21200 Beaune.

13 acres of Beaune Cru in Teurons, Grèves, Cent Vignes, Toussaints, Bressandes and Marconnets. 4.5 acres of Savigny-Vergelesses 'Clos la Bataillère'. Mlle Françoise-Guigone Choppin has recently taken over responsibility from her brother Guy, for making the wines. A fine property to discover the characters of top-level Beaune Premiers Crus.

Domaine Georges Mugneret
Vosne-Romanée, 21700 Nuits-St-Georges.

There are 7 growers called Mugneret in Vosne. This 11-acre domaine, run by the widow and daughter of the late Dr. Georges, includes less than an acre each of Grand Cru Clos de Vougeot and Ruchottes-Chambertin. They have 3 acres of Nuits Premier Cru; the rest is Chambolle-Musigny Premier Cru. The yield is low and the wine serious.

Mugneret-Gibourg
Vosne-Romanée, 21700 Nuits-St-Georges
Run by the same family as Domaine Georges Mugneret, it covers 12 acres, 2.4 of which are Echézeaux Grand Cru. 9.5 acres are in Vosne-Romanée.

Domaine Mugneret-Gouachon
Prémeaux-Prissey, 21700 Nuits-St-Georges.
Bernard Mugneret runs his father's property in Vosne-Romanée and his father-in-law's in Nuits – a total of 26 acres, of which 8.5 are his 'monopole' Premier Cru Les Perdrix in Prémeaux. He has 3 acres each of Echézeaux and Vosne-Romanée and over 8, producing 750 cases, of Bourgogne Rouge. Les Perdrix is a splendid wine regularly bought and shipped to the USA since 1959 by the late Frank Schoonmaker and his successors.

Domaine André Mussy
21630 Pommard
Very much a family concern – the present proprietor, André Mussy, is twelfth generation and he is assisted by his son-in-law and his nephew. The domaine of 14.8 acres includes 1.8 acres of Pommard Epenots Grand Cru, and the same of Pommard Premier Cru, 2.47 acres of Beaune-Epenottes Premier Cru and 3.7 of Beaune-Montremenots Premier Cru. 75% of the wine is exported.

Maison Naigeon-Chauveau
21220 Gevrey-Chambertin
Good-quality négociant house under the same direction (J-P Naigeon) as Domaine de Varoilles (q.v.).

Hospices de Nuits-St-Georges
Rue Henri Challand, 21700 Nuits-St-Georges.
The lesser-known and smaller Nuits counterpart of the great Hospices de Beaune, founded in 1634 and now endowed with 31 acres. They include 14 of Nuits Premier Cru and 5.5 of Nuits 'Village'. The rest is Bourgogne and Bourgogne Grand Ordinaire, which is sold in bulk. The best *cuvées* are sold by auction in March. The Cuvée des Soeurs Hospitalières is Nuits (Village) Les Fleurières; the Cuvée Les Sires de Vergy is Les St-Georges; the Cuvées Fagon, Duret and Cabet are Les Didiers. All are serious *vins de garde*.

Domaine Parent
21630 Pommard
A 30-acre domaine founded in 1750, best known for its Pommard, Epenots, Chanlins, Fremiers, Chaponniers and Clos Micault, but also with vineyards in Corton, Volnay, Beaune, Ladroix and Monthélie. His Clos Micault 1977 showed what a good grower can make of a bad year.

Patriarche Père & Fils
Couvent des Visitandines, 21200 Beaune.
Possibly the biggest firm in Burgundy (it claims to have the biggest cellars) with a history going back to 1780. Patriarche has a paradoxical image: on one hand proprietor of the excellent Ch. de Meursault and Beaune Premiers Crus totalling 100 acres, regularly the biggest buyer at the Hospices de Beaune auctions and a house of great prestige; on the other a brand which the snob in me would describe as definitely down-market. Perhaps it is the dismal design of their labels. Their greatest success must be Kriter Brut de Brut, created in the early 1960s as a high-quality, non-appellation sparkling wine. The Kriter factory on the road south of Beaune boasts a vast celebratory fountain. Appellation wines account for 60%

of turnover. Brand names include Père Patriarche, Cuvée Jean Baptiste, Noëmie Vernaux.

Jean-Marc Pavelot
21420 Savigny-Les-Beaune
The Pavelots have been growers in Savigny since 1640. Their domaine comprises 32 acres, a little under half of it in the Premier Cru vineyards of the slopes. Their wines are made in modern conditions. They bottle the best, notably Savigny 'Dominode' and 'Guettes', and sell the rest in cask to négociants.

Domaine de la Perrière
Fixin, 21220 Gevrey-Chambertin.
An unusually simple property making only one wine: the famous Fixin Clos de la Perrière, established by the Cistercian monks of Citeaux in the 12th century. The original manor, its cellars and their great press, 700 years old, are still here. The 13 acres produce some 2,000 cases of bold, uncompromising wine, made by long fermentation (up to 3 weeks) in covered vats with most of the stems included. Then long barrel-ageing and no filtration – very much what the monks must have done. The wine has been compared with Cambertin for power, if not for finesse.

Château de Pommard
21630 Pommard.
The château is very much in evidence from the main road, with a label and a sales approach which might lead one to think it is strictly for tourists. In fact it is extremely serious; with 50 acres said to be the biggest single vineyard with one proprietor in Burgundy, and acknowledged to make excellent wine from a high proportion of old vines. Despite being a 'Village' wine, it is made like a good Premier Cru. The owner, Jean-Louis Laplance, uses new barrels every year, keeps the wine 2 years in wood and does not filter. The tourists are important too: a major portion of his sales is direct to private clients, 40% is exported, 25% within Europe.

Maison Pierre Ponnelle
Abbaye St-Martin, 53 avenue de l'Aigue, 21200 Beaune.
One of the smaller négociants, evidently thriving, with new premises outside Beaune and a new shop in the town. The present director, Bruno Ponnelle, is the great-grandson of the founder. Their domaine is only 12 acres, but includes parcels of Musigny, Bonnes Mares, Charmes-Chambertin, Clos Vougeot, Corton Clos du Roi and Beaune Grèves. Their wine list is remarkable in quality and diversity and in the old stocks they offer. In my experience Ponnelle wines are true to type and very long-lived: a 1950 Clos Vougeot (not a famous year) was in good condition in 1980.

Domaine Jean-Marie Ponsot
Morey St-Denis, 21220 Gevrey-Chambertin.
An 18-acre domaine over a century old, all in Morey St-Denis except for a small parcel of Latricières-Chambertin. Half of the total is in the splendid Clos de la Roche, making concentrated, long-lived wine difficult to distinguish from Chambertin. White Premier Cru Morey 'Monts Luisants' is Ponsot's other speciality; one of the few whites of the Côte de Nuits, grown on high trellising 'Swiss-style' on the steep upper slopes.

Poulet Père & Fils
12 rue Chaumergy, 21200 Beaune.

A firm of négocants with a long history, known for sturdy wines rather than finesse. It is now owned by Chauvenet.

Domaine de la Pousse d'Or
Volnay, 21190 Meursault.

A domaine of 32 acres entirely in the Premiers Crus of Volnay, Pommard and Santenay. Its reputation is as high as any in the Côte de Beaune. Almost every three-star restaurant offers its wines. The domaine has 3 'monopoles' in Volnay: Clos de la Bousse [sic] d'Or, Clos des Soixante Ouvrées and Clos d'Audignac. The first and last are typically gentle and sociable Volnay, delicacy and elegance that reaches its peak in the 'Bousse d'Or'; the '60 Ouvrées', however, is a prime piece of the Caillerets, more forceful wine demanding maturity. (An *ouvrée* is one twenty-fourth of a hectare: 60 = 2.5 hectares = just over 7 acres.) Another parcel of Caillerets of the same size produces lighter wines. Two similar plots in Santenay's best Premiers Crus (Tavannes and Gravières) and 2.5 acres of Pommard Jarollières complete the domaine. Gérard Potel, the director, ferments his wine for 12 to 14 days, looking, he says, 'for long life but finesse, with subtle and delicate perfumes. Ideally wine with the maximum freshness and maximum *nervosité*.' Few Côte de Beaune wines mature longer than his.

Domaine Jacques Prieur
Rue des Santenots, 21190 Meursault.

One of Burgundy's most remarkable properties, including parts of both Chambertin and Montrachet, with all its 34.5 acres in great vineyards. Its architect was Jacques Prieur, one of the prime movers of the Chevaliers de Tastevin, whose grandson Martin now runs it. In 1988, 50% of the shares were acquired by Financiers des Grands Vignobles de Bourgogne, represented by Sté Antonin Rodet (*see* under Mercurey). The vines include 2.4 acres in Chambertin and Clos de Bèze, 2 in Musigny, 3 in Clos de Vougeot, 4.5 in Beaune (Clos de la Féguine), 6 in the Volnay Premiers Crus Santenots, Clos des Santenots and Champans, 8 in Meursault Clos de Mazeray (red and white), 4.5 in Puligny Les Combettes and Chevalier-Montrachet and 1.4 (making 2,000 bottles) of Le Montrachet. All the wines (some 5,000–8,000 cases a year) are made in Meursault in modern conditions. The domaine has a fading reputation for both red and white wines which Antonin Rodet intends to restore.

Charles Quillardet
21220 Gevrey-Chambertin

An enterprising grower of the northern *côtes* with 40 acres of vines between Gevrey and Dijon, including a parcel of Chambertin, vines in Fixin and Marsannay (where he makes a Bourgogne Rosé) and in the suburbs of Dijon itself, at Larrey, where he has restored an ancient vineyard with the Rabelaisian name of Montre Cul, 'Show your backside' – from the posture of the workers on the steep slope.

Ramonet-Prudhon
Chassagne-Montrachet, 21190 Meursault.

A distinguished old name in Chassagne. Half of the 34-acre domaine is white, including Bâtard- and Bienvenues-Bâtard-Montrachet, racy Chassagne Premier Cru Les Ruchottes, and Chassagne 'Village'. Their red wines are less famous but remarkably fine: Clos de la Boudriotte, Clos St-Jean and red Chassagne 'Village' are as good as any red wines of the southern Côte de Beaune. Father and son, Pierre and André, share the domaine. Pierre labels his wine Ramonet-Prudhon; André uses his own name.

Rapet Père & Fils
Pernand-Vergelesses, 21420 Savigny-Les-Beaune.

A highly reputed 40-acre domaine including parcels of Corton-Charlemagne and (red) Corton Grand Cru, Pernand-Vergelesses Premier Cru and Bourgogne (red and white). The enigmatic Monsieur Rapet's motto is '*Le moins on en dit, le mieux on se porte*' – in other words, 'My wine speaks for itself.' Not 5-star quality, but good value.

La Reine Pédauque
21200 Beaune

A well-known commercial house owned by Pierre André. They own 62 acres including the 10-acre Clos des Longres, 5 acres in Corton-Renards and 5 of Corton Charlemagne.

Remoissenet Père & Fils
21200 Beaune

A small domaine of 6 acres in Beaune Premier Cru (where Grèves and Toussaints make their own best wines) but an important broker and négociant who supplies burgundies to the French firm of Nicolas the Bristol one of Avery's. Through the latter I have had many good bottles, particularly of white wines.

Henri Remoriquet & Fils
25 rue de Charmois, 21700 Nuits-St-Georges.

An established family of growers in Nuits with 3.7 acres in Premiers Crus Les St-Georges, Rue de Chaux, Les Buosselots and Les Damodes and 7 Nuits 'Villages', including 2 acres in Les Allots, a good '*climat*' on the road to Vosne-Romanée, which is domaine-bottled and the house speciality. M. Remoriquet was a pioneer of the Hautes Côtes de Nuits with an acre at Chaux, 2 miles west on top of the hill.

Domaine Bernard Rion Père & Fils
21700 Vosne-Romanée

An emerging reputation. 30 acres in Vosne-Romanée, Nuits, Chambolle-Musigny and Clos Vougeot. Wines tending to firmness, made to last.

Domaine Daniel Rion
Prémeaux, 21700 Nuits-St-Georges

Patrice Rion, cousin of Bernard, has been known longer for his luscious yet elegant wines from Clos Vougeot, Vosne-Romanée and several Premiers Crus of Nuits.

Domaine de la Romanée-Conti
Vosne Romanée, 21700 Nuits-St-Georges.

See Romanée-Conti – A Great Burgundy Estate, pages 118 and 119.

Ropiteau Frères
21190 Meursault

The firm are négociants handling the output of their own Domaine Ropiteau-Mignon and other wines. The domaine is the biggest in Meursault with 12 acres of Premiers Crus in Genevrières, Perrières and 4 other '*climats*', and 32 in the 'Village' vineyards. 4 acres each of Premier Cru Puligny and Monthélie make them strong in fine white wines. Their red holdings are small parcels in Volnay, Monthélie, Pommard, Beaune (Grèves), Clos

Vougeot, Echézeaux and Chambolle-Musigny. The top Ropiteau whites are ideal white burgundy, balancing oak and grape flavours and needing time to develop.

Domaine Philippe Rossignol
21220 Gevrey-Chambertin

Another young man's tiny domaine achieving finer quality with new ideas than many bigger, more traditional, ones.

Joseph Roty
21220 Gevrey-Chambertin

A small but impeccable grower in Charmes-Chambertin, Gevrey Premier Cru and Villages. Even his Bourgogne Rouge is a noble wine.

Domaine Guy Roulot
1 rue Charles Giraud, 21190 Meursault.

A family domaine of 31 acres, 16 in Meursault (including Perrières, Tessons, Luchets, Les Meix Chavaux and Charmes), 3.7 in Auxey-Duresses red, with a quantity of Monthélie, of Passe-tout-grains, Bourgogne Chardonnay and Pinot. Also a still making Fine de Bourgogne (brandy) and Marc de Bourgogne. For both whites and reds they use the unusual phrase *'garde garantie 10 ans'*. Serious, well-judged wines. Guy Roulet died in 1982. His widow runs the firm and a nephew makes the wine.

Domaine G. Roumier
Chambolle-Musigny, 21220 Gevrey-Chambertin.

Jean-Marie Roumier directs the family property, started in 1924, with 35 acres; 18 in Chambolle-Musigny, 6 in Morey St-Denis, 6 of very old vines in Bonnes Mares, 2.5 in Clos de Vougeot and about 1 each in Le Musigny and Les Amoureuses. His brother Alain is cellar master at the Domaine de Vogüé. The family's wines are classics of depth and harmony. They even include a little Corton-Charlemagne.

Domaine Armand Rousseau
21220 Gevrey-Chambertin

The most respected grower of Chambertin. The founder's son, Charles Rousseau, now owns 19 acres, including 4 of Chambertin, 2 of Clos de Bèze, and parcels in Mazis and Charmes-Chambertin as well as in the Clos de la Roche in Morey and (his particular pride) 5.5 acres of Gevrey Clos St-Jacques on the hill above the village. His wine is vatted for 2 weeks. No one makes bigger, more gutsy burgundies. His '85s are a triumph.

Domaine Roux Père & Fils
St-Aubin, 21190 Meursault.

A competent proprietor whose 50 acres in St-Aubin, Meursault, Santenay Premiers Crus, Chassagne- and Puligny-Montrachet can be relied on for the true taste of their respective villages. He is also known for good Passe-tout-grains. The family are also négociants.

Domaine St-Michel
21590 Santenay

An estate jointly run by Michel Gutrin and the Santenay négociant Pierre Maufoux (q.v.). They own 74 acres, mainly in Santenay 'Village', Premier Cru Comme and Clos Rousseau, and in Puligny-Montrachet for white wines. Also a 20-acre vineyard at Pouilly-sur-Loire. Their Bourgogne Rouge St-Michel is good value. Most sales are to private clients in France.

Domaine Etienne Sauzet
Puligny-Montrachet, 21190 Meursault.

Etienne Sauzet (who died in 1975) was the third of the 5 generations who have built up a reputation for richly flavoured white burgundies. Many critics consider the domaine second only to Leflaive. The house style is to keep the wines on their lees for a year to develop flavour and 'fat'. Their main holding is 12.5 acres in Puligny Premiers Crus, with about 4 each of Combettes (their best-known wine) and Champ-Canet. They have a further 8 acres in Puligny, 2 in Chassagne and small parcels of Bâtard- and Bienvenues-Bâtard-Montrachet.

Maison Séguin-Manuel
Rue Paul Maldant, 21420 Savigny-Les-Beaune.

The date of foundation, 1720, gives this a claim to being the oldest merchant in Burgundy. The small (10-acre) domaine is in Savigny; most of the business is in other appellations, including Beaujolais, Côtes du Rhône, spirits and Oeil de Perdrix sparkling rosé.

Domaine Daniel Senard
21420 Aloxe-Corton

Farms 20 acres of his own land, 13 of them in the Grands Crus of Corton, Clos du Roi and Bressandes, and the entire 5-acre 'Clos Meix'; 6 in (red) Aloxe-Corton and small parcels of Beaune Les Coucherias and Chorey-Les-Beaune. The eighth generation of Senards operate in 14th-century cellars (and a tower). Exceptionally long-lived and well-balanced reds are made by controlling fermentation temperatures. Exports are 85% of sales.

Domaine de Serrigny
21550 Ladroix-Serrigny

Of the 28 acres, 9.4 are in Corton Grands Crus (Clos du Roi, Bressandes, Renardes and Maréchaudes), 1.6 in Aloxe-Corton Premier Cru and nearly an acre in Ladroix Premier Cru.

Robert de Suremain
Château de Monthélie, 21190 Meursault.

A small, old-fashioned but famous estate whose 13 acres of old vines in Monthélie produce a red wine comparable with good Volnays. He also has vineyards in Rully producing both red and white wines.

Roland Thévenin
Dom. du Château, Haut de Santenay, 21590 Santenay.

The dynamic proprietor (and restorer) of the ancient Moulin aux Moines at Auxey-Duresses: mayor of St-Romain (where he also has 12 acres), a passionate writer, collector and white-wine maker. His former property, the Château de Puligny-Montrachet, now belongs to a bank.

Domaine René Thévenin-Monthélie & Fils
St-Romain, 21190 Meursault.

A reputable family domaine since 1868 with 37 acres, half of them white St-Romain and the remainder equally divided between Monthélie and Beaune.

Thévenot Le Brun & Fils
Marey-Les-Fussey, 21700 Nuits-St-Georges.

Maurice Thévenot's father bought an abandoned monastic walled vineyard, the Clos du Vignon, in the Hautes Côtes de Nuits in 1933. Maurice and his sons replanted in 1967 and now have 64 acres making some of the best wine of the Hautes Côtes from Pinot Noir (30 acres), which is mixed with Gamay for his Passe-tout-grains, and Aligoté, which is bottled without racking to be drunk very young and faintly fizzy.

Domaine Tollot-Beaut & Fils
Chorey-Les-Beaune, 21200 Beaune.
A family property since 1880 with impeccable standards, sometimes cited as a model for Burgundy. Of a total of 46 acres, a little under half is at Chorey and half divided among the Premiers Crus of Beaune (Grèves and Clos du Roi, 4.2 acres), Savigny and Aloxe-Corton, with some 400 cases a year of Corton-Bressandes, 250 of Le Corton and 125 of Corton-Charlemagne (white). No secrets but careful traditional wine-making, plunging the 'cap' twice a day and controlling the temperature. The special pride of the house is in Corton-Bressandes and Beaune Clos du Roi.

Domaine Tollot-Voarick
Chorey-Les-Beaune, 21200 Beaune.
A 42-acre domaine based at Chorey, just north of Beaune, where it also owns a restaurant, Le Bareuzi. The bulk of its vineyards are outside the grander areas of the Côte, growing Pinot Noir, Gamay and Aligoté at Chorey, Ladoix-Serrigny and Comblanchien. Nearly 9 acres, however, are in Aloxe-Corton and 2 in Pernand Premier Cru Les Vergelesses. Two are in Savigny and 2 in Beaune Clos du Roy. A well-equipped property which takes intelligent pains and every opportunity of making *vins de garde*, in new barrels where the wine warrants the expense.

Domaine Tortochot
21220 Gevrey-Chambertin
A 27-acre family property. They own parcels of between 1 and 2 acres in the Grands Crus Charmes- and Mazis-Chambertin, a similar piece of Lavaux St-Jacques on the hill above the village and considered worthy of Grand Cru standing, some good land in Morey St-Denis and a half acre in Clos Vougeot.

Domaine Louis Trapet
53 route de Beaune, 21220 Gevrey-Chambertin.
Five generations of Trapets have worked to build up a domaine of 30 acres, including nearly 5 of Chambertin, over 4 in Latricières and Chapelle-Chambertin, 2.5 in Gevrey Premiers Crus and 12.5 in the Gevrey 'Village' vineyards. Jean Trapet's great-grandfather started his success by being one of the first in the Côte d'Or to graft vines during the phylloxera epidemic of the 1870s. The pride of the house is its Chambertin, made in the traditional way but not as massive as Rousseau's (q.v.).

Domaine des Varoilles
11 rue de l'Ancien Hôpital, 21220 Gevrey-Chambertin.
A 30-acre domaine with one of the highest reputations in Burgundy for serious *vins de garde* that really must be matured. It takes its name from its 15-acre Clos des Varoilles, planted on the south-facing hill above Gevrey by monks from Langres in the 12th and 13th centuries. The Clos du Couvent, Clos du Meix des Ouches and La Romanée are other 'monopoles' in Gevrey, besides 2 acres of Charmes- and Mazoyères-Chambertin, 1.3 of Bonnes Mares and 6.5 of Clos de Vougeot. The director, Jean-Pierre Naigeon, makes some of Burgundy's firmest, best-structured wines, selecting from old vines and constantly mixing in the skins during fermentation. He quotes the gourmet-critic Gaston Roupnel on Varoilles wines: 'Only age can tame its almost savage force . . . and give it at last the scents of violets and spring.' Amen.

Domaine Charles Vienot
21700 Prémeaux Prissey
The 9.8-acre property (now owned by J.-C. Boisset) is scattered between 11 different parcels in a number of communes including Nuits-St-Georges (2 Premiers Crus), Gevrey-Chambertin (1 Premier Cru), Corton and Clos de Vougeot.

Henri de Villamont
Rue du Docteur Guyot, 21420 Savigny-Les-Beaune.
Negóciants and growers founded by the huge Swiss firm of Schenk in 1964, when they bought the 15-acre Domaine Marthenot at Savigny and the 10-acre Domaine Modot in Chambolle-Musigny and Grands-Echézeaux. In 1969 they bought the business of Arthur Barolet in Beaune. The name Barolet figures largely in their annals since they found and marketed the extraordinary hoard of fine old burgundies of the late Dr. Barolet in 1968. 70% is exported.

Domaine Michel Voarick
21420 Aloxe-Corton
A 22-acre family 'exploitation' which includes farming the famous 6-acre Corton Cuvée Dr. Pest for the Hospices de Beaune. Voarick owns 5 acres of Corton Grand Cru (Clos du Roi, Bressandes, Languettes, Renardes) and 3 of Corton-Charlemagne, besides 6 acres in Pernand-Vergelesses and 7 in Aloxe-Corton. A total of some 3,850 cases of red and 500 of white. Old-fashioned methods include fermenting stalks-and-all in oak *cuves* to make *vins de garde*.

Domaine Comte Georges de Vogüé
Chambolle-Musigny, 21220 Gevrey-Chambertin.
Considered by some the finest domaine in Burgundy, descended by inheritance since 1450. The name de Vogüé appears in 1766. Splendid vaulted cellars under the 15th-century house hold the production of 30 acres. 15 are in Le Musigny, 6.5 in Bonnes Mares, 1.5 in the Premier Cru Les Amoureuses and 5 in the appellation Chambolle-Musigny, 3,000 Chardonnay vines in Musigny produce some 100 cases a year of a unique Musigny Blanc. After a flat patch in the 1970s and early '80s the wines are once again superlative. The names Vieilles Vignes is given to the best wine, which is burgundy at its grandest and yet most subtle – beyond description. 75% is exported.

Cave Coopérative des Grands Vins Rosés
21 rue de Mazy, 21160 Marsannay-La-Côte.
One of the few growers' cooperatives of the Côte d'Or, founded in 1929 and now counting 19 members whose properties vary between 2 and 35 acres. The wines are Bourgogne Rouge and their speciality, Rosé de Marsannay, which is largely sold to passing tourists in summer.

André Ziltener Père & Fils
Chambolle-Musigny, 21220 Gevrey-Chamberlin
Swiss-owned merchant and proprietor of a domaine that includes a Château de Chambolle-Musigny (there are two) and a restaurant in the village. Ziltener offers a full range of good sturdy examples of both red and white burgundies, including a well-oaked Chablis.

THE COTE CHALONNAISE

Santenay brings the Côte d'Or to a close at its southern end. There is scarcely time for lunch at the luxurious Lameloise at Chagny before the wine scout has to be alert again for the five villages that make up the Côte Chalonnaise. In fact, Chalon-sur-Saône has little to do with the district today and the tendency is to refer to the Région de Mercurey, the biggest and best known of the wine parishes. But in antiquity Chalon was one of the great wine ports of the Empire. It was the point where wine coming or going north to or from Paris or the Moselle had to be transshipped from river to road – 25,000 amphoras were found in one dredging operation in the Saône at Chalon.

A new appellation, Bourgogne Côte Chalonnaise, was introduced in 1990 which will distinguish the wines of the Côte Chalonnaise from the greater appellation of Bourgogne which is rather large and undefined. The Côte from Chagny southwards is less distinct and consistent than from Santenay northwards. So is its wine. Rising demand and prices have only recently made wine-growing profitable rather than marginal, and encouraged replanting of land abandoned after phylloxera, or whose owners were killed in World War I. Although its best wines are up to minor Côte de Beaune standards, it is hard to pin them down with a regional character. They vary remarkably from village to village.

Mercurey and Givry are dedicated 90 per cent to red wine, which should be firm and tasty Pinot Noir at least on a level with, say, a good Côte de Beaune-Villages; if anything harder and leaner, with Givry, traditionally the bigger, demanding longer keeping.

Rully is split equally between red wine and white. Here the white at its best is marvellously brisk with a touch of real class. The red, at least as most growers make it today, can be rather thin compared with Mercurey. High acidity in Rully whites makes them ideal for sparkling wines.

Montagny is entirely a white-wine appellation, with the peculiarity that all its wines of 11.5 degrees alcohol or more are entitled to be labelled Premier Cru – which seems scarcely fair to the carefully limited Premier Crus of the other villages. Montagny whites tend to have a little more body and less finesse than those of Rully. The one most often seen abroad, a selection by the Beaune négociant Louis Latour, is quite a fat dry wine.

The fifth appellation of the Côte Chalonnaise is the only specific one of the Aligoté grape in Burgundy. The village of Bouzeron, between Rully and Chagny, has made a speciality of a normally plain, sharp café wine. In 1979 it was granted the appellation Bourgogne Aligoté de Bouzeron.

Besides these specific appellations the Région de Mercurey makes a considerable quantity of honourable Bourgogne Rouge, most of which is sold in bulk. But a few growers in Bouzeron and St-Désert bottle it. Like all red burgundy, it should be kept a minimum of two years in bottle.

The other regional speciality is Crémant de Bourgogne, sparkling wine whose quality will amaze those who think that champagne is first and the rest nowhere. (*See* note on page 132.)

Three sizeable producers account for most of the Crémant. They are Delorme at Rully, R. Chevillard at La Rochepot on the road to Paris, and Parigot-Richard at Savigny-Les-Beaune.

To summarize the region:

Mercurey			1988 crop 302,000 cases, 90% red, 10% white
Givry	,,	,,	84,850 cases, 90% red, 10% white
Rully	,,	,,	150,900 cases, 40% red, 60% white
Montagny	,,	,,	87,000 cases, 100% white
Bourgogne Aligoté de Bouzeron	,,	,,	361,000 cases, 100% white

Tasting from the cask

MAJOR PRODUCERS

Chateau de Chamirey
See Antonin Rodet

Emile Chandesais
Château St-Nicolas, 71150 Fontaines.
A négociant, based in the Côte Chalonnaise, with a reputation for wines from the Région de Mercurey. From their own 27 acres of vineyards they produce 7,000 cases of Bourgogne AC and Rully Les St-Jacques.

Domaine Chanzy-Daniel
Domaine L'Hermitage, Bouzeron, 71150 Chagny.
One of the two considerable domaines in Bouzeron with some 27 acres in that village, 30 in Rully and 6 in Mercurey. Over half of the Bouzeron vineyard is planted in Aligoté, which is considered Burgundy's best. Chanzy's Bourgogne (i.e. Pinot Noir and Chardonnay) vineyards in Bouzeron are called Clos de la Fortune. His biggest production is of Rully Rouge (2,500 cases from 19 acres). His Premier Cru Mercurey vineyards are called Clos du Roy. Daniel Chanzy is insistent that red burgundy must be kept 3 or 4 years in bottle to show its personality.

Jean-François Delorme
Domaine de la Renard, Rully, 71150 Chagny.
The most remarkable enterprise in the region; an estate of 163 acres built up from scratch in 30 years, largely by reclaiming former vineyards abandoned long ago and turned to scrub. Delorme is equally well known as one of Burgundy's best specialists in sparkling wine, for which the very clean, slightly austere whites of Rully are excellent. 64 acres of the domaine in Rully are Chardonnay; 57 are Pinot Noir. Varot is the 44-acre vineyard that gives Delorme's best white, which is notable for freshness and finesse. Its austerity brings it closer in character to Chablis than, say, a Mâcon white. Domaine de la Renarde red is also delicate, 'nervous' and without surplus flesh. A comparison with his Mercurey (he has 12 acres) shows the Mercurey to be plumper and to have more substance. He also has 11 acres of Givry, 4.2 of Bouzeron Aligoté and 12 at La Rochepot. 37,500 cases of Crémant de Bourgogne are made from Pinot Noir and Chardonnay in an impressive new cellar; it is a real alternative to champagne – a *cuvée* that is tasty without being coarse; delicate without being timid.

Michel Derain
St-Désert, 71390 Buxy.
A small-scale producer of 'serious' Bourgogne Rouge and Givry Blanc from 14 acres.

Du Gardin
71640 Givry.
Owners of the 15-acre 'monopole' Clos Saloman in Givry for over 300 years. Very sound wine.

Michel Goubard
Basseville, 71390 St-Désert.
An example of how good Bourgogne Rouge without a specific appellation can be in this part of the Côtes Goubard also bottles some 7,250 cases of Côte Chalonnaise.

Paul & Henri Jacqueson
71150 Rully
Father and son together take great pride in this small domaine of 17 acres making wine in the old way. The reds are trodden by foot, stems and all, fermented for up to 22 days and raised in new barrels every year. 5 acres of Rully Premier Cru are called 'Les Clouds' (red) and 'Grésigny' (white). The other wines are (red) Mercurey and Rully, and some Aligoté and Passe-tout-grains. Their label is seen in some very smart restaurants.

Domaine Michel Juillot
71640 Mercurey
One of the best Mercurey makers, regularly carrying off gold medals for the red Clos des Barraults from his 69 acres (of which 11.8 are Chardonnay). He destems all his grapes, ferments in open vats and buys one third of his barrels new each year. He also owns vines in Aloxe-Corton and Montagny.

Paul and Yves de Launay
Clos du Château de Montaigu, Mercurey, 71640 Givry.
A traditional small property around the ruins of the Château de Montaigu, making Mercurey red and some Aligoté.

Jean Maréchal
71640 Mercurey
Maréchals have made Mercurey for 300 years. 17 of their 22 acres are in the Premiers Crus, almost all red. The aim is to produce long-lived wines, especially his 'Cuvée Prestige'.

Armand Monassier
Domaine du Prieuré, Rully, 71150 Chagny.
The property of a Paris restaurateur (Chez Les Anges, one-star, Boulevard Latour-Maubourg), born in Rully, who since 1958 has assembled a total of 18 acres, 11 of Rully Rouge (5 are Premier Cru) and 5 of Rully Blanc (half Premier Cru). With a little red Mercurey, he also makes Crémant de Bourgogne, Passe-tout-grains, *marc* and *fine*.

E. and X. Noël-Bouton
Domaine de la Folie, Rully, 71150 Chagny.
A substantial property with 1,000 years of history, in the parish of Chagny but in the appellation of Rully. The 44 acres are in one block around the house, with Chardonnay in a majority, producing some 3,300 cases a year of Rully Blanc Clos St-Jacques; Pinot Noir making 2,500 cases of Rully Rouge Clos de Bellecroix; and a smaller patch of Aligoté. Xavier Noël-Bouton buys as much as 40% of his barrels new each year to make aromatic wines with the potential to develop. A leader of the commune.

Domaine Maurice Protheau & Fils
Mercurey, 71640 Givry.
A major domaine of 110 acres, including 15.5 in Clos L'Evêque, 11 in La Fauconnière and 10 in the Clos des Corvées. Négociants François Protheau market the wines.

Domaine Ragot
Poncey, 71640 Givry.
A small domaine in its fourth generation with a dignified château, with 10 acres of Givry Rouge and 5 of Givry Blanc out of a total of 18. The proportion of white is unusually high for Givry and the keeping qualities of the wine are remarkable – particularly in years of high acidity. Ripe vintages, says M. Ragot, are best drunk sooner. His red and white are both regular gold-medal winners.

Antonin Rodet
Mercurey, 71640 Givry.

An important négociant as well as proprietor in Mercurey. The fourth generation of the Rodet family is represented by the Marquis de Jouennes d'Herville, the present head of the firm, whose name appears on the domaine's label, Château de Chamirey. The 66-acre vineyard consists of nearly the whole of the Mercurey Premier Cru Clos du Roi and produces some 8,500 cases of red and 1,500 of white. To many, the red Château de Chamirey is the archetypal Mercurey.

Antonin Rodet deals in wines from all parts of Burgundy, taking special pride in its Bourgogne Rodet, Mercurey, Meursault and Gevrey-Chambertin.

Domaine Saier
Mercurey, 71640 Givry.

Purchasers, in 1979, of the 22-acre Grand Cru Clos des Lambrays in Morey St-Denis. 7.4 acres of the 62-acre domaine are in Mercurey Premier Cru Les Champs Martin. There are 27 more acres of red Mercurey and 7.4 of white.

Domaine Château de la Saule
Montagny-Les-Buxy, 71390 Buxy.

A 32-acre property almost entirely devoted to making fresh, vigorous, white Montagny. The grapes are pressed as quickly as possible after picking, the juice fined and fermented in big oak barrels, to be bottled the following June. While freshness is the main aim, the 'big' vintages have been known to improve for 8 or 10 years.

Hugues de Suremain
Mercurey, 71640 Givry.

A leading proprietor and President of the growers' syndicate of Mercurey, whose own 30 acres are known for concentrated and age-worthy wines.

Société Divile du Domaine Thénard
71640 Givry

Much the grandest estate of Givry, with 50 acres in the village (almost all red Premiers Crus) but better known to the world as the owner of the second-biggest single plot of Le Montrachet, 4.5 acres, as well as 2 acres each of Corton Clos du Roi, Iles des Vergelesses and 1.4 of Grands-Echézeaux. The property has been in the family for 200 years. All the wine is made in the atmospheric oak-beamed *cuverie* and cellars at Givry. Three Givry Premiers Crus, all robust *vins de garde*, are sold under their vineyard names: Boischevaux, Cellier aux Moines and Clos St-Pierre.

A. and P. de Villaine
Bouzeron, 71150 Chagny.

A grower better known as coproprietor of the Domaine de la Romanée-Conti, but equally proud to have helped bring Bouzeron from obscurity to having its own appellation in 5 years (1973–78) of impeccable wine-making. He treats Aligoté as a noble grape, using half barrels (for finesse) and half tanks (for fruit). His Bourgogne Rouge is similarly made, with selective pickings, long fermentation with the stems, and no rackings. His 25 acres of Aligoté produce about 4,350 cases a year. 8 acres of Chardonnay are called Bourgogne Blanc Les Clous and 13.5 acres of Pinot Noir are called by their vineyard names, La Digoine and La Fortune. Bourgogne Rosé is made in suitable years.

Caves des Vignerons de Buxy
Les Vignes de la Croix, St-Gengoux Le Nuit, 71390 Buxy.

The important and very modern growers' cooperative for Buxy and Montagny, founded in 1931 but re-equipped recently. Its members own 580 acres of vines, less than half of which now have generic appellations (Bourgogne Rouge, Passe-tout-grains. Aligoté and Bourgogne Grand Ordinaire are its principal productions.) The remainder include white Montagny, with some Premier Cru, Rully, red Côte Chalonnais, and Crémant de Bourgogne.

MACON

Say 'Mâcon' to most wine drinkers today and their knee-jerk response will be 'Blanc'. The region is riding high on the reliability and uncomplicated pleasantness of its Chardonnay whites. They have the advantage of being recognizably white burgundy but half the price of Côte d'Or wines, and marvellously easy to choose – since most of them are made by skilful cooperatives and marketed by their efficient central Union des Coopératives Vinicoles de Bourgogne de Saône-et-Loire.

The Mâconnais is a widespread and disjointed region, taking its name from the important commercial city on the Saône just outside its limits to the east. It has little of the monoculture of Beaujolais; its mixed farming land is more attractive, and in places geologically spectacular. Pouilly-Fuissé is its only appellation with Grand Vin aspirations.

Most Mâcon wine used to be red, made of Gamay but grown on heavy chalky soil which prevents it from ripening to Beaujolais softness and vitality.

Mâcon Rouge was indeed merely *vin ordinaire* with an appellation until Beaujolais methods of fermentation were introduced. Recently there have been some much better wines up to Beaujolais-Villages standards.

Pinot Noir from the Mâconnais can aspire no higher than the appellation Bourgogne Rouge or (mixed with Gamay) Passe-tout-grains.

Chardonnay now occupies two thirds of the vineyards, including (in the more northerly communes in particular) a strain of Chardonnay known as the 'Musqué' for its decidedly richer, melony-musky flavour. Used to excess it can produce a blowsy, unsubtle wine. In due proportion it adds a hint of richness to otherwise rather straight dry white; undoubtedly an element in the popularity of Mâcon-Villages or with the name of a particular village.

Pouilly-Fuissé rises higher in the quality league, for local reasons of soil and situation – but not as much higher as its price infers. The four villages in the appellation area have been prominent over the centuries, partly for their proximity to Mâcon, partly as a tourist attraction for the mighty limestone bluffs that dominate them and the prehistoric traces that litter the district, partly for the chalky clay and sunny slopes that make their wine at least as good as any south Burgundy white.

Pierre Bréjoux describes it as 'masculine and long-lived', but variable according to the precise location of the vineyard in a country that is all bumps and dips. Such variations are not easy to follow where there are very few domaines of more

than a few acres. The best I have tasted have been full-bodied and dry but rather half-hearted in flavour compared with, say, Meursault or a good Chablis. The growers' cooperative of Chaintré is much the biggest source of Pouilly-Fuissé.

The fact that wines of more or less equal value are produced in the surrounding area has given rise to two other appellations. The smaller Pouilly-Vinzelles (which includes Pouilly-Loché) has somehow failed to catch the public's eye. The much larger St-Véran, which scoops in eight villages, including the northern fringe of the Beaujolais country, was added in 1971 and now offers extremely good value.

THE APPELLATIONS OF MACON

The Mâconnais has five appellations of its own and shares the right to five more with the rest of Burgundy. Its own appellations are:

FOR WHITE WINES

Mâcon Blanc. Chardonnay wine from delimited areas with a minimum 10 degrees of natural alcohol. This wine can also be labelled Pinot Chardonnay de Mâcon.

Mâcon Supérieur. The same with one more degree of alcohol.

Mâcon-Villages (or Mâcon- followed by the name of one of 43 villages in the eastern half of the region). The best known of these are Clessé, Prissé, Lugny, Viré and Chardonnay – the village with the credit for finding the noblest white grape of France. The minimum degree is 11, as for Mâcon Supérieur.

St-Véran. The same as for Mâcon-Villages but from 8 of the southernmost communes, overlapping into Beaujolais at St-Amour. The 8 are Chânes, Chasselas, Davayé, Leynes, Prissé, St-Amour, St-Vérand [sic] and part of Solutré, which is not in the appellation Pouilly-Fuissé. Davayé and Prissé lie to the north, the rest are to the south of Pouilly-Fuissé but offer very similar wines, which can also be sold as Beaujolais Blanc, Mâcon-Villages or Bourgogne Blanc if the customer prefers one of these names. If a particular vineyard is named on the label the minimum degree is 12, with the implication that the wine is better and more concentrated.

Pouilly-Fuissé. Chardonnay wine of 11 degrees from specified parts of the villages of Pouilly, Fuissé, Solutré, Vergisson and Chaintré. If a vineyard name is used it must have 12 degrees.

Pouilly-Vinzelles. The same rules as for Pouilly-Fuissé, but wine from the 2 villages of Vinzelles and Loché to the east – marginally less good but more than marginally cheaper.

FOR RED WINES

Mâcon Rouge. Gamay red wine of at least 9 degrees. It can also be made pink and offered as Mâcon Rosé.

Mâcon Supérieur. The same with an extra degree of alcohol and from certain specified zones. It can also be labelled as Mâcon- (followed by a village name), but *not* Mâcon-Villages.

GENERAL APPELLATIONS

Aligoté. As in the rest of Burgundy.

Bourgogne. For Chardonnay whites and Pinot Noir reds.

Bourgogne Grand Ordinaire. For whites.

Crémant de Bourgogne. As in the rest of Burgundy.

Passe-tout-grains. For Gamay and Pinot Noir (2:1) reds.

The Chante-Flûte

The region of Mercurey has its own equivalent of the Confrérie des Chevaliers de Tastevin which sits in judgement on wines submitted for their special approval. Approved wines, which are always among the best of the region, wear a special label to signify that they have been 'Chante-Flûte.'

Enjoying Mâcon and Beaujolais

White Mâcon is as adaptable as any French white wine for all-purpose use. Well chilled it is a good apéritif. Slightly less cold it serves the same purposes as more prestigious white burgundies. Beaujolais Nouveau, though often served alone, slightly chilled, as a party wine, can be very fatiguing and thirst-making – especially when (as often happens) its alcoholic degree is particularly high. Its cheerful properties are better appreciated with terrines or cheeses, picnic or kitchen food. Beaujolais crus of good vintages aged 3 or 4 years in bottle often begin to resemble fine Rhône wines – more rarely Côte d'Or wines. They are best served at the same temperature as red burgundy and with similar food.

MACON PRODUCERS

The great bulk of Mâcon, both white and red, is produced by the 18 growers' cooperatives of the area. The best known are those of Chaintré (for Pouilly-Fuissé), Lugny (for Mâcon-Lugny and Mâcon Rouge Supérieur), Prissé (Mâcon-Prissé and St-Véran) and Viré (Mâcon-Viré).

All except those marked with an asterisk are distributed by the Union des Coopératives Vinicoles de Bourgogne de Saône-et-Loire, Charnay-Les-Mâcon, 71008 Mâcon, which also offers a good Crémant de Bourgogne under various labels, among them Prince de Chardonne.

The following are the few individual producers with more than a local reputation. The average holding is about 10 acres, producing 2,000–3,000 cases a year.

Pouilly-Fuissé
Château de Beauregard, Fuissé, owner Georges Burrier
Clos de Bourg, Fuissé, owner Maurice Luquet
Joseph Corsin, Fuissé
Roger Duboeuf, Chaintré
Château de Fuissé, owner Marcel Vincent. The outstanding grower of the area.
Claude-Guérin, Vergisson
Pouilly-Vinzelles
Jean Mathias, Chaintré
Mâcon-Clessé
Jean Thevenet, Quintaine-Clessé, Lugny
St-Véran
Lycée Agricole, Davayé
Georges Chagny, Leynes
Andre Chavet, Davayé
R. Duperron, Leynes
Mâcon-Viré
Clos du Chapitre, Viré, owner Jacques Depagneux
Château de Viré, Viré, owner Hubert Desbois
In addition very good wines are offered by several of the négociants well known for their Beaujolais; notably Georges Duboeuf, Thorin and Piat, and by Louis Latour, Robert Drouhin and Louis Jadot of Beaune.

CAVES COOPERATIVES

Production figures are for AOC wines only. Most of these coops also make a limited amount of *vin de table*, which is mostly sold in bulk.
Aze*
71260 Lugny. 511 acres; 125 members; 110,000 cases.
Bissey-sous-Cruchaud
71390 Buxy. 121 acres; 80 members; 27,900 cases.
Buxy*
71390 Buxy, 1,200 acres; 203,600 cases.
Chaintré
71570 La Chapelle de Guinchay. 487 acres; 187 members; 117,300 cases.
Chardonnay*
71700 Tournus. 538 acres; 113 members; 119,000 cases.

Charnay-Les-Mâcon
71000 Mâcon. 160 acres; 73 members; 33,000 cases.
Genouilly
71460 St-Gengoux Le National. 151 acres; 185 members; 22,800 cases.
Igé*
71960 Pierreclos. 593 acres; 102 members; 166,000 cases.
Lugny*
71260 Lugny. 2,359 acres; 505 members; 678,000 cases.
Mancey
71240 Sennecey-Le-Grand. 1,010 acres; 180 members; 59,000 cases.
Prissé
71960 Pierreclos. 882 acres; 234 members; 245,000 cases.

Sennece-Les-Mâcon*
71000 Mâcon. 91 acres; 84 members; 20,300 cases.
Sologny
71960 Pierreclos. 459 acres; 145 members; 107,000 cases.
Verzé
71960 Pierreclos. 2,067 acres; 91 members; 122,000 cases.
'La Vigne Blanche'
Clessé, 71260 Lugny. 293 acres; 83 members; 73,000 cases.
Vinzelles
71145 Vinzelles. 311 acres; 133 members; 76,000 cases.
Vire*
71260 Lugny. 692 acres; 245 members; 200,000 cases.

The hills of Beaujolais rise from the plain of the Saône to a height of more than 1,500 feet.

BEAUJOLAIS

The Beaujolais region is no more complex than its lighthearted wine. Twelve appellations take care of the whole 55,000 acres and the 13 million cases of wine they make every year. They could really be reduced to half a dozen without greatly grieving anyone but the gastronomes of Lyon. What is needed is a grasp of the essential grades of quality and a good address list – which need not be long.

The great majority of Beaujolais is made either by a growers' cooperative or by tiny properties. Two thousand five hundred Beaujolais makers have between two and ten acres – enough to make, say, up to 3,000 cases each. Another 1,400 have between 10 and 18 acres – which it will keep their clients supplied, but scarcely make a reputation.

The details given here are therefore a guide to the major sources of Beaujolais, the merchants and cooperatives of the region, and a very short selection of some standard-setting properties.

The world's perception of Beaujolais today is very different from what it was 20 or so years ago. Beyond its own region and Paris, where it was *the* café wine, it used to be traded as a cut-price burgundy, imitating the weight of the Pinot Noirs of the Côte d'Or; by dint of picking as ripe as possible and adding plenty of sugar, achieving strength without grace. I have always been mystified by mid-nineteenth-century figures showing Beaujolais crus with 15 degrees of alcohol (while Médocs had 9 or 10 degrees). Very few red wines need anything like that strength, and least of all Gamay, which lacks the flavour to countenance it. The Gamay of Beaujolais has no great fruity flavour; well made and in the modern manner it lures you in with its sappy smell and a combination of soft juiciness and a slight nip – the perfect recipe for quenching thirst.

HOW BEAUJOLAIS IS MADE

The secret of the fresh grape fruitness of Beaujolais lies in the way the Gamay – a grape of modest pretentions to quality – is handled and fermented. Wine making in the Beaujolais combines the classic method of burgundy with *macération carbonique* – the activity of enzymes inside an uncrushed grape which, provided it is surrounded by carbon dioxide, causes an internal fermentation and the extraction of colour and flavour from the inner skin.

The trick is to fill the fermenting vat with grapes in their whole bunches, on their stalks, as little crushed and damaged as possible. In a modern Beaujolais *cuverie* a common way is to load the vat with a belt-elevator carrying the bunches to an opening in the top. The weight of the upper grapes crushes the lower ones, which start a normal fermentation with their natural yeasts. The carbon dioxide given off by this (helped along with gas from a bottle, if necessary) blankets off the air from the uncrushed upper layers. Here the grapes quietly feed on themselves, many of them splitting in the process. After six or seven days the vat is about one third full of wine. The liquid is then run off, the solid pressed and the two products blended together. In normal red-wine making the *vin de presse* is in a minority (and may not be used at all). In the Beaujolais method it accounts for between to thirds and three quarters of the total. At this stage the juice still has unfermented sugar in it. Fermentation has to finish before it is stable enough to be called wine. The law says that this will happen by the third Thursday in November, but in years when the harvest is late some fairly brutal methods of stabilization are needed to 'finish' the wine in time.

THE APPELLATIONS OF BEAUJOLAIS

Most basic is plain Beaujolais, from the southern half of the region, south of Villefranche, where the Gamay is encouraged to produce large quantities on heavy soil. (Although there is nothing to stop growers anywhere in Beaujolais using the appellation.) This is essentially now-or-never wine, originally destined to be sold on draught in local cafés and by the carafe in restaurants. It is best drunk as young as possible. The date after which it can be sold *en primeur* is the third Thursday in November. The term *nouveau*, while often used with the same intention, really only means the wine of the last harvest, until the next. The minimum alcoholic degree is 9, but this is regularly exceeded either naturally or by adding sugar. For this reason the appellation Beaujolais Supérieur, only different in requiring 10 degrees, is litle used. 'Beaujolais' applies to red, white or rosé, but the great majority is red.

Total area is 22,035 acres; average production 7,000,000 cases a year.

GROWERS

Alain Bidon
Chessy-Les-Mines, 69380 Lozanne, with 30 acres.
Robert Doat
Domaine de Bois Franc, Jarnioux, 69640 Denice, with 53 acres.
Jean Garlon
Beauvallon, Theizé, 69620 Le Bois d'Oingt, with 7.5 acres.
Régis Manus
'La Paisible', 69480 Anse, with 16 acres.

Raymond Mathelin & Fils
Domaine de Sandar, 69380 Chatillon d'Azergues, with 10 acres.
Jean Pagnon
Morance, 69480 Anse, with 15 acres.
Antoine Pein
Theizé, 69620 Le Bois d'Oingt, with 30 acres.
Member of the Eventail de Vignerons Producteurs is Jacques Montagne at Leynes.

COOPERATIVES

Bois d'Oingt
69620 Bois d'Oingt, with 139 members, 543 acres and 356,000 cases.
Soc. Viticole Beaujolaise
Liergues, 69400 Villefranche, with 1,160 acres and 240 members.
Beau Vallon
Theizé, 69620 Le Bois d'Oingt, with 951 acres.

BEAUJOLAIS-VILLAGES

The northern half of the region, or Haut-Beaujolais, has steeper hills, warmer (because lighter and more sandy) soil, and makes better wine. Beaujolais-Villages is the appellation that covers the whole of this area, 39 villages in all, but 10 small zones in the north, identified by combinations of slopes and soils that are peculiar to themselves, are singled out as the Beaujolais 'crus' – the aristocrats.

Beaujolais-Villages makes a better *vin de primeur* than plain Beaujolais, except in untypically hot vintages. It has a minimum of 10 degrees alcohol and more backing of fruit and body – more flavour, in fact – to complement the rasp of new fruit juice. It is almost always worth its fairly modest premium both *en primeur* and even more when it has been or will be kept. Good Villages is at its best in the summer after the vintage, and can hold for another year. Besides the 'crus', the region as a whole has some producers whose wines are regularly up to 'cru' standards.

Total area is 15,800 acres; average production 4,000,000 cases a year.

GROWERS

Patrick Giloux
Clos de Creuze Naire, 71570 Chanes, 22 acres.
Etienne Jambon
Château Thulon, Lantigné, 69430 Beaujeu, with 30 acres.
Claude & Michelle Joubert
Lantigné, 69430 Beaujeu, with 20 acres.
Durieu de Lacarelle
Dom. de Lacarelle, St-Etienne-des-Oullières, 69830 St-Georges de Reneins, with 345 acres.
René Miolane
Le Cellier, Salles, 69830 St-Georges de Reneins, with 34 acres.
Monternot
'Les Places', Blace, 69830 St-Georges de Reneins, with 20 acres.
Gilles Perroud
'Le Basty', Lantigné, 69430 Beaujeu, with 30 acres.
Jean-Charles Pivot
Quincie-en-Beaujolais, 69430 Beaujeu, with 30 acres.

The slatted wooden press and cylindrical vats typical of Beaujolais

André Vernus
'Le Pouzet', St-Etienne-La-Varenne, 69830 St-Georges de Reneins, 20 acres.
Cave Coopérative (Soc. Viticole Beaujolaise)
Liergues, 69400 Villefranche-Sur-Saône

(Appellation Beaujolais), with 240 members and 1,161 acres.
Members of the Eventail de Vignerons Producteurs include:
Jacques Montagne, **Roger** and **Jean-Luc Tissier** and **Francis Crot** at

Leynes, **André Jaffre** at Charentay and **Jean Verger** at Blacé.

THE 'CRUS' OF BEAUJOLAIS

The map shows that between the railway along the Saône valley and the 450-metre contour line in the Beaujolais mountains to the west, from just south of Belleville to the boundary with the Mâconnais, the vine has the landscape to itself. Sandy, stony or schistous granite-based soils without lime give the Gamay a roundness and depth of flavour it lacks elsewhere. Here it is pruned hard and trimmed plant by plant as an individual. The minimum strength of the wine is the same as for all the Villages, but when it is sold with a vineyard name the required minimum is a degree higher.

Cru Beaujolais can be offered *en primeur*, but not until a month after Beaujolais and Villages, from 15 December. It would be a pity to prevent it being poured for Christmas. The best crus are never treated in this way; they are kept in barrel or vat until at least the March after the vintage. Their full individuality and sweet juicy smoothness take anything from six months to six years in bottle to develop. Three of the crus, Morgon, Chénas and above all Moulin-à-Vent, are looked on as *vins de garde*, at least by Beaujolais standards.

BROUILLY

The southernmost and the largest of the crus, enveloping areas in 5 villages (Odenas, St-Lager, Cercié, Charentay, St-Etienne-La-Varenne and Quincié) grouped around the isolated Mont de Brouilly (*see* Côtes de Brouilly). The word 'typical' is most often used for Brouilly – not surprisingly for the biggest producer lying in the very heart of the region. This means the wine is full of grapey flavour and vigour but not aggressive in its first year.

Total area is 3,000 acres; average production 800,000 cases a year.
Château de Briante
Mme de Buttet, St-Lager, 69220 Belleville.

Château de la Chaize
M. de Roussy de Salles, Odenas, 69830 St-Georges de Reneins. The biggest estate in Beaujolais with 360 acres.
Philippe Dutraive
Dom. des Combes, Charentay, 69220 Belleville.
Claude Geoffray
Le Grand Vernay, Charentay, 69220 Belleville.
Alain Michaud
Cedex, 69220 St Lager.
Château de Nervers
M. de Chabannes, Odenas, 69830 St-Georges de Reneins.
Château de Pierreux
Marquise de Toulzouet, Odenas, 69830 St-Georges de Reneins.

Cave Coopérative de Bel-Air
St-Jean d'Ardières, 69220 Belleville, with 300 members and 1,080 acres (*see also* Côtes de Brouilly).
Members of the Eventail de Vignerons Producteurs are **André Ronzière** at Bonnège, Charentay; **André Large** at Odenas; **Lucien** and **Robert Verger**.

CHENAS

The smallest cru, sheltered from the west by a wooded hill (Chénas is derived from *chêne*, an oak) and including part of the commune of La Chapelle-de-Guinchay. Certain Chénas wines achieve formidable strengths, but its vineyard sites are too varied for the appellation to be readily identifiable or its style reliable.

Total area is 625 acres; average production 164,000 cases a year.

Domaine Champagnon
Les Brureaux, Chénas, 69840 Chénas.
Fernand Charvet
Le Bourg, Chénas, 69840 Juliénas.
Château de Jean Loron
Gabriel Desvignes, 71570 La Chapelle-de-Guinchay.
Emile Robin
Le Bois Retour, Chénas, 69840 Juliénas.
Cave du Château Chénas (Coopérative)
Chénas, 69840 Juliénas, with 278 members and a total of 674 acres. Members of the Eventail de Vignerons Producteurs are Georges Rossi of La Chapelle-en-Guinchay and the Château de Chénas.

CHIROUBLES

All southeast facing on the higher slopes, making some of the best-balanced and most prized Beaujolais in limited quantities. This is the first cru to be 'supple and tender' for the eager Paris restaurateurs.

Total area is 790 acres; average production 203,000 cases a year.

Domaine Emile Cheysson
Les Farges, 69115 Chiroubles, with 54 acres.
Château Javernand
M. Fourneau, 69115 Chiroubles, with 47 acres.
Domaine du Moulin
Mlle Dory, Le Bourg, 69115 Chiroubles, with 42 acres.
Château Les Pres
Héritiers de Raousset, 69115 Chiroubles, with 25 acres.
Cave Coopérative (Maison des Chiroubles)
69115 Chiroubles, with 63 members and 217 acres.
Cave Coopérative Vinicole
69115 Chiroubles.
Members of the Eventail de Vignerons Producteurs are **René Savoye**, **Georges and Alain Passot** at Grosse Pierre and **Philippe Govet**.

COTE DE BROUILLY

The slopes of the Mont de Brouilly give a stronger, more concentrated wine than the surrounding appellation Brouilly, but in smaller quantities. The minimum degree here is 10.5 – the highest in Beaujolais. They are said to develop the high-toned scent of violets after 2 or 3 years in bottle. After warm vintages they benefit from keeping that long.

Total area is 860 acres; average production 198,000 cases a year.

Château Delachanal
M. Leffert, Odenas, 69830 St-Georges de Reneins.
Château Thivin
Mme Geoffray, Odenas, 69830 St-Georges de Reneins.
Mme Veuve Joubert
La Poyebade, Odenas, 69830 St-Georges de Reneins.
Cave Coopérative de Bel-Air
St-Jean d'Ardières, 69220 Belleville, with 300 members and 1,080 acres (appellation Brouilly, Côte de Brouilly, Morgon, Beaujolais and Villages).

FLEURIE

The pretty name, a substantial supply and a singular freshness of flavour all contribute to making this the most memorable and popular Beaujolais cru. Fleurie is often irresistible in its first year, with the result that the full, sweet silkiness of its maturity at 3 or 4 years is little-known.

Total area is 2,100 acres; average production 467,000 cases a year.

M. Darroze
Clos des Quatre Vents, 69820 Fleurie.
Château de Fleurie
Mme Roclore, Mâcon 71000.
Logis du Vivier
Mlle Yvonne Couibes, 69820 Fleurie.
Société Civile du Château de Poncié
69820 Fleurie.
Marcel Rollet
69820 Fleurie.
Cave Coopérative des Grands Vins de Fleurie
69820 Fleurie, 323 members, 983 acres. The member of the Eventail de Vignerons Producteurs is **Maurice Bruone** at Montgenas, who produces about 1,000 cases a year.

JULIENAS

With St-Amour, the northernmost cru (the *département* boundary between Rhône and Saône-et-Loire runs between them). Substance, strong colour and vigour, even tannin, mean that Juliénas needs 2 years or more to age. It is considered mealtime Beaujolais rather than a thirst quencher.

Total area is 1,450 acres; average production 363,000 cases a year.

Ernest Aujas
69840 Juliénas.
Château des Capitans
Bernard Sarrau, 69840 Juliénas.
M. Foillard
Dom. de la Dime, 69830 St-Georges de Reneins.
Château Juliénas
M. Condemine, 69840 Juliénas.
M. J. Perrachon
Dom. Bottière, 69840 Juliénas.

M. P. Poulachon
71000 Mâcon.
Domaine de la Vieille Eglise
Héritiers Paul Loron, Pontanevaux, 71570 La Chapelle-de-Guinchay.
Cave Coopérative des Grands Vins de Juliénas
69840 Juliénas.
Members of the Eventail de Vignerons Producteurs are the **Domaine René Monnet** and **André Pelleire**.

MORGON

The wide spread of vineyards around Villié-Morgon, between Brouilly and Fleurie, are credited with a character so peculiar that '*morgonner*' has become a verb for a way that other wines sometimes (when they are lucky) behave. The soil here is schistous, and the peculiarity is described as a flavour of wild cherries. I have not found them so identifiable as this suggests, but they are among the bigger and longest-lasting wines of Beaujolais.

Total area is 2,750 acres; average production 675,000 cases a year.

Paul Collonge
Domaine de Ruyère, 69910 Villié-Morgon.
Jean Ernest Demont
Javernière, 69910 Villié-Morgon, with 10 acres.
Louis Desvignes
Le Bourg, 69910 Villié-Morgon, with 20 acres.
G.F.A. Domaine Lièven, Château de Bellevue
69910 Villié-Morgon, with 29 acres.
Pierre Piron
Morgon, 69910 Villié-Morgon, with 30 acres.
Domaine du Py
Pierre Savoye, Les Micouds, 69910 Villié-Morgon, with 33 acres.
Général Jacques de Zelicourt
Le Bourg, 69910 Villié-Morgon.
Members of the Eventail de Vignerons Producteurs are **Georges Brun** and **Louis Desvignes** at Villié-Morgon.

MOULIN-A-VENT

There is no village of Moulin-à-Vent, but a sailless windmill among the hamlets between Romanèche-Thorins and Chénas gives its name to the most 'serious' and expensive Beaujolais appellation. Moulin-à-Vent *en primeur* is almost a contradiction in terms. It should be firm, meaty and savoury wine that has less of the surging scent of Beaujolais in its first year but builds up a bouquet resembling burgundy in bottle. Some growers age it briefly in small oak barrels to add to the structure that will preserve it. Moulin-à-Vent is always served last in a Beaujolais meal, often with the cheeses, which will dominate the lighter wines (and it, too, as often as not).

Total area is 1,650 acres; average production 412,000 cases a year.

Propriété Bourisset
Fermier des Hospices de Romanèche, Romanèche-Thorins, 71570 La Chapelle-de-Guinchay.

Château des Jacques
Dom. J. Thorin, Romanèche-Thorins, 71570 La Chapelle-de-Guinchay.

Propriété Laburyère
Romanèche-Thorins, 71570 La Chapelle-de-Guinchay.

Domaine Monrozier
Les Moriers, 69820 Fleurie.

Château du Moulin-à-Vent
The Bloud family, Romanèche-Thorins, 71570 La Chapelle Pontanevaux.

Domaine de la Tour du Bief
Chénas, 69840 Juliénas.

Cave du Château de Chénas
Chénas, 69840 Juliénas. (Appellation Chénas and Moulin à Vent), with 278 members and 674 acres. Members of the Eventail de Vignerons Producteurs are

Pierre Belicard at Lancié and **Jean Brugne** at Vivier and Fleurie.

REGNIE

The newest Beaujolais cru to the west of Brouilly and Morgon from the commune of Regnié-Durette. While it shows a particular resemblance to Brouilly, it nonetheless has a personality of its own with its well-defined aroma of red fruits.

Total area is 18,000 acres: average production 390,000 cases a year. Member of the Eventail de Vignerons Producteurs is **Jean-Charles Braillon**.

ST-AMOUR

The one Beaujolais appellation in the Mâconnais – its white wine is entitled to the appellation St-Véran. The power of suggestion is strong, so its promising name may have some bearing on my predilection for this wine. I find it next to Fleurie and Chiroubles in delicacy and sweetness – pleading to be drunk young, yet tasting even better after 2 or

3 years in bottle. As one of the smallest areas it is, alas, not often seen.

Total area is 700 acres; average production 182,000 cases a year.

Domaine des Billards
Mme Jèan Teissier, Les Charmilles, 71000 Mâcon; and Mme Jean Barbet, Pontanevaux, 71570 La Chapelle-de-Guinchay.

Domaine Jacky Janodet
Jacky Jadonet has 9 acres in Moulin-à-Vent and 7 acres in Morgon.

M. Perrichon
Dom. de la Pirolette, St-Amour-Bellevue, 71570 La Chapelle-de-Guinchay.

Château de St-Amour
M. Siraudin, St-Amour-Bellevue, 71570 La Chapelle-de-Guinchay.

Paul Spay
Au Bourg, St-Amour-Bellevue 71570 La Chapelle-de-Guinchay.

Cave Coopérative du Bois de la Salle
69840 Juliénas (Appellation Juliénas and St-Amour), with 286 members and 847 acres.
Member of the Eventail de Vignerons Producteurs is **Patissier**.

MERCHANTS OF BEAUJOLAIS AND MACON

Aujoux & Cie
St-Georges de Reneins.
A Swiss-owned company which supplies a great deal of Beaujolais in bulk to Switzerland. Their own vineyards surround their cellars. The Aujoux label is seen particularly in Scandinavia.

Paul Beaudet
Pontanaveux, 71570 La Chapelle-de-Guinchay.
Fourth-generation family firm run by Paul's son Jean, well known in top restaurants and in the USA for its own Domaine Chénas and other good wines.

Bouchacourt
Le Fief, Chénas, 69840 Juliénas.
A small merchant with a good reputation. His wines are often seen in Paris restaurants.

Caves de Champclos
Route de Beaujeu, 69220 Belleville.
A small firm dealing in quality wines.

Chanut Frères
Romanèche-Thorins, 71570 La Chapelle-de-Guinchay.
A family company of moderate size, recently expanding into the supermarket business.

Chevalier Fils
Charnay Les Mâcon, 71000 Mâcon.
An old-established family company dealing in above-average quality wines in both bottle and bulk; also make sparkling wine under their own label.

David & Foillard
69830 St-Georges de Reneins.
Reputedly the biggest firm of négociants

in the Rhône, with wide international trade.

Georges Duboeuf
Romanèche-Thorins, 71570 La Chapelle-de-Guinchay.
A young, dynamic and skilful company, leader in the café, hotel and restaurant (not supermarket) business. Duboeuf is widely regarded as 'Mr. Beaujolais'.

Pierre Ferraud
31 rue Maréchal Foch, 69220 Belleville.
A small company with one of the highest reputations for quality.

Jacquemont Père & Fils
Romanèche-Thorins, 71570 La Chapelle-de-Guinchay.
Not a label you will see, but the biggest *commissionaires* or middlemen in Beaujolais.

Gobet
69460 Blaceret.
Owned by Reine Pedauque. They have wines from all the crus of Beaujolais.

Labouré-Roi
A small négociant firm which owns Domaine Roland Piquard, where they make Morgon and Domaine du Griffon, where they make Cotes du Brouilly.

Loron & Fils
Pontanevaux, 71570 La Chapelle-de-Guinchay.
A large, high-quality family business, formerly mainly dealing in bulk but now selling more and more in bottle, under several brand names. Offers some good domaine wines and good-value, non-appellation *vins de marque*.

Mommessin
La Grange St-Pierre, 71009 Mâcon.
Until recently a very traditional family business, now diversifying into *vins de marque* as well as Beaujolais, where it has exclusive arrangements with several good domaines. The house also owns the Grand Cru Clos de Tart in the Côte de Nuits.

Ph. Moreau
4 rue G. Lecomte, 71000 Mâcon.
A small family company of good repute.

François Pacquet
St-Lager, 69840 St-Georges de Reneins.
A family firm which started with simple *vins de café*, now stronger in Beaujolais and Mâconnias appellation wines.

Pasquier-Desvignes
St-Lager, 69220 Belleville.
A company with a long history but modern ideas, diversified into *vins de pays* and VDQS wines as well as Beaujolais, particularly in supermarkets. Their Beaujolais brand is Le Marquisat.

Pellerin
A subsidiary of Rivat, a major Lyon *vin de table* specialist. Owners of Château des Capitans, Juliénas, where they also make their own Fleurie and Morgon.

Piat
71570 La Chapelle-de-Guinchay
Founded in Mâcon in 1849. Now one of the biggest firms, especially in export, belonging to International Distillers and Vintners. Moved to very modern premises in 1980. Uses a special 'Piat' bottle, based on the traditional 'pot' of

The Eventail de Vignerons Producteurs

This establishment at Corcelles-en-Beaujolais is a group of conscientious small producers from all parts of the region and the southern Mâconnais who make their own wine but collaborate in bottling and marketing it. Their average holdings are between 12 and 25 acres. Their central cellars offer a fascinating range of the products of the region. The names of members of the Eventail (the word means 'fan') are given below those of other recommended producers under each appellation.

Beaujolais, for a classic range of Beaujolais and Mâcon wines, including a good standard Beaujolais and Mâcon-Viré. Also red and white branded table wines 'Piat d'Or'.

Sarrau
St-Jean d'Ardières, 69220 Belleville.
A dynamic and imaginative young company, both growers and merchants. They have a branch on La Réunion!

Louis Tête
St-Didier sur Beaujeu, 69430 Beaujeu.
A specialist in the high-class restaurant trade, particularly well known in Switzerland.

Thorin
Pontanevaux, 71570 La Chapelle-de-Guinchay.
A traditional family company; owners of

the superb Château des Jacques in Moulin-à-Vent and Ch. de Loyses, Beaujolais Blanc. Trade is largely in bottle wines. Their supermarket brand is Faye.

Trenel Fils
Le Voisinet, Charney Les Mâcons, 71000 Mâcon.
A small family affair with a very good local reputation, particularly in Mâcon restaurants. They also produce delectable crème de cassis and framboise.

Valette
77 route de Lyon, 71000 Mâcon.
A subsidiary of the Société des Vins de France, the same company as Lionel J. Bruck in Nuits St-Georges.

JURA

Connoisseurs of the French countryside each have their favourite corner. I hope never to be forced to make a final choice, but I have a shortlist ready, and the Jura is on it.

These limestone mountains (they give their name to a whole epoch of geology – the Jurassic) roll up towards Switzerland from the plain of the Saône in Burgundy. Halfway in a straight line from Beaune to Geneva you come to the delicious timbered and tiled little town of Arbois, where Pasteur lived, then Poligny, then Château-Chalon, the heart of a completely original wine country. The Jura vineyards are small (much smaller than they once were; currently 3,400 acres and growing). But their origins are as old as Burgundy's, their climate and soil singular and their grapes their own.

Jura producers are fond of making a wide range of wines, from *méthode champenoise* sparkling to *vin jaune*. The overall appellation is Côtes du Jura. This appellation covers a long strip of country from north of Arbois to south of Cousance. Arbois is another general AC with higher alcohol stipulated. L'Etoile covers whites and *vins de paille* from the valley around the village of L'Etoile to the south of the region.

The vineyard sits on a band of heavy clay, rich in lime, exposed along the mountain slopes between 900 and 1,350 feet high. Woods, bovine pastures and limestone cliffs constantly interrupt the continuity of the vines. Unlike Alsace to the north, which lies in the rain shadow of the Vosges, the west-facing Jura is often deluged by summer rain. Hail is a frequent problem here. But September and October are usually sunny. Jura grapes have been

selected because they thrive in deep damp soil, given a good sun-warmed slope. The most widespread is the Poulsard – a pale red which is the nearest thing to a rosé grape. Another obscure red, the Trousseau, is grown with it to stiffen its too 'supple' wine. Pinot Noir is increasingly added to give more colour and backbone to red wine – but red is in a minority: most of the wine is rosé, fermented on its pale skins as though intended to be red.

Nowadays the Chardonnay is the standard grape for light white wines; it performs well here (under the alias of Melon d'Arbois or Gamay Blanc) but certainly not spectacularly. Much of it is made into sparkling wine. But the real speciality is a local variant of the Traminer called the Savagnin or Nature. Savagnin is a late ripener and a small cropper, but its wine is powerful in alcohol and flavour. Used merely for topping up barrels of Chardonnay it gives them, as they age, a marvellously rustic style. Used alone it behaves in a most peculiar way that makes it comparable with fino sherry. The young wine is left in old barrels with a history of making *vin jaune*, not filled to the top but in the normal perilous state of 'ullage'. A flor yeast, presumably residing in the barrel wood, rapidly grows as a film on the surface of the wine, excluding direct contact with oxygen. The wine is left thus, for a statutory minimum of six years, without being topped up. At the end of six years, a miraculous stability has (or should have) come over it. A finished *vin jaune* is an impressive apéritif, intense in flavour, obviously slightly oxidized but long and fine and altogether worthwhile. The commune (not château) of Château-Chalon is famous for the best,

Arbois

although good *vins jaunes* are made all over the area. Wine produced in such restricted quantities (and by no means every year), then aged for six years, is inevitably expensive. Like Tokay it comes in smaller than standard bottles that help to disguise the price. (The *clavelin* of the Jura, long-necked and hunch-shouldered, holds 64 centilitres.) I cannot pretend it is anything like as good value, as reliable, or even as delicious, as a first-class fino sherry. But it exists – and as wine lovers we should be grateful for variety and support it, especially in such time-honoured forms as this.

Another time-honoured regional speciality, *vin de paille*, has virtually disappeared – at least in its authentic form. It was made by hanging bunches of grapes in the rafters (or laying them on straw – *paille* – mats) to dry and concentrate their sweetness in the manner of Italian Vin Santo.

The Jura vineyard was decimated by phylloxera and took many years to recover. Today it thrives – largely on the tourist trade and faithful private customers in France. There are 1,000 growers, but only 200 who make more than 330 cases a year, and only about a dozen with more than 30 acres.

JURA PRODUCERS

Château d'Arlay
Arlay, 39140 Bletterans.

The Jura's one lordly estate, descended in the same family since the 12th century, when it was a Hapsburg stronghold, and at various times in the hands of the Prince of Orange, William the Silent, the English King William III and almost but not quite Frederick the Great of Prussia. The present owners, the Count and Countess Renaud de Laguiche, can claim indirect descent not only from this galaxy of monarchs but also have family ties with the Marquis de Laguiche of Montrachet, the de Vogüés of Champagne and Chambolle-Musigny, and the Ladoucettes of Pouilly-Fumé. Some 69 acres of vines are 50% Pinot Noir, 20% Savagnin, 12% Chardonnay. They produce a pale Pinot Noir red, the usual Jura rosé, white wine of Chardonnay toped up with Savagnin, and *vin jaune*. As négociants they use the names Comte de Guichebourg (NV wines) and Baron de Proby.

Caves Jean Bourdy
Arlay, 39140 Bletterans.

A cornerstone of the Jura wine industry, dating back to the 16th century, with bottles of such famous vintages as 1820 and 1784 still in the cellars. Jean Bourdy retired in 1979 after 52 years to be succeeded by his son Christian. Their model Jura wines come from 1 acre in Château-Chalon (all Savagnin) and 12 in Arlay, where they make red, rosé and Chardonnay white as well as *vin jaune*. Sales of 2,500 cases are 85% in France – like most Jura *vignerons*, mainly to private clients.

Hubert Clavelin
Le Vernois, 39210 Voiteur.

The proprietor of 38 acres between Château-Chalon and
L'Etoile, highly regarded by his neighbours for his Côtes
du Jura red, white and 'yellow', and his *méthode champenoise*
Brut. His name recalls the unique long-necked pint bottle
used uniquely for *vin jaune*.

Château Gréa
Rotalier, 39190 Beaufort.

A mere 16 acres, but the pride of the Gréa family for nearly
300 years. Their descendants the de Boissieus have owned
it since 1962 and made it the quality leader of the southern
Côtes du Jura.

Their specialities are a brut *méthode champenoise*, Le
Chanet, a blend of Chardonnay with Savagnin which
gives a much more forceful *vin de garde*, a red called Sur La
Roche and a *vin jaune* of pure Savagnin, En Cury.

Henri Maire
Château-Montfort, 39600 Arbois.

Very much the biggest producer and marketer of Jura
wines and a principal force behind the reestablishment of
what was a dwindling wine region. Imaginative and
aggressive sales strategy has made Maire a household
name. The very modern Maire domaines, with wide-
spaced vines, cover some 750 acres, of which the chief are
Montfort (150 acres), Grange Grillard (125), Sorbief (150)
and La Croix d'Argis (200). They produce a vast range of
wines under all the Jura appellations, plus many other
wines. Sparkling Vin Fou is perhaps the best known; its
name is on street corners all over France. One of my
favourites is the pale dry rosé, or *vin gris*, called Cendré de
Novembre. Some of the reds are distinctly sweet – not to
my taste. Up to 90% of annual sales of over 400,000 cases
is by mail order and door-to-door salesmen in France.
Henri Maire has also been a regular buyer of fine
burgundies at the Hospices de Beaune auction, and ships
Souverain wines from California to France.

Désiré Petit & Fils
Pupillin, 39600 Arbois.

Gérard and Marcel are the two Petit '*fils*' who own and
operate this old family property of nearly 30 acres, divided
into 11 little parcels in the sheltered coomb of Pupillin,
and neighbouring Arbois and Grozon. The property was
modernized in 1979: stainless steel and old casks stand side
by side. The vines are 40% Poulsard, 30% Chardonnay,
15% Pinot Noir, 13% Savagnin and 2% Trousseau. 1985
was a great vintage for them.

Domaine de la Pinte
39600 Arbois

A modern estate created by Roger Martin in 1955 on
abandoned vineyard land of the chalky clay loved by the
Savagnin. Thirty of his 62.5 acres are white grapes, 27
Poulsard for rosé and the rest Trousseau and Pinot Noir
for red. All is appellation Arbois if it reaches the necessary
alcoholic degree (11.5° for rosé, 12° for white and 14° for
vin jaune). 20% of 8,300 cases is exported.

J. Reverchon & Fils
GAEC de Chantemerle, 39800 Poligny.

A third-generation family of growers with only 15 acres
(appellation Côtes du Jura) but a typically wide range of
hand-made wines in small quantities – including *vin jaune*,
méthode champenoise and *Macvin*, as well as many small
lots of red, white and rosé, in a grand total, of 2,000

cases. Dispatch is no problem: tourists take it all away
with them.

Rolet Pere et Fils
Montigny-lès-Arsures, 39600 Arbois

One of the most important producers in Jura after Henri
Maire. Founded in 1968, they have now expanded to 124
acres. Now in streamlined, modern premises, they
concentrate on single-grape variety wines including
Chardonnay and Trousseau. They also make a *vin jaune*
and a sparkling wine.

Jacques Tissot
Montigny-les-Arsures, 39600 Arbois.

Thirty acres owned by André and Mireille Tissot making
good Arbois wines of all colours including *vin jaune*.

Vandelle Père & Fils
Chteau de l'Etoile, GAEC, 39570 Lons le Saunier.

The Château de l'Etoile exists no more, but the Vandelle
family have 40 acres of its land in production and 17 more
planted. Their specialities are Vin Blanc de l'Etoile of
Chardonnay, *vin jaune*, *Macvin*, the local 'ratafia' of grape
juice and brandy, and *méthode champenoise* Brut. Rosé is
made from Poulsard alone and red from a mixture of
Trousseau, Gamay and Pinot Noir, both in wooden vats.
Very few of their annual 80,000 bottles leaves France.

CAVES COOPERATIVES

Arbois
2 rue des Fossés, 39600 Arbois.

Founded 1906. 152 members; 481 acres; 58,000 cases AOC
wines: Arbois red, white and rosé and *méthode champenoise*.
The oldest and biggest of the Jura coops.

Château-Chalon et Côtes du Jura
39120 Voiteur

Founded 1958. 68 members; 158 acres; 20,000 cases AOC
wines: Côtes du Jura white and rosé, Château-Chalon
Jaune, Côtes du Jura Jaune. The only cooperative
producing Château-Chalon.

L'Etoile
L'Etoile, 39570 Lons-Le-Saunier.

Founded 1912. 18 members; 25 acres; 2,500 cases AOC
wine: L'Etoile. A little white-wine-only cellar.

Poligny, Caveau des Jacobins
39800 Poligny

Founded 1907. 12 members; 61.7 acres; 9,000 cases AOC
wine: Côtes du Jura red, rosé and white. Perhaps the
prettiest cooperative in France, occupying a splendid old
deconsecrated church in the centre of the lovely little
town. Huge barrels stand under the soaring vaulted
pillars. By modern standards, however, the wine barely
passes muster.

Pupillin
39600 Arbois

Founded 1909. 25 members; 100 acres; 16,500 cases AOC
wines: Arbois-Pupillin white, red and rosé and Papillette
mousseaux. Pupillin is a perfect little example of a Jura
country village, with only 192 inhabitants, all living by
and for the vine.

SAVOIE

The wine country of Savoie follows the river Rhône south from the Lake of Geneva, then lines the Lac du Bourget around Aix-les-Bains, then hugs the sides of the valley south of Chambéry and turns the corner eastwards into the Val d'Isère. It exists more as opportunistic outbreaks than as a cohesive vineyard. Its appellations are consequently complicated: more so than its simple, fresh and invigorating wine.

Three-quarters of Savoie wine is white, based on half a dozen different grapes. Along the south shore of the Lake of Geneva (Haute Savoie) it is the Chasselas, the grape the Swiss know as Fendant. Crépy is the best-known cru, with Marignan, Ripaille and Marin, all light and often sharp wines. Ayze has a name for its sharpish *pétillant*.

Seyssel is your opportunity to win a bet. Few people realize or remember that it is France's northernmost Rhône wine. The grapes here are Roussette (alias Altesse) for still wines and Molette for fizz. Roussette, the aristocrat of Savoie, reaches a relatively high degree of sugar, body and flavour; Molette is a mild little thing. Seyssel has built an international reputation by developing its naturally fizzy tendency into fully fledged *méthode champenoise* sparkling. The firm of Varichon & Clerc, who are the specialists, produce a singularly delicate and delicious *cuvée* – quite one of France's best – but demand seems to have outrun supply; they have been forced to buy grapes outside the area and relabel it Blanc de Blanc Mousseux.

Still or *pétillant*, dry or sometimes slightly sweet Roussette wines with local reputations are made along the Rhône valley and Lac du Bourget at Frangy, Marestel and Monthoux. Occasional supervintages put them on a level with Vouvray.

The third principal white grape, and the commonest of the region, is the Jacquère. South of Seyssel, still on the Rhône, the district of Chautagne, centred on its cooperative at Ruffieux, makes Jacquère white and the grape dominates the vineyards south

of Chambéry: Chignin, Apremont, Abymes and Montmélian. Chignin has the best southern hillside exposure. Its Jacquère fetches a franc or two more a bottle than its neighbours, Apremont and Les Abymes. Red Gamay, Pinot Noir and Mondeuse are also important.

Suburbia is invading these lovely vineyards fast. Montmélian, a little alpine village a few years ago, is now hideous with housing estates. So far the red-wine vineyards on the slopes of the Val d'Isère are almost intact, but I suspect not for long. Their centre is the *cave coopérative* at Cruet, serving Cruet, Arbin, Montmélian and St-Jean de la Porte. Much its best wine, to my mind, is its Mondeuse (especially that of Arbin). Gamay costs a little more, and Pinot Noir more again, but Mondeuse is the character: a dark, slightly tannic, smooth but intensely lively wine that reminds me a little of Chinon, the 'raspberry' red of the Loire.

There are other local specialities too: Roussette is the highest priced white of the Cruet cooperative; a yellow, full-bodied, slightly bitter wine you might take for an Italian. And Chignin grows the Bergeron, either a rare local grape or (say some) the Roussanne of the (lower) Rhône. This is the only Savoyard white wine that ages with distinction.

Savoie's AOCs are shadowed by the VDQS Bugey to the west on the way to Lyon, with an even more complex set of names, hard to justify in reality. The white VDQS is Roussette de Bugey, although the rules only demand Roussette grapes if a village name is used (the 'crus' are Anglefort, Arbignieu, Chanay, Langieu, Montagnieu and Virieu-Le-Grand). Plain Roussette de Bugey can contain Chardonnay as can Roussette du Savoy. Jacquère, Aligoté and Chardonnay are allowed in Vin de Bugey Blanc. VDQS Vin de Bugey is red, rosé or white and also has its crus: Virieu-Le-Grand, Montagnieu, Manicle, Machuraz and Cerdon. Cerdon, in turn, is also an individual VDQS for sparkling *mousseux* and merely fizzy *pétillant*.

SAVOIE PRODUCERS

ABYMES
Cave Coopérative 'Le Vigneron Savoyard', 73190 Apremont (also for Apremont, Gamay, Mondeuse, Vin de Pays de Grésivaudan).

APREMONT
Cave Coopérative 'Le Vigneron Savoyard' (as above),

Pierre Boniface, 73800 Les Marches.
Jean-Claude Perret, 73800 Les Marches, and many others.

AYZE
Marcel Fert, 74130 Marignier.

CHIGNIN
J-F Girard-Madoux, 73800 Chignin.

CHIGNIN AND CHIGNIN-BERGERON
The Quénard family (5 separate branches: André, Claude, Jean-Pierre, Raymond, René) 73800 Chignin.

CHAUTAGNE
Cave Coopérative de Chautagne, 73310 Ruffieux.

CREPY
L. Mercier & Fils, 74140 Douvaine.

CRUET
Cave Coopérative de Vente des Vins Fins, 73800 Cruet (also for Chignin, Roussette de Savoie, Gamay, Mondeuse, Pinot, Arbin, *mousseux* and *pétillant*).

FRANGY
Jean Neyroud & Fils, 74270 Designy.

MARESTEL
Henri Jeandet, 73170 Jongieux.

MARIGNAN
Canelli-Suchet, La Tour de Marignan, 74140 Sciez.

MARIN
Claude Delalex, 74200 Marin.

MONTERMINOD
Château de Monterminod, 73190 Challes-Les-Eaux.

MONTHOUX
Michel Million Rousseau, 73170 St-Jean-de-Chevelu.

MONTMELIAN
Cave Coopérative de Vente des Vins Fins, 73800 Montmélian (also Abymes, Apremont, Chignin, Marestel, Chignin-Bergeron, Gamay, Mondeuse, Arbin, Chautagne).
Louis Magnin, 73800 Arbin (also red Arbin).

RIPAILLE
Fichard (négociant), Grands Chais Léman/Mont-Blanc, 74170 Chens-sur-Léman.
Château de Ripaille

SEYSSEL
Etablissements Donati (J. Quénard), 73000 Barberaz.
Georges Mollex, 01420 Corbonod. Domaine de la Taconnière, 01420 Seyssel.
J. Perrier & Fils, 73800 Les Marches.
Varichon & Clere (négociants: sparkling specialists). 014120 Seyssel. General négociants for Savoie wines.

LOIRE

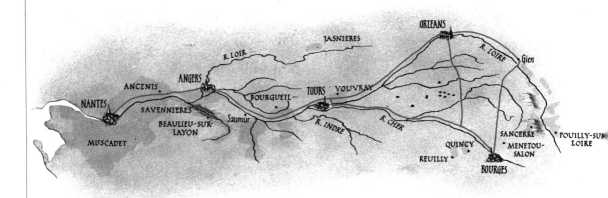

It is marvellous with what felicity, what gastronomic *savoir-vivre*, the rivers Rhône and Loire counterbalance one another on their passage through France. For 100 miles or so they even run parallel, flowing in opposite directions 30 miles apart.

They decline the notion of rivalry: in every way they are complementary. The Rhône gives France its soothing, warming, satisfying, winter-weight wines. The Loire provides the summer drinking.

The Loire rises within 100 miles of the Mediterranean. Wine is made in earnest along some 250 miles of its course and on the banks of its lower tributaries. It is a big stretch of country, and one might expect a wide variety of wines. The long list of the appellations encourages the idea, but it is not difficult to simplify into half a dozen dominant styles based on the grape varieties.

The Loire has three principal white grapes and two red (but only one that gives fine wine). Among the whites, the centre stage is held by the Chenin Blanc (alias Pineau de la Loire). It dominates in Touraine and even more so in Anjou, its produce ranging from neutral/acidic base material for sparkling Saumur to toffee-rich, apparently immortal, dessert wines. It is so versatile because it has little identifiable flavour: its qualities lie more in balance and vitality. It keeps a high acid content even when it ripens (which it can do) to extremely high levels of sugar. Aromatically it is noncommittal – until it matures. Even then it has fruit salad and *crème brûlée* both within its repertoire.

Downstream from Anjou the dominant white grape is the Muscadet – again a low-profile variety. Early ripening and (in contrast) low acidity, rather than any great aroma, makes it ideal for instant drinking with *fruits de mer*.

Upstream in Touraine and beyond to Pouilly and Sancerre is the country of the Sauvignon Blanc, in this climate one of the most intensely aromatic grapes in France.

The Cabernet Franc is the quality red grape of the Loire, at its very best at Chinon in Touraine and almost equally successful in parts of Anjou. It is shadowed everywhere by the Gamay, which can make a fresh one-year wine but no more in this climate. Both are responsible for very large quantities of more or less amiable rosé, one of the region's great money-spinners.

Two or three other grapes are to be found named on Loire labels: the white Gros Plant of the Muscadet region (a sharp grape which might be described as its Aligoté); the Pinot Noir, grown to make red wine in Sancerre; Chardonnay in Haut-Poitou. One or two are traditional and accepted: a white variety called Romorantin gives the thin wine of Cheverny; the red Groslot gives café rosé everywhere. The peasants of the region used to grow a great number of ignoble plants, but in the last 30 years they have been slowly ousted from the vineyards in favour of the principal types and an understudy cast of Cabernet Sauvignon, Malbec (here called Cot), Pinot Meunier, and such local characters as Arbois and Pineau d'Aunis and even Furmint from Hungary and Verdelho from Madeira.

As with grapes, so with regions, the Loire is simply divisible into its upper waters, above Orleans, which with their hinterland near Bourges produce Sauvignon Blanc whites, its famous slow-moving centre, where it passes in infinite procession among the châteaux of Touraine and Anjou, and its broad maritime reaches, where the wind carries the hint of shrimps far inland.

LOIRE WINES

All Loire AOC and VDQS wines are listed below. The production figures for each wine are given in cases. Most of these figures are an average of four crops, but in some cases only one year's total is available. Crops vary widely in the Loire and the figures should be considered approximate.

Coteaux d'Ancenis
(red) VDQS. Lower Loire. 237,000 cases. Light Gamay, occasionally Cabernet, reds from the north bank opposite Muscadet.

Coteaux d'Ancenis
(white) VDQS Lower Loire. 1,200 cases. A tiny quantity of Malvoisie (Pinot Gris), Verdelho, Chardonnay, etc.

Anjou
(red) AC. West central. 1,122,000 cases. Light, mainly Cabernet Franc reds from a wide area (an alternative to Saumur).

Anjou
(white) AC. West central, 736,000 cases. Mainly Chenin Blanc and often slightly sweet – no special quality.

Anjou Pétillant and Anjou Mousseux
(white) AC. West central. Slightly and semi-sparkling wines from Chenin Blanc.

Anjou Coteaux de la Loire
(white) AC. West central. 13,300 cases. A limited area along both banks of the river west of Angers, including the superior Savennières. Chenin Blanc of variable quality, normally dry.

Anjou Gamay
(red) AC. West central. 206,000 cases.

Light reds for first-year drinking.

Anjou-Villages
(red) AC. West central. 156,000 cases. There are 46 communes entitled to this appellation for the production of Cabernet Franc and Cabernet Sauvignon.

Cabernet d'Anjou
(rosé) AC. West central. 1.4m cases. The best-quality rosé, normally rather sweet; at its best from Martigné, Tigné and La Fosse-Tigné in the Coteaux du Layon.

Cabernet de Saumur
(rosé) AC. West central. The upstream equivalent of the above.

Rosé d'Anjou
(rosé) AC. West central. 1.8m cases. The biggest production of the Loire; pale sweet rosé from Gamay, Groslot, Cabernet, Cot, Pineau d'Aunis.

Coteaux de l'Aubance
(white) AC. West central. 19,400 cases. Chenin Blanc, often semi-sweet or nearly dry, from the south bank opposite Angers, north of the (superior) Coteaux du Layon.

Côtes d'Auvergne
(red) VDQS. The extreme upper Loire. 214,000 cases. Near Clermont-Ferrand, formerly famous as Chanturgues, Châteaugay, Corent. Made principally from Gamay.

Côtes d'Auvergne
(white) VDQS. The extreme upper Loire. Very little made. Very light Chardonnay, superseding the red.

Bonnezeaux
(white) AC. West central. 19,900 cases. 250-acre Grand Cru of Chenin Blanc in the Coteaux du Layon, Anjou. In fine

years with noble rot a great sweet wine; otherwise 'nervy' and fine.

Bourgueil
(red) AC. Central, 678,000 cases. Excellent red of Cabernet Franc from the north bank opposite Chinon, Touraine. For drinking young and cool or maturing like Bordeaux.

Châteaumeillant
(red) VDQS. Upper Loire, 5,950 cases. Minor area of Gamay and Pinot Noir south of Bourges. Light reds or very pale *gris* rosés.

Cheverny
(red) VDQS. East central. 77,100 cases. Small but growing supply of light Gamay red and rosé from south of Blois.

Cheverny
(white) VDQS. East central. 67,000 cases. Sharp white from the local Romorantin, south of Blois, giving way to the better-known Loire grapes.

Chinon
(red) AC. Central. 952,000 cases. Fine Cabernet Franc red, sometimes superb and capable of ageing many years, but generally drunk young and cool. The most important Loire red.

Chinon
(white) AC. Central. 4,170 cases. Practically extinct Chenin Blanc, Rabelais' *vin de taffeta*.

Fiefs-Vendéens
(red, a little white) VDQS. West. Promoted vins de pays from the estuary vineyards. Drink young.

Côtes du Forez
(red) VDQS. Extreme upper Loire. 95,000 cases. The southernmost Loire

vineyards, south of Lyon: good Gamay, Beaujolais-style.

Coteaux du Giennois
(red) VDQS. Upper Loire. 51,200 cases. Very light reds, Pinot Noir and Gamay, from just downstream of Pouilly/ Sancerre towards Gien.

Coteaux du Giennois
(white) VDQS. Upper Loire. 8,800 cases. Chenin Blanc and Sauvignon from the same area; a dying breed.

Haut-Poitou (vin du)
(red) VDQS. South central. 100,000 cases. Flourishing largely Gamay vineyard south of Anjou.

Haut-Poitou (vin du)
(white) VDQS. South central. 80,000 cases. Expanding production of Sauvignon and Chardonnay.

Jasnières
(white) AC. North central. 8,700 cases. Small Chenin Blanc area north of Tours. Wine like Vouvray, if less rich. Ages very well.

Coteaux du Layon
(white) AC. West central. 418,000 cases. The biggest area of quality Chenin Blanc, south of Angers, generally semi-dry or -sweet; it includes the Grands Crus Quarts de Chaume and Bonnezeaux.

Coteaux du Layon Chaume
(white) AC. West central. 18,800 cases. A superior appellation for Coteaux du Layon with an extra degree of ripeness, comparable to a 'Villages' AC in the Rhône.

Coteaux du Loir
(red) AC. North central. 10,000 cases. Small area of Pinot Noir and Gamay north of Tours on the Loir, a tributary of the Loire.

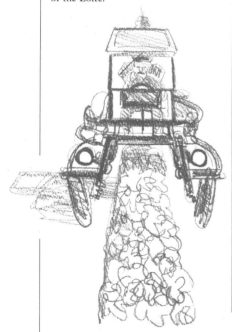

Coteaux du Loir
(white) AC. North central. 3,800 cases. Chenin Blanc from the Loir. The best is Jasnières.

Crémant de Loire
(red) AC. General 13,500 cases. Recent appellation for high-quality sparkling wine – little used for red.

Crémant de Loire
(white) AC. General. 195,500 cases. Recent appellation for high-quality sparkling wine.

Rosé de Loire
(rosé) AC. General. 261,000 cases. An appellation for dry rosés with 30% Cabernet – not widely used, but can be good.

Ménétou-Salon
(red) AC. Upper Loire. 47,000 cases. A minor rival to Sancerre with similar light Pinot Noir.

Ménétou-Salon
(white) AC. Upper Loire. 62,000 cases. Like the red, a rival to Sancerre with Sauvignon Blanc.

Montlouis
(white) AC. East central. 88,000 cases. The reflected image of Vouvray across the Loire: dry, semi-sweet and occasionally sweet wines.

Montlouis Mousseux
(white) AC. East central. 52,000 cases. The sparkling version of Montlouis Blanc.

Muscadet
(white) AC. Lower Loire. 1.5m cases. A large area but a small part of Muscadet production. (*see* Muscadet de Sèvre et Maine).

Muscadet des Coteaux de la Loire
(white) AC. Lower Loire. 191,000 cases. The smallest section of Muscadet, on the Loire upstream of Muscadet de Sèvre et Maine.

Muscadet de Sèvre et Maine
(white) AC Lower Loire. 6m cases. Much the biggest Loire AC: the best part of Muscadet, east of Nantes.

Gros Plant du Pays Nantais
(white) VDQS. Lower Loire, 2.5m. cases. Sharp white of Gros Plant (or Folle blanche) from the Muscadet area.

Orléannais (vin de l')
(red) VDQS. Upper Loire. 62,000 cases. Light reds of Pinot Meunier, popular in Paris, particularly as vinegar.

Orléannais (vin de l')
(white) VDQS. Upper Loire. 6,900 cases. Very minor whites, largely of Chardonnay.

Pouilly Fumé
(white) AC. Upper Loire. 497,000 cases. Powerful aromatic Sauvignon Blanc from opposite Sancerre.

Pouilly sur Loire
(white) AC. Upper Loire. 38,000 cases. Adequate white of Chasselas from the same vineyards as Pouilly Fumé – *must*

be drunk young.

Quarts de Chaume
(white) AC. West central. 6,200 cases. 112-acre Grand Cru of the Coteaux du Layon. In certain years, glorious rich wines of Chenin Blanc.

Quincy
(white) AC. Upper Loire. 51,000 cases. Small source of attractive Sauvignon Blanc west of Bourges.

Reuilly
(red) AC. Upper Loire. 13,500 cases. Light Pinot Noir reds.

Reuilly
(white) AC. Upper Loire. 14,300 cases. Sauvignon Blanc.

Côte Roannaise
(red) VDQS. The extreme upper Loire. 53,600 cases. Minor Gamay region not far from Beaujolais, in distance or style.

St-Nicolas de Bourgueil
(red) AC. Central. 468,000 cases. Neighbour to Bourgueil with similar excellent Cabernet Franc.

St-Pourçain-sur-Sioule
(red) VDQS. The extreme upper Loire. 269,000 cases. The famous local wine of Vichy: largely Gamay from chalk soil – good café wine.

St-Pourçain-sur-Sioule
(white) VDQS. The extreme upper Loire. 55,100 cases. Vichy's equally famous white of Tresallier and other Loire grapes – generally rather sharp.

Sancerre
(red) AC. Upper Loire. 276,000 cases. Light Pinot Noir red and rosé from chalky soil better known for white.

Sancerre
(white) AC. Upper Loire. 1,2m. cases. Fresh, eminently fruity and aromatic Sauvignon Blanc.

Saumur
(red) AC. West central. 444,000 cases. Light Cabernet reds from south of Saumur – can also be sold as Anjou.

Saumur
(white) AC. West central. 339,000 cases. Crisp Chenin Blanc – sometimes even sour. Most is made into sparkling wine.

Cabernet de Saumur
(rosé) AC. West central. 29,700 cases. The local Saumur appellation for pure Cabernet rosé.

Saumur-Champigny
(red) AC. West central. 653,000 cases. The best Cabernet reds of Anjou, from the northern part of the Saumur area just east of the city.

Coteaux de Saumur
(white) AC. West central. 4,700 cases. Chenin Blanc, often dry, from a similar but larger area than Saumur-Champigny.

Saumur Moussex
(red) AC. West central. 86,700 cases. *Méthode champenoise* red of Cabernet and Gamay.

Saumur Mousseux
(white) AC. West central. 682,600 cases.
Méthode champenoise Chenin Blanc;
increasingly popular and sometimes
excellent.
Savennières
(white) AC. West central. 27,000 cases.
Sometimes splendid, powerful, long-
lived, dry Chenin Blanc from west of
Angers. It includes the Grands Crus
Roche aux Moines and Coulée de
Serrant.
Thouarsais (vin de)
(red) VDQS. South central. 2,100 cases.
A tiny enclave of Gamay south of
Saumur.
Thouarsais (vin de)
(white) VDQS South central. 3,650
cases. The Chenin Blanc of Thouars,
often rather sweet.
Touraine
(red) AC. East central. 1,846,000 cases.
The label will name the grape, normally
Gamay, here made into a passable
substitute for Beaujolais – at least in
warm years.
Touraine
(white) AC. East central. 1,651,000

cases. The label names the grape, usually
Sauvignon blanc in a tolerable imitation
of Sancerre – but it can be painfully
unripe.
Touraine-Amboise
(red) AC. East central. 88,800 cases.
Light reds of Gamay, Cabernet and Cot
from just east of Vouvray.
Touraine-Amboise
(red) AC. East central. 26,900 cases.
Chenin Blanc, sometimes capable of
Vouvray-like quality.
Touraine-Azay-Le-Rideau
(red) AC. East central. 9,300 cases. A
minor outpost of Groslot for rosé
between Tours and Chinon.
Touraine-Azay-Le-Rideau
(white) AC. East central. 17,500 cases.
Tiny Chenin Blanc vineyard renowned
for its Saché, occasionally as rich as
Vouvray.
Touraine-Mesland
(white) AC. East central. 95,000 cases.
Less important dry white of Chenin
Blanc and Sauvignon.
Touraine-Mesland
(red) AC. East central. 16,000 cases.
Rather good Gamay from the north

bank of the Loire opposite Chaumont.
Touraine Pétillant & Mousseux
(white) AC. East central. Semi and
sparkling versions.
Valençay
(white) VDQS. Upper Loire. 6,900
cases. An outpost of Gamay on the
eastern border of Touraine.
Valençay
(red) VDQS. Upper Loire. 59,300 cases.
Dry white of Chenin Blanc, Sauvignon
and others.
Coteaux du Vendômois
(red) VDQS. North central. 34,000
cases.
Coteaux du Vendômois
(white) VDQS. North central. 5,800
cases.
Vouvray
(white) AC. East central. 543,000 cases.
Dry, semi-sweet or sweet Chenin Blanc
of potentially superb quality, according
to the vintage.
Vouvray Pétillant Mousseux
AC. East central. 769,000 cases. The
sparkling versions of Vouvray.

MUSCADET

It is hard to resist the notion of Muscadet as Neptune's own vineyard: nowhere is the gastronomic equation quite so simple and clear cut – or appetizing. Britanny provides the *fruits de mer*; the vineyards clustering south and east of Nantes provide oceans of the ideal white wine.

Muscadet is both the grape and the wine – and the zone. The grape came from Burgundy (where it is still sometimes found as the Melon de Bourgogne) as an early ripener that was satisfied with thin stony soil. Early ripening (about 15 September) gets it in before the autumn rain in this often cloudy and windswept vineyard. The Muscadet (or Melon) has low natural acidity that makes it particularly vulnerable in contact with air. To avoid oxidation and to bottle the wine as fresh and tasty as possible, the local tradition is to leave the new wine in its barrel at the end of fermentation, lying on its own yeasty sediment (*sur lie*) and to bottle it in March or April directly from the barrel – racking it, as it were, straight into bottles without fining or filtering. A certain amount of carbon dioxide is still dissolved in the wine and helps to make it fresh and sometimes faintly prickly to the tongue. With modern quantities and economics such careful bottling barrel by barrel is becoming rare, but the aim is still the same – except among certain growers who look for a more fully developed wine for further ageing.

Thus there are different styles of Muscadet, but it is hard to pin them down except by tasting each producer's wares. The extremes are a very light, fruity but essentially rather mild wine or, by contrast, one with a pungently vegetable and somehow 'wild' flavour, which can be very exciting with oysters or clams. The latter style can mature surprisingly well: I have had a five-year-old bottle (of 1976) which had achieved a sort of quintessential soft dryness I found delectable with turbot.

Much the greatest concentration of Muscadet vineyards is just east of Nantes and south of the Loire, in the area named for the rivers Sèvre and Maine. Eighty-five per cent of the 27,000 acres of vineyards are Sèvre et Maine; the rest is divided between the Coteaux de la Loire with 1,200 acres scattered eastwards towards Anjou, and plain Muscadet with 2,400 acres dotted over a wide area south of Nante.

All three appellations are interspersed with plantations (7,400 acres in all) of the secondary white grape of the area, the Gros Plant or Folle Blanche, which stands in relation to Muscadet as Aligoté does to Chardonnay: an acknowledged poor relation, but with a faithful following of its own. Gros Plant du Pays Nantais is a VDQS, not an appellation wine like Aligoté. It is always sharp, often 'green', sometimes coarse, but can be made by a sensitive hand into a very fresh if fragile wine. It would be a natural Breton progression to drink a bottle of Gros Plant with oysters, then Muscadet with a sole. Gros Plant has a minimum alcoholic degree of 9; Muscadet a maximum of 12. Controling the maximum degree is unusual, but particularly necessary in a region where chaptalization is normal and natural acidity low. Oversugared Muscadet would be a graceless brute.

For red wine the region has very little to offer. Seven hundred acres among the Muscadet vineyards of the Coteaux de la Loire around the town of Ancenis grow Gamay and a little Cabernet for light red and rosé, sold as VDQS Coteaux d'Ancenis.

The regional Vin de Pay, Jerdin de la France, is increasingly used for wines such as Chardonnay and Gamay.

MUSCADET PRODUCERS

Château d'Amour
La Grenaudière, 44690 Meisdon-sur-Sèvre

A pretty place, a true castle beside the river, producing soft, earthy wine from 45 acres.)

Gautier Audas
Haut Goulaine, 44115 Basse Goulaine

A moderate-size négociant, selling 83,000 cases a year, with his own domaine of 57 acres and local estates such as the respected Domaine Haut-Perniéres. He believes in bottling and drinking Muscadet as young as possible, but says the time to buy it is in either April/May or October/November; not at the height of summer.

Domaine du Bois Bruley
La Chesnaie, 4415 Basse Goulaine.

A 23-acre farm belonging to one of the Chéreau family, producing Muscadet de Sèvre et Maine *sur lie* and Gross Plant du Pays Nantais, distributed by Chéreau-Carré.

Louis de Bruc
12 rue de Roi, 44330 Vallet

Négociant with very sound wines, including the Château de la Mercredière.

Château de Chasseloir
St-Fiacre-sur-Maine, 44690 La Haie Fouassière.

A 42-acre estate on the banks of the river Maine belonging to the Chéreau family, making about 10,000 cases of Muscadet de Sèvre et Maine bottled *sur lie* at the property, distributed by Chéreau-Carré whose HQ is at Chasseloir. Various cuvées include Comte Leloup.

Château du Coing de St-Fiacre
44690 St-Fiacre-sur-Maine, La Haie Fouassière

A 57-acre estate at the confluence of the rivers Sèvre and Maine, belonging to one of the Chéreau family. Its Muscadet de Sèvre et Maine, bottled at the Château *sur lie*, is distributed by Chéreau-Carré. An oak-aged cuvée is their latest project.

Donatien-Bahuaud & Cie
Château de la Cassemichère, La Loge, 44330 La Chapelle-Heulin.

High quality négociants for wines from the whole Loire who use an original house-style of bottle. Their Château de la Cassemichère is a modern vineyard of 37 acres. The wine is fresh and very attractive. Another 12-acre plot is planted with Chardonnay, officially only a *vin de table*, but very good, called Le Chouan. Ch. de la Turmeliere is another property. In 1985 Bahaud launched 'Le Master de Donatien', a Muscadet cuvée chosen by a 'jury gourmet' and sold in a special bottle.

Domaine des Dorices
44330 Vallet.

A fine sloping vineyard run with great care by Léon Boullault & Fils to produce Muscadet in 2 styles, both bottled *sur lie* but one for drinking young, the other for 2 or 3 years' ageing. The Boullaults have 68 acres of Muscadet and 8 of Gros Plant, from which they also make a little *méthode champenoise* sparkling wine called Leconte.

Joseph Drouard

Domaine des Hauts Pémions, La Hallopière, 44620 Monnières.
A 32-acre property making full-bodied Muscadet deSèvre et Maine of great character. Although it is bottled *sur lie* it benefits by a year in bottle.

Le Cellier des Ducs

Rue de Sèvre et Maine, 44450 La Chapelle Basse Mer.
Négociants distributing Château de la Bigotière, Domaine des Morines, Château de Richebourg and other quality Muscadets. Total sales 83,000 cases, 30% exported.

R.E. Dugast

Domaine des Moulins, Monnières, 44690 La Haye-Fouassière.
A small (22-acre) family estate with a high reputation for very fresh and clear Muscadet de Sèvre et Maine *sur lie*. The second label is Cuvée des Grands Quarterons. Also small amounts of *méthode champenoise* brut from Gros Plant, which M. Dugast says should be drunk at 3°–5°C.

Domaine de l'Ecu

La Bretonnière, 44430 Le Louroux-Bo Hereau
Guy Brosserd's 42-acre estate pioneered organic cultivation in the Sèvre et Maine in the 1970s. The Hermine d'Or cuvée shows the ability of his wines to develop in bottle.

B. Fleurance & Fils

Les Gautronnières, 44330 La Chapelle-Heulin.
The Fleurance family cultivate 50 acres, three-quarters of it producing an excellent Muscadet de Sèvre et Maine *sur lie*, the rest Gros Plant and a red *vin de pays* of Gamay and Cabernet. The Muscadet's distinct character is best seen, they say, at Christmas of the year following the harvest.

Château des Gillieres

44690 La Haie-Fouassière
Large (82-acre) estate producing classic, easy *sur lie* Muscadet.

Marquis de Goulaine

Château de Goulaine, Haute-Goulaine, 44115 Basse-Goulaine.
The showplace of Muscadet; westernmost of the great Renaissance châteaux of the Loire. It is now an efficient example of the stately home trade, with rooms available for functions, and its own wine as the inevitable choice. Grapes from 76 estate acres plus bought-in wine produce very good examples of the modern style. 30% of the

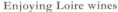

Enjoying Loire wines
The wide range of Loire wines covers almost every gastronomic eventuality. For apéritifs there are the excellent sparkling wines (and even better *crémants*) of Saumur and Vouvray, or the pungent dry Chenin Blanc wines of Savennières.

For seafood there is the incomparable match of Muscadet; for charcuterie Gros Plant du Pays Nantais or a young Pouilly Fumé, for richer fish dishes with sauces either more and better Muscadet or a Sancerre or Pouilly Fumé 2 or 3 years old.

For entrées Chinon, Bourgueil and Saumur-Champigny provide either Beaujolais-style young wines, freshly fruity, or the weight of riper vintages with 5 or 6 years' maturity. Mature Savennières or Vouvray sec or demi-sec can make an interesting alternative to white burgundy for certain richly sauced creamy dishes.

Sancerre is the inevitable local choice with strong cheeses, with milder ones the sweet wines of the Coteaux du Layon can be excellent.

Light young Coteaux du Layon, appley sweet and very cold, can be a remarkable picnic wine. The nobly rotten sweet wines of Bonnezeaux and Quarts de Chaume are some of France's finest dessert wines. Like the great German sweet wines they are complete in themselves – perhaps better alone than with any food.

Bringing in the harvest at Domaine de Chasseloir

Muscadet is bottled *sur lie*. Gros Plant is also made. The 'Cuvée du Millénaire' is from a vineyard of old vines called Montys near the château. It celebrates 1,000 years of family occupation of the estate. The Montys name is also use on a regular bottling. The Marquis quotes the old proverb 'two months, two years' which means do not drink Muscadet earlier than 2 months, nor later than 2 years, after bottling.

Guilbaud Frères
Les Lilas, Mouzillon, 44330 Vallet

Négociants producing above-average Muscadets under various names, including their own wines from Domaines de la Moutonnière and de la Pingossière. Methods are traditional and vineyard distinctions carefully preserved. Their well-known brand Le Soliel Nantais maintains a good standard.

Grand Fief de la Cormeraie
La Bournoire, 44690 Monnières.

A little 12-acre property of one of the Carré family. Its Muscadet de Sèvre et Maine *sur lie* is a gold-medal winner, distributed by Chéreau-Carré. Grand Reserve du Commandeur is a special cuvée from old vines.

Jacques Guindon
La Couleverdière, St-Géréon, 44150 Ancenis.

A family firm of growers who offer soft, exceptionally fine Muscadet des Coteaux de la Loire and the VDQS Coteaux d'Ancenis (Gamay red and rosé) and malvoisie (Pinot Gris). Production of 20,000 cases is sold 65% in France, 35% in Britain and other export markets.

Pierre Lusseaud
Château de la Galissonnière, 44330 Le Pallet.

One of the outstanding estates for full-flavoured Muscadet, using the names La Galissonnière and Château de la Jannière for Muscadet, Gros Plant and *vins de pays*. The 96 acres are picked with mechanical harvesters and every modern method is used to make the liveliest wine without losing the *goût de terroir* of Muscadet.

Pierre & Joseph Landon
Domaine de la Louvetries Les Brandières, 44690 La Haye-Foussière

Growers with a well-sited 55-acre property using the Domaine names, plus special cuvées including one from a select riverside slope within the estate, the Coteaux du Briel.

Martin-Jarry
Domaine du Champ aux Moines, 44450 La Chapelle Basse Mer.

A long-established family firm of négociants handling some 80,000 cases (but much of it in bulk) largely on the export market. Their Muscadet de Sèvre et Maine is bottled *sur lie*. Other wines are Gros Plant and a white *vin de table*, Crustacés.

Gilbert Métaireau
44140 Aigrefeuille-sur-Maine

A 47-acre farm, three-quarters Muscadet, one quarter Gros Plant. Traditionalist in method and style, bottling appropriate wines *sur lie*.

Louis Métaireau
St-Fiacre-sur-Maine, 44690 La Haye-Foussière.

A unique enterprise formed by 9 producers, led by Louis Métaireau, who all sell their wine under his label. They act as a selection panel, tasting all their wines together, 'blind', and only accepting those they all mark higher than 15 out of 20. Then each grower bottles his own wine, *sur lie*, without filtering and brands the cork with his initials. Together they own 188 acres. Seven of the nine have also bought the 68-acre 'Grand Mouton' estate, which they operate together. All Métaireau wines are classic fresh Muscadets without exaggerated flavour. He insists on 'finesse'. Grand Mouton wines are made deliberately slightly underripe, *très sauvage* for the first 1 or 2 years (when they go well with shellfish). At 3 or 4 years they mellow enough to partner sole.

Moulin de la Gravelle
44190 Gorges

A 29-acre vineyard in the Chéreau family stable making Muscadet de Sèvre et Maine bottled *sur lie*.

Château La Noë
44330 Vallet

A lordly domaine, unusual in Muscadet, with a stately neoclassical mansion and the biggest single vineyard in the area, covering 148 acres. The family of the Comte de Malestroit de Bruc have owned it since 1740. The present count (who is equally well known as an author) makes an unusual full-bodied Muscadet with small crops, not bottled *sur lie* but intended for 2 or 3 years bottle-ageing.

Château de l'Oiselinière
44120 Vertou

A 20-acre property of the Carré family, on the Sèvre. There is another château of the same name at Gorges, belonging to the Aulanier family.

Henri Poiron
Domaine les Quatres Routes, 44690 Maisdon-sur-Sèvre.

A nurseryman with 50 acres of Muscadet vines producing wine in the 'wilder', more earthy and solid style; less finesse and more meat than many modern makers.

Marcel Sautejeau
Domaine de l'Hyvernière, Le Pallet, 44330 Vallet.

One of the larger Muscadet négociants, family-run, with 2 properties at Le Pallet (l'Hyvernière and Clos des Orfeuilles) and the Domaine de la Botinière at Vallet. The Muscadet is mechanically harvested and bottled *sur lie* to be drunk within 2 years. Total turnover of wine from the whole Loire valley is more than 1 million cases a year (30% exports).

Sauvion & Fils
Château du Cléray, 44330 Vallet.

A flourishing family firm of growers and négociants. Their estate is the historic Château du Cléray, with 62 acres of Muscadet. The domaine wine *sur lie* is light and attractive. Several wines are bottled for individual producers and labelled as such. A special prestige *cuvée* chosen by a committee of restaurateurs and others is called Cardinal Richard. Lauréat is a prize-winning new Muscadet, Carte d'Or is a brand name for wine made from purchased grapes. Their flower and fruit labels are becoming well known.

Jean Nicholas Schaeffer
Domaine de la Haute Maison, 44860 St-Aignan.

Growers with 3 properties totalling 50 acres: Le Rafou-

Tillières, La Bourdelière, Les Chaboissières. The traditional methods are carried out with very modern equipment. Good Muscadet de Sèvre et Maine *sur lie* and Gros Plant for drinking in the first year.

Gabriel Thébaud
Domaine de Hautière, 44690 St-Fiacre-sur-Maine.

A long-established family estate and négociant business with a high reputation for its domaine wine, La Hautière, and its branded Muscadet de Sèvre et Maine *sur lie*, Les Doyennes. They describe their Muscadet as 'light, lively and gay', and their Gros Plant as 'dry, fruity and slightly sharp'. Production is about 20,000 cases (50%, exports).

André Vinet SA
44330 Vallet

One of the big négociants of the region, with a turnover of more than 400,000 cases, 80% sold in France. His brands include Scintillant, the 57-acre Château La Touche, Château de la Cormerais Cheneau and Domaine de la Croix.

Cave Coopérative La Noëlle
Cana, St-Géréon, 44150 Ancenis

Founded 1955; 150 members with 1,100 acres producing 170,000 cases, 35% exported. Wines are Anjou, Coteaux Ancenis, Cabernet; VDQS Gros Plant and Gamay (rosé); Domaine des Hautes Noelles is a brand name for Muscadet; Ch de la Varenne for AC Coteaux de Loire.

ANJOU-SAUMUR

Muscadet is the most single-minded of all French vineyards. Anjou, its neighbour to the east, has a gamut of wines as complete as any region of France. Its biggest turnover is in rosé, but its sparkling wine industry at Saumur is second only to Champagne in size, its best reds are considerable Cabernets, and its finest wines of all, sweet and dry Chenin Blanc whites, rank among the great apéritif and dessert wines of France. The wonderful 1989 vintage has brought them back squarely into the public eye.

Rosé is the great money-spinner. Rosé d'Anjou is a sweetish light pink from which nobody expects very much – a blend of Cabernet, Cot and Gamay with the local Groslot and Pineau d'Aunis. Cabernet d'Anjou is also rosé (not red) but an appellation to treat with more respect: the Cabernet Franc (here often called the Breton) is the best red-wine grape of the Loire; its rosé is dry and can be full of its raspberry-evoking flavour, too. The best examples come from Martigné-Briand, Tigné, and La Fosse de Tigné in the heart of the Coteaux du Layon – which is also the most important district for Chenin Blanc white wines with an inclination to sweetness.

With one exception all the considerable vineyards of Anjou lie along the south bank of the Loire and astride its tributaries the Layon, the Aubance and the Thouet. The exception is Savennières, the local vineyard of the city of Angers, which interprets the Chenin Blanc in its own way: as a forceful and intense dry wine. Savennières contains two small Grands Crus, La Roche aux Moines and La Coulée de Serrant. The wines of these, or of any of the top-quality Savennières growers, are awkward and angular at first with high acidity and biting concentration of flavour. They need age, sometimes up to 15 years, to develop their honey-scented potential. When they reach it they are excellent apéritifs. Drunk younger, they need accompanying food.

Savennières faces Rochefort-sur-Loire across the broad river, complicated with islands. Rochefort is the gateway to the long valley of the Layon, where the Chenin Blanc may be dry (and acid and pernicious) but where all the fine wines are at least crisply sweet like an apple, and the best deeply and creamily sweet with the succulence of Sauternes. The district contains two substantial Grands Crus, Quarts de Chaume and Bonnezeaux, where noble rot is a fairly frequent occurrence and sheer concentration pushes the strength of the wine up to 13 or 14 degrees. Yet curiously these sweet wines are never aged in barrels. They are in a sense the vintage port of white wines: like vintage port bottled young (in their case in their first spring) to undergo all their development with minimum possible access to oxygen. The eventual bouquet is consequently as clean, flowery and fresh-fruity as the grape itself, with the resonance and honeyed warmth of age. Great old Vouvray is so similar that it would be a brave man (or a native) who could claim to know them apart. Like German wines of fine vintages they perform a balancing-act between sweetness and sustaining acidity. But few German wines of modern times can hold their balance for half as long.

Saumur's sparkling wine industry is built upon Chenin Blanc, which has the acidity to produce successful *méthode champenoise* wines. The main producers, many of which are also négociants dealing in a range of Loire wines, are listed on pages 168–169.

Saumur is the centre of eastern Anjou, with a set of appellations of its own, for dry or medium-dry white wines of Chenin Blanc (usually blended with some Sauvignon and/or Chardonnay), for sparkling and *crémant* versions of the same, and for red and rosé wines of Cabernet Franc and Pineau d'Aunis. The red-wine vineyards are scattered to the south of the city. The appellation Saumur-Champigny (which covers three-quarters of them) has enjoyed a recent leap to fame and fashion, with its light, savoury, herby reds. Anjou-Villages is the AC for the top four dozen red-wine communes. The exceptional vintages of 1976 and 1989, when such wines as the Château de Chaintré took on deeper tones of real richness, were great boosts to their popularity. In normal years such concentration is hard to attain.

To the south of Saumur, the Thouet valley has its own VDQS for Gamay red and Chenin white, called Vins de Thouarsais after their country town.

ANJOU-SAUMUR PRODUCERS

Clos de l'Abbaye
Le-Puy-Notre-Dame, 49260 Montrieul-Bellay
Saumur red and white from a cellar in ancient chalk quarries near Saumur.

Clos de l'Aiglerie
St Aubin-de-Luigne, 49190 Rochefort-sur-Loire.
A typical Layon family property of 38 acres, owned by the widow and sons of Guy Gousset. Also red wines.

Maison Aubert Frères
La Varenne, 49270 St-Laurent des Autels.
A grower (in Muscadet and Anjou) and négociant. Five estates in Muscadet, Les Hardières at St Lambert du Lettay, where Côteaux du Layon, Anjou reds and Sauvignon Anjou Blanc are produced, and Domaine de Mirleau in Anjou, producing good Gamay.

Domaine des Baumard
Logis de la Giraudière, 49190 Rochefort-sur-Loire.
Jean Baumard is a senior figure of the Loire, from a family going back to 1634 at Rochefort, former Professor of viticulture at Angers and now president of the Union of Syndicats AOC de la Loire. Fifty acres of the 70-acre domaine is Chenin Blanc in Quarts de Chaume, Savennières (including part of the Clos du Papillon) and Coteaux du Layon (Clos de Ste-Catherine). Ten acres of Cabernet Franc and 5 of Cabernet Sauvignon produce Anjou Rouge Logis de la Giraudière. Five acres of Chardonnay go, with Chenin, to make Crémant de Loire. Baumard uses no wood 'to avoid oxidation'. He calls Savennières 'the Meursault of the Loire' and Quarts de Chaume its 'Yquem', preferring Savennières young and Chaume either before 3 years or after 8. Between 3 and 8, he says, it goes through an eclipse. Clos de Ste-Catherine is hard to classify: neither sweet nor dry but very lively – recommended with summer fruit or as an apéritif.

Jean Baumard's son Florent will take over soon on his father's retirement. Complete re-equipment of the *chais* is also planned.

Domaine Beaujeau
Champ-sur-Leyon, 49380 Thouarcé
A long-established family estate making award-winning Coteaux du Layon from 25 acres.

Albert Besombes 'Moc-Baril'
St-Hilaire-St-Florent, 49404 Saumur.
The fourth generation of a family company of négociants in all the main Loire appellations, especially red wines of Anjou and Touraine and white and rosé *pétillant naturel*, slightly fizzy wine developed by M. Besombes.

Bouvet-Ladubay
St-Hilaire-St-Florent, 49416 Saumur.
A major producer of sparkling Saumur (see page 168) and also a producer of non-appellation wine from Anjou and Touraine. Their sparkling rosé is one of the best. The firm are also négociants for all Loire wines. Bouvet-Ladubay became part of the Taittinger group in 1974. Over half the production is exported.

Claude Branchereau
Les Barres, St-Aubin-de-Luigńe, 49190 Rochefort-sur-Loire.
Red wine grower with 15 acres making agreeable wine.

Château de Chaintre
Dampierre-sur-Loire, 49400 Saumur.
Owner: Baron Gaël de Tigny. A charming old country house, once a priory, and notable producer of Saumur-Champigny from its 50 acres. The low underground barrel-cellars were used up to the 1978 vintage, and wood as well as stainless steel is still used. The '76 was a splendid wine. Baron de Tigny thinks highly of his '85.

Jean-Pierre Chéné
Impasse de Jardins, Beaulieu-sur-Layon, 49190 Rochefort-sur-Loire.
52 acres of vines belonging to an old Beaulieu family, recently taken over by a new generation. Twenty-five are Chenin Blanc, 20 Cabernet. The best sweet Coteaux du Layon-Beaulieu comes from 3 vineyards: Clos du Paradis Terrestre, Clos des Mulonnières and Clos des Ontinières. Up to 3 months slow, cool fermentation in barrels preserves aromas (and results in alcohol as high as 15° plus 3° remaining in the wine as sugar). Even the Cabernet d'Anjou (rosé) is 12° plus 2° of sugar. Chéné intends to make more red Cabernet and brave the tannin to get a *vin de garde*.

Domaine du Closel
Savennières, 49170 St-Georges-sur-Loire.
A 35-acre estate producing classic white Savennières, concentrated wine fermented in wood, and a little (5 acres) Cabernet (appellation Anjou or Anjou Village) also fermented in barrels. Mme Michelle Bazin de Jessey is the great-granddaughter of Napoleon's *aide-de-camp* Emmanuel de Las Cases, who returned here in 1820 from St-Helena to write his famous memoirs.

Claude Daheuiller
Domaine des Varinelles, Varrains, 49400 Saumur.
A long-established family of predominantly red-wine makers with 56 acres of Cabernet in Saumur-Champigny, now made with modern methods and winning medals in Paris. Their Vielles Vignes selection spends more time in wood. The Daheuillers also make a little Saumur *méthode champenoise* from Chenin Blanc grown on very chalky soil.

Château d'Epiré
Epiré, 49170 St-Georges-sur-Loire.
Following the death of Armand Bizard in 1984 the estate has been run by his children, with daughter Mme Litzow in charge. Family ownership of this 25-acre estate dates back to 1749. Barrels are used, picking is by hand. The aim is Savennières made for long ageing, full-bodied and dry – a *vin de garde*. In addition to Chenin the estate has a little Cabernet for Rosé d'Anjou and Anjou Village. Rosé de la Loire is also made.

Château de Fesles
49380 Thouarcé.

Jacques Boivin is the fourth generation to make remarkable Bonnezeaux at this ancient property. He owns 32 acres of the Grand Cru and another 45 of Cabernet, Groslot and Gamay for red and rosé, with an unusual 6 acres of Chardonnay – which here is a mere *vin de pays*. His Bonnezeaux is selected (when possible – as in 1983) for noble rot and fermented in small barrels. Many find it the best of the appellation.

Paul Filliatreau
Chaintres, Dampierre-sur-Loire, 49400 Saumur.

One of the growers who has brought Saumur-Champigny to prominence. His 74 acres of Cabernet include some century-old vines; vinified separately as '*Vieilles Vignes*'. Another cuvée, Lena, is from gravel as opposed to Limestone soil. His vats are stainless steel but the wine is aged in wood and designed to age. The 1983 was very good. Five more acres make dry white.

J-L & B. Foucault
Chacé, 49400 Saumur

Two brothers run a century-old red wine producer, with vintages in the cellars going back six decades. They buy their *barriques* from Château Margaux and age their wine in wood for 18 months.

Grosset-Château
49190 Rochefort-sur-Loire

Oak-aged Cabernet and Rochefort Layon in the traditional style from a traditionalist family.

Domaine de Haute Perche
St-Melaine-sur-Aubance, 49320 Brissec-Quincé

A 20-acre estate devoted to classic Cabernet reds. Owner Christian Pepin is gaining renown as Anjou reds revive.

Mme A. Joly
Château de la Roche-aux-Moines, 49170 Savennières.

A beautiful little estate in an outstanding situation, chosen by monks in the 12th century. The main vineyard is the 17-acre Coulée de Serrant, run by Mme Joly's son Nicolas Joly, an ex-merchant banker, whose highly individual methods of growing vines and making wine are based around a theory of biodynamism. He uses no fertilizers or artificial pesticides and no modern technological equipment; the results are wines of unusual ageing qualities. Madame Joly also owns 5 acres of La Roche aux Moines called the Clos de la Bergerie and 5 acres of Cabernet for Château de la Roche. Chenin Blanc here makes some of its most intense dry (or off-dry) wines of extraordinary savour and longevity. With a yield of only about 1,700 cases the wine is on allocation, at a suitably high price.

A. Laffourcade
Château de Suronde, 49190 Rochefort-sur-Loire.

The principal proprietor of Quarts de Chaume with 50 of the 112 acres of the Grand Cru. The great sweet wine is made Sauternes-style with a crop of between 20 and 25 hectolitres a hectare picked as the grapes shrivel with noble rot. Fermentation, formerly in 4,000-litre *foudres*, or great barrels, now takes place in stainless steel. Another Laffourcade owns Château de la Echarderie which is the same appellation.

Jacques Lalanne
Château de Bellerive, 49190 Rochefort-sur-Loire.

A major proprietor of the Grand Cru Quarts de Chaume with 42 acres surrounding the château. Almost Yquem-like methods are used, accepting a tiny crop from old vines pruned hard (12 hectolitres a hectare) and picking only nobly rotten grapes in successive *triers* around the vineyard. Fermentation in barrels takes most of the winter. The great difference between this and Sauternes (apart from the grapes) is that bottling is done at the end of April 'when the moon is waxing' and all maturation takes place in bottle rather than barrel.

The wine can scarcely be appreciated for 5, sometimes 10, years – and lasts for 50.

Sylvain Mainfray
rue Jean Jaurès, 49400 Saumur.

A small family firm (founded 1901) of quality négociants, handling some 30,000 cases of appellation wines of Anjou, Saumur and Touraine, mostly bottled at the growers. Mme Mainfray also owns the 25-acre Château d'Aubigné.

Domaine de Montgilet
Juigné-sur-Loire, 49130 Les-Ponts-de-Cé

Jean-Yves Lebreton has a name for red wines from this 17-acre estate: his '85 won prizes.

Domaine de la Motte
49190 Rochefort-sur-Loire

A 40-acre family property run by a son, André Sorin, whose total involvement shows in the quality of his wines (and whose sense of humour shows in the name of his Anjou Sec: Clos des Belles Mères – Mothers-in-law). Coteaux du Layon Rochefort is the appellation of his sweetest and best white. He grows a little Chardonnay as well as the usual local grapes for white, red and rosé.

Vins Mottron
rue d'Anjou, 49540 Martigné-Briand.

A family of négociants and growers with a long history but a very modern outlook; originators of a PVC-packed single-glass portion of table wine. They own 62 acres of Grolleau, Cabernet, Chenin Blanc and Sauvignon and use cold fermentation for a range that includes 40% appellation wines, the rest *vins de table* in the fresh Loire style. Production is about 80,000 cases.

De Neuville
St-Hilaire-St-Florent, 49400 Saumur.

Négociants and sparkling wine producers in the chalk caves of Saumur, with 100 acres principally in Chenin Blanc for their high-quality *mousseux*, a regular medal winner.

Rémy Pannier
St-Hilaire-St-Florent, 49400 Saumur.

The 'maison leader de la Loire' as general négociants, with a big turnover in all Loire wines and a good reputation for quality. The director, Philippe Treutenaere, is a member of the family that started the house in 1885. As growers they own 100 acres of Cabernet for Cabernet d'Anjou and Chenin for Anjou Blanc. Their methods are modern, blends well-made and marketing imaginative.

René Renou
Place du Champ-de-Foire, 49380 Thouarcé.

The sixth generation to bear the same name has 45 acres, one third in the Grand Cru Bonnezeaux and a third each of

Cabernet and Groslot for red and rosé respectively. Renou is the president of the Bonnezeaux *Syndicat*. His son will be the seventh René Renou.

Domaine Richou
Chauvigné, Mozé-sur-Louet, 49190 Rochefort-sur-Loire
Red and white wines, including a *Vieilles Vignes* cuvée of Anjou Rouge from 5 acres which demands bottle-age.

Domaine des Rochettes
Mozé-sur-Louet, 49190 Rochefort-sur-Loire.
Proprietor Gérard Chauvin. 49 acres of Cabernet Sauvignon, Cabernet Franc and Chenin Blanc; also land in Coteaux de l'Aubance.

Domaine du Sauveroy
St-Lambert-du-Lattay, 49190 Rochefort-sur-Loire
Pascal Cailleau is winemaker at this family estate which is leading the way in advanced winemaking for Anjou reds.

Pierre & Yves Soulez
Château de Chamboureau
Savennières, 49170 St-Georges-sur-Loire.
One of the most successful Anjou growers, fully modernized and using steel and temperature control in a way which seems quite alarming on the Loire. He acquired the Château de la Bizolières to enlarge his property to 59 acres, 52 in Savennières, 7 in AOC Anjou Rouge (half-and-half Cabernet Franc and Cabernet Sauvignon). Bottling is done as early as the beginning of January in an effort to capture the maximum fruit flavours. The Savennières is very dry and often rather prickly with carbon dioxide. Young it is not very appealing: a few years in bottle give it dimensions. Château de Chamboureau is another Soulez Savennières, from 25 acres of rocky land on a bluff above the Loire.

Château de Targé
Parnay, 49730 Montsoreau.
A four-towered *manoir*, in the Pisani-Ferry family since 1655, with 50 acres of Cabernet (90% Franc, 10% Sauvignon) for Saumur Champigny. Temperature-controlled stainless steel fermentation then ageing in new oak.

Pierre Yves Tijou
Domaine de la Soucherie, 49190 Rochefort-sur-Loire.
Tijou's parents bought this 75-acre domaine in 1952. Most is in Coteaux du Layon in Chenin Blanc, with

Cabernet and Gamay for red and rosé. His top Coteaux du Layon, Beaulieu is from 90-year-old vines. No wood is used for the white. An Anjou Blanc has 20% Sauvignon added to Chenin Blanc for aroma.

Les Vins Touchais and Les Vignobles Touchais
49700 Doué La Fontaine
One of the biggest growers and négociants of the Loire and recently one of the most celebrated. Les Vignobles Touchais own 400 acres, of which 120 are Chenin Blanc in Coteaux du Layon and Anjou Blanc, 180 are Cabernet and 100 Groslot for red and rosé. The Touchais family have been growers for centuries and have amassed astonishing stocks of fine old sweet Layon wines – the best, sold as Moulin Touchais, maturing almost indefinitely. Wines in stock include 1985, '79, '78, '77, '75, '71, '69, '64, '59, '55, '49, '45, '43, '42, '37, '33, '28, etc. At 20 years the '59 was full of vigour and deep honeyed flavour – a very great dessert wine. The bulk of the business of Les Vins Touchais (founded 1947) is in rosé and other popular regional wines. Cuisse de Bergère – Shepherdess's Thigh – is appropriately sweet and blushing.

Compagnie de la Vallée de la Loire
49260 Montreuil-Bellay
A big-scale general négociant for the Loire with many wines and brands, in bulk and bottle, mostly using the name of the founder, Henri Verdier, or one of his family. Total sales approach 1.25m. cases, one-third to England.

CAVES COOPERATIVES

Les Caves de la Loire
49320 Brissac
A union of 3 cooperative cellars, at Brissac, Beaulieu-sur-Layon and Tigné, producing some 300,000 cases of the general Anjou appellations with modern equipment. As much as half of their production is exported.

Les Vignobles de la Cour de Pierre
49190 Rochefort-sur-Loire
A sales cooperative with 10 members, all small growers in Rochefort, who make their wine personally but band together to sell it on the export market. There are only 33,000 cases but it is well received; especially the *moelleux* Coteaux du Layon Rochefort.

SPARKLING SAUMUR

The in-built acidity of Chenin Blanc is the cause and justification of the Saumur sparkling-wine industry, which is based in the chalk caves of St-Hilaire-St-Florent, just west of Saumur. It uses the champagne method to produce cleanly fruity, usually very dry wines at half champagne prices, less characterful and complex but just as stimulating.

Major producers
Ackerman-Laurance
St-Hilaire-St-Florent, 49416 Saumur.

The original and probably still the biggest firm, founded in 1811 when Ackerman, a Belgian, introduced the *méthode champenoise* to the Loire. Still a leader with the new extra-quality Crémant de Loire. 292,000 cases.
Maison Veuve Amiot
49400 Saumur. Founded 1884, now owned by Martini & Rossi. 250,000 cases of sparkling Saumur, Anjou and Crémant du Roi (Crémant de Loire).
Bouvet-Ladubay
St-Hilaire-St-Florent, 49416 Saumur.

The second oldest (1851) of the sparkling-wine houses. Excellent sparkling Saumurs include Brut de Blanc, Extra Dry Blanc, Carte Blanche demi-sec and the luxury Crémant Saphir. Also vintage Crémant de Loire and Crémant Rosé.
Etablissements Gratien, Meyer & Seydoux
Ch. de Beaulieu 49400 Saumur. A twin company to the Champagne house of Alfred Gratien. 40 acres of vineyards (Chenin Blanc and Cabernet) over the

cellars. Products are sparkling Saumur, Crémant de Loire Brut, Anjou Rosé and Rouge Dry (also sparkling). Gratien and Meyer is a touch more full-bodied than most Saumurs. Other brands are Rosset and Henri d'Alran, and an apéritif G & M Royal.

Langlois-Château
St-Hilaire-St-Florent, 49416 Saumur. This old house merged with Bollinger in 1973. Principally producers of fine sparkling Saumur but also négociants in the major Loire wines.

De Neuville
St-Hilaire-St-Florent, 49416 Saumur. Producer of quality sparkling Saumur from 100 acres.

Vignerons de Saumur à St-Cyr en Bourg
49260 Montreuil Bellay. The Saumur growers' cooperative for sparkling (and other) wines, uniting some 1,000 acres, half Chenin Blanc and half red grapes. Their Saumur Brut Cuvée de la Chevalerie and Crémant de Loire Prince Alexandre are particularly well thought of. Other wines in a total of 87,000 cases include Saumur-Champigny, Anjou Rosé, etc., under the name of Bonnamy.

Remuage in Saumur

TOURAINE

It is hard to define Touraine more precisely than as the eastern half of the central Loire, with the city of Tours at its heart and a trio of goodly rivers, the Cher, the Indre and the Vienne, joining the majestic mainstream from the south.

Almost on its border with Anjou it produces the best red wines of the Loire. Chinon and Bourgueil lie on the latitude of the Côte de Beaune and the longitude of St-Emilion – a situation that produces a kind of claret capable of stunning vitality and charm. The Cabernet Franc, with very little if any Cabernet Sauvignon, achieves a sort of pastel sketch of a great Médoc, smelling sweetly of raspberries, begging to be drunk cellar-cool in its first summer, light and sometimes astringent, yet surprisingly solid in its construction: ripe vintages behave almost like Bordeaux in ageing, at least to seven or eight years.

Much depends on the soil: sand and gravel near the river produce lighter, faster-maturing wine than clay over *tuffeau* limestone on the slopes (*coteaux*). These differences seem greater than those between Chinon and Bourgueil; certainly than any between Bourgueil and its immediate neighbour on the north bank, St-Nicolas de Bourgueil, although this has a separate appellation of its own.

Touraine's other famous wine is Vouvray, potentially the most luscious and longest lived of all the sweet Chenin Blanc whites, though, like German wines, depending more on the vintage than the site for the decisive degree of sugar that determines its character. The best vineyards are on the warm chalky *tuffeau* slopes near the river and in sheltered corners of side valleys. A warm dry autumn (1989

was optimal; one of the historic great years) can overripen the grapes here by sheer heat, or a warm misty one can bring on noble rot to shrivel them. In either case great sweet Vouvray will be possible, with or without the peculiar smell and taste of *botrytis cinerea*. Cool years make wines of indeterminate (though often very smooth and pleasant) semisweetness, or dry wines – all with the built-in acidity that always keeps Chenin Blanc lively (if not always very easy to drink). The solution to overacid wines here, as in Saumur, is to make them sparkle by the *méthode champenoise*.

It is an odd coincidence that each of the great Loire wines comes with a pair across the river: Savennières with Coteaux du Layon, Bourgueil with Chinon, Sancerre with Pouilly and Vouvray with Montlouis. Montlouis, squeezed between the south bank of the Loire and the north bank of the converging tributary Cher, is not regarded, except by those who make it, as having quite the authority and attack of great Vouvray. Its sites are slightly less favoured and its wines softer and more tentative. They can sparkle just as briskly, though, and ripen almost as sweet.

Outside these four appellations Touraine, with its simple but all-purpose AOC Touraine, has only a modest reputation; no popular drink such as Anjou Rosé to give it identity. I suggest that the future lies with the general (and self-explanatory) Sauvignon and Gamay de Touraine; reasonably priced substitutes for – respectively – Sancerre and Beaujolais, two of France's most fashionable and overpriced appellations. They are not as fine as either, but an awful lot cheaper.

TOURAINE PRODUCERS

Domaine Allias
le Petit Mont, Vouvray

Daniel Allias and his sister, Denise, farm 25 acres of hilltop vines over the rock-cut cellars. Concentrated, classic dry, demi-sec and *moelleux* Vouvrays.

Claude Ammeux
Clos de la Contrie, St-Nicolas de Bourgueil, 37410 Bourgueil.

A charming 11-acre property at the foot of the coteaux, almost in Bourgueil. M. Ammeux feeds his very old vines on seaweed and looks for flavour and alcohol at the expense of big crops.

Audebert & Fils
37140 Bourgueil

One of the biggest producers of Bourgueil and St-Nicolas de Bourgueil with 74 acres and modern equipment. His production of over 40,000 cases is sold under 2 labels: Domaine du Grand Clos and Vignobles Les Marquises – easy wines for drinking cool in their youthful prime.

Marcel et Hubert Audebert
Caves St-Martin, Restigné, 37140 Bourgueil.

A long-established family with 25 acres in Restigné, appellation Bourgueil. Their wine is fermented and aged in wood and they also keep stocks for ageing in bottle.

M. Berger
Caves des Liards, 37270 Montlouis-sur-Loire.

A third-generation property of 50 acres, 80% in Chenin Blanc for still, sparkling and *pétillant* Montlouis, the rest in Sauvignon for Touraine Blanc and Cabernet Franc for Touraine Rouge. The wine is all bottled in spring and aged in bottle – about 8,300 cases a year.

Aimé Boucher
Huisseau-sur-Cosson, 41350 Vineul.

A family firm of négociants founded in 1900, widely regarded as setting the highest standards in Touraine and the upper Loire. The director, Claude Kistner, chooses wines from growers and moves them to the firm's own cellars in each area. Specialities include Vouvray (still and sparkling), Sancerre and Crémant de Loire. Chinon and Bourgueil spend 1 year in wood. Production 42,000 cases.

Bougrier
St-Georges-sur-Cher, 41400 Montrichard.

A century-old family firm of growers (with 37 acres, the Domaine Guenault) and négociants. The domaine produces Sauvignon, Cabernet Franc, Gamay and Chenin Blanc, all AOC Touraine. Sixty per cent of the total turnover of 375,000 cases in all Loire wines is exported.

Marc Brédit
Rochecorbon, 37210 Vouvray

Négociants with hospitable cellars in the rock caves below Rochecorbon. The firm belongs to the de Ladoucette concern of Pouilly. The wines are all Vouvrays, in both still and sparkling forms. Brédit invented Vouvray Pétillant in the 1920s. The standards are commendably high.

Caslot-Galbrun
La Hurolaie, Benais, 37140 Bourgueil.

One of the oldest established families of growers in Bourgueil, whose 37 acres seem to produce some of the juiciest, deepest coloured, most age-worthy wine. The walled Clos de la Gaucherie at Restigné is theirs. Fermentation is in stainless steel, but methods and standards are unchanged.

Caslot-Jamet
Domaine de la Chevalerie, Restigné,
37140 Bourgueil.

Paul Caslot, married to a Jamet daughter, farms 25 acres of old Cabernet on the hill and makes firm deep-toned Bourgueil, aged up to 18 months in wood and intended to age a further 3, 4, or more years.

Pierre Chainier
Château de la Roche, 37530 Amboise.

A flourishing négociant business, selling some 330,000 cases of a full range of Loire wines, specializing in Touraine. Pierre Chainier also owns the Château de Pocé, with 80 acres of Gamay, Côt, Sauvignon and Chardonnay, on a south slope facing the Château of Amboise across the Loire (Appellation Touraine-Amboise). Other Chenier estates, both growing Sauvignon, are Domaine du Grand Moulin at Châteauvieux and Domaine des Roussières.

Château de Chenonceau
Chenonceaux, 37150 Blere

The estate belonging to the most beautiful of Loire showplace châteaux has 30 acres of vines, and a well-equipped little winery in a courtyard. A range of wines is made.

Couly-Dutheil
12 rue Diderot, 37502 Chinon.

A grower of Chinon and négociant for other Loire wines, founded in 1910 by B. Dutheil, developed by René Couly and now run by his sons Pierre and Jacques and Bertrand, son of Pierre. Their 125 acres of Chinon are divided between wines of plain and plateau, sold as Domaine de Turpenay and Domaine René Couly, and the (better) wines of the *coteaux*, the Clos de l'Echo and Clos de l'Olive. Equipment is modern, with temperature control and automatic turning of the skins in the stainless steel vats. The object is wine drinkable by the following Easter but able, as Chinon is, to age in bottle for several years. The top wine is a selection labelled Baronnie Madeleine.

Hubert Denay
le Breuil, 37400 Amboise

A family estate with 23 acres, making classic Touraine Amboise, in particular the straight Cot.

Deletang Père et Fils
St-Mertin-le-Beau, 37270 Montlouis-sur-Loire

Good Montlouis from Chenin Blanc, and Touraine AC wines, from 35 well-placed acres.

Dutertre Père & Fils
Limeray, 37400 Amboise.

A 66-acre family property run by father (Gabriel) and son (Jacques). Fifty-odd acres are Cabernet, Malbec, Gamay and Pinot Noir for red and rosé Touraine-Amboise. They also make sparkling and still dry whites in their rock-cut cellar.

A. Foreau
Clos Naudin. 37210 Vouvray.

The Foreau family own 30 acres of prime vineyards and aim to age their wine for as long as possible before selling it – an expensive procedure but essential to let its character develop. Ten years is a good age for a 'new' Vouvray. Their output is about 3,300 bottles of sweet, dry, demi-sec and sparkling.

André Freslier
'La Caillerie', 37210 Vouvray.

M. Freslier and his son Jean-Pierre make serious dry Vouvray from 20 acres, fermenting the wine in old 600-litre casks ('*demi-muids*'). He recommends 4–5 years ageing in bottle. Also dry fizzy Vouvray *pétillant*.

Domaines Girault-Artois
7 Quai des Violettes, 37400 Amboise.

A thoroughly modern property of Touraine-Mesland, specializing in softly fruity reds under the names Château Gaillard (30 acres) and Domaine d'Artois (50 acres): 'Jeunes Vignes' is Gamay, 'Vielles Vignes' a blend of Gamay. Cabernet Franc, Côt and Malbec are given six months in wood and made as a *vin de garde*. White and rosé wines are also made.

René Gouron & Fils
37500 Chinon

The Gouron family have 43 acres at Cravant Les Coteaux, producing some 5,000 cases of outstanding Chinon and a little Touraine rosé *pétillant*.

Gaston Huet
Domaine du Haut-Lieu, 37210 Vouvray.

Perhaps the most respected name in Vouvray, a family of growers for 3 generations making wine of the highest quality from 3 vineyards, Le Haut-Lieu, Le Mont and Le Clos du Bourg, sweet or dry, still or sparkling according to the season. M. Huet is mayor of Vouvray.

Pierre Jamet et Fils
Les Fondis, St-Nicholas de Bourgueil

There are several families of Jamets herabouts: this branch has 50 acres of gravel soil making characterful wines which gain from a little Cabernet Sauvignon to spice the Franc.

Charles Joguet
Sazilly, 37220 L'Ile Bouchard.

An artist-*vigneron*, painter and sculptor as well as farmer of 30 acres of Chinon and one of its best wine makers. His best old vines are in the Clos de la Dioterie. Clos du Chêne Vert is another noted vineyard of his. His up-to-date cellar has automated *pigeage* of juice and skins in stainless steel vats followed by ageing for up to 18 months in *barriques*.

Lamé-Delille-Boucard
Ingrandes de Touraine, 37140 Bourgueil.

A considerable property of 65 acres, divided almost equally between 4 communes with the appellation Bourgueil: Ingrandes, St-Patrice, Restigné and Benais. The grouping is recent, although M. Lamé comes from an old *vigneron* family. He uses wooden vats and describes his wines as ranging from succulent to fragile, depending on the vintage.

Jean-Claude Mabileau
St-Nicolas de Bourgueil, 37140 Bourgueil.

A grower with 24 acres, all beside his house. He makes as much as 2,000 cases of light red with the typical raspberry aroma, which he claims will keep for 7 years even in 'medium' vintages, and up to 30 in great ones.

Paul Maître
SCEA Domaine Raguenières, Benais, 37140 Bourgueil.

A 30-acre Bourgueil property making a little rosé as well as nearly 5,000 cases of clean, fairly tannic, marvellously scented red compared by M. Maître with Bordeaux – especially in its keeping properties.

Henri Marionnet
Domaine de la Charmoise, Soings, 41230 Mur de Sologne.

A modern-minded grower with a new 110-acre vineyard of Gamay and Sauvignon Blanc. He uses *macération carbonique* to get a Beaujolais effect in his Gamay de Touraine, and strives for round and fruity Sauvignon.

Château Moncontour
Rochecorbon, 37210 Vouvray.

Vouray's largest estate, with 270 acres, now in the hands of businessman Charles Rolin. Sparkling and still wines of good quality.

J.M. Monmousseau
41400 Montrichard.

The Taittinger group of Champagne owns this century-old sparkling-wine house, but the director is still Armand Monmousseau. Their own 150 acres of vines at Azay-Le-Rideau, Monlouis and St-Georges-sur-Cher provide a quarter of the grapes for a fine light *méthode champenoise* sparkler. Production is about 100,000 cases, plus 40,000 of still wines of other Loire regions. The Vouvray estate of Château de Gaudrelle is under Monmousseau ownership: fine still wines are made.

Claude Moreau
La Taille, St-Nicolas de Bourgueil, 37140 Bourgueil.

Moreaus abound in St-Nicolas. They go back 5 generations, and Claude Moreau has 5 *vigneron* sons. His own vineyard is 15 acres; his aim, by keeping the wine in barrels for 1 year, is to make it durable as well as fragrant. But he has no old stocks – the customers take it fresh from the bottling line.

Dominique Moyer
Husseau, 3720 Montlouis-sur-Loire.

A respected old family of growers (since 1830) with 30 acres of very old vines (30% are over 70 years old). The Moyers go to the length of successive pickings to crush nothing but ripe grapes, making sec and demi-sec as ripe and round as possible. A little sparkling wine now made.

Gaston Pavy
Saché, 37190 Azay-Le-Rideau.

The best-regarded name in this little appellation, with 5 acres of Chenin Blanc making notably intense semi-sweet Chenin Blanc and 2.5 acres of Groslot and Malbec for a surprisingly durable dry rosé.

J.B. Pinon
Caves aux Tuffières, L'homme, 72340 La Chartre-sur-le-Loir.

An old family of growers from Vouvray, now leading producers of dry Jasnières (as well as Vouvray *pétillant*). They also grow Pineau d'Aunis and Gamay for red and rosé Coteaux du Vendômois (VDQS). Jasnières needs bottle-age to soften its bite.

Prince Poniatowski
Le Clos Baudoin, 37210 Vouvray.

Maker of some immortal Vouvray from 2 Grand Cru vineyards, Clos Baudoin and Aigle Blanc. The fine vintages have what the Prince calls 'race' – breeding – that takes 25 or 30 years to reach its full flowering. The 1854 in the cellar is apparently excellent. The estate is 54 acres, 52 of Vouvray and 2 of Touraine, used for *méthode champenoise* Brut de Brut. Half of some 12–13,000 cases a year is exported.

Clos des Quarterons
St-Nicolas de Bourgueil, 37140 Bourgueil.

A property of 50 acres well distributed on the lighter soils of St-Nicolas. A property of the Amirault family. 8,000 cases of lightly fruity wine sold to restaurants and private clients.

Jean Maurice Raffault
La Croix, Savigny-en-Véron, 37420 Avoine.

In 20 years M. Raffault, whose family have been *vignerons* since 1693, has expanded his vineyards from 12 to 73 acres with parcels scattered over 6 communes, all in the appellation Chinon. He makes the wines of different soils separately. His Clos des Lutinières comes from gravel. Les Galluches from sandier soil, Les Picasses and Isore for the local *taffeau* and Clos de Galon from chalky clay. All the grapes are destalked, then fermented for up to 40 days before being aged for 1 year in *barriques*. He is one of the very few Chinon growers still using *barriques*, aiming for stable, tannic wine which will keep 10 years. His current production is 17,000 cases. 30% is exported.

Olga Raffault
Savigny-en-Véron, 37500 Chinon.

One of several Raffaults in and around this village at the western end of the Chinon appellation. (Another, Raymond, owns Château Raifault [sic.]). The estate is 37 acres, with fermentation in steel vats, then ageing in wooden ones, keeping the wine of different sites separate. Clients (who include the famous restaurant Barrier at Tours) can choose from a range of generally fruity and fairly full-bodied wines.

Joel Taluau
Chevrette, St-Nicolas de Bourgueil, 37140 Bourgueil.

Twenty-two acres of St-Nicolas and 3 of Bourgueil producing 1,500 cases of fragrant light red. Since 1985, Taluau has phased out wood ageing and enforced a severe pruning regime.

Jean-Paul Trotignan
10 rue des Bruyères, 41140 Noyers sur Cher.

A small supplier of the Paris market with carefully made Sauvignon, Gamay and Cabernet (which he considers a *vin de garde*), all AOC Touraine. About 3,000 cases.

Jean Vrillon
Faverolles-sur-Cher, 41400 Montrichard.

A long-established grower with a small business in *méthode champenoise* AOC Touraine and red and white Vin de Pays du Jardin de la France. 1,250 cases, sold in Brittany and Paris.

CAVES COOPERATIVES

Haut-Poitou
86170 Neuville de Poitou.

The VDQS zone of Haut-Poitou is well south of the Loire on the road to Poitiers, where 47 communes on the chalky soil of a plateau used to supply distilling wine to Cognac. In 1948, a coop was founded and succeeded in raising standards to the point where in 1970 the region was promoted to VDQS. Full AOC status now cannot be far away.

Today the coop has 1,200 members farming 2,250 acres, growing by 125 acres a year. Sauvignon Blanc yields a highly characteristic and aromatic dry white, Gamay a light red and Cabernet Franc a dry rosé. New plantings of Chardonnay have been a great success, producing something like featherweight Chablis. All wines are bottled and should be drunk very young. Production 850,000 cases, including *vins de table* and Vin de Pays du Jardin de la France.

La Confrèrie des Vignerons de Oisly et Thesée
Oisly, 41700 Contres.

A young (1961) cooperative with 60 members, which is making great efforts to create a new style and image for the valley of the Cher in eastern Touraine. Their aim is to design a well-balanced light red and white using a blend of grapes. The white is Sauvignon, Chenin Blanc and Chardonnay, the red Cabernet Franc, Cot (Malbec) and Gamay. The cooperative's brand for their selection of each is Baronnie d'Aignan. Production of bottled wine is about 160,000 cases. All AOC wines. The coop also makes wine for les Vignernons de la Vallée du Cher, an informal group of growers led by Michel Sebéo which is pitching at the quality end of the market.

THE UPPER LOIRE

It might well surprise the *vignerons* of Sancerre and Pouilly, the uppermost of the mainstream Loire vineyards, to learn what a profound influence their produce has had on forming modern tastes in white wine. It is an area of generally small and unsophisticated properties – with one or two well-organized exceptions. But it has an easily recognizable style of wine, pungent and cutting, with the smell and acidity of Sauvignon Blanc grown in a cool climate.

Although Sauvignon is planted on a far larger scale in Bordeaux its wine never smelt and tasted so powerfully characteristic there as it does on the Loire. The Bordeaux tradition is to blend it with the smoother and more neutral Sémillon. But since

Château du Nozet

Bordeaux has seen the world paying white burgundy prices for the assertive (some say obvious) Loire style, it is paying it the sincerest form of flattery. Californians, with vastly different growing conditions, have adopted the term Fumé to indicate that their Sauvignon Blanc aims at the Loire flavour (rather than the broader, riper, to some *passé*, style of Graves). One might say that the world discovered the Sauvignon Blanc and its singular flavour through the little vineyard of Sancerre and the even smaller one of Pouilly-sur-Loire.

What is the flavour? It starts with the powerful aroma, which needs no second sniff. 'Gunflint,' suggesting the smell of the sparks when flint strikes metal, is a traditional way of characterizing it. In unripe vintages tasters talk of cats, and I have been reminded of wet wool. Successful Sancerres and Pouilly Fumés have an attractive smell and taste of fresh blackcurrants, leaves and all, and a natural high acidity which makes them distinctly bracing. Sancerre normally has more body and 'drive' (and higher acidity) than Pouilly Fumé; consequently it can benefit from two or three years' ageing, where Pouilly needs only a year or so.

For reasons of tradition the Pouilly vineyards also contain a proportion of the neutral Chasselas grape, which cannot be sold as 'Fumé' but only as Pouilly-sur-Loire – a pale, adequate, rather pointless wine, which must be drunk very young.

Sancerre, on the other hand, is almost as proud of its Pinot Noir red and rosé as its Sauvignon white. They never achieve the flavour and texture of Burgundy. In fact, they frequently have the faintly watery style of German Spätburgunder (the same grape). Nor do they age satisfactorily. But they are highly appreciated at source.

SANCERRE PRODUCERS

Pierre Archambault
Caves du Clos la Perrière, Verdigny, 18300 Sancerre.
A family firm of growers (74 acres) and négociants producing 50,000 cases of Sancerre a year (white, red and rosé) and Pouilly Fumé, and a white *vin de table* Les Roches Blanches. Their best Sancerre is called Clos la Perrière.

They use modern equipment in spacious natural rock cellars. M. Archambault particularly recommends his Sancerre with the local goats'-milk cheese: Crottin de Chavignol.

Bernard Bailly-Reverdy & Fils
La Croix St-Laurent, Bué, 18300 Sancerre.

M. Bailly is a distinguished traditional grower with 37 acres in no less than 15 different sites including the famous Clos du Chêne Marchand. Eight acres are Pinot Noir, producing a worthwhile red Sancerre. His white from other vineyards is called Domaine de la Mercy Dieu. He looks for (and finds) a balance of fruit and finesse, particularly in his white wine.

Domaine Joseph Balland-Chepuis
La Croix St-Laurent, Bué, 18300 Sancerre.

An enthusiastic young descendant of a long line of growers with 42 acres. He sells 3 excellent whites, Grand Chemarin, Clos Le Chêne Marchand and Clos d'Ervocs, and a red and rosé, Les Marnes. His cuvée prestige is called Comte Thibault. His style of white is very fresh, sweet-smelling and long on the palate.

Philippe de Benoist
Domaine du Nozay, 18300 Sancerre.

A small high-quality domaine started in 1970 by the brother-in-law of Aubert de Villaine, co-owner of the Domaine de la Romanée-Conti. He is making Sancerre as delicately rounded as possible.

Etablissements Cordier
Domaine de la Poussie, Bué, 18300 Sancerre.

The great Bordeaux house of Cordier has a well-known Sancerre estate of 70 acres, producing white Clos de la Poussie, red Guche Pigeon and rosé Orme aux Loups. All 3 are fresh and fragrant wines of low acidity designed to be drunk very young (even the red).

Francis & Paul Cotat
Chavignol, 18300 Sancerre.

A very small, totally traditional and most prestigious grower making only about 1,000–1,500 cases. The Cotat brothers do everything themselves, use an old wooden press, ferment in casks and never fine or filter: instead they bottle at the full moon in May when the wine is clear and still. Bottles from the 1930s in their cellar are still in good condition.

Lucien Crochet
Bué, 18300 Sancerre.

A family holding of 50 acres, 37 in Sauvignon, the rest Pinot Noir. Crochet also buys in grapes for his modern, efficient cellars. Classic methods produce excellent wine, particularly his Clos du Chêne Marchand from his 17 acres there.

André Dezat
Chaudoux, Verdigny, 18300 Sancerre.

An old-school grower, mayor of the village, who works in clogs and a beret and loves his red wines as they age – though I prefer them young. One third of his 30 acres is Pinot Noir. His whites are extremely fine, even elegant.

Gitton Père & Fils
Chemin de Lavaud, Ménétréol, 18300 Sancerre.

A family estate of 72 acres, almost entirely Sauvignon, developed since 1945. Gitton makes his wine in many different batches according to different soils – no less than 11 Sancerre cuvées with different labels – Les Belles Dames, Gelinot, les Romains and so on – and 2 Pouilly Fumés (les Chant-al-ouettes is the best). The whites are fermented in barrels and aged 8 months in cuves, the reds fermented in cuves, then aged 2 winters in barrels. Altogether an original house with a style of its own.

A. Mellot
18300 Sancerre

Growers, négociants and propagandists for Sancerre with an important holding of 104 acres in good sites, particularly his Domaine la Moussière (82 acres). The Mellot family, now headed by Alphonse, date back to the 16th century.

Lucien Picard
Bué, 18300 Sancerre.

Picard's Clos du Chêne Marchand is one of the most solid Sancerres, with style and vigour to keep it going 3 or 4 years. His Clos du Roy is scarcely less remarkable. The two account for 8 of his 17.5 acres; 4.5 are Pinot Noir.

Paul Prieur & Fils
Domaine Prieur, Verdigny, 18300 Sancerre.

A prominent family of growers for generations with 30 acres in several good sites, including Les Monts-Damnés (which is chalky clay) and the stonier Pichon, where an unusually high proportion (10 acres) of their property is Pinot Noir. Their white is made to age 2 or 3 years; the rosé of Pinot Noir mysteriously seems to share its quality – even its Sauvignon flavour. The red is made like very light burgundy. They make some 6,500 cases, half of which is exported.

Jean Reverdy & Fils
Domaine des Villots, Verdigny, 18300 Sancerre

A succession of Reverdys since 1646 have farmed about 18 acres, now 13.5 Sauvignon and 4.5 Pinot Noir. They have installed modern equipment in the cellar but make fine classic wines, particularly their Clos de la Reine Blanche white, which can mature for 3 or 4 years.

Domaine Vacheron
18300 Sancerre

A particularly welcoming family of growers whose wines can be tasted in summer in the centre of Sancerre at Le Grenier à Sel. Jean Vacheron, who died in 1988, is succeeded by his sons Jean-Louis and Denis. They own 45 acres, two thirds of it Sauvignon, and offer Le Paradis white, red Les Cailleries and rosé Les Romains. Their equipment and ideas are modern, but the red ages a year in Burgundian casks. Another 25 acres are to be planted.

André Vatan
Chaudoux, 18300 Sancerre.

A respected old family of growers with 10 acres, all Sauvignon. Exports to Britain and Belgium.

Cave Coopérative des Vins de Sancerre
18300 Sancerre

Founded 1963. 182 members; 88,000 cases, 98% AOC. A serious producer of typical Sancerre under a variety of labels.

POUILLY PRODUCERS

Bernard Blanchet
Les Berthiers, St-Andelain, 58150 Pouilly-sur-Loire.
The third generation of Blanchets has 10 acres of Sauvignon and 2.5 of Chasselas. M. Blanchet racks his wine once in January and bottles it early, scorning any treatment to prevent the formation of tartrate crystals, which he says his clients understand.

Gérard Coulbois
58150 Pouilly-sur-Loire.
Old family property with 13 acres of Pouilly-Fumé, 3 of Chasselas. Classic methods but cement vats, no barrels.

Serge Dagueneau
Les Berthiers, 58150 Pouilly-sur-Loire.
A 25-acre family vineyard with a high reputation for typically fruity and full-flavoured Pouilly-Fumé. Dagueneau uses no fining but filters before bottling early in spring.

Paul Figeat
Les Loges, 58150 Pouilly-sur-Loire.
A *vigneron* family for 200 years, respected for fresh Pouilly-Fumé, which is made to be drunk young. Of their 20 acres a small and decreasing fraction is Chasselas for plain Pouilly-sur-Loire.

Jean Claude Guyot
58150 Pouilly-sur-Loire.
A third-generation small producer from 20 acres of Sauvignon for Pouilly-Fumé and a little Chasselas. He uses tanks of steel and cement and some 600-litre casks.

Pascal Joliver
18 rue Ferdinand Gambon, 58150 Pouilly-sur-Loire.
Well-regarded négociant handling domaine and other wines of Pouilly and Sancerre.

J.M. Masson-Blondelet
58150 Pouilly-sur-Loire.
The Masson and Blondelet families (united by marriage in 1974) work 27 acres of Sauvignon and 3 of Chasselas with great skill to produce 5,000 cases of Pouilly-Fumé and Sancerre and a little Pouilly-sur-Loire. Their best vines, in Bascoins and Criots, and vinified separately. 'Tradition Cullus' is their *cuvée prestige*. Great winners of medals.

Château du Nozet
58150 Pouilly-sur-Loire.
The major producer and promoter of the fine wines of Pouilly with a production of over 85,000 cases, largely from company-owned vineyards of 150 acres. The Baron Patrick de Ladoucette is the head of the family firm, which has 3 labels: Pouilly-Fumé de Ladoucette, Sancerre Comte Lafond (from bought-in grapes) and a prestige *cuvée* Pouilly-Fumé Baron de L. Half the total production is exported, the other half is sold in France exclusively to the grander restaurants.

Michel Redde & Fils
La Moynerie, 58150 Pouilly-sur-Loire.
One of the best-known producers of Pouilly-Fumé, from 67 acres in the heart of the appellation. A modern installation with stainless steel vats, operated by the sixth generation of Reddes in succession. They have built splendid modern *caves* and plan new vineyards. Cuvée Majorum is their top wine.

Guy Saget
La Castille, 58150 Pouilly-sur-Loire.
A fifth-generation growers' family affair run by the brothers Saget, expanded since 1976 into a négociant business with a production of 200,000 cases, but still based on their large holding of family vines, including 10 acres in les Loges. Their technique is long cool fermentation with minimum disturbance of the wine and no malolactic fermentation to reduce the high natural fruity acidity.

Château de Tracy
58150 Pouilly-sur-Loire.
The family of the Comte d'Estutt d'Assay has owned the Château, on the Loire just downstream from Pouilly, since the 16th century. Sixty acres produce superb Pouilly-Fumé by traditional methods.

OTHER SANCERRE PRODUCERS

Cave des Chanvières
Verdigny, 18300 Sancerre. Négociants and growers: Paul and Claude Fournier. 37 acres.

Vincent Delaporte
Chavignol, 18300 Sancerre. 32 acres.

Pierre & Alain Dezat
Maimbray, 18300 Sancerre. Brothers with a growing reputation for impressively full-bodied Sancerre from some 20 acres.

Domaine des Garmes
Chaudoux, Verdigny, 18300 Sancerre. Michel and Jacques Fleuriet. 25 acres. Also uses the name Clos du Carroy Maréchaux.

Michel Girard
Verdigny, 18300 Sancerre. 15 acres. Respected red, white and rosé.

Château de Maimbray
Sury-en-Vaux, 18300 Sancerre. George Roblin. 30 acres, Sancerre whie, red (the house speciality) and rosé.

Paul Millérioux
Champtin, Crazancy-en-Sancerre, 18300 Sancerre. 27 acres.

Roger Neveu
Verdigny, 18300 Sancerre. 25 acres (5 Pinot Noir) in Clos des Bouffants.

Pierre & Etienne Riffault
Verdigny, 18300 Sancerre. 25 acres.

Jean-Max Roger
Bué, 18300 Sancerre. 32 acres (7 Pinot Noir) in Clos du Chêne Marchand and Le Grand Chemarin, plus 10 acres in Menetou-Salon. Also a négociant. Traditional techniques.

Château de Sancerre
18300 Sancerre, Marnier-Lapostolle family. 46 acres.

OTHER POUILLY PRODUCERS

Bailly Père et Fils
Les Loges. 30 acres of Pouilly-Fumé.

Jean-Claude Chatelain
Les Berthiers. 25 acres including the Domaine de St-Laurent-l'Abbaye et St-Laurent. Exports to UK & USA.

Didier Dagueneau
St-Andelain. Forward-looking wine-maker; varying cuvées of Pouilly-Fumé.

Didier Pabiot
58150 Pouilly-sur-Loire. 11 acres of Sauvignon and Chasselas; more planted.

Robert Pesson, Les Caissiers, St-Andelain. 15 acres, producing Pouilly-Fumé with some Pouilly-sur-Loire.

Cave Coopérative Pouilly-sur-Loire
Les Moulins à Vent, 58150 Pouilly-sur-Loire. 62,000 cases, 88% are AOC. Pouilly Fumé and Pouilly-sur-Loire.

MINOR REGIONS

The success of Sancerre and Pouilly has encouraged what were dwindling outposts of vineyards in less favoured situations to the west of the Loire to expand their plantings. The names of Ménétou-Salon, Quincy and Reuilly are now accepted as Sancerre substitutes at slightly lower prices (but longer odds against a fine ripe bottle).

Much higher up the river where it cuts through the Massif Central several scattered vineyard areas relate less to the Loire than to southern Burgundy and the Rhône. The most famous is St-Pourçain-sur-Sioule, once a monastic vineyard. Its wine is almost all consumed today to mitigate the effects of treatment at the spa of Vichy – but it is hard to see how it could ever have had more than a local following. Price is so far the main thing in favour of the remaining VDQS areas of the heights of the Loire. The Côtes Roannaise and de Forez and the Côtes d'Auvergne grow the right grapes for quality – Gamay, Chardonnay, some Pinot Noir and Syrah.

REUILLY PRODUCERS

Robert Cordier & Fils
36260 Reuilly. A family with 15 acres, 10 of Sauvignon for Reuilly and 5 of Pinot Noir and Gamay. Pinot Noir makes a Reuilly rosé.

Olivier Cromwell
36260 Reuilly. This grower's remarkable name descends, he thinks, from Scottish guards of Charles VII and Louis XI. His reputation rests on Reuilly rosé of Pinot Noir (5 acres) and Sauvignon (8 acres).

Claude Lafond
Bois St-Denis, 36260 Reuilly. A 17-acre estate divided into Sauvignon Blanc for very dry white, Pinot Noir for pale red and some Pinot Gris, which goes into a rather sweet rosé, which M. Lafond likes to age up to 5 years.

MENETOU-SALON PRODUCERS

Domaine de Chatenoy
18110 St-Martin d'Auxigny. The ancestors of Bernard Clément have owned this estate since 1560. 42 acres produce 6,500 cases of red, white and rosé Ménétou-Salon. Despite their freshness, his wines sometimes reach 13°of alcohol. He recommends them as apéritifs as well as table wines.

Georges Chavet
Les Brangers, 18110 St-Martin d'Auxigny. A 35-acre property which regularly wins gold medals, particularly for its rosé of Pinot Noir, which has been described as the best dry rosé in France. 18 months in bottle round out its flavour.

Jean-Paul Gilbert
18110 St-Martin d'Auxigny. A leading family of growers of Ménétou-Salon since the 18th century. From some 40 acres they produce Sauvignon white and Pinot Noir red and pale rosé – the red made with *chapeau immergé* and up to 3 weeks in the vat.

Jean Teiller
Ménétou-Salon, 18110 St-Martin d'Auxigny. A small but growing property with 18 acres divided equally between Sauvignon and Pinot Noir. The proprietor ferments in cement tasks and 600-litre wooden casks, bottles the white in spring, the red the following September.

Bringing in the harvest in the Loire

QUINCY PRODUCERS

Claude Houssier
Domaine du Pressoir, 18120 Quincy. *Vigneron* with 20 acres all in Quincy, producing Sauvignon only. Houssier avoids chaptalization if possible and aims for long-lived serious dry wines. His production of 2,500 cases is almost all sold in France.

Maison Meunier-Lapha
18120 Quincy. An old family of growers with 28 acres, half in Quincy planted with Sauvignon for its racy white, half of Vin de Pays du Cher of Pinot and Gamay. Their 3,500 cases are snapped up locally and by Parisians.

Raymond Pipet
Quincy, 18120 Lury-sur-Arnon. Carefully made Quincy from 32 acres. M. Pipet de-stems his Sauvignon and looks for finesse and moderate acidity.

COTES DU FOREZ

Cave Coopérative
Trelins, 42130 Boen. Founded 1962. 257 members; 988 acres; 113,000 cases, 55% VDQS Côtes du Forez and 25% Vins de Pays d'Urfe. The grape is the Gamay, this coop the dominant producer.

ST-POURÇAIN

Union des Vignerons
03500 St-Pourçain-sur-Sioule. The cooperative (founded 1952) dominates this once famous 'central' vineyard, formerly a monastic stronghold. 350 members farm 750 acres of Sauvignon, Sacy, Aligoté, Chardonnay and Tressalier whites and Pinot Noir and Gamay reds. Modern methods make 50,000 cases of white, 28,000 of rosé (decreasing) and 80,000 of red (increasing). The red is made either *en primeur* or aged in vats for 8 months. *Cuvée speciale* white is 40% Sauvignon, 60% Chardonnay, cold-shouldering the once dominant local Tressalier.

CHAMPAGNE

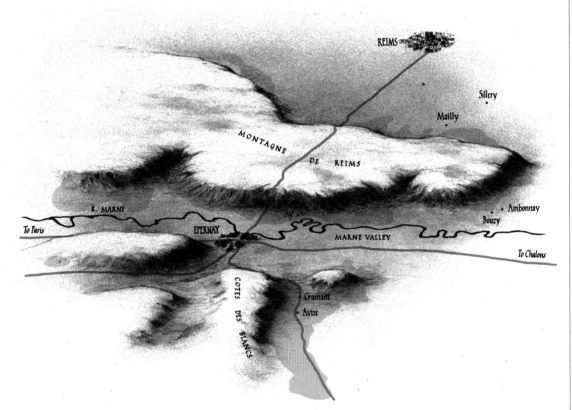

Champagne is the wine grown in the northernmost vineyards of France. The champagne method is something that is done to the wine to make it sparkling – and can be done to any wine. Other sparkling-wine makers would like us to believe that the method is all that matters. What really matters is the wine. It was one of the best in France long before the method was invented. The difference between the best champagne and the merely good (bad is hard to find) is almost entirely a matter of the choice and treatment of grapes, their variety, their ripeness, their handling and the soil that bears them. The difference between champagne and other sparkling wines is the same, only more so.

Most of the grapes of Champagne are grown by small farmers or even part-timers with other jobs. Some sell their grapes to big houses, some to cooperatives and some make wine themselves. Some buy back wine from cooperatives to label and sell as their own. Any merchant buying champagne can think up a name (a 'Buyer's Own Brand') and print a label. So there is no limit to the number of brands. In itself this lends strength to the score or so

of houses with the best-known names and the widest distribution; they are often bought simply as safe bets. But size and wealth also allow them to buy the best materials, employ the best staff and stock their wine longest. (Time is vital to develop the flavours.) The great houses push to the limit the polishing and perfecting of an agricultural product.

The 'method' began 200 years ago with the genius of a Benedictine monk, Dom Pérignon of Hautvillers, apparently the first man to 'design' a wine by blending the qualities of grapes from different varieties and vineyards to make a whole greater, more subtle, more satisfying than any of its parts. This blend, the *cuvée*, is the secret patent of each maker. The best are astonishingly complex, with as many as 30 or 40 ingredient wines of different origins and ages, selected and balanced by nose and palate alone. Houses with their own vineyards tend to stress the character of the grapes they grow themselves: the heavier Pinot Noir of the Montagne de Reims or the lighter Chardonnay of the Côtes des Blancs – each village is subtly different. Very few have enough to supply all their needs; in years of shortage competition for the best grapes is intense. Prices are fixed by a percentage system explained on page 186.

It was not Dom Pérignon, but his contemporaries who discovered how to make their wine sparkling by a second fermentation in a tightly corked bottle – a process with dangers and complications that took another century to master completely. The principle is outlined on pages 180 and 181.

The sparkle is caused by large amounts of carbon dioxide dissolved in the wine. The '*mousse*' or froth in the glass is only part of it – you swallow the greater part. Carbon dioxide is instantly absorbed by the stomach wall. In the bloodstream it accelerates the circulation, and with it the movement of the alcohol to the brain. This is where champagne gets its reputation as the wine of wit and the natural choice for celebration. Other sparkling wines made by the same method can justifiably claim to have the same effect. But not the same taste.

THE PRINCIPAL CHAMPAGNE HOUSES

Besserat de Bellefon
Murigny. Founded 1843. Owned by Pernod-Ricard since 1976. Visits: appt. only.
NV: Cuvée Blanc de Blancs, Brut, Crémant des Moines Blanc and Rosé. Vintage: Brut Intégral, Crémant Blanc and Rosé.
An outstanding success of the last 2 decades, rebuilt with the most modern plant to produce very fine light wines much appreciated in top French restaurants.
Brut Intégral is a totally dry wine in the lastest fashion. France takes 80% of the total sales of 1.8m. bottles a year. Switzerland and Belgium are chief export markets.

J. Bollinger
51160 Aÿ. Founded 1829. Privately owned. Associated companies: Langlois-Château (Loire), Atlas Peak (California), Petaluma (Australia). Visits: appt. only.
NV: Spécial Cuvée Brut. Vintage: Année Rare, Brut, Grande Année, Rosé, Tradition R.D., Vieilles Vignes Françaises. Still wines: Red Aÿ, Côte aux Enfants.
A top-quality traditionalist house making full-bodied masculine champagne with body, length, depth and every other dimension. Wines are kept on their yeast as long as possible; in the case of R.D. about 10 years, giving extra breadth of flavour. A tiny patch of ungrafted prephylloxera Pinot Noir in Aÿ gives Vieilles Vignes Françaises: very rare, expensive and powerfully flavoured.
60% of grapes from Bollinger's own 346 acres, average rating 97%. Remainder bought from Côte des Blancs and Verteuil, Marne valley. Production: 1.5m. bottles a year. Stock: 6–7 years'. Exports, often by restricted quota, make up 80% of sales. UK is largest market.
Madame Bollinger (d. 1977) directed the company for 30 years. *See page 180.*

Canard-Duchêne
1 rue Edmond Canard, 51500 Ludes. Founded 1868. Public company, controlled by Veuve Clicquot, since 1989 part of the Louis Vuitton Moët Hennessy group. Visits: at regular hours, appt. only.
NV: Brut, Rosé. Vintage: Charles VII. Coteaux Champenois is made in limited quantities in prolific years.
The non-vintage is a good lively party wine, finely frothy, not notably impressive in scent but with a definite fragrance of flavour.
Vineyards at Ludes supply a small proportion of needs. Production: 2.5m. bottles a year. Stock is 7m. bottles. 90% of production is sold within France.

Deutz
51160 Aÿ. Founded 1838. Family owned. Subsidiary and associated companies: Delas (Rhône), L'Aulée (Loire), Deutz & Geldermann Sektkellerein (Germany), Pressoir Deutz (California) and companies in Argentina and S. Korea. Visits: invitation only.
NV: Brut, Demi-Sec. Vintage: Brut, Blanc de Blancs, Rosé, Réserve George Mathieu, Cuvée William Deutz.
The house style is roundly fruity without sweetness, the high percentage of Aÿ wines in the *cuvées* and long ageing on the yeast. Exceptionally good Cuvée William Deutz.
Grapes come from 104 acres of own vineyards in Marne valley (mostly Aÿ) and other areas, averaging 97%. Grapes (never wine) are bought in from best crus of the same areas. Production: over 1m. bottles a year. Deutz aim to have $3\frac{1}{2}$–4 years' stock but previous small harvests have reduced this to 3 years (2.3m bottles). Sales in France 50%; USA is the largest export market with 15%.
A deliberately small house, a founder member of the 'Grandes Marques' of Champagne.

Charles Heidsieck
51100 Reims. Founded 1851. Owned by Rémy Martin. Visits: appt. only.
NV: Brut Réserve, Demi-Sec. Vintage: Brut Millésimé, Blanc de Blancs, Champagne Charlie, Rosé.
The original Charles Heidsieck was the 'Champagne Charlie' of the song, who made a fortune in the USA but almost lost it in the Civil War. After a decade of ownership by Henriot, Rémy Martin bought a majority shareholding in 1985. All grapes are bought in to make over 300,000 cases a year. Exports take 60% of this. The non-vintage stresses black grapes (only 15% Chardonnay) and is light, soft and satisfying (also good value). Cuvée Champagne Charlie is a vintage prestige *cuvée* with a higher proportion of Chardonnay: an extremely elegant, racy wine.

Heidsieck Monopole
83 rue Coquebert, 51054 Reims. Founded 1785. Public company linked with Mumm (owned by Seagram) since 1972. Visits: at regular hours.
NV: Dry Monopole, Red Top Sec, Green Top Demi-Sec, Rosé. Vintage: Dry Monopole, Monopole Brut Rosé, Diamant Bleu, Diamant Rosé.
A fairly small house famous for powerful, full-bodied, long-lived wine in the 'grand noir' style, i.e. with more black than white grapes. Diamant Bleu is one of Champagne's real luxury *cuvées*; a powerful character to mature for years. Sales are about 2m. bottles a year, largely supplied by the firm's own 270 acres (average rating 97%) plus leased vineyards. Stocks are about 6m. bottles. Exports go to 139 countries, with Germany and Switzerland taking more than half. The firm owns the historic Moulin de Verzenay, a windmill used as a field HQ in World War I, now used for receptions.

Henriot

51066 Reims. Founded 1808. Owned by the LVMH group. Visits: appt. only. NV: Blanc de Blancs, Crémant Brut Souverain. Vintage: Reserve Baron Philippe de Rothschild, Brut Rosé, Cuvée Baccarat.

Until 1985 Henriot owned Charles Heidsieck, but now Heidsieck has been sold to Rémy Martin and Henriot, having gained control of Veuve Clicquot, is now part of the Louis Vuitton Moët Hennessy group.

Henriot's 248 acres of vines provide 80% of the grapes needed to make 100,000 cases a year. Of the two prestige *cuvées*, Baccarat is mostly Chardonnay and Philippe de Rothschild stresses black grapes. Both they and the straightforward vintage wines are long-lived and classic in style. The non-vintage wines are known for their dryness.

Krug

5 rue Coquebert, 51100 Reims. Founded 1843. Privately owned, linked with Rémy Martin, Cognac. Visits: appt. only.

Grande Cuvée is a blend of 7 to 10 vintages and 20 to 25 different growths. The Vintage is made (since 1979) in very small quantities. Recent additions are rosé and Clos de Mesnil single-vineyard vintage.

Grand Cuvée has a high proportion of Chardonnay brilliantly blended for great finesse, very dry, elusively fruity, gentle yet authoritative at the same time. The Vintage tends to be more powerful, with great ageing qualities. Both are among the finest of all champagnes, but the Krug brothers make a point of preferring 'Grande Cuvée'.

Grapes come from 37 acres of 100%-rated Krug vineyards in Aÿ (Pinot Noir) and Le Mesnil sur Oger (Chardonnay). The other 80% of grapes needed come from the La Marne district, including Aÿ (Pinot Noir), Le Mesnil-sur-Oger (Chardonnay) and Leuvrigny (Pinot Meunier). All 3 grapes go into each blend, except for the Clos de Mesnil which is solely Chardonnay.

All fermentation is still carried out in traditional, small 205-litre oak casks. Ageing is long and the whole cellar process is supervised by Henri Krug, a fifth-generation Krug. Sales of 500,000 bottles are based on stock of 3m.,

giving an exceptionally high ratio of 1:6. 70% is exported, Italy and UK being the largest markets. Krug's wines are sold only by specialist outlets and supplies are limited.

Lanson

12 boulevard Lundy, 51100 Riems. Founded 1760. Owned by the BSN group. Visits: appt. only. NV: Black Label Brut, Demi-Sec, Rosé. Vintage: Brut, Millésime Brut, Noble Cuvée. Small quantities of Coteaux Champenois blanc and rouge, also ratafia and marc de Champagne.

Black Label is extremely popular for its vivid, tingling style. Lanson vintage is one of the more delicately fruity. Noble Cuvée (since 1979) is fuller-bodied and excellent.

Production: 5-6m. bottles a year, almost half from the firm's own 501 acres in 12 scattered prime sites (average 97%), including Bouzy, Ambonnay, Dizy, Cramant, Avize and Oger, with the balance from neighbouring growers. Stocks are about 22m. bottles.

Sales are 50% in France, with UK the largest export market with 10%. The company is directed by a fifth-generation Lanson, but the emphasis today is on modernity in techniques and marketing.

Laurent-Perrier

51150 Tours-sur-Marne. Founded 1812. Privately owned by the Nonancourt family. Close links with Cordier in Bordeaux, and a joint-venture in California. Visits: during working hours. NV: Brut, Cuvée Grand Siècle, Ultra Brut, Rosé Brut. Vintage: Brut Millésme. Still wines: white Blanc de Blancs de Chardonnay, red Pinot Franc.

Laurent-Perrier's non-vintage Brut may have been seen in too many airline quarter-bottles, where it seems a lean, fruitless wine. Under better conditions it is still appley and light, but freshly fruity and an understandable success. Ultra Brut is a completely dry, totally sugarless wine. The real triumph of the house, though, is vintage Millésime Rare; and above all its sumptuous, stylish and long-maturing Cuvée Grand Siècle.

Grapes come from about 2,000 acres either owned or under long-term contract. Supplies come from the Mt de Reims (Pinot Noir), Côte des Blancs (Chardonnay) and

Choosing champagne

The knowledge essential for buying champagne to your own taste is the style and standing of the house and the range of its wines. Other relevant points included in the entries on these pages are the ownership and date of foundation, whether you may visit the cellars, where most of the grapes come from, the annual sales and size of stock and the principal markets of the house. To some extent you may deduce style and quality from the sources of grapes and their standing in the percentage table on page 186, in conjunction with the average age of the wine (the stocks divided by the annual sales). Most houses offer wines in the following categories:

Non-vintage (NV). A *cuvée* maintained, as near as possible, to exactly the same

standard year after year: usually fairly young. The standard gauge of the 'house style'.

Vintage. Best-quality wine of a vintage whose intrinsic quality is considered too good to be hidden in a non-vintage *cuvée*. Normally aged longer on the yeast than non-vintage; more full-bodied and tasty, with the potential to improve for several more years.

Rosé. A blend of a small quantity of still red wine from one of the Pinot Noir villages (often Aÿ or Bouzy) with white sparkling champagne. In many cases entrancingly fruity and fine and one of the house's best *cuvées*.

Blanc de Blancs. A *cuvée* of white (Chardonnay) grapes only, with great grace and less 'weight' than traditional champagne.

Blanc de Noirs. A *cuvée* of black grapes only, sometimes faintly pink or '*gris*' and

invariably rich and flavoury.

Cuvée de Prestige (under many names). A super-champagne on the hang-the-expense principle. Moët's Dom Pérignon was the first; now most houses have one. Fabulously good though most of them are, there is a strong argument for two bottles of non-vintage for the price of one *cuvée de prestige*.

Crémant. A half-pressure champagne, preferred by some people who find a normal one too gassy – particularly with food.

Coteaux Champenois. Still white or red wine of the Champagne vineyards, made in limited quantities when supplies of grape allow. Naturally high in acidity but can be exquisitely fine.

Brut, Extra Dry, etc. What little consistency there is about these indications of sweetness or otherwise is shown on page 182.

BOLLINGER

The Making of a Great Champagne

Although champagne was invented in the seventeenth century the industry as we know it is pre-eminently a product of the nineteenth. Most of the great houses were founded between 1780 and 1880. Architecturally and technologically champagne is high Victorian in concept and style.

The Bollinger establishment at Aÿ is typical in its impressive but compact plan; its buildings and cellars grouped around and under the original owner's house.

As in a Bordeaux château, the agricultural operations are based here, the grapes are brought in and crushed, the wines are fermented and racked and bottled. But the same premises are also a factory for the elaboration of the bottled wine into sparkling champagne, requiring a considerable labour force and huge cellars. The Bollinger house employs 60 people in its 346 acres of vineyards (which produce about three quarters of the wine processed), and 60 in the cellars (apart from an office staff of 20).

Bollinger champagne, in brief, is made like this: harvesting is done with great care to reject split grapes and avoid breaking whole ones. Prematurely crushed grapes give colour to the juice. If necessary the crop is sorted by hand before pressing.

The grapes are pressed, black and white separately, in very large, square, vertical presses taking four tons at a time – the best way to extract the juice gently. They are pressed three or four times, the cake of skins and stalks being cut up and redistributed each time. Only the first and sometimes part of the second pressings are kept for the house *cuvées*.

The greater part of the must is fermented in well-aged 205-litre oak barrels. Overacid must is fermented in large steel tanks that encourage a secondary, malolactic, fermentation that reduces acidity. The wine is racked two or three times during the winter to clean it. In March it is tasted and sorted into lots for blending to make the *cuvées*. At this stage in making, the non-vintage blend wine from previous vintages, stored in the cellars in magnums under slight pressure, barely *crémant*, is added in a proportion of up to one third. The *cuvée* is then bottled with a little fresh yeast and a precisely measured addition of sugar that, when fermented, will add one per cent to the alcoholic content and produce a gas pressure of six atmospheres. (In times past a high proportion of bottles used to burst in the cellars.) Non-vintage wine is sealed with a metal cap, vintage with a cork held in place by a metal clamp. The bottles are well shaken, then stacked in the cold (40°F/4°C) limestone cellars; the non-vintage for two years, the vintage for four or five and the house speciality, Tradition Récemment Dégorgé, for as long as ten years.

The fermentation of the added sugar, although slow at the low temperature, is finished within one and a half to three months. The object of leaving the wine long beyond that time is to mature it in contact with the yeast, which adds another dimension to the flavour.

When the wine is aged enough there comes the problem of removing the yeast. The bottles are moved to racks, where they stand cork downwards at an angle of 45 degrees. Every day for up to three months each bottle is slightly shaken, slightly twisted and tipped slightly nearer the vertical by skilled '*remueurs*' who each handle some 30,000 bottles a day. At each *remuage* the sediment of yeast cells slips closer to the cork.

When all the sediment is resting on the cork the bottles are moved upside down to an icy brine bath, where the ends of their necks containing the sediment are frozen solid. The skilled process of 'disgorging' consists of removing the cork (or cap), letting the pressure in the bottle blow out the plug of frozen sediment, then topping up the bottle and immediately recorking it, with a wire 'muzzle' to hold the cork in. The bottles are then cellared again for at least several months before being washed, labelled, and boxed for dispatch.

Most of these stages have been ingeniously mechanized by the big champagne houses, the latest development being the 'very large machine', a tilting palette, that performs the *remuage* mechanically. Bollinger's director Christian Bizot is not averse to efficiency, but he considers that a house with a firm grasp of the very top of the market, selling only one million bottles a year, has too much to lose to risk any short cuts.

other scattered sites; the average rating is 96%. Sales are 7.5m. bottles a year, 48% in France, with Belgium the leading export market.

Under the direction of Bernard de Nonancourt, Laurent-Perrier has risen from ninety-eighth position in the champagne sales league in 1945 to become one of the top 4 in the 1980s. It is now the biggest privately owned house.

Mercier

75 avenue de Champagne, 51200 Epernay. Founded 1858, now owned by Möet-Hennessy. Visits: at regular hours.
NV: Extra Rich (for UK only), Demi-Sec, Demi-Sec Réserve, Brut, Brut Millésime, Brut Réserve. Vintage: Brut Réserve, Brut Réserve Rosé, Réserve de l'Empereur.

Mercier like the rest of the Moët group, has the virtue of size: consistency of supply means reliability. The stress is on dry, brut champagne, with blends tailored for individual markets.

Grape source: *see* Moët & Chandon. Sales average 4m. bottles a year (over 5m. in 1989), and are mainly within France.

Always known for their clever publicity, the firm's best stunt was unplanned: in 1900 a tethered balloon, in which the public could taste the wines, broke loose and carried a waiter and 9 involuntary passengers across the German border where customs fined them 20 crowns for failing to declare the champagne.

Moët & Chandon

20 avenue de Champagne, 51200 Epernay. Founded 1743. Part of the Louis Vuitton Moët Hennessy group. They are owners of Mercier and Ruinart (qq.v.), Domaine Chandon in California, Australia and Spain, the Simi winery in California and Christian Dior perfume, and wine producers in Brazil, Argentina and Portugal. Visits: at regular hours.
NV: White Star Demi-Sec, White Star Extra-Dry, Première Cuvée (for UK only), Brut Imperial, Crémant Demi-Sec.
Vintage: Brut Imperial and Rosé, Dry Imperial and Rosé (UK), Dom Pérignon and Dom Pérignon Rosé.
Still wines: Saran (still white Chardonnay), Bouzy Rouge, for domestic use only, produced only 5 times in the last 35 years.

Moët's various *cuvées* maintain a light, dry style which rounds out nicely with age. Very wide sources of supply ensure consistency of the huge quantities of NV, which often scores high in comparative tastings for polish and balance. Dom Pérignon is almost as fine as its reputation, with a distinguished almost almond-like flavour, crisp and very long-lived.

The group owns vineyards in 10 out of the 12 Grand Cru communes. Total holding is 2,146 acres (nearly 2% of the total Champagne vineyard), with about 1,660 acres in production. Grapes from these vineyards supply Ruinart and Mercier as well as Moët.

Sales average 18m. bottles a year. Exports are to 154 countries, the biggest markets being UK and USA, in both of which Moët have a third of the champagne market. 25% of all champagne exported comes from Moët and its associated companies.

Moët was the favourite of Napoleon, hence the Brut Imperial brand. The firm owns the Abbey of Hautvillers, where a highly-entertaining museum makes the quite unjustified claim that Dom Pérignon discovered the principles of champagne making. More important is its advanced technical research, which it generously shares with the champagne industry at large.

Mumm

29 rue du Champ de Mars, 51100 Reims. Founded 1827. Public company. Majority shareholder Seagram, Canada. Mumm owns Perrier-Jouët and Heidsieck Monopole (qq.v.), and Domaine Mumm, a joint venture with Seagram in California. Visits: at regular hours.

NV: Cordon Vert (demi-sec), Double Cordon (sec), Extra-Dry (mainly for N. American market), Cordon Rouge. Vintage: Cordon Rouge, René Lalou, Cordon Rosé. Also Crémant de Cramant Blanc de Blancs (brut).

Light and well-balanced wines from a preponderance of Pinot Noir. Cordon Rouge is very correct but has been almost too light, perhaps lacking a little character, recently. The vintage Rosé and lightly sparkling Crémant, made from Chardonnay grapes from the village of Cramant, are both excellent. René Lalou is a very presentable top *cuvée* in a full-bodied style.

Grapes come from 538 acres of owned vineyards, producing 20% of the firm's needs, and on contract from 35-45 different vineyards according to the year. Mumm's own holdings are spread across the region, with the biggest concentrations in Mailly, Ambonnay, Bouzy, Vaudemanges, Avenay, Aÿ, Avize and Cramant. The average rating of the Mumm vineyards is 95%.

Annual production is about 9.5 m. bottles, and stocks are 3 years of sales. North America takes 36% of exports, with Italy the next-biggest customer at 20%.

Joseph Perrier

51000 Châlons-sur-Marne. Founded 1825. Family owned. Visits: appt. only.

NV: Cuvée Royale Brut, Brut Blanc de Blancs, Demi-Sec, Crémant, Rosé. Vintage: Brut, Cuvée du Cent-Cinquantenaire. Still red: Cumières Rouge. Still whites: Chardonnay (blend of Grands Crus) and Coteaux Champenois Blanc de Blancs.

The house style is for lightness and freshness (the non-vintage is particularly pretty) but the wines age admirably.

One third of the grapes come from their 49 acres at Cumières, Damery, Hautvillers and Verneuil, rated on average at 90%. Sales around 650,000 bottles a year with 3 years' stock in reserve for the NV and 5 years' for the vintage wines. 56% of exports are split between Belgium, UK and Germany. The house supplied Queen Victoria and Edward VII and today concentrates on restricted quantities, high quality, and a traditional approach.

Perrier-Jouët

24-28 avenue de Champagne, 51200 Epernay. Founded 1811. Owned by Mumm (q.v.). Visits: appt. only.

NV: Grand Brut. Vintage: Brut, Rosé. Luxury *cuvées*: Blason de France and Belle Epoque.

Respected for first-class, very fresh and crisp but by no means light NV and luxury *cuvées* with plenty of flavour. Blason de France is their rarest wine, complex and age-worthy. The much better-known Belle Epoque, in its flower-painted bottle, is the flagship of the house: a prestige *cuvée* of consistently rich and harmonious style.

They own 267 acres of vineyards, 100 in Cramant and Avize. Grapes also come from some 30 other crus. Sales average 2.7m. bottles a year from stocks of at least 8m. Half the production is exported, 20% to the USA.

Piper Heidsieck

51 boulevard Henry Vasnier, 51100 Reims. Founded 1785. (Same foundation as Heidsieck Monopole.) Owned since 1988 by Rémy Martin. Visits: open.

NV: Brut, Demi-Sec. Vintage: Brut Millésimé, Rosé, Brut Sauvage, Champagne Rare.

Well-regarded, relatively delicate wines. Florens Louis is the luxury *cuvée*, produced only in the best vintages and only from the 12 top communes. Brut Sauvage is totally dry with no dosage but extra age in the blend.

A medium-sized Grande Marque selling about 5m. bottles a year with UK, Italy and USA the main export markets. The firm owns no vineyards and buys mainly in the Mt de Reims and Côte des Blancs. Stocks are about 5 years' shipments, and sales are around 5m. bottles a year, 2m. in France.

The firm is committed to modern technology and was the first to use *gyropalettes*, which are now used for all the wine they make. They own Piper-Sonoma in California, and the linked Champagne Technologie consultancy has advised sparkling wine makers in India and the Americas.

Pol Roger

1 rue Henri-Lelarge, 51206 Epernay. Founded 1849, still family-owned and run. Visits: appt. only.

NV: White Foil, Brut. Vintage: Brut, Rosé, Blanc de Chardonnay. Luxury *Cuvées*: Sir Winston Churchill and Réserve Spéciale P.R.

Serving and enjoying champagne

When. For celebrations any time, as an apéritif, very occasionally with light meals, with dessert (sweet 'demi-sec' only), in emergencies, as a tonic.

How. At 45°-50°F/7°-10°C, colder for inexpensive champagne, up to 54°F/ 13°C for very fine mature ones. In a tall, clear glass, not a broad, shallow one. To preserve the bubbles, pour slowly into a slightly tilted glass.

How much. Allow half a bottle (three glasses) per head for an all-champagne party. Allow half as much when it is served as an apéritif before another wine.

What to look for. Plenty of pressure behind the cork, total clarity, abundance of fine bubbles lasting indefinitely, powerful but clean flavour and finish, and balance – not mouth-puckeringly dry or acid, not cloyingly sweet. Above all it should be moreish. House styles will become apparent with experience.

Who makes champagne?

In 1970 there were 2,900 growers making their own champagne. By 1980 the figure was over 5,000, dropping to 4,600 in 1985. The proportion of sales represented by grower-producers and cooperatives rose from a quarter in 1970 to over a half in 1980, falling to a third by 1985. Most of this growth was within France and represents direct sales and mail-order. The *maisons* continue to dominate the export trade.

Dosage, dryness and sweetness

When champagne is disgorged the loss of the frozen plug of sediment needs making good to fill the bottle. At this stage the sweetness of the finished wine is adjusted by topping up (*dosage*) with a '*liqueur d'expédition*' of wine mixed with sugar and sometimes brandy. A few firms make a totally dry wine, topped up with wine only and known by names such as Brut Nature or Brut Intégral. The great majority have some sugar added. The following are the usual amounts (grams/litre) of sugar in the *dosage* for each style (although they vary from house to house):

Brut: 0-15g/l. very dry. *Extra Dry:* 12-20g/l. dry. *Sec:* 17-35g/l. slightly sweet. *Demi-sec:* 33–50g/l. distinctly sweet. *Doux:* over 50g/l. very sweet.

The landscape of Champagne: vines on the Montagne de Reims at Villedommange

Fairly small house consistently regarded among the best half-dozen and a personal favourite of mine for 30 years. Outstandingly clean and crip NV; stylish long-lived vintage, one of the best rosés and soft, 'tender' Chardonnay. 'Sir Winston Churchill' is shamelessly sumptous, exotically scented and satin-textured.

45% of grapes come from the firm's 185 acres, average 93%, mainly in the Côte des Blancs. Production about 1.4m. bottles; stock about 6m. bottles. Sales 55% France, then UK, Italy, USA, Belgium, Switzerland, etc. The brand is particularly associated with Sir Winston Churchill, after whom the new luxury *cuvée* has been named. On his death the Pol Roger label was given a black border.

Pommery & Greno

5 place General Gouraud, 51100 Reims. Founded 1836. Part of the BSN group. Visits: at regular hours.
NV: Brut Royal, Carte Blanche (demi-sec), Drapeau Sec, Rosé.
Vintage: Brut, Rosé Special. Luxury *cuvée*: Louise Pommery.
After several years of genteel coasting under old family management, a takeover by the dynamic Gardinier family in 1980 brought new ideas and an expansion to double the production. The firm's tradition is for very fine and notably dry champagnes, complex and yeasty rather than fruity. The rosé is almost excessively dry. Louise Pommery (since 1979) has been a revelation of Pommery quality: stylish, crisp, deeply winey and well-structured.

Grapes from 741 acres of vineyards in the Côte des Blancs and the Montagne de Reims, average over 99%. Further supplies from small growers. Production: 5.7m. bottles, with stocks of 3 years' supply. Exports take 68%, with West Germany and Switzerland the largest markets.

Pommery's cellars comprise 9 miles of Roman chalk-pits, some decorated with bas-reliefs. Madame Pommery, who took over the running of the firm in 1858, invented a special *cuvée* for Britain which is still sold there. The marque was represented in Britain by André Simon. Madame Pommery built the company's famous offices to a plan concocted from those of several British castles.

Louis Roederer

21 boulevard Lundy, 51100 Reims. Founded 1776. Privately owned. Visits: appt. only.
NV: Brut, Extra Dry, Brut Premier, Rosé Demi-Sec, Carte Blanche (sweet). Vintage: Brut, Blanc de Blancs, limited quantities of Cristal Brut (in clear bottles), Brut Rosé and Cristal Rosé.
The house style is notably smooth and mature, epitomized by the excellent full-bodied non-vintage and the fabulous Cristal, one of the most luscious champagnes, racy but deeply flavoured. Recent vintages have aged more rapidly than earlier ones.

80% of grapes come from the house's own 445 acres of vines (Côtes des Blancs 185, the rest in Mt de Reims and Marne Valley: all rated over 95%). Production is dictated by these supplies: 1.5–1.8m. bottles a year. Stock: 6m. bottles. Sales in France 40%, with USA the leading export market with 20%. Up to 1916 half of the sales were in Russia, where Czar Alexander III demanded crystal bottles. Roederer have recently opened a new sparkling wine house in California.

Ruinart Père & Fils

4 rue Crayères, 51100 Reims. Founded 1729 – one of the older Champagne firms. Now owned by Moët-Hennessy. Visits: Monday-Friday by appt.
NV: "R" de Ruinart, Dom Ruinart Blanc de Blancs, Dom Ruinart Rosé. Vintage: Brut "R" de Ruinart, Rosé. Still wine: Chardonnay (white).
Extremely stylish among the lighter champagnes both in non-vintage and vintage. The luxury Dom Ruinart is among the most notable blanc de blancs. (The '79 was perfection in '89.) Dom Ruinart Rosé is equally outstanding.

Source of grapes: *see* Moët & Chandon. Sales average 1.5m. bottles a year. France is the major market.

Napoleon's Josephine enjoyed Ruinart – but unfortunately refused, after her divorce, to honour the bills she ran up as Empress.

Salon

Le Mesnil-sur-Oger, 51190 Avize. Founded 1920. Private company owned by Laurent-Perrier. The sole house to produce only vintage blanc de blancs champagne. They have declared just 17 vintages in the last 52 years.

Salon pioneered blanc de blancs wines and still leads in quality if not quantity, with light, extremely delicate and totally dry wine; really for connoisseurs. 15 years is a good age for them.

All grapes come from Côte des Blancs commune of Le Mesnil, rating 100%. The house owns vines and buys from a few growers, the same ones since early this century.

Production is only 50,000 bottles a year, yet stock is around 500,000 bottles (10 years' supply) – one of the biggest sales/stock ratios in Champagne. Sales to European and USA markets are rationed. Techniques are described as 'artisan' – everything done by hand. Marketing is entirely by personal recommendation.

Taittinger

9 place St-Niçaise, 51061 Reims. Founded 1734 as Forest Fourneaux, name changed to Taittinger in 1931. Public company controlled by Taittinger family.
Visits: appt. only.
NV: Brut Réserve, Demi-Sec. Vintage: Brut, Comtes de Champagne (blanc de blancs), Comtes de Champagne Rosé.
Still white: La Marquetterie Coteaux Champenois (all Chardonnay).

The style of the Brut wines derives from the dominance of white grapes in the blend. Comtes de Champagne is one of the most delicate, exquisitely luxurious prestige *cuvées*.

Taittinger own 618 acres and also buy from other growers, mostly on the Côte des Blancs. Main sources of grapes are Avize, Chouilly, Cramant, Mesnil and Oger. Sales around 4m. bottles; stock: 15m. bottles. France drinks about 45%; Italy leads the export market with 13% followed by the USA, Belgium, Switzerland and UK.

Taittinger's cellars, parts of which date from Roman times, belonged in the 13th century to the monks of St-Niçaise, who traded in Champagne wines.

Veuve Clicquot-Ponsardin

12 rue de Temple, 51100 Reims. Founded 1772. Since 1989 part of the Luis Vuitton Moët-Hennessy group. Visits: by appt.
NV: Yellow Label, White Label Rich. Vintage: Gold Label, Rosé, La Grande Dame.

Large, prestigious and influential house making classic 'big' champagne in a firm, rich, full-flavoured style, an outstanding rosé that ages superbly, and the 'biggest' prestige *cuvée*, the buxom Grande Dame.

690 acres of vineyards are widepread, average 97%. Production: about 10m. bottles; stock about 4 years' supply. Exports dominate, especially to Italy, UK, Venezuela, Scandinavia, Australia.

The company's success was founded by 'The Widow' Clicquot, who took over the business in 1805 at the age of 27, when her husband died. She invented the now universal '*remuage*' for clarifying the wine and produced the first rosé champagne.

OTHER PRODUCERS

Ayala, Aÿ
Traditionalist house with 74 acres of vines making nearly 1m. bottles of weighty, old-style wines. Also a lighter blanc de blancs. Once highly fashionable and still respected. Montebello is another label.

Barancourt, Bouzy
Small house with some 120 acres specializing in a rather heavy vintage blanc de noirs, rosé and still red Bouzy.

Billecart-Salmon, Mareuil-sur-Aÿ
NV: Brut and Brut Rosé. Vintage: Brut Cuvée N.F. Billecart, Blanc de Blancs and Grande Cuvée. Family-owned house, founded 1818. Concentrates on Brut NV and on French market (80% of sales). The blend contains a high proportion of Pinot Noir to Chardonnay (60:30). All but 2% of their grapes are bought in. Slow, cool fermentation produces a light, fresh style. Sales: 500,000 bottles a year.

Boizel, Epernay
Family business founded 1834; also uses the names Krémer and Camuset. The prestige *cuvée* is Joyau de France. No vineyards. Production: 1.8m. bottles a year, half of which is exported.

Bonnet, Oger
Small family firm with 25 acres specializing in blanc de blancs.

De Castellane, Epernay
NV: Brut Blanc de Blancs, Brut Croix de St André. Vintage: Brut, Brut Blanc de Blancs, Rosé Brut, Commodore Cuvée. Still white and red wines in prolific years. A family firm, though Laurent-Perrier now has a 40% interest. Production: 3m. bottles a year, of which 70% is sold in France, much of it as Maxim's own-label champagne.

A. Charbaut & Fils, Epernay
NV: Brut, Rosé, Blanc de Blancs. Vintage: Millésime Brut, Certificate Blanc de Blancs. Family-owned house. Specializes in blanc de blancs. Owns 138 acres of 90% vineyards supplying a third of its needs. Sales are 1.2m. bottles a year, 40% exported. Stockists include many great restaurants of N. France, Pan-Am and TWA. They also have links with an Indian sparkling-wine cooperative situated near Bombay.

De Courcy Père & Fils, Epernay
NV: Brut Crémant Blanc de Blancs, Rosé. Vintage: Brut; also Coteaux Champenois. Family-owned house linked with Charbaut (q.v.). Pioneers in export markets of the *crémant* (lightly sparkling) style.

Giesler, Avize
Now owned by the giant Marne & Champagne concern (q.v.). The brand is popular in the south of France, but little is exported. Wines made are NV: Extra Superior Brut. Vintage: Giesler, Rosé, Blanc de Blancs, Cuvée Grande Origin. Despite their origin within the Marne company, these wines show individuality of style.

Gosset, Aÿ
Gosset has good claim to being the oldest champagne house: the firm is now run by the 13th and 14th generations in descent from the founder, Pierre, who was mayor of Aÿ in 1584. Wines produced are: NV: Brut Réserve, Brut Rosé, Grand Réserve. Vintage: Grand Millésime and Grand Millésime Rosé. All show the Aÿ 'grands noirs' style. Production: 700,000 bottles a year.

Georges Goulet, 2/4 avenue du General Giraud, 51055 Reims. Founded 1867. Owned by Les Grands Champagnes de Reims (which includes Abel Lepitre [q.v.] and St-Marceaux). Visits: appt. only.
NV: Demi-Sec, Extra Quality Brut, 'G' (Blanc de Blancs). Vintage: Extra Quality Brut, Crémant Blanc de Blancs, Rosé Brut, Cuvée Centenaire. Still wines: Bouzy Rouge, Blanc de Blancs. NV with a high proportion of Pinot Noir, and smooth and drinkable Crémant, recommended by the firm for 'les lunchs'.
No vineyards. Production: 1m. bottles a year, with stocks of 3.5-4m. Exports to many countries, especially South America and Africa.

Alfred, Gratien Epernay
Small traditionalist house linked with Gratien & Meyer at Saumur. Makes excellent very dry wines fermented in small barrels; among the outstanding

smaller houses of France.

Jacquesson & Fils, Dizy, Epernay
NV: Perfection Brut, Blanc de Blancs, Rosé Brut. Vintage: Perfection Brut. Founded 1798, one of the 9 oldest Champagne firms. Sole proprietor: Famille Chiquet. Their 76 acres of 95% vineyards principally at Dizy, Aÿ, Hautvillers and Avize supply more than half their requirements. Characterized by a high proportion of Chardonnay – the blanc de blancs is made entirely from their 27 acres at Avize. The result is soft and highly swallowable. The prestige *cuvée*, 'Signature', is half Chardonnay and half Pinot Noir. Production: 400,000 bottles a year, 60% sold in France.

Abel Lepitre, Reims
Well known in French restaurants for its Crémant Blanc de Blancs. Its prestige *cuvée* is Prince A. de Bourbon Parme. No vineyards. Linked with George Goulet (q.v.) and St-Marceaux is Les Grands Champagnes de Reims, a group with total sales of 700,000 bottles a year.

Mailly Grand Cru, Mailly-Champagne
Major cooperative, founded in 1929, now with 70 members owning 173 acres in highly rated (100%) chiefly Pinot Noir, vineyards. Top wines: Cuvée des Echansons and Cuvée 60 Anniversaire. Sales approx. 500,000 bottles a year, including exports in Europe. 4 years in stock.

Marne & Champagne, Epernay
One of the giants of the industry with 16km of cellars and a stock of 74m. bottles. The name is hidden behind many brands and BOBs. The best known is A. Rothschild with its prestige Réserve Grand Trianon.

Massé Père & Fils, Reims
Owned by Lanson and bottled at their premises. Massé is sold only in France.

Montebello *see* Ayala

Oudinot, Epernay
Family firm with some 150 acres producing 1.2m. bottles, the best labelled Cuvée Particulière Blanc de Blancs or Rosé. Also owns the brand A. G. Jeanmaire.

Bruno Paillard, Reims
The youngest classic champagne house, the creation of the almost fanatical M. Paillard over the past 20 years. His wines have been consistent models of elegance and refinement, very dry, almost austere, and built to last. Sales are around 400,000 bottles a year; stock runs at over 3 years.

Philipponat, Mareuil-sur-Aÿ
Small family house best known for its fine full-bodied vintage Clos des Goisses. 450,000 bottles a year. Now linked with Gosset (q.v.).

St-Gall *see* Union Champagne
St-Marceaux *see* Abel Lepitre

St-Micel *see* Union Champagne
Trouillard, Epernay
The other half of De Venoge (q.v.) similarly specializing in BOBs and since 1980 a part of the Heidsieck/Henriot group.

Union Champagne, Avize
Giant modern cooperative representing 1,000 growers through 10 smaller coops. Stock of 10–12m. bottles, annual production 5m. Supplies many BOBs, also wines under St-Michel and St-Gall labels. Four fifths of the wine are returned to growers for sale under their own labels.

De Venoge, Epernay
Important house specializing in BOBs, linked with Trouillard.

MINOR PRODUCERS

The number of champagne houses is growing and has now passed 150. Many produce 'Buyer's Own Brands' for overseas shippers and hotel chains, others only export to one or two markets, or may only sell within France. However, such companies are not necessarily small.

Bauget-Jouette, Epernay
Beaumet Chaurey, Epernay
Paul Berthelot, Dizy
Bichat, Reims
Billiard, Gaétan, Epernay
Bouché Père & Fils, Pierry
Château de Boursault, Boursault
Bricout, A., & Co, Avize
Brun, Edouard, & Co, Aÿ
Brun, René, Aÿ
Bur, Vve Paul, Reims
Burtin, Epernay

de Castelnau, Epernay
de Cazanove, Charles, Epernay
Chanoine Frères, Rilly-la Montagne
Collery, Aÿ
Compagnie Française des Grands Vins, Reims
Comptoir Vinicole de Champagne, Reims

Defond, Marcel, Reims
Delamotte Père & Fils, Avize
Desmoulins, A., & Co, Epernay
Doré, Noël, Rilly-la-Montagne
Driant, Emile, Aÿ
Driant, Robert, Aÿ
Dubois, Michel, Epernay
Dueil, Reims
Duval-Leroy, Vertus

Eliniaux, Roland, Aÿ

Fournier & Co, Reims
France Champagne, Epernay

Gardet & Co, Rilly-la-Montagne
Gentils, Lucien, Dizy
Gentils, René, Epernay
Germain, H., & Fils, Rilly-la-Montagne
Gobillard, Paul, Epernay
Guy, Roger, Reims

Hamm, Emile, & Fils, Aÿ

Ivernal, Bernard, Aÿ

Jacquinot & Fils, Epernay
Jamart & Co, Saint-Martin-d'Ablois
Jardin & Co, Le Mesnil-sur-Oger

Kruger, Louis, Epernay

Legras, R. & L., Chouilly
Lemoine, J. Rilly-la-Montagne
Lenoble, Damery, Epernay

Mansard Baillet, Epernay
Martel, G.H., & Co, Epernay
Medot & Co, Reims
Michel, Emile, Verzenay
Monvillers, Aÿ
Morel, G., Fils, Reims

Paillard, E.M., Reims
Pierlot, Jules, Epernay
Pierre, Marcel, Reims
Ployez-Jacquemart, Rilly-la-Montagne

Ralle, Eugène, Verzenay
Rapeneau, Ernest, Epernay
Roederer, Théophile, Reims
Rohrbacher, Jean, Epernay

Sacotte, Epernay
Sacy, Verzy
S.A.M.E., Epernay
Société Générale de Champagne, Ay
Société Vinicole Golden Roy, Epernay

Tarin, Le Mesnil-sur-Oger
Tassin, Bernard, Celles-sur-Ource
de Telmont, J. & Co, Damery

Valentin, Epernay
Vaudon, Pierre, Avize
Vazart, Lucien, Chouilly

Waris, Jean, Avize

The politics of scarcity

Champagne suffers from a chronic shortage of wine that has pushed the price of grapes up from 22 francs a kilo in 1986 to 32 francs a kilo in 1990 – a price that means that the grapes for each bottle cost over 40 francs. A new economic structure was agreed in early 1990 which will allow prices to be agreed between individual growers and merchants, though the percentage rating system still remains all-important.

There are 71,300 planted acres of vineyard within the appellation Champagne (which was determined in 1927 and has a delimited area of 86,500 acres). It has been planned to extend the total area under vine by about 12,000 acres over a period of years during the '80s and '90s, at a rate of 6-700 acres per year.

Total sales in 1988 were 237 million bottles, about two-thirds of which were sold by the merchant houses and the remainder by growers. Growers have greatly increased their share of the market in recent years (in 1949 it was only 11 per cent). They operate mainly in France at 'direct' prices, thus reducing the stocks available for export by the merchants (who maintain the highest standards and the international prestige of champagne).

Of the 237 million bottles in 1988, 147 million were drunk in France and only 90 million were exported. France's amazing thirst for champagne, and the growers' willingness to supply it rather than sell to merchants, means that the exporters are having to retrench in foreign markets for lack of stock. Where they retreat, other sparkling wines step in. For all the present prosperity of Champagne there is a feeling of impending crisis.

The percentage system

Each harvest, the price a grower gets for his grapes is determined by a committee made up of C.I.V.C. officials, growers, producers and a government representatitive. The C.I.V.C. – Comité Interprofessionel du Vin de Champagne – is the official body that controls, promotes and defends the industry. The vineyards of the region are rated on a quality scale ranging downwards from 100 to 80%. There are 17 Grand Cru vineyards, with ratings of 100% (see table). The average percentage rating of a champagne house's grape supplies is a key figure, for it establishes the quality of the firm's raw materials. Where this figure is available it is given in the entries. While each vineyard has a percentage rating, this is based on a notional good quality harvest and the prices may be lowered across the board

if the quality of grapes in a particular year is low. Or they may be increased in times of shortage, as they were in 1980 by no less than 10 francs a kilo.

Producers of grapes from 100% vineyards can ask the full price, others *pro rata*.

The leading vineyards, with their percentage ratings, are as follows:

Marne Valley

Aÿ	100% black grapes
Mareuil-sur-Aÿ	99% ,,
Bisseuil	95% ,,
Dizy-Magenta	95% ,,
Avenay	93% ,,
Champillon	93% ,,
Cumières	93% ,,
Hautvillers	93% ,,
Mutigny	93% ,,

Côte d'Ambonnay

Ambonnay	100% black grapes
Bouzy	100% ,,
Louvois	100% ,,
Tauxières-Mutry	99% ,,
Tours-sur-Marne	100% ,,
Tours-sur-Marne	90% white grapes

Côte d'Epernay

Chouilly	100% white grapes
Chouilly	95% black grapes
Pierry	90% ,,

Côte des Blancs

Avize	100% white grapes
Cramant	100% ,,
Le Mesnil-sur-Oger	100% white grapes
Oger	100% ,,
Oiry	100% ,,
Cuis	95% ,,
Grauves	95% ,,
Cuis	90% black grapes
Grauves	90% ,,

Côte de Vertus

Vertus	95% black grapes
Bergères-Les-Vertus	95% white grapes
Bergères-Les-Vertus	90% black grapes

Montagne de Reims

Beaumond-sur-Vesle	100% black grapes
Mailly	100% ,,
Puisieulx	100% white grapes
Sillery	100% black grapes
Verzenay	100% ,,
Verzy	100% ,,
Trépail	95% white grapes
Villers-Marmery	95% ,,
Chigny-Les-Roses	94% black grapes
Ludes	94% ,,
Montbré	94% white grapes
Rilly-La-Montagne	94% black grapes
Villers-Allerand	90% white grapes

Champagne and food

There is no single classic dish for accompanying champagne, but champagne makers like to encourage the idea that their wine goes with almost any dish. Vintage champagne certainly has the fullness of flavour to go with most, but many people find sparkling wine indigestible with food. Champagne is the apéritif wine *par excellence*, and marvellously refreshing after a rich meal. Meanwhile there is the less fizzy Crémant, the still Coteaux Champenois, white or red (notably Bouzy Rouge) – and of course Bordeaux and burgundy.

Rosé des Riceys

Within the borders of Champagne lies one of France's most esoteric little appellations, specifically for a Pinot Noir rosé. Les Riceys is in the extreme south of Champagne. Most of its

production is champagne, but in good ripe vintages the best Pinot Noir grapes, with a minimum natural 10°, are selected. The floor of an open wooden vat is first covered with grapes trodden by foot. Then the vat is filled with whole unbroken bunches. Fermentation starts at the bottom and the fermenting juice is pumped over the whole grapes. At a skilfully judged moment the juice is run off, the grapes pressed and the results 'assembled' to make a dark rosé of a unique sunset tint and, as its makers describe it, a flavour of gooseberries. The principal practitioner used to be Alexandre Bonnet; his sons now continue this tradition. Since 1981 they have made it only in 1983 and 12,000 bottles in 1985.

The postcode is 10340 Les Riceys.

ALSACE

After all the regions of France whose appellation systems seem to have been devised by medieval theologians, Alsace is a simple fairy tale.

A single appellation, Alsace, takes care of the whole region. Alsace Grand Cru is for chosen sites.

Nor are there Germanic complications of degrees of ripeness to worry about. Alsace labelling is as simple as Californian: maker's name and grape variety are the nub. The difference is that in Alsace a host of strictly enforced laws means that there are no surprises. The grapes must be 100 per cent of the variety named, properly ripened and fermented dry with no sweetening added. The wines are correspondingly predictable and reliable. Their makers would like them to be considered more glamorous. In order to have their wines named among the 'greats' they are laying increasing emphasis on late picking, on wines from Grand Cru and selected sites – on 'Cuvées de Prestige' of various kinds. What matters more to most drinkers is that Alsace guarantees a certain quality and a certain style more surely than any other wine region. It makes brilliantly appetizing, clean-cut and aromatic wine to go with food, and at a reasonable price.

The region is 70 miles long by one or two miles wide: the eastern flank of the Vosges mountains in the *départements* of the Haut-Rhin and the Bas-Rhin where the foothills, between 600 and about 1,200 feet, provide well-drained southeast- and south-facing slopes under the protection of the peaks and forests of the Vosges. The whole region is in their rain-shadow, which gives it some of France's lowest rainfall and most sustained sunshine.

On the principle that watersheds are natural boundaries, Alsace should be in Germany. It has been, but since the Rhine became the frontier it has been French. Its language and architecture remain Germanic. Its grape varieties are Germanic, too – but handled in the French manner they produce a different drink.

What is the difference? The ideal German wine has a certain thrilling balance of fruity sweetness and acidity. It has relatively little alcohol and resulting 'vinosity', which allows the tension of this balance to stand out in sharp relief. The components in all their complexity (or lack of it) can clearly be tasted.

Most cheaper German wines are ingeniously, often excellently, made to reproduce this artificially. After fermentation the missing element is the sweet fruitiness. So it is supplied by adding grape juice. The wine is filtered to prevent further fermentation and the balance holds up in the bottle.

By contrast, an Alsace wine is given its extra or artificial ripeness in the form of sugar before fermentation. The natural ripeness must reach a level that in most parts of Germany would give it 'Qualitätswein' status. It can then be chaptalized with dry (not dissolved) sugar to produce an extra 2.5 degrees of alcohol. The minimum permitted natural alcohol being 8.5 degrees, the resulting wine has 11 degrees, which is the strength that the French are accustomed to in most of their white wines. All the added sugar being totally fermented, the wine is completely dry. The aromatic (or otherwise) character of its grapes stand out cleanly and clearly.

Although most of the best Alsace wines are still fermented in oak the barrels are antiques, thickly lined with tartrate crystals that prevent any flavours of wood or oxidation. So the wines start very simple and straight. They are bottled as soon as possible in the spring (or latest in the autumn) after the vintage. Most are drunk young – which is a pity. Bottle ageing introduces the elements of complexity which are otherwise lacking. A good Riesling or Gewurztraminer or Pinot Gris is worth at least four years in bottle and often up to ten.

Late picking, Vendange Tardive, is the means by which Alsace growers are scaling the heights of prestige which Burgundy and Bordeaux have so far monopolized. A hot summer (1989 was the latest famous example) provides such high sugar readings in the grapes that fermentation can stop with considerable natural sweetness still remaining. The wines reach an alcohol level usually greater than that of a German Auslese. The resulting combination of strength, sweetness and concentrated fruity flavour is still peculiar to Alsace. The Hugel family of Riquewihr was instrumental in creating what has become the Vendange Tardive legislation. Very ripe grapes with a high concentration of sugar, usually sweetened by noble rot, produce wines of enormous power, which are classified as '*Sélection des Grains Nobles*'.

The centre of the finest area lies in the Haut-Rhin, in the group of villages north and south of Colmar with Riquewihr an extravagantly half-timbered and flower-decked little town, as its natural wine capital; a sort of St-Emilion of the Vosges.

The climate is warmest and driest in the south, but scarcely different enough to justify the popular inference that Haut-Rhin is parallel to, let us say, Haut-Médoc. There is no suggestion of lower quality in the name Bas-Rhin; it is simply lower down the river Rhine. Even farther down, going directly north, are the German Palatinate vineyards, producing the richest and some of the greatest of all German Rieslings.

Human nature being what it is many truckloads of Bas-Rin Grapes are taken south at harvest time to go into blends with Haut-Rhin labels.

More important are the individual vineyard sites with the best soils and microclimates. Thirty or 40 Vosges hillsides have individual reputations, which in Burgundy would long ago have been enshrined in law. Alsace hovered on the brink of listing certain vineyards as 'Grands Crus' for many years and finally began to do so in 1983, with 25 names. A further 22 were added to the list in 1985, but not all have been finally accepted so far.

A few of these names are used often enough on labels to be familiar already. Schoenenberg at Riquewihr is particularly noted for its Riesling;

Kaysersberg's Schlossberg, Guebwiller's Kitterlé, Turckheim's Eichberg and Brand, Beblenheim's Sonnenglanz are other examples.

Ownership of these vineyards is noted in the following list of producers.

In 1983 the first two dozen site-names were officially delimited and recognized for the first time. They are expected to be followed by another dozen or so in due course. Almost every village in Alsace wants to have its best hillside recognized as a Grand Cru.

The wine from these Grands Crus 'Lieux-dits' (or sites) will only have to fulfil the same technical standards as a Grand Cru did without a site-name. The wine will not necessarily be better – but it will have to come from the slope in question – and in due course such slopes will no doubt come to be known as characters with a certain style.

GROWERS AND COOPERATIVES

The vineyards of Alsace are even more fragmented in ownership than those of the rest of France. With 9,200 growers sharing the total of 32,000 acres the average individual holding is just over three acres.

The chances of history established a score or more leading families with larger estates – still rarely as much as 100 acres. With what seems improbable regularity they trace their roots back to the seventeenth century, when the Thirty Years' War tore the province apart. In the restructuring of the industry after the wars of this century these families have grouped smaller growers around them in a peculiar pattern consisting of their own domaine plus a

wine-making and merchanting business. They contract to buy the small growers' grapes and make their wine – very often using their own domaine wines as their top-quality range. As the following details of these larger houses show, the pattern is repeated all over Alsace.

The small grower's alternative to a contract with a grower/négociant (or just a négociant) is the local cooperative. Alsace established the first in France, at the turn of the century, and now has one of the strongest cooperative movements. Their standards are extremely high and they often provide the best bargains in the region.

Alsace grapes
Area of grapes occupied is expressed as a percentage of the total Alsation vineyard.

Chasselas (3.8%) (In German Gutedel, in Swiss Fendant.) Formerly one of the commonest grapes, rarely if ever named on a label, but used for its mildness in everyday blends, including the so-called 'noble' Edelzwicker.

Clevner or Klevner A local name for the Pinot Blanc (q.v.).

Knipperlé Like the Chasselas, a common blending grape not named on labels.

Gewurztraminer (19.3%) Much the most easily recognized of all one-wine grapes, whose special spicy aroma and bite epitomizes Alsace wine. Most Alsace Gewurztraminer is made completely dry but intensely fruity, even to the point of slight fierceness when it is young. With age remarkable citrus fruit smells and flavours, suggesting grapefruit, intensify. Gewurztraminer of

a fine vintage, whether made dry or in the sweet Vendange Tardive style, is worth maturing almost as long as Riesling. The fault of a poor Gewurztraminer is sometimes softness and lack of definition, or alternatively a heady heaviness without elegance. In a range of Alsace wines Gewurztraminer should be served last, after Rieslings and Pinots.

Pinot Blanc (19.3%) An increasingly popular grape, giving the lightest of the 'noble' wines; simply fresh and appetizing without great complexity. This is the base wine for most Crémant d'Alsace.

Pinot Gris or Tokay d'Alsace (5.3%) After Riesling and Gewurztraminer the third potentially great wine grape of the region. First-class Tokay has a dense, stiff and intriguing smell and taste which is the very opposite of the fresh and fruity Pinot Blanc. It is almost frustrating to taste, as though it were concealing a secret flavour you will

never quite identify. Tokays mature magnificently into broad, rich deep-bosomed wines whose only fault is that they are not refreshing.

Pinot Noir (6.8%) A grape that is made into both red and rosé in Alsace, but it is sometimes necessary to read the label to know which is which. The must is often heated to extract colour, but the result is never more than a light wine, without the classic Pinot flavour found in, for example, Bouzy Rouge from Champagne.

Riesling (21%) The finest wine grape of Alsace, as it is of Germany, but here interpreted in a totally different way. Alsace Rieslings are fully ripened and usually fully fermented, their sugar all turned to alcohol, which gives them a firmer and more definite structure than German wines. Dryness and the intensity of their fruit flavour together make them seem rather harsh to some people. I have found a prejudice against Alsace Riesling in California. In fact,

LEADING ALSACE PRODUCERS

Caves J. Becker
Zellenberg, 68340 Riquewihr

The Beckers have been growers at Riquewihr since 1618. Their 20 acres are in the Zellenberg vineyard halfway to Ribeauvillé. Oak barrels but modern controls make them a typical small firm of growers/merchants, buying grapes to make up a total of 20,000 cases a year (30% exports). They also own the brand Gaston Beck.

Léon Beyer
68420 Eguisheim

A family firm founded in 1880, now directed by Léon Beyer and his son Marc. Their 45 acres of vines are in Eguisheim (Gewurztraminer, Riesling, Pinots Blanc, Gris and Noir and Muscat). Beyer's best wines are full-bodied and dry, clearly designed to go with food and often seen in top restaurants in France. I have seen some remarkably preserved 10- and even 20-year-old examples. Riesling Cuvée des Ecaillers and Gewurztraminer Cuvée des Comtes d'Equisheim are their principal brands.

Domaine Paul Blanck & Fils
68240 Kientzheim

Top-quality estate founded in 1953 and now producing some 55 wines each year, entirely from its own 56 acres of vineyard. The holdings include part of the Kientzheim Grands Crus, Schlossberg and Furstentum. Fermentation is in stainless steel and temperature-controlled, with splendid results from Riesling and Pinot Gris in 1988. The whole range of Blanck wines earns high praise, the most notable of recent years the Gewurztraminer Grand Cru Furstentum 1989. Total annual sales are about 16,000 cases of which 65% is exported.

E. Boeckel
67140 Mittelbergheim

Grower and négociant (founded 1853) with 50 acres in and around Mittelbergheim, regarded as a steady producer of traditional wines. His standard Sylvaner, Riesling and Gewurztraminer are labelled Zotzenberg; Brandluft and Wibelsberg are selected Rieslings; Château d'Isembourg his best Gewurztraminer. Exports are 55% of a total of 35,000 cases.

Dopff 'Au Moulin'
68340 Riquewihr

Another family firm of 17th-century origins, with the largest vineyard holdings of central Alsace. A total of 185 acres, principally in the Schoenenberg at Riquewihr for Riesling and Eichberg at Turckheim for Gewurztraminer, with Pinot Blanc in the Hardt vineyards near Colmar grown specifically for Crémant d'Alsace, which Dopff pioneered at the turn of the century. *Crémant* is an increasing part of their business, which is known for delicate and individual wines. Special Fruits de Mer is a good blend. Total sales 200,000 cases, 30% exported.

Dopff & Irion
'Château de Riquewihr', 68340 Riquewihr

One of the biggest grower/merchants of Alsace, still run by members of the Dopff and Irion families whose forebears have made wine at Riquewihr for 3 centuries, combining in 1945. They own 87 acres in Riquewihr, producing some 17,000 cases of their own Riesling Les Murailles (from the Schoenenberg), Gewurztraminer Les Sorcières, the very attractive Muscat Les Amandiers and Pinot Gris Les Maquisards. In addition they produce 270,000 cases from the grapes of 500 small growers under contract, representing 1,100 acres. Their main brands are very dry Crustaces and the fuller Crystal; also a Crémant d'Alsace. 45% of sales are exports.

Théo Faller
Domaine Weinbach, 68240 Kaysersberg

A distinguished domaine of 54 acres of former monastic land, the Clos des Capucins, now run by the widow and son of the late Théo Faller, who is buried amongst his vines. The family policy is to harvest as late as possible and

---

they range from light refreshment in certain years to some of the most aromatic, authoritative and longest-lasting of all white wines.

Muscat (2.9%) Until recently Alsace was the only wine region where Muscat grapes were made into dry wine. The aroma is still hothouse sweet but the flavour is crisp and very clean, sometimes with a suggestion of nut kernels. It is light enough to make an excellent apéritif.

Sylvaner (19.3%) Steadily being pushed out by Pinot Noir but at its best (at Mittelbergheim, for example) a classy, slightly '*pétillant*', flavoursome wine, which ages well.

Alsace appellations

One of the 'noble' grape names, or the term Edelzwicker, which means a blend of grapes, is usually the most prominent word on Alsace labels.

Appellation Alsace Wine from any permitted grape variety with a maximum crop of 100 hectolitres a hectare and a minimum natural degree of 8.5 alcohol.

Appellation Alsace Grand Cru Wine from one of the 'noble' grape varieties, growing in a designated Grand Cru site, with a maximum crop of 70 hectolitres a hectare and a minimum natural degree of 10 for Riesling and Muscat, 11 for Gewurztraminer and Pinot Gris (Tokay).

Alsace prices

Hugel & Fils quoted the following ex-cellar prices, per bottle, in 1990: Sylvaner 1989, 31.90 francs; Pinot Blanc 1989, 38.60 francs; Gewurztraminer 1988, 54.10 francs; Riesling 1988, 46.70 francs; Pinot Noir 1988, 53.40 francs;

Tokay Pinot Gris Cuvée Tradition 1988, 57.90 francs; Muscat Cuvée Tradition 1987, 44.30 francs; Gewurztraminer Cuvée Tradition 1988, 66.90 francs; Riesling Cuvée Tradition 1988, 69.20 francs; Tokay Pinot Gris Réserve Personnelle 1988, 101.80 francs; Gewurztraminer Réserve Personnelle 1988, 90.10 francs; Riesling Réserve Personnelle 1988, 95.30 francs; Pinot Noir Réserve Personnelle 1988, 101.80 francs.

use full maturity to give the wines maximum character, structure, length on the palate and the potential to age. Cuvée Théo is the standard label for Riesling and Gewurztraminer, with Vendanges Tardives in certain vintages (e.g. 1983). The Domaine Weinbach label is a superb piece of calligraphy: the best Alsace label. Total production is about 13,000 cases (14% exported).

Maison Louis Gisselbrecht
67650 Dambach-La-Ville

The Gisselbrecht family formed two separate businesses in 1936. This is the smaller one, proprietors of 24 acres at Dambach-La-Ville and elsewhere planted with Riesling, Gewurztraminer, Pinots Blanc and Noir, Sylvaner and Tokay. Riesling is the real speciality of the house; very clean, dry and balanced. Grapes are also bought to make a total of 60,400 cases. 85% is exported.

Willy Gisselbrecht & Fils
67650 Dambach-la-Ville

The larger of the two Gisselbrecht houses, owning 37 acres in and near Dambach-la-Ville and buying grapes to make a total of 125,000 cases a year (35% exported). Regular exhibitors and medal winners at the Paris and Mâcon fairs, particularly with Gewurztraminer.

Heim
68250 Westhalten

A substantial wine maker using the grapes of a group of growers with 222 acres in total. The vineyards include parts of 3 particularly good sites: Strangenberg for Pinot, Zinnkoepflé for Gewurztraminer and Bollenberg for Riesling (sold as Les Eglantiers). Top wines are fermented in oak; other methods are modern. Products include Imperial Brut, a good Crémant d'Alsace; a range of wines under the names Heim, Meyer, Anne Koehler, Anne d'Alsace; Mittnacht. Production 125,000 cases, 40% exported.

Hugel & Fils
68340 Riquewihr

The best-known Alsace label in the Anglo-Saxon world. A combination of grower and grape négociant, in the family since 1639, with 62 acres in Riquewihr producing their top wines. Of these 13 are in the Schoenenberg and 21 in the Sporen vineyards. 42% is Gewurztraminer, 43% Riesling, 13% Pinot Gris and 2% is Pinot Noir. The house style is full, round and 'supple', fermented dry but less apparently so than some houses. The speciality that Hugels have pioneered is late-gathered wines to the level of German Beerenausleses. The quality ladder for Riesling, Gewurztraminer, etc., goes Regular, Cuvée Tradition, Jubilee Vendange Tardive (big wines with definite sweetness) and in certain years (1983, '88, '89) Sélection de Grains Nobles (very sweet). Other registered names made of purchased grapes are Flambeau d'Alsace, Fleur d'Alsace, Cuvée les Amours and (Pinot Blanc) Les Vignards. Sales about 83,000 cases a year, 80% exported.

Domaines Klipfel
67140 Barr

A leading family domaine combined with a négociant business (André Lorentz). 99 acres including the Grands Crus Kirchberg (Riesling), Kastelberg (Pinot Gris) and Wiebelsberg (Gewurztraminer) – all traditionally oak-fermented and matured, with occasional Vendanges Tardives. Bought-in grapes are vinified in tanks for Lorentz label. Sales are largely to French restaurants and private customers. 30% is exported, mainly to Germany.

Domaine Marc Kreydenweiss
67140 Andlau

From 26 acres including holdings in the Grands Crus Wiebelsberg, Kastelberg, and Moenchberg, Kreydenweiss produces beautifully made, concentrated wines. The Rieslings from 25- to 45-year-old vines in the steep Kastelberg site are made to last. Fermentation is temperature controlled and the wines are allowed to stay on their lees until shortly before bottling. Unusually, the domaine produces a late-picked Pinot Blanc. As the law prevents it from being sold as Vendange Tardive, it is offered under the vinyard name *Kritt*, linked with the old Alsatian name for Pinot Blanc, *Klevner*. 5,000 cases are produced annually of which 60% is exported.

Kuehn
68770 Ammerschwihr

Growers and négociants founded in 1675. Their 26 acres of vines are mainly in Ammerschwihr, partly in the famous Kaefferkopf vineyard, with all the usual varieties. In addition there are Riesling holdings in two other Grand Cru vineyards – Sommerberg at Niedermorschwihr and Florimont at Ingersheim. The vines in the Sommerberg are new and planted on a steep site. The wines are made in wood in the 17th-century cellars, much as they have been for 300 years. Other brand names are Baron de Schiele and St-Hubert. 50% is exported.

Kuentz-Bas
68420 Husseren-Les-Châteaux

A family firm of growers and négociants, owning 30 acres of Riesling, Muscat and Gewurztraminer, Pinots Blanc, Gris and Noir in Husseren, Eguisheim and Obermorschwihr. There are holdings in the Grands Crus Eichberg and Pfersigberg at Equisheim. Regular prize winners with firm and dry, well-balanced and elegant wines. The wines have excellent acidity, and the vendange tardive wines are superb. 60% exported.

Jos. Meyer & Fils
68920 Wintzenheim

A family of growers and négociants since 1854, with 35 acres under vine at Wintzenheim and Turkheim. The full flavoured Gewurztraminers are particularly successful. 70% of the annual production of 33,000 cases is exported.

Maison Michel Laugel
67520 Marlenheim

Perhaps the biggest of Alsace wine makers, with annual sales of 330,000 cases. Their popular brand is Pichet d'Alsace, a blend of 85% Pinot Blanc, 10% Riesling and 5% Gewurztraminer – an excellent Edelzwicker at a reasonable price. Their main varieties are well-made, quite light wines for drinking fresh. The Laugel family owns a 12-acre vineyard of Pinot Noir in Marlenheim from which they make a well-known rosé.

Gustave Lorentz
68750 Bergheim

150-year-old family firm of growers and négociants, among the biggest producers and exporters with 250,000 cases a year, half exported. They own 79 acres with their best vines in the Altenberg and Kanzlerberg sites at Bergheim.

Muré
68250 Rouffach

A family of growers dating back to 1630, owners since 1928 of a historic vineyard at Rouffach, the old monastic

Clos St-Landelin of 45 acres. All the usual vines are planted in the Clos, which has warm, stony and limey soil and notably low rainfall. Its wines are full in character and round in style, intended (except the Sylvaner and Pinot Noir) as *vins de garde*. Muré also has a négociant business with a different label, selling some 50,000 cases a year.

Domaine Ostertag
67680 Epfig

24-acre estate with a 5-acre holding in the Muenchberg Grand Cru vineyard (Riesling and Pinot Gris). An expressed desire to move from the technology to the "poetry" of wine does not exclude Pinot Blanc aged in barrique. 70% of annual sale of 5,800 cases is exported.

Preiss-Henny
68630 Mittelwihr

One of the larger growers as well as négociants with 45 acres distributed in 4 communes between Riquewihr and Colmar. The Preiss family use traditional wine-making methods. Their top wines are Riesling Cuvée Marcel Preiss and Gewurztraminer Cuvée Camille Preiss. 45% of sales are exported.

Preiss-Zimmer
68340 Riquewihr

300-year old firm of négociants producing consistently fine wines, particularly Gewurztraminer, from vineyards around Riquewihr, including the Grands Crus Sporen and Schoenenbourg.

Domaines Schlumberger
68500 Guebwiller

The biggest domaine in Alsace, family owned, with 346 acres at Guebwiller and Rouffach at the southern end of the region. Guebwiller's warm climate, sandy soil and sheltered sites allied with old-style methods, relatively small crops and ageing in wood make Schlumberger wines some of the richest and roundest of Alsace, with sweet and earthy flavours of their own. The best are from the Kitterlé vineyard and repay several years' bottle-ageing. Total production is about 81,000 cases, 55% exported.

Albert Seltz & Fils
67140 Mittelbergheim

A family of growers and négociants with 16th-century origins, particularly known for the Sylvaner from its 7 acres in the Grand Cru Zotzenberg. Owner Pierre Seltz, who studied oenology in California, describes his wine making as traditional Alsatian. Many successes in the 1989 vintage.

Domaine Sick-Dreyer
68770 Ammerschwihr

A 30-acre domain, with 12.5 acres in the Kaefferkopf vineyard, famous for its Gewurztraminer. Sick-Dreyer produces a fine, concentrated example from grapes that

Georges and Jean ('Johnny') Hugel, two of the trio of brothers at the head of this ancient house

are almost late-picked, as well as the complete range of classic Alsace wines from the Côtes d'Ammerschwihr. Annual production is about 6,500 cases – all domaine bottled. 20% is exported.

Pierre Sparr & ses Fils
68240 Sigolsheim

Another family firm of growers and merchants dating back to the 17th century. Their own vines cover 74 acres in 6 communes between Turkheim and Bennwihr, including Riesling in the Schlossberg (Kaysersberg) and Altenberg vineyards, and Gewurztraminer in Brand at Turckheim and Mambourg at Sigolsheim. These are the company's top wines. Total sales 166,600 cases, 45% of which is exported.

F.E. Trimbach
68150 Ribeauvillé

A historic (1626) family domaine and négociant house with a reputation for particulary fine and delicate dry wines. They own 49 acres planted 27% in Riesling , 22% in Gewurztraminer. Their special pride is the Hunawihr Riesling Clos Ste-Hune, one of the most stylish Alsace wines. A fascinating tasting of old vintages showed it at its best after about 7 years. Each variety is made in the recently modernized cellar at 3 quality levels: standard (vintage), Réserve and Réserve Personnelle. The prestigious Riesling Cuvée Frédéric Emil, and Gewurztraminer Cuvée des Seigneurs de Ribeaupierre are very fine. 81% of a total production of 63,000 cases is exported.

Alsace Willm
67140 Barr

A very traditional firm with a high reputation, taken over in 1980 by Roger Bahl. It is best known for its Gewurztraminer vineyard of 18 acres, Clos Gaensbroennel, and its 10 acres of Riesling in the Kirchberg. The Gewurztraminer is well ripened and fermented completely dry, making it a firm and impressive *vin de garde*. Its delicate Riesling and very clean, fresh Sylvaner (also Clos Gaensbroennel) are both very attractive. Total sales are about 40,000 cases, 90% exported (Canada is the biggest buyer).

Domaine Zind-Humbrecht
Wintzenheim, 68930 Wintzenheim

The domaines of the Humbrechts of Gueberschwihr (since 1620) and the Zinds of Wintzenheim united in 1959 and are now run by Léonard and Olivier Humbrecht. Humbrecht is a fanatic for the individuality of each vineyard's soil and microclimate, and a pioneer believer in low-temperature (15°C/60°F) fermentation. He makes highly individual wines from 4 Grand Cru vineyards: Brand at Turckheim (which makes light and fruity wines, especially Riesling), Goldert at Gueberschwihr (full-bodied Gewurztraminer), Hengst at Wintzenheim (more full-bodied *vins de garde*) and Rangen at Thann, where his 10-acre Clos St-Urbain gives top-quality Rieslings. The whole domaine is 96 acres of Gewurztraminer, Riesling and other usual varieties. 80% of his 23,000-case (average) production is exported.

ALSACE COOPERATIVES

Andlau-Barr
67140 Barr. 197 members with a total area of 321 acres in 9 communes. Specialities are Zotzenberg and Klevner de Heiligenstein.

Bennwihr
68630 Bennwihr-Mittelwihr. 260 members with a total area of 864 acres in 5 communes. Specialities are Riesling, Rebgarten and Gewurztraminer Côtes de Bennwihr. Brands are Poème d'Alsace and Rêve d'Alsace.

Dambach-La-Ville
67650 Dambach-La-Ville. 160 members with a total area of 358 acres in 7 communes.

Union Vinicole Divinal
67210 Obernai. A union of 7 cooperatives using the brand name Divinal on the usual range of wines, drawn from all over Alsace. Its total production amounts to 1 bottle in 20 of all Alsace wine. Total 500,000 cases (20-25% exports).

Eguisheim
68420 Eguisheim. Cooperative Vinicole with 470 members and a total area of 1,425 acres in 10 communes. Specialities are Gewurztraminer Cuvée St-Léon IX, Riesling Cuvée des Seigneurs, Pinot Noir Prince Hugo, Blanc de Blancs brut (*méthode champenoise*). Total production is 460,000 cases (15% exports), all sold with the brand name 'Wolfberger'.

Caves de Hoen
68980 Beblenheim. 617 acres in 8 communes. Top wines come from the Grand Cru Sonnenglanz. Brands used include Cave de Beblenheim, Eugène Deybach, Baron de Hoen. Total production 200,000 cases (20% exports).

Ingersheim et Environs
68000 Colmar. 210 members, 642 acres in 5 communes. Methods are traditional. 250,000 cases (30% exports).

Kientzheim-Kaysersberg
68240 Kaysersberg. 150 members with a total area of 345 acres in 4 communes. Specialities include Riesling Schlossberg and Gewurztraminer Kaefferkopf.

Orschwiller
67600 Selestat. 141 members with a total of 271 acres in 5 communes. Production is about 100,000 cases, sold mainly in France.

Pfaffenheim-Gueberschwihr
68250 Rouffach. Has 200 members, with a total area of 494 acres in 7 communes. Specialities include a Crémant d'Alsace, Hartenberger, and Gewurztraminer from the Gand Cru Goldert. Total production 125,000 cases (25% exports).

Ribeauvillé et Environs
68150 Ribeauvillé. The oldest growers' cooperative in France (founded at the turn of the century) now has 90 members with 385 acres in 5 communes. The speciality is Le Clos du Zahnacker. Total 150,000 cases (30% exports).

Sigolsheim et Environs
68240 Kayersberg. 690 acres, all in the commune of Sigolsheim. Specialities include a Crémant d'Alsace. Comte de Sigold, and Gewurztraminers of up to *Grains Nobles* quality. Total 250,000 cases (50% exports).

Traenheim et Environs
67310 Wasselonne. 263 members, 543 acres in 14 communes. Brands used include Le Roi Dagobert and Cuvée St-Eloi.

Turckheim
68230 Turckheim. 261 members with a total area of 470 acres in 7 communes. Specialities are Gewurztraminer Baron de Turckheim, Pinot Côtes du Val St-Grégoire.

Vieil-Armand
68360 Soultz-Wuenheim. 150 members, 395 acres in 6 communes. Brands include Château Ollwiller (Riesling and Pinot Noir).

Westhalten et Environs
68111 Westhalten. 168 members, 617 acres in 3 communes and also Gundolsheim, Orschwihr, Steinbach-près-Cérnay. Specialities are Gewurztraminer and Sylvaner Zinnkoepfle and Vorbourg, Muscat, Pinot Blanc Bollenberg. Production about 200,000 cases (20% exports).

RHONE

After many years of virtually ignoring the Rhône valley and its wines the wine trade has recently begun to find in it all sorts of virtues. More perhaps than stand up to dispassionate examination.

Its finest wines, Côte Rôtie and Hermitage, have suddenly been 'discovered', especially in the U.S.A., and their prices forced up to scarcely realistic levels, while great quantities of what is scarcely more than high-strength *vin ordinaire* have climbed to the price of Bordeaux. It would be wrong to discount my personal taste in this. I admit to not liking, except on very rare occasions, wines of the strength of Châteauneuf-du-Pape. But strength aside, it seems to me that common grapes can never make better than common wine. Most of the grapes of the Rhône are either coarse or neutral in flavour. At their best they are grown in soil that exalts their qualities by men of taste who are aware of the flavours they are producing. More often, I feel, the well-worn eulogies of scents of truffles and woodlands, violets and raspberries are pure wishful thinking. Or (more charitably) that they only apply to wines far older than we are now accustomed to drinking. It is hard not to contrast the Rhône with California and the progress that has been made there in the last 15 years.

You will find that I wax more enthusiastic when talking about particular wines.

NORTHERN RHONE

The characteristic of the northern Rhône is dogged single-mindedness: one grape, the Syrah, grown on rocky slopes that need terracing to hold the soil. The red wines are all Syrah (alias Sérine), a grape with concentrated fruity flavour but so darkly tannic that the custom is to add between 2 and 20 per cent of white grapes to leaven it.

The northernmost appellation, Côte Rôtie, used to be a mere 250 acres of terraced hill above the village of Ampuis. Somewhat controversially, the appellation has been enlarged to include up to 750 acres of plateau land behind the Côte proper. Côte Rôtie means 'roasted hill'; two sections of the hill, with paler (more chalky) and darker soil, are known respectively as the Côte Blonde and the Côte Brune. Their wines are normally blended by growers who have only a few acres in total. If no 'Côte' is credited, expect 'plateau' wine. The Syrah here is grown and mixed with up to 20 per cent (but usually less) of Viognier. Partly from this aromatic component, but probably more from the singular soils of the hill, it

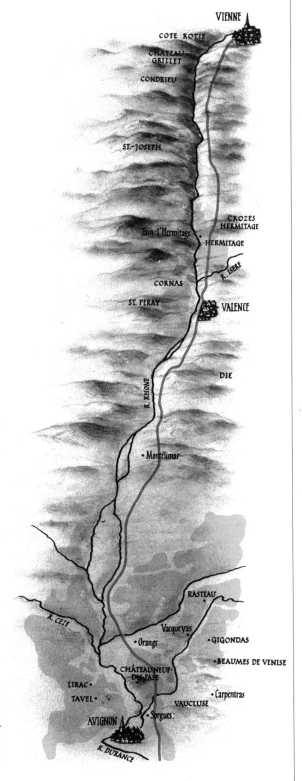

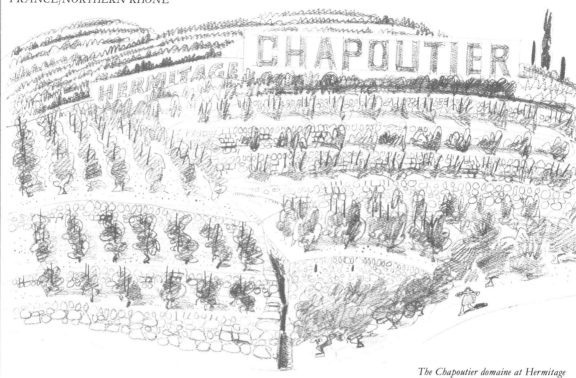

The Chapoutier domaine at Hermitage

draws a delicacy that makes Côté Rôtie eventually the finest, if not the most powerful, of all Rhône wines. Between 10 and 20 years of age it moves closer to great Bordeaux than any other French wine, with an open, soft-fruity, perhaps raspberry bouquet that recalls the Médoc, yet with a warmer texture. Recent development include perhaps more stress on new-oak flavours than the wine will stand.

Condrieu, where the rare Viognier makes white wine, is only three miles downstream from Ampuis on the same south-facing right bank. St-Joseph covers a 30-mile, 750-acre stretch of the same river bank and its immediate hinterland with some very good sites but no consistency. A good example (such as Jaboulet's Grand Pompée) is clean, dark and sufficiently fruity Syrah without the grip or depth of Hermitage; wine to drink at four or five years.

The same in general is true of Crozes-Hermitage, the appellation for the east bank around Tain-L'Hermitage, without the advantage of the great upstanding mass of granite to help grill its grapes. Again, it is uneven in quality, ranging from near-Hermitage to an uninspiring commercial wine.

Few famous vineyards are as consistent as Hermitage. Its whole 310-acre surface faces full south at an angle that maximizes the warmth of the sun. Four fifths are planted with Syrah, the rest with two white grapes, Roussane and Marsanne, that produce a wine as splendid in its way as the red. A century ago white Hermitage (than all Roussanne) was reckoned the best white wine in France,

keeping 'much longer than the red, even to the extent of a century'. It is surprising to find white wine of apparently low acidity keeping well at all. Yet at ten years (a good age for it today) it has a haunting combination of foursquare breadth and depth with some delicate, intriguing, lemony zest.

St-Joseph and Crozes-Hermitage, incidentally, also make white wines of the same grapes which can be excellent. When they are aged they are best served cool, not chilled.

Red Hermitage has the frankest, most forthright, unfumbling 'attack' of any of the Rhône wines. Young, it is massively purple-black, uncomplicated by smells of new oak, powerfully fruity, almost sweet beneath a cloak of tannin and takes years to lose its opacity. Many people enjoy it in this state, or so it seems, because mature bottles are rare.

Cornas concludes the red-wine appellations of the northern Rhône with a sort of country cousin to Hermitage – another dark Syrah wine which only becomes a drink for fastidious palates after years in bottle. The area under vines is expanding and now stands at almost as much as Hermitage.

South of Cornas the appellation St-Péray is a surprising one – for a *méthode champenoise* sparkling wine of Marsanne and Roussanne grapes which, providing you forget the finesse of champagne or the *crémants* of northern France, has much to be said for it. It is a heavy-duty sparkler of almost sticky texture, even when it is dry. With age it develops a very pleasant nutty flavour.

Rhône prices are on page 199.

NORTHERN RHONE PRODUCERS

G. et P. Barge
Ampuis, 69420 Condrieu.

Forward-looking growers of fine Côte-Rôtie and a little Condrieu from 11 acres.

Guy de Barjac
07130 Cornas.

A 5-acre family vineyard going back to the 14th century. Old-fashioned 100% Syrah wine needs 18 months in wood and several years in bottle. The label is La Barjasse.

Madame A. Bégot
Le Village, Serves-sur-Rhône, 26600 Tain L'Hermitage.

Madame Bégot and her son keep up the traditions of Albert Bégot (d.1985), using only 'biological' methods – no chemicals – to cultivate 12 acres of red and white Crozes-Hermitage. 1,000 cases, 30% exported.

J.F. Chaboud
07130 St-Péray.

The fourth generation of the Chaboud family has 20 acres of Marsanne and Roussane. 80% of production is champagne method St-Péray. The *sec* is pure Marsanne.

Emile Champet
Le Port, 69420 Ampuis.

The Champet family has an international reputation on the strength of a mere 4 acres of Côte Rôtie: up to 800 cases a year of sternly tannic red.

M. Chapoutier
26600 Tain L'Hermitage.

Founded in 1808, this is one of the most distinguished names of the Rhône both as growers and négociants. Their 176-acre domaine consists of 75 acres of Hermitage (red and white), 6.6 of Côte Rôtie, 12 of Crozes-Hermitages Les Meysonniers, 13.5 of St-Joseph Deschants red and white and 70 of Châteauneuf-du-Pape (red and white) La Bernardine. Methods are wholly traditional, even to treading the grapes. Their domaine wines are aged in small barrels of either oak or sweet chestnut. Everyone should taste their white Hermitage Chante Alouette at 10 or more years old – a revelation after most modern whites. Total sales 80,000 cases; 65% exported. 'Grand Cuvées' (NV) are wonderful wines. A recent addition is a range of prestige cuvées, also non-vintage, but blended from Chapoutier's best wines.

J.L. Chave
Mauves, 07300 Tournon-sur-Rhône.

Gérard Chave in 1981 celebrated 500 years of direct succession in his 27 acres of Hermitage. His red and white are among the best and longest-lived wines of France. His tiny production – no more than 3,000 cases of Hermitage and 250 of St-Joseph – trails far behind his fame.

Auguste Clape
07130 St-Péray, 07130 Cornas.

A grower with 10 acres of Cornas and 2.5 of St-Péray. His Cornas is dark purple, almost black, intensely tannic – the perfect wine for Roquefort, he says. Techniques are very traditional: no filters, no fining. Certainly it is the leader of the appellation.

Pierre Coursodon
Mauves, 07300 Tournon-sur-Rhône.

Family property of 19 acres of very old vines on the better slopes of St-Joseph. Red and white wines both demand to be aged.

Delas Frères
07300 Tournon-sur-Rhône.

Long-established growers and négociants now owned by Champagne Deutz and recently moved to modern premises. They have 50 acres of vineyards, half in Hermitage (red and white), 12 in Cornas, 6 in Côte Rôtie and 5 in Condrieu. Delas wines are marginally cheaper than their rivals but seem to lack nothing in character and staying power. Delas Hermitage is notably good. Their Cornas is called Chante-Perdrix.

Albert Dervieux-Thaize
Ampuis, 69420 Condrieu.

One of the small growers of Côte Rôtie with 7.5 acres in 3 parcels, making 3 different wines: La Garde in the Côte Blonde, the Côte Brune and a patch he calls Viaillère. The bouquet of the wine, he says, varies from violets to raspberries depending on the soil. He avoids new oak, preferring to let his precious vines express themselves. It needs at least 5 or 6 years and lasts for 20.

Desmeure Père & Fils
26600 Tain L'Hermitage.

Family property of about 40 acres in Hermitage and Crozes-Hermitage, making red and white wines in bulk by traditional methods. Three-quarters of their production goes to private clients.

Pierre Dumazet
07340 Serrières.

A tiny trickle of Condrieu (from an acre of vines) to very smart restaurants and private clients. He is planting more Viognier at enormous expense. Thus, he explains, the price of his Condrieu.

Jules Fayolle & ses Fils
Gervans, 26600 Tain L'Hermitage.

A family property of 17.5 acres in Crozes-Hermitage and 2.5 red Hermitage, founded in 1870. The reds are old-fashioned, 3 years aged in wood; the Marsanne white (from 6 acres) is bottled young and fresh. The red Hermitage is from a vineyard called les Dionnières at the eastern end of the slope.

Domaine Ferraton & Fils
26600 Tain L'Hermitage.

Ten acres of Hermitage, plus vines in Croze, making solid, traditional wines. The red Hermitage spends at least 2 years in wood.

Château Grillet
42410 Verin.

The smallest property in France with its own Appellation Contrôlée, owned by the Neyret-Gachet family since 1830. The vineyard is 7.5 acres of perilous terraces forming a suntrap 500 feet above the bank of the Rhône. 22,000 Viognier vines yield on average 600 to 800 cases a year of highly aromatic wine which is aged 18 months in oak. Opinions are divided about whether any sort of ageing improves Viognier wine.

Bernard Gripa
Mauves, 07300 Tournon-sur-Rhône.

A traditionalist producer of St-Joseph. His 12 acres is 80% red, fermented with stems and aged a year in wood. His whites are 90% Marsanne, made crisp and deliciously refreshing.

Jean-Louise Grippat
La Sauva, 07300 Tournon-sur-Rhône.

The eighth generation of Grippats struggles with the terraces of St-Joseph (11 acres, mainly red) and Hermitage (4 acres, mainly white) to produce a total 2,000 cases a year. Their St-Joseph red is a good 5-year wine, but their Hermitage white is worth 10 years.

E. et M. Guigal
Ampuis, 69420 Condrieu.

The Guigal family are the leading producers of Côte Rôtie, which they grow themselves on 30 acres and buy as grapes from 40 other small growers. They ferment the whole bunches in a closed vat for up to 3 weeks, then age it in new oak barrels for 3 years, avoiding both fining and filtration if possible. The object is extremely long-lived wines. Their 4 labels are La Mouline, La Landonne, La Turque Côte Brune, and Cotes Brune et Blonde. La Landonne is a 3½-acre plot in the Côte Brune. La Turque was only launched with the 1985 vintage. Fierce debate centres on whether Guigal's oak-scented style is true to the nature and traditions of Côte Rôtie. It certainly attracts extravagant praise – and prices. In 1985 the Guigals bought the firm of Vidal-Fleury (q.v.). Guigal also produces Condrieu and Hermitage, Tavel and Côtes de Rhône. Total production is 10,000 cases.

Paul Jaboulet Aîné
26600 Tain L'Hermitage.

Growers and négociants since 1834, now run by 3 members of the founding family with Gérard Jaboulet in charge. The house is a pacesetter for the whole Rhône both as grower and merchant. Their domaine of 160 acres is in Hermitage (44 acres red, 17 white) and Crozes-Hermitage (74 red, 15 white). All 4 are among the best each year; the red Hermitage La Chapelle in great vintages ('61, '78, '83 '85) is one of France's greatest wines, maturing over 25 years or more. The vines which produce La Chapelle are on average 35 years old. Each Jaboulet wine has a name as well as an appellation, as follows: Hermitage (red) La Chapelle; (white) Le Chevalier de Stérimbourg. Crozes-Hermitage (red) Domaine de Thalabert (white) Mule Blanche. St-Joseph Le Grand Pompée. Côte Rôtie Les Jumelles. Tavel L'Espiègle. Châteauneuf-du-Pape Les Cedres and a very full and fruity Côtes du Rhône Parrallèle 45 (also rosé and white). There is also a Cornas. Another label is Jaboulet-Isnard. Total sales are about 125,000 cases, 55% exported.

Robert Jasmin
69420 Ampuis.

A famous name, though a small property, with vines averaging 25–30 years old. Six acres of Côte Rôtie (increasing to 7.5). 1,000 cases produced per annum. Traditional vinification, adding 5–10% of white Viognier to the black Syrah and ageing in barrel for 18–24 months. The yearly production of his La Chevalière d'Ampuis is about 1,100 cases.

Marcel Juge
07130 Cornas.

A small grower of hearty red Cornas from 7.5 acres. Methods are traditional, the wine 'structured and fruity' – but not as fruity as his neighbour Clape's. Cuvée 'C' is the top wine here.

Robert Michel
07130 Cornas.

A simple old-fashioned family holding of 12 acres, partly on the hills giving the typically tough red, partly lighter wine from the foot of the slope. Neither is fined nor filtered before bottling. The former is at least a 10-year wine. 'La Gaynole' is the top wine, from old vines on terraces facing due south.

Paul Multier
Château du Rozay, 69420 Condrieu.

Among the few producers of Condrieu, with a reputation as high as any. He is slowly adding to his 5.7 acres of precipitous terraces. Fermentation is in large, well-used casks, where the wine stays until its second fermentation is finished. Maximum production at present is 580 cases a year, plus some Côtes-du-Rhône red.

Paul-Etienne Père & Fils
07130 St-Péray.

A family firm of négociants and producers of sparkling St-Péray for 160 years. Wines of traditional style from all parts of the Rhône. Sales 42,000 cases, 80% in France.

Domaine Sorrel
26600 Tain L'Hermitage.

A family property with 8.6 acres of Hermitage, mostly red, for a select cuvée called Le Gréal (formerly Le Méal) and a straightforward wine. The white is labelled Les Roucoules. Le Gréal can be very good.

Georges Vernay
69420 Condrieu.

The leading figure in Condrieu today with 15 acres of Viognier, mostly planted on reclaimed abandoned terraces. His wine is bottled in its first spring (or even winter) for freshness – and because demand outruns supply. A small amount spends longer in wood and becomes Coteaux de Vernon, a distinctly superior wine. He also has 4.5 acres of Côte Rôtie and small vineyards in St-Joseph and Côtes du Rhone.

J. Vidal-Fleury
69420 Ampuis.

The oldest (established 1781) and biggest domaine of Côte Rôtie terraces with a princely 20 acres, bought in 1985 by the Guigal family (q.v.). They make wines from the 2 Côtes, Brune and Blonde, separately and also together. Total annual production of these is 2,500 cases. It takes 10 years for the real finesse of these wines to emerge. In addition, the firm has a full line of *négoce* wines of fair to fine quality.

Alain Voge
07130 Cornas.

The Voge family, in its fourth generation here, makes Cornas from 15 acres by old methods and sparkling St-Péray, from 7.5 acres of Marsanne, by the champagne method.

OTHER NORTHERN RHONE PRODUCERS

Albert Dervieux-Thaise
Côte-Rôtie in the traditional style from 8 acres. Some of the most potent, tannic and long-lived.
Gentaz-Dervieux
Côte Rotie. Only three acres of Côte

Brune, made the old way: no new oak, no filters, old vines, two years in wood before bottling. Ten years are needed to maturity.
Joseph Jamet
Côte Rotie. Excellent, traditional wine

from 9 acres: it needs time.
René Rostaing
Côte Rotie. Only 500 cases of dramatic wine in the new, oak-aged style.

SOUTHERN RHONE

The catch-all appellation for the huge spread of southern Rhône vineyards is Côtes du Rhône. It is not a very exigent title: big crops of up to 52 hectolitres a hectare are eligible so long as they reach 11 degrees of alcohol. The area covers a total 99,000 acres in more than 100 communes north of Avignon, describing a rough circle among the low hills surrounding the widening Rhône. It leaves out only the alluvial bottom land around the river itself. In an average year, it makes more than twice as much wine as the appellation Beaujolais – indeed considerably more than the whole of Burgundy and over two thirds the Bordeaux crop. Ninety-nine per cent of it is red or *rosé*. In such an ocean of wine there are several estates that set standards of their own, and good négociants choose and blend well. The thing to bear in mind is that Côtes du Rhône is for drinking young, while it is reasonably fruity.

There is a tradition in the area of making a very light café wine known as *vin d'une nuit* – vatted for one night only. It has been more or less superseded by the adoption of Beaujolais tactics to make a Rhône *primeur* with some of the qualities of new Beaujolais – but not with the exciting smell of the new Gamay. Regular red Côtes du Rhône is unpredictable, but compared with basic Bordeaux as a daily drink it is more warm and winey, less fresh and stimulating.

Côtes du Rhône-Villages is the inner circle. Forty years ago growers in two communes east of the valley, Gigondas and Cairanne, and two to the west, Chusclan and Laudun, raised their sights to making stronger, more concentrated *vin de garde*. Limiting their crop to 35–42 hectolitres a hectare (according to the vintage) and ripening their grapes to give 12.5 degrees alcohol 'they made better wine and got better prices. A number of their neighbours followed suit. In 1967, the appellation Côtes du Rhône-Villages was decreed for a group of what has now risen to 17 communes totalling 12,350 acres. Gigondas and Vacqueyras have been promoted to be appellations, and this seems likely to happen to others in the group as they establish their identity and build their markets. The full list is given on page 199.

Certainly Vacqueyras deserves its promotion. As an example of the style of the area it might be compared with Gigondas. Tasted together the Gigondas is fuller and rounder, with more 'stuffing'; the Vacqueyras is more 'nervous', harsh at first but developing a very pleasant dusty, slightly spicy, bouquet. (The Gigondas has very little.) Both are emphatically *vins de garde*: at five or six years they still need decanting a good 12 hours ahead – or keeping another three years.

Of the communes which are not -Villages, Uchaux and Châteauneuf-de-Gadagne are areas of apparent promise. On about the same quality level as Côtes du Rhône comes the appellation Coteaux du Tricastin, inaugurated in 1974, for vineyards higher up the east bank of the river.

Notes on Tavel and Lirac are given on page 203.

SOUTHERN RHONE PRODUCERS

Pierre Amadieu
Gigondas, 84190 Beaumes de Venise.
Growers and négociants with 300 acres on the hills of Gigondas and 87 in the Côtes du Ventoux (where they make red, white and rosé). They also handle Châteauneuf-du-Pape, Côtes du Rhône and -Villages. Brand names Font Gelado, Bois de Candale, Le Goutail and Romane Machotte – a total of 83,000 cases a year. The largest of the Gigondas producers.

Domaine des Anges
84570 Mormoiron.
Malcolm Swan, an English ex-advertising man, has 20 acres of Grenache, Syrah, Cinsaut and Carignan and makes 2,300 cases of full-flavoured 'Beaujolais-type' Côtes du Ventoux for drinking young.

Arnoux & Fils
84190 Beaumes de Venise.
Use bought-in grapes (mainly Grenache, Cinsaut, Syrah) to make a total of 29,000 cases of Côtes du Rhône and

-Villages, Gigondas, Vacqueyras, Côtes du Ventoux and Vin de Pays du Vaucluse. A name to inspire confidence in the Côtes du Rhône, particularly for their Vacqueyras.

Château d'Aqueria
30126 Tavel.
A 17th-century property owned by the Olivier family since 1919. 135 acres are in Tavel, a few in Lirac, producing up to 20,000 cases p.a. By ageing the Tavel in big casks for a few months they aim to stiffen it a little to survive longer in bottle.

Domaine Assémat
30150 Roquemaure.
The achievement, since 1963, of Jean-Claude Assémat, a young oenologist with modern ideas. He has created two properties: Domaine Les Garrigues of 40 acres (all Lirac) and Domaine des Causses et St-Eymes (85 acres in Lirac, 15 in Laudun). His wines range from Rouge d'Eté *en primeur* to a Syrah made by adding fresh Syrah to the pulp left after macerating his rosé – a double dose of skins, giving wine which will stand up, he says, 'even to thyme and rosemary'. They are lively wines made with flair and gastronomic awareness.

Bellicard d'Avignon
Château de Piot, 84000 Avignon.
A century-old négociant with a good solid reputation for wines from the whole Rhône, now owned by Piat of Mâcon and part of the Grand Metropolitan empire.

Domaines Georges Bernard
30126 Tavel
The Bernards have two properties totalling 101 acres; Domaine de la Genestière in Tavel and Lirac and Domaine de Longval in Tavel. The Tavel is made with a short maceration (12–24 hours) on the skins followed by fining the must (not the wine).

Domaine des Bernardins
84190 Beaumes de Venise
Madame Maurin runs a third-generation family domaine of 40 acres producing some 2,200 cases of fresh and luscious Muscat de Beaumes de Venise and twice as much red wine, largely Côtes du Rhône but about 700 cases of Côtes du Rhône-Villages Beaume. The red is Grenache and Syrah with a little Carignan, aged 6 months in wood.

Romain Bouchard
Domaine du Val des Rois, 84600 Valréas.
The Bouchards have a family tree as tall as that of the Bouchards of Beaune – and curiously enough they compare their wine to Beaune. They are growers with 38 acres of Valréas (Côtes du Rhône-Villages), where they aim to achieve brilliance and harmony rather than rude rustic wine. Despite its relative lightness and no barrel-ageing, they say it will live 15 years (and 'evoke the Côte de Beaune'). Grapes are Grenache 70% and Syrah 30%. Bottling is done in a plant shared by neighbours in the Enclave des Papes. The label is Domaine du Val des Rois. They also make Marc des Côtes du Rhône.

Domaine Brusset
Cairanne, 84290 St-Cécile-les-Vignes.
Daniel Brusset's Cuvée des Templiers, made from 104 acres, is a traditional Cavanne and one of the village's best.

Edmond Burle
La Beaumette, Gigondas, 84190 Beaumes de Venise.
The fourth generation of the Burles still have 60-year-old Grenache vines in their vineyards in Gigondas and Vacqueyras – about 40 acres in scattered parcels. Vinification is 'modernized traditional' with concrete vats and a hydraulic press. Gigondas Les Pallierondes is their *vin noble*, which M. Burle likes to deliver to clients personally.

Domaine de Castel Oualou
30150 Roquemaure.
An important Lirac property of 126 acres developed over the past 20 years by the Pons-Mure family. Madame Pons-Mure wins medals for her splendid Lirac Rouge, which contains Syrah and Mourvèdre. She also makes a little pleasant white of Ugni Blanc, Clairette and Picpoul, and rosé containing Clairette on a basis of Cinsaut and Grenache.

Chambovet & Fils
Château de l'Estagnol, 26130 St-Paul Trois Châteaux.
The Chabovet family have built up a vineyard of 200 acres, 16 miles north of Orange on sandy slopes that give Côtes du Rhône of warm piney and herbal character. The vines are Syrah, Grenache, Cinsaut and Mourvèdre in approximately equal proportions; the Syrah is fermented by *macération carbonique*. A special *cuvée* with extra Syrah, more colour and body is called La Serre Du Prieur.

Maurice Charavin
Domaine du Char-à-Vin [*sic*], 84110 Rasteau.
A family property going back to the years of the French Revolution; 37 acres making the classic sweet Rasteau, entirely from Grenache, and an old-style red from Grenache, Syrah and Carignan aged 1 year in oak barrels and bottled without filtering. Some of the barrels are 100 years old. Only his rosé is given modern treatment.

Domaine du Devoy
30126 St-Laurent-des-Arbes.
Owners the Lombardo brothers. An excellent property of 100 acres, planted in Grenache, with Cinsaut, Mourvèdre and Syrah. Full-coloured, distinguished, even elegant reds with no wood-ageing. Also a little rosé.

Domaine Durban
84190 Beaumes de Venise.
Jacques Leydier is a reticent but excellent producer of both Muscat de Beaumes de Venise and red Côtes du Rhône-Villages from 86 acres.

Domaine du Grand Montmirail
Gigondas, 84109 Beaumes de Venise.
An 80-acre Gigondas estate owned by Denis Cheron (*see* Pascal). Low production from old Grenache vines has been adapted with more Syrah, white Mourvèdre and Cinsaut also used to make more assertive wines for longer life in a new winery. The 5,500-case production has 3 names: Domaine du Roucas de St Pierre, Domaine de St Gens and Domaine du Pradas.

Domaine de Grangeneuve/Domaine des Lones
Roussas, 26230 Grignan.
The Bour family were pioneers of the new appellation Coteaux du Tricastin in the 1970s, when they planted 250 acres with 50% Grenache, 30% Syrah and 20% Cinsaut. Their first wine under the domaine label was in 1974. Red

(and a very little rosé) are made in stainless steel and aged up to 2 years before bottling. The straight Syrah is their best wine.

Domaine Malby
30126 Tavel.

A family property of 250 acres, half in Tavel, where they make the wine as fresh as possible by the old method, a quarter in Lirac for 'big' reds and a quarter Côtes du Rhône for light red.

Château de Manissy
30126 Tavel.

A Tavel property of 74 acres run by the missionary fathers of the Sainte-Familie. They make a deep-coloured rosé aged in wood for up to 18 months.

Establissement Gabriel Meffre
84190 Gigondas.

A major modern domaine of 1,680 acres in Châteauneuf, Gigondas and the Côtes du Rhône. The Meffre family have 12 Rhône and Provence properties; including Château du Vaudieu, 173 acres of Châteauneuf-du-Pape making a *vin de garde*; the Domaines des Bosquets, Raspail and la Daysse in Gigondas (Bosquet fruitier, Raspail more powerful); the Domaine du Bois des Dames of 250 acres at Violes and the huge and historic Château de Ruth with 285 acres at Ste-Cecile des Vignes. The last two make good fruity Côtes du Rhône red, and the Château de Ruth a light fresh white as well.

A. Ogier & Fils
84700 Sorgues.

The great-grandsons of the founder run this Avignon firm of négociants, dealing in most southern Rhône appellations. They have exclusive rights in 2 Côtes du Rhône estates, Domaine Romarin at Domazan and Château St-Pierre d'Escarvaillac at Caumont, and with Domaine de la Gavotte at Puyloubier, Côtes de Provence. They also market several brands of table wine. Total sales exceed 150,000 cases a year.

Pascal SA
Vacqueyras, 84190 Beaumes de Venise.

A 60-year-old merchant house revitalized by its recent owner and wine maker, Denis Cheron. Pascal own 8 acres of Vacqueyras and buy grapes for a total of 85,000 cases of Vacqueyras, Gigondas, Côtes du Rhône and -Villages, Côtes du Ventoux and Vins de Pays de Vaucluse. Cheron looks for roundly fruity wines with depth and vitality, removing all stalks and fermenting 5–8 days. Good selection and technique make him a quality leader. 50% of production is exported, some under the name Augustin Peyrouse. Cheron also owns the Domaine du Grand Montmirail (q.v.).

Domaine Pelaquié
30290 Laudun.

The grandsons of Joseph Pelaquie, one of the *vigerons* who first promoted the Côtes de Rhône, run a small estate, principally in Laudun with a little Lirac (more to come). Very old vines make it a good example of the region.

Domaine Rabasse-Charavin
Cairanne, 84290 St-Cecile-les-Vignes.

A top producer of Cairanne, Corinne Couturier farms 50 acres to make several wines, including a straight Syrah and the Cuvée d'Estavenas from old vines.

Les Fils de Gabriel Roudil
Le Vieux Moulin, 30126 Tavel.

This family property (since 1870) is run by three brothers, with 150 acres, 112 of them in Tavel with some in Lirac and some in Côtes du Rhône. Some 190,000 cases of Tavel Domaine du Vieux Moulin are their main product. The formula is 60% Grenache, 25% Cinsaut, 10% Picpoul, and 5% Carignan, macerated on the skins for between 12 and 24 hours, fermented dry and bottled at 6 months. Red Lirac has Syrah and Mouvèdre in addition for colour, macerates for 8–10 days and spends 1 year in wood. The same traditional method is used for red Côtes du Rhône. Another label for Roudil's Tavel is Réserve de Carvaillons.

Domaine Louis Rousseau
Les Charmettes, 30290 Laudun.

The Rousseaus have 60 acres in Lirac for red and 10 in Laudun for Côtes du Rhône-Villages red and rosé. Like many growers in the area they settled from Algeria in the early 1960s. Their wine-making is 'traditional', but without barrels. Several wines are named for notable Popes.

Les Fils de Hilarion Roux
Domaine Les Pallières, Gigondas, 84190 Beaumes de Venise.

The family wine in the manner of Châteauneuf-du-Pape since the year of Waterloo. Low yields, long macerating of the bunches, 3 years oak-ageing make tannic wine for patient clients – 80% in France. 60 acres produce 6,500 cases.

Château St-Estève
Uchaux, 84100 Orange.

The Français-Monier family have owned the 130-acre estate for 200 years. Uchaux lies on a sandy ridge north of Orange which gives ripe, warm wines with body and character. From 50% Grenache, 18% each Syrah and Cinsaut and a little Mourvèdre, Roussane and even Viognier. The property produces 7 wines including St-Estève Grande Reserve red *vin de garde*, St-Estève Tradition, a light Friand de St-Estève *en primeur*, a rosé, a Viognier white and a *méthode champenoise* blanc de blancs.

Côtes du Rhône-Villages
The 17 communes entitled to this apellation are: Drôme: Rochegude, Rousset-Les-Vignes, St-Maurice-sur-Eygues, St Pantaléon-Les-Vignes. Vinsobres. Vaucluse: Cairanne, Rasteau, Roaix, Sablet, Séguret, Vacqueyras, Valréas, Visan, Beaumes-de-Venise. Gard: Chusclan, Laudun, St-Gervais.

Rhône prices:
Négociants Paul Jaboulet Ainé quoted the following ex-cellar prices, a bottle, in late 1990 (for the 1989 wines): Côtes du Rhône: Red 17.70, White 18.40; Vacqueyras 21.80; Côtes du Ventoux (Red) 14.70; Crozes Hermitage 25.00; Domaine de Thalabert 29.50; Côte Rotie les Jumelles (Red), 1989 80.00; Cornas 55.40; Gigondas 34.80; Chateauneuf du

Pape les Cèdres 40.90; Muscat de Beaumes de Venise 43.50; St. Joseph 34.50; Hermitage La Chapelle 1000.00

Domaine St-Gayan
Gigondas, 84190 Beaumes de Venise.

The Meffre family (Roger, father, and Jean-Pierre, son) claim to have 600 years of Gigondas *vigneron* forebears. They produce much-appreciated tannic Gigondas up to 14.5 degrees alcohol, reeking (they say) of truffles and crushed fruit, from ancient vines. Also big-scale Côtes du Rhône – Villages in Sablet and Rasteau.

Château St Maurice-L'Ardoise
30290 Laudun.

An ancient estate on the site of a Roman temple of Jupiter, owned by André Valat. 250 acres, principally Côtes du Rhône-Villages with some *vins de pays* and a little Lirac. 18% Syrah gives the wine some body and style.

Château St-Roch
30150 Roquemaure.

The 100-acre Lirac property of Antoine Verda, making good warming red Lirac intended to age in bottle, some 'supple' rosé and a trace of soft white. The top wine is the Cuvée Ancienne Vigverie, which gets an extra year in wood. The same proprietor has started the new Domaine Cantegril-Verda, also at Roquemaure, with 45 acres of Côtes du Rhône red and a little white. The crop is 25% higher than in Lirac and the wine correspondingly lighter, for drinking young.

Domaine Ste-Anne
Les Celettes-St Gervais, 30200 Bagnols sur Cèze.

A 64-acre estate making Côtes du Rhône and -Villages red and white; the reds by *macération carbonique*.

Château de Ségriès
30126 Lirac.

The 50-acre estate is owned by Comte de Regis de Gatimel, whose family inherited it in 1804. He makes a tannic red *vin de garde*, fermenting stalks and all and ageing 2 years in concrete tanks. His rosé is also aged but his white, picked just before ripeness, is bottled as young as possible. Notwithstanding the whites apparently age well in bottle for up to 5 years.

Domaine de la Tour d'Elyssas
26290 Donzère.

Pierre Labeve is a dynamic pioneer of the Coteaux du Tricastin who arrived from the north of France in 1965, bulldozed 2 barren hilltops and planted 360 acres of Greanche (150 acres), Cinsaut (100), Syrah (75) and Carignan. The varieties are vinified separately in an ultramodern gravity-fed system. Production is 100,000 cases a year of 3 main types: Syrah (unblended) aged 2 years in vats, Cru de Meynas, one third Syrah, a *vin de garde*, and Cru de Devoy, largely Grenache but no Syrah, for drinking young.

Domaine de la Tour de Lirac
30150 Roquemaure.

An 80-acre estate developed over the last generation specializing in red Lirac, aged 1 year in tanks and intended to be drunk young and lively. They also produce some light rosé.

Domaine des Coteaux des Travers
Rasteau, 84110 Vaison-la-Romaine.

Robert Cheravin (one of several producers of the same name) makes Rasteaux which pleases tasters and is worth bottle-age.

Château du Trignon
Gigondas, 84190 Beaumes de Venise.

An old (1898) family estate with modern ideas making excellent wine. Charles Roux uses *macération carbonique* to make rich and savoury Gigondas, more fruity and less tannic in youth than the old style, maturing up to, say, 8 years. His 120 acres are divided between Gigondas and Sablet and Rasteau.

Château de Trinquevedel
30126 Tavel.

François Demoulin, with 64 acres, is one of the leading growers of Tavel, with interesting ideas on adapting his methods to the state of the crop, using partly old techniques and partly new (chilling and *macération carbonique*). He believes a little bottle-age improves his Tavel.

Domaine de Verquière
84110 Sablet.

A staunchly traditionalist family property of 120 acres in three 'Villages' – Sablet, Vacqueyras and Rasteau. 70% is Grenache, for both reds and Rasteau VDN. Louis Chamfort still keeps his best Villages reds in oak until he judges them ready – which can be five or six years later.

La Vieille Ferme
84100 Orange.

The négociant brand of the Perrin family of Chateauneuf-du-Pape. They make a fine red Côtes du Ventoux made as a *vin de garde* and a delicate white from high vineyards on the Montagne de Lubéron. Also good value Côtes-du-Rhone.

SOUTHERN RHONE COOPERATIVES

There are more than 60 coops producing Côtes du Rhône and the other wines of the region. A few have gained a reputation equal to that of the best private growers and négociants. These include:

Cairanne
84290 St-Cecile-les-Vignes. Founded 1929. 260 members; 2,950 acres. Réserve des Voconces is their top wine, a solid mouthful that tops 14°.

Chusclan
30200 Bagnols-sur-Cèze. Founded 1939 – 137 members: 1,850 acres producing 200,000 cases of Côtes du Rhône and – Villages (Chusclan). Painstaking methods include vinifying each variety (there are 9) separately by both traditional vatting and *macération carbonique*. M. Rivier, the founder, was very specific about the attributes of his wines: reds 'scented with ripe plums and bay leaves', rosé 'perfumed with acacia and wild strawberries'. The white, merely described as 'young and fruity', is in fact a technical achievement; a well-balanced wine with plenty of flavour. Brand names are Seigneurie de Gicon. Cuvée des Monticaud, Prieuré St-Julien.

La Courtoise
St-Didier, 84210 Pernes-Les-Fontaines. Founded 1924. 350 members; 2,500 acres producing 280,000 cases, of which 95,000 are AC Côtes de Ventoux. More Syrah is being grown to stiffen the previously pale and light reds.

Gigondas
Gigondas, 84190 Beaumes de Venise. Founded 1955. 120 members; 617 acres

producing Gigondas and Côtes-du-Rhône. Three-quarters of the grapes are Grenache; Syrah and Mourvèdre add colour and grip. The wine is bottled after 18 months in wood.

De Orgnac-L'Aven
07150 Vallon-Pont-d'Arc. Founded 1924. 83 members; 1,100 acres producing 29,000 cases, of which half is VDQS Côtes du Vivarais. Syrah, Cinsaut, Grenache and Clairette make light but firm reds, rosés and whites, 'which perfectly reflect our wild and arid hills'. A year in bottle is enough.

Rasteau
84110. Vaison-La-Romaine. Founded 1925. 180 members; 1,850 acres producing sweet *vin doux naturel* (red and white), Côtes du Rhône-Villages, plain Côtes du Rhône and *Vin de Table* Festival du Crutat. By far the biggest producer of Rasteau.

Tavel
30126 Tavel. Founded 1937. 130 members; 1,000 acres producing 83,000 cases. They use the traditional local method of macerating the skin, cold fermentation to avoid tannins, then sell (and drink) as soon as possible.

Union des Vignerons de l'Enclave des Papes
84600 Valreas. Union of 800 growers marketing Côtes du Rhône from 9,000 acres under the Enclave des Papes label.

CLAIRETTE DE DIE

Clairette de Die is like a sorbet between the substantial main dishes of the northern and southern Rhône. The energy of the local cooperative has revived a fading appellation. Clairette de Die is at its best when made sparkling, but one or two traditional growers make a satisfying nutty still wine.

Albert Andrieux
26340 Saillans. Small grower of sparkling and still Clairette de Die, of which his Domaine du Plot is a good example.

Buffardel Frères
26150 Die. An old family firm making an annual 17,000 cases of Clairette de Die, but by the *méthode champenoise*.

Cave Coopérative de Clairette de Die
26150 Die. Three-quarters of the appellation is handled by this 529-member coop producing 273,000 cases of Brut, Tradition and still wines from 2,000 acres. The Brut is a dry sparkling wine of Clairette grapes 'with an aroma of lilac and lavender'. Tradition is a sweet fizz of Muscat de Frontignan. The method involves fermentation in bottle (but, unlike champagne, of the original grape-sugar), then filtering and decanting to another bottle under pressure. Other wines are Gamay red and Aligoté/Chardonnay white, for which they have their own AOC Châtillon en Diois.

CHATEAUNEUF-DU-PAPE

Châteauneuf-du-Pape is much the biggest and most important specific Rhône appellation. If its 7,900 acres of vines produced as plentifully as those of its neighbours there would be almost as much Châteauneuf-du-Pape as Côtes du Rhône-Villages. But small crops are mandatory. Concentration is the very essence of this wine. Its vines grow in what looks like a shingle beach of big, smooth, oval stones that often cover the whole surface of the vineyard. Each vine is an individual low bush.

Where all other French appellations specify one or two, at most four, grape varieties of similar character, the tradition in Châteauneuf-du-Pape is to grow a dozen with widely different characteristics. It is not clear whether this is primarily an insurance policy, or simply accumulated tradition. Some growers assert that each of them, even the coarse or simply neutral ones, adds to the complexity of the wine. New plantations, however, are tending to cut down the number to four or five. The base, always in the majority and sometimes as much as 80 per cent, is Grenache. The other essentials are Cinsaut, Syrah, Mourvèdre, and the white Clairette or Pipoul, or both. Varieties that could be described as optional are (red) Cournoise, Muscardin, Vaccarèse and (white) Piccardan, Roussanne, Terret Noir and Bourboulenc. The white varieites are used in the red wine as well as made into white Châteauneuf-du-Pape on their own.

Grenache and Cinsaut are described as providing strength, 'warmth' and softness; Mourvèdre, Syrah, Muscardin and Vaccarèse as adding structure, colour, 'cut' and refreshment to the flavour, and the ability to live for long enough to develop a bouquet. The white grapes are there for mildness and (optimistically) finesse. Although the legal minimum is 12.5 degrees of alcohol, 13.5 degrees is considered the lowest acceptable by the best growers, who are happy to see 14.5 degrees.

And the result? We have all had great, dull, headachy wines called Châteauneuf-du-Pape. There is no distinct 'varietal' handle by which to grasp either the aroma or the flavour. Commercial examples are usually made to be very warm and 'giving' and slightly fruity. The best estates, however, make *vins de garde* that are quite impenetrable at under five years and difficult under ten. When a bouquet does start to develop it is still elusive. It is rather part of a glowing roast-chestnut warmth about the whole wine. Eventually, in the best examples, latent finesse and the essential sweetness of a great wine will emerge. Much the best I have ever drunk was a 1937, in perfect condition in 1981.

White Châteauneuf-du-Pape, formerly a long-lived wine, rich and elusive, is today more often made for drinking within three years at most.

Château des Fines Roches

CHATEAUNEUF-DU-PAPE PRODUCERS

A. Amouroux
Clos de l'Oratoire, 84230 Châteauneuf-du-Pape.
A well-reputed grower making a total of 8,000 cases from 120 acres, including red and a little white Châteauneuf-du-Pape and a Vin de Pays de Vaucluse with some Cabernet Sauvignon.

Père Anselme
84230 Châteauneuf-du-Pape.
The name recalls a wise old ancestor of the founder of this firm of négociants and wine makers, producing most of the Rhône appellations with a total sale of 170,000 cases a year. Brands include La Fiole du Pape, Marescal Côtes-du-Rhône-Villages and Petit Duc Côtes-du-Rhône; they also own the Mule du Pape restaurant at Châteauneuf and a famous old nougat factory, Arnaud-Soubeyran, at Montelimar. Négociants Jean-Pierre Brotte are part of the same concern. Other ventures include a wine museum visited by 40,000 people a year and experimental winemaking from 20 acres.

Château de Beaucastel
84350 Courthézon.
Brothers Jean-Pierre and Francois, the fourth generation of the Perrin family, make one of the best wines of the region on this big property dating back to the 17th century. Their Châteauneuf vineyard is 173 acres, plus 75 of Côtes du Rhône. All 13 authorized grapes, with relatively high proportions of Syrah and Mourvèdre, a 25 hectolitre a hectare crop, 15-day fermentation in the traditional square stone vats and 2 years' ageing in oak give the wine depth and durability. Organic methods are used in the vineyards. A small amount of delicious white Châteauneuf is made of 80% Roussane and 20% Gre-

nache Blanc. The Côtes du Rhône is called Cru de Coudoulet. See also their Côtes du Ventoux La Vieille Ferme.

Domaine de Beaurenard
84230 Châteauneuf-du-Pape.
Paul Coulon represents the seventh generation on this family property of 75 acres. He also owns 110 acres of Côtes du Rhône at Rasteau. Both are planted with the same mixture of 70% Grenache and 10% each of Syrah, Cinsaut and Mourvèdre. He stresses careful, bunch-by-bunch selection in the vineyard and *cuvaison à l'ancienne* – long, carefully-controlled vatting – in the cellar.

Caves Bessac
84230 Châteauneuf-du-Pape.
A century-old firm of négociants with a good name for traditional Châteauneuf-du-Pape, Tavel, Côtes du Rhône and -Villages. Also Côte Rôtie and Hermitage. Sales are 200,000 cases a year. Huge stocks of Châteauneuf-du-Pape are still kept in barrels.

Domaine Chante Cigale
84230 Châteauneuf-du-Pape.
The name means 'the song of the cicada' – if song is the right word. Noël Sabon with his son-in-law Christian Favier is the third generation to own this 100-acre property, now considered among the 10 best of Châteauneuf. The vineyards are 80% Grenache, 10% Syrah and 5% each of Mourvèdre and Cinsaut – no white grapes and no white wine. Old-style vinification and at least 18 months in cask make serious *vin de garde*.

Jean Deydier
Les Clef d'Or, 84230 Châteauneuf-du-Pape.
One of the smaller of the leading estates with 62 acres; a low yield and 2 years wood-ageing giving *vins de garde*. Also a very successful white in small quantities.

Félicien Diffonty
84230 Châteauneuf-du-Pape.
A 42-acre Châteauneuf family property making strong old-style wine, Cuvée du Vatican, fermented on the skins for up to 25 days. Also Côtes-du-Rhône and white and 'cerise' Vins de Pays du Gard, Mas de Bres, from 36 acres.

Château Fortia
84230 Châteauneuf-du-Pape.
The family estate of the instigator of the system of Appellations Contrôlées, Baron Le Roy de Boiseaumarié, who in 1923 first defined the best vineyard land of the region in terms of the wild plants, thyme and lavender, growing together; an early ecologist. Today the best 7,000 cases from the 70 acres are château bottled; the rest sold in bulk. Methods are traditional, using 75% Grenache and as many old vines as possible. The present owner favours the local Counoise in preference to Syrah. The wine is aged in wood and sold at 3 years, intended for maturing up to 15 years, 10% of the production is white Châteauneuf-du-Pape.

Château de la Gardine
84230 Châteauneuf-du-Pape.
A family property of 250 acres, half of them in Châteauneuf-du-Pape, the remainder in Côtes du Rhône and Villages at Rasteau and Roaix. Both the Châteauneuf (red and white) and Côtes du Rhône-Villages carry the château name. The Brunels aim for a reasonably 'supple and elegant' wine rather than a pugilist, ageing their Châteauneuf 3 years in wood.

Domaine de Mont-Redon
84230 Châteauneuf-du-Pape.
The biggest single vineyard (235 acres) in Châteauneuf, with a long history, bought in 1921 by Henri Plantin and now run by his grandsons M. Abeille and M. Fabre. From its immensely stony ground comes some of the toughest Châteauneuf, macerated for 3 weeks to stiffen its spine, and aged for between 2 and 3 years in 10,000-litre oak barrels. The only change with the times, says Jean Abeille, is in not being able to age the wine for clients in bottle as well – a necessary process they must do themselves. Exactly the same wine is sold in some markets under the following names: Cuvées des Felibres, Vignoble Abeille, Vignoble Fabre and Les Busquières. 87 acres of Côtes du Rhône at Roquemaure have been added to the estate. Mont-Redon is the largest producer of white Châteauneuf.

Société Louis Mousset
84230 Châteauneuf-du-Pape.
One of the biggest Rhône estates, built up by 5 generations of the Mousset family to a total of over 600 acres, 260 in Châteauneuf-du-Pape including the Ch. des Fines Roches (112 acres), Dom. de la Font du Roi (62), Dom. du Clos St-Michel (25) and Dom. du Clos du Roi (62). Four Côtes du Rhône estates are called Ch. du Bois de la Garde, Ch. du Prieuré, Dom. de Tout-Vent and Dom. du Grand Vaucroze. They also have 3 brand names: Cigalière, Les Trois Couronnes and Tourbillon. The headquarters is the Ch. des Fines Roches, one of the great names of the area.

Société du Domaine de Nalys
84230 Châteauneuf-du-Pape.
Estate of 120 acres growing the classic 13 grapes to make one of the fresher examples of Châteauneuf, aged only up to a year in wood before bottling. Also small amounts of white.

Domaine de la Nerthe
84230 Châteauneuf-du-Pape.
One of the great names of Châteauneuf, quoted in the 19th century as a separate and slightly better wine than Châteauneuf itself. The estate today has 145 acres (5 for white wines) with a rather simplified planting (Grenache, Mourvèdre, Cinsaut, Syrah and Clairette). Vinification is traditional; the wine is aged 2 or 3 years in wood.

Clos des Papes
84230 Châteauneuf-du-Pape.
A property in direct descent from father to son for more than 300 years. Paul Avril has 80 acres, 70% Grenache with Syrah, Mourvèdre, Muscardin and Vaccarèse. His aim is power and structure. He is not afraid of tannin and believes Châteauneuf needs years in bottle. 10% of his 9,000-case total is white.

Tavel and Lirac
A similar area to Châteauneuf-du-Pape a few miles west, on the other side of the Rhône, has traditionally been famous for its rosé, made with the same grapes. Tavel has a unique reputation for full-bodied dry rosé, made not by fermenting the wine briefly on its (red) grape skins, as most other rosés are made, but by a period of up to 2 days of maceration before fermentation starts. (The yeasts have to be inhibited by sulphur dioxide, or in modern cellars by cooling.) The wine is then pressed and fermented like white wine. I have never been attracted by this powerful, dry rather orange-pink wine, any more than by similar rosés from Provence. It is regarded, though as one of the classics. Like Racine, it should be re-read from time to time.

Lirac, the northern neighbour to Tavel, has been specializing more recently in red wines, which at their best are very pleasantly fruity and lively, and in other cases strong and dull.

Ventoux and Lubéron
Where the Rhône valley merges with Provence to the east, the appellation Côtes du Ventoux has forged ahead in volume, now far out-producing the united Côtes du Rhône-Villages. Among some very reasonable reds the outstanding wine is that of Jean-Pierre Perrin, brother of the owner of Ch. de Beaucastel. He is also experimenting with a Chardonnay from Lubéron. The Côtes du Lubéron, the hills along the north of the Durance valley (famous throughout France for its asparagus), also makes a substantial contribution to this great source of red wine. Lubéron is still only a VDQS, but its reds (and whites) may appeal more for their relative lightness than some of the more pedestrian efforts of the Rhône. There is some very adequate sparkling white Lubéron.

North of the Lubéron near Manosque, the VDQS Coteaux de Pierrevert is a further extension of these Rhône-style vineyards, making light wine.

Domaine Pierre Quiot
Château Maucoil, 84100 Orange.

Possibly the oldest named estate of Châteauneuf-du-Pape, producing the traditional style of wine on 75 acres (with a second lable, Quiot St-Pierre). Also 35 acres of Gigondas under the name of Pradets and 15 of Côtes du Rhône Patriciens.

Château Rayas
84230 Châteauneuf-du-Pape.

A small but outstanding property often cited as the best of Châteauneuf. The Reynaud family have 38 acres (5 are white grapes), planted with 90% Grenache, the balance Cinsaut and Syrah. They age the red for 2 or 3 years in wood depending on the vintage. The white is outstanding for long ageing. Ch. Fonsalette (Côtes du Rhône) is also made at Rayas.

Les Fils de Joseph Sabon
Clos Mont Olivet, 84230 Châteauneuf-du-Pape.

The 3 sons of Joseph Sabon are the fourth generation to make wine they describe as 'well-structured, highly aromatic and long in the mouth' – traditional Châteauneuf – from 59 acres. Another 20 acres at Boltère (Vaucluse) produces Côtes-du-Rhône.

Caves St-Pierre-Sefivin
84230 Châteauneuf-du-Pape.

A very large family company of proprietors and négociants with a stable of well-known names, including 4 Châteauneufs: St-Pierre, Ch. St-André, Dom. des Pontifs and Dom. Condorcet and the Lirac Ch. de Ségriès. Their bottling company, the Socété des Vins Fins de la Vallée du Rhône, handles an annual 500,000 cases.

Domaine de la Solitude
84230 Châteauneuf-du-Pape.

The Lançon family make their wine by *macération carbonique* – a style of Châteauneuf ready to drink much younger than the traditional tough wine. Their 100 acres are planted in a simplified mixture of Grenache, Cinsaut and Syrah. Also Côtes-du-Rhône from 100 acres at Château des Vallonières, Sabran.

Domaine du Vieux Télégraphe
84370 Bedarrides.

A long-established 120-acre estate taking its name from the old signal tower on the hill. The third and fourth generations of the Brunier family make 5,800 cases of a really conservative Châteauneuf; dark, tannic and unyielding for years. The vines are 80% Grenache, 10% Cinsaut and 5% each of Syrah and Mourvédre. The stony soil, a yield of only 34 hectolitres per hectare and long fermentation of the whole bunches account for the concentration of the wine.

Caves Reflets de Châteauneuf-du-Pape
84230 Châteauneuf-du-Pape.

A collaboration between growers for bottling and distribution. The chief members are: Lucien Brunel, Les Cailloux, Pierre Lancon, La Solitude, Guy Nicolet, Chante Perdrix, Joseph Sabon, Clos du Mont-Olivet.

Université du Vin

The crenellated towers of the ancient château of Suze-La-Rousse house the Rhône's Université du Vin, founded in 1978. The first institution of its kind in the world, it is open to professionals – growers, négocians, restaurateurs – and amateurs.

From October to April, courses are run for growers; for the rest of the year others in the wine business and amateurs study tasting, the whole spectrum of viticulture and wine-making and 'the art and civilization of wine'.

Highly sophisticated laboratories and tasting rooms ('with the calm ambience that allows the necessary concentration') serve the University and the official bodies of the Rhône. The laboratories have the latest electronic equipment for wine, vine and soil analysis. Other amenities are an *oenothèque* and a museum.

Université du Vin, Château de Suze-La-Rousse, 26130 Suze-La-Rousse.

A négociant assesses the crop

OTHER PRODUCERS

Bèrard & Fils
84370 Bédarrides. Merchants and proprietors with 300 acres, including the Domaine Terre Ferme. Locally highly regarded, especially for their fresh white and solid, spicy even massive red.

La Bernardine
The 70-acre property of the négociants Chapoutier (*see* northern Rhône). Big old-style wine.

Théophile Boisson & Fils
Domaine du Père Caboche, 84230 Châteauneuf-du-Pape. An old family of growers including the current president of the Châteauneuf *syndicat*. Their 75 acres are 80% Grenache. The wine is made in stainless steel in the lighter style.

Bosquet des Papes
Maurice Bouron. Traditional wine from 57 acres of very old vines.

Domaine les Cailloux
André Brunel.

Domaine de Cabrières
Louis & Guy Arnaud. 138 acres. Depending on the vintage, the wine here spends between 1 and 5 years in wood before bottling.

Les Cèdres
The excellent brand-name Châteauneuf of Paul Jaboulet (*see* northern Rhône).

Domaine Chante-Perdrix
84230 Châteauneuf-du-Pape. Remy & Guy Nicolet. A 47-acre property to the south of Châteauneuf, not far from the Rhône. Very concentrated high-strength wine which spends 3 years in wood.

Remy Diffonty
Domaine du Haut des Terres Blanches. 84230 Châteauneuf-du-Pape. Owner of some 80 acres, producing fine *vins de garde* by old methods, including 3 years in oak.

Château de la Font du Loup
84350 Courthézon. Owner: J. R. Melia. A small (40-acre) estate with old vines and methods making fine aromatic wine.

Domaine du Grand Tinel
84230 Châteauneuf-du-Pape. A traditionalist estate of 180 acres, the property of M. Elie Jeune, the former mayor of the commune.

Château La Grande Gardiole
84350 Courthézon. The property of André Rey of Gigondas, distributed by Mommessin of Beaujolais.

René Jouffron & Fils
Réserve des Cardinaux, 84230 Châteauneuf-du-Pape. A 40-acre property making wines distinguished for long ageing and eventual complexity.

Domaine Jean Trintignant
85 acres of Châteauneuf, plus Côtes du Rhône. Good red wine in the lighter style and sometimes admirable white.

Château de Vaudieu
84230 Châteauneuf-du-Pape. 180 acres, part of the large Gabriel Meffre properties based at Gigondas. Sound wines from an admirably situated vineyard near Ch. Rayas.

PROVENCE

Until recently it was just as well to approach Provence, as most people do, in an indolent frame of mind with serious judgement suspended. Most of its wine was passable at best; sun-glass rosé with too much alcohol and too little taste. There were a few reds of character, and careful wine makers even made white wine that was almost refreshing, but the quality rarely justified the price. Wines as good could be found in the Rhône, and even in the hills of the Midi, for less money.

Provence depended for too long on its captive audience of holiday makers. It still makes nearly twice as much rosé as red, and only a trickle of white. I have tried, but always failed, to enjoy strong dry rosé made from the non-aromatic grapes of the region, the same Carignan, Cinsaut and Grenache as the Rhône, with an even smaller proportion of Syrah and Mourvèdre to give flavour. There are sometimes aromas of herbs and pines – the heady sunbaked smell of the land. But only recently have better grapes been planted and modern controls implemented. 1977 was the year when Côtes de Provence was promoted from a VDQS to an AOC. For a few estates it was recognition of their real quality. For the majority it was more in anticipation and encouragement of progress to come.

Change is coming, but in pockets, as individual growers capitalize on the California-like climate and the wider availability of classic grape varieties. In Provence, the estate or growers' name is all. Appellations are of little use as a guide to quality.

Côtes de Provence is an alarmingly wide area for an appellation, including the coast from St-Tropez to beyond Toulon to the west, and a great stretch of country inland, north of the Massif des Maures back to Draguignan and the first foothills of the Alps.

Before all this became an AOC, however, there were already four little local appellations where the wine was considered consistently above average.

The biggest and unquestionably the best is Bandol, a ten-mile stretch of coast and its hinterland just west of Toulon. The production is some 200,000 cases, and Bandol red can have a quality that has traditionally been rare in Provence: tannic firmness that makes it a two-year wine at least, lasting without problems up to six or seven years. The law requires it to spend 18 months in cask. The reason is a high proportion (legal minimum 50%) of the 'aromatic' Mourvèdre, which apparently appreciates the heat of rocky terraces. There is also Bandol rosé and white.

Farther west along the coast, almost in the outskirts of Marseille, the fishing port of Cassis is known for its (relatively) lively and aromatic white, for which the bouillabaisse restaurants of Marseille see fit to charge Grand Vin prices.

The wines of the district of Aix-en-Provence, north of Marseille, come under the AOC Coteaux d'Aix-en-Provence. The area was VDQS until 1985. The microscopic enclave of Palette, an appellation area just east of Aix, is dominated by Château Simone (q.v.). Aix-en-Provence includes one of the best red-wine estates in Provence, Château Vignelaure (q.v.). Others, such as the Château de Fonscolombe (q.v.), are probably behind only by the length of time it takes their newly planted Cabernet vines to reach maturity. Coteaux des Baux-en-Provence is another, smaller area which is a sub-region of Coteaux d'Aix-en-Provence.

Behind Nice in the hills at the extreme other end of Provence the 100-acre appellation of Bellet is justified by wine that is considerably better than the generally dismal prevailing standard of its neighbours; the whites are better than the reds. The Côte d'Azur seems to disprove the theory that a sophisticated clientele spurs wine makers to make fine wine.

Some 20 estates in Provence use the title 'cru classé': this dates back to the 1950s and an attempt to raise local quality standards. The term should not be taken too seriously.

PROVENCE PRODUCERS

Jean Bagnis & Fils
83390 Cuers

A family company of growers and négociants with 32 acres (making 6,600 cases) at Château de Crémat in the tiny appellation Bellet above Nice in the hills. Expensive wine but distinctly tastier than their standard Côtes de Provence, the ubiquitous brand L'Estandon.

Domaine la Bernarde
83340 Le Luc

M. and the late Mme Meulnart did a California-style switch from industry to wine-making *par amour du vin* and took over this old 210-acre farm 1,000 feet up north of the Maures. Results include a special Cabernet Sauvignon/Syrah Cuvée, Clos Bernarde St-Germain red – best vintages only, long fermentation, wood-aged then matured in bottle – which has won a run of medals at Mâcon. Also good rosé; Clos la Bernarde, a lighter red, and a white. 16,500 cases.

Commanderie de Peyrassol
83340 Le Luc

The Commanderie was founded by the Templars in 1204 and acquired by the Rigord family in 1890. 160 acres produce 33,000 cases of two ranges: Cuvée Eperon d'Or and Cuvée Marie Estelle from older vines. Both reds have substantial percentages of Cabernet Sauvignon and Syrah, and new oak is used for ageing. Their white wine includes Sémillon.

Domaine de la Croix
83420 La Croix-Valmer

Century-old Cru Classé of 285 acres near Cavalaire-sur-Mer, stressing red *vins de garde* and vinifying special unblended *cuvées* of Cabernet Sauvignon and Mourvèdre sold as such. Production 45,000 cases.

Domaine de Curebeasse
83600 Fréjus

Jean Paquette's 44 acres produce 6,600 cases of Côtes de Provence, half rosé. M. Paquette, a partisan for his region's wines, stresses the contribution of volcanic soil. The whites are especially well thought of.

Mas de la Dame
Les Baux de Provence, 13520 Maussane

Jacques Chatin, son-in-law of estate founder Robert Faye, produces one of the best wines from les Baux from 134 acres.

Domaine des Féraud
83550 Vidauban

Owned by the Laudon-Rival family for 3 generations. Paul Rival, the former owner of Château Guiraud, Sauternes, ran the property for 25 years until 1955 then handed over to his nephew Bernard Laudon, who is still in charge. 100 acres of AOC Côtes de Provence. Médoc-inspired Cabernet Sauvignon, Syrah and Grenache red, whites from Sémillon, also rosé. Production 14,700 cases.

Château de Fonscolombe
13610 Le-Puy-Ste-Réparade

The Marquis de Saporta has two Coteaux d'Aix AOC properties north of Aix – this (410 acres) and the Domaine de la Crémade (250 acres). Both have been in his family since 1720. A noble Renaissance château now notable for upgrading local wine quality, especially in whites. Modern techniques for whites and rosés and traditional oak vinification for reds. The Cuvée Spéciale red has 15–20% Cabernet.

Bernard Gavoty
83340 Le Luc

A grouping of 3 domaines – Domaine du Grand Campdumy, proprietor P. Gavoty (136 acres), Domaine du Petit Campdumy, proprietor B. Gavoty (136 acres), and Domaine des Pomples, proprietor J. Brusse (49 acres). Half the reds are *macération carbonique*, the rest traditional. Syrah and Cabernet spice the Mourvèdre and Grenache.

Château Grand'Boise
13530 Trets

A handsome and ambitious estate of 105 acres around a 17th-century château, belong to the Gruy family. The oak-aged red has won gold medals at the Mâcon fair.

Château Minuty
Gassin, 83990 St-Tropez

Gabriel Farnet and Etienne Mattan run this property near St-Tropez which has a fine house and a serious reputation for its oak-aged red. Production 13,000 cases from 100 acres. Second label: Domaines Farnet.

Clos Mireille
83250 La Londe-Les-Maures

123-acre coastal vineyard, owned by Ott (q.v.) of Cru Classé status producing 16,500 cases of full-flavoured blanc de blancs from Sémillon and Ugni Blanc.

Moulin des Costes
83740 La Cadière d'Azur

The brothers Bunan, Paul and Pierre, have 74 acres of steep vineyards at La Cadière and at nearby Le Castellet (Mas de la Rouvière). Most is rosé AOC Bandol, but some excellent long-lived red is made. Production 10,000 cases.

Domaines Ott
06601 Antibes

Founded 1896 by a native of Alsace, now the owner of 3 properties producing top-quality Provence wines by traditional, organic methods: limited yield, no sulphur, oak ageing. It has also introduced new grape varieties to the area. 25% of production exported to 50 countries. *See* Clos Mireille, Château Romasson, Château de Selle.

Domaine des Planes
83520 Roquebrune-sur-Argens

Swiss Christopher Rieder, who with his oenologist wife Ilse farms 62 Côtes de Provence acres in the Argens valley, is a graduate of both Geisenheim and Montpellier and owns vineyards in Germany and Switzerland. 12,500 cases include unblended Muscat, Grenache, Mourvèdre and Cabernet Sauvignon wines, plus AOC Côtes de Provence red, white and rosé. The Mourvèdre is a conspicuous success.

Les Maitres Vignerons de la Presqu'ile de St-Tropez
Gassin, 83990 St-Tropez

This semicoop choose *cuvées* made by member producers, including 12 sizeable estates, bottles the wine and markets it. Production 225,000 cases. Uses brands Ch. de Pampelonne and St-Roch les Vignes, plus Cuvée de Chasseur and Carte Noir for the top reds.

Château Romasson
Le Castellet, 83150 Bandol

Old property of 123 acres now belonging to Ott (q.v.) producing 16,500 cases of white, red and 3 rosés.

Domaine de St-André de Figuière
83250 La Londe-Les-Maures

Father and son André and André-Daniel Connesson farm 40 acres between St-Tropez and Toulon. New underground cellars produce 7,000 cases of red and rosé. Biological cultivation and careful vinification have earned a run of gold medals at Mâcon.

Château de Selle
Taradeau, 83460 Les Arcs

Owners: Domaines Ott (q.v.) 100 acres planted with Sémillon, Ugni Blanc, Cabernet Sauvignon, Cinsaut and Grenache. 13,500 cases of Côtes de Provence red, white and rosé, rated Cru Classé. The Cuvée Spéciale red is worth attention.

Château Simone
Palette, 13100 Aix-en-Provence

One of two properties in the tiny AOC Palette. 33 acres provide local restaurants with a very satisfactory speciality: wines that really taste of the herbs and pines of the countryside. The red ages well; the white could be considered an acquired taste. Owner: René Rougier.

Domaine Tempier
Le Plan du Castellet, 83330 Le Beausset

Lucien Peyraud and his 2 sons are the staunchest champions of Bandol, making remarkably flavoury and long-lived red and rosé from 62 acres. The red (two thirds of production) is 60% Mourvèdre, the rest Grenache, Cinsaut and a little Carignan from very old vines. It is aged 2 years in oak.

Terres-Blanche
13210 St-Rémy-de-Provence

Quality red, white and rosé by M. Noël Michelin from a leading les Baux AOC estate with 111 acres.

Domaine de Trevallon
13150 St-Etienne-du-Grés

Half Cabernet Sauvignon, half Syrah, this 40-acre domaine is only 12 years old yet already has a name for the best wine in the les Baux appellation. M. Eloi Durrbach, a Parisian, plans further planting. A white wine may follow.

Château Vannières
83740 La Cadière d'Azur

A leading Bandol producer on an estate of 67 acres dating back to 1532. Besides excellent Bandol, the total production of 12,500 cases includes Côtes de Provence red, rosé and white. 40% is exported.

Château Vignelaure
83560 Rians

The first estate to demonstrate to the world that Provence could produce very good wines of more than local interest. Georges Brunet had already restored Château La Lagune in the Médoc when he came here in the 1960s and planted Cabernet Sauvignon, being the local vines. The 136 acres make wine in a class above most other wines of Provence or farther afield. The wine spends two years in cask and can age for a decade. Production is about 13,000 cases.

OTHER PRODUCERS

Domaine du Bagnol
Cassis. Mme Lefèvre's small estate produces good whites and an excellent rosé.

Domaine de la Bastide Neuve
Le Cannet des Maures, 83340 Le Luc. René Brochier makes his reds the old-fashioned way – *pas de ciment* – and ages them in small acacia casks. 4,100 cases from 30 acres near Le Luc, including a pure Grenache red Pavillon Rouge.

Château de Beaulieu
13840 Rognes. A large (740-acre) estate in the Coteaux d'Aix-en-Provence AOC region. Reds contain 20% Cabernet Sauvignon, whites are half Sauvignon Blanc. Vinification in its new cellars is traditional. The proprietors, R. Touzet & Fils, produce 125,000 cases.

Château de Bellet
St Romain de Bellet, 06200 Nice. Mme Rose de Charnacé's 25-acre property is one of only two sizeable ones in the tiny AOC Bellet. The other is Ch. de Crémat (see Bagnis).

Mas Calendal
13260 Cassis. Jean-Jacques Bodin-Bontoux's property produces AOC Cassis rosé and white. A local pioneer of domaine bottling.

Château Clarettes
83460 Les Arcs. Old property with 30 acres in production and more, including Cabernet Sauvignon, being planted. Red *vin de garde*, also AOC white and rosé and Dom. de Fantroussière *vin de table*.

Domaine de Clastron
83920 La Motte. A new (1980) start for a large old farm in the Argens valley making Côtes de Provence of all 3 colours and red and rosé Vin de Pays du

Var. Traditional varieties plus Cabernet Sauvignon. Cool fermentation whites and rosés, traditional reds.

Château de Gairoird
83390 Cuers. Philippe Deydier de Pierrefeu makes 6,500 cases, mostly red, some rosé, from 74 acres northeast of Toulon, using modern methods. Other label: Domaine St-Jean. The rosé leads his exports, especially to the US.

Château La Gordonne
Pierrefeu du Var, 83390 Cuers. A 284-acre estate owned by Domaines Viticoles des Salins du Rhône (q.v. Bouches du Rhône) producing red, white and rosé Côtes de Provence from shale soil on the Maures foothills. Cabernet Sauvignon grown is 77,000 cases.

Domaine de la Grande Lauzade
13400 Aubagne. Jean-François Brando makes 9,000 cases of traditional-style red (stressing Syrah) and rosé from 52 acres near Le Luc.

Domaine de la Jeanette
83400 Hyères. The Moutte family make classic reds from 15 acres.

Château de Mentone
83510 Lorgues. Traditional property west of Draguignan, 150 years in Mme Perrot de Gasquet's family. Côtes de Provence from 74 acres. Total production 2,900 cases.

Château Montaud
Pierrefeu du Var, 83390 Cuers. Family company (Vignobles François Ravel) with 1,000 acres AOC Côtes de Provence and 150 Vin de Pays des Maures inland from Hyères. Wines include an unblended Cabernet Sauvignon. Production 160,000 cases AOC, 40,000 *vin de pays*. Other labels: Ch. de Guiranne, Ch. Garamache.

Domaine de Nestuby
Cares, 83570 Cotignac. Jean Roubaud's 100 acres in the upper Argens valley yield up to 33,000 cases of well-built white and red Côtes de Provence.

Pradel
06270 Villeneuve Loubet. Merchant dealing in Côtes de Provence, Bellet and Bandol wines. Annual production 110,000 cases, 75% exported.

Domaine Christianne Rabiega
83300 Draguignan. 45-acre property. Traditional methods produce medal-winning Côtes de Provence.

Domaine Richeaume
13114 Puyloubier. The German proprietor, M. Hoesch, ages his Cabernet-based reds in oak for 2 years. 3,300 cases from 54 organically farmed acres on the slopes of Mt. St-Victoire, east of Aix-en-Provence.

Domaine de Rimauresq
83790 Pignans. A family property in the Maures of 64 acres, rated Cru Classé. Hubert Isnard began bottling the wine

in 1981 after a 20 year gap. He keeps the wine in *foudres* for up to three years.

Establissements Bernard Camp Romain
83550 Vidauban. Leading négociant founded in 1910, today doing worldwide business in Provence wines, such as 'Bouquet de Provence'. Sales 290,000 cases.

Domaine du Château du Rouet
83490 Le Muy. Bernard Savatien's 30,000-case production from 148 acres in the Argens valley comprises Côtes de Provence of all colours and Vin Mousseux Le Rouet made by both *cuve close* and *méthode champenoise*.

Domaine de St-Antoine
83990 St-Tropez. 3,000 cases of red and rosé from 17 acres of very old vines.

Clos Ste-Magdelaine
13260 Cassis. Proprietor François Sack has 25 acres of vines right on the Mediterranean producing 4,200 cases of classic white Cassis and 25 rosé.

Château St-Martin
Taradeau, 83460 Les Arcs. A handsome old house with deep cellars, in the Rohnan Chagbot family since the 17th century. The proprietor, Comtesse de Gasquet, makes 13,000 cases of Côtes de Provence Cru Classé from 99 acres.

Domaine de la Tour
13600 La Ciotat. Traditional 37-acre property making 8,300 cases of Côtes de Provence red, rosé and blanc de blancs (the white is the best).

Domaine de la Tour Campanets
13610 Le Puy Ste-Reparade. A newly created 65-acre vineyard in the region north of Aix. Marcel Laffourges has built a gravity-fed tower *cuverie* that does away with pumps, which he feels injure the wine. 11,500 cases.

Les Vins Breban
83170 Brignoles. Négociants and large-scale makers of *cuve close* sparkling wine, also Côtes de Provence, Domaine de Paris; and Coteaux Varois, Domaine de Fontlade and Domaine de Merlançon.

CAVES COOPERATIVES

Vinicole l'Ancienne
83490 Le Muy. Côtes du Provence and Vin de Pays du Var, all colours, from a coop founded in 1913. 139,000 cases.

Vins de Bandol
Moulin de la Roque. 83740 La Cadière-d'Azur. Founded 1950. 183 members with 608 acres of AOC Bandol red, white and rosé. Production 102,000 cases. This 'serious' coop competes with Bandol's private estates, producing quality wines at sensible prices.

De Pierrefeu-du-Var
83390 Cuers. Founded 1922, 284 members farming 2,129 acres, production of AOC wines: 341,000

cases, producing AOC Côtes de Provence and *vins de pays*.

Les Vignerons Provençaux
Château de Beaulieu, 13840 Rognes. A 'SICA' uniting a growers' coop, the Union des Cooperatives Vinicoles des Bouches du Rhône, the Château de Beaulieu (q.v.), and a distributor, Touzet. produces Côtes de Provence, Coteaux d'Aix-en-Provence, *vins de pays* Bouches-du-Rhône and 'Perlaire' *vin de table*.

La Vidaubannaise
83550 Vidauban. 455 members farm 2,700 acres of AOC Côtes de Provence 3,446 and *vins de pays* in the Argens valley. Production 728,000 cases.

THE MIDI

The arc of country from the Spanish border to the mouth of the Rhône may well be France's oldest vineyard. It is certainly its biggest. Uncountable quantities of unwanted wine are pumped from its plains to the despair of politicians all over Europe. Until recently there was not a great deal more to say. Traditions of better wine-growing persisted in the hills, but at such economic disadvantage that there seemed little future for them. Such traditions are being grafted onto new techniques to produce – at last – some memorable Midi wines. Interest and investment from Australia has made the locals take notice.

There was no demand and no premium for extra effort until the 1960s, when educated wine makers and merchants began to realize that it was only the grapes that were wrong: the soils and climates of hundreds of hill villages have enormous potential. The penny dropped at the same time as California rose from its slumber. In the Midi, low morale, bureaucracy, peasant conservatism, typically complicated land ownership have all been brakes on progress. Otherwise there would by now be famous Cabernets from the Corbières. If California can do it, why not the South of France? But the French way is to move cautiously along established lines. To improve wines, not to change them.

Upgrading started with the wine-making process. The introduction of *macération carbonique* was the vital first step. It extracted from dull grapes juicy flavours that nobody knew were there. The process is now a long way down the road, and a handsome list has begun to emerge of properties and cooperatives with good wine to offer, and better on the way as they hasten to replant with the 'aromatic' grapes that the public want.

The Midi of quality wine divides into four distinct regions. Following the right-hand curve of the coast north from the Spanish border, they are the Roussillon in the Pyrenean foothills, most famous for sweet apéritif and dessert wines; the Corbières, red-wine country; the smaller Minervois in the southernmost foothills of the Cevennes, also best known for red wine; and the scattered Coteaux du Languedoc, producing decent red, white and rosé as islands in an ocean of *vin ordinaire*.

Precisely what constitutes a quality area and which are the 'right' grapes for it is studied here with as much Gallic precision as on the slopes of Beaune. It is not long since VDQS was the senior rank in these parts. Now many areas have been promoted to AOC (and others are about to matriculate). More detailed gradings will be needed, by which some areas will be '*villages*' or '*supérieurs*'. Layer upon layer of legislation is the French way.

This is also the country of the *vins de pays*. Pages 230–234 give details of the innumerable 'country wine' districts. But to sell your wine as a *vin de pays* is also an interesting alternative to growers who find the panoply of appellation too oppressive. There is a danger of the situation arising which Italy already knows, where the bright pioneer believes (and rightly) that his wine is more important than its label. Some of the best wines of the Midi are sold as *vins de pays* because Cabernet or Merlot is not cricket under the existing rules.

In most areas, cooperative cellars dominate. They vary widely in size, sophistication and quality. The best produce wine as good as the best growers. The coop ranking system used in this book is explained on page 211.

ROUSSILLON

Of all the endless vineyards of the Midi, the Roussillon is most firmly planted in Frenchmen's minds as a place of promise. It has the prestige of an ancient and unique product, its *vin doux naturel*, practically unknown outside France but so proud of its origins that it looks on port (an approximate equivalent) as an imposter.

Its sheltered seaside hills around Perpignan and inland up the valleys of the Agly and the Tet also make some formidable red wines; the biggest and most highly coloured of the many based on the

Carignan around the coast. The 'Côtes du Roussillon' and their superior 'Villages' (the northern third) were promoted to full *appellation contrôlée* status in 1977. The best examples, stiffened with superior 'aromatic' grapes, have some of the structure of, for example, Châteauneuf-du-Pape, though with more roundness and a softer texture. Many are best young when their fruit flavour is at its peak, but more and more growers are deliberately ageing in oak and sometimes in bottle too, to add complexity to sheer beef. Better grapes are making headway: Syrah and Mouvèdre, taken together, make up 20% of the vineyard.

One small red-wine area at the seaside resort of Collioure on the Spanish border has had its own appellation since 1949 for a singular concentrated wine in which Carignan plays little part, a blend principally of Mourvèdre and Grenache Noir with intense flavours unlike anything else north of the Spanish border. Two other villages 20 miles inland from Perpignan, Caramany and Latour-de-France, acquired their own appellations in 1977 but as a part of Côtes du Roussillon Villages. The activities of the extremely modern cooperative at Montalba-Le-Château in the same 'Villages' zone between the Agly and Tet valleys are creating more and more interest in this area.

The vins doux naturels apparently owe their origin to the revered figure of Arnaldo da Villanova, the thirteenth-century sage and doctor of Montpellier,

who introduced the still from Moorish Spain. It was he who first added eau de vie to naturally very strong wine to stop the fermentation and maintain a high degree of natural sugar – hence the term 'doux naturel'. But whereas in port the eau de vie represents a quarter of the volume and more than half the alcoholic strength, in vins doux naturels it is limited to ten per cent of the volume, while the natural strength of the wine has by law to reach no less than 15 degrees. It is not for a foreigner, with the privilege of an education in port, to hold forth on the qualities of VDNs. Aged, they acquire an oxidized flavour known by the Spanish term rancio. A few producers age them in 30-litre pear-shaped glass jars known as bonbonnes (from the Spanish bombonas). Vin doux naturel is made in three styles; the best of which is solely from Muscat grapes and called Muscat de Rivesaltes. There is a major attempt to promote this abroad.

ROUSSILLON PRODUCERS

Mas Amiel
664060 Maury. Owner: M. Dupuy. Wine consultant: M. Mayol. Produces vintage VDN using traditional methods for sale at 6 or, best of all, 15 years old. 345 acres; 35,000 cases of Maury from Grenache Noir.

Paul Baillo
66300 Thuir. Major replanting and macération carbonique have improved this property. 123 acres; 20,000 cases of Muscat de Rivesaltes, Rivesaltes and Côtes du Roussillon.

Domaine de Caladroy
Belesta, 66720 Latour-de-France. Owner: Arnold Bobo. 296 acres; 30,000 cases of Muscat de Rivesaltes, Rivesaltes and Côtes du Roussillon.

Domaine de Canterrane
Trouillas, 66300 Thuir. Owner: Maurice Conté. One of the finest estates in Roussillon, with stock of more than 1m. bottles. Vintages back to 1976 are very impressive. 395 acres; 80,000 cases of Rivesaltes. Muscat de Rivesaltes and Côtes du Roussillon.

Château Cap de Fouste
Villeneuve de la Raho, 66200 Elne. Bought in 1979 by the local growers' mutualité agricole and extensively replanted to good effect. 148 acres; 20,000 cases of Côtes du Roussillon, using the name St-Galderic for their best reds.

Cazès Frères
66600 Rivesaltes. Modernized and replanted with Grenache, Syrah and Mouvèdre and Malvoisie. Macération carbonique, oak-ageing and bottle-ageing in air-conditioned cellars. 370 acres; 27,500 cases of Rivesaltes, Muscat de Rivesaltes, Côtes du Roussillon, Côtes

du Roussillon Villages and vin nouveau. Vin de pays accounts for two thirds of their production; the best wine being Le Canon du Maréchal.

Mas Chichet
Chemin de Charlemagne, 66200 Elne. Owner: Paul Chichet. A pioneer with Cabernet and Merlot in assoiciation with Grenache and Syrah – and also remarkable pure Cabernet aged in oak. 74 acres; 15,500 cases of Vin de Pays. Catalan red and rosé.

Château de Corneilla
66200 Corneilla-del-Vercol. Owner: M. Philippe Jonquéres d'Oriola. Wine consultant: M. Mayol. 148 acres producing AOC red. Grape varieties are Carignan, Grenaché Noir, Merlot, Cabernet Sauvignon and Syrah. The property was built in 1150 and the Jonquères d'Oriola family have been there since 1485.

Mas de la Dona
66310 Estagel. Owner: Jacques Baissas. 185 acres; 8,500 cases of Côtes du Roussillon Villages from a splendid schist vineyard.

Château de l'Esparrou
Canet-Plage, St-Nazaire, 66140 Canet. Owner: Jean-Louis Rendu. Replanted with stress on Mourvèdre and Syrah, making excellent Côtes du Roussillon by macération carbonique and barrel-ageing. 247 acres; 60,000 cases of Rivesaltes, Muscat de Rivesaltes, Côtes du Roussillon and vins de pays.

Château de Jau
Cases de Péné 66600 Rivesaltes. Wine maker: M. Robert Dontres. Improving vines and macération carbonique make some of the best Côtes du Roussillon on this 500-acre estate. Also outstanding

Muscat and good whites of Malvoisie and Macabeu. Grape var: Syrah, Mourvèdre, Grenache Noir and Carignan.

Jaubert and Noury
St-Jean Lasseille, 66300 Thuir. Old Carignan vineyards replanted with Syrah and Mourvèdre, and Malvoisie for white, which are flourishing in the sea wind. Good Côtes du Roussillon, Château de Planères, also light vin nouveau, by macération carbonique. 173 acres; 38,500 cases of Rivesaltes, Muscat de Rivesaltes, Côtes du Roussillon.

Domaine du Mas Blanc
66650 Banyuls-sur-Mer. Owners: Dr. André and M. Jean-Michel Parse. The leading producer of AOC Collioure. 10 acres of schist: 40% Mourvèdre, 40% Syrah, 20% Grenache. Long fermentation and 2 years in wood give remarkable wine. 25 acres of Banyuls VDN (90% Grenache Noir, 10% Carignan) aged either in wood or in bottle.

Le Moulin
66330 Cabestany. Owner: Vidal Rossines. An old estate with a fine reputation, particularly for aged Banyuls. 118 acres; 26,500 cases of Rivesaltes, Muscat de Rivesaltes, Banyuls and Côtes du Roussillon.

Mas Péchot; Mas Balande
66600 Rivesaltes; 66000 Perpignan. Owner: Henri Lacassagne. Mas Péchot is one of the best vineyards of Muscat 'petits grains' in the region. 370 acres; 66,500 cases of Muscat de Rivesaltes and Côtes du Roussillon Villages.

Mas Rancoure
Laroque-des-Albères, 66740 St-Genis-des-Fontaines. Owner: Dr. Perdineille.

A small (20-acre) red wine property producing a dramatic Cuvée Vincent.

Château de Rey
St-Nazaire, 66140 Canet. Owner: Mme Georges Sisqueille, 247 acres; 30,000 cases of Muscat de Rivesaltes, Rivesaltes and Côtes du Roussillon.

Domaine de Roquebrune
St-Nazaire, 66140 Canet. Owner Marcellin Casenobe cherishes his old Carignan vines. Very sound *macération carbonique* reds. 64 acres; 16,500 cases of Rivesaltes and Côtes du Roussillon.

Domaine du Mas Rous
66740 Montesquieu. Owner: José Pujol. 124 acres. 20,000 cases of well-made Côtes du Roussillon, Rivesaltes, Muscat de Riversaltes and *vin de pays*.

Domaine St-Luc
Passa Llauro Torderes, 66300 Thuir. Owner: M. Talut. 100 acres; 15,000 cases of Rivesaltes and Côtes du Roussillon.

Domaine de Sau
66300 Thuir. Owner: Albert Passama. 222 acres; 50,000 cases of Côtes du Roussillon and *vins de pays*.

Tresserre
66300 Thuir. Owner: M. Vaquer. Well-made red, rosé and white are fermented long and cold; reds are aged in bottle up to 6 years before being released. 86 acres; 12,000 cases of *vin de table* rosé, red and white.

Château de Villeclare
Palau del Vidre, 66700 Argeles-sur-Mer. Owners: Héritiers Jonquères d'Oriola. 520 acres; 40,000 cases of Côtes du Roussillon.

CAVES COOPERATIVES

L'Agly
66600 Rivesaltes. Rating: 13. Founded 1942. 103 members; 785 acres producing 46,600 cases of AOC Côtes du Roussillon and Villages, Rivesaltes Doré and Muscat de Rivesaltes; 53,900 cases *vins de table*.

Baixas
66390 Baixas. Rating 13. Founded 1923. 450 members; 26,000 acres producing 454,000 cases of AOC Rivesaltes; Muscat de Rivesaltes; Côtes du Roussillon; Côtes du Roussillon Villages; plus 416,800 cases Vin de Pays Côtes Catalanes and *vins de table*. Cuvée Dom Brial is their top Côtes du Roussillon.

Banyuls 'L'Etoile'
66650 Banyuls-sur-Mer. Rating: 12. Founded 1921. 60 members; 420 acres producing 36,500 cases of AOC Banyuls, Banyuls Grand Cru and Collioure; plus 300 cases of *vins de table*.

Caramany
66720 Latour-de-France. Rating: 13. Founded 1925. 106 members; 800 acres producing 109,600 cases of AOC Côtes du Roussillon Villages Caramany red and Côtes du Roussillon red, plus 55,200 cases *vins de pays* and *vins de table*.

Cellier des Capitelles Cassagnes
Cassagnes, 66720 Latour-de-France. Rating: 12. Founded 1924. 81 members; 988 acres producing 96,000 cases of AOC Côtes du Roussillon Villages, Rivesaltes and Muscat, plus 87,300 cases Vin de Pays Val d'Agly, Pyrénées-Orientales and *vins de table*.

Les Vignerons Catalans
66011 Perpignan. A thriving 'union' with wines from Château Cap de Fouste, Villeneuve, and other properties. their 'Taichat' brand is reliable for whites and rosés.

Lesquerde
66220 Lésquerde. Rating: 13. Founded 1923. 72 members, 1,040 acres producing 86,500 cases of AOC Rivesaltes, Côtes du Roussillon and Villages, plus 87,200 cases *vins de table*.

Les Vignerons de Maury
66460 Maury. Rating: 14. Founded 1910. 350 members; 4,199 acres producing 455,500 cases of AOC Maury red, Côtes du Roussillon and Villages, plus 133,000 cases *vins de table*.

Montalba-Le-Château
66130 L'Ile-sur-Tet. Rating: 10. Founded 1924. 86 members; producing 122,100 cases of AOC Côtes du Roussillon red plus *vins de pays*.

Montner
66720 Latour-de-France. Rating: 14. Founded 1919. 107 members; 1,111 acres producing 92,300 cases of Côtes du Roussillon Villages, Rivesaltes red and white, Muscat de Rivesaltes white, plus 109,300 cases Vin de Pays Val d'Agly and *vins de table*.

Pezilla-La-Rivière, 66370 Pezilla-La-Rivière 475 members, 1,890 acres. Their 'Cuvée Blanes' white has been well received.

Planezes
66720 Latour-de-France. Rating: 12. Founded 1923. 41 members: 450 acres producing 86,300 cases of AOC Côtes du Roussillon and Villages red and Rivesaltes, plus *vins de table*.

Rasiguères
66720 Rasiguères. Rating: 13. Founded 1919. 81 members 790 acres producing 137,600 cases of AOC Rivesaltes; Muscat de Rivesaltes; Côtes du Roussillon Villages red, plus *vins de table*.

Tarerach
Tarerach, 66320 Vinca. Rating: 12. Founded 1928. 18 members; 400 acres producing 20,000 cases of AOC Côtes du Roussillon red plus 61,100 cases Vin de Pays Coteaux du Fenouillèdes and *vins de table*.

Tautavel 'Les Maîtres Vignerons'
66720 Tautavel. Rating: 13. Founded 1927. 189 members producing 155,100 cases of AOC Rivesaltes; Muscat de Rivesaltes; Côtes du Roussillon and Villages red: plus 67,200 cases Vin de Pays Côtes Catalanes and *vin de table*.

Terrats
66300 Terrates. Rating: 13. Founded 1932. 150 members; 1,867 acres producing 182,000 cases of AOC Muscat de Rivesaltes, Rivesaltes and Côtes du Roussillon red and white, plus 244,200 cases Vin de Pays Catalan and *vins de table*.

Terroir de Cerbère
66290 Cerbère. Rating: 12. Founded 1931. 100 members; 203 acres producing 15,800 cases of AOC Banyuls.

OTHER COOPERATIVES

'Aglya', 66310 Estagel
Bages, 66670 Bages
Banyuls-dels-Aspres, 66300 Thuir
Belesta, 66720 Latour-de-France
Le Boulou, 66160 Le Boulou
'La Cabestanyenca', 66330 Cabestany
Elne, 66200 Elne
Feilluns, 66220 St-Paul-de-Fenouillet
Fourques, 66300 Fourques
Lamsac, 66720 Latour-de-France

Cooperatives
In most cases, the cooperative cellars listed have been selected on a system rating them with up to 15 points; five each for quality of terrain, grape varieties planted and wine-making technique. Comparison of the ratings of different areas shows that coops in some zones, such as Roussillon, get consistently higher scores than others, indicating environmental advantages.

As the foundation dates show, most of the cooperatives were started between the wars as a response to depressed wine prices.

Collioure
From 125 acres of rocky vineyard comes a mere 22,000 cases of this AOC. Top producers include the Banyuls Coop, using the name Guy de Berlande; Les Celliers du Tete-Vin of Perpignan, Domaine du Mas Blanc and the Domaine de la Rectorie.

CORBIERES

Justice has been slow in coming to the Corbières, until overdue promotion in 1985 the biggest VDQS area in France, now *appellation contrôlée*. It is a huge region, stretching from Narbonne inland almost to Carcassonne and the same distance south to the borders of the Roussillon. It rises and rolls in parched hills of pale limestone suddenly embroidered in bold patterns with the green stitches of vines. The neutral red Carignan has long been dominant but must not now exceed 60% of the blend. Syrah, Mourvèdre and Grenache are blended with it.

A good site, restraint in cropping and careful wine-making made solid enough wines, but with little flavour and no future. Improvements are taking the form of wine-making with *macération*

carbonique, to coax at least an illusion of fruitiness from the grapes, and more radically replanting with 'aromatic' (i.e. not neutral) varieties.

There are some big properties as well as the thousands of growers who contribute to the cooperatives. Two areas in the southeast corner of Corbières, largely coop country, have long enjoyed the appellation Fitou for their reds, on the grounds that they are more age-worthy than the rest. Corbières Superieurs is an AOC for 39 villages where the yield must be held down to 40 hl/ha. The following list describes the best properties, district by district, together with some of the promising ones: names to look out for in the future.

The total production of the Corbières averages 6.7 m. cases.

CORBIERES PRODUCERS

Château Aiguilloux
M. & F. Lemarie, 11200 Thezan des Corbieres. François Lemarié runs this 81 acre estate, producing 6,600 cases of structured, tannic wine.

Château la Baronne.
Dr. André Liguière, 11700 Fontcouverte. Carignan, Grenache and small amounts of Syrah and Mourvèdre are hand-picked for *macération carbonique* in this vineyard outside the village of Fontcouverte. 74 acres of Corbières, 37 of *vin de pays*. Château des Lanes is the export label.

Château de Beauregard
Simone Mirouse, 11200 Bizanet. High-quality Syrah rosé – one of the top Corbières properties. Also a Cabernet Sauvignon *vin de pays*. 107 acres; 28,500 cases.

Château Le Bouis
Pierre Clement, 11430 Gruissan. Well-made medal-winning rosés and white wine. 89 acres; 17,500 cases.

Château de Bouquignan
J. B. Benet. Harsh, strong soil gives concentrated and aromatic wines even from the commoner grapes. 66.5 acres; 16,500 cases.

Bringuier
Coustouge, 11200 Boutenac. A small property on excellent soil that makes good wine even of the dominant Carignan. 39.5 acres; 13,500 cases.

Château de Caraguilhes
M. Faivre, 11220 St Laurent de la Cabrerisse. 150 acres producing 9,000 cases of dark, warming *macération carbonique* wine from an organic vineyard.

Cassignol
11360 Villeneuve-les-Corbières. One of

the few private producers of AOC Fitou. Recent replanting. 112 acres; 16,500 cases.

Domaine des Amouries
Alain Castex, 11330 Davejean. Bought by the present owner in 1981, this estate produces floral, fruity elegant wines combining *macération carbonique* and traditional techniques.

Château du Grand Caumont
Mme Rigal, 11200 Lezignan Corbières. 27 acres producing 5,000 cases a year. This old estate close to the autoroute near the river Orbieu is being energetically modernized.

Château de Comigne
La Grappe d'Alaric, 11700 Comigne. Typical Corbières property, with well developed wines. 1,600 cases a year.

Château Etang des Colombes
H. Gualco, 11200 Lezignan Corbières. The average age of the vines here is 90 years. M. Gualco produces a variety of wines with a total production of 3,000 cases. Pretty painted bottles.

Domaine les Fenals
Mme Roustan, 11510 Fitou. 62 acres producing Fitou, Corbières, Muscat de Rivesaltes and *vin de pays* under the hand of Andrée Roustan-Fontanel.

Domaine de Fontsainte
Yves Laboucarie, 11200 Boutenac. Some of the best land in the Corbières and very good wine-making. Maceration and wood-ageing for splendid reds, and a very pale rosé *gris de gris*. 104 acres; 41,000 cases.

Mlle Huc
11200 Fabrezan. A big well-situated estate with a high proportion of 'aromatic' varieties, capable of making very good wines. 197 acres; 16,500 cases.

Château de Lastours
J.M. Lignieres, 11490 Portel des Corbières. 40 acres producing 5,000 cases a year. This château is a centre for the disabled and employs 60 of them. The Cuvées Simone Descamps and Arnaud de Berre are serious, complex reds with ageing potential.

Château de Mandourelle
E. Latham, 11360 Villesque. 172 acres; 6,000 cases. Eric Latham, who runs this château, has named one of the wines after his grandfather Henri de Monfreid. The red wine is complex and aromatic.

Domaine de Montjoie
M. Guiraud. St-André-de-Cabrerisse. Replanting and modern methods; stylish, full-flavoured wine. 83 acres deep in central Corbières.

Château de Nouvelles
Robert Daurat-Fortes, 11350 Tuchan. One of the finest estates in the region. Part has the appellation Fitou. Also Rivesaltes VDN. 217 acres.

Château des Ollieux
Mme. Surbezy Cartier. A very good vineyard being replanted with 'aromatic' varieties. Up-to-date maceration methods are making good wine. 106 acres; 26,500 cases.

Château Les Palais
M. de Volontat. St-Laurent-la-Cabrerisse, 11220 Lagrasse. The best-known Corbières estate, a pioneer with *macération carbonique* in the 1960s. Excellent and reliable quality. 252 acres; 54,000 cases.

Château de Pech Latt
Antoine André, 11220 Lagrane. A fine ex-monastery property with a wide range of red, rosé, white and VDNs. 250 acres; 43,000 cases.

Peresse
Campagne de Ciceron, 11220 Ribaute. Small and modern with 'aromatic' varieties producing white, red and pale *gris de gris*. 54 acres; 11,000 cases.

Château de Quilhanet
Marie Terral. Bizanet, 11200 Lezignan. A Grenache and Carignan vineyard, sensibly undercropped. *Macération carbonique* and barrel-ageing. 270 acres; 41,500 cases.

Domaine du Révérend
M. Eric Français. Cucugnan, 11350 Tuchan. 133 acres with another 100 to be planted. This estate is run by Agnès Français and her husband Eric; he is the technician; she makes the wines. Red, white and rosé are all excellent and typical.

Roque Sestieres
Jean Berail, 11200 Ornaisons. 18 acre estate producing 1,600 cases a year. Jean and Isabel Bérail spend much time promoting the wines of Languedoc. Their white wine is 80% Maccabeu.

Prieuré de St-Amans
Mme. Thomas. Bizanet, 11200 Lezignan. One of the best red Corbières, made by *macération carbonique* followed by ageing in oak barrels. 27.5 acres; 7,000 cases.

Château St-Auréol
Claude Vialade. Vineyard outside Lagrasse, experimenting with adding Marsanne to Malvoisie and Grenache Blanc in their white wine. Reds are Syrah, Grenache and Carignan.

Château de Vaugelas
M. Bouffet, 11200 Camplong. A substantial estate with low yields producing good wine. 258 acres; 41,000 cases.

Domaine de Villemajou
Georges Bertrand, 11200 Boutenac. One of the best technicians of the region with a fine vineyard. Reds (maceration and wood-ageing) and dry rosés are full of character. 124 acres; 32,000 cases.

Château la Voulte Gasparet
P Reverdy, 11200 Boutenac. Ideal soil and first-class techniques of *macération carbonique* and wood-ageing. 125 acres; 27,000 cases.

CAVE COOPERATIVES

'L'Avenir'
Villeseque des Corbières, 11360 Durban Corbières. Rating: 9. Founded 1932. 165 members; 1,052 acres producing 144,000 cases of AOC Corbières red and rosé, plus 133,500 cases Vin de Pays Vallée du Paradis red and *vins de table*.

'Cap Leucate'
11370 Leucate. Rating: 9. Founded 1921. 221 members; producing 70,000 cases of AOC Fitou red; Muscat de Rivesaltes white; Rivesaltes white; AOC Corbières red, white and rosé; plus 43,000 cases *vins de table*.

Cascastel
11360 Durban Corbières. Rating: 12. Founded 1926. 80 members; 1,099 acres producing 95,000 cases of AOC Fitou red; Muscat de Rivesaltes; VDN Rivesaltes white; AOC Corbières red, white and rosé; plus Vin de Pays de l'Aude red and *vins de table*.

Cave Coopérative 'La Corbière Bizanetoise'
Bizanet, 11200 Lézignan Corbières. Founded 1935. 280 members; 1,623 acres producing 7,200 cases of AOC Corbières plus 76,500 cases Vin de Pays Val d'Orbieu red and *vins de table*.

Les Vignerons de Cucugnan
Chemin du Malpas, 11350 Cucugnan. 50 members. 481 acres. Run by Mme. Pescarou, this cave produces good Corbières red, white and rosé.

Durban
11360 Durban Corbières. Rating: 9. Founded 1913. 279 members; 1,986 acres producing 2,400 cases of AOC Corbières red, white and rosé, plus 50,000 cases Vin de Pays Vallée du Paradis red and white, and 130,000 cases of *vins de table*.

Embrès & Castelmaure
11360 Durban Corbières. Rating: 13. Founded 1921. 123 members; 686 acres producing 170,000 cases of AOC Corbières red, white and rosé; plus Vin de Pays de L'Aude and *vins de table*

Fitou
11510 Fitou. Rating: 9. Founded 1933. 185 members; 1,408 acres producing 140,000 cases of AOC Fitou red; Muscat de Rivesaltes white; VDN Rivesaltes; AOC Corbières red, white and rosé, plus 70,000 cases *vins de table*.

Fraisse Les Corbières
11360 Durban Corbières. Rating: 9. Founded 1920. 123 members; 741 acres producing 70,000 cases of AOC Corbières red, white and rosé, plus 74,000 cases Vin de Pays Vallée du Paradis red and *vins de table*.

Cave Coopérative Lagrasse
11220 Lagrasse. Rating: 10. Founded 1952. 112 members; 482 acres producing 25,000 cases of AOC Corbières and Montagne d'Alaric, plus 44,000 cases Vin de Pays Val d'Orbieu red and *vins de table*.

Cave Coopérative Montseret
11200 Lézignan Corbières. Rating: 9. Founded 1949. 160 members; 1,500 acres producing 82,700 cases of AOC Corbières plus 95,600 cases Vin de Pays l'Aude red and *vins de table*.

Cave Coopérative Mont Tauch
11350 Tuchan. Rating: 11. Founded 1931. 550 members; 2,507 acres producing 249,000 cases of AOC Fitou red: Rivesaltes red and white: Muscat de Rivesaltes red and white; AOC Corbières red, white and rosé; plus 167,900 cases Vin de Pays Coteaux Cathares red and *vins de table*.

Paziols
11530 Paziols. Rating: 10. Founded 1913. 256 members; 1,773 acres producing 190,000 cases of AOC Fitou red; Rivesaltes white; Muscatel, AOC Corbières red and white; plus cases Vin de Pays Coteaux Cathares red and *vins de table*.

Cave Coopérative 'Pilote de Villeneuve Les Corbières'
Villeneuve Les Corbières, 11360 Durban Corbières. Rating: 10. Founded 1948. 82 members; 1,032 acres producing 131,000 cases of AOC Fitou red and white; Muscat de Rivesaltes red and white; Rivesaltes red and white; AOC Corbières white, red and rosé; plus 55,800 cases *vins de pays* and *vins de table*.

Portel
11490 Portel des Corbières. Rating: 9. Founded 1924. 290 members; producing 190,000 cases of AOC Corbières red, plus 140,000 cases Vin de Pays Coteaux du Littoral Audois red and 170,000 cases of *vins de table*.

Chateau de Queribus
Cucugan, 11350 Tuchan. Rating: 11. Founded 1928. 58 members; 482 acres producing 7,100 cases of AOC Corbières red, plus 92,000 cases Vin de Pays Cucugnan red plus 2,400 cases of *vins de table*.

Château de Ribaute
Cave de Ribaute, 11220 Ribaute. The wines from this coop on the Montagne d'Alaric are set to age well. This is one to watch.

St-Martin
11540 Roqueforte des Corbières. Rating: 9. Founded 1949. 236 members; 1,561 acres producing 155,000 cases of AOC Corbières red, white and rosé, plus 115,000 cases Vin de Pays l'Aude red and 56,000 cases *vins de table*.

Les Vignerons de St Roch
Cave de Padern, 11350 Padern. 500 acres. 120 members. Small coop using a high proportion of Maccabeu in its wines. They are making efforts to increase production and to this end they are negociating a merger with the nearby coopérative de Paziols.

BLANQUETTE DE LIMOUX

The most unexpected and original of all the wines of the Midi is the high-quality sparkling wine of Limoux, tucked away behind the Corbières on the upper reaches of the river Aude above Carcassonne. There is substantial evidence that this lonely area of hilly farms produced France's first sparkling wine, about 200 years before Champagne.

It uses the Mauzac (alias Blanquette), the white grape 'with a slight smell of cider' which is the base for the rustic bubbly of Gaillac. (Gaillac was a Roman wine town; its antiquity may be immense.) Whatever its origins, the traditional Limoux formula is Mauzac for sprightliness plus Clairette for mildness, originally just *pétillant*, but now made by the *méthode champenoise* to full pressure and extremely high standards of delicate blending. Chenin Blanc now also plays a part. The latest development is the addition of

Chardonnay in the best *cuvées* for fuller flavour; if Blanquette has a fault, it is a slightly pinched, lemony finesse which can benefit by plumping out. The rules now insist on at least 10% Chenin or Chardonnay.

Sixty per cent of the entire production of the 8,000 acres under vines is in the hands of the vast, ultra-modern cooperative. Founded in 1946, the coop now has 550 members and produces around 425,000 cases of Blanquette a year. Rating: 14.

A few Coopérateurs take back their wine to 'finish' it themselves, but the remarkably high standards of the cooperative make it hard to improve on their product – and certainly not in value for money.

Crémant de Limoux is a new gently-sparkling version which must have 30% Chenin or Chardonnay.

Recently the coop has added to its repertoire a selection of the best red

wine from its members' vineyards, which include a surprising proportion of Cabernet and Merlot. It offers a very pleasant full-bodied and soft brand called Sieur d'Arques, an excellent Vin de Pays de la Haute Vallée de l'Aude under the name Fécos, and an astonishingly Bordeaux-like *cuvée* called Anne des Joyeuses – one of the best non-appellation coop wines in France.

Another coop, at Gardie, near St-Hilaire, makes small quantities of Blanquette de Limoux from 250 acres.

There are also a number of individual producers, such as the 200 acre Domaine de Martinolles near St-Hilaire, which sells some grapes to the coop as well as making its own wines.

A new ruling, which will come into effect in 1994, prohibits the use of the term *méthod champenoise* on labels of wines that do not come from the Champagne district. The new labelling phrase is likely to be *méthode traditionelle*.

MINERVOIS

The river Aude parts the last wrinkles of the Pyrenees from the first of the Massif Central, and the Corbières from the Minervois. The Minervois is a 40-mile stretch of its north bank, encompassing both the gravelly flats along the river and the very different hills behind, topped by a plateau at 600 feet. Rivers have cut deep ravines in its soft brown rock, in one place leaving a mid-river island for the tiny town of Minerve. The plateau is dry, treeless *garrigue* where the vine struggles and even the Carignan makes wine with nerves and sinews. Modern wine-making in the high Minervois has produced some deliciously vital, well-engineered wines with a structure not of old oak beams, as the word *charpente* seems to imply, but more like an airframe; delicately robust.

The commercial centre of the region is below, on the plain. A SICA, a group of ten cooperatives,

produces large quantities of Vin de Pays de Peyriac to the specification of Chantovent, one of the biggest table-wine companies. But Chantovent is also the owner of an estate at La Livinière in the foothills which produces some of the best Miner-vois, going to the length of ageing it in retired Médoc *barriques*, and the cooperative in the same village has followed suit. AOC status was granted to the Minervois in 1985 and a slow upgrading of the permitted grapes is taking place.

Area: 85,000 acres (half is potential AOC but only 10,000 is fully qualified with the right grape varieties). Production: 2.6m. cases of Minervois, 14,000 of the deliciously sweet Muscat de St-Jean-de-Minervois VDN.

The Minervois is semi-officially divided into five zones, distinguished by topography and weather conditions, listed below with their best producers.

MINERVOIS ZONES AND PRODUCERS

ZONE 1
Around Ginestas in the east, on the plain with relatively high rainfall. Its light reds are for drinking young. There are also some clean modern white wines.
Mme. Dominique de Bertier
Château de Paraza, 11200 Lézignan Corbières. The reds are classic and the rosés fine and fruity. 173 acres; 37,000 cases of red and rosé.

Christian Bonnel
Domaine de la Lecugne, Bize Minervois, 11120 Ginestas. 22.5 acres; 4,500 cases of red.
Bernard Mazard
Château du Vergel, 11120 Ginestas. 34 acres; 9,000 cases of red and white.
Jacques Meyzonnier
Pouzols-Minervois, 11120 Ginestas. Very good medal-winning *macération*

carbonique wine with the label 'Domaine Meyzonnier'. 25 acres; 5,400 cases of red Minervois.
Château de Paraza
11200 Lézignan Corbières. The 2 reds are 'Tradition' (classic) and 'Cuvée Speciale' (carbonic maceration) and the rosés fine and fruity. 427 acres; 37,000 cases of red and rosé.

Guy Rancoule
Domaine de l'Herbe Sainte, Mirepeisset, 11120 Ginestas. A good varied vineyard; the rosés and whites are fine and fruity. 99 acres; 5,000 cases of red, white and rosé.
Caves Coopératives
'Les Coteaux de Pouzols Minervois'
Pouzols Minervois, 11120 Ginestas. Rating: 10. Founded 1936. 136 members; 995 acres producing 512,000 cases, of which 70,000 are AOC. Their Comte de Pouzols cuvée is well thought of.
'Les Crus de Montouliers'
Montouliers, 34310 Capestang. Rating: 8. Founded 1937. 106 members; 768 acres producing 420,000 cases, of which 34,000 are AOC red and rosé.

ZONE 2
The south-central area on the plain of the Aude is hottest and driest with richer reds, also for drinking young.
Jean Barthes
Château de St-Julia, 11800 Trebes. 33 acres; 7,500 cases of red and white.
Jean Baptiste Bonnet
Domaine de Gibalaux, Laure Minervois, 11800 Trebes. 59 acres; 13,500 cases of red.
Bernard de Crozals
Domaine de Homs, Rieux, Minervois, 11160 Caunes, Minervois.
Christian Ferret
Château de Badens, Badens, 11800 Trebes. 35 acres; 10,000 cases of red.
Alfred Keim
Domaine de Prat Majou, Laure Minervois, 11800 Trebes. 25 acres; 5,500 cases of red.
Soc. Mesnard Bellissen
Domaine de Millegrand, 11800 Trebes. 101 acres; 22,500 cases of red.

Jean-Pierre Ormières
Château de Fabas, Laure Minervois, 11800 Trebes. 84 acres; 22,000 cases of red.
Guy Panis
Château du Donjon, Bagnoles, 11600 Conques-sur-Orbiel. 42 acres; 10,500 cases of red.
Aymard de Soos
Château de Russol, Laure Minervois, 11800 Trebes. 74 acres; 20,000 cases red.
Jean de Thelin
Château de Blomac, Blomac, 11700 Capendu. 80 acres; 18,000 cases of Minervois, traditional red wine, well made with 10% Syrah. Also 175 acres of *vins de table* vineyard where experiments are being made with Cabernet, Merlot and the Spanish Tempranillo. One of the grandest cellars of the region.
Caves Coopératives
'Les Coteaux de Minervois'
Pépieux, 11700 Capendu. Rating: 7. Founded 1951. 265 members; 2,595 acres producing 800,000 cases, of which 53,000 are AOC red, white and rosé.
Laure Minervois
11800 Trebes. Rating: 7. Founded 1929. 288 members; 3,088 acres producing 1m. cases, of which 181,000 are AOC red, white and rosé.
Peyriac Minervois
11160 Caunes Minervois. Rating: 7.

Founded 1930. 234 members; 1,338 acres producing 494,000 cases, of which 34,000 are AOC red, white and rosé. Peyriac and its district have given their name to France's biggest-selling *vins de pays*, produced for Chantovent by a group of cooperatives.

ZONE 3
The north-central area in the foothills; makes the best-structured reds for keeping.
Gérard Blanc
Domaine de Ste-Eulalie, La Livinière, 34210 Olonzac. 30 acres; 7,000 cases red.
Mme. Suzanne de Faucompret
Domaine de la Senche, La Livinière, 34210 Olonzac. 39 acres; 8,750 cases red.
Soc. Gourgazaud
Château de Gourgazaud, La Livinière, 34210 Olonzac. The extremely influential pioneering property of Chantovent, the huge table-wine company. Success with *macération carbonique* encouraged investment in the area, including the SICA Coteaux de Peyriac for *vins de pays* and the Domaine de Gourgazaud for experimentsl Vin de Pays de l'Hérault. 168 acres; 441,600 cases of red.
Marcel Julien
Château de Villerambert-Julien, 11160 Caunes Minervois. 10,000 cases of red.
Paul Mandeville
Domaine de Vaissière, Azille, 11700 Capendu. A pioneering property with modern vineyards including Cabernet Sauvignon, Merlot and even Bleu Portugais. Its Vin de Pays de l'Aude (or de l'Oc) is sold by Chantovent.

Gruissan, a wine village south of La Clape

Jacques Maris
La Livinière, 34210 Olonzac. Domaine Maris is an expanding property (now 175 acres) in hand-picked sites around La Livinière, chosen for soil and microclimate. The Carte Noir is his best red.

Mme Moureau & Fils
Château de Villerambert-Mourau, Château de Villegly, 1160 Cannes Minervois. 198 acres; 20,000 cases of red and rosé.

Domaine du Pech d'André
Azillanet, 34210 Olonzac. 47 acres; 6,600 cases of red, rosé and white made by Marc Remaury at a 300-year-old estate.

J. A. Tallavignes
Château de Paulignan, Trausse Minervois, 1160 Caunes Minervois. Recognized locally as a highly original and competent wine maker, Jacques Tallavignes sadly died a few years ago and his sons have not shared his enthusiasm. The estate has been recently sold. 34.5 acres; 5,700 cases of red and white.

Caves Coopératives d'Azillanet
Azillanet, 34210 Olonzac. Rating: 8. Founded 1922. 235 members; 1,700 acres producing 635,000 cases, of which 38,000 are AOC red and rosé.

'Les Costos Roussos'
Trausse, 1160 Caunes Minervois. Rating: 8. Founded 1937. 209 members, 1,630 acres producing 570,000 cases, of which 111,000 are AOC. The Mourvèdre does well here, as the coop's wines attest.

'Coteaux du Haut Minervois'
La Livinière, 34210 Olonzac. Rating: 8. Founded 1924. 190 members; 1,358 acres producing 480,000 cases, of which 110,000 are AOC red, white and rosé. The best red, Jean d'Alibert, is made by *macération carbonique* and aged in Bordeaux barrels.

'Felines Minervois'
34210 Olonzac. Rating: 7. Founded 1922. 187 members; producing 399,000 cases, of which 20,900 are AOC red.

'La Vigneronne'
11160 Caunes Minervois. Rating: 10. Founded 1922. 438 members; 1,820 acres producing 650,000 cases, of which 31,000 are AOC red and rosé.

ZONE 4
The high plateau around Minerve has the harshest climate and makes the strongest and biggest wine. St-Jean-de-Minervois in this zone has its own appellation for Muscat *vin doux naturel*.

Mme. Jacqueline Le Calvez
La Caunette, 34210 Olonzac. Well situated on the sunny hillsides of La Caunette. Replanting is making a first-class vineyard. Very good vinification. 30 acres, 5,750 cases of red.

Caves Coopératives de Vinification d'Aigne
Aigne, 34210 Olonzac. Rating: 8. Founded 1948. 147 members; 1,235 acres producing 287,000 cases, of which 60,000 are AOC red and white.

St-Jean-de-Minervois
34360 St-Chinian. Rating: 12. Founded 1955. 55 members; 566 acres producing 113,600 cases, of which 17,300 are AOC white Muscat de St-Jean-de-Minervois. The main cellar for this little sweet-wine appellation.

ZONE 5
The western zone; has the highest rainfall and least distinguished wines.

Caves Coopératives 'La Grappe'
Villeneuve Minervois, 11160 Caunes Minervois. Rating: 7. Founded 1925. 362 members; 2,272 acres producing 717,300 cases, of which 75,200 are AOC red, white and rosé.

'Malves Bagnoles'
Malves-en-Minervois, 11600 Conques-sur-Orbiel. Rating: 7. Founded 1948. 123 members; 988 acres producing 383,000 cases, of which 33,300 are AOC red, white and rosé.

Villalier
11600 Conques-sur-Orbiel. Rating: 8. Founded 1934. 140 members; 988 acres producing 329,000 cases, of which 12,500 are AOC red, white and rosé.

COTEAUX DU LANGUEDOC

The stress in this name is on the Coteaux. The plains of the Languedoc between Narbonne and Montpellier are the notorious source of calamitous quantities of low-strength blending wine. But certain of its hillsides have AOC status and hardly less potential for quality than Corbières and Roussillon. In general their wines are lighter and harsher – but not necessarily so. A dozen separate areas, confusingly scattered across the map, produce named and worthwhile wines.

The concentration is to the north of Béziers, in the first foothills of the Cevennes where the river Hérault leaves its torrents to become placid and poplar-lined. Cabrières, Faugères, St-Saturnin are such foothill vineyards. The best known of them, the only ones with an international reputation of their own, are Faugères and St-Chinian, in the hills to the west towards the Minervois. Their reds can be full-bodied, distinctly savoury wines, admirably suited to vinification by *macération carbonique*. St-Chinian, partly on chalky clay and partly on dark purple schist full of manganese, is worth careful study. The variety of soils in these hills gives character to their wine. The Berlou valley, on the purple schist, is outstanding for riper, rounder reds than the rest of the region.

The most individual, and an area with exciting potential, is La Clape, the isolated limestone massif like a beached island at the mouth of the river Aude, between Narbonne and the sea. Soil and climate conditions on La Clape have shown that they can produce highly distinctive white wines. Cool sea breezes give the hills a microclimate of their own. Blanc de la Clape, made of standard southern grapes, or better from Malvoisie (alias Bourboulenc), is clean if unexciting when young. But real character comes with ageing: at five or six years it can have some of the style of a good Rhône white. Better grape varieties may make magnificent wines. Several domaines have planted Chardonnay.

Many growers in the Coteaux now make use of the Vin de Pays regulations to make non-conforming wines. You will discover Merlots and Chardonnays: look for 'Domaine' names on labels otherwise identical to those of reputable châteaux. 'Château' must not by law appear on a Vin de Pays label.

COTEAUX DU LANGUEDOC DISTRICTS AND PRODUCERS

CABRIERES
In the Cevennes foothills. Best known for light *rosé de goutte*, made without pressing, but recently joining the trend towards Syrah-spiced reds.

Cave Coopérative 'Les Coteaux de Cabrières'
34800 Clermont-l'Hérault. Rating: 10. Founded 1937. 131 members: 965 acres producing 230,000 cases of AOC Coteaux du Languedoc Cabrières and Clairette du Languedoc. Brand names include L'Estable, and Cuvée Cabanon for a 90% Syrah red.

COTEAUX DE VERARGUES
Near Lunel, between Montpellier and Nimes. *See* Muscat de Lunel page 219. Vérargues has some useful reds from the Lunel-Viel coop, which has planted Merlot, and from estates including Château de Beaulieu.

FAUGÈRES
Westernmost of the Cevennes foothill districts with some very competent producers of red and instant rosé. An AOC in its own right since 1982, covering 7 communes. Rules insist on at least 10% Syrah or Mourvèdre from 1990's vintage onwards.

Domaine du Fraisse
Autignac, 34480 Magalas. Jacques Pons created this 50-acre estate out of barren hillsides over the last 20 years. Growing in flavour as the vines mature.

Domaine de la Grange des Aires
Cabrerolles, 34480 Magalas. Mme. Platelle's estate has classic red vine varieties for solid, long-lived wine.

Bernard Vidal
La Liquière, Cabrerolles, 34480 Magalas. Ideally situated with 74 acres of the best grape varieties for red, rosé and white with real finesse. Uses *macération carbonique*.

Vidal-Gaillard
Château de la Liquière, Cabrerolles 34480 Magalas. Good grape varieties on excellent schist soil. Well-managed wine-making by *macération carbonique*.

Caves Coopératives
'Les Crus Faugères'
34600 Bedarieux. Rating: 11. Founded 1961. 180 members; 1,482 acres producing 351,000 cases, of which 134,600 are AOC Faugères.

Laurens
34480 Magalas. Rating: 10. Founded 1938. 380 members; 3,939 acres producing 24,000 cases, of which 165,000 are AOC Faugères.

LA CLAPE
Seaside limestone hills near Narbonne, best for white and rosé.

Soc. Aupècle
Domaine des Monges-Schaefer, Château de Capitoul, 11100 Narbonne. A substantial estate in the centre of La Clape, using traditional methods.

J. Boscary
Château de Rouquette-sur-Mer, 11100 Narbonne. A remarkable 800 acre (130 planted) site on the rocky slopes of La Clape near the sea. The most modern wine-making for high-quality red, white and rosé; perhaps the best of the area. The reds are aged in oak barrels.

Robert Bottero
11560 Fleury d'Aude. Small but high-quality white-wine grower.

Combastet
Château de Ricardelle de la Clape, 11100 Narbonne. Part of the estate is up on the limestone of La Clape and makes good traditional wines from a variety of grapes.

Egretier
Château de Complazens, Armissan, 11110 Coursan. Good grapes and situation on La Clape. Well-made wines.

Philippe Hue
Château de Salles, Salles d'Aude, 11110 Coursan. Classic 'Clape' reds of Carignan, Grenache and Syrah come from part of the estate. M. Hue also makes an interesting *vin de pays* of Merlot and a dry rosé of Cinsaut.

J. B. Jousseaume
Domaine de Ricardelle de la Clape, 11100 Narbonne. Good quality white wines.

Yves Lignères
Domaine de Vires, 11100 Narbonne. A property of 175 acres steadily improving both in grape varieties and wine-making. At present the best wines are *macération* reds, including the superior Cuvée Saphir which mingles traditional and *macération*.

Domaine de Pech-Redon
11100 Narbonne. A restored old estate in a lovely situation high on La Clape but near the sea. A wide variety of vines on 94 acres make good *macération* red, white and excellent dry rosé.

de St-Exupery
Château de Pech-Celeyran, Salles d'Aude, 11110 Coursan. 222 acres. A largely Cabernet and Merlot vineyard producing some good wine.

Jean Ségura
Domaine de Rivière La Haut, 11560 Fleury d'Aude. 32 acres. A leading protagonist in the area of high-quality white wine based on Bourboulenc grapes – the long-lived speciality of La Clape.

Vaille
Des Ruffes, Salleles du Bose, 11110 Coursan.

LA MEJANELLE
Obscure little region near the sea, east of Montpellier.

De Colbert
Château de Flaugergues, 34000 Montpellier. 131 acres. A family property for 300 years with a name for gentle, elegant reds. Henri de Colbert is head of a group of local growers, 'La Domitienne' which aims for quality.

Delbez
Mas de Calage, St-Aunès, 34130 Mauguio.

Teissier
Domaine de la Costière, 34000 Montpellier.

MONTPEYROUX
Northern district for reds near the famous Gorges de l'Hérault.

Cave Coopérative Les Coteaux du Castellas
34150 Gignac. Rating: 10. Founded 1950. 285 members; 4,088 acres producing 455,600 cases, of which 133,300 are AOC Coteaux du Languedoc and Montpeyroux.

PIC ST-LOUP
2,000-foot peak due north of Montpellier. The AOC here limits Carignan to a maximum of 50% in reds.

Arles
Domaine de Lascours, Sauteyrargues, 34270 St-Mathieu-de-Tréviers.

Castries
Château de Fontmagne. Baron Durand de Fontmagne. AOC and *vin de pays* reds and whites, including a Sauvignon Blanc.

Lauriol
Domaine de la Roque, Fontanes, 34270 St-Mathieu-de-Tréviers.

Recouly
Domaine de Cantaussels, Les Matelles, 34270 St-Mathieu-de-Tréviers.

Domaine de Villeneuve
Claret, 34270 St-Mathieu-de-Tréviers.

Caves Coopératives
Les Coteaux de Montferrand
34270 St-Mathieu-de-Tréviers. Rating: 9. Founded 1950. 167 members: 1,680 acres producing 600,000 cases, of which 82,000 are AOC Coteaux du Languedoc Pic St-Loup.

Les Coteaux de St-Gely-du-Fesc
14980 St-Gely-du-Fesc. Rating: 9. Founded 1939. 167 members; 776 acres producing 251,000 cases, of which 19,000 are AOC.

Les Coteaux de Valflaunes
34270 St-Mathieu-de-Tréviers. Rating: 9. Founded 1939. 140 members; 1,530 acres producing 518,000 cases, of which 115,000 are AOC Coteaux du Languedoc and Pic St-Loup.

PINET (PICPOUL DE)
Pleasant dry white with 12° of alcohol
and a touch of freshness.
Cave Coopérative de Pinet
500 acres. Founded 1923. Largest
producer of wine in the area.
C. Gaujal
Château de Pinet, 34850 Pinet. 173
acres. Extremely carefully made Picpoul
white and *vins de pays* from Merlot.

QUATROURZE
A neglected little zone near Narbonne.
Yvon Ortola
Château Notre Dame du Quatourze.
11100 Narbonne. 111 acres producing a
good Cinsaut-flavoured red.

ST-CHINIAN
The biggest and most important zone,
now a cru of Coteaux du Languedoc
since it became an AOC in 1982. It is in
the Cevennes foothills to the west.
Potentially excellent solid and smooth
reds. At least 10% of reds must come
from Syrah or Mouvèdre..
F. Guy & S. Peyre
Château de Coujan, 34490 Murviel Les
Béziers. A substantial (250-acre)
property making 3 excellent wines:
Coteaux de Murviel from Merlot and
Cabernet, classic St-Chinian (Cinsault,
Grenache and Syrah) by *macération
carbonique*, and Cabernet rosé.
Domaine des Jougla
Prades-sur-Vernazobre, 34360 St-
Chinian. A family estate since 1580 in
the Cevennes foothills, now with
modern equipment and new oak.
Libes-Cavaille
St-Nazaire de Ladarez, 34490 Murviel
Les Béziers.
Miquel
Cazal-Viel, 34460 Cessenon.
Pierre Petit
Villespassans, 34360 St-Chinian. A first-
class St-Chinian property using
macération carbonique.
Caves Coopératives
Causses & Veyran
34490 Murviel-Les-Beziers. Rating: 10.
Founded 1946. 215 members; 1,790
acres producing 514,000 cases, of which
59,200 are AOC and Coteaux du
Languedoc Lou Coulinadou.
Les Couteaux de Cebazan
34360 St-Chinian. Rating: 10. Founded
1965. 167 members; 1,647 acres
producing 461,000 cases, of which
68,000 are AOC Coteaux du Lanuedoc.
Coteaux du Creissan
34370 Cazouls-Les-Beziers. Rating: 9.
Founded 1951. 180 members; 874 acres
producing 347,000 cases, of which 6,700
are AOC Coteaux du Languedoc.
Les Coteaux du Rieu Berlou
34360 St-Chinian. Rating: 13. Founded
1965. 102 members; 1,430 acres

producing 320,000 cases, of which
200,000 are AOC Coteaux du
Languedoc. The best wine is produced
under the brand name 'Schisteil'. Their
'Berloup Prestige' cuvée is also noted.
Les Crus Cazedarnais
34460 Cessenon. Rating: 9. Founded
1954. 140 members; producing 385,000
cases, of which 52,000 are AOC Coteaux
de Languedoc and St-Chinian.
Quarante
34310 Capestang. Rating: 9. Founded
1934. 423 members; 2,754 acres
producing 1m. cases, of which 1,200 are
AOC St-Chinian.
Les Vins de Roquebrun
34460 Cessenon. Rating: 13. Founded
1967. 148 members; 988 acres, 233,000
cases, of which 114,000 are AOC
Coteaux du Languedoc and St-Chinian.

ST-CHRISTOL
In a group with Verargues and St-
Drèzery north of Lunel. No notable
activity.
Domaine Martin Pierrat
St-Christol, 34400 Lunel. 94 acres.
Medal winning wines include a Syrah/
Grenache red and a Chardonnay *vins de
pays*.
**Cave coopérative Les Coteaux de
St-Christol**
34400 Lunel. Rating: 9. Founded 1940.
190 members; 1,596 acres producing
514,900 cases.

ST-DREZERY
See St. Christol
Spitaleri
Mas de Carrat, St-Drézery, 34160
Castries. 114 acres, including some
Merlot for vins de pays.
**Cave Coopérative de les Coteaux de
St-Drézery**
34160 Castries. Rating: 9. Founded
1939. 207 members; 1,530 acres
producing 480,000 cases. The top red
carries the Carte Noir label.

ST-GEORGES-D'ORQUES
On the western outskirts of Montpellier,
once fashionable with English tourists
interned by Napoleon. Red wine, largely
of Cinsaut.
Grill
Château de l'Engarran, Laverune, 34430
St-Jean-de-Vedas. 130 acres. AOC reds
and an Ugni Blanc *vin de pays* white.
**Caves Coopérative de
St-Georges-d'Orques**
34680 St-Georges-d'Orques. Rating: 9.
Founded 1947. 400 members; 1,386
acres. Chateau Bellevue is their name for
a *barrique*-aged red.

ST-SATURNIN
Active vineyards in the *garrigue* of the
Cevennes foothills with rather good

lively reds and very light 'Vin d'une
Nuit'. Neighbour to Montpeyroux.
Cave Coopérative de St-Saturnin
34150 Gignac. Rating: 11. Founded
1951. 183 members; 1,010 acres
producing 604,000 cases, of which
270,00 are AOC St-Saturnin and
Coteaux du Languedoc red and rosé.
Their 'Le Lucian' rosé displays its Syrah
to effect.

OTHER PRODUCERS
J. M. Bonnevialle
St-Jean de La Balaquière, 34700 Lodève.
Château de la Condamine Bertrand
34120 Lézignan la Cete. Particularly
well-made and successful white wine
from Clairette grapes.
Daniel Delclaud
Domaine de St-Jean d'Aumières, 34150
Gignac.
B. Gaujal
Château de Nizas, Nizas, 34320 Roujan.
André Heulz
St-André-de-Sangonis, 34150 Gignac.
Mas de Daumas Gassac
Aniane, 34150 Cignac. Perhaps the best,
certainly the most famous, 'new' wine of
the Languedoc. The red is 85%
Cabernet Sauvignon from a vineyard
planted over the past two decades high
up in the hills behind Montpellier. The
white is more of an acquired taste.
Professor Peynaud was the original
consultant.
Domaine du Parc
34120 Bézenas. Owner: M. Henri
L'Epine. A 105-acre vineyard bounded
by a 17th-century wall, producing Vin
de Pays de l'Hérault from Carignan,
Merlot and Cabernet Sauvignon.
Prieuré de St-Jean-de-Bébian
Owner: Alain Roux. 80 acres. Highly
distinctive wine produced from all 13
Châteauneuf-du-Pape grape varieties. It
is entitled only to *vin de pays* status, but
deserves far better.
Caves Coopératives St-Felix de Lodez
34150 Gignac. Rating: 9. Founded 1942.
250 members; 1,753 acres producing
541,000 cases, of which 125,000 are
AOC Coteaux du Languedoc and 3,900
are AOC Clairette du Languedoc.
St-Jean-de-la-Blaquière
34700 Lodève. Rating: 10. Founded
1947. 263 members; 2,110 acres
producing 511,000 cases of which
144,000 are AOC Coteaux du
Languedoc.

THE MUSCATS OF LANGUEDOC

Three small zones along the central south coast, between the wine port of Sète and the marshes of the Camargue, have appellations (and an antique reputation) for sweet Muscat *vins doux naturels*.

Frontignan is the biggest and best known. The Muscat vineyards stretch along the coast through Mireval (the second appellation) towards Montpellier. The grape is the '*muscat à petits grains ronds*'; its wine powerfully aromatic, brown and sticky, but lacking (at least as it is made today) the freshness and finesse of Muscat de Beaumes de Venise. An independent producer, Yves Pastourel at Château de la Peyrade has been working to improve this situation for the last 10 years and has succeeded in producing a lighter and more refined wine. The third area is Lunel, halfway between Montpellier and Nimes, just inland from the Camargue.

The cooperatives of Frontignan and Lunel are the major producers. One other big grower of Frontignan and Mireval is M. Robiscau, who created Le Mas Neuf des Aresquiers at Vic La Gardiole (34110 Frontignan) 20 years ago, ripping up 200 acres of rocky terrain where desultory vines were growing to make a modern vineyard.

Caves Coopératives
Muscat de Frontignan
34110 Frontignan. Rating: 13. Founded 1915. 340 members; 1,642 acres producing 200,000 cases.
Muscat de Lunel
Verargues, 34400 Lunel. Rating: 12. Founded 1956, 69 members; 555 acres; 82,000 cases of AOC Muscat de Lunel.
Muscat de Mireval – Cave de Rabelais
34840 Mireval. Rating: 12. Founded 1961. 77 members: 304 acres producing 39,100 cases.

CLAIRETTE DU LANGUEDOC

A scarcely merited AOC for a generally dull and dispiriting dry white from Clairette grapes grown in several communes along the Hérault. Much of it is fortified as a cheap apéritif and sold under such names as 'Amber Dry'.
Domaine de la Condamine
34230 Paulhan. M. Jany runs a very new property which has 84 acres of Clairette of unusually good quality.

Caves Coopératives
Adissan
34230 Paulhan. Rating: 8. Founded 1929. 285 members; 1,853 acres; 680,000 cases, of which 13,100 are VDQS Coteaux du Languedoc red and 8,700 are AOC Clairette du Languedoc.
La Clairette d'Aspiran
34800 Clermont-l'Hérault. Rating: 9. Founded 1932. 295 members; 2,200 acres of AOC Coteaux du Languedoc and Clairette du Languedoc.

La Fontesole
34320 Roujan. Rating: 9. Founded 1930. 298 Members; 1,600 acres; 604,500 cases, of which 20,000 are VDQS Coteaux du Languedoc and 8,900 are AOC Clairette du Languedoc.
Peret
34800 Clermont-l'Hérault. Rating: 6. Founded 1932. 196 members; 1,300 acres producing 458,000 cases, of which 1,200 are AOC Clairette du Languedoc.

BOUCHES-DU-RHONE

This *département* of the Rhône delta was almost a vinous blank, a pause between the mass production of the Languedoc and the scattered vineyards of Provence, until modern technology stepped in. It has now been made a separate AOC. Only in one area south of Nimes, the Costières de Nimes, a deep deposit of pebbles from the former river bed provides good ripening conditions, officially recognized by a VDQS for Rhône-style reds and rosés in 1951 with the name Costières du Gard. This was changed in 1989 to the present name. For some strange reason a corner of this area even has an AOC for its white Clairette de Bellegarde.

Technology took an unexpected form. The massively wealthy Compagnie des Salins du Midi, the producer of a large proportion of France's salt from the seawater lagoons of this coast, began experimenting with vines in the sand flats along the shore. Their original wines were made with inferior varieties, but today the Vins des Sables du Golfe du Lion (under the trademark Listel) include such '*améliorateurs*' as Cabernet and Sauvignon Blanc.

COSTIERES DE NIMES PRODUCERS

Château Roubaud
Gallician, 30600 Valivert. Owner: Mme. Annie Molinier. Founded 1902. 173 acres producing Costières de Nimes. Total production 12,500 cases.
Mas St-Louis La Perdrix
30127 Bellegarde. Owner: Mme. Lamour. Run by the Lamour family for the past 30 years. 348 acres planted with Carignan, Cinsaut, Grenache, Cabernet, Syrah and Clairette de Bellegarde produce 44,500 cases. 80% of production is Costières de Nimes. The rest is *vins de table*.
Cave Coopérative de Bellegarde
30127 Bellegarde. President: M. Darboux. 260 members; 2,099 acres producing 797,800 cases a year, of which 32,700 are AOC.

OTHER PRODUCERS
Domaine de l'Amarine
30127 Bellegarde. Nicolas Godepski.
Domaine de St-Benezey
30800 St-Giles du Gard. M. Pohe.
Château St-Vincent
Jonquièrs St-Vincent, 30300 Beaucaire.

VINS DES SABLES DU GOLFE DU LION
Domaines Viticoles des Salins du Midi (Listel)
34063 Montpellier. Founded 1856. Sales 1.6m. cases. The biggest wine estate in France, with 4,200 acres, largely in the sand dunes of the Gulf of Lions. Salins du Midi is a vast salt company. In the 19th century it started ploughing its profits into pioneering vineyards in the phylloxera-free sand. It has maintained the highest standards and made the Vins de Pays des Sables du Golfe du Lion a sort of appellation of its own, led by its Domaines de Villeroy, de Jarras and du Bosquet, under the management of Pierre-Louis Jullien who retired in 1986.

It uses sand as an almost neutral growing medium, excludes seawater with dykes of fresh water, fertilizes and fixes the sand with winter cereals and produces wines of remarkable clarity, simplicity and charm of flavour at moderate prices. As well as the sand vineyards 600 acres in the Var at Pierrefeu and Ollières produce Côtes de Provence and Vins de Pays de Maures and Coteaux Varois, a VDQS.

CORSICA: L'ILE DE BEAUTE

The importance of France's dramatically mountainous island of Corsica is almost entirely as a producer of bulk material for table-wine blends. When France lost Algeria, its wine growers flooded into the island to plant the plains of the east coast with the basic grapes of Algeria and the Midi – Carignan, Grenache and Cinsaut. In the period 1960–1973 the island's vineyards expanded from 20,000 to 77,000 acres. Then came a period of retrenchment, with 9,000 acres being pulled up again. So the vast majority of Corsica's vineyards are young, in common grapes and on relatively big properties formed for quantity rather than quality – with an average yield over the island of 76 hl/ha.

The appellation Vin de Corse was instituted in 1976 as an encouragement to limit crops. The specific interest of Corsican wine, such as it is, lies in *crus* of Vin de Corse and two more limited appellations (Patrimonio and Ajaccio) relating to the best vineyards, which retain traditional grape varieties. These include the red Nielluccio and Sciacarello, and the white Vermentino or Malvoise de Corse and Trebbiano (Ugni Blanc).

Patrimonio in La Conca d'Oro in the north of the island is relatively long-established for rosé and red made primarily of Nielluccio and whites from Vermentino, with one degree higher minimum alcohol (12.5) than the rest of the island's wines.

Ajaccio, the capital, has Sciacarello red and rosé and Vermentino white. Calvi and the region of Balagne in the northwest have a relatively high proportion of AOC wine. Cap Corse specializes in dessert wines, including sweet Muscat.

Porto-Vecchio and Figari and the flat southeast have more vineyards, but using a good proportion of Nielluccio. Sartène, around Propriano in the southwest, is the area with the highest proportion of appellation wines (75 per cent), of Corsican grapes – mainly Sciacarello – and of traditional-style small growers working on good hill slopes. On the whole, the south is the place to look for the most interesting wine. There have been recent plantings of Cabernet Sauvignon, Merlot, Chardonnay and Chenin Blanc on the eastern plain south of Bastia and these are included in Vin de Pays de L'Ile de Beauté.

PRINCIPAL CORSICAN PRODUCERS

Albertini Frères, Clos d'Alzeto 20151 Carri-d'Orcino
Couvent d'Alzipratu, Zilia
Clos Capitoro, 20166 Porticcio
Dominique Gentile, 20217 St-Florent
Clos Nicrosi, 20247 Rogliano
Domaine de Paviglia, 2000 Ajaccio
Comte Peraldi, 20167 Mezzavia
Domaine La Ruche Foncière, 20215 Arena-Vescovato

Domaine de Torraccia, 20137 Lecci de Porto Vecchio
Caves Coopératives
Agione, 20255 Aghione
Aleria, 20270 Aleria
Calenzana, Coteaux de Balaone Suare, 20214 Calenzana

La Marana Ruisgnani, 20290 Lucciana
Patrimonio, 20253 Patrimonio
Sartène, 20100 Sartène
SICA de Figari, 20131 Pianottoli

Corisca is entitled to the Vin de Pays name L'Ile de Beauté

THE SOUTHWEST

The southwest corner of France exists in calm self-sufficiency. Its rich food and notable wines seem, like its beauty and tranquility, to be its private business. To the east lie the great vineyards of the Languedoc; to the north Bordeaux; Spain lies beyond the towering Pyrenees. In their foothills and the river valleys of the Tarn, the Garonne, the Lot, the Gers, the Adour and the Gave, a different race of wines is grown, bearing no relation to the Midi and remarkably distinct from Bordeaux. Historically some of these wines, notably Cahors and Gaillac, were exported via Bordeaux and known as the wines of the *Haut-Pays*, the high country. Some use the Bordeaux grapes. But all except those closest to the Gironde, such as Buzet, have real character of their own to offer. A variety of grapes with extraordinary local names, some of them Basque, give a range of flavours found nowhere else. The world is beginning to discover them and encourage the expansion of a depleted vineyard. Fashion is swinging towards the regional idiosyncrasies the southwest has to offer.

BERGERAC

The wily law-givers of the seventeenth century were never short of dodges for discouraging rivals to their main interests. Bergerac is a happily situated region with fine slopes and soil as far inland as shipping can easily penetrate up the river Dordogne. To prevent it competing on equal terms with Bordeaux it was compelled by the Bordeaux *Parlement* to use smaller barrels, which carried a higher tax. Apparently the Dutch were the only nation partial enough to its wines to ignore the tax and keep buying. Hence a virtual monopoly of the region's trade, which inclined it towards Dutch taste: sweet white wines and thin dry ones for distilling. The sweet ones became and remained the pride of the region. Monbazillac is its most famous name. But in this century medium-sweet and thin dry wines have been hard to sell. So the Bergeraçois tried red. Demand has switched to and fro between red and white with Bergerac tending to be a step behind. Recent plantings have been largely in the Bordeaux red grapes, which perform excellently here, with Merlot in the majority. Now there is a shortage of dry white in Bordeaux. With a current near-equilibrium between red and white grapes, Bergerac should at last be well placed for the campaign it is waging to become better known.

It is not one simple appellation, but like Bordeaux an all-embracing one with subsections determined by slopes, soil and microclimates. Bergerac unqualified is light (minimum 10 degrees) red, unmistakably claret-like by nature; an indistinguishable substitute for many light Bordeaux reds, at a slightly lower price. It need not be so light, as some 12-degree wines from the chalky northern part of the region with the appellation Pécharmant bear witness. Young vines may account for the picnic style of much of the red at present. Côtes de Bergerac is a little weightier with 11 degrees.

The dry white is sold as Bergerac Sec. Several skilful and enterprising growers, not least at the cooperatives, have introduced a firm flavour of Sauvignon into wine that is still predominantly Sémillon and the lesser Bordeaux varieties. With cool, clean fermentation in stainless steel, they are making a Sancerre-style wine with more substance than its imitators in Touraine.

Château de Panisseau, Thénac

No less than five little appellations apply to sweet and semi-sweet whites (which rely on Sémillon and hope for a degree of 'noble rot'). Just south of the town of Bergerac, Monbazillac, with its operatic château (the property of the local cooperative), is capable of truly luscious and powerful (15-degree) wines, obviously related to Sauternes. They only lack the miraculous harmony of fruity acidity that makes a great Sauternes – but this does not shorten their lives. I have lingered long over 40-year-old Monbazillac that had turned a fine tobacco colour.

Saussignac is a scarcely used appellation for similar, slightly less rich wine from the slopes to the west of Monbazillac.

To the north of the Dordogne, Montravel is a slightly superior Bergerac Sec, but the distinctions between the appellations Côtes de Montravel (*Moelleux*), Haut-Montravel (sweeter) and Rosette (which is practically non-existent), all for dry to semi-sweet wine with a certain body, seem to complicate matters unnecessarily. However, all *demi-sec* or *Moelleux* wines are usually called Côtes de Bergerac which simplifies this somewhat. Total production: 4.0m. cases.

BERGERAC PRODUCERS

Châteaux Belingard, du Chayne, Boudigand
Pomport, 24240 Sigoulès.
Owner: Comte de Bosredon. 210 acres. 3 properties in Monbazillac run together to produce 2 red Côtes de Bergerac. Châteaux du Chayne and Boudigand, dry white Château du Chayne and sweet Château Belingard Monbazillac.
Reds are made by *macération carbonique* for drinking unaged; the dry white is a sharpish Sauvignon. Monbazillac ages 2 years in wood. A *méthode champenoise* Brut is also named Belingard. The property contains traces of druidical doings which the Count is pleased to discuss.

Château du Bloy
Bonneville, 24230 Vélines.
Owners: The Guillermier brothers. 116 acres. Red: one quarter each Merlot, the 2 Cabernets and Malbec; white, Sauvignon, Sémillon, Muscadelle and Muscadet.
A recent (1967) appellation Montravel property making a full, rather rich red with no wood-ageing, a dry white of pure Sauvignon, another an unusual blend of Muscadet, a little Sémillon and Muscadelle. Dry whites are not aged; red and sweet whites are kept 2 years in cement vats.

Château La Borderie
Monbazillac, 24240 Sigoulès.
Owner: Dominique Vidal. 155 acres. Monbazillac: Muscadelle, Sauvignon and Sémillon. Red: Merlot and the 2 Cabernets.
The Vidals have 2 properties in Monbazillac. La Borderie, bought in 1968, has 87 acres of Monbazillac, aged in large oak vats for up to 4 years. Red from 42 acres is kept 1 year in stainless steel, 1 in cask. Dry white from 17 acres is pure Sauvignon, bottled in spring. Château Treuil de Nailhac, their older, smaller estate, has recently been replanted for red and Sauvignon white as well as Monbazillac.

Château Le Caillou
Rouffignac, 24240 Sigoulès.
Owner: Pierre Eymery. 62 acres: 37 white, mainly Monbazillac (Sémillon 70%, Sauvignon and Muscadelle 15% each); 25 red (Merlot 50%, Cabernet Franc and Sauvignon 25% each).
Half the red is over the Gironde border and therefore appellation Bordeaux. Apart from some Bergerac Sec made of almost pure Sauvignon, M. Eymery uses very traditional methods, ageing reds and sweet Monbazillac up to 3 years in mature barrels.

Domaine Constant
Castang, Lamonzie St-Martin, 24130 La Force.
Owner: Jean-Louis Constant. 50 acres of Monbazillac (Château Lavaud), 30 of Bergerac red, rosé and white.

Usual grape varieties, but rosé is pure Cabernet Sauvignon, dry white pure Sauvignon Blanc. The Monbazillac is aged 2 years in wood and in a good year ages well in bottle.

Château Court-Les-Mûts
Razac de Saussignac, 24240 Sigoulès.
Owner: Pierre-Jean Sadoux. 58 acres of white (Sémillon 75%, Sauvignon 25%) and red (Merlot 42%, Cabernet Sauvignon 33%, Cabernet Franc 26%).
The young oenologist Sadoux has established a modern winery with a good reputation, one of the few producing sweet Saussignac *moelleux* as well as dry white Bergerac, semi-sweet Côtes de Bergerac and a soft fruity red (no barrels), all winning medals. 'Vin de Fête' is a *méthode champenoise* Brut.

Château Le Fagé
Pomport, 24240 Sigoulès.
Owner: François Gérardin. 100 acres: 25 red producing 6,500 cases, 65% Merlot and 15% each Cab.Sauv. and Cab.Franc; 75 white producing 1,500 cases dry Sauvignon, 1,500 Monbazillac, largely Sémillon with Sauvignon, Muscadelle and a little rosé.
Family-owned estate for 200 years. Wine-making without barrels is traditional for the region: ageing is in enamelled vats – Monbazillac for 3–4 years. Red, like dry white, is bottled in spring unaged. Another label is Ch. de Geraud.

Domaine de Haut Pécharmant
24100 Bergerac.
Owner: Mme. Vve. André Roches. 57 acres; Merlot 30%, Cabernet Franc 20%, Sauvignon 40%, Malbec 10%. 12,500 cases.
Pécharmant is made with modern materials but very traditional ideas, fermenting with stems and no filtration. The result is aggressively full-flavoured wine to age 7 or 8 years in bottle.

Domaine de la Jaubertie
Colombier, 24560 Issigeac.
Owner: Henry Ryman. 114 acres, half red (Merlot 50%, Cabernets 40%, Malbec 10%); half white (Sauvignon 55%, Sémillon 45%, a little Muscadelle).
Ryman, well known in Britain for his stationery shops, bought the property in 1973. He uses Australian-inspired cold fermentation in stainless steel to make crisply fruity 100% Sauvignon white, bottled as soon as possible, a 'Tradition' white and a Réserve, both 70% Sémillon and a 100% Muscadelle. Reds are bottled after about 18 months, including 3–4 months in barrels. 2 or 3 years in bottle brings out their character. The standard red is 75%

Merlot, the Réserve 70% Cabernet.) Also a little Monba-zillac, a rosé and a *méthode champenoise*.

Château de Monbazillac
Monbazillac, 24240 Sigoulès.
The showplace of the region, owned by the local cooperative association. *See* UNIDOR.

Château de Michel Montaigne
24230 Vélines.
Owners: The Mähler-Besse family. 37 acres. Merlot, Cabernet Sauvignon, Cabernet Franc.
The home of the great 16th-century philosopher (his study tower can be visited) and the country retreat of a distinguished Bordeaux négociant.

Château de Panisseau
Thénac, 24240 Sigoulès.
Owners: The Becker family. 125 acres. 250,000 cases. Red: one third each Cabernet Sauvignon, Cabernet Franc, Merlot. White: half Sauvignon, half Sémillon.
A stunning little 11th-century fortress, developed since 1958 as a modern wine estate, offering a pure Sauvignon dry white of great finesse and an original, more full-flavoured dry blend of Sémillon with 10% Sauvignon. The red is less exciting.

Château Poulvère
Monbazillac, 24240 Sigoulès.
Owner: Jean Borderie. 212 acres.
One of the biggest properties in the area, producing 17,000 cases of Monbazillac, 11,000 of red Bergerac and a very small quantity of rosé and dry white. Barrels are used only for Monbazillac, and only for 8–12 months.

Château Thénac
Le Bourg, Thénac, 24240 Sigoulès.
Owner: Jean-Pierre Cazalis. 62 acres.
An old château bought in 1976, restored and now making

a red Bergerac of one third each Merlot and the two Cabernets, plus a white of Sauvignon and Sémillon. Both are intended to be drunk young.

Domaine Theulet et Marsalet
St-Laurent-des-Vignes, 24100 Bergerac.
Owner: René Monbouché. 80 acres producing 10,000 cases of Monbazillac (one third each Sauvignon, Sémillon, Muscadelle), 6,000 cases red Bergerac and about 5,000 Bergerac Sec.
M. Monbouché at his 17th-century property makes 3 wines. The Gendre Marsalet red is 50/50 Merlot/Cabernet, Grand Conseil white is mostly Sauvignon, the Monbazillac carries the Theulet et Marsalet label.

Château Tiregand
24100 Creysse.
Owner: Comtesse de St-Exupéry. 82 acres: 75 red (Merlot 35%, Cabernet Sauvignon 35%, Cabernet Franc 21%, Malbec 11%); 7 white (Sauvignon 65%, Sémillon 35%). 14,500 cases.
The biggest property in Pécharmant, dating from the 13th century and in the same family since 1831. A south slope on chalky soil gives the wine body for up to 2 years' barrel-ageing and sometimes up to 10 in bottle. The small white vineyard makes a Bergerac Sec, Les Galinoux.

UNIDOR (Union des Coopératives Vinicole de la Dordogne)
24100 St-Laurent-des-Vignes. 10,000 acres.
The Union of 9 Bergerac cooperatives and 4 in Lot-et-Garonne is much the biggest factor in the local scene, making and marketing 40% of all the wines of the appellation up to a very tolerable standard. Its reds, like its grapey dry whites, are made to drink young. One member, the Monbazillac cooperative, also operates Château Monbazillac, making a good standard of sweet wine but without the expensive refinements of wine-making that could make it very fine. The Union is based at St-Laurent-des-Vignes in the Montbazillac region just south of the town of Bergerac.

CAHORS

Cahors is certainly the most celebrated red wine of the scattered regions of the southwest. The ancient town on the river Lot with its famous fortified bridge is linked in the public mind with dramatic-sounding 'black wine'. The Lot took its produce down to the Garonne and the Garonne to Bordeaux, where it was either used to colour claret or shipped abroad under its own sombre colours. The legendary blackness of Cahors came from the Malbec, a grape grown in Bordeaux more for big crops than quality. But in its Cahors manifestation (where it is known as the Auxerrois) it is a horse of quite a different colour. On the rocky limestone *causses* above the winding Lot its crops are small and its skin thick. The old method of long fermentation (and often boiling some of the must to concentrate it) produced a darker wine than Bordeaux claret.

Cahors was destroyed by phylloxera in 1880 and again by the great frost of 1956 and struggled back very slowly, with little to raise it above the second

class of VDQS until the 1960s and 1970s, when a business-like cooperative and a handful of estates pulled the region together. It was promoted to appellation status in 1971, not for wines of any extraordinary colour or concentration but for well-balanced, vigorous and agreeable reds. The Auxerrois is now 70 per cent of the vineyard, blended with Merlot and Tannat (as in Madiran), supported by Dame Noire (alias Jurancon Noir) and minute quantities of Gamay.

Most of the vineyard is now on the alluvial valley land, which is very gravelly in places, although there have recently been plantings on the *causses*. Some say that a blend of valley and *causse* wine has more qualities than either alone. That of the *causse* is naturally harder and longer lived, but the trend today is to keep the wine relatively light and drink it much younger, even after two years, making a point of its appetizing 'cut'. Most growers advise drinking it cool. Total production: 800,000 cases.

Cahors: the bridge

CAHORS PRODUCERS

M. Baldès
Clos Triguedina, 46700 Puy-L'Evêque.

The eighth generation of the Baldès family own 100 acres and produce Cahors of 2 qualities – Clos de Triguedina is made to drink young; Prince Probus is aged for 3 years in new oak casks and needs another 2 or 3 years in bottle. The vineyard is 70% Auxerrois, 20% Merlot and 10% Tannat.

Château de Cayrou
46700 Puy-L'Evêque.

The Jouffreau family has owned the famous 25-acre Clos de Gamot at Prayssac for 300 years. The vines are all Auxerrois, many of them the original post-phylloxera replantation. In 1972 Jean Jouffreau bought the 75-acre Château de Cayrou, now planted with 70% Auxerrois, 20% Merlot, 7% Tannat and 3% Jurançon. He ferments for up to 4 weeks in stainless steel and ages in big and small barrels for up to 5, 8 or more years – an individualist whose wines, always worth tasting, can last 20 years.

Château de Chambert
Floressas, 46700 Puy-L'Evêque.

Marc Delgoulet of the Caves St-Antoine has rebuilt and replanted this property of 126 acres. The first harvest was 1978, and the wine, which wins medals, is now among the more concentrated, fruity and balanced of the area.

Les Côtes d'Olt
Parnac, 46140 Luzech.

Founded in 1947, this cooperative now has 500 members and with 3,700 acres is the largest producer of Vin de Pays des Coteaux de Quercy. Following a slump in the '70s, new methods and equipment are improving quality. The wines are found under a variety of names including Château Caix, Château Lagrezette and Château de Parnac, where Côtes-d'Olt have their cellars. Their new brand is called Impernal.

Durou & Fils
Gaudou, Vire-sur-Lot, 46700 Puy-L'Evêque.

A fifth-generation family estate that survived the lean years and now makes spicy and stylish wine from 50 acres aged in wood 2 years.

Domaine des Garriques
Vire-sur-Lot, 46700 Puy-L'Evêque.

Roger Labruyere's 42 acres make 8,000 cases of Cahors by firmly traditional methods.

L. E. Reutenauer
Pech d'Angely and Château Peyrat, 46002 Cahors.

Luc Reutenauer is president of the syndicate of Cahors growers and one of the most dynamic promoters of their wine. He himself owns 28 acres but his principal role is as négociant, with a turnover of 80,000 cases of wines designed for specific markets. Recently he has added an estate wine, Domaine des Vignals. All, he insists, should be served at cellar, not room, temperature.

Rigal & Fils
Château de St-Didier, Parnac, 46140 Luzech.

A family firm of négocians and owners of the Château de St-Didler with 173 acres planted. Rigal distributes a number of other domaine wines (incl. Le Castelas, Soullaillou, du Park, Domaine Eugénie) who subscribe to a charter which requires certain standards of yield and quality. He also distributes his own brands of Tradition and Carte Noire (vintage) and other wines of the southwest.

Caves St-Antoine
19102 Brive La Gaillard

Major producers and négociants of both Cahors and Gaillac, founded in 1963 by Marc Delgoulet. His Cahors properties are Château de Chambert (q.v.), Domaine du Single and Clos des Batuts, which are distributed by Menjucq. In Gaillac they own the Domaine de la Martine.

Domaine Des Savarines
46090 Trepoux

Ten acres. Danielle Biesbrouck bought this 10 acre estate (which once belonged to a counsellor of Louis XVI) in 1970. Without any formal training she has more or less single-handedly planted vines and produced her first vintage in 1978, with superb results. Her wine is aged in wood for 12–15 months and is rich, tannic and perfumed. She ferments her Auxerrois and Merlot separately and blends them during the winter.

Georges Vigouroux
Château de Haute Serre, Cieurac, 46003 Cahors.

Both as grower and négociant, M. Vigouroux has invested enormous energy in Cahors. The Château de Haute Serre is the culmination of his work; a stony hilltop site of 150 acres, 4 miles south of Cahors, reclaimed from scrub since 1970 with a winery big enough to ferment and age its wine as slowly as necessary. The varieties are 70% Auxerrois. 15% Tannat and 15% Merlot. Fermentation is in stainless steel for up to 3 weeks and ageing in barrels for 18 months. The good vintages – 1976, 1982, 1988 – last well in bottle. The name Caves du Roc is also used.

OTHER PRODUCERS

Jean Bernède
Clos la Coutale, Vire-sur-Lot, 46700 Puy-L'Evêque.
Henri Bessières
Peyebos, 46220 Prayssac.
André Bouloumié
Les Cambous, 46220 Preyssac.
Charles Burc
'Courbenac', 46700 Puy-L'Ev'que.

Burc & Fils
Roques, Leygues, 46700 Puy-L'Evêque.
Colette Delfour
Gaillac, 46140 Luzech.
Dumeaux & Fils
Vire-sur-Lot, 46700 Puy-L'Evêque.
Jacques Jouves
'Cournou', St-Vincent-Rive-d'Olt, 46140 Luzech.
Roger Labruyère
'Garrigues', Vire-sur-Lot, 46700 Puy-L'Evêque.

Mathieu Lescombes
Domaine de Paillas, Floressas, 46700 Puy-L'Evêque.
M J-C Valière
Domaine de Boliva, 46001 Cahors.
Charles Verhaegue
Domaine du Cedre, Vire-sur-Lot, 46700 Puy-L'Evêque
SCEA de Quattre et Treilles
Domaine de Quattre, Bagat en Quercy, 46800 Montcuq.

GAILLAC

Gaillac is one of the most productive and economically important of the scattered vineyards of the southwest. Historically it has supplied not only Albi, the capital of its *département*, the Tarn, but places much farther away – its reds having a name for amazing transportability and longevity. Some believe that it was established as a vineyard area before Bordeaux, when the Romans were still based on the Midi. It lies at the highest navigable point on the river Tarn, which flows to the sea through the Garonne, past Bordeaux. Its unheard-of indigenous grape varieties encourage the idea of extreme antiquity. Its reds are the Duras, the Brocol, the Fer-servadou and its white the Mauzac, the Ondenc and the Loin de l'Oeil (or l'En de l'El).

A century ago it was considered necessary to keep Gaillac reds 8 years in barrel and 12 years in bottle.

The Mauzac was favoured because it makes sweet, or fairly sweet, wine with a 'faint smell of cider'. The modern reconstruction of the industry, based on enormous cooperatives, has opted for less exotic ideas. A tradition of bottling white wine before its original fermentation was over, to make a sort of rustic champagne, has been modified. Sauvignon, Merlot, Syrah and Gamay have been brought in. All the wines are now lighter and more neutral than they used to be; the whites today are either plain and dry, or dry with a fizzy freshness induced by keeping them on their lees and bottling under pressure to make Gaillac Perlé, or *moelleux* (semi-sweet with 2 degrees of sugar unfermented). The reds are fairly firm and well-structured but otherwise unremarkable. Total production: 625,000 cases.

GAILLAC PRODUCERS

Jean Albert
Domaine de Labarthe, 81150 Marsac-sur-Tarn.
One can hardly say typical when there are so few private producers on any scale in the region, but M. Albert makes a representative range: a full-weight red of local grapes, Duras, Brocol and the Fer-servadou, a very light Gamay *vin de primeur*, sweet white of Mauzac and dry white of Sauvignon blended with Loin de l'Oeil and recently a sparkling wine.

Jacques Auque
Mars Pignou, 81600 Gaillac.
A family estate of 50 acres specializing in traditional dry white Gaillac (no sweet, no sparkling); a blend of Sauvignon and Loin de l'Oeil, and its red opposite number, made of Duras, Brocol, Merlot and Cabernet Franc, aged for 1 year in big wooden casks and best bottle-aged for 5 years.

Boissel-Rhodes
Château de Rhodes, 81600 Gaillac.

A century-old estate of 75 acres now mainly concerned with *méthode champenoise* (1,800 cases under the name René Rieux) and red, both Gamay *primeur* and *vin de garde* of the area, brewed from Duras, Syrah, Fer-servadou or Brocol and Gamay. Some sparkling wine is also made by the '*méthode gaillaçoise*' – bottled before the first fermentation is finished, then treated as in the champagne method.

Jean Cros
Domaine Jean Cros. Cahuzac-sur-Vère, 81140 Castelnau-de-Montmiral.

One of the most important personalities in the area, Jean Cros has a reputation for quality here, and in his second estate Ch. Larroze, which is well deserved. He makes many different wines using for reds at Ch. Larroze, Duras, Merlot and Cabernet Sauvignon; and at Domaine Jean Cros, Duras, Syrah and Fer Servadou. Whites are made from Mauzac and the *perlé* from Loin de l'Oeil and Mauzac which is produced by the *méthode gaillaçoise*.

Domaine des Très Cantous
Très-Cantous, 81140 Castelnau-de-Montmiral

Robert Plageoles is the owner of this unconventional estate with just 32 acres of vines, which nevertheless produces seven different wines. He is moving against the Gaillac fashion of blending red varieties and is making a varietal white wine. He is considering ageing in new barrels. He makes a sparkling wine by traditional methods and dry Sauvignon, a Mauzac and a Mauzac *moelleux*.

Gaillac et du Pays Cordais
Labastide de Lévis, 81150 Marssac-sur-Tarn.

The major producer of Gaillac, founded in 1949, with 543 members farming some 5,000 acres, half of it Gaillac AOC and half Vin de Pays du Tarn. Its wines have gained some character and charm – qualities they used to lack – and have improved. A considerable amount is sparkling, but their Gaillac Perlé, a very fresh half-fizzy dry white, is more original and better value. The red *vin de pays* made by carbonic maceration is another good buy. The GIVISO group exports a part of the 1,400,000-case production.

Rabastens
81800 Rabastens

Rabastens is southwest of Gaillac, making similar wine. This 1953 coop has 516 members farming 4,125 acres of Gaillac AOC and Vin de Pays du Tarn.

Técou
81600 Gaillac

A smaller rival to the coop at Labastide de Lévis, founded in 1953, with 571 members. The best of the 3 coops in the area.

Union Vinicole Coopérative
81600 Gaillac

The original coop of the region, founded in 1926, with 480 members but only a small amount of AOC Gaillac. Most of its wine is *vin de table*.

BUZET

When Bordeaux was firmly limited to the *département* of the Gironde, one of the upcountry sources of claret to be hardest hit was the hills south of Garonne in the north of the Armagnac country: the Côtes de Buzet, now called simply Buzet. Happily, white wine for distillation was an alternative crop, but the gravel and chalky clay on good southeast slopes had long produced very satisfactory red wine. In the last 30 years they have been reconstituted and are doing better than ever.

The cooperative at Damazan dominates the area, making red wine to good Bordeaux standards.

BUZET PRODUCERS

Domaine de Janicot
A 20-acre estate contracted to the négociants Menjucq.

Domaine Padère
Ambrus, 47160 Damazan.

The unexpected enterprise of a distinguished citizen of Beaujolais, M. Bloud of the Château de Moulin-à-Vent, who wanted to try his hand at something new and since 1973 has planted more than 100 acres of Buzet, with 58 more projected. The château is 150 years old but only had a scrap of vineyard. At present M. Bloud uses no barrels, preferring the flavour of fruit uncomplicated, but he will be experimenting with 3 months in barrels and 12 in vats before bottling.

Château Pierron
47160 Damazan

One of the few old-established estates of Buzet, owned by M. Hérail since 1932. 66 acres, half red grapes (50% Merlot, 25% each of the Cabernets) and half white for Armagnac. He ages his Buzet 12–18 months in Bordeaux *barriques*.

Caves Réunis des Côtes de Buzet
Buzet-sur-Baize, 47160 Damazan.

The overwhelming majority of Buzet comes from this model cooperative (with its own cooper), which has steadily expanded and improved the vineyards of the area since 1954 and can claim the credit for its promotion to appellation status in 1973. The man responsible, Jean Mermillo, was a former manager of Château Lafite. 450 members farm 2,900 acres, 98% in the Bordeaux red grapes: 40% Merlot and 30% each of the Cabernets. The wine must be described as a light but round and satisfying claret. A splendidly tasty special selection from older vines on the best soils (some gravel, some chalky clay) is labelled Cuvée Napoléon. Another label is Château de Geuyze, a 75-acre estate making fine wine for keeping. A little dry white wine is made, also of the classic Bordeaux grapes. All wines are aged in wood, the lighter ones for about three months, the best ones in new wood for six months followed by six months in older wood.

MADIRAN

Madiran is the wine that came back from the dead. Forty years ago the vineyard in the Vic Bilh hills on the southern edge of the Armagnac country, 25 miles north of Pau, had dwindled to a dozen acres. Today there are 2,000 and some would claim that Madiran is the best red of the southwest, Cahors included. If it lacked the advantages of Cahors, fame and accessibility, it also avoided the identity crisis which still bothers the better-known wine. The name of 'black wine' lingers, while the reality is merely a healthy red.

The peculiar quality of Madiran is to start life with a disconcerting bite, then to mellow quite rapidly into claret with a most singular style and texture. The bouquet has the teasing qualities of a good Médoc or Graves. When I was looking for the right word for a nine-year-old 1973 from the main cooperative of the region, I was so struck by its silkiness on the tongue that I hesitated over the rather lame 'liquid', then tried 'limpid'. Later I looked Madiran up in Paul de Cassagnac's *French Wines*, a little-known but extremely rewarding work of 1936. 'An infinitely fluid savour' were the first words that struck my eye. So Madiran is consistent, despite its near demise; across 55 years it still caresses the palate in a seductively swallowable way.

This is the more odd in that de Cassagnac fulminates against 'the inferior Tannat', a 'common grape' being introduced to replace the Cabernet in the region for the sake of its bigger crop. All real Madiran, he says, is Cabernet. Yet today its producers tell us the secret of its character is the grape that sounds like tannin, and gives all the harshness its name implies; a smaller-berried cousin of the Malbec, Cot or (in Cahors) Auxerrois. A high proportion of Tannat, they say, is essential. I should like to taste a wholly Cabernet Madiran to judge for myself.

The Vic Bilh hills, a sort of very *piano* rehearsal for the soaring Pyrenees, parallel to the south, give their name to the produce of the Pacherenc, a local white grape. Pacherenc du Vic Bilh is grown by the same growers as Madiran and consists of a complicated blend with Mansengs, Sémillon, Sauvignon, Courbu (alias Sarrat), and Arrufiat. Traditionally it is as sweet a wine as the autumn permits, but some growers make it dry, and some bottle it straight from its lees in spring like Muscadet.

The same growers also produce red, rosé and white wines for the appellation Béarn, which meet their fate in the excellent local restaurants.

MADIRAN PRODUCERS

Château d'Aydie
64330 Garlin. The top Madiran of M. Laplace is 100% Tannat, and some of his huge old vines survived the phylloxera. Another version has 40% Cabernets. His 100-acre vineyards also produce a fresh Pacherenc.

Domaine Barréjat
Maumusson, 32400 Riscle. An old Capmartin family estate of 37 acres, planted in half Tannat and half Cabernet Franc. The wine is kept in oak for 8 months and needs 4 or 5 years in bottle to soften.

Alain Brumont
Domaine Boucassé, Maumusson, 32400 Riscle. An important and expanding estate, whose 54 acres have recently been almost tripled by the purchase of Ch. Montus (62 acres) and a part share in another 37 acres. The grapes are half Tannat and one-quarter each of the Cabernets. Eight to ten years is a good age. Also Pacherenc white.

Château de Peyros
Corbères Abères, 64350 Lembeye. Denis de Robillard has 57 acres planted in this very old vineyard, with 45% Tannat and 50% Cabernet Franc plus Cabernet Sauvignon. His friends call his wine 'Le Bordelais du Madiran'; the relatively high proportion of Cabernet makes it rounder and more 'elegant', with a more pronounced bouquet than its neighbours.

Domaine de Sitère
A 40-acre vineyard of very old vines, mostly Tannat. Distributed by Menjucq.

August Vignau
Domaine Pichard, Soublecause, 65700 Maubourguet. A 25-acre estate, half Tannat and half Cabernets, locally considered one of the best of Madiran.

Caves Coopératives
Union des Producteurs Plaimont
St-Mont, 32400 Riscle. A union of 3 cooperatives, at St-Mont, Aignan and Plaisance, founded in 1974. Producing 1,667,000 cases of fine Madiran, VDQS Côtes de St-Mont and Vin de Pays Côtes de Gascogne (the very successful Cépage Colombard).

Tursan
40320 Geaune. Tursan is a VDQS neighbour of Madiran. The cooperative (founded 1957, with 350 members and 865 acres) is the biggest producer of these interesting country wines.

Vic-Bilh-Madiran
Crouseilles, 64350 Lembeye. The principal producer of Madiran, making nearly half the total. Founded 1950. 200 members have 1,200 acres. Half the current production of 267,000 cases is AOC Madiran, white Pacherenc, Béarn red and rosé, the rest *vin de pays*, Vin des Fleurs. Certain old bottles are very fine indeed.

Vinicole de Bellocq
64270 Salies-de-Bearn. Salies takes its name from its salty spring, provider of the necessary preservative for curing the famous jambon de Bayonne. Its cooperative of 250 members, 432 acres, is the chief source of Béarn appellation red, rosé and white, 111,000 cases a year.

des Vins d'Irouléguy et du Pays Basque
64430 St-Étienne-de-Baïgorry. The sole source today of the Basque wine, Irouléguy, which tastes different from, but is made to a recipe almost identical to Madiran: half and half Tannant and Cabernet. Founded 1954. 210 members; 277 acres producing some 31,300 cases of AOC Irouléguy.

JURANÇON

All references to Jurançon start with the story of the infant King Henri IV, whose lips at birth, in Pau in 1553, were brushed with a clove of garlic and moistened with Jurançon wine – a custom said still to be followed in the Bourbon family, though without such spectacular results. The point is that Jurançon is strong, not just in alcohol but in character. Its highly aromatic grapes ripen on the Pyrenean foothills south of Pau in autumns warmed by south winds from Spain. Its flavour is enhanced by small crops (36 hectolitres a hectare for dry wine and 28 for sweet). The sweet *moelleux* is, or should be, made by harvesting very late, in November, when hot days and freezing nights have shrivelled the grapes (*passerillage*) and concentrated their juice.

The two principal grapes are the Gros and Petit Manseng, the latter not only smaller but tastier. Both give wines of high degree with a remarkably 'stiff' and positive structure in your mouth, almost fierce when young but maturing to scents and flavours variously described as like such exotic fruits and spices as mangoes, guavas and cinnamon. Colette provided tasting notes I will not presume to rival: 'I was a girl when I met this prince; aroused, imperious, treacherous as all great seducers are – Jurançon.'

JURANÇON PRODUCERS

Alfred Barrère
Clos Camcaillau, Lahourcade, 64150 Mourenx. The Barrère property of 38 acres goes back to 1580 – its name is Basque for *champs de cailloux*, the stony field, and is now run by Alfred Barrère's daughter. 42% is planted in Gros Manseng, 33% in Petit Manseng and Courbu, bottled in spring. *Moelleux* is made in 2 qualities, *crème de tête*, picked in successive selections of the most shrivelled Petit Manseng, sometimes with noble rot, and a standard quality, both aged 2 winters in oak.

Jean Chigé
64110 Jurançan. The Chigés have owned their 12-acre Cru Lamouroux for 250 years. They grow the Gros Manseng for dry Jurançon and the Petit for sweet, which they control with sulphur when the fermentation has left 60 grams a litre (6%) of the natural sugar. Both wines are aged for 18 months in oak or chestnut casks. Private customers buy almost all of it.

Alexis Guirouilh
Domaine Guirouilh, Lasseube, 64290 Gan. The 20-acre Clos Guirouilh has been in the family since 1670. 60% is planted with Gros Manseng for dry wine, which is bottled in its first spring, the rest in Petit Manseng, which is picked very late, partly dried on the vine and freezing cold, to ferment very slowly into *moelleux*, either alone or with a proportion of Gros Manseng. The sweet wine is kept in oak for up to 2 years before bottling and will keep up to 20 in bottle.

Cave Coopérative de Gan-Jurançon
64290 Gan. The Gan cooperative (founded in 1950) dominates the increasing production of this famous old white wine making a dry Brut Océan and Cuvée Quatrième Centenaire. They have recently taken over Château les Astros and now have 350 members who farm 988 acres.

Charles Hours
Clos Uroulat, 64360 Monien. 22 acre estate set in an amphitheatre of hills. Charles Hours is experimenting with wood ageing for his *moelleux* which is elegant and delicious.

Château Jolys
Ch. Jolys, 64290 Gan. Robert Latrille bought Château Jolys in 1958 and spent the next six years replanting and started making his own wine in 1983, having formerly sold all his grapes to a négociant. He uses stainless steel vats and modern methods to produce his wine. He makes Jurançon Sec and *moulleux* which are improving with experience.

Henri Ramonteu
Domaine Cauhapé, 64360 Monien. Grapes for the *moelleux* wine made at Henri Ramonteu's vineyard are left on the vines until well into the autumn, a process which makes the juice more concentrated. The wine is fermented for up to a month. His Jurançon Sec grapes are picked in October. He grows Gros Manseng, Petit Manseng and Courbu.

CÔTES DE DURAS

The Côtes de Duras has the misfortune, like Bergerac, to lie just over the departmental boundary from Bordeaux – more particularly from Entre-Deux-Mers. Its wine is in every way comparable: most of it fresh, sometimes rather thin dry white made to taste as far as possible of Sauvignon, though the greater proportion of the grapes are Sémillon, and small amounts of Ugni Blanc, Colombard and Mauzac. One-third is red, with as much as 60 per cent Cabernet Sauvignon, 30 per cent Merlot and a little Cabernet Franc and Malbec.

The red, however, does not seem to have the potential of the more recently recognized appellation Buzet. Much of it is made by *macération carbonique* to produce a fleetingly fruity effect. The majority of growers belong to cooperatives over the border in Entre-Deux-Mers. Duras itself has only had a coop since 1960.

Société Coopérative Agricole de Duras
47120 Duras. Competent but relatively small cooperative, founded in 1965. 94 members farm 939 of the 5,000-odd acres of the appellation to produce 170,000 cases of Côtes de Duras, two-thirds of it white, which is marketed by UNIDOR (q.v.).

COTES DU FRONTON

The slopes around Fronton, 15 miles north of Toulouse and only 20 west of Gaillac, achieved appellation status in 1975 for their ripely fruity red, which up to then had been a secret kept by the people of Toulouse. The local red grape is called the Négrette, a relation of the Tannat of Madiran, the Auxerrois of Cahors and the Malbec of Bordeaux. For those who cannot resist the infinite complications of ampelography I should add that the Négrette turns up in the Charente (of all places) as Ragoutant.

Château Bellevue-La-Forêt
31620 Fronton. The outstanding property of a hitherto obscure region. Since 1974 Patrick Germain has re-planted 215 acres of orchard with the traditional grapes of the area: 50%
Négrette, 25% Cabernets and 25% Syrah and Gamay. The different varieties are fermented separately, then blended to make a roundly fruity wine of immediate appeal, which will presumably get even better as the vines mature. Already half his 55,000-case production is exported.

Cave Coopératives
'Les Côtes du Fronton'
31620 Fronton. The biggest coop of the Côtes du Frontonnais and one of the biggest in France, founded 1947. 586 members (including two estates whose wines are vinified seperately, Château Marguerite and Château de Craussac) now producing nearly 456,000 cases of red and rosé appellation wine and 822,000 of *vin de table*.

GIVISO
47000 Agen. The initials stand for Groupement d'Intérét Economique de Vignerons du Sud Ouest. The organization was started in 1975 to represent 7 leading cooperatives of southwestern areas with increasing production and rising standards. The members are the cooperatives of Buzet, Côtes d'Olt at Parnac (Cahors), Gaillac et Pays Cordais at Labastide, G-Jurançon, Vic Bilh-Madiran and Busca-Maniban (Armagnac).

COTES DU MARMANDAIS

The Côtes du Marmandais lies right on the fringes of Bordeaux. Its light red (its major product) certainly comes under the general heading of 'claret', and its Sauvignon/Sémillon white is comparable to everyday Bordeaux. Two cooperatives make nearly all the wine, marketed through UNIDOR at Monbazillac, and have been inspiring more and better planting by the multitude of small growers. They have now reached the delimitation required but have not yet received an appellation. Average production: 1,160,000 cases.

Cave Coopérative Intercommunale de Cocumont
47250 Bouglon. Younger (1957) and more progressive than its brother-cooperative, producing Vin de Pays de l'Agenais and *vins de table*, and VDQS Côtes du Marmandais. Members are replanting with good advice; wine-making is very modern. 670,000 cases a year. 340 members.

Société Coopérative Vinicole des Côtes du Marmandais.
47200 Marmande. The older (1948) of the two considerable cooperatives that make 159,500 cases of Côtes du Marmandais and about twice as much Vin de Pays de l'Argenais and *vins de table*. There are 430 members and 1,700 acres, now mainly planted with Merlot and Cabernet for the reds, but where such obscure local varieties as Abouriou and Bouchalés may still be found but only in *Van de Pays*. The Marmandais red is like soft lightweight claret, ageing well up to about 4 years.

M. Laugauzère
Beaupuy. Independent grower in the Côtes du Marmandais, with 50 acres. He makes red and white wines of great character in rustic conditions.

VINS DE PAYS

Throughout 1981 and 1982 a stream of decrees flowed from Paris, signed by the Minister of Agriculture, setting out the regulations for newly coined *vins de pays*. The object was to give pride to local production that has hitherto had no identity. Wines that were previously used entirely for blending, or at best to go labelless to the local bars, are now made to minimum standards and in regulated quantities.

This list of *vins de pays* is still changing, a decade after the pioneers were promulgated. Some have been raised to VDQS and AOC status. New *vins de pays* have appeared. This list sets out the ground rules for wines that will build reputations, for some that have already started – and no doubt also for others that nobody will ever hear of again.

The first essential information is the area delimited. Some are as local as three or four parishes; some as sweeping as the whole of the Loire valley (Vins de Pays du Jardin de la France). One may perhaps assume that a small area represents a positive local tradition which is worth nurturing (or a strong local lobby).

The second important control is over the grape varieties to be grown. In some cases one or more classic grapes are prescribed as obligatory, while a number of others are tolerated up to a percentage. Some areas do not specify varieties at all.

The last two indicators are the minimum natural alcoholic strength required (of which you can broadly say the higher the strength the better the wine is likely to be) and the maximum crop allowed. Most *vins de pays* are allowed 80 hectolitres a hectare, which would be high in an *appellation contrôlée* area but low in the *vin de table* vineyards of Languedoc.

The entries are organized in the following way. The name of the *vin de pays* is followed by the *département* or region, whichever is most familiar. Next comes the date of establishment. Then the area delineated with, where possible, a central town and some indication of the type of terrain.

Maximum crop is only given when it differs from 80 hl/ha, and minimum alcohol when it differs from the almost universal 10.5 to 11 degrees. Grape varieties are listed where specified. Where the rules do not specify the grape varieties it can be assumed that the standard grapes of the region are used. The colour of wine is only given when all three colours are not made. Occasionally technical details such as planting density, pruning and training methods, sugar levels and minimum acidity are regulated, and this is noted in the entries. The producers whose names are given have been recommended by local experts. Most *vins de pays* production comes from *caves coopératives* although there are some notable exceptions.

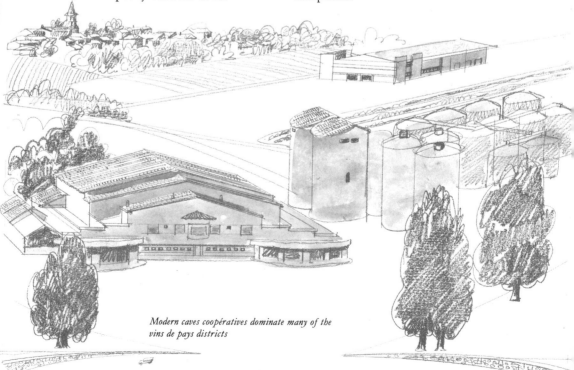

Modern caves coopératives dominate many of the vins de pays districts

RHONE AND PROVENCE

Most of the wine growing areas of the Rhône and Provence are entitled to the wide-ranging Côtes du Rhône or Provence AOCs. The *vins de pays* cover outlying, often interesting, districts and one or two zones within the AOC areas. Bouches-du-Rhône has its own *vin de pays*.

Coteaux de l'Ardèche

Ardèche. 1981. 14 communes in the Ardèche and Chassezac valleys in the southern Ardèche, in the foothills of the Cevennes. 10°. Grapes, red: 70%, minimum of one or more of Cabernet Franc, Cabernet Sauvignon, Carignan, Cinsaut, Counoise, Gamay, Grenache, Merlot, Pinot Noir, Picpoul, Syrah. White: 70% minimum of one or more of Aligoté, Bourboulenc, Chardonnay, Marsanne, Roussanne, Sauvignon, Viognier, Picpoul Gris. Producers: M. Dupre, Lagorce, 07150 Vallon Pont d'Arc; GAEC Brunel, St-Remèze, 07700 Bourg St-Andeol. 6 coops including Ruoms, 07120 Ruoms. 156,000 expected to rise to 222,000 cases.

d'Argens

Provence. 1981. 17 communes around Draguignan in the Argens valley, mostly land also entitled to the AOC Provence. 167,000 to 222,000 cases.

Coteaux des Baronnies

Rhône. 1981. Area around Rémuzat and Rosans, north of Mont Ventoux in the Alpine foothills. Grapes, red and rosé: Cinsaut, Grenache, Gamay, Syrah, Pinot Noir plus up to 30% others. White: Rhône varieties plus Aligoté and Chardonnay. 3 coops including Nyons (26110) and Puymeras (84110). 222,000 to 333,000 cases.

Comté de Grignan

Rhône. 1981. 9 cantons around Vinsobres and Grignan in the lower Rhône. 10°. Grapes, red and rosé: Grenache, Syrah, Cinsaut, Mourvèdre, Gamay, Pinot Noir plus up to 30% others. White: normal Rhône varieties. 2 coops at Suze La Rousse, 26130 and St-Marice-sur-Eygues, 26110 Nyons. 222,000 to 278,000.

Maures

Provence. 1982. In the Var *département*, east and southeast of Maures mountain range extending east to Estérel mountains. Grapes, red, rosé: two thirds red, one third rosé and a little white. Producers: coopératives Gonfaron, Puget Ville, Le Luc, Pierrefeu, La Londe, Grimaud, Carnoules, Cogolin, Ramatuelle, Plan de la Tour, La Crau, Cannet des Maures, Pignans, Vidauban, Les Arcs, Collobrières, Le Muy, Fréjus-Roquebrue. 778,000 to 889,000 cases.

Mont-Caume

Provence. 1982. 12 communes around Bandol. Producers: Vincent Racine, Hubert Jouve, La Cadière d'Azur (83740). Coop at St-Cyr-sur-Mer (83270). 222,000 to 278,000 cases.

Principauté d'Orange

Rhône. 1981. Cantons of Bollène, Orange, Vaison-La-Romaine and Valréas, east of the Rhône in the Côtes-du-Rhône Villages country: Min. alch: 10.8, max 11.8. Pruning methods specified. 89,000 to 133,000 cases.

Petite Crau

Bouches-du-Rhône. 1982. 4 communes in the Petite Crau hills south of Avignon. Min. alch: 11°, no more than 12.5° for white and 13° for red and rosé. Pruning systems regulated. 1 coop at Noves (13550). 56,000 to 67,000 cases. It may rise to 111,000 cases.

Collines Rhodaniennes

Central Rhône. 1981. Parts of 4 *départements* on both banks. 10°. Grapes, red and rosé: Syrah, Gamay, plus Pinot Noir, Merlot and Cabernet Franc in some districts, plus secondary grapes up to 30%. White: traditional Rhône varieties plus Chardonnay in some districts. 4 coops including St-Désirat, 07340 Serrières. 167,000 cases.

Coteaux Varois

Provence. 1981. One of the first *vins de pays*, this area is dominated by coop-eratives, although the best wines are produced by the private estates. The main production is Vin du Pays du Var and the main varieties are Carignan, Cinsaut, Grenache, Mourvèdre and Syrah.

THE GARD

The *département* of the Gard stretches from the Rhône at Avignon west into the hills of the Cevennes. The chief town is Nimes. Most of the *département* is wine-growing country, and there is a *vin de pays* for the whole area: Vin de Pays du Gard. 11 other *vins de pays*, covering areas of varying size, are listed below. No specified grape varieties.

Mont Bouquet

Gard. 1982. 19 communes around Vézenobres, northwest of Nimes. 2 coops at Brouzet Les Alès, 30580 Lussan, and St-Maurice-de-Cazevieille, 30190 St-Chaptes. 222,000 cases.

Coteaux Cévenols

Gard. 1981. 24 communes northeast of Alès in the Cevennes foothills. Producers: M. Silhol, St-Victor de Malcap, 30500 St-Ambroix. 4 coops including Rochegude, 30430 Barjac. 56,000 cases.

Coteaux de Cèze

Gard. 1981. 46 communes on the west bank of the Rhône around Bagnols-sur-Cèze and Roquemaure. 4 coops including Pont St-Esprit (30130) and Roquemaure (30150). 278,000 cases.

Serre de Coiran

Gard. 1982. 23 communes south of Alès in the Cevennes foothills. 6 coops including Cardet, 30350 Ledignan. 89,000 to 133,000 cases.

Coteaux Flaviens

Gard. 1981. 9 communes to the southwest of Nimes. Producers: Domaine de Campuget, 30129 Manduel. Domaine de Cassagnes, 30800 St-Gilles. Coops at Beauvoisin (30640) and Bouillargues (30230). 389,000 cases.

Coteaux du Pont du Gard

Gard. 1981. 19 communes around Remoulins, between Nimes and Avignon. 8 coops including Vers-Pont-du-Gard, 30210 Remoulins. 444,000 to 556,000 cases.

Coteaux du Salavès

Gard. 1981. 28 communes around St-Hippolyte-du-Fort in the west of the *département*. Producers: M. Pieyte, Mandiargues, 30170. 4 coops including Moulezan, 30350 Ledignan. 11,000 to 22,000 cases.

Uzège

Gard. 1981. 26 communes around Uzès, north of Nimes. Producers: M. Reboul, Sagues, 30700 Uzès. 5 coops including St -Quentin-La-Poterie, 30700. 89,000 to 111,000 cases.

Vaunage

Gard. 1982. 14 communes to the west of Nimes. 3 coops including Clarensac (30870). 56,000 cases.

Vistrenque

Gard. 1982. Northeast of the Gard in the Plaine du Vistre. 11,000 to 22,000 cases.

Côtes du Vidourle

Gard. 1982. 15 communes around Sommières, west of Nimes. Producers: Marcel Granic, Aspères (30860). 3 coops including Villevieille, 30250 Sommières. 78,000 to 111,000 cases.

HÉRAULT

The Hérault is the biggest wine-producing *département* in France. Vin de Pays de l'Hérault covers the whole area. 27 local districts have individual sets of regulations. Some of the areas cover land which is in the St-Chinian and Minervois AOC zones, and other include communes entitled to the Coteaux du Languedoc AOC. *See the chapter on the Midi (pages 209–219) for more details.*

Adrailhou

Hérault. 1982. Area around southernmost part of Hérault *département* at the mouths of the Hérault and Orb. Producers: caves coopératives at Portiragnes, Vias, Villeneuve-les-Béziers, Sèrignan. 44,000 cases red.

Vicomté d'Aumelas

Hérault. 1982. 14 communes south of Gignac in the Hérault valley. Technical restrictions. 6 coops, including

Vendémian and Puilacher, 34230 Paulhan. 444,000 to 556,000 cases.

Mont Baudile
Hérault. 1981. Hérault *département* around St-Jean de la Blaquière at the foot of the Causses du Larzac and the Saint-Baudile mountain. Two thirds production red, rest rosé and some white. The leading coopérative is at Saint-Felix-de-Lodez. 144,000 to 278,000 cases.

Beňovie
Hérault. 1982. 15 communes in the extreme east of the *département*. Coop at Beaulieu, 34160 Castries. 133,000 cases.

Bérange
Hérault. 1982. 7 communes around Castries and Lunel in the southeast of the *département*. Producers: M. de Forton, Baillargues (34670). 2 coops at Baillargues and Montaud, 34160 Montaud Castries. 17,000 to 45,000 cases.

Bessan
Hérault. 1981. Commune of Bessan, inland from Agde. Producers: René Fulcrand; Clarou L'Epine, both at Bessan (34550). Coop at Bessan. 56,000 to 167,000 cases.

Côtes du Brian
Hérault. 1982. 13 communes around Minerve and Olonzac in the Minervois. Producers: Robert Caffort, Minerve; Aimé Fraisse, St-Jean de Minervois; Laurent Mari, Aignes; Luc Mondie, Aigues-Vives; M. Marcon, St-Jean de Minervois. 9 coops including 'La Vigneronne Minervoise', 34210 Olonzac. 556,000 cases.

Cassan
Hérault. 1982. 4 communes around Roujan in the central Hérault. 75hl/ha. Coop at Roujan (34320). 22,000 to 45,000 cases.

Caux
Hérault. 1982. Commune of Caux, north of Pézanas. Producers: Henri Collet, Dom. de Daurion. Coop at Caux, 34720. 222,000 to 333,000 cases.

Côtes du Ceressou
Hérault. 1981. 15 communes near Clermont L'Hérault. 70hl/ha. Producers: M. Servent, Dom. de Fabregues, Aspiran; GFA Pages Renouvier, Nizas; Bernard Jany, Dom. de la Condamine, Paulhan (34230); SCA St-Pierre de Granonpiac, St-André de Sangonis. 8 coops including Aspiran, 34230 Pauhan. 33,000 cases.

Cessenon
Hérault. 1982. Commune of Cessenon, east of St-Chinian. Coop at Cessenon (34460). 333,000 cases.

Coteaux de Bessiles
1987. 130,000 cases.

Coteaux d'Enserune
Hérault. 1981. 11 communes west of Béziers. Producers: Dom. d'Auveille et Montels, Capestang; Dom. de la

Garrigue, Nissan Les Enserune; Dom. de la Grande Carmargue, Montady. 6 coops including Nissan Les Enserune (34440). 222,000 to 445,000 cases.

Coteaux de Fontcaude
Hérault. 1982. 6 communes south of St-Chinian. Producers: Pierre Comps, Puisserguier, B. Farret d'Asties, Dom. de Carlètes, Quarante, 34310 Capestang. 111,000 to 278,000 cases.

Sables du Golfe du Lion
Hérault and Gard. 1982. Sand dunes and coastal strips in parts of 12 communes to the west of the mouth of the Rhône. Grapes, red and rosé: Cabernet Sauvignon, Cabernet Franc, Carignan, Cinsault, Grenache, Lledoner Pelut, Merlot, Syrah and up to 30% others. White: Ugni, Clairette, Carignan, Muscats, Sauvignon and up to 30% others. Producers: Cave Coopérative d'Aigues Mortes, 30220 Aigues Mortes; Compagnie des Salins du Midi, 34000 Montpellier. 111,000 to 156,000 cases.

Monts de la Grage
Hérault. 1982. 6 communes in the hills around St-Chinian. 1 coop at St-Chinian (34360). 220,000 cases.

Gorges de l'Hérault
Hérault. 1982. 3 communes in the upper Hérault valley around Gignac. Wine-making restrictions. White and rosé 11°, red 10.5°. 2 coops including Gignac (34150). 56,000 to 89,000 cases.

Coteaux de Laurens
Hérault. 1982. 10.5°. Min. acidity specified. 7 communes around Laurens and Faugères. 1 coop: Laurens, 34480 Magalas. 278,000 cases.

Coteaux du Libron
Hérault. 1982. 6 communes around Béziers. Technical specifications. Producers: G. Vidal, Béziers; Norbert Alker, Dom. Les Bergeries, Béziers; Georges Gaujal, Dom. de Libouriac, Béziers. 5 coops including Béziers (34500). 445,000 to 567,000 cases.

Val de Montferrand
Hérault. 1982. Parts of 5 cantons north of Montpellier. Technical specifications. Producers: M. Pagevy, Dom. du Viviers, 34170 Jacou; GAEC de Brunet, Causse de la Selle (34380). 9 coops including Assas, 34160 Castries. 445,000 to 556,000 cases.

Collines de la Moure
Hérault. 1982. 27 communes around Frontagnan and Mireval. Producers: P. Leenhard, Dom. de Lunac, Fabregues; H. Artignan, Vic La Gardiole; M. de Gaulard d'Allaines, Abbaye de Valmagne. 10 coops including Montarnaud, 34570 Pignan. 1m. cases.

Coteaux de Murviel
Hérault. 1982. 9 communes in the Orb valley. 6 coops including Murviel, 34490 Murviel des Béziers. 223,000 to 334,000 cases.

Haute Vallée de l'Orb
Hérault. 1982. 31 communes in the northwest of the *département*. 70hl/ha. 10.5°. 2 coops including Bousquet d'Orb (34260). 220,000 cases.

Littoral Orb-Hérault
Renamed Adrailhou (q.v.)

Pézenas
Hérault. 1982. Commune of Pézenas. Coop at Pézenas (34210). 89,000 to 111,000 cases.

Coteaux du Salagou
Hérault. 1981. 20 communes around Lodève in the hills. 70hl/ha. Technical specifications. 3 coops including Octon, 34800 Clermont-l'Hérault. 56,000 to 67,000 cases.

Côtes de Thau
Hérault. 1981. 5 communes around Florensac, near the coast at Agde. Technical specifications. 5 coops including Pomérols (34810). 389,000 to 667,000 cases.

Côtes de Thongue
Hérault. 1982. Red and white. 14 communes around Sevrain, north of Béziers. 8 coops, including Montblanc, 34290 Servian and Domaine de l'Arjolle in the village of Ponzolles. 333,000 to 556,000 cases.

AUDE

The entire *département* of the Aude, which stretches inland from Narbonne, is entitled to Vin de Pays de l'Aude.

Haute Vallée d'Aude
Aude. 1981. 55 communes around Lomous. Min. 11°. Max. 12°, 70hl/ha. Grapes, red and rosé: Cabernet Sauvignon, Cabernet Franc, Cot, Merlot. White: Chenin, Chardonnay, Sémillon, Terret Blanc, Terret Gris. Pruning systems regulated. 2 coops at Couiza (11190) and Rouffiac-d'Aude, 11250 St-Hilaire. 222,000 cases.

Hautervie en Pays d'Aude
Aude. 1982. 8 communes in the Corbières and the Orbieu valley. Grapes: wide range. 6 coops. 333,000 to 444,000 cases.

Coteaux du Littoral Audois
Aude. 1981. Communes of Gruissan, Bages, Fitou, Lapalme, Leucate, Peyriac-de-Mer, Port-La-Nouvelle, Sigean, Caves, Feuilla, Portel and Treilles, on the coast east of the Corbières hills, 100hl/ha. 4 coops including Gruissan, (11430). 333,000 to 444,000 cases.

Hauts de Badens
Aude. 1982. Commune of Baden, south of the Minervois. Producers: Jean Poudou, Jacques Hortola, Gérald Branca, all at Baden, 11300 Trèbes. 110,000 to 167,000 cases.

Coteaux de la Cabrerisse
Aude. 1981. 3 communes around Thézan in the Corbières. Grapes: only

Carignan, Cinsaut, Grenache, Syrah, Mourvèdre, Terret, Clairette, Cabernet Franc, Cabernet Sauvignon, Merlot, Lladoner Pelut, Alicanté-Bouschet. 2 coops at Thézan and St-Laurent, 11200 Lezignan. 200,000 to 222,000 cases.

Coteaux de la Cité de Carcassonne
Aude. 1982. 11 communes around Carcassonne. 10.5°. 70hl/ha. Grapes, red and rosé: Carignan, Alicanté-Bouschet, Cinsaut and Grenache with minimum of 10% Cabernet Sauvignon, Cabernet Franc or Merlot. White: wide range. Planting density and acidity controlled. Producers: Pierre Castel, Pennautier; Louis Gobin, Cavanac; André Castel, Rustiques; Yves Barthez, Pennautier. 5 coops. 222,000 to 333,000 cases.

Cucugnan
Aude. 1982. Commune of Cucugnan in the Corbières. Grapes: any. 1 coop at Cucugnan, 11350 Tuchan. 67,000 to 77,000 cases.

Val de Cesse
Aude. 1981. Canton of Ginestas, Minervois, northwest of Narbonne. Producers: Jean Gleizes, Ouveillan; Pierre Calvet, Ouveillan; Pierre Fil, Mailhac; Jacques Mayzonnier, Pouzols. 4 coops including St-Nazaire d'Aude, 11120 Ginestas. 445,000 cases.

Val de Dagne
Aude. 1981. 13 communes in the northern Corbières. 70hl/ha. Grapes: usual local varieties. 3 coops at Montlaur, Monze and Servies-en-Val (11220). 167,000 to 222,000 cases.

Côtes de Lastours
Aude. 1981. 21 communes in the Cabardès and the Fresquel valley on the slopes of the Montagne Noir north of Caracassonne. Grapes: wide range. Producers: Mmer Vve Cazaux, Villemoustaussou; M. Gianesini, Dom. Jouclary, Conques-sur-Orbiel; Antoine Maurel, Conques-sur-Orbiel. Coop at Salsigne, 11600 Conques-sur-Orbiel. 78,000 to 89,000 cases.

Coteaux du Lézignanais
Aude. 1981. 10 communes around Lézignan north of the Corbières. Red. Grapes: wide range. 4 coops. 445,000 cases.

Côtes de la Malepère
Now VDQS.

Coteaux de Miramont
Aude. 1981. 9 communes around Capendu in the valley east of Carcassone. Producers: M. Lemaire, Capendu; Mme Yve Achille Marty, Douzens; Mme Alice Loyer, Fonties; Mme Hélène Gau, Barbaira. 5 coops including Capendu (11700). 445,000 cases.

Coteaux de Narbonne
Aude. 1982. 4 communes near Narbonne. 3 coops. 167,000 cases.

Val d'Orbieu
Aude. 1982. 12 communes in the Orbieu valley west of Narbonne. Grapes, red and rosé: Carignan, Cinsaut, Grenache, Alicante-Bouschet, Picpoul, Terret Noir. White: Clairette, Macabeu, Bourboulenc, Carignan Blanc, Grenache Blanc. Producers: Jacques Berges, Boutenanc; M. Baille, Fabrezan; Armand Sournies, Camplong d'Aude; Honoré Deu, St-André Roquelonge; Mme Marie Rouanet, St-André Roquelonge; Mme Marie Huc, Fabrezan. 4 coops. 333,000 cases.

Côtes de Pérignan
Aude. 1981. 5 communes in the area around La Clape at the mouth of the Aude. 3 coops including Fleury d'Aude (11560). 133,000 to 222,000 cases.

Coteaux de Peyriac
Aude and Hérault. 1982. 17 communes in the Minervois. 9 coops. 28,000 cases, mostly sold by Chantovent.

Côtes de Prouille
Aude. 1982. 39 communes around Razès, southwest of Carcassonne. Grapes: wide range. Producers: Château de Malviès, 11240 Belvèze du Razès. 2 coops at Arzens (11290) and Routier, 11240 Belvèze du Razès. 67,000 to 89,000 cases.

Coteaux de Termènes
Aude. 1982. 9 communes in the Corbières around Termènes. Grapes, red and rosé: Carignan, Cinsaut, Grenache, Syrah, Merlot, Cabernet, Cot, Terret, Alicante-Bouschet, Gamay. White: usual varieties. 1 coop at Villerouge Termènes, 11330 Mouthoumet. 111,000 cases.

Du Torgan
Aude. 1981. 10 communes around Tuchan. Grapes: wide range, red and rosé. 8 coops. 222,000 to 333,000 cases.

Vallée du Paradis
Aude. 1981. 11 communes in the southern Corbières. Producers: M. Amiel, M. Mique, M. Bringuier and M. Navarro all at Coustouge; M. Caziniol at Fraisse-Corbières. 7 coops including Cascatel, 11360 Durban Corbières. 167,000 to 278,000 cases.

ROUSILLON AND THE CORBIERES

The Corbières hills, which the Pyrénées-Orientale *département* shares with the Aude to the north, have several interesting *vins de pays* that are listed here and under the Aude. The country to the south, consisting of plains and the foothills of the Pyrenees, uses the Catalan name for its 2 defined districts.

Val d'Agly
Corbières. 1982. 15 communes around St-Paul de Fenouillet. 8 coops including Belesta, 66720 La Tour de France. 133,000 to 167,000 cases.

Catalan
Roussillon. 1981. Area stretching inland from Perpignan and Argelès. Producers: Michel Cases, Ste-Colombe (66300); Dom. de Casinobe, Trouillas (66300). 20 coops, SICA at Perpignan. 1m. to 1.5m. cases.

Côtes Catalanes
Roussillon. 1981. Area north and west of Perpignan. Producers: Cazes Frères, Rivesaltes (66600); Maurice Puig, Claira (66530). Mas Chichet, Perpignan. 10 coops. 444,000 to 556,000 cases.

Côteaux des Fenouillèdes
Corbières. 1982. 17 communes in the Corbières north of Prades. 11 coops including Arboussols (66320). 167,000 to 222,000 cases.

Côtes Vermeilles
1986. Roussillon. Area around Collivre on the coast. 675,000 cases.

THE SOUTHWEST

The *départements* of the Landes and Pyrénées-Atlantique have their own *vins de pays*. Local zones range from the Lot southwestwards and cover some interesting areas also holding AOC or VDQS rank. The name Comté Tolosan covers the entire Southwest.

Agenais
Southwest. 1982. Most of the *départment* of Lot-et-Garonne. 70hl/ha. Grapes: wide range including Cabernets, Gamay and Sauvignon. 4 coops, including Côtes du Marmandais, Beaupuy, 47200 Marmande. 89,000 to 133,000 cases.

Bigorre
Hautes-Pyrénées. 1985. In Hautes-Pyrénées *département* in the region of Castelnau-Rivière Basse and Vic-en-Bigorre. Grapes, red and rosé: Tannant, Cabernet Franc 90%. White: Arrufiac, Ugni Blanc, Colombard. Producers include Alain Brumont at Château Boucassé. 11,000 to 17,000 cases.

Côtes du Brulhois
Now VDQS.

Condomois
Southwest. 1982. Area borders on Côtes de Gascogne and Côtes de Montestruc in Gers *département*, with four communes of Lot-et-Garonne. Grapes, red: Tannant, Merlot, Cabernets 60%. White: Colombard, Ugni 40%. 55,000 cases.

Côtes du Gascogne
Southwest. 1982. Almost the entire *départment* of the Gers (the Armagnac country). Grapes: wide range of traditional and quality varieties. Producers: M. Esquiro, Dom. de la Higuère, Mirepoix (32540); M. Ribel, Pitre à Montestruc (32390). 7 coops including Lagrualet Gondrin, 32330 Gondrin. 550,000 cases.

Coteaux de Glanes
Southwest. 1981. 7 communes in the upper Dordogne valley, *département* of the Lot. 70hl/ha. 10°. Red and rosé. Grapes: at least 70% Gamay or Merlot. GAEC at Glanes, 46130 Bretenoux.

Coteaux et Terrassès de Montauban
Southwest. 1981. 14 communes between Cahors and Montauban in the cantons of Montauban, Monclar-de-Quercy Negrepelisse and Villebrumier, Lot-et-Garonne. 10°. Main varieties: Gamay, Merlot, Syrah, Cabernet Franc, Cabernet Sauvignon and Tannat. Secondary varieties: up to 30% of Gamay teinturier de Bouze and Gamay teinturier de Chaudenay. Abouriou, Jurançon, Alicante-Bouschet and Cot are only permitted until 1995. Minimum density of vines: 3,000 per hectare. 22,000 to 33,000 to rise to 56,000 cases.

Coteaux du Quercy
Southwest. 1982. The southern part of the Lot and the north of Tarn-et-Garonne, between Cahors and Lafrançaise. 10°. Grapes: at least 70% Cot, Gamay, Cabernets, Merlot or Tannat. Producer: Arlès Belon, Puylaroque 82240. 133,000 to rise to 222,000 cases.

Côtes du Tarn
Southwest. 1981. Wide area of the Tarn around Gaillac and Cordes. Grapes: wide range. Producers: Jean Labert, Castanet; M. de Faramond, Ch. Lastours, L'Ille-sur-Tarn. 4 coops including Gaillac (81600). 1.6m. cases.

Comté Tolosan
11 *départements* in southwest France. 1982. 222,000 cases.

Montestruc
Southwest. 1982. An area in Ger *département* encompassed by the Côtes de Gascogne area, in the Haut Armagnac south of Lectoure and north of Auch. Grapes, red: Jurançon Noir, Cot, Fer, Gamay. 11,000 cases.

Saint Sardos
Southwest. 1982. Area: from left bank of Garonne in the Lomagne area, southwest of Tarn-et-Garonne *département*, including a few communes in the northwest of Haut-Garonne. Grapes, red: Syrah, Tannant, Cabernets, Abouriou, Jurançon Noir. 55,000 to 67,000 cases.

Terroirs Landais
Landes. 1986. In the Adour valley, in the Tursan VDQS country. Producers: Coop de la Haute-Chalosse, 40250 Mugran. 12,000 cases.

Thézac – Pérricard
Lot and Garonne. 1988.

LOIRE

Marches de Bretagne
Lower Loire. 1982. Area to the south of the Loire east of Nantes. Producers: Marcel Chiron, 'La Moranderie', Mouzillon, 44430 Vallet; Joseph Chiron, La Chapelle St-Florent, 44410 St-Florent Le Vieil; Georges Fleurance, 'L'Anière', La Chapelle Heulin, 44330 Vallet; Mme Yve Odette Barre, 'Bonne Fontaine', 44430 Vallet; Gabriel Perraud, 'La Vérignonière', 44190 Clisson. Coop at Ancenis. 167,000 to 222,000 cases.

Pays Charentais
Charente and Charente-Maritime. 1981. Entire *départements*. 70hl/ha. 11° red, 11.5° white. Grapes, red; Cabernet Franc, Cabernet Sauvignon, Merlot, Tannat (on the Ile de Ré only) plus up to 20% others. White: Chenin Blanc, Colombard, Folle Blanche, Muscadelle, Sauvignon, Sémillon, Ugni Blanc. Sugar and acidity regulated. 56,000 to 333,000 cases.

Coteaux du Cher et de l'Arnon
Upper Loire. 1981. 10 communes around Quincy and Reuilly. Grapes, red and rosé: Gamay, Pinot Noir, Pinot Gris, plus 30% others. White: Chardonnay, Sauvignon, plus 30% others. 90,000 cases.

Jardin de la France
Loire. 1981. Most of the Loire basin. Producers: Jean Motheron, 49450 Martigue-Briand; Georges Lalanne, Ch. de Tigné, 49770 Tigne; Bore Frères, 49620 La Pommeraye; Pierre Moreau, La Vernell, 36600 Valencay; Jean-Claude Barbellion, Marcé à Oisly, 41700 Contres; Jacky Preys, Meusnes, 41130 Selles-sur-Cher. Négociants. SA Bougrier, St-Georges-sur-Cher, 41400 Montrichand; Société Vinicole de Touraine, Cour-Cheverny, 41700 Contres. 2.2m. cases.

Retz
Lower Loire. 1982. Area to the south of the Loire west of Nantes. Producers: André Choblet, 44830 Bouaye; Adolphe Richer, St-Cyr en Retz, 44580 Bourgneuf-en-Retz; Pierre Gout, St-Pierre Château de la Tour, 44710 Port St-Père. Coop at Ancenis (44150). 166,000 cases.

Urfé
Loire. 1982. A wide area in the *département* of Loire, in the upper Loire valley. Grapes, red and rosé: at least 70% Gamay and Pinot Noir. White: Chardonnay, Aligoté, Pinot Gris, Viognier, Gamay. 17,000 to 56,000 cases.

Fiefs Vendéens
Now VDQS.

CENTRAL FRANCE

Bourbonnais
Allier. 1986.

Coteaux Charitois
Nievre. 1986.

Coteaux Coiffy
Haute Marne. 1989.

Gorges & Côtes de Millau
Aveyron. 1981. 25 communes in the Tarn valley. 60hl/ha. 4 types of wine made: 2 reds based on Gamay and Syrah, rosé 50% Gamay, white from Chenin and Mauzac. Coop at Agnessac (12520). 33,000 cases.

SOUTHERN FRANCE

L'Ile de Beauté
Corsica. 1981. Entire island. Min. 10.5°. Max. 12°. Grapes: many, with Carignan and Cinsaut not to exceed 25% and 50% respectively of planted area. Producers: M. René Touboul, Domaine de Pojale, 20270 Aléria. Domaine de San Giovanni, 20270 Aléria. Mme Jeanne Salvat, Linguizetta, 20230 San Nicolao. Mme Raymond Guidicelli, Domaine de Liccetto, 20270 Aléria. 7 coops. 1.3m. cases.

Pays d'Oc
Midi and Provence. 1981. Ardèche, Aude, Vouches-du-Rhône, Gard, Hérault, Pyrénées-Orientales, Cabernet Sauvignon, Chardonnay, Var and Vaucluse. Detailed technical specifications, but no yield restrictions. 889,000 to 1m. cases.

JURA AND SAVOIE

Allobrogie
Savoie. 1981. Communes in the two Savoie *départements*, around Grenoble, and in the Ain around Seyssel. Grapes, red: Gamay, Mondeuse at least 5%. White: Chardonnay, Chasselas, Molette, Jacquère together 95%. 380,000 cases, should soon rise by 50%.

Balmes Dauphinoises
Savoie. 1982. Northern part of the *département* of the Isère, around Morestel and Crémieu. Min. alch: 9.5°. Grapes, red and rosé: at least 70% Gamay, Pinot Noir, Syrah, Merlot or Mondeuse. White: at least 70% Chardonnay or Jacquère. 11,000 to 17,000 cases.

Franche-Comté
Jura. 1982. *Départements* of Jura and Haute Saône. 9° for red and rosé, 9.5° for white. Grapes: only Chardonnay, Auxerrois, Pinot Noir, Pinot Gris and Gamay. 17,000 to 33,000 cases. Coop at Champlitte.

Coteaux du Grésivaudan
Savoie. The Isère valley around Grenoble. 9.5°. Grapes, red and rosé: at least 70% Gamay, Pinot Noir or Etraire de la Dui. White: at least 70% Jacquère, Chardonnay or Verdesse. 2 coops. 50,000 cases.

GERMANY

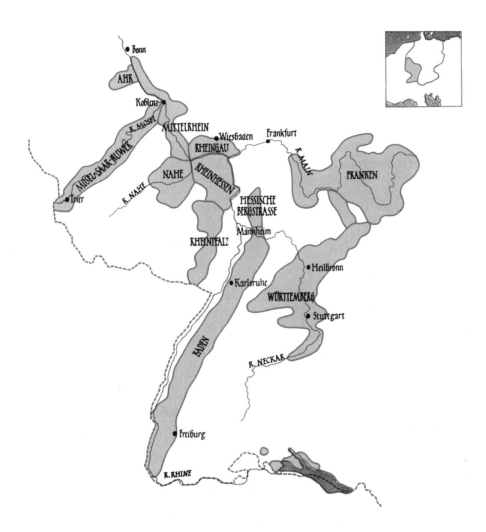

I have sometimes wondered why there is no Chair of German Wine Studies at any of our universities. The subject has just the right mixture of the disciplined, the recondite and the judgemental to appeal to academic minds.

It can be approached as geographical, historical, meteorological, legislational, chemical-pastoral, pastoral-gastronomical, chemical-comical . . . there are enough departments to fill a college.

The German way with wine has a different logic from the French, the Italian or that of any other country. It is highly structured and methodical, making its full explanation a daunting task, but it has – or had until recently – a unity of purpose which made the principle, if not the practice, easy to grasp.

In Germany ripeness is all. All German quality criteria (at least the government-regulated ones) are based on the accumulated sugar in the grapes at harvest time. There is no official ranking of vineyards as in France; no specific recipes for varieties of grapes as in Italy. German labels, at least those of quality wines, make unequivocal statements. Despite the difficulties of Gothic type they are the world's most consistent and informative – up to a carefully calculated point. Beyond that point you need either an elephantine memory or a good clear reference book to delve further.

The wine laws of Germany were radically reformed in 1971 and since then have been subject to further revisions. But their strategy remains unaltered. They divide all German wine into three strata. The lowest, Tafelwein, of tolerable quality, low strength, subject to relatively few controls, is correspondingly barred from claiming any specific vineyard origin. It is assumed to be a blend of wines that have required additional sugar. The only important, potentially confusing, point to remember is the difference between Deutscher Tafelwein, which must be German in origin, and Tafelwein without the qualification, which may contain wine from other European countries (normally Italy). A low-strength neutral base wine is easily cleaned up and given some superficial German characteristics by using very aromatic 'sweet reserve'. The use of heavily Gothic labels has obviously been intended to encourage the innocent to believe that the wine is indeed German. A new category of Tafelwein, called Landwein, with stricter rules (see pages 242 and 288) was introduced in 1982 as a sort of German vin de pays. It has yet to match its French counterparts in popularity or enterprise.

The second category of German wine was christened Qualitätswein bestimmter Anbaugebiete: QbA for short. The term means 'quality wine from a designated region'. To a German the difference between this and the top category of wine, Qualitätswein mit Prädikat, is doubtless clear and simple. Unfortunately the legislators did not take non-Germans into account. It must be stressed to them continually that the two classes of Qualitätswein are far apart, distinguished by a basic difference. The first is made with added sugar; the second is what used (before 1971) to be called, much more directly and succinctly, natur or natuirrein. In other words the grapes had enough natural sugar to make wine. 'Mit Prädikat' is hard to translate. 'With special attributes' is the stilted official version. It certainly does not reflect the status of QmP wines as the top category in which, without exception, all the best wines of Germany are included.

Qualitätswein mit Prädikat all carry a designation of maturity of their grapes as part of their full names, in the following order; simply ripe grapes of the normal harvest are Kabinett; late-gathered (therefore riper) are Spätlese; selected very ripe grapes are Auslese. The precise sugar content (or 'must weight') and therefore potential alcohol required for each category in each region is stipulated in the regulations (see opposite).

At this point most wines begin to retain distinct natural sweetness. If an Auslese is fermented fully dry it will be noticeably high in alcohol by German standards. Two levels of ripeness and selectivity beyond Auslese remain: Beerenauslese, in which the individual berries are selected for extreme ripeness and concentration, and Trockenbeerenauslese, in which only berries dried and shrivelled by noble rot (occasionally by unseasonal heat) are selected. Sugar levels in such wines are commonly so high that fermentation is seriously hampered and may be reluctant to take place at all. TBAs' (to use the current American abbreviation) are usually a stable conjunction of very modest alcohol level (even as low as 5.5%) and startlingly high sugar. They are less than half as strong as Château d'Yquem, which is made in much the same way, and correspondingly twice as sweet. It could, incidentally, be much less confusing for the consumer if the well-tried old term Edelbeerenauslese were used for this category of wine. 'Trocken' means dry, the word is used to describe wines with virtually no sugar. 'TBAs' are made from more-or-less dried-up grapes: a totally different proposition. Much confusion would be saved if 'Edel' – meaning 'noble' and referring to the 'noble rot' – were substituted for 'Trocken', making 'EBAs'.

One further category of QmP wine deserves to be considered separately because of the way it is made: Eiswein is made by crushing grapes that have frozen solid on the vine. Crushing before they thaw means that the almost pure water which constitutes the ice is separated from the sugar, acids and other constituents, which have a lower freezing point. The result, like a TBA, is intensely concentrated, but much less ripe and more acidic. It can be extraordinary, its high acid giving it the potential for almost limitless ageing.

The name and ranking of a QmP wine is conventionally set forth on its label in the same order. First comes the town or village (Gemeinde) name; then the vineyard; then the grape (in some classic Reisling areas this is inferred and omitted); then the category of ripeness – Kabinett, Spätlese and so on.

Only one complicating factor, and the major fault in the 1971 German law, prevents this formula from being crystal clear. It is the concept of the Grosslage, or extended vineyard. Unfortunately labels do not, and are not allowed to, distinguish between a precise vineyard site, known as an Einzellage, and a group of such sites with very much less specificity: a Grosslage. Grosslage groupings were made with the idea of simplifying the sales of wines from lesser-known Einzellagen. Notoriety comes more easily to bigger units. But their names are in no way distinguishable from Einzellage names and I have never met a person who claims to have memorized them. The consumer is therefore deprived of a piece of information to which he has a right. As a further confusing factor, in some areas Einzellagen are also groups of separate vineyards deemed to have a common personality. There is thus no truly clearcut distinction between the categories. In the pages that follow some regions are described in terms of their villages (Germeinden) and some on the basis of their Grosslagen, according to the ruling local practice. The names of the Einzellagen producing the finest wines will be found in the entries for each region's producers.

One exceptional use of the Grosslage name must, however, be mentioned. In the making of Trockenbeerenausleses, picking tiny quantities of dried berries, a single Einzellage often fails to produce enough to fill even a small cask. Trockenbeerenausleses are therefore sometimes the sum of grapes from several sites and use the Grosslage name.

The often-quoted rule of thumb, based on the Kabinett-Spätlese-Auslese scale, is 'the sweeter the wine the higher the quality'. While it is still true to say that quality is directly related to ripeness, the question of sweetness is now very much at the discretion of the wine maker (and the consumer). Sweetness in most modern German wines is adjusted to suit the market, by adding (or not adding) unfermented grape juice to fully fermented, fully dry wine just before bottling. The grower looks for a harmonious balance between acidity, alcohol and fruity sweetness in his wine. In the past he achieved it by stopping the fermentation while some natural sweetness remained (not difficult in a cold cellar, using sulphur dioxide). Today he ferments his wine to full dryness and natural stability, but keeps some of the must in its fresh, sweet, unfermented state for later blending.

There is also a growing demand for fully dry, unsweetened wines, to accompany food. To be so described, as 'trocken', on the label, these must contain less than 9 grams of sugar per litre. In tasting *trocken* wines it soon becomes clear how much a little 'sweet reserve' adds to the charm, balance and drinkability of most German wines: they have to have unusually good figures to survive such naked scrutiny. On the other hand, this is the area in which most progress has recently been made by the most ambitious producers. They have tapped a lucrative new restaurant market in Germany which is insatiable for well-made, harmonious and fruity but very dry wines. A halfway category, *halbtrocken*, with up to 18 grams of sugar per litre, more often achieves the right balance of fullness and bite to make satisfactory mealtime wine. Wines with less than 4 grams of sugar per litre may be able to be labelled '*Für Diabetiker geeignet*', although it should be drunk by diabetics only with their doctor's assent.

German growers produce astonishing quantities. France, Italy and other countries make low yields a precondition for their appellations. In Germany only 'must weight' counts. A big crop is simply taken as evidence of a healthy vineyard. Average crops have grown from 25 hectolitres a hectare in 1900 to 40 (about the French AOC level) in 1939, and in the 1970s were averaging over 100. 1982 hit a record: 173 hl/ha average, with a maximum close to 400.

Without this high productivity German wines would have priced themselves out of the market. The remarkable achievement of the best growers is to have quadrupled their yield while maintaining, and even in some cases improving, their quality. A typical crop on one of the finest sites today is about 70 hl/ha (about twice that of a top Bordeaux château). What has been lost is the concentration of flavours that gave the best of the old low-yield wines the ability to mature for decades. Yet nobody could complain at the condition of the great 1971 vintage (average yield 79.8 hl/ha) two decades later. The almost equally splendid 1976 produced an average of 100 hl/ha throughout Germany. A welcome move was made in 1989 by the government of Rheinland-

Statutory sugar levels Regions	Table wine	Quality wine	Kabinett	Spätlese	Auslese	Beerenauslese/ Eiswein	Trockenbeeren-auslese
The first figure is potential percentage alcohol; the second figure is degrees Oechsle (for Riesling)							
Ahr	5°/44	6°/50	8.6°/67	10°/76	11.1°/83	15.3°/110	21.5°/150
Hessische-Bergstrasse	5°/44	7°/57	9.5°/73	11.4°/85	13°/95	17.7°/125	21.5°/150
Rheingau	5°/44	7°/57	9.5°/73	11.4°/85	13°/95	17.7°/125	21.5°/150
Central Rhein	5°/44	6°/50	8.6°/67	10°/76	13°/95	15.3°/110	21.5°/150
Mosel-Saar-Ruwer	5°/44	6°/50	8.6°/67	10°/76	11.1°/83	15.3°/110	21.5°/150
Nahe	5°/44	6.5°/53	9.1°/70	10.3°/78	11.4°/85	16.5°/120	21.5°/150

Pfalz (which controls two thirds of German wine production) to tighten the law and prevent excessive production and resulting watery wine. It set maximum permitted yields according to region, grape variety and quality classification. The Mosel-Saar-Ruwer was given an overall limit of 130 hl/ha for Müller-Thurgau; 120 hl/ha for Riesling. Other regions were given a sliding scale: Nahe growers, for example, can produce 120 hl/ha of table wine, 110 hl/ha of QbA wine but only 85 hl/ha of Prädikat wine.

On the other hand many have doubted the serious intent of a law that permits over-production in one vintage to be held over to the next. It appears that the political will to frustrate over-production is far from resolute. Meanwhile all serious growers attempting high-quality wines impose their own limits at a level well below the legal maximum.

Another serious concern is that the current law, in setting simple minimum ripeness standards for Ausleses and the other top categories, simply invites growers to achieve that minimum and no more. The old rules allowed eager wine makers to differentiate between their standard and better-than-standard Ausleses, such terms as 'Feine' or 'Feinste Auslese' carrying considerable premiums. If the terms were open to abuse, they also rewarded the patient and ambitious perfectionist. Today he will still signal to his clients which are his best casks of wine, but often in an obscure semaphore of coloured capsules, no less open to abuse because it is closed to the uninitiated.

The official answer to any doubts about the standards or authenticity of quality QbA and QmP German wines is that each wine is both analysed and tasted officially before being issued with a unique Amtliche Prüfungsnummer (A.P. number) which appears on every label. All official tastings employ a standard points scheme, which is also used for the awarding of the gold, silver and bronze medals at both national (D.L.G.) and regional levels. But here again it is the self-imposed criteria of top growers who really set the standard. Regional voluntary organizations ('Charta' in the Rheingau is the prototype) abide by maxima of production and minima of must-weight far stricter than those decreed by government. It is on them and the pride of their members that the future of Germany's high-quality wine industry depends.

THE REGIONS

Germany's finest wines come from hillside vineyards facing the southern half of the compass. In this northern climate the extra radiation on land tilted towards the sun is often essential for ripeness. Other factors also come into account: the climate-moderating presence of water; shelter from wind; fast-draining and heat-retentive soil.

Fine German wines, in fact, come from almost every type of soil from slate to limestone, clay to sand – given other optimal conditions. The effects of different soils on the character of wines from one grape, the Reisling, is a fascinating subplot of German oenology. But climate and microclimate, orientation and angle of hill come first.

Germany has 11 broadly designated wine regions (bestimmate Anbaugebiete) divided into 34 more narrowly defined Bereichs. The Bereichs are in turn divided into Gemeinden (villages) and the villages into Einzellagen (single sites, or vineyards). The latter are also grouped, several sites and often several villages at a time, as Grosslagen. In most cases a Grosslage name remains more or less permanently attached to the name of a single village, the best known within its radius, which is known as its Leitgemeinde. Niersteiner Gutes Domtal is the perfect example of a highly successful Leitgemeinde/Grosslage in the public eye and memory.

Top-quality wines are almost always pinpointed as narrowly as possible by their makers, and therefore come to market under their Einzellage names. There are some 2,600 Einzellagen (since the 1971 laws abolished a figure close to ten times this number). Even this rule, though, is changing rapidly as forward-looking producers rely more and more heavily on their own reputations. Brand-building, more confined to down-market wines, is seen today as the way forward for top estates too. In future we can expect something closer to the Bordeaux château-system where it is the regulation of the estate, rather than the Einzellage, that determines the price of the bottle.

The 11 principal wine regions fall into five broad divisions. The most important is the Rhine valley, including its lesser tributaries, from Rheinpfalz (the Palatinate) in the south, past Rheinhessen, the Hessische Bergstrasse, the Rheingau and the Nahe, the Mittelrhein and finally to the little tributary Ahr near Bonn in the north. Second comes the Mosel, flowing north with its tributaries the Saar and the Ruwer to meet the Rhine at Koblenz. Third comes the vast but scattered region of Baden in the south, from Heidelberg all the way to the Swiss border. Fourth comes Franken (or Franconia), the vineyards of the Main valley in Northern Bavaria. Fifth, and rarely spoken of outside Germany, comes the disjointed and diverse region of Württemberg.

On the export market the first two are far and away the most important. The picture in Germany is rather different, with great loyalty (and high prices) for the wines of the last three. Foreigners tend to meet German wine either as a commercial blend ('Liebfraumilch') or as the produce of one of the many great historic estates of the Rhine or Mosel. Only rarely have the wines of the smaller local grower been offered abroad. Yet very often this small farmer-cum-innkeeper (for most of them sell their wine 'open' by the glass in their own cheerful little Weinstube) epitomizes the style and vitality of his region. His wines are generally less fine than those of sophisticated noble estates. But they have character, often charm, and sometimes brilliant dash and fire.

LEADING EXPORT HOUSES

Deinhard & Co.
Koblenz. Owners: Hanns-Christof and Rolf Wegeler. Estates in Mosel, Rheingau and Rheinpfalz producing quality wines and sparkling wine. Exports to more than 90 countries.

Louis Guntrum Weinkellerei
Nierstein Rhein. Family company. Principals: Lorenz and Hanns Joachim Guntrum. Merchants with their own estates in Rheinhessen producing mostly Riesling.

Arthur Hallgarten GmbH
London and Geisenheim. Established in the Rheingau in 1898, and in London by Fritz Hallgarten in 1933. Now run by his son Peter. Specialities: individually selected estate wines and regional wines of all regions, especially Mosel-Saar-Ruwer.

Hermann Kendermann OHG
Bingen. Owners: European Cellars (Germany) Ltd., London. Specialities are Black Tower Liebfraumilch, Green Gold Moselle, German generic and estate-bottled wines.

Langenbach & Co.
Worms. Owners: European Cellars (Germany) Ltd., London. Wines from estates in Liebfauenstift-Kirchenstück Worms, and Waldrach, Ruwer. Also of other districts and foreign countries. Sparkling wines: speciality 'Kalte Ente'. Large exports.

Sigmund Loeb GmbH
Trier. Owners: Christopher M. Jevell, London, and Josef Steinlein, Trier. Wines of Mosel-Saar-Ruwer. Rheinhessen, Rheinpfalz; particularly fine qualities. 100% export.

Rudolf Müller GmbH
Reil an der Mosel. Principals: Walter Müller, Dr. Richard Müller, Margit Müller-Berggraef. Own estates in Mosel and wines from other estates. Also sparkling wines. Exports 65%.

Franz Reh & Sohn KG
Leiwen. Owners: The Reh family. Principal: Herbert Reh.

Scholl & Hillebrand GmbH
Rüdesheim. Owner: Bernhard Breuer and Partner. A family firm of wine merchants established in 1880, selling wine from its own holding in the Rüdesheimer Berg Roseneck Einzellage, as well as estate-bottled wines from elsewhere in the Rheingau, and wines that it buys in bulk. There is a strong emphasis on elegant Rieslings and the well-balanced brand wine, Riesling Dry QbA.

St Ursula Weinkellerei GmbH
Bingen. Own estates in Rheinhessen. Producers of Goldener Oktober and other brands. (*See* Weingut Villa Sachsen, Rheinhessen producers.)

H. Sichel Söhne
Alzey. Managing directors: Riquet Hess, Friedrich Weidmann, Peter and Ronald Sichel. Exports approx. 1.5m. cases of German wine annually (about 10% of total German exports), best known for Blue Nun Liebfraumilch.

Walter S. Siegel
Wachenheim an der Weinstrasse. Owner: Walter Siegel Ltd., London. Rhine and Mosel wines; also Weingut Dr. Loosen, Bernkastel and Weingut Gunderloch-Usinger. Nackenheim.

Zimmermann-Graef GmbH & Co KG
Zell an der Mosel. Owners: Paula and Johannes Hübinger. Speciality is 'Zeller Schwarze Katz'. Typical Mosel Riesling of all qualities. Exports more than 50%.

Germany in round figures
The total vineyard area of Germany is 246,000 acres, farmed by 89,500 growers. In 1964 there were 122,000 growers, but both the acreage and the numbers of vintners have declined steadily, while modern methods have greatly increased productivity. The total harvest fluctuates widely with weather conditions: 1982, the biggest to date, produced nearly double the modern (10-year) annual average of 8,500,000 hectolitres (94,440,000 cases). Production in recent years with yield per hectare:

1985	5,400,000 hl	(60,000,000 cases)
	58.1 hl/ha	
1986	10,000,000 hl	(111,100,000 cases)
	108.1 hl/ha	
1987	9,000,000 hl	(100,000,000 cases)
	95.9 hl/ha	
1988	9,000,000 hl	(100,000,000 cases)
	99.6 hl/ha	
1989	13,000,000 hl	(144,000,000 cases)
	140.8 hl/ha	

The regional acreage figures below indicate the percentage of the 1989 crop yielded by the four biggest regions:

Rheinhessen	56,349 acres	23.8%
Rheinpfalz	51,285 acres	21.4%
Baden	36,938 acres	13.6%
Mosel-Saar-Ruwer	30,330 acres	15.6%

The principal export markets for German wine in 1989 (of total exports of 2,674,216 hl were:

Great Britain	1,523,522
Netherlands	224,373
USA	196,152
Japan	134,998
Canada	92,402
Denmark	90,620
Sweden	87,205
Norway	59,121
Belgium/Luxembourg	43,409
Mexico	40,222
Others	182,192

Since 1985, the Great Britain figure has increased, the USA figure fallen by 60%, Japan more than doubled.

Serious wine tasting takes place in the cellars around a 'Karossel'. The owner, his wine maker and cellarmen appraise the vintage.

GLOSSARY OF GERMAN WINE TERMS

For details of the main German white and red grape varieties, *see* pages 18–19 and 26–27.

Abfüllung bottling (*see* Erzeugerabfüllung).

Amtliche Prüfung certification of standard quality by chemical analysis and tasting. Compulsory since 1971 for all QbA and QmP wines (qq.v.). Each wine is given an A.P. number which must be displayed in the label.

Anbaugebiet the broadest category of wine region, of which (for 'quality' wines) there are 11 (e.g. Mosel-Saar-Ruwer, Baden).

Anreichern 'enriching' – adding sugar to the must to increase the alcohol, the equivalent of the French chaptalization. In Germany no sugar may be added to wines in the QmP categories (q.v.) but all Tafelwein and QbA wine may be assumed to have been 'enriched'.

Auslese literally 'selected': the third category of QmP wines, made only in ripe vintages and usually naturally sweet. Ausleses often have a slight

degree of 'noble rot' which adds subtlety to their fruity sweetness. Good Ausleses deserve ageing in bottle for several years to allow their primary sweetness to mellow to more adult flavours.

Beerenauslese literally 'selected grapes': the category of QmP wine beyond Auslese in sweetness and price, and theoretically in quality. Only very overripe or 'nobly rotten' grapes are used to make intensely sweet, often deep-coloured wines which age admirably.

Blau 'blue'; when used of grapes, means 'red' or 'black'.

Bereich one of 34 districts or subregions (e.g. Bereich Bernkastel) within the 11 Gebiets. Bereich names are commonly used for middling to lower quality wines (they are legal for Tafelwein and QbA as well as QmP) blended from the less-distinguished vineyards of the district.

Bundesweinprämierung a national wine award presented by the D.L.G. (q.v.) to wines selected from regional prize

winners. The tastings are held at Heilbronn in Württemberg. 3.5 points out of 5 wins a bronze medal, 4 a silver medal and 4.5 a 'Grosser Preis'. Winners normally display their achievement on a neck label on bottles of the wine in question.

Deutsche(r) 'German'; distinguishes Tafelwein grown in Germany from inferior mixtures of the wines of 'various E.E.C. countries', often sold with pseudo-German labels.

Deutsches Weinsiegel a seal of quality awarded by the D.L.G. (q.v.) for wines that achieve a set level of points higher than the standard required to obtain an Amtliche Prüfungsnummer (q.v.). The standard seal is red, but there is a green seal for medium-dry wines and a yellow for dry wines, including Diabetiker-Weins that meet D.L.G. standards.

Diabetiker-Wein the driest category of German wines, with less than 4 grams of unfermented sugar per litre. It should be drunk by diabetics only after medical approval is given.

D.L.G. The German Agricultural

Society (Deutsche Landwirtschafts Gesellschaft), the body that judges and presents the national wine awards. *See* Bundesweinprämierung.

Domäne 'domain' – in Germany a term used mainly to describe the estates owned by Federal German States (e.g. in the Rheingau, Franken, Nahe).

Edelfäule 'noble rot'. For a full explanation *see* Ch. d'Yquem, page 80.

Eigenem 'own'. 'Aus eigenem Lesegut' means 'from his own harvest'.

Einzellage an individual vineyard site. There are some 2,600 Einzellagen in Germany. Before 1971 there were 10 times as many. Officially the minimum size for an Einzellage is 5 hectares (12.3 acres) although there are a number much smaller than this. Not all Einzellagen are therefore in contiguous parcels, particularly in Baden and Württemberg. A Grosslage (q.v.) is a unit of several Einzellagen supposedly of the same quality and character. The Einzellage or Grosslage name follows the village (Gemeinde) name on the label.

Eiswein wine made by pressing grapes that have been left hanging on the vine into mid-winter (sometimes January) and are gathered and pressed in early morning, while frozen solid. Since it is the water content of the grape that freezes, the juice, separated from the ice, is concentrated sugar, acidity and flavour. The result is extraordinarily sweet and piquant wines with almost limitless ageing capacity, less rich but more penetrating than Beeren- or Trockenbeerenausleses, often fetching spectacular prices.

Erzeugerabfüllung 'estate bottled'; the equivalent of the French *mis au domaine* or *mis au château*.

Erzeugergemeinschaft a producers' association, usually for sales purposes, as distinct from a cooperative for making wine.

Fass a barrel. 'Holz-fasse' are oak barrels, the traditional containers in German cellars.

Flasche bottle – the same word as the English 'flask'.

Flurbereinigung the term for the Government-sponsored 'consolidation' of vineyard holdings by remodelling the landscape, a process that has revolutionized the old system of terracing in most parts of Germany, making the land workable by tractors and rationalizing scattered holdings.

Füder the Mosel barrel, an oak oval holding 1,000 litres or about 111 cases.

Gebeit region.

Gemeinde village, parish or commune. The village name always comes before the vineyard on German labels.

Grosslage a 'collective vineyard',

consisting of a number of Einzellagen (q.v.) of similar character and quality. The 34 German Bereichs contain 152 Grosslagen divided into 2,600 Einzellagen – although a few Einzellagen are not attached in this way. Unfortunately the wine law does not permit the label to distinguish between a Grossalage and an Einzellage name. Grosslage names are normally used for wines below the top quality, but also sometimes for such wines as Trockenbeerenausleses when a single Einzellage cannot produce enough grapes to fill even a small barrel.

Jahrgang vintage (year).

Halbtrocken 'semi-dry' – wine with no more than 18 grams of unfermented sugar per litre, therefore drier than most modern German wines but sweeter than a *trocken* wine (q.v.).

Kabinett the first category of natural, unsugared, Qualitätswein mit Prädikat (*see* page 237 for formal ripeness requirements). Fine Kabinett wines have qualities of lightness and delicacy which make them ideal refreshment, not inferior in the right context to heavier (and more expensive) Spätlese or Auslese wines.

Kellerei wine cellar; by inference a merchant's rather than a grower's establishment (which would be called a Weingut).

Landespreismünze regional wine prizes, which act as the 'heats' for the National Bundesweinprämierung (q.v.)

Landwein a category of *trocken* or *halbtrocken* Tafelwein introduced in 1982. *See* page 288.

Lesegut crop.

Liebfraumilch a much-abused name for a mild 'wine of pleasant character' officially originating in Rheinpfalz, Rheinhessen, Rheingau or Nahe. It must be in the QbA category and should be mainly of Riesling, Silvaner or Müller-Thurgau grapes. Since neither its character nor quality is remotely consistent, varying widely from shipper to shipper, its popularity can only be ascribed to its simple and memorable name.

Mostgewicht 'must weight'. The density or specific gravity of the grape juice, ascertained with a hydrometer, is the way of measuring its sugar content. The unit of measurement is the 'degree Oechsle' (q.v.).

Natur, naturrein terms for natural, unsugared wines, obsolete since 1971 when the present QmP categories came into being.

Neuzüchtung new (grape) variety (*see* page 27).

Oechsle the specific gravity, therefore sweetness, of German must is measured by the method invented by Ferdinand

Oechsle (1774–1852). Each gram by which a litre of grape juice is heavier than a litre of water is one degree Oechsle. The number of degrees Oechsle ÷ 8 is the potential alcoholic content of the wine if all the sugar is fermented. *See* page 237.

Ortsteil a suburb or part of a larger community with a standing independent from its Gemeinde or village. For example, Erbach in the Rheingau is an Ortsteil of the town of Eltville. Certain famous estates (e.g. Schloss Vollrads) are allowed to omit the names of their villages from their labels.

Perlwein slightly fizzy Tafelwein, often artificially carbonated under pressure. A small measure of acidic carbon dioxide freshens up dull wines.

Pokalwein wine served 'open' in a large glass (Pokal) in a café or Weinstube.

Prädikat see QmP.

Prüfungsnummer the individual A.P. number given to each 'quality' wine after testing. *See* Amtliche Prüfung.

QbA Qualitative bestimmter Anbaugebiete: 'quality wine of a designated region'. The category of wine above Tafelwein and Landwein but below QmP (q.v.). QbA wine has had its alcohol enhanced with added sugar. It must be from one of the 11 Anbaugebiete (unblended), from approved grapes, reach a certain level of ripeness before sugaring and pass an analytical and tasting test to gain an A.P. number. In certain underripe vintages a high proportion of German wine comes into this category and can be very satisfactory, although never reaching the distinction of QmP wine.

QmP Qualitätswein mit Prädikat. 'Quality wine with special attributes' is the awkward official description of all the finest German wines, beginning with the Kabinett category and rising in sweetness, body and value to Trockenbeerenauslese. The ripeness requirements for each region are listed on page 237. QmP wines must originate in a single Bereich (q.v.) and are certified at each stage of their career from the vineyard on.

Rebe grape (Rebsorte: grape variety).

Restsüsse 'residual sugar': the sugar remaining unfermented in a wine at bottling, whether fermentation has stopped naturally or been stopped artificially. The minimum, in a wine for diabetics, is about 4 grams a litre. In a Trockenbeerenauslese it may reach astonishing figures of more than 180 grams a litre, with very little of the sugar converted to alcohol.

Roseewein, Roséwein pale pink wine from red grapes.

Rotling pale red wine from mixed red and white grapes.

Rotwein red wine.

Säure acidity (measured in units per 1,000 of tartaric acid). The essential balancing agent to the sweetness in German (or any) wine. As a rule of thumb a well-balanced wine has approximately one unit per 1,000 (ml.) of acid for each 10 degrees Oechsle (q.v.). Thus an 80° Oechsle wine needs an acidity of approximately 0.8.

Schaumwein sparkling wine – a general term for low-priced fizz. Quality sparkling wines are called Sekt.

Schillerwein a pale red (Rotling) of QbA or QmP status, produced only in Württemberg.

Schloss castle.

Schoppenwein another term for Pokalwein – wine served 'open' in a large glass.

Sekt Germany's quality sparkling wine, subject to similar controls to QbA wines. *See* also page 257.

Spätlese literally 'late-gathered'. The QmP category above Kabinett and below Auslese, with wines of a higher alcoholic degree and greater body and 'vinosity' than Kabinetts. Also often considerably sweeter but not necessarily so. A grower must notify the authorities of his intention to pick a Spätlese crop, and tasting panels establish a consensus of what constitutes proper Spätlese style in each vintage and region.

Spitzen 'top', a favourite German term, whether applied to a vineyard, a grower or a vintage.

Stück the standard traditional oak cask of the Rhine, holding 1,200 litres or about 133 cases. There are also Doppelstücks, Halbstücks and Viertel (quarter) stücks.

Süssreserve unfermented grape juice with all its natural sweetness, held in reserve for 'back-blending' with dry, fully fermented wines to arrive at the wine maker's ideal of a balanced wine. This sweetening (which also lowers the alcoholic content) is often overdone, but a judicious hint of extra sweetness can enhance fruity flavours and make an average wine more attractive.

Tafelwein 'table wines', the humblest category of German wine. (Without the prefix Deutsche it might not be German, however Gothic the label.) The origin, alcohol content and grape varieties are all controlled but Tafelwein is never more than a light wine for quenching thirst.

Trocken 'dry' – the official category for wines with less than 9 grams of unfermented sugar a litre. Trocken wines have become fashionable for use with meals, but frequently taste arid, hollow and unbalanced compared with *halbtrocken* (q.v.) versions of the same wines, adjusted with Süssreserve (q.v.)

Trockenbeerenauslese 'selected dried grapes' (frequently shortened to TBA). Ironically the precise opposite of the last entry, the 'dry' here referring to the state of the overripe grapes when picked in a shrivelled state from 'noble rot' and desiccation on the vine. Such is the concentration of sugar, acid and flavours that Oechsle readings of TBA must (never in more than minute quantities) can reach more than 300°. TBA wines are reluctant to ferment and rarely exceed 6% alcohol, the remaining intense sweetness acting as a natural preservative and slowing down maturation for many years. Only Eisweins (q.v.) mature more slowly.

VdP Verband Deutscher Prädikats-und Qualitätsweingüter, an association of premium growers.

Weingut wine estate. The term may only be used by growers who grow all their own grapes.

Weinprobe wine tasting.

Weinstein the thick deposit of potassium tartrate crystals forming a glittering rock-like lining to old barrels.

Weissherbst a rosé wine of QbA or QmP status made from red grapes of a single variety, the speciality of Baden, Württemberg and Rheinpfalz, but also the fate of some sweet reds of other regions which fail to achieve a full red colour. ('Noble rot' attacks the pigments and often makes red Ausleses excessively pale.)

Winzer wine grower.

Winzergenossenschaft, Winzerverein growers' cooperative.

Zuckerrest the same as Restsüsse (q.v.).

MOSEL-SAAR-RUWER

One regional (Gebiet) name covers the long and tortuous route of the Mosel from Luxembourg to the Rhine and both its wine-growing tributaries. It is justified by the wine. To a surprising degree the wines of the Mosel (Upper, Middle and Lower), of the Saar and the Ruwer are homogeneous in style, however widely they vary in quality. They are the brightest, briskest, most aromatic and yet most hauntingly subtle of all the fruit of the Riesling. This is essentially Riesling country, and no soil or situation brings out the thrilling harmony of the finest of all white grapes to better effect.

Low-priced Mosels, sold under such popular labels as Zeller Schwarze Katz or Kröver Nacktarsch, or under the generously wide Bereich name of Bernkastel, can be mean and watery wines. They are not Riesling but Müller-Thurgau. The finer sites all grow Riesling, and all go to great pains to identify themselves precisely (*see* Producers' entries). The complications of nomenclature can become excruciating, but the rewards are sublime.

The Mosel wears its first few tentative vineyards in France, flows through Luxembourg, then enters Germany near Trier to be joined by the rivers Saar and Ruwer. It is their side valleys, rather than the main stream, that have the first great Mosel vineyards. Upper Mosel ('Obermosel') wines at their best are light and refreshing. A good deal of the pleasantly neutral, rather sharp Elbling grape is grown on sites where Riesling fails to ripen. Riesling also has difficulty ripening on the Saar and Ruwer. But when it does, on their best slopes, the results are unsurpassed anywhere on earth: quintessential Riesling, clean as steel, haunting with the qualities of remembered scents or distant music.

One Bereich name, Saar-Ruwer, covers the Saar and Ruwer, with two Grosslagen: Scharzberg for the Saar, Römerlay for the Ruwer. The Upper Mosel has two Bereichs: Obermosel, divided into two Grosslagen, Gipfel and Königsberg; and Moseltor. Below it the Saar valley begins the catechism of Germany's great vineyards.

SAAR

Serrig
The uppermost wine village of the Saar (still higher up are steelworks). Steel is also the appropriate metaphor; Serrig has problems ripening Riesling and makes much excellent acid base-wine for Sekt. The State Domain is its principal estate. In exceptionally warm autumns its wines become fables. 207 acres.

Irsch, in a side valley to the north of Serrig, is a minor wine village with the same problems as Serrig.
Growers Schloss Saarstein. Bert Simon. Staatlichen Weinbaudomänen. Vereinigte Hospitien.

Saarburg
The principal town of the area, with several good growers on slopes that are capable of great finesse in good years. 38 acres.
Growers Fischer. Geltz Zillikin. Rudolf Müller. Rheinart. Freiherr von Solemacher.

Ockfen
The first of the noble Saar vineyards is the great hump of the Bockstein in Ockfen, owned by the State Domain and many others. Again, a dry autumn is needed for balanced wines, 249 acres.
Growers Duhr. Fischer. Geltz Zillikin. Milz Laurentiushof. Rudolf Müller. Reverchon. Rheinart. Hermann Freiherr von Solemacher. Staatlichen Weinbaudomänen.

Ayl
The village faces the whale-like ridge of its Kupp vineyard across a flat valley. Thrillingly sweet-and-sour wines at their best. 151 acres.
Growers Bishöflichen Weingüter. Rheinart.

Wawern
A small village with no site name to conjure with, but excellent wines in the true Saar style. 52 acres.
Grower Fischer.

Wiltingen
The hub of the Saar region, surrounded by major vineyards and giving its name to most Saar Grosslage wines ('Wiltinger Scharzberg'). Its best estate, Scharzhofberg – remember the essential 'hof' – is considered so important that it dispenses with the name of Wiltingen on its label.

A galaxy of the top producers own land in the dozen first-rate vineyards, which often produce some of Germany's most delectably elegant, balanced, age-worthy wine. 474 acres.
Growers Bischöflichen Weingüter. Le Gallais. Reichsgraf von Kesselstatt. Revershon. Rheinart. Schlangengraben. H. Schmitz. Hermann Freiherr von Schorlemer. Vereinigte Hospitien. Bernd van Volxem.

Kanzem
Just downstream from Wiltingen, Kanzem evokes only slightly less superlatives for its much smaller area of steep vineyards dropping to the river.

Wines with teasing hints of earth and perhaps spice. 141 acres.
Growers Bischöflichen Weingüter. Rudolf Müller. Reverchon. Vereinigte Hospitien.

Oberemmel
In a side valley east of Wiltingen, Oberemmel has some superb sites, including Hütte and Rosenberg, and considerable land of rather less distinction. 521 acres.
Growers Bischöflichen Weingüter. von Hövel. Oberemmeler Abteihof. Reverchon. Bernd van Volxem.

Filzen
Towards the mouth of the Saar, Filzen has a smaller reputation but some good growers. 128 acres.
Growers Max-G. Piedmont. Reverchon.

Konz
The town at the meeting place of Saar and Mosel includes in its boundaries the place names Falkenstein (known for its 45-acre Hofberg), Filzen and Mennig.
Growers Reverchon. Friedrich-Wilhelm-Gymnasium .

RUWER

Trier
Trier's own vineyards and those of the tiny river Ruwer (pronounced Roover) together make up only a drop in the ocean, yet one of the most precious drops of all. Ruwer wines are feather-light, often *spritzig*; on the face of it scarcely more serious than *vinho verde*. Yet if the pure essence of Riesling is made anywhere it is here; frail but tenacious, even dry wines poised in balance for years and sweet ones growing subtly harmonious for decades.

The boundaries of Trier now include the vineyards of Avelsbach, brilliantly exploited by the State Domain and the Cathedral estates (Hohe Domkirche) to make the most of their perfume, despite a tartness that dogs them in all but the ripest years.
Growers Bischöflichen Weingüter. Staatlichen Weinbaudomänen. Thiergarten. Vereinigte Hospitien.

Waldrach
The first Ruwer wine village coming downstream, and the least celebrated, though its wines have almost the potential of Kasel. Growers include Bischöflichen Weingüter.

Kasel
The 'capital', tiny as it is, of the Ruwer. Its best site, Nies'chen, performs wonders of delicacy, charm and perfume. 104 acres.
Growers Bischöflichen Weingüter. Reichsgraf von Kesselstatt. St. Irminenhof. Bert Simon, Wegeler-Deinhard.

Mertesdorf
Known entirely for the one magnificent estate, Maximin Grünhaus, that faces it across the little valley.
Growers von Schubert. Bert Simon.

Eitelsbach
Almost equally identified with one estate, the Karthäuserhofberg. These last two in their different styles are the 'first-growths' of the Ruwer, and hold that rank in comparison with any properties in Germany.
Growers Bischöflichen Weingüter. Karthaüserhof. Bert Simon.

MIDDLE MOSEL

Bereich Bernkastel

The Bereich Bernkastel, still known to old-timers by its pre-1971 name of Mittelmosel, contains all the best vineyard sites of the main stream, now slowed and broadened by locks to make it a noble river, winding in matchless beauty through alternating cliffs of vineyard to right and left. Whichever side confronts the river with a high hill and makes it bend, offers vines the inclination they need towards the sun.

Bernkastel is the natural centre of the region; a major crossing point, (to Kues opposite) an irresistible architectural museum in its huddle of tall timbered houses, and the producer of its most celebrated wine.

Authors differ on where the villages of noteworthy quality upstream and downstream begin and end. The conservative view limits the classic Mittelmosel to the stretch from Trittenheim to Ürzig. But excellent estates extend much farther upstream and downstream in the best sites. Those on the extremities are more dependent, like the Saar and Ruwer, on exceptional seasons. But lovely, lively, classic Riesling is within their grasp and their names should be remembered along with the more obvious Piesport, Bernkastel and Wehlen.

The first villages below Trier to present good south-facing slopes to the Mosel are Longuich and (across its bridge) Schweich, then the hamlets of Longen 'and Lörsch, all in the Grosslage (Longuicher) Probstberg. No particularly distinguished growers have illuminated their names, but in first-class vintages they can make notable wine. The majority of the vines here are Riesling, the first essential for fine Mosel.

Mehring

Mehring is somewhat better-known, partly because of its size, no doubt partly because the famous Friedrich-Wilhelm-Gymnasium is among the owners of its south slope. Here the Grosslage St. Michael applies to the better sites. Those facing northeast round the river bend have the Grosslage name Probstberg again, making a more modest commodity. 1,000 acres.

Growers Friedrich-Wilhelm-Gymnasium. Licht-Bergweiler. St. Nikolaus Hospital.

Pölich to Rivenich

The little village of Pölich, with its best vineyard the 255-acre Held, marks the next sharp kink in the river. The Grosslage St. Michael continues here all round the next sweeping right-hand bend through the villages of Detzem, Schleich, Ensch, Thörnich, Bekond and Rivenich (these two lying back in western side valleys) to the relatively celebrated little town of Klüsserath.

Klüsserath

The Einzelage Bruderschaft (brotherhood) not only has a pleasant name; its 600-odd acres are planted with 90% Riesling. This can be taken as a starting point for the Middle Mosel. The Grosslage is St. Michael.

Grower Franz Reh.

Köwerich

Köwerich lies on the south bank of the river, facing the steep and narrow Einzellage Laurentiuslay (100% Riesling) across the water. Its other vineyards are not in the same class. Grosslage St. Michael.

The landscape of the Mosel

Leiwen

Leiwen also lies on the south bank and shares the name of Laurentiuslay with Köwerich, but for a detached fragment of vineyard on the opposite side of the river with a different exposure. Leiwen's other vineyards are not so privileged. 1,125 acres in Grosslage St. Michael.
Growers Domklausenhof. Loewen. Reh.

Trittenheim

Trittenheim occupies the centre of a splendid oxbow bend, with equally fine sites on both sides of the river. Although its vines seldom if ever produce wine of great body, they achieve classic Riesling finesse in a more delicate style. Poor vintages find them thin. From Trittenheim north the Grosslage is (Piesporter) Michelsberg. 805 acres.
Growers Bischöflichen Weingüter, Dünweg. Friedrich-Wilhelm-Gymnasium. Milz Laurentiushof. Reh.

Neumagen-Dhron

Neumagen lies on a straight south-north stretch of the river; Dhron in the valley of the tributary Dhron behind the hill. There are good but not outstanding sites in both villages, on both sides of the river, the best being the Hofberger, steep and sheltered in the Dhron valley. Rosengärtchen and Sonnenuhr are the best-placed sites in Neumagen. 778 acres in Grosslage Michelsberg.
Growers Bischöflichen Weingüter (Dhron). Domklausenhof (Neumagen). Dünweg (Neumagen and Dhron). Friedrich-Wilhelm-Gymnasium (Neumagen and Dhron). Haart (Dhron). Matheus-Lehnert (Neumagen and Dhron). Milz Laurentiushof (Neumagen). Reh (Dhron).

Piesport

The village lies in the middle of the biggest south-facing horseshoe of the steepest vineyards on the river. All the north-bank vineyards are fine, although Goldtröpfchen is much the most famous. These Piesporters are the most succulently pleasing of all Mosels, uniting ripeness and a touch of spice with the underlying 'nerve' that gives lasting power and style. They are seldom very full-bodied, even by Mosel standards, yet they leave a glowing, golden impression. The number of top-class growers with property here is both cause and effect. Piesport's flat land on the south bank is the Einzellage Treppchen. It is not in the same class. 956 acres in Grosslage Michelsberg.
Growers Bischöflichen Weingüter. Domklausenhof. Dünweg. Haart, Reichsgraf von Kesselstatt. Matheus Lehnert. Reh. Tobias. Vereinigte Hospitien.

Minheim

Minheim lies on an oxbow bend, a replica of Trittenheim but without its good fortune in the steepness or orientation of its slopes. 383 acres in Grosslage Michelsberg.

Wintrich

Wintrich echoes the geography of Neumagen, its best site, Ohligsberg, lying by the river to the south of the village. Here the Bernkastel Grosslage Kurfürstlay takes over from (Piesport) Michelsberg. 675 acres.

Kesten

Kesten has vineyards on both sides of the Mosel as it turns again to flow east, but only one outstanding site, Paulinshofberger, facing south across the river. 299 acres in Grosslage Kurfürstlay.
Growers Kies-Kieren. Weingut Paulinshof. Wegeler-Deinhard.

Monzel and Osann

These two villages lie behind Kesten in the hills with no remarkable sites but some fair ones. Their wine is as likely to be sold as Bernkasteler Kurfürstlay as by their own little-known names.

Brauneberg

Brauneberg, on the south bank, faces its proudest possession, the Juffer, across the water. Before the Doctorberg in Bernkastel rose to fame, this was the highest-priced Mosel; robust wine of body and full of fruit which aged admirably, in the style of the time, to amber pungency. The name of Brauneberg's hamlet, Filzen, is sometimes seen on good-value bottles. 756 acres in Grosslage Kurfürstlay.
Growers Karp-Schreiber. Licht-Bergweiler. Weingut Paulinshof. Pauly-Bergweiler. St Nikolaus Hospital. Thanisch.

Maring-Noviand

Lying in a side valley north of the river opposite Brauneberg, Maring-Noviand has some well-sheltered if not ideally exposed sites, the Honigberg forming a southwest-facing arc in imitation of a river bend but unfortunately one hill back from the all-important river.

Veldenz and Mülheim

These villages carry the vineyards back from the Mosel up a southern side valley; again useful sources of fair-quality wines, rising to heights only in great vintages.

Lieser

Lieser has a position as prime as Brauneberg's Juffer, without its great reputation. The soil seems to mark it with a stong tang of its own. 504 acres in Grosslage Kurfürstlay.
Growers St Nikolaus Hospital. Schloss Lieser. Hermann Freiherr von Schorlemer. Wegeler-Deinhard.

Bernkastel-Kues

This is the hub of the Middle Mosel: Kues, the larger town, on flat land on the left bank; Bernkastel across the bridge, crammed up against its precipitous vineyards, with the most famous of them, the Doctor, apparently on the point of sliding straight into its streets. Bernkastel's best wines bring together all the qualities of the Mosel: delicacy and drive, force and grace, honey and earth. Riesling, in other words, and pure grey slate. A suggestion of a flinty edge often distinguishes them from their neighbours.

The vineyards are divided into two Grosslagen: Kurfürstlay for the herd (which includes many vineyards upstream from the town boundaries) and Badstube for the select few Einzellagen that share the best hill with the Doctor. 879 acres.
Growers Friedrich-Wilhelm-Gymnasium. Josephshof. Lauerberg. Licht-Bergweiler. Meyerhof. Otto Pauly. Pauloy-Bergweiler. Pfarrkirche. J. J. Prüm. S. A. Prüm Erben. Richter. St Nikolaus Hospital. Hermann Freiherr von Schorlemer. Selbach-Oster. Studert-Prüm Maximinhof. Thiergarten. Vereinigte Hospitien. Wegeler-Deinhard. Zentralkellerei Mosel-Saar-Ruwer.

Graach

Bernkastel melts into Graach, Graach into Wehlen and Wehlen into Zeltingen along the five-mile hill of uninterrupted vines that starts with the Doctorberg. It rises over 700 feet above the river, hardly deviating from its ideal vertiginous tilt or its steady orientation south-southwest.

It may well be the single largest vineyard of sustained superlative quality in the world.

Graach has a major share of this treasure: all its vines are sandwiched between Bernkastel and Wehlen's greatest site, the Sonnenuhr. Its wines can achieve similar intensity and richness; they belong firmly in the top flight of the Mosel, 242 acres in Grosslage Münzlay.

Growers Christoffel. Friedrich-Wilhelm-Gymnasium. Josephshof. Kies-Kieren. Lauerberg. Licht-Bergweiler. Meyerhof. Otto Pauly. Pauly-Bergweiler. Pfarrkirche. J. J. Prüm. S. A. Prüm Erben. St Nikolaus Hospital. Clemens Freiherr von Schorlemer, Hermann Freiherr von Schorlemer. Selbach-Oster. Studert-Prüm Maximinhof. Thanisch. Vereinigte Hospitien. Wegeler-Deinhard. Weins-Prüm. Zentralkellerei Mosel-Saar-Ruwer.

Wehlen

Another of the villages whose growers have the pleasure of admiring their best vineyard across the river. The Sonnenuhr, with the sundial that gives the vineyard its name conspicuous among the vines, lies directly opposite the village centre. The other Wehlen vineyards are on the south bank and have less to offer. (Klosterberg is the best.) The fame of Wehlen hangs entirely on its one great site and the honeyed quintessence of Riesling it can produce, 380 acres in Grosslage Münzlay.

Growers Christoffel. Licht-Bergweiler. Meyerhof. Nicolay. Pauly-Bergweiler. J. J. Prüm. S. A. Prüm Erben. Richter. St Nikolaus Hospital. Schneider. Hermann Freiherr von Schorlemer. Selbach-Oster. Studert-Prüm Maximinhof. Thanisch. Vereinigten Hospitien. Wegeler-Deinhard. Weins-Prüm.

Zeltingen

The village is called Zeltingen-Rachtig, being a union of two small settlements, again with land on both sides of the river. This is the biggest wine-growing commune on the Mosel, and consequently often met with. It is also one of the best, with a Sonnenuhr vineyard only slightly less renowned than Wehlen's, and the excellent Scholssberg above it giving powerful, beautifully balanced, rather earthy wines. The famous name of Himmelreich is one of those which has been extended to embrace sites of very uneven quality, facing several points of the compass. On the opposite shore, Deutschherrenberg tend to less ripeness but foreshadows the famous spicy flavour of its neighbour, Ürzig. 440 acres in Grosslage Münzlay.

Growers Friedrich-Wilhelm-Gymnasium. Josephshof. Nicolay. Pauly-Bergweiler. J. J. Prüm. S. A. Prüm Erben. Clemens Friherr von Shorlemer. Hermann Freiherr von Schorlemer. Schneider. Selbach-Oster. Vereinigte Hospitien.

Ürzig

Ürzig tucks all its modest parcels of vineyards into a sheltered bend of the river facing southeast, on deep slaty soil mixed with red clay in snug crannies where the Riesling ripens to a high level of spicy intensity. Würzgarten means 'spice garden'. Its wines have strong character and should be among the most identifiable of the great Middle Mosels. From Ürzig downstream to Kröv the Grosslage is Schwarzlay. 150 acres.

Growers Bischöflichen Weingüter. Christoffel. Benedict Loosen-Erben. Rudolf Müller. Nicolay. Vereinigten Hospitien. Weins-Prüm.

Erden

The village lies opposite Ürzig, surrounded by the broad, gentle slopes of its Einzellage Busslay, a Müller-Thurgau

rather than a Riesling site, comparable to Piesport's Treppchen. Erden's fine vineyards lie on the opposite bank next to Ürzig. The tiny Prälat is the best, and the last of the truly great vineyards of the Mosel on this downstream route – although Erdener Treppchen, alongside, and Herrenberg, above, are also excellent Riesling sites. 247 acres in Grosslage Schwarzlay.

Growers Bischöflichen Weingüter. Christoffel. Kies-Kieren. Loosen-Erben. Nicolay. Pauly-Bergweiler. Vereinigten Hospitien. Weins-Prüm.

Kinheim

Kinheim, on the north bank, has one fine site, Hubertuslay, but here the soil is beginning to change to a less outrageously slaty mixture and the chance of superlative wine-making to diminish. 284 acres in Grosslage Schwarzlay.

Growers Kies-Kieren.

Kröv

Kröv makes its reputation and its fortune more on its Grosslage name Nacktarsch (and the accompanying label showing a little boy being spanked with his pants down) than on its Einzellagen, good though their wine can be in a freshly fruity style that foreshadows the lower reaches of the Mosel. 842 acres.

Traben-Trarbach

The next across-the-river pair of settlements, these share yet another mighty oxbow bend. But here the riverside slopes have moderated and the best steep sites are back in the folds of the hills in the side valley behind Trarbach. 494 acres in Grosslage Schwarzlay.

Grower Richter.

Enkirch

As the river recovers its northward course, Enkirch has a site that recalls Neumagen and Dhron, with the steep riverfront facing west and a side valley (Steffensberg) facing south. Riesling here makes wines of balanced, deft lightness and spiciness which deserve a higher reputation. 400 acres in Grosslage Schwarzlay.

Growers Carl Aug. Immich-Batterieberg.

Reil

The next major left-bank centre, Reil has good sheltered slopes for Riesling. The best are Goldlay, across the river, and Sorentberg, tucked into a side valley. These produce light wines, capable of gulpable fruitiness in good vintages. The Grosslage is Vom Heissen Stein.

Grower Rudolf Müller.

Pünderich

The steep slopes are dying away here, and Riesling sites are limited. Nonnengartern makes softly fruity Rieslings; the huge Marienburg lighter and more flowery wine. Grosslage Vom Heissen Stein.

LOWER MOSEL

Zell

The best-known wine community (and the Bereich name) of the Lower Mosel, due in some measure to its memorable Grosslage name Schwarze Katz and the inevitable black cat on the label. Zell and Zell-Merl, immediately downstream, both have steep slopes with slaty soil, planted largely in Riesling and capable of very tempting, light but aromatic and flowery wines. 1,800 acres. *Grower* Michel Schneider.

Bullay

A small community, little-known to the outside world, with limited but very worthwhile steep slaty slopes producing fine light Riesling. Kroneberg, sheltered in a side valley, gives particularly satisfying wine, 130 acres in Grosslage Grafschaft.

Neef

Little Neef, on the right bank at the next bend below Bullay, rejoices in one very fine steep slope in the classic Mosel style: the 98-acre Frauenberg. The Grosslage is Grafschaft. *Grower* Ewald Theod. Drathen.

Similar favoured sites occur less and less frequently as the Mosel flows tortuously on past Senheim, Mesenich, Ellenz and Cochem, then takes a straighter course north towards Koblenz, vines still hugging its immediate banks. The Grosslage names for this lower section are Grafschaft, Rosenhang, Goldbäumchen and finally Weinhex. The best-known village of the final reaches is Winningen, with its Einzellagen Uhlen, Hamm and Domgarten growing fine Rieslings almost within sound of the bells of Koblenz.

LEADING MOSEL-SAAR-RUWER PRODUCERS

Weingut Zach. Bergweiler-Prüm Erben

See Weingut Dr. Pauly-Bergweiler.

Verwaltung der Bischöflichen Weingüter Trier

Gervasiusstrasse 1 (Ecke Rahnenstrasse), 5500 Trier.
Director: Wolfgang Richter. About 260 acres in the Middle Mosel, Saar and Ruwer.

The biggest estate under one management in the Mosel-Saar-Ruwer was formed by the union in 1966 of 3 independent charitable properties: the Bishop's Seminary (Priesterseminar), the Trier cathedral (Domkirche) estates and the Bishop's Hostel (Konvikt). It has now also leased 4 other small church estates. The vineyard management and the pressing are carried on independently of the 3 main charities' press houses; all the juice is then brought to the 400-year-old central cellar in Trier for fermentation and cask-ageing. 98% of the whole estate is Riesling.

The Priesterseminar originates from a gift in 1773 by the Prince-Bishop Clemens Wenceslaus (a great promoter of Riesling over lesser vines). Its 84 acres are in 7 villages. In the Middle Mosel: Erdener Treppchen (7.7); Ürziger Würzgarten (1); Dhroner Hofberger (6); Trittenheimer Apotheke (4.2); and Altärchen (4.2). On the Ruwer: Kaseler Nies'chen (16). On the Saar: Kanzemer Altenberg (21.2); Scharzberg (planted 1.25 acres with Spätburgunder for red wine); Wiltinger Kupp (12.8); Ayler Kupp (10).

The Hohe Domkirche has only 2 holdings: 25 acres at Wiltingen on the Saar (19.5 in the Scharzhofberg, 5.4 in the Rosenberg) and 34 at Avelsbach on the outskirts of Trier (sole ownership of the 24 acre Altenberg and 10 acres of Herrenberg).

The Bischöfliches Konvikt is the biggest of the three, dating back to 1653, with 97 acres. On the Ruwer 47 acres of Eitelsbacher Marienholz and 10 of Kaseler Kehrnagel; on the Saar 15.3 acres of Ayler Kupp and 11.4 (solely owned) of Ayler Herrenberger; 5.7 acres at Avelsbach by Trier and far down the Mosel at Piesport 7 acres of Goldtröpfchen.

The leased church properties are at Oberemmel on the Saar, Waldrach and Eitelsbach on the Ruwer, and in Trier – a total of 20 acres.

All this wine is superbly well-made, emphasizing lightness and finesse, with a high proportion of dry and medium-dry wines. If anything, the Priesterseminar properties have the highest reputation of all.

Jos. Christoffel Jr.

Moselufer 1–3, 5564 Ürzig.
Owners: Kurt & Karl Jos. Christoffel and Annekatrin Christoffel-Prüm. Einzellagen: Ürziger Würzgarten; Wehlener Sonnenuhr; Erdener and Prälat Treppchen; Graacher-Domprobst.

A small family estate with holdings in excellent sites. (Christoffels have been vine growers for more than 300 years.) A list of some 120 wines includes a 1971 Ürziger Würzgarten Beerenauslese. 100% ungrafted Riesling.

Gutsverwaltung Deinhard

See Gutsverwaltung Wegeler-Deinhard.

Weinkellerei & Weingut Ewald Theod Drathen GmbH & Co. KG

Auf der Hill, 5584 Alf. Owners: Ewald Theod Drathen KG.
Einzellage; Neefer Frauenberg (7).

A family merchant house founded in 1860 with a small estate that includes part of the remarkable Frauenberg, which is 100% Riesling. Drathen's Frauenberg is not quite a great wine, but has overwhelming simple charm.

Weingüter Dr. Fischer

Bocksteinhof, 5511 Ockfen-Wawern. Owner: Hans-Henning Fischer. 60.5 acres. Einzellagen: Ockfener–Bockstein (18.5), Herrenberg (4) and Geisberg (6); Saarburger Kupp (6); Wawerner Herrenberger (25.5 acres, solely owned).

A principal Saar estate with 2 centres: the Bocksteinhof in the vines at the foot of the great towering Bockstein and an 18th-century former monastic property in a meadow below the Herrenberg, the best site in Wawern. 98% is Riesling. Dr. Fischer's wines are admirable examples of the freshness and drive of good Saar Rieslings.

Stiftung Staatliches Friedrich-Wilhelm-Gymnasium

Weberbachstrasse 75, 5500 Trier. Director: Benedikt Engel. 86.5 acres. Saar Einzellagen: Falkensteiner Hofberg. Mosel Einzellagen: Mehringer–Blattenberg, Goldkupp and Zellerberg; Trittenheimer–Altärchen and Apotheke; Neumagener Rosengärtchen; Dhroner Hofberger; Graacher–Domprobst and Himmelreich; Zeltingen–Himmelreich, Sonnenuhr and Schlossberg; Bernkasteler–Bratenhöfchen and Graben.

Another of the great institutions of Trier, the (formerly Jesuit) school was founded in 1561. The vineyards (87%

Riesling) are beautifully maintained and in prime condition; cellar techniques are excellent and the wines generally among the Mosel's best.

Weingut Le Gallais
5511 Kanzen. Owner: Mme Rochon de Pons, 6 acres.
Einzellage: Wiltinger Braune Kupp and Kupp.
Herr Egon Müller of Scharzhof, with his immensely high standards, runs this little property for the French owner. Only QmP wines are sold as Braune Kupp; the Grosslage name Scharzberg is for QbA wine, some of which comes from Müller's own estate. The Kabinett wines are light; higher qualities are aromatic and spicy. 100% Riesling.

Weingut Forstmeister Geltz Zilliken
Heckingstrasse 20, 5510 Saarburg. Director: Hans-Joachim Zilliken. 25 acres. Einzellagen: Saarburger–Rausch (11), Antoniusbrunnen (5) and Bergschlösschen (6); Ockfener–Bockstein (2.5).
The family estate of the much-respected Master Forester of the King of Prussia, Ferdinand Geltz (1851–1925), now run by his great-grandson Hans-Joachim Zilliken. The wines are made very traditionally, in casks, and designed for long age in bottle. A 1979 fully dry Spätlese is outstanding. Beerenausleses from the estate have broken auction price records. 100% Riesling, some ungrafted.

Weingut Fritz Haag
Dusemonder Hof, 5551 Brauneberg. Owners: Wilhelm and Thomas Haag. 13.6 acres. Einzellagen: Brauneberger-Juffer-Sonnenuhr, Juffer and Mandelgraben; Burgener Römerberg; Graacher Himmelreich.
Distinguished estate whose history can be traced back to 1605. It is one of the top addresses for perfectly-made, elegant, cask-matured Riesling wines. No Süssreserve is used. Only their QmP wines bear the name of individual Einzellage, but the QbA is nonetheless a model of what it should be; particularly the Fritz Haag Riesling Halbtrocken. Sales are via wine merchants and to restaurants. Fritz Haag is a leading member of the *Grosser Ring*.

Weingut Freiherr von Heddesdorff
5406 Winningen. Owner: Andreas von Canal. 10 acres.
The top grower of this excellent but little-known site, with origins in the 15th century. Vines are 100% Riesling producing carefully made wine.

Weingut von Hövel
Agritiusstrasse 5–6, 5503 Konz-Oberemmel. Owner: Eberhard von Kunow. 30.5 acres. Einzellagen: Oberemmeler Hütte (solely owned), Rosenberg and Agritiusberg; and Scharzhofberg.
A former part of the monastic St. Maximin estate with Romanesque cellars and a beautiful old farmhouse. Von Hövel's Hütte is exceptionally fine and elegant even by Saar standards; a light but lovely wine. 95% Riesling.

Weingut Christian Karp-Schreiber
5551 Brauneberg. Owner: Alwin Karp. 12 acres. Einzellagen: Brauneberger–Juffer, Juffer Sonnenuhr and Mandelgraben.
A family property since 1664, making prize-winning Rieslings matured in oak; sold mainly to private customers.

Gutsverwaltung Karthäuserhof
(Formerly H. W. Rautenstrauch), Karthäuserhof 1, 5500 Trier-Eitelsbach. Owner: Christof Tyrell. 47 acres. Einzellage: Eitelsbacher Karthäuserhofberg.

A beautiful old manor of the Carthusian monks in a side valley of the Ruwer, bought by the ancestor of the present owner when Napoleon secularized church land. The wines can be fabulous in great vintages, but tend to have harsher acidity (and are usually made drier) than the only comparable Ruwer estate, Maximin Grünhaus (*see* von Schubert). The bottle is unmistakable with only a narrow label on the neck, none on the body. 90% Riesling.

Weingut Reichsgraf von Kesselstatt
Liebfrauenstrasse 9–10, 5500 Trier. Owners: Günther and Käthi Reh. 160 acres in many of the best villages.
This was the greatest private estate of the Mosel-Saar-Ruwer when it was bought in 1978 by Günther Reh, son of Carl Reh of Leiwen. From 1978 the Reh empire expanded to include several high-quality estates, but these have now either become independent or have been closed down. Despite fluctuations in the size of the estate it has retained its character, all sites are still individually cultivated, and general standards remain high. The entire estate is planted with 100% Riesling; between 60 and 70 percent of the wines are *trocken* or *halbtrocken*. The estate makes a point of guaranteeing that its wines will last 10 years; if they don't, they will refund customers.
The splendid baroque Kesselstatt palace in Trier, from which the Counts promulgated the planting of Riesling in the 18th century, is the headquarters. The estate is in 4 parts, each with its own press house and cellars. (Although all the wines since 1987 have been made in a new cellar at Schloss Marienlay between Waldrach and Morscheid on the Ruwer.) The most famous part of the estate is the Josephshof at Graach, which owns the whole Einzellage of 6 hectares at the foot of the hill between the greatest vineyards of Bernkastel and Wehlen.
The following 4 Weingüter were bought around 1820 and constitute the main estate:
Weingut Domklausenhof Piesport/Mosel. Einzellagen: Piesporter-Domherr, Grafenberg and Goldtröpfchen; Brauneberger Juffer; Leiwener Laurentiuslay; Neumagener-Häs'chen and Sonnenuhr.
Weingut Josephshof Graach/Mosel. Einzellagen: Graacher-Josephshöfer, Domprobst and Himmelreich; Bernkasteler-Lay, Graben and Doctor; Zeltingener Sonnenuhr.
Oberemmeler Abteihof Oberemmel/Saar. Einzellagen: Niedermenniger-Herrenberg and Euchariusberg; Oberemmeler-Karlsberg, Rosenberg, Agritiusberg and Raul; Wiltingener-Braunfels, Kupp, Gottesfuss and Scharzhofberg.
Weingut St. Irminenhof Kasel/Ruwer. Einzellagen: Kaseler-Neis'chen, Herrenberg, Kehrnagel and Hitzlay; Waldracher Heiligenhäuschen.

Weingut Kies-Kieren
Hauptstrasse 22, 5550 Graach. Owner: Ernst Kies, 10 acres.
Einzellagen: Kinheimer–Hubertuslay and Rosenberg; Graacher–Himmelreich and Domprobst; Kestener Paulinshof.
The Kies family has been growing vines since the 17th century. The concentration today is on Rieslings which have won the highest awards at national competitions; also production of dry and half-dry specialities.

Weingut J. Lauerburg
5550 Bernkastel. Owners: Karl-Heinz Jacob and Karl Patrik Lauerburg. 10 acres. Einzellagen: Bernkasteler–Schlossberg, Johannisbrünnchen, Mattheisbildschen, Lay, Graben, Bratenhöfchen and Doctor; Graacher Himmelreich.
A small but very prestigious family estate founded in 1700

(when the cellars were dug under the vineyards). The oldest owner in the Doctor site. 100% Riesling, making wines intended for considerable bottle-ageing.

Maximin Grünhaus
See C. von Schubert.

Moselland eG Winzergenossenschaft
5500 Bernkastel-Kues. Director: Dr. Rudolf Rinck. The central coperative for the Mosel-Saar-Ruwer; handles daunting quantities, 3.3m cases, but maintains remarkably high standards. 5,200 growers deliver their grapes from 7,400 acres: 55% Riesling, 23% Müller-Thurgau and 9% Elbling. Most of the wines are QbA but some very fine Ausleses have been made.

Rudolf Müller GmbH & Co. KG
Postfach 20, 5586 Reil. Owners: Dr. Richard Müller, Magrit Müller-Burggraef and Barbara Rundquist. 15 acres. Einzellagen: Reiler-Mullay-Hofberg, Sorrentberg, Goldlay and Falklay; Ockfender-Bockstein, Herrenberg and Geisberg; Saarburger-Antoniusbrunnen and Scharzhof; Kanzemar Sonnenberg; Ürziger Würzgarten.
Best known for its brand of Bereich Bernkastel. 'The Bishop of Riesling'. The *trocken* and *halbtrocken* Saar wines have been much in demand in recent years.

Weingut Egon Müller-Scharzhof
5511 Wiltingen. Owner: Egon Müller.
See next page.

Weingut Peter Nicolay
Gestade 15, 5550 Bernkastel-Kues. Owner: Helga Pauly-Berres. 10 acres. Einzellagen: Ürziger-Würzgarten and Goldwingert (solely owned); Erdener-Treppchen, and Prälat; Zeltinger-Himmelreich and Deutschherrenberg; Wehlener Klosterberg.
Peter Nicolay was a famous innkeeper of a century ago. The Berres family are his descendants, now connected by marriage to the Paulys who own Dr. Pauly Bergweiler of Bernkastel. 100% of the estate is on steep slopes; 100% is Riesling. The wines are matured as individuals in oak and offer the full spectrum of styles that come from the bend in the Mosel from Wehlen to Erden.

Weingut Dr. Pauly-Bergweiler
Gestade 15, 5550 Bernkastel-Kues. Owner: Dr. Peter Pauly. 25 acres. Einzellagen: Bernkasteler-Graben, Lay, Matheisbildchen, Schlossberg and Johannisbrunnchen; Graacher-Himmelreich and Domprobst; Wehlener Sonnenuhr; Zeltinger Himmelreich; Erdener Busslay; Braunebeger-Juffer Sonnenuhr and Juffer.
Inheritors of a fine part of the famous Prüm properties. 50% of the estate is on the steepest slopes, 25% on moderate slopes and 25% on level ground. The wide range of wines is made in both stainless steel and oak, emphasizing vineyard character as far as possible. The estate prefers to use physics rather than chemistry in its winemaking. Süssreserve is not used and no blue fining takes place. The wines have a 'breath of carbon dioxide' – naturally, I assume. 92% Riesling and, unusually, 5% Spätburgunder.

Weingut der Pfarrkirche
Bernkastel, 5501 Leiwen. Owner: Kath. Kirchengemeinde. About 15 acres. Einzellagen: Bernkasteler-Graben, Lay, Bratenhöfchen, Schlossberg and Johannisbrünnchen; Graacher Himmelreich.

The old estate of the parish church. The wines are on the steep slaty slopes which give a particular smack of the soil to good Bernkastel.

Weingut Otto Pauly KG
Bernkastelerstrasse 5–7, 5550 Graach. Owners: Otto-Ulrich and Axel Pauly, 7.5 acres. Einzellagen: Graacher-Domprobst, Himmelreich; Wehlener Sonnenuhr; Bernkasteler-Lay, Johannisbrünnchen.
The vineyards lie on steep slopes, planted 95% with Riesling, in the heart of the Middle Mosel. The wines, full in character, racy and elegant, are sold exclusively via the estate's own merchant company, Weinkellerei Otto Pauly GmbH. The Pauly's, growers since 1620, also own the small but well-sited estate Weingut Abteihof in the Mosel.

Weingut J. J. Prüm
5550 Bernkastel-Wehlen. 35 acres. Owners: Dr. Manfred and Wolfgang Prüm. Einzellagen: Wehlener-Sonnenuhr, Klosterberg and Nonnenberg; Graacher-Himmelreich; Zeltinger Sonnenuhr; Bernkasteler-Badstube and Lay.
The most famous family of growers of the Middle Mosel, with records going back to the 12th century. The estate house, down by the river, looks up to the great Sonnenuhr vineyard, of which it has one of the largest holdings, across the water. The huge sundials among the vines here and in Zeltingen were built by an earlier Prüm. The estate's signature is wine of glorious fruity ripeness, setting off the raciness of Riesling grown on slate with deep notes of spice and honey.

Weingut S.A. Prüm Erben, S.A. Prüm
Uferallee 25–36, 5550 Bernkastel-Wehlen. Owners: Raimund and Erika Prüm. 16 acres. Einzellagen: Wehlener-Sonnenuhr, Klosterberg, Rosenberg and Nonnenberg; Bernkasteler-Lay, Graben, Schlossberg and Johannisbrünnchen; Graacher-Himmelreich and Domprobst; Zeltinger-Schlossberg and Sonnenuhr.
Part of the great Prüm estate which became separate in 1911, was divided in 6 parts in 1964 but has since been partially reconstituted and enlarged. The wines are made with great emphasis on the character of each cask. The biggest holding (3.7 acres) is Wehlener Sonnenuhr – a dry Spätlese of 1979 was outstanding.

Franz Reh & Söhn
Römerstrasse 27, 5501 Leiwen. President: Herbert Reh. Two estates with about 32 acres. Einzellagen: Leiwener-Laurentiuslay and Klostergarten; Trittenheimer-Apotheke and Altärchen; Piesporter-Goldtröpfchen, Gärtchen (solely owned), Günterslay and Treppchen; Dhroner Hofberger.
A highly successful merchant house with the brands Kellerprinz, Klosterprinz and Hockprinz. Also the owners of 2 estates, Josefinengrund at Leiwen and Marienhof at Piesport.

Weingut Edmund Reverchon
Saartalstrasse 3, 5503 Konz. Owners: Eddie and Nicole Reverchon. 67.5 acres. Einzellagen: Filzener-Steinberger, Urbelt and Herrenberg (solely owned); Wiltinger-Gottesfuss and Klosterberg; Okfener-Bockstein and Geisberg; Kanzemer Altenberg; Konzer-Karthäuser, Klosterberg and Euchariusberg; Oberemmeler Altenberg.
The friendly family estate of the Reverchons, based at Konz. Light, *spritzig* wines with high acidity, 92% Riesling, Filzener Herrenberg is the pride of the house – from Sekt to Gold-capsuled Ausleses.

EGON MÜLLER

A great Saar estate

German wine-making at its highest level can best be described as wine for wine's sake. In a fine vintage the producer is almost passive, like a painter before a sunset. Rather than try to mould the vintage to his preconceived ideal he is dedicated to interpreting what nature provides. If one estate embodies this approach to wine it is Egon Müller's Schwarzhofberg. Egon Müller is the owner of the Scharzhof Manor at Wiltingen on the Saar and 27.5 acres of the steep Scharzhofberg above it. His late-picked wines regularly fetch the highest prices at the annual auction of 'The Ring' of the best Mosel growers at Trier. Egon Müller's great-great-grandfather bought the estate, formerly church land like so much of Germany's best, when it was secularized under Napoleon. It is very much the old family house, its hall lined with trophies of the chase and its library with leather-bound books. A tasting of the new vintage with Egon Müller takes place in the half-light of the hall, standing at a round table with a ring of green bottles and little tumblers.

The Riesling he grows on the steep grey schist of the Scharzhofberg is Riesling in its naked purity. Only Kabinett and better wines are made with the estate name, and each is fermented apart in its own cask. The samples at the tasting are of different casks. As the late part of the harvest approaches the differences between casks increase. The Kabinetts will probably all be bottled as one wine, but Spätleses may be kept in separate lots, and there may be five or six different Ausleses as each day's ripening intensifies the honeyed sweetness of the latest wines. It is very rare in the cold Saar vineyards to have grapes ripe enough for a Beerenauslese; Trockenbeerenausleses are rarer still. But a gold-topped Auslese (once called a feinste Auslese) from Egon Müller has as much penetrating perfume, vitality and 'breeding' as any wine in Germany. Its measured sweetness is matched with such racy acidity that the young wine may almost make you wince. Yet time harmonizes the extremes into a perfectly pitched unity, a teasing, tingling lusciousness that only Riesling, only the Saar, only the Scharzhofberg can achieve.

Weingut Adolf Rheinart Erben

In der Botacht 4,5501 Longuich. 29.6 acres. Einzellagen: Schodener–Saarfeilser Marienberg; Ockfener–Bockstein and Herrenberg; Ayler Kupp; Wiltinger Schlangengraben; Saarburger Antoniusbrunnen.

A well-known name on the Saar with some 26 acres, all on good sloping sites. 100% Riesling. Ockfener Bockstein and Saarfeilser Marienberg produce the estate's best wine.

Michel Schneider Nachf.

Merlerstrasse 28, 5583 Zell. Owners: the Schneider family. 123.5 acres. Einzellagen: Wehlener–Abtei and Hofberg; Zeller–Marienburger; Merler–Königslay-Terrassen, Adler and Klosterberg; Zeltinger Deutschherrenberg.

Half the property is in Wehlen and half divided between Zell and Merl on the Lower Mosel. The Schneider family, growers in Zell since 1869, bought and painstakingly restored an old Cistercian property, Kloster Machern at Wehlen, in 1969. The Wehlen estate is 100% Riesling and the entire property 75% Riesling, 15% Müller-Thurgau and 10% new varieties.

Weingut Max Ferd. Richter

Hauptstrasse 37/85, 5556 Mülheim. Owners: Horst and Dr. Dirk Richter. 37 acres. Einzellagen: Traben-Trarbacher Ungsberg; Wehlener Sonnenuhr; Graacher–Domprobst and Himmelreich; Bernkasteler Schlossberg: Brauneberger–Juffer and Juffer-Sonnenuhr; Mülheimer Helenenkloster (solely owned) and Sonnenlay; Veldenzer Elisenberg.

Family estate that dates from the 1680s, producing fine cask-matured Reislings, including dry and medium-dry. Also outstanding Eiswein.

Weingut St. Johannishof

5500 Bernkastel-Kues. Owner: Ernst F. Loosen. 19.8 acres. Einzellagen: Bernkasteler–Lay and Schlossberg; Erdener–Prälat and Treppchen; Graacher Himmelreich; Urziger Würzgarten; Wehlener–Klosterberg and Sonnenuhr.

Innovative winemaker Ernst Loosen is renowned for superb concentrated Riesling (96%) and *barrique*-aged Müller-Thurgau.

Hermann Freiherr von Schorlemer Weingüterverwaltung GmbH

5550 Bernkastel-Kues. Holdings in the Mosel and Saar with 5 estates in Lieser, Zeltingen and Graach, Wehlen and Bernkastel, Wiltingen and Ockfen.

One of the largest old family estates on the Mosel, with 5 separate properties (listed below). 98% is Riesling; all the wines are made in oak. Schloss Lieser, the vast Victorian mansion of the von Schorlemers in their glory, has its best sites in the steep Niederberg-Heldenberg. The estate also produces Riesling Sekt from individual vineyards.

Weingut Clemens Freiherr von Schorlemer Zeltingen and Graach.
Weingut Schloss Lieser Lieser.
Weingut Meyerhof Graach, Wehlen and Bernkastel.
Weingut Franz Duhr Nachf. Ockfen.
Weingut Schlangengraben Wiltingen.

C. von Schubert, Maximin Grünhaus

5501 Grünhaus/Trier. Directors: Andreas and Dr. Carl von Schubert 76.6 acres. Einzellagen: Maximin Grünhäuser Bruderberg 7, Herrenberg 42, Abtsberg 27.

The outstanding estate of the Ruwer and one of Germany's greatest, with a unique undivided hill of vines dominating the beautiful, formerly Benedictine-owned manor house, whose cellars go back to Roman times and whose records start in AD 966. It was bought by the von Schubert family in 1882. The estate does not use the local Grosslage name Römerlay but offers all its wines under its own singularly beautiful label bearing the name of the village, Maximin Grünhaus. The sweet Ausleses of good vintages are sublime: infinitely subtle but surprisingly spicy and powerful, ageing 20 years or more. Even the lesser wines are a revelation.

Bert Simon, Weingut Herrenberg

5512 Serrig-Saar. Owner: Bert Simon. 80 acres. Einzellagen: Serriger–Herrenberg, Würtzberg and König Johann Berg (each 16 acres solely owned) and Antoniusberg (2.2); Staadt Maximiner Prälat (12 solely owned); Niedermenniger Sonnenberg (1.2); Eitelsbacher Marienholz (3); Mertesdorfer Herrenberg (1.7); Kaseler–Kehrnagel (10), Neis'chen (0.5) and Herrenberg (0.5).

A dynamic young estate started in 1968 with the purchase of the old von Schorlemer vineyards in Serrig, and enlarged since with 4 more small estates in excellent sites. Has enormous success in the USA. 90% is Riesling, the balance is Müller-Thurgau and Weissburgunder, unusual on the Saar. The small percentage of Weissburgunder is made unblended as a dry wine.

Weingut Freiherr von Solemacher

5510 Saarburg Bez. Owner: Baron Raitz von Frentz. 13.5 acres. Einzellagen: Saarburger–Bergschlösschen, Antoniusbrunnen and Rausch (12.35); Ockfener–Bockstein and Herrenberg (1.25).

The Baron lives in a castle in the Eifel mountains shown on his label. The Weingut, which was destroyed in World War II, had been in the family for 100 years. 90% is Riesling, 10% Optima and Kerner. The wines are lively and *spritzig* with natural carbon dioxide, changing character completely in great keeping years such as 1976.

Verwaltung der Staatlichen Weinbaudomänen

Deworastrasse 1, 5500 Trier. Director: Peter Hoffman. 173 acres. Einzellagen: Avelsbacher–Hammerstein. Rotlay; Ockfener–Bockstein; Serriger–Vogelsang. Heiligenborn; Trierer–St. Maximiner Kreuzberg, Deutschherrenberg and Deutschherrenköpfchen (25).

The immensely impressive estate founded by the King of Prussia in 1896, and bearing his eagle on the label, was largely carved out of oak woods in the Saar valley. 80% of the vineyards are on steep slopes of up to 70° gradient, 88% of the vines are Riesling. Visitors can see the precipitous Serrig estate from a narrow-gauge railway.

The wine is still made in 1,000-litre casks: the splendid vaulted cellars contain 400 of different sizes, as well as bottles going back to the great 1921 vintage, and a dank, mossy chamber where the Director conducts tastings. The range of qualities is wide (it includes Sekt made of Serriger Riesling). There are great stylish steely wines and some rather ordinary ones.

Weingut Wwe. Dr. H. Thanisch

5550 Bernkastel-Kues. Owners: the Thanisch family. 16 acres. Einzellagen: Bernkasteler–Doctor, Badstube, Graben, Schlossberg and Lay; Brauneberger Juffer Sonnenur; Graacher–Himmelreich and Domprobst.

The family estate (with roots going back to 1650) that made the worldwide reputation of the famous Doctor vineyard at the turn of the century when King Edward VII, visiting Bad Homburg, took a fancy to the name. The cellars are dark dripping caves 100 feet under the slate of the vineyards that produce the most famous Mosel. The standard of wine-making remains impeccable.

Weingut Thiergarten

Im Tiergarten 12, 5500 Trier. Owners: George-Fritz von Nell. 39.5 acres chiefly in Trier. Einzellagen: Trierer–Benediktinerberg 12.4, Kurfürstenhofberg 12.4, Thiergarten unterm Kreuz 11 and Thiergarten Felsköpfchen 1.2; also 1.2 acres in the Saar and 0.6 in Bernkastel.

A former Benedictine manor, bought in 1803 by the von Nells, whose descendants run the small estate personally. Enthusiastic producers of excellent and individual, light and potentially long-lived wines, 80% Riesling. 60% of the wines are *trocken* or *halbtrocken*.

Güterverwaltung der Vereinigten Hospitien

Krahnenufer 19, 5500 Trier. Director: Dr. Hans Pilgram. 136 acres. Vineyards in Serrig, Wiltingen, Scharzhofberg and Kanzem on the Saar; and in Trier, Piesport, Bernkastel, Graach, Wehlen, Zeltingen, Ürzig and Erden on the Mosel.

One of the great charitable institutions of Trier, occupying Germany's oldest cellars, built as a Roman warehouse. Napoleon united ('Vereinigte') the numerous charities of Trier in the Benedictine abbey of St. Irminen, which continues to be a free hospital like the Hospices de Beaune, financed by its vineyards and other considerable estates. It takes its label, a gold figure of Sanctus Jacobus (St. James of Compostela) from the medieval hospital incorporated by Napoleon. 90% of the vines are Riesling. The wines are made and mainly matured in cask and include some fine and typical Mosels and Saars. 25% are dry or medium-dry.

Weingut Bernd van Volxem

5516 Wiltingen. Owner: Heinz-Peter von Volxem. 22.5 acres Einzellagen: Wiltinger–Gottesfuss, Klosterberg, Braunfels, Schlangengraben and Schlossberg; Oberemmeler Rosenberg; Scharzhofberger.

A fourth-generation family estate planted with 80% Riesling, 10% Weissburgunder and 5% Ruländer. The finest wines are the Scharzhofbergers and Wiltinger Gottesfuss. The range includes *trocken* and *halbtrocken* wines up to Spätlese level, generally light crisp and true to Saar style.

Gutsverwaltung Wegeler-Deinhard

Martertal 2, 5550 Bernkastel-Kues. Manager: Norbert Kreuzberger. 69 acres in the villages of Bernkastel, Graach, Wehlen, Kesten, Lieser and Kasel. Einzellagen: Bernkasteler–Doctor (2.7), Graben (7), Lay (2), Bratenhofchen (9), Mattheisbildchen (0.7), Johannisbrunnchen (6.4), Alte Badstube am Doctorberg (0.5) and Schlossberg (0.2); Graacher Himmelreich (2.5); Wehlener–Sonnenuhr (12.4), Klosterberg (6), Nonnenberg (1) and Rosenberg (1); Kestener–Paulinsberg (1.2) and Paulinshofberger (1.7); Lieser Schlossberg (2.7); Kaseler-Nies'chen (5.7), Hitzlay (8), Kehrnagel (1) and Herrenberg (2.2).

The Mosel estate of the famous Koblenz wine merchants started in 1900 with the sensational purchase of part of the Doctor vineyard for 100 gold marks a square metre. Further acquisitions totalled some 33 acres in 1981, when a long lease of vineyards in Wehlen from the Dr. Zach. Bergweiler-Prüm estate more than doubled their Mosel holdings. 89% is on steep slopes and 92% is Riesling. The cellars, press house and a villa now occupied by the manager are in Kues near the railway station.

Deinhard's Mosels are perfectly true to type with little sweetening: classic wines to show the subtle differences of the terrain. Bernkasteler Doctor concentrates all the qualities, but all their Middle Mosel Kabinetts and better are serious wines for bottle-ageing, and the Kasel wines from the Ruwer are distinctly brisk and piquant.

OTHER PRODUCERS

Weingut Eduard Bremm
Moselferstrasse 4, 5581 Neef. Owner: Eduard Bremm. 7.4 acres. Einzellagen: Neefer–Frauenberg and Rosenberg; Kinheimer–Rosenberg and Hubertuslay. A 400-year-old Mosel wine-making family, now well-known for its 100% Riesling wines from classic steep slate vineyards. All the wines are vinified and mature in 'Fuder' (1000-litre casks) and all are dry. Also Riesling Sekt.

Weingut Otto Dünweg
Moselstrasse 5–7, 5507 Neumagen-Dhron. 16 acres. Einzellagen: Neumagener–Rosengartchen, Laudamusberg and Engelgrube; Dhroner–Hofberger and Grosser Hengelberg (solely owned); Trittenheimer Apotheke; Piesporter–Goldtröpfchen, Treppchen and Kreuzwingert (solely owned). The Dünweg family has owned this estate since 1837. They also own a merchant's business. The estate is 94% Riesling, the cellars damp, with oak casks, regularly producing medal-winning wines.

Weingut Grans-Fassian
Römerstrasse 28, 5501 Leiwen. Owner: Gerhard Grans. 24.7 acres. Einzellagen:

Dhroner Hofberger; Leiwener–Klostergarten and Laurentiuslay; Piesporter–Goldtröpfchen and Treppchen; Trittenheimer–Altärchen and Apotheke. A 17th century property producing wines from steep sites with the minimum use of artificial fertilizers. Careful grape selection and exceedingly gentle pressing lead to wines with little tannin and good acidity. No cultured yeasts are used. The reputation of this estate is increasing steadily. Planted 85% Riesling.

Weingut Johann Haart
St. Michaelstrasse 47, 5555 Piesport. Director: Gerd Haart. 14.8 acres. Einzellagen: Piesporter–Goldtröpfchen, Falkenberg, Günterslay, Grafenberg, Domherr and Treppchen. Dhroner Roterd. One of the larger Piesport family estates, going back to 1337. Half the property (Treppchen) is on gentle slopes planted with Müller-Thurgau and new varieties. The other half is 100% Riesling and makes classic ripe and honeyed Goldtröpfchen, Falkenberg and Günterslay.

Weingut Graf zu Hoensbroech
See Weingut Hubert Schmitz.

Carl Aug. Immich-Batterieberg
5585 Enkirch. Owners: Georg Immich. 15 acres. Einzellagen: Enkircher–Ellergrub, Zeppwingert, Sterffensberg and Batterieberg (solely owned). The Immichs have been growers in Enkirch since 1425. Georg Immich qualified at the Geisenheim Wine School and stoutly defends the Mosel traditions of Riesling and oak.

Weingut Schlosskellerei Freiherr von Landenberg
Moselweinstrasse 60, 5591 Ediger-Eller. Owners: Baroness Nelly von Landenberg and family. 24 acres. Einzellagen: Ellerer–Bienenlay. Engelströpfchen, Höll, Pfirsichgarten and Calmont; Ediger–Osterlämmchen and Elzhofberg. A popular estate with a wine museum in the old manor house. Vines are 95% Riesling, making full-bodied, positively fruity wine.

Weingut P. Licht-Bergweiler Erben
Bernkasterlerstrasse 33, 5551 Brauneberg. Owner: Ria Licht. About 30 acres. Einzellagen: Brauneberger–Juffer, Mandelgraben and Klostergarten; Wehlener Sonnenuhr; Graacher Domprobst; Bernkasteler

Johannisbrünnchen. The Licht family inherited this 200-year-old property with traditional methods and cellars. Their finest wines are from the Juffer and Sonnenuhr.

Weingut Carl Loewen
Mathiasstrasse 30, 5559 Leiwen. Owner: Karl Josef Loewen. 12 acres. Einzellagen: Lerwener–Laurentiuslay and Klostergarten; Detzemer Wurzgarten and Maximiner Klosterlay; Policher Held. The Loewens bought the once monastic land when it was secularized by Napoleon. It includes a very steep slope in the Laurentiuslay where Reisling ripens magnificently. The speciality is really full, dry Riesling made in the style of centuries ago.

Weingüter Benedict Loosen-Erben
Würzgartenstrasse 1, 5564 Ürzig. Owners: Hanni Müller and family. Small growers with 6 acres in the best sites of Erden and Ürzig (they own Ürzig's sundial, set in the Würzgarten).

Weingut J. Matheus-Lehnert
in der Zeil 1, 5507 Neumagen-Dhron. Owners: Ferdinand and Dorothea Krebs-Matheus. 13.5 acres. Einzellagen: Piesporter Goldtröpfchen; Dhroner–Hofberger and Roterd; Neumagener Rosengärtchen. A fine small property: 90% Riesling and 90% steep slopes. Wood-aged Ausleses from his old vaulted cellar win gold medals.

Weingut Milz Laurentiushof
5501 Trittenheim. Owner: Karl Josef Milz. About 20 acres. Einzellagen: Neumagener, Rosengärtchen and Nusswingert (solely owned); Dhroner Hofberger; Trittenheimer–Altärchen, Apotheke, Felsenkopf and Leiterchen (last two solely owned); Ockfener Geisberg. A family house by the church, Milz property since the 17th century. All Riesling, the wines well-balanced

towards dryness.
Weingut Paulinshof
5561 Kesten b. Bernkastel. Owners: Klaus and Christa Jüngling. Einzellagen: Kestener–Herrenberg, Paulinsberg, Paulins-Hofberger, Brauneberger Juffer-Sonnenuhr, Juffer and Kammer. Small, one-time monastic estate (records go back to 936), 90% Riesling. Light *spritzig* wines, built to last. A 1988 Auslere trocken was a Mosel classic – in an old-fashioned, wax-capsuled bottle, too.

Ökonomierat Max-G. Piedmont
Saartal 1, 5503 Konz-Filzen. Owner: Klaus Piedmont. 15 acres. Einzellagen: Filzener–Pulchen, Urbelt and Steinberger. A fourth-generation family estate in the narrow valley of the lower Saar. 90% is Riesling, 10% Weissburgunder; stylish dry wines matured in oak.

St. Nikolaus Hospital
Cusanusstift, Cusanusstrasse 2, 5550 Bernkastel-Kues. 20 acres. Einzellagen: Wehlener Sonnenuhr; Graacher Himmelreich; Bernkasteler–Weissenstein, Graben; Kueser Kardinalsberg; Lieser Süssenberg; Brauneberger Juffer. The foundation of the 15th-century theologian and philanthropist Cardinal Nikolaus Cusanus of Kues, whose library is still in the old hospital by the bridge. Purist Rieslings from some superb sites.

Weingut Schloss Saarstein
5512 Serrig. Owners: Dieter and Christian Ebert. 27 acres. Einzellagen: Serriger–Antoniusberg and Schloss Saarsteiner. Typically light and racy Saar Riesling.

Weingut Hubert Schmitz
Klosterbergstrasse 108, 5511 Wiltingen. Owner: Christoph Schmitz. 10 acres. Einzellagen: Wiltinger–Kupp, Braunfels

and Klosterberg. The Schmitz family has farmed the old Hoensbroech land since 1948 and bought it in 1968. Almost 100% Riesling, with a tiny plot of Optima in the Klosterberg. The best Auslese comes from the Kupp.

Weingut Geschwister Selbach-Oster
Uferallee 23, 5553 Zeltingen. Owners: Hans and Johannes Selbach. 15 acres. Einzellagen: Zeltinger–Himmelreich, Schlossberg and Sonnenuhr; Wehlener-Sonnenuhr and Klosterberg; Graacher Domprobst; Bernkasteler–Schlossberg. Selbachs have been growers since 1661. The wines are oak matured, generally dry and lively.

Weingut Studert-Prüm Maximinhof
5550 Bernkastel-Wehlen. Owners: Stephan and Elisabeth Studert. 15 acres. Einzellagen: Wehlener–Sonnenuhr, Nonnenberg; Graacher–Himmelreich, Domprobst; Bernkasteler Graben. The Studert family, which has been growing vines since the 16th century, acquired the Wehlen vineyard holdings of the Benedictine St. Maximin Abbey in Trier in 1805. Today the wines are traditional in style, elegant and fruity. 90% of the vines are Riesling.

Oskar Tobias
5555 Piesport. An outstanding specialist in Piesporter Goldtröpfchen, of which he has some of the finest plots, planted entirely with Riesling.

Weingut Dr. F. Weins-Prüm (Selbach-Weins)
Uferallee 20, 5550 Bernkastel/Wehlen. Owner: Herr Selbach-Weins. 11 acres. Einzellagen: Graacher–Himmelreich and Domprobst; Wehlener–Sonnenuhr and Klosterberg; Ürziger Würzgarten; Erdener–Treppchen and Prälat. The cellars of this property date back to 1560. Its Sonnenuhr and Prälat Rieslings are in particular demand.

AHR AND MITTELRHEIN

Ahr
Perverse as it seems, Germany's northernmost wine region specializes in red wine. The Ahr is a western tributary of the Mittelrhein, not far south of Bonn, whose steep sides are clothed almost continuously in vines for ten miles: 1,000 acres, of which two-thirds are Spätburgunder, Portugieser and other red grapes, and one-third is Riesling, Müller-Thurgau and a little Kerner.

The white wines, when ripe, have a distinct aromatic lilt which is very attractive. Real ripeness for red grapes is almost impossible here. The wine is pale and thin, often made distinctly sweet, and

would probably be extinct were it not for the beauty of the valley, the nearness of large rich centres of population, and the German fondness of a walk in the vineyard followed by an evening in a snug little restaurant drinking the proprietor's wine.

No less than 900 small growers till the soil, most of them banded into seven cooperatives, but a hundred or so making and selling their own wine. There is only one Grosslage name: Klosterberg.

Mittelrhein
A more logical name for this spectacular but dwindling wine region would be the Lower Rhine.

It is exactly analogous to the Lower Mosel – the part of the river downstream from the classic sites, where custom (and extraordinary effort) maintain a narrow necklace of vineyards on the immediate riverside slopes – and sometimes cliffs. There are 1800 acres of vines along some 60 miles of river, starting near Oberdiebach on the left bank, almost opposite Assmannhausen, the last of the Rheingau, and wriggling north on either or both sides of the river as far as Königswinter.

Riesling is the principal grape of the morsels of vineyard that cling to the hills. It makes good, usually austere and even sharp wine, used in good vintages in the Weinstuben of its growers and in poor ones for processing a Sekt.

The Mittelrhein has 11 Grosslagen, in order following the river: Schloss Reichenstein (villages: Trechtingshausen, Niederheimbach, Oberheim-bach); Schloss Stahlech (villages: Oberdiebach, Manubach, Bacharach, Bacharach-Steeg); Herrenberg (villages: Kaub, Dörscheid); Schloss Schön-burg (villages: Perscheid,. Langscheid, Dellhoten, Oberwesel, Damscheid, Niederburg, Urbar); Lore-leyfelsen (villages: Bornich, St. Goarshausen, Patersberg, Nochern, Kestert, Kamp-Bornhofen); Burg Rheinfels (villages: St. Goar, St. Goar-Werlau); Gedeonseck (villages: Boppard, Spay, Brey, Rhens); Marksburg (villages: Filsen, Osters-pai, Braubach, Lahnstein, Koblenz, Koblenz-Ehrenbreitstein, Urbar, Vallendar); Lahntal (vil-lages: Obernhof, Weinähr, Nassau, Dausenau, Bad Ems, Fachbach); Hammerstein (villages: Leutes-dorf, Hammerstein, Rheinbrohl , Bad Hönningen, Leubsdorf, Dattewnberg, Linz, Kasbach, Unkel); Petersberg (villages: Rhöndorf, Königswinter, Nie-derdollendorf, Oberdollendorf).

AHR AND MITTELRHEIN PRODUCERS

Weingut J. J. Adeneuer
Max-Planckstrasse 8, 5483 Bad Neuenahr-Ahrweiler. Owners: Marc and Frank Adeneuer. 9.4 acres. Einzellagen: Walporzheimer–Gärkammer and Domlay; Ahrweiler Forstberg; Nenenahrer–Schieferlay and Sonnenberg; Heimersheimer Burggarten. A completly red-wine specialist with 500 years of tradition in the family. 76% Spätburgunder, 21% Portugieser. Wines as stylish as any on the Ahr.

August Perll
Oberstrasse 81, 5407 Boppard. Mittelrhein. 12 acres Einzellage: Bopparder Hamm. A small grower of Riesling and Spätburgunder on the vertiginous slopes of the Boppard bend of the Rhine. Dry wines of character.

Jakob Sebastian Nachf.
Brückenstrasse 2, 5481 Rech Ahr. 10 acres. Einzellagen: Heppinger Berg; Neuenahrer Schieferlay; Ahrweiler Daubhaus; Recher–Hardtberg, Blume and Herrenberg; Mayschosser–Silberberg. An old wine-growing family with a complicated little red-wine estate (of which it owns 70%). The Mayschoss vines are rented from Fürst von Arenberg. Heppingen, with heavier soil, produces the 'biggest' wines; most are Kabinetts ranging from very light to quite firm and dry. The Sebastians are also wholesale merchants.

Staatliche Weinbaudomän Kloster Marienthal Ahr
Klosterstrasse, 5487 Marienthal Ahr. 45.7 acres. Einzellagen: Marienthaler–Klostergarten and Stiftsberg; Walporzheimer–Kräuterberg; Ahrweiler–Rosenthal and Silberberg. Dernauer Hardtberg, Grosslage:

Klosterberg. Vines are 60% Spätburgunder, 10% Portugieser, and many experimental red-wine varieties. An Augustinian convent from the 12th to the 19th century; now the model Ahr estate producing the most prestigious reds, including many Ausleses.

Weingut Meyer-Näkel
Hardtbergstrasse 20, 5487 Dernau. Owners: Werner and Willibald Näkel. 13.6 acres. Einzellagen: Ahrweiler–Forstberg, Riegelfeld and Rosenthal; Neuenahrer Sonnenberg; Dernauer–Goldkaul, Hardtberg and Pfarrwingert; Marienthaler Trotzenberg. A small family estate that emerged in the 1980s, producing cask- and *barrique*-matured, dry red wines, softened by malolactic fermentation. 80% Spätburgunder, 5% Portugieser, 5% Dornfelder, 5% Riesling. Average yield 50 hl/ha. 80% is sold directly to the consumer, and the balance to top restaurants, including the well-known 'Ente vom Lehel' in Wiesbaden, and the 'Schiffchen' in Düsseldorf.

Weingut J. Ratzenberger
Blüchestrasse 167, 6533 Bacharach-Steeg, Mittelrhein. Owner: Jochen Ratzenberger. 12 acres. Einzellagen: Steeger St. Jost; Bacharacher–Wolfshöhle and Kloster Fürstental. A small family estate and source of excellent, racy Rieslings – both still and sparkling – produced with an average yield of 65 hl/ha from steep slate slopes. The cask matured Spätburgunder is similar to that of Assmannshausen.

Weingut Jean Stodden
Rotweinstrasse 7–9; 5481 Rech/Ahr. 11 acres. Einzellagen: Mayschosser Mönchberg; Dernauer Burggarten;/ Recher–Blume, Hardtberg and

Herrenberg. A little estate, merchant-house and distillery for four generations; 30% Portugieser, 53% Spätburgunder, 15% Riesling, 2% Muller-Thurgau. Its Portugieser is very light, Spätburgunder in good years warm and 'fiery' (the best is stored in oak), Riesling quite sharp and Müller-Thurgau mild. Steep slopes and slate are the secret of the best sites.

Weingut Heinrich Weiler
Mainzerstrasse 2–3, 6532 Oberwesel am Rhein. Mittelrhein. 12 acres. Einzellagen: Oberweseler–Römerkrug and St. Martinsberg; Engeholler Goldemund; Kauber–Backofen and Rossstein (solely owned). Perhaps the best-known property of this lovely part of the Rhine valley, 80% Riesling, 8% Müller-Thurgau with steeply terraced slaty vineyards capable of full-flavoured, even fruity Riesling.

RHEINGAU

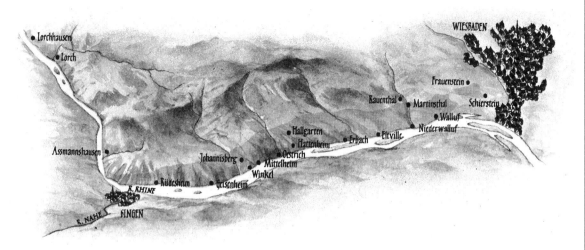

The Rheingau can add to the inherent quality of its wines the merits of consistency and coherence. It is the tidiest major German wine region; 20-odd miles of monoculture along the north bank of the Rhine, the whole of the short stretch where it flows southwest instead of north, deflected by the tall and sheltering Taunus mountains.

The extremities of the area are Hochheim at the upstream end, overlooking not the Rhine but the tributary Main joining from the east, and Lorch downstream. The heart of it, where vines and urbanization battle it out along the river's busiest shore, is the 12-mile stretch from Walluf to the Rüdesheimer Berg, a towering prow of hill that churns the river into rapids as it fights to turn north once more. The entire region has the Bereich name Johannisberg with ten Grosslagen, including Daubhaus (for the Hochheim extension), Stein-mächer, Deutelsberg, Erntebringer and Burgweg.

In the minds of its purists (and promoters) Rheingau and Riesling are inextricably linked. Although 18 per cent of its vineyards are planted with lesser grapes, the Rheingau owes entirely to the Riesling the force, the cut, the drive and follow-through that make its fine wines the best of the Rhine.

The purest magic is when all this vitality is captured in the relative delicacy and miniature scale of a Kabinett wine. It is not so difficult to be impressive with forceful late-gathered Spätleses or Ausleses. It is when the region is judged on what it can pack into its lightest category of wine that the Rheingau, along with parts of the Mosel, the Nahe and the Rheinpfalz (Palatinate), stands out as one of the world's greatest vineyards.

Hochheim
The vineyards are separated from the main Rheingau by Wiesbaden and many an autobahn. The isolated hillside owes its survival to the strength of character of the wines; full-bodied to the point of coarseness (and immensely long-lived) in hot years, but generally combining Riesling finesse with a soft earthiness of their own. The English term 'hock', meaning any Rhine wine, is a contraction of 'hockamore' – an early attempt at pronouncing Hoch-heimer. 595 acres in Grosslage Daubhaus.
Growers Allendorf. Aschrott. Staatsweingüter Eltville. Stadt Frankfurt. Königin Victoria Berg. Ress. Schönborn. Werner.

Wiesbaden
Wiesbaden is not normally seen as a wine name except on the labels of its 11-acre Neroberg. The wines of the rest of its 371 acres are normally bottled under the Grosslage name: Rauenthaler Steinmächer.

Walluf
The little-known village stretches back from the river front up the valley of its stream. Most of its wines, which can be full-flavoured and keep excellently, take advantage of the Grosslage name Rauenthaler Steinmächer.
Growers J. B. Becker. Frankensteiner Hof.

Martinsthal
The altitude, soil, shelter and orientation of Martinsthal, 600 feet up and a good mile from the river, facing south, are very similar to those of its more famous neighbour Rauenthal. Rauenthal's best sites are steeper, but Martins-thal also makes wines of full, spicy flavour in good vintages. The Grosslage name Steinmächer has not overwhelmed its identity. 193 acres.
Growers J. B. Becker. G. Breuer. Frankensteiner Hof.

Rauenthal

The Leitgemeinde of the Grosslage Steinmächer lies high on the hill above its skirt of highly prized vineyards. From Baiken and Gehrn the State Domain and others coax bottles of smoothly measured, spicy, notably firm yet almost low-key Ausleses. Drier wines, including Kabinetts, are less distinctive in different vintages. 242 acres.
Growers J. B. Becker. G. Breuer. Staatsweinguter Eltville. Eser. Frankensteiner Hof. Langehof. Schloss Rheinhartshausen. Schloss Schönborn, Freiherrlich Langwerth von Simmern. Sturm.

Eltville

The most substantial town of the Rheingau waterfront, the headquarters of the State Domain and several other important estates, with ample gently sloping vineyards just below the first class in soil and situation, and correspondingly often a better bargain than more exclusive names. 593 acres in Grosslage Steinmächer.
Growers Allendorf. J. B. Becker. Belz Erben. G. Breuer. Staatsweinguter Eltville. Landgräflich Hessiches. J. Fisher. Freiherr zu Knyphausen. Robert von Oetinger. Richter-Boltendahl, Freiherrlich Langwerth von Simmern, Weil.

Kiedrich

The atmospheric old village lies 2 miles up a little valley from Eltville and the river. Thanks to a Victorian English benefactor, its Gothic church of rosy stone is still resplendent with Gregorian sounds. Vinously, Kiedrich occupies a place just behind Rauenthal, also needing the ripeness of a good vintage to give the ultimate vitality to its flavour. 425 acres in Grosslage Heiligenstock.
Growers Schloss Groenesteyn. J. Fischer. Freiherr zu Knyphausen. Landgräflich Hessiches. Lamm-Jung. Hans Lang. Nikolai. Robert von Oetinger. Schloss Reinhartshausen. Balthasar Ress. Tillmanns Erben. Dr. R. Weil.

Erbach

The town is like a western continuation of Eltville, but lapped round with vineyards on every side. Strangely, here it is not the apparently best-sited vineyards tilting up behind the town by the river (and the railway) with deep, fat, marly soil, suggesting by its position that it is both a frost trap and a swamp after rain. It is neither, but bears the name of Marcobrunn; for centuries a synonym for luxuriously full and high-flavoured hock. In fact, the drainage is excellent, the 5-degree slope sufficient and the whole of this stretch of riverbank a suntrap. Ebrach used to share the vineyard, then simply known as Marcobrunner, with its neighbour Hattenheim. They now share the Grosslage name Deutelsberg. 666 acres.
Growers C. Belz. Freiherr zu Knyphausen. Lamm-Jung. Nikolai. Robert von Oetinger. Schloss Reinhartshausen. Richter-Boltendahl. Balthasar Ress. Freiherrlich Langwerth von Simmern. Tillmanns Erben. Weil.

Hattenheim

The name of Hattenheim is not as celebrated as its great vineyards deserve. Down by the river, round the lovely little timbered town, Mannberg, Wisselbrunnen and Nussbrunnen share the suntrap qualities of Marcobrunn. High on the hill behind is perhaps the most famous vineyard in Germany, the Steinberg. (As an Ortsteil it omits the Gemeinde name. Behind the Steinberg, up the wooded coomb of the purling Erbach, lies Kloster Eberbach, the great Cistercian monastery belonging to the State Domain, now effectively the ceremonial headquarters of the German wine industry.)

The wines of Hattenheim thus range from the sensuous, smooth and subtly spicy products of the riverside to the martial harmonies of the Steinberg. The great walled vineyard was chosen 700 years ago by the monks for its exposure high on the flank of the hill on stony ground. They were looking for power and concentration, which with Riesling means steel as well as scent. The State Domain has recently been testing some of the new grape varieties in the Steinberg, producing wines of almost outrageous perfume. Steinberger Riesling needs time. Its harshness sometimes fights with sweetness for years before the harmonies emerge. 568 acres in Grosslage Deutelsberg.
Growers Staatsweinguter Eltville. Engelmann. August Eser. Vereinigte Winzergenossenschaft Hallgarten. Freiherr zu Knyphausen. Hans Lang. Robert von Oetinger. Schloss Reinhartshausen. Balthasar Ress. Schloss Schönborn. Schumann-Nägler. Freiherrlich Langwerth von Simmern. Tillmans Erben.

Hallgarten

Hallgarten continues the succession of upland villages from Rauenthal and Kiedrich, here rising to the Rheingau's highest point: vines in the Hendelberg are up to 700 feet above the river. With less mist and less frost than below, cooler nights, more sunshine and wind, combined with alkaline clay in the soil, Hallgarten wines are big-bodied and slow to develop – certainly below the first rank in charm but with some of the attack of Steinbergers.

The Grosslage name for these 516 acres of vineyards is Mehrhölzchen.
Growers Allendorf. Engelmann. August Eser. Vereinigte. Winzergenossenschaft Hallgarten. Hans Lang. Nikolai. Riedel. Wegeler-Deinhard. Weil.

Oestrich

Nestling snugly along its wharves, Oestrich is the biggest vineyard commune and one of the most reliable names of the middle rank, rising to star quality in Ausleses from the best growers in the Lenchen; wines of sinful, almost oily lusciousness. 1,094 acres in Grosslage Gottesthal.
Growers Allendorf. Altenkirch. Engelmann. August Eser. Vereinigte. Winzergenossenschaft Hallgarten. Hupfeld Erben. Kühn. Balthasar Ress, Schloss Schönborn. Wegeler-Deinhard.

Mittelheim

Mittelheim is squeezed between Oestrich and Winkel, while its wines are half in the Winkel Grosslage of Honigberg and half in Erntebringer, going to market as Johannisbergers. Its reputation thus dispersed, wines that proudly bear the name Mittelheim are likely to have character at a reasonable price. 413 acres in Grosslagen Erntebringer and Honigberg.
Growers Allendorf. August Eser. Vereinigte Winzergenossenschaft Hallgarten. Hupfeld Erbgen. Kühn. Wegeler-Deinhard.

Winkel

Winkel continues to line the river road with a hugger-mugger blend of buildings and vineyards at the foot of the slopes that lead up to two of the greatest sites on the Rhine: Schloss Johannisberg, obvious on the skyline, and Schloss Vollrads, sheltering discreetly in a fold of the hill at the back of the parish. Schloss Vollrads is the great name of Winkel, but an Ortsteil which sheds no reflected glory on its neighbours. The flag-carrying vineyard for Winkel is its Hasensprung (Hare leap), the eastern flank of the hill of Schloss Johannisberg. It gives very lovely, perfumed and almost delicate wines of infinite nuance and distinction. 650 acres in Grosslagen Erntebringer and Honigberg.

Growers Allendorf. Basting-Gimbel. Baron von Brentano. August Eser. Landgräflich Hessisches. Hupfeld. Johannishof. G. H. von Mumm. Balthasar Ress. Schloss Schönborn. Schuman-Nägler. Wegeler–Deinhard. Freiherr von Zwierlein.

Johannisberg

Johannisberg is the village behind the famous Schloss. It is also the Bereich name for the entire Rheingau. California vintners call their Rieslings after it. In fact, it must be the most borrowed name in Germany. What is its special quality? The situation of Schloss Johannisberg, dominating the river from a sort of saluting base of its own, explains itself.

The wines of Schloss Johannisberg inevitably have a hard time living up to their reputation. The competition from the neighbours, moreover, could hardly be fiercer in this area where ancient and noble estates are the rule rather than the exception. There is considerable justice in looking on Johannisberg as the epitome of the Rheingau; the place where all its qualities of vitality, spice, delicacy and grace come together. 290 acres in Grosslage Erntebringer.

Growers Fritz Allendorf. Basting-Gimbel. Landgräflich Hessisches. Hupfeld Erben. Schloss Johannisberg. Johannishof, G. H. von Mumm. Balthasar Ress. Schloss Schönborn. Wegeler–Deinhard.

Geisenheim

The riverside town below Johannisberg is known by name as much for its research and teaching institute, the H.Q. of German viticulture, grape breeding and oenology, as for its excellent vineyards, only a little, if at all, below the best in potential. The Rothenberg, a modest mountain above the centre of the town, has produced Rieslings whose perfume has driven me almost to ecstasy. Fuchsberg (where the experimental plots of the Institute are) and Mäuerchen, higher on the hill on the way to Rüdesheim, have almost ideal situations and soil - though Fuchsberg can be struck by untimely frosts. 1,057 acres in Grosslagen Burgweg and Erntebringer.

Growers Allendorf. Basting-Gimbel. Hessische Forschungsanstalt. Landgräflich Hessisches. Johannishof. G. H. von Mumm. Balthasar Ress. Schloss Schönborn. Schumann-Nägler. Wegeler-Deinhard. von Zwierlein.

Rüdesheim

Rüdesheim brings the main block of the Rheingau to a triumphant close. Here the crest of the Taunus mountains closes in on the river and squeezes the vineyards into steeper and steeper formation. The town is the tourist centre of the Rheingau, with a summer population it is pleasanter to avoid (but with a very useful car ferry to Bingen).

The vineyards west of the town, becoming steeper and narrower as they approach the river bend, carry the distinctive name of Berg after Rüdesheimer and before their individual names. Until recently they were terraced in tortuous steps and ramps, impossible to work except by hand. An astonishingly bold Flurbereinigung relandscaped the whole hillside. For a while bulldozers looked as if they would roll into the river. Now all is orderly and the Berg wines once more the ripest, strongest, most concentrated (if not the subtlest) of the Rhine. 808 acres in Grosslage Burgweg.

Growers Allendorf. Altenkirch. G. Breuer. Staatsweinguter Eltville. August Eser. Frankensteiner Hof. Hessische Forschungsanstalt. Schloss Groenesteyn. Landgräflich Hessisches. G. H. von Mumm. Nägler. Schloss Reinhartshausen. Balthasar Ress. Schlotter. Schloss Schönborn. Schumann-Nägler. Wegeler-Deinhard.

Assmannshausen

Everything changes at the Rüdesheim bend – even the colour of the wine. The village of Assmannshausen, with its sheltered valley of vines giving west on to the river, is two thirds planted with Spätburgunder. Most of the red wines have been pallid in the past. However, young growers are now introducing wines of quite a different structure. These reds have little appeal to foreigners, but the German cognoscenti dote on them.

The State Domain (at Eltville) is the principal producer, obtaining remarkable prices for sweet Ausleses of a disconcerting colour. The sweetness helps to mask the lack of a kernel of real Pinot Noir flavour. 430 acres in Grosslage Steil.

Growers Allendorf. Staatsweinguter Eltville. G. H. von Mumm. Schlotter.

Lorch and Lorchhausen

These villages are the transition from Rheingau to Mittelrhein. The best growers produce very creditable Riesling even without the natural advantages of the Rheingau. 449 acres.

Growers Altenkirch. Graf von Kanitz.

Sekt

Germany has found a way of turning her awkward excess of under-ripe wine, the inevitable result of her northerly situation, into pleasure and profit. They make the ideal base material for her national sparkling wine, Sekt. Sekt may be either fermented in bottle or in tank, may be made from any grapes from any region and may even include imported wines.

All the better Sekts, however, fall within the new (1986) German wine law as either Deutscher Sekt, which means that the wine must be from 100% German-grown grapes, or Deutscher Sekt bA, entirely from German grapes from one of the 11 designated wine-growing regions.

Many of the best specify that they are entirely Riesling wines and some specify their exact origins. There is, in fact, a huge range of qualities from the banal to the extremely fine. The best examples have nothing in common with champagne except bubbles: their flavour is essentially flowery and fruity with the inimitable Riesling aroma in place of champagne's mingled fruits and yeast and age. The principal producers include: Deinhard & Co., Koblenz. Faber Sektkellerei Faber, Trier. Fürst von Metternich, Johannisberg. Henkell & Co., Wiesbaden. Peter Herres, Trier. Christian Adalbert Kupferberg, Mainz. Matheus Müller, Eltville, Schloss Böchingen, Böchingen. Schloss Saarfels, Sektkellerei Spicka, Serrig/Saar.

RHEINGAU PRODUCERS

Geheimrat Ashrott'sche Erben Weingutsverwaltung

Kirtchstrasse 38, 6203 Hochheim am Main. Director: Holger Schwab. 49.4 acres. Einzellagen: Hochheimer–Kirchenstück, Domdechaney, Hölle, Stielweg and Reichstal.

A major all-Hochheim property. 96% Riesling. The wines are typical Hochheimers: powerful and succulent from their fertile soil and southern slopes. The Aschrott family established itself in 1823, but the 4 owners now live in England and Australia.

Baron von Brentano'sche Gutsverwaltung Winkel

Am Lindenplatz 2, 6227 Oestrich-Winkel. Owner: Udo Baron von Brentano. 22.7 acres. Einzellagen: Winkeler–Hasensprung, Jesuitengarten, Gutenberg and Dachsberg. Grosslage: Honigberg.

A relatively small family estate since 1804, entirely in Winkel, proud of its historic associations with Goethe, Beethoven and the romantic literary and artistic life of the Rhine in Imperial times. Goethe's profile appears in blue on the label of selected 'Goethewein' from the Hasensprung and Jesuitengarten. The estate is 96% Riesling and 4% Spätburgunder (partly for red wine and partly for Weissherbst) and maintains old-fashioned high standards in a museum-like atmosphere.

Weingut des Hauses Deinhard

See Wegeler-Deinhard.

Verwaltung der Staatsweingüter Kloster Erbach

Schwalbacherstrasse 56–62, 6228 Eltville. Director: Karl Damm. 464 acres in Assmannshausen (exclusively for red wine), Rüdesheim, Hattenheim, the Steinberg, Rauenthal, Eltville, Hochheim and Bensheim/Heppenheim (the last outside the Rheingau on the Hessische Bergstrasse between Darmstdt and Heidelberg). Einzellagen: Assmannshäuser Höllenberg (56.8 acres); Rüdesheimer–Berg Schlossberg, Berg Rottland, Berg Roseneck and Bischofsberg (total 56.8); Hattenheimer–Engelmannsberg and Mannberg (22.2); Erbacher–Marcobrunn, Siegelsberg and Honigberg (14.8); Steinberger (76.6); Rauenthaler–Baiken, Gehrn, Wülfen and Langenstück (86.5); Eltviller–Taubenberg, Langenstück and Sonnenberg (29.6); Hochheimer—Domdechaney, Kirchenstück, Stein, Hölle and Berg (42); Bensheimer–Streichling and Kalkgasse, Schönberger Herrnwingert, Heppenheimer Steinkopf and Centgericht (total 79).

The Rheingau State Domain at Eltville is the biggest and perhaps the most prestigious domain in Germany, based on monastic vineyards which were ceded to the Duke of Nassau under Napoleon, thence to the Kingdom of Prussia and now to the State of Hessen, whose capital is nearby Wiesbaden. The 7 estates are administered from an unromantic headquarters at Eltville by Karl Damm, the long-standing representative of his predecessor Dr. Hans Ambrosi.

For its ceremonial H.Q. the Domain has the magnificent and perfectly preserved Cistercian abbey of Kloster Eberbach (1135), in a wooded valley behind Hattenheim, and the most famous of its vineyards, the Steinberg, a walled 'clos' comparable to the Clos Vougeot (but unlike Vougeot still in one ownership). Kloster Eberbach is the scene of annual auctions of the wines of the Domain and certain of its distinguished neighbours; also of the German Wine Academy, which runs regular courses for amateurs and professionals. It was here that the word 'Cabinet' was first used (for the vintage of 1712) to designate reserve-quality wine – a meaning totally altered by modern laws.

The estates are planted with 88% Riesling, 10% Spätburgunder, 2% others. Wine-making methods are extremely modern; there is more stainless steel than oak and wines are bottled very young.

The Domain is immensely impressive and impeccably run, and must be counted as one of the greatest wine estates on earth. Its wines fetch high prices at auction, particularly the Eisweins, which it has made a speciality, and the predominantly dry or semi-dry Assmannshausen reds – although these are rarely seen outside Germany.

Using a budget of 10 million DM, the vast cellars have been renovated and extended, with the aim of giving each wine greater individual attention and combatting criticisms of uniformity and lack of inspirational quality in the wines.

Schloss Groenesteyn

Postfach 1180, 6229 Kiedrich. Owner: Baron von Ritter zu Groenesteyn. 79 acres. Einzellagen: Kiedricher–Gräfenberg, Wasseros, Sandgrub and Klosterberg; Rüdesheimer–Berg Rottland, Berg Roseneck, Berg Schlossberg, Bishofsberg, Kirchenpfad, Klosterlay and Magdalenenkreuz.

Another of the lordly estates of the Rheingau, dating from the 15th century, held by the Barons von Ritter zu Groenesteyn since 1640 and based at their great baroque mansion (the schloss) in Kiedrich, with its cellars in Rüdesheim. Vines are 92% Riesling, the rest Spätburgunder and Müller-Thurgau. The wines are kept in the old way in individual barrels to encourage variety and nuance, the Kiedrichers delicate and scented; the Rüdesheimers (especially from the Berg sites) fruity and spicy. A wide variety of wines is available from the cellars.

Landgräflich Hessisches Weingut

6222 Geisenheim am Rhein. The estate now consists of 123.5 acres in Einzellagen Rüdesheimer–Bishofsberg, Berg Rottland; Geisenheimer–Fuchsberg, Mäuerchen and Kläuserweg; Johannisberger–Goldatzel, Hölle, Klaus and Vogelsang; Winkeler–Gutenberg, Jesuitengarten, Dachsberg and Hasensprung; Eltviller–Langenstück, and Sonnenberg; Kiedricher Sandgrub and Rauenthal (where the Grosslage name, Steinmächer, is used).

The Count (Landgraf) of Hessen bought this estate in 1958 from the family of Kommerzienrat Krayer. 88% of the vines are Riesling, with a little Spätburgunder and an unusual (for the Rheingau) speciality, a plot of the spicy Scheurebe in Winkeler Dachsberg, planted by the former manager, Heinz Scheu, son of the famous breeder who introduced the grape in the Rheinpfalz. 'Kurhessen' is the brand name for Sekt. The range of wines is wide and the quality is high.

Schloss Johannisberg

Fürst von Metternich–Winneburg'sche Domäne. 6222 Geisenheim–Johannisberg. Owner: Paul Alfons Fürst von Metternich. 86.5 acres.

The most famous estate of the Rhine, whose name is often used to designate the true Riesling vine. Its first planting is credited to Charlemagne; the first monastery was built on its hilltop comanding the Rhine in 1100; full flowering came in the 18th century under the Prince-Abbot of Fulda. Its vintage of 1775 was the first to be gathered overripe (the Abbot's messenger having arrived late with permission to pick): the term Spätlese and the appreciation of noble rot are said to have started with this incident.

The estate was secularized under Napoleon and presented in 1816, after the Treaty of Vienna, by the Austrian Emperor to his Chancellor, Prince Metternich, for his diplomatic services. His descendant Prince Paul Alfons von Metternich-Winneberg is still nominally the owner, although the wine business is now part of a group belonging to the Sekt producer Henkell and Söhnlein, together with the neighbouring von Mumm estate.

In 1942 the monastery-castle (but not its cellar) was destroyed in an air raid. It is now totally rebuilt. The vineyard, in one block on the ideally sloping skirts of the castle hill, is planted entirely in Riesling. Technically it is an Ortsteil – a local entity which needs no Einzellage name. Average production is 70 hl/ha, a potential total of some 25,000 cases. The varying qualities within this mass of wine are designated by two different labels and 10 coloured capsules as well as the usual terminology. The capsules were originally wax – in German, *Lack*; thus Rotlak equals red seal, Grünlack, green seal, etc. (Coincidentally, the characteristic bouquet of mature Johannisberg is said to be a smell of burning sealing wax.)

At their best Schloss Johannisberg's wines are extraordinarily firm in structure, concentrated and long-lived, with every quality of classic Riesling grown on an exceptional site. I have drunk an 1870 which at a century old was still vigorous and bore traces of its original flavour. Recent wines, like those of several of the great lordly estates, have shown signs of commercialization: lightness and lack of 'grip'. The defence is that few people intend to keep them for maturing.

The majority of Schloss Johannisberg is now drunk abroad and, I fear, by people who have no yardstick to judge it by. Ausleses of 1971 and 1976 were quite properly superb, but this is only as it should be.

Weingut Graf von Kanitz
Rheinstrasse 49, 6223 Lorch. Owner: Count Carl Albrecht von Kanitz. 42 acres. Einzellagen: Lorcher–Schlossberg, Kapellenberg, Krone, Pfaffenwies and Bodental-Steinberg.
An ancient family property on steep slopes of varying soils, from slaty to sandy loam, giving fine but milder, softer wines than the main Rheingau. 95% is Riesling, 2.5% Müller-Thurgau and 2.5% Ehrenfelser. The inheritance, dating from the 13th century, includes the earliest Renaissance building of the area, the Hilchenhaus in Lorch, now a Weinstube.

Weingut August Kesseler
Lorcherstrasse 16, 6220 Rüdesheim-Assmannshausen. Owner: August Kesseler. 32 acres. Einzellagen: Assmannshausen, Höllenberg, Frankenthal and Hinterkirch; Rüdesheimer–Berg Schlossberg, Berg Roseneck, Berg Rottland and Bischofsberg.
A remarkable young estate producing four wines, all fully fermented, including an outstandingly successful, deep-coloured Spätburgunder matured in *barriques*, and a Riesling. Wines of potential Kabinett quality are enriched and sold as QbA. The prices are high but the wines have been taken up enthusiastically by top-quality restaurants and private customers. The vineyards are planted 93% Spätburgunder and 3% Riesling.

Weingut Freiherr zu Knyphausen
Klosterhof Drais, 6228 Eltville. Owner: Gerko, Baron zu Knyphausen. 50 acres. Einzellagen: Erbacher–Marcobrunn, Siegelsberg, Hohenrain, Steinmorgen and Michelmark;

Hattenheimer Wisselbrunnen; Kiedericher Sandsgrub; Eltviller Taubenberg.
A former monastic estate of the Cistercians of Kloster Eberbach, brought in 1818 by the Baron's forebears. 92% is Riesling, 4% Spätburgunder and 4% Ehrenfelser. The property is run on traditional and personal lines, making full-flavoured wines, 70% dry or medium-dry.

Weingut Königin Victoriaberg
Rheingaustrasse 113, 6227 Oestrich-Winkel. Owners: the Hupfeld family. 27.2 acres. Einzellagen: Mittelheimer–Edelmann and St. Nikolaus; Oestricher–Lenchen and Klosterberg; Winkeler–Jesuitengarten and Hasensprung; Johannisberger–Hölle and Vogelsang.
Queen Victoria stopped to watch the vintage in this fortunate vineyard on the lower slopes of Hochheim in 1850. The then owners, the Pabstmann family, were not slow to commemorate the visit, getting the Queen's permission to rename the vineyard after her, erecting a Gothic monument and designing the most tinselly (now quite irresistible) label. Deinhards, who sell the wine abroad, go to great lengths to maximize its quality. It is not Hochheim's finest, but full, soft, flowery and just what Queen Victoria might well have enjoyed. The label is printed in black and white for QbA wines, yellow and gold for Trocken wines and glorious Technicolor for QmP wines.

Weingut Krone
Rheinuferstrasse 10, 6220 Rüdesheim–Assmannshausen. Owner: Dr. Irene Hufnagel-Ullrich. 11 acres. Einzellagen: Assmannshausener–Frankenthal and Höllenberg; Rüdesheimer Berg Schlossberg.
The estate of probably the most famous hotel on the Rhine, the 'Krone'. The 100% Spätburgunder wine is matured in either tank, cask or *barrique* and needs time to develop in the bottle. It is serious and expensive wine.

Weingut Franz Künstler
Freiherr-vom-Stein-Ring 3, 6203 Hochheim. Owner: Franz Künstler. 12.4 acres. Einzellagen: Hochheimer Herrnberg, Hölle, Hofmeister, Kirchenstück and Reichestal.
The Künstler family began growing vines in Moravia (Czechoslovakia) in the 17th century and only moved to Hochheim after 1945. The estate has been very successful in recent years at national (DLG) competitions with its fresh, long-lasting wines, many of which are dry or medium-dry. Riesling is 84% and Spätburgunder 10%, plus small plantations of Scheurebe and Ehrenfelser.

Weingut Fürst Löwenstein
Schloss Vollrads, 6227 Oestrich-Winkel. Director: Count Erwein Matuschka-Greiffenklau. 44.5 acres. Einzellagen: Hallgartener–Schönhell, Hendelberg and Jungfer.
Estate leased by Count Matuschka-Greiffenklau since 1979. Vineyards are planted 99% Riesling. The wines are stylish, full of flavour, excellently-made yet without the ultimate thrilling fruit-acidity of Matuschka's Schloss Vollrads.

G. H. von Mumm'sches Weingut
Schulstrasse 32, 6222 Geisenheim. Owner: Rudolf August Octker. 173 acres. The Weingut is sole owner of Johannisberger–Hansenberg (10 acres) and Schwarzenstein (10). Other Einzellagen: Johanisberger–Vogelsang (12.4), Hölle (7.4), Mittelhölle (14.8) and Klaus (2.5); Rüdesheimer–Bischofsberg, Berg Rottland (2.5), Berg Schlossberg (4) and Berg Roseneck (7.4); Assmannshauser–Höllenberg,

Hinterkirch and Frankenthal; Geisenheimer–Mönchspfad, Mäuerchen, Kilzberg and Kläuserweg; Winkeler Dachsberg. An estate founded on the profits of the legendary 1811 'Comet' vintage, when the banker Peter Mumm of Frankfurt bought the whole crop of Schloss Johannisberg (which was temporarily in the hands of one of Napoleon's marshals, Kellermann). Mumm bought land in Johannisberg and the neighbourhood. In 1957 Rudolf August Oetker of Bielefeld, famous for his grocery products, bought 173 acres. 20 acres are planted in Spätburgunder in Assmannshausen; the balance of vines is 100% Riesling.

The same owners control Schloss Johannisberg. The technical wine-making side of both properties is now handled at the Mumm cellars; the administration at Schloss Johannisberg.

The Mumm wines have evolved in a modern style with the emphasis on dry and semi-dry categories. The better qualities are still wood-matured and well-balanced to age moderately. The estate owns a restaurant at Burg Schwarzenstein, high above Johannisberg, where its wide range of wines is on offer.

Schloss Reinhartshausen

6229 Erbach. Owners: the Princes of Prussia. 165 acres between Erbach and Hattenheim. Einzelagen: Erbacher–Marcobrunn, Schlossberg (solely owned), Siegelsberg, Rheinhell (solely owned), Hohenrain, Steinmorgen, Michelmark and Honigberg; Hattenheimer–Wisselbrunnen and Nussbrunnen; Kiedricher Sandgrub; Rauenthaler–Wülfen; Rüdesheimer Bischofsberg.

The riverside estate of the Prussian royal family; the mansion is now a luxury hotel facing the tranquil green island of Mariannenaue (Rheinhell) across the Rhine. 80% of the estate is Riesling; the rest is divided between Weisburgunder for full-bodied dry wine, Spätburgunder for light red and Weissherbst (rosé), and Gewürztraminer and Kerner (aromatic wines for the table).

The rich loam of Erbach, especially Marcobrunn, gives notably full-bodied wines. The island's wine is also soft and rich. The estate uses traditional casks and maintains a balance between top-quality wines (recently particularly good) and commercial lines.

Balthasar Ress

Hattenheim, 6228 Eltville 3. Owner: Stefan B. Ress. Some 59.3 acres scattered among good sites. Einzellagen: Rüdesheimer–Berg Rottland, Berg Schlossberg, Bischofsberg, Kirchenpfad, Klosterlay and Magdalenenkreuz (7); Geisenheimer Kläusweg (6.4); Hattenheimer–Wisselbrunnen, Nussbrunnen, Hassel, Heiligenberg, Schützenhaus, Engelmannsberg and Rheingarten (17); and small sites in Johannisberg, Winkel, Oestrich, Erbach, Kiedrich and Hochheim.

A century-old family firm of growers and merchants (under the name Stefan B. Ress). Vines are 90% Riesling, 7% Spätburgunder. In 1978 Ress rented the 10-acre Schloss Reichartshausen, originally Cistercian property but latterly neglected. Ress wines are cleanly made, bottled very early for freshness, balanced in sweetness for modern taste.

Each year a modern artist is commissioned to paint a label for a selected Auslese of top quality (e.g. Hattenheimer Wisselbrunnen, Oestricher Doosberg).

Domänenweingut Schloss Schönborn

Hauptstrasse 53, Hattenheim, 6228 Eltville. Owner: Count Dr. Karl von Schönborn-Wiesentheid. 188 acres. Einzelagen:

Hattenheim–Pfaffenberg (14.8, sole owner), Nusbrunnen (5), Engelmannsberg, Schützenhausen; Erbacher Marcobrunn (5); Rauenthaler Baiken; Oestericher Doosberg (32); Winkeler Hasensprung; Johannisberger Klaus (10); Geisenheimer–Schlossgarten (5), Mäuerchen (2.5), Rothenberg and Kläuserweg; Rüdesheimer–Berg Schlossberg, Berg Rottland (3.7) and Bishofsberg; Hochenheimer–Domdechaney (3.7), Kirchenstück (6.2), Hölle (7.4). Stielweg.

The biggest privately owned estate in the Rheingau, since 1349 in the hands of a family of great political and cultural influence. The present owner lives in his Franconian castles of Pommersfelden and Wiesentheid. The same Director, Domänenrat Robert Englert, has run the wine estates for more than 20 years and his signature appears on the labels.

Critics are divided over the recent performance of Schönborn wines. Some find them beautifully balanced – the ultimate in finesse. Others have described them as the 'Rubens of the Rheingau', while others have found them heavy and oversweetened. They come in vast variety from the central Marcobrunn to Lorch at the extreme west of the region and Hochheim at the extreme east. 90% of the estate is Riesling, 6% Spätburgunder, 1% Weissburgunder (made into a fully dry wine), 0.5% Müller-Thurgau and 2.5% others. All the wines are stored in small casks and should repay keeping in bottle. Commercialism may have affected parts of the range, but the best Schönborn wines are undoubted Rheingau classics.

Freiherrlich Langwerth von Simmern'sches Rentamt

Langwerther Hof, Kirchgasse, 6228 Eltville. The present Baron Friedrich owns a property held by his family since 1464, now amounting to 106.2 acres (92% Riesling, 7% Spätburgunder) in the best sites of Erbach, Hattenheim, Rauenthal and Eltville, including Erbacher Marcobrunn (4); Hattenheimer–Nussbrunnen (12), Mannberg (15.5) and Rheingarten (30); Rauenthaler–Baiken (3.7) and Rothenberg (2); Eltviller Sonnenberg (15.5).

The Gutshaus is the beautiful Renaissance Langwerther Hof in the ancient riverside centre of Eltville – one of the loveliest spots in the Rheingau. The richly heraldic (if scarcely legible) red label is one of the most reliable in Germany for classic Riesling, whether dry or sweet, balanced to age for years.

Schloss Vollrads

6227 Oestrich-Winkel. Owner: Graf Matuschka-Greiffenclau. Erweiun Matuschka-Greiffenclau, an impressively involved young man who presides over this magnificent old estate in the hills a mile above Winkel, is the 29th in a line of Grieffenclaus who have owned estates in Winkel since at least 1100. Their original 'Grey House' in Winkel, the oldest stone-built dwelling in Germany, is now a wine-restaurant. In about 1300 the family built the castle, whose great stone tower symbolizes their estate, accepted as an Ortsteil, a separate entity which uses no commune or Einzellage name. The 123 acres are 98% Riesling, 2% Ehrenfelser, of the old Rheingau strain that gives the 'raciest', relatively light but very long-lived wines. Schloss Vollrads specializes in dry wines with as little residual sugar as possible. On average about half the production of some cases is QmP wine, Kabinett or better (34% Kabinett, 10% Spätlese, 2% Auslese and very sweet wines).

Since 1979 the estate has rented the Weingut Fürst Löwenstein, a 42-acre neighbouring princely estate in

Hallgarten (Einzellagen Jungfer, Schönhell and Hendelberg), which produces relatively riper, mellower and more aromatic wines than the austere Vollrads style. Georg Senft, the cellar-master at Vollrads, makes both. The Löwenstein wines are more immediately pleasing: the Vollrads need several years' bottle-age.

The estate works closely with the Suntory winery in Japan, with whom Graf Matuschka-Grieffenclau bought Weingut Robert Weil. Visitors to Vollrads wine bar can taste a wide range and by booking can take part in sumptuous 'Lukullische' tastings with appropriate meals from the 'Graues Haus' restaurant. Count Matuschka leads this gastronomic match-making personally.

Gutsverwaltung Wegeler-Deinhard

Friedenplatz 9, 6227 Oestrich-Winkel. 148.2 acres. Einzellagen: Oestricher–Lenchen, Doosberg and Klosterberg (42.7 acres); Hallgarten Schönhell (2.5); Mittelheimer–Edelmann and St. Nikolaus (17.5); Winkeler–Hasensprung and Jesuitengarten (13.6); Johannisberger Hölle (2.2); Geisenheimer–Rothenberg, Kläuserweg and Schlossgarten (45); Rüdesheimer–Magdalenenkreuz, Bishofsberg, Berg Rottland, Berg Schlossberg and Berg Roseneck (23.5).

The very substantial Rheingau estate of the Koblenz merchant house of Deinhard, assembled by Geheimer Rat (counsellor) Wegeler, a Deinhard partner and cousin, a century ago. 97.4% is Riesling, 1% Scheurebe, 4% Müller-Thurgau and 0.7% others. 30% of the estate is on steep slopes. The average production is 40,000 cases.

Deinhards are known for their old-fashioned devotion to quality. Norbert Holderrieth is in charge. The Wegeler wines are true individuals; the best (especially from Oestricher Lenchen, Winkeler Hasensprung, Geisenheimer Rothenberg and the vineyards on the Rüdesheimer Berg) are often long-lived classics. Eisweins are a house speciality.

Altogether one of the biggest and most reliable Rheingau producers. The dry Spätlese wine, Geheimrat 'J', is much admired in Germany.

Weingut Robert Weil

Muhlberg 5, 6229 Kiedrich. Owner: Suntory Limited and Count Erwein Matuschka-Greiffenclau. 87 acres. Einzellagen: Kiedericher–Sandgrub (12.4), Wasseros (19.8), Gräfenberg (10), and Klosterberg (2.5); Eltviller–Sonnenberg (5), Rheinberg (5) and Taubenberg (2.5); Erbacher–Steinmorgen (2.5), Michelmark (5) and Honigberg (7.4); Hallgartener–Schönhell (2.5), Jungfer (10) and Würzgarten (2.5).

The leading estate of Kiedrich and one of the ten largest estates in the Rheingau. The Weils bought the property in 1868, partly from an Englishman, Sir John Sutton, still remembered as a benefactor by the village where he restored the splendid Gothic church and its famous organ. The estate is planted almost entirely with Riesling and complemented by a small proportion of Spätburgunder. New ownership in 1988 (see Schloss Vollrads).

Domdechant Werner'sches Weingut

Rathausstrasse 30, 6203 Hochheim. 30 acres. Einzellagen: Hochheimer–Domdechaney, Kirchenstück, Hölle, Stielweg, Stein and Reichestal.

The Werner family bought this superbly sited manor, overlooking the junction of the Rhine and Main, from the Duke of York in 1780. The buyer's son, Dr. Franz Werner, was the famous Dean (Domdechant) of Mainz who saved the cathedral from destruction by the French. The same family (now called Werner Michel) still owns and runs the estate, making some of the most serious, full-flavoured Hochheimers from the mingled soils of the old river terraces, sloping fully south. Traditional barrel-ageing makes essentially dry but long-flavoured and long-lived wines. 97% are Riesling.

COOPERATIVES

Vereinigte Winzergenossenschaft Hallgarten/Rhg.eG

Hattenheimerstrasse 15, 6227 Oestrich-Winkel-Hallgarten. 300 members. 308.8 acres in the excellent Einzellagen Hallgartener–Schönhell, Jungfer, Würzgarten and Hendelberg. Oestricher–Lenchen and Doosberg; Mittelheimer Edelmann and in Hattenheim. The Grosslage names used are Mehrnhölzchen and Deutelsberg.

A recent amalgamation of two local growers' cooperatives of Hallgarten.

Gebeitswinzergenossenschaft Rheingau eG

Erbacherstrasse 31. 6228 Eltville. 330 members. 371 acres scattered through the whole region.

The major cooperative of the Rheingau. 80% of their vines are Riesling, 8% Müller-Thurgau, 10% new white varieties, 2% Spätburgunder. Total production averages 1.3 million litres over 144,000 cases. 10% sold abroad via export houses.

OTHER PRODUCERS

Weingut Fritz Allendorf
Winkel. Owner: Fritz Allendorf. A very old Winkel wine-growing family, more recently established as a substantial estate with 62 acres and 37 more rented in Assmannshausen, Rüdesheim, Johannisberg, Geisenheim, Winkel, Oestrich, Mittelheim, Hallgarten, Eltville and Hochheim, planted with 80% Riesling, 10% Spätburgunder, 6% Müller-Thurgau, 4% various others. The biggest holding is 17 acres of Winkeler Jesuitengarten. The wines are full-flavoured and generally dry or medium-dry.
Weingut Friedrich Altenkirch
Bingerweg 2, 6223 Lorch. Owner: Peter Breuer. 36.3 acres. Einzellagen:

Lörcher–Schlossberg, Kappellenberg, Krone, Pfaffenwies and Bodenthal-Steinberg; Rüdesheimer–Berg Rottland and Magdalenenkreuz. Oestricher Doosberg. The former cellars of the Schwan Hotel, immensely deep and long, were taken over in 1973 by Herr Breuer, who has established a successful merchant house and estate. 81% of the latter is Riesling, 18% Spätburgunder, which is increasingly popular. The commercial lines include Altenkirch Sekt.
Weingut Basting-Gimbel
Hauptstrasse 70–72, 6227 Winkel. Owner: Gerhard Hofmann. A 400-year-old family estate with about 25 acres in Winkeler–Dachsberg, Gutenberg and

Hasensprung; Geisenheimer–Rothenberg, Mönchspfad and Maüerchen; Johannisberger Goldatzel. 86% is Riesling. QbA wine is sold as (Grosslage) Johannisberger Erntebringer. Serious little commercial house with a good Weinstube.
Weingut Weinhandel J. B. Becker
Rheinstrasse 5–6, 6229 Walluf. Owners: The Becker family (Johann-Josef and Maria). The Becker family of Walluf are well-known as brokers as well as growers, the third generation also owning the handsome old Hotel Schwan, with a garden by the river and excellent cooking. Their vineyards now amount to 37 acres in Einzellagen: Wallufer–Walkenberg, Berg-Bildstock

and Oberberg; Martinsthaler Rödchen; Rauenthaler Wülfen; Eltviller Sonnenberg, Rheinberg and Taubenberg. 80% is Riesling, 15% Spätburgunder (made into powerful dry red wine in Wallufer Walkenberg) and 5% Müller-Thurgau. Specialities are dry wines that have great character with remarkable keeping powers.

Weingut C. Belz K. Ries
Kiedricherstrasse 20, 6228 Eltville. Karl Ries took over his grandfather's estate in 1966 and enlarged it to 19.8 acres. Einzellagen: Eltviller–Sonnenberg, Taubenberg, Kalbspflicht and Langenstück; Erbacher Honigberg. 80% is Riesling, 20% Kerner. Riesling makes powerful, aromatic and sweetish wines.

Weingut G. Breuer
Grabenstrasse 8, 6220 Rüdesheim am Rhein. Owners: Heinrich and Bernhard Breuer. 38.3 acres in Rüdesheim: 6.2 in Berg Schlossberg, the rest divided between other Berg sites and the 'Oberfeld'. 81% is Riesling. The Breuers aim for the fine steely acidity the 'Berg' can give. They are also partners in the well-known merchant house of Scholl and Hillebrand (founded 1880) in Rüdesheim.

Weingut Diefenhardt
Hauptstrasse 9–11, 6229 Eltville 4. Owners: The Seyffardt family. 32 acres. Einzellagen: Rauenthaler–Rothenberg and Langenstück; Martinsthaler–Wildsau, Langenberg and Rödchen: Eltviller Taubenberg. A long-established firm (which furnished the first round-the-world Zeppelin ride in 1929) with 17th-century cellars. 85% is Riesling, 10% Spätburgunder (increasingly popular as a full dry red), 5% others. Medium-dry Riesling Kabinett, made for bottle-ageing, is characteristic of the house. The Seyffardt family plan to increase the number of wines matured in cask.

Weingut Karl Fr. Englemann
Hallgartenerplatz 2, 6227 Hallgarten. Owner: Karl Josef Nass. Einzellagen: Hallgartener–Schönhell, Jungfer and Würzgarten; Hattenheimer Schützenhaus. Oestricher Doosberg. A small estate of only about 16 acres, but producing Hallgarten wines (esp. Jungfer Riesling Kabinett) of classic quality.

Weingut August Eser
Friedensplatz 19. 6227 Oestrich-Winkel. Owner: Joachim Eser. A family estate since 1759, now consisting of 14.8 acres. Einzellagen: Oestricher–Doosberg, Lenchen and Klosterberg; Winkeler–Hasensprung and Gutenberg; Mittelheimer–Edelmann and St. Nikolaus; Rüdesheimer Bischofsberg; Hallgartener Schönhell; Hattenheimer Engelmannsberg; Rauenthaler–Gehrn and Rothenberg. 92% Riesling, 8% Ehrenfelser. Joachim Eser makes a full range from dry to sweet, presenting QmP wines with an 'expertise' – a document carrying a full analysis. The approach is modern, energetic and wins many prizes.

Frankensteiner Hof Weingut Espenschied
Marktstrasse 14, 6229 Walluf 2. Owner: Klaus Kludas. 11 acres. Einzellagen: Rüdesheimer–Berg Roseneck, Berg Rottland, Berg Schlossberg and Burgweg; Wallufer–Walkenberg, Fitusberg and Berg Bildstock; Rauenthaler–Langensrück and Steinmächer; Martinsthaler–Rödchen and Wildsau. The Espenschied family started in Rüdesheim in the 1780s and bought the Frankenstein house in Walluf at the other end of the Rheingau in 1845. The present owner bought the estate in 1975 and has enlarged it with more vines in Walluf and Rauenthal. 85% is Riesling. The wines are wood-matured, have firm acidity and regularly carry off prizes.

Weingut Ökonomierat J. Fischer Erben
6228 Eltville. Owner: Frau Fischer. A small fourth-generation property founded in 1880. Einzellagen: Eltviller–Sonnenberg, Langenstück Kalbspflicht and Taubenberg; Kiedricher Sandgrub. Vines are 90% Riesling. The Fischers' wines are outstanding models of conservative Rheingau taste, weighty and rich in flavour and made to keep a decade. The wines are ready to drink after 3–5 years.

Weingut der Stadt Frankfurt am Main
Limpuvgeugasse 2, 6000 Fraukfurt. 62 acres. Einzellagen: Hochheimer–Reichestal, Stielweg, Domdechaney, Kirchenstück, Sommerheil, Hofmeister, Holle and Stein; Frankfurter Lohrberger Hang. The wine estates of the city of Frankfurt were taken over from a Carmelite nunnery and a Dominican monastery in 1803. They include the largest holdings in Hochheim and the only vineyard in Frankfurt. QbA and Kabinett wines are 'hearty, *spritzig* and lively'. Spätlese and upwards are dignified with 'noble' flavours. 85% is Riesling.

Hessische Forschungsanstalt für Wein-, Obst- und Gartenbau
6222 Geisenheim. The horticultural and viticultural departments of the Hessen Technical School have holdings in Geisenheimer–Rothenberg, Kläuserweg, Mäuerchen and Fuchsberg (89 acres) and Rüdesheimer–Magdalenenkreuz, Klosterberg, etc. More than half the vines are Riesling, but much experimenting is done with new varieties, although still using the traditional cask. Standards are extremely high and the wines are reliably true to type – indeed sometimes outstanding.

Weingut Hupfeld Erben
Rheingaustrasse 113, 6227 Oestrich-Winkel. Owners: the Hupfeld family. 27.2 acres. Einzellagen: Mittelheimer Edelmann and St. Nikolaus; Oestricher–Lenchen and Klosterberg; Winkeler–Jesuitengarten and Hasensprung; Johannisberger–Hölle and Vogelsang. Planted with 90% Riesling; the rest consists of Spätburgunder and Grauburgunder. Wine growers since 1907 and merchants before that. Since the 1940s the Hupfelds have established themselves as a top-quality small estate, aiming for medium-dry balance, and winning regular medals. The Hupfeld family also own the well-known Königin Victoriaberg estate at Hochheim.

Weingut Johannishof, Eser
6222 Johannisberg. Owner: Hans Hermann Eser. 44.5 acres. Einzellagen: Johannisberger–Hölle, Klaus, Vogelsang, Schwarzenstein and Goldatzel; Winkeler–Jesuitengarten, Hasensprung and Gutenberg; Geisenheimer–Kläuserweg and Kilzberg. The estate is conspicuous on the road up to Johannisberg for its huge 18th-century wine press by the door. Herr Eser comes from an old growers' family and has made a reputation for powerful and full-flavoured wines. The deep cellars, 10 metres under the hill, are traditional; cold and damp with dark oval casks for maturing wine of character.

Weingut Robert König
Landhaus Kenner, 6220 Rüdesheim-Assmannshausen. Owner: Robert König. 14.8 acres. Einzellagen: Assmannshausener-Höllenberg, Frankenthal and Hinterkirch; Rüdesheimer Berg Schlossberg. A 99% Spätburgunder estate, offering cask-matured wines typical of the vine variety and vintage, including diabetic wine.

Weinbau Heinrich Kühn
Beinerstrasse 14, 6227 Oestrich-Winkel. Owner: Heinrich Kühn and sons. 4 acres. Einzellagen: Oestricher–Lenchen and Doosberg; Mittelheimer–Edelmann and St. Nikolaus. A tiny part-time business, but a maker of serious prize-winning wines (100% Riesling) specifically for long bottle-ageing.

Weingut Lamm-Jung
Eberbacherstrasse 50, 6228 Erbach. Owner: Josef Jung. 20.3 acres. Einzellagen: Erbacher–Honigberg, Hohenrain, Steinmorgen and Michelmark; Kiedricher Sandgrub. The

vineyards are 86% Riesling, followed by Spätburgunder, small parcels of Ruländer and Gewürztraminer. A high proportion of the wines are dry or medium-dry. In the wine bar 25 different vintages can be tasted, including Weissherbst (rosé), and the increasingly popular red wine from the Spätburgunder.

Weingut Hans Lang
Rheinallee 6, 6228 Eltville-Hattenheim. 29.5 acres. Einzellagen: Hattenheimer–Nussbrunnen (0.5), Schützenhaus (12.3), Heiligenberg (2.5), Wisselbrunnen (2.5) and Hassel (5); Hallgartener–Jungfer (5) and Schönhell (1.2); Kiedricher Sandgrub (0.5). A nurseryman, merchant and (since 1959) grower who has expanded rapidly. His style is robust with plenty of character and acidity. 80% Riesling and 10% Spätburgunder, matured in *barrique*.

Weingut Langehof
Martinsthalerstrasse 4. 6228 Eltville Rauenthal. Owners: Josef and Marianne Klein. 5 acres. Einzellagen: Rauenthaler–Langenstück, Wülfen, Rothenberg and Baiken. Small but very keen grower with 80% Riesling and 20% Gutenborner on good slopes. Wines mainly dry or medium-dry. A 1976 Rothenberg Beerenauslese was a considerable medal winner.

Weingut Dr. Heinrich Nägler
Friedrichstrasse 22. 6220 Rüdesheim. Owner: Dr. Heinrich Nägler. A distinguished small estate specializing in fine Rüdesheimer since the 19th century. 17.3 acres. Einzellagen: Rüdesheimer–Berg Rottland (2), Berg Schlossberg (2), Berg Roseneck (3), Bischofsberg (2.2). Drachenstein (6), Klosterlay (1) and Magdalenenkreuz (1.2). 86% is Riesling, 8% Ehrenfelser, 6% Spätburgunder. Nägler goes to great lengths to achieve concentrated wines of character, thinning the grapes and nursing small individual lots. Rather dry wines to accompany food, but makes some luxurious polished Spätleses and Ausleses.

Weingut Heinz Nikolai
Ringstrasse 16, 6228 Erbach. 17 acres. Einzellagen: Erbacher–Steinmorgen, Hohenrain, Michelmark and Honigberg; Kiedricher Sandgrub; Hallgartener Jungfer. A fourth-generation grower with 85% Riesling, 5% Scheurebe and Kerner, 10% Spätburgunder. His aromatic Scheurebe and fruity Kerner are popular. 70% of his output are *trocken* or *halbtrocken* wines.

Robert von Oetinger'sches Weingut
Rheinallee 1–3, 6228 Eltville–Erbach. Owner: Eberhand von Oetinger. 22.8 acres. Einzellagen: Erbacher–Hohenrain, Steinmorgen, Honigberg, Michelmark, Seigelsberg and

Marcobrunn; Kiedricher Sandgrub; Hattenheimer–Hassel and Heilenberg; Eltviller Sonnenberg. An old Erbach family in new premises (since 1966) by the Rhine, with Weinstube and garden. Their speciality is dry wines with pronounced acidity and powerful flavour, mainly drunk in the neighbourhood.

Weingut Fritz Perabo
Schauerweg 57, 6223 Lorch. Owner: Christof Perabo. 12 acres. Einzellagen: Assmannshäuser Höllenberg; Lorcher–Bodental–Steinberg, Kapellenberg, Krone, Pfaffenwies, Schlossberg. The Perabo family has been established in Lorch since the early 17th century. The small estate produces good, firm Rieslings in the modern style. 70% are dry or medium dry. There is also a small amount of traditionally made Spätburgunder.

Weingut Richter-Boltendahl
Walluferstrasse 25, 6228 Eltville. 3 acres. Einzellagen: Eltviller–Taubenberg, Langenstück, Sonnenberg and Rheinberg; Erbacher–Honigberg and Steinmorgen; Kiedricher Sandgrub. 86% Riesling, 7% Müller-Thurgau, 5% Spätburgunder, 2% Scheurebe. A century-old family estate. The buildings are an old barge-house stable by the Rhine. The wines are fresh and fruity, with Eltville Rheinberg, Riesling and Scheurebe Kabinett, and Weissherbst (rosé) as specialities.

Weingut Jakob Riedel
Taunusstrasse 1, 6227 Hallgarten. Owner: Wolfgang Riedel. 7.4 acres. Einzellagen: Hallgartener–Jungfer, Hendelberg Schönhell and Würzgarten. A 17th-century property making full-bodied wines with good acidity, bottled very young and intended for long maturing. 100% Riesling. (Ehrenfelser is used only for 'sweet reserve'.)

Weingut Valentin Schlotter
Lorcherstrasse 13, 6220 Rüdesheim. Owner: Karl-Heinz Runck. 23.5 acres. Einzellagen: Rüdesheimer–Berg Rottland, Berg Schlossberg, Berg Roseneck, Bischofsberg, Kirchenpfad, Klosterlay, Klosterberg, Drachenstein and Magdalenenkreuz (13.5); Assmannshäuser–Höllenberg and Hinterkirch (10). A well-established grower of both white and red wines. The cellars are next door to the famous inn Zur Krone in Assmannshausen. His red wines are light and flowery with a hint of almonds; his Rüdesheimer 50% *trocken* or *halbtrocken*, particularly good in 'off' vintages.

Weingut Schönleber-Blümlein
Kirchstrasse 39, 6227 Winkel. Owners: Karl and Gerda Schönleber. 12.4 acres. Einzellagen: Mittelheimer–Edelmann and St. Nikolaus; Oestreicher–

Klosterberg and Lenchen; Winkeler–Gutenberg and Hasensprung. Small estate with high standards, concentrating on Riesling (80%) and Spätburgunder (12%). Sales are exclusively to private customers.

Weingut Schumann-Nägler
Nothgottesstrasse 29, 6222 Geisenheim. Owners: Karl and Fred Schumann. 30 acres. Einzellagen: Rüdesheimer Magdalenenkreuz; Geisenheimer–Mäuerchen, Mönchspfad, Kilzberg, Kläuserweg; Winkeler Dachsberg; Hattenheimer–Schützenhaus, Hassel and Wisselbrunnen. A high proportion (97%) of Riesling, planted on sloping sites is the characteristic of this estate. The owners have been making Rheingau wine since 1438, and are at present increasing their holdings. The wines are typical of the region – good acidity and fruit. All are matured with individual attention in wood.

Weingut Georg Sohlbach
Oberstrasse 15, 6229 Kiedrich. Owner: Georg Sohlbach. 15 acres. Einzellagen: Kiedricher–Sandgrub, Wasseros, Klosterberg and Gräfenberg. An old estate, with a 450-year-old ancient cask cellar in the centre of Kiedrich. Einzellage names are used only for Riesling – other grapes have the Grosslage name Heiligenstock. 70% is mainly dry or semi-dry, as fresh and flowery as possible. Red wine from Spätburgunder has been made since 1983.

Tasting from the cask

Weingut Sturm & Sohn
Hauptstrasse 31, 6228 Eltville 5. Owner:
Walter Sturm. 9.1 acres in Rauenthaler–
Baiken, Wülfen, Langenstück, Gehrn
and Rothenberg. Growers in Rauenthal
since 1653 and much respected for their
typically spicy, cask-matured wines with
a long life. The largest holding is
Wülfen and the best Baiken. 70% is
Riesling, the rest consists of Kerner,
Ehrenfels and Portugieser. The 1976
TBA won the top German prize for that
great vintage.

**Weingutsverwaltung H. Tillmanns
Erben**
Hauptstrasse 41, 6228 Eltville 2 –
Erbach. Owner: Willi Leibbrand. 35
acres. Einzellagen: Erbacher–
Hohenrain, Michelmark, Honigberg,
Steinmorgen; Kiedricher Sandgrub;
Hattenheimer Wisselbrunnen. Ancient
cellars once owned by Kloster

Eberbach. 91% is Riesling. Half his
production is dry or semi-dry. Erbacher
Hohenrain is his speciality.

Weingut Troitzsch
Haus Schöneck, Bächergrund 12, 6223
Lorch. Owner: Otto Troitzsch. 9 acres.
Einzellagen: Lorcher Schlossberg;
Kapellenberg, Krone, Pfaffenwies and
Bodental-Steinberg. This estate, under
the resolute hand of Otto Troitzsch, has
been making fully fermented wines for
over 40 years. They are matured in
wood and sold to about 100 private
customers. 55% Riesling and 10% each
of Weissburgunder and Silvaner, plus
others.

Weingut Wagner-Weritz
Eberbacherstrasse 90–94, 6228 Eltville-
Erbach. Owner: Jakob Weritz. 18.5
acres. Einzellagen: Erbacher–
Michelmark, Honigberg, Hohenrain,
Siegelsberg and Steinmorgen;

Hattenheimer Hassel; Kidreicher
Sandgrub. The old Wagner property has
been enlarged by the present owner,
who also bought the 'Erbacher Hof' in
1971. Substantial, firm wines, over 95%
Riesling, particularly from the
Steinmorgen vineyard.

Weingut Freiherr von Zwierlein
Schloss Kosakenberg, Bahnstrasse 1,
6222 Geisenheim. Owner: Frau Gisela
Wegeler. The Schloss, built by the
Prince-Bishop of Mainz, took its name
from a Cossack regiment in Napoleon's
time. The present property is about 30
acres. Einzellagen: Geisenheimer-
Kläuserweg, Mäuerchen, Rothenberg
and Schlossgarten; Winkeler
Jesuitengarten. 100% Riesling. The
finest wines are from the Kläuserweg,
made rather dry, slightly tannic and
intended to last a good 10 years.

NAHE

The river Nahe (the 'a' is long) is a minor tributary
of the Rhine, joining its broad floor from the south
at Bingen, opposite the vineyards of the Rheingau.
Its vineyards are thus placed centrally between the
Middle Mosel, the best of Rheinhessen, the Saar and
the Rheingau. Its upper reaches have some of the
most perfect vineyard sites in Germany. Yet only
within the last century has Riesling been planted
here, and the region's full reputation as the producer
of some of the world's most perfect white wines is
even now scarcely established. The whole area is not
large, with 11,300 acres, and its Riesling vineyards
are less than a quarter of the total. Much of its
output is unexceptional, to be compared or confused with standard Rheinhessen wine. The outstanding wines come from a mere five-mile stretch
of the north bank of the upper river where it flows
east, from its capital town of Bad Kreuznach, and
from singular spots on southern slopes abutting the
river between Kreuznach and Bingen.

The conventional way of describing Nahe wines,
not surprisingly, is as being transitional between
Mosel and Rhine; some say specifically between Saar
and Rheingau. This is true of the weight and
balance, body and structure of the fine wines of the

upper Nahe: they do have the 'nerve', the backbone
of the Saar with some of the meat of the weightier,
more densely flavoured Rheingau. The soil, however, seems to add a certain singularity; to me the
great Nahe wines often have a suggestion of ethereal
Sancerre, a delicate hint of the blackcurrant leaf with
a delicious mineral undertone. In their delicacy yet
completeness they make hypnotic sipping, far into
the night.

The whole region is divided into two Bereichs:
Schlossböckelheim for the upper half, Kreuznach
for the lower. Schlossböckelheim contains three
Grosslagen: Burgweg (the best and most restricted,
containing the core of the riverside vineyards);
Paradiesgarten, and Rosengarten (almost always
associated with the village of Rüdesheim – one
suspects in the hope of confusion with the famous
Rüdesheim of the Rhine). Kreuznach contains four
Grosslagen: Kronenberg, Sonnenborn, Schlosskapelle and Pfarrgarten.

The upper (southern) Nahe region is fragmented
into scattered villages with no pattern and no
famous names, although reasonable wines are made
at, for example, Kirschroth, Meddersheim, Monzingen, Odernheim and Duchroth.

Schlossböckelheim

Schlossböckelheim is the first great name of the upper
Nahe. It is the Bereich name, it is also a village, and its
most famous vineyard, the Kupfergrube, was planted and
is exploited by the impeccable State Domain at Niederhausen, the Domain buildings overlooking their prize site
across a defile in the hills. Kupfergrube was a copper mine
until the beginning of this century; the diggings are still

discernible. Felsenberg, next door on the hill, has an
almost equally ideal slope and orientation; In den Felsen
and Königsfels only marginally less so. Down to Altenbamberg the Grosslage name is Burgweg.
Growers August E. Anheuser. Paul Anheuser. Crusius. Nahe-
Winzer Kellereien. Von Plettenberg. Schlink. Staatlichen
Weinbaudomäne.

Niederhausen

The space between Schlossböckelheim and Niederhausen is occupied by a gentle bend in the river, offering every inclination from southwest to east to a hill of vines. The finest are in the Steinberg around the State Domain cellars, but Hermannsberg, Hermannshöhle, Klamm, Kertz and the rest are all magnificent Riesling sites.
Growers August E. Anheuser. Paul Anheuser. Schneider. Staatlichen Weinbaudomänen.

Norheim

The much-divided vineyards of Norheim vary from steep to flat, lending themselves to a range of varieties, with fine Silvaner in Klosterberg and some well-flavoured Müller-Thurgau on the other sites. The best Riesling is found in Dellchen, Kirschheck and Kafels.
Growers August E. Anheuser. Paul Anheuser. Crusius. Von Plettenberg. Schneider. Staatsweingut Weinbau.

Traisen

Traisen is equally variable, from the sloping Nonnengarten, largely Müller-Thurgau, to the supreme Bastei, an extraordinary little ramp of Riesling at the foot of the immense red porphyry cliff of the Rotenfels. The Einzellage Rotenfels, also entirely Riesling, makes almost equally distinguished wine. The words 'race' or 'breeding' are quite unequal to its balance of finesse and fire.
Growers Hans Crusius & Sohn.

Bad Münster

The Nahe turns the corner northward at the town of Bad Münster. Its vineyards, though excellent, are infinitesimal compared with those of Münster-Sarmsheim farther downstream. Münsterer Felseneck and Steigerdell, though rarely seen, produce exceptional Rieslings worth searching for. Ebernburg, with its ancient castle over the river, also has three fine steep slopes: Schlossberg, Erzgrube and Feuerberg.

Altenbamberg

Altenbamberg lies in a side valley two miles south of the Bad Münster bend. The hills around offer several steep and sheltered slopes, largely planted with Riesling, here lighter and tauter than on the classic riverside sites, but also some notable Müller-Thurgau and Silvaner.
Growers Paul Anheuser. Staatlichen Weinbaudomäne.

Bad Kreuznach

The hub of the Nahe is the little spa-cum-commercial city of Kreuznach. Its name is known all over the wine world for its Seitzwerke, the factory where filter technology has reached perfection. The spa section of the town is quietly pretty, made interesting (and presumably salubrious) by an ambitious system of creating ozone by pouring salt water on to vast drying frames; a bizarre feature of the road into town.

Kreuznach gives its name to the lower Nahe Bereich. It also musters the enormous total of 2,500 acres of vineyards – approaching a quarter of the Nahe region. They lie almost all round the town, the best of them coming close to the centre on the northwest. Kahlenberg, Krötenpfuhl and Brückes are considered top sites, but several others, including Steinberg, Narrenkappe, Forst and Kauzenberg are excellent vineyards for Riesling.

On a more modest level, and with other grape varieties, the Einzellage wines of Kreuznach, in the Grosslage Kronenberg, are generally a safe bet and often a very pleasant surprise.

Using a refractometer to measure sugar levels of ripening grapes

Growers August E. Anheuser. Paul Anheuser. Finkenauer. Nanh-Winzer Kellereien. Von Plettenberg. Schlink. Rheingräfenberg. Staatsweingut Weinbau.

Winzenheim

Winzenheim continues the left-bank vineyards of the Nahe without a break from Kreuznach. Its Einzellagen Rosenheck, Honigberg and Berg are all slopes with good potential, now included with Bad Kreuznach.

Bretzenheim

The vineyards flow on from Winzenheim with increasingly loamy, fertile soil, Silvaner and Müller-Thurgau becoming more prominent than Riesling. Grosslage Kronenberg.
Growers Dr. Josef Höfer. Von Plettenberg.

Langenlonsheim

The next community of the northward-flowing Nahe has another huge vineyard area taking advantage of a south slope of sandy loam at right angles to the river. The Steinchen is largely planted with Müller-Thurgau and Silvaner, which give fairly full-bodied and aromatic wines, but a far cry from the upstream classic. The best site is the Rothenberg. Langenlonsheim is in the Grosslage Sonnenborn.
Growers Nahe-Winzer Kellereien. Pallhuber. Schweinhardt. Erbhof Tesch.

Laubenheim

Laubenheim, again on the river, has similar loamy slopes; none of outstanding reputation. The Grosslage here is Schlosskapelle.

Growers Erbhof Tesch. Schlossmühle.

Dorsheim

Dorsheim lies immediately west of Laubenheim, facing the community of Burg Layen and the Rümmelsheim across a little valley. Its best sites lie on the Burg Layen side, stonier and steeper than Laubenheim, with a high proportion of Riesling of real style. Goldloch and Pittermännchen are the best slopes. Grosslage Schlosskapelle.

Growers Diel auf Burg Layen. Dr. Josef Höfer. Staatlichen Weinbaudomäne. Erbhof Tesch.

Burg Layen and Rümmelsheim

Burg Layen and Rümmelsheim are effectively one village, with vineyard conditions similar to Dorsheim, reaching their best, for notable Silvaner and Müller-Thurgau as well as Riesling, in the Schlossberg and Hölle. Grosslage Schlosskapelle.

Growers Diel auf Burg Layen. Dr. Josef Höfer. Nahe-Winzer Kellereien.

Münster Sarmsheim

Münster Sarmsheim brings the Nahe vineyards to an end just before Bingen, with slopes angled southeast away from the river. The Nahe State Domain has demonstrated that these gentle inclines of stony loam are capable of ripening magnificent Riesling, more full-bodied and robust than their beautiful wines from Schlossböckelheim and Niederhausen. Dautenpflänzer is the best of the Einzellagen. Grosslage Schlosskapelle.

Growers Diel auf Burg Layen. Dr. Joseph Höfer. Nahe-Winzer Kellereien. Staatlichen Weinbaudomäne.

A number of villages west of the river contribute worthy wines to the Nahe contingent. Weinsheim, Sponheim, Roxheim, Wallhausen, Dalberg and Guldental all have above-average sites.

Growers Paul Anheuser. Dr. Josef Höfer. Nahe-Winzer Kellereien. Prinz zu Salm-Dalborg. Schlink.

NAHE PRODUCERS

Weingut Ökonomierat August E. Anheuser

Brückes 53, 6550 Bad Kreuznach. Owner: Ökonomierat August E. Anheuser. 117.3 acres. Einzellagen: Kreuznacher–Brückes, Hinkelstein, Hofgarten, Kahlenberg, Krötenpfuhl, Mönchberg, St. Martin, Narrenkappe, Steinberg (solely owned), Winzenheimer Rosenheck; Norheimer Kafels and Dellchen.

The Anheuser family dominate the best sections of the Kreuznach vineyards, with roots going back to the 17th century. The company (founded 1869) also owns Anheuser and Fehrs, who are merchants, not growers. Vines are 74% Riesling and 13% Müller-Thurgau, the rest being Scheurebe, Ruländer, Silvaner and Weissburgunder. The heroic rock-cut cellars are a treasure house of old vintages in vast variety. The Anheuser family is also famous in American brewing for Anheuser-Busch and Budweiser beers.

Weingut Paul Anheuser

Strombergerstrasse 15–19, 6550 Bad Kreuznach. Owner: Rudolf Peter Anheuser. The present estate consists of 136 acres. Einzellagen: Kreuznacher–Brückes, Forst, Hinkelstein (15), Kahlenberg, Kapellenpfad, Krötenpfuhl (15), Mönchberg, Mollenbrunnen, Monhard, Narrenkappe, Osterhöll, St. Martin and Tilgesbrunnen; Schlossböckelheimer–Felsenberg, Heimberg, In den Felsen (12.5 acres), Königsfels (27) and Mühlberg; Niederhäuser–Felsensteyer (12.5) and Pfingstweide; Altenbamberger–Kehrenberg, Rotenberg, Schlossberg and Treuenfels; Norheimer–Dellchen and Kafels; Roxheimer–Berg and Höllenpfad; Mönzinger Halenberg.

A family concern tracing its origins to 1627. Rudolf Anheuser, the occupier in the 1880s, was the first to introduce Riesling to the Nahe. His descendants stress variety and vineyard character in their wines, which mature in wood in deep, cool cellars. The aim is freshness and fruit. 70%° is Riesling, 7% each Müller-Thurgau, Ruländer, Kerner and Weissburgunder (with some others, but not Silvaner). The speciality of the house is Riesling Kabinett *halbtrocken* with the singular Nahe character.

Weinkellereien Anheuser & Fehrs

Brückes 41, 6550 Bad Kreuznach.
Wine merchants (*see* August Anheuser).

Weingut Hans Crusius & Sohn

Hauptstrasse 2, 6551 Traisen.
Owners: Hans and Peter Crusius.

See opposite

Schlossgut Diel auf Burg Layen

6531 Burg Layen, Kreis Bad Kreuznach. Owner: Armin Diel. 29.6 acres. Einzellagen: Burg Layener–Schlossberg, Rothenberg, Hölle and Johannisberg; Dorsheimer–Goldloch, Honigberg, Pittermännchen and Klosterpfad.

The Diel family has farmed the manor surrounding the ruins of Burg Layen castle for 200 years. Radical changes have recently been made. Herr Diel has increased his Riesling to 80% and is maturing some of his wines in new oak. All the wines are now *trocken* except for the Beerenauslesen and Eiswein. The range is well made as well as wide: Dorsheimer Auslesses can be spendid.

Weingut Hermann Dönnhof

Bahnhofstrasse 11, 6551 Oberhausen. Owner: Helmut Dönnhof. 21.2 acres. Einzellagen: Bad Kreuznacher Mollenbrunnen; Niederhausener Hermannshöhle; Oberhausener–Brücke (solely owned), Felsenberg, Kieselberg and Leistenberg; Schlossböckelheimer Felsenberg.

Very old estate now producing wines with high acidity which are very much in the modern German taste. 60% of production is dry and many achieve Kabinett status. 73% Riesling, 12% Müller-Thurgau, plus others.

Weingut Carl Finkenauer

Salinenstrasse 60, 6550 Bad Kreuznach Rhld. Owners: Frau Elisabeth Finkenauer–Trummert and Hans–Georg Trummert–Finkenauer. 76.6 acres. Einzellagen: Kreuznacher–Brückes, St. Martin, Gutental, Narrenkappe; Winzenheimer Rosenheck; Roxheimer Mühlenberg.

The sixth generation of the family runs this estate in the attractive spa area of Bad Kreuznach. 53% is Riesling, 10% Müller-Thurgau, 8% Silvaner. Other varieties are

HANS CRUSIUS
A great Nahe estate

Hans Crusius of Traisen in the upper Nahe is the type of German grower who quietly achieves perfection, without apparent ambition to do more than till the land that his family has owned since the 16th century.

The Crusius property is 30 acres, 22 of them in the Einzellage Traiser Rotenfels, with small parcels in Norheim,. Niederhäuser Rosenberg, Schlossböckelheimer Felsenberg and a precious acre in the sandstone suntrap of Traiser Bastei. 72% is Riesling, 12.5% Müller-Thurgau, 7.5% Weissburgunder, 5% Kerner and 3% Spätburgunder.

Hans and his son Peter work in their traditional vaulted cask-cellar to produce wines of extraordinary quality and character, to my taste among the best in Germany. Each vineyard has its own character. They ascribe the remarkable delicacy of their Felsenberg and Rosenberg to the rare 'melaphyr' soil. Bastei is pungent; the steep Norheimer Kirschheck powerfully scented. Rotenfels is more scattered and variable – yet always firm with a racy clarity of flavour that is never neutral.

Scheurebe, Kerner, Spätburgunder, Grauburgunder, Weissburgunder, Gewürztraminer and Dornfelder for red wine. Good vigorous Nahe wines, particularly in the dry range – extending to an unusual dry Auslese.

Weingut Dr. Josef Höfer Schlossmühle
6531 Burg Layen. Owner: Dr. Thomas Höfer. 86 acres. Einzellagen: Rümmelsheimer (Ortsteil Burg Layen) – Johannisberg, Schlossberg and Hölle; Dorsheimer–Goldloch and Trollberg; Münsterer–Trollberg; Winzenheimer Rosenheck; Bretzenheimer Pastorei; Laubenheimer Fuchsen.

A family estate since 1775, producing mellow, aromatic wines, including dry ones, from many varieties (16% Silvaner, 20% Müller-Thurgau, 42% Riesling and 12% Grauburgunder, Weissburgunder and Spätburgunder). Some wines are bottled only after 1–2 years in the cellar. Riesling and Silvaner are seen as the wines of the future. Only the best wines are sold bottled.

Weingut Kruger-Rumpf
Rheinstrasse 47, 6538 Münster-Sarmsheim. Owner: Stefan Rumpf. 32 acres. Einzellagen: Dorsheimer–Burgberg and Goldloch; Münster-Sarmsheimer Dautenpflänzer, Kapellenberg, Pittersberg and Rheinberg.

This estate has become well-known in Germany for concentrated, firm wines of great style from top-quality sites. A high proportion are dry. 65% Riesling, 15% Silvaner, plus Müller-Thurgau, Weissburgunder, Spätburgunder, Gewürztraminer and, as a sign of the owner's youthful exuberance, Chardonnay. All the wines can be tasted in the estate's wine bar.

Staatsweingut Weinbaulehranstalt
Rüdesheimerstrasse 68, 6550 Bad Kreuznach. Director: Dr. Kadisch. 61.8 acres. Einzellagen: Kreuznacher–Forst, Hinkelstein, Kahlenberg, Mollenbrunnen, and Vogelsang; Norheimer–Dellchen, Kafels and Kirschheck.

Founded in 1900 as the provincial wine school; now owned by the State of Rheinland-Pfalz and regarded as one of the best research and educational stations in Germany. Its vineyards (20% on steep sites, 40% on slopes and a small proportion on terraces, rare in the Nahe) are concentrated in Kreuznach and Norheim. The main vine variety is Riesling, but much experimenting is done with new varieties, trying to catch the Nahe style. Controlled fermentation under CO_2 pressure was developed here. One of the most respected Nahe labels, regularly winning high awards.

Weingut & Weinkellerei Maximilian Pallhuber GmbH

An den Nahewiesen, 6536 Langenlonsheim. Owners: Karl-Heinz Paul and Heinz Pallhuber.

A substantial wine merchant with a small estate: 30% Riesling, 30% Müller-Thurgau, 20% Silvaner and 20% others. Kerner and Bacchus with their aromatic flavours are very popular.

Weingut Reichsgraf von Plettenberg

Winzenheimerstrasse, 6550 Bad Kreuznach. Owners: The Counts Wolfgang and Egbert von Plettenberg. 86.5 acres. Einzellagen: Bretzenheimer–Vogelsang, Pastorei and Felsenköpfchen; Winzenheimer–Rosenheck and Berg; Kreuznacher–Brückes, Forst, Kapellenpfad, Hinkelstein, Narenkappe, Mollenbrunnen, Osterhöll, Kahlenberg, St. Martin, Hofgarten and Mönchberg; Roxheimer–Höllenpfad, Berg and Mühlenberg; Norheimer Götzenfels; Schlossböckelheimer–Kupfergrube and Felsenberg.

A family domain since the 18th century, known by this name since 1912. Now a modern winery with little romantic appeal but excellently placed vineyards, and a wide selection of some of the Nahe's best wines, the most outstanding from Kreuznach. 60% of the vines are Riesling, 20% a mixture of Burgunders and 20% Müller-Thurgau, Portugieser and Kerner.

Prinz zu Salm-Dalberg'sches Weingut

Schloss Wallhausen, 6511 Wallhausen. Owner: Prinz zu Salm-Salm. 20 acres. Einzellagen: Wallhauser–Johannisberg, Mühlenberg and Felseneck; Dalberger–Schlossberg and Ritterhölle Sommerlocher–Sonnenberg, Steinrossel and Ratsgrund; Roxheimer Berg.

An estate dating from 1200, claiming to be the oldest in West Germany in the uninterrupted ownership of one family. No use is made of Grosslage names and the wines are made and matured individually in cask, with elegance and fruity acidity being the aim. Vines are Riesling (70%), followed by Müller-Thurgau, Silvaner, Ruländer, Scheurebe, Kerner and Spätsburgunder.

Weingut Günther Schlink

Planigerstrasse 154, 6550 Bad Kreuznach. Owner: Günther Schlink. 123.5 acres. Einzellagen: Kreuznacher–Narrenkappe, Hinkelstein, Osterhöll, and Brükes; and at Roxheim and Schlossböckelheim.

Several estates, including Herf and Gutleuthof, united by the present owner Günther Schlink. Vines are 35% Riesling, other varieties include 23% Weissburgunder and 8% Grauburgunder.

Weingut Jakob Schneider

Winzerstrasse 15, 6551 Niederhausen. Owner: Jakob Schneider, Jr. A mixed farm with 30 acres of vineyards on fine slopes. Einzellagen: Niederhäuser–Hermannshöhle (6.2), Rosenheck (7.5), Klamm (5), Steinwingert (4) and Rosenberg (2.5); Norheimer Kirschheck (5).

The wines are 90% Riesling and Herr Schneider uses farm manure and every natural method to produce intense wines with flavour and finesse. 60% are dry.

Weingut Bürgmeister Willi Schweinhardt Nachf.

Heddesheimerstrasse 1–3, 6536 Langenlonsheim. Owner: Wilhelm Schweinhardt. 59 acres. Einzellagen: Langenlonsheimer–St. Antoniusweg, Steinchen, Königsschild, Rothenberg, Bergborn, Lauerweg and Löhrer Berg; Guldentaler Rosenteich.

A very old family of growers, producing medium – sweet as well as dry wines with up to 13% alcohol. The grapey, light and charming wines are largely sold in Berlin.

Verwaltung der Staatlichen Weinbaudomänen

Niederhausen-Schlossböckelheim, 6551 Niederhausen. Director: Dr. Werner Hofäcker. The vineyards total 111 acres. Einzellagen: Schlossböckelheimer Kupfergrube (27) and Felsenberg (2.5); Niederhäuser–Hermannshöhle (5), Kertz (2.5), Hermannsberg (15) (solely owned) and Steinberg (10); Traiser Bastei (2.5); Altenbamberger Rotenberg (17); Ebernburger Schlossberg (2.5); Münsterer.Sarmsheim–Dautenpflänzer (5), Pittersberg (5), Liebehöll (2.5), Königsschloss (2.5), and Kappellenberg (2.5); Dorsheimer–Burgberg (5), Goldloch (2.5) and Honigberg (2.5).

The Nahe State Domain, which many consider the finest in Germany, was founded in 1902 by the King of Prussia and pioneered viticulture on steep slopes above the now-famous site of a former copper mine (Kupfergrube) to grow Riesling. By 1920 its wines were acknowledged superlative. In 1927 more land was added at Münster and Dorsheim in the lower Nahe and in 1953 more at Altenbamberg. The State of Rheinland-Pfalz, on its creation in 1946, took over the estate. The vineyards are planted 90% in Riesling.

Luxembourg

Luxembourg has some 3,000 acres of vines along the upper Mosel, above Trier. There are 1,200 small growers, but two thirds of the country's wine is made in cooperatives. The grape varieties are Rivaner (Riesling × Silvaner) about 50 per cent, Elbling about 25 per cent, Riesling and Auxerrois about 10 per cent, with a little Gewürztraminer, Pinot Gris and Pinot Blanc. Elbling produces very weak juice and is mostly converted to sparkling wine. Rivaner is reliable, Auxerrois occasionally extremely tasty, Riesling always lean but sometimes classic.

The industry is highly organized and controlled. All vines are graded in one of five qualities: non admis (not passed), Marque Nationale, Vin Classé, Premier Cru or Grand Premier Cru.

The major producers are Caves Bernard-Massard at Grevenmacher (for sparkling wines) and Vinsmoselles S.C. at Stadtbredimus (the organization of cooperatives). Others are Caves Gales & Cie at Bech-Kleinmacher, Caves St. Martin and Caves St. Remy at Remich (which is also the H.Q. of the Government Viticultural Station), Caves Krier Frères at Remich, Feipel-Staar at Wellenstein, and Thill Frères at Schengen.

For a demonstration of the subtlety and finesse of great German wine, ranging from fine-drawn floweriness to sumptuous elegance, this estate's wines can rarely be beaten. Schlossböckelheimers are the most stylish and delicate: Niederhäusers fuller and more seductive; Traisers big, ripe and long-lived; the lower Nahe full-bodied and spicy. The label is the black eagle of Prussia.

Weingut Erbhof Tesch
Naheweinstrasse 99, 6539 Langenlonsheim bei Bingen/Rhein. Owner: Hartmut Tesch. 99 acres. Einzellagen: Laubenheimer–Karthäuser, St. Remigiusberg, Krone; Langenlonsheimer–Löhrer Berg, Konigsschild, Steinchen, St. Antoniusweg; Dorsheimer Goldloch.

A principal grower of the lower Nahe valley, established since 1723; much extended and improved since 1960. The organically maintained vineyards are on some of the best slopes of the region: the first 4 named, totalling 48 acres, are all Riesling. Of the others, Königsschild (8 acres) is Spätburgunder, Steinchen (17.5), Müller-Thurgau and St. Antoniusweg (9) Silvaner. Crisp, 'extrovert' Laubenheim Rieslings with considerable *spritz* are the pride of the house, which consistently wins medals with them. Sales are to private customers in Germany.

COOPERATIVES

Nahe-Winzer eG
Winzenheimerstrasse 30, 6551 Bretzenheim.
The union of 3 cooperatives, founded in 1935 and now numbering more than 882 members with 1,804 acres. A new cellar was built recently in Bretzenheim and a crushing plant in Langenlonsheim. The main Grosslagen are Rosengarten, Burgweg, Kronenberg, Schlosskapelle, Pfarrgarten, Sonnenborn, Paradiesgarten. The Einzellagen names used are principally in the following communes: Kreuznach, Langenlonsheim, Guldental, Wallhausen, Monzingen, Kirschroth, Odernheim, and Münster-Sarmsheim.
Vines are 20% Silvaner, 40% Müller-Thurgau, 20% Riesling, 20% miscellaneous. The top-quality wines are true to type, very well made and good value. The annual turnover is over 600,000 cases, with 35% of the wines exported.

Weinzergenossenschaft Rheingräfenberg eG
Naheweinstrasse 63, 6553 Meddersheim.
120 members with 385 acres in Meddersheim, Merxheim, Sobernheim, Kirshroth, Hargesheim and Bad Kreuznach.

A top-quality cooperative with 55% Riesling, but also using Müller-Thurgau, Kerner and Bacchus, based at Meddersheim, upstream from Schlossböckelheim. The best Einzellagen are Meddersheim Rheingräfenberg and Sobernheimer Marbach. Many wines are sold under the Grosslage names Paradiesgarten and Kronenberg and all wine is sold in bottle – not bulk.

Throughout the chapter on Germany, names of the Einzellagen producing the finest wines will be found in the Producers' entries.

RHEINHESSEN

Anonymity behind the *nom de verre* of Liebfraumilch is the fate of most Rheinhessen wine. The heart of the wine-growing Rhineland specializes in soft, sufficiently flowery Müller-Thurgau, blunt, often rather insipid Silvaner, and the aromatic new varieties that offer the thrills of flowery bouquet with the chance of a better balance (and a better crop) than the Müller-Thurgau. Only seven per cent of its 61,000-odd acres is planted with Riesling, concentrated in its few outstanding sites. Of these by far the most important is the 'Rheinterrasse', the riverside communities from Dienheim to Mettenheim, with Nierstein as their centre. A little Spätburgunder and Portugieser is also grown.

Frank Schoonmaker points out in his classic book *The Wines of Germany* that of the 160-odd villages producing wine in Rheinhessen no less than 120 have names ending in 'heim' – home. They are scarcely a rarity anywhere in Germany, but this stress on domesticity seems especially fitting for Rheinhessen, an area of bland, fertile farmland whose very monotony makes it seem bigger than its mere 20 by 30 miles. The Rhine curls protectingly around its eastern and northern boundaries; the Nahe guards its western limits. The cities of Worms (in the south), Mainz, Bingen and Kreuznach mark its corners.

There are only three Bereich names which divide the whole area: Nierstein, Bingen and (for the south) Wonnegau, which means – more or less – the happy country.

Bereich Nierstein
Bereich Nierstein stretches from Mainz down the eastern half of the region to Mettenheim, including almost all the vineyards that are known by name outside Germany. The best-known Gemeinden are listed following the course of the Rhine northwards.

Alsheim
Alsheim is just north of Mettenheim, lying well back from a low-lying bend in the Rhine. Its importance has increased recently with the spread of new vine varieties, although Riesling and Gewürztraminer both grow well here, in sandy loam. Riesling makes substantial dryish wines.

Alsheim and Mettenheim are both divided between the Grosslage Krötenbrunnen (a very wide area of mixed quality) for the flat land, and Grosslage Rheinblick, confined to the hilly vineyards with their view (Blick) of the distant Rhine.
Growers Rappenhof. Sittmann.

Guntersblum

Guntersblum continues the quality vineyards northward, the hills drawing nearer to the river. Like Alsheim it has two Grosslage names, Krötenbrunnen for its flat land, Vogelsgärtchen for the slopes with a chalk content in their sandy loam, which naturally makes better wine – though oddly enough in Guntersblum it seems to be the flat land which has a higher reputation. The name Krötenbrunnen itself is much used on labels – usually in conjunction with the better-known name of Oppenheim, the next Gemeinde.

This is a prime example of the confusion arising from Grosslage names. Wine labelled Oppenheimer Krötenbrunnen sells well. The name is available to growers in the relatively unknown Guntersblum. They naturally tend to swallow their pride in their best Einzellagen and use the Grosslage name.

Guntersblum includes the village of Ludwigshöhe, with flat vineyards.

Growers Dr. Dahlem. Rappenhof. Schmitt-Dr. Ohnacker.

Dienheim

Dienheim is almost attached to Oppenheim, shares its Grosslage and two of its Einzellage names, and seems content to subsume its reputation in that of its more famous neighbour.

The enormous Herrengarten Einzellage is on flat sandy land along the Rhine, which skirts the town of Oppenheim. This is Grosslage Krötenbrunnen. The best vineyards of both Dienheim and Oppenheim are in the Grosslage Güldenmorgen.

Growers Baumann. Braun. Dr. Dahlem. Carl Koch Erben. Rappenhof. Gustav Adolf Schmitt. Heinrich Seip, Kurfürstenhof. Sittmann. Staatsweingut Oppenheim.

Oppenheim

The first of the 'Rhein-front' wine towns going downstream, although it stands back from the river at a respectful distance on a low hill out of reach of floods. This is the end of the chalky ridge coming north from Alsheim and has its best vineyards.

Roughly half the vines are Riesling, but all real Oppenheimers (recognizable by their Einzellagen names) are capable of the extra concentration and finesse that singles out Rheinterrasse wines. They are always softer and broader than (for example) Rheingau wines. Their excellence lies in a vitality, a backbone that keeps them from being formless or flabby. The Oppenheimer Krötenbrunnen wines from the flat fields do not necessarily share this quality.

Growers Baumann. Dr. Dahlem. Guntrum. Carl Koch Erben. Geschwister Schuch. Heinrich Seip, Kurfürstenhof. Rappenhof. Sittmann. Staatsweingut Oppenheim.

Nierstein

The best-known name in Rheinhessen and one of the most popular in Germany and abroad, the centre of the Rheinterrasse and an attractive little town full of wine merchants. The name of Nierstein is also a caution to those who find the fine print of vineyard names too much trouble. It can legally be used not only for its whole Bereich (one third of Rheinhessen) but also for the Grosslage name Gutes Domtal, which is available to 15 villages lying inland to the west of Nierstein, but only to one 85-acre vineyard in Nierstein, Pfaffenkappe (which in any case is in the hamlet of Nierstein-Schwabsburg and not in Nierstein itself). Thus tenuous is the link between Nierstein and its most famous product.

All the fine wines of Nierstein, and there are many, lie in three small Grosslagen hugging the town and within sight of the Rhine. The Grosslage Spiegelberg embraces all the Einzellagen on the hills above some 300 feet, just north and south of the town. Of these Hölle, Paterberg and Brückchen, south of the town, are generally considered the best. Auflangen embraces a line of steeper south-facing but lower-lying vineyards, starting at the river and running inland just north of the town along a narrow valley. Kranzberg, on the Rhine, with its sub-divisions Bergkirche, Glöck and Zehnmorgen, is the best of these. Rehbach, the third Grosslage, embraces three famous steep little Einzellagen directly on the riverfront to the north, running on into the next village, Nackenheim.

The quality of the best Niersteiners is velvety softness with a kernel of fire. Dry wines are the exception; the ripeness of Ausleses happens in most vintages. In very hot years, the Spiegelberg vineyards tend to overripen and lose their 'nerve' and elegance, particularly with grapes other than Riesling.

Growers Anton Balbach Erben. Baumann. Guntrum. Freiherr Heyl zu Herrnsheim. Rappenhof. Gustav Adolf Schmitt. Schneider. Geschwister Schuch. Heinrich Seip, Kurfürstenhof. Sittman. Staatsweingut Oppenheim. Strub. Wehrheim.

Nackenheim

The little village concludes the steep line of sandstone hills of the Rheinterrasse with its famous Rothenberg, named for the redness of its sandy loam. Rothenberg and Engelsberg, higher and on flatter land, are in the Nierstein Grosslage Spiegelberg. The rest of Nackenheim's small acreage, away from the river, is included in the Grosslage Gutes Domtal.

Growers Gunderloch-Guntrum. Heinrich Seip, Kurfürstenhof.

Bodenheim

Bodenheim continues the line of worthy vineyards northwards towards Mainz; good slopes but without the advantages of the riverside. Its sandy loam vineyards look eastward over the town. The Grosslage name is St. Alban.

In the interior of the Bereich Nierstein few villages are known by name. 'Gutes Domtal' is well established. The other Grosslagen not mentioned above are Domherr, with no remarkable production, and Petersberg, which abuts the better part of the Bereich Wonnegau to the south.

Albig and Gau-Odernheim

Albig, just north of Alzey, has lately produced some fresh and pleasing wines. Gau-Odernheim lies to the northeast of Alzey.

Growers in Albig: Köster-Wolf.

Bereich Bingen

The western half of Rheinhessen (excluding its southern fringe) is all included in the Bereich Bingen. Although it abuts the excellent vineyards of the Nahe between Bingen and Kreuznach it has nothing of that quality to offer, except from the isolated Scharlachberg, the hill above Bingen itself, which looks north over the Rhine to Rüdesheim and south over an ideally sited vineyard.

Bingen

The best of Bingen's wines are Riesling, of body and firmness that recalls the Rheingau more than Rheinhessen. The Grosslage is St. Rochuskapelle.

Growers Ohler. Villa Sachsen.

Ockenheim

The southeastern neighbour of Bingen, Ockenheim (also in Grosslage St. Rochuskapelle) has a certain reputation for both white and Spätburgunder light red wines.

Ingelheim

The city of Ingelheim, facing the Rheingau across the river a few miles east of Bingen, has an ancient reputation for its red wines – though you would probably have to go there to find an example.

The rest of Bereich Bingen is a useful source of easygoing, soft and sometimes aromatic wines (depending on the grape variety). The new crossings are widely used, along with Müller-Thurgau. The central Rheinhessen cooperative cellars at Gau-Bickelheim supply wine under the names of many of the villages, without any of them distinguishing itself above the rest.

The Grosslagen names are St. Rochuskapelle (for Bingen), Abtey, Rheingrafenstein, Adelberg, Kurfürstenstück and Kaiserpfalz. Some of the better-known towns and villages are Ockenheim, Wörrstadt, Armsheim, Flonheim, Bornheim, Gau-Algesheim, Wöllstein and Sprendlingen.

Flonheim

Growers Koehler-Weidmann (also at Bornheim). Köster-Wolf.

Bereich Wonnegau

The happy land of Wonnegau stretches in bucolic bliss from the city of Worms on the Rhine to the city of Alzey in the hilly country known as the Hügelland where the three Bereichs of Rheinhessen meet.

Alzey

Alzey is the centre of the Grosslage Sybillenstein, and has under its wing the villages of Weinheim (promising name) and Heimersheim (which seems to carry domesticity a little too far even for Rheinhessen). This is a district of many new grape varieties and a mixture of soils, with some respectable slopes. Sandstone, slate, marl, chalk and loam are all present.

Although few of its wines are widely known at present, many of them have the essential vitality and freshness to make them worth exploring.
Growers Weingut der Stadt Alzey.

The wines tend to become heavier and less fresh as the Wonnegau spreads out south and east towards Worms. The Grosslage names here are Pilgerpfad (with a restricted inner Grosslage called Gotteshilfe), Bergkloster, Burg Rodenstein, Domblick and, around the city of Worms, Liebfrauenmorgen. The most notable towns and villages are Bechtheim and Osthofen (Grosslagen Pilgerpfad and Gotteshilfe), which form the link between Worms and Alsheim (*see* Bereich Nierstein) on a vein of chalky clay running north to the Rheinterrasse and Flörsheim-Dalsheim (Grosslage Burg Rodenstein), on the same vein just west of Worms (which is itself on sandy loam and loess: alluvial soil from the Rhine).
Growers in Bechtheim: Beyer. Brenner. Johann Geil.
In Osthofen: Ahnenhof, Hermann Müller. Glaser. May-Weissheimer.
In Flörsheim-Dalsheim: Bezirks-Winzergenossenschaft Nierstein. Müller-Dr. Becker. Schales.

Worms

Worms still maintains, in the centre of a city destroyed in World War II and rebuilt, the famous patch of vines beside the church of Our Lady, which apparently gave the name to Liebfraumilch. Their wine is well made but by no means outstanding. Grosslage Liebfrauenmorgen.
Growers Schlosskellerei Adam Hemer. Langenbach (*see* p.239).

RHEINHESSEN PRODUCERS

Weingut Bürgermeister Anton Balbach Erben

Mainzerstrasse 64, 6505 Nierstein. Owner: Frau Charlotte Bohn. 44.5 acres, 58% in the Grosslagen Rehbach and Auflagen, the rest in Spiegelberg. Einzellagen: Niersteiner–Hipping, Pettenthal, Ölberg, Kranzberg, Klostergarten, Rosenberg and Bildstock.

The best known of several Balbachs who were Burgermasters of Nierstein since the 17th century was Anton, who cleared woods from what is now the famous Pettenthal vineyard. The estate, down by the Rhine, with Victorian cellars now full of stainless steel, is planted with 80% Riesling, 6% Müller-Thurgau, 7% Kerner, 1% Weissburgunder and 1% Grauburgunder. It produces some of the finest, raciest Rieslings of Rheinhessen.

Weingut Gunderloch

Carl-Gunderloch Platz 1, 6506 Nackenheim. Owner: Agnes Hasselbach-Usinger. 29.6 acres. Einzellagen: Nackenheimer–Rothenberg, Engelsberg and Schmittskapellchen; Niersteiner–Paterberg, Hipping and Pettenthal.

This estate, founded in 1890, has won much praise from the German press in recent years. The average yield is low (45 hl/ha) and the wines, particularly the Riesling from the steep Rothenberg site, concentrated, cask-matured and wonderfully fresh – they are undoubtedly amongst the very best on the prestigious 'Rheinterrasse'. The vineyards are planted 80% Riesling, 10% Silvaner (producing strongly flavoured wines from the red Nackenheim soil) and 5% Müller-Thurgau. A classic Rheinhessen dry Riesling-Silvaner blend was bottled as the 'Jubiläums-Cuvée' in 1989. The wine bar offers good food, and the estate's own Sekt and still wines.

Weinkellerei Louis Guntrum

Rheinallee 62, 6505 Nierstein. Director: Hanns Joachim Louis Guntrum. 133.4 acres in the Grosslagen Rehbach, Auflangen and Spiegelberg. Einzellagen: Nackenheimer Rothenberg; Niersteiner–Pettenthal. Rosenberg, Klostergarten, Hölle, Ölberg, Heiligenbaum, Orbel and Paterberg; Oppenheimer–Schloss, Herrenberg, Sackträger, Schützenhütte, Kreuz; Dienheimer Tafelstein.

The family business was started in 1824 in the present buildings, lying right on the Rhine. About 40% of the business is in estate-bottled wines; the vines are 33% Riesling, 26% Müller-Thurgau, 11% Silvaner, 9% Scheurebe, 9% Kerner, 2% Gewürztraminer, 4% Bacchus. The estate wines are particularly ripe and lively with a wide range of flavours, each variety and site being made individually. The 4th and 5th Guntrum generations now direct the estate and a merchant house with many bread-and-butter lines such as Liebfraumilch Seagull, Bereich Nierstein Goldgrape and a catalogue of other growers' wines from Rheinhessen and elsewhere.

Weingut Freiherr Heyl zu Herrnsheim

Mathildenhof, Langgasse 3, 6505 Nierstein. Owners: The von

Weymarn family. 61.8 acres. Einzellagen: many, including the solely owned Brudersberg (3.2 acres), Pettental, Hipping and Oelberg in Grosslagen Rehbach, Spiegelberg, Auflangen, Gutes Domtal, Güldenmorgen and Krötenbrunnen.

A dignified manor, its gardens full of experimental vine plots, in the heart of Nierstein. The estate has been inherited for 5 generations. 60% is Riesling, particularly fine in the Rehbach and Auflangen vineyards; 16% is Silvaner, which in Ölberg makes a powerful dry wine; 20% is Müller-Thurgau, very popular from Spiegelberg. The wines are matured in cask and often need a couple of years before they are ready to drink.

Weingut Kurfurstenhof

See Heinrich Seip.

Weingut Koehler-Weidmann

Hindenburgring 2, 6509 Bornheim. Owner: Wilhelm Weidmann. 46 acres. Einzellagen: Bornheimer–Hähnchen, Hütte-Terrassen, Schönberg and Kirchenstück; Flonheimer–Klostergarten and Roche.

Both traditional grapes and new crossings/experimental grapes figure in the wide range of vines grown on this estate, now in its 9th generation. The Riesling, however, sells out first of the dozen varieties offered. The list includes a Trockenbeerenauslesen and, usually, a 1988 Rüländer Eiswein. Modest cropping makes intense wines.

Weingut Rappenhof

Bachstrasse 47–49, 6526 Alsheim. Owner: Dr. Reinhard Muth. 98.8 acres. Einzellagen: Alsheimer–Fischerpfad, Frühmesse, Sonnenberg and Goldberg; Guntersblumer–Bornpfad, Himmelthal, Kreuzkapelle, Steinberg and Eiserne Hand; Dienheimer–Tafelstein and Siliusbrunnen; Niersteiner Rosenberg; Oppenheimer–Sackträger, Herrenberg and Kreuz.

A very old family estate, among the best of its district, well known particularly for dry wines. 50% is Riesling, 21% Burgunder (Pinot) family, 10% Kerner, 3% Gewürztraminer, plus others. Sekt and red and white *barrique*-aged wines are a speciality.

Gustav Adolf Schmitt'sches Weingut

Wilhelmstrasse 2, 6505 Nierstein. Owner: Beatrix Carolyn Schmitt. About 250 acres including Einzellagen: Niersteiner–Pettenthal, Ölberg, Hipping and Kranzberg; Dienheimer Falkenberg; Oppenheimer–Herrenberg and Kreuz; Dexheimer Doktor.

Growers since 1618, merchants since about 1920. 75% of the very big estate is planted in standard vine varieties with an emphasis on the Riesling, and about 25% in crossings such as Scheurebe, Kerner, Ehrenfelser and Bacchus. The range of wines is wide, including very fine intense and full-bodied QmP wines from the best sites. Two thirds of turnover is in branded regional wines and dry Niersteiner.

Weingut Geschwister Schuch

6505 Nierstein. Owners: Diether and Michael Günther. 39.5 acres. Einzellagen: Niersteiner–Ölberg, Pettenthal, Findling Orbel, Hipping, Rosenberg, Klostergarten and Heiligenbaum; Oppenheimer Sackträger; Dienheimer Falkenberg.

One of the most respected old family estates of Nierstein, founded by the Schuchs in 1817. Planted with 50% Riesling, 15% Scheurebe, 10% red-wine varieties; 25% other varieties, such as Müller-Thurgau, Silvaner and Kerner. The wines are models of the gentle but distinctive 'Rhein-front' style, particularly in dry and semi-dry Riesling.

Heinrich Seip, Kurfürstenhof

Nierstein. Owner: Heinrich Seip. 86.5 acres in Nierstein. Einzellagen: Niersteiner–Paterberg, Bildstock, Kirchplatte, Findling, Rosenberg, Klostergarten, Pettenthal, Hipping, Kranzberg, Ölberg, Heiligenbaum, Orbel, Schloss Schwabsburg and Goldene Luft (sole owner); Oppenheimer Schloss; Dienheimer–Tafelstein, Kreuz and Falkenberg; Nackenheimer Engelsberg.

An ancient royal estate bought by the Seip family in 1950 and now regarded as a leader in wines from the new grape varieties, which occupy 15% of its vineyards. One of the specialities, a grape called Jubiläumsrube, ripens so early that it rarely fails to make Auslese and Beerenauslese, in the rather low-acid Ruländer style. Seip's cellar techniques combine old casks with modern ideas, aiming at aromatic sweet wines of real quality and character.

Weingüter Carl Sittmann

Wormserstrasse 61, 6504 Oppenheim. Owner: Dr. Liselotte Sittmann. Nearly 200 acres. Einzellagen: Alsheimer–Goldberg, Frühmesse, Römerberg; Oppenheimer–Herrenberg, Sackträger; Dienheimer–Falkenberg, Paterhof. Einzellagen also in Nierstein.

The biggest private estate in the district, inherited by the granddaughter of the founder, who also runs a big merchant house under the name Dr. Itschner. The vines are 20% Müller-Thurgau, 16% Silvaner, 14% Kerner, 12% Riesling. Wines from the best sites are matured in casks: Oppenheimer Sackträger makes splended Ausleses. Weissherbst (rosé) under the name Alsheimer Rheinblick is a speciality.

Staatsweingut der Landes-Lehr- und Versuchsanstalt

Zuckerberg 19, 6504 Oppenheim. Director: Dr. Fuchss. 61.8 acres. Einzellagen: Oppenheimer–Sackträger, Kreuz, Herrenberg and Zuckerberg; Niersteiner–Paterberg, Ölberg, Glöck and Pettenthal; Dienheimer Tafelstein; Bodenheimer Reichsritterstift.

The regional wine school, founded in 1895 by the Duke of Hessen and now considered an exemplary college for wine makers, using the most modern methods. In 1980 the school opened a new German wine museum in the heart of Oppenheim. 40% of the estate is on steep slopes and half is Riesling, but only Niersteiner Pettenthal is 100% Riesling. Among the many other varieties planted, a large proportion are experimental vines. The school produces relatively few dry and semi-dry wines but regularly wins medals with balanced, distinctive and clean sweet ones. It formerly made some of the finest wine from the steepest sites in Nackenheim and Bodenheim as well, but has now sold this land.

Weingut J. & H. A. Strub

Rheinstrasse 42, 6505 Nierstein. Owner: Walter Strub. 44.5 acres in Grosslagen Rehbach. Auflangen and Spiegelberg. Einzellagen: Niersteiner Hipping, Ölberg, Heiligenbaum, Orbel, Brückchen, Paterberg, Findling and Bildstock; Dienheimer Falkenberg.

An old family estate with a good name for gentle, mellow wines from the best parts of the 'Rhein-front'. Vines are 55% Riesling, 15% Silvaner, 25% Müller-Thurgau, 2% Spätburgunder, 2% Scheurebe, 1% Ortega and Siegerrebe.

Weingut Villa Sachsen

Mainzerstrasse 184, 6530 Bingen. 67 acres. Einzellagen: Bingener–Scharlachberg (19.8), Kirchberg (16.5), Schlossberg

Schwätzerchen (6.7), Osterberg (4), Kapellenberg (2.5), Rosengarten (1.2) and Bubenstück (0.7). The Victorian villa starred in a bestseller of 1869. *The Country House on the Rhine*, was bought by a prince of Hessen in 1879, became a model wine estate and in 1963 was bought by St. Ursula, the big wine merchants of Bingen. Over 50% is Riesling; also Müller-Thurgau, Silvaner, Kerner, Weissburgunder, Grauburgunder and others. The Scharlachberg is the best site, producing stylish, manly Rieslings, particularly dry and semi-dry types. Full-bodied Silvaner and mild Müller-Thurgau are also popular.

Weingut Eugen Wehrheim

Mühlgasse 30, 6505 Nierstein. Owner: Klaus Wehrheim. 25.5 acres. Einzellagen: Niersteiner–Orbel, Ölberg, Hipping, Paterberg, Pettenthal, Klostergarten, Brückchen, Bildstock and Findling.

Specialists in Nierstein since 1693; 44% Riesling, 23% Silvaner, 12% Müller-Thurgau, 21% other varieties. The Rieslings are light and sprightly; more serious wines are sweet, aromatic and heavy, for example Ruländer and Huxelrebe Beerenauslese.

OTHER PRODUCERS

Weingut der Stadt Alzey

Schlossgasse 14, 6508 Alzey. Director: U. Kaufmann. 37 acres. Einzellagen: Rotenfels, Kapellenberg, Kirchenstück and Römerberg, all in the Grosslage Sybillenstein. The town of Alzey in central Rheinhessen is unusual in possessing (since 1916) its own wine estate, planted with one sixth each of Riesling, Müller-Thurgau and Silvaner; the remaining half with a score of other varieties. The wines are among the best of their district.

Weingut Friedrich Baumann

Friedrich-Ebert-Strasse 55, 6504 Oppenheim. Owner: Friedrich Baumann. About 20 acres. Einzellagen: Oppenheimer–Sackträger, Herrenberg, Kreuz, Paterhof, Daubhaus and Herrengarten; Niersteiner–Pettenthal and Findling; Dienheimer–Falkenberg and Tafelstein. A long-established family business remodelled in the 1970s but still using barrels and 40% Riesling, aiming for fresh, sprightly wines which win prizes. A quarter of the property is in the excellent Einzellage Oppenheimer Sackträger, from which a brut Riesling is now being made.

Brenner'sches Weingut

Pfandturmstrasse 20, 6521 Bechtheim. Owner: Bürgermeister Christian Brenner. About 30 acres. Einzellagen: Bechtheimer–Geyersberg, Rosengarten, Hasensprung, Heiligkreuz and Stein; Osthofener Hasenbiß. A family estate since 1877 and the principal grower of Bechtheim, using old methods: wooden casks in spacious cellars with an emphasis on substantial dry wines. 15% Silvaner, 15% Müller-Thurgau, 15% Riesling, 35% Weissburgunder, 20% Spätburgunder. Weissburgunder, Riesling and red wines are made absolutely dry – even Ausleses. Also dry Riesling Sekt.

Sanitätsrat Dr. Dahlem Erben KG

Rathofstrasse 21-25, 6504 Oppenheim. Owners: The Dahlem family. 62 acres. Einzellagen: Oppenheimer–Sackträger, Herrengerg, Schloss, Kreuz and Herrengarten; Dienheimer–Tafelstein, Paterhof and Falkenberg;

Guntersblumer Kreuzkapelle. An old family estate (since 1702) among the most reliable for traditional Rheinhessen wines. The vineyards are 60% on slopes; the vines 25% Riesling, 20% each Silvaner and Müller-Thurgau, 8% Bacchus; 27% others, including new varieties. The wines are barrel-aged.

Bürgermeister Carl Koch Erben

6504 Oppenheim. Owner: Carl Hermann Stieh-Koch. 30 acres. Einzellagen: Oppenheimer–Sackträger, Kreuz, Herrenberg, Schloss, Paterhof and Herrengarten; Dienheimer Tafelstein. In the family since 1824, concentrating on Oppenheimer Sackträger, from dry to TBA. 35% Riesling, 14% Müller-Thurgau, 20% Silvaner, 5% Kerner, 7% Weissburgunder, 5% Gewürztraminer, etc.

Weingut Köster-Wolf

6509 Albig. Owners: Werner Köster and Manfred Wolf. 59.4 acres. Einzellagen: Albiger–Hundskopf and Schloss Hammerstein; Flonheimer–Rotenpfad and Klostergarten; Heimersheimer Sonnenberg. Grosslagen: Petersberg, Adelberg, Sybillenstein. A 400-year-old vintner family. Their best Riesling is from 2.5 acres of steep slope in Flonheim; of particular pride are dry Silvaner and a highly successful Dornfelder red wine.

Weingut Müller-Dr. Becker

6523 Flörsheim-Dalsheim. Owner: Klaus Becker. 55.5 acres. Einzellagen in Flörsheim-Dalsheim: Hubacker, Steig, Sauloch and Bürgel. Grosslage: Burg Rodenstein. Very varied and differentiated 'varietals', two thirds dry or semi-dry, made as fruity and flavoury as possible. 20% Müller-Thurgau, 20% Riesling, 10% each of Silvaner, Kerner, Weissburgunder, Spätburgunder and Grauburgunder, plus others. Sauloch in particular makes good Riesling Kabinett.

Kommerzienrat P. A. Ohler'sches Weingut

Gaustrasse 10, 6530 Bingen. Owner: Bernhard Becker. 17 acres. Einzellagen: Bingener–Schlossberg-Schwätzerchen,

Rosengarten and Scharlachberg; Münsterer–Kapellenberg and Dautenpflänzer; Ockenheim–Klosterweg and St. Jakobsberg. Since the 17th century a small estate in the centre of Bingen with parcels of the best surrounding vineyards, aiming for racy, spicy, aromatic Kabinetts and Spätlese, especially from Riesling, Kerner and similar vines.

Weingut Ohnacker

Neustrasse 2, 6524 Guntersblum. Owner Walter Ohnacker. 33 acres in Guntersblum and Ludwigshöhe. Best Einzellagen: Guntersblumer–Steig-Terrassen and Himmeltal. The vines are 20% Müller-Thurgau, 25% Riesling, 20% Silvaner, 2% each of Scheurebe and Ruländer, 5% Spätburgunder and Portugieser, 3% Gewürztraminer. 150 years of family ownership; now one of the best specialists in the village, with wines ranging from Himmelthal Riesling (full-bodied and slow to develop) to light-drinking Müller-Thurgau, largely aged in cask, in cellars cut into the hill out of reach of Rhine floods. The yield from about a quarter of the vineyards is sent to a cooperative.

Weingut Schales

6523 Flörsheim-Dalsheim. Owners: The Schales family: 89 acres. Einzellagen: Flörsheimer-Dalsheimer–Hubacker, Steig, Bürgel, Sauloch and Goldberg. Grosslage: Burg Rodenstein. A seventh-generation family with a private wine museum, making the usual wide range of aromatic wines from the limestone soil of Dalsheim. No Einzellage or Grosslage names are used. 25% Riesling, 17% Müller-Thurgau, 11% Weissburgunder, 7% Siegerrebe, 6% Kerner, 5% Silvaner, 6% Spätburgunder, 5% Huxelrebe, 5% Bacchus, 4% Scheurebe, 3% Gewürztraminer etc.

Weingut Georg Albrecht Schneider

6505 Nierstein. Owner: Albrecht Schneider. 37 acres entirely in Nierstein with holdings in all the principal Einzellagen. A modest, conscientious and candid specialist in fine Niersteiner; the seventh generation of a family of

growers. He aims for fruity, 'nervous' wines: i.e. not too mild or sweet, bottling only the best, mainly Rieslings, under his own label.
Weingut Oberst Schultz-Werner
Bahnhofstrasse 10, 6501 Gaubischofsheim über Mainz. Owner: Hans-Christoph Schultz. About 30 acres. Einzellagen: Gau-Bischofsheimer–Herrnberg, Kellersberg and Pfannenweg. Grosslagen: Gutes Domtal

and St. Alban. A family firm since 1833, with 37% Riesling, 19% Müller-Thurgau, plus Gewürztraminer, Silvaner, etc. Dry and medium-dry wines of good flavour, including dry Portugieser red and rosé. Now the estate makes *méthode champenoise* Sekt using its own wines.
Zentralkellerei Rhein. Winzer. eG
6551 Gau-Bickelheim. Central cooperative cellars, established in 1946,

receiving the crop from 7,400 acres of the Rheinhessen and Rheingau, covering no less than 622 Einzellagen. 32 different vine varieties are grown, of which the most significant are Müller-Thurgau (25%), Silvaner (20%), Scheurebe (15%) and Bacchus (10%). All the wines are sold as 'estate bottlings' – as the law permits.

RHEINPFALZ

Germany's most fertile, sunniest and most productive wine region takes its English name, the Palatinate, from the former Counts Palatine of the Holy Roman Empire. It stretches in a narrow 50-mile band along the eastern flank of the Haardt mountains, from the southern edge of Rheinhessen to the French frontier, where the Haardt become the Vosges. At the border, in an extraordinary sudden switch, the wines change from the flowery sweetness and lively attack of Germany to the savoury vinosity of Alsace.

With 56,000 acres of vines, Rheinpfalz is marginally second in acreage to Rheinhessen – though frequently a bigger producer. The southern half of the region, from Neustadt south, known as the Bereich Südliche Weinstrasse, is Germany's most up-to-date and intensive vineyard. The last two decades have seen formidable progress – in vine varieties, reorganization of vineyards and cellar technology.

Natural conditions are so favourable here that the city of Landau was once Germany's biggest wine market. Sadly, because it was almost entirely a Jewish enterprise, it was destroyed in 1935 by the Nazis, who then invented the Deutsche Weinstrasse

and obliged each German city to adopt a wine village as its supplier of bulk wine. More than half was shipped in tanks to the Mosel for blending – a practice that continued until 1971. No wine was bottled in the region until after World War II. Judgements based on its history and reputation are therefore likely to be wide of the mark. The Südliche Weinstrasse has no history as a producer of great wine, few well known estates, yet its potential is formidable and its wines represent some of the best value in Germany – indeed in Europe.

The prestige of Rheinpfalz is mainly centred on the half-dozen villages at the centre of its northern half, known as the Mittelhaardt. The 1971 wine law divided the entire region into only two Bereichs: Südliche Weinstrasse for the south and Mittelhaardt-Deutsche Weinstrasse for the north, with the city of Neustadt between them. It thus gave the prestige of the Mittelhaardt to a wide range of vineyards in the north of the region which have nothing in common with it. There should be a third Bereich name for what was formerly called the Unterhaardt. (The Südliche Weinstrasse was formerly called the Oberhaardt, making a logical trio which might well have been preserved.)

Bereich Mittelhaardt-Deutsche Weinstrasse
The northernmost vineyards of Rheinpfalz, hardly separated from the southernmost of Rheinhessen, produce little wine of note or distinction.

Grosslage Schnepfenflug vom Zellertal
This Grosslage name, often attached to the village of Zell, is as insignificant as it contrives to be ponderous. Needless to say this Zell, despite having an Einzellage called Schwarzer Herrgott, is distinct in every way from the famous Zell of the Lower Mosel with its Grosslage Schwarze Katz.

Grosslage Grafenstück
The town of Bockenheim is the centre of this productive area. A certain amount of pale red Portugieser as well as Müller-Thurgau, Silvaner, a little Riesling and Kerner make reasonable wines on some good sloping sites.

Grosslage Höllenpfad
The city of Grünstadt marks the beginning of the Rheinpfalz vineyards in earnest. Here they fan out from the hills with good south and east slopes down on to the sandy plain towards the Rhine. Kleinkarlbach (with its little neighbour Neuleiningen) is the first of the line of Haardt villages that reaches a climax at Forst and Deidesheim. Already here the Riesling is distinctly clean and stylish, and TBA can be extraordinarily fine.
Growers Emil Hammel. Georg Fr. Spiess.

Grosslage Schwarzerde
Growers Emil Hammel.

Grosslage Rosenbühl
Weissenheim am Sand, down on the plain five miles east, is in complete contrast. The dry sand gives a small crop of very light but clean and agreeable wine – an understate-

ment that suits such aromatic grapes as Kerner but makes Riesling almost neutral. Phylloxera is only a recent arrival here and makes slow progress in the sandy ground. The Portugieser (30% of the vineyard) ripens well and gives a firmer, more savoury red wine than usual.

Grosslage Kobnert
The first famous name of the Mittelhaardt is the Grosslage which was given the former name of a fine Einzellage in Kallstadt. The villages of Dackenheim, Weissenheim am Berg, Herxheim am Berg, Freinsheim, Erpolzheim, Leistadt, Ungstein and Kallstadt now all share in it – which very much lowers its tone. The best vineyards of Ungstein, however, have an exclusive little Grosslage (*see* Honigsäckel).

Kallstadt's best sites are in Saumagen, a chalky slope where both Riesling and Silvaner make remarkably ripe and intense wine. The three Enzellagen of Grosslage Saumagen (Nill, Kirchenstück and Horn) have now been combined into a single new Einzellage called Saumagen, under Grosslage Kobnert. Grosslage Saumagen no longer exists.
Growers Koehler-Ruprecht. Schuster. Stauch.

Kallstadter Annaberg
Kallstadt also boasts one of the few German vineyards which was once sold by its own name alone, the famous Annaberg. Annaberg grows Riesling and Scheurebe with a special intensity of flavour that comes from a sheltered, loamy slope and extremely disciplined wine-making. Confusingly enough. Annaberg, along with the 113-acre Kallstadter Kreidkeller, is in the Grosslage Feuerberg (*see* below), which links it to Bad Dürkheim.
Grower Stump-Fitz'sches Weingut Annaberg.

Grosslage Honigsäckel
Ungstein's best sites (again with a chalky content) also have their own Grosslage name: Honigsäckel. The tiny 7-acre Ungsteiner Michelsberg is included in the Dürkheim Grosslage Hochmess (which just about seems to sum up the whole situation).
Growers Bassermann-Jordan. K. Fitz-Ritter. Pfeffingen. Schuster.

Bad Dürkheim
Bad Dürkheim is the capital of the Mittelhaardt proper, the main town of the district which flows with richer, more fiery and sumptuous wine than any other in Germany. It musters almost 2,000 acres of vineyards, a busy if not precisely fashionable spa, and a famous annual Sausage Fair (at which wine is at least as much the attraction). A good deal of its wine attempts to be red, presumably for the sausages' sake.

Three Grosslage names are given to different parts of Dürkheim (and its neighbours): Feuerberg, Hochmess and Schenkenböhl.

Grosslage Feuerberg
Feuerberg is a long strip of mainly gentle incline which makes white wine of real character (Annaberg being the best) and reasonably well-coloured red.
Growers K. Fitz-Ritter. Johannes Karst. Koehler-Ruprecht. Schuster.

Grosslage Hochmess
This much smaller Grosslage is devoted mainly to Riesling and Silvaner.
Growers K. Fits-Ritter. Johannes Karst. Schaefer.

Grosslage Schenkenböhl
This is a larger area to the south, also embracing the lesser vineyards of Wachenheim.
Growers Bürklin-Wolf. K. Fitz-Ritter. Johannes Karst. Schaefer.

Grosslage Mariengarten
The village of Wachenheim begins the real kernel of the Mittelhaardt, a large part of its vineyard devoted to Riesling by the biggest and best estates in the region. The Einzellagen Goldbächel and Gerümpel, generally considered the best, are 100% Riesling. Rheinpfalz Rieslings are all warmer in their wineyness than those farther north. Rheingaus of the Rüdesheimer Berg, perhaps Marcobrunner and Hochheim, may be comparable in certain vintages. The greater quality of Wachenheim and its neighbours is the elegance (in Wachenheim even the light touch) and the delicacy they deliver with all their ripeness.

In Forst the element of honeyed, velvet ripeness seems more pronounced. The tiny Jesuitengarten in Forst is probably the most famous Rheinpfalz vineyard, although its neighbours on the hill, Ungeheuer, Pechstein, Kirchenstück and Freundstück, share its qualities. The soil here is clay loam, darkened by an outcrop of black basalt, rich in potassium, which in sunny years warms and feeds the ripening grapes to sometimes astonishing concentration of flavours. The greatness of the best wine lies in elegance: however full-bodied, it seems to keep a sort of lilt or lift in your mouth.

As wine producers, Forst and Deidesheim are age-old rivals of really equal standing. As an opera-set wine town, Deidesheim is incomparable. The Rheinpfalz architectural style is dignified rather than quaint: substantial white-walled mansions dressed with rosy sandstone, monumental gateways, trim arcades and cupolas. The indoor style is heavy wainscotting, with lead windows and mighty fireplaces. Deidesheim is lavish with the comfortable accessories for enjoyment. It is to the Rheinpfalz what Bernkastel is to the Mosel, or St-Emilion to Bordeaux.

All its best vineyards lie in the Grosslage Mariengarten. They have rather lighter, faster draining, warmer soil than those of Forst; the principal difference between the two. Black basalt from Forst is also quarried and spread on the Mariengarten vineyards to make them warmer still. The result is often perfect harmony in medium vintages when Forsters lean towards austerity.

It is almost sacrilege to plant anything but Riesling in sites which bring it to such perfection. Even Riesling with its aristocratic restraint sometimes develops flavours and scents of tropical fruit. Ausleses, Beeren- and Trockenbeerenausleses display their lusciousness in colours ranging from full gold to an almost lurid orange tint in some very sweet wines.
Growers in Wachenheim: Von Buhl. Bürklin-Wolf. Schaefer. J. L. Wolf Erben. In Forst: Bassermann-Jordan. Von Buhl. Bürklin-Wolf. Dr. Deinhard. Dr. Kern. Lindenhof. Mosbacher. Winzerverein Forst. J. L. Wolf Erben. In Deidesheim: Bassermann-Jordan. Biffar. Von Buhl. Bürklin-Wolf. Dr. Deinhard. Dr. Kern. Lindenhof. Mosbacher. Wegeler–Deinhard. J. L. Wolf Erben.

Grosslage Schnepfenflug an der Weinstrasse
One substantial vineyard in Wachenheim, three in the little-known neighbouring Friedelsheim on the plain, three in Forst and one in Deidesheim make up this second-ranking (by the highest standards) Grosslage.
Growers Bassermann-Jordan. Von Buhl. Bürklin-Wolf. Lindenhof. Mosbacher. Winzerverein Forst.

Grosslage Hofstück

The great name of Deidesheim is considerably extended through this area of more than 3,000 acres, 300 of them in Deidesheim, on the flat side of town where a good deal of Müller-Thurgau is grown. Few of the neighbouring villages which benefit from this big-hearted policy are ever heard of except under the umbrella name of Deidesheimer Hofstück. The very considerable exception is Ruppertsberg, the next in the north-south line of foothill villages, with magnificent sites of its own.

The best Ruppertsberg Einzellagen deserve better than to be lumped together with the vineyards of the plain. They are Reiterpfad, Spiess (all Riesling), Nussbein, Hoheburg and Gaisböhl. The larger Linsenbusch is less distinguished.
Growers Bassermann-Jordan. Biffar. Von Buhl. Bürklin-Wolf. Dr. Deinhard. Fitz-Ritter. Dr. Kern. Lindenhof. Ruppertsberger Winzerverein 'Hoheberg'. Winzerverein Forst.

Grosslage Meerspinne

The vineyard area south of Ruppertsberg is restricted to the lower slopes of the Haardt range without spilling out into the plain. Two villages, Königsbach and Gimmeldingen have good-quality vineyards at the tail end of the Mittelhaardt, certainly up to the general level of the Grosslage Hofstück. The Grosslage name Meerspinne is justifiably popular, for lighter wines than those of the central Mittelhaardt from a wider range of grape varieties (although Gimmeldingen itself has 50% Riesling). Wines of these villages sold under Einzellage names are certainly worth investigating.
Grower Dr. Deinhard.

Grosslagen Rebstöckel and Pfaffengrund

Growers in Grosslage Rebstöckel (Neustadt an der Weinstrasse, Ortsteil Diedesfeld): Kurt Isler. Dieter Ziegler. In Grosslage Pfaffengrund (Neustadt, Ortsteil Diedesfeld): Bergdolt. Kurt Isler.

Bereich Südliche Weinstrasse

The city of Neustadt is effectively the dividing line between the two Bereichs of Rheinpfalz where Mittelhaardt ends and Südliche Weinstrasse begins (although two Grosslagen to the south, Rebstöckel and Pfaffengrund, are officially in the Mittelhaardt).

From here south to the Alsace border the flourishing vineyard spreads out into the plain, with the city of Landau in its centre, but still, as in the Mittelhaardt, with the spine of hills along its west flank providing all the best sites.

The great majority of wines here are made and marketed by cooperatives, and Grosslage rather than Einzellage names are the rule. Even more common is a grape variety name and the simple appellation Bereich Südliche Weinstrasse.

These wines are steadily increasing in quality and are generally remarkable value for money. There is still a lively tradition of rather harsh and earthy 'Schoppenwein', or wine to be served 'open' by the quarter or fifth-litre glass. After a good vintage the young wine in the cafés and Weinstuben can have as much vitality and local character as any in Germany, and is very much headier than most. The drier versions of Weissburgunder and Grauburgunder are impressive, and sometimes show the signs of maturation in new *barriques*. Gewürztraminer can be close to those of Alsace – indeed Alsace now imports quantities of wine from the 'Süd-Pfalz' in bottle. Riesling is very much in the minority, but can also be good, if not precisely 'fine'. Silvaner is popular as the mildest of the wines. Müller-Thurgau is generally at its best overripened to a good sweet Auslese. Spätburgunder and Portugieser are grown for reds but without great enthusiasm or success.

The Grosslage names – Mandelhöhe, Schloss Lüdwigshöhe, Ordensgut, Trappenberg, Bischofskreuz, Königsgarten, Herrlich, Kloster Liebfrauenberg, Guttenberg – are only vague guides, covering about a dozen villages each. The most notable villages lie in most cases on or near the Haardt foothills, even though their Grosslagen may extend far out into the plains to the east.
Growers Kloster Heilsbruck. Rebholz. Schneider. Gebiets-Winzergenossenschaft Deutsches Weintor.

RHEINPFALZ PRODUCERS

Weingut Dr. v. Bassermann-Jordan

6705 Deidesheim. Owner: Dr Ludwig von Bassermann-Jordan. 99 acres. Einzellagen: Deidesheimer–Hohenmorgen (70% of the whole), Grainhübel, Kieselberg, Kalkofen, Leinhöhle, Herrgottsacker, Paradiesgarten, Mäushöhle and Langenmorgen; Forster–Jesuitengarten, Kirchenstück, Ungeheuer, Pechstein, Freundstück, Stift and Musenhang; Ruppertsberger–Reiterpfad, Hoheburg, Spiess, Nussbien and Linsenbusch; Dürkheimer–Michelsberg and Spielberg; Ungsteiner: Herrenberg. Grosslagen: Hofstück, Mariengarten, Schnepfenflug and Honigsäckel.

A historic house, perhaps the finest to make top-quality wines in the region, under its 18th-century founder Andreas Jordan. His great-grandson, Dr. Friedrich von Bassermann-Jordan, was in turn a legislator of great influence and a famous historian of wine who started an important wine museum in his medieval cellars. The present owner, his son, maintains impeccable, entirely traditional standards and methods, with Rieslings more delicate than many in the Rheinpfalz but no less long-lived. The estate is now entirely Riesling.

Weingut Reichsrat von Buhl

Weinstrasse 16, 6705 Deidesheim. Owner: Georg Enoch, Reichsfreiherr von und zu Guttenberg. Manager: Udo Loos. 148.2 acres. Einzellagen: Forster–Bischofsgarten, Ungeheuer, Pechstein, Kirchenstück, Freundstück and Jesuitengarten; Deidesheimer–Nonnenstück, Paradiesgarten, Kieselberg, Leinhöhle, Mäushöhle and Herrgottsacker; Ruppertsberger–Linsenbusch and Reiterpfad; Wachenheimer Luginsland; Grosslagen: Mariengarten, Schnepfenflug and Hofstück.

One of the biggest and most illustrious wine estates in Germany, founded in 1849 and still in the same family. The vines are 98% Riesling, 2% Müller-Thurgau. The wines are barrel-aged, powerful and full-bodied, and include a bottle-fermented Riesling Sekt brut.

Weingut Dr. Bürklin-Wolf

Weinstrasse 65, 6706 Wachenheim. Owner: Bettina Bürklin–von Guradze. Director: Georg Racquet. 271.7 acres. Einzellagen: Wachenheimer–Gerümpel, Goldbächel, Altenburg, Böhlig, Luginsland, Bischofsgarten, Mandelgarten, Königswingert and Rechbächel (sole owner); Forster–Kirchenstück, Ungeheuer, Jesuitengarten, Pechstein, Bischofsgarten; Deidesheimer–Hohenmorgen, Langenmorgen, Kalkofen, Herrgottsacker; Ruppertsberger–Hoheburg, Reiterpfad, Nussbien, Linsenbusch and Gaisböhl (sole owner).

Grosslagen: Schnepfenflug, Mariengarten, Schenkenböhl and Hofstück.

A magnificent estate in all the best vineyards of the Mittelhaardt, generally acknowledged as the finest in the region and one of the best in Germany. It has been in the family for over 200 years and the cellar goes back to the 16th century. Dr. Albert Bürklin, one of his country's greatest wine men, died in 1979 and his daughter inherited the estate. The Director, Georg Racquet, formerly at the great Nahe State Domain at Niederhausen, is supremely qualified to continue the tradition.

The vines are Riesling, Müller-Thurgau, Weissburgunder, with some Gewürztraminer, Scheurebe, Silvaner, Muskateller and Spätburgunder and Dornfelder for red wine. The style of wine is the most 'racy', deft and harmonious in the Rheinpfalz, from light-vintage dry Riesling Kabinetts, so pure and refreshing that you could drink them for breakfast, to great orange-tinted late-picked wines of amazing spice and expressiveness. Some superb Eisweins (including a very rare 1979) have been made. Technology includes the most modern ideas; many young wine makers have learned their art here.

Gutsverwaltung Deinhard
See Gutsverwaltung Wegeler-Deinhard.

Weingut Dr. Deinhard
Weinstrasse 10, 6705 Deidesheim. Owner: Frau Renate Hoch. Director: Heinz Bauer. Einzellagen: Deidesheimer–Leinhöhle, Grainhübel, Kieselberg, Kalkofen, Paradiesgarten Mäushöhle and Nonnenstück; Ruppertsberger–Reiterpfad and Nussbien; Forst, Neustadt, Gimmeldingen and Mussbach.

A well-known estate built up in the 19th century by Dr. Andreas Deinhard, a founder of the German Winegrowers' Association and an influential legislator. His handsome Gutshaus (built 1848) now houses both this and the estate rented to Deinhards (*see* Gutsverwaltung Wegeler-Deinhard). 75% Riesling, Müller-Thurgau, Scheurebe, Gewürztraminer and Kerner. The wines are mainly trocken and halbtroken, and emphasis is on Kabinett wines with good acidity.

Weingut K. Fitz-Ritter
Leistadterstrasse 1c, 6702 Bad Dürkheim. Owner: Konrad Fitz. 53.1 acres, 10 in Grosslage Schenkenböhl: Einzellagen Dürkheimer–Abtsfronhof (sole owner), Fronhof and Fuchsmantel, and Wachenheimer Mandelgarten; 18.5 acres in Grosslage Hochmess: Einzellagen Dürkheimer–Michelsberg, Spielberg, Rittergarten and Hochbenn; 7.9 acres in Grosslage Feuerberg: Einzellagen Dürkheimer–Nonnengarten and Steinberg; Ellerstadter–Bubeneck and Sonnenberg; 3.4 acres in Grosslage Honigsäckel: Einzellage Ungsteiner Herrenberg; 5 acres in Grosslage Hofstück: Einzellage Ellerstadter Kirchenstück.

A family estate with a fine classical 18th-century mansion (1785) whose park contains the largest maidenhair tree (*Ginkgo biloba*) in Germany, along with other noble trees. The Fitz family also started here (in 1837) one of the oldest Sekt businesses in Germany. 65% of their vines are Riesling, 3% Gewürztraminer, 6% Spätburgunder, 26% others. Most of their wines are QmP (Kabinett or better) with a high reputation for individuality.

Weingut Knipser Johannishof
Hauptstrasse 47, 6711 Laumersheim. Owners: Heinz and Werner Knipser. 34.6 acres. Einzellagen: Grosskarlbacher–Burgweg and Osterberg: Laumersheimer–Kapellenberg, Kirschgarten and Mandelberg.

An estate dating from the 19th century producing fascinating wines which are not only all dry, but fully fermented. The red wines are remarkable and of a far higher quality than the common run – understandably, they are quickly sold out. The list of whites is impressive and includes a 1986 Riesling Auslese Trocken with over 13% alcohol. Of their rarer wines, there is a 1983 Laumersheimer Mandelberg Riesling Trockenbeerenauslese with 10.9% alcohol in practical, half-bottle size. The vineyards are planted 35% Gewürztraminer, 25% Riesling, 15% Scheurebe, plus Spätburgunder, Portugieser, Dornfelder, Schwarzriesling, St. Laurent, plus more besides.

Weingut Müller-Catoir
Mandelring 25, 6730 Neustadt-Haardt. Owner: Heinrich Catoir. 39.5 acres. Einzellagen: Gimmeldingener–Mandelgarten and Schlössel; Haardter–Bürgergarten, Herrenletten, Herzog and Mandelring; Hambacher Römerbrunnen; Neustadter–Grain and Mönchgarten.

This estate, although not in the most fashionable part of the Rheinpfalz, is widely regarded as amongst the very best. Happily, it is not alone in its rise to stardom. Success begins in the vineyard with meticulous grape selection and a delayed harvest. Wines are then individually fermented, matured and bottled, enabling it to produce nearly 40 different wines for the exclusively private customers. Rieslaner (5%) is an unusual speciality; a 1983 Rieslaner Auslese Trocken with 14.7% alcohol is a sensational wine with great length and a dry, fruity flavour. Other varieties grown include Riesling (34%), Scheurebe (15%), Müller-Thurgau (10%), plus Kerner, Weissburgunder, Spätburgunder, Grauburgunder and Silvaner.

Weingut Karl & Hermann Lingenfelder
Hauptstrasse 27, 6711 Grosskarlbach. Owners: the Lingenfelder family. 25 acres. Einzellagen: Grosskarlbacher–Burgweg and Osterberg; Frienshiemer–Goldberg and Musikantenbuckel.

This family estate – in its 13th generation – produces wines high in extract, of considerable individuality and character, that are increasingly successful in international competitions. The vineyards are planted with 30% Riesling, 10% Scheurebe, 20% Spätburgunder, 10% Dornfelder and 12% Kerner. The Spätburgunder, made like a Burgundy, is matured in French oak. Rainer Karl Lingenfelder was the Chief Oenologist of the wine shippers H. Sichel Söhne.

Weingut Pfeffingen
6702 Bad Dürkheim. Owners: Karl Fuhrmann and Günter Eymael. 25.9 acres. Einzellage: Ungsteiner–Herrenberg and Weilberg. Grosslage: Honigsäckel.

A highly regarded consolidated estate, formerly in the Schnell family. 70% is Riesling, 10% Müller-Thurgau, 10% Scheurebe, plus Silvaner and Gewürztraminer. Pfeffingen wines have considerable finesse, the Rieslings often dry and the Scheurebes juicily rich. Even wines from 'off' vintages age long and gracefully.

Weingut Ökonomierat Rebholz
Weinstrasse 54, 6741 Seilbeldingen. Owner: Christine Rebholz. 24.7 acres. Einzellagen: Birkweiler Kastanienbusch; Siebeldinger–im Sonnenschein and Rosenberg. Grosslage: Königsgarten.

The family that pioneered quality wine-making in the area, where steep sites and varied soils give good opportunities. In 1949 Eduard Rebholz (grandfather of the present director, Hansjörg) was the first man to make a Müller-Thurgau TBA, thus making the workhorse grape respectable. The vines are 35% Riesling, 22% Spätburgunder, 13% Müller-Thurgau, 9% Grauburgunder, 7% Weissburgunder, 10% Gewürztraminer. Sweet reserve is never used. The resulting wines are clean, racy and exciting – outstanding in the area.

Gutsverwaltung Wegeler-Deinhard

Weinstrasse 10, 6705 Deidesheim. Owner: Deinhard & Co. KGaA. 44.5 acres in Deidesheim: Herrgottsacker (13.5) and Paradiesgarten (1.5); Ruppertsberg: Linsenbusch (20); Forst: Ungeheuer (9).

The Koblenz merchants Deinhard rented this section of the old Dr. Deinhard estate in 1973. There are said to be old family connections and the two estates are run by the same Director from the same fine sandstone Gutshaus in Deidesheim (see Weingut Dr. Deinhard), but their wines are made apart and labelled differently. Deinhard's wines, like those of their estates in the Rheingau and Mosel, are models of correct and characterful wine-making. Linsenbusch is a relatively light wine from flat land; the others are on slopes, riper and more 'Pfalzy' – Ungeheuer best of all, rarely producing less than Spätleses. 91% is Riesling, 7% Müller-Thurgau, 2% Scheurebe.

Gebiets-Winzergenossenschaft Deutsches Weintor

6741 Ilbesheim.

The massive central cooperative of the Südliche Weinstrasse, symbolized by its great stone gateway, the 'Deutsches Weintor', which stands challengingly on the border of French Alsace at Schweigen. Its 1,255 members farm a total of 28,252 acres in 47 communes, filling its vast vat houses with a total capacity of 40m. litres – said to be the biggest in Europe. 41 varieties of vines are grown, mainly: Müller-Thurgau (28%), Morio-Muskat 15% and Kerner 11%.

The resulting wines are mild and often highly aromatic (especially Morio-Muskat and its blends), mainly sweet, often with good vitality and balance which makes them excellent value. The Weintor has made several Grosslage names almost household words in Germany: e.g. Guttenberg, Kloster Liebfrauenberg, Herrlich, Bischofskreuz, Trappenberg and Königsgarten.

OTHER PRODUCERS

Weingut Josef Biffar
Niederkirchenerstrasse 13, 6705 Deidesheim. Owner: Gerhard Biffar. 29 acres. Einzellagen: Deidesheimer–Nonnenstück, Herrgottsacker, Mäushöhle, Kieselberg, Leinhöhle, Grainhübel and Kalkofen; Ruppertsberger–Nussbien, Linsenbusch and Reiterpfad; Wachenheimer–Altenburg and Goldbächel. Grosslagen: Hofstück and Mariengarten. A well-regarded estate for traditional cask-aged wines of good balance. 87% Riesling, 7% Weissburgunder, 4% Müller-Thurgau and 2% Gewürztraminer.

Emil Hammel & Cie
Weinstrasse Süd 4, 6719 Kirchheim. Owners: Rudolf and Martin Hammel. 135 acres. Einzellagen: Bisserheimer–Goldberg and Held; Kirchheimer–Kreuz, Römerstrasse, Steinacker and Geisskopf; Neuleininger Sonnenberg; Kleinkarlbacher Herrenberg; Dirmsteiner Mandelpfad. Grosslagen: Schwarzerde and Höllenpfad. Growers and merchants with a total production of some 85,000 cases. The company is known for very good carafe wines, mainly semi-dry, with the stress on Müller-Thurgau, Riesling and (red) Portugieser.

Kloster Heilsbruck
Klosterstrasse 170, 6732 Edenkoben. Owners: Karl Ueberle Erben. Manager: Rudolf Nagel. 29.5 acres in Edenkobener–Klostergarten, Heilig Kreuz and Bergel; Ruppertsberger Reiterpfad. Old monastic buildings with the rustic atmosphere of seven centuries ago shelter an enormous range of old oak casks with a total capacity of 480,000 litres. The oak-aged wines keep remarkably: although not particularly fine they are fascinating in representing an almost-lost tradition. 70% is Riesling.

Weingut Johannes Karst & Söhne
Burgstrasse 15, 6702 Bad Dürkheim. Owner: Heinz Karst. 25 acres. Einzellage: Dürkheimer–Fuchsmantel, Spielberg, Hochbenn and Michelsberg. Grosslagen: Feuerberg, Schenkenböhl and Hochmess. A family firm of growers. 80% of the vines are Riesling, 10% Scheurebe. Scheurebe has become something of a speciality; and Huxelrebe is being made into Auslesen, Beerenauslesen and Trockenbeerenauslesen.

Weingut Dr. Kern
Schloss Deidesheim, 6705 Deidesheim. Owner: Gottfried Kern. 14.3 acres. Einzellagen: Deidesheimer–Herrgottsacker, Kieselberg, Leinhöhle, Langenmorgen, Paradiesgarten, Grainhübel and Nonnenstück; Forster Ungeheuer; Ruppertsberger–Linsenbusch and Reiterpfad; Niederkirchener Klostergarten. Relatively small but well-known estate with holdings in some of the best vineyards of the Mittelhaardt. The plantation of Riesling (69%) is high, and other vines grown are Kerner (10%), Müller-Thurgau (4%), Gewürztraminer (8%) and Spätburgunder (9%). The estate is very proud of its dry Rieslings, deliberately bottled late to allow the maximum development in bulk. The result can be tasted in the wine bar.

Weingut Koehler-Ruprecht
Weinstrasse 84, 6701 Kallstadt. Owners: The Philippi family. President: Bernd Philippi. 20.3 acres. Einzellagen: Kallstadter–Saumagen, Steinacker and Kronenberg. Grosslagen: Kobnert and Feuerberg. A family property going back centuries, including the charming hotel 'Weincastell' – all typical antiques and local food. Vines are 68% Riesling, with red Spätsburgunder as another speciality (their 1983 Kallstadter Feuerberg is a great rarity). The Kallstadt vineyards ripen grapes remarkably: Herr Philippi reports that he can always make an Auslese. Cellar methods are traditional, the wines full of flavour.

Weingut Georg Mosbacher
Weinstrasse 27, 6701 Forst. Owner: Richard Mosbacher. 23 acres. Einzellagen: Forster–Ungeheuer, Pechstein, Elster, Freundstück, Musenhang and Stift; Deidesheimer Herrgottsacker. Grosslagen: Mariengarten and Schnepfenflug. The Mosbachers have steadily improved this small estate in the centre of Forst since they first bottled their wine in 1920. 84% is Riesling, 8% Müller-Thurgau, 4% Spätburgunder, 2% each of Gewürztraminer and Scheurebe. They regularly win prizes with fresh flowery wines, particularly dry Riesling Kabinett from Forster Pechstein and Stift. Wines are sold direct or at their own Weinstube.

Weingut K. Neckerauer
Ritter von Geisslerstrasse 9, 6714 Weissenheim. Owners: Klaus and Arnd Neckerauer. 59.3 acres. Einzellagen: Weissenheimer–Hahnen, Hasenzeile, Goldberg, Altenberg, Halde and Burgweg; Grosskarlbacher Osterberg. 89% of the property is under the

Grosslage name of Rosenbuhl and 11% is under Schwarzerde. The third generation (sales in bottle began in 1930), Klaus is a most competent wine maker who matches varieties with soil types to produce intense dry Riesling Kabinetts, aromatic medium Kerner, fruity Müller-Thurgau and light (often 'Weissherbst') Portugieser. The sandy soil and low rainfall make crops small.

Weingut Karl Schaefer
Weinstrasse Süd 30, 6702 Bad Dürkheim. Owner: Dr. Wolf Fleischmann. 42 acres. Einzellagen: Wachenheimer–Gerümpel and Fuchsmantel; Dürkheimer–Michelsberg and Spielberg; Forster Pechstein; Ungsteiner Herrenberg. A family estate established in 1843, now in its fourth generation. The vineyards are planted with Silvaner, Scheurebe, Gewürztraminer, Spätburgunder, Weissburgunder, Muskateller and Kerner, but 75% of the area is under Riesling, nowadays producing much dry wine, fresh in flavour and elegant.

Ludwig Schneider GmbH
Maikammerstrasse 7, 6731 St. Martin. Owners: The Schneider family. 234.7 acres. Einzellagen: St. Martiner–Baron, Kirchberg and Zitadelle; Maikammerer–Kapellenberg, Heiligenberg, Kirchenstück and Immengarten. Grosslagen: Schloss Ludwigshöhe and Mandelhöhe. A merchant house (turnover 125,000 cases a year) handling the produce of the 'St. Martinus' Producers' Cooperative. It owns a beautiful old inn, one of the prettiest timbered Renaissance buildings of the Südliche Weinstrasse. The style of wines is light, extrovert and *spritzig*.

Weingut Eduard Schuster
Neugasse 21, 6701 Kallstadt. Owner: Detlev Schuster. 37 acres. Einzellagen: Kallstadter–Saumagen, Steinacker,

Kronenberg and Kreidkeller; Ungsteiner–Herrenberg, Weilberg, Nussriegel and Osterberg; Dürkheimer Spielberg; Herxheimer Honigsack; Freinsheimer Goldberg. Grosslagen: Kobnert, Honigsäkel and Feuerberg. Wine growers since 1590. 56% Riesling, 13% Silvaner with a wide variety of other vines, including Muskateller. Tasty, authentic and enjoyable wines. All are made in oak (100 years old) in vaulted sandstone cellars.

Kommerzienrat Georg Fr. Spiess
Kleinkarlbach. Owners: The Spiess family. 49 acres. Einzellagen: Keinkarlbacher–Herrenberg and Herrgottsacker; Neuleiningen Schlossberg. 50% Riesling plus a Müller-Thurgau, Kerner and Scheurebe. A flourishing estate with high standards. Direct sales only. Fine Rieslings include a clean, light, vintage Sekt.

Weingut Lindenhof Eugen Spindler
Weinstrasse 55, 6701 Forst. 33.3 acres. Einzellagen: Forster–Jesuitengarten, Ungehever, Pechstein, Musenhang, Elster and Stift; Deidesheimer–Grainhübel, Leinhöhle, Herrgottsacker, Langenmorgen and Nonnenstück; Ruppertsberger–Nussbien, Reiterpfad and Hoheburg. Widely respected family-owned estate whose vines consist of 75% Riesling, 5% Müller-Thurgau, 3% each Kerner and Scheurebe, 5% Dornfelder and 9% others.

Weingut Hartmut Stauch
Weinstrasse 130, 6701 Kallstadt. Owner: Alfred Stauch. 16 acres in Einzellagen: Kallstadter–Steinacker and Kronenberg. Small estate with a high proportion for the Rheinpfalz of Riesling (68%). Other wine varieties are 12% Gewürztraminer, 4% Scheurebe, 4% Muskateller, 4% Ruländer, 8% Spätburgunder. The Rieslings are particularly good, full-flavoured, fruity wines.

Weingut J. L. Wolf Erben
Weinstrasse 1, 6706 Wachenheim. Owners: Dieter and Ingrid Müller. 44.5 acres. Einzellagen: Wachenheimer–Belz (solely owned), Königswingert, Gerümpel, Altenburg and Goldbächel; Forster–Ungeheuer, Jesuitengarten and Pechstein; Deidesheimer–Herrgottsacker and Leinhöhle. The vines are 90% Riesling. The wines are well made and racy, from dry to medium sweet.

COOPERATIVES

Winzerverein Deidesheim
Prinz Rupprechstrasse 8, 6705 Deidesheim. 475 members with 526 acres. Einzellagen: Deidesheim, Ruppertsberg, Forst, Niederkirchen, Meckensheim and Wachenheim. Some 78% is planted with Riesling; as high a proportion as in the commune as a whole. Standards are in keeping with the wine capital of the Rheinpfalz.

Winzerverein Forst
Wienstrasse 57, 6701 Forst. Founded 1918. 114 members with 158 acres in Forst, Deidesheim, Wachenheim and Ungstein. Grosslagen: Schnepfenflug, Mariengarten and Hofstück. The highly regarded cooperative of Forst, with 109 acres of Riesling in fine sites. Half the sales are in bottle and and half in cask.

Ruppertsberger Winzerverein 'Hoheburg'
Hauptstrasse 74, 6701 Ruppertsberg. 209 members with 504 acres. Einzellagen: Ruppertsberg, Königsbach, Meckenheim, Mussbach, Deidesheim and Gimmeldingen. Grosslagen: Hofstück and Meerspinne. 45% of the vines are Riesling. Apart from the usual Silvaner and Müller-Thurgau, Kerner and Portugieser have an important share. The top Ruppertsberg Rieslings can be excellent.

HESSISCHE BERGSTRASSE

Germany's smallest wine region lies across the Rhine from Worms, in steep, even terraced hills north of Heidelberg with a westerly outlook over the Rhine valley. Its fame today lies largely in the fact that the Hessen State Domain, based at Eltville in Rheingau, has vineyards here, at Bensheim and Heppenheim.

The region is divided into two Bereichs: Umstadt, a remote minor area, away from the Rhine east of Darmstadt, principally Müller-Thurgau, and Starkenburg, a north-south hillside 10 miles long. Starkenburg is warm enough, with its light sandy loam on its west slopes, to ripen the Riesling which dominates its vineyards, giving Rheingau-like wines without the finesse of the more famous region.

From south to north the Grosslagen are Schlossberg (for Heppenheim), Wolfsmagen (for Bensheim) and Rott (for Schönberg, Auerbach, Zwingenberg and Alsbach). Seeheim is a one-vineyard village to the north with no Grosslage name. The total area under vine is some 960 acres.

Most of the wine is made in the two cooperatives, the Bergstrasse Gebietswinzergenossenschaft at Heppenheim and the Odenwälder Winzergenossenschaft at Gross Umstadt. Both have Weinstubes, as do a score of small growers and the State Domain.

Weingut der Stadt Bensheim
6140 Bensheim. Director: Axel Seiberth. The town of Bensheim has a small estate of about 29.6 acres in the Grosslage Wolfsmagen, mainly Riesling but with 17% Rotberger made into rosé. The estate makes its own Sekt from Weissburgunder and Grauburgunder.

Staatsweingut Bergstrasse
Grieselstrasse 34-36, 6140 Bensheim. Director: Dr. Ambrosi. 90 acres. Einzellagen: Heppenheimer–Centgericht (sole owner) and Steinkopf; Bensheimer–Steichling and Kalkgasse; Schönberger Herrnwingert (sole

owner). Much the largest estate in this region and in fact part of the old Prussian State Domain now administered from Eltville in the Rheingau (*see* page 258). The best site is Steinkopf in Heppenheim. 86% of the wines are *trocken* or *halbtrocken*. Eiswein has been produced successfully every year since 1977. Vines are 73% Riesling, 8% Müller-Thurgau, 7% Grauburgunder, 6% Weissburgunder, 4% Spätburgunder and 2% Gewürztraminer.

Weingut H. Freiberger OHG
Hermannstrasse 16 And Lehrstrasse 15, 6148 Heppenheim. Owners: Herbert and

Heinz Freiberger. 32 acres. Einzellagen: Heppenheimer–Maiberg, Steinkopf, Eckweg, Guldenzoll and Stemmler. Grosslage Schlossberg. The leading private estate of the district, making a broad spectrum of powerful, uninhibited, dry to medium wines of all qualities for local consumption. Now has a Riesling Sekt from its own base wine. Vines are 58% Riesling, 14% Müller-Thurgau, 13% Ruländer, 6% Ehrenfelser and 9% Gewürztraminer, Kerner, Spätburgunder and Silvaner. The late-harvest Ruländers have great character and reach TBA sweetness.

FRANKEN

Fifty miles east of the Rheingau, beyond the city of Frankfurt, the river Main, flowing to join the Rhine at Hochheim, scribbles a huge drunken W through the irregular limestone and red marl hills of Franken (Franconia), the northern extremity of Bavaria.

The centre of the region is the baroque city of Würzburg. Its most famous vineyard, sloping down to the Main within the city itself, is Würzburger Stein. The name Stein has been traditionally borrowed by foreigners to describe Franconian wine generically (as the English shortened Hochheim to 'hock' for all Rhine wines). 'Steinwein' comes in fat flagons called Bocksbeutels, thus distinguishing itself from almost all other German wines, which come in elegant bottles. This is probably the extent of popular knowledge. Franken wine is a specialized subject, not least because its rarity value and local popularity keep the price higher than we are accustomed to pay for more famous names from the Rhine and Mosel. Most 'Frankenwein' is drunk in Bavaria, particularly in Munich, or in the wealthy cities of northern Germany. Besides, the area is exceptionally diffuse and hard to comprehend. Vineyards are only found on exceptional south slopes. The climate is harsh and serious frosts are common; the season is too short for regular success with Riesling.

Traditionally Franken has made its best wine with the Silvaner, only here and occasionally on the Rheinterrasse in Rheinhessen a better-than-moderate variety. Silvaner here can produce full-bodied

dry wines (and occasionally sweet ones) with a noble breadth and substance; dense, even sticky in their intensity. They are regularly compared with white burgundy, not for their flavour but for their vinosity and ability to match rich food at table.

Unfortunately the Müller-Thurgau has now gained the upper hand. It works well, when not overproduced, and make stylish, flavourful wines; though it rarely matches the remarkable low-key stylishness of Silvaner. Scheurebe and the new Perle can do better. Bacchus tends to be aggressively aromatic; out of keeping for the region. Kerner is also too aromatic, although many people find it acceptable. In a ripe year Rieslaner is a good compromise, making excellent Ausleses with the breadth of a Silvaner and the depth of a Riesling. 1976 in the Steigerwald produced some extraordinary wines with a bouquet like salty honey.

The rambling region is divided into three Bereichs: Mainviereck for its lower reaches towards Frankfurt; Maindreieck for its heart, the district of Würzburg; and Steigerwald for its eastern extremities with the sternest climate of all. The Bereich names are frequently used, partly because a great number of the scattered vineyards are included in no Grosslage.

A high percentage of wine, as in Baden, is made by cooperatives. Würzburg itself, however, boasts three of the oldest, biggest and best wine estates in Germany–the Bürgerspital, the Juliusspital and the Staatlicher Hofkeller.

Bereich Mainviereck
Bereich Mainviereck extends across the famous Spessart forest from Aschaffenburg in the northwest down to Kreuzwertheim in the first trough of the W described by the Main. The very limited vineyard area is all close to the river with the exception of Rück, in a little eastern side

valley. The soils are largely sandstone based and loamy. Two Grosslagen: Reuschberg (Hörstein) and Heiligenthal (Grossostheim) and 15 villages where no Grosslage name applies.
Growers Staatlicher Hofkeller. Juliusspital. Winzergenossenschaft Thüngersheim.

Bereich Maindreieck

Bereich Maindreieck includes Homburg and Lengfurt, next door to Kreuzwertheim, but then leaps over the central ridge of the W to an isolated area of vines on the tributary river Saale around Hammelburg. Here the soil is limestone (Muschelkalk), the soil of all the best Franconian vineyards. Eleven Grosslagen: Burg (Hammelburg), Rosstal (Karlstadt), Ravensburg (Thüngersheim), Marienberg (Würzburg), Ewig Leben (Randersacker), Ölspiel (Sommerhausen), Teufelstor (Eibelstadt), Markgraf Babenberg (Frickenhausen), Hofrat (Kitzingen), Honigberg (Dettelbach) and Kirchberg (Volkach).

The first isolated Maindreieck vineyards, grouped around Homburg and Lengfurt, have no Grosslage name. The Grosslage Hammelburger Burg, to the northeast, includes all the vineyards of the river Saale.
Growers Schloss Saaleck. Winzergenossenschaft Hammelburg.

Würzburg

The eastern trough of the W is the centre of Franconian wine production, with Würzburg at its heart. The main concentrations of vines are in the villages north and south of Würzburg along the river, all on limestone, down to Frickenhausen, the foot of the trough, and north again in the bends in the river higher up around Escherndorf and Nordheim, still on limestone but here with an overlay of marly clay. The famous hill of Escherndorfer Lump makes great Silvaners from this soil structure.

The wines of all the principal vineyards can be tasted and compared at the big, bustling Weinstuben of the three great Würzburg estates. The Juliusspital, the Bürgerspital and the Staatliche Hofkeller all maintain wonderfully comfortable and convivial cafés for the appreciation of their wines in a city which is infiltrated with vineyards to its very heart. You can look up from its famous baroque statue-lined bridge (on feast days one long café from end to end) to see the steep vine-ramp of the Leiste supporting the Marienberg Castle. The celebrated Stein vineyard covers the best parts of the south-facing hill overlooking the city – a skyline now sadly marred by ugly and intrusive new buildings. Steinwein begins to have real meaning when you have sipped a stiff Silvaner Spätlese at the Bürgerspital and gone on to marvel at Tiepolo's ceilings in the Residenz.
Growers Bürgerspital. Gebhardt. Herpfer. Juliusspital. Müller. Staatlicher Hofkeller. Winzergenossenschafts Nordheim, Randersacker, Sommerach and Thungersheim.

Bereich Steigerwald

Wine communities to the east of the Main form this much smaller Bereich. The best known are Iphofen, Rödelsee and Castell, all on heavier marly clay soil which demands a fine summer but can deliver both full-bodied and nicely nuanced wines. Eight Grosslagen: Schild (Abtswind), Herrenberg (Castell), Schlossberg (Rödelsee), Burgweg (Iphofen), Schlosstück (Frankenberg), Ipsheimer Burgberg (Iphofen), Kapellenberg (Zeil) and Steige.
Growers Bürgerspital. Fürstlich Castell. Herpfer. Juliusspital. Müller. Ernst Popp. Staatlicher Hofkeller. Wirsching. Winzergenossenschafts Franken and Sommerach.

FRANKEN PRODUCERS

Bürgerspital zum Heiligen Geist

Theaterstrasse 19, 8700 Würzburg. Director: Heinz Zeller. 346 acres. Einzellagen: Würzburger–Stein (56), Pfaffenberg (106), Abtsleite (46.5) and Innere Leiste (6.5); Randersackerer–Teufelskeller (16), Marsberg (3.7) and Pfülben (5); Veitshöchheimer Sonnenschein (12), Thüngersheimer Scharlachberg (5.5); Michlelauer Vollburg (24); Gössenheimer Homburg-Arnberg (18.5); Leinacher Himmelberg (18). (No Grosslage names are used.)

A splendid charity founded in 1319 for the old people of Würzburg by Johannes von Steren, and although now somewhat overshadowed by the even richer ecclesiastical upstart, the Juliusspital (q.v.), still the fourth-biggest wine estate in Germany, with the biggest share of Würzburg's famous Stein and other good south slopes. The vineyards are 25% Riesling, 20% each Silvaner and Müller-Thurgau, the rest include Kerner, Scheurebe, Spätburgunder and several new varieties.

Hearty, full-flavoured and dry Rieslings are the pride of the house, though a tasting at the huge 500-seater Weinstube in the venerable hospital buildings leaves an impression of powerful and flavoury wines from almost any variety. Dry Silvaner and Weissburgunder, particularly Spätlesen, are a speciality.

Fürstlich Castell'sches Domänenamt

Schlossplatz 5, 8711 Castell. Owner: Prince Albrecht zu Castell-Castell. 155.6 acres. Einzellagen: Casteller–Schlossberg, Kugelspiel, Bausch, Hohnart, Kirchberg, Trautberg, Reitsteig and Feuerbach (the last 2 for red wine). Neundorfer–Hüssberg, Sonnenberg, Wonne and Mönchsbuck.

A gem of an operatic princely estate with classic palace in a village on a hill, the vineyards sloping up to perfectly kept oakwoods – the princes' other pride. The Castell wines are admirably balanced. Müller-Thurgau accounts for 31%, Silvaner 21% and there is a catholic range of newer varieties; also admirable Sekt ('Casteller Herrenberg'). The new varieties tend to taste more or less *'schmalzig'* and trite beside the dignified soft earthiness of the classic Silvaner. Scheurebe is successfully spicy; Rieslaner excellent for Silvaner-style Ausleses. Visitors to this remote spot can taste the wines in a beautiful tasting room decorated with *trompe l'oeil*, or in the 'Weinstall', a stable-turned-restaurant.

Weingut Sektkellerei Ernst Gebhardt

Hauptstrasse 21-23, 8701 Sommerhausen. Owners: the Hügelschäffer family. 37 acres. Einzellagen: Sommerhausener–Reinfenstein and Steinbach; Eibelstadter Kapellenberg; Frickhausener–Fischer and Markgraf Babenberg (the latter now absorbed into the Frickenhausen Einzellage Kapellenberg, under the new Grosslage Markgraf Babenberg); Winterhausener Kaiser Wilhelm; Randersacker–Teufelskeller and Sonnenstuhl; Marktbreiter Sonnenberg.

An 18th-century family estate bought in 1888 by the Hügelschäffer family, who are also wine merchants. They make somewhat fruitier and sweeter wines than the old Franconian style with great skill, especially from their best sites: Steinbach and the famous Teufelskeller. 26% is Silvaner, 26% Müller-Thurgau, 20% Scheurebe (a favourite, distinctly blackcurrant), 6% Bacchus and 6% Riesling. Their Weinstube in the Flemish baroque style is a well-known attraction, as is Gebhardt Sekt.

Weinbau-Weinkellerei Christoph Hs. Herpfer

Paul-Eberstrasse 5-7, 8710 Kitzingen.
Director: Peter Herpfer.

A most unusual democratically run producers' association

(not a cooperative) with members in Escherndorf, Volkach, Nordheim, Sommerach, Kitzingen, Rödelsee, Obreisenheim, Randersacker and elsewhere. The object is individual wines made by modern methods, entirely protected from oxygen, dry in the regional style but with very distinct fruitiness. Silvaners from the limestone of Würzburg, Randersacker and Escherndorf are probably their finest wines, with Scheurebes for the richest wines in ripe vintages.

Juliusspital-Weingut

Klinikstrasse 5, 8700 Würzburg 1. Director: H. Kolesch. 403 acres. Einzellagen: Würzburger–Stein (52), Pfaffenberg, Innere Leiste and Abtsleite; Randersackerer–Teufelskeller and Pfülben (12.3); Escherndorfer Lump (5); Iphöfer–Julius-Echter-Berg (22) and Kronsberg; Rödelseer Küchenmeister (15); Volkacher Karthäuser; Thüngersheimer Johannisberg; Bürgstädter Mainhölle. (No Grosslage names are used.)

A charitable foundation on a scale even grander than the Hospices de Beaune, founded in 1576 by the Prince-Bishop Julius Echter von Mespelbrunn and now the third-largest wine estate in Germany, supporting a magnificent hospital for the people of Würzburg. Its low-vaulted cellar, 250 metres long, was built in 1699 under the great classical 'Fürstenbau' wing by Antonio Petrini. The vineyards are 35% Silvaner, 22% Müller-Thurgau, 18% Riesling. The remaining 30% includes Gewürztraminer, Ruländer, Weissburgunder, Muskateller, Scheurebe, Spätburgunder (in Bürgstadt) and several new varieties. All are matured in oak (some of the casks are over 100 years old). Aside from the classic Silvaners, the Riesling and Rieslaner are particularly fruity, extrovert and powerful. The white wines have black labels and the red wines, red labels. The wines can be tasted in the hospital's own Weinstube.

Staatlicher Hofkeller

Residenzplatz 3, 8700 Würzburg. Owner: The State of Bavaria. Director: Dr. A. Schmitt. 407.6 acres. Einzellagen: Würzburger–Stein (67) and Innere Leiste (17); Randersaker–

Pfülben (5) and Marsberg (15); Hörsteiner Abtsberg (30); Handthaler Stollberg (17); Abtswinder Altenberg (17); Thüngersheimer Scharlachberg (32).

The superlative vineyards of the lordly Prince-Bishops of Würzburg, orginating in the 12th century, are now (since 1814) the Bavarian State domain, run by the Bayerische Landesanstalt für Weinbau and Gartenbau. The great cellar under the baroque Residency at Würzburg is one of the most stirring sights in the world of wine. The vines, all on steep or sloping sites, on many different soils, are 26% Müller-Thurgau, 25% Riesling, 12% Silvaner, 8% Rieslaner (a Silvaner × Riesling cross), 8% Kerner and many others in small quantities, including Spätburgunder in the 7.5-acre Bischofsberg vineyard. The object is wines of true Franconian style, balancing high acidity with powerful flavours, all either dry or semi-dry (except for Ausleses, etc.). The '76 Spätleses of Riesling and Rieslaner were the estate's ideal: highly concentrated and aromatic dry wines, matured, like all the estate's wines, in wood. The estate has a college at Veitshochheim and restaurants in Würzburg, Schloss Aschaffenburg (another cellar) and Stollberg in the Steigerwald.

Weingut Hans Wirsching

Ludwigstrasse 16, 8715 Iphofen. Owners: Hans and Dr. Heinrich Wirsching. 128 acres. Einzellagen: Iphofener–Julius-Etcher-Berg, Kronsberg and Kalb; Rödelseer Küchenmeister. Grosslagen: Burgweg and Schlossberg.

A family firm since 1630 with its original Gutshaus and cellars, as well as modern ones outside the village. Silvaner, Müller-Thurgau and Riesling are predominant; Kerner, Scheurebe, Bacchus and Portugieser are also grown, with a little Traminer. Half the wines are full dry; the rest not greatly sweetened. Most of their business is direct to consumers but a little is also exported to the UK, USA, Netherlands and other countries.

Throughout the chapter on Germany, names of the Einzellagen producing the finest wines will be found in the Producers' entries.

Ageing German wines

Good-quality German wines have a much longer lifespan, and benefit much more by being kept in bottle, than fashion suggests or most people suppose. The wine industry and trade have little to gain from older bottles and have tacitly agreed that German wines are ready to drink within months of being bottled. With the enormous crops (and hence the high water content) of standard-quality modern wines there is indeed no gain from keeping bottles more than 6 months or a year. But almost all the superior-grade (QmP) wines, delectable as they may taste in their flower and fruity youth, have the potential to put another dimension of flavour with maturity. When they are first offered for sale they are at their most brisk and lively, with acidity and fruitiness often tending to cancel each other out in a generally tingling and exciting effect. Some fine wines

(particularly Rieslings) at this stage have remarkably little aroma.

Sometimes after a year or two in bottle the first rapture goes without maturer flavours taking its place; the wine you bought with enthusiasm seems to be letting you down. Be patient. The subtle alchemy takes longer. It may be 4 or 5 years before the mingled savours of citrus and spice and oil emerge.

Each vintage has its own timespan, but as a generalization Kabinett wines from a first-rate grower need at least 3 years in bottle and may improve for 7 or 8, Spätleses will improve for anything from 4 to 10 years, and Ausleses and upwards will benefit from 5 or 6 years up to 20 or even more.

Liebfraumilch

For most foreigners the great stumbling block to the full enjoyment of German wines is the German language. It certainly takes dogged persistence for a non-German speaker to master the polysyllabic names and categories. It is little comfort to be told that they form a logical national system by which everything can be unravelled – and still less to discover that the vaunted logic often lapses into local exceptions.

Small wonder then that most non-Germans shrug their shoulders and settle for the one name they know: Liebfraumilch – a name that guarantees nothing. The law requires only that the wines should be 'of pleasant character', with more than 18 grams per litre of unfermented sugar, and be made of certain grapes in certain regions – those which in any case produce the greatest volumes of wine.

OTHER PRODUCERS

Weingut Rudolf Fürst
Hohenlindenweg 46, 8768 Bürgstadt.
Owner: Paul Fürst. 24 acres.
Einzellagen: Bürgstadter
Centgrafenberg; Grossheubacher
Bischofsberg. Fine deep-coloured red
wines from Spätburgunder, Domina,
Portugieser and Frühburgunder; full-
bodied whites with high acidity from
Müller-Thurgau and Rieslaner.

Weingut Müller
Nordheim. 15 acres in Iphofen,
Nordheim, Sommerach,
Frankenwinheim. A typical 300-year-old
family property making fresh and
charming Silvaner, pleasant Müller-
Thurgau, slightly earthy Riesling and
excellent crisp and spicy Scheurebe.

Weingut Ernst Popp KG
8715 Iphofen. Owners: Michael Popp.
34.5 acres plus 49.5 on contract to
Iphofen and Rödelsee. Einzallagen:
Iphofener–Julius-Echter-Berg, Kalb and
Burgweg; Rödelseer–Schwanleite,
Küchenmeister and Schlossberg;
Frankenberger Schlosstuck. A respected
family firm since 1878 making dry,
'nutty' wines of character, typical of the
region. 25% Silvaner and 70%
Müller-Thurgau.

**Weingut-Weinkellerei Bernhard
Völker**
8710 Kitzingen. Owner: Bernhard
Völker. 8 acres. Vineyards in Kitzingen,
Sulzfeld, and Rödelsee. The estate,
which was recently taken over from
Knoll and Reinhardt by Bernhard
Völker, has cultivated vines since 1665.
It has extensive old cellars and matures
the majority of its wines in wooden
casks. Supplies are supplemented with
bought grapes. Varieties used are
Müller-Thurgau, Silvaner, Riesling,
Kerner, Schwarzriesling, Domina and
Spätburgunder. A speciality is the top
quality wine from the Kitzinger
Eselsberg, which is almost exclusively
marketed by the Völker family.

**Schloss Saaleck-Städt, Weingut
Hammelburg**
Postfach 1220, 8783 Hammelburg.
Director: Joseph Kastner. 74 acres.
Einzellagen: Saalecker Schlossberg;
Hammelburger–Heroldsberg and
Trautlestal; Feuerthaler Kreuz;
Westheimer Längberg. The ancient
Schloss Saaleck and its estate are the
property of the town of Hammelberg,
down the Main west of Würzburg. The
vineyards are 50% Müller-Thurgau,
20% Silvaner, 10% Bacchus (which the
director particularly favours) and other
new varieties. The wines are for the
most part dry with powerful fruit
flavours.

COOPERATIVES

**Gabietswinzergenossenschaft
Franken eG**
8710 Kitzingen. 2,800 members. The
massive union of 18 cooperatives. 57%
Müller-Thurgau, 23% Silvaner; small
quantities of several other varieties are
grown, red and white. 1,400 different
wines are produced annually.

Winzergrenossenschaft Hammelburg
Marktplatz 11, 8783 Hammelburg.
Director: Heer Baier. 62 acres in
Hammelburger–Trautlestal and
Heroldsberg, both part of Grosslage
Burg. A tiny local cooperative offering
principally Silvaner.

Winzergenossenschaft Nordheim
8711 Nordheim/Main. 251 members;
741 acres. Einzellagen: Escherndorfer–
Lump and Fürstenberg; Nordheimer–
Vögelein and Kreuzberg;
Sommeracher–Katzenkopf and
Rosenberg. The principal cooperative
for the upper Main wine villages: 55%
Müller-Thurgau, 22% Silvaner plus
various others – mainly new varieties –
and 3% red-wine grapes. The wine is
happily drunk up in Bavaria.

Winzergenossenschaft Randersacker
Maingasse 33, 8701 Randersacker. 258
members; 302 acres in Randersacker

(210), Sommerhausen (49.5) and
Würzburg (15). Einzellagen:
Randersacker–Sonnenstuhl, Marsberg,
Pfülben, Dabug and Teufelskeller;
Sommerhäuser Steinbach and
Reifenstein; Würzburger–Abtsleite and
Kirchberg; Gerbrunner–Alter Berg and
Neuberg; Rimparer Kobersberg;
Theilheimer Altenberg; Leinacher
Himmelberg. The cooperative of one of
the best areas in Franken with high
standards. Müller-Thurgau and Silvaner
are the two main grapes with only 2%
Riesling. Good as the wines are, 80% is
consumed locally.

Winzergenossenschaft Sommerach
Zum Katzenkopf 1, 8711 Sommerach/
Main. The oldest cooperative cellar in
Franken, established in 1901 in the
'Kingdom of Bavaria', as it was then
called. 250 members supply grapes from
420 acres in villages from a wide area
surrounding the town of Volkach.
Amongst the best known of the 16
Einzellagen are the Iphöfer Kalb,
Escherndorfer Lump, and Volkacher
Ratsherr, but the largest holdings are at
Sommerach (Rosenberg and
Katzenkopf) covering 102 hectares. 45%
of the vineyards are planted with
Müller-Thurgau, 25% with Silvaner and
13% with Bacchus. No exports.

Winzergenossenschaft Thüngersheim
Untere Hauptstrasse 1, 8702
Thüngersheim. 364 members. 553 acres.
Einzellagen: Thüngersheimer–
Johannisberg and Scharlachberg;
Retzbacher Benediktusberg;
Veitshöchheimer Sonnenschein;
Erlabrunner Weinsteig; Himmelstadter
Kelter; Rück–Jesuitenberg and Schalk;
Karlstadter Rosstal (Grosslage);
Leinacher; Himmelberg. The major
cooperative of the scattered wine
villages of the lower Main. More than
half of its vines are Müller-Thurgau.
Silvaner, Scheurebe, Kerner and
Bacchus are also important, and some
red wine is also produced. Many of the
wines win medals. Only 6% exported.

WÜRTTEMBERG

The old principalities of Baden and Württemberg
are united as a state, but remain separate as wine
regions. Baden is much the bigger producer of the
two, but Württemberg would say that it was the
better. What is certainly true is that Württemberg
cannot even satisfy its own demand. The hardwork-
ing, productive Württembergers are also some of
Germany's great wine drinkers, and they prefer
Württemberg wine. As a result it is scarcely ever

exported and the best bottles (which are expensive)
almost never.

The land-locked regions of Germany only take
on comprehensible shapes as they are encompassed
and traversed by rivers. The river Neckar is almost a
Mosel in Württemberg, ambling through the hills
and fed by tributaries that provide the essential
south slopes for vineyards. Württemberg, like the
Mosel, concentrates on Riesling for its fine white

wines. But its real speciality is red and rosé made of its own indigenous grape the Trollinger, and to a lesser extent the Lemberger (or Limberger), the Portugieser, the Schwarzriesling (the Pinot Meunier in French, with the German alias of Müllerrebe), and the Spätburgunder (Pinot Noir). Red plantings make up half the total; if the red is not fully red it is mixed with white wine to make Schillerwein – a true local speciality. A pale pink rosé, Weissherbst, is also made. This must be made from a single grape variety, usually either Spätburgunder or Portugieser.

Bereich Remstal-Stuttgart
Four thousand acres of vines are divided into five Grosslagen. Hohenneuffen is the uppermost of the river, round Neuffen, Frickenhausen and Metzingen. There is no Riesling here but light Silvaner, Müller-Thurgau and (for red) largely Schwarzriesling.

Weinsteige is the Grosslage of Stuttgart, a city where the appearance of vineyards in its midst (or at least in its suburbs Bad Cannstatt, Mühlhausen and Zuffenhausen) is particularly surprising. The vines here are mainly Trollinger and Riesling, the best-known Einzellagen Berg, Steinhalde and Zuckerle, and in Fellbach, facing west over the Neckar towards Stuttgart, Wetzstein, Goldberg, Lämmler (entirely red wine) and Hinterer Berg.
Growers Weingut Graf Adelmann. Weingärtnergenossenschaft Bad Cannstatt. Weingärtnergenossenschaft Felbach. Württembergische Hofkammer-Kellerei.

The valley of the Rems (Remstal) has three Grosslagen: Kopf centred round Schörndorf, with a good deal of Trollinger but also some fair sites for Riesling; Wartbühl round Weinstadt and Korb, with Riesling and other white grapes in the majority; and Sonnenbühl south of Weinstadt and the Rems, which specializes in robust Trollinger.

Bereich Württembergisch Unterland
Much the biggest area, with 24,200 acres of Württemberg's vines. The Bereich, with nine Grosslagen, spreads across the Neckar valley north of Stuttgart from Baden to the Bottwar valley in the east.

Grosslage Schalkstein
The first Grosslage, following the Neckar north, stretches from Ludwigsburg to Hessigheim, the wine centre, with red grapes in the majority, their best wines well-coloured and full-bodied.
Grower Felsengärtenkellerei, Besigheim.

Grosslage Stromberg
A widely dispersed collection of Einzellagen along the tributary Enz valley to the west, with Mühlhausen and Vaihingen as centres, stretching down the Neckar valley to Kirchheim and Bönnigheim. Two thirds are red vines, with considerable Lemberger.
Grower Stromberg Kellerei, Bönnigheim.

Grosslage Heuchelberg
A more intensive viniferous district just north of Stromberg to the west of the Neckar. The centres are Cleebronn and Schwaigem, responsible for some of the area's best Rieslings from lime-rich soil.
Grower Graf von Neipperg.

As in Baden, the great majority of the production is by the cooperatives, with only a handful of relatively modest private estates. But even the cooperatives cannot simplify the complexity of a region with five Bereichs and 16 Grosslagen. The best way to understand it is to follow the northwards flow of the Neckar. On the analogy of the Mosel picture, the huge car-factory city of Stuttgart is its Trier. Here and along the tributary Rems, flowing in from the east like the Ruwer to the Mosel, are the first and some of the best Württemberg vineyards, the Bereich Remstal-Stuttgart.

Grosslage Kirchenweinberg
This is the real kernel of Württemberg's wine region. It includes the huge 1,140-acre Katzenbeisser at Lauffen. Talheim and Flein, on the outskirts of Heilbronn, are its other centres. Schwarzriesling is the most popular grape in a predominantly red-wine area.
Growers Bentzel-Sturmfeder. Felsengärtenkellerei, Besigheim. Staatliche Lehr-und Versuchsanstalt Weinsberg.

Grosslage Wunnenstein
A limited district east of the Neckar, including the town of Grossbottwar, mainly dedicated to red grapes.
Grower Weingut Graf Adelmann.

Grosslage Schozachtal
A small area just north of Wunnenstein, around Abstatt and Untergruppenbach. White wines are in the majority. Some good Riesling is grown here.

Grosslage Salzberg
An important area east of Heilbronn, noted for some of Württemberg's best Rieslings. The 12 Einzellagen are spread between Eberstadt, Lehrensteinsfeld, Willsbach, Affaltrach, Eichelberg, Obersulm and Löwenstein.
Growers Schlosskellerei Affaltrach. Weingärtnergenossenschafts Eberstadt, Lehrensteinsfeld and Mittleres Weinsberger.

Grosslage Lindelberg
A more scattered region of mainly white wine, northeast of Heilbronn round the Brettach valley between Bretzfeld and Untersteinbach.

Grosslage Staufenberg
Heilbronn is an important wine centre with a first-class cooperative. Its vineyards and those of the Neckar downstream are in the Grosslage Staufenberg, which has Einzellagen divided almost equally between white grapes and red. The main centres are Gundelsheim, Erlenbach, Weinsberg and Heilbronn itself.
Growers Genossenshaftskellerei Heibronn-Erlenbach-Weinsberg. Staatliche Lehr-und Versuchsanstalt Weinsberg.

Bereich Kocher-Jagst-Tauber
The northern Württemberg Bereich is much the smallest, with 1,000 acres, and the only one to specialise (90%) in white wine. It straddles the valleys of the Kocher and Jagst, Neckar tributaries from the east, and the Tauber.

Grosslage Kocherberg
The southern half of the Bereich includes Ingelfingen and Niedernhall on the Kocher.
Grower Weingärtnergenossenschaft Niedernhall.

Grosslage Tauberberg

The isolated Tauber valley vineyards are centred on Bad Mergentheim, Weikersheim and Niederstetten. Both the limy soil and the use of Silvaner and Müller-Thurgau recall the fact that Franken is not far away.
Grower Fürstlich Hohenlohe Lagenburg.

WÜRTTEMBERG PRODUCERS

Weingut Graf Adelmann, 'Brüssele'

Burg Schaubeck, 7141 Steinheim-Kleinbottwar. Owner: Count Michael Adelmann. A 37-acre estate: 30 acres in Kleinbottwar (Einzellagen Oberer Berg and Süssmund, solely owned); 7 in Hoheneck.

One of the best-known estates in Württemberg, instantly recognized by its pale-blue 'lacey' label with the name 'Brüssele' (after a former owner). Burg Schaubeck is a small but towering and venerable stronghold, apparently with Roman origins, owned by the Adelmanns since 1914. The vines are 48% red: 22% Trollinger, also Samtrot, Limberger, Muskat-Trollinger; 52% white: 27% Riesling, also Traminer, Ruländer, Müller-Thurgau, Kerner, Muskateller and Silvaner.

Kleinbottwar is red marl, Hoheneck limestone; both are sloping sites.

The wines are originals, with distinct characters and yet notable delicacy that makes them sometimes almost timid. Acidity tends to be low but flavours dry and complex (90% is *trocken*): the estate is now aiming for higher acidity in its white wines. Specialities include Weissherbst and red wine from Muskat-Trollinger – a table grape elsewhere, making slightly raisiny wine; Samtrot (a Pinot Meunier mutation); a mature Auslese (which reminded

me of Valpolicella); Muskateller, delicate and long despite its obvious spicy character; and a soft, low-key, smoky but elegant Riesling. The quality is as high as the wines are unusual.

Weingüter und Schlosskellerei Graf von Neipperg

7103 Schwaigern. Owner: Count Karl-Eugen zu Neipperg. 77 acres. Einzellagen: Schwaigerner Ruthe; Neipperger Schlossberg; Klingenberger Schlossberg.

Documents prove the family to have been making wine here since 1248, shortly after the building of Burg Neipperg, the original castle. There is now a Weinstube in Schloss Schwaigern over the cellars. Vines are 59% red: 23% Limberger, 17% Schwarzriesling (Pinot Meunier), 11% Spätburgunder, 8% Trollinger; the whites are 26% Riesling, 2% Traminer, 5% Muskateller and 8% Müller-Thurgau. The Neippergs introduced the Limberger (or Lemberger) to make red wine of colour and tannin; their other speciality is spicy Traminer, although their Riesling is highly thought of. 97% of the wines are *trocken*. Count Neipperg is also the owner of properties in St-Emilion: Châteaux Canon-La-Gaffelière and La Mondotte.

Staatliche Lehr-und Versuchsanstalt für Wein- und Obstbau Weinsberg

Traubenplaz 5, 7102 Weinsberg. Director: Dr. Gerhard Götz. 140 acres. Einzellagen: Abstatter Burg Wildeck (solely owned); Weinsberger–Ranzenberg and Schemelsberg (solely owned); Talheimer Schlossberg; Gundelsheimer Himmelreich; Lauda–Altenberg and Kirchberg; Lauffener Katzenbeisser.

The largest wine estate in Württemberg and the oldest wine school in Germany (founded in 1866). Rebuilt in the mid-1980s, and there are plans for a new cellar to be built by 1992. Experimentation and development form a major part of its work.

Of the circa 109 acres in production, about 23% is Riesling, 17% Müller-Thurgau, 14% Kerner, 9% Spätburgunder, 8% Limberger (or Lemberger). A wide variety is in areas of more than 5 acres. Methods are very modern and hygienic, aiming at maximum aroma by excluding air and avoiding sulphur. The wines are generally dry and full-bodied and the reds (especially Limberger) a good colour. Visits and tastings (by arrangement) are encouraged; both the vineyards and the wine are a great advertisement for Württemberg.

Württembergische Hofkammer-Kellerei

7140 Ludwigsburg, Schloss Monrepos. Owner: Carl, Herzog von Württemberg. 103.7 acres in 7 scattered areas at Eilfingerberg (42 acres), Steinbachhof (35 acres), Stuttgart–Untertürkheim, Stetten, Asperg, Hohenhaslach and Mundelsheim.

Almost half the vines are Riesling, with smaller parcels of Trollinger, Limberger, etc. The grapes are pressed locally and the must brought to the medieval ducal cellars in Ludwigsburg for fermentation in oak casks. The wines are classically made and the estate is generally considered to be the flagship of Württemberg wines.

Control panel at a giant South German cooperative

Schlosskellerei Affaltrach

7104 Obersulm. Owner: Thomas Baumann. 24.7 acres. Einzellagen: Affaltracher Dieblesberg planted with a wide variety of red and white grapes. Originally a 13th-century foundation, bought by the present owners in 1928 and now consisting of a small estate and an associated company buying grapes from some 200 small growers to make wine and Sekt. The estate wines are dry, intended for use at table and made to improve in bottle when possible. Eisweins and Trockenbeerenausleses with some of the highest must weights in the country are produced here.

Gräf von Bentzel-Sturmfeder-Horneck'sches

7129 Ilsfeld-Schozach. Owner: Count Benedikt von Bentzel-Sturmfeder-Horneck. 43.5 acres. Einzellage: Schozacher Roter Berg. An estate with 14th-century origins and 18th-century cellars. The vineyards are 32% Riesling, 22% Spätburgunder, 18% Samtrot (a Pinot Meunier mutation), 10% Schwarzriesling (Pinot Meunier) etc., on

clay slopes which give body to the wines. The wines last well, even when the acidity is relatively low, with barrel-ageing giving them stability. Noble rot is a rare occurrence; most of the wines are dry, much appreciated in local restaurants.

Weingut Burg Hornberg

6951 Neckarzimmern. Owner: Baron Hans-Wolf von Gemmingen-Hornberg. 36 acres. Einzellagen: Burg Hornberger–Götzhalde and Walmauer. An ancient steep vineyard site owned by this family since the 17th century, with 35% Riesling, 15% Spätburgunder, 12% Weisburgunder, 10% Silvaner and some Muskateller, Gewürztraminer and Ruländer. The wines are made by traditional methods to extract the maximum from the warm site; the best are full-bodied and impressive. A restaurant provides a chance to taste a wide range.

Fürstlich Hohenlohe Langenburg'sche Weingüter

6992 Weikersheim im Schloss. Director: Karl-Heinz Schäfer. 64 acres.

Einzellagen: Weikersheimer–Karlsberg (42 acres solely owned) and Schmecker (57); Tauberrettersheimer Königin (which is over the Württemberg border in Franken, 7). The ancient cellars of Schloss Weikersheim are used for very modern wine-making. The limestone vineyards give light, aromatic wines with a certain 'bodenton' or *gout de terroir*. This is the transition from Württemberg to Franken. Vines are 30% Müller-Thurgau, 17% Riesling, 15% Kerner, 10% Silvaner, etc.

Fürst zu Hohenlohe-Öhringen'sche Schlosskellerei

7110 Ohringen, Schloss. Owner: Prince Kraft zu Hohenlohe-Öhringen. 54 acres. Einzellage: Verrenberger Verrenberg (solely owned). A princely estate since the 14th century, with 17th-century cellars (and even a cask dated 1702). The Verrenberg is unusual in being one sweep of vines, producing almost uniformly dry whites, which they claim contain less than 2 grams/litre of sugar. The vines are 60% Riesling, 2% Limberger, 10% Spätburgunder and 7% Kerner.

BADEN

Baden is the new force in German wine – at present only domestically, but soon no doubt on the world stage. Its vineyards have undergone no less than a revolution in recent years: they have been almost entirely rationalized and remodelled by Flurbereinigung, have doubled in size and now lie fourth in yield in Germany, behind Rheinpfalz, Rheinhessen and the Mosel-Saar-Ruwer.

Baden faces Alsace across the Rhine. It is Germany's warmest (although not necessarily its sunniest) wine region, with correspondingly ripe, high-alcohol and lower in acid wines: the diametric opposite of Mosels in style and function. The best Mosel wines are for analytical sipping. Baden makes mealtime wines with a warm vinosity that approaches the French style. It is the choice of grape varieties and the taste for a trace of sweetness that distinguishes them from Alsace wines. The difference is reinforced by a slightly less favourable climate than the suntrap of the Vosges foothills.

Eighty per cent of Baden's vineyards lie in an 80-mile strip running from northeast to southwest, from Baden Baden to Basel, in the foothills of the Black Forest where it meets the Rhine valley. The balance is of purely local importance. The vineyards lie southeast on the banks of the Bodensee (alias Lake Constance), north of Baden in the minor

regions of the Kraichgau and Badischer Bergstrasse, respectively south and north of Heidelberg (but now united in one Bereich with both names), and far north on the border of Franken, a little region known logically enough as Bereich Badlisches Frankenland. The main thrust of Baden viticulture is thus along the Rhine from where it leaves the Bodensee to where it enters Rheinpfalz.

Baden is, even more than the southern Rheinpfalz, the land of the cooperative. More than 100 cooperatives process nearly 90 per cent of the crop, and half of all their output finds its way to the huge Badischer Winzerkeller central cellars in Breisach on the Rhine. The cooperative, formerly called the ZBW (they've dropped the 'Zentrale') bottles some 400–500 different types of wine. Baden has no powerful preference for one grape variety. The Müller-Thurgau is the workhorse, with more than one third of the acreage. Spätburgunder for red and light rosé (Weissherbst) comes second with one fifth. Then come Ruländer (Pinot Gris), Gutedel (Chasselas), Riesling, Silvaner, Weissburgunder and Gewürztraminer. Baden's taste is clearly not for the highly aromatic new varieties: the vast majority of its white wine is made of relatively 'neutral' grapes. Its best, however, is made of Riesling and Ruländer.

The Kaiserstuhl

Bereich Bodensee

The Bodensee and the Rhine which flows from its western end marks the German-Swiss border. The lake (Germany's biggest) counteracts the considerable altitude (about 1,500 feet above sea level) to produce a mild climate in which Spätburgunder and Müller-Thurgau both give refreshing, lightly fruity wines. The whites are often *spritzig*, the Spätburgunder either pale red or (its most attractive form) made into Weissherbst, the often very lively pale rosé which is the true local speciality. The region has less than 800 acres and only one Grosslage name: Sonnenufer. The main centres are on or near the lake shore: Bermatingen, Birnau, Kirchberg and Meersburg. Hagnau on the lake and the Erzingen farther down the Rhine also have cooperatives.
Growers Schloss Salem. Staatsweingut Meersburg.

Bereich Markgräflerland

Markgräflerland is the unexciting orchard corner of Germany between Basel and Freiburg, a district with its own taste in wine, marvellous cakes and very passable distillations of its abundant fruit. Its favourite grape is the Gutedel, the local name for what the Swiss call Fendant and the French Chasselas – in all cases a mild, not to say neutral wine maker, yet somehow very agreeable in its innocent freshness, dry and often *spritzig*. A cross between Gutedel and Silvaner called Nobling shows real promise, with surprising aroma and finesse. Otherwise the predominant grapes are Müller-Thurgau (here pleasantly aromatic) and Spätburgunder – often made as Weissherbst.

The Bereich is divided into three Grosslagen, listed here from south to north (down the Rhine).

Grosslage Vogtei Rötteln

Efringen-Kirchen is the seat of the considerable cooperative, which uses most of the Einzellage names contained in the Grosslage. Weil am Rhein is another centre.
Grower Bezirks-Kellerei 'Markgräflerland'.

Grosslage Burg Neuenfels

Auggen, Bad Bellingen, Badenweiler, Müllheim. Laufen and Schliengen are centres of this hillier district.
Growers Fritz Blankenhorn. Freiburger Jesuitenschloss. Schlumberger. Erste Markgrafler Winzergenossenschaft.

Grosslage Lorettoberg

This Grosslage includes the southern outskirts of the lovely city of Freiburg. Its centres include Bad Krozingen, Ebringen, Pfaffenweiler and Ehrenkirchen.
Growers Freiburger Jesuitenschloss. Winzergenossenschaft Pfaffenweiler.

Bereich Kaiserstuhl

Northwest of Freiburg the Rhine is briefly diverted from its northward course by a volcanic outcrop from the plain, an advance guard for the Black Forest hills ranged along the eastern skyline. There are two lumps, the modest Tuniberg on the doorstep of Freiburg, then the dignified flat-topped hill of the Kaiserstuhl – 'the King's Seat'. Breisach, seat of the great central cooperative, is the Rhine port and bridge-town to France. This is the climax of the Baden wineland, with a quarter of all its vines and a good share of its best wine concentrated on its volcanic slopes.

The Kaiserstuhl slopes have been the subject of a spectacular relandscaping to convert them into modern vineyards. The whole broad hill now has a distinctly man-made look. One third of the whole district is planted with Müller-Thurgau, then follow Spätburgunder and Ruländer. The latter performs exceptionally well on these iron-rich volcanic slopes. In its dry, crisp form Rülander is called Grauburgunder.

Much of the Spätburgunder is made into Weissherbst but the warmest vineyards, notably in Ihringen, Achkarren, Bickensohl and Oberrotweil on the south of the Kaiserstuhl, take pride in their red wines. Some of the best sites are also planted with Silvaner to good effect.

Growers In Grosslage Vulkanfelsen: Freiherr von Gleichenstein. Badischer Winzerkeller.

Bereich Tuniberg

A smaller repetition of the Bereich Kaiserstuhl, rising out of the Rhein plain south of Breisach. Practically all the crop is processed by the Badische Winzerkeller. The vine varieties are the same as those grown in Kaiserstuhl but the slightly cooler and wetter climate makes the wines less alcoholic.

Bereich Briesgau

Breisgau is the name for the backdrop of Black Forest foothills running north from Freiburg almost to Offenburg. It has three Grosslagen: Schutterlindenberg for its northern section centred on Lahr; Burg Lichteneck running south to Emmendingen; and Burg Zähringen for the hills just north of Freiburg. The best known Eizellage is the steep little 15-acre Roter Bur in Glottertal, planted with 75% Spätburgunder to produce a particularly lively Weissherbst.

Growers In Grosslage Schutterlindenberg: Gräflich Wolff-Metternich. In Grosslage Burg Lichteneck: Freiburger Jesuitenschloss.

Bereich Ortenau

The Black Forest foothills continue north from Offenburg to Baden-Baden, the mixture of vineyard and forest with old villages and feudal castles producing unforgettable pictures. There are two Grosslagen: Fürsteneck for the southern half of the Ortenau; Schloss Rodeck for the northern. Durbach, near Offenburg, is the most distinguished of its villages by reason of its lordly ownership and the Riesling (here called Klingelberger) and of its steep sand and granite slopes. Durbach has all or part of 10 of the 12 Einzellagen contained in the Grosslage Fürsteneck, Ortenberg has four and Oberkirch most of the 765-acre Einzellage Renchtäler.

The best-known Einzellagen in Schloss Rodeck are Yburgberg and Stich den Buben at Steinbach near Baden-Baden, Mauerberg at Neuweier in the same hills, farther south the Alde Gott at Sasbachwalden, Hex vom Dasenstein at Kappelrodeck and Pfarrberg at Waldulm.

Ortenau is Spätburgunder country. From somewhere in its heart comes a large supply of a popular light red called Affenthaler, distinguished only by the moulded figure of a monkey clutching the bottle. Much its best wines are its Klingelbergers and Ruländers, with some respectable Gewürztraminer and adequate Müller-Thurgau.

Growers In Grosslage Fürsteneck: Markgräflich Badis'ches Weingut. Freiburger Jesuitenschloss. Andreas Mannle. Freiherr von Neveu. Gräflich Wolff-Metternich.

Bereich Badische Bergstrasse/Kraichgau

The northernmost section of the Baden vineyards of the Rhine is so diffuse that its union in one Bereich looks like a measure of desperation. The Kraichgau is the area south of Heidelberg between the Rhine and the converging River Neckar, flowing northwest from Heilbronn in Württemberg. The Badische Bergstrasse is a southern extension of the Hessische Bergstrasse, a narrow ridge of vineyards running north–south and straddling the university city of Heidelberg.

The Kraichgau boasts three Grosslagen: Hohenberg in the south around Pforzheim, Stiftsberg to the east and Mannaberg in the northwest (and including the southern villages of the Bergstrasse: the chief of these is Wiesloch). The northern Bergstrasse has its own Grosslage: Rittersberg. Its principal town is called, simply, Weinheim.

The whole Bereich has some 4,900 acres of vineyard. 40% of its vines are Müller-Thurgau, only 10% are red; the exceptional sites, such as they are, are planted with Riesling (20%) and Ruländer (13%).

Growers In Grosslage Stiftsberg: Freiherrlich von Göler. Reichsgraf & Marquis zu Hoensbroech.

Bereich Badisches Frankenland

But for political boundaries this remote outpost of Baden wine-growing would be attached to its natural ally, Franken. It produces wines in the Franken style, mainly from Müller-Thurgau, and bottles them in Franconian flagons. The whole area, with some 1,700 acres of vines, is one Grosslage, Tauberklinge, and its centres are the towns of Lauda, Tauberbischofsheim and Wertheim on the Main.

Landwein

This new (1982) category of German table wine was introduced as a response to the success of French *vins de pays* – as standard drinking but of some local character, with more style and flavour than the totally anonymous Tafelwein. 15 acres with new names but roughly corresponding to the well-known basic regions of Germany have the right to christen a Landwein if the wine in question meets certain simple requirements. The alcohol content, for example, must be 0.5% higher than that of Tafelwein. An important regulation is that the sugar content should not be more than 18 grams a litre (the upper limit for the *halbtrocken* or halfway category). Landwein is therefore intended as a relatively dry and briskly acidic wine suitable for mealtimes

The 15 Landwein areas are as follows:
Ahrtaler Landwein Ahr
Starkenburger Landwein Hessiche Bergstrasse
Rheinburgen-Landwein Mittelrhein
Landwein der Mosel Mosel and Ruwer
Landwein der Saar Saar
Nahegauer Landwein Nahe
Altrheingauer Landwein Rheingau
Rheinischer Landwein Rheinhessen
Pfälzer Landwein Rheinpfalz
Fränkischer Landwein Franken
Regensburger Landwein a minuscule area on the Danube.
Bayerischer Bodensee-Landwein a small area near Lindau on Lake Constance (Bodensee), which in QbA terms is part of Württemberg, although politically it belongs to Bavaria.
Schwäbischer Landwein Württemberg
Unterbadischer Landwein northern part of Baden.
Südbadischer Landwein southern part of Baden.

BADEN PRODUCERS

Badischer Winzerkeller eG
Zum Kaiserstuhl 6, 7814 Breisach.
Directors: Manfred J. Weber, Armin Göring and Heinz Trogus.

The mammoth central cooperative of Baden, uniting no less than 100 local cooperatives at one of the largest and most modern plants in Europe at Breisach on the Rhine. The vineyards are scattered all over Baden's seven Bereiche – from Badisches Frankenland by the River Main to the banks of the Bodensee in the south – and they amount to 9,139 acres. Altogether some 8,900 growers are involved. The vines are 42% Müller-Thurgau, 30% Spätburgunder, 13% Ruländer, 4.5% Weissburgunder, 3% Gutedel and 2% each of Gewürztraminer and Riesling. Each vintage some 400–600 different wines are produced under 50 different Einzellage and Grosslage names, with their grape varieties and qualities. Over 4 million cases are exported annually, and distribution is country-wide. Exports are mainly to the UK, USA, the Benelux countries and Scandinavia. It is impossible to generalize about the output of this great organization more than to say that its wines are well-made and true to type and class across the whole spectrum.

Weingut Fritz Blankenhorn KG
7846 Schliengen. Owner: Klaus Blankenhorn. 41 acres. Einzellagen: Schlienger Sonnenstück; Mauchener Sonnenstück; Müllheim; Reggenhag; Badenweiler Römerberg; Auggener Schäf. Grosslage: Burg Neuenfels.

A well-known producer of the light, juicy Gutedel and typical dry red of the region. Vines are 30% Gutedel, 10% Riesling, 10% Spätburgunder, 10% Weissburgunder and 10% Grauburgunder.

Staatliches Weinbauinstitut
Merzhauserstrasse 119, 7800 Freiburg. Owner: the State of Baden-Württemberg. Director: Dr. Günter Staudt. 104 acres. Einzellagen: Freiburger–Schlossberg, Jesuitenschloss (22); Müllheimer Reggenhag (4); Blankenshornberger Doktorgarten (62); Hecklinger Schlossberg (7.5); Durbacher Steinberg (6, solely owned).

The institute of the state of Baden-Württemberg, founded in 1920 and including the 19th-century estate of the Blankenhorn brothers at Ihringen, known as Balankenhornsberg (q.v.), the most considerable on the Kaiserstuhl. The vineyards are planted with a variety of vines, including Traminer (often known as Clevner in Baden's Bereich Ortenau, and labelled as such at the institute). The wines are made with exemplary care.

Staatliches Weinbauinstitut Freiburg Blankenhornsberg
7817 Ihringen. Director: Erich Meinke. 86.5 acres. Einzellage: Blankenhornsberg Doktorgarten (solely owned).

See Freiburger Jesuitenschloss for ownership. The outstanding Kaiserstuhl estate, on steep volcanic slopes, planted with 21% Spätburgunder, 16% Riesling, 15% Müller-Thurgau, 10% Weissburgunder, 9% Ruländer and 29% other varieties. Up to 87% of the wines are normally made dry, but with powerful acidity and flavours. 1976 was an exception, an *annus mirabilis* for sweet wines.

Staatsweingut Meersburg
Seminarstrasse 6, 7758 Meersburg. Director: Helmut Häussermann. 146 acres. Einzellagen: Meersburger–Lerchenberg, Bengel, Sängerhalde, Jungfernstieg, Rieschen, Chorherrenhalde and Fohrenberg; Hohentwiel bei singener Olgaberg; Gailingen am Hochrheiner Ritterhalde. Grosslage: Sonnenufer

Formerly the estate of the Prince-Bishops of Meersburg. In 1802 it became Germany's first state domain, largely in Meersburg on the banks of the Bodensee (Lake Constance). The vineyards at Hohentwiel bei Singen are 530m above sea level – the highest in Germany. In 1956 frosts destroyed the vineyards and total reconstitution brought them up to date in varieties and methods. The vines are 47% Spätburgunder, 34% Müller-Thurgau, 5% Weissburgunder, 4% Ruländer and Grauburgunder, 3% each of Traminer and Riesling, 4% other varieties. More red varieties are to be planted. The specialities are Müller-Thurgau of the gentler kind and pinky-gold *spritzig* Spätburgunder.

Markgräflich Badis'ches Weingut, Schloss Staufenberg
7601 Durbach. Owner: H.M. Max, Margrave of Baden. 67 acres, Durbacher Schloss Staufenberg (which belongs exclusively to the Weingut).

A homely old manor on a hill with skirting vineyards, 45% Riesling (alias Klingelberger), 25% Spätburgunder, 15% Müller-Thurgau, 8.3% Traminer (alias Clevner), some Ruländer, Weissburgunder and Scheurebe. A place of great charm, with delicate and distinguished Rieslings. Two thirds of the wines are dry; one third medium-sweet. The Margrave also owns Schloss Salem (q.v.), and Schloss Eberstein-Murgtal (28 acres), whose Spätburgunder is made at Schloss Staufenberg.

OTHER PRODUCERS

Weingut Freiherr von Gleichenstein
Bahnhofstrasse 12, 7818 Oberrotweil. Owner: Hans Joachim von Gleichenstein. Einzellagen: Oberrotweiler–Eichberg, Henkenberg and Käsleberg; Amolterner Steinhalde. Grosslage: Vulkanfelsen. The vines are 25% Müller-Thurgau, 35% Spätburgunder, 20% Weissburgunder, 10% Grauburgunder, 5% Riesling and the rest are Silvaner, Traminer, Muskateller, Nobling and Findling. Estate founded in the 17th century, in even older buildings, making

conservative wines, 95% dry, the reds fermented on the skins, tannic, dry and full of character. Dry Weissherbst Spätlese, pale but full of flavour, is the speciality of the house.

Weingut Albert Heitlinger
Am Mühlberg, 7524 Oestringen-Tiefenbach. Owner: Erhard Heitlinger. 59.3 acres. Einzellagen: Tiefenbacher–Schellenbrunnen and Spiegelberg; Ubstadter Weinhecke. A relatively new estate with vineyards run along ecological lines. Vines are planted 46% Riesling, 17% Spätburgunder and 13%

Müller-Thurgau. Additional varieties include Weissburgunder, Grauburgunder, Silvaner and Dornfelder. Most Kabinett wines are enriched and sold as QbA. 80% of production is dry. Wines are mainly sold to private customers and restaurants.

Weingut Reichsgraf & Marquis zu Hoensbroech
6921 Angelbachtal-Michelfeld. Owner: Rüdiger, Reichsgraf und Marquis zu Hoensbroech. 42 acres. Einzellagen: Michelfelder Himmelberg and Sonnenberg; Eichelberger Kapellenberg.

Grosslage: Stiftsberg. A small lordly estate of the Kraichgau, south of Heidelberg in north Baden. Powerful dry wines are made of Weissburgunder (35%), Riesling (25%) and Silvaner (20%): also Spätburgunder, Grauburgunder, Gewürztraminer, Rivaner and Blauer Limberger. Dry Kabinett wines constitute the main produce.

Weingut Andreas Männle
Heimbach 12, 7601 Durbach. Director: Alfred Männle. 18.2 acres. Einzellage: Durbacher Bienengarten. The vines are 34% Spätburgunder, 30% Riesling, 12% each of Müller-Thurgau and Clevner (Traminer), 4% Weisburgunder and 2% each of Grauburgunder, Scheurebe, Kerner and Gewürztraminer. On the face of it a simple guesthouse wine farmer, but a specialist in fine sweet wines with some remarkable successes including extraordinary Weissherbst Eiswein. 70% of the wines are dry. The sweet reds are a very German taste.

Weingut Freiherr von Neveu
7601 Durbach. Owner: Heinrich, Freiherr von Neveu. 37 acres. Einzellagen: Durbacher–Josephsberg (solely owned) and Ölberg; Ortenberger Schlossberg. A neighbour of Schloss Staufenberg with similarly stylish wines, perhaps more full-blooded with good acidity. 44% Riesling, 18% Müller-Thurgau, 18% Spätburgunder, 14% Clevner. The wines are made and matured at the estate but bottled and distributed by Badischer Winzerkeller, the cooperative at Breisach.

Weinbauversuchsgut Schloss Ortenberg des Ortenaukreises
Burgweg 19a, 7601 Ortenberg. Director: Herbert Dresel. 18.5 acres. Einzellage: Ortenberger Schlossberg. Established in 1950 on former castle land, with a modern cellar and exemplary standards. 21% Riesling, 19% Müller-Thurgau, 15% Spätburgunder and several other varieties. The best wines are 'Klingelbergers' (Riesling), whether 'slim' and refreshing or splendidly ripe and sweet.

St. Andreas Hospital Fonds Weingut der Stadt Offenburg
Steingrube 7, 7601 Ortenberg. Director: Alfons Decker. 74 acres. Einzellagen: Ortenberger Andreasberg; Offenburger Spitalhalde; Fessenbacher Bergle; Zell-Weierbacher Abtsberg. A medieval almshouse taken over by the town of Offenburg in 1936 as an inn. 36% Müller-Thurgau, 17% Riesling, 17% Spätburgunder, 6.6% Kerner, 5% Gewürztraminer and Traminer, 4.3% Scheurebe, 2.1% Muskateller, 1.6% Ruländer, 1.5% Weissburgunder and about 5% others. Its standard drinking

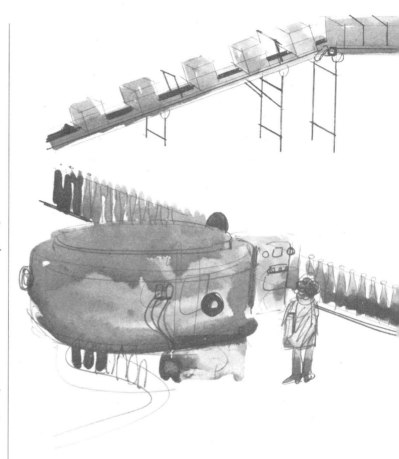

is principally Müller-Thurgau; Riesling Kabinetts are the speciality, as are the Beerenauslesen.

Schloss Salem
7777 Salem. Owner: Max, Markgraf von Baden. Holdings in three estates: Birnau, Schloss Kirchberg and Bermatingen, all specializing in Müller-Thurgau and Spätburgunder Weissherbst. Schloss Salem is the Bodensee residence of the Margrave of Baden and the modern cellar of the widespread estate. *See* also Markgräflich Badis'ches Weingut, Schloss Staufenberg.

Weingut Hartmut Schlumberger
Weinstrasse 19, Laufen, 7811 Sulzburg. Owner: Hartmut Schlumberger. 18.5 acres. Einzellage: Laufener Altenberg. Grosslage: Burg Neuenfels. An old family manor between Freiburg and Basel in the heart of the Markgräflerland, planted with 40% Gutedel, 25% Spätburgunder, 12% Weissburgunder, 10% Müller-Thurgau and 13% other varieties. The wines, generally dry and refreshing, are 'made with love and developed in wood'.

Weingut Rudolf Stigler
Bachenstrasse 29, 7817 Ihringen.

Owner: Rudolf Stigler. 12 acres. Einzellagen: Ihringer Winklerberg (11.8 acres) and Oberrotweiler Eichberg. One of the best private estates in Baden, known particularly for its Rieslings from the most famous Einzellage in Kaiserstuhl. Besides Riesling (35%), Spätburgunder (21%), Silvaner and Müller-Thurgau (both 11%), Traminer, Weissburgunder, and Ruländer are also grown. The style is concentrated, full, mainly dry, and most impressive.

Weingut Schwarzer Adler
Badbergstrasse 23, 7818 Vogtsburg-Oberbergen. Owner: Franz Keller. 35 acres. Einzellagen: Jechtingener Eichert; Oberbergener-Bassgeige and Pulverbuck; Oberrotweiler-Eichberg and Kirchberg. For many years Franz Keller has been a strong opponent of Süssreserve; all his wines are allowed to ferment to dryness or come to a natural halt. His ideas on wine-making appear to be more French than German; the 'Schwarzer Adler' restaurant, one of the best in Baden, with its magnificent list of French wines, bears witness to this. *Barrique*-ageing has also been a feature for some years, with a number of wines being sold (at a very high price) as

Tafelwein. Viticulture and wine-making are 'green'. The vineyards are planted with 25% Müller-Thurgau, 25% each of Spätburgunder and Grauburgunder, 15% Weissburgunder, plus others.

Gräflich Wolff-Metternich'sches Weingut

7601 Durbach. Owner: Count Paul Josef Wolff-Metternich. A 68-acre hillside estate in Durbach and Lahr, of ancient origin, particularly proud of its late harvest and aromatic wines. 32% Riesling, 23% Spätburgunder, 17% Weissburgunder and Grauburgunder, 15% Müller-Thurgau, 9% Traminer and Gewürztraminer and 4% other varieties.

Cooperative Bezirkskellerei 'Markgräflerland'

Winzerstrasse 2, 7859 Efringen-Kirchen. 708 members in 27 villages. Einzellagen: Hornfelsen, Schlipf, Sonnhohle, Weingarten, Kapellenberg, Wolfer, Kirchberg, Ölberg, Steingässle. Grosslage: Vogtei Rötteln. Vines are 52% Gutedel, 26% Müller-Thurgau, 12% Spätburgunder. The major coop of the region, exporting significant quantities of its typical light dry wine.

The bottling hall at the Baden cooperative's cellar at Breisach, which handles the wines of 25,000 Baden growers

ITALY

In sheer quantity of wine made, Italy now regularly surpasses even France as the vine's own country. Every one of her 20 regions is in the wine business to a greater or lesser extent. Her geography, essentially a mountain range reaching south and east from the Alps towards the subtropics, offers as wide a range of vine-worthy sites and microclimates as nature has devised in any country.

It should come as no surprise that some of the world's best wines come from Italy. And yet it does. During the two and a half centuries when France was building the formidable structure and reputation of her quality-wine industry, and selecting and propagating her superlative vines, Italy was doing no such thing. Wine, like loyalty,

remained very much a local, even a family, affair. Like bread, it was no less important for being taken for granted. But it was not measured even by national, let alone international, standards until well into this century. And when it was, Italy was inevitably judged simply as a source of low-priced wine, either for cheap and cheerful drinking or to be passed off as something else. To this day an almost incredible quantity, about half Italy's total wine exports, slinks anonymously out of the country in tankers to other parts of the E.E.C. — principally to France. High-quality wine depends entirely on demand, and nobody demanded it in Italy. It is still, to their own loss, the practice of many foreign wine merchants to list a token handful of the best-known Italian names rather than to investigate at first hand what Italy offers.

In the merchants' defence it must be said that the Italians seem to rejoice in giving their wines complicated labels. Access to them for non-Italians, even the most interested, is often blocked by a lilting litany of tuneful polysyllables in which not just the name of the wine and its maker but that of his property, and often an additional fantasy name for good measure all appear equally important. In writing tasting-notes on Italian wines it often takes me as long to identify them in my notebook as to taste and judge them.

Recent years have seen some dramatic changes in attitude and practice. The best wine makers are increasingly experimenting with untraditional ideas, grape varieties and techniques. They are offering distinctive wines with designer labels at high-fashion prices (which are not always justified by their quality). This producer-led revolution circumvents, or even ignores, the rules enshrined in the DOC system described below.

A new development at official level could prove equally important. New blood in the bureaucracy promises an end to the scandal of deliberate wine surpluses; grapes grown to be distilled into unwanted industrial alcohol. More DOC wine is promised, with revisions of the law to move towards the French 'pyramid' concept of regional appellations, with smaller, higher-quality, zones within them. Those DOCs which are virtually unused may be revoked. *Vini Tipici* – a new concept akin to *Vins de Pays* – may emerge as a new kind of quality wine at the good-value level. Single vineyards may be officially recognized with DOCs.

All these are plans, not yet implemented. And Italy's wine laws are awash with past good intentions. But such proposals are the best blueprint yet for necessary change.

The method of access to the essentials in the following pages tries to make the problems of identifying and judging Italy's wines as simple as possible. This is how it works.

The country is divided into 20 regions. Each is treated separately, in two parts: first the names and descriptions of the wines, then a wide selection of the better and bigger wine makers, with brief accounts of their standing, methods, size and a list of the wines they offer. If you know the name of the wine or the maker but not the region, the only place to start is the index. If you know the region, go straight to the wine or the maker. Cross-referencing goes from maker to wine but not (to avoid endless repetitive list) the other way round. The only list of producers, for example, of Chianti Classico is the list of wine

makers in Tuscany, in which you will find that many Chianti makers also make other wines.

On the face of it, there is a radical division between officially controlled ('DOC') wines and others. The DOC (*Denominazione di Origine Controllata*) was instituted in 1963 as the very necessary regulatory system for Italian quality wines – an approximate equivalent to the French AOC. At present between 10 and 12 per cent of the country's total crop is thus regulated, depending on the harvest.

A DOC is a very detailed legal stipulation as to the precise character, origin, grapes, crop levels, strength, methods and ageing of a particular wine or group of wines agreed between the consortium of its producers and an expert committee in Rome. Since 1966, when the first DOC decree was signed by the President, more than 230 have been declared. A summary of the DOC regulations for each of them is given in the following pages. It states the colour(s) of the wine(s), the province(s) within the region, the principal village(s) or a summary of the zone, the permitted grape varieties and their proportions, the maximum yield, the minimum alcohol level, the total annual production and any regulations concerning ageing – for example, when it may be sold as a *riserva*. The maximum crop is expressed in this book in hectolitres per hectare to make it comparable with those of other countries, although the DOC regulations stipulate both the number of quintals (100 kilograms) of grapes that may be picked and also what percentage of that weight may be processed into wine – the idea being to control the maker's urge to press every last drop out of his grapes. These listings do not include the stilted official descriptions of the style of the wine or the technical data on acidity, 'extract' and the rest.

In addition, an equal number of wines are listed that are not DOC and have no official delimitation. It is the great paradox of Italian wine today that a DOC freezes a type of wine in a historical moment. A DOC is essentially the definition of a tradition – at the very moment when wine technology has reached a pitch undreamed of before, when California (the outstanding example) is using its freedom to experiment to produce more exciting wine every year.

Not surprisingly, Italy's best wine makers are as eager to try new ideas as anyone. They therefore either ignore DOC regulations or add to their traditional wares unconsecrated products representing their aspirations for the future. However good these are – and they include almost all the great new wines of Italy – they must suffer the indignity of being officially classed as *vino da tavola* – table wine – the basic E.E.C. category for the blended wine of every day.

A potentially useful new compromise is signalled by a new unofficial classification of wines from the hills of central Tuscany, which has been pioneered by a few leading producers, led by Ambrogio Folonari of Ruffino. The category of Predicato (*see* Tuscany p.334) would not qualify under DOC regulations, but it is an attempt to bring the most definable of the new-style wines into line for official recognition. The reader of this book, therefore, should make no absolute distinction between DOC and other wines beyond the fact that a DOC is 'traditional' and subject to official regulation.

A further step in the regulation of certain DOCs has been instigated with an additional category: DOCG. The G stands for *Garantita*; the inference being that such wines are officially guaranteed as Italy's best. The first four DOCGs were Barbaresco, Barolo, Brunello di Montalcino and Vino Nobile di Montepulciano. Albana di Romagna was the next to be added to the list. Anyone who tastes it may be forgiven for asking how seriously the 'G' is to be taken. The latest candidates, Carmignano and Torgiano, go a long way to restoring faith.

It is scarcely possible to summarize the state of Italian wine-making at present. Enormous recent investments in modern equipment and new ideas have already produced some wonderful results, but on the other hand some have stripped old friends of their character. So far the modern movement has succeeded in making both the most boring and the most brilliant of Italian wines. There is a balance to be found between tradition and technology (in grapes, in cellaring, in every aspect of wine-making). As the following pages show, Italy is very busy looking for it.

PIEDMONT

For uninhibited exploration of the varieties of grape juice and what can be made of them, no part of Europe can compare with Piedmont. The vermouth of Turin witnesses that a good brew-up is part of local tradition. For ingredients the hills of Piedmont offer such an assortment of indigenous grapes that the accepted international varieties have scarcely been planted at all. Each of the local grapes is a character with something to offer. Each is made into wine unblended, often in several styles, and also mixed with others in brews which may be traditional or experimental, conventional or idiosyncratic. The former are frequently blessed with DOCs and DOCGs, the latter not – but this has no bearing on their respective qualities.

The emphasis is all on red wine. Only one Piedmont white has any history of other than local success before the last decade – and that is Asti Spumante. The Cortese is a good white grape now proving itself, but the catechism of important Piedmont wines must start with a list of the red grapes that enjoy the harsh climate of this subalpine area.

Nebbiolo comes first in quality. It takes its name from the fog (*nebbia*) that characterizes autumn here, not only closing Milan airport but creating quintessentially mellow fruitful pictures of gold-leaved vines tilting up to the grey hilltop villages.

The 1,600-foot Langhe hills south of the town of Alba on the river Tanaro provide the slopes, shelter, soil, sunshine and humidity that bring Nebbiolo to perfection in Barolo (southwest of Alba) and Barbaresco (to its east). The style of Barolo, a wine of the maximum concentration, tannin and alcohol, has no very ancient history. But it has conviction, and its growers' palates are ready for as much power as their vines will give them. The inexperienced, the timid and the claret lovers should start with Nebbiolo in its less explosive manifestations.

Barbera comes first in quantity. But it too, unlike the common grapes of the south of France, carries conviction. It can be clumsy, but good Barbera is plummy and astringent in just the right measure.

Dolcetto is quite different. No other red grape succeeds in conveying such an impression of softness while being sometimes startlingly dry. It sounds odd, but with rich food it makes a tantalizing meal opener. Dolcetto is not normally for ageing.

In complete contrast Freisa is inclined to be sweet and fizzy, and again in contrast Grignolino tends to the pale, mild but teasingly bitter style of wine which is common in northeast Italy. Add the lively light Bonarda and the Croatina and Vespolina and the range of possible cocktails is almost limitless.

The following list reflects the complexity of the region with more DOCs and DOCGs than any other – and lots of unofficial 'table' wines besides.

Would that there were space for more than a low bow towards the best fare of Italy; the truffles, the fonduta, the game and all the simple but sensuous things that give these wines their proper context.

The 14th-century castle of Cavour houses the Piedmont wine institute.

DOC AND OTHER WINES

Arengo

Made of excess Barbera and other red grapes, this wine was conceived by 18 producers acting in concert.

Barbaresco

DOCG. Red wine. Province: Cuneo. Villages: Barbaresco, Neive, Treiso, part of Alba. Grape: Nebbiolo. Max. crop: 56 hl/ha. Min. alch: 12.5°. Aged for a minimum of 2 years, of which 1 is in wood, 3 years for *riserva*. Annual production: 220,000 cases.

The immediate neighbour of Barolo, sharing most of its qualities of power and depth, youthful harshness and eventual perfumed sweetness. Great Barbaresco has a style and polish it is hard to define; it is tempting, though inaccurate, to call it the Côte Rôtie to the Hermitage of Barolo. Neither lives as long or develops so sumptuously as the best Rhône wines; but recent bottlings (particularly the wines from Gaja's special vineyards) have added new superlatives to Italy's wine vocabulary: the most luxurious, the most vigorous, silky, incisive and memorable.

Barbera d'Alba

DOC. Red wine. Province: Cuneo. Villages: many around Alba. Grape: Barbera. Max. crop: 70 hl/ha. Min. alch: 12° (12.5° for *superiore*). Aged for 1 year in oak for *superiore*. Annual production: 440,000 cases.

Barbera wines are ubiquitous in Piedmont, but the best of them fall into one of three DOCs. Alba is considered the best area for full-bodied Barbera apt for ageing – though the style is entirely at the producer's discretion.

Barbera d'Asti

DOC. Red wine. Provinces: Asti and Alessandria. Villages: from Casale Monferrato to Acqui Terme. Grape: Barbera. Max. crop: 63 hl/ha. Min. Alch: 12° (12.5° for *superiore*). Aged

1 year for *superiore* in oak or chestnut barrels. Annual production: 1.3m cases.

Critics disagree on whether this or Alba gives the best Barbera. This may be expected to be less of a 'character', with less bite. Many prefer it so.

Barbera del Monferrato

DOC. Red wine. Provinces: Alessandria and Asti. Villages: a large part of the above provinces. Grapes: Barbera 85–90%, Freisa, Grignolino and Dolcetto 10–15%. Max. crop: 70 hl/ha. Min. Alch: 12°. *Superiore* is aged for 2 years. Annual production: 910,000 cases.

The optional addition of other grapes allows this to be the most frivolous of the DOC Barberas – though none of them demands to be taken too seriously.

Barengo

Red and white table wine from Barengo in the Novara hills. The red is comparable to Boca and Faro (qq.v); the white, of Greco grapes, can be dry or sweet.

Barolo

DOCG. Red wine. Province: Cuneo. Villages: Barolo, Castiglione Falletto, Serralunga d'Alba, part of Cherasco, Diano d'Alba, Grinzane Cavour, La Morra, Monforte d'Alba, Novello, Roddi, Verduno. Grape: Nebbiolo. Max. crop: 56 hl/ha. Min. alch: 13°. Aged in wood for at least 2 years (and in bottle for 1), 5 years for *riserva*. Annual production: 500,000 cases.

If Barolo gives the palate a wrestling match it makes its eventual yielding all the more satisfying. It takes practice to understand this powerful and astringent wine. For several years all flavour and most smell are masked and inaccessible. What is hidden is an extraordinary spectrum of scents (tar, truffles, violets, faded roses, incense, plums, raspberries have all been found).

Notes on a 1974 in 1981 show how slow the process can be: 'Still a deep blackish plum colour, smelling harsh and indistinct. Strong and hard to taste, full of glow but ill-defined. More study reveals sweetness and fruit flavours, if not depth; sweetness and a genial roast-chestnut warmth grow with acquaintance (and air). Still no real development.' With such traditional Barolos maturity comes on quite suddenly at about 10 years and little is gained by keeping bottles beyond 15. The current trend, though, is for more generous, though by no means easy, wines whose softer tannins make them more accessible sooner without shortening – indeed probably adding to – their long-term potential.

The best vineyards are often signalled on the labels with the dialect words *sori* (a steep sheltered slope) or *bricco* (a ridge). La Morra makes the earliest developing wines, Monforte and Serralunga the slowest.

Barolo Chinato
Permitted under DOCG. A domestic tradition among Barolo growers is to brew apéritifs and cordials with their wine. This, the best-known 'Amaro', is made bitter with an infusion of *china* bark. Another recipe includes green walnuts, tansy, garlic, cloves and cinnamon.

Boca
DOC. Red wine. Province: Novara. Villages: Boca, Gattinara, part of Maggiora, Cavallirio, Prato Sesia, Grignasco. Grapes: Nebbiolo (Spanna) 45–70%, Vespolina 20–40%, Bonarda Novarese (Uva Rara) up to 20%. Max. crop: 63 hl/ha. Min. alch: 12°. Aged 3 years (2 in wood). Annual production: 3,300 cases.
One of several dry reds from the hills north of Novara where Nebbiolo is called Spanna. Blending with other grapes lightens this one.

Bonarda Piemontese
Bonarda is a light red grape mostly grown in north Piedmont for blending. It can be fresh and pleasant on its own.

Brachetto d'Acqui
DOC. Red wine. Provinces: Asti, Alessandria. Villages: Acqui Terme, Nizza Monferrato and 24 others. Grape: Brachetto; Aleatico, Moscato up to 10%. Max. crop: 56 hl/ha. Min. alch: 11.5°. Annual production: 19,000 cases.
A light sweet fizzy red with more than a touch of Muscat in the aroma. That made by Villa Banfi is a marvel; one of the best examples of Italian tradition up-dated for modern times.

Bramaterra
DOC. Red wine. Province: Vercelli. Villages: Massarano, Brusnengo, Cruino Roasio, Villa del Bosco, Sostegno and Lozzolo. Grapes: Nebbiolo (Spanna) 50–70%, Croatina 20–30%, Bonarda and/or Vespolina 10–20%. Max. crop: 49 hl/ha. Min. alch: 12°. Aged 2 years (18 months in wood); *riserva* 3 years (2 in wood). Annual production: 10,000 cases.
A 1979 DOC for a big solid blended red from the Vercelli hills, increasing in production and evidently improving with age. Sold in Bordeaux-style bottles.

Bricco del Drago
A Nebbiolo/Dolcetto blend from one grower near Alba.

Bricco Manzoni
A Nebbiolo/Barbera blend; the excellent invention of one grower at Monforte d'Alba.

Bricco dell'Uccellone
A single grower's highly successful interpretation of Barbera, aged in new oak casks.

Caramino
A Spanna (Nebbiolo) blend from Caramino in Fara (q.v.). Well worth ageing up to 10 years.

Carema
DOC. Red wine. Province: Torino. Village: Carema. Grape: Nebbiolo (here called Picutener, Pugnet or Spanna). Max. crop: 56 hl/ha. Min. alch: 12°. Aged 4 years, of which 2 are in barrel. Annual production: 9,000 cases.
A variety from the borders of Piedmont and Valle d'Aosta; a relatively lightweight Nebbiolo which can add in finesse what it loses in power. The terrain is steep and terraced, the high climate cool, and prices (especially in ski resorts) can be excessive.

Colli Tortonesi
DOC. Red and white wine. Province: Alessandria. Villages: Tortona and 29 others. Grapes: (red), Barbera 100%, or with up to 15% Freisa, Bonarda and Dolcetto; (white) Cortese. Max. crop: 63 hl/ha. Min. alch: 12° (red), 10.5° (white). Red aged 2 years (1 in oak or chestnut barrels) for *superiore*. Annual production: 145,000 cases.
A good-quality Barbera blend with ageing potential, and a very light dry Cortese white tending to sharpness and sometimes fizzy.

Cortese dell'Alto Monferrato
DOC. White wine. Provinces: Asti and Alessandria. Villages: A large part of the above provinces. Grapes: Cortese 85%, other secondary white grapes – not aromatic ones – 15%. Max. crop: 70 hl/ha. Min. alch: 10°. Annual production: 100,000 cases.
An increasingly popular DOC for dry Cortese white, still or sparkling, at a humbler level than that of Gavi (q.v.).

Dolcetto d'Acqui
DOC. Red wine. Province: Alessandria (vinification is also permitted in Asti). Villages: Acqui Terme and 24 others. Grape: Dolcetto. Max. crop: 56 hl/ha. Min. alch: 11.5°. Aged 1 year for *superiore*. Annual production: 89,000 cases.
Dolcetto from here can be expected to be light everyday red of good colour and certain character.

Dolcetto d'Alba
DOC. Red wine. Province: Cuneo. Villages: Alba, Barolo, Barbaresco, La Morra and 30 others. Grape: Dolcetto. Max. crop: 63 hl/ha. Min. alch: 11.5°. Aged 1 year for *superiore*. Annual production: 533,000 cases.
Generally considered the best DOC of Dolcetto, partly because the most skilful growers are concentrated here. The style varies from the traditional soft but dust-dry to something more fruity and refreshing. In most cases youth is a virtue.

Dolcetto d'Asti
DOC. Red wine. Province: Asti. Villages: Calamandrana, Canelli, Nizza Monferrato and 21 others. Grape: Dolcetto. Max. crop: 56 hl/ha. Min. alch: 11.5°. Aged 1 year for *superiore*. Annual production: 66,600 cases.
Less widely seen but not consistently different from Dolcetto d'Acqui.

Dolcetto delle Langhe Monregalesi

DOC. Red wine. Province: Cuneo (vinification is also permitted in Imperia and Savona). Villages: Briaglia, Castellio Tanaro, Igliano, Marsaglia, Neilla Tanaro, part of Carru, Mondovi, Murazzano, Piozzo, S. Michele Mondovi and Vicoforte. Grape: Dolcetto. Max. crop: 49 hl/ha. Min. alch: 11°. Aged 1 year for *superiore*. Annual production: 2,200 cases.
A rarely used DOC established in 1974 for a lightweight Dolcetto said to have more aroma than most.

Dolcetto di Diano d'Alba

DOC. Red wine. Province: Cuneo. Village: Diano d'Alba. Grape: Dolcetto. Max. crop: 56 hl/ha. Min. alch: 12°. Aged 1 year for *superiore*. Annual production: 66,600 cases.
A premium Dolcetto, generally stronger, 'thicker' and less brisk than Dolcetto d'Alba.

Dolcetto di Dogliani

DOC. Red wine. Province: Cuneo. Villages: Bastia, Belvedere, Langhe, Clavesana, Ciglie, Dogliani, Farigliano, Monchiero, Rocca de Ciglie and part of Roddino and Somano. Grape: Dolcetto. Max. crop: 56 hl/ha. Min. alch: 11.5°. Aged 1 year for *superiore*. Annual production: 134,000 cases.
Possibly the original Dolcetto; often a good one with more 'grip' (or less soft) than some.

Dolcetto di Ovada

DOC. Red wine. Province: Alessandria (vinification is also permitted in Asti, Cuneo, Torino, Genoa and Savona). Villages: Ovada and 21 others. Grape: Dolcetto. Max. crop: 66 hl/ha. Min. alch: 11.5°. Aged 1 year for *superiore*. Annual production: 189,000 cases.
The best producers in this DOC make very lively wine, as fruity to smell as every Dolcetto and capable of developing in bottle like good Cru Beaujolais.

Erbaluce di Caluso, Caluso

DOC. White wine. Provinces: Torino and Vercelli. Villages: Caluso and 35 others. Grapes: Erbaluce; *passito* with up to 5% Bonarda. Max. crop: 84 hl/ha. Min. alch: 11°; 13° for *passito*. *Passito* is aged at least 5 years.
This is the northern Piedmont equivalent of the Ligurian Cinqueterre and Sciacchetrà: a pleasant dry white with a tendency to sharpness and a sweet *passito* made by half-drying the same grapes. The *passito* is sometimes boosted with alcohol and then called *liquoroso*.

Fara

DOC. Red wine. Province: Novara. Villages: Fara and Briona. Grapes: Nebbiolo (Spanna) 30–50%, Vespolina 10–30% and Bonarda Novarese (Uva Rara) up to 40%. Max. crop: 77 hl/ha. Min. alch: 12°. Aged 3 years with 2 in barrel. Annual production: 10,000 cases.
Fara, Boca and their neighbour Sizzano, similar reds of the same quality, were all early applicants for DOCs, recognized in 1969 (Boca and Sizzano) and 1976 (Fara) but still limited in production.

Favorita

This white, dry wine grown in the Roeri and Langhe hills has recently made a comeback. Best drunk young. DOC requested.

Freisa d'Asti

DOC. Red wine. Province: Asti. Area: the hills of Asti. Grape: Freisa. Max. crop: 56 hl/ha. Min. alch: 11°. Aged 1 year for *superiore*. Annual production: 56,000 cases.
A cheerful fruity sharpish red, sometimes sweet and often fizzy. It can be immensely appetizing, though the non-DOC Freisa d'Alba is often better made.

Freisa di Chieri

DOC. Red wine. Province: Torino. Villages: Chieri and 11 others. Grape: Freisa. Max. crop: 56 hl/ha. Min. alch: 12°. Aged 1 year for *superiore*. Annual production: 5,600 cases.
Chieri on the outskirts of Turin specializes in the sweeter style of Freisa, often fizzy, which makes good café wine.

Gabiano

DOC. Red wine. Province: Alessandria. Villages: Gabiano and Montecestino. Grapes: Barbera 90–95%, Freisa and/or Grignolino 5–10%. Max. crop: 56 hl/ha. Min. alch: 12°. (12.5° for *riserva*). *Riserva* aged 2 years. Annual production: 2,200 cases.
From the Gabiano village in the Monferrato Casalese hills north of Asti. A very long-lived Barbera.

Gattinara

DOC. Red wine. Province: Vercelli. Village: Gattinara. Grapes: Nebbiolo (Spanna) with up to 10% Bonarda. Max. crop: 63 hl/ha. Min. alch: 12°. Aged 4 years (2 in wood). Annual production: 44,000 cases.
The best-known Spanna (Nebbiolo) of the hills north of Novara, a quite separate enclave from Barolo and the Langhe with a broader, juicier, less austere style of wine. Few if any Gattinaras reach top Barolo standards, but they are both impressive and easy to like. The area is restricted. Prestige consequently often exceeds quality.

Gavi or Cortese di Gavi

DOC. White wine. Province: Alessandria. Villages: Gavi, Carrosio, Bosio, Parodi S. Cristoforo. Grape: Cortese. Max. crop: 70 hl/ha. Min. alch: 10.5°. Annual production: 445,000 cases.
A recent international star, DOC'd in 1974 and led to distinction by the La Scolca estate under the name Gavi di Gavi. It does not quite reach the standards of mingled acidity and richness that say 'white burgundy'; several taste castrated by too-cold fermentation. But this area can grow this grape superbly well.

Ghemme

DOC. Red wine. Province: Novara. Villages: Ghemme and part of Romagnano Sesia. Grapes: Nebbiolo (Spanna) 65–85%, Vespolina 10–30%, Bonarda Novarese (Uva Rara) up to 15%. Max. crop: 70 hl/ha. Min. alch: 12°. Aged 4 years with 3 in barrel. Annual production: 16,700 cases.
A very similar wine to Gattinara, generally reckoned slightly inferior, though some (like me) may prefer the rather finer, less hearty style. The best bottles at 5 or 6 years incline towards a claret-like texture.

Grignolino d'Asti

DOC. Red wine. Province: Asti. Villages: 35 communes in Asti. Grapes: Grignolino 100%, or with up to 10% Freisa. Max. crop: 52 hl/ha. Min. alch: 11°. Annual production: 156,000 cases.
Good Grignolino is refreshing and lively, slightly bitter, pale but not pallid.

Grignolino del Monferrato Casalese

DOC. Red wine. Province: Alessandria. Villages: 35 communes (in the Monferrato Casalese). Grapes: Grignolino 100%, or with up to 10% Freisa. Annual production: 100,000 cases. Max. crop: 45 hl/ha. Min. alch: 11°.

An additional Grignolino area to the north DOC'd a year after Grignolino d'Asti.

Lessona

DOC. Red wine. Province: Vercelli. Village: Lessona. Grapes: Nebbiolo (Spanna) and up to 25% Vespolina and Bonarda. Max. crop: 56 hl/ha. Min. alch: 12°. Aged 2 years with 1 in wood. Annual production: 3,300 cases.

This remarkably fine claret-weight Nebbiolo blend is scarce. 6 years is a good age for it.

Malvasia di Casorzo d'Asti

DOC. Red and *rosato* wine. Provinces: Asti and Alessandria. Vilages: Casorzo, Grazzano Badoglio, Altavilla Monferrato, Olivola, Ottiglio and Vignale Monferrato. Grapes: Malvasia Nera di Casorzo 100% or with up to 10% Freisa, Grignolino and Barbera. Max. crop: 77 hl/ha. Min. alch: 10.5°. Annual production: 14,400 cases.

A rare sweet sparkling light red (or *rosato*) for café work.

Malvasia di Castelnuovo Don Bosco

DOC. Red wine. Province: Asti. Villages: Castelnuovo Don Bosco, Albugnano Passerano, Marmorito, Pino d'Asti, Berzano and Moncucco. Grapes: Malvasia di Schierano 100%, or with up to 15% Freisa. Max. crop: 77 hl/ha. Min. alch: 10.5°. Annual production: 17,800 cases.

Similar to Malvasia di Casorzo d'Asti, either gently bubbly or fully sparkling.

Moscato d'Asti-Asti Spumante

DOC. White sparkling or still wine. Provinces: Asti, Cuneo and Alessandria. Villages throughout the communes. Grape: Moscato Bianco. Max. crop: 82.5 hl/ha. Min. alch: (Moscato) 10.5°; (Spumante) 12°. Annual production: 6m. cases.

Often effectively the base of Asti Spumante, but the regulations allow it to be slightly sweeter and lower in alcohol. Some of the best non-DOC Moscato comes from Strevi. Still or only slightly fizzy Moscato is often made with great pains to be swooningly aromatic, sweet and swallowable. It *must* be drunk as young as you can get it. Asti Spumante itself is one of Italy's true and inimitable classics: sweet, buxomly fruity but girlishly giggly with its scented froth. It is a major industry dominated by big names in the vermouth field, normally produced in tanks, rarely bottle-fermented, and hence moderate in price.

Möt Ziflon

A Nebbiolo/Bonarda/Vespolina blend. Lighter than most of its area in the Gattinara country, developing bouquet after 3–4 years.

Nebbiolo or Nebbiolo del Piemonte

An alternative title for any Nebbiolo wine. Not classified as DOC or DOCG. Ordinary to excellent wines.

Nebbiolo d'Alba

DOC. Red wine. Province: Cuneo. Villages: Alba and 16 others. Grape: Nebbiolo. Max. crop: 63 hl/ha. Min. alch: 12°. Annual production: 133,000 cases.

For those who can do without the stern majesty of Barolo but love the character of its grape this is the DOC to tie up in. 4 years is usually enough to develop a delicious bouquet of fruit ranging from plums to raspberries and, with luck, truffles.

Nebbiolo delle Langhe

Name used for *vino da tavola* by Barolo and Barbaresco for second selection wines, some good, some ordinary.

Pinot

Pinot Nero, Bianco and Grigio are all grown in parts of Piedmont. Fontanafredda (q.v.) makes a good dry white by blending them.

Roero-Arneis del Roero

DOC. Red and white wine. Province: Cuneo. Villages: 19 in the province of Cuneo. Grapes: (red) Nebbiolo 95–98%, Arneis 2–5%, and a max. of 3% of other grape varieties recommended for Cuneo; (white) Arneis. Red aged 18 months, white *superiore* 1 year. Max. crop: 56 hl/ha. Min. alch: 11.5°.

A new category for red from Nebbiolo but growers may still opt to produce Nebbiolo d'Alba or Roero. This zone makes attractive red wines, good young but sometimes capable of ageing beyond 5–6 years. The white is a dry table wine from the local Arneis grape grown in the Roeri hills north of Alba. Soft, richly textured and a bitter almond finish.

Rubino di Cantavenna

DOC. Red wine. Province: Alessandria. Villages: Gabiano, Moncestino, Villamiroglio, Cantavenna, Camino. Grapes:

Italy glossary

The keys to deciphering Italian labels and wine lists are given below. For grape names, see the notes in the colour section on Italian grape varieties on page 23. For DOC regulations see the introduction on pages 293.

Abboccato slightly sweet.
Amabile a little sweeter than *abboccato*.
Amaro bitter.
Annata the year of the vintage.
Asciutto totally dry.
Azienda (on a wine label) a wine estate.
Bianco white.
Botte cask or barrel.
Bottiglia bottle.
Cantina wine cellar.
Cantina sociale or *cooperativa* a growers' cooperative cellar.

Casa vinicola a wine firm, usually making wine from grapes it has not grown on its own estate.
Cascina northern term for a farm or estate.
Chiaretto 'claret' – meaning very light red or even rosé.
Classico the 'classic' heart of a DOC zone, by implication (and usually) the best part.
Consorzio a consortium of producers of a certain wine, who join forces to control and promote it.
Dolce fully sweet (technically, with between 5% and 10% residual sugar).
Enoteca 'wine library' – Italy has many establishments with wide national or regional reference collections of wine.
Etichetta label.
Fattoria Tuscan term for a farm or

wine estate.
Fiasco (plural *fiaschi*) flask; the traditional straw-cased Chianti bottle.
Frizzante slightly fizzy, but with much less pressure than sparkling wine.
Gradazione alcoolica (grad. alc.) alcoholic degree in % by volume.
Imbottigliato (or *messo in bottiglia*) *nel'origine* (or *del produttore all'origine*) estate bottled.
Liquoroso strong, often but not necessarily fortified, wine, whether sweet or not.
Marchio depositato registered brand.
Metodo tradizionale or *classico* the champagne method.
Nero black or very dark red.
Passito wine made from grapes half-dried to concentrate them; strong and usually sweet.

Barbera 75–90%, Grignolino and/or Freisa up to 25%. Max. crop: 70 hl/ha. Min. alch: 11.5°. Aged 1 year. Annual production: 4,500 cases.
A minor DOC for a respectable local dry red.

Ruchè de Castagnole Monferrato

DOC. Red wine. Province: Asti. Villages: Castagnole Monferrato, Grana, Montemagno, Portacomaro, Refrancore, Scurzolengo, Viarigi. Grapes: Ruchè; with up to 10% Barbera Brachetto. Max. crop: 63 hl/ha. Min. alch: 12°.
A rare red grape found only in the sub-Alps above Castagnole Monferrato where it makes a tannic wine that ages to something perfumed and fine. Also known as Ruchè, Rouchè or Rouchet.

Sizzano

DOC. Red wine. Province: Novara. Village: Sizzano. Grapes: Nebbiolo (Spanna) 40–60%, Vespolina 15–40%. Bonarda Novarese (Uva Rara) up to 25%. Max. crop: 70 hl/ha. Min. alch: 12°. Aged 3 years with 2 in barrel. Annual production: 4,500 cases.
Considered by many the best of the north Piedmont Spanna (Nebbiolo) blends, to be compared with Boca and Fara. Potentially a 10-year wine.

Spanna

The alias of the Nebbiolo grape in the Novara and Vercelli hills of north Piedmont, also used as a wine name for Gattinara-style wines.

Vinòt

The brand name of a pioneering Beaujolais-Nouveau style of instant red made of Nebbiolo with *macération carbonique* by Angelo Gaja.

PIEDMONT PRODUCERS

Elio Altare

La Morra, 12064 Cuneo.
DOC: Barolo Vigneto Arborina, Dolcetto La Pria. Other: Barbera, Nebbiolo. Despite the small size (12 acres) of this vineyard, the wines have made international impact.

Antichi Vigneti di Cantalupo

Ghemme, 28074 Novara.
Owners: Alberto and Maurizio Aulunno. DOC: Ghemme. Other: Agamium *vino da tavola*. One of northern Piedmont's best producers.

Antoniolo

Gattinara, 13045 Vercelli.
Owner: Rosanna Antoniolo. DOC: Gattinara. Other: Spanna. A leading name in Gattinara, if anything improved in recent years.

Villa Banfi

Strevi, 15019 Alessandria.
Founded: 1960. Piedmont branch holdings in Italy replaced V.B. Bruzzone winery whose president Giuseppina Viglierchio is still the administrator. Chief wine maker: Ezio Rivella. DOC: Asti Spumante, Brachetto d'Acqui, Dolcetto d'Acqui, Gavi. Other: Moscato di Strevi, Banfi Brut *champenoise*; Brut Pinot *charmat*. The Gavi Principessa Gavia is a particularly good example of a cold-fermentation modern white.

Produttori del Barbaresco

Barbaresco, 12050 Cuneo.
Italy's most admired cooperative, with 65 growers, revived in 1958 by the families that founded the original winery in 1894. Director: Celestino Vacca. DOCG: Barbaresco. A remarkable array of *cru* Barbarescos vinified from individual plots. Some 42,000 cases of Nebbiolo *vino da tavola* are also made.

Marchesi di Barolo

Barolo, 12060 Cuneo.
One of the larger Barolo houses, founded in 1861, formerly owned by Marchesa Giulia Falletti, whose family originated Barolo wine. Now a corporation. DOC: Asti Spumante, Barbaresco, Barbera d'Alba, Barolo, Cortese di Gavi, Dolcetto d'Alba, Freisa d'Asti, Nebbiolo d'Alba. The house owns 90 acres and buys from 400 more. Its collection of old vintages is probably unique.

Pastoso medium (not very) dry.
Podere a farm or wine estate.
Produttore producer.
Riserva, riserva speciale DOC wines that have been matured for a statutory number of years (the *speciale* is older). *See* DOC entries.
Rosato rosé.
Rosso red.
Secco dry.
Semisecco semi-dry (in reality, medium-sweet)
Spumante sparkling.
Stabilimento the company's premises.
Stravecchio very old (a term regulated under DOC rules, not permitted elsewhere).
Superiore superior in any one of a number of ways specifically designated by DOC rules. *See* DOC entries.

Tenementi or *tenuta* holding or estate.
Uva grape.
Vecchio old. *See* DOC entries for regulations.
Vendemmia the vintage, also used in place of *annata* on labels.
Vigna, vigneto vineyard.
Vignaiolo, viticoltore grape grower.
Vin or *vino santo* wine made from grapes dried indoors over winter.
Vino da arrosto 'wine for a roast' implying a red of full body and maturity – 'Sunday best'.
Vino cotto cooked (concentrated) wine.
Vino novello the wine of the current year, now used in the same sense as Beaujolais 'Nouveau'.
Vino da pasto everyday wine.
Vino da taglio blending or 'cutting' wine, of high degree and concentration.

Vino da tavola the regulation term for non-DOC Wines, the equivalent of French *vin de table* but not (such is the E.E.C.) of German *Tafelwein*.
Vite vine.
Vitigno grape variety.

Batasiolo
La Morra, 12060 Cuneo.

Winemaker: Mario Monchiero. Formerly Kiola and Fratelli Dogliani, this winery is rapidly improving using nearly 300 acres of some of the best vineyard potential in Barolo. DOC: Barolo, Moscato d'Asti. Other: Dolcetto, Chardonnay.

Bersano (Antica Podere Conti della Cremosina)
Nizza Monferrato, 14049 Asti.

Founded in 1896 by the Bersano family. The firm, bought by Seagrams in 1967, was recently resold. DOC: Barbaresco, Barbera d'Alba, Barolo, Cortese di Gavi, Dolcetto d'Alba, Moscato d'Asti, Oltrepò Pavese Pinot Spumante. A large firm, its 100,000 cases come from its own land and other grapes bought in DOC zones. Some vineyards have been bought by Zonin. The wine museum created by the late Arturo Bersano is open 5 days a week. Its new, Italian, ownership is intent on restoring its former glory.

Braida-Giacomo Bologna
Rocchetta Tanaro, 14030 Asti.

Owner: Giacomo Bologna. Oenologist: Giancarlo Scaglione. DOC: Brachetto d'Acqui, Grignolino d'Asti, Moscato d'Asti. Others: Bricco dell' Uccellone, Bricco della Bigotta. More than a talented wine maker, Bologna is a prominent figure in Italian wine. I must single out his Moscato as one of Italy's most ravishing throatfuls.

Caudrina-Dogliotti
Castiglione Tinella, 12053 Cuneo.

Owners: Redento and Romano Dogliotti. DOC: Dolcetto d'Alba, Moscato d'Asti. Other: Freisa. One of the best Moscato producers, with 35 acres.

Ceretto
Alba, 12051 Cuneo.

Founded: 1935. Owners: Bruno and Marcello Ceretto. DOC: Barbaresco, Barbera d'Alba, Barolo, Dolcetto d'Alba, Nebbiolo d'Alba. The Ceretto brothers have expanded the family firm to include model estate wineries of Bricco Asili in Barbaresco, Bricco Rocche in Barolo and the Blangé estate in the Roeri hills where they make stylish Arneis. They are also part owners of I Vignaioli di Santo Stefano (for Asti and Moscato d'Asti) and the new Cornarea estate.

Pio Cesare
Alba, 12051 Cuneo.

A pillar of tradition in the Alba area, founded in 1881 by Pio Cesare, great-grandfather of Pio Boffa, who has given the winery a modern touch. DOC: Barbaresco, Barbera d'Alba, Barolo, Dolcetto d'Alba, Gavi, Nebbiolo d'Alba. Other: Grignolino. Pio Cesare owns 20 acres in Barolo, 15 in Barbaresco and selects grapes from regular suppliers to make some of the best Piedmont wines.

Michele Chiarlo (Duca d'Asti)
Calamandrana, 14042 Asti.

Oenologist: Roberto Bezzato. DOC: Barbaresco, Barbera d'Asti, Barbera del Monferrato, Barolo, Gavi, Grignolino del Monferrato Casalese. Other: Nebbiolo-Barbera *vino da tavola*, Granduca Brut *champenoise*. The owner is currently developing key properties in Barolo and other zones. Prestige wines will carry the name of Michele Chiarlo, and others Duca d'Asti.

Francesco Cinzano
10121 Torino

Founded in the 18th century, Cinzano became a corporation in 1922. Chief wine maker: Ezio Mignone. DOC: Asti Spumante. Other: Cinzano Brut and Principe di Piemonte Blanc de Blancs *champenoise*. The renowned vermouth firm, with affiliated bottling plants in other countries, also produces sparkling wines, table wines, spirits and soft drinks. Cinzano controls the wine houses of Florio in Marsala and Col d'Orcia in Montalcino.

Tenute Cisa Asinara dei Marchesi di Gresy
Barbaresco, 12050 Cuneo.

Founded in the last century on the site of a Roman villa. Owner: Alberto di Gresy. Wine maker: Paolo Torchio. DOC: Barbaresco, Dolcetto d'Alba. Other: Nebbiolo della Martinenga. From 80 acres of the prized Martinenga and Palazzina vineyards, di Gresy makes big, angular Barbaresco, lighter Nebbiolo and austere Dolcetto.

Le Colline (Monsecco)
Gattinara, 13045 Vercelli.

Founded in the early 1950s by Don Ugo Ravizza, who formed a corporation in 1974. Now run by Bruno Cervi. DOC: Barbaresco, Gattinara, Ghemme, Moscato d'Asti. 45 acres in Gattinara, Ghemme and Treiso (for Barbaresco). The long-lived Monsecco demonstrates just how good Gattinara could be.

Aldo Conterno
Monforte d'Alba, 12065 Cuneo.

DOC: Barbera d'Alba, Barolo, Dolcetto d'Alba. Other: Freisa, Grignolino (Arneis and Chardonnay soon). Conterno's skills as grower and wine maker stem from 5 generations of forebears. He served in the US army before taking up the family tradition of making wine with passion and humour. His Dolcetto is soft, his Freisa brisk and his Barolo notably harmonious, despite its massive chassis of tannin.

Giacomo Conterno
Monforte d'Alba, 12065 Cuneo.

Founded: 1770. Owner: Giovanni Conterno. DOC: Barbera d'Alba, Barolo, Dolcetto d'Alba. Brother of Aldo (see above), Conterno is most noted for his Barolo Monfortino, chosen from the best vintages and aged 8 years in casks.

Giuseppe Contratto
Canelli, 14053 Asti.

Founded in 1867, the firm is headed by Alberto Contratto. Wine maker: Remo Cattaneo. DOC: Asti Spumante, Barbaresco, Barbera d'Asti, Barolo, Cortese dell'Alto Monferrato, Dolcetto d'Alba, Freisa d'Asti, Grignolino d'Asti, Nebbiolo d'Alba. Other: *méthode champenoise* sparkling wines. Though the firm makes still wines, some from family vineyards, it is most noted for champagne-method Asti Spumante, Brut Riserva, Reserve for England, Bacco d'Oro, Riserva Novecento and semi-sweet Imperial Riserva Sabauda.

Coppo
Canelli, 14053 Asti.

Owners: Fratelli Coppo. DOC: Asti Spumante, Barbera d'Asti, Gavi, Grignolino d'Asti. Other: Chardonnay, Brut Riserva *champenoise*. An established *spumante* house which is now earning new respect with its high quality DOC wines.

Luigi Einaudi
Dogliani, 12063 Cuneo.

Founded in 1907 by Luigi Einaudi, who later became president of Italy. Owners: Mario, Roberto and Giulio Einaudi. DOC: Barolo, Dolcetto di Dogliani. Other: Barbera, Nebbiolo. From 60 acres, reliable though unadventurous wine with emphasis on Dolcetto and traditional-style Barolo.

Luigi Ferrando
Ivrea, 10015 Torino.

Oenologist: Gaspare Buscemi. DOC: Carema, Erbaluce di Caluso. Other: Gamay-Pinot Nero della Valle d'Aosta; Nebbiolo. Quality Carema, bottled with a special black label for fine vintages (e.g. '82, '85); and small amounts of unclassified sweet wines, such as his *barrique*-aged Solativa, from 7.5 acres in the Caluso zone.

Fontanafredda (Tenimenti di Barolo e di Fontanafredda)
Serralunga d'Alba, 12050 Cuneo.

The most impressive wine estate of Piedmont, founded in 1878 by Conte Emanuele Guerrieri, son of King Victor Emmanuel II, and Contessa Rosa di Mirafiori; now owned by the Monte dei Paschi di Siena bank. Wine maker: Livio Testa. DOC: Asti Spumante, Barbaresco, Barbera d'Alba, Barolo, Dolcetto d'Alba. Other: Nebbiolo, Contessa Rosa and Gattinara Spumante *champenoise*, Noble Sec Spumante, Pinot Bianco. A major producer of Barolo and Asti. The winery has been perfecting production from 250 acres of estate and bought-in grapes. Admirable *vino da tavola* as well as DOC wines.

Gaja
Barbaresco, 12050 Cuneo.

Founded: 1859. Owner: Angelo Gaja. Barbaresco, Barbera d'Alba (Vignarey), Barolo, Dolcetto d'Alba (Vignabaja), Nebbiolo d'Alba (Vignaveja). Other: Nebbiolo del Piemonte, Vinòt. *See* below.

Fratelli Gancia
Canelli, 14053 Asti.

A family firm that pioneered the champagne method in Italy. Founded in 1850 by Carlo Gancia, now headed by Piero and Vittorio Vallarino Gancia. Wine makers: Giancarlo Scaglione and Giorgio Grai. DOC: Asti Spumante, Barolo, Oltrepò Pavese Pinot and Riesling della Rocca. Other: Gran Riserva Carlo Gancia Brut *champenoise*, Il Brut, Pinot di Pinot. Now also a producer of vermouth and spirits, Gancia remains a leader in sparkling wine with more than 1.5 m. cases a year. They have recently acquired vineyards in Piedmont and Apulia and are bottling wines under the Mirafiori brand and Barolo Chinato under Castello di Canelli.

Bruno Giacosa
Neive, 12057 Cuneo.

Founded: 1890. DOC: Barbaresco, Barbera d'Alba, Barolo, Dolcetto d'Alba, Grignolino d'Asti, Nebbiolo d'Alba. Other: Arneis, Freisa, Spumante, Brut *champenoise*. Bruno Giacosa is one of Piedmont's best wine makers, admired for powerful Alba reds that age with grace, and an excellent *champenoise* made from Chardonnay and Pinot Nero. He buys all the grapes he needs from his pick of well-sited vineyards.

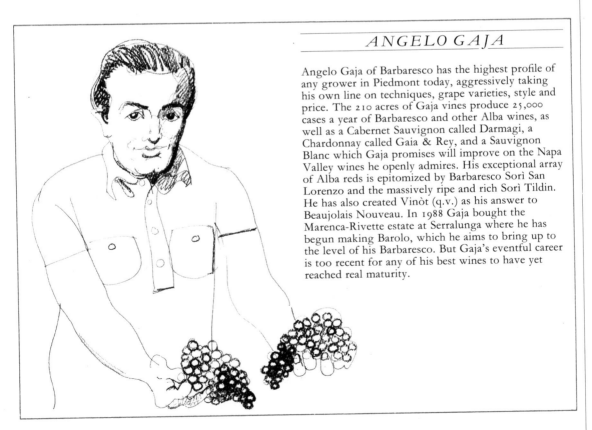

ANGELO GAJA

Angelo Gaja of Barbaresco has the highest profile of any grower in Piedmont today, aggressively taking his own line on techniques, grape varieties, style and price. The 210 acres of Gaja vines produce 25,000 cases a year of Barbaresco and other Alba wines, as well as a Cabernet Sauvignon called Darmagi, a Chardonnay called Gaia & Rey, and a Sauvignon Blanc which Gaja promises will improve on the Napa Valley wines he openly admires. His exceptional array of Alba reds is epitomized by Barbaresco Sorì San Lorenzo and the massively ripe and rich Sorì Tildin. He has also created Vinòt (q.v.) as his answer to Beaujolais Nouveau. In 1988 Gaja bought the Marenca-Rivette estate at Serralunga where he has begun making Barolo, which he aims to bring up to the level of his Barbaresco. But Gaja's eventful career is too recent for any of his best wines to have yet reached real maturity.

Marcarini-Cogno
La Morra, 12064 Cuneo.
Owners: Elvio Cogno and Anna Marcarini. DOC: Barolo, Dolcetto d'Alba. Despite its small size Elvio Cuneo's winery is a leading force in the area. The excellent Dolcetto, carrying his name, is made partly from the pre-phylloxera vines of Boschi di Berri; the luscious, Burgundy-like Barolo is labelled Marcarini after the vineyard owner.

Martini & Rossi
10125 Torino
Founded in 1863. Martini & Rossi IVLAS is now part of the international conglomerate General Beverage Corporation. Wine maker: Giovanni Cavagnero. DOC: Asti Spumante. Other: Riserva Montelera Brut *champenoise*. The world-famous (and world-leading) vermouth firm is a major producer (about 1.5m. cases) of sparkling wines.

Bartolo Mascarello
Barolo, 12060 Cuneo.
Founded in 1919 by Giulio Mascarello. The owner and wine maker is Bartolo Mascarello. DOC: Barolo, Dolcetto d'Alba. Other: Nebbiolo delle Langhe. A tiny Barolo maker, steadfastly relying on traditional methods to produce his remarkable, polished wines.

Giuseppe Mascarello & Figlio
Monchiero, 12060 Cuneo.
Founded 1881. Owner and wine maker: Mauro Mascarello. DOC: Barbaresco, Barbera d'Alba, Barolo, Dolcetto d'Alba, Nebbiolo d'Alba. The excellent Barolo Monprivato comes from a 6.8-acre family vineyard. Other grapes are bought from choice plots.

Monfalletto-Cordero Montezemolo
La Morra, 12064 Cuneo.
Owners: Giovanni and Enrico Cordero. DOC: Barolo, Dolcetto d'Alba. The sons of the founder are carrying on the family tradition, building consistently on their father's reputation. With a total of about 40 acres of their own vineyard, they produce in particular a fine Barolo, Enrico VI, made for relatively young drinking, without losing depth and intensity. The estate name became Monfalletto after the construction of new cellars there.

Produttori Nebbiolo di Carema
Carema, 10010 Torino.
DOC: Carema. An admirable small cooperative founded in 1959. Run by Luciano Clerin, with 45 members. Their best wine is the barrel-aged Carema Carema.

Castello di Neive
Neive, 12057 Cuneo.
Owner: Italo and Giulio Stupino. DOC: Barbaresco, Barbera d'Alba, Dolcetto d'Alba, Moscato d'Asti. Other: Arneis. Small winery first made famous in 1862 when French oenologist Louis Oudart won a gold medal for his Neive wine at the London Exposition. Still produces some of the best Barbaresco.

Luigi & Italo Nervi
Gattinara, 13045 Vercelli.
DOC: Gattinara. Other: Nebbiolo. House producing respectable wines, run by Giorgio Aliata. There are two good single-vineyard bottlings, Molsino and Valferana, from 52 acres in all.

Harvesting in Piedmont.

Alfredo Prunotto
Alba, 12051 Cuneo.
Founded in 1904 as a cooperative, acquired by Alfredo Prunotto in 1920 and then by oenologists Giuseppe Colla and Carlo Filiberti, who moved to a handsome new establishment on the edge of Alba. Controlling interest has now been acquired by Antinori-Whitbread. DOC: Barbaresco, Barbera d'Alba, Barolo, Dolcetto d'Alba, Nebbiolo d'Alba. Very careful traditional wine-making produces benchmark Alba wines: gentle, plummy Nebbiolo and complex Barolo are first class. All wines are bottle-aged for a year before sale.

Renato Ratti (Abbazia dell'Annunziata)
La Morra, 12064 Cuneo
Founded in 1962 in the cellars of the ancient abbey, which date from 1479. DOC: Barbaresco, Barbera d'Alba, Barolo, Dolcetto d'Alba, Nebbiolo d'Alba. The founder, the late Renato Ratti, was president of the consortium of Asti Spumante, member of the national DOC committee, author, lecturer and curator of the wine museum in the abbey. His sons and nephew continue to make beautifully clear and deep, typically astringent wines from 12 acres of own vineyard and grapes from committed friends. The family also owns the Villa Pattono near Asti.

Riccadonna
Canelli, 14053 Asti.
Founded in 1921, now headed by Ottavio Riccadonna. DOC: Asti Spumante. Other: President Brut Riserva Privata and President Extra Brut (both *champenoise*), President Reserve Crystal Extra Secco, President Reserve Rosé. The large vermouth and marsala firm also markets the Valfieri line of Piedmont and Alto Adige wines in which it now has a controlling interest.

Rocche di Manzoni
Monforte d'Alba, 12065 Cuneo.
Founded: 1974. Owner: Valentino Migliorini. DOC: Barbera d'Alba, Barolo, Dolcetto d'Alba. Other: Bricco Manzoni, Trabense, Valentino Brut *champenoise*. The innovative Migliorini and his oenologist, Sergio Galetti, make Alba reds from 114 acres, including his original and excellent Bricco Manzoni of Nebbiolo blended with Barbera and aged in *barriques*. His sparkling dry Trabense and Valentino Brut come from the Colli Piacentini and Oltrepò Pavese.

Luciano Sandrone
Barolo, 12060 Cuneo.
DOC: Barolo, Dolcetto d'Alba. The owner and his brother Luca produce slight quantities of top-ranked Barolo and admired Dolcetto from a tiny (3-acre) vineyard. They are planning to bring out a Barbera.

Antica Casa Vinicola Scarpa
Nizza Monferrato, 14049 Asti.
One of the outstanding Piedmont firms founded in the mid-19th century; now directed by Mario Pesce. DOC: Barbaresco, Barbera d'Asti, Barolo, Grignolino d'Asti, Nebbiolo d'Alba. Other: Brachetto, Dolcetto, Freisa, Rouchet. Scarpa's wines are all models of their genre, from Barolo to Barbera to his unique soft, rich red Rouchet or (a bargain) his smooth Nebbiolo. Mario Pesce also owns the Cascina Pesce estate nearby.

Paolo Scavino
Castiglione Falletto, 12060 Cuneo.
DOC: Barbera d'Alba, Barolo, Dolcetto d'Alba. An outstanding small grower. His Barolo Bric dël Flasc gets top ratings.

La Scolca
Rovereto di Gavi, 15066 Alessandria.
Owner: Giorgio Soldati. DOC: Gavi. Other: Pados Spumante *champenoise*. A 50-acre estate now run by the son of its founder, whose Gavi di Gavi made the world take the Cortese grape seriously. At best it has the body and balance of good white burgundy.

Sella
Lessona, 13060 Vercelli.
Founded: 1671. Owners: The Sella family. DOC: Bramaterra, Lessona. Others: Orbello, Piccone. The Lessona and Bramaterra estates (27 and 22 acres respectively) have recently combined into a single unit under the name Sella, managed by Fabrizio and family. The style of the Lessona wine is light, for quicker consumption; Piccone is its younger brother. Bramaterra is a medium-weight blended Nebbiolo, Orbello a lighter version. Altogether a much-admired enterprise.

Cascina La Spinetta-Rivetti
Castagnole Lanze, 14054 Asti.
Owners: The Rivetti family. DOC: Barbera d'Asti, Moscato d'Asti. The family makes a fine Barbera, and their Moscato is often considered the finest in the zone.

Castello di Tassarolo
Castello di Tassarolo, 15060 Alessandria.
Owner: Marchesi Spinola. Wine maker: Giancarlo Scaglione. DOC: Gavi. The first quality is smooth, soft and excellent. A second pressing (in Bordeaux bottles) was rougher but full of character.

Vietti
Castiglione Falletto, 12060 Cuneo.
Owner-wine maker: Alfredo Currado, son-in-law of founder Mario Vietti. DOC: Barbaresco, Barbera d'Alba, Barolo, Dolcetto d'Alba, Nebbiolo d'Alba. Other: Arneis, Freisa, Grignolino, Moscato. Currado has recently been joined by daughter Elisabetta and son-in-law Mario Cordero. Young wines are intensely vital and even fragrant; old vintages mellow and luxurious. For carefree zing their Freisa is hard to beat.

Roberto Voerzio
La Morra, 12064 Cuneo.
DOC: Barbaresco, Barbera d'Alba, Barolo, Dolcetto d'Alba, Nebbiolo d'Alba. Other: Arneis, Dolcetto, Freisa. Owner Roberto Voerzio has recently split from the family winery (now Gianni Voerzio, his brother) to open his own operation, which is rapidly on the rise.

OTHER PRODUCERS

Accademia Torregiorgi
Neive, 12057 Cuneo. Owner: Mario Giorgi. DOC: Barbaresco, Barolo, Barbera d'Alba, Dolcetto d'Alba.
Accomasso
La Morra, 12064 Cuneo. DOC: Barolo, Dolcetto d'Alba.
Vecchia Cantina Sociale di Alice Bel Colle
Alice Bel Colle, 15010 Alessandria. Cooperative. Director: Paolo Ricagno. A wide range of Acqui, Asti and Monferrato DOCs.
Azelia
Castiglione Falletto, 12060 Cuneo. Owners: Lorenzo and Alfonso Scavino. DOC: Barolo, Dolcetto d'Alba. 25 acres.
Baracco
Castellinaldo, 12050 Cuneo. DOC: Barbera d'Alba, Nebbiolo d'Alba.

Fratelli Barale
Barolo, 12060 Cuneo. Founded: 1870. DOC: Barbera d'Alba, Barolo, Dolcetto d'Alba. A respected name in Barolo.
Cascina La Barbatella
Nizza Monferrato, 14049 Asti. Owner: Angelo Sonvico. Barbera and Grignolo *vino da tavola*.
Terre del Barolo
Castiglione Falletto, 12060 Cuneo. A big cooperative with high standards. DOC: Barbera d'Alba, Barolo, Dolcetto d'Alba, Dolcetto di Diano d'Alba, Nebbiolo d'Alba. Members have holdings in some of Alba's best vineyards; the wines are reliable and often tasty.
La Battistina
Novi Ligure, 15067 Alessandria. DOC: Gavi. A relatively new estate with 54 acres of Cortese vines. A Gavi to watch:

already a prize winner.
Bava
Cocconato d'Asti, 14023 Asti. Owners: The Bava family. DOC: Barbera d'Asti, Freisa d'Asti, Barolo. Other: Malvasia di Castelnuovo Don Bosco.
Bera-Cascina Palazzo
Neviglie, 12050 Cuneo. Owners: Fratelli Bera. DOC: Barbera d'Alba, Dolcetto d'Alba; a rising star with Moscato d'Asti-Asti Spumante.
Nicola Bergaglio
Rovereto di Gavi, 15066 Alessandria. A widely admired maker of DOC Gavi.
A. Bertelli
Costigliole d'Asti, 14055 Asti. Owners: Fratelli Bertelli. DOC: Barbera d'Asti. Other: Traminer, barrel-fermented Chardonnay.
Bianco & Figlio
Barbaresco, 12050 Cuneo. Owner: L.

Bianco. DOC: Barbaresco, Barbera d'Alba, Dolcetto d'Alba.

Alfiero Boffa
San Marzano Oliveto, 12050 Asti. DOC: Barbera d'Asti. Emerging grower.

Carlo Boffa & Figli
Barbaresco, 12050 Cuneo. DOC: Barbaresco, Dolcetto d'Alba.

Vittorio Boratto
Piverone, 10010 Torino. DOC: Caluso Passito. Excellent, rare, expensive.

Giacomo Borgogno & Figli
Barolo, 12060 Cuneo. Owners: The Boschis family. DOC: Barbera d'Alba, Barolo, Dolcetto d'Alba. A major Barolo firm, also owning the small and prestigious house of E. Pira & Figli.

Serio & Battista Borgogno
Barolo, 12060 Cuneo. DOC: Barolo.

Bosca
Canelli, 14053 Asti. Founded: 1831. Owners: The Bosca family. DOC: Asti Spumante, Barbaresco, Barbera d'Asti, Barbera del Monferrato, Dolcetto d'Alba, Gavi, Grignolino d'Asti. Other: Chardonnay and *champenoise* Brut Nature and Riserva del Nonno. With ample funds from the recent sale of Canei, the firm may emerge with some interesting wines. 370 acres are being devoted to quality wines.

Gianfranco Bovio
La Morra, 12060 Cuneo. DOC: Barolo, Dolcetto d'Alba.

Antiche Cantine Brema
Incisa Scapaccino, 14045 Asti. DOC: Barbera d'Asti, Grignolino d'Asti. Carlo Brema's Barbera is outstanding.

Brezza
Barolo, 12060 Cuneo. DOC: Barbera d'Alba, Barolo, Dolcetto d'Alba. Other: Nebbiolo.

Poderi Bricco Mondalino
Vignale Monferrato, 15049 Alessandria. Owner: Amilcare Gaudio. DOC: Barbera d'Asti, Barbera del Monferrato, Grignolino del Monferrato. A winery with high standards.

Luciano Brigatti
Suno, 28019 Novara. Lone producer of Möt Ziflon *vino da tavola*. Also Bonarda.

Fratelli Brovia
Castiglione Falletto, 12060 Cuneo. DOC: Barbera d'Alba, Barolo, Dolcetto d'Alba.

G. B. Burlotto
Verduno, 12060 Cuneo. DOC: Barbera d'Alba, Barolo, Dolcetto d'Alba.

Piero Busso
Neive, 12057 Cuneo. DOC: Barbaresco.

Ca' Bianca
Alice Bel Colle, 15010 Alessandria. DOC: Barbera d'Asti, Bracchetto d'Asti, Moscato d'Asti. 50 acres.

Ca' Roma
Barbaresco, 12050 Cuneo. Owner: Romano Marengo. DOC: Barbaresco (highly praised Maria di Brun).

Luigi Calissano & Figli
Alba, 12051 Cuneo. Founded in 1872, now under Coltiva-Gruppo Italiano Vini complex. Produces and sells Piedmont DOC and other wines and vermouth.

Cantina Sociale di Canelli
Canelli, 14053 Asti. Cooperative. DOC: Asti Spumante, Moscato d'Asti.

Carbonere
Santo Stefano Belba, 12058 Cuneo. Owner: Amerio Agostino. DOC: Moscato d'Asti.

Giorgio Carnevale
Rocchetta Tanaro-Cerro, 14030 Asti. A distinguished family firm founded in 1880. DOC: Barbaresco, Barbera d'Asti, Barolo, Brachetto d'Acqui, Freisa d'Asti, Grignolino d'Asti, Moscato d'Asti. Other: Cortese, Dolcetto, Nebbiolo. Carnevale selects, ages and bottles some of Asti's most impressive wines.

Tenuta Carretta
Piobesi d'Alba, 12040 Cuneo. Owners: The Veglia family. DOC: Barbera d'Alba, Barolo, Dolcetto d'Alba. Nebbiolo d'Alba. Other: Bianco dei Roeri, Bonarda, Brachetto, Freisa. An interesting range of wines from 4 vineyards.

Castellari Bergaglio
Roverato di Gavi, 15066 Alessandria. Owner: Wanda Castellari Bergaglio. DOC: Gavi. 17 acres.

Antica Contea di Castelvero
Castel Boglione, 14040 Asti. Cooperative. DOC: Barbera d'Asti, Barbera del Monferrato, Dolcetto d'Asti, Freisa d'Asti.

Cascina Castlét
Costigliole d'Asti, 14055 Asti. Owner: Mario Borio. DOC: Barbera d'Asti. Other: Barbera Policalpo and Passum *vino da tavola*.

Fratelli Cavallotto
Castiglione Falletto, 12060 Cuneo. Owners: Olivio and Gildo Cavallotto. DOC: Barbera d'Alba, Barolo, Dolcetto d'Alba. Other: Favorita, Grignolino, Nebbiolo. Good value in Barolo but drifting.

La Chiara
Vallegge di Gavi, 15066 Alessandria. Owners: Ferdinando and Roberto Bergaglio. DOC: Gavi.

Quinto Chionetti & Figlio
Dogliani, 12063 Cuneo. DOC: Dolcetto di Dogliani. Top Dolcetto producer.

Fratelli Cigliuti
Neive, 12057 Cuneo. DOC: Barbaresco, Barbera d'Alba, Dolcetto d'Alba. 7.5 acres.

Clerico
Monforte d'Alba, 12065 Cuneo. Owner: Domenico Clerico. DOC: Barbera d'Alba, Barolo, Dolcetto d'Alba. Other: Freisa, *barrique*-aged Arte di Nebbiolo.

A rising star in Barolo.

Colle Manora
Quargnento, 15044 Alessandria. DOC: Barbera d'Asti. Other: Sauvignon Mimosa, Cabernet. On the rise.

Colué
Diano d'Alba, 12055 Cuneo. Owner: Massimo Oddero. DOC: Barbaresco, Barbera d'Alba, Barolo, Dolcetto d'Alba, Nebbiolo d'Alba.

Conterno-Fantino
Monforte d'Alba, 12065 Cuneo. DOC: Barolo, Dolcetto d'Alba. Other: Nebbiolo, Nebbiolo-Barbera *barrique* wine Monprà.

Cora
10129 Torino. DOC: Asti Spumante. Other: Pinot del Poggio Spumante, Royal Ambassador Brut *champenoise*.

Cornarea
Canale, 12043 Cuneo. Owner: Francesco Rapetti. DOC: Roero, Arneis di Roero. Other: *Passito*.

Giuseppe Cortese
Barbaresco, 12050 Cuneo. DOC: Barbaresco, Dolcetto d'Alba.

De Forville
Barbaresco, 12050 Cuneo. Owners: Paolo and Walter De Forville. DOC: Barbaresco, Dolcetto d'Alba. Other: Chardonnay. 25 acres.

Luigi Dessilani & Figlio
Fara, 23073 Novara. Founded: 1924. Wine maker: Enzo Lucca. DOC: Fara, Gattinara. Other: Barbera, Bonarda, Caramino, Cornaggina, Spanna. Reliable, if coasting somewhat. The Caramino and Gattinara are most admirable.

Cascine Drago
San Rocco Seno d'Elvio, 12051 Cuneo. Founded: 1721. Owner: Luciano de Giacomi. DOC: Dolcetto d'Alba. Other: Bricco del Drago (Dolcetto-Nebbiolo), Campo Romano (Freisa-Pinot Nero), Pinot Nero. De Giacomi is a virtuoso red-wine maker.

Cantina Sociale di Fara Novarese
Fara, 28073 Novara. Cooperative. DOC: Fara. Other: Barengo Bianco, Bonarda, Caramino.

Eredi Virginia Ferrero
Serralunga d'Alba, 12050 Cuneo. DOC: Barolo.

Umberto Fiore
Gattinara, 13045 Vercelli. DOC: Gattinara.

Forteto della Luja
Loazzolo, 14050 Asti. Wine makers: Giancarlo Scaglione, Giacomo Bologna. Acclaimed sweet wine. The estate is leading the move for a new Loazzolo DOC for Moscato *passito*.

Franco Fiorina
Alba, 12051 Cuneo. Founded: 1925. Owner: Elsa Franco. DOC: Barbaresco, Barbera d'Alba, Barolo, Dolcetto d'Alba, Nebbiolo d'Alba. Other: Bianco

Fiorina, Freisa, Grignolino, Favorita del Roeri, Moscato Naturale, Primaticcio Vino Novello. A slightly declining house that buys all the grapes it needs.

Castello di Gabiano
Gabiano Monferrato, 15020 Alessandria. Owner: Cattaneo Giustiniani. DOC: Barbera d'Asti, Gabiano, Grignolino d'Asti. Somewhat fading.

Gastaldi
Neive, 12057 Cuneo. DOC: Barbaresco, Dolcetto d'Alba.

Gatti
Santo Stefano Belbo, 12058 Cuneo. DOC: Moscato d'Asti.

Fratelli Giacosa
Neive, 12057 Cuneo. Owners. Leone, Renzo and Valerio Giacosa. DOC: Barbaresco, Barbera d'Alba, Barolo. Recently much improved.

Gillardi
Farigliano, 12060 Cuneo. DOC: Dolcetto di Dogliani.

Cantina del Glicine
Neive, 12057 Cuneo. Owner: Roberto Bruno. DOC: Barbaresco, Barbera d'Alba, Dolcetto d'Alba. A minuscule wine house of consistent good quality.

La Giustiniana
Rovereto di Gavi, 15066 Alessandria. DOC: Gavi.

Elio Grasso
Monforte d'Alba, 12065 Cuneo. DOC: Barbera d'Alba, Barolo, Dolcetto d'Alba, Nebbiolo d'Alba.

Domenico Ivaldi
Strevi, 15019 Alessandria. DOC: Brachetto d'Acqui. Other: Moscato di Strevi, excellent Moscato *passito* Casarito.

Ermenegildo Leporati
Casale Monferrato, 15040 Alessandria. DOC: Barbera del Monferrato, Grignolino del Monferrato.

Eredi Lodali
Treiso, 12050 Cuneo. Owner: Rita Lodali. DOC: Barbaresco, Dolcetto d'Alba.

Malabaila di Canale
Canale, 12043 Cuneo. DOC: Arneis, Nebbiolo d'Alba, Roero. 19 acres.

Malvirà
Canale, 12043 Canale. Owners: Roberto and Massimo Damonte. DOC: Arneis, Roero. Others: Favorita, *barrique*-aged San Guglielmo from Nebbiolo and Barbera.

Marenco
Strevi, 15019 Alessandria. DOC: Brachetto d'Acqui, Dolcetto d'Acqui, Moscato d'Asti.

La Meirana
Gavi, 15066 Alessandria. Owner: Gian Piero Broglia. DOC: Gavi.

Moccagatta
Barbaresco, 12050 Cuneo. Owners: Franco and Sergio Minuto. DOC: Barbaresco. Other: Chardonnay and

Barbera in *barriques*.

Moncucchetto
Casorzo, 14032 Asti. DOC: Barbera d'Asti, Freisa, Grignolino d'Asti. Other: Malvasia Nera.

Nuova Cappelletta
Vignale Monferrato, 15049 Alessandria. Owners: The Arzani family. DOC: Barbera d'Asti, Barbera del Monferrato, Grignolino del Monferrato Casalese.

Fratelli Oddero
La Morra, 12064 Cuneo. Founded: 1878. Owners: Giacomo and Luigi Oddero. DOC: Barbaresco, Barbera d'Alba, Barolo, Dolcetto d'Alba, Nebbiolo d'Alba. Other: Freisa. Respected family winery with 57 acres of their own vines. Recent single-vineyard bottlings show promise.

Orsolani
San Giorgio Canavese, 10010 Torino. Owner: Francesco Orsolani. DOC: Erbaluce di Caluso, Caluso Spumante *champenoise*.

I Paglieri Roagna
Barbaresco, 12050 Cuneo. DOC: Barbaresco, Dolcetto d'Alba. Owner: Alfredo Roagna.

Armando Parusso
Monforte d'Alba, 12050 Cuneo. Owner: Marco Parusso. DOC: Barbera d'Alba, Barolo, Dolcetto d'Alba.

Secondo Pasquero-Elia
Bricco di Neive, 12057 Cuneo. DOC: Barbaresco, Dolcetto d'Alba, Moscato d'Asti. Other: Chardonnay. The Barbaresco of the Sori d'Paytin vineyard has Barolo depth and structure.

Luigi Pelissero
Treiso, 12050 Cuneo. DOC: Barbaresco, Barbera d'Alba, Dolcetto d'Alba.

Luigi Perazzi
Roasio, 13060 Vercelli. DOC: Bramaterra.

I Vignaioli Elvio Pertinace
Treiso, 12050 Cuneo. Cooperative. DOC: Barbaresco. An impressive grouping of Barbaresco growers.

Pianpolvere Soprano
Monforte d'Alba, 12065 Cuneo. Owner: Riccardo Fenocchio. DOC: Barbera d'Alba, Barolo, Dolcetto d'Alba, Grignolino d'Alba.

Armando Piazzo
San Rocco Seno d'Elvio, 12050 Cuneo. A range of Alba DOCs.

Vinicola Piemontese
La Morra, 12064 Cuneo. Owner: Marco Ferrero. DOC: Barbaresco, Barolo, Dolcetto d'Alba.

Castello del Poggio
Portacomaro, 14037 Asti. Owner Zonin makes DOC Barbera d'Asti, Grignolino d'Asti and Moscato d'Asti, and is developing the estate.

Cantina della Porta Rossa
Diano d'Alba, 12055 Cuneo. Owners. Berzia and Rizzi. DOC: Barbaresco,

Barbera d'Alba, Barolo, Dolcetto di Diano d'Alba, Moscato d'Asti. Other: Nebbiolo. A noteworthy new house.

Punset
Neive, 12057 Cuneo. Owners: Marina and Renzo Marcarini. DOC: Barbaresco, Barbera d'Alba, Dolcetto d'Alba.

Renato Rabezzana
San Desiderio d'Asti, 14031 Asti. DOC: Barbera d'Asti, Grignolino d'Asti.

Tenuta dei Re
Castagnole Monferrato, 14030 Asti. Owners: The Re family. DOC: Grignolino d'Asti.

Francesco Rinaldi & Figli
Barolo, 12060 Cuneo. Owners: Luciano and Michele Rinaldi. DOC: Barbaresco, Barbera d'Alba, Barolo, Dolcetto d'Alba.

Rizzi
Treiso, 12050 Cuneo. Owner: Ernesto Dellapiana. DOC: Barbaresco, Barbera d'Alba, Dolcetto d'Alba.

Bruno Rocca-Cascina Rabajà
Barbaresco, 12050 Cuneo. DOC: Barbaresco, Dolcetto d'Alba. Other: Nebbiolo.

Rocche Costamagna
La Morra, 12064 Cuneo. Owner: Claudia Ferreresi Locatelli. DOC: Barbera d'Alba, Barolo, Dolcetto d'Alba. Other: Nebbiolo.

Roche
Alba, 12051 Cuneo. Owner: Raffaele Ferrero. Wine maker: Carlo Brovia. DOC: Barbaresco, Barbera d'Alba, Barolo, Dolcetto d'Alba, Dolcetto di Diano d'Alba.

Gigi Rosso
Castiglione Falletto, 12060 Cuneo. Owner: Gigi Rosso. DOC: Barolo, Dolcetto d'Alba, Dolcetto di Diano d'Alba.

Castello di Salabue
Ponzano Monferrato, 15020 Alessandria. Owner: Carlo Cassinis. DOC: Barbera del Monferrato.

Tenuta San Pietro
Gavi, 15066 Alessandria. Owner: Maria Rosa Gazzaniga. DOC: Gavi. 37 acres.

I Vignaioli di Santo Stefano
Santo Stefano Belbo, 12058 Cuneo. Cooperative with 62 acres. DOC: Moscato d'Asti.

Saracco
Castiglione Tinella, 12053 Cuneo. DOC: Moscato d'Asti. Top traditional Moscato.

Cascina Scarsa Olivi
San Lorenzo di Ovada, 15076 Alessandria. DOC: Dolcetto d'Ovada. A fanatical maker of lively Dolcetto, which he claims will keep for 10 years.

Giorgio Scarzello & Figli
Barolo, 12060 Barolo. Owners: Giorgio and Gemma Scarzello. DOC: Barolo, Dolcetto d'Alba.

Scrimaglio

Nizza Monferrato, 14049 Asti. DOC: Barbera d'Asti, Barbera del Monferrato.

Cantine Sebaste
Barolo, 12060 Barolo. Owner: Mauro Sebaste. DOC: Barolo, Dolcetto d'Alba. Other: Arneis, Freisa, Nebbiolo. Label: Sylla Sebaste.

La Spinona
Barbaresco, 12050 Cuneo. Owner-wine maker: Pietro Berutti. DOC: Barbaresco, Barbera d'Alba, Dolcetto d'Alba. Other: Freisa, Grignolino, Nebbiolo.

Castello di Tagliolo
Tagliolo Monferrato, 15070 Alessandria. Owner: Olberto Pinelli Gentile. DOC: Barbera d'Alba, Dolcetto d'Alba, Cortese di Gavi.

Terre da Vino
Moriondo, 10020 Torino. *Négociant*

operation with several Piedmontese DOCs.

Travaglini
Gattinara, 13045 Vercelli. DOC: Gattinara. 42 acres.

Tre Castelli
Montaldo Bormida, 15010 Alessandria. Cooperative. A range of DOC wines including good Dolcetto di Ovada.

Renato Trinchero
Agliano, 14041 Asti. DOC: Barbera d'Asti.

G.D. Vajra
Barolo, 12060 Barolo. Owner: Aldo Vajra. DOC: Barbera d'Alba, Barolo, Dolcetto d'Alba. Increasingly praised.

Antonio Vallana & Figlio
Maggiora, 28014 Novara. Owner-wine maker: Bernardo Vallana. DOC: Boca. Other: Barbera, Bianco, Bonarda,

Grignolino, Spanna. Producers of long-lived Spanna and reliable Boca.

Castello di Verduno
Verduno, 12060 Cuneo. Owners: The Burlotto family. The former property of the Italian royal house. DOC: Barolo. Other: Pelaverga.

Gianni Voerzio
La Morra, 12064 Cuneo. DOC: Barbera d'Alba, Barolo, Dolcetto d'Alba. Other: Arneis, Freisa. Recently split with more illustrious brother Roberto (q.v.), Gianni now runs the family winery.

Cantine Volpi
Tortona, 15057 Alessandria. Wine house specializing in Colli Tortonesi sparkling wines and Monferrato DOCs.

VALLE D'AOSTA

The Valle d'Aosta is France's umbilical cord to Italy (and vice versa). It's narrow confines lead to the Mont Blanc Tunnel and Saint Bernard Passes. Small vineyards perched in south-facing crannies along the valley manfully carry winemaking almost all the way from Piedmont to Savoie, with a corresponding meeting of their respective grapes: Nebbiolo and Barbera from the south join Gamay and Petit Rouge (which tastes suspiciously like Mondeuse) from the north, with Swiss Petit Arvine, some Moscato and Malvoisie (Pinot Gris) and two indigenous grapes, Blanc de Valdigne and red Vien de Nus.

Quantities are very small: the skiers of Courmayeur help the townsfolk of Aosta prevent exports from the region. In 1986 Italy's most comprehensive regionwide DOC was established. Valle d'Aosta or Vallée d'Aoste takes in 18 types of wine with their names in two languages. But even if classified, Aostan wines are interesting *sur place* but do not currently represent good value for money.

VALLE D'AOSTA PRODUCERS

Caves Cooperative Donnaz
Donnaz, 11025 Aosta. Cooperative. DOC Donnaz. 25 acres.

Antoine Charrère et Fils
Aymaville, 11010 Aosta. Aymaville La Sabla. A fine red *vino da tavola* made from Petit Rouge.

Co-Enfer Arvier
Arvier, 11011 Aosta. Cooperative. DOC Enfer d'Arvier.

Delfino Grosjean
Quart, 11020 Aosta. Torrette and Pinot Noir in *barrique*, Blanc d'Ollignan *vino da tavola*.

Institut Agricole Régional
11100 Aosta. Experimental cellars of the regional agriculture school founded in 1969 and directed for years by Joseph Vaudan, a priest. Malvoisie de Cossan, Petit Rouge, Riesling-Sylvaner, Sang des Salasses (Pinot Noir), Vin des Chanoines (Gamay), Vin du Conseil (Petite Arvine). Oenologist Grato Praz directs wine making at the school,

producing some of the best wines of Aosta.

Le Cave du Vin Blanc de Morgex et de la Salle
Morgex, 11017 Aosta. Growers with 37 acres specializing in Blanc de Morgex and Blanc de la Salle. At 3,400 feet their vineyards are some of the highest in Europe. The wine has rarity value, but is light and can be sharp, though recent new cellars should mean an improvement in quality.

La Crotta de Vegneron
Chambave, 11023 Aosta. Cooperative directed by Yves Burgay. Impressive DOC Chambave and Nus.

La Kiuva
Arnad, 11020 Aosta. Cooperative. DOC Arnad-Montjovet.

Malga-Dayné
Villeneuve, 11018 Aosta. Owner: Marisa Dayné. Small vineyard making Torrette and Müller-Thurgau.

Alberto Vevey
Morgex, 11017 Aosta. Despite Alberto Vevey's death his sons continue to make the most widely admired Blanc of this zone.

Ezio Voyat
Chambave, 11023 Aosta. Voyat's wines have an élite following in Italy. They are classic Chambave wines but he sells them as *vino da tavola* under non-DOC names: Rosso Le Muraglie (Chambave Rouge), La Gazzella (Moscato di Chambave) and Passito Le Muraglie (Moscato Passito) – the latter superb.

LIGURIA

The crescent of the Ligurian coast, linking France and Tuscany, is scarcely regarded as a wine region and has never been an exporter. But in the centre of the crescent lies Italy's greatest port, and one of its most cosmopolitan cities, Genoa. Genoa demands, and gets, much better than ordinary whites for its fish and reds for its meat from the scattered vineyards of the hilly coast.

There are now four DOC zones in Liguria: white Cinqueterre in the seaside vineyards to the east towards Tuscany, the red Rossese di Dolceacqua on the borders of France, the Riviera Ligure di Ponente (red: Ormeasco and Rossese; white: Pigato and Vermentino) grown on the western Riviera, and the new white Colli di Luni in the lower Magra and Vora valleys.

Liguria's wine list is a much longer one than its list of DOC's, but if the officially ranked wines are rarely exported, much less are the individualistic productions of its many small wine makers.

DOC AND OTHER WINES

Buzzetto di Quiliano
A very light, often scarcely ripe, dry white (Buzzetto is the grape) from west of Genoa.

Cinqueterre
DOC. White wine. Province: La Spezia. Villages: Riomaggiore, Vernazza, Monterosso, La Spezia. Grapes: Bosco min. 60%, Albarola and/or Vermentino up to 40%. Max. crop: 63 hl/ha. Min. alch: 11° for Cinqueterre, 17° for Cinqueterre Sciacchetrà. Aged 1 year for Sciacchetrà. Annual production: Cinqueterre 42,000 cases; Sciacchetrà 500 cases.
The largely legendary dry white of the beautiful Ligurian coast southeast of Genoa. It should be cleanly fruity. Sciacchetrà is made with the same grapes shrivelled in the sun to achieve concentration and sweetness. It is worth a detour, but not a journey.

Colli di Luni
DOC. Red and white wines. Provinces: La Spezia, Massa e Carrara. Villages: 15 communes in La Spezia; Aulla, Fosdinovo and Podenzana in Massa e Carrara. Grapes: (red) Sangiovese 60–70%, Canaiolo/Polera Nera/Ciliegiolo min. 15%, other reds up to 25%; (white) Vermentino, Trebbiano Toscano. Max. crop: 70 hl/ha. Min. alch: (red) 11.5°; (white) 11°.
Wine has been made in this area since Roman times, but it has only recently (1989) been elevated to DOC status. Good reds are made from Sangiovese-based blends, whites that can almost rival those of Riviera di Ponente predominantly from Vermentino. Leading wine makers of the zone are investing heavily in new equipment and expertise, and look set to demand some respect in the future.

Riviera Ligure di Ponente
DOC. Red and white wine. Province: Savona and Imperia. Villages: 67 communes in Imperia, 46 communes in Savona, plus 2 communes in Genoa. Grapes: (red) Rossese, Ormeasco; (white) Pigato, Vermentino. Max. crop: 63 hl/ha for Ormeasco, Rossese; 77 hl/ha for Pigato, Vermentino. Min.

Professional tasting panels are an important part of the DOC system.

alch: 11°. Ormeasco aged 1 year for *superiore*.

The red and white wines of this relatively new DOC are grown between Savona and Imperia. The whites are best drunk young, the reds gain with age.

Rossese di Dolceacqua or Dolceacqua

DOC. Red wine. Province: Imperia. Villages: Dolceacqua, Ventimiglia and 13 others. Grape: Rossese. Aged 1 year for *superiore*. Max. crop: 63 hl/ha. Min. alch: 12°. Annual production: 27,000 cases.

The claret of the coast near the French frontier – a country wine with a good balance of fruit and bite, best after 2–5 years, when it can develop a real bouquet to linger over.

Terizzo

Red wine made from Sangiovese and Cabernet grown at Castelnuovo Magra. It will last at least 3–4 years.

Vermentino

The commonest white grape of the coast, grown particularly to the west of Savona (west of Genoa). Standards vary, but an example from Giuncheo was slightly green, yet with an almost oily softness. It should be faintly aromatic and dry: in fact a good fish wine. DOC in Riviera di Ponente, Colli di Luni and in Cinqueterre blend.

LIGURIA PRODUCERS

Luigi Anfossi
Bastia d'Albenga, 17031 Savona. Good Pigato and Rossese.
Riccardo Bruna
Ranzo Borgo, 18028 Imperia. Some of the zone's finest Pigato, produced in small quantity.
Cane
Dolceacqua, 18035 Imperia. Owner: Giobatta Cane. Small production of admired Rossese.
Cascina du Feipù
Bastia d'Albenga, 17031 Savona. Owners: Pippo and Bice Parodi. Superb Pigato di Albenga, legend in the area, and a fresh Rossese.
Colle dei Bardellini
Sant'Agata d'Imperia, 18100 Imperia. Fine DOC Vermentino; some Rossese.
Cooperativa Agricola di Cinqueterre
Riomaggiore, 19017 La Spezia. Oenologist: Nello Capris. Consistently good range of dry white DOC Cinqueterre, the best being the Sciacchetrà.
Conte Picedi Benettini
Baccano di Arcola, 19021 La Spezia.

Good DOC Colli di Luni Vermentino del Chioso.
Enoteca Bisson
Chiavari, 16043 Genoa. Owners: Pier Luigi and Wally Lugano. Fine Vermentino di Verici.
Forlini Capellini
Manarola, 19017 La Spezia. A family vineyard producing a full-bodied, noteworthy DOC Cinqueterre.
Enzo Guglielmi
Soldano, 18030 Imperia. DOC Rossese di Dolceacqua, consistently good.
Michele Guglielmi
Soldano, 18030 Imperia. DOC Rossese di Dolceacqua. At 3 years 'Colli di Soldano' has a claret-like 'cut' and real style.
La Colombiera
Castelnuovo Magra, 19030 La Spezia. Owner: Francesco Ferro. A leading maker of fine DOC Colli di Luni and Vermentino; also *vino da tavola* Albachiara and Terizzo from Sangiovese and Cabernet respectively.
Ottaviano Lambruschi
Castelnuovo Magra, 19030 La Spezia.

Good DOC Colli di Luni Vermentino.
Lupi
Pieve di Teco, 18026 Imperia. Owners: Tommaso and Angelo Lupi. Oenologist: Donato Lanati. Ormeasco di Pornassio, Pigato, Vermentino, Rossese di Dolceacqua. The region's top producer. Their Ormeasco di Pornassio from mountain vineyards shows uncommon finesse for a Dolcetto and ages well, up to 6 years or more.
Mario Maccario
San Biagio della Cima, 18030 Imperia. His Dolceacqua has outstanding potential.
Podere Boiga
Finale Ligure, 17024 Savona. Owner: Domenico Boiga. Good DOC Vermentino and *vino da tavola* Lumassina.
Andrea Vercelli
Cisano sul Neva, 17035 Savona. Good Vermentino.
Pippo Viale
Soldano, 18030 Imperia. Consistently good Dolceacqua.

LOMBARDY

Lombardy has always kept a low profile in the world of wine. It has no world-famous name. Oltrepò Pavese, its productive and profitable viticultural heart, is scarcely a name to conjure with. Valtellina, the last alpine valley before Switzerland, commands more respect with its hard Nebbiolo reds. The lakeside wines of Garda have romantic associations. But a region needs a flag carrier which embodies its special qualities, and this Lombardy has not yet provided.

Efforts to create a memorable name, particularly in the Oltrepò Pavese, have resulted in a confusion

of faintly comic-sounding brands (Red Arrow, Spitfire, Judas' Blood). In contrast to Piedmont, with its proliferation of DOCs, Lombardy has a mere thirteen, but those of Oltrepò Pavese in particular, and Valtellina to a lesser degree, are umbrellas for a number of regulated brands or types of wine.

The grapes of Piedmont and the grapes of the northeast are all grown here, and frequently blended. It is inescapably a zone of transition with rich possibilities but no clear identity to bank on.

DOC AND OTHER WINES

Barbacarlo
An enclave of the Oltrepò Pavese (q.v.) near Broni well known for its unusual full-bodied *frizzante* red, which can be dry or semi-sweet but always finishes faintly bitter. Unlike other fizzy reds Barbacarlo is often aged in bottle for 1½ years.

Barbera
One of the commonest red grapes of Lombardy, used both blended and alone. In Oltrepò Pavese it can be DOC.

Bonarda
Another red grape with DOC rights in the Oltrepò Pavese. Dark, soft and bitter in the finish.

Botticino
DOC. Red wine. Province: Brescia. Villages: Botticino, Brescia, Rezzato. Grapes: Barbera 30–40%, Schiava Gentile 20–30%, Marzamino 15–25%, Sangiovese 10–20%. Max. crop: 84 hl/ha. Min. alch: 12°. Annual production: 11,000 cases.
A fairly powerful and sweetish red; the local red-meat wine, preferred with 3–4 years of maturity.

Buttafuoco
A forceful concentrated red of blended Barbera, Uva Rara and Croatina produced near Castana (under the umbrella DOC Oltrepò Pavese). 2 years' barrel-age does not prevent it fizzing when it is poured.

Capriano del Colle
DOC. Red and white wine. Province: Brescia. Villages: Capriano del Colle and Poncarale. Grapes: (red) Sangiovese 40–50%, Marzemino 35–45%, Barbera 3–10%; (white) Trebbiano. Max. crop: 87.5 hl/ha. Min. alch: 11°. Capriano del Colle-Trebbiano is a white from Trebbiano di Soave grapes. Annual production: 11,100 cases.
A recent DOC for light local wines, unknown before.

Cellatica
DOC. Red wine. Province: Brescia. Villages: Brescia, Gussago, Cellatica, Collebeato, Rodengo-Saiano. Grapes: Schiava Gentile 35–40%, Barbera 25–30%, Marzemino 20–30%, Incrocio Terzi n.l. (Barbera × Cabernet Franc) 10–15%. Max. crop: 84 hl/ha. Min. alch: 11.5°. Annual production: 16,700 cases.
A respectable mild red, best within 2–4 years which has been enjoyed in the area since the 16th century.

Colle del Calvario
Potentially good Merlot/Cabernet red and Pinot white from Grumello, a town in the hills east of Bergamo.

Colli Morenici Mantovani del Garda
DOC. Red, white and *rosato* wine. Province: Mantova. Villages: Castiglione delle Stiviere, Cavriana, Monzambano, Ponti sul Mincio, Solferino and Volta Mantovana. Grapes: (white) Garganega 20–25%, Trebbiano Giallo 20–25%, Trebbiano Nostrano 10–40%; (red and *rosato*) Rossanella 30–60%, Rondinella 20–50%, Negrara Trentina 10–30%. Max. crop: 65 hl/ha. Min. alch: 11°. Annual production: 38,900 cases.
Lightweight local wines, though with a long history. Virgil mentioned them. The white could pass for Soave.

Franciacorta
DOC. Red, white and rosé wine. Province: Brescia. Villages: 23 communes south of Lake Iseo. Grapes: (red) Cabernet Franc 40–50%, Barbera 20–30%, Nebbiolo 15–25%, Merlot 10–15% other reds up to 15%; (white) Pinot Bianco; Chardonnay; (rosé) Pinot Bianco, Chardonnay, Pinot Nero obligatory up to 15%. Max. crop: (red) 87.5 hl/ha; (white, spumante) 85 hl/ha. Min. alch: 11° (11.5° for spumante). Annual production: 378,000 cases.
Red Franciacorta is very pleasant light wine of some character. The Pinot is used to make *spumante* of splendid potential: Brut, Crémant or a rosé. Ca' del Bosco Franciacorta is one of Italy's best sparkling wines.

Groppello
A local red grape of southwest Garda.

Grumello
A subregion of Valtellina Superiore (q.v.).

Inferno
Another subregion of Valtellina Superiore (q.v.).

Lambrusco Mantovano
DOC. Red wine. Province: Mantova. Region: zones around the R. Po and the border of Emilia-Romagna. Grapes: Lambrusco Viadanese and other subvarieties; Ancellotta/Fortana (Uva d'Oro) up to 15%.
A fairly new DOC (1987) making Lambrusco from the local Viadanese subvariety; robust in the west, lighter towards the east of the zone. Wines are dry or *frizzante*, and can hold their own with their counterparts from Emilia.

Lugana
DOC. White wine. Provinces: Brescia and Verona. Region: the south end of Lake Garda between Desenzano and Peschiera. Grapes: Trebbiano di Lugano 100%, or with other light grapes up to 10% (but not aromatic types). Max. crop: 87.5 hl/ha. Min. alch: 11.5°. Annual production: 211,000 cases.
Formerly a glamorous rarity to be sought out in such lovely spots as 'olive-silvery' Sirmione. Now a very pleasant light dry white, scarcely distinguishable from an upper-class Soave.

Merlot
Increasingly grown as a 'varietal' wine in Lombardy. Very satisfactory, though not included in a DOC. Part of blend in Franciacorta and Valcalepio.

Moscato di Scanzo
A great rarity from Bergamo: an excellent tawny dessert Muscat.

Müller-Thurgau
The German grape is successfully grown in the Oltrepò Pavese, though not admitted in its DOC.

Narbusto
Made from the Oltrepò red grapes, this is a long-lived table wine (aged at least 8 years).

Oltrepò Pavese
DOC. Red and white wine. Province: Pavia. Area: Oltrepò Pavese. Grapes: (red) Barbera up to 65%, Croatina min. 25%, Uva Rara and/or Ughetta up to 45%; (white) Pinot Grigio or

Riesling Renano, others up to 15%. Max. crop: 71 hl/ha. Min. alch: 11.5°. Annual production: (total): 2.8m. cases.

The DOC for general reds from the Oltrepò Pavese. Most of the more distinctive wines of the area are either specifically named (e.g. Barbacarlo, Buttafuoco) or have a specified grape variety dominant (e.g. Barbera, Pinot).

Pinot

Pinot Nero, Grigio and Bianco are all widely grown in Lombardy. The Oltrepò Pavese is a major supplier of base wines of Pinot for *spumante* made in Piedmont and elsewhere.

Riesling

The Oltrepò DOC includes both Italian and Rhine Rieslings without distinguishing them. Both grow well here.

Riviera del Garda Bresciano

DOC. Red and *rosato* wine. Province: Brescia. Villages: 30 communes on western and southwestern shore of Lake Garda. Grapes: Groppello 50–60%, Sangiovese 10–25%, Barbera 10–20%, Marzemino 5–30%. Max. crop: 85 hl/ha. Min. alch: 11°. Aged for at least 1 year for *superiore*. Annual production: 167,000 cases.

The mirror image of Valpolicella and Bardolino from the other side of the lake. Commercial qualities at least are similar, although classic Valpolicella is far deeper in flavour. The village of Moniga del Garda makes a pale Chiaretto which is lively and good when very young.

San Colombano al Lambro or San Colombano

DOC. Red wine. Provinces: Milan and Pavia. Villages: San Colombano al Lambro, Graffignana, S. Angelo Lodigiano. Grapes: Croatina 30–45%, Barbera 25–40%, Uva Rara 5–15%; other reds up to 15%. Annual production: 16,500 cases.

Relatively recent DOC makes hearty reds on the slopes around San Colombano. Best ready for drinking after 2–4 years.

Sangue di Giuda

A fizzy, often sweet red called 'Judas' Blood' is the sort of wine that makes 'serious' wine lovers turn their eyes to heaven. It should be tried without prejudice. There are good ones.

Sassella

A subregion of Valtellina Superiore (q.v.).

Sfursat or Sfurzat or Sforzato

Valtellina's equivalent of the Recioto of Valpolicella in

the Veneto; a strong (14.5°) red made of semi-dried grapes, in this case Nebbiolo. Age certainly improves it as it turns tawny, but whether the final result pleases you is a personal matter.

Tocai di San Martino della Battaglia

DOC. White wine. Provinces: Brescia and Verona. Villages: Sirmione, Desanzano, Lonato, Pozzolengo, Peschiera. Grape: Tocai Friulano. Max. crop: 81 hl/ha. Min. alch: 12°. Annual production: 44,500 cases.

A distinctive character among Garda wines; dry, yellow and tasty with something of the typical local bitterness in the finish. It is best drunk as young as possible.

Valcalepio

DOC. Red and white wine. Province: Bergamo. Villages: 15 in the Calepio valley. Grapes: (white) Pinot Bianco 55–75%, Pinot Grigio 25–45%; (red) Merlot 55–75%, Cabernet Sauvignon 25–45%. Red aged 2 years. Max. crop: (white) 58 hl/ha; (red) 65 hl/ha. Min. alch: (white) 11.5°; (red) 12°. Annual production: 27,800 cases.

A small production, principally red, of light wines with an ancient name but modern grape varieties. The red is aged 2 years in wood, the white not at all.

Valgella

A subregion of Valtellina Superiore (q.v.).

Valtellina and Valtellina Superiore

DOC. Red wine. Province: Sondrio. Subdistricts: Sassella, Grumello, Inferno and Valgella for *superiore*, 12 communes for Valtellina. Grapes: Nebbiolo (called Chiavennasca) 70%, plus Pinot Nero, Merlot, Rossola, Brugnola or Pignola Valtellinese max. 30%. *Superiore* is 95% Nebbiolo. Max. crop: 84 hl/ha. Min. alch: 11° for Valtellina, 12° for Valtellina Superiore. Aged for not less than 2 years, of which 1 is in wood, 4 years for *riserva*. Annual production: 500,000 cases.

The most successful excursion of Nebbiolo outside its home region of Piedmont. Plain Valtellina can be expected to be a fairly 'hard' light red. The named *superiores* develop considerable character as dry, claret-weight wines with hints of autumnal mellowness. It is hard to discern consistent differences between Sassella, Inferno, etc., but the first is generally considered the best. Switzerland (St-Moritz is just over the mountain) is a principal consumer. *See also* Sfursat.

Maurizio Zanella

Cabernet Sauvignon and Franc with Merlot blend grown in Franciorta.

LOMBARDY PRODUCERS

Guido Berlucchi

Borgonato di Cortefranca, 25040 Brescia.
President: Guido Berlucchi. Wine maker: Franco Ziliani. Cuvée Imperiale Berlucchi. Brut, Grand Crémant, Max Rosé, Pas Dosé, all *champenoise*. This firm is Italy's largest producer of champagne-method wines – more than 400,000 cases. Berlucchi also owns Antica Cantine Fratta and produces *champenoise* under that label.

Bellavista

Erbusco, 25030 Brescia.
Owner: Vittorio Moretti. Wine maker: Mattia Vezzola. DOC: Franciacorta *rosso* and *bianco*. Other: 5 types of *champenoise*. The sparkling wines are stylish and very highly regarded, particularly the pure Chardonnay Gran Cuvée Crémant Millesimato and the still wines are elegant. This estate is Ca' del Bosco's closest competitor.

Ca' del Bosco
Erbusco, 25030 Brescia.

Founded: 1968. Owners: The Zanella family. Wine maker: Maurizio Zanella. DOC: Franciacorta Pinot, Rosso. Other: Ca' del Bosco, Chardonnay, Pinèro, Maurizio Zanella, Cabernet-Merlot, Vino Novallo di Erbusco. One of Italy's best sparkling-wine makers. Their production from 150 acres is dominated by Brut, Crémant and remarkably fine Dosage Zèro from Pinot and Chardonnay plus the recently issued vintage 1980. Recent issues of Chardonnay, Pinèro and the highly acclaimed Maurizio Zanella confirm high standards in the still wines field as well.

Tenuta Castello/Perlage
Grumello del Monte, 26064 Bergamo.

Wine maker: Carlo Zadra. Valcalepio (labelled as Colle del Calvario), excellent wood-aged Chardonnay called Aurito, 3 types of *spumante*, the most recent being a soft velvety *champenoise*.

Cavalleri
Erbusco, 250030 Brescia.

Owner: Giovanni Cavalleri. DOC: Franciacorta. Other: *Champenoise* Brut, Pas Dosé and Rosé; barrel-fermented Chardonnay Seradina, and a French-style Cabernet-Merlot blend, Tajardino. This family estate, with 40 acres of vines, is continuing to make a name for itself with both its still and sparkling wines.

Fondazione Fojanini
23030 Sondrio

DOC: Valtellina Superiore. The cellars and research centre are run by Alberto Baiocchi, a leader in Valtellina wine. He makes a fine Sassella sold under the label La Castellina.

Tenuta Mazzolino
Corvino San Quirico, 27043 Pavia.

Owner: Roberto Piaggi. Consultant: Giancarlo Scaglione. A fine range of DOC Oltrepò wines, as well as an excellent *barrique*-aged *vino da tavola* called Noir.

Monte Rossa
Bornaro, 25040 Brescia.

Owner: Paola Rovetta. DOC: Franciacorta. Admirable Brut, Brut Non Dosato and Rosé *champenoise* made by the owner and her son Emanuele Rabotti from 40 acres of vines.

Nino Negri
Chiuro, 23030 Sondrio

Founded: 1897. Now part of the Coltiva-Gruppo Italiano Vini complex. DOC: Valtellina, Valtellina Superiore. The zone's largest cellars, benefiting from advanced technology and under the direction of oenologist Casimiro Maule, remain a leading force. Their *riserva* is issued as 'Le Botti d'Oro'.

Premiovini
25100 Brescia

Founded: 1825. This is the quality part of the Folonari operation (q.v.). The firm bottles or distributes numerous DOC wines from several regions under the trade or company names Anforio, Contessa Matilde, Della Staffa, Nozzole, Pegaso, Plauto, Poggetto, San Grato, Torre Sveva. Consistent, sometimes excellent, quality.

Cantina Sociale di Santa Maria della Versa
Santa Maria della Versa, 27047 Pavia.

A respected cooperative, founded in 1905, directed by Antonio Duca Denari. Its 700 members own nearly 5,000 acres of vines and produce nearly 80,000 cases. DOC: Oltrepò Pavese. It sells a fraction of the production under its own label, most notably Gran Spumante Brut *champenoise*.

Visconti
Desenzano del Garda, 25015 Brescia.

A family firm founded in 1908; now headed by Franco Visconti. Oenologist: Gian Franco Tonon. DOC: Bardolino, Lugana, Oltrepò Pavese Moscato, Riviera del Garda Bresciano. Other: Merlot, Pinot Grigio, Riesling, Verduzzo. Visconti's skilled use of modern techniques makes him the quality leader in Lugana.

OTHER PRODUCERS

Giacomo Agnes
Rovescala, 27040 Pavia. DOC: Oltrepò Pavese Rosso. Other: Gaggiarone from Bonarda and Barbera.
Anteo
Rocca de'Giorgi, 27043 Pavia. Consultant: Beppe Bassi. *Champenoise* Anteo Brut Rocca de'Giorgi and Nature from Chardonnay and Pinot Nero. 82 acres.
Franco Balgera
Sondrio. Good DOC Valtellina Superiore.
Fratelli Berlucchi
Borgonato di Cortefranca, 25040 Brescia. DOC: Franciacorta Pinot, Rosso. Other: Pinot Grigio. Still and sparkling wines.
Tenuta Il Bosco
Zenevredo, 27049 Pavia. DOC: Oltrepò

Pavese. Zonin property, along with San Zeno at Stradella, becoming the base of a major *spumante* operation.
Ca' dei Frati
25019 Lugana di Sirmione. DOC: Lugana. Other: Merlot Rosato, Rosso dei Frati.
Comincioli
Puegnago, 25080 Brescia. DOC: Riviera del Garda.
Conti Sertoli Salis
Tirano, 23037 Sondrio. Ancient house revived with the '89 vintage is aiming at the top in Valtellina.
Cornaleto
Adro, 25030 Brescia. Owner: Luigi Lancini. DOC: Franciacorta Rosso. Also admired *champenoise*. 45 acres.
Costaripa
Moniga del Garda, 25080 Brescia.

Owners: Bruno Vezzola and sons. DOC: Riviera del Garda. Other: Groppello red *vino da tavola*. 10 acres.
Doria
Montalto Pavese, 27040 Pavia. Owners/wine makers: Adriano and Bruno Doria, Beppe Baddi. DOC: Oltrepò Pavese Pinot Nero (*barrique*-aged), Roncorosso, Bonarda, Riesling. Other: *Charmat* Querciolo.
Sandro Fay
San Giacomo di Teglio, Sondrio. Good Valgella Ca' Moreí.
Folonari
Persico Dosimo, 26043 Cremona. Founded: 1825. Part of the Gruppo Italiano Vini complex. From a family firm this has grown to become one of Italy's largest table wine producers, producing 4.5m. cases a year of DOC

wine (mainly Verona) and *vino da tavola* of middling to economy class. Main cellars are near Cremona. *See* also Premiovini.

Fontanachiara
Stradella, 27049 Pavia. Owner: Angelo Maggi. Wine makers: Marco Maggi, Beppe Bassi. Fine *champenoise* Fontanachiara Brut and Riserva from Pinot Nero and Chardonnay.

Frecciarossa
Casteggio, 27045 Pavia. A 50-acre estate founded in the early 1920s 'in imitation of Château Lafite' by the late Giorgio Odero, and now owned by his daughters, Anna and Margherita. DOC: Oltrepò Pavese. Odero had great influence in improving wine in Lombardy.

Castello di Luzzano
Rovescala, 27040 Pavia. Owners: Giovannella and Maria Giulia Fugazza. DOC: Oltrepò Pavese Rosso. 150 acres. Also produce Colli Piacentini wines in Emilia.

Cascina Madonna Isabella
Casteggio, 27045 Pavia. Owner: Giulio Venco. DOC: Oltrepò Pavese. Rosso della Madonna Isabella (800 cases) is a gem of the Oltrepò.

Lino Maga
Broni, 27043 Pavia. Owner: Lino Maga. DOC: Oltrepò Pavese. Other: Montebuono. The estate originated Barbacarlo (now a proprietary wine), one of Italy's most praised and most durable bubbly reds.

Mairano
Mairano di Casteggio, 27045 Pavia. Owner: Fernando Bussolera. DOC: Oltrepò Pavese.

Villa Mazzucchelli
Ciliverghe, 25080 Brescia. Owner: Piero Giacomini. *Champenoise* Brut, Pas Dosé and Riserva del Conte.

Monsupello
Torricello Verzate, Pavia. Founded: 1893. Owner: Carlo Boatti. DOC: Oltrepò Pavese Rosso, Pinot Nero. 30 acres.

Cella di Montalto
Montalto Pavese, 27040 Pavia. Owners: The Canegallo family. DOC: Oltrepò Pavese Riesling Italico.

Montelio
Codevilla, 27050 Pavia. Founded: 1848. Owner: A. Mazza Sesia. DOC: Oltrepò Pavese. Other: Merlot, Müller-Thurgau.

La Muiraghina
Montù Beccaria, 27040 Pavia. Owner: Anna Gregorutti. Excellent *vino da tavola* of Riesling, Barbera and Malvasia.

Nera
Chiuro, 23030 Sondrio. Founded: 1936; headed by Pietro Nera. DOC: Valtellina, Valtellina Superiore. 110,000 cases from 370 acres. The Valtellina Superiore Signorie is outstanding.

Tenuta di Oliva
Oliva Gessi, 27050 Pavia. DOC: Oltrepò Pavese Riesling. 72 acres.

Pasini Produttori
Raffa di Puegnago, 25080 Brescia. Owner: Diego Pasini. DOC: Riviera del Garda. Other: Groppello.

M. Pasolini
Mompiano, 25060 Brescia. Owner: Mario Pasolini. Ronco di Mompiano red.

Cascina La Pertica
Picedo di Polpenazze, 25080 Brescia. Owner: Ruggero Brunori. DOC: Riviera del Garda. Other: barrel-aged Chardonnay. Labels: Il Colombaio and Le Sincette. Ambitious producer.

Ricci Curbastro
Capriolo, 25031 Brescia. DOC: Franciacorta Rosso, Bianco and *champenoise*.

Fratelli Triacca
Madonna di Tirano, 23030 Sondrio. Winery run by Domenico and Gino Triacca. Heavy investment has produced much improved Valtellina Superiore.

Tronconero
Casteggio, 27045 Pavia. DOC: Oltrepò Pavese led by a fine Bonarda. Other: Chardonnay.

Uberti
Erbusco, 25030 Brescia. DOC: Franciacorta, including *champenoise* Francesco 1 Brut and Pas Dosé. Other: Cabernet Sauvignon called Rosso dei Frati Priori.

Luigi Valenti
Cigognola, 27045 Pavia. DOC: Oltrepò Pavese. The house specializes in *frizzante* Sangue di Giuda.

Enologica Valtellinese
Sondrio. DOC: Valtellina Superiore. Other: Roccascissa (Nebbiolo white), Rossola (red).

Pietro Vercesi
Rovescala, 27040 Pavia. Good Bonarda and *rosso*.

TRENTINO-ALTO ADIGE

The valley of the river Adige is Italy's corridor to the Germanic world; a narrow, rock-walled but surprisingly flat-bottomed and untortuous trench among high peaks which has carried all the traffic of millennia over the Brenner Pass from the land of olives to the land of firs and vice versa.

So Germanic is its northern half, the Alto Adige, that more than half its inhabitants know it as the Südtirol and think of Italy as a foreign country. Much of its wine goes north to market labelled in German.

The Trentino has a more southern culture, but even Trento feels only halfway to Italy. The region's wines are correspondingly cosmopolitan, using most of the international grape varieties.

The Alto Adige has made more and more successful interpretations of the white classics. The shelter and warmth of its best slopes counterpoised by its altitude give excellent balance of ripeness and acidity.

Farther south in the Trentino the trend is also towards whites. But happily, local taste still maintains the survival of the native reds. The Schiava, Lagrein and Teroldego all seem to be mountain-bred versions of the grapes of Valpolicella. In slightly different ways they all share the smooth inviting start and the lingering bitter finish which you could call the *goût de terroir* of northeast Italy.

DOC AND OTHER WINES

Alto Adige (Südtirol)
DOC: Red, *rosato* and white wine. Province: Bolzano.
Villages: 33 communes with vineyards up to 700 metres
for red grapes and 1000 metres for white.
Grapes: 95% of any of the following:
Moscato Giallo (Goldenmuskateller),
Pinot Bianco (Weissburgunder), Pinot Grigio (Ruländer),
Riesling Italico (Welschriesling), Riesling × Sylvaner
(Müller-Thurgau), Riesling Renano (Rheinriesling),
Sylvaner, Sauvignon, Traminer Aromatico (Gewürztraminer),
Cabernet, Lagrein Rosato (L. Kretzer), Lagrein Scuro
(L. Dunkel), Malvasia (Malvasier), Merlot, Moscato Rosa
(Rosenmuskateller), Pinot Nero (Blauburgunder), Schiava
(Vernatsch), Chardonnay, plus 5% of any other; 85% Schiava
and 15% of any other. Max. crop ranges from 98 hl/ha (for
Schiava and Lagrein) down to 56 hl/ha (for Moscato Giallo).
Min. alch: 11° for Moscato Giallo and Bianco, Riesling Italico,
Riesling Renano, Riesling × Sylvaner, Sylvaner,
Merlot, Chardonnay: 11.5° for Pinot Grigio, Sauvignon,
Traminer Aromatico, Cabernet, Lagrein Rosato,
Lagrein Scuro, Malvasia, Pinot Nero; 12.5° for Moscato Rosa;
10.5° for Schiava. Annual production: 1.78m. cases.
Alto Adige Lagrein Scuro, Merlot, Pinot Nero aged for
1 year is *riserva*; Cabernet aged for 2 years is *riserva*.

The general DOC for a large zone following the Adige and Isario valleys through the mountains, and including the Bolzano basin with altitudes ranging from 250 m. to 1,000 m. Of the 19 varieties allowed, the classic international grapes form the majority, several of them doing as well here as anywhere in Italy. Cabernet, Gewürztraminer, Pinot Bianco and Rheinriesling can all be outstanding. The local characters are the Lagrein, red or rosé, which makes a fruity, rich, smooth and flowing wine with a bitter twist, and the Schiava, which could be described as a jolly junior version of the same thing. The Traminer is also very much a local character, having its birthplace at Tramin (Termeno) just south of Bolzano.

The same geographic area has several more restrictive DOCs (Santa Maddalena, for example) but they are not necessarily superior in quality. Alto Adige is one of Italy's biggest suppliers of export-quality wine.

Caldaro or Lago di Caldaro or Kalterersee
DOC. Red wine. Provinces: Bolzano and Trento.
Villages: 9 communes in Bolzano and 8 in Trento.
Grapes: Schiava 85–100%, Pinot Nero and
Lagrein 15%. Max. crop: 98 hl/ha.
Min. alch: 10.5° (11° for Auslese or 'Scelto').
Annual production: 2.38m. cases.

The German name Kalterersee is more common than the Italian on this light and often sweetish red, originally grown around the lake southwest of Bolzano (now designated on labels as 'Classico'). Like all Schiava it has a bitter finish which helps to make it refreshing, though some of the bottles shipped to Germany are so revoltingly sweet and mawkish that the freezer is the only way of making them drinkable.

Castel San Michele
One of the most highly regarded reds of the region, a Cabernet-Merlot blend from the regional agricultural college at San Michele, north of Trento. It needs 5–6 years or more bottle-age.

Casteller
DOC. Red wine. Province: Trento. Villages: 27 communes,
slopes no higher than 600 m. Grapes: Schiava at least 30%,
Lambrusco up to 60% and Merlot Langrein, Teroldego 20%.
Max. crop: 112 hl/ha. Min. alch: 11.5°. Annual
production: 722,000 cases.

The light dry everyday red of the southern half of the region from Trento to Lake Garda but rarely seen outside.

Colli di Bolzano or Bozner Leiten
DOC. Red wine. Province: Bolzano. Villages: Laives,
Terlano, S. Geneiso, Bolzano, Renon, Fie, Cornedo.
Grapes: Schiava 90%, Lagrein and Pinot Nero 10%.
Max. crop: 91 hl/ha. Min. alch: 11°.
Annual production: 33,000 cases.

A similar light wine to Caldaro (q.v.) but more often dry.

Kolbenhofer
A superior Schiava red made at Tramin by Hofstätter.

Meranese di Collina or Meraner Hügel

DOC. Red wine. Province: Bolzano, Villages: around Merano, on both sides of the Adige river. Grapes: Schiava (Grossa, Media, Piccolo, Gentile, Grigia, Tschaggele). Max. crop: 87.5 hl/ha. Min. alch: 10.5°. Annual production: 122,000 cases.
The local light red of Merano, for the young and hot to drink young and cool.

Nosiola

DOC Trentino native white grape. The wine is aromatic, fruity, dry and (surprise!) finishes with a bitter note. It is also the base of Vin Santo.

San Leonardo

One of the successful Cabernet-Merlot reds of the Trentino. *See* San Leonardo (Gonzaga) under Producers.

Santa Maddalena or St Magdalener

DOC. Red wine. Province: Bolzano. Villages: the hills to the north, above Bolzano (Classico is from Santa Maddalena itself). Grapes: Schiava (Grossa, Media, Grigia, Tschaggele); Langrein, Pinot Nero up to 10%. Max. crop: 87 hl/ha. Min. alch: 11.5°. Annual production 333,000 cases.
An obvious relation to Caldaro but from better vineyards, more concentrated and stronger. Under Mussolini it was absurdly pronounced one of Italy's three greatest wines (Barolo and Barbaresco were the others). This and Lagrein Dunkel must be considered the first choice among typical reds of Bolzano.

Sorni

DOC. Red and white wine. Province: Trento. Villages: Lavis, Giovo and S. Michele all'Adige, north of Trento. Grapes: (red) Schiava 70%, Teroldego 20–30% and Lagrein up to 10%, (white) Nosiola 70% and others 30%. Max. crop: 98 hl/ha. Min. alch: 10° white; 10.5° red, 11° is 'Scelto' or Auslese. Annual production: 22,000 cases.
DOC for reds and whites from around the village of Sorni. Both are light dry wines for summer drinking.

Trelano or Terlaner

DOC. White wine. Province: Bolzano. Villages: Terlano, Meltina, Nalles, Andriano, Appiano, Caldaro (Terlano and Nalles are 'Classico'). Grapes: Chardonnay, Müller-Thurgau, Pinot Bianco, Riesling Italico, Riesling Renano, Sauvignon, Sylvaner 90%, plus other DOC grapes of the same colour and the blend known as Terlano or Terlaner (Pinot Bianco 50%, Riesling Italico/Riesling Renano/Sauvignon/Sylvaner/ Müller-Thurgau up to 50%, other whites up to 5%). Max. crop: 91 hl/ha. Min. alch: 11.5° for Terlano, Riesling Renano and Sylvaner; 10.5° for Riesling Italico; 11° for Pinot Bianco and 12° for Sauvignon. Annual production: 122,000 cases.
The best whites of the Alto Adige are grown in this part of the valley, particularly just west of Bolzano where Terlano has excellent southwest slopes. Pinot Bianco, Riesling Renano, Sauvignon and sometimes Sylvaner can all make wines of real body and balance, occasionally in the international class. Terlano without a grape name is a Pinot Bianco blend and often a good buy.

Teroldego Rotaliano

DOC. Red wine. Province: Trento. Villages: Mezzocorona, Mezzolombardo, S. Michel all'Adige (all on the Campo Rotaliano). Grapes: Teroldego. Max crops: 91 hl/ha. Min. alch. 11.5° (12° aged 2 years is *superiore*). Annual production: 244,000 cases.
Pergola-trained Teroldego vines on the alluvial gravel of the Campo Rotaliano give the best of the typical (smooth, well-fleshed, finally bitter) reds of the region.

Trentino

DOC. Red and white wine. Province: Trento. Villages: a long zone from Mezzocorona north of Trento to 15 miles north of Verona. Grapes: (red) 50–85% Cabernet and 15–50% Merlot; (white) 50–85% Chardonnay and 15–50% Pinot Bianco, Moscato (Giallo and Rosa), Müller-Thurgau, Nosiola, Pinot (Grigio and Nero), Riesling (Italico and Renano), Traminer Aromatico, Lagrein, Marzemino. Max. crop varies from 63 to 87 hl/ha. Min. alch: 10.5° for Nosiola, Riesling Italico; 11° for Cabernet, Chardonnay, Lagrein, Marzemino, Merlot, Müller-Thurgau, Pinot, Riesling; 11.5° for Pinot Nero, Moscato Giallo, Traminer Aromatico; 12.5° for Moscato Rosa. Annual production: 1.27m. cases. Aged 2 years (*riserva*) for Lagrein, Marzemino, Merlot, Pinot Nero, Cabernet; 3 for Vino Santo.
The southern counterpart of the DOC Alto Adige, with almost as great a range of wines but more emphasis on reds. Cabernet is well established here with excellent results; Lagrein gives some of the best examples of the regional style. Merlot is common – best in its blends with Cabernet. Pinot Bianco and Traminer are the best of the dry whites, Moscato is potentially excellent dessert wine.

Valdadige or Etschtaler

DOC. Red and white wine. Provinces: Trento, Bolzano and Verona. Villages: 38 communes in Trento, 33 in Bolzano and 4 in Verona. Grapes: (red) Schiava and/or Lambrusco 30% and the rest, Merlot, Pinot Nero, Lagrein, Teroldego and/or Negrara up to 70%; (white) Pinot Bianco, Pinot Grigio, Riesling Italico or Müller-Thurgau 20%; the rest, Bianchetta Trevigiana, Trebbiano Toscano, Nosiola, Vernaccia up to 80%. Max. crop: 98 hl/ha. Min. alch: white 10.5°, red 11°. Annual production: 1.02m. cases.
The catch-all DOC for most of the Adige valley from Merano to Verona. No high standards are imposed, but producers who add 'varietal' names self-impose them.

Valle Isarco or Eisacktaler

DOC. White wine. Province: Bolzano. Villages: parts of 12 communes in the Isarco valley northeast of Bolzano to Bressanone (Brixen). Grapes: Traminer Aromatico, Pinot Grigio, Veltliner, Sylvaner or Müller-Thurgau. Max. crop: ranges from 70 to 91 hl/ha. Min. alch: 11° for Traminer Aromatico, Pinot Grigio; 10.5° for Veltliner, Sylvaner, Müller-Thurgau. Annual production: 100,000 cases.
The white wines of this alpine valley are all light and need drinking young in contrast to the 'stiffer' wines of Terlano to the west.

TRENTINO-ALTO ADIGE PRODUCERS

Abbazia di Novacella (Stiftskellerei Neustift)
Bressanone, 39042 Bolzano.
A lovely 12th-century monastry with 120 acres. DOC: Valle Isarco. Bottles Müller-Thurgau and Sylvaner entitled to the designation Brixner.

Càvit (Cantina Viticoltori Trento)
38100 Trento.
Founded: 1957. A consortium of 15 cooperatives with no less than 4,500 growers, who produce about 75% of the wine of Trento province. Only a select part is issued under

the Càvit label. Chief wine maker: Giacinto Giacomini. DOC: Casteller, Teroldego Rotaliano, Trentino, Valdadige. Other: Chardonnay, Pinot Grigio, 4 Vicariati, Firmanto *champenoise*, table wines. This immense but effective cooperative is unbeatable for quality at a reasonable price. Notable are Gran Spumante Càvit Brut Brut (*charmat*) and 4 Vicariati (Cabernet-Merlot). A new project is a series of estate wines called Collezione di Càvit.

Conti Bossi Fedrigotti-Foianeghe
Rovereto, 38068 Trento.

A family firm founded about 1860. DOC: Trentino. Other: Foianeghe Bianco, Rosso, Schiava Rosato, Teroldego della Vallagarina. Best known for Foianeghe Rosso (Cabernet-Merlot).

Ferrari
38040 Trento

A family firm founded in 1902 in the heart of Trento; long the leading name in Italian champagne-method wines. The firm is now run by Franco, Gino and wine maker Mauro Lunelli. Ferrari Brut, Brut de Brut Millesimato, Brut Rosé, Extra Dry, Giulio Ferrari Riserva del Fondatore, Ferrari wines have great finesse, to the point of austerity.

Gaierhof
Rovere della Luna, 38030 Trento.

Founded: 1976. Owner: Luigi Togn. DOC: Caldaro, Sorni, Teroldego Rotaliano, Trentino, Valadige. Togn is actively building production, here and at his Maso Poli estate.

Giorgio Gray
Appiano, 39100 Bolzano.

Owner-wine maker: Giorgio Gray. DOC: Alto Adige. The elusive Giorgio Gray (who designed a dozen or so wines in other regions) best demonstrates his gifts in some of Alto Adige's most convincing wines – red and white – now bottled under his own name rather than under the Bellendorf, Herrnhofer and Kehlburg labels of the past.

J. Hofstätter
Tramin, 39040 Bolzano.

Founded: 1907. Now owned and operated by Paolo Foradori. DOC: Alto Adige, Cadaro. Other: de Vite, Kolbenhofer. An outstanding assortment of South Tyrolean wines partly from 86 acres of family vines. The Pinot Nero from Barthenau is highly rated.

Instituto Agrario Provinciale San Michele all'Adige
San Michele all'Adige, 38010 Trento.

The agricultural college built around Castel San Michele is a national leader in viticultural research. There has been a revival in recent years under the guidance of wine maker Professor Salvatore Maule. From 100 acres of vines, the college makes several wines both for experiment and commerce, including the excellent Castel San Michele (a Cabernet-Merlot blend). There are single vineyard bottlings for Pinot Grigio, Chardonnay, Riesling Renano, Pinot Bianco and Sauvignon Blanc.

Kettmeir
Caldaro, 39052 Bolzano.

One of the biggest firms of the region. The controlling interest was recently sold to Santa Margherita of the Veneto, though Franco Kettmeir remains as manager.

DOC: Alto Adige, Caldaro, Santa Maddalena, Terlano. Other: Chardonnay, Grande Cuvée Brut, Gran Spumante Rosé, Merlot Siebeneich, Moscato Atesino.

Lagariavini
Volano, 38060 Trento.

Founded in 1972, a union of two older wineries. DOC: Teroldego Rotaliano, Trentino. Other: Chardonnay, Mori Vecio (Cabernet-Merlot), Moscato, Müller-Thurgau. A considerable establishment making each major type of wine, plus some Brut di Concilio *champenoise*.

Alois Lageder
39100 Bolzano

Founded: 1855. DOC: Alto Adige, Caldaro, Santa Maddalena, Terlano. This well-known family winery owns 50 acres and buys from growers with another 1,000 acres to make some of the region's finest varietals. Lageder recently founded the Partico dei Leoni cellars to produce oak-aged Chardonnay and other *avant garde* wines.

Conti Martini
Mezzocorona, 38016 Trento.

Founded: 1977. Owners: The Martini family. Wine maker: Christina Martini. DOC: Teroldego Rotaliano, Trentino. Other: Müller-Thurgau, Pinot Grigio. A new 25-acre estate producing wines of exceptional class.

Pojer & Sandri
Faedo, 38010 Trento.

Founded: 1975. Owners: Mario Pojer (oenologist) and Fiorentino Sandri (viticulturist). Chardonnay, Müller-Thurgau, Nosiola, Pinot Nero, Schiava, Vin dei Molini. The youthful producers, with 30 acres, use what they call 'technologically advanced artisan methods' to make about 2,000 cases each of Müller-Thurgau and Schiava, less of the others – all remarkable for a delicately floral scent and fruity crispness. The Schiava is pale and pretty.

Vinicola Santa Margherita
Caldora, Bolzano.

A new winery created next door to Kettmeir which this Veneto company has recently taken over. There is a new prestige line of Alto Adige DOCs, Ca'd'Archi Chardonnay, Cabernet Sauvignon and Müller-Thurgau.

Armando Simoncelli
Navicello di Rovereto, 38060 Trento.

A leading estate with a fine Marzemino among the DOCs. Other: Simoncelli Brut Trento Classico and Navesel, a Cabernet-Merlot blend.

J. Tiefenbrunner (Schloss Turmhoff)
Entiklar, 39040 Bolzano.

Owner and chief wine maker: Herbert Tiefenbrunner. DOC: Alto Adige, Caldaro. Others: Feldmarschall, table wines. This established family winery produces some of the South Tirol's most exciting white wines. The Feldmarschall comes from vineyards of 3,250 ft above sea level, the region's highest.

Roberto Zeni
Grumo di San Michele all'Adige, 38010 Trento.

Founded: 1882. Run by Roberto Zeni. DOC: Teroldego Rotaliano, Trentino. Other: Chardonnay, Rosé di Pinot. 800–1,200 cases of each type from 10 acres. Zeni is an excellent wine maker; his Chardonnay and Pinot Bianco are perfumed, his Teroldego harmonious and rounded.

After DOC?

A monumental effort of organization and definition produced, within 20 years from 1962, 200-odd DOCs covering some 450 styles of wine. It was precisely the discipline that Italy needed, both to concetrate her producers' minds on quality and to convince the rest of the world that she was in earnest; that her labels were to be trusted.

The DOCs are accurate records of the regional practice of the time when they were promulgated. Whatever a consensus of growers agreed as normal and satisfactory within the traditions of their area was, after consultation with Rome, engraved on the tablets.

What is not often clearly understood is that the practices being followed and approved were in many, if not most, cases far from optimal. In the matter of grape varieties the DOC enshrined what the farmers had planted in their vineyards, not what they should, or might, have planted to produce the best wine. It allows for example, a proportion of white grapes in Chianti which can almost make it a *rosato*.

The growers in most cases allowed themselves crops far larger than could be consistent with fine wine. Since surplus is a perpetual headache in Italy this was short-sighted. They also set high minimum alcohol levels based on their old fear of unstable wine – whereas with modern techniques lower alcohol is both practicable and desirable.

Again, in their search for stability (and with their inherited taste for wines aged almost to exhaustion in oak) they set minimum ageing limits which run clean counter to the modern trends for clearly fruity and fragrant, or else bottle-aged and complex, wines. For the time being the only alternative, for producers who are unwilling to be bound by ideas they reject, is to label their wine *vino da tavola*.

Abate Nero
Gardolo, 38100 Trento. Abate Nero Brut is first-rate *champenoise*.

La Vinicola Sociale Aldeno
Aldeno, 38060 Trento. Cooperative. Founded: 1910. DOC: Casteller, Trentino. Other: San Zeno, Degli Aldü Brut Trento Classico.

Riccardo Battistotti
Nomi, 38060 Trento. Range of DOCs includes fine Marzemino.

Bolognani
Lavis, 38015 Trento. A quality producer of white Nosiola, Müller-Thurgau and Chardonnay.

La Cadalora
Ala, 38061 Trento. A 10-acre estate producing Marzemino, Pinots and Chardonnay.

Maso Cantanghel
Civvezzano, 38045 Trento. Fine, barrel-fermented Chardonnay Vigna Piccola and Pinot Nero from 5 acres.

Remo Calovi
Faedo, 38010 Trento. DOCs Trentino. A miniscule production of particularly good Müller-Thurgau and Chardonnay.

Barone de Cles
Mezzolombardo, 38017 Trento. Owners: Leonardo and Michele Cles. DOC: Teroldego Rotaliano, Trentino. Other: Chardonnay, Dama delle Rosé, Pinot Grigio.

Cantina Sociale Colterenzio (Kellereignossenschaft Shreckbichl)
Cornaiano, 39050 Bolzano. A go-ahead group of 360 growers with a range of Alto Adige, Terlano, St. Magdalener and Kalterersee DOCs with some single vineyard bottlings. The Cornell label is used for selected wines aged in *barriques*.

Cantina Sociale Cornaiano (Kellereignossenschaft Girlan)
Cornaiano, 39050 Bolzano. Wine maker: Hartmuth Spitaler. A specialist in Kalterersee plus good Riesling, Gewürztraminer and Pinot Nero under the Optimum label.

Anton Dissertori-Plattenhof
Termino, 39040 Bolzano. Noted for Gewürztraminer.

Donati
Mezzocorona, 38016 Trento. Owner: Pierfranco Donati. DOC: Teroldego, Trentino.

Fratelli Dorigati
Mezzocorona, 38016 Trento. Owners: The Dorigati family. DOC: Teroldego, Trentino. Other: Rebo and Grener (from Teroldego with Cabernet).

von Elzenbaum
Tramin, 39040 Bolzano. Wine has been made on the estate since at least 1533. Owner: Anton von Elzenbaum. DOC: Alto Adige. Other: Edelweisser, Blauburgunder (Pinot Nero),

Gewürztraminer and Rheinriesling. The Gewürztraminer is Italy's most highly regarded – appropriately, since Tramin gave its name to the grape.

Fratelli Endrizzi
San Michele all'Adige, 38010 Trento. Founded: 1885. Owners: Franco and Paolo Endrizzi. DOC: Trentino, Valdadige. Other: Teroldego di San Michele.

Giuseppe Fanti
Pressano di Lavis, 38015 Trento. Known for fine, dry Nosiola. Also a good Chardonnay.

Foradori
Mezzolombardo, 38017 Trento. DOC: Teroldego Rotaliano, Trentino. Often the best Teroldego. Also a fine Gewürztraminer from their Alto Adige Maso Foradori.

Alphons Giovanett-Castelfelder
Egna, 39044 Bolzano. Alto Adige DOCs, notably Gewürztraminer.

Anton Gojer-Glogglehof
39100 Bolzano. Good St. Magdalener and *barrique*-aged Langrien Dunkel.

Haderburg
Salorno, 39040 Bolzano. Owners: the Ochsenreiter family. Respected Haderburg Brut and Nature *champenoise*. Work has begun on promising still wines.

Josepf Huber-Pacherhof
Bressanone, 39042 Bolzano. Excellent Müller-Thurgau from high vineyards.

Catina Sociale di Isera
Isera, 38060 Trento. Cooperative. DOC: Trentino. Other: Marzemino di Isera.

Graf Eberhard Kuenburg-Schloss Sallegg
Caldaro, 29052 Bolzano. First-class late-harvest Rosenmuskateller and fine Kalterersee.

Lagariavini-I Vini del Concilio
Volano, Trento. A range of DOCs plus Mori Vecio, a Cabernet-Merlot blend. Grand Bleu Pinot *frizzante* and Concilio Brut Trento Classico.

Cantina Sociale Lavis-Sorni-Salorno
Lavis, 38015 Trento. Cooperative. DOC: Caldaro, Sorni, Casteller.

Le Brul
Mezzocorona, 38016 Trento. Owner: Salvatore Maule. Trentino's leading consultant produces his own Gran Le Brul *champenoise*.

Letrari
Nogaredo, 38060 Trento. Founded: 1976. Owner: Leonello Letrari. DOC: Trentino. Other: Maso Lodron (Cabernet-Merlot).

Longariva
Rovereto, 38068 Trento. Owner: Marco Manica. Admired DOCs plus Tre Cesure, a Cabernet-Merlot table wine and a Rülander.

Madonna della Vittoria
Arco, 38062 Trento. A promising new estate with a range of DOCs.
Conti Martini
Mezzocorona, Trento. An old family estate making fine Teroldego and Lagrein and a perfumed, dry Moscato Bianco.
Karl Martini & Sohn
Cornaiano, 39050 Bolzano. A range of DOCs including a good Kalterersee.
Cantina Mezzocorona
Mezzocorona, 38016 Trento. DOC: Teroldego Rotaliano, Trentino, Valdadige. Other: Chardonnay, Pinot Grigio, Rotari Brut *champenoise*.
Equipe Trentina Spumanti
Mezzolombardo, 38017 Trento. Owner: Letrari & C. Wine maker: Pietro Turra. This respected specialist in *champenoise* uses the trademark Equipe 5 on Brut, Brut Riserva, Extra Dry, Rosé Brut and Sec.
Klosterkellerei Muri-Gries
39100 Bolzano DOC: Alto Adige, Santa Magdalena, Terlano. Other: Malvasier di Gries. The ancient cellars of the Benedictine monastery of Gries produce marvellously typical wines.
Fratelli Pedrotti
Nomi, 38060 Trento. DOC: Casteller, Trentino, Teroldego Rotaliano, Valdadige. Other: Morlacco, Trento Classico Pedrotti Brut.
Fratelli Pisoni
Pergolese Sarche, 38070 Trento. DOC: Trentino. Other: Gran Spumante Pisoni Brut *champenoise*, San Siro Bianco, Rosso.
Giovanni Poli
Santa Massenza, 38070 Trento. Elegant, luscious Vino Santo though aged in stainless steel tanks.
Maso Poli
San Michele all'Adige, Trento. Owner: Luigi Togn. An old estate producing good Sorni Bianco and Pinot Nero.
Portico di Leoni
Magré, Bolzano. Owners: Alois Lageder and Luis von Dellemann. Wine maker: Maurizio Castelli. Fine barrel-fermented Chardonnay.
Praeclarus
San Paolo-Appiano, 39057 Bolzano. Owner: Johann Ebner. Noted *champenoise* Praeclarus Brut and Extra Brut.
Baroni a Prato
Segonzano, 38047 Trento. Chardonnay, Pinot Nero and Cabernet from an estate high in the Cembra valley.
Luigi Raffaelli
Volano, 38060 Trento. Good range of DOCs plus the table wine Salengo from Cabernet-Merlot.
Castel Rametz
Merano, 39012 Bolzano. DOC: Alto Adige, Meranese di Collina, Santa

Magdalena.
Cantine Cooperativa Rotaliana
Mezzolombardo, 38017 Trento. Admirable Teroldega along with Lagrein and Trentina DOCs.
Hans Rottensteiner
39100 Bolzano. A sound range of DOCs including good St. Magdalener.
Heinrich Rottensteiner
39100 Bolzano. A dedicated grower making excellent St. Magdalener.
Schloss Sallegg
39100 Bolzano. Owner: Eberhard Kuenburg. DOC: Alto Adige, Caldaro. Kuenburg's lightly sweet Moscato Rosa 'Rosenmuskateller' is exquisite.
Tenuta San Leonardo
Avio. Trento. Owner Carlo Gonzaga is using *barriques* to bring new finesse to Cabernet Sauvignon and the Cabernet-Merlot blend of Campi Sarni.
Cantina Sociale San Michele (Kellereigenossenschaft St. Michael)
San-Michele-Appiano, 39057 Bolzano. A good range of Alto Adige DOCs with *spumante* and Kelterersee.
San Rocco
38100 Trento. Creator of the excellent Novecento Brut *champenoise*.
Schloss Schwanburg (Rudolf Carli Eredi)
Nalles, 39010 Bolzano. Founded: 1884. DOC: Alto Adige, Caldaro, Santa Maddalena, Terlano. Other: *barrique*-aged Castel Schwanburg from Cabernet and Merlot.
Enrico Spagnolli
Isera, 38060 Trento. A range of Trentino DOCs including a fine Marzemino and Müller-Thurgau.
Giuseppe Spagnolli
Aldeno, 38060 Trento. Producer of the outstanding *champenoise* Spagnolli Brut – a blend of Chardonnay and Pinot Nero.
de Tarczal
Marano d'Isera, Trento. An admirable range of Trentino DOCs with an exemplary Marzemino d'Isera.
Cantina Sociale Terlano (Kellereigenossenschaft Terlan)
Terlano, 39018 Bolzano. DOC: Alto Adige, Terlano.
Cantina Sociale di Termeno (Kellereigenossenschaft Tramin)
Tramin, 39040 Bolzano. DOC: Alto Adige, Caldaro. Other: Hexenbichler.
Vallarom
Avio, 38063 Trento. Owners: the Scienza family. Attilio Scienza is the director of CS San Michele. Good Marzemino, Pinot Nero, Merlot, Cabernet Sauvignon and an admired late-harvest Chardonnay.
Cantina Sociale Valle d'Isarco (Eisacktaler Kellereigenossenschaft)
Chiusa, 39043 Bolzano. DOC: Valle Isarco. A respected cooperative making fine Isarco whites.

Vivaldi
Meltina, 39010 Bolzano. Owner: Josef Reiterer. Makes exemplary *champenoise* Brut and Extra Brut and has acquired prized vineyards at Mazzon for still wines.
W. Walch
Tramin, 39040 Bolzano. Owners: The Walch family. DOC: Alto Adige, Caldaro, Santa Magdalena, Terlano.

VENETO

The hinterland of Venice is one third mountain, two thirds plain. Its northernmost boundary is with Austria, high in the Dolomite; in the south it is the flat valley of the Po. All the important wines of the Veneto are grown in the faltering alpine foothills and occasional hilly outcrops in a line eastwards from Lake Garda to Conegliano. Verona, near Lake Garda, is the wine capital, with a greater production of DOC wine from its vineyards of Soave, Valpolicella and Bardolino than any other Italian region. So important are these three in the export market that Verona has a claim to being the international wine capital of the whole of Italy. The nation's biggest wine fair, Vinitaly, takes place in Verona in April.

To the east Conegliano has another claim: to be the nation's centre of viticultural technology and research.

The Verona and Conegliano areas have strong traditions of using grape varieties peculiar to themselves: Garganega, the Soave grape, the Corvina of Valpolicella and the Prosecco, which makes admirable sparkling wine at Conegliano, are unknown elsewhere. But less established and self-confident areas, such as the Berici and Euganean hills and the Piave, prolific flatland vineyards on the borders of Friuli-Venezia Giulia to the east, try their luck with a range of international varieties: Pinots, Cabernets and their kin. Merlot is the standby red of the region and rapidly improving from acceptable to delicious.

DOC AND OTHER WINES

Amarone
See Valpolicella.

Bardolino
DOC. Red and rosé wine. Province: Verona. Villages: Bardolino and 15 others. Grapes: Corvina Veronese 35–65%, Rondinella 10–40%, Molinara 10–20%, Negrara up to 10%, Rossignola, Barbera; Garganega and Sangiovese up to 15%. Max. crop: 91 hl/ha. Min. alch: 10.5°. Aged 1 year for *superiore*. Annual production: 2.33m. cases.

A pale red and even paler Chiaretto; a lighter version of Valpolicella with the same quality (in a good example) of liveliness. Bardolino is on glacial deposits which do not warm up as well as the limestone of Valpolicella. Like Valpolicella it is briskest and best in the year after the vintage. Guerrieri Rizzardi (*see* Producers) makes a sort of Bardolino Recioto called Rosso San Pietro.

Bianco di Custoza
DOC. White wine. Province: Verona. Villages: Grapes: Trebbiano Toscano 35–45%, Garganega 20–40%, Tocai Friulano 5–30%, Cortese, Riesling Italico, Malvasia Toscano 20–30%. Max. crop: 97 hl/ha. Min. alch: 11°. Annual production 722,000 cases.

The southern neighbour of Soave, this white is increasingly seen, especially a *spumante* (usually *charmat*).

Breganze
DOC. Red and white wine. Province: Vicenza. Villages: Breganze and Maróstica, and parts of 13 other communes. Grapes: Breganze Bianco: Tocai, plus Pinot Bianco, Pinot Grigio, Riesling Italico, Sauvignon and Vespaiolo, max. 15%. Breganze Rosso: Merlot, plus Marzemino, Groppello, Cabernet Franc, Cabernet Sauvignon, Pinot Nero and Freisa, max. 15%. Breganze-Cabernet: Sauvignon or Franc. Breganze-Pinot Nero: Pinot Nero. Breganze-Pinot Bianco: Pinot Bianco and Pinot Grigio. Breganze-Pinot Grigio: Pinot Grigio. Breganze-Vespaiolo: Vespaiolo. Max. crop: 91 hl/ha. Min. alch: 11° for white, red, 11.5° for Cabernet, Pinot Nero, Pinot Bianco, Pinot Grigio and Vespaiolo. Annual production: 278,000 cases.

Light and agreeable 'varietal' wines from the birthplace of the great architect Palladio. Pinot Bianco and Cabernet are the best (*see* Maculan under Producers).

Cabernet di Pramaggiore
See under Lison-Pramaggiore.

Campo Fiorin
An unusually serious interpretation of Valpolicella by Masi (*see* Producers). The wine is macerated with the skins of Recioto Amarone (q.v.) after pressing. The prototype for *ripasso* wines.

Capitel San Rocco
A similar serious red to Campo Fiorin from Tedeschi (*see* Producers). Also a clean, fairly pale-bodied dry white.

Colli Berici
DOC. Red and white wine. Province: Vicenza. Villages: 28 communes south of Vicenza. Grapes: 7 varieties, with limited (10–15%) admixture of other local grapes. The range is Garganega (comparable with Soave), Tocai Bianco, Sauvignon, Pinot Bianco, Merlot, Tocai Rosso (sharp fruity young red), Cabernet. Cabernet is aged for 3 years for *riserva*. Max. crop: 78 hl/ha. Min. alch: 10.5° for Garganega, 11° for Tocai Bianco, Sauvignon, Pinot Bianco, Merlot and Tocai Rosso. Annual production: 522,000 cases.

These hills between Verona and Padua have clear potential for quality, best demonstrated by their Cabernet.

Colli Euganei
DOC. Red and white wine. Province: Padua. Villages: 17 communes south of Padua. Grapes: (red) Merlot 60–80%, Cabernet Franc, Cabernet Sauvignon, Barbera and Raboso Veronese 20–40%; (white) Garganega 30–50%, Serprina 10–30% Tocai and/or Sauvignon 20–40%, Pinella, Pinot Bianco and Riesling Italico max. 20% (Moscato) Moscato Bianco. Max. crop: 98 hl/ha. Min. alch: 10.5° for white and Moscato, 11° for red, 11.5° for Cabernet. Annual production: 356,000 cases.

Euganean wine, despite its long history is generally rather dull. The best at present is the non-DOC Cabernet and a branded red, Sant'Elmo.

Gambellara
DOC. White wine. Province: Vicenza. Villages: Gambellara, Montebello Vicentino, Montorso and Zermeghedo. Grapes: Garganega 80–90%, Trebbiano di Soave up to 20%. Max. crop: 98 hl/ha. Min. alch: 10.5° for Gambellara (11.5° for *superiore*); 12° for Recioto di Gambellara; 14° for Vin Santo di Gambellara. Vin Santo di Gambellara aged for at least 2 years. Annual production 611,000 cases.

Soave's eastern neighbour, worth trying as an alternative. Its Recioto version is sweet (and sometimes fizzy). Vin Santo is sweet and strong.

Lessini Durello
DOC. White wine. Provinces: Verona and Vicenza. Area: 7 communes in Verona and 21 in Vicenza. Grape: Durello min. 85%, Garganega, Trebbiano di Soave, Chardonnay, Pinot Nero up to 15%. Max crop: 112 hl/ha. Min. alch: 10°.

Recent DOC approved zone, making 'steely dry wines, both still and sparkling' (Burton Anderson).

Lison-Pramaggiore
DOC. Red and white wine. Provinces: Venice, Pordenone, Treviso. Area: 11 communes in Venice, 2 in Treviso and 5 in Pordenone. Grapes: Cabernet (Franc and Sauvignon), Chardonnay, Merlot, Pinot (Bianco and Grigio), Refosco del Peduncolo Rosso, Riesling Italico, Sauvignon, Tocai Italico and Verduzzo. Aged: (Cabernet) 3 years for *riserva*; (Merlot) 2 years for *riserva*. Max. crop: 91 hl/ha. Min. alch: 11°. Annual production 611,000 cases.

A relatively new DOC comprising the areas of Tocai di Lison, Cabernet and Merlot di Pramaggiore. The wine list includes 12 types; the Pinot Bianco and Riesling Italico may also be *spumante*.

Merlot
The major red grape of the eastern Veneto, included in the major DOC zones but often found as a 'table wine' which may be the sign of an individualist product of quality. (See Villa dal Ferro-Lazzarini under Producers.) Its best wines are dark and nicely fruity, often ending with an astringent note.

Merlot di Pramaggiore
See under Lison-Pramaggiore.

Montello e Colli Asolani
DOC. Red and white wine. Province: Treviso. Villages: 17 communes in the province. Grapes: Prosecco for white, Cabernet or Merlot for red (up to 15° blending allowed). Max. crop: 70 hl/ha. Min. alch: 10.5° for white; 11° for Merlot; 11.5° for Cabernet. Aged: (red) 2 years (1 in wood) for *superiore*. Annual production: 88,900 cases.

DOC with a small supply of Cabernet and more of Merlot and Prosecco, which is usually fizzy and often sweet. The hills around Asolo were a resort during the Renaissance, famous for Palladio's villas. The most famous wine estate of the area is Venegazzù (*see* Venegazzù-Conte Loredan-Gasparini under Producers).

Piave
DOC. Red and white wine. Provinces: Venice, Treviso. Villages: from Conegliano to the Adriatic sea. 50 communes in Treviso, 12 in Venice. Grapes: Cabernet, Merlot, Pinot Bianco, Pinot Grigio, Pinot Nero, Raboso, Tocai or Verduzzo. Max. crop: 91 hl/ha. Min. alch: 11° for Merlot, Pinot Bianco, Tocai, Verduzzo, 11.5° for Cabernet, Pinot Grigio, Pinot Nero, Raboso. Aged: (Cabernet) 3 years for *riserva*; (Merlot) 3 years for *vecchio*; (Pinot Nero) 2 years for *riserva*. Annual production 1.5m. cases.

The river Piave flows through flat country to the sea north of Venice (at Jesolo). Cabernet and Merlot both thrive here, making rather dry wines that benefit from ageing. The whites need drinking young.

Pinot Bianco, Grigio, Nero
All three Pinots are found in the Veneto; none achieves the quality found farther east in Friuli-Venezia Giulia. Some good Pinot Spumante is made by Maculan and Chardonnay Spumante by Venegazzù-Conte Loredan-Gasparini (*see* Producers).

Pramaggiore
See under Lison-Pramaggiore.

Prosecco di Conegliano-Valdobbiadene
DOC. White wine. Province: Treviso. Villages: Valdobbiadene, Conegliano, Vittorio Veneto plus 12 other communes. Grapes: Prosecco, Verdiso, Pinot Bianco, Pinot Grigio, Chardonnay up to 15%, or Verdiso alone up to 10%. Max. crop: 84 hl/ha. Min. alch: 10.5°. Annual production: 1.55m.

The native Prosecco grape gives a rather austere and charmless yellowish dry wine but responds well to being made fizzy, whether *frizzante* or *spumante*, particularly in its semi-sweet and sweet forms. Valdobbiadene is a restricted zone where the wines have a finer texture, greater length on the palate and the right to the title Superiore di Cartizze.

Raboso del Piave
The local Raboso grape makes an astringent red wine which is worth meeting, especially with 4 or 5 years' bottle-age.

Recioto
See under Valpolicella.

Soave and Recioto di Soave
DOC. White wine. Province: Verona. Villages: Soave and 12 others. Grapes: Garganega 70–90%, Trebbiano di Soave and Trebbiano Toscano up to 30%. Max. crop: 98 hl/ha. Min. alch: 10.5° for Soave, 11.5° for Soave Superiore. Aged 8 months for *superiore*. Annual production: 5.55m. cases

The most popular of all Italian white wines. Its simple name seems to express its simple nature: it is smooth, light and easy to drink. When it is well made and above all fresh it is hugely tempting. The zone is immediately east of Valpolicella, making Verona a singularly well-watered city.

A central zone of Soave is entitled to the term Classico, which in this case is worth an extra hundred lire or two. To taste the wine at its best, look for Pieropan (*see* Producers), though Bolla and the colossal cooperative are reliable. Recioto di Soave is a concentrated, semi-sweet and rich-textured version made of semi-dried grapes.

Tocai di Lison
See under Lison-Pramaggiore.

Valpolicella – Recioto della Valpolicella-Amarone

DOC. Red wine. Province: Verona. Villages: 19 communes in the hills north of Verona, the westernmost 5 of which are the 'Classico' zone. Grapes: Corvina Veronese 40–70%, Rondinella 20–40%, Molinara 5–25%, Rossignola, Negrara, Barbera, Sangiovese up to 15%. Max. crop: 84 hl/ha. Min. alch: 11°. Recioto must have 14° potential alcohol of which at least 12° is actual. Aged 1 year for *superiore*. Annual production 4.11m. cases.

Valpolicella, like Chianti, has too wide a range of qualities to be easily summed up. At its best it is one of Italy's most tempting light reds, always reminding one of cherries, combining the smooth and the lively and ending with the bitter-almond hallmark of almost all northeast Italian reds. In commerce it can be a poor, pale, listless sort of wine. Part of the secret lies in its age and condition: the youngest is always best, no matter what its makers or the DOC regulations may say. 'Classico' is also better; the pick of the villa-dotted vineyards are in the hills skirted to the south and west by the river Adige, divided by the river from Bardolino. Soave lies at the opposite, eastern, end of the zone.

At any Veronese gathering the last bottle to be served is Recioto, either in its sweet form or its powerful, dry, velvety but astringent and bitter Amarone. Recioto is made by half drying selected grapes to concentrate their sugars, then giving them a long fermentation in the New Year. If the fermentation is allowed to go on to the bitter end the result is Amarone. Many critics find it one of Italy's greatest red wines. My advice is to keep a glass of young Valpolicella at hand to quench your thirst. Recioto is also made in a fizzy form.

Venegazzù della Casa

The estate of Conte Loredan (*see* Producers) in the DOC Montello-Colli Asolani, but most famous for its non-DOC Cabernet-Merlot blend in the Bordeaux style, comparable perhaps to a powerful rustic St-Emilion, and its *méthode champenoise spumante*.

VENETO PRODUCERS

Allegrini
Fumane di Valpolicella, 37022 Verona.

Owners: The Allegrini family for 3 generations. DOC: Valpolicella, Recioto, Amarone. Other: Pelara. The late Giovanni Allegrini's 3 children, Walter, Marilisa and Franco, now run the estate which has about 50 acres of choice plots in Valpolicella Classico. Their increasingly admired wines include some of the most persuasive Valpolicella Classico Superiore and Amarone.

Anselmi
Monteforte d'Alpone, 37032 Verona.

Owner: Roberto d'Anselmi. DOC: Soave, Valpolicella. Other: Cabernet Sauvignon. With 62 acres of his own vineyard and 74 under contract, Anselmi has become a major force in the area, expressing the versatility of Soave. He also makes a widely admired *barrique*-seasoned Recioto.

Bertani
37121 Verona.

Founded: 1857; now headed by Gaetano and Giovanni Bertani. DOC: Soave, Valpolicella-Valpantena, Recioto, Amarone. Other: Bertarosé, *barrique*-aged Chardonnay, red *ripasso*. From 500 acres of family vines and 500–600 acres belonging to suppliers, this venerable house makes model wines, notably Secco-Bertani Valpolicella and aged Amarone. Always reliable, it is now reasserting signs of leadership in Verona.

Bolla
37100 Verona.

Founded in Soave in 1883, the firm – FRABO S.P.A. – is now run by the Bolla brothers. DOC: Soave, Valpolicella, Recioto, Amarone. Other: Cabernet Sauvignon, Chardonnay. Grapes acquired from more than 400 growers are processed in ultra-modern plants in the Verona area to make nearly 2.5m. cases. Bolla, synonymous with Soave in the United States, is a leader in viticultural research through the Sergio Bolla Foundation. They also control the firm of Valdo, which makes sparkling wines at Valdobbiadene.

Carpenè Malvolti
Conegliano, 31015 Treviso.

A family firm, founded in 1868 by Antonio Carpenè. His descendant Antonio Carpenè still directs and makes the wine. DOC: Prosecco di Conegliano. Other: Carpenè Malvolti Brut *champenoise*. With production of 300,000 cases at two cellars, a leading name in Italian sparkling wine.

Guerrieri-Rizzardi
Bardolino, 37011 Verona.

A family estate going back to the 18th century, with a small but interesting museum. Owner: Cristina Guerrieri-Rizzardi. DOC: Bardolino, Soave, Valpolicella. Other: Bianco San Pietro red Castello Guerrieri, medium dry Moscato. From 370 acres in Bardolino, Valpolicella and Soave come splendid, gracious Verona wines. The Bardolino is admirably lively – one of the best of the pale breed. After a static period the firm is now undergoing a revival.

Lamberti
37017 Lazise sul Garda, Verona.

Part of the Gruppo Italiano Vini complex. DOC: Bardolino, Lugana, Riviera del Garda Bresciano, Soave, Valpolicella. Special bottlings include Bardolino Le Primule, Valpolicella Le Primule and Soave I Ciliegi. Other: Turà *vino da tavola*. From extensive company vineyards in Bardolino and purchases elsewhere, Lamberti produce wines of good commerical quality. They are also a pioneer of Bardolino *novello*.

Maculan
Breganze, 36042 Vicenza.

Founded: 1937. Owners: Fausto and Franca Maculan. DOC: Breganze. Other: Costa d'Olio Rosato, Torcolato, Ferrata Chardonnay and Cabernet Sauvignon, Prado di Canzio, *charmat* Accademia Brut. From 75 acres, including family property, superb examples of each of 12 types of wine. The Breganze Cabernet Fratta and sweet white Torcolato (a *barrique*-aged *recioto*) have given this small winery a great reputation.

Masi
Gargagnago, 37020 Verona.
The firm is run by the Boscaini family, producers of wine for 6 generations. Wine maker: Lanfranco Paronetto. DOC: Bardolino, Soave, Valpolicella, Recioto, Amarone. Other: Campo Fiorin *ripasso*, white Masianco. Unerring selection (partly from their own vineyards) and ingenious techniques have made this medium-large winery a touchstone for Verona wines. But best of all is the youngest vintage of Valpolicella.

Pieropan
Soave, 37038 Verona.
Owner: Leonildo Pieropan (whose grandfather won a prize for Soave in 1906). DOC: Soave, Recioto di Soave. Other: Riesling Italico. Pieropan produces what is generally rated the best Soave Classico from his own and rented vines. His wines are colourful and flavoursome, partly due to his minimal use of filtering and other interventions.

Giuseppe Quintarelli
Cerè di Negrar, 37024 Verona.
Founded in 1924 by the current owner's father. DOC: Valpolicella, Recioto, Amarone. Other: Alzero red. Rich complex wines processed under traditional methods with unsurpassed devotion, from 25 acres. Some consider this Amarone the finest.

Le Ragose
Arbizzano, 37020 Verona.
Founded: 1969. Owners-wine makers: Maria Marta Galli with her husband Arnaldo. DOC: Valpolicella, Recioto, Amarone. Other: Montericco. The Gallis meticulously select grapes from their 26 acres for some of Valpolicella's very best wines.

Castello di Roncade
Roncade, 31056 Treviso.
Owner: Vicenzo Ciani Bassetti. DOC: Piave. Other: Villa Giustinian Riserva, *spumante*. An impressive fortress with a worthy Cabernet/Merlot blend.

Santa Margherita
Fossalta di Portogruaro, 30025 Venezia.
Owners: The Marzotto family. Director: Arrigo Marcer. Wine maker: Giorgio Mascarin. DOC: Alto Adige, Grave del Friuli, Piave, Pramaggiore, Prosecco de Conegliano, Tocai di Lison. Other: Chardonnay Atesino, Pinot Brut, Rosé Brut. An *avant-garde* winery: Italy's undisputed leader in the Pinot Grigio field. Also owns Kettmeir in the Alto Adige and Cantine Torresella.

Serègo Alighieri
Garganego, 37020 Verona.
The owner, Pieralvise Serègo Alighieri (a descendant of Dante Alighieri), grows vines on 74 acres of ground surrounding his ancient villa. His grapes are bought by Masi (q.v.). His own DOC Valpolicella, Amarone and Recioto wines have considerable finesse due partly to their ageing in cherry wood casks.

Cantina Sociale di Soave
Soave, 37038 Verona.
Among several claimants to be the largest cooperative in Europe, but certainly the biggest producer of Soave. Founded in 1930, it has 630 members with more than 6,000 acres of vines, 80% in the Soave DOC zone. DOC: Bardolino, Soave, Valpolicella. Production is more than 3m. cases, mostly of Soave, some under the Cantina's label, some to bottlers and shippers. It also makes Valpolicella, Bardolino and *spumanti*.

Fratelli Tedeschi
Pedemonte, 37020 Verona.
Founded: 1884. Owners: Renzo Tedeschi and family. DOC: Bianco di Costoza, Soave, Valpolicella, Recioto, Amarone. Other: Capitel San Rocco Bianco, Rosso delle Lucchine, white Vin de la Fabriseria. From 20 acres of their own vines and discreet purchases the Tedeschi family makes some of the area's best wines.

Tommasi
Pedemonte, 37020 Verona.
Owner: Dario Tommasi. DOC: Bardolino, Bianco di Custoza, Soave, Valpolicella, Recioto, Amarone. Recently much improved, this estate of 87 acres makes an Amarone that can hold its own with the best.

Venegazzù-Conte Loredan-Gasparini
Venegazzù del Montello, 31040 Treviso.
The estate was founded in 1940 by Piero Loredan, descendant of Venetian doges, and bought by Giancarlo Palla in 1974. DOC: Prosecco del Montello e dei Colli Asolani. Other: Brut *champenoise*, Pinot Bianco, Pinot Grigio, Venegazzù Della Casa, Venegazzù Etichetta Nera, Venegazzù Rosso. From 148 acres, wines include the famous reserve Della Casa, a Bordeaux-style blend of great character and class, like a big, not exactly genteel, St-Emilion. The estate seems to be drifting lately.

Zonin
Gambellara, 36053 Vicenza.
The Zonin family firm, founded in 1821, claims to be Italy's largest private winery with production of nearly 3.2m. cases, of which about a third is exported. DOC: Bardolino, Gambellara, Recioto di Gambellara, Valpolicella. Other: *Spumante* and table wines. The firm bases its production on vineyards in the Veneto; it has a growing range of estates, including Pian d'Albola in Chianti Classico, Ca'Bolani in the Friuli; San Gimignano in Tuscany, Bersano in Piedmont and Il Giangio in Gambellara; and employs a staff of 16 oenologists. It also makes wine in Barbersville, Virginia, USA.

OTHER PRODUCERS

Adriano Adami
Colbertaldo di Vidor, 31020 Treviso. DOC: Prosecco, Superiore di Cartizze.
Arvedi d'Emelei
Cavalcaselle, 37066 Verona. DOC: Bardolino, Bianco di Custoza. Ancient family estate with 30 acres.

Astoria Vini
Crocetta del Montello, 31035 Treviso. DOC: Prosecco, Cartizze. Other: Astoria Brut.
Desiderio Bisol & Figli
Santo Stefano di Valdobbiadene, 31040 Treviso. DOC: Cartizze, Prosecco di Valdobbiadene. Other: *Champenoise* Bisol Brut Riserva.
Paolo Boscaini & Figli
Valgatara, 37020 Verona. DOC: Bardolino, Soave, Valpolicella, Recioto, Amarone. Other: Chardonnay, Pinot Grigio.

Brigaldara
San Floriano, 37020 Verona. DOC:
Valpolicella, Amarone.

Ca' Bruzzo
San Germano dei Berici, 36040 Vicenza.
Owners: Aldo Bruzzo and Sarah
Wallace. DOC: Range of Colli Berici,
particularly good Tocai Rosso. Other:
Chardonnay and 'California Blush'.

Ca' del Monte
Negrar, 37024 Verona. Owner: Luigi
Zanconte. DOC: Valpolicella, Amarone.

Adamo Canel & Figli
Col San Martino, 31010 Treviso. DOC:
Cartizze, Prosecco di Valdobbiadene.

Canevel
Valdobbiadene, 31049 Verona. DOC:
Cartizze, Prosecco.

Cardinal
Pieve di Soligo, 31053 Treviso. Wine
maker: Gianni Bignucolo. DOC:
Cartizze, Pinot Bianco *spumante*. Other:
bright pink Cardinal Brut.

Le Case Bianche
Pieve di Solido, 31053 Treviso. Owner:
Alvise Orlandi. DOC: Sparkling
Prosecco. Other: Wildbacher, Camoi
(Cabernet Sauvignon-Wildbacher).
Estate wines also sold under the Orlandi
label.

Cavalchina-Piona
Sommacampagna, Verona. DOC:
Bardolino, Bianco di Custoza. Other:
Pinot Bianco. Among the better whites
of Verona.

Cecilia di Baone
Terralba di Baone, 35030 Padova. DOC:
Range of Colli Euganeis. Other:
Moscato Fior d'Arancio (sweet,
sparkling), Don Noè Spumante Brut.

Colle dei Cipressi
Calmasino di Bardolino, 37010 Verona.
DOC: Bardolino.

Cantina dei Colli Berici
Lonigo and Barberana, 36045 Vicenza.
Following 1989 merger of two
cooperatives, now Europe's second
largest wine production unit, producing
over 8m. cases a year from nearly 10,000
acres. Mainly *vino da tavola*. DOC: Colli
Berici.

**Cantina Sociale Cooperative dei Colli
Euganei**
Vò Euganci, 35030 Padova. DOC: Colli
Euganei. Other: *Vino da tavola, spumante.*

Ferrari
Gargagnago, 37020 Verona. DOC:
Valpolicella, Recioto, Amarone.

Villa dal Ferro-Lazzarini
San Germano dei Berici, 36040 Vicenza.
The vineyards and cellars of his 16th-
century villa have been renewed in the
last 20 years by Alfredo Lazzarini.
DOC: Colli Berici. All varietals carry
individual vineyard names.

Foss Marai
Valdobbiadene, 31049 Treviso. DOC:
Prosecco, Cartizze.

Fratelli Fraccaroli
San Benedetto di Lugana, Verona.
Owners-wine makers: Francesco and
Giuseppe Fraccaroli. Good DOC
Lugana.

Nino Franco
Valdobbiadene, 31049 Treviso.
Founded: 1919. Wine maker: Primo
Franco. DOC: Cartizze, Prosecco di
Valdobbiadene (sparkling and still). A
leader in Prosecco production.

Cantina Sociale di Gambellara
Gambellara, 36053 Vicenza.
Cooperative. DOC: Colli Berici,
Gambellara.

Villa Girardi in Cariano
San Pietro in Cariano, 37029 Verona.
DOC: Bardolino, Soave, Valpolicella,
Recioto, Amarone. Now owned by
Tommasi (q.v.).

Girasole
Lazise, 37017 Verona. Good DOC
Bardolino and Valpolicella.

Gorgo
Custoza, 37066 Verona. Owner:
Roberto Bricolo. DOC: Bardolino,
Bianco di Custoza. 74 acres.

Gregoletto
Premaor di Miane, 31050 Treviso.
DOC: Prosecco di Conegliano.

Liasora
Ponte di Piave, 31047 Treviso. DOC:
Piave. Other: Semi-sweet white
Buschino. 99 acres.

Marcato
Roncà, 37030 Verona. DOC: Lessini
(still and *champenoise*), Soave.

Maschio
Visnà, 31050 Treviso. DOC: Prosecco.
Other: *Champenoise* Maschio dei
Cavalieri.

Il Maso
Negrar di Valpolicella, Verona. Owner:
Zonin (q.v.). DOC: Valpolicella,
Amarone.

Merotto
Col San Martino, 31049 Treviso. DOC:
Cartizze, Prosecco. Other: Merotto Brut
champenoise.

La Montanella
Monselice, 35043 Padova. DOC: Colli
Euganei. Other: Moscato Fior
d'Arancio. 32 acres.

Montecorno
Sona, 37060 Verona. DOC: Bardolino,
Bianco di Custoza. 57 acres.

**Cantina Sociale La Montelliana e dei
Colli Asolani**
Montebelluna, 31040 Treviso.
Cooperative. DOC: Montello e Colli
Asolani.

Montresor
37100 Verona. DOC: Bardolino, Bianco
di Custoza, Soave, Valpolicella, Recioto,
Amarone.

Abazia di Nervesa
Nervesa della Battaglia, 31040 Treviso.
DOC: Montello e Colli Asolani.

Opere Trevigiane
Crocetta del Montello, 31035 Treviso.
Owners: The Moretti family. Fine
spumante classico and Prosecco DOC.
Label is La Gioiosa.

Fratelli Pasqua
37100 Verona. DOC: Bardolino, Soave,
Valpolicella, Recioto, Amarone. Other:
Cabernet Morago.

Fratelli Poggi
Affi, 37010 Verona. DOC: Bardolino. 99
acres.

**Ponte (Cantina Sociale Cooperative
di Ponte di Piave)**
Ponte di Piave, 31047 Treviso.
Cooperative. DOC: Piave. Other: Pinot
Bianco, Pinot Grigio, Riesling Italico,
Raboso, Rosato, Sauvignon. A large
supplier of Veneto wines.

Graziano Pra
Monteforte d'Alpone, 37032 Verona.
DOC: Soave Classico.

Rechsteiner
Piavon di Oderzo, 31046 Treviso.
Owner: Baroni Steski-Doliwa. DOC:
Piave. Other: Chardonnay. 110 acres.

Luigi Righetti
Marano, 37020 Verona. DOC:
Valpolicella, Amarone.

Castello di Roncade
Roncade, 31056 Treviso. Owner:
Vicenzo Ciani Bassetti. DOC: Piave.
Other: Villa Giustinian Riserva,
spumante. An impressive fortress with a
worthy Cabernet/Merlot blend.

Russolo
Pramaggiore, 30020 Venezia. Owner: I.
Russolo. DOC: Lison-Pramaggiore.
Other: Excellent Borgo di Peuma and
Casali Bearzi *vini da tavola*.

Sanpereto
Negrar, 37024 Verona. Owner: Roberto
Mazzi. DOC: Valpolicella, Recioto,
Amarone. 17 acres. Rising quality.

Le Vigne di San Pietro
Sommacampagna, 37066 Verona.
Owner: Carlo Nerozzi. DOC:
Bardolino, Bianco di Custoza. Other:
Good Cabernet Sauvignon Refolà. 12
acres. Other: Zardetto Brut, made
by a modified *charmat* process
which prolongs the yeast
fermentation; tastes like a good
champenoise.

Santa Sofia
Pedemonte, 37020 Verona. DOC:
Bardolino, Bianco di Custoza, Soave,
Valpolicella, Recioto, Amarone. Since
the estate has been sold the name is used
for a line of commercial wines.

Tenuta Sant'Anna
Loncon di Annone Veneto, 30020
Venezia. Owner: Agricola Rus S.p.A.
DOC: Grave del Friuli, Lison-
Pramaggiore. Other: Pinot Grigio,
Prosecco, *spumante*. The firm owns more
than 600 acres of vines in the Veneto
and some 250 acres in Grave del Friuli.

Santi
Illasi, 37031 Verona. Founded in 1843, the winery is now part of the Gruppo Italiano Vini complex. DOC: Bardolino, Soave, Valpolicella, Recioto, Amarone. Other: Carlo Santi Brut *champenoise* Turà.

Sant'Osvaldo
Loncon di Annone Veneto, 30020 Venezia. DOC: Lison-Pramaggiore. Other: Pinot Bianco, Pinot Grigio, Raboso, Refosco, Sauvignon.

Sartori
Negrar, 37024 Verona. DOC: Bardolino, Soave, Valpolicella, Recioto, Amarone.

Scamperle
Fumane di Valpolicella, 37022 Verona. Large bottler of Verona wines.

Scarpa
Trevignano, 31040 Treviso. Corbulino Bianco (Pinot Bianco-Chardonnay) and

Rosso (Pinot Nero blend). Label: Giorgio Grai.

Villa Sceriman
Vò Euganei, 35030 Padova. Owners: The Soranzo family. DOC: Colli Euganei. Other: Moscato Fior d'Arancio. 62 acres.

Viticola Suavia
Soave, 37038 Verona. Owner: Giovanni Tessari. DOC: Soave. A rising star with his single-vineyard Soave Monte Carbonare.

Cantine Torresella
See Santa Margherita.

Tramanal
Arbizzano di Negrar, 37024 Verona. Owner: Domenico Vantini. DOC: Valpolicella, Amarone, Recioto. A gem in Valpolicella.

Valdo
Valdobbiadene, 31049 Treviso. DOC: Prosecco, Cartizze. *See* Bolla.

Cantina Sociale di Valdobbiadene
San Giovanni di Bigolino, 31030 Treviso. Cooperative. DOC: Cartizze, Prosecco di Valdobbiadene.

Massimo Venturini
San Floriano, 37020 Verona. DOC: Valpolicella, Amarone.

Zardetto
Conegliano, 31015 Treviso. Founded in 1969 by oenologist Pino Zardetto. DOC: Cartizze, Prosecco di Conegliano.

Zenato
San Benedetto di Lugana, Verona. DOC: Bardolino, Bianco di Custoza, Lugana, Riviera del Garda Bresciano, Tocai di San Martino della Battaglia, Valpolicella, Amarone. 40 acres.

FRIULI-VENEZIA GIULIA

There is a tidiness about the DOC arrangements in Friuli-Venezia Giulia which is due to their recent emergence as an important part of Italian viticulture. There was little folklore to get in the way of a simple carve-up into geographical zones whose wines are named for their grape varieties.

With six zones and some dozen varieties, as well as the brand names that some growers insist on adding, the combinations still reach a head-spinning number. It helps to distinguish between them if you are clear that there is one very big DOC that embraces most of the region, two superior hill zones with Colli in their names, and three smaller and newer DOCs of less significance in a row along the coastal plain.

The big zone is Grave del Friuli, DOC for the whole wine-growing hinterland from the Veneto

border east to beyond Udine where the Alps reach down towards Trieste. The hills of Gorizia, right on the Yugoslav border (otherwise just known as the 'Collio'), are the oldest-established and best vineyards of the region. To their north is the separate DOC of the Colli Orientali del Friuli ('the eastern hills of Friuli') with similar growing conditions.

The coastal DOCs from west to east are Aquilea, Latisana and Isonzo; the last, adjacent to the Gorizian hills, apparently having the greatest potential for quality. The coastal vineyards tend to stress red wine, whereas the reputation of the hills is mainly based on white – whether such traditional grapes as Tocai Friulano, Malvasia, Picolit or Verduzzo, or more recent imports: the Pinots, Sauvignon Blanc and Rhine Riesling.

DOC AND OTHER WINES

Aquileia
DOC. Red and white wine. Province: Udine. Villages: Aquileia and 17 others. Grapes: Merlot, Cabernet, Refosco, Tocai Friulano, Pinot Bianco, Pinot Grigio, Riesling Renano, Sauvignon, Traminer Aromatico, Verduzzo. Max. crop: 91 hl/ha. Min. alch: 10.5° for Merlot, Refosco, Tocai Friulano, Pinot Grigio, Riesling Renano, Rosato; 11° for Cabernet, Pinot Bianco, Sauvignon, Traminer Aromatico, Verduzzo. Annual production: 278,000 cases.
A DOC for the varied production of the cooperative at Cervignano, named after a Roman city. The land is flat, the climate temperate and efforts at quality production only recent, but signs are that it will come, particularly with Cabernet and Merlot.

Carso
DOC. Red and white wine. Provinces: Trieste and Gorizia. Area: 6 communes in Gorizia and 6 in Trieste. Grapes: Terrano (85%), Pinot Nero, Piccola Nera up to 15%; Malvasia Istriana (85%), other authorized light grapes up to 15%. Max. crops: 70 hl/ha. Min. alch: 10.5%.
Annual production: 7,800 cases.
Carso and Carso Terrano are virtually the same, both based on the Terrano (relative of Refosco) grape. Carso Malvasia is similar to other DOC Malvasia Istriana types. Terrano del Carso was historically the table wine of Trieste and supposedly builds blood because of high malic acid.

Collio Goriziano or Collio

DOC. White and red wine. Province: Gorizia.
Villages: west of Gorizia. Grapes: Riesling Italico,
Sauvignon, Tocai Friulano, Traminer Aromatico,
Malvasia Istriana, Merlot, Pinot Bianco, Cabernet Franc,
Pinot Grigio, Pinot Nero, Cabernet, Cabernet Sauvignon,
Chardonnay, Müller-Thurgau, Picolit, Ribolla Gialla,
Riesling Renano. Max. crop: 77 hl/ha. Min. alch: Collio
Bianco 11°; Malvasia 11.5°; Cabernet Franc, Merlot,
Pinot Grigio, Riesling Italico, Tocai Friulano, Traminer 12°;
Pinot Bianco, Pinot Nero, Sauvignon 12.5°.
Annual production: 890,000 cases.

A DOC of such diversity of wines and styles that
California comes to mind. Fruity early-developing reds of
the Bordeaux varieties are less interesting than the white
specialities, particularly the aromatic Tocai Friulano and
Pinot Bianco and Grigio, which at their best balance
Hungarian-style 'stiffness' and strength with real delicacy.
Collio without a varietal name is a light dry white of
Ribolla and other local grapes. 'Pinot Bianco' sometimes
includes Chardonnay and can develop burgundian rich-
ness with barrel-age.

Colli Orientali del Friuli

DOC. White and red wine. Province: Udine.
Villages: 14 communes in the province. Grapes: Tocai
Friulano, Verduzzo, Ribolla, Pinot Bianco, Pinot Grigio,
Sauvignon, Riesling Renano, Picolit, Merlot, Cabernet,
Pinot Nero, Refosco, Malvasia Istriana, Ramandolo
(Classico), Rosato, Schioppettino. Max. crop: 77 hl/ha.
Min. alch: mainly 11°; Pinot Bianco, Pinot Grigio,
Verduzzo Friulano 11.5°; Ramandolo 14°; Picolit 15°.
Merlot, Cabernet, Pinot Nero, Refosco and Picolit are *riserva*
after 2 years' ageing. Annual production: 780,000 cases.

The neighbouring DOC to Collio, with similar white
wines, perhaps slightly less prestigious except in its native
Verduzzo (q.v.) and its rare dessert white Picolit (q.v.).
The splendid rustic red Refosco and Cabernet are better
than Collio reds.

Grave del Friuli

DOC. Red and white wine. Provinces: Udine, Pordenone.
Area: Udine and Pordenone. Grapes: Merlot, Cabernet,
Refosco, Tocai, Pinot Bianco, Pinot Grigio, Verduzzo,
Riesling Renano, Pinot Nero, Sauvignon, Traminer
Aromatico, Chardonnay. Max. crop: 91 hl/ha. Min. alch: 10.5°
for Chardonnay; 11° for Merlot, Refosco, Tocai, Pinot Grigio,
Verduzzo, Cabernet, Pinot Nero, Pinot Bianco, Riesling
Renano, Sauvignon, Traminer Aromatico. Annual production
2m. cases.

The largest DOC of the region: biggest source of Merlot,
which accounts for half of its production. Grave Merlot is
soft, dark and dry with a hint of grassiness; not as good as
its Cabernet, which has more personality and life, nor as
memorable as its fruity bitter Refosco. Grave Pinot
Bianco (sometimes Chardonnay) and Tocai can be as good
as Collio wines.

Isonzo

DOC. White and red wine. Province: Gorizia. Area: 20
communes around Gradisca d'Isonzo. Grapes: Tocai,
Sauvignon, Malvasia Istriana, Pinot Bianco, Pinot Grigio,
Verduzzo Friulano, Traminer Aromatico, Riesling Renano,
Merlot, Cabernet, Chardonnay, Franconia, Pinot Nero,
Refosco dal Peduncolo Rosso, plus a Bianco, Rosso and Pinot
Spumante. Max. crop: 91 hl/ha. Min. alch. 10.5° for Tocai,
Malvasia Istriana, Verduzzo Friulano and Merlot; 11° for
Pinot (Bianco and Grigio), Sauvignon, Traminer Aromatico,
Riesling Renano and Cabernet. Annual production:
600,000 cases.

The DOC zone between the Collio and the Gulf of Trieste
also specializes in Merlot, which can be better than that of
Grave del Friuli and Cabernet for drinking young. Its
whites are light and pleasant; rarely to Collio standards.

Latisana

DOC. Red and white wine. Province: Udine. Area: 12
communes in the province. Grapes: Merlot, Cabernet,
Refosco, Tocai Friulano, Pinot Bianco, Pinot Grigio,
Traminer Aromatico, Chardonnay and Verduzzo Friulano.
Max. crop: 91 hl/lha. Min. alch: 11° for Latisana Merlot,
Refosco, Tocai Friulano, Pinot Grigio and Verduzzo Friulano;
11.5° for Cabernet, Pinot Bianco. Annual production:
100,000 cases.

This DOC is dominated by Merlot, Cabernet and Tocai,
but Refosco is more robust and durable.

Picolit

A native grape of the Colli Orientali del Friuli and its
dessert wine, one of the almost-lost legends of the 19th
century along with Romania's Cotnari and the (really lost)
Constantia of the Cape. It is a powerful, smooth, even
dense-textured wine, not necessarily very sweet, and
ending in the regional style, slightly bitter. Bottles I have
tasted have clearly been too young to have developed the
glorious bouquet and flavour that others report. It is rare
and extremely expensive.

Ramandolo Classico

A restricted name for sweet Verduzzo from vineyards at
Ramandolo in the commune of Nimis in the Colli
Orientali del Friuli. However, producers elsewhere in the
zone may use the name Ramandolo alone for sweet
Verduzzo.

Schioppettino

A native red grape of the Colli Orientali del Friuli, giving
wine with some of the rasping fruitiness of a good Barbera
from Piedmont.

Verduzzo

A native white grape made either into a fresh dry white
'fish' wine or a sort of Recioto, an *amabile* of partly dried
grapes – *see* Ramandolo.
N.B. Verdiso is a different but similar white grape,
occasionally seen as a dry wine. Mainly in the Veneto.

FRIULI-VENEZIA GIULIA PRODUCERS

Abbazia di Rosazzo
Rosazzo, 33040 Udine.

The estate winery occupies an 11th-century abbey.
Manager: Silvano Formigli. Wine maker: Franco Bernabei. DOC: Colli Orientali del Friuli. Other: Ronco dei
Roseti, Ronco delle Acacie, Ronco di Corte, Pignolo. The
reasonable range of Friulia varietals is enhanced by Ronco
dei Roseti red from Franconia, Tazzelenghe, Refosco,
Cabernet, Merlot and Pignolo, and Ronco delle Acacie
white from Tocai, Pinot Grigio and Ribolla.

Collavini
Corno di Rosazzo, 33040 Udine.
Manlio Collavini is the third generation of wine makers. DOC: Colli Orientali del Friuli, Collio, Grave del Friuli. Others: Conte di Cuccanea (a barrel-aged white), sparkling Il Grigio, *charmat lungo* Ribolla Gialla, *champenoise* Applause Nature. Collavini sparkling wines round out an impressive period.

EnoFriulia-Puiatti
Gorizia.
Two establishments, both owned and run by wine maker Vittorio Puiatti and his son Giovanni. EnoFriulia (founded in 1967 as EnoJulia) makes a range of good quality Friuli wines, mainly *vino da tavola*. On the family estate at Farra d'Isonzo Puiatti makes prestigious Collio DOC. Also notable are the stylish white Nuvizial and Puiatti Bianco table wines, as well as a *champenoise*, Puiatti Extra Brut.

Livio Felluga
Brazzano di Cormons, 34070 Gorizia.
Livio Felluga's sons Maurizio and Andrea represent the fifth generation of wine makers. DOC: Colli Orientali del Friuli, Collio. From 5 estates with nearly 300 acres of vines, Felluga makes internationally-acclaimed wines. A Pinot *spumante champenoise* is in preparation. The white *vino da tavola* Terre Alte is highly esteemed.

Marco Felluga-Russiz Superiore
Gradisca d'Isonzo, 34072 Gorizia.
Marco (brother of Livio) Felluga founded his wine house in 1956, the Russiz Superiore estate in 1967. DOC: Collio. The Marco Felluga label consists of the usual Collio varieties from grapes purchased from regular suppliers in Collio. Russiz Superiore, a model of its kind, consists of 170 acres of terraced vines. Two white table wines are highly acclaimed: dry Roncuz and a light, subtly oaky Verduzzo. Felluga also bottles some wine under the Villa San Giovanni label.

Stelio Gallo
Mariano del Friuli, 34070 Gorizia.
Now run by Stelio's son Gianfranco, who has turned the 12 acres of densely-planted, low-yielding vineyard into a model estate. His Isonzo DOC wines and *vino da tavola* Chardonnay are consistently among the region's top rated, and his Sauvignon is frequently outstanding.

Francesco Gravner
Oslavia, 34170 Gorizia.
DOC: Collio. A rising star in Collio. As well as superb DOC wines, Josko Gravner (whose 27 acres of vineyard stray in places over the border into Yugoslavia) makes interesting *vino da tavola*, including the red Rujno (Cabernet-Merlot) and the white Vinograd Breg. He ages most of his wines in wood, producing Chardonnay and Sauvignon of particular character.

Jermann
Villanova di Farr, 34070 Giorzia.
A family estate founded in 1880; now run by Sylvio Jermann. Other: Engel Rosé, Picolit, Engelwhite, Vinnae, Vintage Tunina. Jermann makes first-rate now entirely non-DOC wines, including the very special Vintage Tunina (from Chardonnay, Sauvignon, Malvasia, Ribolla, Picolit) from 57 acres of vines. Taste Tunina if you are a sceptic about Italian whites. Jermann's most recent release is a formidably expensive, barrel-aged Chardonnay called 'Dreams'.

Mario Schiopetto
Capriva del Friuli, 34070 Gorizia.
Founded in 1969 by Mario Schiopetto on property belonging to the Archbishopric of Gorizia since 1859. DOC: Collio. Other: Cabernet, Merlot, Ribolla, Riesling Renano. Schiopetto is one of the most skilled and courageous wine makers of Italy. His whites (including Rhine Riesling) are perhaps the most exceptional.

Torre Rosazza
Poggiobello di Manzano, 33044 Udine.
DOC: Colli Orientali del Friuli. This historical 207-acre estate is being developed by the Generali insurance group under the supervision of wine maker Walter Filiputti. Both DOC and table wines are promising, notably Ronco della Torre (Cabernet-Merlot). The *barrique*-aged Ronco delle Magnolie (Pinot Bianco-Chardonnay) and L'Altremerlot (a pure varietal) are also interesting.

Volpe Pasini
Togliano di Torreano, 33040 Udine.
A 74-acre estate owned by the Volpe Pasini family who make some of the zone's best wines. Tocai and Pinot Bianco are frequently the finest of their DOC (Colli Orientali) wines, which are labelled Zuc di Volpe. Of their table wines, white Le Roverelle (Tocai, Sauvignon, Pinot Bianco, Verduzzo) and red Le Marne (Cabernet, Refosco, Pinot Nero) are noteworthy.

OTHER PRODUCERS

Angoris
Cormons, 34071 Gorizia. Founded: 1648. Owners: The Locatelli family. Wine maker: Flavio Zuliani. DOC: Colli Orientali del Friuli, Isonzo. Other: Modolet Brut *champenoise*, Spirfolét *spumante*. Angoris also owns Fattoria Casalino in Chianti Classico.

Conti Attems
Lucinico, 34070 Gorizia. Owner: Douglas Attems Sigismondo, who carries on a centuries-old family tradition. DOC: Collio, Isonzo. Other: Rosato di Lucinico. Quality slipped

badly, but recent collaboration with wine maker Collavini may restore class.

Mario Arzenton
Cividale, 33043 Udine. DOC: Colli Orientali del Friuli. 27 acres.

Duchi Badoglio Rota
Codroipo, 33033 Udine. DOC: Grave del Friuli. Other: Il Blanc-Blanc *spumante*.

Fabio Berin
Mossa, 34070 Gorizia. Owner: Fabio Berin. DOC: Collio. Other: Chardonnay. A small winery attracting critical attention (though unknown in Italy).

Fratelli Buzzinelli
Cormons, 34071 Gorizia. An excellent family winery. The Buzzinelli brothers have been bottling wine since 1955. DOC: Collio. Other: Müller-Thurgau.

Ca' Bolano
Cervignano del Friuli, 33052 Udine. Owner: Zonin (q.v.) of the Veneto, who also owns nearby Ca' Vescovo. The two estates together have 445 acres and mainly produce a stylish Aquileia DOC. Other wines include a Müller-Thurgau table wine, Chardonnay *frizzante* and Conte Bolani Brut Riserva *champenoise*.

Ca' Ronesca
Dolegna del Collio, 34070 Gorizia.
Owner: Sergio Comunello. Wine maker:
Fabio Coser. DOC: Collio, Colli
Orientali del Friuli. Other: Merlot-based
Sariz. Decidedly on the rise.

Ca' Vescovo
See Ca' Bolani.

La Castellada
Oslavia, 34170 Gorizia. Owners:
Giorgio and Nicolò Bensa. DOC:
Collio.

**Cantina Produttori Vini del Collio e
dell'Isonzo**
Cormons, 34071 Gorizia. Cooperative.
Cellarmaster: Luigi Soini. DOC: Collio,
Isonzo. Other: *Spumanti*, Vino della
Pace.

G. B. Comelli
Nimis, 33045 Udine. Owner: G. B.
(Filippon) Comelli. DOC: Colli
Orientali del Friuli. A tiny estate
renowned for Ramandolo Classico.

Borgo Conventi
Farra d'Isonzo, 34070 Gorizia. The
former walled convent, founded in
1876, is owned by Gianni Vescovo.
DOC: Collio. Other: Tocai Italico.
Good Sauvignon Blanc and Pinot
Bianco.

Fratelli Coos
Ramandolo, 33045 Udine. Noted for
Ramandolo Classico.

Marina Danieli
Buttrio, 33042 Udine. Stylish DOC
Grave and Colli Orientali del Friuli.
Other: Red Faralta (Cabernet-
Tazzelenghe), Müller-Thurgau, Brut
Mus *spumante*.

Girolamo Dorigo
Vincale di Buttrio, 33042 Udine. DOC:
Colli Orientali del Friuli. Other: Red
Montsclapade, *champenoise*, white and red
Ronc di Juri.

Giovanni Dri
Ramandolo di Nimis, 33045 Udine.
DOC: Colli Orientali del Friuli. Dri's
Ramandolo Classico is a highly prized
rarity; a lovely wine.

Le Due Terre
Prepotto, 33040 Udine. DOC: Colli
Orientali del Friuli. Recently much
improved.

Fantinel
Buttrio, 33042 Udine. DOC: Collio,
Grave del Friuli. Gianfranco Fantinel
also owns Santa Caterina where he
makes impressive Collio DOC.

Conti Formentini
San Floriano del Collio, 34070 Gorizia.
The 16th-century castle and property
have long belonged to the Formentini
family, after whom the Furmint grape of
Hungarian Tokay is said to be named.
Owner: Michele Formentini. DOC:
Collio. Splendid stiff Pinot Grigio from
250 acres. The castle contains an *enoteca*,
restaurant and wine museum.

Villa Frattina
Ghirano, 33080 Pordenone. DOC:
Grave del Friuli.

Viticoltori Friuliani-La Delizia
Casarsa della Delizia, 33072 Pordenone.
Cooperative. Director: Noè Bertolin.
DOC: Aquileia, Grave del Friuli. Other:
Spumanti. Annual production is more
than a million cases from 3,700 acres.

Silvano Gallo
Mariano del Friuli, 34070 Gorizia.
DOC: Isonzo. 12 acres.

Gradnik
Plessiva di Cormons, 34071 Gorizia.
Wanda Gradnik maintains a century-old
family tradition. DOC: Collio. A
stalwart among Collio's small producers.

Isola Augusta
Palazzolo della Stella, 33056 Udine.
Owners: The Bassani family. DOC:
Latisana reds and local. Other: *Spumante*.
A leading estate in Latisana.

Edy Kante
San Pelagio, 34011 Trieste. DOC:
Carso. Other: Sauvignon, white
Vitovska. A new leader in Carso.

Vigneti Le Monde
Prata, 33080 Pordenone. Owners: The
Pistoni family. DOC: Grave del Friuli.
Good Cabernet Sauvignon.

Dorino Livon
Dolegano, 33048 Udine. A rising force
in DOC Collio and Colli Orientali del
Friuli. Also DOC Grave del Friuli.
Other: *Spumante*.

Borgo Magredo
Tauriano, 33097 Pordenone. Owner:
Generali insurance group. Wine maker:
Walter Filiputti. DOC: Grave del Friuli.

Giovanni Marin
Fornalis di Cividale, 33043 Udine.
DOC: Colli Orientali del Friuli. Two
outstanding small estates.

Nascig
Corno di Rosazzo, 33040 Udine. DOC:
Colli Orientali del Friuli. Other:
Franconia, Vigna del Broili.

Francesco Pecorari
San Lorenzo Isontino, 34070 Gorizia.
DOC: Isonzo, Collio. Young Alvaro
Pecorari makes *vino da tavola* Pinot
Grigio, Chardonnay and Sauvignon to
compare with the best in Collio.

Lina & Paolo Petrucco
Buttrio, 33042 Udine. An emerging
estate.

Fratelli Pighin
Risano, 33050 Udine. Founded: 1963.
Owners: The Pighin family. DOC:
Collio, Grave del Friuli. Other:
Gallorosé, Picolit, Pinot Nero, Soreli
(Tocai, Pinot Bianco, Sauvignon), red
Baredo.

Vigneti Pittaro
Rivolto di Codroipo, 33033 Udine.
Owner: Piero Pittaro, who heads Italy's
oenologists and Friuli's wine
development board. DOC: Grave del

Friuli. Other: *Champenoise*, red Agresto,
sweet, white, Chardonnay-based Apicio.

Plozner
Spilimbergo, 33097 Pordenone. DOC:
Grave del Friuli. Other: Chardonnay,
Pinot Nero, Traminer. Plozner's
Chardonnay is building an international
reputation.

Prà di Pradis
Pradis di Cormons, 34071 Gorizia. An
emerging estate.

Doro Princic
Pradis di Cormons, 34071 Gorizia.
Owners: Doro and Sandro Princic.
DOC: Collio. This tiny family winery
makes gorgeous Tocai.

Radikon
Oslavia, 34170 Gorizia. DOC: Collio.
Other: Saltnik *vino da tavola* from
Chardonnay, Tocai and Sauvignon.

Rocca Bernarda
Ipplis, 33040 Udine. The old Perusini
family estate, which recently became the
property of the Sovrano Militare Ordine
di Malta (Knights of Malta). DOC: Colli
Orientali del Friuli.

Roncada
Cormons, 34070 Gorizia. Owners: Silvia
and Lina Mattioni. DOC: Collio. Other:
Red Franconia.

Ronchi di Cialla
Prepotto, 33040 Udine. Owners: Paolo
and Dina Rapuzzi. DOC: Colli Orientali
del Friuli. Other: Schioppettino. This
small winery excels with obscure
classics: Picolit, Schioppettino,
Verduzzo.

Ronco del Gnemiz
San Giovanni al Natisone, 33048 Udine.
Owner: Enzo Palazzolo. DOC: Colli
Orientali del Friuli. Other: Müller-
Thurgau, Chardonnay, Ronco del
Gnemiz (Cabernet Sauvignon-Franc).

Rubini
Spessa di Cividale, 33043 Udine. DOC:
Colli Orientali del Friuli.

Villa Russiz
Capriva del Friuli, 34070 Gorizia.
Founded: 1869 by a French nobleman,
La Tour. It now supports the A. Cerruti
orphanage. Director and wine maker:
Edino Menotti. DOC: Collio. Other:
Picolit.

San Cipriano
Sacile, 33077 Pordenone. Owners: The
Lot family. DOC: Grave del Friuli.
Other: White Truola, red Fondreta.

Santa Caterina
See Fantinel.

Specogna
Rocca Bernarda, 33040 Udine. DOC:
Colli Orientali del Friuli. Recent tastings
indicate Leonardo Specogna to be
rapidly on the rise. Especially good
DOC Picolit.

Castello di Spessa
Spessa di Capriva, 34070 Gorizia. Estate
with potential to equal its neighbour

Schiopetto (q.v.).
Subida di Monte
Cormona, 34070 Gorizia. DOC: Collio.
17 acres.
Borgo del Tiglio
Brazzano di Cormons, 34070 Gorizia.
Owner: Nicola Manferrari. DOC: Colli
Orientali del Friuli. Especially good
Tocai and Malvasia. Fine *vino da tavola*
Rosso della Centa (Merlot-Cabernet).
Vinicola Udinese
33100 Udine. DOC: Colli Orientali del
Friuli, Collio, Grave del Friuli, Carso.
Other wines include *spumanti* as well as
still *vino da tavola*.

Valle
Buttrio, 33042 Udine. Owner: Luigi
Valle. DOC: Colli Orientali del Friuli,
Collio. Other: Franconia, Araldica
range.
Redi Vazzoler
Mossa, 34070 Gorizia. Owner: Redento
Vazzoler. Wine maker: Walter Filiputti.
DOC: Collio. Other: White Ghiaie
Bianche (Tocai, Pinot Bianco,
Müller-Thurgau).
Venica
Dolegna del Collio, 34070 Gorizia.
DOC: Collio.

La Viarte
Novacuzzo, 33040 Udine. Owner:
Giuseppe Ceschin. DOC: Colli Orientali
del Friuli.
Vigne dal Leon
Rocca Bernada, 33040 Udine. Owner:
Tullio Zamò. DOC: White Colli
Orientali del Friuli. Other:
Schioppettino, Tacelenghe, Rosso di
Vigne dal Leon (Merlot-Cabernet), oak-
aged Pinot Bianco.
Tenuta Villanova
Farra d'Isonzo, 34070 Gorizia. DOC:
Isonzo, Collio.

EMILIA-ROMAGNA

It is ironic that Italy's greediest culinary region, by all accounts, should put the emphasis on quantity rather than quality in its wine. Any ambition to produce better than simple thirst quenchers is recent and limited to an elect few.

Bologna, the cooks' capital, is the hub of the region and the meeting place of its two component parts. Most of the land is the flat Po valley, following it to the Adriatic between Ravenna and Venice. All the wine regions of interest lie in the foothills, however tentative, of the Apennines to the

south, dividing the province from Tuscany.

Fizzy red Lambrusco leads, not just in Emilia but in the whole of Italy, for volume production of a distinct type of wine. It is an ingenous and profitable way of achieving notoriety in deep valley soils where more conventional quality is unlikely.

Romagna has nothing so exceptional. Its best-known wine is the white Albana, which has yet to distinguish itself. It is in the Colli Bolognesi and Piacentini, the hill areas nearest to Bologna and Piacenza, that progress is being made.

DOC AND OTHER WINES

Albana di Romagna
DOCG. White wine. Provinces Ravenna, Forli and Bologna.
Villages: 23 communes between Bologna and Rimini. Grape:
Albana. Max. crop: 91 hl/ha (70 hl/ha for Passita). Min. alch:
Secco 11.5°, Amabile and Dolce 12°, Passita 15.5°. Annual
production 390,000 cases.
The standard white of Bolgna and east to the coast. The
Albana is a mild, not to say neutral, grape whose dry wine
tend to flatness, finishing bitter to satisfy local taste. It
gains more character when made *amabile* and/or *spumante*
but these may only be classed as DOC, not DOCG.

Barbarossa di Bertinoro
A vine not found elsewhere, cultivated on a small scale at
Bertinoro, the centre of the Romagna vineyards, for a
good full-flavoured red with ageing potential.

Barbera
The ubiquitous red grape is popular in the area of
Piacenza and in the Colli Bolognesi, where it is given
DOC dignity.

Bianco di Scandiano
DOC. White wine. Province: Emilia-Romagna. Villages:
commune of Scandiano plus 5 others southwest of Reggio.
Grapes: Sauvignon (locally Spergola or Spergolina) up to
85%, Malvasia di Candia and Trebbiano Romagnolo up to
15%. Max. crop: 84.5 hl/ha. Min. alch: Frizzante 10.5°,
Spumante 11°. Annual production: 89,000 cases.

A white alternative to Lambrusco (q.v.) made either semi-
dry or distinctly sweet, sometimes fizzy and sometimes
fully frothy.

Bosco Eliceo
DOC. Red and white wine. Provinces: Ferrara and Ravenna.
Villages: six communes in the Bosco della Mésola and the
Bertuzzi and Commacchio Lagoons. Grapes: Trebbiano
Romagnolo; Sauvignon/Malvasia di Candia up to 30%.
Fortana, Merlot and Sauvignon allow other varieties up to
15%. Max. crop: 105 hl/ha. Min. alch: 10.5° (Sauv. 11°).
The Fortana is a rustic red from this new DOC from
reclaimed marshland.

Cagnina di Romagna
DOC. Red wine. Province: Forli and Ravenna. Villages: 16
communes in Forli, five in Ravenna. Grapes: Caragnina, other
varieties up to 15%. Max. crop: 85.5 hl/ha. Min. alch. 11°.
A sweet red wine which was classified as DOC in 1989. It
is enjoyed locally as an accompaniment to roast chestnuts.

Chardonnay
Strictly an outlaw in the region, but was planted with
striking success by the late Enrico Vallania at Terre Rosse
near Bologna.

Colli Bolognesi – Monte San Pietro-Castelli Medioevali

DOC: Red and white wine. Province: Bologna. Villages: 10 communes southwest of Bologna. Grapes: (white) Albana 60–80%, Trebbiano Romagnolo at least 20%, other whites up to 20%. For named varieties: Barbera, Merlot, Riesling Italico, Pinot Bianco, Cabernet Sauvignon, Sauvignon 85%, with 15% neutral grapes allowed. Max. crop: 70–91 hl/ha. Min. alch: 11.5° for Barbera, Merlot; 12° for Sauvignon, Cabernet Sauvignon, Pinot Blanc, Riesling Italico; 11° for Bianco. Barbera and Cabernet Sauvignon must be 3 years old, 1 in wood, for *reserva*. Annual production 145,000 cases.

An umbrella DOC for the everyday wines of Bologna. More remarkable wines are being made in the same vineyards by growers experimenting with better grapes, including Sauvignon, Cabernet Sauvignon and Chardonnay. Growing conditions are excellent.

Colli di Parma

DOC. Red and white wine. Province: Parma. Villages: 14 communes in the Apennine foothills south and west of Parma. Grapes: (red) Barbera 60–75% with Bonarda or Croatina 25–40%, other dark varieties up to 15%; (Malvasia) Malvasia di Candia 85–100%, Moscato Bianco up to 15%; Sauvignon 100%. Max. crop: red 70 hl/ha, Malvasia 71.5 hl/ha, Sauvignon 49 hl/ha. Min. alch: red 11%, Malvasia 10.5%, Sauvignon 11.5%. Annual production: 78,000 cases.

In this DOC, the red resembles Otrepò Pavese Rosso, the Malvasia may be either dry or *amabile*, usually *frizzante*; the Sauvignon usually still.

Colli Piacentini

DOC. Red and white wine. Province: Piacenza. Villages: There are four sub-zones: Gutturnio (in three sectors and nine communes in the Tidone, Nure, Chero and Arda valleys); Monterosso Val d'Arda (in six communes in the Arda valley); Trebbianino Val Trebbia (in five communes along the Trebbia); Val Nure (in three communes in the Nure Valley. Grapes: (white) 30–50% Malvasia di Candia, 20–35% Ortrugo, 20–35% Trebbiano Romagnolo; Barbera, Bonarda, Malvasia, Ortugo, Pinot Grigio, Pinot Nero, Sauvignon. Max. crop: 63 to 84 hl/ha. Min. alch: white 11°, Malvasia, Ortugo 10.5°, Pinot Grigio, Pinot Nero, Sauvignon, Bonarda 11.5°. Annual production: 1m. cases.

Three former DOCs – Gutturnio dei Colli Piacentini, Monterosso Val d'Arda and Trebbianino Val Trebbia with the newly approved Val Nure – plus seven others (mainly varietal wines) are included in this large zone.

Gutturnio dei Colli Piacentini

See under Colli Piacentini.

Lambrusco

Lambrusco from Emilia was the smash hit of the Italian wine industry in the 1970s, selling like Coca-Cola (in more senses than one) in the United States. It is simply a sweet, semi-sweet or occasionally dry fizzy red (or pink or occasionally white) wine such as any wine maker could produce who had the foresight to see the demand. The common qualities are scarcely drinkable by a discerning wine drinker, but this misses the point. The market is elsewhere. Some see it as the training ground for future connoisseurs. Such discerning palates will choose one from a named region, of which the best is Sorbara.

Lambrusco Grasparossa di Castelvetro

DOC. Red wine. Province: Modena. Villages: 14 communes south of Modena. Grapes: Lambrusco Grasparossa 85%, other Lambrusco and Uva d'Oro 15% . Max. crop: 98 hl/ha. Min. alch: 10.5°. Annual production: 500,000 cases.

Lambrusco Reggiano

DOC. Red and rosé wine. Province: Reggio Emilia. Area: 20 communes in the province. Grapes: Lambrusco Marani, Salamino, Montericco and Maestri either singly or together. 20% Ancellotta also allowed. Max. crop: 97.5 hl/ha. Min. alch: 10.5°. Annual production: 2m. cases.

Commonest, lightest and usually fizziest Lambrusco.

Lambrusco Salamino di Santa Croce

DOC. Red wine. Province: Modena. Villages: Carpi and 10 other communes north of Modena. Grapes: Lambrusco Salamino 90%, other Lambrusco and Uva d'Oro 10%. Max. crop: 105 hl/ha. Min. alch: 11°. Annual production: 722,000 cases.

Salamino di S. Croce is a local subvariety of the Lambrusco grape with a bunch said to resemble a little salami.

Lambrusco di Sorbara

DOC. Red and rosé wine. Province: Modena. Villages: 10 communes north of Modena, including Sorbara. Grapes: Lambrusco di Sorbara 60%, Lambrusco Salamino max. 40%. Max. crop: 98 hl/ha. Min. alch: 11°. Annual production: 1m. cases.

Good Lambrusco di Sorbara is a delight; juicy, racy, tingling and extraordinarily drinkable – a childish wine perhaps, but marvellously thirst quenching with rich food. The pink froth is a pleasure in itself. Alas, offputting chemical flavours are all too common, even in this premium Lambrusco. Do not on any account store bottles of this, or any of them.

Merlot

Is widely grown in Emilia-Romagna mostly for blending. In the Colli Bolognesi it is DOC.

Monterosso Val d'Arda

See under Colli Piacentini.

Montuni del Reno

DOC. White wine. Province: Bologna. Villages: five communes in Modena. Grapes: Montuni; other non-aromatic grapes up to 15%. Max. crop: 126 hl/ha. Min. alch: 10.5°. Can be dry or semi-sweet and usually *frizzante*.

Pagadebit di Romagna

DOC. White wine. Provinces: Forli and Ravenna. Villages: 24 communes in Forli, five in Ravenna. Grapes: Pagadebit; other whites up to 15%. Max. crop: 98 hl/ha. Min. alch. 10.5° (11.5° for Bertinoro).

A rare white vine enjoying revival and modernization around Bertinoro in Romagna. Gentle dry wine and an *amabile*. The commune of Bertinoro rates as a special subdenomination.

Picòl Ross

An esoteric dry Lambrusco of high quality from one grower, Moro of Sant'Ilario d'Enza near Reggio.

Pinot Bianco

Widely grown in Emilia-Romagna; DOC in Colli Bolognesi.

Pinot Grigio
Increasingly being grown, Pinot Grigio is DOC in Colli Piacentini. *See* Terre Rosse (Producers).

Sangiovese di Romagna
DOC. Red wine. Provinces: Ravenna, Bologna, Forli. Villages: 42 communes in all three provinces. Grape: Sangiovese di Romagna. Max. crop: 71.5 hl/ha. Min. alch: 11.5°. Aged 2 years for *riserva*, 6 months for *superiore*. Superiore only from certain specified zones. Annual production 1.1m. cases.

Romagna has its own strain of the red Sangiovese, distinct from the Tuscan one which is the basis of Chianti. It makes pleasant light to medium-weight red, often with a slightly bitter aftertaste, produced in enormous quantities and enjoyed young as the Sunday wine of the region.

Sauvignon
A coming white grape in this part of Italy, possibly the best of the DOC Colli Bolognesi and the major partner in the 1977 DOC Bianco di Scandiano.

Trebbianino Val Trebbia
See under Colli Piancentini.

Trebbiano di Romagna
DOC. White wine. Provinces: Bologna, Forli, Ravenna. Villages: 54 communes in all 3 provinces. Grape: Trebbiano di Romagna. Max. crop: 84 hl/ha. Min. alch: 11.5° Annual production: 666,000 cases.

Taking over the area as the everyday white. Its style is clean tasting and unobtrusive.

EMILIA-ROMAGNA PRODUCERS

Castelluccio
Modigliana, 47012 Forli

Owner and wine maker: Gian Matteo Baldi. Table wines known as Ronco Casone, Ronco dei Ciliegi and Ronco delle Ginestre from Sangiovese and Ronco del Re from Sauvignon Blanc are fashioned by young Baldi into some of Romagna's finest bottlings although there are doubts over the estate's future.

Cavacchioli
San Prospero, 41030 Modena

Owners: Franco Cavacchiolo and brothers. DOC: Lambrusco di Sorbara, Lambrusco Grasparossa di Castelvetro, Lambrusco Salamino di Santa Croce. Other: Lambrusco Bianco. This medium-large winery is a quality leader for Lambrusco.

Chiarli-1860
41100 Modena

Founded in 1860 and still run by the Chiarli family. DOC: Lambrusco di Sorbara, Lambrusco Grasparossa di Castelvetro, Lambrusco Salamino di Santa Croce.

Corovin (Consorzio Romagnolo Vini Tipici)
47100 Forli

A consortium of cooperatives founded in 1968. Corovin groups 12,000 growers in 23 wineries; they consign 235m. kilograms of grapes – enough for 155m. litres. DOC: Albana, Sangiovese and Trebbiano di Romagna. Other: Lambrusco and numerous table wines.

Giacobazzi
Nonantola, 41015 Modena

DOC: Lambrusco di Sorbara, Lambrusco Grasparossa di Castelvetro, Lambrusco Salamino di Santa Croce. One of the largest producers, bottlers and shippers of Lambrusco but now moving more into light fizzy wines.

Coltiva-Gruppo Italiano Vini
41100 Modena

This Coltiva consortium of cooperatives, which includes the giant Riunite of Reggio Emilia, CIV of Modena and Le Chiantigiane of Chianti, in 1986 acquired Gruppo Italiano Vini the former Swiss Wine Food Group of mainly privately operated wineries. The consortium, which groups 45,000 growers in 103 cooperatives around Italy, accounted for more than 7m. hectolitres a year of wines sold under 150 wines or labels. The merger added some premium wines from Bigi in Umbria; Calissano in Piedmont; Forlani and Negri in Lombardy; Lamberti and Santi in the Veneto; Conti Serristori and Melini in Tuscany and Fontana Candida in Latium. The complex makes more than 10% of the nation's production, apparently ranking third in volume among the world's wine producers after E.N.J. Gallo of California.

Fattoria Paradiso
Capocolle di Bertinoro, 47032 Forli

A historic estate (founded in 1880) has been shaped into a viticultural paradise by Mario Pezzi and his family. DOC: Albana, Sangiovese and Trebbiano di Romagna. Other: Barbarossa, Cagnina, Pagadebit. From 45 acres, Pezzi makes 13,300 cases of exemplary wine, including the unique red Barbarossa (of a vine only he grows) and white semi-sweet Pagadebit ('debt payer'). An *enoteca*, museum and *tavernetta* are open to the public.

Riunite
42100 Reggio Emilia

Founded in 1950, Riunite is one of the world's largest wine-making operations, grouping 26 cooperatives, including 7 outside the province of Reggio, with 2 bottling plants. Walter Sacchetti presides over the complex which includes 9,934 growers and 368 winery employees. DOC: Lambrusco Reggiano Lambrusco di Sorbara and Bianco di Scandiano. Other: White and rosé table wine and *spumante* and a sulphur-free table wine for the U.S. market.

Spalletti-Tenuta di Savignano
Savignano sul Rubicone, 47039 Forli

The heirs of Conte G. Battista Spalletti own this winery in the 16th-century Castello di Ribano. Director-wine maker: Luigi Bonfiglioli. DOC: Sangiovese di Romagna. Rocca di Ribano *riserva* is commonly considered the best Sangiovese di Romagna.

La Stoppa
Anarano di Rivergaro, 29029 Piacenza

A leader in Colli Piacentini owned by Raffaele Pantaleoni. There is La Stoppa, an impressive red table wine and the *champenoise* Pantaleoni Brut.

Terre Rosse (Vallania)
Zola Predosa, 40069 Bologna

Founded in 1965 by the late Enrico Vallania, a physician, whose genius and tenacity charted new directions in Italian viticulture. DOC: Colli Bolognese. Other: Cabernet Sauvignon, Chardonnay, Malvasia, Pinot Grigio. The Vallania family are still coming up with new creations including an impressive white from Viognier.

Fattoria Zerbina
Marzeno Faenza, Ravenna

A family winery, run by Vincenzo Geminiani and daughter Cristina with guidance from oenologist Vittorio Fiore, which has quickly become a top estate in Romagna. Their Scaccomatto is the best Albana DOCG. They also make Marzeno di Marzeno '87 from Sangiovese with a little Cabernet, as well as a promising white called Vicchio, from Chardonnay with Trebbiano.

OTHER PRODUCERS

Tenuta Amalia
Villa Verrucchio, 47040 Forli. Good Sangiovese Superiore.

Conte Otto Barattieri
Vigolzone, 29010 Piacenza. Good Colli Piacentini DOC and table wine.

Francesco Bellei
Bomporto, 41030 Modena. Highly regarded Lambrusco di Sorbara DOC and Pinot-Chardonnay *champenoise*.

Tenuta Bissera
Bruno Negroni makes good Colli Bolognesi DOC and *spumanti*.

Le Calbane
Meldola, 47014 Forli. Good Sangiovese Superiore and Calbanesco, a red table wine from a mystery variety discovered in the vineyards of this small estate.

Camarone
Biancanigo di Castelbolognese, 48014 Ravenna. Good range of Romagna DOCs and *spumanti*.

Much of Emilia-Romagna's production is typical cafe wine, drunk where it is made.

Cansetto dei Mandorli
Predappio Alta, 47010 Forli. Good range of Romagna DOCs including Sangiovese and Cagnina.

Casetta dei Frati
Modigliana, 47015 Forli. Good Sangiovese and the unique Rosso della Trafila from an unknown variety found in 25 acres of wines.

Cesari
Castel San Pietro, 40024 Bologna. DOC: Albana, Sangiovese and Trebbiano di Romagna. The Sangiovese *riserva* is delicious, the Rèfolo *frizzante* fun.

Colombini
Castelvetro, 41014 Modena. Medium-large house respected for Lambrusco.

Comune di Faenza
Faenza, 48018 Ravenna. DOC: Albana, Sangiovese and Trebbiano di Romagna.

Stephano Ferrucci
Castelbolognese, 48014 Ravenna. Founded: 1931. Owner: Francesco Ferrucci. DOC: Albana, Sangiovese and Trebbiano di Romagna. A quality leader.

Fini
Solara, Bomporto 41030 Modena. DOC: Lambrusco di Sorbara. The well-known family of restaurateurs have their own Lambrusco.

Cantina Sociale di Forli
47100 Forli. Good Sangiovese Superiore DOC.

Carla Foschi
Cesena, 47023 Forli. Fine Sangiovese Superiore.

Fugazza
Ziano Piacentino, Piacenza. Giovanna and Maria Fugazza also own Castello di Luzzano in Oltrepò Pavese, Lombardy. They make Gutturnio from vineyards in Colli Piacentini.

Guarini Matteucci
San Tomé, 47100 Forli. Owner: Domenico Guarini Matteucci. DOC: Albana, Sangiovese and Trebbiano di Romagna.

Oreste Lini & Figli
Correggio, 42015 Reggio Emilia. DOC: Lambrusco Reggiano.

Malaspina
Bobbio, 29022 Piacenza. Owners: The Malaspina family. DOC: Trebbianino Val Trebbia. Other: Cabernet, Merlot.

Contessa Matilde
41 Modena. Established Lambrusco house which is now part of the Premiovini group.

Giancarlo Molinelli
Ziano, 29010 Piacenza. DOC: Gutturnio dei Colli Piacentini. Other: Barbera, Bonarda, Malvasia, Molinelli, Müller-Thurgau.

Tenuta del Monsignore
San Giovanni in Marignano, 47048 Forli. Owner: Maria Sarti Bacchini.

DOC: Sangiovese and Trebbiano di Romagna.

Moro
Calerno di Sant'Illaio d'Enza, 42049 Reggio Emilia. Owner-wine maker: Rinaldini. DOC: Lambrusco Reggiano. Other: Amarone del Partitore, Picòl Ross, Sauvignon.

Mossi
Ziano, 29010 Piacenza. Owner: Luigi Mossi. DOC: Gutturnio dei Colli Piacentini. Other: Müller-Thurgau.

Bruno Negroni (Tenuta Bissera)
Monte San Pietro, 40050 Bologna. DOC: Colli Bolognesi. Other: Bruno Negroni Brut *champenoise*.

Pasolini Dall'Onda
Montericco di Imola, 44026 Bologna. Wine makers since the 16th century, the Pasolini Dall' Onda family owns properties in Romagna and Tuscany. DOC: Albana, Sangiovese and Trebbiano di Romagna, Chianti.

Al Pazz
Monteveglio, 40050 Bologna. DOC: Colli Bolognese. Other: Rosso Montebudello.

Villa I Raggi
Predappio Alta, 47010 Forli. Sangiovese Superiore.

Fratelli Rizzi
Castell'Arquato, 29014 Piacenza. Good Monterosso Val d'Arda.

Cantine Romagnoli
Villo di Vigolzone, 29010 Piacenza. A complete range of Colli Piacentini DOCs plus *spumanti*.

Cantina Sociale Ronco
Ronco, 47010 Forli. Range of Romagna DOCs including single vineyard bottlings.

Samori
Bertinoro, 47032 Forli. Promising new house producing Romagna DOCs.

San Patrignano
Ospedaletto di Coriano, 47040 Forli. Good Sangiovese Superiore and Trebbiano as well as table wine and *spumanti*, made by young people at a drug rehabilitation centre.

La Tosa
Vigolzone, 29010 Piacenza. An emerging estate making good Colli Piacentini wines.

Tre Monti
Imola, 40026 Bologna. The Tarsallo label is used for good Albana.

Venturini & Baladini
Roncolo di Quattro Castella, Modena. Fine, full-bodied Lambrusco Regiano and Cuvee di Pinot *champenoise*.

Zerioli
Ziano Piacentino, 29010 Piacenza. The Zerioli family make a complete range of Colli Piacentini DOCs plus table wines and the *champenoise* Zerioli Brut.

TUSCANY

To find a national identity in such a federation of disparities as Italy is not as difficult as it sounds. The answer is Tuscany. For foreigners at least, the old Tuscan countryside of villas and cypresses, woods and valleys where vine and olive mingle is Italy in a nutshell.

And so is its wine. Nine out of ten people asked to name one Italian wine would say 'Chianti'. They would have many different ideas (if they had any at all) of what it tastes like – for if ever any wine came in all styles and qualities from the sublime to the gorblimey it is Chianti – and this despite being the earliest of all regions, possibly in all Europe, to start trying to define and defend its wine. Certainly in modern times the Consorzio of its producers paved Italy's way to its DOC system.

Chianti started in the Middle Ages as a small region of constant wars and alarms between Florence and Siena. It is now the biggest and most complex DOCG in Italy. There is a real unity and identity, despite its varied soils, traditions and microclimates, because they all grow the same basic red grape, or versions of it. The Sangiovese is what

holds Chianti together. On the other hand, Chianti is a blended wine, and individual inclinations can show up strongly in the balance of the blend, the type of fermentation, the use or neglect of the 'governo', the method and time of ageing.

Chianti has many departments and subregions. It also has several neighbours who claim superiority for their not-dissimilar wine: most notably Brunello di Montalcino and Vino Nobile di Montepulciano. Above all it is the firing range for the army of ambitious producers who believe that a dose of Cabernet, some new oak barrels and a designer bottle and label add up to The Great New Italian wine. Their Field Marshal, Piero Antinori, has demonstrated that it can.

White wine is a relative stranger here. There is no white Chianti. But several small traditional supply points have been encouraged by the world's swing to white and others have been instigated recently. Of the former, Vernaccia di San Gimignano, Montecarlo and Elba are the most important; of the latter, Galestro and Bianco della Lega – and various excellent non-DOC brands.

DOC AND OTHER WINES

Bianco dell'Empolese

DOC. White wine. Province: Florence. Villages: communes of Empoli, Cerreto Guido, Fucecchio, Vinci, Capraia e Limite, and Montelupo Fiorentina. Grapes: Trebbiano Toscano min. 80%, other whites up to 20%, Malvasia del Chianti up to 8%. Max. crop: 84 hl/ha. Min. alch: 10.5°.

Recent DOC, not well-known outside the hills of Empoli.

Bianco Pisano di San Torpé

DOC. White wine. Provinces: Livorno and Pisa. Villages: 17 in Pisa and Collesalvetti. Grapes: Trebbiano Toscano 75%, other whites up to 25%. Max. crop: 84 hl/ha. Min. alch: 11°. Vin Santo aged 4 years in *caratelli*. Annual production: 167,000 cases.

DOC named after a (very) early martyr – beheaded in AD 68 at Pisa. A pale dry wine with some body and a touch of bitterness.

Bianco di Pitigliano

DOC. White wine. Province: Grosseto. Villages: Pitigliano, Sorano, part of Scansano and Manciano. Grapes: Trebbiano Toscano 65–70%, Greco (Grechetto), Malvasia Bianca Toscana and Verdello 30–35% together but no more than 15% each. Max. crop: 87.5 hl/ha. Min. alch: 11.5°. Annual production: 330,000 cases.

Pitigliano is in the extreme south of Tuscany near Lake Bolsena, the home of Est! Est!! Est!!! (*see* Latium). Its soft, dry, slightly bitter white has no particular distinction.

Bianco della Valdinievole

DOC. White wine. Province: Pistoia. Villages: communes of Buggiano, Montecatani Terme and Uzzano. Grapes: Trebbiano Toscano min. 70% , Malvasia del Chianti, Canaiolo Bianco, Vermentino max. 25%, other whites up to 5%. Max. crop: 75 hl/ha. Min. alch: 11°. 3 years is required for Vino Santo. Annual production: 22,000 cases.

A small production of plain dry, sometimes slightly fizzy, white from west of Florence. Production of Vin Santo is smaller still.

Bianco Vergine Valdichiana

DOC. White wine. Provinces: Arezzo and Siena. Villages: 6 communes in Arezzo and 4 in Siena. Grapes: Trebbiano Toscano 70–85%, Malvasia del Chianti 10–20%, others 5–10%. Max. crop: 91 hl/ha. Min. alch: 11°. Annual production: 367,000 cases.

A satisfactory though pretty mild mid-dry white from eastern Tuscany often used as an apéritif in Chianti. A slightly bitter finish gives it some character. At least one producer (Avignonesi) makes it throughly crisp and tasty with additional Grecheto grapes.

Bolgheri

DOC. White and rosé wine. Province: Livorno. Villages: Bolgheri and neighbouring communes. Grapes: (white) Trebbiano Toscano 75–90%, Vermentino 10–25%, others up to max. 15%; (red) Sangiovese 80–95%, Canaiolo 5–20%, other reds up to 15%. Max. crop: 70 hl/ha. Min alch: 10.5°. Annual production: 28,000 cases.

Within this DOC zone are vineyards for Antinori's Rosé di Bolgheri and Sassicaia. Sassicaia is not covered by the DOC.

Brunello di Montalcino

DOCG. Red wine. Province: Siena. Village: Montalcino. Grape: Brunello di Montalcino. Max. crop: 52 to 56 hl/ha. Min. alch: 12.5°. Aged for at least 4 years (3-5 in wood); 5 years for *riserva*. Annual production: 278,000 cases.

A big dry red produced for many years by the Biondi-Santi family on 'the Petrus principle' – that nothing is too much trouble. But sold more in the spirit of Romanée-Conti – no price is too high. Made DOCG in 1980, the Brunello is a strain of Sangiovese which can be disciplined in this soil to give dark, deeply concentrated wines. Long (3-5 years) barrel-ageing and – the more vital – long bottle-age are used to coax a remarkable bouquet into its rich, brawny depths. Now several dozen growers make it, with inevitably varying standards.

Burton Anderson cites the following as the current leaders: Altesino, Biondi-Santi, Fattoria dei Barbi, Tenuta Caparzo, Tenuta Il Poggione, Villa Banfi (*see* Producers). A younger wine from young vines is also sold as Rosso dei Vigneti di Brunello.

Candida dei Colli Apuani

DOC. White wine. Province: Massa-Carrara. Villages: communes of Carrara, Massa and Montignoso. Grapes: Vermentino Bianco 70–80%, Albarola 10–20%. Max. crop: 56 hl/ha. Min. alch: 11.5° Annual production: 5,550 cases.

A DOC whose white wine is rarely seen outside the marble-quarry coast.

Carmignano

DOCG (1990). Red wine. Province: Florence. Villages: Carmignano, Poggio a Caiano (10 miles northwest of Firenze). Grapes: Sangiovese 45–65%, Canaiolo Nero 10–20%, Cabernet 6–10%, Trebbiano Toscano, Canaiolo Bianco and Malvasia del Chianti 10–20%, other varieties 5%. Max. crop: 56 hl/ha (77 for rosato). Min. alch 11.5°, rosso 12.5°. Aged 20 months for Carmignano, 3 years (2 in wood) for Carmignano Riserva.

Best described as Chianti with a just-tastable dollop of Cabernet, justified to the authorities by the fact that the Bonacossi family introduced it from Bordeaux generations ago. Carmignano is consistently well made and justifiably self-confident. Posterity may well thank it for the inspiration to aim all quality Chianti in this direction.

Chianti

DOCG. Red wine. Provinces: Siena, Florence, Arezzo, Pistoia, Pisa. Villages: 103 communes: 19 in Arezzo, 34 in Florence, 16 in Pisa, 8 in Pistoia, 26 in Siena. Grapes: Sangiovese 75–90%, Canaiolo Nero 5–10%, Trebbiano Toscano, Malvasia del Chianti 5–10%. Max. crop: 75 hl/ha Chianti. Min. alch: 11.5° for Chianti, 12.5° for *riserva*. Aged 6 months, 3 years for *riserva*. Annual production: 10.5m. cases.

There are 2 basic styles of Chianti: that made as fruity and fresh as possible for local drinking in its youth (still often bottled in *fiaschi*, whether covered with straw or plastic) and drier, more tannic and serious wine aged in barrels or tanks and intended for bottle-ageing; therefore bottled in Bordeaux bottles which can be stacked. The traditional grape mixture is the same for both – basically Sangiovese but with variable additions of dark Canaiolo, white Trebbiano and Malvasia. The *governo* is a local tradition of adding very sweet dried grape must (usually Colorino) to the wine after its fermentation to make it referment, boost its strength, smooth its astringency and promote an agreeable fizz which can make young *fiasco* Chianti delicious. Few producers now use the *governo* for wine that is to be aged before bottling.

Fine old Chianti Riserva has marked affinities with claret, particularly in its light texture and a definite gentle astringency which makes it feel very much alive in your mouth. Its smell and flavour are its own – sometimes reminding me faintly of mulled wine with orange and spices, faintly of chestnuts, faintly of rubber. I have also found a minty 'lift' in its flavour like young burgundy. Its mature colour is a distinct, even glowing garnet. The future of Chianti is under constructive debate. Few serious producers now use any white grapes in their wine. Many have experimented with a little seasoning of Cabernet, and with new, rather than often reused, barrels. But most seem agreed that the ultimate Chianti will be made when the ultimate strain of Sangiovese has been identified (as it has in Montalcino), propagated and its use mastered. Chianti is betting its future on the qualities of its ancestral grape variety.

Chianti Classico

The original zone between Florence and Siena, including the towns of Castellina, Radda, Gaiole, Greve and San Casciano. Most of its best producers are members of the very active Consorzio di Chianti Classico, based in Florence, and seal their bottles with its badge, a black rooster. Many are the country residences of ancient noble families with names familiar from the Renaissance (*see* Producers). Most of the best Chianti is Classico.

Chianti Putto

The Consorzio grouping the 6 other Chianti zones surrounding Chianti Classico uses a pink cherub (*putto*) for its seal. The term is generally used for their wines, although not all producers belong to the Consorzio, which is a voluntary group accounting for less than half of Chianti production. The six zones are:

Chianti Colli Aretini
The country to the east in the province of Arezzo; a good source of fresh young wines.

Chianti Colli Fiorentini
The zone just north of Chianti Classico around Florence, especially east along the river Arno. Several estates here are at least on a level with the best Classicos.

Chianti Colli Pisane
A detached area south of Pisa making lighter, generally less considerable wine.

Chianti Colli Senesi
A fragmented and inconsistent zone including the western flank of the Classico area south from Poggibonsi, the southern fringes around Siena and the separate areas of Montepulciano and Montalcino to the south. A wide range of styles and qualities.

Chianti Montalbano
The district west of Florence that includes the separate DOC of Carmignano. Also good Chiantis, though lesser known.

Chianti Rufina
A small area 15 miles east of Florence. Rufina is a village on the river Sieve, a tributary of the Arno. The hills behind, where the magically named Vallombrosa is hidden, contain some of the best Chianti vineyards (*see* Frescobaldi under Producers).

Colline Lucchesi

DOC. Red and white wine. Province: Lucca. Villages: Lucca, Capannori and Porcari. Grapes: (red) Sangiovese 45–60%. Canaiolo 8–15%, Ciliegiolo and Colorino 5–15%, Trebbiano Toscano 10-15%, Vermentino-Malvasia Toscana 5–10%; (white) Trebbiano. Max. crop: (red) 84 hl/ha;

(white) 77 hl/ha. Min. alch: (red) 11.5°; (white) 11°. Annual production 82,000 cases.
A cousin of Chianti from nearer the coast, also made in both first-year and *riserva* styles. The white is as yet an unknown entity.

Elba

DOC. White and red wine. Province: Island of Elba. Grapes: (white) Trebbiano Toscano (known as Procanico) 90%, other whites up to 10%; (red) Sangiovese at least 75%; Canaiolo, Trebbiano Toscano and Biancone 25%. Max. crop: (white) 67.5 hl/ha; (red) 63 hl/ha. Min. alch: 11° for white, 12° for red. Annual production: 66,000 cases.
The island off the south Tuscan coast, like a stepping stone to Corsica, has ideal dry white to wash down its fish and Chianti-style red from some highly competent producers.

Galestro

An ultramodern white produced by a group of Chianti makers using cold fermentation to instil zip and fruity freshness into Trebbiano white (which often lacks it). The name derives from a specific soil type. It is the only Italian wine to have a ceiling on its alcoholic degree: 10.5°.

Monte Antico

Chianti-style red, from the hills south of Siena. The Trebbiano white is not as remarkable.

Montecarlo

DOC. White and red wine. Province: Lucca. Villages: hills of Montecarlo. Grapes: (white) Trebbiano Toscano 60–70%, Semillon, Pinot Gris, Pinot Bianco, Vermentino, Sauvignon and Roussanne 30–40%; (red) Sangiovese 50–75%, Canaiolo Nero 5–15%, Ciliegolo, Colovino, Malvasia Nera, Syrah 10–20%. Max. crop: 70 hl/ha. Min. alch: 11.5°. Annual production: 105,000 cases.
A good example of the improvements possible to Tuscan wines by allowing some more aromatic grapes to elaborate the essentially neutral Trebbiano. Montecarlo's smooth, unaggressive but interesting white can develop a very pleasant bouquet with 2 or 3 years in bottle. DOC has expanded to include a red Sangiovese (not yet established).

Montescudaio

DOC. Red and white wine. Province: Pisa. Villages: Montescudaio and 6 other communes. Grapes: (red) Sangiovese at least 75%, Trebbiano Toscano and Malvasia 15–25%, other reds up to 10%. (white) Trebbiano Toscano 70–85%, Malvasia del Chianti and Vermentino 15–30%, other whites up to 10%. Max. crop: 84 hl/ha. Min. alch: 11.5° (17° for Vin Santo). Annual production: 89,000 cases.
Light red and white from near the coast west of Siena. The most distinguished is the strong white Vin Santo.

Morellino di Scansano

DOC. Red wine. Province: Grosetto. Villages: Scansano and 6 other communes in the very south of Tuscany. Grapes: Sangiovese plus up to 15% other red grapes. Max. crop: 84 hl/ha. Min. alch: 11.5° (12° with 2 years' ageing is *riserva*). Annual production: 189,000 cases.
DOC for an all-Sangiovese red. The only other one is the famous Brunello di Montalcino. The intention is clearly to build up this burly wine into something notable.

Moscadello di Montalcino

DOC. White wine. Province: Siena. Village: Montalcino. Grapes: Moscato, plus max. 15% other white grapes. Max. crop: 65 hl/ha. Min. alch: 10.5°. Aged 6 months from fortification for *liquoroso*.

This sweet Moscato has been revived as a DOC due largely to Villa Banfi. There is also a still and sweeter *liquoroso* version, though rarely seen.

Parrina

DOC. Red, white and rosé wine. Province: Grosseto. Villages: the commune of Orbetello. Grapes: (red and rosé) Sangiovese 80%, Canaiolo Nero, Montepulciano, Colorino up to 20%; (white) Trebbiano 80%, Ansonica and/or Malvasia del Chianti up to 20%. Max. crop: (white) 84 hl/ha; (red and rosé) 77 hl/ha. Min. alch: 11.5° for white; 12° for red; 11° for rosé. Annual production: 33,300 cases.

Lively wines, both red and white, from near the Argentario peninsula in south Tuscany. Parrina Bianco caught young, can be a good glass with seafood.

Pomino

DOC. Red and white wine. Province: Firenze. Village: Pomino in the commune of Rufina. Grapes: (white) Pinot Bianco and/or Chardonnay (60–80%), Trebbiano max. 30%, other whites up to 15%; (red) Sangiovese 60–75%, Canaiolo and/or Cabernet Sauvignon and/or Cabernet Franc 15–25%, Merlot 10–20%; (Vin Santo) Sangiovese, Trebbiano and others. Max. crop: 73.5 hl/ha. Min. alch: Bianco 11°, Rosso 12°, Vin Santo 15.5°. Red aged 1 year; 3 years (18 months in wood) for *riversa*; 3 years in *caratelli* for Vin Santo. Annual production 45,000 cases.

The move for this DOC was led by Frescobaldis. It applies to Pomino Bianco which is based on Pinot Bianco and Chardonnay with Trebbiano. The zone was cited in 1716 by Grand Duchy of Tuscany as one of the best wine areas.

Predicato

A new category of red wine from the hills of central Tuscany which does not qualify under DOC regulations but carries a high prestige. There are four Predicato categories:

Predicato del Muschio: for white wine from Chardonnay or Pinot Bianco with up to 20% Riesling, Müller-Thurgau or Pinot Grigio.

Predicato del Selvante: for white wine from Sauvignon Blanc with up to 20% Riesling, Müller-Thurgau or Pinot Grigio.

Predicato di Biturica: for red wine from Cabernet with up to 30% Sangiovese and 10% other red grapes.

Predicato di Cardisco: for red wine from Sangiovese with up to 10% other red grapes.

Rosso di Cercatoia

A handmade, barrel-aged red in the style of Chianti Riserva from Montecarlo, near Lucca, best known for its white. *See* Buonamico under Producers.

Rosso di Montalcino

DOC. Red wine. Province: Siena. Village: Montalcino. Grape: Brunello di Montalcino. Max. crop: 70 hl/ha. Min. alch: 12°. Aged for 1 year. Annual production: 145,000 cases.

A DOC made from Brunello grapes at Montalcino not aged long enough to qualify as Brunello di Montalcino. Rosso di Montalcino is lighter than Rosso dei Vigneti di Brunello without the wood ageing, but can be strikingly good value.

Rosso di Montepulciano

DOC. Red wine. Province: Siena. Village: the commune of Montepulciano. Grapes: Sangiovese (Prugnolo Gentile) 60–80%, Canaiolo Nero 10–20%, other varieties up to 20% though no more than 10% white. Max. crop: 70 hl/ha. Min. alch: 11°. Aged for 6 months. No production figures yet.

New DOC, which is enabling producers to make Vino Nobile a lighter red to drink young.

Sassicaia

An eccentric wine that has proved the most influential of all in the shape of Tuscan wine-growing. The late Marchesi Incisa della Rocchetta grew pure Cabernet Sauvignon on the coast at Bolgheri, south of Livorno – outside any recognized wine zone. What started as a whim became a sensation. He aged it in *barriques* like Bordeaux. His cousin Antinori of Florence used to bottle and sell it but his son, Niccolò, has moved the bottling to Bolgheri, and sells about 8,300 cases a year. A bottle should be surreptitiously slipped into top level Cabernet tastings.

Tignanello

The firm of Antinori are leading modern thinking about Chianti with this exceptional wine (and their Chiantis). It is non-DOC because it has 10% Cabernet (allowed only in Carmignano, not in Chianti). Wine-making and ageing are done Bordeaux-style with *barriques*. Tignanello is the obvious link between the eccentric Sassicaia and the traditional Chianti. It started the Tuscan revolution of the '80s.

Val d'Arbia (formerly Bianco della Vall d'Arbia)

DOC. White wine. Province: Siena. Villages: 10 along the Arbia river between Radda in Chianti and Buonconvento. Grapes: Trebbiano Toscano 75–85%, Malvasia del Chianti 15–25%, a max. 15% other grapes also allowed (not Moscato Bianco). Max. crop: 84.5 hl/ha. Min. alch: 11°. Annual production: 77,700 cases.

A DOC for a crisp, light, typically Tuscan white made in Chianti Classico country.

Val di Cornia

DOC. Red, white and rosé wines. Provinces: Livorno and Pisa. Villages: Campiglia Marittima, San Vincenzo, Piombino and Suvereto (including Sassetta and Monteverdi Marittimo) in hills drained by the Cornia stream in southwestern Tuscany. Grapes: (red and rosé) Sangiovese 70–100%, Canaiolo Nero, Ciliegiolo, Cabernet Sauvignon and/or Merlot at max. 30% but not more than 15% each; (white) Trebbiano Toscano 60–70%, Vermentino 15–30%, other white varieties up to 20%. Max. crop: 68 hl/ha for red and rosé, 82 hl/ha for white. Min. alch: 11.5° for red (12.5° for *riserva*, which must be aged 2 years), 10.5° for white, 11° for rosé. No production figures yet available.

A newly approved DOC.

Vernaccia di San Gimignano

DOC. White wine. Province: Siena. Villages: the communes of San Gimignano. Grape: Vernaccia di San Gimignano. Max. crop: 77 hl/ha. Min. alch: 11° (aged 1 year for *riserva*). Annual production: 433,000 cases.

Old-style Vernaccia was made as powerful as possible, fermented on its (golden) skins and aged in barrels for gently oxidized flavours to emerge. This was the wine Michelangelo loved. It can still be found like this, or in a modernized pale version which can be good but is hard to identify.

Vinto Santo

Wine of grapes dried in the loft until Christmas (to shrivel and sweeten them) is found all over Italy, but most of all at every farm in Tuscany where it is enjoying a resurgence. It can be red or white, but white is more common. Under several DOCs it is defined and regulated, but farmers make it regardless. It should be at least 3 years old, and may be sweet or dry. A few producers age it in small barrels under the roof tiles to produce a madeira-like effect. The results can be sensational.

Vino Nobile di Montepulciano

DOCG. Red wine. Province: Siena. Villages: the commune of Montepulciano. Grapes: Sangiovese (Prugnolo Gentile) 60–80%, Canaiolo 10–20%. Other varieties up to 20%, though no more than 10% white. Max. crop: 56 hl/ha. Min. alch: 12.5. Aged 2 years in wood; 3 years for *riserva*. Annual production: 267,000 cases.

Montepulciano would like to rival Montalcino, also in the south of the Chianti country. It is highly debatable whether it has anything as exceptional as Brunello to offer. This is essentially Chianti but professional wine makers have come to the fore and the DOCG is justified by some excellent examples.

TUSCANY PRODUCERS

Castello d'Albola
Radda, 53017 Siena.

Zonin's base in Chianti Classico, a 10th century castle with 128 acres. He also produces DOC Bianco Val d'Arbia, a *novello* called Sant'Ilario, and a new red *vino da tavola* called Acciaiolo.

Altesino
Montalcino, 53024 Siena

Director: Claudio Basla. Wine makers: Angelo Solci and Pietro Rivella. DOC: Brunello di Montalcino, Rosso di Montalcino. Other: Bianco di Montosoli, Palazzo Altesi, Alte d'Allesi (a Brunello-Cabernet Sauvignon mix), and Ambro d'Altesi (a Moscadello *passito*). Increasingly respected small producer. The *vino da tavola* Palazzo Allesi is *barrique*-aged, to produce an almost Burgundy-like suppleness and fruitness.

Fattoria di Ama
Amma in Chianti, 53010 Siena

DOC: Chianti Classico. Other: Collino di Ama, Pinot Grigio, Sauvignon, Chardonnay. Former manager Sivano Formigli brought this estate into the front rank of Chianti Classico and wine maker Marco Pallanti maintains high quality with first-rate single-vineyard Chiantis, as well as Merlot and Pinot Noir.

Marchesi L. & P. Antinori
50123 Firenze

Owner: Piero Antinori (succeeding Antinoris since 1385). DOC: Chianti Classico, Orvieto Classico. Other: Aleatico, Brut Nature *champenoise*, Galestro, Rosé di Bolgheri, San Giocondo, Tignanello, Villa Antinori Bianco, Vin Santo. *See* next page.

Argiano
Montalcino, 53024 Siena

The ancient estate of the Lovatelli family, now part of the stake of the Cinzano group in Brunello and reduced to 50 acres. Wine maker Maurizio Castelli makes noteworthy DOC Brunello di Montalcino and Rosso Argiano *vino da tavola*.

Avignonesi
Montepulciano, 54045 Siena

The 16th-century Palazzo Avignonesi, over its 13th-century cellars in the heart of Montepulciano, houses the family's barrel-aged Vino Nobile. The firm is run by the 3 Falvo brothers, whose experiments with Cabernet and Chardonnay are showing great promise. A second estate near Cortona makes exceptional dry Bianco Vergine della Valdichiana, a good dry Malvasia *vino da tavola*, a

Chardonnay called Il Marzocco and a Sauvignon Blanc called Il Vignola. A tiny amount of excellent Vin Santo is made, called Occhio del Pernice. At the recently acquired Sovana estate near Pitigliano they are making a fine sweet Aleatico.

Badia a Coltibuono
Gaiole, 53013 Siena

DOC: Chianti Classico. Other: *bianco, rosato* and Vin Santo. The monks of this magical 11th-century abbey in the woods might have been the original growers of Chianti. The buildings, cellars and gardens (with an excellent restaurant) are perfectly preserved by the Stucchi-Prinetti family, owners since 1846. The hills are too high here for vines; the 150 acres of vineyards are at Monti, to the south, half-way to Siena. There are few more consistently first-class Chiantis, as *riservas* back to 1958 prove.

Villa Banfi
Montalcino, 53024 Siena

Founded in 1977 by the House of Banfi, the largest US importer of wine. DOC: Brunello di Montalcino, Chianti Classico, Moscadello di Montalcino, Rosso di Montalcino. Other: Tavernelle Cabernet Sauvignon, Fontanelle Chardonnay, San Angelo Pinot Grigio, Santa Costanza Vino Novello, Sauvignon Blanc Fumaio, and the unusual Castello Banfi from Brunello, Cabernet Sauvignon, Petite Syrah and Pinot Nero. The firm, under the direction of Ezio Rivella and Pablo Hari, is developing vineyards and cellars on its vast Poggio all'Oro estate at Montalcino which has expanded through the purchase of the neighbouring Poggio alle Mura estate. From almost 2,000 acres, Banfi is producing growing quantities of premium red and white wines, as well as the bubbly and sweet Moscadello, plus Cabernet Sauvignon, Chardonnay and Rosso di Montalcino. In Piedmont, Banfi is producing Asti Spumante Brachetto d'Acqui, which makes a *spumante champenoise* and Charmat Banfi Brut; also from Gavi, Principessa Gavia-Banfi. Rivella, Italy's foremost oenologist, is using Montalcino as his base for leading Italian wine into the future. *See* page 342.

Fattoria dei Barbi
Montalcino, 53024 Siena.

Owner: Francesca Colombini Cinelli. Wine maker: Giancarlo Arrigoni. DOC: Brunello di Montalcino. Other: Bianco del Beato, Brusco dei Barbi, Moscatello, Vin Santo. The Barbi estate has an old reputation. It makes excellent Brunello, selected from good vintages.

A̅NTINOR̅I

Charting Tuscany's future

The Marchese Piero Antinori may well be to 21st-century Chianti what the Barone Ricasoli was to the Chianti of the 19th and 20th – the man who wrote the recipe. Antinori is persuasive with the eloquence of an aristocrat who does not have to raise his voice. He and his wine maker Giacomo Tachis have made this ancient Florentine house, based in the Renaissance Palazzo Antinori, Piazza Antinori, Florence, the modern pacesetter, not only for exemplary Chianti (and Orvieto) but more prophetically for Tignanello, which is Sangiovese blended with 10% Cabernet Sauvignon and aged, Bordeaux style, in new oak *barriques*. By replacing the currently obligatory 10% of white grapes in Chianti with Cabernet he has set a precedent that others are now following in droves – whether or not they are permitted to call the result Chianti.

The Antinori family has over 900 acres under vines in Tuscany (Santa Cristina, Peppoli, Badia a Passignano and Chianti Classico at Bolgheri) and Umbria (Castello della Scala). Extra grapes are bought under contract. The ultramodern winery is at San Casciano (near Santa Cristina) and the Palazzo Antinori in Florence has tasting facilities. The splendid Villa Antinori, portrayed on labels of the vintage Chianti Classico (which is made by the rule book) was destroyed in World War II. Antinori and Tachis are also in the forefront of white (including sparkling) wine-making in Italy, buying Pinot and Chardonnay grapes in Lombardy for their excellent sparkling Brut. Tachis himself is the great authority on Vin Santo. *See also* Sassicaia.

Berardenga-Fattoria di Felsina
Castelnuovo Berardenga, 53019 Siena.

Under manager Giuseppe Mazzocolin and wine maker Franco Bernabei, this estate is emerging as a leader for Chianti, especially with its *riserva* Vigneto Rancia. The Sangiovese *vino da tavola* Fontalloro is first-rate, as is the barrel-fermented Chardonnay I Sistri.

Biondi Santi – Il Greppo
Montalcino, 53024 Siena.

Founded in 1840 by Clemente Santi, whose grandson, Ferruccio Biondi Santi, is credited with originating Brunello di Montalcino. A controlling interest in the family firm was bought in 1989 by Pierluigi Tagliabue (of the neighbouring Poggio Salvo estate), but Franco Biondi Santi and son Jacopo remain in charge at Il Greppo. DOC: Brunello di Montalcino. 4,000 cases of some of Italy's most esteemed and expensive wine come from Il Greppo and its 30 acres of old vines. Sometimes described as 'Italy's first *grand cru*'.

Poderi Boscarelli
Cervognano di Montelpulciano, 53045 Siena.

Founded: 1963. Owner: Paola de Ferrari Corradi. DOC: Chianti Colli Senesi, Vino Nobile de Montepulciano. The little (22-acre) estate is considered the best in Montepulciano; its Vino Nobile has more depth, tone and muscle than its rivals. Fine *vino da tavola* Boscarelli is made with the aid of wine maker Maurizio Castelli.

Brolio Barone Ricasoli
50123 Firenze.

Owners: The Ricasoli family since 1141, though a major share is now held by the Australian firm of Thomas Hardy's (since 1990). DOC: Chianti, Chianti Classico, Orvieto. Other: Arbia, Brolio Bianco, Galestro, Rosé, Torricella, Vin Santo; Barone Ricasoli Brut *champenoise*, Vernaccia di San Gimignano. The great grim brickbuilt stronghold where the great grim Bettino Ricasoli, second Prime Minister of Italy in the 1850s, 'invented' Chianti – or at least the blend of grapes and method of production. The 620-acre Brolio estate is where the current Barone Ricasoli grows vines on some of Chianti's finest plots. Its former 'first-growth' reputation is in eclipse today as the pace becomes faster, but chief oenologist Luigi Casagrande is working to restore it to its former position.

Fattoria del Buonamico
Montecarlo, 55015 Lucca.

Founded: 1954. Owner: Rina Berti Grassi. Wine maker: Vasco Grassi. DOC: Montecarlo Bianco and Rosso. Other: Superb Sangiovese blend Rosso di Cercatoia. A leading Montecarlo maker, started by the well-known Turin restaurant Al Gatto Nero.

Castello di Cacchiano
Monti, 53010 Siena.

A 12th-century estate near Gaiole, owned by the Ricasoli Firidolfi family and Elisabetta Ricasoli Balbi Valier. DOC: Chianti Classico. A steady producer of good vintages; becoming one of Chianti's top estates. A fine new *vino da tavola* is called 'FR'. The second label is Castello di Montegrossi.

Tenuta Caparzo
Montalcino, 53024 Siena.

Manager: Nuccio Turone. Wine maker: Vittorio Fiore. DOC: Brunello di Montalcino, Rosso di Montalcino.

Other: Ca' del Pazzo, Le Grance Chardonnay, Rosso dei Vigneti di Brunello. A Brunello of growing quality and importance; particularly fine single-vineyard Brunello La Casa.

Tenuta di Capezzana
Carmignano, 50042 Firenze.

Founded in the 15th century. Owned and run by Ugo Contini Bonacossi and his family. DOC: Carmignano, Chianti Montalbano. Other: Capezzana Bianco, Ghiaie della Furba, Vin Ruspo, Vin Santo. The ex-Medici villa of the Bonacossis, with its 260 acres of vines, may be the first place Cabernet Sauvignon was grown in Tuscany. The excellence of their Carmignano assured the establishment of what seemed an alien DOC in the heart of Chianti (the finest is selected and sold as Villa Capezzana and Villa di Trefiano; named after the 2 estates where it is made). Other innovations include the rosé Vin Ruspo and red Barco Reale, and a Cabernet-Merlot blend called Ghiaie della Furba. A still Chardonnay has been introduced, along with a blended *champenoise* called Villa di Capezzana Brut.

Case Basse
Montalcino, 53024 Siena.

Owned by Milanese stockbroker Gianfranco Soldera, this tiny (15½-acre) estate makes exceptional Brunello that often comes out top in tastings. A *vino da tavola*, Intistieti, is also notable.

Castelgiocondo
Montalcino, 53024 Siena.

The estate with the largest tract of Brunello vines (395 acres of a total 543) is owned by the Frescobaldi family. DOC: Brunello di Montalcino, Rosso di Montalcino. Production, which began with the 1975 vintage, includes various table wines, such as the oaky Sauvignon Blanc Vergena.

Castelgreve
Mercatale Val di Pesa, 50024 Firenze.

The Castelli del Grevepesa cooperative is the largest Chianti Classico producer: 335,000 cases from growers with more than 1,600 acres. DOC: Chianti Classico. Other: Coltifredi, Valgreve Bianco, Vin Santo. Some of the Chianti Classico is bottled under the Castelgreve label, the rest as Lamole, Monte Firidolfi, Panzano, Sant'Angelo Vico L'Abate, and Selezione Vigna Elisa.

Castellare di Castellina
Castellina in Chianti, 53011 Siena.

Owners: Paolo and Fioretta Panerai. Wine maker Maurizio Castelli. DOC: Chianti Classico. Other: Castellare Bianco, I Sodi di San Niccolò in Santo, Canonico Chardonnay, Spartito Sauvignon Blanc. A fine Chianti in the *barrique*-aged I Sodi di San Niccolò. Maurizio Castelli has built a sterling reputation for this small estate. The *vini da tavola* are particularly successful, including a new pure Cabernet called Coniale.

Castell'in Villa
Castelnuovo Berardenga, 53053 Siena.

Founded in 1968 by Riccardo and Coralia Pignatelli della Leonessa (the wine maker). Excellent Chianti Classico, Bianco Val d'Arbia and good Vin Santo. Also an impressive Sangiovese *vino da tavola* called Balastrada.

Luigi Cecchi & Figli & Villa Cerna
Castellina in Chianti, 53011 Siena.

Owner: The merchant house of Luigi Cecchi & Figli. Founded: 1893. DOC: Chianti, Chianti Classico. Other: Bianco della Lega, Galestro, Sarmento, Spargolo. 550,000 cases a year.

Agricoltori del Chianti Geografico
Gaiole in Chianti, 53013 Siena.

Cooperative. Wine maker: Vittorio Fiore. DOC: Chianti Classico. About 220,000 cases are selected and bottled with the respected Contessa di Radda and *riserva* Tenuta Montegiachi labels. Other DOC wines include Vernaccia di San Grimignano and Bianco Val d'Arbia; table wines include Galestro and Sarmento.

Col d'Orcia
Montalcino, 53024 Siena.

A considerable estate bought by Cinzano in 1973 and managed by Edoardo Virano. DOC: Bruno di Montalcino, Chianti Colli Senesi, Moscadello di Montalcino. Other: Rosso Col d'Orcia, Novembrino *novello*, Vin Santo. One of the largest and best Brunello producers, progressing with Maurizio Castelli as wine maker.

Colli al Matrichese-Poderi Emilio Constanti
Montalcino, 53024 Siena.

Owner: Costanti family. Wine maker: Vittorio Fiore. DOC: Brunello di Montalcino, Chianti Colli Senesi. Other: Albatro (white), Vermiglio. A 17-acre property, whose 1,600 cases include some of the grandest and longest-lived Brunello.

Fattoria di Cusona
San Gimignano, 53017 Siena.

Owners: Girolamo Strozzi and Robert Guicciardini. DOC: Chianti, Vernaccia di San Gimignano. Other: Vin Santo, *spumante*, Sangiovese Sòdole. Leading producer of Vernaccia, dating back to the 16th century, now being revitalized with the aid of wine maker Vittorio Fiore.

Ricardo Falchini-Il Casale
San Gimignano, 53037 Siena.

Founded: 1965. Falchini makes some DOC Chianti, and is a principal producer of admired Vernaccia. He also makes good Vin Santo, a *champenoise* called Falchini Brut, and a fine Sangiovese-Cabernet blend called Paretato. He has recently expanded the property to 79 acres and is making notable Cabernet and Chardonnay *vino da tavola*, including an outstanding pure Cabernet Sauvignon called Campora.

Castello di Fonterutoli
Castellina in Chianti, 53010 Siena.

Owners: the Mazzei family since 1435. DOC: Chianti Classico. Other: Bianco della Lega red Concerto. Lapo Mazzei is president of the Classico Consortium, and a modest but wholly convincing champion of true Chianti. His sons Filippo and Francesco, with oenologist Franco Bernabei, are excelling with the *riserva* Ser Lapo and the *vino da tavola* Concerto, a Cabernet-Sangiovese blend.

Fontodi
Panzano, 50020 Firenze.

Owners and wine makers: Domizano and Dino Manetti. DOC: Chianti Classico. Other: Flaccaniello della Pieve. Fine Chianti and outstanding *barrique*-aged Flaccaniello (pure Sangiovese) make this small estate a quality leader in Tuscany.

Marchesi de' Frescobaldi
50125 Firenze.

Owners: the Frescobaldis since 1300, now 3 brothers: Vittorio (president), Ferdinando (manager for Italy), Leonardo (export manager). Wine maker: Luciano Boarino. DOC: Chianti Rufina, Pomino. Other: Frescobaldi Brut *champenoise*, Galestro, Nuovo Fiore, Villa di Corte Rosé, Vin Santo. Like the Antinoris, an ancient noble house leading the way for Tuscany with wines of outstanding quality, reliability, value and originality. All Frescobaldi wines come from their 8 estates east of Florence in Rufina, totalling 1,300 acres. Castello di Nipozzano is their most famous red (a superior selection is called Montesodi). Other estate Chiantis are Pomino and Poggio a Remole. Pomino Bianco is an excellent white seasoned with Chardonnay. Frescobaldi also manages Castelgiocondo (q.v.) at Montalcino.

Grattamacco
Castagneto Carducci, 57022 Livorno.

Owner: Pier Mario Meletti Cavallari. DOC: Bolgheri. A small estate making artisan wines, first making its name with Grattamacco Bianco from Trebbiano and Malvasia. The recent Grattamacco Rosso, made from Sangiovese and Malvasia with Cabernet Sauvignon, is highly regarded in Italy and can hold its own with Sassicaia.

Isole e Olena
Barberino Val d'Elsa, 50021 Firenze.

Owned by the de Marchi family since 1954. DOC: Chianti Classico. On this increasingly admired 90-acre estate wine maker Paolo de Marchi makes a fine Sangiovese *vino da tavola* called Cepparello, excellent Vin Santo, Chardonnay and a recent Cabernet Sauvignon. 1989 was the first vintage of a unique Syrah.

Melini
Gaggiano di Poggibonsi, 53036 Siena.

Founded: 1705. Now part of the Coltiva Gruppo Italiano Vini complex, and managed by Nunzio Capurso. In the 1860s, Laborel Melini devised the strengthened Chianti flask which enabled shipping, thus becoming one of the best-known names abroad. DOC: Chianti, Chianti Classico, Orvieto, Vernaccia di San Gimignano, Vino Nobile di Montepulciano. Other: Lacrima d'Arno Bianco and Rosato, Spumante Brut, Vin Santo, red Coltri and Chardonnay Granio. Melini owns vineyards of about 310 acres.

Monsanto
Barberino Val d'Elsa, 50021 Firenze.

Founded: 1962. Owner: Fabrizio Bianchi. Distinguished DOC Chianti includes Il Poggio *riserva* and Sangioveto Grosso. As well as good Vin Santo the estate produces a Sangiovese-Cabernet *vino da tavola* called Tinscvil, and a pure Cabernet called Nemo.

Monte Vertine
Radda, 53017 Siena.

Owned and run by Sergio Manetti; with consultant Giulio Gambelli. A fastidiously tended little vineyard producing Chianti (no longer under the DOC) – and Le Pergole Torte, an oak-aged all-Sangiovese red of unusual quality and also an interesting white and a first-rate Vin Santo.

Ornellaia
Bolgheri, 57020 Livorno.

Foreward-looking estate developed by Lodovico Anti-

The ancient monastic estate of La Badia a Coltibuono.

nori, with cellars designed by California's André Tchelist-cheff, and advisers including viticulturalist Mario Fregoni, Antinori wine maker Giacomo Tachis and French oenologist Jacques Puisais. The resident wine maker is Federico Staderini, whose white Poggio alle Gazze (Sauvignon Blanc with Sémillon), first issued in 1988, is highly praised. The red Ornellaia *vino da tavola* (Cabernet Sauvignon, Merlot and Cabernet Franc) is set to rival (though not imitate) Sassicaia, and the '86 may even surpass it.

Tenuta Il Poggione
Montalcino, 53024 Siena.
Founded: 1890. Owners: Clemente and Roberto Francheschi. Wine maker: Fabrizio Bindocci. DOC: Brunello di Montalcino, Rosso di Montalcino. Other: Moscadello di Montalcino, Rosso dei Vigneti di Brunello, Vin Santo. One of the biggest Montalcino estates of consistently good quality. The Brunello is for drinking young.

Poliziano
Montepulciano, 53045 Siena.
Owned by Federico Carletti who, with the help of Maurizio Castelli, makes admired Chianti, Bianco Vergine and Vin Santo. Carletti is turning this estate into a first-class Vino Nobile producer. Impressive table wines include Elegia, a pure Sangiovese, and Cabernet-based Le Stanze. New vineyards are planned for Rosso di Montepulciano. Second label: Carletti della Giovampaola.

Fattoria La Querce
Impruneta, 50023 Firenze.
Owner: Gino Marchi and Grazia Montorselli. Wine maker: Attilio Pieri. DOC: Chianti. In some eyes (and some vintages) the best-made wine of Chianti.

Castello dei Rampolla
Panzano in Chianti, 50020 Firenze.
Owners and wine makers: Di Napoli family. DOC: Chianti Classico. Other: Sammarco, Trebbiano. Sammarco blend (Cabernet with Sangiovese) has become a major new table wine.

Riecine
Gaiole, 53013 Siena.
Founded in 1971 by an Englishman, John Dunkley, and his wife Palmina Abbagnano. DOC: Chianti Classico. Other: Riecine Bianco, La Gioia di Riecine. Dunkley proved himself a perfectionist from his first vintage. His attitude and his excellent, truly typical, Chianti have helped to make the British more attentive.

Rocca delle Macìe
Castellina in Chianti, 53011 Siena.
Founded in 1974. A respected producer, with 543 acres in Chianti. Their top wines are the *riserva* Chianti Fizzano and the red *vino da tavola* Ser Gioveto. They also produce Orvieto Classico, Galestro, Rubizzo and Decembrino.

Rocca di Castagnoli
Castagnoli, 53013 Siena.
Owner: Calogero Calì. Manager: Walter Filiputti of Friuli. DOC: Chianti, Val d'Arbia. Other: Chardonnay, Sangiovese, Cabernet. This estate is very much on the rise under Calì and Filiputti, who also make wine from the La Capriaia estate at Castellina.

I. L. Ruffino
Pontassieve, 50065 Firenze.

Founded: 1877. Owners: The Folonari family. DOC: Chianti, Chianti Classico, Orvieto. Other: Galestro, Sarmento, Predicato, Rosatello. One of the largest Chianti houses with vast holdings in the Classico zones, Ruffino has been moving smartly to upgrade its already solid image with Predicato wines devised by Ambrogio Folonari. The Ducale is the classic among Chianti *riserva* and the Cabreo Sangiovese/Cabernet blend and Chardonnay have rapidly become models of the new style Tuscan Predicato wines. A Pinot Nero, called Nero del Tondo, is also impressive. Their holdings in Chianti Classico are the source of the respected Riserva Ducale. They also own the Nozzole estate at Greve.

San Felice
San Gusmè, 53030 Siena.

Owner: The Agrel corporation. Manager: Enzo Morganti. DOC: Chianti Classico, Val d'Arbia. Other: Galestro, Chardonnay, Vigilio, Vin Santo, Vigorello (pure Sangiovese), Predicato di Biturica. A steadily improving estate making fine Chianti, and special red Vigilio from some 470 acres. They also own neighbouring La Pagliaia, Campogiovanni near Sant'Angelo, and the small Poggio Rosso estate, from which young wine maker Leonardo Bellacini styles some of the region's finest reds.

San Giusto a Rentennano
Monti, 53010 Siena.

Owner Francesco Martini di Cigala and family make Chianti, Percarlo (strong, pure, *barrique*-aged Sangioveto) and Vin Santo that are among the best.

Tenuta San Guido-Sassicaia
Bolgheri, 57020 Livorno.

Owner: Niccolò Rocchetta. DOC: none. The late Marchese Mario Incisa della Rocchetta planted Cabernet Sauvignon on his seaside estate near Bolgheri, Tenuta San Guido, in 1942. His Sassicaia emerged in the late 1960s as Italy's finest Cabernet. The wine is made and aged at Bolgheri, and used to be distributed by his cousins the Antinoris of Florence; since Mario Incisa's death in 1983 his son Niccolò has taken personal control of selling the 8,300 cases produced annually. *See also* Sassicaia, page 334.

Castello di San Polo in Rosso
Gaiole, 53013 Siena.

Cesare and Katrin Canessa, with oenologist Maurizio Castelli make fine Chianti Classico, and a superb pure Sangioveto *vino da tavola* called Cetinaia, plus Bianco and Rosato d'Erta.

Selvapiana
Pontassieve, 50065 Firenze.

Founded: 1840. Owner: Francesco Giuntini. DOC: Chianti Rufina. An old family property brought to the top ranks in Chianti with the help of wine maker Franco Ernabei.

Conti Serristori
Sant'Andrea in Percussina, 50026 Firenze.

Part of the Gruppo Italiano Vini complex. DOC: Chianti, Chianti Classico, Orvieto, Vernaccia di San Gimignano. Other: Bianco and Rosato Toscano, Galestro, Vin Santo. The property includes the country house where Machiavelli lived in exile.

Teruzzi & Puthod – Ponte a Rondolino
San Gimignano, 53037 Siena.

Founded in 1975 by Enrico Teruzzi and Carmen Puthod. DOC: Chianti Colli Senesi, Vernaccia di San Gimignano. Other: Galestro, Terra Peperino, Sarpinello *champenoise*. The estate is expanding; 84 acres provide exemplary Vernaccia and wood-aged *riserva* known as Carmen and Terra di Tufo respectively.

Castello di Uzzano
Greve, 50022 Firenze.

Owner: Briano Castelbarco Alabani Masetti, whose family has owned the property since the 17th century. DOC: Chianti Classico. One of the greatest names of Chianti, whose 14th-century cellars (the walls are 27 feet thick) slowly mature wines of sweet harmony and long life. As well as Castello di Uzzano, Castelbarco and friend Marion de Jacobert make an impressive *vino da tavola* called Vigna Niccolò da Uzzano, from more than 100 acres of vines.

Val di Sugga
Montalcino, 53024 Siena.

DOC: Brunello di Montalcino, Rosso di Montalcino. The first of Milanese Lionello Marchesi's 3 estates; he also owns Tenuta Trerose in Montepulciano and San Leonino in Chianti Classico, making him a major force in Tuscan estate wines. From 57 acres he produces wines of good quality and is steadily improving.

Vecchie Terre di Montefili
Greve, 52022 Firenze.

Owner: Roccaldo Acuti. Wine maker: Vittorio Fiore. Fine DOC Chianti wines, and an interesting white *vino da tavola* called Vigna Regis, made from Chardonnay, Sauvignon Blanc and Traminer. With its red Bruno di Rocca, this estate is a rising star in Chianti.

Castello Vicchiomaggio
Greve, 50022 Firenze.

Owner: John Matta since 1968. DOC: Chianti Classico. Others: Ripa delle More, Ripa delle Mimose. A 9th-century castle in a super site with 54 acres of vines. Under the guidance of wine maker Vittorio Fiore the estate has seen a rapid improvement, and is now the scene of some excellent modern wine-making.

Vignamaggio
Greve, 50022 Firenze.

Owner: Gianni Nunziante. Wine maker: Franco Bernabei. DOC: Chianti Classico. Other: Sangiovese Gherardino. The beautiful 15th-century villa where Mona Lisa probably lived, home of Michelangelo's biographer and one of the most prestigious Chiantis, but rather light in style. The new owner is aiming to bring this historical estate back to Chianti's front ranks.

Castello di Volpaia
Radda in Chianti, 53017 Siena.

Owners: Giovannella and Carlo Stianti Mascheroni. Wine maker: Maurizio Castelli. DOC: Chianti Classico, Bianco Val d'Arbia. Other: Balifico, Coltassala, Torniello, Vin Santo. The medieval castle and its hamlet were high on the list of 15th-century *crus*. Its refined wines include the new delicately sweet and fruity Coltassala of Sangioveto and Mammolo, and the revelatory oak-aged Torniello.

OTHER PRODUCERS

Aiola
Vagliagli, 53010 Siena. Owner: Giovanni Malagodi. DOC: Chianti Classico, Bianco Val d'Arbia. Other: Logaiolo.

Fattoria Ambra
Carmignano, 50040 Firenze. Owners: The Rigoli family. DOC: Carmignano. 15 acres.

Amorosa
Sinalunga, 53046 Siena. Owners: Carlo Citterio. DOC: Chianti Colli Senesi. Other: Borgo Amorosa, Amorosa Bianca.

Artimino
Artimino, 50040 Firenze. The 16th-century Medici villa, once surrounded by a 32-mile wall, is one of Tuscany's most impressive wine estates. DOC: Carmignano, Chianti. Other: La Ferdinanda da Bianco and Rosso, Vin Ruspo, Vin Santo. Recent administrative changes have left wines in decline and the future in doubt.

Fattoria di Bacchereto
Bacchereto, 50040 Firenze. Owner: Carlo Bencini Tesi. DOC: Carmignano, Chianti.

Baggiolino
La Romola, 50020 Firenze. Owner: Ellen Fantoni Sellon. DOC: Chianti. Other: Poggio Brandi. 37 acres.

Erik Banti
Montemerano, 59050 Grosseto. DOC: Morellino di Scansano called Ciabatta, Aquilaia and Piaggie. Other: Alicante. 26 acres.

Jacopo Banti
Campiglia Marittima, 57021 Livorno. Leader of the new Val di Cornia DOC, with red Ciliegolo and white Corniello.

Bibbiani
Capraia e Limtie, 50050 Firenze. DOC: Chianti Montalbano.

Rudolf Bindella
Montepulciano, 53045 Siena. Important Swiss importer makes fine Vino Nobile and has bought an estate in Chianti.

Fattoria di Bossi-Marchese Gondi
Pontassieve, 50056 Firenze. DOC: Chianti Rufina, Vin Santo. 41 acres.

La Brancaia
Castellina, 53010 Siena. Owners: Bruno and Brigitte Widmer. DOC: Chianti. 12 acres.

Brugnano
San Casciano Val di Pesa, 50026 Firenze. Owner: Conte Lodovico Guicciardini. DOC: Chianti.

Villa Cafaggio
Panzano, 50020 Firenze. Owner and wine maker: Stefano Farkas. DOC: Chianti Classico. Other: Solatio Basilica, San Martino. Fine austere wine.

Caggiolo
Castellina, 53010 Siena. Owners: Ezio

and Pietro Rivella. Often excellent Chianti Classico.

Villa Calcinaia
Greve, 50022 Firenze. Owned by the Caponi family since 1523. DOC: Chianti. 99 acres.

Le Calvane
Montagnana Val di Pesa, 50025 Firenze. DOC: Chianti. Other: Sorbino (white). 35 acres.

Camigliano
Montalcino, 53024 Siena. Owners: The Ghezzi family. DOC: Brunello di Montalcino. Other: Bianco, Rosso dei Vigneti di Brunello.

Campogiovanni
See San Felice.

Candialle
Panzano, 50020 Firenze. Owner: Gerd von Bentheim. DOC: Chianti. 7.5 acres.

Podere Capaccia
Radda, 53017 Siena. Wine maker: Vittorio Fiore. DOC: Chianti. Other: Sangioveto Querciagrande. 7.5 acres.

Capannelle
Gaiole, 53013 Siena. Owner: Raffaele Rossetti. A tiny 'boutique' winery, rare in Tuscany, making Capannelle Rosso, Bianco and Chardonnay *vini da tavola*, much prized but over-priced.

Caprili
Montalcino, 53024 Siena. Owner: Alfo Bartolommei. Excellent DOC Brunello and Rosso di Montalcino. 17 acres.

Carmignani G. 'Fuso'
Montecarlo, 55015 Lucca. DOC: Montecarlo Bianco. Other: Red Sassonero (from Sangiovese, Syrah and Malvasia Nera), white Pietrachiara. 10 acres.

Carpineto
Dudda, 50020 Firenze. Owner: Giovanni Carlo Sacchet. Reliable Chianti, Orvieto and *vini da tavola*.

Fattoria Le Casalte
Montepulciano, 53045 Siena. Owner: Paolo Silvestri. DOC: Chianti, Vino Nobile.

Casanova dei Neri
Montalcino, 53024 Siena. Rising star in Montalcino with Brunello and Rosso. The new label carries the family name. 30 acres.

Casavecchia di Nittardi
Castellina in Chianti, 53011 Siena. Owner: Anstalt Nittardi. DOC: Chianti Classico. 5 acres.

Fattoria Casenuove
Panzano, 50020 Firenze. Owner: Pietro Pandolfini. DOC: Chianti Classico. 59 acres.

Castello di Cerreto
50122 Firenze. The estate near Castelnuovo Berardenga belongs to the dress designer Marchese Emilio Pucci. DOC: Chianti Classico. Pucci also owns

the Granaiolo and Coiano estates in Chianti Colli Fiorentini.

Castiglion del Bosco
Montalcino, 53042 Siena. Wine maker: Maurizio Castelli. DOC: Brunello and Rosso di Montalcino. 86 acres.

Cennatoio
Panzano, 50020 Firenze. Owner: Leandro Alessi. Wine maker: Alfonso Garberoglio. DOC: Chianti. Second label: Luca della Robbia.

Fattoria del Cerro
Montepulciano, 53045 Siena. Owner: SAI Agricola insurance company. DOC: Chianti, first-rate Vino Nobile. Second label: Cantine Baiocchi. 289 acres.

Le Chiantigiane
Tavarnelle Val di Pesa, 50028 Firenze. Group of 10 cooperatives, and part of the Coltiva Gruppo Italiano Vini complex. DOC: Chianti (some Classico) and a range of others. Other: Galestro. 1.5m. cases.

La Chiesa di Santa Restituta
Montalcino, 53024 Siena. Owner: Roberto Bellini. Oenologist: Pietro Rivella. DOC: Brunello and Rosso di Montalcino. Steady improvement puts this among the best Brunello. 40 acres.

Chigi Saracini
Castelnuovo Berardenga, 53033 Siena. DOC: Chianti Colli Senesi, Bianco Val d'Arbia. The ancient estate was bequeathed to the Chigiana Musical Academy of Siena by Conte Guido Chigi. 99 acres.

Tenuta La Chiusa
Magazzini di Portoferraio-Elba, 57037 Livorno. Owner: Giuliana Foresi. DOC: Elba. Dignified wines from 12 acres.

Ciacci Piccolomini d'Aragona
Montalcino, 53024 Siena. Old estate emerging with fine Brunello di Montalcino.

Villa Cilnia
Owner: Giovanni Bianchi. DOC: Chianti Colli Aretini. Other: Whites include Poggio Garbato, barrel-aged Camp del Sasso, sweet Sassolato, fizzy Le Bizze, and Predicato del Muschio; rosé Poggio Cicaleto; reds Vocato and Le Vignacce.

Colognole
Rufina, 50068 Firenze. Owner: The Marchesa Spalletti (formerly of Poggio Reale). DOC: Chianti Rufina.

La Colonica
Montepulciano, 53045 Siena. Owner: Fernando Cattani. Good Vino Nobile and Bianco Vergine. 74 acres.

Contucci
Montepulciano, 53045 Siena. DOC: Vino Nobile di Montepulciano, Chianti, Vin Santo. Recent modernization has improved style.

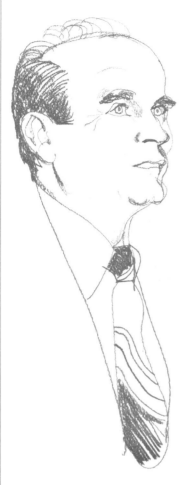

Ezio Rivella
As the wine director and chief
oenologist for Villa Banfi, the largest
exporters of Italian wine to the United
States. Ezio Rivella (Piedmont-born, a
man of startling competence and
vitality) has fabulous resources at his
disposal. His chief preoccupation is the
vast Banfi development at Montalcino in
the south of Tuscany, where in the '70s
the company acquired no less than 2,000
acres for planting. The principal goal is
Brunello on a scale never contemplated
before. Rivella has succeeded in making
available to a world-wide public a fine
example of one of Italy's rarest and most
splendid wines. But his ambitions have
gone much further: Cabernet,
Chardonnay and Pinot Grigio have been
striking successes, and he is
experimenting with Sauvignon Blanc,
Pinot Nero, Petite Syrah – and no doubt
other varieties. Meanwhile the simple
Rosso di Montalcino sold as Centine
epitomizes Rivella's and Banfi's policy
of offering value for money to everyone.

Fattoria Il Corno
San Casciano Val di Pesa, 50026 Firenze.
Owners: Antonio and Maria Teresa
Frova. DOC: Chianti. *Barrique*-aged
Sangovese Fossespina. 148 acres.

Dievole
Vagliagli, 53010 Siena. Great potential
from 237 acres of vines being developed
slowly.

Fanetti
Montepulciano, 53045 Siena. DOC:
Chianti Colli Senesi, Vino Nobile di
Montepulciano.

Tenuta di Farneta
Sinalunga, 53046 Siena. Good Chianti
and a fine pure Sangiovese *vino da tavola*
called Bongoverno.

Fassati
Pieve di Sinalunga, 53046 Siena.
Founded 1913. Owned since 1969 by
Fazi-Battaglia (*see* Marches). Wine
maker: Amadeo Esposito. DOC:
Chianti, Chianti Classico, Vino Nobile
di Montepulciano. A new property at
Graccianello improves quality potential.

Le Filigare
San Donato in Poggio, 50020 Firenze.
Wine maker: Gabriella Tani. DOC:
Chianti. Other: Stylish red Podere Le
Rocce.

Fattoria di Fognano-Talosa
Montepulciano, 53045 Siena. Manager:
Ottorino De Angelis. DOC: Vino
Nobile (single-vineyard Talosa), Chianti.

Fossi
50133 Firenze. Owners: Andrea and
Gianfranco Fossi. DOC: Chianti
Classico. 4,400 cases, including some
fine *riserva*.

Castello di Gabbiano
Mercatale Val di Pesa, 50024 Firenze.
DOC: Chianti Classico. Other:
Impressive pure Sangiovese Ania,
Sangiovese/Cabernet/Merlot 'R&R',
Chardonnay Ariella. Wine maker
Bernabei has recently left and the estate
may be for sale.

Il Greppone Mazzi
The Folonari family make good Ruffino
Brunello from 20 acres.

Fattoria di Grignano
Pontassieve, 50026 Firenze. Owner: The
Marchesi Gondi. DOC: Chianti Rufina.
99 acres.

Carla Guarnieri
Pozzolatico, 50023 Firenze. DOC:
Chianti. Other: Highly praised
Sangiovese Terricci.

Lamole di Lamole
Owners: The Toscano family. DOC:
Chianti Classico. A small estate at
Lamole near Greve, highly reputed for
splendid old vintages.

Lilliano
Antella, 50011 Firenze. DOC: Chianti.
52 acres.

Lilliano
Castellina in Chianti, 53011 Siena.

Owners: The Berlingieri and Ruspoli
families. DOC: Chianti Classico.
Distinguished wines from 120 acres.

Lisini
Montalcino, 53024 Siena. Owners: The
Lisini brothers. DOC: Brunello and
Rosso di Montalcino. Wine maker:
Franco Bernabei. Ranks with the best in
some years.

Podere Lo Locco
Carmignano, 50040 Firenze. Owners:
The Pratesi family. DOC: Carmignano.

Tenuta di Lucciano-Spalletti
Quarrata, 51039 Pistoia. Chianti
Montalbano and table wines. 110 acres.

Mantellassi
Magliano in Toscana, 58051 Grosseto.
DOC: Morellino di Scansano.

Fattoria di Manzano
Manzano di Cortona, 52042 Arezzo.
Owner: Massimo D'Alessandro. DOC:
Bianco Vergine. Other: Vigna del
Vescovo.

Le Masse di San Leolino
Panzano, 50020 Firenze. Owner:
Scotsman Norman Bain. Wine maker:
Franco Bernabei. DOC: Highly praised
Chianti Classico.

Mastroianni
Montalcino, 53024 Siena. Owners:
Gabriele and Antonio Mastroianni.
Wine maker: Pino Zardetto. DOC:
Brunello and Rosso di Montalcino.

Fattoria Michi
Montecarlo, 55015 Lucca. DOC:
Montecarlo. Other: Roussanne white. 42
acres.

Miscianello Tomarecchio
Vagliagli, 53010 Siena. DOC: Chianti,
Val d'Arbia. 17 acres.

Mocenni
Vagliagli, 53010 Siena. DOC: Chianti,
Val d'Arbia. 45 acres.

Montagliari
Panzano, 50020 Firenze. Owner:
Giovanni Capelli. DOC: Chianti. Other:
Brunesco di San Lorenzo, Vin Santo.

Fattoria Montellori
Fucecchio, 50054 Firenze. Owner:
Giuseppe Nieri and son Alessandro.
DOC: Chianti. Other: *Barrique*-aged
Castelrapiti Rosso, *champenoise*
Montellori Brut. 120-acre estate where
ambition sometimes exceeds results.

Montemaggio
Radda, 53017 Siena. Owner: Giampaolo
Bonechi. Oenologist: Vittorio Fiore.
DOC: Chianti. 32 acres.

Montenidoli
San Gimignano, 53037 Siena. Owner:
Elisabetta Fagiuoli. DOC: Chianti Colli
Senesi and Vernaccia. Other: white
Vinbrusco, *rosato*.

Vecchia Cantina di Montepulciano
Montepulciano, 53045 Siena. A
cooperative founded in 1937, now with
some 300 growers. DOC: Bianco
Vergine della Valdichiana, Chianti, Vino

Nobile di Montepulciano. The zone's largest producer of Montepulciano, but of no particular repute.

Pagliarese
Castelnuovo Berardenga, 53033 Siena. Owner: Alma B. Sanguineti. DOC: Chianti, Bianco Val d'Arbia. Other: red Camerlengo, Vin Santo.

Fattoria Pagnana
Rignano sull'Arno, 50067 Firenze. DOC: Chianti. Other: Bianco, Vin Santo.

Parri
Montespertoli, 50025 Firenze. Owner: Luigi Parri. DOC: Chianti.

La Parrina
Albinia di Orbetello, 58010 Grosseto. Owner: Franca Spinola. DOC: Parrina Bianco, Rosso. Other: Albinia Rosato. The principal producers of this dry white 'Vino Etrusco' from the coast near Orbetello.

Pasolini Dall'Onda-Enoagricola
Barberino Val d'Elsa, 50021 Firenze. Owners: The Pasolini family. DOC: Chianti (noteworthy *riserva*, Montòli). 148 acres.

Peppoli
Mercatale Val di Pesa, 50024 Firenze. Owner: Antinori. DOC: Excellent, traditional Chianti seasoned in large casks.

Fattoria di Petriolo
Rignano sull'Arno, 50067 Firenze. Good Chianti and a fine Merlot.

Fattoria di Petroio
Vagliagli, 53010 Siena. Owners: Pamela and Gian Luigi Lenzi. On the rise with their fine Chianti.

Le Pici
San Gusmè, 53030 Siena. Owner: Gunnar Lüneburg. DOC: Chianti Classico. 22 acres.

Pietrafitta
San Gimignano, 53030 Siena. Oenologist: Sergio Conforti. DOC: Chianti. Vernaccia di San Gimignano. 99 acres.

Pietraserena
San Gimignano, 53037 Siena. DOC: Vernaccia (outstanding Vigna del Sole). 41 acres.

Cantina Cooperativa di Pitigliano
Pitigliano, 58017 Grosseto. DOC; Bianco di Pitigliano. The cooperative (Tuscany's largest) includes most of Pitigliano's 1,000 registered growers.

Tenuta di Poggio
Rufina, 50068 Firenze. Owner: Vittorio Spolveri. DOC: Chianti Rufina.

Poggio al Sole
Sambuca Val di Pesa, 50020 Firenze. Owner: Aldo Torrini. Oenologist: Gabriella Tani. DOC: Chianti Classico. Other: Vino della Signora, Vin Santo. 17 acres.

Poggio Romita
Tavarnelle Val di Pesa, 50028 Firenze. Owner: Angiolo Sestini. DOC: Chianti.

Il Poggiolino
Sambuca Val di Pesa, 50020 Firenze. Owners: Carlo and Maria Grazia Pacini. DOC: Chianti. Other: Sangiovese Roncaia.

Il Poggiolo
Poggiolo di Monteriggioni, 53035 Siena. Owners: The Bonfio family. DOC: Chianti Colli Senesi. 46 acres.

Fattoria Il Poggiolo
Carmignano, 50042 Firenze. Owner: Giovanni Cianchi Baldazzi. DOC: Carmignano. Other: Vin Ruspo, Vin Santo.

Poggio Rosso
See San Felice.

Castello di Poppiano
Montespertoli, 50025 Firenze. Owner: Ferdinando Guicciardini. DOC: Chianti Colli Fiorentini.

Fattoria Le Pupille
Magliano in Toscana, 58051 Grosseto. DOC: Morellino di Scansano.

Castello di Querceto
Lucolena, 50020 Firenze. Manager-wine maker: Alessandro François. DOC: Chianti Classico. Other: Sangiovese La Corte, white Le Giuncaie, Vin Santo.

Fattoria Querciabella
Greve, 50022 Firenze. DOC: Chianti. Other: Red Camartina.

Querciavalle
Vagliagli, 53010 Siena. Owners: The Losi brothers. DOC: Chianti, Bianco Val d'Arbia.

Castello de Rencine
Castellina in Chianti, 53011 Siena. DOC: Chianti Classico.

Rodano
Castellina, 53010 Siena. Owner: Vittorio Pozzesi. DOC: Chianti. 45 acres.

Fattoria di Sammontana
Montelupo, 50056 Firenze. Owners: Andrea and Michele Dzieduszycki, whose noble Polish ancestors acquired the estate in 1870. DOC: Chianti. 74 acres.

San Cosma
San Gusmé, 53030 Siena. Owner: Bent Myhre. DOC: Chianti. 15 acres.

San Fabiano Calcinaia
Poggiobonsi, 53036 Siena. Wine maker: Giuseppe Bassi. DOC: Chianti. Other: Cerviolo (red Cabernet, white Chardonnay-Sauvignon). This and nearby Cellole are being developed together, with great potential.

San Filippo dei Comunali
Montalcino, 53024 Siena. Owner: Ermanno Rosi. DOC: Brunello and Rosso di Montalcino.

Fattoria San Leonino
Castellina in Chianti, 53011 Siena. Owner: Lionello Marchesi – one of his 3 Tuscan estates. 123 acres.

San Vito in Fior di Selva
Montelupo Fiorentino, 50056 Firenze. Owners: Laura and Roberto Drighi.

DOC: Chianti. White *vini da tavola*.

Santa Valeria
Vagliagli, 53010 Siena. Owner: Alberto Procovio. Wine consultant: Carlo Ferrini. DOC: Chianti. 15 acres.

Villa La Selva
Bucine, 52020 Arezzo. The ancient estate is owned by the Carpini family. Oenologist: Vittorio Fiore. DOC: Chianti, Vin Santo.

Fattoria di Selvole
Vagliagli, 53010 Siena. DOC: Chianti Classico.

Setriolo
Castellina, 53010 Siena. Owner: Desmond and Antoinette Crawford. DOC: Chianti. 5 acres.

Soiana
Terricciola, 56030 Pisa. Young Bruno Moos is leading a revival in Chianti Colline Pisane from his castle and handsome estate.

Sorbaiano
Montecatini Val di Cecina, 56040 Pisa. Owner: Febo Picciolini. Wine maker: Vittorio Fiore. DOC: Montescudaio (single-vineyard Rosso del Miniere, barrel-fermented Lucestraia Bianco), Vin Santo.

La Suvera
Pievescola, 53018 Siena. Owner: Marchesi Ricci Paracciani Bergamini. Wine maker: Vittorio Fiore. Oddly fascinating wines include the Chianti-like Rango Rosso and Bianco, sparkling Cuvée Italienne Brut.

Talenti-Pian di Conte
Montalcino, 53024 Siena. Owner: Pierluigi Talenti (formerly wine maker at Il Poggione). First-rate DOC Brunello and Rosso di Montalcino. 6.5 acres.

Terrabianca
Vagliagli, 53010 Siena. Owner: Swiss Roberto Guldener. Wine maker: Vittorio Fiore. DOC: Chianti Scassino and Vigna della Croce. Other: Campaccio (Cabernet-Sangiovese), Piano della Cappella (Chardonnay). A rapidly rising estate.

Torre a Cona
San Donato in Collina, 50012 Firenze. Owners: The Rossi di Montelara family of Martini & Rossi. DOC: Chianti. 27 acres.

Torre a Decima
Molino del Piano, 50065 Firenze. DOC: Chianti Colli Fiorentini. Other: Dolce Amore Bianco. A dramatic 13th-century castle built by the Pazzi family.

Travignoli
Pelago, 50060 Firenze. Owners: Giampiero and Giovanni Busi. DOC: Chianti Rufina.

Fattoria dell'Ugo
Tavarnelle Val di Pesa, 10028 Firenze. Owner: Franco Amici Grossi. DOC: Chianti. 94 acres.

Castello di Verrazzano
Greve, 50020 Firenze. Owner: Luigi
Cappellini. DOC: Chianti Classico.
Other: Red Sassello. The castle where
the explorer Giovanni da Verrazzano
was born in 1485.
Villa Vetrice
Rufina, 50068 Firenze. Owner: Fratelli
Grati. DOC: Chianti Rufina, Vin Santo.
250 acres.
Vignavecchia
Radda, 53017 Siena. Owner: Franco

Beccari. DOC: Chianti Classico,
including a small quantity of sought-
after *riserva*. Other: Red Canvalle.
Vignole
Panzano, 50020 Firenze. Fine,
reasonably-priced Chianti Classico.
Vinattieri
Gaiole, 53013 Siena. Founded 1983.
Wine makers: Maurizio Castelli and
Roberto Stucchi-Pinetti. A négociant
making Vinattieri Rosso from
Sangiovese and Vinattieri Bianco from
Chardonnay.

Vistarenni
Gaiole, 53013 Siena. Owners: The
Tognana family. Director: Elisabetta
Tognana. Oenologist: Gaspare Buscemi.
DOC: Chianti, Vin Santo and Bianco
Val d'Arbia. Other: Red Codirosso. 99
acres.
Viticcio
Greve, 50022 Firenze. DOC: Chianti.
Other: Pure Sangiovese Prunaio. 37
acres.

UMBRIA

If Umbria figured on a discerning wine buyer's
shopping list in the past it was purely for Orvieto, its
golden, gently sweet and occasionally memorable
speciality. Today it is more likely to be for Rubesco,
the noble red of Torgiano near Perugia, one of the
best wines and best bargains in Italy.

If Torgiano can make such good wine, so surely
can other hills in this inland region. New DOCs are
appearing. With 15 percent DOC this is above the
national average. They should allow for the maximum latitude in the choice of grapes, since those of
the north and the south could both do well here, and
there is no good reason for planting (say) Trebbiano
if you could plant Sauvignon Blanc.

DOC AND OTHER WINES

Colli Altotiberini
DOC. Red, white and *rosato* wine. Province: Perugia. Villages:
a wide sweep of country in northern Umbria, including
Perugia and 8 other communes in the province. Grapes (red
and *rosato*) Sangiovese 55–70%, Merlot 10–20%, Trebbiano
and Malvasia 10%; (white) Trebbiano Toscano 75–90%,
Malvasia up to 10%, others up to 15%. Max. crop: 77 hl/ha.
Min. alch: 10.5° for white; 11.5° for red and *rosato*. Annual
production: 67,000 cases.
Recent DOC from the hills of the upper Tiber. Production in the area is increasing. All its wines, including its
dry red with Merlot, are intended for drinking young.

Colli Amerini
DOC. Red, white, rosato and novello wine. Province: Terni.
Villages: Amelia, Narni and 11 others along the Tiber and
Nera valleys between Orvieto and Terni. Grapes: (red, rosato
and novello) Sangiovese 65–80%, Montepulciano, Ciliegiolo,
Canaiolo, Barbera and/or Merlot 20–35% (but no more than
10% Merlot); (white) Trebbiano Toscano 70–85%, Grechetto,
Verdello, Garganega and/or Malvasia Toscana 15–30% (but
no more than 10% Malvasia); (Malvasia) Malvasia Toscana
85–100%. Trebbiano Toscano and/or other white varieties up
to 15%. Max. crop: 84 hl/ha. Min. alch. 11° for red, white,
rosato and novello, 11.5° for Malvasia, 12° for rosso superiore.
Production began only in 1990 and while all signs are
promising, so far no reliable judgement can be made.

Colli Martani
DOC. Red and white wine. Province: Perugia. Villages: From
Bettona as far south as Spoleto; Gualdo Cattaneo, Giano
dell'Umbria and parts of 12 other communes. Grapes:
Grechetto; other whites up to 15%; Trebbiano Toscano;
Sangiovese; other reds up to 15%. Max. crop: Grechetto 77
hl/ha, Trebbiano and Sangiovese 84 hl/ha. Min. alch: 12° for
Grechetto, 11° for Trebbiano, 11.5° for Sangiovese.
This is the newest of Perugia's DOCs and the wines so far

are promising. Of the three varietals, Grechetto seems to
offer the brightest prospects.

Colli Perugini
DOC. Red, white and *rosato* wine. Provinces: Perugia and
Terni. Villages: 6 communes in Perugia province; San
Vananzo in Terni province. Grapes: (red and *rosato*)
Sangiovese 65–85%, Montepulciano, Ciliegiolo, Barbera and/
or Merlot 15–35% (but no more than 10% Merlot); (white)
Trebbiano Toscano 65–85%, Grechetto, Verdicchio,
Garganega and/or Malvasia del Chianti 15–35% (but no more
than 10% Malvasia). Max. crop: 84 hl/ha (72 hl/ha *rosato*).
Min. alch: 11.5° for red and *rosato*, 11° for white. Annual
production: 89,000 cases.
DOC from the area between Perugia and Todi, which
makes good wine at Marscino and Colli Marteni.

Colli del Trasimeno
DOC. White and red wine. Province: Perugia. Villages: 9
communes around Lake Trasimeno. Grapes: (white)
Trebbiano Toscano 60–80%, Malvasia del Chianti, Verdicchio
Bianco, Verdello and Grechetto up to 40%; (red) Sangiovese
60–80%, Gamay, Ciliegiolo up to 40%, Trebbiano Toscano;
Malvasia di Chianti up to 20%. Max. crop: 87 hl/ha. Min. alch:
11° for white, 11.5° for red. Annual production: 220,000 cases.
The red and white of this zone on the borders of Tuscany
are both average. Gamay and Ciliegiolo give spirit to the
red and Grechetto gives the white a slight edge of acidity
essential for freshness.

Grechetto or Greco
A 'Greek' white grape which plays an increasingly
important role here and in DOC in Colli Martani farther
south. Unblended its wine is somewhat more fruity, firm
and interesting than Trebbiano.

Montefalco and Sagrantino di Montefalco
DOC. Red wine. Province: Perugia. Villages: the commune of
Montefalco and parts of 4 others. Grapes: Sangiovese 65–
75%, Trebbiano Toscano 15–20%, Sagrantino 5–10%, others
up to 15%; for Sagrantino: 100% with up to 5% Trebbiano.
Max. crop: 91 hl/ha. Min. alch: 11.5° (12.5° for Sagrantino, 14°
for *passito*). Annual production: 55,500 cases.
Recent DOC for a small area south of Asissi where the
local Sagrantino grape makes very dark red wine,
described as tasting of blackberries. The true speciality is
the sweet and strong *passito* version, a notable dessert
wine which is aged for a year. Dry it is tough and tannic
but may yet command respect. Plain Montefalco red uses
Sagrantino as seasoning in a less original but still smooth
and agreeable wine.

Orvieto
DOC. White wine, Province: Orvieto, Terni and Latium.
Villages: Orvieto and surrounding area; 11 commues in
Terni province and 5 in Latium's province. 'Classico' is from
Orvieto itself. Grapes: Trebbiano Toscano (Procanico) 40–
65%, Verdello 15–25%, Grechetto, Drupeggio and other
whites 20–30%, Malvasia Toscana up to 20%. Max. crop: 71
hl/ha. Min. Alch: 12°. Annual production: 1.22m. cases.
The simple and memorable name that used to mean
golden, more or less sweet wine now suffers from the same
identity crisis as many Italian whites. The taste for highly
charged, then gently oxidized wines has gone. Modern

vinification answers the problem with pale, clean but
almost neuter ones. Not long ago (perhaps still) you could
see huge barrels in Orvieto with their glass fermentation
airlocks still occasionally breaking wind after 2 years or
more. The wine, laboriously fermented dry, was then
resweetened with a dried-grape *passito* to be *abboccato*. If
you found a good one it was memorably deep and velvety,
but probably none too stable – like Frascati, a poor
traveller.

Modern Orvieto is nearly all pale, but should still have a
hint of honey to be true to type. Much is dry and frankly
dull. Chianti shippers put their names to several, Antinori
to one of the better ones.

Torgiano
DOC. Red and white wine. Province: Perugia. Village:
Torgiano. Grapes: (red) Sangiovese 50–70%. Canaiolo 15–
30%, Trebbiano Toscano 10%, Ciliegiolo and/or
Montepulciano 10%; (white) Trebbiano 50–70%, Grechetto
15–35%, Malvasia or Verdello up to 15%. Max. crop: 81 hl/
ha. Min. alch: 12° for red; 11.5° for white. Annual production:
167,000 cases. Aged 3 years for *riserva*.
Virtually a one-man DOC; local tradition reshaped in
modern terms by Dr. Giorgio Lungarotti (*see* next page
and Producers). This was Umbria's first DOC and its
reputation was built on the Lungarotti brands of Rubesco
and Torre di Giano.

UMBRIA PRODUCERS

Fratelli Adanti
Arquata di Bevagna, 06031 Perugia.
DOC: Montefalco Rosso, Sagrantino. Others: Rosso
d'Arquata, Bianco d'Arquata, Rosato D'Arquata, Vin
Santo. The Arquata estate is the quality leader for DOC
Sagrantino di Montefalco. All wines, especially the non-
DOC Bianco d'Arquata, the Sagrantino and the vdt Rosso
d'Arquata have been consistently improving but Alvaro,
the talented wine maker responsible, has now left.

Barberani-Vallesanta
Orvieto, 05018 Terni.
Owner: Luigi Barberani. Wine maker: Luigi Castelli.
DOC: Orvieto Classico. Others: Lago di Corbara.
Castagnola, Pulicchio, and Calcaia (with impressive noble
rot). One of the best old firms in Orvieto, modernized and
maintaining high standards.

Luigi Bigi & Figlio
Ponte Giulio di Orvieto, 05018 Terni.
Founded: 1881. Part of the Gruppo Italiano vini complex.
DOC: Orvieto, Est! Est!! Est!!!, Vino Nobile di Monte-
pulciano. Other: Rosso di Corbara. One of the best-
known producers of several popular DOCs. Single
vineyard Orvieto Torricella and Orzalume both notable.
Annual production: over 3m. cases.

Val di Maggio-Arnaldo Caprai
Montefalco, 06036 Perugia.
Drawn from 62 acres, Montefalco DOCs include a

consistently fine, dry Sagrantino. Grechetto dell'Umbria
vdt and bubbly wines also produced.

Giorgio Lungarotti
Torgiano, 26089 Perugia.
Founded as a corporation in 1960. Owners: The Lungarotti family. DOC: Torgiano. Others: Cabernet Sauvignon
di Miralduolo, Castel Grifone Rosato, Chardonnay,
Rondo, Rosciano, Solleone. The creator of Torgiano as a
DOC and one of Italy's greatest wine makers, though
quality seems a little less reliable of late. Giorgio's
daughter Teresa and oenologist Corrado Cantarelli now
share the credit for continuing innovation. About half the
production is DOC Torgiano. The Rubesco Riserva
Monticchio is the cream of this. Torre di Giano is the
white. Cabernet (in a blend called San Giorgio) and
Chardonnay are highly promising. Solleone is a sherry-
style apéritif. Annual production 270,000 cases, of which
over half is exported. *See also* DOC Torgiano and next
page.

Castello della Sala
Sala, 05016 Terni
Run independently by Renzo Cottarella Antinori's
Umbrian castle has 74 acres of vines. 'Castello della Sala'
are vdt wines, the best being Cervaro della Sala and Borro
della Sala 'Fumé'. Also a botrytised sweet wine, Muffato
della Satta, and a sweet Gewurztraminer. Red Pinot Noir
being considered.

OTHER PRODUCERS

Antonelli
Montefalco, Perugia. DOC: Montefalco,
including Sagrantino and Grechetto.

Castello di Ascagnano
Pierantonio di Umbertide, 06015
Perugia. Colti Altotiberini DOC and

spumanti – from 90 acres of vines. Not
all 90 acres' produce is bottled.

DR. GIORGIO LUNGAROTTI

The saturnine face of Dr. Giorgio Lungarotti masks one of Italy's most original wine makers, a man of extraordinary energy and sagacity who has pursued his vision of great wine independent of any historic reputation. His creation is now the DOC Torgiano. The little hill-town across the young Tiber from Perugia is the Lungarotti republic, from its modern winery to its excellent wine museum and its beautifully restored and greatly enlarged hotel, the Tre Vasselee (where each October the Umbrian government holds an all-Italian wine championship).

Lungarotti's red, Rubesco di Torgiano, is like a first-rate, unusually concentrated Chianti. Its *riserva* from the Monticcio vineyard even more so, deserving 10 years in bottle. In the 1970s he introduced Cabernet Sauvignon in a *riserva* called San Giorgio. His stylish, oak-aged, Torre di Giano is Trebbiano enlivened with Grechetto to be crisp and fragrant. In 1981 he introduced a Chardonnay, and also has Gewürztraminer in his 620 acres of vineyards. His Solleone is one of Italy's rare sherry-style dry apéritif wines made by *solera*. His daughter Teresa follows in the family footsteps.

Fattoria Belvedere
Villastrada Umbria. Castiglione del Lago, 06060 Perugia. Owner: Angelo Illuminati. DOC: Colli del Trasimeno.
Domenico Benincasa
Capro di Bevagna, 06031 Perugia. DOC: Sagrantino di Montefalco. Others: Capro/Bianco, Rosso, all from 18 acres.
Casole
Otricoli, Terni. Elio and Alberto Carccarini, and Trentino's Salvatore Maule make Casole Bianco and Rosso vdt here.
Cantina Colli Amerini
05022, Ternio Fornule di Amelia. DOC Orvieto Classico.
Colle del Sole-Polidori
Pierantonio di Umbertide, 06015 Perugia. Owner: Carlo Polidori. DOC: Colli Altotiberini. Others: Rubino, Verdello.
Co.Vi.P. (Consorzio Vitivinicolo Perugia)
Ponte Pattoli, 06080 Perugia. DOC: Colli del Trasimeno, Orvieto, Torgiano. Others: Bianco and Rosso d'Umbria. The consortium comprises 6 cooperatives and bottles wine from all 6 Perugia DOC zones.
Dubini-Locatelli
Orvieto, 05019, Terni. In 1988, Giovanni Dubini began vinifying the entire production from 44 acres under the Palazzone label. The vineyards are at Rocca Ripesena and in Orvieto Classico.

La Fiorita
Macchie di Castiglione del Lago, 06060 Perugia. 185 acres of vines for Colli del Trasimeno DOC (led by the red Sangue di Miura), rosé vdt and *spumante*.
Conti Fiumi Petrangeli
Orvieto, 05019 Terni. Orvieto Classico and red vdt, both served at their restaurant La Badia.
Castello di Montoro
Montoro di Narni. Montoro Umbro, 05020 Terni. DOC: none. Others: Castello di Montoro Bianco, (disappointing) Rosato, and Rosso. The outstanding red is blended from Sangiovese, Merlot, Barbera and Montepulciano. All from 370 acres.
Pieva del Vescovo
Corciano, 06036 Perugia. DOC: Colli del Trasimeno.
La Querciolana
Panicale, 06064 Perugia. Owner: Roberto Nesci. DOC: Colli del Trasimeno. The excellent red sold under the name Grifo di Boldrino.
Rocca di Fabri
Montefalco, 06036 Perugia. DOC: Montefalco. Also vdt including Grechetto dell'Umbria.
Sasso Rosso
Capodacqua, 06082 Perugia. DOC: None. Other: vdt Rosso di Assisi, a prizewinner which may well become one of the classic reds of central Italy.
Cantina Sociale del Trasimeno
Castiglione del Lago, 06061 Perugia.

Cooperative. DOC: Colli del Trasimeno.
Cantina Sociale Tudernum
Todi, 06059 Perugia. Cooperative. Greco di Todi, Tudernum Bianco, Rosso.
Tenuta Le Velette
Orvieto Stazione, 05019 Terni. DOC: Orvieto Classico. Other: Rosso Le Velette. A 16th-century estate restored and replanted in the 1960s.
Tili
Capodacqua, 06082 Perugia. Assisi vdt and a good Grechetto dell'Umbria from 32 acres. More consistent class than Sasso Rosso.
Cantina Sociale del Trasimeno
Castiglione del Lago, Perugia. DOC: Colli del Trasimeno, and vdt. From growers with over 2,200 acres.
Cantina Sociale Tudernum
Todi, Perugia. Grechetto di Todi and other vdt from 1,600 acres.
Conti Vaselli
Castiglione in Teverina, 01024 Viterbo. Orvieto Classico and vdt red Santa Guilia have vastly improved.
Ruggero Veneri
Spello, Perugia. A limited but very good production of Merlot and Gran Merlot di Spello vdt.
Cantina Coopertiva Vitivinicola
Orvieto, 05019 Terni. The best of this, the largest producer of Orvieto Classico, is bottled under the Cardeto trademark.

THE MARCHES

The central slice of the Adriatic coast, from the latitude of Florence to that of Orvieto, is probably even better known for its dry white Verdicchio than for the beaches and fishing boats that give the wine such a perfect context. The historic cities of Urbino in the north and Ascoli Piceno in the south of the region draw a proportion of its visitors inland, but the eastern lanks of the Apennines hardly rival the cultural crowd-pulling quality of Tuscany.

So the red wines of the Marches, potentially (sometimes actually) of good Chianti quality, are less well known than they should be. The Montepulciano grape gives them a quality missing in most of those in Romagna to the north.

DOC AND OTHER WINES

Bianchello del Metauro

DOC. White wine. Province: Pesaro. Villages: 18 communes in the valley of River Metauro. Grapes: Biancame (Bianchello) 95%, Malvasia 5%. Max. crop: 98 hl/ha. Min. alch: 11.5°. Annual production: 200,000 cases.

A pleasant sharp plain white from the north of the region, for drinking young with fish.

Bianco dei Colli Maceratesi

DOC. White wine. Provinces: Macerata and Ancona. Villages: Loreto and all of Macerata. Grapes: Trebbiano Toscano 50–70%, with Maceratino; Malvasia Toscana and Verdicchio 15% Max. crop: 98 hl/ha. Min. alch: 11°. Annual production: 45,000 cases.

A minor DOC for another local dry seafood wine. Macerata is halfway from Ancona south to Ascoli Piceno.

Falerio dei Colli Ascolani

DOC. White wine. Province: Ascoli. Villages: all of province of Ascoli Piceno. Grapes: Trebbiano Toscano 80%, Passerina, Verdicchio, Pinot Bianco, Pecorino up to 25%, Malvasia Toscana up to 7%. Max. crop: 84 hl/ha. Min. alch: 11.5° Annual production 112,000 cases.

Another of the local dry whites associated with restaurants on the beach.

Lacrima di Morro d'Alba

DOC. Red wine. Province: Ancona. Villages: Morro d'Alba, Monte San Vito, San Marcello, Belvedere Ostrense, Ostra and Senigallia. Grapes: Lacrima Montepulciano/Verdicchio up to 15%. Max. crop: 98 hl/ha. Min. alch: 11°. Annual production: 5,500 cases.

A DOC from around the ancient town of Morro d'Alba, south of Senigallia.

Montepulciano

Important in the Marches as a constituent grape of the best red wines, also sometimes sold unblended.

Rosso Cònero

DOC. Red wine. Province: Ancona. Villages: 5 communes in Ancona and part of 2 others. Grapes: Montepulciano 85%, Sangiovese 15%. Max. crop: 98 hl/ha. Min. alch: 11.5°. Annual production: 233,000 cases.

A full-strength, full-flavoured red from Monte Cònero, near the Adriatic just south of Ancona. One of the most flourishing of central and eastern Italy, with fruit to mellow and tannin to sustain it. Chianti methods are sometimes used to enrich and liven up the wine.

Rosso Piceno

DOC. Red wine. Provinces: Ancona, Ascoli Piceno, Macerata. Villages: a large number in the above provinces. Grapes: Sangiovese 60%, Montepulciano 40%, Passerina/Trebbiano up to 15%. Max. crop: 84 hl/ha. Min. alch: 11.5°. *Superiore*, from a limited zone to the south, has 12°. Annual production: 500,000 cases.

The standard red of the southern half of the Marches, varying widely in quality from unremarkable to hand-made and worth ageing, both in barrel and bottle. At its best it has Chianti-like weight and balance.

Sangiovese dei Colli Pesaresi

DOC. Red wine. Province: Pesaro. Villages: 30 communes and part of 6 others in and around Pesaro. Grapes: Sangiovese 85%, Montepulciano and/or Ciliegiolo 15%. Max. crop: 77 hl/ha. Min. alch: 11.5°. Annual production: 178,000 cases.

A little-used DOC for a red of limited character. Sangiovese is frequently used for non-DOC reds.

Verdicchio dei Castelli di Jesi

DOC. White wine. Provinces: Ancona. Villages: 17 communes and part of 5 others around the town of Jesi. Grapes: Verdicchio 85%, Trebbiano Toscano and Malvasia up to 15%. Max. crop: 105 hl/ha. Min. alch: 11°. Annual production 1.78m. cases.

The great commercial success of the Marches. Straightforward, dry, well balanced and clean; one of the earliest Italian whites to taste modern and international, thanks to the skill of its promoters, the firm of Fazi-Battaglia (*see* Producers). Their marketing flair produced the distinctive amphora-shaped bottle now seen among the fishnets in every Italian restaurant abroad. The Verdicchio is a tricky grape to grow but clearly has quality. The wine is short-lived, however, and bottles held too long in stock are often undrinkable. There is also a *champenoise* sparkling version.

Verdicchio di Matelica

DOC. White wine. Provinces: Macerata and Ancona. Villages: Matelica and 7 others. Grapes: Verdicchio 85%, Trebbiano Toscano and Malvasia up to 15%. Max. crop: 91 hl/ha. Min. alch: 12°. Annual production: 167,000 cases.

Verdicchio from higher ground farther inland, said to be superior, but hardly ever seen abroad. Another (non-DOC) with a similar reputation is Verdicchio di Montanello.

Vernaccia di Serrapetrona

DOC. Red wine. Province: Macerata. Villages: Serrapetrona and part of Belforte del Chianti and San Severino Marche. Grapes: Vernaccia di Serrapetrona; Sangiovese, Montelpulciano, Ciliegiolo up to 15%. Max. crop: 70 hl/ha. Min. alch: 11.5°. Annual production 16,600 cases.

A locally popular, normally sweet, sparkling red which has been made since the 15th century.

MARCHES PRODUCERS

Brunori
Jesi, 60035 Ancona.

Owners: Mario and Giorgio Brunori. DOC: Verdicchio dei Castelli di Jesi. A few hundred cases of splendid Verdicchio from the tiny San Nicolò vineyard, planted in 1972.

Fratelli Bucci
Ostra Vetere, 60010 Ancona.

Owned by Ampelio Bucci. Wine maker: Giorgio Grai. DOC: Verdicchio dei Castelli di Jesi. Other: Tenuta di Pongelli. Grai's master touch is sensed in the fine Verdicchio.

Cocci Grifoni
San Savino di Ripatransone, 63030 Ascoli Piceno.

Owner: Guido Cocci Grifoni. An admirable producer whose Rosso Piceno is one of the best and whose Falerio has no rivals.

Colonnara
Cupramontana, 60035 Ancona.

Cantina Sociale di Cupramontana now goes under the name Colonnara and is making some of the best Verdicchio, still and sparkling, under wine maker Carlo Pigini.

Faxi-Battaglia "Titulus"
Castelplano Stazione, 60032 Ancona.

Founded in 1949 by the Angelini family. DOC: Rosso Cònero, Rosso Piceno, Verdicchio dei Castelli di Jesi. Others: Rosato delle Marche, Sangiovese delle Marche. The house that devised the green amphora bottle that made Verdicchio famous. From 570 acres of company vines plus extra grapes bought in, Fazi-Battaglia makes about 400,000 cases of Verdicchio of which roughly 40% is exported.

Garofoli
Loreto, 60025 Ancona.

Founded: 1871. Now run by 2 generations of Garofoli. Wine maker: Carlo Garofoli. DOC: Rosso Cònero, Verdicchio dei Castelli di Jesi. A high-quality producer with the excellent single vineyard Verdicchio Macrina and oak-aged Serra Fioresa as well as sparkling versions by both tank and *champenoise* methods.

Mecvini
Fabriano, 60044 Ancona.

Enzo Mecella is one of the region's most skilled and inspired wine makers with a good range of DOCs and innovative table wines.

Monte Schiavo
Moie di Maiolati Spontini, 60032 Ancona.

A cooperative backed by the farm machinery manufacturers, Pieralisi.

It competes in quality with top private wineries. From 35 growers with 360 acres come Verdicchio Classico and *spumante* as well as a Rosso Cònero.

Villa Pigna
Offida, 63035 Ascoli Piceno.

Founded about 1960. Owners: Constantino and Elio Rozzi. DOC: Falerio dei Colli Ascolani, Rosso Piceno. Others: Rosato, Villa Pigna Vellutato.

With 150,000 cases from more than 600 acres of vines, Villa Pigna quickly emerged as a model large-scale estate. A modern winery was built in 1979. Rosso Piceno Superiore is almost like claret. The Vellutato table wine from Montepulciano is even better.

Umani Ronchi
Osimo Scalo, 60028 Ancona.

Founded in 1960 by Gino Ronchi, now managed by the Bernetti brothers. DOC: Rosso Cònero, Rosso Piceno, Verdicchio dei Castelli di Jesi. Others: Rosato delle Marche, Sangiovese delle Marche, Spumante Brut. One of the best-distributed brands of the Marches, producing 100,000 cases of good-quality estate-bottled wines from 180 acres of Verdicchio and 75 of Rosso Cònero. Other wines are made of bought-in grapes. Wines are exported under the trade name Bianchi.

Cantina Sociale Val di Nevola
Corinaldo, 60013 Ancona.

Cooperative. DOC: Rosso Piceno, Verdicchio dei Castelli di Jesi. Others: Montepulciano, Rosato, Sangiovese and Trebbiano delle Marche, Rosso di Corinaldo, *spumante*, table wines.

Villamagna
Contrada Montanello, 62100 Macerata.

Founded: 17th century. Owner and wine maker: Valeria Giacomini Compagnucci-Compagnoni. DOC: Bianco dei Colli Maceratesi, Rosso Piceno. Others: Mosanulus and Verdicchio di Montanello. The family company built new cellars in 1973 and has since made a name for some of the finest Rosso Piceno and Verdicchio on the market.

About 2,200 cases of each wine are produced from 37 acres.

OTHER PRODUCERS

Anzillotti Solazzi
Bonta di Saltara, 61030 Pesaro. Owners: Guglielmo Anzilotti and and Giovanni Solazzi. DOC: Bianchello del Metauro, Sangiovese dei Colli Pesaresi.
Fratelli Bisci
Matelica, 64024 Macerata. The Bisci brothers occasionally make magnificent Verdicchio di Matelica.
Castellucci
Montecarotto, 60036 Ancona. Owners:

Armando and Corrado Castellucci. DOC: Verdicchio dei Castelli di Jesi.
Fattoria dei Cavalieri di Benedetti
Matelica, 64024 Macerata. DOC: Verdicchio di Matelica.
Attilio Fabrini
Serrapetrona, 62020 Macerata. DOC: Bianco dei Colli Maceratesi, Vernaccia di Serrapetrona *champenoise*. Others: Pian delle Mura Rosso, Verdicchio (still and *champenoise*).

Marchetti
60125 Ancona. DOC: Rosso Cònero.
La Monacesca
Civitanova-Marche, 62012 Macerata. Owner: Casimiro Cifola. DOC: Verdicchio di Matelica.
Fattoria di Montesecco
Montesecco di Pergola, 61045 Pesaro. Owner-wine maker: Massimo Schiavi. No DOC. Other: Tristo di Montesecco. A unique, complex, dry, wood-aged

white from Trebbiano, Malvasia, Riesling and Pinot Grigio.

Moroder
Montacuto, 60029 Ancona. Alessandro Moroder produces a good Rosso Cònero from his small estate.

Picenum (Consorzio Agrario Ascoli Piceno)
63100 Ascoli Piceno. Cooperative. DOC: Falerio dei Colli Ascolani, Rosso Piceno.

Serenelli
60125 Ancona. Alberto Serenelli makes typical Rosso Cònero, plus a special selection known as Varano aged in small oak barrels.

Tattà
Porto San Giorgio, 63017 Ascoli

Piceno. Good Rosso Picenco DOC and Montepulciano table wine.

Le Terrazze
Numana, 60026 Ancona. Paolo Terni makes good Rosso Cònero. The pink *champenoise* Donna Giulia from Montepulciano grapes is a revelation.

Le Terrazze di Roncosambaccio-Giovanetti Fano, 61032 Pesaro. Good Bianchello and Sangiovese DOC.

La Torraccia
Passo Sant'Angelo, 62020 Macerata. Owner: Piero Costantini. DOC: Bianco dei Colli Maceratesi, Rosso Piceno. Others: Bianco Anitori, Cabernet, Villa Simone Frascati.

Cantina Sociale Val di Nevola
Corinaldo, Ancona. Verdiccio Classico

and Rosso Piceno DOC plus Rosso di Corinaldo table wine.

Cantina Cooperative tra Produttori del Verdicchio
Montecarotto, 60036 Ancona. Sound Verdicchio Classico.

Vnimar (Associazione Cantine Cooperative Marche)
Camerano, 60021 Ancona. A group of cooperatives bottling and selling all the region's DOC wines under the name Vinimar.

Fratelli Zaccagnini
Staffolo, 60039 Ancona. Verdicchio Classico, including the single vineyard Salmagina.

LATIUM

Rome can be compared with Vienna, as a capital city with wine so much in its veins that such artificial obstructions as bottles and corks have traditionally been foreign to it. The wine makers' taverns of Rome are slightly farther out of town than the *beurigen* of Vienna, but even more tempting as a summer outing, to the cool of the wooded Alban hills, or 'Castelli Romani' south of Rome. Frascati, the hub of the hills and their wine, has the air of a holiday resort. The spectacular Villa Aldobrandini and its beautiful gardens in the heart of Frascati show that the taste is patrician as well as popular.

Latium, both north and south of Rome, is pockmarked with volcanic craters, now placid lakes. The volcanic soil is highly propitious to the vine. The choice of grape varieties, presumably based on the Roman taste for soft young wines, has determined that they should remain local. The low acidity of the Malvasia, the grape that gives character to Frascati, makes it prone to disastrous oxidation once out of its cold damp cellar, without such processes as pasteurization and, more recently cold treatments, which have restored the balance of modern wines.

DOC AND OTHER WINES

Aleatico di Gradoli
DOC. Red wine. Province: Viterbo. Villages: Gradoli, Grotte di Castro, San Lorenzo Nuovo, Latera (in the hills above Lake Bolsena). Grapes: Aleatico. Max. crop: 63 hl/ha. Min. alch: 12°. Annual production: 5,500 cases.
A limited production of a local speciality: sweet red wine with a faintly Muscat aroma made at both normal strength and *liquoroso* (fortified to 17.5° alcohol).

Aprilia
DOC. Red, white and *rosato* wine. Provinces: Latina and Roma. Villages: Aprilia and Nettuno. Grapes: (red) Merlot, (rosé) Sangiovese, (white) Trebbiano. Max. crop: Merlot 91 hl/ha; Sangiovese 84 hl/ha; Trebbiano 90 hl/ha. Annual production 335,000 cases.
A vineyard area established by refugees from Tunisia after World War II. Merlot is reckoned its best product at 2 or 3 years of age. Although one of the first DOCs the wines scarcely merit the dignity, however recent experiments in vineyards and cellars are aimed at notable improvements.

Bianco Capena
DOC. White wine. Province: Roma. Villages: Capena, Fiano Romano, Morlupo, Castelnuovo di Porto. Grapes: Malvasia di Candia, del Lazio and Toscana 55%, Trebbiano Toscano, Romagnolo and Giallo 25%, Bellone and Bombino up to

20%. Max. crop: 112 hl/ha. Min. alch: 11° (*superiore* 12°). Annual production: 56,000 cases.
Similar white wine to that of the Castelli Romani (e.g. Frascati) but from just north of Rome instead of south.

Castelli Romani
An umbrella (non-DOC) name for the verdant region, otherwise known as the Colli Albani, where Frascati and its peers are grown.

Cerveteri
DOC. Red and white wine. Province: Roma. Villages: Cerveteri, Ladispoli, Santa Marinella, Civitavecchia, part of Allumiere, Rome, Tolfa and Tarquinia. Grapes: (red) Sangiovese and Montepulciano 60%, Cesanese Comune 25%, Canaiolo Nero, Carignano and Barbera 30%; (white) Trebbiano (Toscano, Romagnolo and Giallo) 50%, Malvasia 35%, Verdicchio, Tocai, Bellone and Bombino 15%. Max. crop: 108 hl/ha for white, 95 hl/ha for red. Min. alch: 11° for white, 12° for red. Annual production: 278,000 cases.
South standard dry wines from the country near the coast northwest of Rome. A noteworthy cantina (coop).

Cesanese di Affile
DOC. Red wine. Province: Roma. Villages: Affile and Roiate, and part of Arcinazzo. Grapes: Cesanese di Affile and/or

Cesanese Comune min. 90%; Sangiovese, Montepulciano, Barbera, Trebbiano Toscano, Bombino Bianco 10%. Max. crop: 81 hl/ha. Min. alch: 12°.

Neighbour to Cesanese del Piglio. No wine has been made in recent years.

Cesanese di Olevano Romano

DOC. Red wine. Province: Roma. Villages: Olevano Romano and part of Genazzano. Grapes: Cesanese di Affile and/or Cesanese Comune min. 90%, Sangiovese; Montepulciano, Barbera, Trebbiano Toscano, Bombino Bianco 10%. Max. crop: 81 hl/ha. Min. alch: 12°. Annual production: 22,000 cases.

A little closer to Rome but otherwise not to be distinguished from the other Cesaneses. All 3 were made DOCs in an excess of bureaucratic enthusiasm in 1973.

Cesanese del Piglio

DOC. Red wine. Province: Roma. Villages: Piglio and Serrone, Acuto, Anagni and Paliano. Grapes: Cesanese di Affile and/or Cesanese Comune min. 90%; Sangiovese, Montepulciano, Barbera, Trebbiano Toscano or Bombino Bianco 10%. Max. crop: 81 hl/ha. Min. alch: 12°. Annual production: 56,000 cases.

Dry or sweet, still or sparkling red from a zone just to the left of the Autostrada del Sole, heading southeast 40 miles out of Rome, where Anagni sits on its hilltop.

Colle Picchioni

Surprisingly good dry red of blended Merlot, Cesanese, Sangiovese and Montepulciano grapes, made in the traditionally white (i.e. Marino) country of the Castelli Romani. The superior Vigna del Vassallo is a Cabernet-Merlot blend.

Colli Albani

DOC. White wine. Province: Roma. Villages: Ariccia and Albano, part of Rome, Pomezia and Castelgandolfo. Grapes: Malvasia Rossa (or Bianca di Candia) 60%, Trebbiano Toscano, Romagnolo, di Soave and Giallo 25–50%, Malvasia del Lazio 5–45%, Bonvino and Cacchione up to 10%. Max. crop: 115 hl/ha. Min. alch: 11° (*superiore* 12.5°). Annual production: 1.05m. cases.

The local white of the Pope's summer villa (and that of the Emperor Domitian, too, on the same superb site with views west to the sea and east down to Lake Albano). Dry or sweet, still or fizzy.

Colli Lanuvini

DOC. White wine. Province: Roma. Villages: Genzano and part of Lanuvio. Grapes: Malvasia Bianca di Candia and Puntinata max. 70%, Trebbiano Toscano, Verde and Giallo 30%, Bellone and Bonvino 10%. Max. crop: 101 hl/ha. Min. alch: 11.5°. Annual production: 167,000 cases.

A lesser-known but recommended dry white of the Castelli Romani. Genzano is on Lake Nemi, south of Lake Albano.

Cori

DOC. White and red wine. Province: Latina. Villages: Cisterna and Cori. Grapes (white) Malvasia di Candia up to 70%; Trebbiano Toscano up to 40%; Trebbiano Giallo, Bellone up to 30%; (red) Montepulciano 40–60%, Nero Buono di Cori 20–40%, Cesanese 10–30%. Max. crop: 112 hl/ha. Min. alch: 11° for white, 11.5° for red. Annual production: 28,000 cases.

Cori is south of the Castelli Romani where the country flattens towards the Pontine marshes. The red is soft and pleasant and, along with the white, is rarely seen.

Est! Est!! Est!!! di Montefiascone

DOC. White wine. Province: Viterbo. Villages: Montefiascone, Bolsena, San Lorenzo Nuovo, Grotte di Castro, Gradoli, Capodimonte and Marta. Grapes: Trebbiano Toscano 65%, Malvasia Bianca Toscana 20%, Rossetto 15%. Max. crop: 91 hl/ha. Min. alch: 11°. Annual production: 24,500 cases.

Large quantities of unpredictable wine take advantage of this the earliest example of what is now called a fantasy name. The emphatic 'It is' was the first 3-star rating in history, antedating the Michelin guide by some 800 years. More recent inspectors have had less luck, but now modernization of techniques and taste is producing an acceptable, usually dry, white.

Falerno or Falernum

The most famous wine of ancient Rome, from the borders of Latium and Campania to the south. Then sweet and concentrated, now a good strong red of Aglianico and Barbera and a pleasant low-acid white. The red has a DOC in Compania.

Fiorano

The best of Rome's own wines, from one producer (*see* page 351) on the ancient Appian Way south of Rome. The red is Cabernet and Merlot like Bordeaux, the whites Malvasia di Candia and Sémillon. The wines are aged in wood and set a standard far above the local DOCs.

Frascati

DOC. White wine. Province: Roma. Villages: Frascati, Montecompartri, Monteporzio Catone and Grottaferrata. Grapes: Malvasia Bianca di Candia and Trebbiano Toscano min. 70%, Malvasia del Lazio and Greco max. 30%. Max. crop: 105 hl/ha. Min. alch: 11° (*superiore* 11.5°). Annual production: 2.16m. cases.

In legend and occasionally in fact the most memorable Italian white wine, though possibly the one that originated the notion of wines that 'do not travel', even the 20 miles to Rome. Malvasia on volcanic soil gives a splendid sensation of whole-grape ripeness, a golden glow to the wine, encouraged by fermenting it like red on its skins. The dry variety should be soft but highly charged with flavour, faintly nutty and even faintly salty. Sweeter (*amabile*) and sweeter still (*cannellino*) versions can be honeyed, too but I would not count on it.

These are tasting notes made in a cool damp Frascati cellar. Notes on the bottled wine vary from neutral and sterile with no character to flat and oxidized to (occasionally) an approximation to the real thing. The best way to learn the difference between old-style and new-style Italian whites is to go to a restaurant in Frascati and order a bottle of a good brand, and also a jug of the house wine. Sadly the luscious qualities of the latter are the ones that do not travel. The best producers manage a very satisfactory compromise.

Marino

DOC. White wine. Province: Roma. Villages: Marino and part of Rome and Castelgandolfo. Grapes: Malvasia Rossa 60%, Trebbiano Toscano, Verde and Giallo 25–55%. Malvasia del Lazio 15–45%, Bonvino and Cacchione 10%. Max. crop: 115.5 hl/ha. Min. alch: 11.5° (*superiore* 12.5°). Annual production: 889,000 cases.

First cousin to Frascati, preferred by many Romans who dine out at Marino to drink it fresh and unbottled.

Montecompatri-Colonna
DOC. White wine. Province: Roma. Villages: Colonna, part of Montecompatri, Zagarolo and Rocca Priora. Grapes: Malvasia 70%, Trebbiano 30%, Bellone, Bonvino 10%. Max. crop: 108 hl/ha. Min. alch: 11.5° (*riserva* 12.5°). Annual production: 50,000 cases.
Another alternative to Frascati in the Castelli Romani.

Torre Ercolana
The highly recherché speciality of one producer (*see* Colacicchi) at Anagni (*see* Cesanese del Piglio). A red of Cesanese with Cabernet and Merlot, powerful in personality and maturing to outstanding quality.

Velletri
DOC. White and red wine. Province: Latina and Roma. Villages: Velletri, Lariano and part of Cisterna di Latina.

Grapes: (white) Malvasia 70%, Trebbiano 30%, Bellone and Bonvino 10%; (red) Sangiovese 20–45%, Montepulciano 30–35%, Cesanese Comune 15%, Bombino Nero, Merlot and Ciliegiolo 10%. Max. crop: 104 hl/ha. Min. alch: 11.5° for white, 12° for red. Aged 2 years for *riserva*. Annual production: 333,000 cases.
South of the Frascati zone of the Castelli Romani, Velletri has a DOC for both its pleasant white and its mild red.

Zagarolo
DOC. White wine. Province: Roma. Villages: Zagarolo, Gallicano. Grapes: Malvasia 70%, Trebbiano 30%. Bellone and Bonvino up to 10%. Max. crop: 108 hl/ha. Min. alch: 11.5° (*superiore* 12.5°). Annual production: 5,500 cases.
The smallest producer of the Frascati group, with similar white wine.

LATIUM PRODUCERS

Colli di Catone
Monteporzio Catone, 00040 Roma.
Antonio Pucini makes good Frascati Superiore under the Colli di Catone, Villa Catone and Villa Porzina labels. His two special versions of Frascati are both made from pure Malvasia, one, the single vineyard Colle Gaio, is made only in good years from low yielding wines.

Cantina Colacicchi
Anagni, 03012 Frosinone.
A family winery, made famous by the late Luigi Colacicchi, now run by his nephew Bruno. No DOC. Others: Romagnano (white), Torre Ercolana (red). The splendid red of Cabernet, Merlot and Cesanese, intense, long-lived and long on the palate, is one of Italy's rarest. Only about 700 cases are made from 8½ acres.

Fiorano
Divino Amore, 00134 Roma.
Founded in 1946 by Alberico Boncompagni Ludovisi, Principe di Venosa. No DOC. Others: Fiorano Bianco, Rosso. A perfectionist 5-acre estate which has proved that exceptional wine can be made in Rome. Fiorano Bianco is made of Malvasia di Candia grapes and Fiorano Rosso of Cabernet Sauvignon and Merlot. There is also a little Fiorano Sémillon. All are splendid but rare.

Fontana Candida
Monteporzio Catone, 00040 Roma.
DOC: Frascati. Part of the Coltiva-Gruppa Italiano Vini complex owning extensive vineyards, cellars and bottling plants in the Frascati DOC zone. The production of more than 600,000 cases includes a choice parcel of Vigneti Santa Teresa, one of the best of all Frascatis.

Cantina Produttori Frascati (San Matteo)
Frascati, 00044 Roma.
The central Frascati cooperative. DOC: Frascati. San Matteo is the label of the cooperative's selected wine sold in bottle – a reliable brand in the modern style.

Cantina Sociale Cooperativa di Marino (Gotto d'Oro)
Frattocchie di Marino, 00040 Roma.
Founded: 1945. A cooperative whose members have about 2,700 acres of vines. DOC: Frascati, Marino. Others: Rosata and Rosso Rubino dei Castelli Romani. Wine maker Manlio Erba produces consistent quality Frascati and Marino, sold under the Gotto d'Oro label.

Paola di Mauro (Colle Picchioni)
Marino, 00040 Roma.
This small estate is run by Paulo di Mauro and son Armando. DOC: Marino. Other: Colle Picchioni Rosso. From 10 acres they produce a remarkable traditional Marino and one of Rome's rare fine reds.

Villa Simone
Monteporzio Catone, 00040 Roma.
Piero Constantini selects from 15 acres of vines to make an impressive, full-scale Frascati Superiore, including the single vineyard Vigneto Filonardi, and the rare *cannellino*.

Conte Zandotti-Tenimento San Paolo
00132 Roma.
Founded in 1734 by the Zandotti family and now run by Enrico Massimo Zandotti. Modern methods are used in the cellars carved into the vaults of an ancient Roman water cistern beneath the San Paolo villa. There are 62 acres of vines used for a superb, dry Frascati Superiore.

OTHER PRODUCERS

Cantina Sociale Colli Albani (Fontana di Papa)
Cecchina, 00040 Roma. Cooperative. DOC: Colli Albani and Marino. Others: Castelli Romani, Rosato, Rosso. Bottled wine is Fontana di Papa.
Cantina Sociale Colli del Cavaliere
Aprilia, 04010 Latina. Cooperative.

DOC: Aprilia. Others: Colli del Cavaliere Bianco, Rosso.
Casale del Giglio
Borgo Montello, 04010 Latina. DOC: Aprilia. Good Trebbiano and Merlot made from 450 acres. New varieties and training methods are being studied on an experimental genetic engineering

project.
F. Cenatiempo & C.
Formia, 04023 Latina. No DOC. Others: Cècubo, Falerno, Falernum. The modern versions of the ancient wines.
Cantina Sociale Cooperative Cerveteri
Cerveteri, 00052 Roma. Large production of Cerveteri DOC.

Cantina Sociale Cesanese del Piglio
Piglio, Frosinone. Sound Cesanese del
Piglio DOC.
Villa Clemens
Velletri, 00049 Roma. A new winery
founded by the oenologist Ivo-Straffi.
Exemplary Velletri Bianco and Frascati
DOC and a red vdt called Zeus.
Collefiorito
Rocca Sinibalda, 02026 Rieti.
Englishman Colin Fraser is proving that
good wines can be made in untried
places. From 12 acres he produces light
appealing vdt. A Pinot Bianco called
Rigogolo and the red Nibbio from
Sangiovese and Montepulcianco.
Coopertiva Enotria
Aprilia, 04010 Latina. A huge
cooperative, members have 2,200 acres
of vines. DOC: Aprilia. Other: table
wines. Aprilia Merlot, Sangiovese and
Trebbiano are sold with the Enotria
label.
Falesco
Montefiascone, 01027 Viterbo. Good
Est! Est!! Est!!!

Cantina Sociale Cooperativa Feronia
Capena, 00060 Roma. Good Bianco
Capena DOC.
Cantina Sociale Cooperativa Gradoli
Gradoli, 01010 Viterbo. Cooperative.
DOC: Aleatico di Gradoli. Other:
Greghetto.
Il Marchese
Frascati, 00044 Roma. Good Frascati
Superiore from 100 acres.
Massimi Berucci
Piglio, 03010 Frosinone. Good
Cesanese DOC under Casal Cervino
label.
Italo Mazziotti
Bolsena, 01023 Viterbo. An old family
winery. DOC: Est! Est!! Est!!! di
Montefiascone. Other: Bolsena Rosso.
Mazziotti is a keen oenologist and
grower.
Conte Moncada-Monte Giove
Cecchina, 00040 Roma. Owner:
Raimondo Moncada. DOC: Colli
Lanuvini. A good estate wine.
Cantina di Montefiascone
Montefiascone, 01027 Viterbo.

Cooperative. DOC: Est! Est!! Est!!! di
Montefiascone. Others: Colli Etrusco
Bianco, Rosso.
Principe Pallavincini
Colonna, 00030, Roma. Good Frascati
Superiore from 136 acres and table wine
under Marmorelle label.
**Cantine Sociale Cooperative San
Tommaso**
Genzano, 00045 Roma. Good Colli
Lanuvini DOC.
Cooperative La Selva
Genzano, 00045 Roma. Sound Colli
Lanuvini DOC.
Colli di Tuscolo
Frascati, 00044 Rome, Cooperative.
DOC: Frascati. Frascati Superiore under
the De Sanctis and Vigneti Carlo Micara
labels.
Consorzio Produttori Vini Velletri
Velletri, 00049 Roma. Cooperative.
DOC: Velletri Bianco, Rosso. Other:
Castelli Romani Rosato.

ABRUZZI

The Apennines rise to their climax in the 9,000-foot
Gran Sasso d'Italia, which towers over L'Aquila
('The Eagle'), the capital of the Abruzzi. Mountains
only subside close to the sea, where Pescara is the
principal town. Close as it is to Rome, the Abruzzi is
a backward region with simple ideas about wine.
One of them, attachment to the red Montepulciano
as chief grape, is a good one. Here and in the even
more rural Molise to the south this grape makes
wine of vigour and style, if not refinement. Whites
at present are not remarkable, but only because the
Trebbiano is the standard grape.

DOC WINES

Cerasuolo
See Montepulciano d'Abruzzo.

Montepulciano d'Abruzzo
DOC. Red wine. Provinces: Chieti, Aquilia, Pescara, Teramo.
Villages: many communes throughout the 4 provinces.
Grapes: Montepulciano, plus Sangiovese up to 15%. Max.
crop: 98 hl/ha. Min. alch: 12°. Aged for 2 years or more is
vecchio. Annual production: 2.17m. cases.
The production zone for this excellent red stretches along
most of the coastal foothills and back into the mountains
along the valley of the river Pescara (where Sulmona has a
particular reputation for its wine). Standards in this large
area vary widely, but Montepulciano at its best is as

satisfying, if not as subtle, as any Italian red – full of
colour, life and warmth. Cerasuolo is the name for its
DOC *rosato* – a pretty wine with plenty of flavour.

Trebbiano d'Abruzzo
DOC. White wine. Province: throughout the Abruzzi region.
Villages: suitable vineyards (not exceeding 500–600 metres) in
the whole region. Grapes: Trebbiano d'Abruzzo, and or
Trebbiano Toscano; Malvasia Toscana, Coccociola and
Passerina up to 15%. Max. crop: 122 hl/ha. Min. alch: 11.5°.
Annual production: 933,000 cases.
A standard mild dry white, except in the case of Valentini
(*see* Producers).

ABRUZZI PRODUCERS

Emidio Pepe
Torano Nuovo, 64010 Teramo.
DOC: Montepulciano and Trebbiano d'Abruzzo. Pepe
runs his family winery with almost eccentric devotion.
Grapes crushed only by foot.and aged entirely in bottle.

Casal Thaulero
Roseto degli Abruzzi, 64026 Teramo.
Cooperative. DOC: Montepulciano and Trebbiano
d'Abruzzo. Sound quality Montepulciano including the
special bottlings of Orisetto Oro. Abbazia di Propezzano
is a pure Montepulciano aged in small barrels.

Cantina Sociale di Tollo
Tollo, 66010 Chieti.

DOC: Montepulciano and Trebbiano d'Abruzzo. Oenologist Umberto Svizzeri has made this large cooperative a top cellar for quality and price.

Edoardo Valentini
Loreto Aprutino, 65014 Pescara.

DOC: Montepulciano and Trebbiano d'Abruzzo. Valentini selectes the best grapes from his 150 acres in the best years (selling the rest) to make artisan wine of the highest order, including a singular aged Trebbiano and a sumptuous Montepulciano.

Ciccio Zaccagnani
Bolognano, 65020 Pescara.

A small but increasingly admired estate acclaimed for fine Montepulciano Castello di Salle.

OTHER PRODUCERS

Vinicola Casacanditella (Rosso della Quercia)
Casacanditella, 66010 Chieti. Founded in 1975 by Giuseppe di Camillo and Ilio Mauro. DOC: Montepulciano d'Abruzzo. 'Rosso and Rosa della Quercia' from selected grapes.

Duchi di Castelluccio (Scali Caracciolo)
Scafa, 65027, Pescara. DOC: Montepulciano and Trebbiano d'Abruzzo. Lively and satisfying wines; the red has more to say that the white.

Barone Cornacchia
Torano Nuovo, 64010 Teramo. Owner: Piero Cornacchia. DOC: Montepulciano and Trebbiano d'Abruzzo.

Guardiani Farchione
Tocco da Causaria, 65028 Pescara. DOC: Montepulciano.

Filomusi Guelfi
Tocca da Causaria, 65028. A newly emerging estate with Montepulciano of power and grace.

Lucio di Giulio (Cantalupo)
Tocco di Casuria, 65028 Pescara. DOC: Montepulciano d'Abruzzo.

Dino Illuminati (Fattoria Nicò)
Controguerra, 64010 Teramo. DOC: Montepulciano and Trebbiano d'Abruzzo. Also *champenoise* Diamante d'Abruzzo.

Elio Monti
Controguerra, 64010 Teramo. Elio took over from his father Antonio in 1990. Good Montepulciano DOC.

Camillo Montori
Controguerra, 64010 Teramo. DOC: Montepulciano, Trebbiano d'Abruzzo.

CAMPANIA

The region of Naples and the Sorrento peninsula may have been cynical about the taste of tourists in the past, and left some of its visitors with a nasty taste in their mouths, but in many ways it is superbly adapted for wine-growing. Volcanic soils, the temperate influence of the sea and the height of its mountains give a range of excellent sites. Its own grapes have character and perform well. The red Aglianico (the name comes from Hellenico) and white Greco both refer in their names to the Greeks who presumably imported or at least adopted them in pre-Roman times. Quality wines are made at Ravello on the Sorrento peninsula, on the island of Ischia, and above all in the Irpinian hills north of Avellino, east of Naples, where the Mastroberardino winery has done more than anyone for the reputation of the region. Good wine is still very much in a minority, but it deserves recognition.

DOC AND OTHER WINES

Aglianico del Taburno
DOC. Red and rosé wines. Province: Benevento. Villages: Monte Taburno Torrecuso and 10 other communes. Grapes: Aglianico min. 85%, Piedirosso/Sciascinoso/Sangiovese up to 15%.

Recent DOC in an area where conditions are particularly suited to Aglianico. The wines are still rarely seen.

Capri
DOC. White and red wine. Province: Naples. Area: the island of Capri. Grapes: (white) Falanghina and Greco, plus Biancolella up to 20%; (red) Piedirosso, plus others up to 20%. Max. crop: 84 hl/ha. Min. alch: 11° for white, 11.5° for red. Annual production: 3,300 cases.

A small supply of adequate dry white and a minute supply of light red to drink young are lucky enough to have this romantic name.

Cilento
DOC. Red and rosé wines. Province: Salerno. Villages: Agropoli and 60 other communes. Grapes: (Aglianico) Aglianico; other reds up to 15%; (red) Aglianico 60–75%, Piedirosso/Primitivo 15–20%, Barbera 10–20%, other reds up to 10%; (rosé) Sangiovese 70–80%, Aglianico 10–15%, Primitivo/Piedirosso 10–15%; (white) Fiano, 60–65%, Trebbiano Toscano 20–30%, Greco Bianco/Malvasia Bianco 10–15%; other whites up to 10%.

Approval has been granted for types of wine including a red from Aglianico.

Falerno del Massico
DOC. Red and white wine. Province: Caserta. Villages: Mondragone, Sessa Aurunca and 3 other communes. Grapes: (red) Aglianico 60–80%, Piedirosso 20–40%, Primitivo, Barbera up to 20%; (white) Falanghina.

These wines, from a new DOC, show promise. Revived in their original area, they bear little similarity to their forbears but are worth watching.

Fiano di Avellino
DOC. White wine. Province: Avellino. Villages: Avellino and 25 nearby communes. Grapes: Fiano min 85%, Greco, Coda di

Volpe Bianco and Trebbiano Toscano up to 15%. Max. crop: 70 hl/ha. Min. alch: 11.5°. Annual production: 6,700 cases.
One of the best white wines of the south, light yellow and nutty in scent and flavour with liveliness and length. It also goes by the name of Apianum, a Latin reference to bees, which apparently appreciated either its flowers or grapes – or juice.

Greco di Tufo

DOC. White wine. Province: Avellino. Villages: Tufo and 7 other communes. Grapes: Greco di Tufo 80–100%, Coda di Volpe Bianco up to 15%. Max. crop 70 hl/ha. Min. alch: 11.5°. Annual production: 50,000 cases.
White wine of positive character, a little neutral to smell but mouth-filling with a good 'cut' in the flavour which makes it highly satisfactory with flavoursome food. Some bouquet develops with 2–3 years in bottle. It leads all the Campania DOCs in volume, nearly all of it made by Mastroberardino. It can also be made *spumante* (rarely seen).

Ischia

DOC. Red and white wine. Province: the island of Ischia. Villages: throughout the island. Grapes: (red) Guarnaccia 50%, Piedirosso (alias Per'e Palummo) 40%, Barbera 10%; (white) Forastera 65%, Biancolella 20%, others 15%; (Bianco Superiore) Forastera 50%, Biancolella 40%, San Lunardo 10%. Max. crop: 72 hl/ha. Min. alch: 11° for white, 11.5° for red. Annual production: 8,900 cases.
The standard red and white of this green island in the Bay of Naples are made to drink young and fresh. The white should be sharp enough to quench thirst. Bianco Superiore is sometimes fermented in the old way on its skins and becomes substantial, dry, golden and rather striking. Don Alfonzo (*see* Perrazzo under Producers) is a good non-DOC brand from the island.

Lacrimarosa d'Irpinia

A very pale coppery *rosato* of good quality, aromatic to smell, faintly underripe to taste, made of Aglianico by Mastroberardino (*see* Producers).

Lettere

DOC requested for quite mild but well-made dry red from the Sorrento peninsula.

Per'e Palummo

The alternative name of the Piedirosso grape, meaning 'dove's foot', applied to one of Ischia's best reds, refreshingly tannic and a shade 'grassy' to smell.

Ravello

Surely a future DOC. Red, white and *rosato*, each good of its kind, from the terraced vineyards leading up to the ravishing hilltop town of Ravello. Sea mists, I suspect, keep the wines fresh. The Caruso family also provide the entrancing Hotel Belvedere in which to enjoy the wines.

Solopaca

DOC: Red and white wine. Province: Benevento. Villages: Solopaca and 10 neighbouring communes. Grapes: (red) Sangiovese 45–60%, Piedirosso 20–25%, Aglianico 10–20%, Sciascinoso 10%; (white) Trebbiano Toscano 50–70%, Malvasia di Candia 20%–40%, Malvasia Toscano and Coda di Volpe 10%. Max. crop: 105 hl/ha. Min. alch: 11.5° for red, 12° for white. Annual production: 38,900 cases.
A little-known DOC zone north of Naples with decent red but rather dreary white.

Taurasi

DOC. Red wine. Province: Avellino. Villages: Taurasi and 16 other communes in the Irpinia hills east of Naples. Grapes: Aglianico min 80%, Piedirosso, Sangiovese and Barbera max. 30%. Max. crop: 77 hl/ha. Min. alch: 12°. Aged for not less than 3 years (1 in wood), 4 for *riserva* (1 in wood). Annual production: 14,500 cases.
Possibly the best red of southern Italy, at least as made by Mastroberardino (*see* Producers). Aglianico ripens late in these lofty vineyards to make a firm wine of splendidly satisfying structure, still dark in colour even when mature at 5 years. It has a slightly roasted richness without being at all port-like. First class but impossible to pin down by comparisons.

Vesuvio (Lacryma Christi)

DOC. White, red and rosé wine. Province: Naples. Villages: Boscotrecase, Trecase and San Sebastiano al Vesuvio, plus part of 12 other communes in Naples. Grapes: (white) Coda di Volpe and Verdeca; (red) Piedirosso; Sciascinoso up to 50%, Aglianico up to 20%. Max. crop: 70 hl/ha. Min. alch: 11° for white, 10.5° for red and rosé. Annual production: 38,900 cases.
Recent DOC, Vesuvio applies to the basic white, rosé and red while Lacryma Christi del Vesuvio applies to four superior versions which are capable of ageing 3–6 years or more. The white may also be sparkling.

Molise

Molise, a slice of central Italy stretching from the Apennines to the Adriatic, is a newcomer to Italy's wine map. Bottles with labels on are a relative novelty in a land of bulk production.

The first Molise DOCs date from 1983. They are Biferno, for red and white wine from 42 communes in Campobasso province and Pentro, for red and white wines from 16 communes in the hills around Isernia. Both specify Montepulciano for red, in Biferno it is the dominant variety, in Pentro it is used half and half with Sangiovese.

Both whites are based on Trebbiano Toscano. Both allow the addition of Bombino, in Biferno Malvasia Bianco may also be added.

One outstanding Molise winery, and one of the most modern in Italy, is **Masseria di Majo Norante-Ramitello** (Campomarino, 86023 Campobasso). Owned by Luigi di Majo, the property is managed by his son Alessio. His Montepulciano is as good as the best of Abruzzo, and Ramitello is a bargain in tasty everyday reds. He also makes Trebbiano del Molise, *Rosato* and Frizzante.

Other Molise producers include:
Cantina Cooperativa Valbiferno Guglinoesi, 86024 Campbasso. Biferno DOC and vdt. Bianco and Rosso di Molise, Valbiferno. The region's largest winery, processing some 8m. litres a year.
VI.TA-Viticoltori del Tappino Gambatesa, 86013 Campobasso. Biferno DOC with the Serra Meccaglia and Rocca del Falco brands, as well as Vernaccia di Serra Meccaglia white and other vdt and *spumante*.

CAMPANIA PRODUCERS

D'Ambra Vini d'Ischia
Forio d'Ischia, 80070 Napoli

Founded in the late 19th century by Francesco d'Ambra. DOC: Ischia. Others: Amber Drops, Biancolella, Forastera, Per'e Palummo. After a lapse in the firm's quality and prestige, the late Mario D'Ambra brought about a revival, introducing a new style to Ischia DOC and to the vdt Sparkling Kalimera, created by Andrea d'Ambria. The Amber Drops and Forastera are both well made.

Mastroberardino
Atripalda, 83042 Avellino.

Founded in 1878 as a continuation of a long-standing business; now run by Antonio and Walter Mastroberardino and sons Carlo and Paolo. DOC: Fiano di Avellino, Greco di Tufo, Taurasi and Vesuvio Lacryma Christi. Others: Irpinia Bianco, Rosso, Lacrimarosa d'Irpinia. From 250 acres of family-owned vines and 370 acres of others under contract, Tonino the oenologist makes 75,000 cases. Cellars were renovated and expanded after being destroyed in the earthquakes of 1980. The subsequent installation of ultramodern equipment signalled a new approach to the style of their white Fiano and Greco, now made in temperature-controlled stainless steel tanks.

Antonio Mastroberardino, who with his brother Walter has proved conclusively with their Taurasi, Greco di Tufo and Fiano di Avellino that Campania can make wines of distinct and excellent character

OTHER PRODUCERS

P. Caruso
Ravello, 84010 Sorrento. Founded: 1896; owned by the Caruso family. No DOC. Others: Gran Caruso Ravello Bianco, Rosato, Rosso. Well-made red and a 'fish' white of style.
CS del Cilento
Rutino, 84070 Salerno. Cilento DOC.
Cantine Episcopio-Pasquale Vuilleumier
Ravello, 84010 Salerno. Founded: 1860; owned by the Vuilleumier family. No DOC. Others: Episcopio Ravello Bianco, Rosato, Rosso.
La Guardiense
Guardia Sanframondi, 82034 Benevento. Large producer of Solopaca DOC, vdt and *spumante* from growers with almost 3,700 acres of vines.

Villa Matilde
Cellole, 81030 Caserta. Very drinkable Falerno del Massico DOC and vdt.
Michele Moio
Mondragone, 81034 Caserta. Substantial Primitivo will come under Falerno del Massico DOC.
Mustilli
Sant'Agata dei Goti, 82019 Benevento. Good vdt from typical Campania varieties under the Santa Croce label. Aglianico matches Flanghina and Greco.
Perrazzo Vini d'Ischia
Ischia Porto, 80077 Napoli. Founded in 1880 by Don Alfonzo Perrazzo. DOC: Ischia. Others: Don Alfonzo Bianco, Rosato, Rosso. The Ischia Bianco Superiore is noteworthy.

Saviano 1760
Ottaviano, 80044 Napoli. Vesuvio DOC and vdt, including some Gragnano.
Giovanni Struzziero
Venticano, 83030 Avellino. The Fiano, Greco and especially Taurasi DOC can be impressive from this emerging wine maker.
Pasquale Venditti
Castelvenere, 82030 Benevento. The quality of Solopaca DOC and red and white vdt is improving.
Volla
Solopaca, 82036 Benevento. The dedicated Maria Teresa Perlingieri produces fine Solopaca Rosso DOC from 20 acres of vines.

APULIA

The heel and hamstrings of Italy are its most productive wine regions. Their historic role has been to supply strength and colour for more famous but frail wines in blending vats farther north. The reds are very red indeed, very strong and often inclined to portiness. The whites are the faceless background to vermouth. This is the one region where the best wines until recently were the rosés – or at least some of them.

The Salento Peninsula, the heel from Taranto southeastwards, is the hottest region. A few producers here are learning to moderate the strength and density of their reds to make good-quality winter-warming wines – though a bottle still goes a long way. Their grapes are the Primitivo (possibly California's Zinfandel) and the Negroamaro – 'bitter black'. North of Taranto the hills have well-established DOCs for dry whites, originally intended as vermouth base-wines, but with modern techniques increasingly drinkable as 'fish' wines on their own. As elsewhere in Italy the existence of a DOC is better evidence of tradition than of quality. There is more interest in the fact that even in this intemperate region successful spots have recently been found to plant superior northern grapes – even Chardonnay (*see* Favonio under Apulia Producers).

Much the best-known DOC is Castel del Monte, and this is largely due to the crisp *rosato* of Rivera – for many years one of Italy's best. The list of producers shows that things are changing: Apulian reds are no longer ashamed of their origin.

DOC AND OTHER WINES

Aleatico di Puglia

DOC. Red wine. Provinces: Bari, Brindisi, Foggia, Lecce, Taranto. Area: the whole of Apulia. Grapes: Aleatico 85%, Negroamaro, Malvasia Nera and Primitivo 15%. Max. crop: 52 hl/ha. Min. alch: 13° plus 2° of sugar for *dolce naturale*; 16° plus 2.5° of sugar for *liquoroso*. Aged 3 years for *riserva*. Annual production: *liquoroso* 17,000 cases, *dolce naturale* limited production.

A dessert wine, approaching ruby port in its fortified (*liquoroso*) version. Small supply, and of local interest only.

Alezio

DOC. Red and *rosato* wine. Province: Lecce. Villages: Alezio, Sannicola, plus parts of Gallipoli and Tuglie. Grapes: Negroamaro, plus Malvasia Nera di Lecce, Sangiovese and Montepulciano up to 20%. Max. crop: (red) 98 hl/ha; (*rosato*) 49 hl/ha. Min. alch: 12°. Annual production: 15,500 cases.

A DOC for the red and *rosato* of the tip of Italy's heel, made from Negroamaro and Malvasia Nera and every inch a southern red, dark and powerful. It is moot whether to try ageing it or to take it on the chin as it is. Like many Apulian *rosatos* the paler wine has more immediate appeal.

Brindisi

DOC. Red and *rosato* wine. Province: Brindisi. Villages: Brindisi and Mesagna, just inland. Grapes: Negroamaro, others up to 30%. Max. crop: 105 hl/ha. Min. alch: 12° (12.5° and 2 years' ageing for *riserva*). Annual production 22,000 cases.

The local red of Brindisi can age for 5–10 years or more. Also makes a pleasant rosé.

Cacc'e Mmitte di Lucera

DOC. Red wine. Province: Foggia. Villages: communes of Lucera, Troia and Biccari. Grapes: Uva di Troia 35–65%, Montepulciano, Sangiovese and Nera Malvasia 25–35%, others 15–30%. Max. crop: 91 hl/ha. Min. alch: 11.5°. Annual production 38,900 cases.

Scholars tell us that the dialect name refers to a local form of '*governo*', in which fresh grapes are added to the fermenting must.

Castel del Monte

DOC. Red, *rosato* and white wine. Province: Bari. Villages: Minervino Murge and parts of 9 other communes. Grapes: (red) Uva di Troia 70%, Bombino Nero, Aglianico, Montepulciano and Sangiovese 35%; (white) Pampanuto 70%, Trebbiano Toscano, Trebbiano Giallo, Bombino Bianco and Palumbo 35%, (*rosato*) Bombino Nero with up to 35% Uva di Troia, Aglianico, Pinot Nero and Montepulciano. Max. crop: 84 hl/ha. Min. alch: 11.5° for white and *rosato*, 12° for red. Aged 1 year in wood for *riserva*. Annual production: 445,000 cases.

Castel del Monte, the octagonal fortress of the medieval Hohenstaufens, lie 30 miles west of Bari near Minervino Murge. The leading DOC of Apulia deserves its name for an outstanding red and famous *rosato*. The red has a fat, inviting smell and considerable depth and vitality, with a certain bite and long pruney finish. Rivera's Il Falcone is the best example. The pale *rosato* has long been popular all over Italy for balanced force and freshness.

Copertino

DOC. Red wine. Province: Lecce. Villages: Copertino and 5 other communes. Grapes: Negroamaro, plus others up to 30%. Max. crop: 98 hl/ha. Min. alch: 12° (12.5° and 2 years' ageing for *riserva*). Annual production 55,500 cases.

A warmly recommended red made in some quantity south of Lecce on Italy's heel. The *riserva* is said to be smooth with plenty of flavour and a bitter touch.

Five Roses

A powerful dry *rosato* from Leone de Castris (*see* Producers), so named by American soldiers who gave it one more rose than a famous Bourbon whiskey.

Gioia del Colle

DOC. Red, white and *rosato* wine. Province: Bari. Village: Gioia del Colle and 15 neighbouring communes. Grapes: Aleatico, Trebbiano Toscano, Primitivo, Montepulciano, Sangiovese and others.

Gioia is halfway from Bari south to Taranto. The Primitivo gives a pretty brutal red in these hot hills. With age it becomes more politely overwhelming.

Gravina

DOC. White wine. Province: Bari. Village: Commune of Gravina and parts of Altamura and Spinazzola. Grapes: Malvasia del Chianti 40–65%, Greco di Tufo and Bianco d'Alessan 35–60%. Max. crop: 105 hl/ha. Min. alch: 11°. Annual production: 22,000 cases.

Dry white from around Gravina. A *spumante* also permitted.

Leverano

DOC. Red, *rosato*, white wine. Province: Lecce. Villages: commune of Leverano. Grapes: (red and *rosato*) Negroamaro, plus others up to 35%; (white) Malvasia Bianco, plus others up to 35%. Max. crop: 67 hl/ha. Min. alch: white 11°, *rosato* 11.5°, red 12° (12.5° aged 2 years is *riserva*). Annual production: 38,900 cases.

One of the 1980 class of DOCs for Salento wines. The red and the *rosato* stand with Salento's finest.

Lizzano

DOC. Red, white and *rosato* wine. Province: Taranto. Villages: communes of Lizzano, Faggiano and part of Taranto. Grapes: (red and *rosato*) Negroamaro 60–80%, Montepulciano, Sangiovese, Bombino Nero, Pinot Nero max. 40%, Malvasia Nera di Brindisi or Lecce max. 10%; (white) Trebbiano

Toscano 40–60%, Chardonnay, Pinot Bianco min. 30%, Sauvignon, Bianco di Alessano max. 25%, Malvasia Bianca Lugna max. 10%. Max. crop: red 98 hl/ha, *rosato* 91 hl/ha, white 104 hl/ha. Min. alch: 10.5° for white, 11.5° for red and *rosato*. Malvasia Nera and Negroamara Rosso can also be *superiore* at 13°.

Latest Salento DOC with six new, but as yet untried, wines.

Locorotondo

DOC. White wine. Provinces: Bari and Brindisi. Villages: Locorotondo, Cisternino and part of Fasano. Grapes: Verdeca 50–65%; Bianco di Alessano 35–50%; Fiano, Bombino, Malvasia Toscana 5%. Max. crop: 91 hl/ha. Min. alch: 11°. Annual production: 448,310 cases.

Locorotondo is famous for its round stone dwellings. With Martina Franca it lies east of Bari at the neck of the Salento peninsula. Serious efforts are made to keep its white wine fresh and brisk.

Martina or Martina Franca

DOC. White wine. Provinces: Taranto, Bari and Brindisi. Villages: Martina Franca and Alberobello, and part of Ceglie, Messapico and Ostuni. Grapes: Verdeca 50–65%, Bianco di Alessano 35–50%, Fiano, Bombino and Malvasia Toscana 5%. Max. crop: 91 hl/ha. Min. alch: 11°. Annual production: 133,000 cases.

Grapes and wine amount to much the same thing as Locorotondo.

Matino

DOC. *Rosato* and red wine. Province: Lecce. Villages: Matino and part of 7 other communes in the Murge Salentino, at the tip of Italy's heel. Grapes: Negroamaro 70%, Sangiovese and Malvasia Nera 30%. Max. crop: *rosato*. 78 hl/ha, rosso 84 hl/ha. Min. alch: 11.5° for *rosato* and red. Annual production 16,700 cases.

An early (1971) DOC but still obscure.

Moscato di Trani

DOC. White wine. Provinces: Bari and Foggia. Villages: Trani and 11 other communes. Grapes: Moscato di Trani (or 'Reale'), plus other Muscats up to 15%. Max. crop: 58 hl/ha. Min. alch: 13° plus 2° of sugar for *dolce naturale*; 16° plus 2° of sugar for *liquoroso*. Annual production: 2,780 cases.

Sweet golden dessert Muscats of good quality, fortified or not, from the north coast west of Bari. Other Apulian Muscats, particularly those of Salento, can also be very drinkable.

Nardò

DOC. Red and *rosato* wine. Province: Lecce. Villages: Nardò and Porto Cesarco. Grapes: Negroamoro and Malvasia Nera. Annual production: 16,670 cases.

Recent DOC for red and rosé wines. The red is best in 3–6 years.

Orta Nova

DOC. Red and *rosato* wine. Province: Foggia. Villages: Orta Nova, Ordona and parts of Ascoli Satriano, Carapelle, Foggia and Manfredonia. Max. crop: red 105 hl/ha, *rosato* 97.5 hl/ha. Min. alch: 12° for red, 11.5° for *rosato*. Annual production: 1,670 cases.

A DOC for red and rosé wines grown at Orta Nova.

Ostuni and Ottavianello di Ostuni

DOC. White and red wine. Province: Brindisi. Villages: Ostuni, Carovigno, S. Vito dei Normanni, S. Michele Salentino and part of 3 other communes, including Brindisi. Grapes: (white) Impigno 50–85%, Francavilla 15–50%, Bianco di Alessano and Verdeca 10%; Ottavianello: Ottavianello; 4 others up to 15%. Max. crop: 77 hl/ha. Min. alch: 11° for Ostuni, 11.5° for Ottavianello. Annual production: 33,300 cases.

The unusual white grapes give a very pale mild and dry 'fish' wine; Ottavianello is a cheerful cherry-red dry wine, pleasant to drink cool.

Primitivo di Manduria

DOC. Red wine. Provinces: Taranto, Brindisi. Villages: Manduria and 15 other communes along the south coast of Salento. Grape: Primitivo. Max. crop: 63 hl/ha. Min. alch: 14° for Primitivo di Manduria; 13° plus 3° of sugar for *dolce naturale*; 16° plus 1.5° of sugar for *liquoroso dolce naturale*; 15° plus 2.5° of sugar for *liquoroso secco*. Aged 2 years for *liquoroso* types. Annual production: 16,670 cases.

The Primitivo, which may well be the same grape as California's Zinfandel, makes blackstrap reds here, some sweet and some even fortified, as though 14° were not enough. You may age them or not, depending on whether you appreciate full-fruit flavour or just full flavour.

Rosato del Salento

Rosatos are perhaps the best general produce of the Salento peninsula. It is not a DOC but this name is widely used.

Rosso Barletta

DOC. Red wine. Province: Bari and Foggia. Villages: Barletta and 4 other communes. Grapes: Uva di Troia, plus others up to 30%. Max. crop: 105 hl/ha. Min. alch: 12°. 'Invecchiato' if aged for 2 years. Annual production: 16,670 cases.

Some drink this relatively light red young and cool – others age it moderately and treat it like claret.

Rosso Canosa

DOC. Red wine. Province: Bari. Village: Canosa di Puglia. Grapes: Uva di Troia 65%, others 35%. Max. crop: 98 hl/ha. Min. alch: 12° (13° plus 2 years' ageing for *riserva*). Annual production: 22,000 cases.

Canosa, between Bari and Foggia, was the Roman Canusium (an alternative name for the wine). Its wine is in a similar style to Rosso Barletta.

Rosso di Cerignola

DOC. Red wine. Province: Bari. Villages: Cerignola, Stornara, Stornarella, part of Ascoli Satriano (east of Foggia). Grapes: Uva di Troia 55%, Negroamaro 15–30%, Sangiovese, Barbera, Montepulciano, Malbec and Trebbiano Toscano 15%. Max. crop: 98 hl/ha. Min. alch: 12° (13° aged 2 years in wood is *riserva*). Annual production: 5,500 cases.

A big dry heady red with faint bitterness.

Salice Salentino

DOC. Red and *rosato* wine. Provinces: Brindisi and Leece. Villages: Salice Salentino and 6 other communes in the centre of the Salento peninsula. Grapes: Negroamaro; plus others up to 20%. Max. crop: red 84 hl/ha, *rosato* 48 hl/ha. Min. alch: 12.5° (*riserva* after 2 years), 12° for *rosato* (*invecchiato* after 1 year). Annual production: 110,000 cases.

Typically big-scale southern reds have a porty undertone accompanied by a balancing measure of astringency. I have found this a rather clumsy wine, but I am prepared to believe I have been unlucky – other Salento reds are often nicely balanced with an attractively clean finish. The *rosatos* can be fresh and flowery and complex with time and are among the most distinctive of Italian rosés.

San Severo

DOC. White, red and *rosato* wine. Province: Foggia. Villages: San Severo, Torremaggiore, San Paolo Civitate and part of 5 other communes north of Foggia. Grapes: (white) Bombino Bianco and Trebbiano Toscano 40–60%, Malvasia Bianca and Verdeca up to 20%; (red and *rosato*) Montepulciano di Abruzzo 70–100% plus Sangiovese up to 30%. Max. crop: white 98 hl/ha red and *rosato* 84 hl/ha. Min. alch: 11° for white, 11.5° for red and *rosato*. Annual production: 611,000 cases. Inoffensive wines of no special qualities but offering good value.

Squinzano

DOC. Red and *rosato* wine. Province: Lecce. Villages: Squinzano and 8 others. Grapes: Negroamaro plus 30% others. Max. crop: red 98 hl/ha, *rosato* 42 hl/ha. Min. alch: 12.5° (13° aged 2 years is *riserva*). Annual production: 45,000 cases.

Salento wines of moderate quality. The *rosato* is much less tiring to drink than the red.

Torre Quarto

A notable individual estate at Ceriguola east of Foggia, setting itself high standards for a red of Malbec, Uva di Troia and Negroamaro, intended for long ageing. Its purchase by ERSAP, the regional development board, has left its future uncertain.

*Primitive harvesting methods
in Apulia*

Leone de Castris
Salice Salentino, 73015 Lecce.

The ancient estate of the Leone de Castris family, which has a large ultramodern winery, is now directed by Salvatore Leone de Castris. DOC: Locorotondo, Salice Salentino. Others: Albino, Blhiss Frizzante, Five Roses, Il Medaglione, Negrino, Primofiore, Rosato and Rosso del Salento, Spumanti, Ursi, Vini Novelli. Since 1929 the estate of 1,000 acres has bottled some of its (and Apulia's) best wine; rich and heady but not gross reds and (among others) Italy's first bottled *rosato*, Five Roses. 80% Of their grapes are estate-grown and potential production is more than 1m. cases.

Cantina Sociale Cooperativa di Locorotondo
Locorotondo, 70010 Bari.

Founded: 1932. A cooperative grouping of 1,300 growers producing 1.3m. cases. DOC: Locorotondo. Others: Rosso Rubino, Rose de Rosé. Locorotondo DOC is selected and aged briefly in barrels into an impressive, crisp but by no means neutral white wine.

Rivera
Andria, 70031 Bari.

Founded by the De Corato family in the locality of Rivera. Bottling began in the early 1950s. Gancia have acquired half-ownership. Wine maker: Carlo De Corato. DOC: Castel del Monte, Locorotondo, Moscato di Trani. Rivera makes about 90,000 cases of Castel del Monte from family vineyards and grapes from regular suppliers. The popularity of the lively *rosato* overshadows the quality of Il Falcone Riserva, one of Apulia's best-constructed reds. Since the collaboration with Gancia, De Corato has broken new ground with varietal vdt from Pinot, Sauvignon and Aglianico under the Vigna al Monte trademark.

Rosa del Golfo
Alezio, 73011 Lecce.

The Calò family has been selling wine from its estate near Gallipoli since 1938. No DOC. Others: Portulano (Rosso del Salento), Rosa del Golfo (Rosato del Salento). Family and neighbouring vineyards produce wines of consistent class, two thirds of it Rosa del Golfo, one of Italy's most limpid and lovely *rosatos*.

Cosimo Taurino
Guagnano, 73010 Lecce.

Cosimo Taurino is a skilled wine maker who with oenologist Severino Garofano, makes admirable Brindisi and Salice Salento DOC. Others: Patriglione, Notarpanaro, Chardonnay and Salento.

Tenuta di Torrebianco
Andria, 70031 Bari.

A new estate owned by Gancia with Giorgio Grai as consultant wine maker. It has made its debut with Preludio No. 1, a Chardonnay table wine. Sauvignon Blanc, Pinot Bianco, Pinot Nero and Aglianico has also been planted.

Agricole Vallone
72100 Brindisi.

A 350-acre estate owned by Vittoria and Maria Teresa Vallone. They produce fine Brindisi and Salice Salentino DOCs from the Vigna del Salento, and other table wines.

Cantina Sociale Cooperativa Alberobello
Alberobello, 7011 Bari. DOC; Martina Franca.

Barone Bacile di Castiglione
73100 Lecce. Owner: Fabio Bacile di Castiglione. DOC: Copertino.

Cantina Sociale di Barletta
Barletta, 70051 Bari. Cooperative. DOC: Rosso Barletta.

Borgo Canale
Selva di Fasano, 72015 Brindisi. Good Locorontondo and Martina Franca DOCs as well as table wines.

Felice Botta
Trani, 70059 Bari. DOC: Aleatico di Puglia, Castel del Monte, Moscato di Trani.

Michele Calo & Figli
Tuglie, 73058 Lecce. Alezio DOC and Salento vdt.

Francesco Candido
Sandonaci, 72025 Brindisi. DOC: Aleatico di Puglia, Salice Salentino. Others: Bianco, Rosato and Rosso del Salento.

Chiddo Vini
Bitonto, 70032 Bari. DOC: Castel del Monte.

Niccolò Coppola
Alezio, 73011 Lecce. A family estate since 1460, now run by Carlo and Lucio Coppola. No DOC. Others: Alezio, Rosato, Rosso.

Cantina Sociale di Copertino
Copertino, 73043 Lecce. The best coop of Salento with a huge production including good Copertino DOC.

Distante Vini
Cisternino, 72014 Brindisi. DOC: Locorotondo. Others: Negroamaro, Rosato and Rosso del Salento.

Favonio Attilio Simonini
71100 Foggia. No DOC. Many attractive wines.

Lippolis
Alberobello, 70011 Bari. DOC: Aleatico di Puglia, Martina Franca.

Gennaro Marasciuolo
Trani, 70059 Bari. DOC: Castel del Monte, Moscato di Trani.

Miali
Martina Franca, 74015 Taranto. DOC: Martina Franca. Others: Aglianico dei Colli Lucani, Apulia, Rosato.

Fratelli Nugnes
Trani, 70059 Bari. Small production of refined Moscato di Trani Dolce Naturale.

Santa Lucia
Corato, 70033 Bari. Emerging estate with Castel del Monte DOC.

Giovanni Soloperto
Manduria, 74024 Taranto. DOC: Primitivo di Manduria. Others: Bianco, Rosato and Rosso del Salento.

Cantine D'Alfonso del Sordo
San Severo, 71016 Foggia. DOC: San Severo.

Cantina Sociale Svevo
Lucera, 71036 Foggia. Cacc'e Mmitte di Lucera DOC.

Torre Quarto
Cerignola, 71042 Foggia. DOC: Rosso di Cerignola. Others: Torre Quarto Bianco, Rosato, Rosso. Torre Quarto in central Apulia was once one of Italy's greatest estates.

Conti Zecca
Leverano, 73043 Lecce. Owner: A. Zecca. DOC: Leverano. Others: Donna Marzia Bianco, Rosso. The rich red and agreeable white are among the most admired wines of Salento.

CALABRIA

The vast mountainous peninsula that forms the toe of Italy has no famous wines, unless Cirò, with its athletic reputation, can be so called. The local red grape is the Gaglioppo, a variety of deep colour and potentially very high alcohol, but the spots where it is grown to best effect are (with the exception of Cirò) high enough in the Calabrian hills to cool its fiery temper.

The white is the Greco, which is used in the extreme south at Gerace to make a very good dessert wine which ages well and which goes for a high price.

With little established wine making except of the most primitive kind, Calabria, like Sicily, is modernizing in a hurry. Its DOCs, though little known, represent wines that meet up-to-date criteria.

Cirò

DOC. Red, white and *rosato* wine. Province: Catanzaro. Villages: Cirò, Cirò Marina, part of Melissa and Crucoli. Grapes: (red and *rosato*) Gaglioppo, plus 5% Trebbiano Toscano and Greco Bianco; (white) Greco Bianco and up to 10% Trebbiano Toscano. Max. crop: 97 hl/ha. Min. alch: 13.5° for red and *rosato*, 12° for white. Aged 3 years for *riserva* (red only). Annual production: 327,700 cases.
Bruno Roncarati, himself an athlete, tells us that the Italian Olympic team maintain a 2,500-year-old tradition by training on this blockbuster of a wine from the heel of the toe of Italy. Red Cirò is certainly a full diet, but a soporific rather than a stimulating one. Earlier picking and new cellar techniques have reduced its tendency to oxidize though only the *riserva* can be aged beyond 3–4 years. White Cirò, as modernized, is a decent standard dry white to drink young.

Donnici

DOC. Red and *rosato* wine. Province: Cosenza. Villages: 10 around and including Cosenza. Grapes: Gaglioppo 60–90%, Greco Nero 10–20%, Malvasia Bianca, Montonico Bianco and Percorella 20%. Max. crop: 84 hl/ha. Min. alch: 12°. Annual production: 1,100 cases.
A relatively light and fruity red to drink young and fairly cool, from the central western coastal hills of Calabria.

Greco di Bianco

DOC. White wine. Province: Reggio Calabria. Village: Bianco and part of Casignana. Grape: Greco plus other whites up to 5%. Max. crop: 45 hl/ha. Min. alch: 14° plus 3° of sugar. Aged 1 year. Annual production: 1,100 cases.
A smooth, juicy and intriguingly orange-scented sweet dessert wine made of Greco grapes at Bianco, where a few small vineyards make it their speciality. Bianco is on the

south coast of the extreme toe of Italy. More vineyards are expanding production. Bianco also produces a drier, more lemony, barrel-aged dessert or apéritif white called (after its grapes) Mantonico.

Lamezia

DOC. Red wine. Province: Catanzaro. Villages: Part of 10 communes around Lamezia Terme. Grapes: Nerello Mascalese and Nerello Cappuccio (either separately or together) up to 30–50%, Gaglioppo (known locally as Magliocco) 25–35%, Greco Nero (locally called Marsigliana) 25–35%, other varieties up to 5%. Max. crop: 84 hl/ha. Min. alch: 12°. Annual production: 18,900 cases.

A straightforward palish dry red from around the gulf of St. Eufemia on the west coast. Drink it young and cool. Lametina is the name of the local non-DOC sweet or dry white.

Melissa

DOC. White and red wine. Province: Catanzaro. Villages: Melissa and 13 other communes. Grapes: (white) Greco Bianco 80–95%, Trebbiano Toscano and Malvasia Bianca 5–25%; (red) Gaglioppo 75–95%, Greco Nero, Greco Bianco, Trebbiano Toscana, Malvasia Bianca 5–25%. Max. crop: 84 hl/ha. Min. alch: 11.5° for white, 12.5° for red. Aged 2 years for *superiore* (red only). Annual production 15,500 cases.

The light, yellow, dry seafood wine of the heel of the toe of Italy, around the port of Crotone. The wines resemble Cirò but don't match it for quality. Most of it is drunk locally where it represents good value.

Pellaro

Powerful but light red or pink wines of imported Alicante vines grown on the Pellaro peninsula in the extreme south.

Pollino

DOC. Red wine. Province: Cosenza. Villages: Castrovillari, S. Basile, Sarancena, Cassano Ionio, Civita and Frascineto. Grapes: Gaglioppo 60–80%. Greco Nero max. 40%, Malvasia Bianca, Montonico Bianco, Guarnaccia Bianco max. 20%. Max crop: 77 hl/ha. Min. alch: 12°. *Superiore* must be aged 2 years. Annual production: 22,000 cases.

Monte Pollino is a 7,000-foot peak that divides northern Calabria from Basilcata. Its slopes produce a pale but powerful red.

Sant'Anna di Isola Capo Rizzuto

DOC. Red and *rosato* wine. Province: Catanzaro. Villages: Capo Rizzuto and parts of the communes of Crotone and Cutro. Grapes: Gaglioppo 40–60%, Nocera, Nerello Mascalese, Nerelo Cappuccio 40–60%, Malvasia, Bianca and Greco up to 35%. Max. crop: 84 hl/ha. Min. alch: 12°. Annual production: 2,200 cases.

A pale red/*rosato* to drink young and cool, made on the easternmost cape (not an island) of the Calabrian coast.

Savuto

DOC. Red wine. Provinces: Cosenza and Catanzaro. Villages: 14 communes in Cosenza and 6 in Catanzaro. Grapes: Gaglioppo 35–45%, Greco Nero, Nerello, Cappuccio, Maglicco Canino, Sangiovese max. 10%, and up to 25% Malvasia Bianca and Pecorino. Max. crop: 77 hl/ha. Min. alch: 12°. Aged for at least 2 years for *superiore*. Annual production: 44,500 cases.

A recommended red of moderate strength and some fragrance. Worth choosing the *superiore*.

Squillace

A locally popular fresh medium-dry white of Greco Bianco and Malvasia. Squillace is south of Catanzaro.

CALABRIA PRODUCERS

CACIB (Cooperativa Agricola Calabro Ionica Bianchese)
Bianco, 89032 Reggio Calabria. DOC: Greco di Bianco. Other: Mantonico del Bianco.

Caparra & Siciliani
Cirò Marina, 88072 Catanzaro. Founded: 1963. DOC: Cirò. A major Cirò producer. From 445 acres, potential production is 110,000 cases, but careful selection reduces the numbers.

Fratelli Caruso
88063 Catanzaro Lido. DOC: Cirò. Other: Villa Santelia Bianco.

Umberto Ceratti
Caraffa del Bianco, 89030 Reggio Calbria. DOC: Greco di Bianco. Other: Mantonico di Bianco. Minute production of the best dessert white of the south. (Mantonico is an apéritif.)

Enotria Produttori Agricoli Associati
Cirò Marina, 88072 Catanzaro. Cooperative with 70 growers. DOC: Cirò.

Vincenzo Ippolito
Cirò Marina, 88072 Catanzaro. Founded: 1845. Now run by Antonio and Salvatore Ippolito. DOC: Cirò. Potentially 60,000 cases, including a fine white Cirò, from 173 acres.

Cantine Lamezia Lento
Lamezia Terme, 88046 Catanzaro. DOC: Lamezia. Table wines.

Librandi
Cirò Marina, 88072 Catanzaro. Founded in 1950 by Antonio Cataldo Librandi. DOC: cirò. Traditional wines; the red is best.

Ferdinando Messinò
Bianco, 89032 Reggio Calabria. Tiny estate producing non-DOC Greco di Gerace, Bianco's finest wine. Also some Mantonico di Bianco.

Aloisio Nicodemo
Cirò Marina, 88072 Catanzaro. DOC: Cirò.

Giovanni Battista Odoardi
Nocera Terinese, 88047 Cantanzaro. Progressive winery with 150 acres of vines. DOC: Savuto. Table wines: Scavigna red, white and rosé, interesting sweet Moscato called Valeo. Good potential.

Cantina Sociale Vini di Pollino
Castrovillari, 87012 Cosenza. Cooperative. DOC: Pollino. Table wines.

Fattoria San Francesco
Cirò, 88071 Catanzaro. Owners: the Siciliani family are trying hard with their admired Cirò DOC red, white and *rosato*.

Cantina Sociale Vini del Savuto (Giambattista Longo)
Savuto di Cleto, 87030 Cosenza. Cooperative. DOC: Savuto. Table wines.

BASILICATA

This mountainous region of the central south, almost entirely landlocked and chronically poor, would not feature on the wine list at all were it not for its romantically named Aglianico del Vulture, a close relation of Taurasi and one of the best reds of southern Italy.

Aglianico dei Colli Lucani
A worthwhile red, from the Apulia side of Basilicata. It is worth tasting any wine made from this grape.

Aglianico del Vulture
DOC. Red wine. Province: Potenza. Villages: 15 communes north of Potenza. Grape: Aglianico.

Max. crop: 70 hl/ha. Min. alch: 11.5°. Average production: 44,300 cases. Aged 3 years, 2 in wood, is *vecchio*. Aged 5 years, 2 in wood, is *riserva*.

Monte Vulture lies right in the north of Basilicata, not far from the Iripinia mountains where Campania's splendid Taurasi is made. The same grapes grown at high altitudes on volcanic soil give a well-balanced red of firm structure, sometimes offered young, sweet and fizzy, but more often as matured red with real quality and character.

Asprino or Asprinio
A welcome refresher; sharpish, fizzy white without pretensions: Naples' universal café wine.

BASILICATA PRODUCERS

Donato Botte
Barilo, 85022 Polenza. DOC: Aglianico. Other: Moscato.
Giuseppe Botte
Barile, 85022 Polenza. DOC: Aglianico.
Fratelli D'Angelo
Rionero, 85028 Potenza. Founded: 1944; now directed by oenologist Donato d'Angelo with his brother Lucio. DOC: Aglianico del Vulture. Others: Malvasia and Moscato del Vulture (both sparkling). The foremost winery of Basilicata. D'Angelo makes 13–15,000 cases a year of Aglianico DOC from

grapes purchased from high-altitude vineyards; they have also started developing an estate.
Armando Martino
Rionero, 85028 Potenza. DOC: Aglianico del Vulture. Others: Malvasia and Moscato del Vulture *spumanti*.
Fratelli Napolitano
Rionero, 85028 Potenza. DOC: Aglianico del Vulture. Other: Malvasia and Moscato.
Paternoster
Barile, 85022 Potenza. DOC: Aglianico del Vulture. Others: Malvasia and

Moscato del Vulture and *spumante*.
Francesco Sasso
Rionero, 85028 Potenza. DOC: Aglianico. Other: Malvasia.
Società Cooperativa Vinicola del Vulture
Rionero, 85028 Potenza. DOC: Aglianico. Other Malvasia and Moscato.
Consorzio Vitacoltori Assciati del Vulture
Barile, 85022 Potenza. DOC: Aglianico. Table wines.

SICILY

Of all the regions of Italy the island of Sicily has changed most in the past few decades. Thirty years ago it was an almost medieval land. The marriage of dignity and squalor was visible everywhere. Its unsurpassed Greek ruins lay apparently forgotten; Syracuse was still a small city commanding a bay of incredible beauty and purity where you could easily imagine the catastrophic defeat of the Athenian fleet 2,000 years before; Palermo was sleepy, violent, indigent but magnificent. As far as wine was concerned, there was Marsala, a name everyone knew but which nobody drank, and a few small aristocratic estates – the best-known on the ideal volcanic slopes of Mount Etna, and around Syracuse, from which there was a trickle of legendary sweet Moscato. But the general run of wine was almost undrinkable, and the best of it was exported northwards for blending.

An apparently well-directed regional development programme has changed all this. Palermo is now a great semi-modern city and Syracuse has been disfigured by industry. But the wine industry has become the biggest in Italy and one of the most modern. Enormous new vineyards supply automated cooperatives, which churn out 'correct', clean and properly balanced modern wines. Three quarters of the wine is white. Eighty per cent of the colossal total is made in the cooperatives. DOCs are almost irrelevant here; less than five per cent qualifies.' It is a table-wine industry, based not on local traditions but on choosing appropriate grapes, converting cornfields into mechanized vineyards, and making wine with cool efficiency. None of this could have been achieved without New World techniques – and huge government grants.

The industry has grown far faster than its market. Although fair quality, good reliability and modest prices have made one or two brands (above all Corvo) internationally famous, most Sicilian wine stays in bulk looking for a blender to turn it into something else – be it Vermouth or even an apparently German wine.

DOC AND OTHER WINES

Alcamo or Bianco Alcamo

DOC. White wine. Provinces: Palermo and Trapani. Villages: around the town of Alcamo. Grapes: Catarratto Bianco Comune or Lucido plus 20% Damaschino, Grecanico and Trebbiano Toscano. Max. crop: 84 hl/ha. Min. alch: 11.5°. Annual production 266,500 cases.

A straight, fairly full-bodied dry white. Rapitalà is a far superior brand with some nuttiness and some astringency. Rincione Bianco is another similar brand.

Cerasuolo di Vittoria

DOC. Red wine. Provinces: Ragusa, Caltanissetta and Catania. Villages: 11 communes in southeastern Sicily. Grapes: Frappato min. 40%, Calabrese up to 60%, Grosso Nero and Nerello Mascalese up to 10%. Max. crop: 65 hl/ha. Min. alch: 13°. Annual production: 20,370 cases.

An unusual pale 'cherry' red of high strength which the critic Luigi Veronelli recommends keeping for as much as 30 years. Little is made, but its reputation is high.

Corvo

Perhaps the best known of all Sicilian wines today, a highly successful brand from Duca di Salaparuta at Casteldaccia near Palermo (*see* Producers). A green-labelled white is reasonably full-bodied but not over-strong and nicely in balance, a yellow-labelled one is very pale and delicate. The red is a brilliant piece of modern wine design; clean, warm and satisfying without leaving any clear memory of scent or flavour. There are also *spumante* and dry fortified Stravecchio Corvo wines.

Etna

DOC. White, red and *rosato* wine. Province: Catania. Villages: Milo and 20 other communes on the lower eastern slopes of Mt. Etna. Grapes: (white) Carricante at least 60% with Catarrato Bianco 40%, Trebbiano, Minella Bianca and other whites 15%; (red and *rosato*) Nerello Mascalese at least 80% with Nerello Mantellato the other 10%. Max. crop: 63 hl/ha. Min. alch: 11.5° for white; 12.5° for red and *rosato*. Annual production: 88,900 cases.

Until recently this was the only quality table-wine area in Sicily. The volcanic soil of the still-fiery volcano and the cool of its altitude allow both reds and whites of vigour and some refinement. The reds age well to a consistency not far from claret and the whites are brisk and tasty young. The leading estate is Villagrande (*see* Producers).

Faro

DOC. Red wine. Province: Messina. Village: Messina. Grapes: Nerello Mascalese 45–60%, Nerello Cappuccio 15–30%, Nocera 5–10%, Calabrese, Gaglioppo, Sangiovese up to 15%. Max. crop: 70 hl/ha. Min. alch: 12° Annual production: 550 cases.

Limited production of a distinctly superior red, best aged 3 years or so.

Malvasia delle Lipari

DOC. Dessert white wine. Province: Messina. Villages: islands of the Aeolian archipelago, especially Lipari. Grapes: Malvasia di Lipari 95%, Corinto Nero 5–8%. Max. crop: 63 hl/ha. Min. alch: 11.5° (18° plus 6° of sugar for *pasito*, which must be aged 9 months; 20° plus 6° of sugar for *liquoroso*). Annual production: 2,780 cases.

Well-known but scarcely exceptional wines (except in their lovely birthplace). There are many good dessert wines in Sicily; Moscato is much more interesting than Malvasia.

Marsala

DOC. Apéritif/dessert wine. Provinces: Trapani, Palermo and Agrigento. Villages: throughout the provinces but above all at Marsala. Grapes: (*oro* and *ambra*) Carratto and/or Grillo, plus Inzolia up to 15%; (*rubino*) Perricone, Calabrese, Nerello Mascalese, whites up to 30%. Max. crop: 75 hl/ha. for *oro* and *rosato*, 67.5 hl/ha. for *rubino*. Min. alch: 17° by volume for *fine* (or Italia Particolare); 18° aged 2 years for *superiore* (or London Particular, or Superior Old Marsala, or Garibaldi Dolce – or the appropriate initials); 18° by volume aged 5 years for *vergine*. Annual production: 2.44m. cases.

An Englishman, John Woodhouse, started the Marsala industry in 1773. Nelson stocked his fleet with it. In a sense it is Italy's sherry, though without sherry's brilliant finesse or limitless ageing capacity. Its manufacture usually involves concentrated and/or 'muted' (stopped with alcohol) musts, known as *cotto* and *sifone* – but the best, *vergine*, is made with neither, simply by an ageing system similar to the soleras of sherry. *Fine* is normally sweet and rather nasty, *superiore* can be sweet or dry, with a

---

Italy in round figures

Italy holds first place in the world leagues of both wine production and consumption per head. The average harvest for 1985–89 was 67,228,000 hectolitres of wine, or 746 million cases. Average production dropped considerably to just over 60 million hectolitres in 1988, '89 and '90, but the average is still close to 70m. hl. for the decade, due to big crops earlier.

The region with the largest average production is Apulia, closely rivalled in volume by Sicily. Next come Veneto and Emilia-Romagna.

Total production by region, average of years 1984–88, in cases, was:

Piedmont	41,570,000
Valle d'Aosta	444,000
Lombardy	20,213,000
Trentino-Alto Adige	13,919,000
Veneto	94,061,000
Friuli-Venezia Giulia	11,167,000
Liguria	3,141,000
Emilia-Romagna	84,860,000
Tuscany	40,315,000
Umbria	12,210,000
Marches	25,297,000
Latium	55,034,000
Abruzzi	41,725,000
Molise	6,094,000
Campania	27,273,000
Apulia	130,125,000
Basilicata	4,884,000
Calabria	12,576,000
Sicily	121,079,000
Sardinia	24,387,000

DOC production made up a record 14.26% of the total in 1988, well above the average of about 11% in recent years. Of the regions, Veneto produced the largest amount of DOC wine, 19.5 million cases in 1988 or 20.2% of the national total. The next largest contributors to the DOC totals were Piedmont with 13.2 million cases (13.7%), Tuscany (11.9m. cases, 12.3%), Emilia-Romagna (9.6m. cases, 10%) and Trentino-Alto Adige (8m. cases, 8.3%). Only 21.4% of Veneto's crop was DOC, despite the region being the largest DOC producer. Trentino-Alto Adige had the highest proportion of DOC (62.6%).

strong caramel flavour; *vergine* is dry, with more barrel-wood flavour. *Speciali* used to be a strange aberration – Marsala blended with eggs, or even coffee – but is now no longer permitted under DOC regulation. Another recent change to the DOC are the descriptions *oro* (gold), *ambra* (amber) and *rubino* (ruby); the former two refer to the wines based on white grapes, while the latter refers to the darker varieties less often seen. A great deal of Marsala is used for making *zabaglione* (just as France buys volumes of Madeira for *sauce madère*).

Moscato di Noto

DOC. White dessert wine. Province: Siracusa. Villages: Noto, Rosolini, Pachino and Avola. Grape: Moscato Bianco. Max. crop: 81 hl/ha. Min. alch: 11.5° (3.5° of sugar) for *Naturale*; 13° (3.5° of sugar) for Spumante and 22° (6° of sugar) for *Liquoroso*. Annual production 550 cases.

Little of this delicious Moscato is made, but the *liquoroso* is a very good example of this sumptuous genre. The Greeks introduced the Muscat grape here 2,500 years ago.

Moscato and Passito di Pantelleria

DOC. White wine. Province: Trapani. Villages: the island of Pantelleria. Grapes: Zibibbo. Max. crop: 49 hl/ha. Min. alch: 12.5° (4.5° of sugar) for *naturale*; 14° for *Passito*. Annual production 38,900 cases.

The island of Pantelleria is closer to Tunisia than Sicily.

Moscato from its Zibibbo grapes has singular perfume, whether made as *spumante*, *naturale* or best of all *passito* (which can also be fortified). The best quality is known as Extra.

Moscato di Siracusa

DOC. White wine. Province: Siracusa. Village: Siracusa. Grape: Moscato Bianco. Max. crop: 49 hl/ha. Min. alch: 16.5° (min 2.5° of sugar).

The celebrated old Moscato vineyard of Syracuse, once the greatest city of the Greek world, home of Plato, Theocritus and Archimedes, is apparently extinct, like the matchless beauty of its bay before Sicily began to modernize. The fact will not stop a bar selling you a glass of sticky aromatic wine at a high price as 'Siracusa'.

Regaleali

The brand name of a good-quality range of wines, perhaps the island's best brand, from Conte Tasca d'Almerita (*see* Producers). The Riserva Rosso del Conte is as good as any Sicilian red; the white contains Sauvignon Blanc.

Settesoli

The acceptable handiwork of a Cantina Sociale at Menfi on the western south coast. Red and white are both well made, if not memorable.

SICILY PRODUCERS

Giuseppe Coria
Vittoria, 97019 Ragusa.

The ancient estate owned by Giuseppe Coria began bottling its own wine exclusively in 1968. DOC: Cerasuolo di Vittoria. Others: Moscato di Villa Fontane, Solicchiato Bianco, Cerasuolo Villa Fontane, Villa Fontane Perpetuo. Coria is a former army officer, a dedicated wine maker, lecturer and author of books on Sicilian and Italian wines. From 7.4 acres he makes extraordinary wine, including a Cerasuolo Invecchiato (formerly known as Stravecchio Siciliano) aged 40 years in barrel, and Perpetuo, of which bottles are filled annually from a large cask which is then topped up with new wine.

Donnafugata
Contessa Entellina, 90030 Palermo.

Owned by Gabriella Anca and Giacomo Rallo, who are making this into a much-noticed estate. With new cellars and 170 acres of vines, they produce stylish dry *vini da tavola*, including the award-winning Donnafugata Bianco and Rosso. They also make a single-vineyard white called Vigna di Gabri, a rosé, some Chardonnay and the interesting white Damaskino.

Florio
Marsala, 91025 Trapani.

Founded in 1883 by Vincenzo Florio. In 1929 the firm was incorporated along with Ingham, Whitaker and Woodhouse as S.A.V.I. Florio & Co., part of the Cinzano group. DOC: Marsala. Florio was known in his day as 'the king of the historic Marsala'; now this rather lack-lustre company has no vines but still makes Marsala, including the fine *superiori* ACI 1840 and Riserva Egadi. Ingham, Whitaker and Woodhouse are sold under separate labels.

Carlo Hauner
Salina, 98050 Leccena.

Owner and wine maker: Carlo Hauner. DOC: Malvasia delle Lipari. Other: Capo Salina. Milanese Hauner adds new dimensions to the wines of this widespread family of vines; making a unique, acclaimed dessert wine.

Agricoltori Associati di Pantelleria
Pantelleria, 91017 Trapani.

A cooperative of about 1,300 growers on the island of Pantelleria. Director: Vito Valenza. Wine maker: Fiorino Perletto. DOC: Moscato di Pantelleria. Others: table wines. Besides much ordinary wine the cooperative bottles a notable dessert Moscato *passito extra* called Tanit and a growing amount of sparkling Solimano.

Carlo Pellegrino
Marsala, 91025 Trapani.

Founded 1880. DOC: Marsala. Others: Grecanico, Pignatello. Marsala Superiore ranks with the finest.

Nuova Rallo
Marsala, 91025 Trapani.

Founded in 1860 by Diego Rallo. The large family winery is run by his descendants. DOC: Alcamo, Etna, Marsala. Others: Normanno Bianco, Rosso, Royal Club Spumante. Rallo makes about 90,000 cases of Marsala and a significant amount of other wines from 295 acres of company vines, supplemented by farmers. The best wine of the distinguished range is Vergine 1860. Rallo also supplies table wines to the US market.

Rapitalà (Comte de la Gatinais)
Camporale, 90043 Palermo.

Owned by the Adelkam corporation and run by the French Comte Hugues de la Gatinais. The wine maker is Gigi Lo Guzzo. DOC: Alcamo. Other: Rapitalà Rosso.

Racking wine in a traditional Sicilian cellar.

An earthquake destroyed the winery in 1968. It was rebuilt in 1971. With 370 acres it produces 125,000 cases of Alcamo DOC and 40,000 cases of Rapitalà Rosso table wine. Rapitalà adds unaccustomed lustre to the DOC with another dimension of balance and finesse.

Regaleali-Conte Tasca d'Almerita
93010 Vallelunga Caltanissetta

A family estate founded in 1835. Owner: Giuseppe Tasca d'Almerita. No DOC. Others: Regaleali Bianco, Rosato, Rosso, Rosso del Conte; Nozzo d'Oro. 741 acres of estate vineyards produce some of Sicily's finest dry wines, including the excellent Rosso del Conte and the first-rate Nozze d'Oro (a white from Sauvignon Blanc and Inzolia).

Duca di Salaparuta (Corvo)
Casteldaccia, 90014 Palermo.

Founded in 1824 by Edoardo Alliata di Villafranca, Duca di Salaparuta. The modern winery is owned by the region and run by Benedetto Migliore. Chief wine maker: Franco Giacosa. No DOC. Others: Corvo Ala, Bianco, Colomba Platino, Rosso, Spumante, Stravecchio di Sicilia, Vino Fiore (red), Prima Goccia (white). Corvo is the most famous brand of Sicilian wine. Production is about 830,000 cases, prevalently in Corvo Bianco and Rosso and the white Colomba Platino, from grapes bought in the hills of central and western Sicily. New vines of interest are the red Duca Enrico, an aged, pure Nero d'Avola, one of the most successful new reds, not only of Sicily but of all the south, and Bianco Valquarnera from Inzolia and aged in small oak barrels.

Cantina Sociale Settesoli
Menfi, 92013 Agrigento.

A cooperative founded in 1958, now with claims to being Europe's largest winery, with 9,880 acres and 8m. cases. No DOC. Others: Settesoli Bianco, Rosato, Rosso, Bonera, Feudo dei Fiori. California techniques are evident in the light, suprisingly high-acid wines sold as Settesoli. 20% of production is sold in bottle, the rest in bulk.

Vecchio Samperi-De Bartoli
Marsala, 91025 Trapani.

Owners: Marco de Bartoli. DOC: Marsala and Moscato di Pantelleria. De Bartoli selects grapes from 37 acres for a limited production of Vecchio Samperi, an outstanding apéritif wine, a superior virgin Marsala in all but DOC. He also makes a Marsala Superiore Riserva, sweet white Inzolia di Samperi, dry Joséphine Doréo, and Bukkuram *passito*.

OTHER PRODUCERS

V. Giacalone Alloro
Marsala, 91025 Trapani. DOC: Malvasia delle Lipari, Marsala.

Cooperativa Agricola Aurora
Salemi, 91018 Trapani. DOC: Alcamo. Others: Castelvecchio Bianco, Rosso.

Bagni
Santa Margherita, 98020 Messina.

Owner: Giacomo Currò. Lone producer of Faro DOC. 5 acres.

Cantina Colosi
98020 Messina. DOC: Malvasia delle Lipari. Other: Salina Rosso, Bianco.

Vito Curatolo Arini
Marsala, 91025 Trapani. Founded in 1875, the family firm is run by Roberto Curàtolo. DOC: Marsala. Others: Marina Bianco, Rosso.

Fratelli De Vita
Marsala, 91025 Trapani. DOC: Marsala.

Cantina Soicale Enocarboj
Sciacca, 92019 Agrigento. Cooperative. No DOC. Others: Rosso di Sciacca,

Trebbiano di Sicilia. Carboj is the brand name for some very drinkable wines.

Fratelli Fici
Marsala, 91025 Trapani. Oenologist Nicolò Fici runs the family firm. DOC: Marsala. Fine Marsala Vergine from a reliable range.

Fontanarossa
Cerda, 90010 Palermo. Red, white and *rosato* Cerdese table wine.

Cooperativa La Ginestra
Malfa, 98050 Messina. Small group of growers on the island of Salina making DOC Malvasia delle Lipari.

Fratelli Lombardo
Marsala, 91025 Trapani. DOC: Marsala (Superiore). Table wines. 1,050 acres.

Marino Grandi Vini Siciliani
Marsala, 91025 Trapani. DOC: Marsala, Alcamo. Other: White Verdello Siciliano, red Nerello Siciliano.

Mirabella
Marsala, 91025 Trapani. Admirable Marsala Vergine DOC from this dynamic firm, which also uses the Cudia brand.

Fratelli Montalto
Marsala, 91025 Trapani. DOC: Alcamo, Marsala. Others: Grecanico, Malvasia, Moscato, Nerello, Zibibbo.

Salvatore Murana
Pantelleria, 91017 Trapani. Small production of Moscato di Pantelleria DOC and table wine.

Rincione
Calatafimi, 92013 Trapani. Owner: Pietro Papè. DOC: Alcamo. Others: Rincione Bianco, Rosso, Rosato.

Cooperativa Agricoltori Saturnia (Draceno)
Partanna, 91028 Trapani. Draceno Bianco, Rosato, Rosso.

Terre di Ginestra
Sancipirello, 90040 Palermo. Maurizio Miccichè is developing this estate with good *vini da tavola*: white Terre di Ginestra and red Tenuta Casalbaio Rubilio.

Cantina Sociale Sambuca di Sicilia
Sambuca di Sicilia, 92017 Agrigento. Large production of Cellaro red, white and *rosato* table wines.

Cantina Sociale Torrepalino
Solicchiata, 95030 Catania. Cooperative. DOC: Etna. Table wines. 400 acres.

Barone di Villagrande
Milo, 95010 Catania. Owner: Carlo Nicolosi Asmundo, Barone di Villagrande, whose son, Carlo, a professor of oenology, makes the wine. DOC: Etna. A dignified old estate which made Etna wine respectable when little else in Sicily was.

SARDINIA

Sardinia is a strange, timeless island adrift in the centre of things and yet remote, without Sicily's innate drama, without Corsica's majestic mountains or sour social history.

The modern world comes and camps on the coastline of Sardinia, the jet set on the Costa Smeralda, the wine world on the opposite coast at Alghero, where one of Italy's most sophisticated and original wineries takes advantage of ideal natural conditions to break all the rules.

Sardinia's original wines are heroically strong, designed it seems by and for the supermen who built the round fortress houses of colossal stones that dot the island: the nuraghe. The most characteristic wine of the island is Cannonau, an indigenous red with a minimum alcoholic degree of 13.5 and often much more. The traditional practice is to prevent all the sugar from converting to alcohol; to balance strength with sweetness in something faintly reminiscent of port. The sweet red is actually best

liquoroso, fortified with brandy, when it goes all the way to a port-style dessert wine. The Anghelu Ruju of Sella & Mosca is the version of Cannonau most likely to appeal to untrained tastes. Two other grapes, Girò and Monica, make similar sweet and heady reds.

Nor are old-style Sardinian white wines any easier to cope with. Nasco, Malvasia and Vernaccia are three white grapes that all achieve formidable degrees, often tempered, like the reds, with unfermented sugar left to sweeten them.

Sweet Malvasia is a serious speciality that can reach very high quality. Vernaccia, on the other hand, is best fermented dry and aged in the same way as sherry. (It even develops the same *flor* yeast that allows it to oxidize to a nicely nutty maturity.) Old dry Vernaccia needs no apology.

The modern movement in Sardinia consists largely of cooperatives, but is symbolized, and indeed led, by the Sella & Mosca winery at Alghero.

DOC AND OTHER WINES

Arborea
DOC. Red, white and *rosato* wine. Area: many communes in Oristano province. Grapes: (red and *rosato*) Sangiovese min. 85%; (white) Trebbiano Romagnolo or Toscano min. 85%. Max. crop: 126 hl/ha. Min. alch: (red) 11°; (white) 10.5°.
New and unproven DOC, the white also possibly *frizzante* or *amabile*.

Campidano di Terralba
DOC. Red wine. Provinces: Cagliari, Oristano. Villages: Terralba and 22 communes nearby (vineyards not exceeding 400 meters). Grapes: Bovale (others up to 20%). Max. crop: 105 hl/ha. Min. alch: 11.5°. Annual production 11,100 cases.

A lightish dry red, pleasantly soft and best served young and cool.

Cannonau di Sardegna
DOC. Red and *rosato* wine. Province: whole of Sardegna. Grapes: Cannonau, plus 10% Bovale Grande Carignano, Pascale di Cagliari, Monica and 5% Vernaccia di S. Gimignano. Max. crop: 72 hl/ha. Min. alch: 13.5° for Cannonau di Sardegna (1 year old: 3 years for *riserva*); 15° for *superiore* naturale; 18° for *liquoroso*. Annual production: 110,000 cases.

The complicated set of DOC rules means that much Cannonau is sold as Vino di Tavola (without the DOC qualification 'di Sardegna'), and is none the worse for a little less alcohol. It is the basic Sardinian red grape, traditionally both strong and sweet – in fact anything but refreshing, however rich (which it is) in flavour. The most famous old-style Cannonau is that of Oliena, near Nuoro in the eastern centre of the island.

Carignano del Sulcis

DOC. Red and *rosato* wine. Province: Cagliari. Villages: the islands of S. Antioco and S. Pietro on the southwest coast. Grapes: Carignano and up to 15% Monica, Pascale and Alicante-Bouschet and other red varieties. Max. crop: (rosso) 104 hl/ha; (rosato) 88 hl/ha. Min. alch: 11.5°. Annual production: 55,500 cases.

Both reasonable red and a quite smooth and fruity *rosato* are made of the French Carignan in this area of hilly islets and lagoons, known to the ancients as Sulcis. The red will take 1–2 years' ageing.

Girò di Cagliari

DOC. Red wine. Province: Cagliari. Villages: 72 communes in Oristano. Grape: Girò. Max. crop: 72 hl/ha. Min. alch: 14.5° for *dolce naturale*; 14° for *secco*; 17.5° for *liquoroso* and *liquoroso secco*. Aged at least 2 years for *riserva*. Annual production: 2,200 cases.

Girò, like Cannonau, is a traditional red grape of formidable sugar content, most often seen as a sweet wine; impressive rather than attractive when it is made dry.

Malvasia di Bosa

DOC. White wine. Provinces: Nuoro and Oristano. Villages: Bosa, Flussio, Magomadas, Modolo, Suni, Tinnura, Tresnuraghes – near the west coast south of Alghero. Grape: Malvasia di Sardegna. Max. crop: 56 hl/ha. Min. alch: 14.5° plus 0.5° of sugar for *secco*; 13° plus 2° of sugar for *dolce naturale*; 15° plus 2.5° of sugar for *liquoroso dolce naturale*; 16.5° plus 1° of sugar for *liquoroso secco*. Annual production: 3,300 cases.

The most highly prized of several Sardinian amber whites that can best be compared with sherry – at least in function. They go through a shorter and simpler ageing process but acquire smoothness and some depth of flavour, ending in a characteristically Italian bitter-almond note. Dry versions, served chilled, are good apéritifs.

Malvasia di Cagliari

DOC. White wine. Province: Cagliari. Villages: entire province and several in Oristano. Grape: Malvasia di Sardegna. Max. crop: 72 hl/ha. Min. alch: as for Malvasia di Bosa. Aged for 1 year in wood for *liquoroso dolce* and *liquoroso secco riserva*. Annual production: 5,500 cases.

Similar wines to the last but from less exclusively southern vineyards.

Mandrolisai

DOC. Red and *rosato* wine. Province: Nuoro. Villages: Sorgono and 6 other communes. Grapes: Bovale Sardo 35%, Cannonau 20–35%, Monica 20–35%, max. 10% other grapes allowed. Max. crop: 84 hl/ha. Min. alch: 11.5°. Annual production: 8,900 cases.

A new DOC for less than full-power Cannonau and *rosato* from modernized cooperatives.

Monica di Cagliari

DOC. Red wine. Province: Cagliari. Area: throughout the province. Grape: Monica. Max. crop: 72 hl/ha. Min. alch: 14.5° (2.5° of sugar) for *dolce naturale*; 14° for *secco*; 14° for

liquoroso; 17.5° plus 2.5° of sugar for *liquoroso dolce naturale*; 17.5° plus 1° of sugar for *liquoroso secco*. Annual production: 5,500 cases.

The usual range of strengths and sweetness in lighter reds with less character than Cannonau.

Monica di Sardegna

DOC. Red wine. Province: the whole island. Grapes: Monica, other reds up to 15%. Max. crop: 105 hl/ha. Min. alch: 11°; 12.5° for *superiore*. Aged 6 months, *superiore* 1 year in wood. Annual production: 278,000 cases.

A standard dry red table wine of acceptable quality, perhaps more enjoyable rather cool.

Moscato di Cagliari

DOC. White wine. Province: Cagliari. Villages: throughout the province. Grape: Moscato Bianco. Max. crop: 72 hl/ha. Min. alch: 16° (3° of sugar) for *dolce naturale*; 17.5° (2.5° of sugar) for *liquoroso* (fortified). Aged for 1 year for *riserva*. Annual production: 11,000 cases.

The Muscat grape has a stronger tradition in Sicily than Sardinia. What is made here is reasonable local drinking. The fortified *liquoroso* is the most convincing.

Moscato di Sardegna

DOC. White wine. Province: the whole island. Grapes: Moscato Bianco plus 10% others. Max. crop: 91 hl/ha. Min. alch: 11.5° (3.5° of sugar). Annual production: 3,300 cases.

A new DOC for low-strength sweet Muscat *spumante* – in fact the Asti of Sardinia. It can use the geographical term 'Tempo Pausania' or 'Tempio e Gallura' if the grapes are vinified at Gallura in the province of Sassari in the northwest.

Moscato di Sorso-Sennori

DOC. White wine. Province: Sassari. Villages: Sorso and Sennori, north of Sassari. Grape: Moscato Bianco. Max. crop: 14 hl/ha. Min. alch: 13° plus 2° of sugar. It can also be fortified to make a *liquoroso dolce*. Annual production: 1,100 cases.

A local Muscat DOC for a strong sweet white, reputed better than that of Cagliari in the south.

Nasco di Cagliari

DOC. White wine. Province: Cagliari. Villages: throughout the province. Grape: Nasco. Max. crop: 72 hl/ha. Min. alch: 14.5° (2.5° of sugar) for *dolce naturale*; 14.5° (0.5° of sugar) for *secco*; 14° for *liquoroso*; 17.5° (2.5° of sugar) plus 2° of sugar for *liquoroso dolce naturale secco*. Aged at least 2 years in wood for *liquoroso dolce naturale* and *secco riserva*. Annual production: 6,670 cases.

Another rustic island white more appreciated sweet and strong by the locals, but in its modernized, lighter and drier versions by visitors. Sella & Mosca (*see* Producers) spurn the DOC to make the latter.

Nuragus di Cagliari

DOC. White wine. Provinces: Nuoro (part) and Cagliari. Grapes: Nuragus 85–95%, Trebbiano Toscano and Romagnolo, Vermentino, Clairette and Semidano 5–15%. Max. crop: 140 hl/ha. Min. alch: 10.5°. Annual production: 388,900 cases.

A light and essentially neutral dry white wine, the standard resort of those who have been overwhelmed by Sardinia's more characteristic products.

Torbato di Alghero
The fruit of modern technology and intelligent market planning applied to a number of Sardinian white grapes by Sella & Mosca (*see* Producers). Not exactly a thrilling wine, but an extremely well-designed dry white of just memorable personality, and just what is needed with the island's fish. In fact it is a bargain anywhere.

Vermentino di Gallura
DOC. White wine. Provinces: Sassari and Nuoro. Villages: 19 communes in the north of the island.
Grape: Vermentino, max. 5% other grapes allowed.
Max. crop: 98 hl/ha. Min. alch: 12° (13.5° for *superiore*).
Annual production: 166,700 cases.
By tradition the sort of strong dry white with low acidity that does the opposite of quenching your thirst – epitomized by the 14° *superiore*.

Vernaccia di Oristano
DOC. White wine. Province: Cagliari. Villages: 15 communes in the south and west, including Oristano. Grape: Vernaccia di Oristano. Max. crop: 52 hl/ha. Min. alch: 15° (and 2 years in wood). Aged for 3 years in wood for *superiore*, 4 for *riserva*.
Annual production: 100,000 cases.
On first acquaintance I found this the most appealing of all Sardinian wines; a sort of natural first cousin to Spain's Montilla, or an unfortified sherry. The grapes are slightly shrivelled before fermentation, the natural strength slows down oxidation while subtle and distinct flavours develop – including the characteristic Italian bitterness lingering in the finish.

Vermentino di Sardegna
DOC. White wine. Province: the whole island. Grapes: Vermentino, plus other whites up to 15%. Max. crop: 130 hl/ha. Min. alch: 10.5°, *spumante* 11°.
New DOC (1989), not yet established, but not showing much promise of character. Wine is dry white and may also be *amabile* or *spumante*.

SARDINIA PRODUCERS

Attilio Contini
Cabgras, 09072 Oristano.
Founded in the late 19th century. Owners: The Contini brothers. DOC: Vernaccia di Oristano. Other: White Contina, rosé. The most respected of Vernaccia producers, whose *riservas* are a high point for this type of wine.

Sella & Mosca
Alghero, 07041 Sassari.
Founded in 1899 by the Piedmontese Emilio Sella and Edgardo Mosca, now owned by the INVEST group. Chief wine maker: Mario Consorte. No DOC. Others: Anghelu Ruju, Cannonau di Alghero, I Piani, Monica, Nasco, Rosé di Alghero, Torbato di Alghero, Vermentino di Alghero. One of Europe's largest wine estates and a model of contemporary viticulture. 990 acres of vines have a potential production of 420,000 cases. The principal lines are Vermentino, fine dry white Torbato, Cannonau and the port-like Anghelu Ruju.

OTHER PRODUCERS

Giovanni Cherchi
Usini, 07049 Sassari. Table wines. Unique red Cagnulari, and a Vermentino di Usini which is considered top of category.
Cantina Sociale di Dorgali
Dorgali, 08022 Nuoro. DOC: Cannonau di Sardegna. Others: Bianco, Rosato and Rosso di Dorgali. One of the biggest and best producers of Cannonau.
Cantina Sociale Gallura
Tempio Pausania, 07029 Sassari. DOC: Vermentino di Gallura, Moscato di Sardegna. Other: Table wines, including rare Nebbiolo di Luras.
Cantina Sociale Marmilla
Sanluri, 09055 Cagliari. A huge cooperative founded in the early 1950s. DOC: Cannonau di Sardegna, Monica di Sardegna, Nuragus di Cagliari. Others: Malvasia, Nasco, Rosato. Run by oenologist Enzo Biondo.
Meloni Vini
Serlargins, 09047 Cagliari. DOC:

various Cagliari, plus Cannonau and Vermentino di Sardegna.
Gian Vittorio Naitana
Magomadas, 08010 Nuoro. Malvasia della Planargia, selected by wine writer Gilberto Arru.
Cantina Sociale Il Nuraghe
Mogoro, Oristano. DOC: Nuragus di Cagliari and others. Rare white Semicano di Mogoro *vino da tavola* is their speciality.
Cantina Sociale Ogliastra
Tortoli, 08048 Nuoro. Good Cannonau DOC and *vino da tavola*.
Perda Rubia
Tortoli, 08048 Nuoro. Perda Rubia. A good sweet port-like Cannonau.
Produttori Riuniti
Baratili San Pietro, 09070 Oristano. DOC: Vernaccia di Oristano. 120 acres.
Cantina Sociale Regione su Concali
Jerzu, 08044 Nuoro. DOC: Cannonau (under the Jerzu trademark) and table wines.

Cantina Sociale della Riforma Agraria
Alghero, 07041 Sassari. Table wines: Aragosta, Le Bombarde. Aragosta is a good dry Vermentino.
Cantina Sociale di Samugheo
Samugheo, 09020 Oristano. DOC: Mandrolisai, Campidano di Terralba, exquisite, amber Nasco di Ortneri *vino da tavola*.
Cantina Sociale di Sant'Antioco
Sant'Antioco, 09017 Cagliari. DOC: Carignano del Sulcis, Monica di Sardegna. Sardus Pater is the trademark of a notable red Carignano.
Cantina Sociale del Vermentino
Monti, 07020 Sassario. Large output including DOC Vermentino di Gallura, red Abbàia and rosé Thaòra table wines.
Cantina Sociale della Vernaccia
09025 Oristano. Founded: 1953. Vernaccia di Oristano. The best Vernaccia of this large cooperative is the brand Sardinian Gold.

Italy's export trade
Italy's average exports of wine for the 4 years 1986–1989 were 126 million cases, about 17% of the national production. In 1989, 146.5m. cases were exported, of which 33.4m. cases (or 22.7%) were DOC. The total value of exports for 1989 was 1,555,881m. lire. The value of

DOC wine exports was 777,975m. lire, or exactly half of the total.
France is the leading export customer in terms of quantity, taking 53.5m. cases in 1989. Of this, only 1,373,000 cases (2.5%) were DOC. Other major export markets are West Germany 42.6m. cases (24.6% DOC); USA 12.9m. cases

(24.6% DOC); UK 12.2m. cases (32.6% DOC).
In terms of the value of exports, rather than sheer volume, West Germany is by far the most important market, followed by the USA, France and the UK.

SPAIN

To the majority of interested wine drinkers in other countries (South America excepted) Spanish wine of serious quality is scarcely less of a novelty than Californian. Even Spain's finest export-quality table wine, Rioja, was almost unsaleable in fashionable markets 20 years ago. Sherry was the only Spanish wine with international acceptance. Sherry, and cheap strong wine of the most basic kind.

Inside Spain Rioja completely dominated the market for quality wine, not just in the north but nationwide. Not even sherry had the same coverage. Local wines were offered in restaurants in carafes. Most visitors ignored them – not out of snobbery but from bitter experience. A great deal has changed in the last 20 years. First came the international discovery of Rioja. Then the rise of Penedès in Catalonia as its rival. A scattering of individual estates, some far from recognized wine regions, have made their names for wines which are extraordinary in every sense. Sherry, after a period of frenetic expansion, hit a crisis, not of quality but of international recognition, that makes it currently the most undervalued of all the world's classic wines. But the general mood all over the country has been an awakening of local pride.

A slow succession of regions had since the 1920s formed local Consejos Reguladores to control and promote their products. In 1970 the Spanish government passed a statute which drew together the threads of wine law and established national minimum standards. In 1972 it instituted a central controlling body for *Denominaciónes de Origen*. There are now 35 regions with controls broadly analogous to French appellations. *See* pages 28–29. Spain joined the EEC in 1986 and is thus now subject to the Community's laws on labelling and quality control.

Control, however, is not the same as quality. Only a small minority, even of *denominación* wine, is of international interest – and much of that only for its formidable strength combined with minimal character, as good blending material.

Modern cooperatives have done much to raise standards of essential technology and hygiene. Better grape varieties and earlier picking can improve matters radically if they are allowed to. But the great central Spanish well of wine, the region of La Mancha, south of Madrid, and its neighbours Jumilla, Yecla, Utiel-Requena,

Almansa and Manchuela to the east, disposes of its potent produce without difficulty and is only slowly changing its philosophy.

It is surprising to see in the statistics that Spain claims the highest acreage of vineyard in Europe – while coming only third in quantity produced. Spain's vineyards are still in the main old-fashioned, unmechanized and their soil relatively infertile. Crops are very small by French standards, except in the sherry region, where the clay soil allows production at an almost German rate. Average figures for some *denominación* regions show how very little wine even the 'bulk' areas coax out of their land, though the figures rose in the 1980s as new techniques made their mark.

The vineyards of Spain are so widely scattered over the peninsula that only the broadest regional classification or grouping is strictly applicable. Only in one or two instances do the names of the old provinces evoke a style of wine: the *denominaciónes* and other wine areas follow a different logic.

The country can reasonably be divided into three broad latitudinal bands: the north for table wines of quality, or at least character; the centre for bulk wines with high alcohol as their dominant characteristic; the south for *vinos generosos*: apéritifs and dessert wines with sherry as their archetype.

A further, longitudinal, division finds the northwest alone in producing sharp 'green' wines in the manner of Portugal's better-known *vinho verde*; the centre north responsible for most of Spain's best-balanced red wines; and Catalonia in the northeast leading in white table and sparkling wines, with good reds rapidly gaining ground.

The same longitudinal division across the centre of Spain finds the wines at their rudest and most characterful in the west, very strong but sadly lacking in flavour in the centre, and even stronger but with more colour and body in the Levante, towards the Mediterranean.

This is as far as generalization can usefully go. But it gives us a framework for progression from northwest to southeast.

Harvesting, Jerez

SPAIN IN ROUND FIGURES

Spain's vineyards cover just under 4m. acres, making her the country with the largest area under vines in the world (the Soviet Union is second, Italy third and France fourth). Both Italy and France, however, produce more than twice as much wine. The vineyards of Spain produce an average total of 37m. hectolitres a year: the amount fluctuates widely. Of this, only 27m. hl is allowed under EEC quotas to stay as wine: the surplus is distilled. Small crops, such as 1988's 20m. hl and 1989's 26m., do occur, and the yields in hl/ha are affected accordingly. The average crop over recent years is around 20–22 hl/ha, extremely low by modern standards; 1988's figure was only 12.5 hl/ha.

Well over half Spain's vineyards are included in her system of Denominación de Origen. (In contrast only 10% of Italy's wine is DOC.) D.O. status therefore has little to do with quality.

The D.O. regions and their production (in cases) in 1988 are listed on the right:

	cases
Alella	79,266
Alicante	690,955
Almansa	564,977
Ampurdán-Costa Brava	837,500
Campo de Borja	561,166
Cariñeno	3,433,011
Cava	10,805,900
Condado de Huelva	1,646,133
Costers del Segre	1,120,066
Jumilla	5,793,977
La Mancha	8,824,344
Málaga	411,633
Méntrida	840,411
Montilla Moriles	5,285,066
Navarra	4,360,488
Penedès	6,487,355
Priorato	46,966
Rias Baixas	326,888
Ribeiro	1,396,666
Ribera del Duero	358,888
Rioja	11,159,544
Rueda	1,014,644
Somontano	37,933
Tarragona	4,632,155
Terra Alta	1,570,611
Toro	333,100
Utiel-Requena	3,791,344
Valdeorras	294,455
Valdepeñas	9,931,155
Valencia	4,995,333
Yecla	1,929,866

Exports

Exports of D.O. wine in 1988 totalled 2,940,358 hl. After sherry, Cava and Rioja are the most important exports among D.O. wines.

	cases
Jerez-Sherry	11,147,444
Cava	3,939,188
Rioja	3,810,633

The main export markets for sherry, in order of importance are:

		cases
Netherlands	In bottle:	1,713,500
	In bulk:	1,095,500
	Total:	2,809,000
UK	In bottle:	1,273,000
	In bulk:	992,000
	Total:	2,265,000
Germany	In bottle:	1,721,000
	In bulk:	42,500
	Total:	1,763,500
USA	In bottle:	527,500
	In bulk:	—
	Total:	527,500

NORTHERN SPAIN

The Rioja region and its wines, much the most important for quality and consistency in Spain, have a section to themselves on pages 374–375. Catalonia, the quasi-independent province of the northeast, is also described separately on page 380. Recently wines of similar (in one or two cases even better) quality have been developed in the regions to the northeast and southwest of Rioja.

Navarra

Northeast is the old province of Navarra, which actually abuts on Rioja and can claim some of the vineyards of the Rioja Baja. Its limits are Catalonia in the east, the river Ebro in the south and the Pyrenees to the north. The province has some 60,000 acres (44,000 demarcated) of vineyard, using the same grapes as Rioja but with emphasis on the heavy, alcoholic Garnacha. The best lie just south of its capital, Pamplona, where the cooling influence of the Pyrenees can already be felt. The growers are being encouraged to replant with Tempranillo by increasing recognition of the best Navarra estates. Some are also experimenting with small amounts of Cabernet Sauvignon.

Aragón

South and east of Navarra, astride the Ebro lies Aragón, whose climate tends more towards the Mediterranean. Aragón's one well-known *denominación*, Cariñena, is a byword for high-strength dark red wine with a rustic bite, though worth oak-ageing for two years to achieve a pleasantly smooth

Racking in a Rioja bodega

texture. The grape here is again largely Garnacha Tinta, despite the fact that the region gave its name to the great grape of France's Midi, the Carignan.

Cariñena lies in the south of the province of Zaragoza, with 54,000 acres of vineyard in all (50,000 demarcated). A newer and small D.O., Campo de Borja (with 23,000 acres, of which 21,000 are demarcated), lies halfway between Cariñena and the Rioja Baja. Borja (the origin of the Borgias) makes an even more rustic and alcoholic red, more in demand for blending than drinking. Calatayud, south of Borja, makes similar wines and has just been granted its own D.O. A fourth D.O., still little known, lies round Huesca to the north of Zaragoza. Somontano, as it is called, feels the influence of mountain air and gives much lighter reds. Barbastro, east of Huesca, is its centre.

Old Castile
Suprisingly it is the very heart of the high plain of Old Castile, with some of the worst of Spain's savagely extreme climate, that is now producing wines of quality seriously to challenge Rioja. Big hot-country wines that they are, the red table wines of the Portuguese upper Douro and the Spanish Ribera del Duero seem to be kindred in their fine engineering. They have the structure, the cleanness and 'cut' of a massive Bordeaux – something not found (as far as I know) elsewhere in Spain, although well known as the hallmark of Portugal's best wine.

Some of Spain's greatest reds, including her most expensive by far, grow along the Duero banks, the Ribera del Duero, just east of Valladolid towards Peñafiel. This is the 'discovery' of the 1980s. There are 18,500 acres in the *denominación*. Vega Sicilia, aged 10 years in cask, is the crown jewel, but even the *reservas* of the cooperative at Peñafiel echo the underlying quality of the region.

Farther upstream at Aranda de Duero is the Ribera de Burgos, with 25,000 acres; not a D.O. but part of the Ribera del Duero. Its typical *claretes* lack the concentration and class of the Valladolid wines.

It is strange to find an up-and-coming white wine D.O. only 20 miles south of Valladolid, in the country that breeds such massive reds. Rueda made its name with a sort of sherry, a strong *flor*-growing yellow wine of Palomino, grown on chalky clay not unlike the *albariza* of Jerez. Modern white-wine technology has revolutionized Rueda. First the Marqués de Riscal from Rioja, then other investors, have seen enough potential here to call in the best advice from France and invent a new Rueda: a full-bodied crisp dry white of the kind Spain chronically needs.

Every other wine in Old Castile is red. Toro is Rueda's nearest neighbour: a massive wine for blending from the dusty Duero valley between Valladolid and Zamora. Cabreros, from over the mountains to the south between Avila and Madrid, makes powerful *claretes*. Cigales, just north of Valladolid, is another region of rough *clarete* – though pale in colour.

Leon
This sort of alcoholic dark rosé is met with all the way north to León, the capital of Castile's twin province. Benavente, with its castle-parador just south of León, is the centre for a bizarre sort of bodega burrowed in the ground. Among the vineyards of Los Oteros, along the shallow valley of the Tera river, and Valdevimbre nearer León, clusters of these extraordinary earthworks appear like ant cities. The city of León is now the commercial centre for the province. The great VILE bodega dominates the region and is turning its essentially peasant wine traditions to good account.

The last of the named wine areas of León, El Bierzo, lies west of the capital and over the mountains on the borders of cool Galicia. Vilafranca del Bierzo is the centre of a region of 24,000 acres, whose nearest wine-growing neighbour is the Galician *denominación* of Valdeorras. El Bierzo wines are correspondingly the lightest of León, with good acidity and not excessively strong. The Palacio de Arganza is perhaps the best producer of this region.

Galicia
The geography and climate of Galicia make it more like a northern extension of Portugal than part of viticultural Spain. But whereas Portugal's Minho has turned its *vinho verde* into a significant export wine, Galacia's similarly 'green', acidic and more or less fizzy wines remain a local attraction. The best of them (as in the Minho) are made of the excellent, aromatic, Albariño grape, which legend relates to the Riesling. The majority are made of a variety of local grapes adapted to much cooler and rainier conditions than anywhere else in Spain, except the Basque region. Yet even here, as in California, the degree of ocean influence varies widely from place to place with the incidence of coastal hills. Galicia's easternmost wine region, Valdeorras, shares the conditions of El Bierzo in León: moderate rain and a warm growing season. The main white grape is the Palomino; the red, Garnacha.

The other inland region, Monterrey, along the Portuguese border around Verin, shelters from the Atlantic behind the Sierra de Larouca with peaks of 5,000 and 6,000 feet. Monterrey wines are almost as sunbaked as those of León.

But these are the exceptions. The centre of Galician wine-growing is the D.O. Ribeiro, around Rivadavia between Orense and the coast at Vigo. Its cooperative is the biggest wine plant in Galicia, and its produce, particularly its red wines, are in the eccentrically fizzy and rasping style of *vinho verde*.

Strangely, the best wines of Galicia come from the D.O. of Rias Baixas in the Pontevedra province (containing the port of Vigo) immediately north of Portugal. This green coastal zone grows Albariño, notably around Cambados in the north and the Condado de Tea and O Rosal on the Portuguese border.

NORTHERN SPAIN PRODUCERS

Bodegas Julián Chivite
Cintruenigo, Navarra.

The largest private wine company in Navarra, founded in 1860. Its Gran Fuedo is a pleasant, full-bodied and oaky wine; the white Gran Feudo too: able to age 3-4 years with benefit. Older *reservas*, Cibonero and the 10-year-old Parador, are fuller and more fruity. Chivite is a pleasant dry white.

Bodegas Alejandro Fernandez
47315 Pesquera del Duero.

Visits by appt. Grower with 150 acres of vineyard on the north side of the Duero. Alejandro Fernandez has shot to stardom in the 1980s with Pesquera, a red wine made from Tinto Fino grapes, aged for 2 years in new American oak. American critics are particular admirers of his dense chewy style and powerful tannic structure. His reserve of reserves is called 'Janus'.

Bodegas Peñalba López
Aranda de Duero, Burgos.

A small family firm founded in 1903 with 500 acres of vineyard planted with Tinto Fino. It makes fruity and well-balanced Torremilanos wines, relatively light in style and among the best from this up-and-coming region. A big expansion programme, including a new winery and thousands of new *barriques*, is a testament to the Peñalba López family's confidence.

Bodega de Sarria
Puente de la Reina, Navarra.

The finest wine estate in Navarra, unique in the region (almost in Spain) for its château-style approach and almost Bordeaux-like results. The ancient estate was bought by a rich builder, Señor Huarte, in 1952, and taken over by a bank in 1981 which has, since then, rebuilt, landscaped, replanted vines and perfected cellarage. 321 acres of the 2,500-acre estate are vineyard, with Rioja vines in appropriate proportions (60% Tempranillo) and a little Cabernet Sauvignon. Its best *reservas* are better than most Riojas; even the light Cosecha (non-*reserva*) wines are very well balanced, Bordeaux-like to smell with a nice plummy flavour. A 3-year-old red is called Viña Ecoyen and a bigger, full-bodied red Viña del Perdon.

Bodegas Vega Sicilia
Valbuena de Duero, Valladolid.

The most prestigious wine estate in Spain: a legend for the quality (and the price) of its wines. It was founded in 1864 in limestone hills 2,400 feet above sea level on the south bank of the Duero. The founder imported Bordeaux grapes (Cabernet Sauvignon, Merlot and Malbec) to add to the local Tinto Aragonés (a form of Tempranillo) Garnacha Tinata and Albillo. Only 16,500 cases are made. There are plans to expand production to 25,000 cases – but slowly. 20 years ago production was only 2,700 cases. The yield is very low and the wine-making completely traditional. Only the unpressed *vin de goutte* is used, fermented for 15 days and matured in Bordeaux *barricas* for no less than 10 years for the great *reserva* 'Unico' (Vega Sicilia itself) and 3 or 5 for its younger brother Valbuena. The result is a wine combining immense power (13.5% alcohol with formidable fruit) and unmistakable 'breeding'. The raciness of the flavour is astonishing and the perfume intoxicating. Vega Sicilia is one of Europe's noble eccentrics, but if proof were needed of the potential of the Ribera del Duero for fine reds of a more conventional kind Valbuena would be evidence enough.

VILE (Planta de Elaboracion y Embotellado de Vinos SA)
León.

A private consortium growing and buying León wines on a big scale (it owns 2,500 casks) and with modern ideas. Its young Coyanza red and white are well-made everyday wines. Older and *reserva* class include Palacio de Guzman, Catedral de León, Don Suero.

Cooperativa Ribero del Duero
Peñafiel, Valladolid.

A long-established cooperative (founded in 1927) with 230 members, producing red wines worthy of a more famous region, well above normal coop standards. Ribera Duero is their blackberryish red without oak ageing. Peñafiel is slightly oak-aged (they have 2,300 *barricas*) and Protos is a sensational *reserva*, deep in colour and in its oak and mulberry fragrance, at 10 years comparable to an excellent Rioja *tinto*; long, soft and delicious.

OTHER NORTHERN SPAIN PRODUCERS

Albariño de Fefiñanes
Fefiñanes, Pontevedra, Galicia. The aristocrat of Galician wine, made by the Marqués de Figueroa in a small modern bodega in his palace of Fefiñanes, near Cambados. It is 100% Albariño, the best white grape of the region (and Portugal's Minho), aged for up to 6 years (for *reservas*) in oak. It bears no

resemblance to *vinho verde* except in its remarkable freshness.

Albariño de Palacio
Fefiñanes, Pontevedra, Galicia. The brother of the Marqués de Figueroa makes this high-quality, typical fizzy young Albariño – but not in the palace.

Bodegas los Acros
El Bierzo, León. A small family-owned

bodega. Its Santo Rosado has a good reputation.

Bodegas Palacio de Arganza
Villafranca del Bierzo, León. Since 1805 the bodega that occupies the 15th-century palace of the Dukes of Arganza has been the most important in El Bierzo, the best wine area of León. It ages its potent *reservas* in oak casks.

Almena del Bierzo is its considerable red, Vega Burbia a clean crisp white.

Bodegas Cenalsa
31001 Pamplona. Set up with the support of the regional government, Cenalsa selects wine from local growers and coops and bottles it under the Agramont label.

Bodegas Chaves
Barrantes-Ribadumia Pontevedra, Galicia. A small family-run bodega offering typical sharp and fizzy Albariño to a good standard.

Bodegas de Crianza de Castilla la Vieja
Rueda, Valladolid. Started in 1976 as a consortium of local growers to upgrade their wine. Their speciality was a *solera*-aged, sherry-style white. In 1980 Emile Peynaud of Bordeaux was engaged by new owners to make a small quantity of top-class modern white, carrying the name of the owner, Marqués de Griñon. The same nobleman has succeeded admirably with Bordeaux red grapes at Toledo. They also make a sparkling Brut wine called Palacio de Bornos.

Fernandez Cervera Hermanos
36770 O Rosal. Bodega near the Portuguese border making crisp, appley tasting wines (labelled Lagar de Cervera) from 50 acres of their own Albariño vines. The bodega was recently bought by Bodegas La Rioja Alta (q.v.) who have invested large amounts of money updating the winery and vineyard.

Bodegas la Magallonera
Magallon, Zaragoza, Aragón. A small family bodega in the D.O. Campo de Borja, founded in the 1950s by Andrés Ruberte, whose family are well-known wine makers. His typically alcoholic and full-bodied but also acidic red Pagos de Oruña is worth tasting.

Bodegas Magaña
31523 Barillas. This family-owned property has gone further than any other in Navarra in uprooting Garnacha, replanting Cabernet Sauvignon and Merlot grapes. Their wines share more than a passing similarity with good Bordeaux.

Vinicola Navarra
Las Campanas, Navarra. A century-old company with French origins; the biggest exporter of Navarra wines, without great refinement but reliable and increasingly tasty in the better qualities. Las Campanas Extra is a stout plain red; Castillo de Olite is a clean, pleasantly fruity, faintly sweet red and dry white. Castillo de Tiebas is the full-bodied *reserva* with Rioja-like oaky notes.

Bodegas Ochoa
Olite, Navarra. A locally popular privately owned bodega in Olite, once

the capital of the Kings of Navarre. The reds and rosés are soundly made.

Bodega Hnos. Perez Pascuas
09314 Pedrosa de Duero. Visits by appt. Another rising star; the Pascuas brothers own 100 acres of vineyard north of the Duero and buy in grapes from other growers. Viña Pedrosa made entirely from Tinto Fino is full but round from short ageing in oak.

Vinos Santiago Ruiz
36770 O Rosal. Small producer of high quality white wines selling on the Spanish market and commanding a high price. Unusual blend of Albariño, Loureiro and Troixadura grapes makes an especially aromatic, floral dry white.

Bodegas Sanz
Rueda, Valladolid. A small family-run bodega, founded in 1900. Its fresh young rosé is its best wine.

Bodegas Joaquin Soria
Cariñena, Zaragoza, Aragón. A small family firm now over 150 years old, growing its own grapes for its benchmark Cariñena, Espigal *clarete*, made of Garnacha Tinta (Grenache Noir) and white Macabeo.

Vicente, Suso y Pérez
Cariñena (Zaragoza), Aragón. The biggest and best-known private bodega in Cariñena and the largest exporter. It buys grapes from growers, using oak to age the wines. Don Ramon is the standard red and rosé; *reservas* include Comendador and Duque de Sevilla.

Bodegas Vilariño-Cambados S.A.
06633 Cambados. 85 growers cultivating more than 200 acres of vines send their Albariño grapes to an up-to-date stainless steel winery in the Valle de Salnés north of Vigo. Good, clean, fragrant dry wines are bottled under the Martin Codax label.

Vinos Blancos de Castilla
Rueda, Valladolid. A branch of the famous Rioja firm of Marqués de Riscal, founded in 1973 and built with advice from Emile Peynaud of Bordeaux. Riscal make three whites here, Marqués de Riscal blanco (Verdejo + Viura, no oak); Reserva Limousin (the same with a few months in oak); and a 100% Chardonnay.

Cooperative Barco de Valdeorras
El Barco, Orense. A substantial coop bottling very adequate plain still red and white (D.O. Valdeorras) with the name El Barco ('The Boat').

Cooperativa de Monterrey
Verin, Orense. The only bottler of Monterrey wines, founded in 1963. Red and white are both bubble-free; the best are labelled Castillo de Monterrey.

Cooperativa del Ribeiro
Ribadavia, Orense, *Galicia*. Much the biggest cooperative in Galicia, with 800 members and very modern facilities,

producing the equivalent of more than 750,000 cases a year. Its best white is crisp, clean and faintly fragrant, only slightly *pétillant*, like a Portuguese *vinho verde*. The red is fizzy, sharp and an acquired taste. The label for its best wine is Bradomin.

Cooperativa Viticola San José de Aguaron
Aguaron – Cariñena (Zaragoza), Aragón.
A 500-member cooperative founded in 1948. It ages its very sound wines in oak casks. Puente de Piedra is a typical Cariñena red.

Cooperativa San Roque
Murchante, Navarra. The best cooperative of southern Navarra, with powerful but clean reds typical of the warm and fertile region.

Cooperativa San Valero
Cariñena, Zaragoza, Aragón. A large cooperative (1,000 members) with a wide market in Spain for its 'Don Mendo' and Monte Ducay wines. Also a rather superior oak-aged 'Villalta' red and a cold-fermented 'Perçebal' rosé.

Agricola Castellana Sociedad Cooperativa La Seca
Rueda, Valladolid. An important cooperative, founded in 1935, producing from huge stocks both traditional *solera*-aged Rueda whites (e.g. Camp Grande *fino* and Dorado 61) and a modern-style, unaged, fruity dry white, Verdejo Pallido.

RIOJA

As a wine region, Rioja claims a longer history than Bordeaux. Some French historians believe that the Romans may even have found the ancestor of the Cabernet in this part of Spain. Certainly the Romans followed the river Ebro up from the Mediterranean rather as they followed the Rhône, as a corridor of the climate and conditions they were accustomed to into a colder and more hostile land. High in the headwaters of the Ebro, over 2,000 feet up, round its little tributary Rio Oja, they found ideal conditions for wine of good quality – and possibly even the necessary grapes.

The postclassical history of Rioja was similar to that of all the Roman wine regions. Rapid decline (accelerated in Spain by the Moorish invasion), the dominance of the Church, a slow renaissance in the sixteenth century, but no real changes until the eighteenth or early nineteenth century. Then it was the influence of Bordeaux that reached Rioja, the new idea of barrel-ageing the best wines. It was first tried in 1787, was overruled by Luddite reaction, and was finally introduced by reforming aristocratic landowners – in much the same way and at the same time as Chianti was 'invented' by the Barone Ricasoli.

The first commercial bodegas of the modern age of Rioja were founded in the 1860s, by the Marqués de Riscal and the Marqués de Murrieta, with the Bordeaux château system very much in mind. Both used (and still use) grapes from their immediate districts. They sold their wine in bottle and spread the reputation of the region at a most opportune moment. Phylloxera was invading Bordeaux, and French capital and technology were looking for a new region to develop. Before the end of the century a dozen much bigger new bodegas had been built, drawing on grapes from a much wider area – the three regions of Rioja all contributed to their blends.

The railhead at Haro formed the nucleus for this boom, and the bodegas round it remain both physically and spiritually the embodiment of the late-Victorian technology. The cluster of huge, rather raffish buildings almost recalls Epernay, the Champagne capital that grew in the same lush decades.

Phylloxera reached Rioja in the early years of the twentieth century. The disruption, followed by World War I, then the Spanish Civil War, prevented the bodegas from capitalizing on the foreign markets they had successfully opened, despite the fact that in 1926 Rioja became the first wine region

of Spain to set up a Consejo Regulador to supervise its affairs. During this period the region was making and maturing some superlative vintages (examples can still occasionally be found). Yet Rioja remained the staple of connoisseurs only in Spain and Latin America until the international wine boom of the 1970s.

That decade saw the founding of a new wave of bodegas, a flurry of takeovers, and a vast increase in planting and production. It also saw modifications in wine-making techniques which have added new styles to the already wide range produced in the region.

Long ageing in Bordeaux-type barrels is the hallmark of traditional Rioja. It gives the wines, whether red or white, an easily recognized fragrance and flavour related to vanilla. The best wines, with a concentrated flavour of ripe fruit, can support a surprising degree of this oaky overlay. Lesser wines become exhausted by it, losing their fruity sweetness and becoming dry and monotone. Spanish taste leans to emphasis on oak. International taste inclines to less oak-ageing for reds and little or none for whites. Many bodegas have therefore modified their old practice of bottling the wine at what they consider full maturity. By replacing time in barrel with time in bottle they reduce the impact of the oak in favour of the more subtle bouquet of bottle-age.

Red wines make up three-quarters of the total production of the region. The range offered by a typical Rioja bodega includes some or all of the following:

Vinos Blancos
White wines, either in Bordeaux-, burgundy- or German-shaped bottles. Normally very dry and gratifyingly low in alcohol (10–11%). Principally made of the Viura grape (alias Macabeo), with or without Malvasia and/or Garnacho Blanco. They have good acidity and resist oxidation well. Made in the old way they had little grape aroma but often very satisfying structure and balance. The style formerly sold as 'Chablis' was not aged in oak and was stony and austere at first, but responded rather well to four or five years in bottle. Some of these low-price wines may have been blended with strong neutral Valdepeñas. Examples still exist.

Better whites were formerly all aged in old oak barrels for between about three and anything up to 12 years – the best longest. Outstanding examples of these *reservas* remain pale lemon-yellow and keep an astonishing freshness, roundness and vigour beneath a great canopy of oaky fragrance. They can be compared with the best old vintages of white Graves.

Many bodegas now make all or some of their whites by long, slow fermentation followed by almost immediate bottling, the object being to capture primary grape aromas in all their freshness. The Viura makes delicious wine in this style, possibly benefiting from some bottle-age (though Bodegas Olarra make a white 'Reciente', which they recommend be consumed within months of the vintage). Most bodegas also make a compromise, semi-modern white, cold fermented and briefly oak-aged.

Sweet white Riojas are rarely a success. Noble rot is very rare in the dry upland atmosphere. Overripe grapes are simply half-raisined. But exceptional vintages have produced beautiful delicate and aromatic sweet wines of apparently limitless lasting power.

Vinos Rosados
Rosé wines, made in the customary way, normally dry and pale and not oak-aged.

Vinos Tintos
Many bodegas now call all their red wines *tinto*. The former custom was to divide them into *clarete*, light-coloured red wine of fairly low strength (10-11.5%) bottled in Bordeaux bottles, and *tinto* (sometimes called Borgogña) sold in burgundy bottles. *Tinto* in this sense is much darker in colour, more fruity, fuller in body and higher in alcohol. Both are made of a mixture of Tempranillo, the dominant red grape, with the luscious and aromatic Graciano and the alcoholic Garnacha Tinta (the Rhône Grenache), often with some Mazuelo, a cousin of the Carignan of the Midi. A little white Viura is also sometimes used in *claretes*. Both types are equally made up to the level of *reservas* or *gran reservas*, but Rioja's ultimate glories tend to be of the *tinto* type, which resists barrel-ageing better without growing thin and (although less fragrant) can grow marvellously velvety in the bottle.

All wines can be sold either as *sin crianza*, 'without ageing', or *con crianza*. A *vino de crianza* from Rioja is bottled at either three or four years old ('3°año' or '4°año'), of which at least one year must be in *barricas*, or 225-litre Bordeaux barrels. The rest will usually be in bigger oak containers. Wines of modest, medium and good quality are all handled like this. *Reservas* are specially selected wines at least three years old, of which one year was in *barricas*. Now, however, any of the statutory period can be substituted by twice as long in bottle. White *reservas* have a minimum of six months in oak.

Gran reservas are wines of at least five years old, with at least two years in *barricas*, or twice as long in bottle. These requirements for ageing are much less than they were only a few years ago. The reason given is a change in customers' tastes, although commercial necessity points in the same direction. Reputable bodegas will of course only select wines of fine quality to mature as *reservas* and top quality as *gran reservas* – although this is only implied, not required, by the regulations.

The regions
The Rioja district is divided into three regions, with a total vineyard area of more than 100,000 acres, following the valley of the Ebro from the Conchas de Haro, the rocky gorge where it bursts through the Sierra Cantabrica, to its much wider valley at Alfaro, 60 miles east and nearly 1,000 feet lower in altitude.

The highest region, La Rioja Alta, has the city of Logroño as its capital, although the much smaller Haro is its vinous heart. Cenicero, Fuenmayor and Navarrete are the other towns with bodegas. Haro has 14 out of a total of 40. There are 40,000 acres of vineyards. The soils are a mixture of chalky clay, iron-rich clay and alluvial silt. The climate is cool here and the rainfall relatively high. The minimum required strength for Rioja Alta wine is only 10 degrees. Rioja Alta wines have the highest acidity but also the finest flavour and structure, finesse and 'grip' that sometimes allows them to age almost indefinitely.

The Rioja Alavesa, north of the Ebro, along the borders of the county of Alava, has more southern slopes and a more consistently clay soil. Its 18,000 acres of vines are largely Tempranillo, which here gives particularly fragrant, smooth, almost lush light wine, tending to be pale and quick-maturing. The minimum strength is 11-11.5 degrees. A dozen bodegas are based in four villages: Labastida, Elciego, Laguardia and Oyon.

The Rioja Baja ('Lower Rioja'), with 33,000 acres, has much the warmest and driest climate. Its soil is silt and iron-rich clay, its principal grape the Garnacha Tinta and its wine stronger, broader and less fine, with a required minimum strength of 12-12.5 degrees. There are only six bodegas for ageing in the region, but nearly all bodegas buy some of their wine here, and several have been planting the finer grapes in the highest parts of the region.

It is probably true to say that most red Riojas are blends of wines from all three regions, although the old-established bodegas draw most heavily on the areas in which they were founded, and a few in Rioja Alavesa make a particular point of the regional style of their wines.

RIOJA PRODUCERS

AGE Bodegas Unidas
26360 Fuenmayor, Logroño, Rioja Alta.

A large modern bodega, but one with a long history. It was established in 1967 with the joining of Bodegas Romeral (founded in 1881 by Don Feliz Azpilicueta) and Las Veras (set up by Don Cruz Garcia Lafuente in 1926) and it is now owned by the American firm of Schenley and the Banco Español de Credito. Though they own vineyards, most grapes have to be bought in. The best of the reds are the tradicional *reservas*, Marqués del Romeral, Fuentemayor and Siglo Saco, sold in a sacking wrapper. White wines, all made in the new fruity style and bottled at 5 months old, include Romeral, Siglo Saco, Pedregal and Esmerado. The policy is to give the red wines less barrel-age and more bottle-age than formerly. Sales now amount to 1.66m. cases a year.

Bodegas Berberana
Ctra. Elciego, 26350 Cenicero, Rioja Alta.

Back in private hands after a period with Rumasa and then nationalization. Berberana was founded in Ollauri in 1877 and run by the same family until 1967. The huge new bodega in Cenicero (with no less than 34,000 barrels) dates from 1970. Grapes are from their own 130-acre vineyard, though some are still bought in. This impressive pioneering plantation is on high ground near Aldeanueva del Ebro. The classic Tempranillo of the Rioja Alta is thriving here. Preferido is their vigorous cheap *sin crianza* red, Carta de Plata is their big-selling 3° año, Carta de Oro the fuller-bodied 5° año. The *gran reservas* are big and velvety, while the new Berberana white is young and fruity without barrel-age. Sales of 1.8m. cases a year cover Europe and the Americas.

Bodegas Bilbainas
Particular del Norte 2, 48003 Bilbao, and at Haro.

The bodega was founded in 1901 and continues essentially as a family firm. 35% of their grapes are grown in their own 625 acres of vineyards in Haro (Rioja Alta) and Elciego, Leza and Laguardia in Alavesa. They sell nearly 300,000 cases of still and sparkling wines a year. Their aim is a wide choice of wines rather than a strong house style, but all the wines are conservative; rather austere by modern standards. Viña Paceta is a dry white, Cepa de Oro a sweeter white and Brillante a golden dessert wine. Viña Zaco is a high-quality *clarete*, while Viña Pomal is its more full-bodied *tinto* complement. Pomal *reservas* are the biggest and longest-lived wines. Royal Carlton is a *méthode champenoise* wine which they have been making since 1912. They also make a brandy, Imperator.

Bodegas Marqués de Cáceres
Union Viti-Vinicola, Carretera de Logroño, 26350 Cenicero, Rioja Alta.

Founded in 1970 by Enrique Forner (owner with his brother of Château de Camensac in Bordeaux), planned with the help of Professor Emile Peynaud, and recently modernized. Grapes come from 81 local growers, including the Cenicero cooperative. The red wines spend 15-18 months in wood and 15-18 months in bottle (though the Reserva and Gran Reserva spend 36 months in barrel and may be kept for 10 years in bottle). They emerge less oaky than traditional Rioja, but well balanced and fruity. The white Marqués de Cáceres, marketed young and without barrel-ageing, was the first of the new-style whites and, with its fruit and freshness without excess acidity, is still one of the best. The principal brand names are Marqués de Cáceres and Don Sebastian. 70% of the 500,000 cases sold annually are red wines, the rest being white or *rosado*. 45% of production is for the export market.

Bodegas Campo Viejo
26006 Logroño, Rioja Alta.

One of the largest bodegas; owned by Savin and formed in 1963 by the amalgamation of 2 old firms. Capacity in the new premises, built in 1968 and extended in '71, is now 50m. litres. 50% of production is from wine bought from cooperatives and 25% is from grapes bought in for vinification; 25% comes from their own vineyard of 1,200 acres, which include, in addition to the traditional grape varieties, experimental quantities of Cabernet Sauvignon, Pinot Noir, Gamay, Merlot, Chenin Blanc, Sémillon and Chardonnay.

Annual sales amount to 2m. cases. On the domestic market Campo Viejo, Almenar, Castillo de San Asensio and Foncalada are among the most familiar trademarks, accounting for 25-30% of all Rioja sold in Spain. Campo Viejo 4ª año is consistently good value among the less ethereal red Riojas. San Asensio is a robust unaged red. Marqués de Villamagna is the bodega's top *gran reserva*.

CVNE (Compañia Vinicola del Norte de España)
Avda. Costa del Vino 21, 26200 Haro, Rioja Alta.

One of the top half-dozen Rioja houses, founded in 1879 by the Real de Asua brothers and still owned by this family. Though the home market is now their most important – accounting for 85% of annual sales of around 440,000 cases – for the first 60 years they exported all they produced. Their own 1,300 acres under vine provide 65% of the grapes needed for red wine. Other vineyards are under contract. The bodega has a capacity of 17m. litres of steel tanks, as well as 22,000 oak barrels for ageing. They make consistently good wines. Reds include the excellent, vigorous Cune 3°, 4° and 5° años, the velvety Imperial (a *reserva* from the Rioja Alta), and the notably full-bodied, spicy Viña Real from Alavesa (made at Elciego). A new-style no-oak white made from Viura grapes only, and marketed as Cune Lanceros, has been well received, but CVNE is better known for its traditional oak-flavoured white in a Moselle bottle, Monopole – a standard and reliable resource in most good Spanish restaurants.

Bodegas Domecq
Ctra. Villabuena, 9, Elciego, Alava.

Founded in the early '70s by the sherry house of Pedro Domecq and the Canadian giant, Seagram. When the two parted company in 1974, Domecq built a modern, vitrified-steel-equipped bodega (recently expanded by 25%) and began planting new vineyards and buying old ones in Alavesa. They now claim to be the biggest growers in Rioja, with 790 acres in production, but still have to buy in 60% of their grapes. White and red Marqués de Arienzo, the low-priced Viña Eguia and the round, fruity Domecq Domain (labelled Privilegio Rey Sancho for the Spanish market) are their main brands. Domecq Domain and Marqués de Arienzo are also made as *reserva* and *gran reserva*. Annual sales reach 300,000 cases. 30% is exported.

Bodegas Faustino Martinez

Carretera de Logroño, 01320 Oyon, Alava.

Founded in 1860 and still family owned and run. All grapes come from around the Oyon area in Rioja Alavesa, 40% from their own 1,200 acres. Faustino I, the *gran reserva*, and Faustino V, an aromatic, lemony white in the new style, are made largely from their own grapes from first-class vineyards. The reds are given extra age in bottle rather than spending overlong in oak. Faustino V is the red *reserva*; Faustino I is the top wine. Total sales are 580,000 cases, with a high proportion of *reserves* and *gran reservas*. A recent development is the production of some *cava* using their own grapes.

R. Lopez de Heredia Viña Tondonia

Avenida de Vizcaya 3, 26200 Haro, Rioja Alta.

One of the great bastions of Rioja tradition. A family-owned, family-run bodega founded by Don Raphael Lopez de Heredia y Landeta in 1877 and now headed by his grandson, Don Pedro. The premises, on a railway siding at Haro, are a marvel of Art Nouveau design; the underground tasting-room Wagnerian in its lofty cob-webbed splendour; the cellars damp and chilly. Approximately half the grapes come from their own vineyards in Rioja Alta and most of the rest come from small local growers. All the wines are fermented and aged long in oak: the minimum is 3 years. Wines include Tondonia (fine red and white not less than 4° año), Bosconia (a bigger red, at best sumptuous) and Gravonia (an oaky white), and Cubillo, a red, and at 3° año their youngest wine. White wines are important, accounting for a quarter of their annual sales of 1.2m. litres. A 1964 Tondonia Blanco was still brilliantly fresh in 1988. The domestic and European market is their biggest, with exports making up 30% of their sales.

Bodegas Muga

Barrio de la Estacion, 26200 Haro, Rioja Alta.

A small family firm founded in 1932 by Don Isaac Muga. His son, Don Isaac Muga Caño, took over on his father's death in 1969 and 2 years later moved to a new bodega by the famous Haro railway station. Muga claim to be the only producers in Rioja to use American oak exclusively throughout fermentation and ageing. Their own 80 acres under vine provide 40% of their needs; the rest they buy from farmers in the Rioja Alta. Muga wines are almost alarmingly pale and ethereal but very fragrant. Much their best wine to my taste is the darker and richer Reserva Prado Enea, a wine with some of the velvet pungency of burgundy. They also make traditional white and a featherweight *méthode champenoise* with the name of Conde de Haro. Annual sales are 50,000 cases of which 20% is exported.

Marqués de Murrieta

Finca Ygay, Logroño, Ctra. de Zaragoza km 5, Rioja Alta.

With Marqués de Riscal, one of the two noble houses of Rioja, the first 2 bodegas to be founded, still with a special cachet, and remarkably unchanged by time. Don Luciano de Murrieta y Garcia-Lemoine founded this, the second oldest, in 1872. In 1983 control passed to Vicente Cebrian, Count of Creixel. Their own vineyards of 366 acres at Ygay near Logroño supply the majority of grapes and the new owner plans more plantings to make the bodega self-sufficient. Wines are made by wholly traditional methods and maintain a very high standard. The small range includes a fruity 4° año, Etiqueta Blanca, and their extremely rare and expensive Castillo Ygay – the 1934 vintage of which has recently been succeeded by the 1942. The current white Castillo Ygay vintages is 1968.

Bodegas Olarra

Polígono de Cantabria, Logroño, Rioja Alta.

Founded 1972. The most stylish modern bodega in Rioja, owned by a company founded by a Bilbao industrialist, Luis Olarra, and now controlled by the Guibert-Ucin family. The ultra modern winery, formed of 3 wings to symbolize Rioja's 3 regions, would look better in the Napa Valley than on an industrial estate outside Logroño. It owns no vines but has rapidly made a name for typical and stylish wines, red and white (the white very lightly oaked and ageing extremely well in bottle, viz. the '76 in 1982). Cerro Añon is the label of the fatter and darker *reservas*. Reciente is a new-wave white. Añares Crianza is their best-seller of recent years. 40% of their production of 500,000 cases is exported.

Bodegas Federico Paternina

Avda. Santo Domingo 11, 26200 Haro, Rioja Alta.

One of the largest bodegas, now owned by Marcos Equizabal, who also owns Lan and Franco-Españolas. It was founded in Ollauri in 1898 by Don Federico Paternina Josue. The extensive vineyards have been sold, and Paternina now buy in their grapes from cooperatives and growers. Wines include Banda Azul (a variable but popular young red), Viña Vial (full and fruity), a *gran reserva* and a *reserva especial* Conde de los Andes. The white Banda Dorada has recently been joined by Rinsol, a superior white in the fresh, fruity style. Annual sales are 800,000 cases; 35% is exported.

Anastasio Gutiérrez, export manager of López de Heredia

La Rioja Alta
Avda. Vizcaya, 26200 Haro, Rioja Alta.

One of the group of top-quality firms round the station at Haro. Founded in 1890 and with descendants of the founders still on the board. They own 740 acres at various sites in Rioja, and also buy in a varying proportion of grapes from local producers. The reds are more distinguished than the whites. Viña Alberdi is the pleasant *crianza* red, Viña Arana is a fine light red (and a rather dull white) and Viña Ardanza a sumptuous full red worth laying down. The top wines are the Reservas 904 and 890, selected for depth of colour and flavour to withstand respectively 6 and 8 years in American oak and emerge in perfect balance. They have recently acquired a bodega in Galicia, Lagar de Fornelos, producing wine under its label Lagar de Cervera.

Bodegas Riojanas
Estacion 1-21, Cenicero, Rioja Alta.

A substantial and conservative bodega, conceived in 1890 as a sort of château in Spain, by families who still own and manage the company today. The original French staff stayed on until 1936. Some grapes are bought in, the rest come from their own 494-acre holding in Cenicero. Traditional methods are used to produce the *reservas*, Viña Albina, and Monte Real, a most pungent and admirable red. Albina is a semi-sweet white, Medieval a dry one and Canchales a young red. Puerta Vieja and Bori are other brands. Annual sales are 83,000 cases, with Italy among the export markets.

Herederos Marqués de Riscal
Torrea 1, Elciego, Alava.

The oldest existing Rioja bodega, founded in 1860 by Don Camilo Hurtado de Amezaga, Marqués de Riscal. The bodega was designed by a Bordeaux *vigneron*, and most of the wines continue to have a light, elegant, almost claret-like character – the epitome of the Rioja Alavesa.

40% of the grapes come from their own vineyards, 49 acres of which are planted with Cabernet Sauvignon. Cabernet is used in a proportion of about 15% for all *reservas* and above, but occasionally much more. A 1970 *reserva* had 60% and an astonishing 1938, still vigorous in 1982, had 80%. The wines are aged in barrel for up to 4 years, then in bottle for a minimum of 3, often 10 – and no maximum. White Riscal wines are not Riojas, but come from Rueda. *See* Vinos Blancos de Castilla, p.373. Sales of 250,000 cases a year, including wines under the Riscalsa label, go to 82 countries.

OTHER RIOJA PRODUCERS

Lopez Agos y Cia
PO Box 9, Ctra. de Logroño, Fuenmayor, Rioja Alta. Founded in 1972 by a group of businessmen with experience in Riojan bodegas. Half the grapes come from the company's own 99-acre site, the rest from farmers (all in Rioja Alta) under supervision. They market red *reservas* under the Señorio Agos and Viñas Tesos labels, a white *reserva*, Agos Oro, and a *sin crianza* range of red, white and rosé under the bodega name. Annual sales of 100,000 cases.

Bodegas Alavesas
Laguardia, Rioja Alavesa. Founded 1972. Now owned by the group Alter. They own over 900 acres and also buy in some grapes from local growers. They make typically pale, light, fragrant Alavesa wines; *reservas* under the name Solar de Samaniego; other names include Solar de Iriarte and Solar de Berbete.

Bodegas Ramon Bilbao
Avda. Santa Domingo, Haro, Rioja Alta. Founded in 1924; a family-owned company which buys in most of its wine and grapes from private vineyards. Wines under the bodega name include Turzaballa, Monte Blanco, Monte Llano and Monte Rojo.

Bodegas Martínez Bujanda
Campo Viejo de Logroño, Oyón, Alava. A century-old family-owned bodega re-founded in 1988 and already making exceptional wines, especially its Valdemar Reservas, of which Centenario is the sumptuous best. Also fruity *sin crianza* and very fruity rosado.

Bodegas Corral
Carretera de Logroño km 10, Navarrete, Rioja Alta. Owned by Don Florencio Corral Daroca (grandson of the founder) and a group of Riojan friends. Their own 96-acre Rioja Alta vineyard provides 25% of their grape needs, the rest comes from growers in the same area. Traditional methods produce distinctly oaky wines under the Don Jacobo and Corral labels. Annual sales of 80,000 cases.

Bodegas El Coto
Oyon, Alava, Rioja. A young bodega founded in 1970 and expanded in 1977 and 1988. The firm owns 300 acres of vineyards in Cenicero and Mendavia, providing 57% of the red and all the white grapes. Soft fruity reds, Coto de Imaz and El Coto, are made almost wholly from Tempranillo, while El Coto white is made in the new style almost entirely from Viura.

Bodegas Franco-Españolas
Cabo Noval 2, Logroño, Rioja Alta. A big bodega in the city of Logroño, bought after Rumasa ownership by Marcos Equizàbel Ramiriz. Its French and Spanish founders (hence the name) included Monsieur Anglade, a fugitive from phylloxera-devastated France. The vineyards have been sold; they buy in grapes and wine from Rioja Alta and Alavesa. Traditional oak-aged whites, Viña Soledad and Vinã Sole, have now been joined by a young no-oak white Diamante. Traditional reds include a dark and flavoury (if rather coarse) bargain, Rioja Bordon, the Royal *reservas* and Excelso *gran reservas*. Annual production is around 3,500 cases.

Bodegas Gurpegui
Cuevas 38, Haro. One of the largest producers of wine to sell to other bodegas. Founded in 1872. Don Luis Gurpegui Muga is the third-generation proprietor. 10% of production comes from their own 250-acre vineyard, 90% from regular suppliers over many years. 2 of the well-known brands of well-made classic Riojas from this stable are Dominio de la Plana and Berceo (and Gonzalo de Berceo). Annual sales of 208,000 cases.

Martinez Lacuesta Hnos Lda
La Ventilla 71, 26200, Haro, Rioja Alta. A family firm founded in 1895 and now directed by Don Luis Martinez Lacuesta. All grapes, including an unusually high proportion of Garnacha, are bought in from cooperatives. Reds are a very pale and oaky *clarete* and a fuller, still oaky, Campeador (both to be found on Iberian Airlines). A white wine is called Viña Delys. Average production is around 150,000 cases.

Bodegas Lagunilla
26360 Fuenmayor, Rioja Alta. Next door to Lan (see next entry), a modern bodega but a century-old firm (founded in 1885), now owned by IDV. Buys in wine to make fresh whites and reds to age, including a powerful *gran reserva*.

Bodegas Lan
Paraje de Buicio, 26360 Fuenmayor, Rioja Alta. A large and very modern bodega founded in 1973. Tempranillo, Mazuelo and Viura from their own 270

acres in El Cortijo (Rioja Alta) provide some of their requirements. Most of the rest is bought from small growers, principally in Rioja Alavesa. The labels are Lan, Lander and Viña Lanciano (for *reservas*). Production is 150,000 cases and sales are to both national and international markets.

Bodegas Muerza
Plaza Vera Magallon, San Adrian, Navarra. A small bodega founded in 1882. It has changed hands several times and now belongs to the Agronavarra group. Buys in all its grapes from both cooperatives and individual growers. Reds are made in the traditional way, whites and rosés in the no-oak style. There are 2 brand names: Rioja Vega and Señorial.

Bodegas Navajas
Carnino de Balgoraiz 2, Navarrete. Founded in 1978. They have 12 acres but most of the grapes are bought in. There is one white made of 100% Viura but the reds are better, from 70% Tempranillo, 30% Garnacha. They aim to unite the fresh and oaky style of new and old Riojas.

Bodegas Palacio
San Lazaro 1, Laguardia, Alava. Founded by Don Angel Palacio in 1894. Formerly famous for its splendid Glorioso, which is showing signs of regaining its reputation. Now owned by the Seagram group. They have small vineyards in Laguardia where they grow Tempranillo and Viura, but most grapes are bought in for their Glorioso, Portil and Castillo red, white and rosé Riojas.

Bodegas José Palacios
Poligono de Calabria, PO box 1.152, Logroño, Rioja Alta. Founded by Don José Palacios Remondo in 1947 and still in the family. Grapes are bought in, mostly from Alfaro (Rioja Baja). Brands are Eral, Utrero, Copa Remondo and Herencia. Reds are traditional; whites unaged.

Salceda
Carretera de Cenicero km-3, 01340 Elciego, Alava. Founded in 1973. A red-wine-only bodega with 70 acres of its own vineyard, using modern methods to make good wine with a leaning to the soft Alavesa style. Recent expansion has enabled production to be increased. Viña Salceda is the 4-year-old quality; Conde de la Salceda the *reserva*.

Bodegas Carlos Serres
Avda. Santo Domingo 40, 26200 Haro, Rioja Alta. Founded in 1896 by Charles Serres, who arrived in Haro from phylloxera-infected France. Now a limited company. Grapes and wine are bought in from growers and cooperatives. Reds, whites and rosés are made by traditional methods with very modern equipment. Red Carlos Serres *reservas* (the top wines) are good, usually rather light in style.

Cooperative Vinicola de Labastida
Rioja Alavesa. Founded 1965. Its 160-odd members are all in Rioja Alavesa with admirable vineyards, and their cooperative competes on equal terms with the best bodegas. The powerful reds range from the everyday Manuel Quintano and good-value Montebuena to very fine *reservas* and *gran reservas* called Gastrijo and Castillo Labastida (the top of the line). The white is un-oaked, in the modern manner, and one of the best of its sort.

Rioja exports

In 1988, 3.8m. cases of Rioja were exported, out of a production of 14.7m. cases. The main markets, in order of importance were:

Germany	500,000 cases
UK	490,000 ,,
Denmark	450,000 ,,
Netherlands	255,000 ,,
USA	190,000 ,,

Figures are for sales in bottle and in bulk.

Adding wax capsules to bottles

CATALONIA

Your Catalan is only half a Spaniard. He is proud of the autonomy of his privileged province. He basks in a temperate, mild-winter climate without the extremes of most of Spain. Catalonia lies on the same latitude as Tuscany, sheltered from the north by the Pyrenees and their gradually rising foothills, facing southeast into the Mediterranean. It can be considered as a southward extension of the best wine area of France's Midi: the Côtes de Roussillon and their hinterland. They both have the capacity to produce ponderous and potent reds and elaborate luscious dessert wines – and also to surprise with the quality of their white grapes.

Historically most important have been the dessert wines of Tarragona, the warmest part of the Catalan coast. From Priorato, an inland enclave in the same area, came red wines of legendary colour and strength (but also quality) for blending. A century ago the Raventós family of Penedès realized the potential of their native white grapes, naturally high in acid, for the champagne treatment. Today Penedès produces 90 per cent of Spain's sparkling wine.

The latest development, but the most significant of all, has been the successful trial of the classic French and German grapes in the higher parts of Penedès. The Torres family, long-established wine makers of the region, have led the way with a judicious mixture of these exotics and the best of the well-tried Catalan varieties.

Among the native whites Parellada and Xarel-lo are crisply acidic with low alcoholic degrees, Malvasia is broadly fruity, with low acidity, and Macabeo (the Viura of Rioja) is admirably balanced and apt for maturing.

Catalonia shares the best red grapes of the rest of Spain, above all the Tempranillo (here called Ull de Llebre), the Garnacha Tinta and the deep and tannic Monastrell. The Cariñena (alias Carignan) is no more distinguished here than elsewhere.

Seven zones in Catalonia now have *Denominación de Origen* status. They are:

Alella

A coastal valley just north of Barcelona, now reduced to less than 1,000 acres of vines by urban sprawl. Almost all its many small growers take their grapes to the Alella cooperative.

Its best wine is a mildly fruity semi-sweet white made from the fruit of the southern slopes. Also good are its dry whites, which are clean and acidic. The red is passable.

Ampurdán – Costa Brava

The northernmost D.O. centred round Perelada in the province of Gerona, behind the cliffs and beaches of the Costa Brava. The 6,500 acres produced mainly rosé, recently some *primeur*-style red called Vi Novell, and adequate whites, some made sparkling but without the quality of the best Penedès wines.

Costers del Segre

This is the most recent of the Catalonian D.O.s, ratified in 1988, really due to the influence of a single bodega, Finca Raimat (owned by Codorníu). The D.O. is in the rugged, fertile western region of Lleida (Lérida), and is made up of the four geographically disparate sub-zones of Raimat, Artesa, Valls de Riu Corb and Les Garrigues. Grape varieties are mainly traditional, but Cabernet Sauvignon, Merlot and Chardonnay are also to be found. Most of the vineyards are cooperative-owned and devoted to producing the white wine traditional to the area, though modern methods and technological innovations are being introduced. Wines are of varying quality, with Raimat far in the lead.

Penedès

The biggest D.O. of Catalonia ranges from the coast at Sitges back into 2,000-foot limestone hills. Its centres are Vilafranca de Penedès, best known for its table-wine bodegas (among them Torres), and San Sadurní d'Anoia, 20 miles west of Barcelona, the capital of Spanish sparkling wine and headquarters of the vast firm of Cordorníu.

The table wines of Penedès have been revolutionized in the last 20 years and now rival Rioja. The reds are generally darker in colour and fruitier than Riojas, lacking the delicacy and refinement of Rioja at its best, but adding a concentration that Rioja normally lacks. Exceptional wines, especially those with a proportion of Cabernet, reach the best international standards. Modern methods have brought the white wines under total control. There is now a benchmark dry fruity Catalan white, highly satisfactory if not exactly exciting. Unlike the best Rioja whites it does not (at least to my taste) take kindly to ageing in oak. Possibly less concentrated fruit, partly the result of bigger crops, is to blame.

Priorato

The long viticultural course of the river Ebro, starting near Haro in the Rioja Alta, might be said to end without shame in the western hills of Tarragona with this memorable wine, whose true quality is still waiting to be discovered. Priorato is a D.O. within the much greater *denominación* of Tarragona, applying to some 4,600 acres of steep volcanic hillside vines around the little Ebro tributary the Montsant. The fame of Priorato lies in the almost blackness of its wine, a brew of Garnacha and Cariñena that reaches 16 (sometimes even 18) degrees alcohol, with the colour of crushed blackberries and something of their flavour. There is also amber-white Priorato deliberately oxidized to a *rancio* flavour.

Tarragona

The D.O. of Tarragona has almost the same vineyard area as Penedès spread over a wider region. The table wines are normally of blending quality without the extra distinction of Priorato. Its finest products are fortified dessert wines (*see* De Muller under Producers). But the great bulk of Tarragona's exports are of a more humble nature.

Terra Alta

A new D.O. continuing south from that of Tarragona beyond the river Ebro. Mora on the Ebro and Gandesa are the chief centres for the 22,000 acres of vines in the hills that rise to the mountainous province of Teruel. The wine is potent, vigorous and unpretentious, much used, like Tarragona, for blending.

Conca de Barberá

Declared a D.O.P. (provisional D.O.) in 1972, and since then the subject of continuing debate as to its status – still, in fact, provisional. Situated in the hills inland from Penedès, with 25,000 acres largely planted in white grapes for the Penedès sparkling-wine industry. It is to these cooler hills that the Torres company has looked for new sites for classic French grapes.

Cava

Whilst technically a D.O., this is not actually a geograpical region. *Cava* is the official term for champagne-method sparkling wine, and is produced predominantly in Penedès, though there are a few producers elsewhere in Spain.

It may have been characteristic leaness of body of Catalan white wine that inspired the creation of *cava*. Certainly the Xarel-lo, Parellada and Viura (locally called Macabeo) produce high-acid musts of only slight flavour; ideal base material: the flavour of champagne yeast comes through distinctly with its richness and softness. Wines that were stored in wooden vats (some still are) also picked up a very faint tarry taste which added character. Chardonnay is increasingly used both in blends and in premium 'varietal' *cavas*.

The *cavas* of Penedès today range from the extremely deft and delicate to the fat and clumsy. The best can certainly be counted among the world's finest sparkling wines. It is only in the inevitable comparison with champagne that they lose. Where champagne finally triumphs is the vigour of the flavours that it assembles so harmoniously.

CATALAN PRODUCERS

Cavas del Ampurdán

Perelada, Gerona. D.O. Ampurdán-Costa Brava.
Founded in 1925, this is the sister company of Castillo de Perelada, producing very pleasant still red, white and rosé. They buy in all their grapes. The aged reds Tinto Cazador and Reserva Don Miguel are the top wines. 'Pescador' is a refreshing half-sparkling white, very popular in restaurants. Sparkling wines are bulk produced by the *cuve close* method. The company was the defendant in a famous London court case in 1960 when the Champagne authorities succeeded in preventing it from using the term Spanish Champagne.

Masía Bach

Sant Esteve Sesrovires, Barcelona.
Masía means farm. Bach was the name of 2 bachelor brothers who in 1920 used a fortune made by clothing soldiers to build a Florentine folly in Penedès, with garages for 40 cars and a winery which grew in reputation and size until its 1,000 metres of cellars held 8,500 oak casks. It was bought by Codorníu (q.v.) in 1975, but continues to make the house speciality, an oak-flavoured sweet white called Extrísimo Bach, but has added high-quality dry white and a fine light red to the range.

René Barbier

Ctra. S. Quintin km 5, San Sadurní d'Anoia 08770, Barcelona.
An old-established bodega now owned by Freixnet. Its wines are made in the cellars of Segura Viudas (q.v.). Kraliner is the fresh dry white. Reds are made fruity for everyday and oak-aged for Sundays. Sales are about 800,000 cases, almost half of which are exported.

Castell del Remey

Penelles, Lleida (Lerida).
A long-established firm on the inland fringes of Catalonia. Its vineyards include Cabernet Sauvignon and Sémillon and its wines have good reputation.

Bodegas José L. Ferrer

C. Conquistador 75, 07350 Binisalem, Majorca.
The one distinguished bodega of the Balearic islands, founded by Señor Ferrer in 1931 and now owned by the firm Franco Roja S.A. The 165 acres of vineyards are situated in the centre of the island. The local Manto Negro grape makes lively reds. Autentico is the young Ferrer wine. *Reservas* can be extremely good. There is also a dry Blanc de Blancs.

THE TORRES FAMILY

No single family of wine makers has made such an impact on the Spanish scene during the last decade as Miguel Torres Carbó and his son Miguel A. Torres Riera. In 1970 Catalonia was known only for blending wines and, within Spain, for its excellent sparkling *cavas*. Within 10 years the Torres Gran Coronas was being compared with Château Latour and the family, all deeply and enthusiastically involved, to the legendary Mondavis of Calfornia.

The Torres principle is to make uninhibited and innovative use of the wide range of growing conditions offered by the Catalonian coast and the mountains behind. Their base at Vilafranca del Penedès is the traditional centre of the industry, but higher altitudes have provided slower ripening and better conditions for trial lots of French grapes. They have not abandoned the regional varieties but rather improved their performance with careful growing and fermentation, modified the sometimes excessive local use of oak ageing, and when necessary added a seasoning of Cabernet or Chardonnay. The 1980s have also seen the Torres family move into the lead in their new Chilean estates (*see* Chile).

Torres marketing is done with the same uninhibited perfectionism. Miguel's daughter Marimar has demonstrated that Catalonia has nothing to learn from Madison Avenue. To create in 20 years a big-volume brand which is synonymous with quality, in the intensively competitive world of modern wine, is a tough assignment.

J. Friexedas Bové
Avda. Barcelona 87–89, 08720 Vilafranca del Penedès, Barcelona.

A substantial bodega founded in 1897, owning 200 acres but buying the majority of its grapes for rather good sparkling wine and the Santa Marta range of Penedès table wines.

Jean León
Torrelavid, Barcelona.

A California transplant. León is the owner of La Scala Restaurant, Los Angeles. In 1964 he started to plant what is now 150 acres of Cabernet and Chardonnay in Penedès. The wines are first-rate, and excellent value. 60% of the 10,000 cases of Cabernet and 2,000 of Chardonnay are sold abroad.

Marqués de Monistrol
San Sadurní d'Anoia, Barcelona.

A family firm with 740 acres of vines making sparkling wines since 1882, recently bought by Martini & Rossi. Since 1974 they have added still wines, including an attractively lively 'Vin Natur Blanc de Blanc' and traditional-style red reservas, long-aged in oak and bottle.

De Muller
Real 38, 43004 Tarragona.

The great name in the classic tradition of sweet Tarragona wines. A family firm founded in 1851, now a limited company directed by the present Marqués de Muller y de Abadal, still in its old bodegas by the harbour with a vast capacity of oak storage. The pride of the house is its altar wines, supplied to (among others) the Vatican, and its velvety *solera*-aged Moscatel, Pajarete and other dessert wines. The firm has a Priorato bodega at Scala Dei, producing both the massive red of the area and a *solera*-aged dry apéritif, Priorato Rancio Dom Juan Fort. Standard-quality table wines are called Solimar.

Raïmat
Segrià, Lleida (Lérida).

The Raventós family of Cordoníu has replanted the vineyards of the Castle of Raimat, in the arid hill-region of Lleida (Lérida), on a grand (1,700-acre) scale, and reopened a magnificent bodega built early in the century and subsequently abandoned. Cabernet Sauvignon, Merlot and Chardonnay are both blended with native grapes and made 'straight'. The resulting wines are some of the most exciting in Spain.

Cellers de Scala Dei
43379 Scala Dei, Tarragona.

Scala Dei was a great Carthusian monastery, now in ruins. The small modern bodega is in an old stone building nearby, making high-quality oak-aged Priorato, deep, dark, strong (14.5°) but balanced with rich soft-fruit flavours. The labels include Cartoixa Scala Dei, a *Gran Reserva* made of 100% Garnacha Negra.

Viñedos Torres
Vilafranca de Penedès, Tarragona.

An old family company (founded 1870) which has changed the wine map of Spain in the last 20 years, putting Catalonia on a par with Rioja as a producer of really high-quality table wines. The family has 2,000 acres of vineyards, supplying 50% of their needs, and now planted with Chardonnay, Gewürztraminer, Riesling, Sauvignon Blanc, Cabernet Sauvignon, Merlot and Pinot Noir as well as the traditional Penedès varieties. White wines are cold-fermented, reds aged in oak for a mere 18 months, French style, then in bottle. Viña Sol is a fresh Parellada white; Gran Viña Sol a blend with Chardonnay. Green Label is Parellada and Sauvignon Blanc with a little oak age. Of the reds Tres Torres is a full-bodied blend of Garnacha and Cariñena (Carignan), Gran Sangre de Toro an older *reserva* of the same, Coronas either Monastrell or Ull de Llebra (Tempranillo), Gran Coronas Reserva, Tempranillo with some Cabernet Sauvignon. Gran Magdala is Pinot Noir, Viña Las Torres a Merlot, and Gran Coronas Black Label, the top wine, is a Cabernet Sauvignon. Other wines include a semi-sweet Muscat/Gewürztraminer blend, Esmeralda, a Chardonnay, Milmanda, and a successful Riesling, Waltraud. Total sales average well over a million cases per year, 40% of which are exported. (*See* opposite page.)

Bodega Cooperativa Alella Vinícola
Rbla. Angel Guimerà 62, 08328 Alella, Barcelona.
The long-established (1906) cooperative of the dwindling Alella region, which is suffering building blight as

Barcelona pushes north. There are 150-odd members. Its wines, in hock bottles, are labelled Marfil ('Ivory'). The white *semisecco* is pleasant enough; the dry rather dull.

Cooperativa Argicola de Gandesa
Gandesa, Tarragona.
A old-established (1919) coop with 135 members now in the recent D.O. Terra Alta. Grandesa Blanc Gran Reserva is its most remarkable wine.

Cooperativa de Mollet de Perelada
Perelada, Gerona.
A considerable coop with a French-trained wine maker specializing in *primeur* red, white and rosé called Vi Novell – the red modelled on Beaujolais Nouveau. Their Garnacha Blanca dessert white is also attractive and their sparkling wine worth trying.

Union Agraria Cooperativa
Reus, Tarragona.
A federation of all 180 cooperatives in Tarragona, founded in 1962. Tarragona Union and Yelmo are their popular labels but most wine is sold in bulk. The best are *reservas* from the Cooperativa de Gratallops.

OTHER CATALAN PRODUCERS

Alta Alella
Alella, Barcelona. A newcomer causing comment with a good fruity dry white.
Aquila Rossa
Vilafranca del Penedès, Barcelona. A century-old bodega known for its Montgros Penedès table wines and vermouths.
José Lopez Bertran y Cia
Tarragona. A long-established family business supplying such everyday wines as Vinate, Don Bertran and Corrida.

Bodegas Bosch-Guell
Vilafranca de Penedès, Barcelona. A family company founded in 1886, using the name Rómulo for a range of sound Penedès wines.
La Vinicola Iberica
Tarragona. A large old-established bodega in the bulk business.
Bodegas Pinord
Vilafranca de Penedès, Barcelona. A family company with a range of labels: Chatel, Chateldon, Reynal and others.

Bodegas Robert
Sitges, Barcelona. A small company making the (now rare) sweet white Sitges, from Moscatel and Malvasia.
Pedro Rovira
Mora la Nova, Tarragona. An old family firm producing *solera*-aged dessert Tarragona, 'Cream Solera' and 'Dry Solera', as well as everyday wines.
Vinos Jaime Serra
Alella, Barcelona. A small private bodega: brand name 'Alellasol'.

CAVA PRODUCERS

Conde de Caralt
Ctra. S. Quintin km 5, San Sadurní d'Anoia 08770, Barcelona.
A famous old sparkling-wine bodega, now part of the Freixenet group and in the same cellars as Segura Viudas and René Barbier (qq.v.). The name now appears on a range of still wines, including delicate red *reservas*. About 200,000 cases are sold, mainly in the domestic market.

Castillo de Perelada
Perelada, Gerona.
A celebrated *cava* concern in a picturesque castle dating back to the 14th century, now housing a fine library, collections of glass and ceramics and a wine museum – and a casino. Half the grapes come from the firm's vineyards. The best wine, Gran Claustro, is one of Catalonia's most satisfying *cavas*. Others are less notable. A sister company, Cavas del Ampurdán, produces the cheap and cheerful *cuve close* sparkling Perelada.

Codorníu
San Sadurní d'Anoia, Barcelona.
The first Spanish firm to use the champagne method and now the second biggest sparkling-wine house in the world. The Raventós family has made wine in Penedès

since the 16th century. In 1872 Don José returned from Champagne to imitate its methods. The establishment is now monumental, its vast *fin-de-siècle* buildings and miles of cellars, lie in a green park with splendid cedars. They include a considerable wine museum and attract enormous numbers of visitors. A winery has recently been opened in Mexico.

Most of the grapes are bought from 350 local growers, for total sales of some 3m. cases. The wines range from simple and fruity to highly refined – the apogee being the vintage Non Plus Ultra and Gran Codorníu with longer age in bottle; and a 'straight' Chardonnay. Codorníu also owns the Raïmat and Masía Bach bodegas (*see* Catalonia).

Freixenet
C. Jojan Sala, 2 San Sadurní d'Anoia 08770, Barcelona.
The biggest Spanish *cava* house and now the biggest sparkling-wine producer in the world, overtaking the giant Codorníu. Founded by the Bosch family in 1915. The top Friexenet wines are special vintage releases. Brut Barroco and Brut Nature are the best standard lines; Cordon Negro is the best seller. Carta Nevada is a cheaper brand, and a Brut Rosé is also made. Sales total almost 5 million cases, half being exports. Freixenet also owns 50%

of the big *cuve close* sparkling-wine firm L'Aixertell. Its partner is Savin.

Cavas Mascaró

C. Casal 9, Vilafranca del Penedès, Barcelona.

An old family bodega with 170 acres, respected for its *cava* sparkling wines and fine brandy. They have recently acquired the Compañía Vinicola del Penedés, dedicated to making still wines, and a barrel-matured Cabernet Sauvignon is planned for the future.

Segura Viudas

Ctra. S. Quintin km 5, San Sadurní d'Anoia 08770, Barcelona.

The 3 *cava* companies owned by Freixenet all shelter in the same cellars. Segura Viudas is the prestige marque, made in a modern winery surrounded by a 556-acre vineyard that supplies part of its needs. Its best wine, Reserva Heredad, a very delicate production, comes in a horrifically vulgar bottle with a sort of built-in silvery coaster and other distractions. Half of its sales of 360,000 cases are to the export market.

OTHER CAVA PRODUCERS

Gonzales y Dubosc

The sparkling-wine subsidiary of Gonzales Byass (*see* Sherry) now with its own winery.

Cavas Hill

Moja, Vilafranca del Penedès. The English Hill family arrived in Penedès in 1660. In 1884 Don José Hill Ros established this commercial bodega, recently expanded, which now produces both *cava* and still wines. Labels include Blanc Brut dry white and Gran Toc red *reserva*.

Juvé y Camps

San Sadurní d'Anoia, Barcelona. Sizeable family firm making superior and expensive *cava* from grapes grown in its own 920 acres of vineyard and from free-run juice; 40% of its grapes are now bought in from carefully-selected growers. Its Reserva, Reserva de la Familia and Gran Cru are available only in the best shops and restaurants – in the U.K. at Harrods. Some still wines are also produced.

Antonio Mestres Sagues

San Sadurní d'Anoia, Barcelona. A particularly good small family-owned *cava* house founded in 1312.
See also:
Cavas del Ampurdán
J. Freixedas Bové
Marqués de Monistrol
Cooperativa de Mollet de Perelada

CENTRAL SPAIN

By far the greatest concentration of vineyards in Spain lies south and southeast of Madrid in a great block that reaches the Mediterranean at Valencia in the north and Alicante in the south. This central band, with scattered outposts farther west towards Portugal in Extremadura, contained no great names, no lordly estates, no pockets of perfectionism. Its wines combined various degrees of strength with various degrees of dullness – but in the main a generous helping of body. The last ten years have seen changes. Spain's membership of the EEC has exposed the traditional cooperative producers of the region to the realities of competition. Modern market forces – the ever-more-stringent quality demands of northern European customers – have prompted producers to invest in modern technology. Central Spain, like California's Central Valley, has a climate of extremes, but predictable extremes. This allows oenologists to 'design' wines by regulating picking dates and controlling fermentation.

While large-scale cooperatives still make much of the wine, estates and smaller bodegas are emerging. The Marqués de Griñon's Cabernet Sauvignon from Toledo has made a mark, as have wines from Bodegas Saviron and Vinícola de Castilla in La Mancha. Experimental plantings are introducing French grapes; unsuspected flavours being coaxed by skilled wine makers from local varieties.

Central Spain has a long road ahead of it, but it is no longer an unrelieved ocean of mediocrity.

Tierra de Barros, in the province Badajoz, though producing some of the best wine from Extremadura, was never confirmed as a D.O. Its 100,000-odd acres are largely planted with a common white grape, the Cayetana, giving dry low-acid but high-strength wines – the curse of Spain, in fact. Its rarer red wines, however, have some merit; particularly those of Salvatierra de Barros on the Portuguese border, and the eccentric Montánchez, from the northern province of Cáceres, which grows a *flor* yeast like sherry. The same is true of the white of Cañamero.

Toledo province, southwest of Madrid, contains the D.O. of Méntrida, an 80,000-acre spread of Garnacha vines supplying strong red wine.

By far the biggest wine region in the whole of Spain, demarcated or not, is La Mancha, the dreary plain of Don Quixote. It has no less than 1.2 million acres under vine, almost all of a white variety called Airén. The best that could be said of most Airén wine was that it had no flavour beyond that of its 13-14° of alcohol, but some producers have been coaxing agreeable flavours from it by careful wine-making.

The one superior enclave of La Mancha is the D.O. Valdepeñas, 100 miles south of Madrid, where the tradition is to blend the Airén white with a small measure of dark red, made of Tempranillo (here called Cencibel) and Garnacha. So dark is the red that a mere 10 per cent of it makes the wine – known as *aloque* – a *clarete* in colour, though it remains a soft rather spineless wine, low in acid and tannin. The old method is fermentation in the tall clay *tinajas*, obviously descended from Roman or earlier vessels. Modern methods have shown clearly how much better the wine can be. Such producers as Los Llanos and Felix Solin now cool-ferment and oakage their wines with results worthy of the better parts of northern Spain.

The sorry tale continues with the D.O. of Manchuela, east of La Mancha and making both white and red wine on its 20,000 acres.

The smaller D.O. of Almansa around Albacete concludes the toll of the Castilian plain. Its 26,000 acres are planted in dark grapes.

The term Levante embrace five D.O.s of only very moderate interest at present, but some considerable potential as modern methods creep in. To the north on the coast is Valencia (and what was formerly called Cheste), liberal producers of alcoholic white wine and to a lesser degree red. Inland from Valencia lies Utiel-Requena, a hill region of black grapes (the principal one, the Bobal, as black as night) used expressly for colouring wine. The local technique is to ferment each batch of wine with a double ration of skins to extract the maximum colour and tannin: a brew called *vino de doble pasta*. Its by-product, the lightly crushed juice with barely any 'skin contact' or colour, surplus to the double brew, makes the second speciality of the region, a racy pale rosé more to the modern taste.

The D.O. Alicante covers both coastal vineyards producing sweet Moscatel and hill vineyards for red wines, *vino de doble pasta* and rosés. A little local white wine is (relatively) highly prized.

Behind Alicante in the province of Murcia there are two *denominaciós*, Yecla and Jumilla, whose respective cooperatives are struggling with their inky material to teach it modern manners. So far Jumilla seems to be marginally the more advanced of the two, with some wines showing surprising potential to age in bottle.

CENTRAL SPAIN PRODUCERS

Fermin Ayuso Roig
Villarobleda, Albacete. A family concern in Manchuela. Other labels are Armino and Estola.
Bodegas Bleda
Jumilla (Murcia). The son of the founder (in 1935) still runs this pioneer house for Jumilla wine. He matures his powerful reds, Castillo de Jumilla and Oro de Ley, in oak casks.
Casa de Calderón
Requena, Valencia. A small family vineyard and bodega making some of the best Requena. Their *generoso* has some of the flesh and grip of port.
Bodegas Delgado Camara
Valdepeñas. Traditional bodega which wins praise for its Marchante reds.
Bodegas Miguel Carrión
Alpera, Almansa. The best producer of the D.O. Almansa to the east of La Mancha. A small company with a good soft strong Tinto Selecto, aged in oak.
Bodegas Cevisur
Tierra de Barros, Almendralejo, Badajoz. A family concern bottling Tierra de Barros white, as Viña Extremeña.
Bodegas Galán
Montánchez, Badajoz. A little family bodega in a village near Mérida. Of interest because it makes a red wine called Trampal, growing *flor* and tasting like sherry. It has a following in Madrid.
Industrias Vinícolas del Oeste
Almendralejo, Badejoz. Best bodega of this region of *consumo* wines, making red and white Lar de Barros, though not from the typical grapes of the area.
Bodegas Los Llanos
Valdepeñas, Cuidad Real. The first of the houses in Valdepeñas to bottle its wines. The oak-aged *reservas* and *gran reservas* are setting new standards for the region. Señorio de Los Llanos Gran Reserva is a fine, aromatic and silky wine by any standards, and the white Armonioso is clean and fruity. Both are bargains.
Marqués de Griñon
Toledo. The recent enterprise of an ambitious landowner, advised by Emile Peynaud of Bordeaux. He is producing an excellent Cabernet Sauvignon here in Garnacha country.
Luis Megia
Valdepeñas. A very modern mass-production wine factory.
Bodegas Murviedro
Valencia. A long-established little bodega exporting above-average wines, including a reasonable white.
H.L. Garcia Poveda
Villena, Alicante. The 2 considerable bodegas of Alicante are both called Poveda. This is in the hills behind the town, family run and making a range of strong red, white and rosé with the names Costa Blanca and Marquesado.
Bodegas Salvador Poveda
Monavar, Alicante. Perhaps the best Alicante bodega, a family business known especially for its rich dessert Fondillon. Other labels for its strapping wines are Doble Capa and Viña Vermeta.
Bodegas Ruiz
Cañamero, Cáceres. Unique bottlers of the roughish sherry-style Cañamero white, made of Palomino grapes and growing *flor* like sherry. It is the house wine of the Parador at Cañamero.
Bodegas Schenk
Valencia. The Spanish division of the biggest Swiss wine company, shipping from the Levante and La Mancha both blended (e.g. the well-known Don Cortez) and individual wines. Schenk's red Los Monteros, made entirely of the dark Monastrell, is one of the best of the region. Also a Valencian sweet Moscatel and a rosé from Utiel-Requena.
Bodegas Señorio del Condestable
Jumilla, Murcia. A member of the big Savin group of wine companies, best known for its red Condestable, a well-made everyday wine, light in colour and flavour but with a fresh almost cherry-like smell and pleasant texture.
Bodegas Felix Solis
Valdepeñas. Large-scale maker of reds and *rosados* with a reputation for oak-aged reds, especially Viña Albali Reserva.
Vinval
Valencia. A big bulk-wine shipping company founded in 1969. Its great

vaulted brick bodega by the harbour handles the products of several producers under the label Torres de Serrano.

Visan
Santa Cruz de Mudela, Valdepeñas, Ciudad Real. Producer of the agreeable Castillo de Mudela and Viña Tito.

Cooperativa del Campo La Daimieleña
Daimieleña, Ciudad Real. One of the principal white wine producers of La Mancha. The brand is Clavileño.

Grupo Sindical de Colonizacion No. 795
Cebrerors, Avila. Producers of a passable if powerful red, El Galayo, in the undemarcated region west of Madrid.

Cooperativa La Invencible
Valdepeñas, Ciudad Real. The best cooperative of the region, making a clean *clarete*.

Cooperativa Nuestro Padre Jesus del Perdon
Manzanares, Ciudad Real. A large cooperative known particularly for its dry white. The brand name is Yuntero.

Cooperativa La Purisima
Yecla, Murcia. The major producer of Yecla wine. The huge bodega makes efforts to please the educated palate with wines of moderate strength (e.g. Viña Montana) but the result tends to mingle overripe and underripe flavours in rather thin wine.

Cooperativa de San Isidro
Jumilla, Murcia. The major Jumilla

coop, with 2,000 members. All its wines are strong and heavy. Rumor is the best known. Some *reservas* are aged in oak (without achieving distinction).

Cooperativa Santa Rita
Fuenterobles, Valencia. A medium-sized modern cooperative turning out concentrated blending wine, *vino de doble pasta*, but also a remarkably fresh pale rosé, indicating what the region is capable of.

Cooperative Virgen de la Viñas
Tomelloso, Ciudad Real. One of the bigger coops, known by its brand name Tomillar and its Reserva de Cencibel.

SOUTHERN SPAIN

The great fame and success of sherry were achieved to some degree at the expense of the other regions of Andalusia. From their long-established trading base, the sherry makers were able to buy the best from their neighbours to add to their own stock. Sherry may be the best *vino generoso* of Andalucia, but it is not the only one. Montilla can compete with very similar wines, and Málaga with alternatives at the sweeter end of the range.

Málaga
Málaga, on the Costa del Sol, is strictly an entrepôt rather than a vineyard centre. The grapes that make its sweet (occasionally dry) brown wines are grown either in the hills 25 miles to the east or the same distance to the north. East are the coastal vineyards of Axarquia, where the grape is the Moscatel. North around Mollina (in fact towards Montilla) it is the Pedro Ximénez. The rules require that all the grapes are brought to Málaga to mature in its bodegas. Various methods are used to sweeten and concentrate the wines, from sunning the grapes to boiling down the must to *arrope*, as in Jerez. The styles of the finished wine range from a dry white of Pedro Ximénez not unlike a Montilla *amontillado* to the common dark and sticky *dulce color*, thickly laced with *arrope*. The finest quality, comparable in its origins to the *essencia* of Tokay, is the *lagrima*, the 'tears' of uncrushed grapes. The difference is that noble rot concentrates Tokay; in Málaga it is the sun. Other Málagas are Pajarete, a dark semi-sweet apéritif style, the paler semi-*dulce* and the richly aromatic Moscatel. The finer wines are made in a *solera* system like sherry, with younger wine refreshing older. A great rarity, a century-old vintage Málaga from the Duke of Wellington's estate, bottled in 1875, was a superlative, delicate, aromatic and still-sweet dessert wine in 1988.

Montilla-Moriles
Montilla's wines are close enough to sherry to be easily confused with (or passed off as) its rivals. The soil is the same *albariza* but the climate is harsher and hotter and the Pedro Ximénez, grown here in preference to the Palomino, yields smaller crops, producing wines of a higher degree and slightly lower acidity. The wines are fermented in tall clay *tinajas*, like giant amphoras, and rapidly develop the same *flor* yeast as sherry. They fall into the same classifications: *fino, oloroso* or *palo cortado* – the *finos* from the first light pressing. With age *fino* becomes *amontillado*, 'in the style of Montilla'. Unfortunately, however, the sherry shippers have laid legal claim in Britain (the biggest export market for Montilla) to the classic terms. Instead of a Montilla *fino, amontillado* or *oloroso*, a true and fair description, the label must use 'dry', 'medium' or 'cream'.

Montilla has much to recommend it as an alternative to sherry. Its *finos* in particular have a distinctive dry softness of style, with less 'attack' but no less freshness. A cool bottle disappears with gratifying speed as a partner to *hors d'oeuvre*.

Last of the Andalusian *denominaciones*, and most deeply in the shadow of Jerez, is the coastal region of Huelva near the Portugese border. Huelva (known in Chaucer's time as 'Lepe') has exported its strong white wines for 1,000 years. The commercial power of Jerez has effectively kept it in obscurity. Until the 1960s its wine was blended and shipped as sherry. Now that it has to compete with its old paymaster times are not easy and the region is increasingly making light white wines.

Alvear
Maria Auxiliadora 1, Montilla, Córdoba.

An indpendent firm founded by the Alvear family in 1729. Today it is jointly owned and managed by Álvaro de Alvear and his cousin Fernández. They have 308 acres under vine in Montilla-Moriles, much of it in the superior Sierra district, and 17,000 butts of maturing wine in their bodegas. Fermentation in *tinajas* and ageing through the *solera* system are carried out according to the traditions of Montilla, but bottling is done with very modern equipment, producing wines of high quality. Fino CB is their biggest seller and is No. 3 *fino* (behind 2 sherries) in volume terms in Spain. Festival is a slightly fuller *fino* and other names and styles include Marqués de la Sierra, Carlos VII, Pelayo, Asuncion and the *dulce* Pedro Ximénez 1830.

Scholtz Hermanos
Málaga.

The leading bodega in Málaga, founded in 1807 and owned for many years by the German family whose name it bears (though it is now Spanish owned). The wines are made at Mollina in the hills north of Málaga, but matured (as the Consejo requires) in the city, in a modern plant that produces some 220,000 cases a year. Half is exported. The company's most famous wine is Solera Scholtz 1885. It is a light brown dessert wine of 18°, forming a slight 'crust' in its bottle, neither quite like an *oloroso* nor a tawny port, pungent and long-flavoured, starting sweet and finishing dry. I find it slightly more at home before a meal than after one. There are a score of other Scholtz brands of similar quality from dry to sweet; the driest Seco Añejo 10 years old, the sweetest *lagrima* 10 years old.

Hijos de Antonio Barceló
A family run firm founded in 1876, now a major exporter, also branching out into Rioja and Rueda in the north of Spain. The brand name is Bacarles, covering a wide range of typical Málaga styles, including old Moscatel and a very sweet Pedro Ximénez, Gran Málaga Solera Vieja.

Carbonell y Cia
Córdoba. A substantial Montilla producer, equally well known for its olive oil. The bodegas are in the Moorish city of Córdoba. Some fine old *soleras* produce 3 *finos*, Moriles, Serranio and Monte Corto. Moriles Superior is a *fino amontillado* (used for once in the literal sense). Flor de Montilla is an *amontillado pasado*, an older and nuttier wine. 'Nectar' is a fair description of both the *oloroso* and the dark Pedro Ximénez.

Gracia Hermanos
Montilla, Córdoba. A family-run bodega with high standards. Their *fino*, Kiki, is a typically light and refreshing one.

Larios
Málaga. Better known for its gin in Spain, but a Málaga bodega with an excellent sweet Moscatel, Colmenares.

Bodegas Mazaga
Lanzarote, Canary Islands. The one serious bodega in the Canaries, once famous for 'sack'. Its Malvasia Seco of white Malvasia grapes is well made, aged briefly in oak and longer in bottle, in cellars cut in the lava rock. A pleasant apéritif wine.

Bodegas Monte Cristo
Montilla, Córdoba. Large exporters of Montilla, now part of the Rumasa group. They have 60% of exports to the UK, Montilla's biggest export market.

Bodegas Perez Barquero
Montilla, Córdoba. Another Rumasa company. Brand name: Gran Barquero.

Perez Teixera
Málaga. A Málaga bodega making a true *lagrima* wine from the 'tears' of the uncrushed overripe grapes.

Bodegas Miguel Salas Acosta
Bollullos del Condado, Huelva. A family-run company known for above-average sherry-style Huelva wines.

Hijos de Francisco Vallejo
Bollulos del Condado, Huelva. A Huelvan family bodega with good sherry-style wines.

Bodega Cooperativa Vinícola del Condado
Boilullos del Condado, Huelva. The main cooperative of Huelva, responsible for large quantities of brandy, some table wines and some good *solera*-aged sherry-style *generosos*.

The solera system
A *solera* is the bodega's way of achieving complete continuity in its essential stock-in-trade: a range of wines of distinctive character. It is a 'fractional blending' system, in which wine is drawn for use from the oldest of a series of butts, which is then topped up from the next oldest, and so on down to young wine in the youngest *criadera* in the series, which in turn is supplied with young sherry as close in character to its elders as possible. The effect of withdrawing and replacing a portion (normally about a third) of a butt at a time is that each addition rapidly takes on the character of the older wine to which it is added. An incalculable fraction of the oldest wine in the *solera* always remains in the final butt (or rather butts, for the operation is on a big scale, and each stage may involve 50 butts). At the same time, so long as the *solera* is operating, the average age of the wine at every stage (except the new input) is getting gradually greater; thus the individuality of the *solera* more pronounced. Certain famous *soleras* in Jerez, those that produce Tio Pepe, for instance, or San Patricio, were started over a century ago.

Here the word 'produce', however, is misleading. It is more accurate to say 'give character to'. For *solera* wine is rarely bottled 'straight'.

SHERRY

Sampling sherry

Sherry, like many Mediterranean wines, was first appreciated and shipped to the countries of northern Europe for its strength, its sweetness and its durability – all qualities that made it a radically different commodity from medieval claret. By Shakespeare's day, while spirits were still unknown, sack (as it was then called) was hugely popular as the strongest drink available. The warming effect of a 'cup of sack', at perhaps 17 per cent alcohol, was the addiction not just of Falstaff but of very taverngoer. 'Sack' came from Málaga, the Canary Islands, and even from Greece and Cyprus. But the prince of sacks was 'sherris', named for the Andalucian town of Jerez de la Frontera.

Jerez has had an international trading community since the Middle Ages. Until the rise of Rioja it was unique in Spain for its huge bodegas full of stock worth millions. The refinement of its wine from a coarse product, shipped without ageing, to the modern elaborate range of styles began in the eighteenth century. Like champagne (which it resembles in more ways than one) it flowered with the wealth and technology of the nineteenth.

What its makers have done is to push the natural adaptability of a strong but not otherwise extraordinary, indeed rather flat and neutral, white wine to the limit. They have exploited its potential for barrel-ageing in contact with oxygen – the potentially disastrous oxidation – to produce flavours as different in their way as a lemon and a date. And they have perfected the art of blending from the wide spectrum in their paintbox to produce every conceivable nuance inbetween – and to produce it unchanging year after year.

The making of sherry today, folklore apart, differs little from the making of any white wine. A fairly light wine is rapidly pressed and fermented. Its acidity is adjusted upwards, traditionally by adding gypsum or plaster. It is traditionally fermented in new oak barrels (with a violence in the early stages that sends fountains of froth high into the air). Eventually it reaches a natural strength of between 12 and 16 degrees. At this point it is fortified with spirit to adjust the strength to 15 or 18 degrees, depending on its quality and characteristics. This is where sherry's unique ageing process begins.

It is the wayward nature of sherry that different barrels (500-litre 'butts') of wine, even from the same vineyard, can develop in different ways. The essential distinction is between those that develop a vigorous growth of floating yeast, called *flor*, and those that do not. All the young wines are kept in the 'nursery' in butts filled four-fifths full. The finest and most delicate wines, only slightly fortified to maintain their finesse, rapidly develop a creamy scum on the surface, which thickens in spring to a layer several inches deep. This singular yeast has the property of protecting the wine from oxidation and at the same time reacting with it to impart subtle hints of maturity. These finest wines, or *finos*, are ready to drink sooner than heavier sherries. They remain pale because oxygen is excluded. They can be perfect at about five years old. But their precise age is irrelevant because, like all sherries, they are blended for continuity in a *solera* (see page 387).

Young wines of a heavier, clumsier and more pungent style grow less *flor*, or none at all. A stronger dose of fortifying spirit discourages any *flor* that may appear. This second broad category of sherry is known, if it shows potential quality, as *oloroso*, if not as *raya*. These wines are barrel-aged without benefit of *flor*, in full contact with the air. Their maturing is therefore an oxidative process, darkening their colour and intensifying their flavour.

A third, eccentric, class of sherry is also found in this early classifying of the crop – one that combines the breadth and depth of a first-class *oloroso* with the fragrance, finesse and 'edge' of a *fino*. This rarity is known as a *palo cortado*.

These three are the raw materials of the bodega – naturally different from birth. It is the bodega's business to rear them so as to accentuate these differences, and to use them in combinations to produce a far wider range of styles. A *fino* which is matured beyond the life span of its *flor* usually begins to deepen in colour and broaden in flavour, shading from straw to amber to (at great age) a rich blackish brown. Every bodega has one or more *soleras* of old *finos* which have been allowed to move through the scale from a fresh *fino*, to a richer, more concentrated *fino-amontillado*, to an intensely nutty and powerful old *amontillado*.

Commercially, however, such true unblended *amontillados* are very rare. In general usage the term has been more or less bastardized to mean any 'medium' sherry, between dry *fino* and creamy old *oloroso* in style but rarely with the quality of either. All sherries in their natural state, maturing in their *soleras*, are bone dry. Unlike port, sherry is never fortified until fermentation is completely over – all sugar used up. Straight unblended sherry is there-fore an ascetic, austere taste, a rarity in commerce. The only exception is *dulce* – concentrated wine used for sweetening blends.

As it ages in the bodega, evaporation of water increases both the alcohol content and the propor-tion of flavouring elements. Very old sherries still on wood often become literally undrinkable in their own right – but priceless in the depth of flavour they can add to a blend. Classic sherry-blending is very much the art of the shipper, but anyone can try it for himself by acquiring, say a bottle of a very old dry sherry such as Domecq's Rio Viejo or Gonzalez Byass's Duque, and simply adding one small glassful of it to a carafe of an ordinary 'medium' sherry. The immediate extra dimension of flavour in the everyday wine is a revelation.

The former custom was for every wine merchant to have his own range of blends made in Jerez to his own specification, and label them with brand names from his own imagination. In practice this meant that there were far too many indistinguishable (and often undistinguished) blended wines on the market. The more rational modern trend is for the shippers in Jerez to promote their own brands. The best of these will be the produce of a single prized *solera*, usually slightly sweetened with special treacly sweetening wine. A touch of near-black but almost tasteless *vino de color* may be needed to adjust the colour. Possibly a little younger wine in the same style will be added to give it freshness.

A common commercial blend, on the other hand, will consist largely of low-value, minimally aged *rayas* or *entre finos* (the term for second-grade wine in the *fino* style). A small proportion of wine from a good *solera* will be added to improve the flavour, then a good deal of sweetening wine to mask the faults of the base material. It is, unfortunately, wines made to this sort of specification that have given sherry the image of a dowdy drink of no style.

The sad result is that the truly great wines of Jerez, wines that can stand comparison in their class with great white burgundy or champagne, are absurdly undervalued. There is no gastronomic justification for the price of Montrachet being five times that of the most brilliant *fino* – nor, at the other end of sherry's virtuoso repertoire, of the greatest *olorosos* selling at a fraction of the price of their equivalent in madeira.

The sherry region

Jerez lies 10 miles inland from the bay of Cádiz in southwest Spain. Its vineyards surround it on all sides, but all the best of them are on outcrops of chalky soil in a series of dune-like waves to the north and west, between the rivers Guadalete and Guadal-quivir. The Guadalquivir, famous as the river of

Seville, from which Columbus set out to discover America and Pizarro to conquer Peru, forms the northern boundary of the sherry region. Its port, Sanlúcar de Barrameda, Jerez and Puerto are the three sherry towns. The land between them is the zone known as Jerez Superior, the heart of the best sherry country.

There are three soil types in the sherry region, but only the intensely white *albariza*, a clay consisting of up to 80 per cent pure chalk, makes the best wine. It has high water-retaining properties that resist summer drought and the desiccating wind, the 'Levante', that blows from Africa. It also reflects sunlight up into the low-trained bush vines, so that the grapes bask in a slow oven as they ripen.

Barro, a brown chalky clay, is more fertile but produces heavier, coarser wine. *Arena*, or sand, is little used now for vineyards at all.

The distinct, low vineyard hills each has a name: Carrascal, Macharnudo, Añina, Balbaina are the most famous of the *pagos*, as they are called, surrounding Jerez in an arc of *albariza* to the north and west. A separate outbreak of excellent soil gives rise to the *pagos* south and east of Sanlúcar, 14 miles from Jerez, of which the best-known name is Miraflores.

The regulations of the Consejo Regulador, the governing body of Jerez, stipulate that every bodega buys a certain proportion of its wine from the Superior vineyards – a rule scarcely necessary today, since 85 per cent of the whole region is Superior: outlying low-quality vineyards have fallen out of use. The present total area of sherry vineyards is 48,360 acres. In 1970 it was 28,652.

Sherry glossary

Almacenista a wholesaler or stockholder of wines for ageing; also used for the individual old unblended wines he sells which are occasionally offered as collectors' items.

Amontillado literally 'a wine in the style of Montilla'. Not at all so in fact, but a well-aged *fino* that has developed a nutty flavour with maturity in oak. Also loosely used for any medium sherry.

Amoroso the name of a vineyard famous for *oloroso* sherry. Literally 'amorous': not a bad description of the sweet *oloroso* sold under the name.

Añada the wine of one year, kept as such in a butt until (or instead of) becoming part of a *solera*.

Arroba the working measure in a sherry bodega. The standard 500-litre butt holds 30 *arrobas*.

Arrope a *vino de color*: wine reduced by boiling to one fifth of its original volume, intensely sweet and treacly black, used only for colouring and sweetening blends. *Sancocho* is similar.

Bristol the historic centre of the sherry trade in Britain, a name much used on labels to imply quality, but not a reference to any particular style of wine.

Brown sherry sweet sherry blended from *olorosos* and *rayas* to be sweeter and darker than a 'cream'.

Cream sherry a blend of sweetened *olorosos*, with or without *vino de color*. Harvey's Bristol Cream was the original. Croft's introduced the idea of a pale (uncoloured) 'cream' in the 1970s.

Dulce apagado intensely sweet wine made by stopping the fermentation of must by adding brandy. Used only for sweetening 'medium' sherries.

Dulce de almibar a mixture of young wine and invert sugar used for sweetening pale sherries without darkening them.

Dulce pasa dark sweetening wine made by leaving ordinary sherry grapes in the sun to concentrate the sugar, then stopping their fermenting must with brandy. Used for sweetening good quality 'cream'.

East India now a fanciful name for a sweet, usually Brown, sherry. It derives from the former custom of sending sherry (like madeira) to the Indies and back as ship's ballast to speed its maturity.

Entre fino the classification of a young wine which shows *fino* character but not the required quality for the finest *soleras*.

Fino the lightest, most delicate, and literally finest of sherries. It naturally develops a growth of *flor* yeast, which protects its pale colour and intensifies its fresh aroma.

Fino-amontillado a *fino* on the way to maturing as an *amontillado*.

Fino viejo, vijissimo occasionally an old *fino* declines to enter middle age as an *amontillado* and simply intensifies its aristocratic finesse, growing formidably powerful, dusty dry and austere while remaining straw-pale.

Jerez quinado a cordial or apéritif made by mixing quinine with sherry.

Macharnudo the most famous of the *pagos*, vineyard districts, northwest of Jerez; sometimes mentioned on labels.

Manzanilla the speciality of Sanlúcar de Barrameda. Sherries matured in its bodegas by the sea take on a singular sharp and even salty tang that makes them the most appetizing of all. Removed to bodegas elsewhere they revert to normal wines. Most *manzanilla* is drunk as pale and unsweetened *fino*. With age it becomes *pasada*, darker and slightly nutty with an almost buttery richness. Eventually it becomes a deeply nutty *Manzanilla amontillado*; one of the most vivid and intense of all sherries.

Moscatel sweetening wine made of sun-dried Moscatel grapes for giving added sugar and fruity flavour to certain sweet blends.

Oloroso in its natural state, full-bodied dry sherry without the delicacy, fragrance or piquancy of *fino* but with extra richness and depth. It does not develop *flor* to the same extent but picks up colour and oak flavours in the butt. Old unblended *olorosos* are astonishingly dark, pungent and so concentrated that they almost seem to burn your mouth. In practice nearly all *oloroso* is used as the base for sweet sherries, particularly 'creams'.

Palma a classification for a particularly delicate and fragrant fino. Tres Palmas is the brand name of a very fine one.

Palo Cortado an aberrant sherry which shows the good characters of both *amontillado* and *oloroso* at the same time. A highly prized rarity nearly always kept apart and bottled as an unblended *solera* wine with only a little sweetening.

Pata de galina an *oloroso* which in its natural state shows signs of sweetness, derived from glycerine. Occasionally bottled as such, when it is incomparable.

Paxarete an alternative name for *vinos de color*.

Raya the classification for an *oloroso*-type wine of secondary quality; the makeweight in most middle-range blends.

Vino de color colouring wine, e.g. *arrope*.

Vino de pasto 'table wine' light medium-dry sherry of uncertain quality, now rarely seen.

Manuel De Arqueso

PO Box 6, Jerez de la Frontera.

Medium-sized company founded in 1822 by Don Leon de Argueso, from Northern Spain. Good dry *amontillado* and *manzanilla* from a separate bodega in Sanlúcar.

Antonio Barbadillo

Calle Luis de Eguilaz 11, PO Box 25,
Sanlúcar de Barrameda.

The biggest bodega in Sanlúcar with a big stake in the *manzanilla* business and some wonderful old wines. It was founded in 1821 by Don Benigno Barbadillo. 5 generations later, the firm is run by Antonio Barbadillo y Ortiguelo, although Harvey's, which jointly run a vinification centre in the vineyards, have a shareholding. Offices (in the former bishops' palace) and the original bodegas are in the town centre. In the surrounding *albariza* areas of Cádiz, Balbaina, San Julian, Carrascal and Gibaldin, they own 2,000 acres of vines, producing a wide range of *manzanillas* and other sherries: Solear, Eva, Pastora, Tio Rio, Pedro Rodriguez, Principe, La Caridad, Ducado de Sanlúcar and Villareal. Recently they have pioneered with dry white table wines made from Palomino grapes called Castillo de San Diego and Gibalbino.

Hijos de Agustin Blázquez

PO Box 540, Carretera de la Cartuja.

A relatively small high-quality bodega founded in 1795 by the Paul family, now part of the Pedro Domecq group, operated independently under its own name, with 3 vineyards, 2 in the Balbaina district, one in Macharnudo. Stocks are 15,000 butts. Its best-known products are a well-aged *fino*, Carta Blanca, Carta Roja *oloroso* and Felipe II brandy. In smaller quantities, they make a *palo cortado* called Capuchino and a noble old *amontillado*, Carta Oro. They have recently introduced a new range in Spain under the name Balfour. Sales of sherry and brandy go to the Americas, Holland and Italy.

Bobadilla

Ctra Circunvalación, Apartado 217, Jerez de la Frontera.

This large company, which produces brandy as well as sherry, was founded in 1872. The original bodega was part of a monastery in Jerez, though premises are now modern. Wines include Victoria Fino, Alcazar Amontillado and Capitan Oloroso. Stocks are 15,000 butts. The house style is quite dry which makes them more popular in Spain than in the export market. Manuel Fernandez, the other half of the group, exports to Holland and Germany.

John William Burdon

PO Box 6, Puerto de Santa Maria.

Formerly an English-owned bodega founded by John William Burdon, an employee of Duff Gordon (q.v.) who subsequently set up on his own, it was one of the largest bodegas of the middle- to late-19th century and on Burdon's death passed to La Cuesta; it is now owned by Luis Caballero (q.v.). Wines are Burdon Fino, a Puerto style *fino*, Don Luis Amontillado and Heavenly Cream. Wines have improved in recent years.

Luis Caballero

San Francisci 32, Apartado 6, Puerto de Santa Maria.

Founded in the 1830s with a stock of wine from the Dukes of Medina, this is now the sixth-largest firm in Jerez. Still family-run by Don Luis Caballero (the sixth generation), they also make an orange brandy liqueur called Ponche which is the leading brand in Spain. All wines are supplied from their own vineyards; major brands are Burdon and Troubadour of La Cuesta and a range called Benito. Stocks are 17,000 butts. Sound but not outstanding.

Croft Jerez

Rancho Croft, Carretera Madrid, Jerez.

The port shippers (founded 1768) gave their name to the sherry division (formerly Gilbeys) of International Distillers and Vintners in 1970. Rancho Croft is an ambitious development from Gilbeys' simple old bodegas; a huge complex of traditional-style buildings housing the most modern plant and 70,000 butts of sherry. Crofts have planted 865 acres of *albariza* land in Los Tercios and Cuartillos. Market research led them to launch the first pale cream sherry, Croft Original. Croft Particular is a pale *amontillado*, classic medium-dry and Delicado a true *fino*. They also make a *palo cortado* and a brandy called Gourmet. Exports (to 65 countries) are 1.5 m. cases a year.

Diez-Merito

Ctra Nac IV Km 641.750, Jerez de la Frontera.

An amalgamation of bodegas specializing in supplying 'buyers' own brands'. It was founded in France in 1884 as Diez Hermanos and is now controlled by Marcos Eguizábal. The name was changed in 1979 when Diez took over the old house of Merito. Since 1972 expansion has been rapid. Stocks are now 72,000 butts. They have 430 acres of vines in the Jerez Superior area, with a huge new bodega in Jerez and one at Puerto de Santa Maria. Brands include Fino Imperial (a very old *amontillado*), a splendid *oloroso* Victoria Regina and the Diez Hermanos range. After the collapse of Rumasa, Diez-Mérito took over Don Zoilo and Celstino Diez de Morales and now market the very fine 'Don Zoilo' *fino*, *amontillado* and cream.

Pedro Domecq

San Ildefonso 3, Jerez de la Frontera, Cadiz.

Founded 1730. The oldest, largest and one of the most respected shipping houses, founded by Irish and French families and including in its history (as English agent) John Ruskin's father. It owns 3,952 acres of vines and no less than 73 bodegas all over the region. Stocks are 92,000 butts. The present head of the firm, Don José Ignacio Domecq, is recognized world-wide both literally and figuratively as 'the nose' of sherry. The finest wines are the gentle Fino La Ino; Sibarita, an old amontillado, old *oloroso* cross, dating from 1792; Rio Viejo, a dark, rich but bone-dry *oloroso*, Celebration Cream and the luscious Double Century. Domecq also owns La Riva (q.v.).

Duff Gordon

Fernan Caballero 2, El Puerto de Santa Maria.

Founded in 1768 by the British Consul in Cádiz, Sir James Duff, and his nephew Sir William Gordon. It remained in the family for more than a century, before being bought in 1872 by Thomas Osborne, who had been a partner in the firm since 1833. The Osborne company (owners of 618 acres of vines) continue to market the Duff Gordon sherries and brandies for export, but do not sell them in Spain. Their most popular brands are Fino Feria, El Cid *amontillado*, the dry Nina *oloroso*, the fuller Club Dry *oloroso* and Santa Maria cream.

*Don José Ignacio Domecq,
head of the oldest
sherry firm*

Bodegas Jésus Ferris
Avenida San Fernando 118, Rota.

Small firm run from Rota but with a bodega in Puerto de Santa Maria. Owner Don Jésus Ferris Marhuenda has 86 acres and stocks of 8,000 butts. He exports to Europe and the US direct.

Garvey
Bodegas de San Patricio, Divina Pastora, 3, Apartado 12, Jerez de la Frontera.

One of the great bodegas, founded in 1780 in Sanlúcar de Barrameda by an Irishman, William Garvey, who built what for many years remained the grandest bodega in Spain: 558 feet long. A new winery and new maturing bodegas have recently been built on the outskirts of Jerez. Once part of the Rumasa empire, the firm was taken over by the German Coop group in 1985. Garvey's have 740 acres under vine in the *albariza* areas of Maribe, Balbaina, Macharnudo, Carrascal, Montegil and Campix, producing consistently good wines. San Patricio (named after the patron saint of Ireland), a full-flavoured *fino*, is their best-known sherry. Others include Tio Guillermo *amontillado*, Ochavico dry *oloroso*, Long Life medium-dry *oloroso*, La Lidia *manzanilla*, Lanza cream and Bicentenary pale cream. *Fino* accounts for 70% of all production.

Gonzalez Byass
Manuel M. Gonzalez 12, Jerez de la Frontera.

One of the greatest sherry houses, founded in 1835 by Don Antonio Gonzalez y Rodriguez, whose London agent, Robert Blake Byass, became a partner in 1863. The company is still owned and directed entirely by descendants of these two men. They own nearly 15% of the vineyards in the Jerez area and have stocks of 132,000 butts. In addition to the world's biggest-selling *fino*, Tio Pepe, La Concha *amontillado*, Apostoles dry *oloroso*, San Domingo pale cream and Nectar cream are exported throughout the world. There is a range of glorious old sherries including Amontillado Del Duque. They also make very large amounts of brandy (mainly Soberano and Lepanto), and perhaps the greatest of all dessert sherries: Matusalem. Other interests include Bodegas Beronia in Rioja and Gonzalez y Dubosc in Catalonia.

Harvey's of Bristol
John Harvey & Sons (España), Alvar Nuñez 53, Jerez de la Frontera.

The famous Bristol shippers were founded in 1796. In 1822 the first John Harvey joined the firm. In 1968 it was taken over by Allied Breweries, though John Harvey's great-grandson, Michael McWatters, is the present managing director. Another John Harvey, fifth of the name, heads the company's fine-wine business. The firm became famous as blenders of 'Bristol' sweet sherries, above all Bristol Cream, now the world's biggest-selling brand with a reported 20% of the British market and a huge export business. Not until 1970, when they bought McKenzie & Co., did they own their own bodegas or vineyards. Now they have 3,800 acres, all in fine *albariza* land, and stocks of 155,000 butts.

Bristol Cream, once the ultimate luxury sherry, is now merely good. Other brands are Bristol Milk (not sold in the UK), Club Amontillado, Bristol Dry (which is medium) and Luncheon Dry, a dry *fino*. They have recently introduced a mixer sherry called Harvey's II or Tico, and a range called 1796, which includes a *palo cortado*, a dry *oloroso* and dry *amontillado*.

Bodegas Internacionales
PO Box 300, Carr M-Cádiz.

A public company founded in 1974 by Rumasa. Now under new ownership. Said to be the largest bodegas in the world, covering 50,000 square metres and holding stocks of 68,000 butts. These house, in addition to their own Duke of Wellington and B.E.S.T. sherries and Primado, Solaron and Dickens brandies, the wines and *soleras* of the Varela, Bertola and Marqués de Misa companies which were taken over by Rumasa. Vineyards in the Añina district supply a proportion of Bodegas Internacionales' wines.

Emilio Lustau
Plaza del Cubo 4, Jerez de la Frontera.

Founded in 1896, one of the largest independent family-owned producers (with 74 acres and stocks of 20,000 butts) making top-quality sherries under their own and customers' labels. Tomás Abad is a subsidiary company. Their best wines are Dry Lustau *oloroso*, Jerez Lustau *palo cortado* and a selection of rare *almacenista* reserve sherries from small private stockholders. Their newest introduction is a range of Landed Age Rare Sherries of which the Rare Dry *oloroso* and the *amoroso* are particularly fine. One of their two vineyards, Nuestra Señora de la Esperanza in the Carrascal district, was noted by Richard

Ford in his travel journal in 1845, and they have recently built a new bodega here. The original bodegas, just outside the Jerez city walls, include one cellar with a high, vaulted dome, believed to have been the headquarters of the Guard during the Moorish occupation.

Osborne
Calle Fernan Caballero 3, El Puerto de Santa Maria.

A large and expanding, entirely family-owned and run bodega founded in 1772 by Thomas Osborne Mann from Exeter in Devon. The family today is totally Spanish and the title of Conde de Osborne was created by Pope Pius IX. In 1872 Osborne took over Duff Gordon. Today, it is also co-owner of Jonas Torres y Cía (founded in 1980), Osborne de Portugal (founded in 1967) and Osborne de Mexico (founded in 1971), owner of Bodegas Montecillo in Rioja, Coivisa and Osborne Distribuidora. Osborne have 900 acres of vineyards and stocks of 60,000 butts. They are the biggest drinks company in Spain. Among their sherry brands are Quinta *fino*, IORF (or Reserva Familiale), Coquinero *amontillado*, Bailen *oloroso* and Osborne Cream. Their important brandy portfolio includes Veterano, Magno, Independencia and Conde de Osborne.

Palomino y Vergara
Colon 1–25, Jerez de la Frontera.

One of the oldest big bodegas in Jerez, founded in 1765, taken over by Rumasa in 1963, expropriated by the Government in 1983 and now resold to Harvey's, its offices and bodegas (capacity 32,000 butts) in the centre of Jerez are housed in an extraordinary glass-domed building still equipped with the original mahogany and gilt counters. Palomino & Vergara is a name on the domestic market, but is less important in the export field, with no UK distributor at present. Tio Mateo *fino* is their most important sherry. Others include Buleria *amontillado*, Los Flamencos *oloroso* and 1865 Solera cream. Their brandies are also important, especially Fabuloso (3° año) and Eminencia (5° año). The oldest is Gran Reserva.

Zoila Ruiz-Mateos
PO Box 140 La Atalaya, Cervantes 3, Jerez.

Founded in 1857 by Zoilo Ruiz-Mateos and recently run by a descendant of the same name, who was also vice-president of his brother's company Rumasa, the giant concern nationalized in 1983. Zoilo was bought by Diez-Mérito after the demise of Rumasa. The Don Zoilo company has 556 acres of vineyards in the best *albariza* areas of Añina and produces an extremely high-quality (and expensive) Don Zoilo range of *fino*, *amontillado* and cream sherry, and one of Spain's best brandies, Gran Duque de Alba. The bodegas in Jerez contain 200,000 butts of 500 litres each.

Sandeman Hermanos y Cía
Calle Pizarro 10, Jerez.

One of the great port and sherry shippers, founded in London in 1790 by George Sandeman, a Scot from Perth. It now belongs to the Seagram group, but a descendant, David Sandeman, is chairman. After shipping sherries for many years, Sandeman's founded their own bodega and now have 15 vineyards, totalling 1,600 acres, all on *albiriza* soil. Traditional methods produce some fine sherries: Fino Apitiv, Dry Don Amontillado, Armada Cream and a *palo cortado*, Royal Ambrosante. Royal Corregidor and Imperial Corregidor are their rarest.

Williams & Humbert
Nuno de Canas 1, PO Box 23, Jerez.

Founded in 1877 by Alexander Williams. His partner was his brother-in-law, Arthur Humbert. Bought in 1972 by Rumasa, the firm quickly became one of the most important in Jerez and continues to be a major exporter, with markets in North and South America, Europe, Japan and the Far East. Still Government-owned. Vineyards on *albariza* soils in Carrascal, Balbaina and Los Tercios produce good wines. The best known is Dry Sack *amontillado*. Pando is an excellent fresh *fino-amontillado*; other brands are Canasta Cream, Walnut Brown, A Winter's Tale, As You Like It and Cedro.

OTHER SHERRY PRODUCERS

Tomás Abad
Playa del Cubo 4, Jerez. Subsidiary of Emilio Lustau (q.v.), producing a first-rate *fino*, and they have stocks of 2,000 butts.

Herederos de Manuel Baron
Banda Playa 21, PO Box 39, Sanlúcar de Barrameda. A small family firm dating back over 300 years; now comprising Bodegas Tartaneros, Regina, Moninillo, Trabajadero and Carretería, and owning 346 acres of *albariza* vineyards at Viña Atalaya and Martin Miguel. They make a range of sherries under names such as Baron, Atalaya, Pinoviejo, Malva, Lider, Jorge III and Marqués de Casa Trevino.

Bertola
Ca. M. Cádiz, 641–750 Apartado 33, Jerez de la Frontera. Founded in 1911 as the Jerez branch of the port firm of Kopke. It is now owned by Marcos Eguizábal and jointly run with Bodegas Internacionales. Best-known brand is Bertola Cream, and other wines include

a *palo cortado*, an *oloroso* style and a heavy *fino*.

Luis Caballero
Puerto de Santa María. Founded 1830. A family-owned firm amalgamated in 1932 with the famous English house of Burdon and continuing to ship Burdon Fino, Bristol Milk, etc., under the Burdon label, as well as their own *fino* Don Guiso, *fino* Benito and other good-quality wines.

Cuvillo y Cia
Puerto de Santa Maria. Founded 1783. A fine independent bodega of medium size with excellent wines to offer; notably its 'Fino C' Trabajadero dry *oloroso* and a model *palo cortado*.

Delgado Zuleta SA
Carmen 32, Sanlúcar de Barrameda. An independent family firm founded in 1744. Their best-known wine is La Goya, a *manzanilla pasada*. Other wines include a range under the Zuleta name, a *fino* called Don Tomás and also a range

of brandies under the Mateagudo label.

Francisco Garcia de Velasco
Sebastian Elcano 2, Sanlúcar de Barrameda. A realtively small bodega founded in 1803 by Francisco Garcia de Velasco and now owned by Bodegas Barcena. Los 48 *manzanilla* is their most important product, but they make several other sherries under various labels, including El Padre, Los Angeles Diplomatico, Tia Anita and Tres Cañas.

Luis G. Gordon
PO Box 48, Jerez. One of the oldest sherry companies, founded by a Scot, Arthur Gordon, in 1754. Brands include Alexander Gordon, Gordon & Rivero, Marqués de Irun, Doz y Cia. Specialities are Manola *fino* and Royal, an old brandy.

Emilio M. Hidalgo
Clavel 29, PO Box 221, Jerez. A family firm based in the old town of Jerez, now in the fourth generation of the Hidalgo family since it was founded in

1874. They have 346 acres of *albariza* in Añina and Carrascal and have been vinifying their own grapes since 1926. Stocks stand at 8,000 butts. Their principal brands, in addition to the bodega name, are Rodil and Privilegio.

Vinicola Hidalgo y Cia

Banda Playa 24, Sanlúcar de Barrameda. A small bodega founded in 1800 and still owned and run by the Hidalgo family. They have 494 acres of *albariza* vineyards in Balbaina and Miraflores, stock 6,000 butts and sell 30,000 cases a year on the home market. Their principal brands are the fine La Gitana *manzanilla*, Jerez Cortado Hidalgo and Napolean *amontillado*.

Bodegas de los Infantes de Orleans-Borbon

Sanlúcar de Barrameda. Torre Breva, the 543-acre vineyard owned by this company, was turned over to vines in 1886 by Don Antonio de Orleans, Duke of Montpensier, who had until then used it as a shooting estate. Bodegas Infantes was founded much later, in 1943. It now has stocks of 8,000 butts. Their principal sherries are Torre Breva and La Ballena *manzanillas*, Alvaro *fino*, Orleans cream and Fenicio *oloroso*.

Lacave & Cia

Avda A. Alvaro Domecq 9, PO Box 519, Jerez. Founded in Cádiz in 1810; bought and moved to Jerez by Rumasa in 1972. They have 370 acres of *albariza* land in the Jerez Superior area and produce a range of 3 sherries and a brandy under the Lacave name.

B. M. Lagos

Carretera de Sanlúcar, PO Box 440, Jerez. Founded in 1910. From stocks of 5,000 butts they sell 178,000 cases a year; 111,000 of these to Britain. (They have connections with Harvey's.) Their own brands include Señero and Tio Cani *finos*, Las Flores *manzanilla*, Gran Cartel *oloroso* and a range of brandies.

José Medina

Banda Playa 46/50, Sanlúcar de Barrameda. A traditional family firm with 15,000 butts of sherry in its bodegas in Sanlúcar and vineyards in Carrascal.

Rafael O'Neale

Jerez de la Frontera. Founded 1724. The earliest of the several houses founded by Irishmen and still independent. The present director is Señora Casilda O'Neale de la Quintana. The vineyards have been in the female line since 1264. Modest in size but fine in quality. Its labels are Wild Geese, Spanish Arch, Casilda Cream and a good *manzanilla*.

Luis Paez

Jardinillo 2, PO Box 545, Jerez. Family firm with 6,000 butts of stock in Jerez and Sanlúcar, but no vineyards. Brand names are Conqueror, Rey de Oro

Primavera, Verano, Otoño and Invierno.

Hijos de Rainera Pérez Marin, 'La Guita'

Banda Playa 28, Sanlúcar de Barrameda. A small company known for its first-class *manzanillas*, especially La Guita, the name by which the bodega is often known. Other wines include Hermosilla *manzanilla* and Bandera *fino*.

Herederos del Marqués del Rel Tesoro

Calle Pajarete 3, PO Box 27, Jerez. A respected small family firm founded towards the end of the 19th century by the Marqués del Real Tesoro. From fine stocks of 16,000 butts they produce a range of sherries under the bodega name, including the fresh and fragrant Ideal *fino*, and a range under the label Bodegas M. Giles.

La Riva SA

Alvar Nuñez 44, Jerez de la Frontera. An old-established small bodega with some of the finest *soleras* in Jerez, taken over in the 1970s by Pedro Domecq but still operated independently for its lovely *fino* Tres Palmas, *amontillado* Guadalupe and old *olorosos* and *palo cortados* of superlative quality. Vineyards 130 acres and stocks 2,773 butts.

Felix Ruiz y Ruiz

Calle Cristal 4, 6 & 8, Jerez. A small firm founded in 1809; now owning 3 bodegas and selling over 222,000 cases of sherry and brandy each year from stocks of 10,000 butts. They sell 2 ranges of sherries, Don Felix and Ruiz, each with 3 styles (dry, medium and cream) plus brandies of the same names.

Bodegas Sanchez de Alva

Carretera de Arcos Km 2, PO Box 26, Jerez. Founded in 1935 by Manuel Gil Luque and taken over by the Canterero group in 1978, since when turnover has increased considerably, particularly in export. Stocks are now over 10,000 butts, plus a wide range of brandies and liqueurs. Their main sherry names are Deportivo and Alba *finos*, Don Quijote *oloroso* and a range of 5 styles under the Sanchez de Alva label.

Sanchez Romate

Lealas 26–30, 11404 Jerez. A respected small bodega, founded in 1781 by Juan Sanchez de la Torre, a well-known businessman and philanthropist. It remains an independent company owning 200 acres in 4 vineyards. One in Balbaina and 2 in Macharnudo are on *albariza* and the fourth, in the Cuartillo district, is on *barros* soil. Stocks are some 8,000 butts. Brands include Marismeño and Cristal *finos*; Viva la Pepa and Petenera *manzanillas*; NPU (Non Plus Ultra) *amontillado*; Iberia cream and Doña Juana *oloroso*. Cardinal Mendoza brandy (called Cardinal for the USA) is made in limited quantities.

José de Soto

M. A. Jesus Tirado 6, Jerez. Founded towards the end of the 18th century by José de Soto, who acquired Viña Santa Isabel at the same time. They own 6 vineyards covering 370 acres of *albariza* in the finest districts of Balbaina and Macharnudo. Stocks of 10,000 butts go to make Soto and Camper *finos*, Don Jaime and La Uvita *amontillados* and La Espuela *oloroso*. Probably most famous for making the first *ponche* (a sherry-based liqueur) – and still one of the best.

Fernando A. de Terry

Sta. Trinidad 2, Puerto de Santa Maria. Founded 1883. Originally the foundation of an Irish family, now (after Rumasa control) owned by Harvey's. Better known for their Centenario brandy than their sherries. Ultramodern premises house over 50,000 butts. Camborio is their label in Spain. In the UK they supply Marks & Spencer's own-label sherries.

Valdespino SA

Pozodel Olivar 16, PO Box 22, Jerez de la Frontera. Still the property of the Valdespino family. Their Ynocente, named from a single Macharnudo vineyard, is a classic *fino* and Tio Diego one of the driest dark and masculine *amontillados*.

Varela

Ctra Madrid, Cádiz Km 641–750, Jerez. Founded in 1850 by Ramón Jiménez Varela and bought from his descendants by Rumasa in 1960 and since resold to Bodegas Internacionales. The *amontillado* and cream are the best known of the 5 Varela sherries.

Wisdom & Warter Ltd.

Pizarro 7, Jerez. Wisdom and Warter, although apparently a short-cut recipe for bargain sherry, were the two Englishmen who founded the company in 1854. It owns a 173-acre *albariza* vineyard, La Bodogonera, in Los Tercios and has stocks of 20,000 butts. The main brands are Olivar *fino*, Royal Palace *amontillado*, Wisdom's Choice cream, Merecedor *oloroso* and a range under the Wisdom label.

Delgado Zuleta

Carmen 32, Sanlúcar de Barrameda. An independent family firm founded in 1719. Their best-known wine is La Goya, a *manzanilla pasada* (named after a famous flamenco dancer.) Other wines include a range under the Zuleta name, a *fino* called Don Tomás and a range of brandies under the Mateagudo label.

C.A.Y.D.

Sanlúcar de Barrameda. The trading name of the important Sanlúcar cooperative, with 1,000 members and a stock of 50,000 butts. Its speciality is such *manzanills* as Bajo de Guia and Sanluqueña.

PORTUGAL

Portugal, conservative as she is, was the first country in modern times to invent a new style of wine for export, and to get it so spectacularly right that it became one of the biggest-selling brands on earth. The wine, of course, is Mateus Rosé. With its competitors it accounts for a large part of Portugal's wine exports – more than port, her traditional tribute to foreign taste – though it is now officially a 'stable' brand, and its principal producers are busily diversifying away from mono-brands.

Mateus is simply an imaginative development of peasant tradition: *vinho verde*, the sharp and fizzy 'green wine' of the country's northern province, the Minho. It is the measure of Portuguese conservatism that neither the Mateus style, nor even port, has ever caught on in a big way in their home country. There is a developing market, especially in Lisbon and Oporto, for more modern wines – cool-fermented fruity whites and softer, fruitier reds; but Portugal continues to drink predominantly old-fashioned wines. Yet this is no little backwater. Portugal is sixth in the league of wine-producing nations and third in the league of consumption per head (although per capita consumption is declining). The Portuguese drink two thirds of the 9.5 million hectolitres they produce; the remaining third constitutes their largest single export item.

Conservative they may be, but the Portuguese were the first to establish the equivalent of a national system of *appellation contrôlée*: the first delimited area being the Douro in 1756. Then came a wave of demarcations starting in 1908 with *vinho verde*. Portugal had legally defined boundaries, grapes, techniques and standards for all of what were then her better wines.

For many years, unfortunately, these have sat heavily on progress, leading to a distorted picture of where the best wines were really being grown. It is more realistic today to ignore the original list of demarcated regions for all except historical purposes and to consider the regional names in use as being of equal validity. With entry into the European Community, legislation is changing and freeing producers from the rules which stifled enterprise in many demarcated regions.

The snag is that during the long period while the regional system was out of date, many of Portugal's better wine companies took to using brand names without indication of origin. Several of Portugal's most distinguished and reliable wines still come from 'somewhere in Portugal'. Portugal is the only country where a brand without any further clues may lead to the best available wine. This has changed with entry to the European Common Market: 26 new regions have been delimited. They do not yet share the same status as the nine traditional demarcated regions and are therefore referred to as IPRs (*Indicação de Provenencia Regulamentada*) rather than RDs (*Região Demarcada*).

The ascendancy of merchant companies, rather than the primary producers, is another Portuguese peculiarity. Big wine estates are almost unknown, except in the port country where shippers have planted or accumulated considerable vineyards. The newer regions of the south also tend to have larger estates. Only 13 per cent of Portugal's 180,000 growers make more than 1,000 cases a year, and only 4 per cent as much as 3,000 cases or their equivalent. Forty per cent take their grapes to the country's 117 cooperative cellars. Most of the rest who have wine to spare after supplying their families and friends sell it to merchants. Merchants and their brands rather than growers' names are therefore the key to Portuguese wine. Most of the bigger and better merchants buy and bottle wine from each of the major areas: there is little regionality at this level either. The last 15 years has seen the rise of single *quintas* (estates): individual properties growing their own grapes and making their own wine.

The Portuguese practice is to divide all wines into two categories: *verde* or *maduro*. *Vinho verde* is unaged wine, and the use of the term now legally limited to the northern province, the Minho. Sparkling rosés would however logically fit into this category. *Maduro* means mature. It implies long ageing in barrel (or frequently, cement vat) and bottle. It is the natural, indeed the essential, treatment for wines, red or white, made in the traditional manner of every part of Portugal except the Minho. For the Portuguese grow thick-skinned grapes, pick them fully ripe, ferment them stalks and all at a high temperature, and then admire the concentration, the colour, the tannin and the strength rather than looking for fruitiness or finesse in their handiwork.

The very real virtue of Portuguese wine made this way is its structure: it is engineered to last for decades, slowly evolving from gum-withering astringency to the most satisfying texture, when firmness is rounded out to velvet smoothness without losing the feel of the iron fist within. Its vice is lack of flavour, and often only the shyest fragrance for such a potent wine.

Earlier picking, destemming the bunches and cooler fermentation are among the manoeuvres that more modern wine makers are adopting to catch the flavour of their admirable fruit. But in Portugal the old habits die hard.

A peculiar piece of terminology is used for selected and long-aged wines. The word *garrafeira* has much of the meaning of *reserva* but with the added implication that it is the merchant's 'private' best wine, aged for several years in bottle as well as in barrel to be ready for drinking when it is sold. Levels of alcohol need to be at least 0.5% above the legal minimum.

PORTUGUESE TABLE WINES

The wines of Portugal (excluding port) are described here in a progress as nearly as possible from north to south. For port *see* pages 401–406.

The Minho
The single most important table-wine region, accounting for about 20 per cent of the country's harvest, is the northern province of the Minho from Orporto to the Spanish border. Its name is synonymous with *vinho verde*, Portugal's most original and successful contribution to the world's cellar.

What is green about *vinho verde* is not its colour (55% is red and the white is like lemon-stained water). It is its salad-days freshness, which seems to spring straight from the verdant pergolas where it grows in promiscuous polyculture with maize and vegetables. Traditionally, the vines hang in garlands from tree to tree, or are trained on pergolas of granite post and chestnut lintel. Growing the grapes so high above the ground has several advantages: it slows their ripening and produces the desired sugar/acid balance; it counteracts the tendency to fungus diseases in a cool and rainy climate; it also allows for other cultivation below and between. However, modern vineyards are being trained on lower systems, making the operation easier to mechanize as well as producing wines with better acid balance.

The traditional method of making *vinho verde* is to encourage an active malolactic fermentation. The cool climate, the grapes cultivated (*see* pages 28 and 29), and their elevated training result in very high levels of malic acid. The natural bacterial conversion of malic to lactic acid takes the rasp out of the acidity and adds the tingle of its by-product, carbon dioxide. In some country inns the jug wine from barrels is not unlike very dry, fizzy and rather cloudy cider.

Nowadays, however, only a few jug wines are made in the traditional way, and almost no *vinho verde* undergoes malolactic fermentation in bottle, as this creates a sediment. The vast majority of commercial wineries finish the wine to complete bacterial stability and then bottle it with an injection of carbon dioxide to arrive at approximately the same result. The last method also gives the wine maker the option of sweetening his wine (with unfermented must) without the danger of its refermenting. The total dryness and distinct sharpness of 'real'

The traditional means of transporting port down the Douro was by flat-bottomed boats, the barcos rabelos

vinho verde is not to everyone's taste. In the red version, fermented stalks and all, it contrives with high tannin to make an alarmingly astringent drink which foreigners rarely brave a second time.

The merchants' brands of *vinho verde* do not normally specify which part of the wide region they come from. Of the eight subregions, Amarante and Peñafiel, just inland from Oporto, produce the highest proportion of white wine. Braga, the centre of the Minho, has good-quality fresh red and white. Lima, along the river of the same name north of Braga, specializes in slightly more full-bodied reds. Monção, along the river Minho on the Spanish border in the north, is most famous for its single-variety white, its Alvarinho, much the most expensive (and most alcoholic) wine of the region but only by courtesy, if at all, a *vinho verde*. Alvarinho is smooth and still, aged in wood and softly fragrant of apricots or freesias, rather than brisk and tinglingly fruity. Some of the best *vinho verdes* are now being made by single vineyard properties – members of a self-styled group of grower producers called APEVV (*Associacão dos Produtores-Engarrafadores de Vinho Verde*).

Dão

The region of Dão, centred on the old cathedral city of Viseu, 50 miles south of the Douro, is much the biggest and most prosperous producer of *vinhos maduros* under a seal of origin. It is pine-forested country along the valleys of three rivers, the Alva, the Mondego and the Dão, cut through hills of granite boulders and sandy soil. The vast majority of its 38,000 acres of vineyard is planted with black grapes (several of which it has in common with the Douro).

The profile of a red Dão remains, despite the care and skill of several of the merchants who mature it, a rather dry, hard wine reluctant to 'give', excellent palate cleansing with rich food, smooth and inviting to swallow, yet strangely lacking in bouquet or lingering sweetness.

The reason is that until the 1990 vintage nobody except the 10 local cooperatives could make Dão except from his own grapes; the vineyards belong to small farmers, and there is, astonishingly, only one estate-grown Dão on the market – that of the Conde de Santar. The merchant bottlers have had to make the best of what the farmers and cooperatives provide them with. Now that the cooperatives have lost their monopoly, a number of producers have been encouraged by the release of this stranglehold and are starting to buy in grapes and make their own wines. Sogrape, the makers of Mateus Rosé, are probably in the strongest position, having invested about £4 million in a new winery.

Bairrada

Although it remained undemarcated until 1979, some 70 years after the Dão region, Bairrada is a real rival to the Dão in the quality of its wines. The name applies to an area between Dão and the Atlantic north of Coimbra and south of Oporto, with the towns of Mealhada and Anadia as its main centres. Its low hills of heavy lime-rich soil have a slightly greater vineyard area than Dão, and the same overwhelming preponderance of red grapes (90%) over white. But its climate is more temperate, its grape varieties different and its *adgeas* more individual.

Two local grapes not found elsewhere have outstanding qualities. The red Baga is a late-ripening variety high in tannin and acid that gives real authority and 'cut' to a blend. As the dominant variety it needs 15 to 20 years' ageing, but eventually achieves the great fragrance of a fine claret.

The aromatic local white grape is the Bical, which seems to have an outstanding balance of acidity and extract, aromatic of apricots, brisk and long-flavoured. Another grape, called Maria Gomes, a more neutral variety, forms the basis of the sparkling-wine industry of Bairrada, which now has some very palatable products.

Garrafeira wines from almost any Portuguese merchant may contain or be based on Bairrada wines. The following firms are in the area and make good examples: Aliança, Messias, São João and Luis Pato.

The Douro

The mythology of the Douro reports that it was its terrible table wine that forced merchants to lace it with brandy and create port. It may have been so, but today the Douro produces the admirable table wines drunk daily by most port shippers, a number of well-known merchants' *garrafeiras*, and, in the shape of Barca Velha (*see* the entry for A. A. Ferreira under Port Producers on page 404), a great red wine of international stature to put besides Spain's Vega Sicilia, from 100 miles farther up the same river.

Both Trás-os-Montes, north of the Douro, and Beira Alta to its south have well-balanced, not over-strong red wines to offer. Lafões is a recently regulated region in the wetter west of the Beira Alta, producing wine similar in style to *vinho verde*, called *verdasco*; Beiras is farther east, between Dão and the border of Spain.

The Centre and South

Of the four historic wine regions, demarcated with *selos de origem*, clustering round Lisbon, the capital, two are reduced to relics with only a single remaining producer, one is still substantial but dwindling, and only the fourth, Setúbal, across the Tagus estuary, has escaped the attrition of housing development to prosper under modern conditions.

Carcavelos is nearest to extinction. The one remaining vineyard has almost 'given up the ghost', however, a new producer is starting up: wines from Quinta dos Pesos should be launched in 1990/91. The sprawling resort of Estoril seems to have swallowed up the rest of wine-producing Carcavelos. But the quality of the wine justifies the search. It is a light amber, velvety, not oversweet, slightly fortified dessert or apéritif wine like a soft, nutty and buttery Verdelho or Bual madeira.

More is heard of Bucelas, whose 450 acres of vineyards 10 miles due north of Lisbon continue to produce 74,000 cases of a very pleasant, if not very original, dry white of moderate strength, in my experience rather lacking in aroma and not improved by the age in barrel it is often subjected to.

Still more is heard of Colares, not because there is any quantity – 26,000 cases is the average – but because it is a true original, and one of Portugal's most sought-after red wines. Its vineyards are an unplottable sprawl in the sand dunes of the Atlantic coast west of Lisbon, between Sintra and the sea. They grow the Ramisco, a tiny, bloomy dark-blue bullet of a grape whose thick skin would tan an ox-hide. Grown in pure sand (the plants have to be planted at the bottom of deep pits, which are then progressively filled in) it makes wine of quite unreasonable inkiness and astringency. Grafting is unnecessary: phylloxera is baffled by sand.

Much the biggest Lisbon area lies across the Tagus, between the bridge and Setúbal on the far side of the Arrabida peninsula, a region with nearly 50,000 acres of vineyards divided between good plain red wine and the sumptuously aromatic Muscat of Setúbal. Setúbal in this form was apparently the creation of the firm of José-Maria da Fonseca of Azeitão, in the middle of the region, who originally had a quasi-monopoly in the area (there are now three producers). It is a 'muted' wine, its fermentation stopped by the addition of spirit, in which the skins of more Muscat grapes, themselves highly aromatic, are steeped and macerated to give it the precise fragrance of a ripe dessert grape. The wine is barrel-aged and drunk, without further ageing in bottle, either at six years (when it is still amazingly fresh and grapey) or at 25 or more (when it has taken on more piquant notes of fragrance and developed the tobacco hue and satin texture of a fine tawny port).

The biggest undermarcated wine region of Portugal is the central coastal area, north of Lisbon, where Wellington held the famous lines of Torres Vedras. From here eastwards to the far banks of the Tagus beyond Santarem, Ribatejo is bulk-wine country, yet bulk wine which a stranger can drink with pleasure; not over-alcoholic like its equivalent from Spain. How good it can be is demonstrated by Serradayres, the standard produce of Carvalho, Ribeiro and Ferreira, the most prestigious merchant of the region. The Ribatejo concentrates on white wine, but its red has more interest.

The vast area south of the Tagus, the Alentejo, is now being considered a 'discovery' in wine terms as more producers take advantage of almost virgin territory as far as viticulture is concerned. Its brown hills are covered with the dark cork oaks that furnish the world with its best-quality corks. The names of certain areas are establishing themselves for good workaday red wine: notably Portalegre near the Tagus, Vidigueira near Beja, and Redondo and Borba towards Elvas (of the famous preserved plums). These and one other region, Reguengos de Monsaraz, have recently been given IPR status. These regions are almost neighbours of the Spanish Extremadura and their wines correspondingly high in alcohol. So are those of the demarcated Algarve, the south coast, of which only a coarse sherry-style white has any reputation – and that an appalling one! In fact Algarve risks being demoted, given the poor quality of its wines.

Rosés

The fabulous success of Mateus and subsequent Portuguese semi-sweet, semi-sparkling rosés was achieved by applying the idea (not the traditional technique) of *vinho verde* to red grapes from a region where the wine had no particular reputation: the hills of north of the Douro round the town of Vila Real. It did not matter that this was not a demarcated region; rather the reverse: it meant that when the local grapes ran out supplies could be found in other areas. Today, rosés are made of grapes from almost anywhere in Portugal. The principal rosé wine-making areas are Bairrada and the Setúbal peninsula south of Lisbon.

It is a process then, and not a regional identity that characterizes these wines. They are made in the usual rosé fashion, of red grapes with a very short period of skin contact after crushing to extract the pink tinge, then fermented like white wine, the fermentation stopped while about 18 grams per litre of original grape sugar remain intact. This is done by adding sulphur dioxide and removing the yeast with a centrifuge pump. The wine is then blended for consistency and bottled with the addition of carbon dioxide under pressure.

TABLE-WINE PRODUCERS

Caves Aliança – Vinicola de Sangalhos
Sangalhos, 3783 Anadia. Founded 1920. Visits.

One of Portugal's principal table- and sparkling-wine producers. A public company controlled by the Neves family based in the Bairrada but offering *vinho verde* (the good dry Casal Mendes), Dão, and Douro rosé as well as its admirable Bairrada red Aliança Tinto Velho, and very passable *méthode champenoise* sparkling wine.

Borges & Irmão SARL
Avenida da Republica 796, 4401 Vila Nova de Gaia. Founded 1884. Visits.

A substantial company in both the table wine and port trades with a major winery in the Minho. Their best-known brands are Gatão, a rather sweet 'commercial' *vinho verde*, Trovador, a ditto rosé, Gamba, a dry *vinho verde* and Dão wines under the label Meia Encosta, of which the white is a fruity, modern-style wine. They have also shipped 11 vintages of port since 1905.

Carvalho, Ribeiro and Ferreira
Avenida da Republica, 19, 1,000 Lisboa. Founded 1898.

This important table wine merchant has cellars at Vale do Carregado on the edge of the Ribatejo, and vineyards in Colares, Dão, the Douro and Oeste. Some of their best wines are blends from the Ribatejo including Serradayres (a firm claret-weight red) and soft, round *garrafeiras*.

A. A. Ferreira S.A.
Rua da Carvalhosa, 19–103, 4400 Vila Nova de Gaia. Visits.

Barca Velha, launched by port producers Ferreira in the 1950's, has quickly earned itself the reputation as one of Portugal's most prestigious red wines. Grapes, mainly Tinta Roriz, are grown at Quinta do Vale do Meão and trodden in big, stone *lagares* making about 4,000 cases of wine a year. Barca Velha is only released in the best vintages ('65, '66, '78); lesser years are declassified to Ferreirinha Reserva Especial.

José Maria da Fonseca Succs.
The Old Winery, 2925 Azeitão. Founded 1834. Visits.

One of the leading wine companies of Portugal, famous as the largest producers of fortified 'Setúbal' and for a range of quality red table wines. Periquita is the best known, made from a blend of local grapes of the same name; Quinta da Camarate is a ripe blackcurrant blend of Cabernet Sauvignon and Periquita and Tinto Velho from the J. S. Rosado Fernandes *adega* in the Alentejo is a good peppery blend of local grapes fermented in large clay amphorae. The company also owns a winery in Dão which bottles the Terras Altas brand. Fonseca is run by two brothers, Antonio and Domingos Soares Franco, who are descendants of the founder.

J. M. da Fonseca Internacional
The New Winery, 2925 Azeitão. Visits.

Lancers Rosé, formerly made by José Maria da Fonseca, has been hived off to a subsidiary of the American firm Heublein who themselves belong to International Distillers and Vintners, part of Grand Met. Apart from the enormous sales of their semi-sweet, sparkling pink wine, Fonseca Internacional have recently invested in a plant producing sparkling wine by the continuous method first developed in Russia. The management of the firm is headed by a descendant of the original Fonseca family, Antonio Avillez, who also owns João Pires (q.v.).

Palace Hotel do Buçaco
3050 Mealhada

The cellars of this extravagant hotel mature one of Europe's most unusual wines. The hotel's 37-acre vineyards are near Luso on the fringes of the Bairrada region and grow its typical grapes. They are trodden (both red and white) in a 5,000-litre stone *lagar* and their wine made exactly in the manner of the last century; fermented in casks, then only racked; the red bottled at 4-5 years, the white at 2-3. Average production is 5,500 cases of red, 3,300 of white and a little dry rosé. Vintages available in the hotel go back to 1944 white and 1927 red, both still well preserved. The best vintages (e.g. white: 1966, '65, '56; red: 1963, '60, '58, '53) have an exquisite hand-made quality, great fragrance and depth.

João Pires and Filhos, Lda
2955 Pinhal Novo

Australian wine-maker Peter Bright has scored a decisive hit both in Portugal and abroad with a delicious grapey, dry Muscat. Red wines from the João Pires stable include Quinta da Bacalhôa; a minty Bordeaux-like blend of Cabernet and Merlot; Meia Pipa, a blend of Periquita and Cabernet grapes; and Tinto da Anfora, a warming spicy red from the Alentejo. Cova da Ursa, a barrel-fermented Chardonnay, has more than a hint of the New World about it and there's even a Late Harvest dessert wine made from botrytis-affected grapes.

Real Companhia Vinícola do Norte de Portugal
4401 Vila Nova da Gaia. Visits.

Royal Oporto, the old port monopoly company set up in the 18th century, is also known for its wide range of table wines. These include a *vinho verde* called Lagosta; Dão, Colares, Evel reds from the Douro; and a sweet wine called Grandjó. The company was nationalized after the 1974 revolution but has since been returned to private hands: the Silva Reis family together with the Casa do Douro, the regulatory body of port growers.

Sogrape – Vinhos de Portugal SARL
Av. da Boavista, 1163, 4100 Porto. Visits.

Portugal's biggest wine company, the makers of Mateus Rosé, have annual sales of over 3.5 million cases. The founding Guedes family still control the firm, its subsidiary Vinícola do Vale do Dão and have recently bought Ferreira port (see page 404). Mateus Rosé is made from grapes grown all over the north of Portugal, especially Baga from Bairrada where Sogrape have a large winery. Grão Vasco is a good Dão wine made at the company's own winery near Viseu, Vila Regia a ripe Douro red, and Terra Franca a soft, fruity Bairrada. The company also makes a deliciously oaky, dry white Reserva from grapes grown north of the Douro around Vila Real.

Caves Velhas – Companhia Portuguesa de Vinhos de Marca Lda
Rua Fernão Lopes 9, Lisbon. Founded 1939. Visits.

The trading name of Adegas Camilo Alves (founded 1881), one of the few producers of Bucellas wine. The firm owns 220 of the 450 acres remaining in Bucelas and buys the grapes from the rest. Bucellas *garrafeira* is aged 3 years in cask in their grand old barn of an *adega*. Romeira is the name used for red and rosé wines from the Ribatejo; Caves Velhas for their Dãos.

OTHER PRODUCERS

Quinta da Aveleda Lda
PO Box 121, 4002 Porto. Founded 1947. Visits by appt. Makers of the most famous brand of *vinho verde*, Casal Garcia, and a secondary, medium-dry brand called Aveleda. Quinta da Aveleda is a traditional dry white *vinho verde* and Grinalda a wine made from the best grapes grown only on the beautiful family estate at Penafiel.

Solar das Bouças
4720 Amares. One of the best *vinho verde* estates, recently bought by the van Zeller family of Quinta de Noval. 86 acres of vineyard planted predominantly with Loureiro produce 20,000 cases of aromatic, dry, crackling *vinho verde*.

Caves do Casalinho Lda
R. Duque de Saldanha 182, 4300 Porto. A rapidly growing family-owned (the Camelo and Costa families) table-wine company with several *quintas* in the Minho and one (rented) in the Douro. Casalinho is their best brand of dry *vinho verde*, others are Três Marias, Montemar and 5 Cidades. Casalinho Rosé is a lookalike of Mateus. Their Dão brand, Alexandre Magno, can be impressive.

I may have been prejudiced against their prestige line, Ouro Velho, by its absurd fake-dusty lop-sided bottle. I found the red *garrafeira* muddy and the white like oily sherry.

Caves São João
S. João de Anadia, 3780 Anadia. Family-owned merchant with 50 acres of vines in the Bairrada region. Two brothers, Alberto and Luis Costa, age, blend and bottle some of the most impressive red wines from Dão and Bairrada. *Reservas* sporting a cork label have good depth and ageing potential

Casa Agricola Herd. de D. Luis Margaride
2080 Almerim. Two Ribatejo estates, Casal de Monteiro and Convento da Serra, are together planted with nearly 500 acres of vines. Grapes include traditional Portuguese varieties as well as Cabernet Sauvignon, Merlot, Chardonnay and Riesling. Fresh-tasting dry whites and well-balanced reds are bottled under the names of the two estates and the Dom Hermano label.

Vinhos Messias
Apartado 1, 3050 Mealhada. Founded 1926. Growers and merchants with a wide range of different ports (see page 404) and table wines. Quinta do Cachão is a full, spicy Douro red; Quinta do Valdoeiro a fresh-tasting, appley dry white from extensive Bairrada vineyards. Other wines bought in and blended at their cellars include the Santola brand of *vinho verde*, a solid, well-made red Dão, a Bairrada and

good, sparkling *espumantes*.

Vinhos de Monção Lda
4950 Monção. Diminutive producers of the famous (and expensive) Alvarinho white, Cepa Velha, a potential *vinho verde* fermented and aged in wood to achieve a totally different result.

Palacio de Brejoeira
4950 Monção. Minho. The most prestigious producer of the rare Alvarinho white.

Luis Pato
Ois de Bairro, 3780 Anadia. Established grower/wine-maker in Bairrada with 150 acres of vineyard. Good firm-flavoured reds are made mainly from Baga; a small amount of Cabernet produces a softer blackcurranty wine. Whites along with a sparkling *espumante* are clean, fresh and fragrant.

Caves de Raposeira
5100 Lamego. The largest producers of Portuguese sparkling wine by the champagne method. Owned by the Canadian drinks multi-national Seagram. Cool vineyards on the high land south of the Douro produce crisp, well balanced wines. Their Super Reserve includes a proportion of Pinot Noir and Chardonnay in the blend.

Adega Regional de Colares
Colares, 2710 Sintra. The centre of Colares production, although most of its produce is matured and bottled by several firms, including Real Companhia Vinícola and António B.P. da Silva, which labels its wines as Colares Chitas.

Adega Cooperativa de Monção
4950 Monção. The growers' cooperative of Monção makes, besides much *vinho verde*, some 2,000 cases of the rare still white Alvarinho.

Barros Almeida
4400 Vila Nova de Gaia. A family-owned substantial shipper of medium-quality ports, largely in bulk. Also proprietors of Kopke, the oldest brand of all, Feuerheerd, the Douro Wine Shippers Association and several other companies.

J. W. Burmester & Co.
Rua de Belomonte 39, 4000 Porto. Founded in 1750. No visits. A small family-owned, now Portuguese, house of English and German foundation. No vineyards, but well-chosen wines from Pinhão go to make their Tordiz tawny and vintages. Other names used are Jems and Southam's.
Stocks: 4,500 pipes.
Vintages: 1900, '10, '20, '22, '27, '29, '34, '37, '40, '44, '48, '50, '55, '58, '60, '63, '75, '77, '83.

Diez Hermanos Lda
Rua Guilherme Braga 38, 4401 Vila Nova de Gaia. No visits. A small

subsidiary of Offley Forrester (q.v.). Stock: 6,000 pipes.

Feuerheerd Bros. & Co.
4400 Vila Nova de Gaia. Founded 1815. The formerly British-owned company now belongs to Barros Almeida (q.v.).

Martinez Gassiot & Co. Ltd
Rua das Coradas 13, Vila Nova de Gaia. Founded 1790. Visits. The company was bought by Harvey's in 1961 and is now a subsidiary of Allied Breweries; thus allied to Cockburn (q.v.). Its speciality is fine tawnies rather than ruby or vintage-character wines. Stocks: *see* Cockburn. Vintages: 1900, '04, '08, '11, '12, '19, '22, '27, '31, '34, '45, '55, '58, '60, '63, '67, '70 and '75.

Niepoort & Co. Ltd
Rua Infante D. Henrique 39–2, 4000 Oporto. Founded 1842. Visits by appt. A small Dutch family-owned company, unusual in storing its vintage port before bottling in glass demijohns in a cellar, rather than pipes in a lodge.

Rozes Lda
Rua do Choupelo 250, Vila Nova de Gaia. Founded 1853. No visits. A shipper jointly owned by Möet Hennessy and Taylor, Fladgate and Yeatman, specializing in the French market for its tawny, ruby and white ports. Stocks: 6,000 pipes.

Wiese & Krohn
4401 Vila Nova de Gaia. Founded 1866. No visits. A small independent company, originally German, without vineyards. Shipped the vintages of 1957, '58, '60, '61, '63, '65, '67, '70, '75, '78.

PORT

What the English have long known as port, and the Portuguese and other nations as porto, belongs with champagne and sherry in the original trinity of great 'processed' wines. Each is an elaboration on the natural produce of its region to enhance its latent quality. Being capital intensive, requiring the holding of big stocks for long periods, their trade has become concentrated in the hands of shippers. Single-vineyard ports, and even single-vintage ports, are the exceptions in an industry which lives day to day on long-established, unchanging blends.

Unlike champagne and sherry, port was the child of political pressure. In the late seventeenth century the British were obliged by their government to find alternatives to the French red wines they preferred. They turned to Portugal, an old and useful ally, for a convenient substitute for claret. Finding nothing to their liking in the existing vineyards (which is surprising: Lisbon had good wine, if Oporto did not) the enterprising traders pushed inland from Oporto up the valley of the Douro into the rugged hinterland. What they tasted there that made them persevere is hard to imagine. They could hardly have chosen a more difficult and inaccessible place, with a more extreme climate, to develop as a major new wine area. They started around Regua, about 60 miles (or three mule-days) upstream from Oporto where the river Corgo joins the main stream. Gradually, finding that the higher they went the better the wine became, they built terraces up the almost impossible mountains surrounding the Douro and its tributaries: the Távora, the Torto, the Pinhão, the Tua. They dotted the mountainsides with white-walled *quintas* or farms, and demonstrated that once cultivated, the thin arid soil of granite and schist became extraordinarily fertile. Today not just the grapes but the nuts, oranges, almonds and even vegetables of the Douro are famous.

The first port was apparently a strong dry red wine, made even stronger with 'a bucket or two' of brandy to stabilize it for shipping. It got a very cold reception from British claret lovers, who complained bitterly. The shippers tried harder, and at some time in the eighteenth century hit on the idea of stopping the fermentation with brandy while the wine was still sweet and fruity. History is unclear on when this became the standard practice, since as late as the 1840s the most influential British port shipper of all time, James Forrester (created a Portuguese Baron for his services), was urging a return to unfortified (therefore dry) wines. Modern ideas provide surprising justification for Forrester's

notions: today the Douro is indeed providing some of Portugal's best dry red table wine. Sweet or dry, however, port was the most-drunk wine in Britain from the early eighteenth century to the early twentieth.

Today port is one of the most strictly controlled of all wines. A series of statutory authorities regulate and oversee every stage of its making. Every one of 85,000 vineyards, totalling 62,000 acres, is individually clasified for quality on an eight-point scale by the 'Casa de Douro', taking into account its situation, altitude, soil, inclination, grape varieties, standard of cultivation, fertility and the age of its vines. It is then given an annual quota. Only 40 per cent on average of the total Douro crop may be turned into port, the rest is just red wine. The maximum yield, allowed for vineyards classified A on the eight-point scale, is 700 litres to 1,000 vines.

At harvest time, late September in the Douro, bureaucracy seems remote enough. The grinding labour of picking and carrying the crop from the steep terraces to the press-houses is carried on with amazingly cheerful, even tuneful, energy by gangs of villagers who often walk miles over the mountains for their annual 'holiday'. On remote little farms, and with the best-quality grapes at some of the largest *quintas*, the crop is still trodden barefoot by lamplight in open granite *lagars*, then fermented in the *lagars* until it is ready to be 'stopped' with brandy. Much the greater proportion today though is machine crushed and fermented in closed concrete fermenting tanks of a kind introduced from Algeria, with a simple percolating system, operated by the natural build-up of carbon dioxide, to keep the juice constantly churning over the skins.

With either method the moment comes when about half the grape sugar is fermented into alcohol. This is when the half-made wine is run off into barrels one quarter full of brandy. Fermentation stops instantly.

The great majority of the port is moved, after its first racking off its gross lees, to the shippers' lodges to mature. The lodges are huddled together in the Oporto suburb of Vila Nova de Gaia, facing the steep streets of the city across the Douro and linked to it by a remarkable double-decker bridge. The down-river journey can no longer be made by the beautiful Viking-style *barcos rabelos* since the river was dammed for hydroelectric power. What was once a picturesque if perilous river highway is now a series of placid lakes, dotted with windsurfers and occasionally furrowed by water-skiers.

Once in the shipper's lodge, port, like sherry, is classified by tasting and its destiny decided by its quality and potential for improvement. Most ports join a sort of perpetual blending system whose object is an unchanging product.

Simple, fruity and rather light wines without great concentration are destined to become ruby, aged for up to about two years in wood and bottled while their bright red colour and full sweetness show no sign of maturity. This is the cheapest category, very popular in France as an apéritif.

Young wines with more aggressive characters and greater concentration, some outstandingly good, some of only moderate quality, are set aside to develop into tawnies – so-called from their faded colour after many years in wood. Tawnies include some of the greatest of all ports, the shippers' own favourite blends, kept for up to 40 years in cask, then (usually) refreshed with a little younger wine of the highest quality. Tawnies also include some very ordinary mixtures with scarcely any of the character of barrel-age, made by blending young red and white ports. Their price varies accordingly. The best tawnies have an indication of age on the label. Twenty years is old enough for most of them – the high premium for a 30- or 40-year-old wine is seldom worth it. Styles among top tawnies vary from the intensely luscious (e.g. Ferreira's Duque de Bragança) to refinement and dry finish (e.g. Taylor's 20-year-old).

The great majority of port falls into one or other of the above categories, which together are known as 'wood ports'; their whole maturing process takes place in wood.

Vintage port, by contrast, is the product of one of the three or four vintages in a decade which come close to the shipper's idea of perfection – which have so much flavour and individuality that to make them anonymous as part of a continuing blend would be a waste of their potential. Whether or not a shipper 'declares' a vintage is entirely his own decision. It is very rare that all do so in the same year. The Douro is too varied in its topography and conditions.

Vintage ports are blended in the particular style the shipper has developed over many years, using the best lots of wine from his regular suppliers – including invariably his own best vineyards. They are matured for a minimum of 22 and a maximum of 31 months in cask for their components to 'marry', then bottled 'in Oporto' (i.e. in Vila Nova de Gaia) while they are still undrinkably tannic, aggressive and concentrated in flavour. Almost all their maturing therefore happens in the airless 'reductive' conditions of a black-glass bottle with a long cork, designed to protect the wine for decades while it slowly feeds on itself. Its tannins and pigments react

Terraced port vineyards in the Upper Douro

to form a heavy skin-like 'crust' that sticks to the side of the bottle. Its colour slowly fades and its flavour evolves from violently sweet and harsh to gently sweet, perfumed and mellow. Yet however mellow, vintage port is designed to have 'grip', a vital ingredient in wine which should never lose its final bite even in old age.

Between the clear-cut extremes of wood port and vintage port come a number of compromises intended to offer something closer to vintage port without the increasingly awkward need to cellar the wine for between 10 and 30 years. Vintage character (or vintage reserve) is effectively top-quality ruby port whose ingredient wines were almost up to vintage standards, but kept for four or five years in cask. These potent and tasty wines are 'ready' when bottled, but will continue to develop, and even to form a slight 'crust' in bottle if they are kept. The term crusted or crusting port is sometimes used for the same style (though not officially recognized in Portugal).

Late-bottled vintage is similar, but is made of the wine of one 'vintage' year, kept twice as long as vintage port in barrel: i.e. from three and a half to six years. The label 'L.B.V.' carries both the date of the vintage and the bottling, and the wine is lighter in colour and flavour than vintage port but should have some of its firmness. It may or may not form a

deposit in bottle according to its maturity on bottling and the degree to which the shipper has chilled and filtered it for stability.

An increasingly popular compromise with some of the best shippers is single-*quinta* vintage port. In years that are not generally up to vintage standard some wine of excellent quality is often made in the best sites. In several famous cases these belong to eminent shippers. In vintage years they are the backbone of the blend. In less-than-perfect years the shippers sometimes bottle them unblended, with the vintage date. They will mature sooner than classic vintages but often have distinct and charming character. Being bottle-matured they will of course form a crust and need decanting. Some of the best-known single-*quinta* wines occasionally offered are Taylor's Quinta de Vargellas, Graham's Quinta dos Malvedos, Croft's Quinta da Roêda, Cálem's Quinta da Foz.

White port is made in the same way as red port but of white grapes, usually fermented further towards dryness before being fortified with brandy. It is intended as an apéritif rather than a dessert wine, but never achieves the quality or finesse of, say, a *fino* sherry. Its underlying heaviness needs to be enlivened, at least with a lump of ice, and it can be even more enjoyable as a long drink with tonic water, ice and a slice of lemon.

PORT PRODUCERS

Borges E. Irmao
Avenida da Republica 796, 4401 Vila Nova de Gaia. Vintages: 1945, '55, '58, '60, '63, '70, '79, '80, '82, '83 and '85.
Founded in 1884 by the Borges brothers, this port house has major banking connections (Banco Borges e Irmao), and a substantial involvement in table wines. They have two vinification plants, one in Minho for the Vinho Verde and one in Douro for port. Main exports are to Holland, Belgium and France. Best wines are Quinta do Junço, Soalheira and Roncao. Quick-maturing vintages but very average wines.

A. A. Cálem & Filho Lda.
Rue de Reboleira 7, 4000 Porto. Stock: 15,500 pipes. Vintages: 1935, '48, '55, '58, '60, '63, '66, '70, '75, '77, '80, '82, '83 and '85. Visits.
Founded in 1859 by a family already long in the trade, and who still own the firm. The Cálems own the excellent Quinta da Foz and 3 others, in total 125 acres of vineyards, at Pinhão, where they still tread the grapes. They make other ports from bought grapes by 'autovinification'. Their Cálem and da Costa ports are well known in France, Germany, the Netherlands and the UK.

Cockburn
Cockburn Smith & Cia, 13 Rua das Coradas, 4401 Vila Nova de Gaia. Stocks (including Martinez): 32,000 pipes. Vintages: 1900, '04, '08, '12, '27, '35, '45, '47, '50, '55, '60, '63, '67, '70, '75, '77, '83, and '85. Founded 1815. Visits by appt.
One of the greatest names in port, owned by Allied

Breweries but still run by descendants of its Scottish founders. Cockburn vineyard properties are the Quintas do Tua (60 acres), da Santa Maria near Regua (40 acres) and do Val do Coelho and do Atayde near Tua where they are planting 500 acres. 60% of the *quinta* wines is still trodden. Cockburn's wines have a distinctive dry finish, or 'grip'. Their best tawny, Director's Reserve, with Special Reserve Tawny and Fine Old Ruby, make up 38% of port sales in the UK. Martinez Gassiot (q.v.) is an associated company. The '83 and '85 are the best of recent vintages.

Quinta do Cotto
Quinta do Cotto, Citadelha, Vila Real.
The Champalimaud family, who have owned their 271 acres near Regua since the 17th century, are now the best-known of the new breed of grower-bottlers; that is their single-*quinta* vintage is made and matured in the Douro and not moved down to Vila Nova de Gaia for bottling. They also make one of the Douro's best table wines.

Croft & Co.
Largo Joaquim Magalhães 23, Apartado 5, 4401 Vila Nova de Gaia. Stock: 30,000 pipes. Vintages: Croft – 1900, '04, '08, '12, '17, '20, '22, '24, '27, '35, '42, '45, '50, '55, '60, '63, '66, '70, '75, '77, '82 and 85. Quinta da Roêda – 1967, '70, '78, '80, '83 and '87. Morgan –1900, , '04, '08, '12, '20, '22, '24, '27, '42, '45, '48, '55, '60, '63, '66, '70, '77, '82 and '85.
Founded 1678. Visits by appt.
Perhaps the oldest port firm, originally known as Phayre

and Bradley, now owned by International Distillers & Vintners (*see also* Sherry). Owners of the superb Quinta da Roêda with 156 acres at Pinhão, responsible for the distinctive floweriness of their vintage wines regularly among the finest of all. Other wines include the excellent Distinction Tawny, Distinction Finest Reserve, and the sister brands Delaforce (q.v.) and Morgan.

Delaforce Sons & Co.
Apartado 6, 4401 Vila Nova de Gaia. Stock: 15,000 pipes. Vintages: 1908, '17, '20, '21, '22, '27, '35, '45, '47, '50, '55, '58, '60, '63, '66, '70, '75, '77, '82 and '85. Quinta da Corte: '78, '80, '84 and '87.
Founded 1868. No visits.

Still family run by the Delaforces, although since 1968 a subsidiary (like Crofts, q.v.) of IDV. The firm's finest wines, with great freshness and elegance, come from the contracted Quinta de Corte in Rio Torto valley. His Eminence's Choice is a superbly succulent 10-year-old tawny.

Dow's *see* Silva & Cosens Ltd.

A. A. Ferreira, S.A.
Rua da Carvalhosa 19–103, 4400 Vila Nova de Gaia. Stocks: 20,000 pipes. Vintages: 1945, '47, '50, '58, '60, '63, '66, '70, '75, '77, '78, '80, '82, '83 and '85.
Founded 1751. Visits.

A historic Portuguese house, in the mid-19th century the richest in the Douro, then ruled over by the famous Dona António, who built the magnificent Quintas do Vesuvio and do Vale de Meão, colossal establishments in the remotest high Douro. They still own, between the members of the family, many acres of vineyard although the company was sold in 1987 to Sogrape, who produce Mateus Rosé. Today Ferreira sells more bottled port in Portugal than any other house, and none in wood. Sales in 1982 were 3m. bottles. Their vintage wines (though fine) are less well known than their tawnies. Superior, Dona Antonia and above all the superlative Duque de Bragança, are largely made of wines from the great Quinta do Roriz above Pinhão.

Hunt, Roope is a subsidiary company, which in turn ships Tuke, Holdsworth vintage ports. Another close link is with MacKenzie & Co. Ferreira also make, in the cavernous *lagars* at the Quinta do Vale de Meão, almost on the Spanish frontier, some 4,000 cases of one of the finest Portuguese table wines, their Ferreirinha, in its best years (e.g. '65, '66, '78, '79, '80) christened Barca Velha.

Fonseca Guimaraens
Rua Barão de Forrester 404, 4400 Vila Nova de Gaia. Stock: 5,000 pipes. Vintages: 1904, '08, '12, '20, '22, '27, '34, '45, '48, '55, '60, '63, '66, '70, '75, '77, '80, '83 and '85.
Founded 1822. Visits by appt.

Despite their name an English family business for over a century, now linked to Taylors. The firm started in the 18th century as Fonseca and was bought by Manuel Pedro Guimaraens in 1822. It was known as Guimaraens Vinhos and the ports as Fonseca, but in 1988 the names were merged. Their vineyards of Quinta Cruizeiro (160 acres) and Quinta Santo Antonio (100 acres), both in the Val de Mendiz near Alijo, are splendidly sited and still make all their best wines by treading. Fonseca Guimaraens is regularly one of the finest and richest vintage ports and their Bin '27 an admirable youngish tawny. They have recently introduced an LBV and the single *quinta* Quinta do Panascal.

Forrester & Co.
Apartado 61, Rua Guilherme Braga 38, 4401 Vila Nova de Gaia. Vintages: 1945, '50, '54, '60, '62, '63, '66, '67, '70, '72, '75, '77, '80, '82, '83 and '85.

This firm was founded in 1737 by William Offley and joined by James Forrester in 1803. His nephew Baron Joseph James Forrester was famous for mapping the Upper Douro and saving the vineyards from a fungal disease in the 1850s. The company was sold in 1929 and sold again in 1983 to Martini & Rossi. Best wine is Baron Forrester Tawny.

Gould Campbell *see* Smith Woodhouse

W. & J. Graham & Co.
Rua Rei Ramiro 514, 4400 Vila Nova de Gaia. Stocks: 11,000 pipes. Vintages: 1904, '08, '12, '17, '20, '24, '27, '35, '42, '45, '48, '55, '60, '63, '66, '70, '75, '77, '80, '83 and '85.
Founded 1820. Visits by appt.

A shipper renowned for some of the richest and sweetest vintage ports, now part of the empire of the Symington family (with Warre, Silva & Cosens etc, qq.v.). Graham's Quinta dos Malvedos on the Douro near Tua provides exceptionally ripe fruit for vintage port of great colour, body and guts which mellows to a singularly sumptuous wine. Part of the crop is still trodden. Malvedos is also issued as a single-*quinta* wine. Tawny and late-bottled vintage follow the full-bodied, luscious style. Particularly good is the vintage six Grapes ruby.

C.N. Kopke & Co.
P.O. Box 42, Rua Serpa Pinto 183–191, 4401 Vila Nova de Gaia. Vintages: 1934, '35, '42, '45, '52, '55, '58, '60, '63, '66, '70, '74, '75, '77, '78, '79, '80, '82, '83 and '85.
Founded 1638. Visits by appt.

In name at least the oldest of all the port firms, founded by a German. It now belongs to Barros Almeida (q.v.). Kopke has 148 acres of vines and uses the names Quinta São Luiz for vintages, Old World for tawny, Bridge for ruby.

dos Vinhos Messias SARL
Apartado l, 3050 Mealhada, 4401 Vila Nova de Gaia. Stocks: port 8,500 pipes; table and sparkling wines 200,000 cases. Vintages: 1958, '60, '63, '66, '67, '70, '75, '77, '79, '80, '82, '83, '84 and '85. Founded 1926. Visits.

A Portuguese family-run company owning substantial port vineyards, notably the Quinta do Cachão near San João da Pesqueira (250 acres). The *quinta* crops are trodden for vintage and vintage-style wines, which are reputed to have a faint almond flavour. For table wines Messias have an *adega* at Mealhada in the Bairrada in central Portugal.

Quinta do Noval
Rua Cândido dos Reis 575, Vila Nova de Gaia. Stock: 6,000 pipes. Vintages: 1904, '08, '12, '17, '20, '24, '27, '31, '34, '('41 & '42), '45, '50, '55, '58, '60, '63, '66, '67, '70, '78, '80, '82, '83 and '85. Founded 1813. Visits by appt.

Perhaps the most famous, and one of the most beautiful *quintas* on the Douro, perched high above Pinhão. It belongs to the Van Zeller family, who also own the firm of A. J. da Silva, and run by brother and sister, Cristiano and Teresa. A tragic fire in 1982 destroyed the historic records of the company and part of the stock. Old Noval vintages were some of the most magnificent of all ports. The '31 is legendary and the '27 was even better. A small plot of ungrafted vines still makes an astoundingly concentrated

'Nacional' vintage. Most Noval wines have recently been in a lighter, more feminine, very charming style. Noval late-bottled wines, tawnies and white ports are good, though they are not single-*quinta* wines. Quinta do Silval is another property.

Porto Poças Junior, Lda

Rua de Visconde das Devesas 186, 4401 Vila Nova de Gaia. Stock: 7,000 pipes. Vintages: 1960, '63, '70, '75 and '85. Visits by appt.

An independent family company founded in 1918, owning 2 Douro properties, the Quintas das Quartas and Santa Barbara, run on traditional lines. Their brands Poças Junior, Pousada, Terras, Almiro and Pintão have substantial sales in Belgium and France.

Quarles Harris & Co. Lda

Tr. do Barão de Forrester, Apartado 26, 4401 Vila Nova de Gaia. Stock: 4,000 pipes. Vintages 1908, '12, '20, '27, '34, '45, '47, '50, '55, '58, '60, '63, '66, '70, '75, '77, '80, '83 and '85. Founded 1680. Visits by appt.

Together with Warre, Graham, Dow, etc. (qq.v.), now part of the remarkable stable of the Symington family; there are no vineyards, but only contacts with good growers along the Rio Torto maintain a style of very intense full vintage port with a powerful bouquet. Only a small proportion is still trodden. Harris (not Quarles) is the brand for tawnies, ruby and white ports.

Adriano Ramos-Pinto Vinhos

380 Avenida Ramos-Pinto, P.O. Box 65, 4401 Vila Nova de Gaia. Stock: 8,000 pipes. Vintages: 1924, '27, '35, '45, '50, '52, '55, '60, '61, '70, '75, '80, '82, '83 and '85. Visits.

Founded in 1880 and one of the most distinguished Portuguese-owned houses. Their properties include the famous Quinta Bom-Retiro with 104 acres in the Rio Torto valley, the 90-acre Quinta Santa Maria and the smaller San Domingos. Tawnies (including a fine '1937') are their specialities, but they also produce two highly successful white ports. Brazil is their traditional market, although France, Switzerland and Germany are now important. Possible new ownership in 1990.

Real Companhia Vinícola do Norte de Portugal

Rua Azevedo Magalhães 314, 4401 Vila Nova de Gaia. Vintages: 1908, '41, '43, '44, '45, '47, '54, '55, '58, '60, '62, '63, '67, '70, '77, '78, '79 and '80. Founded 1889. Visits.

Founded in 1756 by the Marquis de Pombal to control the port trade, the company now belongs to Senhor da Silva Reis. Its interests are now half in port and half in other wines (of which half are sparkling). Its port Quintas do Corval and do Sibio (near Tua) provide part of its needs for a stock of 8,000 pipes. *See* also under table-wine producers (p.399).

Robertson Bros.

Rua António Granjo 207, 4401 Vila Nova de Gaia. Stocks: 3,100 pipes. Vintages: 1945, '47, '55, '63, '66, '67, '70, '72, '75, '77, '80, '83 and '85. Founded 1847. Visits.

Now a subsidiary of Sandeman. Shippers of Rebello Valente vintage ports, notably robust, tannic and fruity wines still trodden in *lagars*, largely at the Quinta de la Rosa at Pinhão. Robertsons also pioneered new-method vinification for their tawnies: Game Bird, Privateer, Pyramid, Izaak Walton and the splendid Imperial.

Royal Orporto Wine Co.

Rua Azevedo Magalhaes 314, 4401 Vila Noa de Gaia. Vintages: 1945, '53, '54, '55, '58, '60, '61, '62, '63, '67, '70, '77, '78, '79, '80, '82, '83 and '85. Visits March-October.

Started by the Portuguese government as a controlling body for the port trade, this is now the largest port shipper. It is no longer a government-owned monopoly and is involved in table-wines as much as port. Not particularly good wines but produced in enormous quantities. The single-*quinta* tawny Quinta das Carvalhos has character.

Sandeman & Co.

Apartado 2, Largo Miguel Bombarda 3, 4401 Vila Nova de Gaia. Stocks: 53,000 pipes. Vintages: 1904, '08, '11, '12, '17, '20, '27, '34, '35, '42, '45, '47, '50, '55, '60, '63, '66, '67, '70, '75, '77, '80, '82 and '85. Founded 1790. Visits.

One of the biggest shippers of both port and sherry and the first company ever to advertise port, now a subsidiary of Seagrams but still chaired by David Sandeman, a direct descendant of George Sandeman, the founder, a friend of the Duke of Wellington. The firm's vineyards are the Quintas de Confradeiro and Casal at Celeirós (118 acres on the Pinhão river). Quinta Laranjeira (528 acres at Moncorvo) is a big new development in the highest Douro near Spain. Another 60 acres at Vale de Mendiz near Pinhão are rented. Sandeman's view is that their vintage wines are on the dry side, which is not borne out by my experience. I find them fruity, if not as rich as (say) Graham. Their tawnies are nice and nutty, especially the 10-year-old Royal. Associated companies are Robertson, Forrester, Diez Hermanos and Rodriguez Pinho.

Silva & Cosens Ltd. (Dow's Port)

Tr. Barão de Forrester, Apartado 14, 4401 Vila Nova de Gaia. Stock: 15,000 pipes. Vintages: 1904, '08, '12, '20, '24, '27, '34, ('42 & '44), '45, '47, '50, '55, '60, '63, '66, '70, '72, '75, '77, '80, '83 and '85. Founded 1798. Visits by appt.

The proprietors of Dow's brand, named after a Victorian partner. Since 1912 a sister company of Warre, under the control of the ubiquitous Symingtons. The family Quinta do Bomfim at Pinhão is one of the finest on the Douro. Supported by the Quinta Santa Madelana nearby up the Rio Torto it gives mightily tannic and concentrated vintage port, recognized by its dry finish in maturity. Most is now made by 'autovinification'. Dow also sell 'Boardroom' and 30-year-old tawny, and ruby and white ports.

Smith Woodhouse & Co.

Apartado 19, 4401 Vila Nova de Gaia. Stock: 4,000 pipes. Vintages: 1904, '08, '12, '17, '20, '24, '27, '35, '45, '47, '50, '55, '60, '63, '66, '70, '75, '77, '80, '83 and '85. Founded 1784. Visits by appt.

Together with Dow, Warre, etc. (qq.v.), now part of the Symington family property (which altogether stocks some 40,000 pipes). Smith Woodhouse also ship Gould Campbell vintage ports. Both come largely from the Rio Torto (Vale Dona Maria). Gould Campbell vintages are big, dark, powerful and very long-lasting wines; the Smith Woodhouse style is more fragrant and fruity and their tawnies notably so. His Majesty's Choice is a fine 29-year-old. Part of the crop is still trodden and vintages reflect the quality of the year accurately.

Taylor Fladgate & Yeatman

Rua do Choupelo 250, 4400 Vila Nova de Gaia. Stocks: 12,000 pipes. Vintages: 1904, '06, '08, '12, '17, '20, '24, '27, '35, '38, '40, '42, '45, '48, '55, '60, '63, '66, '70, '75, '77, '80, '83 and '85. Founded 1692. Visits.

One of the oldest and consistently one of the best shippers, still owned by descendants of the Yeatman family (Chairman, Alistair Roberston). The style of their tremendous vintage wines, of unrivalled ripeness, depth and every other dimension, is largely derived from their famous Quinta de Vargellas (630 acres), high on the upper Douro above São João de Pesqueira. In 1973 they also bought the Quintas do Panascal at Tabuaço and de Terafeita at Celeiros up the Pinhão valley. Each has 400 acres. Their vintage ports are still trodden by foot, although they are experimenting with stainless steel fermenters at their vinification centre for ruby ports near Regua. In occasional second-quality vintages Vargellas wine is shipped unblended under its own label. Fonseca (q.v.) is an associate company. Taylor's LBV is the biggest selling one on the market. Their tawnies (particularly their 20-year-olds) are also exceptional.

Warre & Co.

Tr. do Barão de Forrester, Apartado 26, 4401 Vila Nova de Gaia. Stock: 13,000 pipes. Vintages: 1904, '08, '12, '20, '22, '24, '27, '34, ('42), '45, '47, '50, '55, '58, '60, '63, '66, '70, '75, '77, '80, '83 and 85. Founded 1670. Visits.

Possibly the oldest English port firm, now one of the largest firms in the group owned by the Symington family. The vintage wines are based on their Quinta da Cavadinha near Pinhão, produced by modern methods. The single-*quinta* Quintra da Cavadinha is a recent introduction. The style is extremely fruity with a fresh, almost herbal bouquet and a firm 'grip' at the finish. Some recent vintages have been beautifully balanced and lingering. Warrior is a good vintage-character wine and Nimrod a tawny. Warre's LBV is particularly good. Cintra is a label for France.

OTHER PRODUCERS

Barros Almeida

Box 39, Ruada Leonor de Freitas 182, 4400 Vila Nova de Gaia. A family-owned substantial shipper of medium-quality ports, largely in bulk. Founded in 1913. Also proprietors of Kopke, the oldest brand of all, Feuerheerd, the Douro Wine Shippers Association and several other companies.

J. W. Burmester & Co.

Rua de Belomonte 39, 4000 Porto. Founded in 1750. Visits by appt. A small family-owned, now Portuguese, house of English and German foundation. No vineyards, but well-chosen wines from Pinhão go to make their Tordiz tawny and vintages. Other names used are Jems and Southam's. Stocks: 4,500 pipes. Vintages: 1900, '10, '20, '22, '27, '29, '34, '35, '37, '40, '44, '48, '50, '55, '58, '60, '63, '70, '77, '80, '84 and 85.

Churchills

Churchill Graham Lda, 63 Rua de Golgota, 4100 Porto. Vintages: 1982 and '85. Founded in 1981 by John Graham, this was first independent port shippers to be set up in 50 years. Wines are splendidly concentrated and full.

Diez Hermanos Lda

Rua Guilherme Baga 38, 4401 Vila Nova de Gaia. No visits. A small subsidiary of Forrester (q.v.). Stock: 6,000 pipes.

Feuerheerd Bros. & Co.

PO Box 39, 4401 Vila Nova de Gaia. Founded 1815. The formerly British-owned company now belongs to Barros Almeida (q.v.).

Martinez Gassiot & Co. Ltd

Rua das Coradas 13, Vila Nova de Gaia. Founded 1790. Visits. The company was bought by Harvey's in 1961 and is now a subsidiary of Allied Breweries; thus allied to Cockburn (q.v.). Its speciality is fine tawnies rather than ruby or vintage-character wines. Stocks: *see* Cockburn. Vintages: 1900, '04, '08, '11, '12, '19, '22, '27, '31, '34, '45, '48, '50, '55, '60, '63, '67, '70, '75, '82 and '85.

Niepoort & Co. Ltd

Rua Infante D. Henrique 39, 4000 Porto. Founded 1842. Visits by appt. A small Dutch family-owned company, currently being run by the fifth generation of Niepoorts. Unusual in storing its vintage port before bottling in glass demijohns in a cellar, rather than pipes in a lodge. Sales amount to 50,000 cases of high quality port a year. Vintages: 1945, '55, '60, '63, '66, '70, '75, '77, '78, '80, '82, '83, '85 and '87.

Rozes Lda

Rua do Choupelo 250, 4400 Vila Nova de Gaia. Founded 1853. No visits. A shipper jointly owned by Moët Hennessy and Taylor, Fladgate and Yeatman, specializing in the French market for its tawny, ruby and white ports. Stocks: 5,600 pipes. Vintages: 1963, '67, '77, '78, '82, '83 and '85.

Wiese & Krohn Sucrs.

Ruade de Serpa Pinto 149, 4401 Vila Nova de Gaia. Founded 1866. No visits. A small independent company, originally German, without vineyards. Shipped the vintages of 1957, '58, '60, '61, '63, '65, '67, '70, '75, '78, '82, '84 and '85.

MADEIRA

The very existence of madeira has been touch and go for a century. No famous wine region has suffered so much the combined onslaught of pests, diseases, disillusioned growers and public neglect. It is doubtful whether any other would have survived as more than a footnote.

What has kept madeira alive is the unique quality its old wines have of going on getting better and better. The remaining bottles of madeira from before its troubles began are proof that the island can make the longest-lived wines in the world. At a century old they have concentrated their flavours into a pungency that would be overwhelming were it not so fresh. They leave the mouth so cleanly and gracefully as you swallow that water could not be more reviving. Harmony between sweetness and acidity can go no further.

Madeira is the largest of three small islands 400 miles west of the coast of Morocco. It was discovered early in the fifteenth century by an eloping Bristol sea captain, who died there with his bride. Their crew sailed on, to be captured by corsairs. In a Moroccan dungeon they told their tale to a Spanish navigator, who in 1419 piloted a Portuguese ship to the island.

. It flourished as a Portuguese colony. Prince Henry the Navigator ordered the sweet Malvasia grapes of Greece to be planted, as well as sugar cane from Sicily. Later, with the discovery of the West Indies, bananas became an important part of the island's harvest. The crops were, and still are, grown in a garden-like mixture on steep terraces that rise half-way up the 6,000-foot island-mountain. As in the north of Portugal the vines are trained on pergolas to allow other crops beneath. With its warm climate Madeira was a natural producer of 'sack', like Jerez and the Canaries. What settled its destiny was a piece of English legislation of 1665, forbidding the export of European wines to British colonies except through British ports and in British ships. Madeira was presumably deemed to be in Africa; at all events it became the regular supplier for American vessels heading west. By the end of the seventeenth century the American and West Indian British colonists used madeira as their only wine.

Far from being spoilt by the long hot voyage across the mid-Atlantic, the wine proved better as a result. Later, with growing British interests in the Far East, it was discovered to benefit even more from a voyage to India. So fine was their sea-matured madeira that casks were shipped as ballast to India and back to give connoisseurs in Europe a yet finer wine. It was during the eighteenth century that brandy was increasingly added, as it was to port, to sweeten and stabilize it.

In America the appreciation of old madeira became a cult – southern gentlemen would meet to dine simply on terrapin and canvas-back duck before 'discussing' several decanters of ancient wine, named sometimes for their grapes, sometimes for the ship that brought them over, sometimes for the families in whose cellars they had rested and become heirlooms. Thus a Bual might be followed by a Constitution, and that by a Francis, a Butler or a Burd. One popular pale blend, still sometimes seen, is known as Rainwater – because, apparently, of a similiarity of taste. Almost the same reverence was paid to its qualities in England – and still is, by the few who have tasted such wines.

Quantities became far too great to transport through the tropics as a matter of course. In the 1790s Napoleon's navy also put difficulties in the way of merchantmen. A practical substitute was found in heating the wines to 45°C (113°F) in hot stores (Portuguese *estufas*) for up to six months: the cheaper wines in large pipe-heated vats; the best wines in casks in the warm space above them.

Four principal grape varieties and three or four others were grown to provide different styles of wine. The original, the Malvasia or Malmsey, made the richest: the Bual a less rich, more elegant but equally fragrant wine; Verdelho a soft, much drier wine with a faintly bitter finish, the Sercial (a clone of Riesling) a fine light wine with a distinct acid 'cut'. Tinta Negra Mole, reputedly a form of Pinot Noir, was planted to make the strong red wine once known as 'Tent'. Bastardo, Terrantez and Moscatel were also grown in smaller quantities.

Madeira was at the peak of prosperity when a double disaster struck. In the 1850s came oidium, the powdery mildew. In 1873 phylloxera arrived. Six thousand acres of vineyard were destroyed, and only 1,200 replaced with true madeira vines. To save grafting the remainder were replanted (if at all) with French-American hybrids whose wine has no claim to be called madeira at all.

Since then, Madeira has lived on its reputation, kept alive by memories, by a meagre trickle of high-quality wines, and by the convenient French convention of *sauce madère*, which is easily enough satisfied with any wine that has been cooked. Half the wine from the island today is destined for sauce-making with no questions asked. Unfortunately even the replanting of the original European vines, the four classics, was neglected in favour of the obliging Tinta Negra Mole. Today 80 per cent of the crop (hybrids apart) is Tinta. It has to do service for the Malmsey, Bual, Verdelho and Sercial (respectively 3.5, 2, 2 and 1.5 per cent of the crop) in all except the most expensive brands. Tinta, in fact, is picked either earlier or later, fortified during or after fermentation, 'stoved' more or less, coloured and sweetened more or less, according to whether it is destined to be sold as Sercial, Verdelho, Bual or Malmsey.

Portugal's entry to the E.E.C. has served notice on this practice. Its regulations require 85 per cent of a wine to be of the grape variety named. 'Malmsey' can no longer be simply a style: it will have to be genuine Malvasia. Taking note of this, the islanders are busy regrafting vines, 100,000 of them a year, to the classic varieties.

It is their only hope. They cannot thrive on cheapness and low quality. They have no cash crop of 'instant' wine; it all needs ageing. The *estufas* are expensive to run (on imported coal). The maintaining of dated *solera* (as in Jerez) used to be standard practice, but is now dying out. However, the Madeira shippers still occasionally declare a vintage – always a rarer occurrence with madeira than with port, and taking place not immediately after the vintage but some 30 years later.

Vintage madeira is kept in cask for at least 20 years, then in glass 20-litre demijohns for another period before bottling – when it is deemed ready to drink. In reality it is still only a young wine at this stage; it needs another 20 to 50 years in bottle to achieve sublimity.

The late Noël Cossart, the fifth generation of the old firm of madeira shippers Cossart Gordon, counselled 'never to buy a cheap Sercial or Malmsey; these grapes are shy growers and must consequently be expensive; whereas Bual and Verdelho are prolific and develop faster and may be both cheaper and good.'

Vintages

The most famous madeira vintages up to 1900, bottles of which are still occasionally found, were 1789, 1795 (esp. Terrantez), 1806, 1808 (Malmsey), 1815 (esp. Bual), 1822, 1836, 1844, 1846 (esp. Terrantez and Verdelho), 1851, 1862, 1865, 1868, 1870 (Sercial), 1880 (esp. Malmsey).

Since 1900 some 13 vintages have been shipped: 1900 (the last year Moscatel was made), 1902 (esp. Verdelho and Bual), 1905 (esp. Sercial), 1906 (esp. Malmsey), 1907 (esp. Verdelho and Bual), 1910, 1914 (Bual), 1915 (Bual and Sercial), 1916, 1920, 1926 (esp. Bual), 1934 (Verdelho), 1940, 1941 (esp. Bual), 1950, 1954 (esp. Bual), 1956.

Madeira Wine Company

Avenida Arriaga 28, 9000 Funchal. In 1913 a number of shippers in the beleaguered trade formed themselves into the Madeira Wine Association to pool their resources and share facilities. Reconstituted in 1981 as the Madeira Wine Company, the group now controls 26 companies and accounts for about 40% of Madeira exports. The main, modern winery is situated in a converted army barracks, and blends corresponding to its 120 different labels are made up in the Company's lotting rooms. One of its picturesque old lodges is next to the Tourist Office in Funchal and open for visits and a tasting.

Companies owned by the Madeira Wine Company include Blandy's, Cossart Gordon, Leacock (qq.v),

Lomelino, Rutherford & Miles (q.v.) and Shortridge Lawton. There are only seven independent firms remaining outside the Company.

Barbeito

Vinhos Barbeito Lda, Apartado 264, Estrada Monumental 145, 9000 Funchal. Founded 1947; the present owner is the daughter of the founder. Independent. They do have an impressive range of vintages in stock, some of which were purchased after the founding of the company. Stocks are 490,000 litres.

Blandy Brothers

Madeira Wine Company, Funchal. Founded 1811 by Berkshire-born John Blandy who first came to Madeira to defend the island against Napoleon in 1807; the family is still involved in the company.

H. M. Borges Sucrs

Rua 31 Janeiro 83, PO Box 92, 9001 Funchal, Independent.

Cossart Gordon

Madeira Wine Company, Funchal. Founded 1745 by Francis Newton and William Gordon after they fled the failure of Bonnie Prince Charlie's Jacobite uprising. They were joined by William Cossart in 1808 and the Cossart family are still an active force in the Madeira trade.

Henriques & Henriques

Rua Dr Joao Brito Camara 32A, 9000 Funchal. Founded 1850. Independent; the largest outside the Madeira Wine Company, and still family-run. It makes 2 year old Madeiras for Harvey's and Sandeman, but their best wines go out under their own name.

Leacock

Madeira Wine Company, Funchal. Founded 1741. Thomas Slapp Leacock is famous in Madeira for saving the island's vineyards from phylloxera by dipping the roots in tar and resin, and organizing a programme of regrafting. Wines include the basic St John range and the Special Reserve 10 year olds.

Pereira D'Oliveira Vinhos

Rua dos Ferreiros 107, 9000 Funchal. Founded 1820. Tiny independent company making excellent wines, with a good stock of old vintages.

Rutherford & Miles

Madeira Wine Company, Funchal. Founded early 19th century.

Veiga França

Avenida Arriaga 73, 9000 Funchal. Independent. Wine produced mainly for export to France and other European countries, where it is mainly used for supermarket own-labels and cooking.

SWITZERLAND

So rare are Swiss wines outside their own country that it is easy to assume that they fall short of international standards and remain the special taste of a blinkered culture.

The assumption is not wholly accurate. Many Swiss are critical and wine-conscious, most have money to spare – which is a good thing, for Swiss wines are expensive by almost any standards. Land prices and the cost of culture of their cliff-hanging vineyards are startlingly high. To justify inevitably high prices there should in principle be every pressure on growers to concentrate on high quality. In practice, the market is cushioned by a series of subsidies and protectionist measures. The chill winds of competition are beginning to blow, however, and talk is for the first time being heard of white wine quotas being liberalized. Change is in the air.

One hundred and fifty years ago the emphasis was on red wines, and the best of them came from Graubünden in the German-speaking east. The best whites came from the north shore of lake Geneva between Lausanne and Montreux in Vaud canton, where the steep south slopes ripened the local Chasselas to perfection. Further up the Rhône valley in the remote mountain area of the Valais there was a largely part-time winegrowing tradition, and vineyards were irregularly planted with obscure grapes chosen for their potentially dazzling sweetness and strength in the dry and sunny alpine climate.

The modern industry began to take shape when Chasselas spread up the Rhône valley, when pressure for the sunny lake slopes of Lake Geneva as building land drove half the wines out of the Vaud, and when selected forms of the Pinot Noir and Gamay began to penetrate from France, via Geneva and then eastwards. Meanwhile the Müller-Thurgau, bred by the eponymous Swiss scientist a century ago at Geisenheim, began to invade the eastern cantons. (Nowadays his name is forgotten and the variety referred to as Riesling-Sylvaner.) In 1945 the Italian-speaking Tessin (Tessino) adapted the Merlot of Bordeaux as its main red grape variety.

Although in the last 100 years the overall vineyard area has diminished considerably, selected areas such as German-speaking Switzerland, the Valais, Vaud and Geneva have put on acreage. Plantings of red varieties are also increasing. The Swiss produce enough white wine to meet (indeed exceed) local demand – hence the stringently low import quotas designed to protect domestic growers. Red wine, for which the import quota is more generous, is imported in large quantities.

The essential information given on the often rather taciturn, though frequently highly decorative, Swiss wine label is laid down by the federal government in the ODA (*Ordonnance sur les Denrées Alimentaires*). Generally speaking, for white wines, if there is no other indication of grape variety, assume Chasselas. Red wines will in the main be Pinot Noir and/or Gamay. Some German-Swiss labels use terms with no international validity – but then they not only never travel abroad, they seldom leave the confines of the canton in which they were grown. Italian-Swiss wine labels are simplicity itself as there are essentially only two types of wine: Merlot and the (fast disappearing) Nostrano, made from a clutch of hybrid grapes.

The maker's name seems to be considered of little importance to the consumer and is often tucked away down at the bottom in small print. Pride of place may be given to a brand name (Les Murailles), estate name (Château d'Allaman) or village name (St Saphorin). It is not always easy to tell which is which.

Though chaptalization is permitted (and quite commonly practised at the lower quality levels), all Swiss wines can be assumed to be dry unless a specific caution is included on the label: *miflétri* or *flétri* (literally 'shrivelled') in the French-speaking cantons, *Spätlese* where German is the lingua franca.

THE FRENCH-SPEAKING CANTONS

All the principal vineyards of the French-speaking cantons (Suisse romande) lie along the south-facing right bank of the Rhône, from its emergence into the Valais (a suntrap sheltered on both sides by towering Alps), round the shores of Lake Geneva (simply a widening of the Rhône) to its departure through the gently rolling farmlands of Geneva canton into France. Also included in this group are the three lakes of Neuchâtel, Biel/Bienne and Morat, each of which enjoys good, south-facing, lake-shore conditions. Three-quarters of all Swiss wine is grown in Suisse Romande, over eighty per cent of it is white.

The Valais

The Valais (which begins, geographically, at the Grimselpass and ends at St Maurice on the right bank, and St Gingolph on the left) has Switzerland's driest and sunniest climate, frequently described as a cross between that of Spain and that of Provence. On its steeper vineyards, terraced on arid mountain slopes, irrigation by means of wooden channels known as *bisses* used to be common practice. Nowadays irrigation is limited to periods of severe drought and this only during the *période végétative*.

Wine-growing starts in earnest somewhere between Visp and Sierre, reaches a crescendo around Sion, the heart (and capital) of the Valais, and begins to wind gradually down after the Rhône has executed its sharp right turn at Martigny. At its upper extremes, the village of Visperterminen above Visp has what are said to be Europe's highest vineyards at around 1,000 metres above sea level. The principal wine growing villages in the upper Valais are Salquenen/Salgesch, Sierre and St Léonard; in the lower Valais, Vétroz, Ardon, Leytron, Chamoson, Saillon and Fully are the most important.

Action has finally been taken in the Valais in response to an urgent awareness of the need for some notion of *crus*. For too long Fendant (i.e. Chasselas), which accounts for the largest quantity of wine produced in the Valais, was sold without mention of village or vineyard name. Since many were of poor quality (and the consumer had no way of differentiating), the result was that all Fendants, whether good, bad or indifferent, tended to be tarred with the same bottom-of-the-market brush. Nowadays there will often be a village or vineyard name appended; the appellation Fendant may even be omitted. Sylvaner, known here as Johannisberg (sometimes Rhin, either Petit or Gros), makes aromatic, fuller-bodied yet dry wines; when late harvested they can be impressive indeed.

Lakes of Chasselas are one thing; the so-called 'specialities' of the Valais, generally considered to be the great undiscovered potential of Swiss wines, are quite another. First comes the incomparable Arvine, its name said to come from the Latin meaning 'pale yellow'. Distinguished by its fine nose and characteristic salty finish, it is usually vinified dry; some growers harvest a small proportion of the crop late to make a *mi-flétri* or *flétri*. Humagne ('vigorous vine' in Latin), is a nervy, stimulating wine traditionally prescribed as a post-partum tonic to young mothers. Its requires the best sites, performs rather irregularly and ripens late – all of which had contributed to a gradual decline over the years, but that decline is happily now in reverse. Amigne, whose favoured sites are concentrated in and around Vétroz, is made in extremely limited quantities into a rich, velvety wine, almost always with some residual sugar but sufficient acidity and backbone to give it good keeping qualities.

Rarer still are a clutch of very old, quaintly-named varieties, found mainly in the upper Valais around Visp. In centuries past they were harvested early to give quite sharp, thirst-quenching wines designed for vineyard quaffing after a hard day's work. Of these, the finest is Heida (or Païen), thought to be a relation either of Savagnin (the same grape as used in *vin jaune*), or of Traminer. Himbertscha, whose name sounds vaguely raspberry-related, apparently means 'trellis-grown' in the upper Valais dialect, referring to the traditional method of training this particular grape, while Lafnetscha turns out to be the Blanchier of Savoie. Both give clean-tasting, rather acidic wines which need plenty of time to mature. Finally comes Gwäss (Gouais blanc), another native of the Jura, sharply reminiscent of cider when young.

Of the non-indigenous but well-established varieties, the Marsanne grape thrives here under the name of Ermitage, giving (especially around Fully) a full-bodied wine with a striking nose and an elusively smokey flavour. Malvoisie (alias Pinot Gris) may be vinified dry (in which case it is often labelled Pinot Gris), or harvested late and made into a sweet wine (and often labelled Malvoisie). Muscat has been grown in the Valais since the sixteenth century, and is made here with all residual sugar fermented out, closer in style to a Muscat d'Alsace than to any other. Tiny quantities of Gewürztraminer, Riesling, Aligoté, Chardonnay, Chenin and Pinon Blanc are also to be found.

Over a third of Valais wine is red and two thirds of this is Pinot Noir, which acquits itself with some distinction, particularly around Sierre. The better growers are experimenting with Burgundy clones and varying proportions of new oak. Pinot Noir is also blended with Gamay and called Dôle, at its lower levels a good lunchtime wine quaffed throughout Switzerland in multiples of the decilitre to accompany uncomplicated meals. (To qualify for the appellation, a Dôle must contain at least 51 per cent Pinot Noir and reach a certain minimum Oechslé level prescribed by the cantonal wine commission; if it misses the mark it is labelled Goron.) Gamay vinified alone is not to be sneezed at, especially from the villages around Martigny.

Of antique red grapes there is Humagne Rouge (no relation of the white Humagne but reckoned by some to be Oriou, from the Valle d'Aosta). It makes robust, pleasantly tannic and appetizing country wine. Cornalin (alias Landroter or Rouge du Pays) is an extremely rare variety whose irregular yield and uneven performance makes it a tricky commercial proposition for most wine growers. Its deep colour, good tannins and superb fruit, however, make it an extremely interesting proposition for interested wine drinkers. Finally, in the upper Valais Eyholzer Roter (the Mondeuse of Haute Savoie) is to be found, which gives a tawny-reddish, rather rough country wine. Syrah, of fairly recent import, deserves special mention, particularly from around Chamoson; some Nebiolo is also being produced.

The Vaud
The canton of Vaud includes all the vineyards of the north shore of Lake Geneva and the Rhône, as high upstream as the border with the Valais at Bex: a 50-mile arc of southern slopes. It is divided into three main zones: Chablais, the right bank of the Rhône between Ollon and the lake; Lavaux, the central section between Montreux and Lausanne; and La Côte, from Lausanne round to Nyon at the border with Geneva. Further north, just short of lake Neuchâtel are the little enclaves of Côtes de l'Orbe and Bonvillars; half the villages in the Vully vineyard on Lake Morat also belong to Vaud. The canton has its own recently introduced AO systems, the term implying here control of origin, grape varieties and Oechslé levels.

Chablais' AOs include the villages of Villeneuve, Yvorne, Aigle, Ollon and Bex, all with good southwest slopes above the Rhône. Yvorne, with its minerally, gunflint character, real vigour, ripeness and length is generally considered to be the greatest of Chablais wines. At its best it is undoubtedly a match for (though subtly different from) the top wines from Lavaux.

Lavaux is certainly Switzerland's most scenic vineyard, piled high in toppling terraces above the lakeside villages. The view from among the vines is superb: the mountains of Savoie a great dark jagged-topped bulk against the sun opposite, the lake surface below gleaming grey, wrinkled by white paddle-steamers gliding from village pier to village pier. Erosion is a serious problem: a brown

Château d'Aigle, in the Chablais district of the Vaud, is now a wine museum.

stain in the lake after a night's heavy rain is bad news for a wine grower.

Lavaux boasts two recently designated *crus* – Dézaley (for centuries considered the high point of Swiss white wine) and nearby Calamin – as well as six of Vaud's 26 AOs. Chasselas from the upper slopes takes on a liveliness and an almost aromatic quality which distinguishes it from the more austere dryness of the lower vineyards. Each village, however, has its committed supporters and the names of Epesses, St Saphorin, Rivaz, Cully, Villette, Lutry, Chardonne and others are writ correspondingly large on the label. (The old appellation Dorin, meaning a Chasselas from the Vaud, has all but disappeared.)

La Côte between Lausanne and Nyon has twelve AOs, the best-known of which are Féchy, Perroy, Mont-sur-Rolle, Tartegnin, Vinzel and Luins. This is a more gentle, often southeasterly sloping vineyard whose wines rarely have the vigour or flavour of those of Lavaux or Chablais, but make deliciously floral pre-prandial quaffing wines.

Chasselas dominates the Vaud vineyard; a very small part is made over to Pinot Gris, Pinot Blanc and Riesling-Sylvaner. Pinot Noir and Gamay are also found vinified singly, or blended and designated Salvagnin (a so-called 'label of quality' which has fallen somewhat into disrepute).

Geneva

The Geneva winegrowers have upstaged the rest of Switzerland by introducing a full-blown AC system (control of origin, varieties, Oechslé levels and yields), the first and so far the only one in Switzerland – though it is hoped and expected that others will follow suit.

The canton is divided into three districts: the biggest – Mandement – to the north on the right bank of the Rhône, includes Dardagny, Russin and above all Satigny. South of the river (and of the city) is the region Arve-et-Rhône, centred around Lully-Bernex. The area which sets off round the other side of the lake is called Arve-et-Lac. Since the slopes are gentle and the vines well spaced out, mechanical harvesting is a possibility, which gives the wines a useful price advantage.

The area has increased its vineyards steadily and is now third in importance after the Valais and the Vaud. Chasselas (often, but not inevitably, known here as Perlan) accounts for about half the wine produced, a light, dry wine usually bottled with a slight prickle to make up for the character it frequently lacks. Some increasingly useful forms of Gamay have been introduced that suit both the conditions of the vineyard and the local taste, shaped by years of massive Beaujolais imports. Riesling-Sylvaner, Pinot Gris, Pinot Blanc, and Gewürztraminer are also to be found; impressive results are being achieved with Aligoté and Chardonnay.

Lakes Neuchâtel, Biel and Morat

Vines grow all along the northern shores of all three lakes, sheltered by the Jura chain which forms the backbone of the route from Geneva up to Basle. The best-known villages on Lake Neuchâtel are Cortaillod, Auvernier, Boudry and St Blaise; on Lake Biel, the names of Schafis and Twann are famous, while on Lake Morat, the Fribourg villages of Praz, Nant and Môtier enjoy a certain renown.

Chasselas reigns here once more to give wines which are light, dry and given to a natural prickle ('*l'étoile*') – a result of their being mainly bottled *sur lie*. There is no Gamay north of Geneva: Pinot Noir is the only permitted red variety. The limestone hills to the north and west of Lake Neuchâtel and the temperate climate seem to bring out some of the elusive finesse of the Pinot Noir grape. Neuchâtel Pinots from reputable growers may be expected to have some distinction; in a good year they may be considered the best Pinots Switzerland can produce. The pale rosé Oeil-de-Perdrix ('partridge's eye') – an appellation native to Neuchâtel, now widely used all over Switzerland – is an appealing *rosé de Pinot Noir*.

VALAIS PRODUCERS

Oscar Chanton AG
3930 Visp. Founded 1944. Owner: Josef-Marie Chanton. 17 acres.

Over 20 different wines can be tasted in the venerable old Chanton cellar on the Junkergasse in Visp, including rarities from the upper Valais like Heida, Himbertscha, Lafnetscha and Gwäss, rescued from oblivion by Josef-Marie Chanton. The Arvine is superb, as are the late harvested Malvoisie and Gewürztraminer.

Gérald Clavien
3961 Miège/Sierre. Owner: Gérald Clavien. 11 acres.

The wines of this young, dynamic grower (who started life as a chef before taking over his father's vineyards) feature on the lists of all the top restaurants in Switzerland. Sierre is the hub of red wine-growing in the Valais: Clavien's straight Pinot Noir and *Tête de Cuvée* are notable, also the Dôle Blanche (a *rosé de Pinot Noir*). Some Chardonnay is also produced.

Traditional signs.

Caves Orsat SA

1920 Martigny. Founded 1874. Owner: Amann Vins Holding, Winterthur. 86 acres.

Didier Joris is the noted oenologist responsible here for the *domaine* wines and the highly esteemed Primus Classicus Arvine. All the usual Valaisan range is produced, and the firm places great importance on the concept of domaine and village wines (Fendant de Martigny, de Fully, de Chamoson etc.). Their reds include Pinot Noir, Dôle, Humagne rouge and Gamay (for which the Martigny area is famous).

Jacques-Alphonse & Philippe Orsat frères

1920 Martigny. Founded 1988. Owners: Jacques-Alphonse Orsat, Philippe Orsat and Antoine Escher. 30 acres.

A newly formed company which rose from the ashes of Alphonse Orsat. All the Valais wines and specialities are made (with the exception of Arvine), with a special accent on *vins d'appellations*: Fendant de Ravanay, Fendant les Marques, Syrah du Clos d'Anzier among others.

Provins Valais

Fédération des Caves des Producteurs du Vins du Valais. 1951 Sion. Founded 1930. Director: Jean Actis.

The enormous, highly regarded central cooperative of the Valais producing some 30% of all Valais wines. Their Capsule Dorée range includes well-known brand names like Pierrafeu Fendant, Johannisberg Rhonegold, Oeil-de-Perdrix Perdrizel (a rosé de Pinot Noir) and Pinot Noir Saint-Guérin. To the usual vast Valaisan spectrum of grapes they add Pinot Blanc, Chardonnay and Cabernet Sauvignon. An exciting new development is their Chasselas St. Léonard, made (exceptionally for Switzerland) without malolactic fermentation, and reserved for *la grande restauration*.

Marc Raymond et fils.

1913 Saillon. Founded 1948. Owners: Marc and Gérard Raymond. 9 acres.

Tiny family business producing top quality Fendant, Johannisberg, Arvine (the pride of the house), Muscat, Malvoisie and Dôle Blanche. Their reds are also noted, particularly Dôle and Pinot Noir. Marc Raymond is one of the few Valaisan growers to make Nebbiolo.

Eloi et Gérard Roduit

1926 Fully. Founded 1952. Owners: Eloi and Gérard Roduit. 15 acres.

A small family (uncle and nephew) business making the full range of Valais wines on some prime sites above the village of Fully. Of especial note are their Ermitage and Arvine (vinified dry and *flétri*), Gamay, Pinot Noir (of which a proportion is oak-aged), and Syrah.

Maurice Zufferey

3964 Muraz/Sierre. Founded 1963. Owner: Maurice Zufferey. 11 acres.

Sierre is red wine country and Maurice Zufferey's are particularly notable (though he also produces many other specialities). Three Pinot Noirs are made (one of them oak-aged), Dôle, Humagne rouge and the tricky but infinitely rewarding Cornalin which Monsieur Zufferey was among the first to revive in the Valais.

Michel Clavien

1962 Pont-de-la-Morge. Founded 1925. Owner: Michel Clavien. 62 acres (37 owned, 25 leased).

A prime mover in the *appellation d'origine* debate and a marketing man to his fingertips, Michel Clavien has worked tirelessly to raise the image of Valaisan wines both within Switzerland and abroad. The wines are elegant, the labels (especially of the Fin Bec line) eye-catching. Le Grand Sion is a blend of Chasselas from a number of *lieux-dits* around Sion; Dôle Fin Bec contains 85% Pinot Noir and 15% Gamay; Pinot Noir de la Follie comes from the vineyard of the same name.

Simon Maye

1956 St Pierre-de-Clages. Owners: The Maye family. 18.5 acres.

A small, quality grower making two highly prized Fendants (Le Fauconnier and La Mouette), Johannisberg, Dôle, Pinot Noir, Humagne rouge, a richly spicy Syrah, plus some Chardonnay, Malvoisie and Arvine.

Domaine du Mont d'Or

1962 Pont de la Morge. Founded 1948. Owners: the shareholders (publicly quoted company). Director: Dominique Favre. 52 acres.

The most famous property of Sion, established on a steep, dry, sheltered hill by a soldier from the Vaud, one Sergeant-Major Masson, who installed the irrigation system by *bisses* which is still in operation. The domaine is best known for its Johannisbergs: du Mont d'Or when vinified dry, or de la St Martin (and more rarely du 1er Décembre) when late harvested. Also produced is a magnificent Arvine, and strong tannic and alcoholic Dôle.

VAUD PRODUCERS

Henri Badoux

1860 Aigle. Founded 1908. Owner: Henri Badoux and family.
123 acres.

A substantial, second-generation family-owned business with vineyards in Yvorne, Aigle, Ollon, Villeneuve, St Saphorin, Féchy, Vinzel and Mont-sur-Rolle. The two wines considered *les moteurs de l'entreprise* are the famous Aigle les Murailles (with the classic lizard label) and Yvorne Petit Vignoble. Diners on the excellent Swiss trains may enjoy Badoux's Aigle Pourpre Monseigneur, a Pinot Noir from the Chablais district.

Jean-Michel Conne

1605 Chexbres. Owner: Jean-Michel Conne. 25 acres.

By dint of wise buying of vineyards outside Lavaux, and by inheritance of the family vineyards, a considerable holding of good sites around Lake Geneva has been built up. Especially famous is their Dézaley Plan Perdu, St Saphorin Le Sémillant and Ollon L'Oisement. The Oeil-de-Perdrix, made exclusively from Pinot Noir, was recently nominated the best Swiss rosé. Several Pinot Noirs (of which the oak-aged is labelled Cartige) are also produced.

Henri Delarze

1867 Verschiez/Ollon. Founded 1696. Owner: Henri Delarze
and son. 8.5 acres.

Unusually for the area, this small estate specializes in (and is renowned for) its red wines which are only commercialized between 2 and 3 years after bottling. Les Colondeys is a Pinot Noir from several different Pinot forms; La Pidance is from Burgundy clones.

Grognuz Frères

1844 Villeneuve. Founded 1848. Owners: Marco and Frédéric
Grognuz. 37 acres.

A medium-sized family firm in the heart of the Chablais, wine makers *de père en fils* for several generations with widely spread, excellently sited vineyards. From Villeneuve come some notable Chasselas and Pinot Noirs; further south from Les Evouettes come Chasselas, Pinot Noir and Oeil-de-Perdrix (rosé); from Lavaux an elegantly smokey St Saphorin. Tiny quantities of Chardonnay and Gewurztraminer complete the picture. Pride of the house is Pinot Noir Selection Sang Bleu, from selected Burgundy Pinot Noir vines, aged in *petites pièces*.

Hammel

1180 Rolle. Founded 1920. Director: Gilbert Hammel Rolaz.
62 acres.

A leading domaine and merchant house of La Côte, producing Chasselas from various Vaudois vineyards: Domaine Les Pierrailles and La Bigaire (La Côte), Domaine de Riencourt (Bougy), Clos du Chatelard (Villeneuve), Clos de la George (Yvorne).

Alain Neyroud

Chardonne. Owner: Alain Neyroud. 17 acres.

A fifth-generation business selling mainly to private clients in German-speaking Switzerland and to restaurants in the area. Their Chasselas is labelled La Petite Combe, Gamay La Perle Rouge, Pinot Noir Au Coin des Serpents. Unusually for a Vaud house, about 50% of their production is red.

Obrist

1800 Vevey. Founded 1854. Owner: the Schenk group.
Director: Emile Saugy. 99 acres.

One of the largest growers of Vaudois white, with a particular reputation for their Yvornes: Clos du Rocher, Clos des Rennauds and Prè Roc. Also famous is their Cure d'Attalens and Salvagnin Domaine du Manoir.

Gérard Pinget

1812 Rivaz. Founded 1884. Administrator: C. Pinget. 25 acres.

A traditional little estate whose top wines are Dézaley Renard (the label sports a fox), St Saphorin and Soleil de Lavaux.

Schenk

1180 Rolle. Founded 1893. Owner: André Schenk. 560 acres.

The giant Swiss wine firm (sometimes referred to as '*le Ciba-Geigy du vin*'). Principal estates are in Yvorne, Mont-sur-Rolle, Vinzel and Féchy. Foreign subsidiaries and companies are in Burgundy, the Midi, Spain, northern Italy, Belgium and the USA.

Jean & Pierre Testuz

1096 Treytorrens-Cully. Founded 1845. President: Jean
Testuz. Administrator: Jean-Philippe Testuz. 486 acres.

The Testuz family (whose premises are actually in Dézaley) date their wine growing from the 16th century. In 1865 they sold the first bottled wine in Switzerland. Their Dézaley, L'Arbalète, is one of the finest of the area. Other Lavaux wines include the fine St Saphorin Roche Ronde and Epesses. Chablais wines include Aigle Les Cigales and Yvorne Haute-Combe. Lavaux and La Côte wines both include some from the vineyards of the City of Lausanne. Reds from the same sites as the whites are good though less distinguished. The red label is Grand Croix.

GENEVA PRODUCERS

Pierre Dupraz

Lully/1233 Bernex. Founded 1909. Owner: Pierre Dupraz. 27
acres.

All wines are labelled varietally (Chasselas, Aligoté, Chardonnay, Gamay and Pinot Noir) with the domaine's name (Domaine des Curiades) appended. Some Chardonnay is oak-aged.

Luc Mermoud

Lully/1233 Bernex. Owners: Luc and Liliane Mermoud. 10 acres.

All the Geneva gamut is produced and wines labelled simply by variety: Chasselas, Aligoté, Pinot Blanc, Gamay

and Pinot Noir. They are particularly proud of their Aligoté, which performs well in the clay/limestone soils and benevolent climate of this corner of Lake Geneva.

Claude Ramu

1282 Dardagny.

A range of mythologically named (and artistically labelled) wines is produced, of which the Pinot Gris Domaine du Centaure stands out. Other whites include Chasselas, Aligoté, Pinot Blanc and Gewürztraminer. Gamay, Pinot Noir (some oak-aged) and a *crémant* labelled *Les Compagnons de Venus* are also produced.

Vin-Union Genève

1242 Satigny. President: Jean Revaclier. Director: Fred Kummer. 365 members.

A federation of 3 cooperative cellars whose members own some 2,400 acres, over 80% of the canton's vineyards. Their members have vineyards in nine out of the recently designated *grands crus*, among them Rougemont (Gamay), La Feuillée (Chasselas) and Côtes de Russin – the favoured child of the house – where red and white are produced. Their Château du Crest from Jussy is mildly fruity, better value for money than many Beaujolais. The label of their Chardonnay Le Bruant (showing a very beautiful bunting) is even more appealing than the bottle's contents.

NEUCHÂTEL PRODUCERS

Samuel Chatenay

2017 Boudry. Founded 1796. Director: J. C. von Buren. 123 acres.

Large quantities of wine (white, pink and red) are produced by this big old house, the best of which come from the 4-acre Domaine de Château Vaumarcus.

Château d'Auvernier

2012 Auvernier. Founded 1603. Owner: Thierry Grosjean. 74 acres.

One of the oldest-established Neuchâtel houses, making a finely nervy Neuchâtel blanc, Oeil-de-Perdrix, Pinot Noir d'Auvernier, Pinot Gris and a little Chardonnay.

A. Porret

2016 Cortaillod. Founded 1858. Owner: Pierre-André Porret.

A fourth-generation family house making Chasselas (Domaine des Cèdres, named after the 200 year-old cedars outside the family house), Pinot Noir Cortaillod, an Oeil-de-Perdrix and (since the '60's) a little Pinot Gris. An experimental planting of Chardonnay is giving some good results in the better vintages.

THE GERMAN-SPEAKING CANTONS

Because the German-speaking cantons favour the same grape varieties and use broadly the same vinification techniques, they tend to be grouped together and called (for some obscure reason) eastern Switzerland. There are the usual concentrations around lakes (Constance, Zurich) and along rivers (Rhine, Aare, Limmat) with the odd microclimate thrown in for good measure (notably the four villages in Graubunden known as the Bundner Herrschaft). In eight of the Swiss-German cantons wine is grown: Graubunden, St. Gallen, Thurgau, Schaffhausen, Zurich, Aargau, Bas35 land and Bern. The most productive cantons today are Zurich (scattered between Wädenswil, home of the Federal School of Oenology and Viticulture, Winterthur and the villages along the north shore of the lake); and Schaffhausen (whose Hallau vineyard is the largest in eastern Switzerland). Consumption of Swiss German-produced wines is almost exclusively local and entirely faithful: most growers are sold out by year's end.

Up here north of the Alps, the colour balance changes and red begins to predominate in the shape of Pinot Noir (alias Blauburgunder, or Clevner on Lake Zurich). Riesling-Sylvaner is the main white variety, which performs well in the right (i.e. secateur-wielding) hands to give suprisingly aromatic, lively wines – frequently of more interest than run-of-the-mill Chasselas from further south. Blauburgunder excels in the Bundner Herrschaft, whose warm autumn climate ripens it to real substance, with colour and a velvet touch. Elsewhere the Swiss Germans exhibit a mystifying fondness for pale, slightly fizzy Blauburgunders, a penchant not inevitably shared by others.

Besides these two (plus a little Gewürztraminer, Pinot Blanc and Pinot Gris) there are some specialities which are confined to the Swiss German cantons. Completer is an extremely rare, late-ripening, late-harvested speciality found in Graubünden (where it is long-matured and liquorous) and on the lakeshore of Zurich (where it is more austere). Its name is linked to the evening office of Compline, after which the monks were said to gratefully quaff a glass or two. Raüschling is an old-established Zurich variety which makes elegant, crisp white wines. Freisamer is a (potentially promising) cross between Sylvaner and Pinot Gris.

SWISS GERMAN PRODUCERS

Schlossgut Bachtobel

8570 Weinfelden. Owner: Hans Ulrich Kesselring. 14 acres.

At the elegant Bachtobel property just outside Weinfelden, 80% of the production is Blauburgunder, about 20% Riesling-Sylvaner plus tiny amounts of Pinot Gris, Chardonnay and rosé. An expensively experimental *méthode champenoise* has resulted in what Herr Kesselring describes as 'probably not the best, but certainly the dearest 'champagne' ever made . . .'

Familie Donatsch
7208 Malans. Owner: Thomas Donatsch. 9 acres.

The beautiful old, wood-panelled *Gasthof zum Ochsen* in the patrician village of Malans has belonged to the family for over 150 years. Thomas Donatsch's superb Blauburgunders (Pinot Noir) and finely structured Chardonnays are found on the wine lists of most of the top Swiss restaurants. Also produced are Riesling-Sylvaner, Pinot Blanc and Pinot Gris.

Ruedi Honegger
8712 Stäf/Mutzmalen. Owner: Ruedi Honegger.

Herr Honegger, at the wonderfully-sited Itzikerhüsli, is one of the relatively small number of growers on lake Zurich who bottles his own wine on the domaine. He makes fine Riesling-Sylvaner, Räuschling, Clevner (Pinot Noir) and rosé.

Hans Jörg Lauber
Gut Plandaditsch, 7208 Malans. Founded 1928. Owners: the Lauber family. 5 acres.

The lovely, onion-domed Gut Plandaditsch is a Malanser landmark, beneath which the Laubers grow both fruit and wine. Especially notable is their deep ruby Blauburgunder, powerfully aromatic Pinot Blanc, late-harvested Freisamer and Pinot Gris. Their mouth-filling Chardonnay, produced in tiny quantities, spends up to seven months in new oak.

Anton Meier
zum Sternen, 5303 Würenlingen. Founded: 1828. Owner: Anton Meier. 12 acres.

Anton Meier is a noted wine grower, landlord of the village pub and owner of one of Switzerland's foremost vine nurseries. He produces an extraordinarily fruity Riesling-Sylvaner, good Pinot Gris, a fine Gewürztraminer, some rosé (Pinot Noir) and, lately, a crisp Crémant. His pride and joy are the Blauburgunders, frequent winners of high-profile comparative (international) tastings of Pinot Noir.

Nussbaumer
4147 Aesch. Founded 1935. Owner: Kurt Nussbaumer. 12 acres.

A small firm making Riesling-Sylvaner, Chasselas, Pinot Gris, Gewürztraminer and Blauburgunder in their Aesch (Kluser) and Arlesheim (Steinbrüchler and Schlossberg) vineyards, a stone's throw from the border with Alsace. A more recent addition is *Chrachmost*, a *méthode champenoise* Chasselas.

Hans Schlatter
8215 Hallau. Founded 1931. Owner: Hans Schlatter. 25 acres.

A well respected grower and merchant of German Switzerland, particularly for Hallauer Blauburgunder Spätlese, 16-Fahre Wy and Tokayer (Pinot Gris).

Hermann Schwarzenbach
8706 Meilen. Founded: 1739. Owner: Hermann Schwarzenbach. 15 acres.

A small house making Riesling-Sylvaner (some late harvested), Freisamer, the special Zurich type Räuschling, Chardonnay, Pinot Gris and – the only grower still to make it on the lake – Completer. Clevner (Blauburgunder) is made both straight and late harvested, fermented in oak vats and recommended as a keeper.

VOLG (Verband Ostschweizer Landwirtschaftliche Genossenschaften)
8400 Winterthur. Founded 1886. Director: F. Rottermann.

A major agricultural cooperative with a chain of stores. Vineyards are in Hallau, Winterthur and Graubunden, including an estate of 74 acres planted with 75% Blauburgunder, 20% Riesling-Sylvaner and 5% specialities. The wines are light, clean and well-made. Hallauer Blauburgunder has a reputation as a wine with keeping qualities.

THE ITALIAN-SPEAKING CANTONS

The Tessin or Ticino divides into four main areas: north and south of Monte Céneri (Sopraceneri and Sottoceneri respectively), the shores of Lake Lugano (Luganese) and the districts of Mendrisiotto. It is a delightfully uncomplicated, mainly red wine area where Merlot holds sway over a bunch of miscellaneous red grapes (Bondola, Freisa, Barbera) blended into everyday table wine labelled Nostrano. The VITI 'label of quality' is awarded by a commission of experts to Merlot wines of one year's bottle age which score 18 points or more (out of 20) in a tasting. A few growers are successfully ageing some Merlots in new oak (often calling the result Riserva). It gives them distinct character, no longer the typical, soft, one-dimensional Merlot del Ticino. Little white wine is grown in the Tessin: the soils are all wrong and the climate far too benevolent, though there is some Semillon, Sauvignon and Pinot Gris to be found. The foxy Americano hybrid is seldom vinified nowadays, but converted mainly into an excellent Grappa del Ticino.

TESSIN PRODUCERS

Angelo Delea
6616 Losone. Founded 1982. Owner: Angelo & Leopoldo Delea. 17 acres.

Restaurateur-turned-wine-grower, Angelo Delea produces some long-macerated, powerful Merlots. Each year he buys in 40 per cent new barels, into which goes his best Merlot (labelled Riserva); the rest is aged in used *pièces*. Also produced is Chasselas del Ticino, Pinot Blanc and – for old times' sake – an Americanello, cherry red and distinctly foxy.

Werner Stucky

6802 Rivera-Capidogno. Founded: 1982. Owners: Werner and Lilo Stucky. 7.5 acres.

One of the young Swiss German pioneers of the region, Werner Stucky produces tiny quantities of Merlot, straight and oak-aged, both of them sold out by year's end to private customers and a handful of top restaurants.

Fratelli Valsangiacomo fu Vittore

6830 Chiasso. Founded 1831. Director: Cesare Valsangiacomo. 55 acres.

Cesare Valsangiacomo is the fifth generation of this distinguished old Tessiner house, producing some of the most respected bottles of the regions: Roncobello, Dioniso, Merlot del Ticino Cuvée Spéciale, Riserva di Bacco, L'Ariete, Pedrinate del Piccolo Ronco (all Merlots), Cagliostro (a Merlot rosé) and two Merlot bubblies: Spumante Metodo Classico and Ronco Grande Extra Brut. A swashbuckling brigand (*un mattirolo*) adorns the label of Valsangiacomo's fruity blend of Chasselas, Semillon and Sauvignon: Il Mattirolo.

Vinattieri Ticinesi

6853 Ligornetto. Founded: 1985. Owner: Signor Zanini. 62 acres.

Zanini have long been known in the area as importers of fine Italian wines; now they have turned their hand to their own production and no expense has been spared in vineyard or cellar. Cocking a snook at the region's VITI 'quality' label, they are shortly to introduce their own DOC system. The best Vinattieri Merlots bear vineyard names (sometimes complete with beautifully contoured sketch maps): Ligornetto, Tenuta ai Ronchi, Redegonda; all are oak-aged to some degree or another. With some good sites with chalky soils Vinattieri even manages to produce a creditable white, labelled simply Bianco Ticinese Vinattieri.

Eredi Carlo Tamborini SA

6814 Lamone. Founded 1944. Owner: Claudio Tamborini. 25 acres.

An important Tessin house whose Merlot is improving constantly. Vigna Vecchia is their best, oak-aged from vines between 30 and 60 years old. Collivo is also good.

AUSTRIA

Austria has re-emerged as a useful, vigorous and well-regulated producer of interesting (mostly white) wines. The trough she has emerged from was the scandal of 1985, when small amounts of poisonous diethylene glycol were found in wines claiming high natural sweetness. Although nobody was poisoned – in contrast to the later Italian scandal – enormous damage was done to many innocent and well-run Austrian businesses. The damage was compounded by the fact that the Austrian wines most admired abroad were the late-harvest sweet whites of the Burgenland, and it was such wines that were implicated in the scandal.

The Austrian authorities responded by rushing through legislation to further control the wine industry. The 1985 wine law was, as originally framed, the strictest in the world. So strict that growers and merchants claimed with justice that it was inoperable. As a result, amendments were made and the law was enacted in 1986.

The new laws continue a process of tightening up which goes back nearly two decades. During this period Austria's image has slowly changed from that of the land of operetta taverns where the wine goes round in jugs. Vienna's *heurigen*, the new-wine taverns of her wine-growing suburbs, and their country cousins the *buschenschenken*, are still major and characteristic elements in Austria's wine economy.

The Austrian passed wine law is similar in many respects to the German. The principal differences arise from the warmer climate which makes Austrian wine generally riper and stronger than German, and the national taste for dry wines. To achieve the Austrian equivalent of German Prädikatswein (unsugared wine) status the must weight, or ripeness, has to be higher, and Süssreserve is not allowed. *See* page 421.

The country has 144,000 acres of vineyards, concentrated entirely in the east, with the regions of Niederösterreich (Lower Austria, north and south of Vienna) and the Burgenland (on the Hungarian border, southeast of Vienna) much the most important for quality and quantity. Niederösterreich has 83,000 acres, or more than half the nation's wines, Burgenland 51,800, Steiermark 7,000 acres and Vienna 1,700 acres.

The finest wines come from the northern part of the Burgenland. Sauternes is the nearest equivalent: an area with frequent (here regular) sunny but misty autumns, the mists of Burgenland arising from the shallow mere of the Neusiedler See on the Hungarian border. Noble rot is a routine occurrence, and sweet wines of Beerenauslese to Trockenbeerenauslese level are made in industrial quantities even by the cooperatives. The principal vines are the Welschriesling, Grüner Veltliner, Müller-Thurgau and Muskat-Ottonel, but superb wines are also made of Rheinriesling, Gewürztraminer, Weissburgunder and Neuburger. The most famous wines are those of Rust, Donnerskirchen and Eisenstadt (where the Esterhazy family still

Harvesting in the Danube Valley

has a palace and cellars) on the west of the lake. Their Weissburgunder and Muskat-Ottonel in particular are among the world's greatest dessert wines. This western part of the Burgenland is now called Neusiedlersee-Hügelland.

The sandy district of the Seewinkel (now the wine region Neusiedlersee) on the eastern shore has less of a great tradition, but the wines made by Lenz Moser (among others) at Apetlon are supremely aromatic and pungent, lacking perhaps only the extraordinary balance (and potential long life) of the other shore. The rest of Burgenland, to the south, has fewer vines and is not influenced by the lake and its microclimate. Until 1986 what is now Southern Burgenland was called Eisenberg.

The sprawling region of Niederösterreich can most conveniently be surveyed using its traditional division into the Donauland (Danube) region, the Südbahn or southern railway out of Vienna (now the Thermenregion), and the Weinviertel or Wine Quarter, which stretches from the Danube north to the Czech border. The last includes Falkenstein-Matzen to the east and Retz to the west (including the important vineyards of Röschitz and Mailberg). This is overwhelmingly Grüner Veltliner country and its wine is light, dry: the very opposite of Burgenland's potent produce.

Of the Danube regions much the most memorable is the Wachau, where the river suddenly looks almost like the Rhine washing the Lorelei rocks. The steep north bank from Weissenkirchen past Dürnstein to Krems is pocked with laborious plots of Grüner Veltliner and Rheinriesling, here making wine as good as any in Austria, ranging from finely tart and harmonious to peppery and full of fire according to the season and the exposure of their 'Ried'.

The word Ried is the Austrian for a vineyard, and under the 1986 law if a Ried, village or other local name is on the label, the wine must be 100% from that place.

The town of Krems, with fine sites facing the river, is linked by the little valley of the Kamp to its northern neighbour, Langenlois. They are grouped together in the new Kamptal-Donauland wine region.

Langenlois in particular, from the soft, deep loess (half-rock, half soil) of the Kamp valley, makes extremely good Rheinrieslings and even reds of deep colour and a certain firmness.

The rest of Lower Austria's viticulture is all so interwoven with the capital and its suburbs that it can be listed in one north–south catalogue. Overlooking Vienna from the north are the vineyards of Klosterneuburg with its great baroque palace-abbey, the Chorherrenstift, Austria's largest individual wine estate. These vineyards and those west along the Danube are in the Donauland-Carnuntum wine district.

Few of the wines of Vienna's own vineyards escape the clutches of its citizens and their guests. There are some 1,000 *heurigen* in the district to dispense them either in the form of *sturm*, the fermenting juice before it even becomes wine, after November 11th as new wine, incredibly lively and dashing, and for older and wiser customers the '*alte*' wine of the previous year. Sievering, Grinzing, Neustift, Nüssdorf are the principal resorts of the thirsty. The *heurige* is a facet of wine that everyone should experience.

The Südbahn runs south from Vienna, its trains stopping at a series of spas-cum-wine-towns of varying charm and reputation, known now, for wine purposes, as Thermenregion. Much the most famous is Gumpoldskirchen, a very pretty resort. The best of its wines, notably from Thallern, are refreshing Rheinrieslings and a piquant, full-bodied speciality blending lively Zierfändler and heavier Rotgipfler. Baden and its neighbour Bad Vöslau are specialists in red wines, principally of Blauer Portugieser, which gives good dark colour but a rather soft bland taste. Vöslau, with chalky soil, also produces white sparkling wines.

The last of Austria's wine provinces, least known in the world's markets, is Steiermark or Styria, the southeastern boundary province with Slovenia (now part of Yugoslavia). This corner of the Alpine foothills has few natural advantages for the vine. The soil is stony on the steep slopes, and although rainfall is high, vines often suffer from drought. South Styria with its capital Leibnitz is the most fertile region, growing Welschriesling, Rheinriesling, Sauvignon Blanc ('Muskat-Sylvaner') and the mild Morillon, a local form of Weissburgunder.

East Styria specializes in Gewürztraminer and Ruländer, making more pungent wines on red volcanic soil.

A recent trend in all districts is the planting of French classic grape varieties. Chardonnay is the favourite, and Cabernet Sauvignon and Merlot are also on the increase. With these go a fashion for *barrique* ageing in place of Austria's traditional giant casks. These modish grapes are in a very small minority, but their acceptance (and success) is in contrast to the German attitude.

AUSTRIA PRODUCERS

Weingut Bründlmayer

3550 Langenlois. Founded 1581. Family owned. 111 acres; 16,500 cases. Grape var: Spätburgunder, Rheinriesling, Grüner Veltliner, St. Laurent, Merlot, Cab.Sauv.

Traditional producer – no chemicals used – specializing in dry Kabinett wines which are kept in acacia casks. The estate has been in family hands since 1650, and is now run by a father and son partnership: the son trained in Germany and Burgundy. Chardonnay is now on the estate's lists. Best site: Zobinger Heiligenstein (Rheinriesling).

Weingut Elfenhof

7071 Rust, Burgenland. Owners: Johannes and Elfriede Holler. Founded 1680. 49 acres in Rust. 13,000 cases. Grape var: various, 80% white.

Old concern re-formed in 1969 and now with the most modern cellar in Rust, producing a range from dry Kabinetts to a Trockenbeerenausleie which gained a Vinexpo medal.

Esterhazy'sche Schlosskellerei

700 Eisenstadt, Burgenland. 106 acres, 75% white; 27,500 cases. Grape var: Welschriesling, Rheinriesling, Grüner Veltliner, Ruländer.

The ancient princely family of Esterhazy, patrons of Haydn and tamers of the Turks, have been making some of the best wine in the Burgenland since the 17th century. Vineyards include experimental plots run with Klosterneuberg college. Commercial vineyards in Rust, St. Georgen, St. Margaretten, Grosshöflein and Eisenstadt itself. 140 great casks line the cellars beneath the castle. The wines they hold are traditional, full and rich in extract. Some of the best dessert wines of the Burgenland carry the Esterhazy label. The estate is part of the Metternich-led grouping of princely estates (see below).

Domäiße Baron Geymüller

3506 Krems. A family property, founded 1811. 59 acres produce 11,000 cases of Grüner Veltliner, Rheinriesling, Müller-Thurgau, etc.

Traditional methods, dramatic 'designer' labels and strict insistence on vineyard and variety origin make this a locally respected conservative house.

Weingut Karl Grabner – Sepp Schierer

2500 Sooss, Gumpoldskirchen. Founded 1950. 35 acres, 8,500 cases. Varieties include Cab.Sauv. and Chardonnay plus local reds and whites.

Consistent medal winner with typical Gumpoldskirchner wines up to Trockenbeerenauslese standard, plus *barrique*-aged French varietals.

Schlossweingut Graf Hardegg

2062 Seefeld-kadolz 100 acres; 28,000 cases. Grape Var: Grüner Veltliner (40%), Rheinriesling, Weissburgunder, Müller-Thurgau.

One of Austria's senior estates, in existance for 350 years, but with a very modern cellar. The stress is on dry wines.

Weingut Franz Hirtzberger

3620 Spitz, Wachau. 17 acres: 5,000 cases. Grape var: Grüner
Veltliner (40%), Rheinriesling, Sylvaner, Müller-Thurgau.

Franz Hirtzberger, Bürgermeister of Spitz, is the fourth
generation to own this old-established, traditionally
minded property, well-known locally for typical dry
Wachau Grüner Veltliner from the noted Rotes Tor and
Tausandeimerberg Riede. His 14th-century cellars, with a
300-year-old working press, are the oldest still in use in
Austria.

Weingut Sepp Hold

7001 St. Georgen, Burgenland. Owner: the Hold family.
Founded 1947. Merchant with 25 acres in St. Georgen.

Large modern premises producing local Tafelwein, QbA
and QmP wines; also bottles wine from other Austrian
regions and abroad. The late Sepp Hold started the
business selling wine from a trailer towed by a bicycle. His
widow, partner and son now run the firm, which produces
a wide range including attractive Ausleses. Top wines
(such as Weissburgunder, which they label Pinot Blanc
are in burgundy-shape bottles. Exports to Germany, UK,
USA.

Weingut Josef Jamek

3610 Joching, Wachau. Founded 1912. 54 acres, plus grapes
bought in; 17,000 cases of estate wines. Grape var:
Rheinriesling, Grüner Veltliner, Weissburgunder, Sylvaner,
Müller-Thugau and red varieties.

Pioneer of totally dry Wachau wines – up to Spätlese
quality they contain only 1 or 2 grams of sugar a litre,
which makes them pungent drinking. The Auslese has a
maximum of 15 grams of sugar a litre. The vineyards
include plots in the best Riede or Joching (Klaus,
Achleiten). The Jamek family also run a good restaurant
in the village.

Johann Kattus
Vienna

Major Vienna merchant dating from 1857, now in the
fourth generation, and specializing in Sekt under the
Hochriegel brand. The founder was caviar merchant to
both the Russian and Austro-Hungarian courts, and
Austrian agent for Veuve Clicquot. Their *méthode champenoise* Alte Reserve, made from Riesling and Grüner
Veltliner, is slightly fruity with a clean finish. Specialities
include Gewürztraminer from Nussberg – in the Vienna
suburbs.

Kelleramt Chorherrenstift Klosterneuburg

3400 Klosterneuburg. Founded 1108.
Monastery. 242 acres: Klosterneuburg (83 acres),
Kahlenbergerdorf (83 acres) and
Tattendorf (76 acres). 63,000 cases.
Grape var: various, 60-40 white–red.

The Augustines of Klosterneuburg have made wine for
nearly 9 centuries, but the operation is now a commercial
company wholly owned by the monastery. Grapes from
the extensive vineyards are augmented by supplies from
small producers in Burgenland and Neiderösterreich.
Weissburgunder and Rheinriesling are wood-aged, late-
bottled, and can be distinguished, especially in QmP
qualities. All wines use the characteristic squat bottle.
Sket – including a pink one – can be delicious.

*The baroque monastery of Klosterneuburg,
atop three tiers of ancient cellars*

The enormous 3-level cellars harbour 3m. bottles, including the Austrian State Wine Archive. Visitors are shown the tidemark a metre above the floor where wine flowed after Russian looters smashed all the casks in 1945.

Klosterneuburg also controls the ancient Deutsch-Ordens-Schlosskellerei in Gumpoldskirchen.

Prinz Liechtenstein'sches Weingut

8522 Gross St. Florian, Steiermark. Owners: E. and M. Müller. Growers and merchants. Founded 1813, bought by the Müllers in 1936. 13.5 acres in Riede Burgegg and Deutschlandsberg. Grape var: Blauer Wildbacher (for Schilcher), Welschriesling, Gewürztraminer, Zweigelt, etc. Grapes are also bought in to make a total of 85,000 cases.

The leading producers of the Schilcher rosé of Steiermark, plus whites and reds, all of QbA standard.

Weingut Mantlerhof

3494 Brunn im Felder. Founded 1814. 30 acres; 5,500 cases. Grape var: Grüner Veltliner 50%, Roter Veltliner 20%, Rheinriesling 15%, Chardonnay 10%.

Traditional methods from an ancient estate, founded in 1365. Kabinett quality, dry wines. The rare and delicious dry Roter Veltliner is a Mantler speciality. Recently they have added Merlot and Chardonnay to the roster. Widely distributed in Tirol hotels.

Weingut Franz Mayer

1190 Vienna. Founded 1683. 74 acres, yielding 44,000 cases in Nussberg, Grinzing and Alsegg. Grape var: Grüner Veltliner, Rheinriesling, Müller-Thurgau, Traminer, Weissburgunder, Chardonnay, red varieties.

Mayer is Vienna's largest grower and owns the Beethovenhaus, probably the best known of all the *heurigen*. His modern cellar produces wines from Heuriger to Spätlese.

Metternich'sche Weingüter

Dominikanerplaz 11, 3500 Krems. 173 acres, 33,000 cases. An alliance of 5 princely estates, the HQ being at the Metternich estate in Krems. This 173-acre estate, at Schloss Grafenegg, is run on ecological principles. Other members are the estates of Prince Starhemberg in Krems (Starhemberg'sches Weingut), Count Abensperg-Traun in Maissau (Schloss Maisau), Prince Khevenhüller-Metsch in Pulkau (Schloss Riegersberg) and the Esterházy'sche Schlosskellerei (q.v.) in the Burgenland.

The wines are made by each estate but marketed jointly under the name 'Erste Österreiche Weingüter-Kooperation.'

Lenz Moser

3495 Rohrendorf bei Krems. Founded 1929. Owner: GHG (a wholesaler). Vineyards at Tohrendorf (148 acres); Mailberg, Retz (148 acres); and Seewinkelhof, Apetlon, Burgenland (136 acres). 2,000 cases. Grape var: many, including Cabernet Sauvignon at Mailberg, Sauvignon Blanc at Seewinkelhof.

Dr. Lenz Moser (d. 1978) founded this winegrower and merchant house. It is now owned by a big drinks group, though Mosers still fill senior posts. Dr. Moser developed a system of growing vines on high trellises much used in Austria and other wine countries. Wines from Lenz Moser's own estate (particularly at Apetlon) include Beeren- and Trockenbeerenausleses of fabulous quality, sometimes reaching a pitch of concentration almost painful to taste. All their wines are well made and most are extremely good value. The 120-acre Malteser Ritterorden estate at Mailberg is leased from the Maltese knights. Here Lenz Moser planted Austria's first Cabernet Sauvignon vineyard in 1982. Lenz Moser now owning Kloster-Keller Siegendorf (q.v.).

Weingut Franz Prager

3610 Weissenkirchen, Wachau. Founded 1715. 25 acres; 7,000 cases. Grape var: Rheinriesling 40%, Grüner Veltliner 30%, others 30%. Holdings in Reide Steinriegl, Hinter der Burg, Ritzling, Durnsteiner Grünchen, Kollmitzberg.

A proud maker of Kabinett wines (Spätlese in good years) by traditional method and low yields (30 hl/ha). All his wines are dry and stress natural acidity and crispness.

Weingut Romerhof

7051 Grosshoflein, Burgenland. Owner: Kollwentz family. Founded 1775. 34 acres of the southwest end of the Leithagebirge hills, west of Rust; 7,200 cases.

Good unblended dry wines (even his Spätleses). Reds include Cabernet Sauvignon, whites Sauvignon Blanc and Chardonnay.

Weingut Robert Schlumberger

2540 Bad Vöslau. Founded 1842.

Robert Schlumberger, son of a branch of the Alsace family, made Austria's first *méthode champenoise* Sekt in 1842 after learning his trade in Champagne (he rose to be manager of Ruinart) and marrying the daugher of a Vöslau grower. Today the family firm makes respected reds from 22 acres. The Sekt business was sold to Underberg in 1973 and is still carried on, making high-quality wines that are unfortunately little exported. The Bad Vöslau reds are made from St. Laurent, Cabernet

---

The Austrian wine law

Labels must show unfermented sugar content of the wine. Trocken is max. 4 grammes/litre (g/l), Halbtrocken 9 g/l, Halbsüss or Lieblich 18 g/l. Higher levels are labelled Süss.

If vintage and/or grape variety are specified, the wine must be 85% from that vintage and variety. If a vineyard (Ried) is specified, the wine must be 100% from that site.

Austria rates sugar content in degrees KMW (Klosterneuburger Mostwaage).

Categories

Tafelwein Landwein: minimum 13° KMW (63 Oechsle). A Tafelwein must come from a single wine area, maximum alcohol 11.5%, max. unfermented sugar 6 g/l.

Qualitätswein: From a single wine area, minimum 15° KMW (73° Oechsle), enriched up to maximum 19° KMW (94° Oechsle), officially tested.

Kabinett: Minimum 17° KMW (83.5° Oechlse), maximum 19° KMW (94° Oechsle), maximum 9 g/l unfermented sugar, no enrichment.

Prädikatswein: Qualitätswein 'of exceptional maturity or vintage': no

enrichment. The grades are:

Spätlese: late-picked grapes with minimum 19° KMW (94° Oechsle).

Auslese: selected late-picked grapes with min. 21° KMW (105° Oechsle).

Eiswein: made from frozen grapes with min. 25° KMW (127° Oechsle).

Beerenauslese: selected late-picked overripe grapes with noble rot, minimum 25° KMW (127° Oechsle).

Ausbruch: over-ripe, nobly-rotten grapes which have naturally dried. Min. 27° KMW (138° Oechsle).

Trockenbeerenauslese: nobly-rotten, raisin-like grapes, min. 30° KMW (150° Oechsle).

Sauvignon, Merlot and Blauer Portugieser. Stress is on Bordeaux-style wines made by classic methods.

Stift Schotlen, Weingut Nussdorf
Hackhofergasse 17, 1190 Wien. 74 acres, 8,000 cases. Grape var: Grüner Veltliner (50%), Riesling, Müller-Thurgau, Blauer Portugieser.

Member of the Vinobilities grouping of quality estates, producing Grüner Veltliner and other wines for sale in bottle and in the estates *heurige* (March to December) which holds 500 people.

Klosterkeller Siegendorf
7011 Siegendorf, Burgenland. Founded 1860. Owners: The Patzenhofer family. Wine maker and manager: Jost Hopler. Visits by appointment. 76 acres, plus grapes and wine bought in from the locality; 80,000 cases. Grape var: the usual.

An ancient monastic estate which has expanded to become one of the Burgenland's largest firms, now owned by Lenz Moser (q.v.) The wine maker has worked in France, Germany and Australia. His wines have distinct varietal character. Cold fermentation, but Weissburgunder, Gewürztraminer and reds (which now include Cabernet and Merlot) age in wood for up to 2 years.

Gräfl. Stubenberg'sches Schlossweingut, Schloss Welkersdorf
3492 Schloss Walkersdorf/Krems. 25 acres, 5,500 cases. Grape var: Grüner Veltliner (60%), Riesling, Sylvaner.

The stress here is on wood-aged, traditional, dry Grüner Veltliner and Riesling. Another Vinobilites estate.

Gräflich Stürgkh'ches Weingut
8493 Klöch. 30 acres. Grape var: Welschriesling, Traminer, Gewürztraminer, Rheinriesling.

Leading Styrian estate, under the control of the Seyffertitz family, who aim for balanced, traditional wines.

Freigut Thallern
2352 Gumpoldskirchen. Founded 1141, owned and farmed since by the Cistercians of Heiligenkreuz. 172 acres at Gumpoldskirchen and Burgenland, usual varieties.

Holdings include land in Ried Wiege, one of Austria's best sites, producing lively, fresh Rieslings and legendary Zierfandler that ages for decades. Traditional techniques; all wines are aged in wood. Long-lived, complex-structured (and good-value) wines result, leading Austria in the field of traditional wine-making.

Ladislaus Torok
7071 Rust, Burgenland. Founded 1626. 30 acres; 6,600 cases. Grape var: the usual reds and whites.

Seventh-generation family concern produces full range from Neuburger diabetic wine to Trockenbeerenausleses. High-culture vineyards; a synthesis of modern and traditional techniques. The firm was selling to the Baltic in the 17th century, and now exports 30% of production.

Schlosskellerei Uhlheim
8262 Ilz, Steiermark. Owner: Dr. Karl Maier. 7 acres in Klöch, Steiermark. 116,000 cases, of which 2,100 cases are estate wines. Grape var: Welschriesling, Müller-Thurgau, Sauvignon Blanc.

Merchant dealing in the wines of Styria and other Austrian districts, exporting 15% of production. Notable wines in a quality range are Rheinriesling from Retz and a gold-medal St. Laurent from the best red-wine district of Austria, Vöslau.

Weingut Undhof, Fritz Saloman
3504 Stein, Wachau. Owner: Fritz Saloman. Founded 1792. 35 acres, plus grapes bought in; 9,000 cases. Grape var: Grüner Veltliner in Riede Undholf-Wieden and Wachtberg, Rheinriesling, in Riede Kögl and Steiner Pfaffenberg, Müller-Thurgau in Riede Steiner Goldberg. Also Weissburgunder (vines brought from Meursault before the war).

One of the first Austrian estates to bottle its own wine. Saloman makes completely dry, powerful, balanced whites which age well. A benchmark of quality in Austria. Now also the seat of a wine academy at Kloster Und. Exports to USA, Germany, UK.

Weingut & Sektkellerei R. Zimmerman
3400 Klosterneuburg. Founded 1920. 10 acres in Klosterneuburg (Reid Buchberg) plus grapes bought in, 2,000 cases. Grape var: Rheinriesling, Weissburgunder, Grüner Veltliner, Müller-Thurgau, St. Laurent.

Grower, Sekt producer and owner of a popular *heurige* in the Vienna village of Grinzing.

Verband Neiderösterreichischen Gebietswinzergenossenschaften
1110 Vienna. Director: Josef Weissböck.

Union of 16 growers' coops in Lower Austria, with two large plants in Vienna and at Walkersdorf. The union has a total of 10,000 members farming 17,250 acres, and also owns the 45-acre Gut Türkenweg in Baden. Production 220,000 cases.

OTHER PRODUCERS

Weingut Peter Dolle
Strass, Kamptal-Donauland. 45-acre estate which does well with Weisser Burgunder and Rheinriesling.
Weingut Feiler-Artinger
Rust, Burgenland. Traditionalist with 42 high-class acres in Rust, making noted Trockenbeerenauslese. In good years half the harvest can attain this quality. Production is 8,000 cases.
Weingut Gunter Haimer
2170 Poysdorf, Falkenstein. Founded 1860. 32 acres. Grape var: Grüner

Veltliner (60%), Rheinriesling, Müller-Thurgau, Gewürztraminer. Traditionally made Grüner Veltliner, up to Spätlese quality.
Franz Heiss
Illmitz, Burgenland. 22 acres in the Seewinkel villages of Illmitz and Apetlon. 5,000 cases a year. Mixed varieties. All qualities up to Eiswein, leaning towards the modern, lighter Burgenland style.
Weingut Just Marienhof
Rust. Owner: Franz Just. 22 acres in

Rust, most in Ried Umriss, on the slopes away from the lake. Production is 13,000 cases.
Weingut Nikolaihof-Geyerhof
3512 Mautern, Wachau. Owners: Nickolaus and Christine Sachs. 45 acres; 6,600 cases. Grape var: Grüner Veltliner, Rheinriesling. Alliance of two estates following ecological principles. Geyerhof wines are from biological vineyards free of sprays.
Weingut Sattlerhof
8462 Samlitz, Steiermark. Founded

Gabled cellar entrances, arranged in a Kellargasse or cellar street, are traditional in the Falkenstein district

1887. 12 acres. 3,000 cases. Grape var: Welschriesling, Muskat, Weissburgunder, Ruländer, Sauvignon Blanc, Kerner.

Franz Schwartz
3492 Etsdorf-Walkersdorf, Krems. Grower and merchant. 50 acres; 17,000 cases from own vineyards.

Alexander Unger Moorhof
St. Margarethen, Burgenland. Grower (32 acres) and merchant, also using names Weingut Moorhof and Weingut Hubertshof. Complete range of colours and styles from rosé to Eiswein. Römerbruch is their label for prädikatswein. (Exports to UK).

COOPERATIVES

Burgenlandischer Winzerverband
Rust, Burgenland. A 'mother coop' heading 28 smaller organizations, founded in 1957. About 6,000 members with a total vineyards area of 17,300 acres. Total storage capacity of the group is 270,000 hl. Wines up to Trockenbeerenauslese quality.

Winzergenossenschaft Gumpoldskirchen
Founded 1907. 350 members. Brands include Gold and Königswein. Austria's oldest active coop, with a name for quality. Total storage capacity is 16,000 hl.

Schlossweingut Graf Hardegg
Seefeld, Weinviertel. 100-acre estate around a baroque castle, producing dry, typical Grüner Veltliner.

Weingut Hans Igler
Deutschkreug, Burgenland Red-wine specialist with 15 acres, wines include *barrique*-aged Blaufränkisch and Cabernet.

Karl Inführ
Klosteneuburg. Sekt specialist whose best wine is the Riesling Rilter von Dümstein.

Winzergenossenschaft Krems
3500 Krems. Founded 1938. 2,700 members. 4,000 acres in Krems, Langenlois and Klosterneuberg; 2.5m. cases. Grape var: Grüner Veltliner 60%; 92% white, 8% red. Largest independent coop in Austria and a consistent medal winner, especially with sekt and 'Kellermeister Private' wines.

Winzergenossenschaft Dinstlgut Loiben
3601 Unter Loiben, Wachau. Founded as a coop 1936, previously privately owned ex-monastic cellars, founded in 1002. 2,960 acres Austria's largest producer of Rheinriesling. Grape var: Grüner Veltliner, Rheinriesling, Müller-Thurgau, Weissburgunder. Brands: Loibner Kaiserwein, Schütt, Burgstall, Rotternberg Rheinriesling Spätlese. Exports 17%.

Winzergenossenschaft St. Martinus
7082 Donnerskirchen, Burgenland. Chairman: Stefan Leeb. 317 members with 4,900 acres in Donnerskirchen, Purbach, Breitenbrunn and Schutzen. 77,500 cases. Grape var: Grüner Veltliner 50%, Welschriesling 15%, Müller-Thurgau 15%, Muskat-Ottonel 39%, Blaufränkisch, Zweigett 10% each, Weissburgunder, Traminer 7% each. The largest quality-wine producer in Burgenland, founded in 1953, taking over the 14th-century cellars of the noble family of Windisch-Graet with storage capacity of 65,000 hl. The first Burgenland Trockenbeerenauslese was

made here, and called *Lutherwein* by a fanatical Protestant proprietor.

Winzergenossenschaft Wachau
3601 Durnstein. Founded 1938. 850 members; 3,750 acres; 400,000 cases. Grape var: Grüner Veltliner, Rheinriesling, Müller-Thurgau. Brandy also made. A traditionally minded coop whose members own some of the best vineyards in the Wachau and whose best wines are not to be despised. Above the cellars is the 1714 Kellerschloss, a miniature baroque château beautifully decorated with frescoes and carvings.

Winzergenossenschaft Wolkersdorf
Founded 1938. Members own 2,200 acres, mostly Grüner Veltliner. 500,000 cases. Brands: Roseneck (Grüner Veltliner QbA), Katzensteiner (Weissburgunder QbA). Makes the altar wine for the Archdiocese of Vienna. Exports through the Lower Austria coops union.

HUNGARY

The Eastern European Revolution of 1989 is having profound effects on wine industries that have been centrally directed for decades. The outcome can only emerge gradually, but it is reasonable to suppose that in the medium to long term the full potential of the vineyards of Central and Eastern Europe will emerge.

Historically, Hungary is incontestably the regional leader. Indeed, in all of Europe only France and Germany have older and more evolved traditions of quality wine-making than Hungary's most famous vineyards. In recent years Bulgaria, starting almost from scratch, has far overtaken Hungary in exports. Whether the Hungarians can recapture their former standing in the world of wine depends in part on whether the world continues to prize the 'international' grape varieties above all others, or whether, as in Italy, there is a real place for authentic ethnic traditions.

The true Hungarian words of appreciation for the country's traditional wines sum up their character and appeal. They call a good white wine 'fiery' and 'stiff' – masculine terms which promise a proper partner for the paprika in the cooking.

Such wines can occasionally still be found in the historical sites of Hungarian viticulture, the hill regions which dot the country from the southwest northwards, skirt the long Lake Balaton, then run up the Czech border from near Budapest to Tokay.

Unfortunately the predictable result of central direction and huge state farms, combined with the low morale of an uncritical market, largely in East Germany, was a vast increase in harvest and loss of this highly desirable concentration. Use of the traditional Hungarian grapes ensures that the wines are still very much individuals, but even within the last 15 years they seem to me to have become milder, less male, Magyar and memorable.

Hungary is rich in indigenous grapes of character that could contribute splendid wines to the world scene but have hardly been tried elsewhere. The most notable of all is the vigorous Furmint, the dominant grape of Tokay, which not only rots nobly but in its dry form gives strongly sappy, velvety and high-flavoured wine. The Hárslevelü or 'lime-leaf' is scarcely less notable: an excellent dry-climate late ripener with abundant crops and good acid levels, resistant to fungus diseases – a model grape for South Africa, Australia or California.

Szürkebarát or 'grey friar' is more familiar than it sounds: it is a form of Pinot Gris (German Ruländer) grown to splendid effect on the volcanic Mt. Badacsonyi. But the Kéknyelü ('blue-stalk') of the same vineyards is purely indigenous, a modest producer of concentrated and complex golden-green wines for the fish course. More widespread are three other white Hungarians (at least by adoption), Ezerjó ('thousand blessings'), which is a good bulk-producer on the Great Plain, making fine wine only at Mor in the north, Leányka ('little girl') whose delicate dry white is probably the best wine of Eger, again in the northern hills, and Mezesfeher ('white honey'), an archetypal description of the national view of a good glass of wine.

Most widespread of all is the international Italian (here 'Olasz') Riesling. The Great Plain makes most of its white from it, and on Mt. Badacsonyi it rises to its maximum flavour and concentration.

The great Hungarian red grape is the Kadarka, which flourishes equally on the Great Plain produc-

---

The classes of Tokay
Tokay Szamorodni
This is Tokay 'as it comes' – i.e. the basic wine, sweet (Edes) or dry (Száraz) according to the vintage.
Tokay Aszú
Aszú is the term for grapes infected with noble rot (*Botrytis cinerea*). Destalked hand-picked Aszú grapes are stored 6–8 days, then kneaded to a pulp which is added to base Tokay wine, or to must, by the *puttony* (hod of 20–25 kilos). The eventual sweetness depends on the number of *puttonyos* added to the 136–140 litre barrels (called Gönci) of one-year-old base wine – usually 3, 4 and 5 *puttonyos*. 6 is exceptional. The sequence then is:

– maceration and stirring for 24–48 hours
– settling and racking the must
– fermentation period depending on number of *puttonyos*
– racking, fining and filtering
– ageing in oak for not less than 3 years
– filtering prior to bottling
– if binned in Tokay cellars bottles are not laid on their sides but stood upright, corks changed every 15–20 years.
Tokay Aszú Essencia
Only individually hand-selected Aszú grapes. Only produced in exceptional years from the best vineyards. Method as for Tokay Aszú, but:
– quality cannot be measure by numbers of *puttonyos* as sugar content is higher

than for 6 *puttonyos*
– fermentation takes several years (special yeast is used – Tokaj 22)
– minimum of 10 years' ageing in oak.
Tokay Essence
Destalked hand-picked Aszú grapes. While grapes are being stored (*see* Tokay Aszú) the pressure of their own weight produces a minute amount of highly concentrated juice at the bottom of the tub (one *puttonyo* yields only 142 millilitres of this Essence). The juice is then allowed to ferment extremely slowly for many years in oak casks. In practice it scarcely ferments at all; the sugar content is too high.

ing light wine with a slight but convincing 'cut', and at Eger and Szekszárd, producing a big stiff spicy red for ageing. Unfortunately the much lighter Kékfrankos (Austrian Blaufränkisch) has been planted more and more as a substitute with predictable results. The Austrian Zweigelt, on the other hand, is a newcomer with different virtues of softness, darkness and a pleasantly sweet scent. There is also a long tradition of growing Pinot Noir (Nágyburgundi) in south Hungary around Vilányi and Merlot (bizarrely called 'Médoc Noir') around Eger in the north.

Added to these are many grapes whose identification causes no problems: Szilváni, Cabernet (Sauvignon and Franc), Rajnairizling, Traminí, Muskat Ottonel or Muskotály.

Each of Hungary's notable wines is called by a simple combination of place and grape name. The place name has the suffix '-i'. Thus Ezerjó from Mor is Morí Ezerjó.

Hungary has almost 400,000 acres of vines. In communist days production was dominated by seven huge regional combinats, run as individual enterprises but owned by the state, and by 100-odd state farms, totalling some 80,000 acres, separately controlled by an enterprise known as Agker. Most of the country's best land was under the state farm regime, although even in Tokay, the most important area of all, many smallholders still owned land and made their own wine. The catch was that they could not bottle and sell their own wine; it became part of the blend made and marketed by one of the government organizations.

Happily already by 1990 liberalization had begun, to the extent that a would-be buyer from abroad could form a joint-enterprise company with a group of smallholders (the first was formed in the village of Mád, in Tokay). Their wines could then be bottled individually, without the intervention of the state cellars. This is the way in which top-quality wines will begin to appear once more on the international market. Meanwhile the vast bulk of Hungarian wine will continue to be made by the combinats and state farms, with the difference that as the Eastern bloc market fades away, and buyers from the West come to the fore, their emphasis too should shift from quantity to quality.

The Great Plain
The Danube divides Hungary almost down the middle. All the old wine regions are either to the west of the river or along the Czech border. East of the Danube lies the sandy Pannonian or Great Plain, a dreary steppe which has found its first useful purpose in this century with the planting of vines. Half of Hungary's wine now comes from there.

A single awesome combinat at Kecskemet has no less than 62,000 acres making one million hectolitres (11 million cases) a year. They are light white wines from Ezerjó, Olaszrizling and Müller-Thurgau with a little Kékfrankos light red. Another at Szeged near the Yugoslav border in the south has 28,000 acres making heavier and sweeter wines of a wider range of grapes: Olaszrizling, Leányka, Kövidinka (a common white), Muskat Ottonel and also Cabernet Franc and Merlot. Other growers' cooperatives on the plain tend to grow Kadarka for their red and Olaszrizling for their white, both low-strength everyday wines which they sell to their local combinat.

The South
The historic wine regions start across the Danube in the south at Siklos and Vilányi where, on hills of stiff loess, the Pinot Noir (with or without some Kékfrankos) gives unmistakably Burgundian wine. Four or five years' bottle-age give Vilányi Burgundi the velvet touch. They continue a little to the north at Pecs in the Mecsék region, producer of very respectable off-dry Olaszrizling, and Pinot Blanc that deserves three years' bottle-age. Farther north again Szekszárd has a historic reputation for a Kadarka red (Vörös) with strength and astringency, traditionally likened to Bordeaux. The Szekszárdi from the state farm is known as Nemes Kadar.

Lake Balaton
Lake Balaton lies across the heart of western, trans-Danubian, Hungary, in the centre of the country's finest white-wine region. The north shore of the 50-mile-long lake has ideal southern slopes on the basalt stumps of very dead volcanoes. The most famous of these, Mt. Badacsonyi, is the source of Hungary's best full-bodied whites, neither fully dry nor very sweet. Dryish Kéknyelü is perhaps the best of all; Szürkebarát is denser and stickier. Badacsonyi and the nearby hills have 6,000 acres of vines.

On the same shore 20 miles east red-sand soil and a slightly warmer microclimate give wines with more roundness and less 'nerve'. This area of 5,000 acres is known as Balatonfüred-Csopak. Olaszrizling and Furmint make notable wines here. The remainder of the Balaton area goes by the simple name of the lake alone, its wines standing in relation to Badacsonyi as, say, other Rheinpfalz wines stand in relation to the Mittelhaardt. The south side of the lake has a major state farm at Balatonboglár, specializing in white wines, Szilváni, Leányka, Traminí, Muskotaly, sparkling Csabagyöngye and table grapes. The wines are much less attractive than the north-shore collection. But Hajos, 20 miles west, has a name for surprisingly good Cabernet.

The Northwest

Three widely separated hills north of Balaton are considered 'classic' areas. Somló, with a mere 1,000 acres, today largely of Furmint and Olaszrizling, used to have a reputation second only to Tokay, not only for flavour but for restorative properties.

Sopron, far north on the border of Austria's Burgenland, is a red-wine district growing Kékfrankos and claiming kinship with Beaujolais, though the resemblance is remote.

Mor, north towards the hills of the Czech border, conjures qualities out of the Ezerjó which are not found elsewhere: aroma and body in a dry wine which is usually neutral. Mor also produces very respectable Rhine Riesling, with both acidity and 'fire'. The credit goes to steep quartz-rich soil on a limestone base which continues north into the newer area of Barsönyös-Csaszar.

Mátraalya

Hungary's greatest concentration of quality vineyards stretches east from here along the hilly border country with Czechoslovakia as far as Tokay. The biggest delimited area surrounds the 'historic' wine-town of Debró, whose Hárslevelü remains one of the country's best medium-sweet aromatic wines. It is now buried in the Mátraalya (or Matravidek) region, of 22,000 acres, including its neighbour Gyöngyös-Visonta.

A wide variety of the commoner grapes, including Chasselas for the table, are grown in the shelter of these hills. But such farms as Gyöngyös also show that Riesling, Grüner Veltliner, and the fragrant Muskotaly thrive here.

Mátraalya leads on into the district of Eger to the east. The baroque city of Eger is the centre of 36,000 acres of both red grapes for its famous Bull's Blood, or Bikavér, and white for its less-known but equally good Leányka, Muskotaly and Olaszrizling. Another 7,000 acres wait to be planted.

Eger

Eger's impressive tufa-quarried state cellars are lined with vast red-hooped casks in which even the white wines are sometimes kept for up to five years without losing freshness. Tufa appears to be the secret of Egri quality. The red grapes for Bull's Blood are Kadarka 70%, Kékfrankos 15% and 'Médoc Noir' (Merlot) 15%. To my surprise the cellar master (in big boots, *gris de travail* and a little military cap) preferred the Médoc Noir straight, with a high degree of unfermented sugar. Bull's Blood built its reputation on potency which it no longer displays. It has become a mere middle-of-the-road red with a memorable name. But one quality it has not entirely lost is its longevity. Full-strength Kadarka benefits enormously from bottle-age, and Bull's Blood ought to be kept at least four years for its warm, almost Italian, character to emerge.

Tokáji

Tokay remains Hungary's one wine still hand-made by ancient painstaking methods to capture a character found nowhere else: a sort of eastern Yquem. Up to 1990 it was all bottled at the state farm of Tokajhegyaljai at Satoraljaujhely which eliminated the individuality of both its producers and their vineyards. Moreover, the state farm wine is pasteurised, which limits its capacity to mature to its optimum. The vineyards amount to 15,000 acres in the worn-down, loess-covered, once volcanic hills on the Soviet border. Its twin secrets are the Furmint grape and the late autumn sun alternating with mist that provokes *Botrytis cinerea*, or noble rot. There are many degrees of sweetness and quality, as there are of rottenness in the grapes. Much confusion has been caused by the cellar techniques which build up the different qualities from whatever the harvest brings. They are most clearly explained in tabular form (*see* page 424).

CZECHOSLOVAKIA

Unlike Hungary (but like Austria) Czechoslovakia has traditionally grown its wine for its own use, rather than for export. Its wine capitals are not Prague (which has its Pilsener) but Bratislava in Slovakia, the eastern half of the country, and Brno in Moravia in the centre. Bratislava lies on the Hungarian border, Brno not far from Austria's Weinviertel.

With 129,000 acres, or nearly a third as many vines as Hungary, the country is no dabbler, little as her produce is seen beyond her borders. Her wines may lack the superficial graces of smart labels (and known names), and sometimes suffer from poor bottles and tiny corks, but are nonetheless the well-made products of a modern and competent industry in the Austro/German style.

Slovakia is the chief producer, with some 90,000 acres. In the Czech system of classifying grape varieties 20% of this is planted with First Class "A" white varieties: Rhine Riesling, Pinot Blanc, Gewürztraminer, Sauvignon Blanc, Rülander, Muscat Ottonel. Half is planted with First Class "B" whites (of which Wälschriesling, Grüner Veltliner and Müller-Thurgau are much the most important.)

About a quarter is red, with Limberger the leading grape and the whole list having an Austrian air – save for some 1,500 acres of Cabernet Sauvignon. Limberger is known as Frankovka, and the state farm at Rāca, just north of Bratislava, produces Slovakia's best-known red, a rather soft and simple wine, under this name. The two other Slovakian state farms with the highest reputations are at Nitra and Pezinok.

Slovakia's other special pride is in possessing a small corner of the Tokay vineyard on the Hungarian border, growing 65% Furmint, 25% Harslevelü and 10% Muscat de Frontignan to produce her own Tokay.

Moravia's 35,000 acres of vineyards lie between Brno and the Austrian border, centred on the state farms and cooperatives of Znojmo (perhaps the best), Blatnice, Hustopeče, Šaldorf and Velké Pavlovice. Although they grow more "B" varieties than "As", their Muller-Thurgaus, Grüner Veltliners, Rülanders and Rieslings are first choice in the "vinarmas", the wine-bars of Prague, and have the spirit of Austria's heurigen when young.

Bohemia, the western province with Prague at its heart, has a mere 2,500 acres, including some Rhine Riesling of fair quality. But full ripeness does not come easily here and Moravian wine is the people's choice.

YUGOSLAVIA

The six republics and two autonomous regions that make up Yugoslavia are all in the wine business: some more traditionally and interestingly than others but all with considerable and growing competence and professionalism. Three are major exporters: Slovenia in the northwest for white wines, Kosovo in the south for red and Serbia in the east for a wide variety of both.

Yugoslavia comes tenth among the world's wine countries and tenth among exporters: a respectable position for a country which had to build its wine industry almost from scratch after World War II. Its roots are as old as Italy's, but long occupation by the Turks removed the sense of continuity. The recent reconstitution of the industry combines the Germanic Austro-Hungarian traditions of the north, the Italian influence down the coast and some truly Balkan traditions in the east and south, with a general move towards adopting the internationally known grapes in place of indigenous characters.

The wine industry is state controlled but consists almost half-and-half of small independent growers and state-owned farms. The small growers normally take their crops to the local cooperatives. These in turn supply the larger regional organizations, which act as négociants, blenders and distributors.

SERBIA

The republic of Serbia was formerly the whole of the eastern, landlocked, third of Yugoslavia from Hungary to Macedonia. Now its northern section, north of the Danube, is the autonomous region of Vojvodina, and a significant southern slice, adjacent to Albania, is also autonomous and known as Kosovo or Kosmet. Both are important wine areas.

Serbia is second to Croatia in vineyard area with 181,000 acres (30% of the national total). Vojvodina has 44,000 (7%) and Kosovo 20,000 (3.3%).

Serbia has been relatively conservative in its grape varieties, with the dark Prokupac as its chief red grape and Smederevka (Smederevo is near Belgrade) as its white. Its oldest and most famous vineyard is Župa, 80 miles south of the capital between Svetozarevo and Kruševac. Župsko Crno ('Župa red') is a Prokupac blend with the lighter Plovdina. Prokupac is also widely used for rosé ('Ružica'). More and more Cabernet, Merlot and Gamay is being planted, but not so far with results as good as those farther south. The Royal Serbian Cellars makes a rather disappointing Cabernet. Farthest east of all, the regions of Timok and Krajina (adjoining Bulgaria) plants mainly Gamay.

Vojvodina has a history of red-wine making (of which Carlowitz was once a famous example). Today a wide range of mainly white grapes is producing nicely aromatic and balanced wines, the best of them in the Fruška Gora hills by the Danube north of Belgrade. Gewürztraminer and Sauvignon Blanc are particularly tasty, though I fear less widely planted than Laskiriesling. Farther north and east, Subotiča and Banat are the areas bordering on Hungary and Romania, both with sandy Great Plain soils and light wines; Subotiča growing the Hungarian red Kadarka and white Ezerjó.

Kosmet (or Kosovo) is extraordinarily successful for a relatively new region. Its Pinot Noir, made sweet for the German taste and labelled Amsel-felder, is one of Yugoslavia's largest exports. Its Cabernet, exported to Britain simply as 'Cabernet from Kosovo', takes bottle-age extremely well. It is a light wine but at six years still retains fresh and faintly exotic aromas of the grape – though oddly enough not recognizably Cabernet: I have found a touch of the apricot smell of Žilavka which makes me wonder whether its lightness is a clever piece of blending. Žilavka is also grown in Kosovo.

SLOVENIA

Slovenia, tucked into the Italian–Austrian–Hungarian northwest corner of the country, makes Yugoslavia's best white wines. Its principal grape is the Italian Riesling, called here Laskiriesling or Graševina. The 47,000 acres of vineyards (8% of the national total) reach their highest quality at Ljutomer, Maribor, Ptuj and Ormož in the extreme north, between the valley of the Mura (which forms the border in places with Austria and Hungary) and the Drava. The combined influences of the Adriatic, the Alps and the Hungarian plain make the climate moderate, while limestone subsoils favour white wine. The hills between Ljutomer and Ormož, only 50 miles from the west end of Lake Balaton, bear a vineyard almost as famous as Mt. Badacsonyi, known by the name of Jerusalem from crusader connections. The majority of the exports from this admirable region are unfortunately of Laskiriesling, although Pinots Blanc and Gris, Gewürztraminer, Sylvaner and Rhine Riesling are also grown. It seems a pity to waste a first-rate vineyard on what is essentially a second-rate grape, however satisfactory

its performance – and some of its late-picked wines here are more than satisfactory. Its wines are usually made dry for the domestic market but sweetened for export.

South of the Drava the Haloze hills produce a similar range of white wines. South again the Sava valley, continuing into Croatia and on to its capital, Zagreb, makes light red Cviček of local grapes.

At the western end of Slovenia on the Italian border four small viticultural regions with a total of 12,000 acres have a mild Mediterranean climate. Their best-known wine is a vigorous but not heavy red called Kraški Teran. Teran is the Italian Refosco and Kraški signifies that it is grown on the rugged limestone 'karst' that stretches up the coast.

Vipava, between Ljubljana and Trieste, grows Cabernet, Merlot, Barbera and dry white Rebula. The tiny part of Istria that is Slovenia's brief sea coast makes some rich Malvasias and Muscats for local consumption, using the same red grapes as Vipava. Slovin of Ljubljana, the country's biggest exporter, is the main Slovenia producer.

CROATIA AND DALMATIA

The old kingdom of Croatia musters the most vineyards of any of the republics, 198,000 acres or very nearly a third (32.5%) of the national total. It falls into two distinct and very different parts: Slavonia, the continental north between Slovenia

and Serbia, between the Drava and the Sava rivers, and the coast, from the Istrian peninsula in the north all the way south to Montenegro, including all Dalmatia and its lovely islands.

Slavonia has half the grape acreage, but its wines

USSR
The Soviet Union is the world's third-largest wine producer, with some 3.5 m. acres of vines, according to some statistics which are neither new nor necessarily reliable. In late Communist times the country was also a considerable net importer. But the Western world has seen few, if any, Soviet wines and remains largely in ignorance of their historical traditions and undoubted potential.

A glimpse of past glories appeared in London in 1990 at an auction by Sotheby's of dessert wines from the private estates of the Tsar's and other

great families in the Crimea. The muscat wines of the Imperial Massandra estate were outstanding among a variety of very well-made old 'ports', 'sherries', 'madeiras' and even 'Cahorski'.

The Russian republic (including the Crimea) is very much the greatest producer of wines of all qualities, with sparkling wine as its great speciality. Russia's sweet tooth is well-known, but the technical competence displayed, especially in drier cuvées, is beyond denial.

Georgia, though tiny in relation to Russia, has a far more ancient and original wine culture, with at least 500

indigenous vine varieties. Georgia's most famous wine region is Kakhetia, east of Tbilisi, where the climate is at its most continental. The princely estate of Tsinandali was developed in the 19th century to make the finest Kakhetian wines, famous for fragrance and bite.

Today Tsinandali is the brand name of an adequate dry white; Gurdzhani and Mukuzani are others. Saperavi, Napareuli and Kindzmarauli are some of the best-known reds – although even in Georgia Cabernet Sauvignon is creeping into the repertoire.

Georgia is also the home of a flourishing sparkling wine industry.

have neither the appeal of Slovenia's whites, close though they are, nor of some of the new wines of Vojvodina to the east. Wine shipped as Yugoslav Laskiriesling without further particulars (e.g. by Slovin) comes from here.

Croatia's best wines come from Istria and Dalmatia. Istria grows the same grapes as western Slovenia: Merlot, Cabernet, Pinot Noir and Terran for reds – the Merlot particularly good. The whites include rich Muscats and Malvasias, and Pinot Blanc, which is the base of the local sparkling wine.

Dalmatia has Yugoslavia's richest array of original characters – mainly red. Plavać Mali (there seems to be no translation) is the principal grape, supported by Plavina, Vranac, Babić, Cabernet, Merlot and 'Modra Frankija'. Plavac has its moments of glory. One is Postup, a concentrated sweet red, aged for years in oak, produced on the Pelješac peninsula north of Dubrovnik. A 15-year-old Postup is still bright red, a strange sort of half-port with more than a hint of retsina, a big (14.2°) well-balanced and structured wine that would appeal to those who like Recioto from Valpolicella. Dingač is very similar. Another is Faros from the island of Hvar, a degree lighter than Postup and softly dry rather than sweet;

a full-bodied, warmly satisfying wine without coarseness. The regular quality of coastal red is simply called Plavać. Some find Babić, when aged three or four years, a better wine. The dry rosé of the coast, made from several grapes, is called Opol.

White Dalmatian wines are in a minority but in greater variety than red. The Maraština is the most widespread white variety and has its own appellation at Čara Smokvica. Grk is the oxidized, sherry-like speciality of the island of Korčula. Pošip (which some equate with Šipon/Furmint) makes heavy but not flat wine. Bogdanuša, especially on the islands of Hvar and Brač, can be surprisingly light, crisp and aromatic. Vugava, grown on the remote island of Vis, is similar. Sometimes they are presented as separate varities, sometimes in blends. It is hard to discover, in fact, whether some are different names for the same grape. But they certainly have old-style character to balance against the predictable correctness of Laskiriesling.

Dalmatia's dessert wines, whether of red or white grapes or both, are known as Prošek. The best Prošek tends to be a family matter, nursed in a little cask and given to guests in a thick tumbler with absolutely appropriate pride.

ROMANIA

The long-established quality and individuality of Romanian wine has suffered badly in the socialist era. The country speaks a Latin-based tongue and has both cultural and climatic affinities with France. Once the wines of Moldavia were drunk in Paris. Today little Romanian wine is seen in Western countries. German terms on the labels serve the needs of the largest Western market. There is some sign that government research stations are producing wines of modern standards.

Romania's vineyards surround the central Carpathian mountains. The main centres are Tirnave, at 1,600 feet on the Transylvanian plateau to the north, Cotnari to the northeast in Moldavia, Vrancea (including the once-famous Odobeşti and Nicoreşti) to the east, Dealul Mare to the southeast and Murfatlar in the extreme southeast by the Black Sea, and in the south Stefaneşti, Drăgăşani and Segarcea. In the west, part of the sandy Banat plain round Minis is planted with both Hungarian and international grapes. The rest of the vineyards are stocked with a mixture of international varieties and Romania's own white Fetească, Grasă and Tămîioasă and red Babeasca and Fetească Neagră.

Cotnari is the best and most individual wine: a pale dessert wine like a distant cousin of Sauternes.

Tirnave produces a reasonable white blend called Perla de Tirnave and more interesting 'varietal' Fetească, Ruländer, Gewürztraminer, Riesling and Muscat Ottonel. Vrancea's most notable wine is the brisk red Băbească of Nicoreşti. Dealul Mare specialises in Cabernet, Merlot and Pinot Noir – in the Russian style. The state experimental station at Valea Călùgărească is the country's most modern, with a wide range including a fairly dry Riesling.

Murfatlar is traditionally a white and dessert wine area. Its Muscat is of good quality, but Chardonnay from here is too heavy for Western palates. In the southern vineyards Stefaneşti and Drăgăşani are better known for whites and Segarcea and Sadova for reds – particularly Cabernet and a rosé.

On the whole the white wines (especially Tirnave) are more acceptable than the red, but Cotnari is the only wine to be sought out for its own sake.

BULGARIA

Of all the countries of what was Eastern Europe, Bulgaria has been most adept at re-programming its wine industry to earn Western currency. Since the late-1970s Bulgarian wine has not been an occasional exotic excursion, but standard fare in several Western markets. It is now the fourth largest exporter behind Italy, France and Spain. Today it offers some of the world's best value for money in familiar flavours – above all in rich Cabernet Sauvignon, which satisfies palates accustomed to red Bordeaux. Bulgaria, according to the official figures, has four times as much vineyard planted with Cabernet Sauvignon as California.

Wine is a major preoccupation of the whole country. Over 400,000 acres, or 4% of the land area, is vineyard. Red and white varieties are evenly balanced. Of the red vineyard 55% (about 90,000 acres) is Cabernet, 20% Merlot, 11% Pamid, most of the rest such other traditional varieties as Gamza (the Hungarian Kadarka) and Mavrud, and a little Pinot Noir and Gamay.

The white vineyard is much more traditional: almost half is Rkatziteli, Red Misket 14%, Dimiat (or Smederevka) 13%, Muscat Ottonel 11% with so far only developing plantings of Chardonnay, Riesling, Aligoté and Ugni Blanc alongside small acreages of Tamianka, Gewürztraminer and Sauvignon Blanc. Nobody can doubt, however, from their progress to date, that the better varieties will be long in taking over. Chardonnay is beginning to show its natural superiority, even without expensive ageing in oak.

Wine growing is divided into five main regions: conditions are cooler and the quality generally higher in the northern regions. Since 1978 20 subregions have been officially recognised as appellations (Controliran Regions) for one or more grapes and the number is increasing as quality and consistency improve. The Controliran Region wines have to comply with regulations issued by the Government which cover grape varieties, cultivation techniques and vinification technology. Levels of alcohol, acidity and sugar are checked and the wines are approved by the National Tasting Committee. In 1985 a new classification was introduced, the Reserve category, for wines with a potential for ageing and which have been matured in oak.

Wine production in Bulgaria has been industrialised and since 1971, enormous state-run agro-industrial complexes have evolved. Bulgaria exports 85 per cent of its wine production, all sold by the state marketing organization, Vinimpex. The recent changes have clouded this simple picture, but it is too soon to be sure what kind of wine industry will emerge.

Eastern Region

This region lies between the mountains and the Black Sea, has 30 per cent of the vineyards of Bulgaria and specialises in white wines, sparkling wines and brandy. The area includes many noted sub-regions, the most notable of which are Varna, Shumen, Targovishte, and Razgad. The main grape varieties are Riesling, Rkatziteli, Aligoté, Chardonnay, Misket, Muscat Ottonel, Ugni Blanc, Dimiat and Fetiaska.

The Varna district bordering the Black Sea was recognised in 1986 as a Controliran Region for Chardonnay and the Shumen district, which is experimenting with fermenting Chardonnay in small oak barrels, has three Controliran Region areas producing Chardonnay, Gewürztraminer and Sauvignon Blanc.

Northern Region

The northern region has the river Danube as its northern boundary. It is known for its quality red wines – the main varieties being Gamza, Cabernet Sauvignon and Merlot. The state wineries of Suhindol, Pleven and Pavlikeni in particular produce good Cabernets. Sparkling wine is another speciality of the region, benefiting from its relatively high acid levels. The area has several Controliran Region wines – the best being the Gamza, Cabernet Sauvignon and Merlot of Suhindol and an Aligoté from Lhaskovetz.

Southern Region

The southern region grows Cabernet and some Pinot Noir and Merlot but also makes some well-known traditional wines such as Mavrud, Bulgaria's pride, a substantial dark Rhône-like wine needing four years' ageing. The winery at Asenovgrad near Plovdiv has a reputation for Mavrud. Another traditional grape variety, Pamid, makes a rather pallid everyday wine.

Southwest Region

A very small and distinct region on the Yugoslav border across the Rhodope Mountains in the southwest of the country. The Melnishki Controliran Region was designated in 1979 for the production of Melnik wine from Harsovo. Bulgarians have the greatest respect for Melnik, its red wine, which they say is so concentrated that you can carry it in a handkerchief. It needs five years' ageing and will last for 15.

Sub-Balkan Region

A narrow strip south of the Balkan range which includes the famous Sungurlare valley where the Red Misket is grown, and the Valley of Roses (the source of attar of roses) which specialises in Muscats – Hemus is the brand name. A fair proportion of Rhakziteli is also grown in this region.

GREECE

The ancient Greeks colonized the Mediterranean and the Black Sea with the vine, exporting their wines in exchange for Egyptian grain, Spanish silver and Caucasian timber. In the Middle Ages the Peloponnese and Crete were valued sources of Malmsey sack for northern Europe. The largely alkaline (in places, volcanic) soils and multifarious microclimates of Greece make her a natural country of the vine. With 403,000 acres of grapes (not all for wine) she is a major producer – but on a level of sophistication far lower than, say, Yugoslavia. Only since 1975, with entry into the EEC imminent, was there a move towards varieties and systems of control that will lead to fine wine. So far only 9 per cent of the crop qualifies for the national appellation quality seal, but there are signs of rapid progress.

Under primitive conditions, with hot fermentations, the best qualities that could be produced were all sweet wines. The Athenian taste remained faithful to what appears to be an ancient tradition of adding pine-resin during fermentation to make retsina. Fifty per cent of the wine of Attica (almost all white) is resinated. It goes too well with Greek cooking to be ignored.

Greece is modernizing her wine industry to take advantage of membership of the EEC

At present Greek wine can usefully be divided into national brands (usually blends), retsina and other traditional and country wines for uncritical first-year drinking, and wines from defined areas now controlled by an appellation system in accordance with EEC law. There are 23 such areas.

The Peloponnese has more than half of Greece's vineyards and produces more than a third of her wine. Patras at the mouth of the Gulf of Corinth is the main wine centre, with four appellations: Muscat, Muscat of Rion, Mavrodaphne and plain Patras. Mavrodaphne can be the most notable of these: a sweet dark red wine of up to 16 per cent alcohol, something in the style of Recioto of Valpolicella, much improved by long maturing. Plain Patras red is for drinking young. Two other appellations of the Peloponnese are better: the region of Nemea for strong red made of the Agiorgitiko (St. George) grape and Mantinia for a reasonable, though rather flat, white. The main Nemea producer is the cooperative, which uses the name Hercules (the conqueror of the dreaded Nemean lion). Their Rhoditis rosé is adequate.

The 45,000 acres of vines in the north of Greece, from Thrace in the east through Macedonia to Epirus, appear to have most potential for quality. Its appellations are Naoussa (west of Thessaloniki) for potent though balanced and nicely tannic red, Aminteion, at 2,000 feet in the mountains of Macedonia, producing lighter red, Sitsa (near Joannina in Epirus) for a light mountain white of Debina grapes, and Metsovo in Epirus, which was replanted after phylloxera with Cabernet Sauvignon. The most important recent development was the planting of the Sithonian peninsula, the middle one of the three fingers of Halkidiki, with Cabernet and other grapes, by the firm of Carras.

The island of Crete is second to the Peloponnese in acreage, but only third in production (Attica has far more productive vineyards). Crete has four local appellations, all for dark and more or less heavy and sweet reds: Daphnes, Archanes, Sitia and Peza – Peza being the seat of the island's biggest producer, its cooperative. The grapes are Kotsiphali, Mandilari and Liatico, old Cretan strains sometimes just called Mavro Romeiko.

Attica (including mainland Boetia and the island of Euboea) is Greece's most productive area, but overwhelmingly for retsina. Experiments with fine grapes on Euboea have not yet materialized. Delphi has a certain reputation for its red Mavroudi.

Next in importance for acreage and quality comes Cephalonia, which with the other Ionian (western) islands musters 25,000 acres. Cephalonia is known for its dry white Robola (exceptional from Gentilini), its red Mavrodaphne, and its Muscat. Zakinthos to the south makes a white Verdea and red Byzantis (which have no appellation, but perhaps merit one).

The central mainland region of Thessaly also has 25,000 acres of vineyards, but only one appellation, Rapsani, a middle-weight red from Mt. Olympus.

The wines of the Aegean islands, the Dodecanese and the Cyclades, have more renown, notably the pale gold Muscat of Samos, the luscious Vino Santo and a curious semi-sparkling white of the volcanic Santorini, the red and the Muscat of Lemnos and the sweet Malvasia and Muscat of Rhodes. (Rhodes' best wines are white Villare and red Cava Emery.)

Malvasia is grown on many islands and is often their best product. Other island wines with esoteric reputations are the very dark Mavro of Paros and the Santa Mavra of Levkas, whose grape, the Vertzani, is unknown elsewhere.

GREEK PRODUCERS

Achaia-Clauss
Patras

At one stage the biggest and most famous Greek wine house, but now experiencing fierce competition from other expanding producers. Their best-known wines are Demestica and Santa Helena. Otherwise, a large variety of dry and sweet wines from vineyards in the Peloponnese and Crete.

Botrys
(Société Hellenique des Vins et Spiritueux), Athens

Négociant specializing in Attica wines including retsina plus those of Nemea, Paros and Patras (Mavrodaphne). Their strength, however, lies in vintage brandy and ouzo. A new campaign to expand these sectors began in 1990.

J. Boutari & Son
Naoussa, Thessaloniki

Old established producer who has grown rapidly in recent years, covering several appellations around the country with own new wineries at each locality. The main winery is in Naoussa specialising in Naoussa wines. Their top red is Grande Reserve Boutari.

Oinoexagogiki, J. & G. Calligas
Athens

A firm with modern marketing ideas, specializing in well-above-average wines from the island of Cephalonia, in well-designed, unusual bottles. The winery produces dry white Robola Calliga, red Montenero, Calliga Ruby and, recently, red and white Château Calliga.

Andrew P. Cambas
Kantza, nr Athens

Old established producer with wineries in Kantza and Mantinia, and a wide range of table and sparkling wines, ouzo and brandy.

Domaine Carras
Sithonia, Halkidiki

Developed mainly in the 1960s this now well-established major estate, created by John Carras with advice from Professor Peynaud of Bordeaux, produces the well-known Château Carras, a blend of Cabernet Sauvignon, Cabernet Franc and Merlot, maturing for 18–20 months in limousin oak and 3 years in bottle. There are several other labels under the appellation Côtes de Meliton and Domaine Carras.

D. Courtakis
Athens

A family merchant house. Brand names are Apollo, Apelia and Kouros. They produce a dark, oaky Nemean red plus large quantities of a good retsina from the Savatiano grape of Attica, which is selling well around the world.

Karelas & Son
Patras

Merchant with a variety of labels including a pale, dry red called Aeolos.

Markopoulo Cooperative
Attica. Founded 1914

Dry whites aged 1 year before bottling, and a blended dark and soft red called Marco.

Peza Cooperative
Crete

Large cooperative producing under the Logado, Regalo and Mantiko labels.

Semeli
Stamata, nr Athens

Small family winery developed in the late 1970s. Produces quality wines both from traditional Greek grapes, like Savatiano and Agiorgitiko, as well as grapes from the Estate's own Cabernet Sauvignon for the Château Semeli.

E. Tsantali
Aios Pavlos, Halkidiki

A second generation Macedonian merchant house which made its name with Olympic ouzo. Grew rapidly in the 1980s, and now competes for one of the few top positions in the Greek wine scene. A wide range of sound wines, some of which originate in Mt. Athos and appear as 'local wines' (vins de pays) under the Agioritiko label, and others originate in various appellation areas around the country.

Samos Union of Cooperatives
Samos

With two wineries, this union of about 300 growers produces remarkable muscat wines which are either naturally sweet or fortified, and exported widely. Top of the range, the Samos Nectar is rich and golden, maturing continuously and darkening in the bottle.

Union of Ioannina Cooperatives
Zitsa, Ioannina

The growers from six mountainous villages in Ipiros cultivate the grape Debina and produce Zitsa, a fine appellation white wine, both still and semi-sparkling. Zitsa, where the modern winery is located, was admired and immortalised by Byron in Childe Harolde's Pilgrimage.

Château Pegasus
Naoussa

The two Markovitis brothers use the native Xynomavro grape to produce, on their small estate, a first-class Naoussa red wine, aged in oak in the winery's cellar.

Naoussa Wine Producers Cooperative
Naoussa

Large cooperative in western Macedonia producing mainly strong, above-average red wines from the Xynomavro grape, under the labels of Naoussa and Vaeni.

Nemea Wine Producers Cooperative
Nemea

Large cooperative in the Peloponnese producing mainly red wines from the Agiorgitiko grape, under the labels of Nemea and Hercules.

CYPRUS

It was the close connection of Cyprus with Britain that put the farthest east of the Mediterranean islands firmly into the business of making wine for export. Not only has she ancient and honourable wine traditions that centuries of Islamic rule somehow failed to extinguish, but British government from 1878 brought stability and a market.

Cyprus has no great range of wines to offer, but what she does she does well, producing low-cost sherries modelled on the Spanish, smooth dry red and white table wines and her own extremely luscious liqueur-wine, Commandaria. Commandaria is to Cyprus what Constantia was to South Africa or Tokay is to Hungary.

Cyprus has until very recently been intensely conservative about grape varieties. Having never been afflicted with phylloxera, and intending to stay untainted, she spurned new-fangled introductions and planted only three grapes: Mavron the black, Xynisteri the white, and Muscat of Alexandria. There is also a traditional red grape called Ophthalmo. Today there are promising experiments with superior grapes that suggest that the Troodos Mountains could be a mini-California.

All the island's quality vineyards lie on the south slopes of the Troodos Mountains, between 1,000 and 2,500 feet. Grape acreage has increased in 10 years by 25%, to 124,000 acres, creating a great island sea of vines on the high plateaux and every pocket of hill-top soil. Some of the best vineyards are on almost pure red sand; others on grey chalk.

The best Commandaria is grown on the south slopes just north of Limassol. One famous village, Khalokhorio, makes it from pure Xynisteri – a light brown wine of considerable finesse which can be drunk young. Others, notably Zoopiyi and Yerasa, use Mavron and Opthalmo to make a dark tawny wine, superb after five or more years in barrel. The grapes are simply sun-dried for 10 days in the vineyard, then pressed. No fortification is used and the wine reaches 13–14° alcohol. The commercial brands tend to be largely youngish Mavron. All the Khalokhorio wine, made in one cooperative, is bought for blending by one firm, Keo.

Four concerns dominate the Cyprus trade, three Limassol-based merchants (all very well equipped and modern) and the Sodap Cooperative. Etko/ Haggipavlu, founded in 1844, produces Emva Cream sherry and some of the Hirondelle table wines for the British Bass Charrington, which owns 35% of the company. Their Semeli is a class Cyprus red. Keo, founded in 1926, makes the smooth traditional Othello red, Aphrodite dry white, St. Pantaleimon sweet white and the pale, slightly fizzy Bellapais. Domaine d'Ahera is a prestige red of lighter character. Mosaic, their brand of sherries, includes a good very dry wine. Their St. John is perhaps the best commercial Commandaria.

Loel is the maker of the fine Negro red and a very clean Palomino dry white as well as Amathus (alias Kykko) table wines, Command sherries and Alasia Commandaria. Sodap is a group of cooperatives with Afames as its flagship Mavron red and Arsinoe its traditional dry white. Salamis and Kolossi are other table-wine brands, St. Barnabas its Commandaria and Lysander its sherry.

TURKEY

If Noah's vineyard on the slopes of Mount Ararat was really the first, Turkey can claim to be the original home of wine. Hittite art of 4000 BC is possibly better evidence that Anatolia (central Turkey) used wine in highly cultivated ways. In relation to such a time span the long night of Islam has been scarcely more of an interruption than Prohibition was in the United States. For since the 1920s Turkey has again been making good wines; much better than her lack of a reputation leads us to expect. One of the most surprising bottles of fine wine I have ever drunk was a 1929 Turkish red – at a friend's house in Bordeaux. I took it for a Bordeaux of that famous vintage.

Turkey's vineyards are the fifth largest on earth (more than twice as great as Argentina's), but only a fraction of their produce is made into wine. Kemal Ataturk founded the twentieth-century wine industry in his drive to modernize the country. The state monopoly, Tekel, is much the biggest producer, with 21 wineries handling wines from all regions and dominating exports, particularly with popular bulk wines to Scandinavia. But there are 118 private wineries, two with very high standards.

The main wine regions are Trakya, the Thrace– Marmara region on the European side of the Bosphorus, the Aegean coast around Izmir, central Anatolia around Ankara and eastern Anatolia.

The majority of the grapes are local varieties whose names are unknown in the West, except in Trakya, where Cinsaut and Gamay and Sémillon (supported by Clairette) make the best-known red and white. A Gamay red, Hosbag (from Tekel), is not remarkable, but Trakya Kirmisi, made of the Turkish Papazharasi and Adakarasi, is a good vigorous wine. *Kirmisi* is Turkish for red and *Beyaz* for white; *Sarap* for wine. Trakya Beyaz (dry Sémillon) is one of the most popular exports.

Kutman's Villa Doluca at Mürefte on the Sea of Marmara is the most distinguished independent local producer. Founded in 1926 (the first in modern Turkey) they now make two qualities of red: Doluca of Cinsaut and Papazharasi and Villa Doluca of Gamay, Papazharasi and Cabernet Sauvignon. In my experience this is the best Turkish red. Doluca also make oak-aged Sémillon, unaged Sémillon and some 'Johannisberg Riesling'.

The Aegean region counts Cabernet and Merlot (known, I believe, as 'Bordo') among its reds, along with Carignan and Calkarasi. Most of the white is made of Sultanye, the seedless table grape with no real wine-making potential. Some Sémillon and Muscat is grown – the Muscat probably the best.

Central Anatolia makes dry white Urgup from Emir grapes and sweet white Narbag from Narince, grown at Tokat. Eastern Anatolia is the home of the best known of Turkish reds, the heavy and powerful Buzbag, made of Bogazkere near Elâzig. This is the produce of Tekel, the state enterprise. Its private enterprise rivals include Yakut and Dikmen, reds aged respectively for four and two years from the largest independent firm, Kavaklidere (who are based in Ankara, but use grapes from as far apart as Thrace and eastern Anatolia). Yakut is said to contain some Cabernet as well as native varieties.

Lebanon

What wine might be in the Levant, were it not for the followers of the Prophet, is a tantalising topic. In 1840 Cyrus Redding had heard tell (he certainly had not been there) that 'Syria makes red and white wine of the quality of Bordeaux'.

But now we have current evidence that the eastern Mediterranean can make great wine. Noah's ancient land of Canaan, now the Bekaa valley, 3,000 feet above sea level at the foot of Mt. Lebanon, emerged in the 1970s as a producer to be compared with Bordeaux, just as Redding had reported.

During the early nineteenth century its reputation was for dry white 'vin d'or' preserved in amphoras. In 1857 the Jesuits founded a vast underground winery at Ksara, with more than a mile of barrel-filled natural tunnels.

The estate which suddenly fluttered the dovecots of the wine trade is Château Musar, at Ghazir, 16 miles north of Beirut. In the 1930s Gaston Hochar founded the property, with vineyards in the Bekaa valley 15 miles to the east. In 1959 his son Serge, after training in Bordeaux, became wine maker. Bottles started appearing in London. In 1982 he showed a range of vintages going back to the 1940s which demonstrated beyond doubt that the region can produce extraordinarily fine and long-lived reds based on Cabernet Sauvignon with some Cinsaut and Syrah, aged in *barriques* – not at all unlike big Bordeaux of ripe vintages. White wines are well made but less fine, clearly needing the coming introduction of better grape varieties. During the Beirut civil war of the 1980s, Hochar, stoically carrying on making fine wine with Syrian tanks in his vineyards, became a figure of heroic legend in the world of wine.

Other Bekaa valley properties with aspirations are Domaine de Tournelles, Naquad and Kefraga.

Israel

The wine industry of Israel was a gift to the state by Baron Edmond de Rothschild, who founded the wineries at Richon-le-Zion near Tel Aviv and Zichron-Jacob on Mount Carmel near Haifa at the end of the nineteenth century. From their original aim of making sweet sacramental wine they have long since developed dry table and sparkling wines, principally with Carignan, Grenache and Sémillon, but latterly experimenting with all the classic varieties. Today there are some 7,000 acres of wine grapes in Israel, divided between the hills of Upper Galilee (an expanding area), Lower Galilee near Nazareth, Samaria, the coast between Haifa and Tel Aviv, Judea (Richon), Jerusalem and the Negev. The Golan in the north is the latest vineyard, high and therefore cool, producing decent Sauvignon Blanc and Cabernet. Carmel is the established brand name on the international Kosher market, but since 1986 the Yarden Winery has made far superior, even oak-aged wines from Golan grapes. 'The President's' sparkling wine is also well made.

Tunisia

The institution of an Office du Vin in 1970 marked the start of Tunisia's coordinated plan to make wines of export quality. Her vineyard area has been reduced from 124,000 to some 61,000 acres, all in the vicinity of Tunis (and ancient Carthage) on the north coast. There are now 13 state-owned, 13 cooperative and 10 private cellars offering a dozen wines for export. Muscats are the most characteristic wines of the country, as they are of the Sicilian islands lying not far off-shore. Reds, rosés and whites are made of French Midi-type grapes, in many cases using modern methods. As in Algeria the pale rosés are often the most attractive.

The biggest producer is the Union des Cooperatives Viticoles de Tunisie (route de Mornag, Djebel Djelloud). The union makes an unusual dry white Muscat, Muscat de Kelibia, from vineyards at the tip of Cap Bon to the northeast. It is highly aromatic, not overstrong at 11.8° but nonetheless a difficult wine to enjoy with a meal. Its best-quality red is Magon, from Tébourba in the valley of the river (Oued) Medjerdah, west of Tunis. Cinsaut and Mourvèdre in this 12° wine give it both roundness and more personality than the standard 11.5° Coteaux de Carthage. Other Union wines are Château Mornag (both red and rosé) from the Mornag hills east of Tunis, a pale dry Gris de Tunisie of Grenache and Cinsaut from the same region, and a dry Muscat-scented rosé called Sidi Rais.

The most notable wines of the state-owned Office des Terres Domaniales are the red Château Thibar, from the hills 85 miles west of Tunis up the Medjerdah valley, and Sidi Salem from Kanguet, near Mornag. Other producers to note are the Société Lomblot for their 12° red Domaine Karim from the Coteaux d'Utique, near the sea north of Tunis, Château Feriani for one of Tunisia's tastiest red wines from the same area, Héritiers René Lavau for their Koudiat, another strong red from Tébourba, and Société des Vins Tardi at Aïn Ghellal, north of Tébourba, for their Royal Tardi, which contains a touch of Pinot Noir. Perhaps better than any of these are the strong sweet dessert Muscats with the appellation Vin Muscat de Tunisie.

Algeria

The biggest and most intensely planted of France's former North African colonies has reduced her wine-grape vineyard from 900,000 acres, its total of the 1960s, to not much more than 378,000 today – and her productivity by an even greater proportion. Most of this has been done by converting the fertile plains to cereals and concentrating on the hill vineyards which produced superior wine in French days. A dozen 'Crus' were indeed given VDQS status before independence.

Seven regions are recognized by the Office Nationale de Commercialisation des Produits Viticoles as quality zones. They are all in the hills about 50 miles inland in the two western provinces of Oran and Alger. Oran has always been the bulk producer, with three quarters of Algeria's vines. The ONCV has standard labels that reveal nothing about the origin of the wine except its region – and in the case of its prestige brand, Cuvée le Président, not even that. Le Président is a matured faintly claret-like wine I have not found as good as the best regional offerings.

The western quality zone, the Coteaux de Tlemcen, lies close to the Moroccan border, covering north-facing sandstone hills at 2,500 feet. Red, rosé and white wines are well made: strong, very dry but soft in the style the Algerians have mastered. The rosés and whites in particular have improved enormously with cool fermentation.

The Monts du Tessalah at Sidi-bel-Abbès to the northeast seem rather less distinguished; certainly less so than the Coteaux de Mascara, whose red wines in colonial days were frequently passed off as burgundy. Mascara reds are powerful and dark with real body, richness of texture and, wood-aged as they are sold today, a considerable aroma of oak and spice. A certain crudeness marks the finish. This I have not found in the Mascara white, dry though it is; it would be creditable in the South of France: pleasantly fruity, not aromatic but smooth and individual – probably as good as any white wine made in North Africa.

At Dahra the hills approach the sea. The former French VDQS Crus of Robert, Rabelais and Renault (now known as Taughrite, Aïn Merane and Mazouna) make smooth, dark and full-bodied reds and a remarkable rosé with a fresh almost cherry-like smell, light and refreshing to drink – a skilful piece of wine-making. Farther east and farther inland, in the province of Al-Jazir, the capital, the Coteaux du Zaccar makes slightly lighter, less fruity wines. Again the rosé, though less fruity than the Dahra, is well made. South of Zaccar and higher, at 4,000 feet, the Medea hills are cooler, and finer varieties are grown along with the standard Cinsaut, Carignan and Grenache. Cabernet and Pinot Noir go into Medea blends, which have less flesh and more finesse than Dahra or Mascara. The easternmost of the quality zones is Aïn Bessem Bouira, making relatively light (11.5°) reds and what some consider Algeria's best rosés.

Morocco

Morocco has the smallest wine-grape acreage of the North African wine countries (56,000 acres) but the tightest organization and the highest standards. The few wines that are 'AOG' (Appellation d'Origine Garantie') have similar controls to French appellation wines, strictly applied. They are produced by a central organization, SODEVI, which includes the important cooperative union of Meknès, and are bottled and sold by a Moroccan company in Brussels, the Comptoir des Vins du Maroc (Avenue des Arts 20, 1040 Bruxelles).

Four regions of Morocco produce fair wines, but by far the best and biggest is the Fez/Meknès area at 1,500–2,000 feet in the northern foothills of the middle Atlas mountains, where the regions of Sais, Beni Sadden, Zerkhoun, Beni M'Tir and Guerrouane are designated. The last two have achieved remarkable reds of Cinsaut, Carignan and Grenache, respectively sold abroad as Tarik and Chantebled (and in Morocco as Les Trois Domaines). Tarik is the bigger and more supple of the two, but both are smooth, long and impressive. Guerrouane also specializes in an AOG *vin gris*, a very pale dry rosé of Cinsaut and Carignan, which substitutes well for the white wines Morocco lacks. SODEVI at Meknès makes sound non-AOG red and rosé under the name Aïn Souala.

A little wine, but none of consequence, is made in the Berkane/Oujda area to the east near the Algerian border. The other principal areas are around Rabat, on the coastal plain, in the regions of Gharb, Chellah, Zemmour and Zaer. The brand names Dar Bel Amri, Roumi and Sidi Larbi, formerly used for pleasant soft reds from these zones, have been abandoned in favour of the regional names.

Farther south down the coast the Casablanca region has three wine zones: Zennata, Sahel and Doukkala. The first produces a solid 12° red marketed as Ourika. South of Casablanca the firm of Sincomar makes the standard drinking of every thirsty visitor, the Gris de Boulaouane. Boulaouane is the archetypal North African refresher: very pale, slightly orange, dry, faintly fruity, extremely clean and altogether suited to steamy Casablanca nights.

UNITED STATES

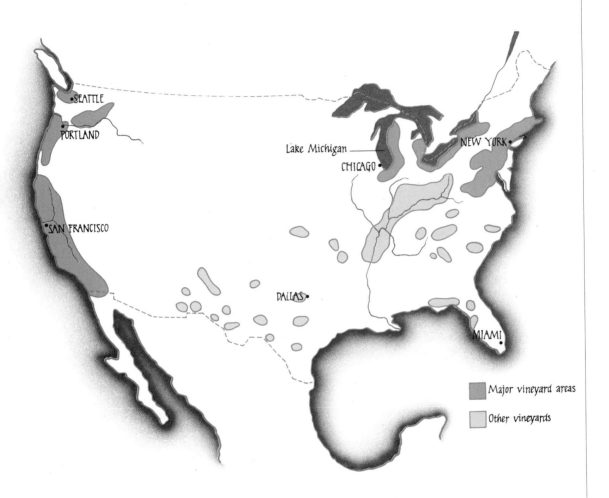

Until the late 1960s it was true to say that wine-growing was an exotic activity that had only succeeded in gaining footholds on the fringes of North America. 90 per cent of all American wine came (as it still does) from California. Its distribution was regulated (as it still is) by the Bureau of Alcohol, Tobacco and Firearms, as though it were an ignitable, if not explosive, substance. Wine-drinking was an infrequent, low-profile, even faintly suspect activity. Prohibition had almost snuffed out the promise of healthy Americans, free of neuroses, freely accepting the happy legacy of Mediterranean culture.

During the past quarter century both the production and consumption of wine have vastly increased. The USA is now fifth or sixth (according to annual fluctuations) in the world

league of wine-producers, and regularly makes approximately a quarter as much wine as France or Italy, the two giants of the wine world. Imports have soared. The per capita consumption has quadrupled from a mere two and a half bottles to almost 11 a year. And perhaps most importantly nine of the 11 bottles are of natural table wines (whereas two of the two and a half were of fortified or dessert wines).

The figure is still modest, and the neurosis certainly has not departed, but interest in wine has spread far beyond its original coastal toeholds. At least 42 of the 52 states now have aspiring winegrowers. Six could be said to have industries. Their enthusiastic experiments point to the possibility of a far more widespread wine culture in some future enlightened age.

CALIFORNIA

It now seems so natural to include California in the shortlist of the world's top winelands that it bears repetition that this status is relatively new. The 1970s was the decade when California decisively took up her position in the world of wine. She had had what proved to be a false start, though a very promising one, a century earlier. An adolescent America was not ready for what she (and wine in general) had to offer. The generation of wine makers that followed the repeal of Prohibition did indispensable groundwork for an industry that appeared to be remarkably friendless. Hardly anyone was prepared for the impact when in the late 1960s Americans started to change their habits, to look outwards for new ideas, to start thinking about their environment, their diet and their health, and to discover that they had a well of the world's most satisfactory beverage in their own back yard.

From the early 1970s on, growth has been so rapid and change so breathless that one of the observers and critics closest to the scene in California, Bob Thompson, has compared an attempt to follow it to 'taking a census in a rabbit warren'. The figures hardly express the changes. In 1970 there were 220 wineries; in 1982, 591, in 1985, 676, in 1990, 700. Wine grape acreage has stabilized at around 300,000 acres, up from 170,000 in 1970. But beneath these figures, impressive as they are, everything was in ferment: grapes, men, priorities, areas, tanks and philosophy. They still are.

Predictably the other-drink businesses – brewers, distillers and soft-drink manufacturers – have moved in to control what they can of the mass-production end of the market. Although Gallo, the company that has done most for wine in America is still run personally by the brothers who started it.

At the other extreme, in what rapidly and rather unkindly became known as boutique wineries, fashion has rocketed about from one winery to another as drinkers even newer to wine than the wine makers tried to make up their minds what they liked, at the same time as discovering who made it – or if he made it again the following year. There are enduring landmarks, but they are few and far between. Essentially this is an industry with no structure and very few rules.

There are four approaches to finding what you want in California, and you need them all. There is no escaping the dominance of the brand or winery name. The grape variety is the only firm information available about what is in the bottle. The area of production is a good clue to the style of the wine, if not its quality. And the vintage date at least tells you how old it is – and often considerably more. Access to the essentials in this chapter is therefore organized into three alphabetical directories: of wineries and brands, of grapes (and wine types) and of areas.

How good are the wines, and where do they fit into an international comparison?

In the last 20 years the top class of handmade wines have proved that they can outshine in blind tastings the very European wines they emulate. The reason why they do this with almost monotonous predictability is inherent in their nature. It is the fully ripe grape, a comparative rarity in France and Germany, that makes California wines comparable with the great vintages and the best vineyards of Europe – the only places with those flavours.

There is also, however, the rate of ripening and the question of soil to consider. Both of these have more bearing on the long-term quality of wine than California is at present inclined to allow. The concomitant disadvantage of the super-ripe grape is the relentless force of flavour that it gives.

Heartiness suits Americans – at least the Americans of today. It suits many wine drinkers everywhere. But it is an important sign of the maturity of the California wine maker that today he is talking in terms of toning it down. Not long ago the terms of highest praise were 'impressive fruit', 'heaps of varietal character', 'distinct notes of French oak'. Today 'delicacy', 'balance', 'harmony' and 'elegance' are becoming fashionable terms of approval. There is new stress on the vineyard: the winery techniques have been mastered, say California's wine thinkers. Now it is time to get the yields right, the ripeness optimum, the chemical content down. Americans now have less assertive wines from the Pacific Northwest to compare with those of California. With what may be considered an over-reaction, some big California wineries started marketing extremely low-alcohol 'soft' wines.

California should not try to be all things to all men. It should make its own style of wine with all the formidable skill and sensitivity it can muster – it has nothing to fear from comparison.

Personal taste is the final arbiter – as I was reminded when I rashly asked a gathering in New York if they would really like all red Bordeaux to have the character of the great champion of modern vintages, 1961. 'Of course,' they said. What a fool I must be, not to want the most concentrated, the most overwhelmingly full-flavoured (but the least refreshing) of all wines with every meal.

THE CLIMATE

California's climate can only be understood in terms of the Pacific Ocean alongside and the effect of the long chain of 2,000-foot mountains that follows the coast. The prevailing northwest sea winds cause currents that bring very cold water from the depths to the surface close inshore. Sea-warmed air passing over the cold water vapourizes. The effect is dense fog just offshore all summer long.

Behind the mountains it is hot and dry. Every day in summer the Central Valley reaches 80° or 90°F (26° or 32°C) its hot air rises and draws colder air in from the sea to take its place. Every gap or pass in the coast range becomes a funnel for the coastal fog to seep inland.

Everyone who has been to San Francisco in spring or autumn has marvelled at the white blanket stealing under the Golden Gate by lunchtime, and by early evening mounting its towers and creeping in wisps over the surrounding hills. In summer the city is often shrouded in fog all day.

The same phenomenon happens far down the coast to the south, and its moderating influence is felt in places many miles inland. The exhilarating air of San Francisco Bay not only cools the Carneros vineyards at the mouth of the Napa Valley to the north. It penetrates, via the flats of the Sacramento River delta, as far inland as Lodi in the Central Valley.

Each coastal valley from Mendocino in the north to Santa Barbara in the south receives its regular draught of clammy air. At Monterey, where the Salinas Valley opens invitingly to the ocean, the chill prevents some grape varieties from ripening at all.

In other words topography, rather than latitude, is the determining factor in the climate of California. Its emerging vineyard areas therefore have to be studied and experimented with individually – a process that in many cases is still only at the beginning of its development.

THE CLIMATE REGION SYSTEMS

The complexities of California's climate have led the Department of Viticulture at the Davis campus of the University of California to devise a climate zone system, to help growers plant grapes suitable to their area.

The basis of the system is 'heat-summation', which is a measure of the total number of 'degree-days' when a vine will be in active growth. The degree-days are arrived at by averaging each day's temperature between 1 April and 31 October, then subtracting 50°F (the temperature at which a vine becomes active).

For example, if the average temperature for ten days was 80°F, the heat summation would be 80–50 = 30 × 10 = 300 degree-days.

The state has been divided into five regions, which are mapped on page 31.

Region 1
The coolest, has 2,500 degree-days or less, the equivalent of such northern European vineyards as Champagne, the Côte d'Or and the German Rhine. Chardonnay, Riesling, Sauvignon Blanc, Cabernet and Pinot Noir are recommended. Region 1 only exists where the influence of the ocean is paramount.

Region 2
Has between 2,500 and 3,000 degree-days – an average temperature similar to Bordeaux. Most Region 1 grapes are also recommended for Region 2, although not so emphatically.

Region 3
Has between 3,000 and 3,500 degree-days, a total comparable to the Rhône valley. Recommended varieties include Sauvignon Blanc, Semillon, Carignane and Ruby Cabernet. Zinfandel does well but only has a qualified recommendation.

Region 4
With 3,500 to 4,000 degree-days, is comparable to the south of Spain and is therefore dessert-wine country, with the exception of Emerald Riesling, Barbera and Ruby Cabernet. Port grapes grow well.

Region 5
Has more than 4,000 degree-days. Souzão, Tinta Madera and Verdelho are highly recommended varieties in this North African-type climate.

The regions are built into the California system and are constantly referred to (e.g. in the notes on grapes that follow). Like all generalizations, however, they are riddled with qualifications and exceptions. California has just as many microclimates as equivalent parts of Europe. And in the ripening of grapes the average temperature may not be nearly so important as the timing of period of unusual heat or cold. For example, the North Coast tends to grow warmer and less foggy towards vintage time, when in Bordeaux the chance of rain increases. The final spurt towards ripeness is therefore normally more rapid – which has a distinct effect on the style of the wine.

THE REGIONS

California is in the process of working out a system of designated American Viticultural Areas, which will be referred to informally as AVAs.

They should in no way be confused with French appellations, which include strict control of grape types, quantities produced and every other aspect of winemaking. California's are purely geographical. The rule is simply that 85 per cent of the grapes in the bottle must come from the viticultural area named on the label.

The broadest area is 'California' – used either for wine from an unprestigious grape-growing region, or for a blend of wines or grapes from several (which may, of course, be of the highest quality). All the grapes used must come from within the state.

More specific are the counties. Their boundaries may or may not have viticultural significance, but at present their names are the only officially recognized areas that cover the whole state. At least 75% of the grapes must come from the county in question.

The Napa Valley. Until quite recently, the deep, fertile soil of the valley floor was cultivated in preference to the rocky slopes. Frost is a danger here: hence the oil heaters and windmills to disperse cold air.

Areas under discussion and being gradually agreed are both more and less specific: as unspecific, for example, as 'North Coast' and as pinpointed as Knight's Valley (a part of Sonoma affecting only 1,000 acres). 'North Coast' causes an argument because it is broad but carries an inference of quality. (It sounds cool.) One lobby wanted six counties included; another only Napa, Sonoma and Mendocino. Surprisingly, it does not seem to have occurred to the folk of Sonoma that Napa is not a coast county at all.

An early decision was taken on the limits of the 'Napa Valley' – virtually the whole of Napa County, minus a rocky fraction on the borders of Lake County. 'Sonoma Valley' is quite different: a tightly drawn area in the south of the county. This is because other parts of Sonoma, notably the Alexander, Dry Creek and Russian River valleys, all have their own AVA's.

The following list includes all the counties with wineries, and grape-growing areas with some claim to being considered individual (and, by implication, above average quality) whose names are used on

CALIFORNIA'S SOIL

labels, whether legislation has defined them or not. You hear surprisingly little about soil in California. With all the official stress on climate, it has been left to individuals to discover the characteristics of their own land – a startling contrast to France, where soil differences are given pride of place.

The assumption here is that any reasonably fertile and well-drained land will produce a good crop of grapes. Fertility is generally high because the land is new to agriculture – at least by European standards – and much of it is volcanic in origin. Drainage is rarely a problem because hardly any rain falls in the growing season. The deep soil of the valley floors can therefore be profitably used – though leaching of minerals by winter rains is proving a problem in some bottom-land vineyards.

The chief argument for planting in more difficult places, the rocky hillsides with their thin topsoil, is that the vine under stress, its crop limited by scarcity of water and nutrients, produces a smaller quantity of more concentrated juice that makes better wine.

Soil temperatures are also higher on the gravelly loam of the hills than on the heavier alluvial land of the valley floor. Whether this, or faster drainage, or better air circulation or any of several other factors is the most important, it is assumed that it is the physical rather than the chemical properties of the soil that determine quality. Chalk soil (such as produces the white wines with the utmost finesse in Europe, notably in Champagne and the sherry country) is rare in California – but at least one vineyard, Chalone, has been planted in an almost inaccessible and waterless spot for the sake of its alkaline properties.

Now more and more perfectionist growers are moving higher and higher into the hills, especially around the Napa Valley. Besides the search for more strenuous soil conditions, the higher they go, the cooler the growing season and the less the chance of early leafing followed by disastrous frost – an annual threat in the valley.

The years to come will bring more discussion of soils and more distinctions between vineyards. Already one winery, Diamond Creek, has three Cabernets distinguished as coming from Red Rock Terrace, Volcanic Hill and Gravelly Meadow.

APPELLATIONS, COUNTIES AND DISTRICTS OF CALIFORNIA

Alameda. East of San Francisco Bay, climate region 3, with 1,700 acres of vineyards. The Livermore Valley, (AVA) is its main district.

Alexander Valley. AVA. Sonoma. Regions 2 and 3. Russian River Valley around Geyserville.

Amador. In the Sierra foothills 100 miles east of San Francisco. Regions 4-5. 1,000 acres, mainly Zinfandel. Shenandoah Valley is the principal vineyard area.

Anderson Valley. AVA. Mendocino. Region 2. Source of white grapes for sparkling wines, also Chardonnays. 582 acres.

Arroyo Grande Valley. AVA. San Luis Obispo.

Arroyo Seco. AVA. Monterey. Now mostly white grapes. 8,500 acres.

Ben Lomond Mountain. AVA. Santa Cruz.

California, Shenandoah Valley. AVA. Amador. The largest district in the county, with Zinfandel and Sauv.Blanc.

Calveras. The county south of Amador. Regions 4-5. 60 acres.

Calistoga. *See* Napa.

Carmel Valley. AVA. Monterey. Cab.Sauv. does well. 200 acres.

Carneros. AVA. Napa and Sonoma. Region 1. Cool conditions at southern end of Napa and Sonoma valleys. Good for Pinot Noir and Chardonnay.

Central Coast. An inexact term for counties between San Francisco and Santa Barbara. The Central Coast Wine Growers Association covers just San Luis Obispo and Santa Barbara.

Central Coast. AVA. San Luis Obispo–Santa Barbara.

Central Valley. A general term for the hot inland region often referred to as the San Joaquin Valley.

Chalk Hill. AVA. Sonoma. Region 2. 1,600 acres. White grapes do well.

Chalone. AVA. Monterey.

Chiles Valley. *See* Napa.

Cienega Valley. AVA. *See* San Benito.

Clarksburg. AVA. San Joaquin Valley.

Clear Lake. AVA. Lake. Region 4.

Cloverdale. *See* Sonoma.

Cole Ranch. AVA. Mendocino–Lake.

Contra Costa. The county south of Alameda. Region 3. 900 acres.

Cucamonga. *See* Riverside.

Dry Creek Valley. AVA. Sonoma. Next valley west from Alexander. Zinfandels, Cab.Sauvs., Sauv.Blancs.

Edna Valley. AVA. San Luis Obispo. Regions 1 and 2. Good Chardonnay. 650 acres.

El Dorado. AVA. Sierra foothills counties north of Amador. Gold country. Regions 3-4. 225 acres.

Fiddletown. AVA. East of Shenandoah Valley.

Fresno. Central San Joaquin Valley. County with 39,000 acres of wine grapes and far more of table. Regions 4-5. Mainly Thompson Seedless, Barbera, French Colombard.

Geyserville. *See* Sonoma.

Greenfield. *See* Monterey.

Green Valley. AVA. Sonoma. Tributary of the Russian River. Chard. and sparkling wines. 800 acres.

Guenoc Valley. AVA. Lake. Region 5.

Guerneville. *See* Sonoma.

Hecker Pass. *See* Santa Clara.

Healdsburg. *See* Sonoma.

Howell Mountain. AVA. Small, hilly district NE of the main valley.

Humboldt. On the coast north of Mendocino. 1 winery but no recorded vineyards.

Kenwood. *See* Sonoma.

Kern. Southern San Joaquin Valley. 38,000 acres of wine grapes in region 5 heat. Mainly Thompson Seedless, Barbera, Chenin Blanc, French Colombard.

Knight's Valley. AVA. Sonoma. East of Alexander and north of Napa. Region 3. 1,000 acres.

Lake. North of Napa, east of Mencocino. Region 3. 2,500 acres, mainly Cabernet Sauvignon, Zinfandel and Gamay. 5 wineries.

Livermore Valley. AVA. Alameda. Sauv.Blanc good. 1,200 acres.

Lodi. AVA. *See* San Joaquin.

Los Angeles. 4 wineries but no recorded vineyards.

Madera. AVA. Central San Joaquin Valley. Region 5. 32,000 acres of wine grapes, mainly Thompson Seedless, Barbera, Carignane, French Colombard. 3 wineries.

Marin. Just north of San Francisco across the Golden Gate. Region 1. 300 acres and 5 wineries.

McDowell Valley. AVA. Mendocino. Region 3. One winery.

Mendocino. The northernmost wine county, on the coast, ranging from regions 1-3. A dozen wineries and 10,000 acres, still largely old plantations of Carignane and French Colombard but increasingly Cabernet and Zinfandel, Chardonnay, Pinot Noir and Johannisberg Riesling.

Mendocino. AVA in Mendocino county.

Merced. Central San Joaquin Valley. Regions 4 and 5. 13,500 acres of wine grapes, mainly Thompson Seedless, Chenin Blanc, French Colombard, Barbera.

Merrit Island. AVA. San Joaquin Valley.

Modesto. *See* Stanislaus.

Monterey. The most important vineyard county of the Central Coast, with 33,000 acres and 12 wineries, chiefly in the Salinas Valley, region 1 at the ocean end, to Soledad, then warming to 3 at King City. (The Greenfield and Arroyo Seco areas come between the two.) Also Carmel Valley, (AVA) region 1, and The Pinnacles (*see* Chalone Vineyards). All the best varieties are grown, led by Cabernet with 3,800 acres – 600 less than 5 years ago: it can have difficulty ripening.

Monterey. AVA in the county of Monterey.

Mount Veeder. AVA. *See* Napa.

Napa. The most concentrated and prestigious vineyard county, with 28,500 acres ranging from region 1 in the south (Carneros, just north of San Francisco Bay) to 3 at Calistoga in the north. Now has about 130 wineries. Appellations or sub-areas include Los Carneros (AVA), Mount Veeder, (AVA) Yountville, Oakville, Rutherford (famous for Cabernet), St Helena, Spring Mountain and Calistoga on the western side, and Stag's Leap, (AVA) Silverado Trail, Howell Mountain (AVA) and Chiles Valley on the east, with Pope Valley tucked away up in the hills northeast. All the best grape varieties are grown: Cabernet leading with 5,900 acres, Chardonnay 5,600, Sauvignon Blanc 2,700, Pinot Noir 2,300, Zinfandel 2,100, Chenin Blanc 2,300, Johannisberg Riesling 1,300.

Napa Valley. AVA in Napa county. Region 1.

North Coast. AVA. Lake, Marin, Napa, Mendocino, Solano, Sonoma.

North Coast. An inexact term for the counties north of San Francisco Bay.

Northern Sonoma. AVA. Sonoma County.

Oakville. *See* Napa.

Pacheco Pass. AVA. San Benito

Paicines. AVA. *See* San Benito.

Paso Robles. AVA. San Luis Obispo. Region 3. Zinfandel traditionally, also Sauv.Blanc.

The Pinnacles. *See* Monterey.

Placer. Sierra foothills county, north of

El Dorado. Regions 3 and 5. 130 acres of wine grapes.

Pope Valley. *See* Napa.

Potter Valley. AVA. Mendocino. Region 1. White grapes. 1,000 acres.

Redwood Valley. Mendocino. Region 3. Cab.Sauv. a speciality. 2,200 acres.

Riverside. The principal wine county of Southern California, east of Los Angeles, with 3,000 acres, mainly Thompson Seedless, but significant new acreages of good varieties at Temecula (AVA), led by Johannisberg Riesling despite being regions 3-4. There are 6 wineries at present.

Russian River Valley. AVA. Sonoma. South of Dry Creek. Regions 1 and 2. Chard., Gewürz. and Pinot Noir plus sparkling wines.

Rutherford. *See* Napa.

Sacramento. Inland county northeast of San Francisco Bay, regions 4-5, with 3,000 acres, mainly of Zinfandel, Chenin Blanc, Cabernet and Gamay.

St Helena. *See* Napa.

Salinas Valley. *See* Monterey.

San Benito. County inland from Monterey, region 3, with 4,600 acres, almost all planted by Almadén in Chardonnay, Cabernet, Pinot Noir, etc. Paicines and Cienega Valley are AVAs, as is Lime Kiln Valley, a single winery.

San Bernardino. Largely desert (region 5) county east of Los Angeles with over 7,000 acres of Zinfandel, Mission, Grenache, Palomino, etc. Cucamonga is the wine district, with 5 wineries.

San Diego. Southernmost coast county, regions 4-5, with 240 acres of mixed vines and 3 wineries.

San Francisco. No vineyards, but at least 2 wineries recorded, 1 of them on a pier in the harbour.

San Joaquin. The Northern county of the central San Joaquin Valley with 37,000 acres of wine grapes. Most is region 5, but Lodi (AVA) is region 4 and specializes in Zinfandel, some 11,000 acres of it. Carignane, Petite Sirah and French Colombard are the other principal grapes. The dozen wineries in the county include the huge Franzia and Guild.

San Lucas. AVA. Monterey–San Benito.

San Luis Obispo. The coastal county south of Monterey, relatively new to wine-growing but with 5,200 acres in 3 areas, Paso Robles/Templeton (region 3), Shandon and the cooler Edna Valley running south from San Luis Obispo city. Cabernet, Zinfandel, Chardonnay and Sauvignon Blanc are the main grapes being grown. There are 20 wineries.

San Mateo. The county immediately south of San Francisco has 6 recorded acres of vines and 3 wineries.

San Pasqual Valley. AVA. Southern California.

Santa Barbara. The southern central coast county, with 2 valleys in regions 2-3 mustering 10,000 acres, mostly of Johannisberg Riesling, Cabernet, Chardonnay and Pinot Noir. The Santa Maria and Santa Ynez valleys are up-and-coming AVAs with 24 wineries.

Santa Clara. South of San Francisco Bay but sheltered from the coast by the Santa Cruz Mountains. The Hecker Pass in south Santa Clara is region 3, the Santa Cruz Mountain AVA region 1. The 1,700 acres are divided between Zinfandel and cool-climate varieties. 30 wineries include the giant Almaden and Paul Masson and many small country ones.

Santa Clara Valley. AVA. Santa Clara County.

Santa Cruz Mountains. AVA. Central Coast county, south of San Mateo. Only 94 acres of wine grapes, but 12 wineries.

Santa Maria Valley. AVA. Santa Barbera.

Santa Ynez Valley. AVA. Santa Barbera.

Sierra Foothills. AVA. Sierra Foothills counties.

Silverado Trail. *See* Napa.

Solano-Green Valley. AVA. San Joaquin Valley.

Sonoma. Large, varied and important county between Napa and the ocean, its 30,000 acres of vines distinctly divide into: Sonoma Valley (AVA), just north of the Bay, region 1 warming up to region 2 at Kenwood; Russian River Valley (AVA), long and diverse, region 1 at the ocean end near Guerneville, to region 3 farther north and inland near Cloverdale; Sonoma/Green Valley (AVA), around Forestville within the Russian River Valley AVA; Dry Creek Valley (AVA), an offshoot northwest from the centre of the Russian River Valley near Healdsburg, regions 2-3; Alexander Valley, the centre of the Russian River Valley between Healdsburg and Geyserville, also regions 2-3; Knight's Valley (AVA), east of Alexander Valley and a shade warmer. *See also* all the above. Sonoma has the biggest plantings in the state of Gewürztraminer, Pinot Noir and high-quality Zinfandel, and important ones of Cabernet and Chardonnay. There are 100 wineries.

Sonoma Coast. AVA. Sonoma County.

Sonoma County. AVA. Sonoma County. Region 5.

Sonoma Mountain. AVA. Sonoma County.

Sonoma Valley. AVA. Sonoma. Southern end of the county, next to Carneros, 5,900 acres.

South Coast. AVA. Southern California.

Spring Mountain. *See* Napa.

Stag's Leap. *See* Napa.

Stanislaus. Central San Joaquin Valley county with 19,000 acres, mostly region 5 and largely Carignane, French Colombard, Chenin Blanc, Grenache and Ruby Cabernet. The one winery, Gallo, at Modesto, is the world's biggest.

Suisun Valley. AVA. San Joaquin Valley.

Temecula. AVA. *See* Riverside.

Templeton. *See* San Luis Obispo.

Tulare. Southern San Joaquin, region 5, with 17,000 acres, largely Barbera, Carignane and French Colombard.

Ukiah Valley. Mendocino's largest district. 4,500 acres.

Ventura. Coastal county just north of Los Angeles with 7 acres and an 1 winery.

Wild Horse Valley. AVA in Napa county.

Willow Creek. AVA. Humbolt, Trinity.

Winery Lake. A much-cited source of high-quality, cool-climate grapes in the Carneros region of Napa.

Yolo. County east of Napa, region 4, with 700 acres, mainly Chenin Blanc, and 1 winery.

York Mountain. AVA. San Luis Obispo. Small district west of Paso Robles.

Yountville. *See* Napa.

Varietals and varieties

The useful word 'varietal' was coined in California as shorthand for a wine that is either made entirely from, or derives its character from, one named grape variety. Up to 1983 the law required that the named variety be 51% of the total. From 1983 the requirement is 75%. Most high-quality varietals have long been closer to 100%.

On a semantic note, varietal is an epithet describing a wine. It is not a noun meaning a specific sort of grape. That noun is variety. The Chardonnay grape is a variety; its wine is a varietal wine.

GRAPES AND GENERIC WINE NAMES

Angelica

A fortified sweet wine traditional to California, usually made from the old Mission grape. Heitz has made the best-known samples.

Barbera

The Italian red variety has good acidity in hot regions; used mainly for blending in California. Increasing acreage in the Central Valley. Recommended for climate regions 3 and 4. Produces 5 to 8 tons an acre. 10,800 acres.

Burgundy

An accepted term for any red wine, with the vague implication that it should be dark and full-bodied (unlike real burgundy). California burgundy is usually slightly sweet. But it is not all low quality; some reputable firms use the term for good wine.

Cabernet Sauvignon (Cab. Sauv.)

Makes California's best red: fruity, fragrant, tannic, full-bodied. Needs maturing in oak, and at least 4 years in bottle. Also makes very pretty rosé or 'blush' wines.

Highly recommended for region 1 and recommended for 2. Crop is 4 to 6 tons an acre. The best comes from the central Napa Valley, parts of Sonoma and of the Central Coast. Total acreage increased from 6,600 in 1977 to 29,700 in 1989.

Carignane (Carig.)

A high-yield – 8 to 12 tons an acre – red blending grape recommended for region 3 and little seen as a 'varietal'.

Carnelian (Carn.)

A new grape produced at Davis to give Cabernet-flavoured wines in hot regions.

Chablis

Despite justified French protests that this is a part of France, it remains the uninformed American's term for (relatively) dry white wine from California, or anywhere else.

Champagne

Until some imaginative new name for California sparkling wine appears, the name of the French region will continue to be used – although not by the French.

Charbono

Little-used Italian red grape produced by 2 Napa wineries.

Chardonnay (Chard.)

California's most successful white grape, capable of great wines in the Burgundian tradition with age, and sometimes fermentation, in oak. Nice judgement is needed not to produce overintense, ponderous wines (especially in Napa). Parts of Sonoma and the Central Coast (Monterey) tend to have a lighter touch. The best examples age for 10 years or more in bottle.

Highly recommended for region 1, recommended for region 2, but surprisingly now also rather good in Central Valley region 3. Acreage has increased from 3,000 to 48,000 acres in 18 years. Yield is 4 to 6 tons an acre.

Chenin Blanc (Ch. Bl.)

A surprisingly popular, usually rather dull white grape recommended for region 1 but adequate in regions 2 and 3, appreciated for its high crop – 6 to 10 tons – and clean, adaptable flavour, pleasant when semi-sweet (although best dry); good in blends; not needing age. Acreage in the state has increased in 18 years from 9,600 to 32,000.

Chianti

The Italian name still occasionally used as a 'generic' for sweetish reds of moderate to poor quality.

Emerald Riesling (Em. Ries.)

An original Davis University white grape (Riesling × Muscat) recommended for enormous crops (6 to 12 tons) and fruity flavours in warm region 4. Scarcely an improvement on (e.g.) French Colombard for popular cheap whites. 2,750 acres.

Flora

Another Davis-bred white derived from Gewürztraminer, moderately recommended for regions 1 and 2. Crops 4 to 7 tons an acre. Makes tolerable sweetish wine. 400 acres.

French Colombard (Fr. Col.)

Very popular white blending grape recommended for regions 3 and 4, where it gives 6 to 10 tons an acre and maintains good fresh acidity. Also used for sparkling wine and sometimes as a 'varietal', although 'weedy' describes its flavour rather well. By far the most widely planted grape in California with over 62,000 acres.

Fumé Blanc (Fumé Bl.)

See Sauvignon Blanc.

Gamay Beaujolais (Gamay Beauj.)

Not the Beaujolais grape but a form of Pinot Noir, productive in cool regions but not recommended anywhere.

Gamay

Growing confusion between Gamay Beaujolais (see above), the real (French) thing, and Napa Gamay, which is not Gamay at all, blights any attempt to sort out which wines are made from which.

Gewürztraminer (Gewürz.)

After a hesitant start, a great success in California, where its wine is oddly softer and less spicy than in Alsace. Recommended for region 1. Crops 4 to 6 tons an acre. 18 years have seen acreage rise from 650 to 2,100 acres. More is planted, but not yet mature.

Golden Chasselas

An alias of the Palomino, the best sherry grape. Produces 6 to 10 tons an acre in region 5.

Gray Riesling (Gray Ries.)

Not a Riesling but a minor French grape Chauché Gris, related to the Trousseau of the Jura. Adequate white table wine, not recommended by Davis. There are some 2,000 acres.

Green Hungarian

A minor white grape, reasonably fruity and acidic, not recommended but offered by a few wineries.

Grenache (Gren.)

The pale red blending and pink-wine grape of the south of France, recommended for region 2. Crops 5 to 9 tons. High sugar content makes it popular for dessert wines in warmer regions. 13,156 acres.

Grignolino (Grig.)

Non-recommended red grape (or grapes), presumably from Italy, used by 1 or 2 wineries in cool regions to make off-beat red or rosé, sometimes distinctly Muscat flavoured.

Johannisberg Riesling (or White Riesling) (J.R.)

Commonly called 'J.R.' for short. The real Rhine Riesling, surprisingly a great success in California's coolest areas (highly recommended in region 1, recommended in 2). The dry equivalents of German Kabinetts are rarely as good as the sweet or very sweet wines. Late-picking with botrytis ('noble rot') is triumphant.

California's faster ripening also seems to hasten the maturing of the wine, which tastes fully developed in 2 or 3 years – much sooner than in Germany. The crop is 4 to 6 tons an acre (much lower than in Germany). There are 6,000 acres.

Malbec

The Bordeaux blending grape. There is very little in California but more is planned.

Malvasia Bianca

The common Italian grape, recommended for dessert wines in regions 4 and 5 but capable of pleasant, soft table wine in cooler areas.

Merlot

The Pomerol grape; a coming thing in California both for blending with Cabernet and as a 'varietal'. Acreage is 10 times the 300 acres of 10 years ago (mainly in Napa, Sonoma and Monterey). Not officially recommended, but best in region 1.

Mission

The coarse old grape of the Franciscan missionaries. Some 3,200 acres are left in regions 4 and 5. Crops 6 to 12 tons an acre, used in dessert wines (*see* Angelica).

Muscat or Moscato

The best is Muscat de Frontignan or Moscato Canelli, recommended for white table wines in regions 2 and 3; for dessert wines in hotter areas. Crop 4 to 6 tons an acre. Its best production is a sweet, low-alcohol wine so unstable that it must be kept refrigerated. There are only 1,400 acres in the state. Muscat of Alexandria is a hot-climate grape grown mainly for eating.

Nebbiolo

Piedmont's noble grape, recently given its first chance in California. Fog is the very thing it likes best.

Petite Sirah (Pet. Sir.)

California's name for a low-grade French grape, Durif. Useful for giving colour and tannin to blends. Recommended for region 2 (4 to 8 tons an acre). Most is grown in Monterey and (oddly) the San Joaquin Valley.

Pinot Blanc (P.Bl.)

Like a low-key Chardonnay, recommended for region 1 but little planted.

Pinot Noir (P.N.)

Burgundy's red grape is widely regarded as the last great hurdle for California's wine makers – early results were over-strong, heavy and dull. Recent years have seen intermittent but increasing success. Recommended for region 1 but only 3 to 4 tons an acre. 9,140 acres.

Pinot St. George (P.St.Geo.)

A minority speciality of very few wineries. Most of the 700 acres are in Monterey. Never exciting wine.

Port

A 'generic' name taken from the Old World for sweet dessert wine which rarely resembles the Portuguese original – although it may well have qualities of its own.

Rkatsiteli

A (white) Russian variety occasionally seen. In cool regions it makes adequate, quite lively dry wine.

Ruby Cabernet (Ruby Cab.)

A Davis-bred Cabernet × Carignane with really useful qualities: a high yield – 6 to 8 tons – of Cabernet-flavoured red from regions 3 and 4, too hot for Cabernet. There are some 7,000 acres, mainly in the San Joaquin Valley.

Sauvignon Blanc (Sauv. Bl.)

Fashionable since the '70s, but always potentially excellent in California. Its best wine is closer to white Graves than Pouilly Fumé, although its frequent alias of Fumé Blanc suggests the Loire. It can be light and 'herbaceous' or oak-aged, solid and of Chardonnay quality. Highly recommended for region 1, recommended for regions 2 and 3. Crops 4 to 7 tons an acre. There are 13,800 acres.

Semillon (Sem.)

Bordeaux's sweet-wine and Australia's dry-wine grape, little exploited yet in California. Recommended for regions 2 and 3. Crops 4 to 6 tons an acre. There are some 2,300 acres.

Sherry

California 'sherry' has never achieved the standard of imitation of the Spanish original found in South Africa. There are some tolerable sweet dessert wines under the name.

Souzão

One of the Portuguese port grapes used for some of California's best sweet dessert wines

Sylvaner (Sylv.)

Once more popular than it is today for poor man's Riesling. Recommended for region 2, though much the best I have had came from Monterey in region 1. Crops 4 to 6 tons. Only 1,400-odd acres.

Syrah

The splendid red of the Rhône and Australia is at last being grown in California although still with a tiny acreage. Regions 2 and 3 may suit it. The first, from Phelps, was excellent. Its devotees are sometimes dubbed Rhône rangers.

Thompson Seedless

A neutral white table, dessert and distilling wine grape never mentioned on the label, but present in many jug whites and perhaps sparklers. One third of the State's total of 250,000 acres (all in the San Joaquin Valley) is crushed for wine.

Zinfandel (Zin.)

California's own red grape, possibly of Italian origin, immensely successful and popular for all levels of wine from cheap blends to fresh light versions and to galumphing sticky blackstrap. The best have excellent balance, a lively raspberry flavour and seem to mature indefinitely. 'White' (blush) Zinfandel is a commercial smash hit. Recommended for region 1 but grown everywhere – 33,300 acres of it. Crops 4 to 6 tons an acre.

Varietals and varieties
The useful word 'varietal' was coined in California as shorthand for a wine that is either made entirely from, or derives its character from, one named grape variety. Up to 1983 the law required that the named variety be 51% of the total. From 1983 the requirement is 75%. Most high-quality varietals have long been closer to 100%.

On a semantic note, varietal is an epithet describing a wine. It is not a noun meaning a specific sort of grape. That noun is variety. The Chardonnay grape is a variety; its wine is a varietal wine.

CALIFORNIA WINERIES

It is a dull (and unusual) week in California when another new winery (or wineries) does not announce itself. The yeast of romance and experiment is so active that any list is out of date before it comes back from the printers.

Like the rest of this book, therefore, the following survey of the California wineries is a record of a moment in history: the winter of 1990–1, with as much hard fact as the wineries cared to make known about themselves and as much explanatory or critical comment as experience and space allows.

Specifically, each entry states (if the information was available) the location of the winery, its ownership, date of foundation, the name of the wine maker (a key figure in determining quality and style), vineyards owned (if any) and the principal wines produced. The most striking feature is the number of wineries founded since 1979. Clearly, any critical evaluation on the basis of a few vintages is extremely tentative: there simply has not been enough time for consistency – or lack of it – to make itself felt. So there are many entries which belong here as a matter of record, but where evaluation must wait.

The Rhine House at the Beringer/Los Hermanos winery in St. Helena reflects the origins and the aspirations of a pioneer German wine-making family a century ago

Acacia
Las Amigas Road, *Napa*. Founded 1979.
Owners: see Chalone. Up to 25,000 cases. 50 acres in Carneros, Napa. Wines: Chard., P.N.
The Pinot Noir from this enterprise has exciting qualities of freshness, the berry smell of Pinot Noir and the soft texture of burgundy – clear indication, since reinforced, that the Carneros district is right for the variety. Up to 5 Chardonnay wines are produced each year, with half of the vintage fermented in French barriques. The former partners sold out to Chalone (q.v.) in 1986.

Ahern Winery
San Fernando, *Los Angeles*. Founded 1978.
Wine maker: Jim Ahern. 6,200 cases. Wines: Chard. Sauv.Bl., Cab.Sauv. and Zin.

Ahlgren Vineyard
Boulder Creek, *Santa Cruz*. Founded 1976.
Wine maker: Dexter Ahlgren. 1,800 cases. Wines: Chard., Cab.Sauv. and Sem.
Ahlgren's first Cabernet was rapturously received by the critics. Since, minute amounts of hand-made wines have been released to more muted acclaim.

Alderbrook Vineyards
Healdsburg, *Sonoma*. Founded 1982.
Visits. 18,000 cases (30,000 planned). 55 acres in Dry Creek Valley and Russian River Valley. Wines: Chard., Sem., Sauv.Bl.
White wine specialist using estate and other grapes for full-flavoured, good-value whites.

Alder Fels
Santa Rosa, *Sonoma*. Founded 1980.
Co-owner: Lila Burford. President and wine maker: David F. Coleman. 26 acres.
7,000 cases. Wines: J.R., Gewürz., Chard., P.N., Sauv.Bl.
A hilltop winery buying in Sonoma grapes to make Chardonnay, Sauvignon Blanc and Gewürztraminer.

Alexander Valley Vineyards
Healdsburg, *Sonoma*. Founded 1975.
Owners: The Wetzel family. Wine maker: Hank Wetzel.
Visits. 50,000 cases. 130 acres in Alexander Valley, Sonoma.
Wines: Chard., Ch.Bl., J.R., Gewürz., Cab.Sauv.
Dry Burgundian-style Chardonnay with life and length, accepted in England as one of California's best and an indication of the ideal climate of the Alexander Valley. Also good-value, well-made Cabernet.

Almadén Vineyards
San Jose, *Santa Clara*. Founded 1852.
Owners: Grand Metropolitan.
Wine maker: Klaus Mathes.
Visits. 8.5 m. cases. 6,500 acres in Monterey and San Benito.
Wines: about 60 different wines under Almadén, Charles LeFranc and Le Domaine labels.
One of the historic names, a pioneer of quality after Prohibition and of the move south down the Central Coast with huge plantings in San Benito in the 1960s. Almadén became the third or fourth largest wine company in America and the largest so-called 'premium' one. In 1987 bought by Heublein which was in turn bought by Grand Metropolitan, which decided to close down or sell all the vineyards and cellars and use the brand for bulk wine.

Alta Vineyard Cellar
Calistoga, *Napa*. Founded 1878, refounded 1979.
Owners: Benjamin and Rose Falk. Wine maker: Jon P. Axhelm. Visits by appt. 2,100 cases. 10 acres in Napa Valley.
The original winery (next door to Schramsberg) was visited by Robert Louis Stevenson. The new one is a Chardonnay specialist.

Amador Foothill Winery
Plymouth, *Amador*. Founded 1980.
Owners: Ben Zeitman and Katie Quinn.
Visits. 12,000 cases. 10.5 acres.
Small Shenandoah Valley vineyard. The winery is below ground for natural cooling. Zinfandel predominates.

Anderson Wine Cellars
Exter, *Tulare*. Founded 1980.
Wine maker: Don Anderson. Visits by appt. 2,000 cases. 20 acres. Wines: Ruby Cab., Chard., Colomb.

S. Anderson Vineyard
Yountville, *Napa*. Vineyard founded 1971, winery 1979.
Owners: Carole and Stanley B. Anderson Jr. (who is also wine maker). Visits by appt. 15,000 cases. 32 acres in Yountville; 68 acres at Carneros. Wines: Chard. and sparkling wine only.
Good Chardonnay and, recently, good sparkling wines: non-vintage Tivoli, vintage Brut and vintage Blanc de Noir.

Arrowood
Sonoma. Founded 1990.
Wines: Chard., Cab.Sauv.
New venture by Chateau St Jean's wine maker. First releases are an '86 Chard. and an '85 Cabernet. To watch.

Arroyo-Sonoma Winery
see Bandiera Winery.

Atlas Peak Vineyards
Foss Valley, *Napa*. Founded 1985.
Owner: Partnership between Whitbread (UK), Piero Antinori (Italy) and Bollinger (Champagne). 300 acres at Altas Park.
Major venture which has yet to release any wines. These will include a Cabernet Sauvignon, a Chardonnay, a Sauvignon/Semillon blend and, perhaps, a Sangiovese varietal. The wine maker, Dr Dick Peterson, was formerly at Monterey Vineyard.

Au Bon Climat
Santa Barbara. Pinot Noir and Chardonnay specialist.

Baldinelli Vineyards
Plymouth, *Amador*. Founded 1979.
Owners: John Millar and Edward Baldinelli. Wine maker: Edward Bladinelli. 70 acres. 16,000 cases. Wines: Zin., Cab.Sauv., Sauv.Bl.

Ballard Canyon Winery
Solvang, *Santa Barbara*. Founded 1978.
Owner: Gene Hallock. Wine makers: Gene Hallock and Fred Holloway. Visits by appt. 10,000 cases. 45 acres in Santa Ynez Valley, Santa Barbara. Wines: Chard., Cab.Sauv., J.R., Muscat, Fumé Bl.

Balverne Winery and Vineyards
Windsor, *Sonoma*. Founded 1980.
President B.J. Bird. Wine maker: Michael Duffy. No visits. 20,000 cases. 200 acres in Chalk Hill area of Sonoma County.

Wines: Chard., Gewürz., Sauv.Bl., Cab.Sauv.
The hillside vineyards are well placed. Chardonnay and other white wines are variable but can be good.

Bandiera Winery
Cloverdale, *Sonoma*. Founded as The California Wine Company in 1937; refounded as Bandiera in 1975. Owner: The California Wine Corporation. President: John B. Merritt Jr. 175,000 cases.

Under its new name, the old California Wine Company continues to produce a wide range of wines, mainly from leased vineyards in Napa and Sonoma. There are 5 labels: Bandiera for good-value generics; Arroyo-Sonoma for Sonoma wines; Sage Canyon for Napa wines; Potter Valley for Mendocino wines; and John B. Merritt for reserve wines.

Bargetto's Santa Cruz Winery
Soquel, *Santa Cruz*. Founded 1933. Owners: The Barghetto family. Visits. 35,000 cases. Wines: Chard., Gewürtz., P.N., Cab. Sauv., Zin.

Grapes from Santa Barbara County are used for varietal whites, of which the Chardonnay and Gewürztraminer have been well received. Late-harvest botrytis Riesling is a speciality.

Beaulieu Vineyard
Rutherford, *Napa*. Founded 1900.
Owners: Grand Metropolitan. Wine maker: Thomas Selfridge. 350,000 cases plus. 745 acres at Rutherford and in the Carneros region. Wines: Cab.Sauv., Chard., Sauv.Bl., Ch.Bl., P.N.

The foundation of a French family, the de Latours, which set the pace for the Napa Valley throughout the 1940s, '50s and '60s under a wine maker of genius, the Russian-born André Tchelistcheff, who retired in 1973. At Beaulieu he pioneered small-barrel ageing and malolactic fermentation for reds, cold fermentation for whites (the basis of most California practice today) and discovered the virtues of the Carneros region south of Napa for cool-climate varieties.

Tchelistcheff's masterpiece (or the one that has lasted best) is the Georges de Latour Private Reserve Cabernet. Bottles from the 1950s and '60s are excellent, and the tradition is continued by his successors. The grapes are grown on Rutherford land still owned by the founding family. Rutherford Cabernet is lighter, Beautour, a good-value Cabernet. Pinot Noir (a Tchelistcheff passion) has never quite reached this standard, but Chardonnays have been brilliant, the standard Cabernet and the Napa burgundy are very good, the Sauvignon Blanc vibrant and there was once a sparkling Pinot Noir rosé I still dream about.

Bellerose Vineyard
Healdsburg, *Sonoma*. Founded 1979.
Owner: Charles Richard. 6,000 cases. 52 acres in Dry Creek Valley. Wines: Cab.Sauv., Merlot, Sauv.Bl.

Quality copies of French wines using grapes from a horse-plowed vineyard.

Belvedere Wince Co
Sonoma. Founded 1980.
Wines: Cab.Sauv., Chard., P.N., Sauv.Bl., Zin.
Single-vineyard wines including Alexander Valley 'Robert Young' Cabernet, Napa 'York Mountain' Cabernet and 'Bacigalupi' Chardonnay from the Russian River. Palatable, enjoyable wines.

Beringer Vineyards
St. Helena, *Napa*. Founded 1876,
Owners: Nestlé. Wine maker: Ed Sbragia. Wine master Emeritus: Myron Nightingale Sr. 400,000 cases. 2,800 acres owned and leased in Carneros, Napa Valley and Knight's Valley, Sonoma. Most table wine varieties plus port, sherry, dessert malvasia and brandy. Wines: Chard., Cab., J.R., Ch.Bl., Fumé Bl., Gewürz., P.N.

One of the great old stone-built wineries of Napa, with coolie-cut tunnels into the hills as its original cellars. Under the Beringers it declined, was bought in 1969 by Nestlé, who fixed it on an upward course. Nightingale is particularly skilful with white wines; his Fumé Blanc, late-harvest Riesling and Chardonnay are setting the pace. Two admirable Chardonnays, the Proprietor Grown and barrel-fermented Private Reserve, are produced, both from Beringer's Napa Valley vineyards. Private Reserve and other Cabernets are impressive. Los Hermanos and Napa Ridge are second labels.

Boeger Winery
Placerville, *El Dorado*. Founded 1973.
Wine maker: Greg Boeger. Visits. 10,000 cases plus. 35 acres owned, 20 leased. Wines: Cab.Sauv., Zin., Ch.Bl., Sauv.Bl. Merlot.

Bogle Vineyards Winery
Clarksburg, *Yolo*. Founded 1979.
President: Warren V. Bogle. Wine maker: Mark Shannon. Visits by appt. 650 acres in Clarksburg. Wines: Chard., Sem., Sauv.Bl., Ch.Bl., Cab.Sauv., Merlot, Zin.

Bonny Doon Vineyard
Santa Cruz Mountains, *Central Coast*. Founded 1981.
Owner: Randall Grahm. 8,000 cases plus. Vineyards: 25 acres of Syrah, Marsanne, Roussanne, Viognier.
Impressive small winery dedicated to making Rhône-style wines from Rhône varieties. Wines released so far include a Mourvedre called Old Telegram and a good Grenache/Mourvedre/Syrah blend called Le Cigare Volant.

Bouchaine
Napa, *Napa*. Founded 1924, refounded 1981.
Owner: David Pollak Jr. Wine maker: Jerry Luper. 20,000 cases. Wines: Chard., P.N., Sauv.Bl.

The first winery in the Carneros district, bought by Beringer in 1955 and the present partners in 1981. The appointment of Jerry Luper (from Chateau Montelena) as wine maker showed high ambitions. Bouchaine Vineyard is the principal label. The oaky Pinot Noir has been followed by equally good Chardonnay and Sauvignon Blanc.

The Brander Vineyard
Santa Ynez, *Santa Barbara*. Founded 1981.
Owner: Fredric Brander. 8,000 cases. Visits. 40 acres.
Fred Brander makes outstanding Sauvignon Blanc, as well as Chardonnay, a Cabernet rosé and a Cabernet Franc/Merlot blend.

David Bruce Winery
Los Gatos, *Santa Cruz Mountains*. Founded 1964.
Principal: David Bruce. Wine maker: Keith Hohlfeldt. 32,000 cases. 25 acres in the Santa Cruz Mountains. Chard., P.N., Cab.Sauv., Zin.

The owner believes in wine on a heroic scale from very ripe grapes. The results can impress or oppress, according to taste.

The Buena Vista Winery at Sonoma was the scene of Agoston Haraszthy's epoch-making experiments with European grape varieties.

Buehler Vineyards
St. Helena, *Napa*. Founded 1978.
Owner: John Buehler. Wine maker: Heidi Peterson Barrett.
20,000 cases. 62 acres. Wines: Cab.Sauv., Zin., Musc.Bl., P.Bl.

Buena Vista Winery and Vineyards
Sonoma, *Sonoma*. Founded 1857, refounded 1943.
Owner: A. Racke. Wine maker: Jill Davis. Visits. 110,000
cases. 1,100 acres in Carneros and Napa.
Historically important as the winery of Agoston Haraszthy, 'the father of California wine'. Restarted in 1943 by Frank Bartholomew, who was ahead of his time but never made great wine here. Things have greatly improved since German owners took over in 1979 and Jill Davis became wine maker in 1981. Good Chardonnay, Sauvignon, Cabernet, Pinot Noir and Riesling are now made, under two labels – Estate and Private Reserve. Prices remain reasonable.

Burgess Cellars
St. Helena, *Napa*. Founded 1972.
Owner: Tom Burgess. Wine maker: Bill Sorenson. Visits by
appt. 30,000 cases. 70 acres owned and 25 leased in Napa
County. Wines: Zin., Cab.Sauv., Chard.
This was the original little Souverain winery where Lee Stewart made great Cabernet in the 1960s. It was bought and rebuilt in the 1970s and is best known for Cabernet Sauvignon, partially barrel-fermented Chardonnay and heady Zinfandel. Bell Canyon Cellars is a second label.

David Bynum Winery
Healdsburg, *Sonoma*. Founded 1965.
President: David Bynum. Wine maker: Gary Farrell. Visits.
28,000 cases. Wines: Chard., Cab.Sauv., P.N., Sauv.Bl., Zin.
Producer of good Artist Series wines, especially Chardonnay and Pinot Noir, and a wide range of other varietals.

Caché Cellars
Davis, *Solano*. Founded 1978.
Wine maker: Charles Lowe. Visits by appt. 4,000 cases.
Part-time wine maker Charles Lowe, (he is a full-time pilot) makes varietals from bought-in Napa grapes.

Cadenasso Winery
Suisun City, *Solano*. Founded 1906.
Wine maker: Frank Cadenasso. Visits. 145 acres. Wines:
Chard., Chenin Bl., Ries., Zin., Cab.Sauv. and P.N.

Cain Cellars
St. Helena, *Napa*. Founded 1981.
Owners: Jerry and Joyce Cain. Visits by appt. 30,000 cases.
110 acres on Spring Mountain. Wines: Cab.Sauv., Merlot,
Chard., Sauv.Bl.
'Cain Five' is an ambitious Bordeaux-style blend using Spring Mountain grapes.

Cakebread Cellars
Oakville, *Napa*. Founded 1973.
Owner: Jack Cakebread. Wine maker: Bruce Cakebread. Visits
by appt. 40,000 cases. Vineyards: 75 acres of Cab.Sauv.,
Cab.Fr. and Sauv.Bl.
Specialists in dry Sauvignon Blanc from their own vines. Two Chardonnays are produced, both from bought-in Napa grapes, as well as rich pungent reds including a Cabernet Sauvignon from 20 acres beside the winery.

Calera Wine Company
Hollister, *San Benito*. Founded 1975.
Owners: Josh and Jeanne Jensen. Wine maker: Steve Doerner.
Visits by appt. 10,000 cases. 24 acres of lime-rich hill in San
Benito. Wines: P.N., Chard.
Specialists in estate-bottled Pinot Noirs and Chardonnays from San Benito, San Luis Obispo and Butte counties.

CHAPPELLET

Donn Chappellet was the second man to build a new winery for the new age of California wine. He started in 1968, two years after Robert Mondavi. The scope of Mondavi's success in combining quality with quantity has no parallel. But the Chappellet property was the prototype for many newcomers. (Chappellet himself was in industrial catering before he heard the call.)

The aim is a limited range of top-class wines made as far as possible from estate-grown grapes. The capacity of the winery matches the size of the vineyard – though both have room for gradual expansion up to perhaps another 10,000 cases a year.

An artist friend designed the strange, church-like, triangular-pyramid winery to sit high on Pritchard Hill east of St. Helena, above the Napa Valley but at the foot of its own steep ramp of vines out of the reach of valley frosts. The roof is of steel protected by its own warm-brown rust, almost the same colour as the iron-rich soil around. One corner of the triangle is full of large and small stainless steel tanks, all with temperature-control jackets, for fermenting, storing and blending. The second

Callaway Vineyard and Winery
Temecula, *Riverside*. Founded 1974.
Owners: Hiram Walker Allied Vintners. Chairman: Ely Callaway. Wine maker: Dwayne Helmuth. Visits. 150,000 cases plus. Vineyards: 720 acres.
The most considerable pioneer of varietal table wine in Southern California. Entirely whites, including Callalees Chardonnay, innocent of oak, and luscious 'botrytized' 'Sweet Nancy' Chenin Blanc.

Caparone
Paso Robles, *San Luis Obispo*. Founded 1980.
Wine maker: Dave Caparone. Visits. 7 acres. 3,000 cases.
Nebbiolo and Brunello have been planted in an interesting attempt to fit these grapes into the California roster.

J. Carey Cellars
Solvang, *Santa Barbara*. Founded 1977.
Owners: Firestone Vineyards. 7,000 cases. Vineyards: 25 acres in the Santa Ynez Valley.
Now owned by Firestone, this winery continues to produce Cabernet, Chardonnay, Sauvignon and Merlot.

Carmenet
Sonoma. Founded 1982. Owners: as Chalone (q.v.).
Wines: Chard., Sauv.Blanc, Cabernet/Merlot, French Colombard.
The Chalone team are aiming for Bordeaux here with Edna Valley Sauvignon Blanc and and a Cabernet/Merlot blend from high above Sonoma town. This Chardonnay comes from Carneros.

Carneros Creek Winery
Napa, *Napa*. Founded 1972.
President: Balfour C. Gibson. Wine maker: Francis Mahoney. Visits by appt. 20,000 cases. 21 acres in Napa Valley, Carneros and Sonoma. Wines: P.N., Chard., Cab.Sauv., Sauv.Bl.
Winery at the south end of the Napa Valley that caused a sensation with its first Pinot Noir. The '77 was the best I had tasted in California, with the combined velvet and carpentry of very good burgundy. The Chardonnay has the same conviction. The named-vineyard Cabernets are equally fine. Merlot is good value.

corner is stacked with French oak barrels. The third is for bottled wine – while the centre space is free for whatever work is in progress.

Chappellet's wines have an austere, built-to-last style quite different from the Napa norm. His Chenin Blanc is the best in California: dry, firm, long-flavoured and truly appetizing. His Chardonnay, fermented partly in barrels, partly in steel, is impressively reined-in. He makes his Cabernet with Château Latour in mind; serious and tannic, balanced for long maturing.

Cassayre-Forni Cellars
Rutherford, *Napa*. Founded 1976.
Owner: Paul Cassayre. Wine maker: Mike Forni. Visits by appt. 10,000 cases. Wines: Zin., Cab.Sauv., Ch.Bl., Chard.
Two third-generation Napa families making Napa Valley appellation wines with the exception of a Zinfandel from Dry Creek Valley, Sonoma.

Caymus Vineyards
Rutherford, *Napa*. Founded 1971.
President and wine maker: Charles F. Wagner. Visits by appt. 30,000 cases. 73 acres. Wines: Cab.Sauv., P.N., Zin., Sauv.Bl., Chard.
Wagner's finest wine is his juicy, even flowery Cabernet, to many tastes the most harmonious and elegant in the Napa Valley. His white wine from Pinot Noir, the palest 'partridge eye', really tastes of the grape. The excellent-value second label in Liberty School.

Chalk Hill (formerly Donna Maria Vineyards)
Healdsburg, *Sonoma*. Founded 1974.
Owner: Frederick P. Furth. Wine maker: Tom Cottrell.

65,000 cases. 310 acres in Chalk Hill, near Windsor, Sonoma County. Visits by appt. Wines: Chard., P.N., Cab.Sauv., Sauv.Bl., Merlot.
The first vintages (80 to 82) went under the name of Donna Maria with Chalk Hill as the second label for bought-in grapes. All wines are now sold under the Chalk Hill label. Chardonnay, Sauvignon Blanc and Cabernet Sauvignon are produced plus a recently introduced Merlot and and a Late Harvest Sauvignon Blanc. All wines now come from the winery's own vines.

Chalone Vineyard
Soledad, *Monterey*. Chairman: Richard Graff. Wine makers: Michael Michaud and Richard Graff. 15,000 cases 174 acres. Wines: Chard., P.Bl., Ch.Bl., P.N.
For 50 years a lonely outpost of viticulture on a droughty limestone hilltop near the Pinnacles National Monument where all water had to be brought up by truck. Then the Graffs stunned California with Pinot Noir successfully modelled on great Côte d'Or burgundies and Chardonnay maturing to the smoky fragrance of the great white wines of the northern Rhône. Pinot Blanc is also doing well on this elevated site. Now also owns Acacia and Carmenet (q.v.). In 1989 Chalone traded shares with Domaines Baron de (Lafite) Rothschild.

Chamisal Vineyard
San Luis Obispo, *San Luis Obispo*. Founded 1972.
Owner: Norman Gloss. Wine maker: Scott Boyd. Visits by appt. 3,000 cases. 57 acres. Wines: Chard., Cab.Sauv.

Chappellet
St. Helena, *Napa*. Founded 1968.
President: Donn Chappellet. Wine maker: Cathy Corison. No visits. 30,000 cases. 110 acres (with more leased) in Napa Valley. Wines: Cab.Sauv., Chard., J.R., Ch.Bl.

Chateau Chevre Winery
Yountville, *Napa*. Founded 1979.
Wine maker: Gerald Hazen. Visits by appt. 4,000 cases. Wines: Merlot, Sauv.Bl.

Chateau de Leu Winery
Suisun, *Solano*. Founded 1981.
Owner/wine maker: Ben Volkhardt. Visits. 5,000 cases. 80 acres.

Chateau Montelana Winery
Calistoga, *Napa*. Founded 1881, refounded 1969.
President: Jim Barrett. Wine maker: James P. 'Bo' Barrett. Visits. 28,000 cases. 100 acres (mainly Cab.Sauv.). Wines: Chard., Cab.Sauv., J.R., Zin.
Old stone winery north of Calistoga, at the foot of Mt. St. Helena, now has a 20-year record of some of the best California Chardonnays and Cabernets from the state vineyard and grapes bought in from Napa. The Napa wines tend to be richer – and so do their drinkers. Two distinguished wine makers have set the style: Mike Grgich up to 1974, Jerry Luper up to 1981 – the first known for elegant discretion, the second for heaps of flavour.

Chateau Souverain (formerly Souverain Cellars)
Geyserville, *Sonoma*. Founded 1973.
Owners: Nestlé Inc. Wine maker: Thomas Peterson. Visits. 400,000 cases. Wines: Sauv.Bl., Cab.Sauv., Chard. and Zin.
Beringer (Nestlé) took over this luxurious Alexander Valley winery in 1986.

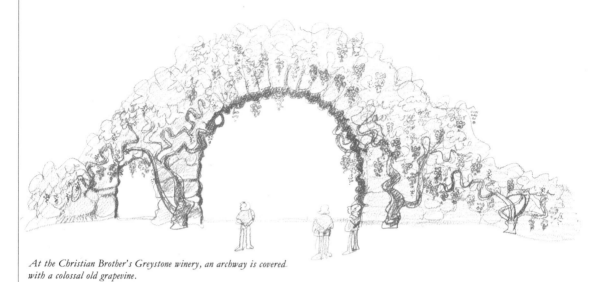

*At the Christian Brother's Greystone winery, an archway is covered
with a colossal old grapevine.*

Chateau St. Jean
Kenwood, *Sonoma*. Founded 1973.
Owner: Suntory International. President: Gregory J. de
Lucca. Winemaster: Richard Arrowood. Winemaster
(sparkling wines): Edgar 'Pete' Downs. 190,000 cases of table
wine and 50,000 cases of sparkling wine. 121 acres. Wines:
Chard., J.R., Gewürz., P.Bl., Fumé Bl., Sem., Cab.Sauv., P.N.
and sparkling wines.

A showplace winery specializing in white wines of the sort
of subtropical ripeness more often associated with the
Napa Valley. Robert Young Vineyard Chardonnay is the
biggest and lushest of all. I often prefer the more easily
drinkable regular bottling. Arrowood also makes formidable sweet, late-harvest Rieslings and Gewürztraminers
up to Trockenbeerenauslese quality and price. Chateau St
Jean's sparkling wine facility at Graton, which released its
first wine in 1983, now makes some of California's best
méthode champenoise sparklers: a dry Brut, a rich Grande
Cuvée Brut Réserve, and a Chardonnay-based Brut Blanc
de Blancs.

Christian Brothers Winery
Mount La Salle, *Napa*. Founded 1888.
Owner: Heublein, Inc., 1.25 m. cases wines, 1.35 m. cases
brandies. 1,200 acres in Napa for table and sparkling. 1,200
acres in San Joaquin for dessert and brandies.

The Christian Brothers (a Catholic teaching order) sold
the winery in 1989. Apart from the hilltop showpiece, the
stone-built Mount La Salle winery, there is the huge old
Greystone winery, 2 others in the Napa Valley, and 2
more in the San Joaquin Valley. The massive production
has been known for consistency and value for money.
Reserve bottlings and vintage dates had recently been
introduced and Heublein appear to be continuing on this
course. My favourites are Napa Fumé Blanc (ripe, dry,
slightly oaked, mature at 1 year); Chardonnay; Cabernet
(the non-vintage is light by Napa standards, but not
simple; the vintage is bigger with the structure to last);
Gamay Noir (sweetly fruity to smell; enjoyable gummy
finish). Others include (to me rather dull) red Pinot St.
George, sweet Pineau de la Loire (Chenin Blanc) and very
sweet Muscat Chateau La Salle, and a Charmat-process
sparkler. Tinta Madeira port and XO brandy are outstanding of their kind.

Cilurzo & Piconi
Temecula, *Riverside*. Founded 1978.
Wine maker: Vicenzo Cilurzo. 10,000 cases. 40 acres. Wines:
Chard., Sauv.Bl., Ch.Bl., Zin., P.N., Cab.Sauv.

Clos du Bois
Healdsburg, *Sonoma*. Founded 1974.
Owner: Hiram-Walker Allied Vintners. President: Terrence
Clancy. Wine maker: Margaret Davenport. Visits. 200,000
cases. 690 acres in Dry Creek and Alexander Valley. Wines:
Chard., Sauv.Bl., Gewürz., Cab.Sauv., P.N., Merlot.

Clos du Bois wines were well established before there was
a winery. The best are boldly winey Gewürztraminer and
an easily drinkable claret-style Cabernet. The Chardonnay
is lively, long and dry, with a hint of green (in both colour
and flavour) that seems to spell Alexander Valley.
Woodleaf (Dry Creek) and Briarcrest (Alexander Valley)
are appellation Cabernets. Winemaker's Reserve wines
are made 'in years when the opportunity to make a limited
amount of unique wine exists'. Named-vineyard wines
(e.g. Calcaire Chardonnay) are very fine.

Clos du Val Wine Co.
Yountville, *Napa*. Founded 1972.
Owner: John Goelet. Wine makers: Bernard Portet and Krimo
Souilah. 265 acres in Yountville, Carneros and Stag's Leap.
60,000 cases. Wines: Cab.Sauv., P.N., Merlot, Zin., Chard., Sem.

Portet was brought up at Château Lafite, where his father
was manager. As in Bordeaux, he blends Merlot with
Cabernet. His wines are reckoned soft and supple by Napa
standards but they are still deep-coloured, juicy, and long
on the palate. They can age beautifully. His Zinfandel is as
strapping as they come. Like all good examples of this
grape, they can be drunk young, sweet and heady or kept
virtually for ever. Taltarni in Victoria, Australia, has the
same owners.

Clos Pegase
Napa. Founded 1987.
Owners: Jan and Mitsuko Schrem.

A major architectural competition was won by the
American architect Michael Graves. The resulting winery
is Napa's most striking post-modernist building to date. It
produces steadily improving Chardonnay and Cabernet.

Concancon Vineyard
Livermore, *Alameda*. Founded 1883.
Owners: Dr Sergio Traverso and Deinhard. Wine maker: Dr Sergio Traverso. Visits. 100,000 cases. 180 acres in Livermore Valley. A wide range of table wines.

Founded to make altar wine in the same year as the other great Livermore Valley winery, Wente Bros., and still estate-bottling some Livermore wine, although also buying grapes in Clarksburg (Yolo County, the Sacramento River delta) and Amador, for 'selected vineyard' bottlings. Specialities include California's first Petite Sirah (from Livermore: a big soft wine) and perhaps its only Rkatsiteli, a crisp white Russian. The Sauvignon Blanc is now dry in style. A vigorous company with one of the steadiest reputations in California.

Congress Springs Vineyards
Saratoga, *Santa Clara*. Founded 1892, refounded 1976.
Owner: Vic Erickson. Wine maker: Daniel Gehrts. Visits. 6,000 cases. 10 acres owned and 50 acres leased in Santa Cruz Mountains. Various vintage varietal table wines.

Well-made, fruity Chardonnay and dry Semillon lead the whites and Cabernet Franc the reds, all from Santa Cruz grapes.

Conn Creek
St. Helena, *Napa*. Founded 1979.
Owners: Ch Ste Michelle (of Washington). Wine maker: Daryl Eklund. Visits by appt. 21,000 cases. 146 acres east of Yountville and north of St. Helena. Wines: Cab.Sauv., Chard., Zin.

A reputation built mainly on stylish Cabernet, distinctly oak-tinged with both plummy and more ascetically herbaceous notes. What I have tasted of the Chardonnay was rather blunt and the Zinfandel meaty with a certain astringency.

R. & J. Cook
Clarksburg, *Yolo*. Founded 1978.
Owners: Roger and Joanne Cook. 50,000 cases. Big-scale grape farmer in the Sacramento River delta.

Their first 'Steamboat' Cabernet was astonishingly fruity. Now specializing in Chenin Blanc.

Corbett Canyon Vineyards
Edna Valley, *San Luis Obispo*. Founded 1978.
Owners: The Wine Group. Wine maker: John Clark. Visits. Over 100,000 cases. Wines: Chard., Sauv.Bl., Cab.Sauv., Zin., P.N.

Purchased in 1988 from Glenmore Distillers by The White Group, who then added a 200 acre vineyard in Santa Barbara County. Over recent years, production has built up decent, well-made varietals. The second label, 'Shadow Creek', is used for *méthode champenoise* wines. Good 'Reserve' wines in small lots.

Cosentino Wine Co.
Yountville, *Napa*. Founded 1980..
Owner: Mitchell Cosentino. Visits Mon-Fri. 12,000 cases, rising to 20,000. Wines: Cab.Sauv., Cab.Fr., Merlot, Chard., P.N., a lightly fortified Muscat-based wine and a sparkling wine.

Cresta Blanca
Formerly an important Livermore, Alameda, winery. Now part of Guild Wineries, using coop members' grapes for 100,000 cases of a wide range of varietal and table wines solely for the Asian Export market.

Cronin Vineyards
Woodside, *San Mateo*. Founded 1980.
Owner/wine maker: Duane Cronin. Visits by appt. 1,200 cases.

John Culbertson Winery
Fallbrook, *San Diego*. Founded 1981.Owners: John and Martha Culbertson. 40,000 cases. Wines: *Méthode champenoise*.

Sparkling specialist using grapes from the unlikely source of Southern California to make a range of wines.

Cuvaison Vineyard
Calistoga, *Napa*. Founded 1970.
Chairman: Alexander Schmidheiny. Wine maker: John Thacher. Visits. 65,000 cases. 400 acres in Napa Valley and Carneros. Wines: Chard, Cab.Sauv., Merlot, Zin.

Swiss owned, with its style set by Swiss-born wine maker Philip Togni (who left in 1982). Togni believed in powerful and austere, even hard wines that need considerable bottle-age, but deserve it. More recently, under new direction, the wines have been softer. The Chardonnay from Carneros vines is their best. Calistoga Cellars is the name on the second label.

John Daniel Society
Napa. Founded 1983.
Owners: Christian Moueix, Marcia Smith, Robin Lail. Wines: Dominus, Daniel Estate Cab.Sauv.

Franco-Napa partnership. Christian Moueix brings the perfectionism and prestige of Petrus; the results are massive, austere and immensely impressive.

Deer Park Winery
Deer Park, *Napa*. Founded 1979.
Wine maker: David Clark. 6,000 cases. 5-acre vineyard east of St. Helena. Wines: Zin., Petite Sirah, Chard., Sauv.Bl.

Dehlinger Winery
Sebastopol, *Sonoma*. Founded 1976.
Owner and wine maker: Tom Dehlinger. 9,000 cases. 31 acres in Sonoma County. Wines: Chard., P.N., Cab.Sauv., Zin.

Highly regarded little winery, offering wines that taste distinctly of the grape, not overstrong or overpriced.

DeLoach Vineyards
Santa Rosa, *Sonoma*. Founded 1975 (winery built 1979).
Owner and wine maker: Cecil O. DeLoach. Visits. 70,000 cases. 74 acres owned, 75 acres leased in Russian River Valley in Sonoma County. Wines: Zin. (red and white), P.N., Fumé Bl., Chard., Gewürz., Sauv.Bl., Cab.Sauv.

The pioneer '79 Pinot Noir was deep in colour and flavour, excellent in youth and apparently fit to age. Chardonnay is impressive. The Zinfandels (including the White Zin.) and the Sauvignon are good too.

DeMoor Winery
Oakville, *Napa*. Owners: Firmin and Jacques Deschepper. Visits. 14,000 cases. 3 acres. Wines: Chard. Sauv.Bl., Cab.Sauv., Zin.

Formerly Napa Cellars. Big strong reds and whites with a soft dry Gewürztraminer a favourite.

Deutz
Arroyo Grande, *San Luis Obispo*. Founded 1983.
Owners: Deutz of Champagne. Increasing to 60,000 cases. Wines: *Méthode champenoise* sparkling wines.

A Franco-American venture which has planted an ambitious 150 acres with Champagne grapes plus Pinot Blanc and Chenin Blanc. Until the vineyards bear fully they are buying fruit in the locality. First release in 1986: a non-vintage blend. Rich, full-flavoured wines.

Devlin Wine Cellars
Soquel, *Santa Cruz*. Founded 1978.
Owner/wine maker: Charles Devlin. 10,000 cases.
Wines: Cab.Sauv., Chard., Gewürz., Sauv.Bl., Mus., W.R., Zin., P.N.

Diamond Creek Vineyards
Calistoga, *Napa*. Founded 1972.
Owner: Al Brounstein. 3,000 cases. 20 acres southwest of Calistoga, Napa. Wines: Cab.Sauv. only.
Cabernet from 3 small vineyards, Volcanic Hill, Red Rock Terrace and Gravelly Meadow, reflects 3 different soils and situations – a subject little enough studied in California. They are all big, tough wines designed for long ageing. Cabernet Franc, Malbec and Merlot are added to the predominant Cabernet Sauvignon.

Domaine Carneros
Carneros, *Napa*. Founded 1986.
Owners: Taittinger, Kobrand Corp. and Ordway. 138 acres.
Initial volume is 4,000 cases, with plans to grow to 40,000 by 1993.
First wines were due in 1990 from Taittinger's highly-visible Carneros cellar.

Domaine Chandon
Yountville, *Napa*. Founded 1973; winery opened 1977.
Owners: Moët-Hennessy (Paris). Wine maker: Dawnine Sample Dyer. Consultant: Edmond Maudière. Visits. 500,000 cases. 800 acres in Napa Valley. Wines: Chandon Napa Valley Brut, Chandon Blanc de Noirs, Reserve Cuvée, Still White, Pinot Noir Blanc and Panache, a sweet apéritif. The second label for non-Napa wines is Shadow Creek.
The spearhead of France's invasion of California, a characteristically stylish and successful outpost of Champagne (but you must not use the word). A wine factory and an entertainment at the same time, with a first-class fashionable restaurant. Both sparkling wines are excellent, the Blanc de Noirs considerably heftier, and marvellous value for money. Out of context, in England, the sheer fruitiness of the Napa grapes make the wines taste rather sweet, technically Brut though they may be. The Reserve cuvée is a showstopper.

Domaine Laurier
Forestville, *Sonoma*. Founded 1978.
Owners: see Lyeth. Wine maker: Merry Edwards. Visits by appt. 17,000 cases. 30 acres in Russian River Valley, Sonoma.
Wines: Chard., Sauv.Bl., P.N., Cab.Sauv.
Beautifully structured wines from the Green Valley AVA. New owners have hired star wine maker Edwards.

Domaine Michel
Dry Creek Valley, *Sonoma*.
Owner: J-J. Michel. Wine maker: Phillip Baxter. 60 acres in Dry Creek Valley.

Domaine Mumm
Calistoga, *Napa*.
Owners: Seagram. Wine maker: Guy Devaux. Wines: *Méthode champenoise*.
One of several incursions by Champagne companies into California. First release was 1986: crisp, fine sparkling wines.

Domaine St George
Healdsburg, *Sonoma*. Founded in 1934 as Cambiaso.
Owners: Four Seas Investment (Thailand). Wine maker: Robert Tredson. 300,000 cases.
Cambiaso was long associated with good cheap jug wines. Under a new name and new owners, it has much increased its output, producing a range of acceptable red and white wines from bought-in grapes.

Dry Creek Vineyard
Healdsburg, *Sonoma*. Founded 1972.
President: David Stare. Wine maker: Larry Levin. 50,000 cases. 105 acres in Dry Creek, Sonoma. Wines: Ch.Bl., Fumé Bl., Chard., Zin., Cab.Sauv., Gewürz., Merlot, P. Syrah, Sauv.Bl.
Maker of one of California's best dry Sauvignon Blancs (Fumé Blanc) with other whites in the same old-fashioned balanced, vital but not-too-emphatic dry style. Reserve Chardonnays are barrel-fermented and aged *sur lie*. The Cabernet Sauvignon was judged to be California's best in 1985. Cabernet Franc is their next target.

Duckhorn Vineyards
St. Helena, *Napa*. Founded 1976.
10,000 cases. 27 acres at St. Helena, newly planted with Sauv.Bl. and Sem.
Wines: Napa Merlot, Cab.Sauv., Sauv.Bl.
One of the wineries provoking great interest in Merlot. Also Sauvignon Blanc.

Dunn Vineyards
Howell Mountain, *Napa*. Owner: Randall Dunn.
Ex-Caymus wine maker now makes small lots of dark, stern Cabernet at his own winery.

Durney Vineyard
Carmel, *Monterey*. Vineyards founded 1968, winery 1977.
Owners: W.W. and D.K. Durney. Wine maker: David Sharp.
Wine consultant: Daniel Lee. Visits by appt. 15,000 cases. 142 acres in hills above Carmel Valley. Wines: Ch.Bl., J.R., Cab.Sauv.
Carmel's first vineyard, on steep slopes not far from the ocean. The Cabernet is ripe, deep and impressive, the Chenin Blanc equally well made.

Duxoup Wine Works
Healdsburg, *Sonoma*. Founded 1981.
Owners: Deborah and Andrew Cutter. 2,000 cases. Wines: Syrah, Napa Gamay, Zin.
Marxist inspiration but serious red wines with a Syrah that has pleased local tasters. Grapes come from Dry Creek vineyards.

East Side Winery
(formerly Oakridge Vineyards)
Lodi, *San Joaquin*. Founded 1934.
Wine maker: Lee Eichele. Visits. A growers' cooperative with 8m. gallons' storage, bottling 450,000 cases under Oakridge Vineyards, Handel and Mettler and Royal Host labels.
Conti Royale is the label for some worthy varietals, dessert wines and brandies.

Edmeades Inc
Philo, *Mendocino*. Founded 1968.
President: Deron Edmeades. Wine maker: Tex Sawyer. Visits. 24,000 cases. 35 acres in Anderson Valley, Mendocino. Wines: Chard., Cab.Sauv., Gewürz., Zin., W.R. and 'Rain Wine'.
Originally a grape grower for Parducci, since 1974 a

winery proud of being (at only 25 miles from the Pacific) in California's rainiest wine region. Hence the name of their generic white. In 1977 they made California's first ice wine, a sweet Colombard from frozen grapes. All this damp and cold, they say, produces intense 'varietal character'.

Edna Valley Vineyard
San Luis Obispo. *San Luis Obispo*. Founded 1980.
Owners: Chalone Vineyard and Paragon Vineyards. Wine maker: Stephen Dooley. 45,000 cases. Vineyards in Edna Valley, San Luis Obispo County, planted with Chard., P.N.
Powerful barrel-aged Chardonnay from vineyards adjoining the winery. Also Pinot Noir and Pinot Noir based 'Vin Gris'.

Evensen Vineyards & Winery
Oakville, *Napa*. Founded 1979.
Wine maker: Richard Evensen. 1,300 cases. 7 acres between Rutherford and Oakville. Wine: Gewürz.
Specialist with an admirable Gewürztraminer.

Far Niente Winery
Oakville, *Napa County*. Founded 1979.
Wine maker: Dirk Hampson. 36,000 cases. 100 acres. Wines: Chard., Cab.Sauv.
A famous pre-Prohibition name reborn in its original stone building with its old vineyard replanted and now bearing. The Chardonnays are very full-flavoured.

Fenestra Winery
Livermore, *Alameda*. Founded 1976.
Owners: Lanny and Fran Replogle. Wine maker: Lanny Replogle. 3,000 cases. Wines: Chard., Sauv.Bl., Cab.Sauv., Zin.

Ferrari-Carano
Healdsburg, *Sonoma*. Founded 1981.
Owners: Donald and Rhonda Carano. Wine maker: George Bursick. Visits. 50,000 cases. Vineyards: 1,000 acres in Alexander Valley, Dry Creek, Knights Valley and Carneros.
Wines: Cab.Sauv., Merlot, Chard. and Fumé Bl.
New and expanding winery. The first whites were released in 1985, reds in 1986.

Gloria Ferrer
Carneros, *Sonoma*. Founded 1984.
Owners: Frexinet S.A. Wine maker: Eileen Crane. 65,000 cases. Visits. Wines: *Méthode champenoise* sparkling Brut (P.N. and Chard. blend).
Catalonia rather than Champagne is the parent of this sparkling wine house, named after the wife of the president of Freixenet. A new winery and 360 acres of Pinot Noir and Chardonnay vineyard spell serious intent. First wines were bought-in, but from the 1986 vintage the Freixenet winery came on stream, producing 65,000 cases a year. Early results promising.

Fenton Acres Winery
see J. Rochioli.

Fetzer Vineyards
Redwood Valley, *Mendocino*. Founded 1968.
President: John Fetzer. Wine maker: Paul Dolan. Visits by appt. 1m. plus cases. 780 acres in Redwood Valley, planted mainly in Cab.Sauv., Sauv.Bl., Ries., Zin. and Chard.
Fast-expanding family-run winery with interesting, reliable and very good value wines, including some outstanding Petite Sirah, Zinfandels of distinct styles from named Mendocino and Lake County vineyards, equally various

ANDRE TCHELISTCHEFF

The California wine world has silently and unanimously bestowed the title of its 'dean' on André Tchelistcheff. His career has spanned the whole history of the industry since Prohibition, for 36 years (1937–73) as wine maker at Beaulieu vineyard and since, from his home in St. Helena, as consultant to many of the best wineries all over California and beyond. Tchelistcheff was born in Russia and trained in Burgundy. He was chosen to make their wine by the French de Latour family, founders of Beaulieu and for many years the royal family of the Napa Valley. In the early 1940s he introduced the idea of ageing red wine in small oak barrels. His reserve Cabernet from the best Rutherford vineyards, named as a memorial to Georges de Latour, has served as a model for California wine makers ever since. Cold fermentation of white wine malolactic fermentation . . . many of the house rules of California were written by Tchelistcheff and his advice continues to point new directions today.

Among the many wine makers who owe at least part of their training to him are such masters as Joe Heitz, Mike Grgich of Grgich Hills, Warren Winiarski of Stag's Leap, Richard Peterson of Monterey Vineyards and Theo Rosenbrand of Sterling.

Rieslings, estate Cabernet Sauvignon and most of the usual varieties. The Barrel Select range is fine value. Attractive jug wines include Fetzer Premium and Bel Arbors.

Ficklin Vineyards
Madera, *Madera*. Founded 1946.
President: Jean Ficklin. Wine maker: Peter Ficklin. Visits by appt. 10,000 cases. Family vineyards grow Portuguese port varieties.
California's most respected specialists in port-style wine, neither vintage nor tawny in character but ages indefinitely like vintage. It needs careful, often early, decanting. Recently Ficklin has revived the issue of vintage-dated wines.

Field Stone Winery
Healdsburg, *Sonoma*. Founded 1976.
Owner: the John Staton family. Wine maker: James Thomson. Visits. 12,000 cases. Vineyards in Alexander Valley, Sonoma. Wines: Gewürz, Pet.Sir., Cab.Sauv.
A gem of a winery, burrowed in the ground among the vineyards, designed by the late Wallace Johnson, who made picking machines. The grapes for white and rosé are crushed in the vineyard. They include a ravishingly pretty, pale pink 'Spring Cabernet', perhaps California's best picnic wine. Also good Petit Sirah.

Filsinger Vineyards & Winery
Temecula, *Riverside*. Founded 1980.
Wine maker: Greg Hahn. Visits. 5,000 cases. 25 acres.
Recently has added sparkling wines to a range of mainstream varietals.

Firestone Vineyard
Los Olivos, *Santa Barbara*. Founded 1974.
Wine maker: Alison Green. Visits. 75,000 cases. 275 acres in Santa Ynez Valley planted in Cab.Sauv., J.R., Chard., P.N., Merlot, Gewürz., Sauv.Bl.
Firestone (of the tyres) in partnership with Suntory, the Japanese distillers, have pioneered the relatively cool Santa Ynez Valley with a handsome Napa-style wooden

winery. The conditions suit Riesling and Gewürztraminer particularly well; also Chardonnay and Pinot Noir. Merlot is preferred to Cabernet by many (although not by me). Ambassador's Vineyard (sweet) Riesling is outstanding and all wines are modestly priced for the quality, which over the range is as high as any to be found in California.

Fisher Vineyards
Santa Rosa, *Sonoma*. Founded 1979.
Wine maker: Fred Fisher. 10,000 cases. 70 acres in Napa Valley and at the winery. Chard., Cab. Sauv.
Whitney's Vineyard is the 'home' Chardonnay.

Flora Springs Wine Co.
St. Helena, *Napa*. Founded 1978.
Owners: The Komes and Garvey families. Wine maker: Ken

Deis. Visits by appt. 15,000 cases. 400 acres in Napa Valley. Wines: Chard., Cab.Sauv., Sauv.Bl.
A new winery in an old stone barn used by Louis Martini to store wine during Prohibition. First-release Chardonnay ('79) won a gold medal at the Los Angeles County Fair. Sauvignon Blanc is equally successful, Cabernet less certain. Trilogy is a new Bordeaux-style blend red.

Folie a Deux
St. Helena, *Napa*. Founded 1981. Owners: Larry and Evie Dismang. Visits. 8,000 cases. 27 acres. Wines: Chard., Ch.Bl., Cab.Sauv.
Small winery with 15 acres. Impeccable Chardonnay, very good Chenin Blanc. Fantasy, a *champenoise* sparkler was launched in 87.

Newton Vineyard has broken entirely new ground, bulldozing forest high on Spring Mountain above the Napa Valley. Mountain vineyards escape destructive late frosts, benefit from alternating hot days and cool nights in the ripening season. Their shallow rocky soil 'stresses' the vine, intensifying the flavour of the grapes

Labels
Two pieces of information included on the label of many good California wines give a helpful indication of what to expect in the bottle.

Alcohol content is measured in degrees or percentage by volume (the two are the same). Traditional wines vary between about 11.5° and 14° enough to make a substantial difference to taste and effect. New-style 'soft' wines go down to 7.5°. But the law allows the labeller a remarkable latitude of 1.5° from the truth. As a practical tip, if you find a he-man Napa Chardonnay, for example, too powerful for you at 13.5°, there is no law against adding a drop of water. Perrier refreshes clumsy wines beautifully.

Residual sugar is most commonly reported on labels of Riesling and Gewürztraminer. It is the unfermented sugar left (or kept) in the wine at bottling. Below 0.5% by weight sugar is undetectable: the wine is fully dry. Above about 1.5% it would be described as 'medium sweet', above 3% as 'sweet' and above 6% as 'very sweet'. A 'selected bunch late harvest' might have 14% and a 'selected berry late harvest' as much as 28%. Measurement in grams per 100 millilitres is the same as measurement in percentages.

California's range
One of the most impressive (and confusing) things about visiting a California winery is the range of products. To a European accustomed to the specialization of old wine areas, it is bewildering to be asked to sample the equivalent of claret, burgundy (red or white). German wines and Italian wines too, with possibly sparkling and dessert wines as well – all in the same tasting. And yet it is hard to tell a wine maker that you are only interested in his Cabernet, or his Riesling – at least on that occasion. Tasting at wineries demands a prodigious effort of concentration.

L. Foppiano Wine Co.
Healdsburg, *Sonoma*. Founded in 1896.
Owner: Louis J. Foppiano. Wine maker: Bill Regan. Visits. 125,000 cases plus. 200 acres in Sonoma County. Many wines.
One of the oldest family-owned wineries, recently refurbished and raising its already respectable standards. Reserve wines are labelled Fox Mountain; Riverside Farm is name for second-rank wines.

Forman Winery
St. Helena, *Napa*. Founded 1980.
Owner and wine maker: Ric Forman. 2,000 cases. 6 acres on Howell Mountain.
The former Sterling wine maker uses grapes from his own hill vineyards, and others down at Rutherford, to make classic 'French-style' Chardonnay and Cabernet.

Fortino Winery
Gilroy, *Santa Clara*. Founded 1970.
Wine maker: Ernest Fortino. Visits. 75 acres. 30,000 cases .
Wines: wide range. Clear-cut, ripe-fruit wines in the Santa Clara Italian style.

Francisan Vineyards
Rutherford, *Napa*. Founded 1973.
Owners: Peter Eckes Co. and Agustin Huneeus. President: A. Huneeus. Wine maker: Gregory Upton. Visits. 100,000 cases. 250 acres at Oakville, Napa; 200 acres in Alexander Valley, Sonoma; 500 acres in Monterey. Wines: sparkling wines, Cab.Sauv., Zin., Merlot., Chard., J.R.
A major new enterprise, founded by the ebullient Justin Meyer and now German owned. Successes so far are sweetish Riesling, oaky Napa Chardonnay, different Cabernets from Napa and Sonoma vineyards and a good burgundy blend, all at fair prices. The good-value Monterey wines come under the Estancia label.

Franzia Brothers Winery
Ripon, *San Joaquin*. Founded 1906.
Owners: The Wine Group. 5 m. cases. Wines: Zin., Ch.Bl., Chablis.
Many generics and a few varietal wines under various names, all traceable by the Ripon address on the label. In recent years the winery has led the bag-in-box market under their Franzia and Summit labels.

Freemark Abbey Winery
St. Helena, *Napa*. Founded 1895, refounded 1967.
Principal: Charles A. Carpy. Wine maker: Ted Edwards.
Visits. 33,000 cases. 260 acres in Napa Valley. Wines: Chard., Cab.Sauv., J.R.
Perfectionist winery just north of St. Helena. Three of the partners (Messr. Carpy, Jaeger and Wood) are leading Napa grape growers. Another (Brad Webb) made history with barrels at Hanzel (q.v.) in the late 1950s. Their Chardonnay is often the best in the valley. My notes on the '79 read: 'generous and complex, round and silky but with good grip and sweet, clean finish.' In 1973 they pioneered sweet botrytis-rotten Riesling, now labelled 'Edelwein'. Cabernet from a Rutherford grower called Bosché (and so labelled) is outstandingly concentrated and balanced, even better than their splendid regular bottling. Their latest success is the exceptional Carpy Ranch Chardonnay.

Frick Winery
Santa Cruz, *Santa Cruz*. Founded 1976.
Owners: Judith and William Frick. Wine maker: William Frick. 3,500 cases.

Fritz Cellars
Cloverdale, *Sonoma*. Founded 1979.
Owner: Donald Fritz. Wine maker: David Hastings. Visits by appt. 15,000 cases. Wines: Chard., Fumé Bl., Cab.Sauv., Zin. 95 acres of Chardonnay and Sauvignon supply grapes for ripe, wood-aged wines. Red wines come from bought-in Alexander Valley grapes.

Frog's Leap Wine Cellars
St. Helena, *Napa*. Founded 1981.
Owners: Larry Turley and John Williams. Approaching 16,000 cases (20,000 planned). Wines: Sauv.Bl., Zin., Chard., Cab.Sauv.
Sauvignon Blanc and Zinfandel were the first wines at this winery on the site of a former frog farm. Chardonnay and Cabernet were added in 1982. Sauvignon and Chardonnay have proved successful during the late 1980s.

E. & G. Gallo Winery
Modesto, *Stanislaus*. Founded 1933.
Principals: Ernest and Julio R. Gallo. 40 m. to 50 m. cases.
Grapes from Healdsburg–Sonoma area, Napa, Fresno, Modesto, Livingston.
The world's biggest wine maker, still run by the brothers who founded it. Everything about Gallo is stupendous. They own the world's 2 biggest wineries to supply their incredible tank farm, which has a capacity of 265 m. gallons, including 1 m. gallon storage tank and a 25-acre warehouse. The bottling line starts with a glass factory. And the whole operation is still growing fast.

Farmers in most parts of California (including the best) supply grapes. The wines are patiently and thoroughly designed for their huge markets.* The long-running favourites are Chablis Blanc (well structured, fragrant, not quite dry, if anything more German than French in style) and Hearty Burgundy (which is more Italian in feeling). In fact, both comparisons are backward looking: they are the archetypes for California. Gallo sparkling wine, sweet sherry and E & J brandy are all equally well designed and good value. The late 1970s saw the introduction of Gallo varietals: Colombard, Barbera, Ruby Cabernet, Zinfandel, Sauvignon Blanc, followed later by Gewürztraminer, Riesling, Cabernet and Chardonnay. Sauvignon Blanc is generally reckoned the best (and very good value). In the 1980s the Gallos swung their immense marketing power fully behind varietal wines. The Cabernet Sauvignon is enjoyable drunk fairly young. Zinfandels can be impressive with bottle age. *Brand names are: The Reserve Cellars of Ernest & Julio Gallo, Gallo, Paisano, Thunderbird, Carlo Rossi, Ripple, Boone's Farm, Madria-Madria, Tyrolia, Spanada. Night Train Express, Brandy: E & J.

Gan Eden
Sonoma. Founded 1985. 25,000 cases.
Wines: Chard., Cab.Sauv., Gamay Beauj., Ch.Bl.
Kosher wines, using only bought-in Sonoma grapes, which win prizes and praise.

Gauer Estate Vineyard
Alexander Valley, *Sonoma*. Vineyards planted from 1970, winery from 1988. President: Allan J. Hemphill. Wine maker: Kerry Damsky.
250 acres of mountain vineyards overlooking the Alexander Valley have recently acquired a winery identity. High quality Chardonnay and later Cabernet etc. will come from designated vineyards.

Geyser Peak Winery
Geyserville, *Sonoma*. Founded 1880.
Owners: The Trione family and Penfolds. Wine maker:
Armand Bussane. Visits. 500,000 cases. 1,100 acres in Sonoma
County. Many table and sparkling wines.

An old bulk-selling winery bought in 1972 by Schlitz Brewery and sold again a decade later. Gewürztraminer and Fumé Blanc are the top choices in a range without peaks. The best wines bear Harry Trione's name and are increasingly from his own vineyards.

Girard Winery
Oakville, *Napa*. Founded 1974.
Owners: the Girard family. Wine maker: Mark Smith. 14,000
cases. 80 acres at Oakville and in the western Napa Valley.
Wines: Chard., Ch.Bl., Cab.Sauv.

Small family-owned winery east of Oakville.

Giumarra Vineyards
Bakersfield, *Kern*. Founded 1946.
Owners: The Giumarra and Corjaro families. Wine maker:
Dale Anderson. Visits. 1 m. cases. 6,000-acre estate in south
San Joaquin Valley.

Produced bulk wines until 1973, when the Giumarra label appeared on good-value generic lines and some vintage-dated varietal reds, under the brand names of Giumarra Vineyards, Breckinridge and Ridgecrest.

Glen Ellen Vineyards & Winery
Glen Ellen, *Sonoma*. Founded 1980.
Owners: Bruno Benziger and family. Visits. 3.8 m. cases. 100
acres, 20 acres leased. Wines: Cab.Sauv., Sauv.Bl., Chard.,
Merlot, Zin.

The modestly priced 'Proprietor's Reserve' series of varietals, using bought in wines from all over the state, accounts for much of the 3.8 m. cases. A new premium range, called Benziger after the founding family, is planned for the 1990s.

Gran Cru Vineyards
Glen Ellen, *Sonoma*. Founded 1886, refounded 1972.
Owners: Walt and Bettina Dreyer. Wine maker: Robert
Magnani. Visits. 60,000 cases. Vineyards in Alexander and Dry
Creek valleys and Yolo County. Wines: Ch.Bl. Gewürz.,
Sauv.Bl., Zin., Cab.Sauv., Chard.

Originally known for one of the country's best Gewürz-traminers – a slightly sweet, very spicy one. Also a syrupy 'botrytized' version. Chenin and Sauvignon Blancs are both highly professional. Recently they have switched the emphases to Chardonnay and Cabernet.

THE GALLO BROTHERS

The brothers Ernest and Julio Gallo have done more to determine the direction and rate of growth of wine drinking in America than anybody else in history. By far the biggest wine producers in America, and probably the world, they still personally, entirely and privately own and direct their company.

The sons of an Italian immigrant grape farmer, they were brought up in Modesto in the heart of the Central Valley, where they still live and work. They started making wine in 1933, when Ernest was 24 and Julio 23. Julio made the wine and Ernest sold it.

They built their first winery in 1935 where the present vast plant now stands, and in 1940 started planting vineyards to experiment with better grapes. They realized the limitations of Central Valley grapes and bought from growers in Napa and Sonoma. They were prepared to outbid rivals. Today they are said to grow or buy one wine-grape in three in California.

In the 1950s the Gallos started a craze for flavoured 'pop' wines with the fortified Thunderbird, to be followed by a series of such enormously advertised and vastly popular gimmicks as fizzy Ripple and Boone's Farm apple wine. In 1964 they launched Hearty Burgundy which, with Chablis Blanc, set a new standard for California jug wines.

The Gallo trend has been slowly but steadily up-market, taking America with it. In 1974 they introduced their first varietal wines, which were much better than they were given credit for at the time. Their first generation of varietals, which included such compromises as Ruby Cabernet and Barbera, was replaced by a second, going all the way with wood-ageing for Chardonnay and Cabernet. In the process they made a two-acre cellar to house some two million gallons in oak.

When the day comes to inscribe a Gallo memorial, the word I would choose for it would be Consistency.

Green and Red Vineyard
St. Helena, *Napa*. Founded 1977.
Wine maker: J. Heminway. 2,000 cases. 17 acres.
Tiny Pope Valley winery with freshly fruity Zinfandel and
a Chardonnay.

Greenwood Ridge Vineyards
Philo, *Mendocino*. Founded 1980.
Owner: Allen Green. Wine maker: Fred Scherrer. 3,000 cases
from 8 acres. Wines: Riesling, Cab.Sauv.

Grgich Hills Cellar
Rutherford, *Napa*. Founded 1977.
Owners: Austin Hills and Mike Grgich. Wine maker: Mike
Grgich. Visits by appt. 40,000 cases. 360 acres in Napa Valley.
Wines: Chard., J.R., Zin., Cab.Sauv.
Hills grows the grapes, Grgich (formerly at Chateau
Montelana, q.v.) has enhanced his reputation for vigor-
ous, balanced wines with more fruit than weight.
Chardonnay and Riesling (especially late-harvest) have
led the way with Cabernet since 1985.

Groth Vineyards & Winery
Oakville, *Napa*. Founded 1982.
Owners: Dennis and Elizabeth Groth. Wine maker: Nils
Venge. Visits by appt. 30,000 cases plus. Wines: Cab.Sauv.,
Chard., Sauv.Bl.
Two vineyards sites totalling 163 acres provide grapes for
some solid, oak-aged wines. New winery under
construction.

Grover Gulch Winery
Soquel, *Santa Cruz*. Founded 1979.
Owners: Dennis Bassano and Rheinhold Banek. 1,000 cases.
Wines: Cab.Sauv., Car., Pet.Sir., Zin.

Emilio Guglielmo Winery
Morgan Hill, *Santa Clara*. Founded 1925.
Wine maker: George E. Guglielmo. 50,000 cases. 115 acres.
Wines: Cab.Sauv.Reserve, Pet.Sir., Chard., J.R., Sauv.Bl.,
Ch.Bl.

Gundlach-Bundschu Winery
Vineburg, *Sonoma*. Founded 1858, refounded 1973.
President: Jim Bundschu. Wine maker: Lance Cutler. 50,000
cases. 375 acres in Sonoma Valley. Wines: Cab.Sauv., Merlot,
P.N., Zin., Chard., Gewürz., J.R., Kleinberger.
A famous San Francisco wine business destroyed by the
1906 earthquake. Grapes from the old vineyards were sold
until 1973, when the winery reopened in a small way with
Zinfandel. An ex-dairyman partner installed stainless steel
milk tanks for fermentation. The range is excellent,
especially Cabernet and Merlot and a crisp, refreshing
Gewürztraminer like an Alsace wine. Chardonnay and
Riesling are also admirable. Most grapes are from 130-
year-old estate vineyards.

Hacienda Wine Cellars
Sonoma, *Sonoma*. Founded 1973.
Owner: Crawford Cooley. Wine maker: Steven MacRostie.
Consultant: Brad Webb. Visits. 25,000 cases. 40 acres at
Sonoma, 70 at Russian River, Sonoma. Wines: Chard.,
Gewürz., J.R., Ch.Bl., Cab.Sauv., P.N., Sauv.Bl.
Part of Haraszthy's original vineyard (*see* Buena Vista),
started by Frank Bartholomew, has made a new repu-
tation for Chardonnay (not too strong) and particularly
Gewürztraminer. The Pinot Noir, from old vines, can be
good.

Handley Cellars
Anderson Valley, *Mendocino*. Founded 1980.
Owner and wine maker: Milla Handley. 12,000 cases. Wines:
Gewürz., Chard., Sauv.Bl., sparkling Brut.
Ex-Chateau St Jean wine maker Handley is winning
praise for Chardonnay, Gewürztraminer and *méthode
champenoise* sparklers.

Hanzell Vineyards
Sonoma, *Sonoma*. Founded 1957.
Owner: Barbara de Brye. Wine maker: Robert Sessions. 3,000
cases. 32 acres. Wines: Chard., P.N., Cab.Sauv.
Scene of revolutionary wine making in the late 1950s,
when James D. Zellerbach set out to make burgundy-
style wines in small French oak barrels. The steep south-
facing vineyard gives high alcohol but the concentration
and balance of both the Chardonnay and the Pinot Noir
still makes them among California's most impressive,
demanding long maturing. The winery is (vaguely) a
miniature Château du Clos de Vougeot. An additional
vineyard has been planted in Cabernet.

Harbor Winery
W. Sacramento, *Sacramento*. Founded 1972.
Owner and wine maker: Charles H. Myers. No visits. 1,000
cases. Grapes from Napa Valley and Amador County. Wines:
Cab.Sauv., Zin., Chard., Mission del Sol.
A university professor's hobby and his friends' delight,
especially Napa Chardonnay and Amador Zinfandel.

Haywood Winery
Sonoma, *Sonoma*. Founded 1980.
Owner: Peter Haywood. Wine maker: Charles Tolbert. Visits.
34,000 cases. 84 acres of Chard., J.R., Cab.Sauv., Zin.
Fine fruity Chardonnay and powerful Zinfandel from the
hills above Sebastini.

Hecker Pass Winery
Gilroy, *Santa Clara*. Founded 1972.
Owners: Mario and Frances Fortino (wine maker). Visits.
5,000 cases. 14 acres in Santa Clara. Wines: Pet.Sir., Zin.,
Carig., Ruby Cab., Gren., Chablis., Fr.Col., sherry.
Stylish reds from southern Santa Clara county.

Heitz Wine Cellars
St. Helena, *Napa*. Founded 1961.
Owners: Joe and Alice Heitz. Wine maker: David Heitz.
Visits. 40,000 cases. 150 acres. Wines: Cab.Sauv., Chard., P.N.,
Grig., Chablis, burgundy, sparkling wine.
Heitz is known worldwide for his Cabernet, more locally
for his Chardonnay, and very locally for his surprisingly
long list of other wines. Yet they all reflect the man; a
sometimes gruff original whose palate has its own logic.
The Heitz's white house and old stone barn in an eastern
side-valley still have an early-settler feeling among far
more sophisticated neighbours. Most of the grapes are
bought from friends, one of whom, Martha May, has
already passed into legend as the name on 'Martha's
Vineyard', Heitz's flagship Cabernet – a dense and gutsy
wine of spicy, cedary and gumtree flavours, somehow
unmistakably the Mouton of the Napa Valley even at the
teeth-staining stage. Bella Oaks vineyard is of similar
stature. Young Heitz Chardonnay (his first was from
Hanzell, q.v., in 1962) stands out in tastings as strong and
dry, its fruit flavour held in check. Grignolino is a
surprising, sweet, Muscat-flavoured red. Angelica is a
California tradition you would expect Joe Heitz to
respect.

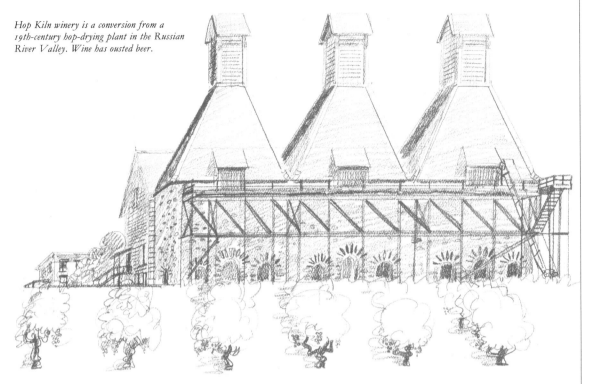

Hop Kiln winery is a conversion from a 19th-century hop-drying plant in the Russian River Valley. Wine has ousted beer.

Hess Collection Winery

Napa, *Napa*. Founded 1982.
Owner: Donald Hess. Visits by appt. 15,000 cases (50,000 planned). 280 acres. Wines: Chard., Cab.Sauv.

William Hill Winery

Napa, *Napa*. Founded 1976.
Owner and wine maker. William H. Hill. 70,000 cases. 700 acres around Atlas Mountain and Mt. Veeder in Napa Valley and in Carneros. Wines: Cab.Sauv., Chard.
One of Napa's biggest vineyard holdings, on high ground promising fine wine. Gold and Silver labels mark expensive and less expensive Cabernets and Chardonnays. Recent vintages have confirmed expectations and sealed a remarkable reputation.

Hop Kiln Winery (at Griffin Vineyards)

Healdsburg, *Sonoma*. Founded 1975.
Owner: Martin Griffin. Wine maker: Steve Strobl. Visits. 10,000 cases. 65 acres in Russian River Valley of Chard., Gewürz., J.R., Cab.Sauv., P.N., Zin. and P.S.
The Petite Sirah and Gewürztraminer are well spoken of. Reds are from Alexander Valley grapes.

Husch Vineyards

Philo, *Mendocino*. Founded 1971.
Owner: Hugo Oswald. Wine maker: Mark Theis. Visits. 164 acres. From Anderson and Ukiah valleys.

Inglenook – Napa Valley

Rutherford, *Napa*. Founded 1881.
Owners: Grand Metropolitan. Wine maker: John Richburg. Visits. 265,000 cases. Vineyard in Napa Valley and elsewhere. Wines: Cab., Chard., Sauv.Bl., Pinot Noir.
Inglenook was one of the handful of vineyards to survive Prohibition. A family property with a tradition of memorable, if not subtle, wines until John Daniel, grand-

nephew of the founder, sold it to United Vintners in 1964.Only the Estate and Reserve levels are bottled under the Inglenook Napa label – the more ordinary wines are bottled under a second label – Rutherford Estate. The estate wines are led by three Cabernets, Charbono (lumbering in youth, enjoyable with age) and a good Gewürztraminer. The original stone winery on the west slopes of the valley is a historic landmark. Inglenook-Navalle has the same owners, but is quite separate. It produces some 3 million cases of bulk wines in the Central Valley.

Iron Horse Vineyard

Sebastopol, *Sonoma*. Founded 1979.
Principal: Audrey Sterling. Wine maker: Forrest Tancer. Visits by appt. 25,000 cases. 192 acres in Sonoma–Green Valley and Alexander Valley. Wines: P.N., Cab.Sauv., Chard., Sauv.Bl.
I took an instant liking to Iron Horse Cabernet, tannic to start, ripely sweet to finish, like good claret. Since then vibrant Chardonnay and even more lively sparkling Iron Horse have stolen the limelight. Latest plans are for a tie-up with Laurent-Perrier of Champagne.

Jekel Vineyards

Greenfield, *Monterey*. Vineyard founded 1972, winery 1978.
Owners: Bill and Gus Jekel. Wine maker: Rick Jekel. Visits. 50,000 cases. 330 acres in Arroyo Seco, Monterey. Wines: Chard. and Ries., J.R., and Cab.Sauv.
The whites (especially Riesling and Chardonnay) are among the best of the region, ripe but not heavy. Cabernet Sauvignon – especially the excellent '83 Private Reserve – has also been a huge critical success.

Johnson's of Alexander Valley

Owners: Tom and Gail Johnson. Wine maker: Ellen Johnson. Visits. 5,000 cases. 45 acres in Alexander Valley, Sonoma. Wines: J.R., Pinot Noir (also P.N. white), Zin., Cab.Sauv.

Johnson-Turnbull
Oakville, *Napa*. Founded 1979.
Wine maker: Lawrence Wara. 2,000 cases. 38 acres. Wines: Cab.Sauv., Chard.

Balanced, distinguished Cabernets from next-door to Mondavi. Red grapes come from estate vines; Chardonnay from a Knight's Valley plot.

Jordan Vineyard and Winery
Healdsburg, *Sonoma*. Vineyard founded 1972, winery 1976.
Owner: Thomas N. Jordan. Wine maker: Robert Davis. Visits by appt. 70,000 cases. 275 acres in Alexander Valley, Sonoma. Wines: Cab.Sauv. (with Merlot), Chard.

At least in folklore the most extravagent tycoon's chateau-in-California yet: a Bordeaux-style mansion and winery deliberately set on producing claret like the Médoc, in a setting of dark oaks and rolling golden grassland beautiful even by Sonoma standards. The first vintage, '76, made in barrels from Château Lafite, was light but very stylish. Now both Cabernet and Chardonnay are regularly among California's most stylish wines.

Kalin Cellars
Novato, *Marin*. Founded 1977.
Wine maker: Terrance Leighton. 6,000 cases.

A scientist-wine maker produces 5 vineyard-denoted Chardonnays plus Semillon and reds.

Karly Wines
Plymouth, *Amador*. Founded 1980.
Wine maker: Lawrence Cobb. 11,000 cases. 20 acres. Wines: Fumé Bl., Zin., Chard., P.Sir.

A subtle touch with Zinfandel and Sauvignon (called Fumé) Blanc plus Chardonnay and (occasionally) Petite Sirah.

Robert Keenan Winery
St. Helena, *Napa*. Founded 1977.
Owner: Robert H. Keenan. Wine maker: Rex Geitner. 9,000 cases. 46 acres in Napa Valley. Wines: Chard., Cab.Sauv., Merlot.

High, cool vineyards on Spring Mountain Road produce Chardonnay, and Cabernet Sauvignon which is blended with Napa Merlot and oak-aged. Could be over-strong and tannic in early vintages; the recent style is more polite.

Kendall-Jackson Vineyard
Lakeport, *Lake*.
Owner: Jess Jackson. Wine maker: John Hawley. 400,000 cases. Wines: Chard., J.R., Sauv.Bl., Cab.Sauv., Zin.

One of the great commercial successes of the 1980s. Grapes are bought-in from local vineyards and coastal counties to augment the crop from 85 acres owned by the company, which is the major force in the emergence of Lake County as a quality region. They also have an interest in large vineyards in Santa Barbara and Sonoma Counties. Special reserves of Chardonnay and Sauvignon Blanc from the estate carry the second label, 'Chateau du Lac'.

Kathryn Kennedy Winery
Saratoga, *Santa Clara*. Founded 1979.
Wine maker: Martin Mathis. 400–800 cases. 5 acres.
Concentrates on solid Cabernet Sauvignon.

Kenwood Vineyards
Kenwood, *Sonoma*. Founded 1906 as Pagani Bros; renamed 1970.

Owners: Lee family. President: John Sheela. Wine maker: Michael Lee. 100,000 cases. 185 acres. Wines: Cab.Sauv., P.N., Zin., Chard., Sauv.Bl., J.R., Gewürz., Ch.Bl.

Wide range of varietals from Sonoma grapes including Jack London Vineyard and Artist's Series Cabernet Sauvignons. Reds are increasingly stylish, and the Sauvignon Blanc is very good.

Kenworthy Vineyards
Plymouth, *Amador*. Founded 1978.
Wine maker: John Kenworthy. 1,000 cases. 7 acres.

Kirigin Cellars
Gilroy, *Santa Clara*. Founded 1976.
Wine maker: Nikola Kirigin Chargin. Visits. 48 acres. 3,000 cases of various varietals.

Kistler Vineyards
Glen Ellen, *Sonoma*. Founded 1978.
President: Stephen Kistler. Wine makers: Stephen Kistler and Mark Bixler. 9,000 cases. 60 acres. Wines: Chard., P.N., Cab.Sauv.

Hilltop vineyards on the Napa/Sonoma watershed produce Chardonnay grapes for artisan-method wines. Subtlety is replacing headiness. Cabernet and Pinot Noir have been added, and more vineyards have joined the Chardonnay roster.

Konocti Cellars Winery
Kelseyville, *Lake*. Founded 1979.
Owners: J. Parducci 50%, Lake County Vintners 50%. Wine maker: William Pease. 40,000 cases. 500 acres (27 Lake County growers with 10 to 20 acres each).

Attractive, consistent Sauvignon Blanc, Cabernet and other wines from this remote northern district.

F. Korbel and Bros.
Guerneville, *Sonoma*. Founded 1882.
President: Gary Heck. Wine maker: Robert Stashak. Visits. 1.2 m. cases, 400 acres owned, 200 leased in Russian River Valley, Sonoma County. Wines: sparkling, brandy and table.

Until Domaine Chandon came on the scene this was the first choice in widely available California 'Champagne'. It is still a reliable bargain, especially the extremely dry Natural. Additions are Blanc de Blancs and Blanc de Noirs and a sweet Sec. The winery is a lovely old place in coastal redwood country.

Hanns Kornell Champagne Cellars
St. Helena, *Napa*. Founded 1952.
President and wine master: Hanns J. Kornell. Visits. 85,000 cases. No vineyards. Wines are all *méthode champenoise* sparkling: Sehr Trocken, Brut.

If Domaine Chandon is France's invasion of Napa, this is Germany's. Germany no longer makes Sekt like Kornell's Sehr Trocken, with burly dry Riesling-and-yeast flavours. His fruity, faintly sweet Brut is more in the refreshing modern Sekt style. The newest wine is a Chardonnay Blanc de Blancs.

Charles Krug Winery
St. Helena, *Napa*. Founded 1861.
President: Peter Mondavi Sr. Visits. 200,000 cases (incl. jug 'C.K.'). 1,200 acres in Napa Valley. Wines: a wide range, including the second label, CK-Mondavi.

C. Mondavi & Sons is the company name at the oldest of Napa's historic wineries. The other son is Robert, who left in 1966 to start his own winery, with spectacular success. Krug led the field with Chenin Blanc as a semi-sweet varietal. Their Chardonnay is Napa at its least reticent – what Bob Thompson calls 'buttered asparagus'. Krug Cabernets also have a fine pedigree; the standard one is lightish and ready-matured but the Cesare Mondavi Selection is the typical deep-flavoured, ripe-fruit-and-dust sort from the Rutherford/Oakville foothills. New Chardonnays from Carneros vineyards, and a Pinot Noir, add depth to the range.

La Crema
Graton, *Sonoma*. Founded 1979.
Owner: Jason Korman. Visits by appt. 80,000 cases of P.N., Chard, Sauv.Bl.

Since taking over in 1985, Jason Korman has dispensed with vineyard designated wines and has introduced reserve bottling. The approach is still broadly French with impressive Pinot Noir. The cellar is about to move to the Russian River Valley.

Lakespring Winery
Napa, *Napa*. Founded 1980.
Owners: the Battat family. Wine maker: Randy Mason. 18,000 cases. 8 acres. Wines: Merlot, Cab.Sauv., Sauv.Bl., Chard.

Making a name for Merlot from bought-in Napa grapes.

Lambert Bridge
Dry Creek Valley, *Sonoma*. Founded 1975.
Owners: Margaret and Gerald Lambert. Wine maker: Ed Killian. 25,000 cases. 119 acres in Dry Creek Valley. Wines: Cab.Sauv., Chard., Merlot.

Lean, powerfully flavoured Chardonnay, if less oaky than formerly, and tannic Cabernet Sauvignon that needs bottle-age.

Landmark Vineyards
Kenwood, *Sonoma*. Founded 1974.
Wine maker: William R. Mabry III. 15,000 cases. 77 acres in the Russian River, Alexander and Sonoma valleys of Chard.

Chardonnay specialist now based at Kenwood. Cypress Lane is the second label.

Laurel Glen Vineyards
Santa Rosa, *Sonoma*. Founded 1980.
Wine maker: Patrick Campbell. 40 acres. 5000 cases of Cab. Sauv.

Sound Cabernet Sauvignon from mountain vineyards, with a little Cab. Franc blended in.

Lazy Creek
Anderson Valley, *Mendocino*. Owner: Hans Kobler. Founded 1979. 20 acres. 2,000 cases. Wines: P.N., Chard. Gewürz.

The Gewürztraminer from this tiny property is highly rated.

Leeward Winery
Oxnard, *Ventura*. Founded 1978.
Wine makers: Chuck Brigham and Chuck Gardner. Visits. 18,000 cases of Chard., P.N., Cab. Sauv.

Ventura (Monterey) Chardonnay, plus other named-vineyard wines, has been a promising beginning for this coastal winery.

Live Oaks Winery
Gilroy, *Santa Clara*. Founded 1912.
Owner: Richard Blocker. Visits. 3,500 cases. 69 acres.

The Czech Korbel brothers built their red brick winery by the Russian River in northern Sonoma in 1886. The 'brandy tower' stands as a symbol for the produce of one of California's most consistent companies

Livermore Valley Cellars
Livermore, *Alameda*. Founded 1978.
Wine maker: Chris Lagiss. Visits. 3,000 cases. 30 acres.

Llords and Elwood Winery
Fremont, *Alameda*. Founded 1955.
Owner: Monticello Cellars. 8,000 cases. Wines: Chard.,
Sauv.Bl., Cab.Sauv., White Zin., 3 sherries, 1 port.
This winery is best known for Great Day Dry Sherry, but
table wines from a Napa winery have been added since the
'85 vintage.

J. Lohr Winery
San Jose, *Santa Clara*. Founded 1974.
Owner: Jerry Lohr. Wine maker: Barry Gnekow. Visits by
appt. 200,000 cases. 1,000 acres in Salinas Valley, Monterey
and Napa Valley. Wines: J.R., Ch.Bl., Fumé Bl., P.Bl., Chard.,
Gam., P.N., Cab.Sauv., Zin., Pet.Sir.
Riesling from Monterey is the best-regarded wine. The
labels are J. Lohr and Jade.

The Lucas Winery
Lodi, *San Joaquin*. Founded 1978.
Wine maker: David Lucas. Visits. 30 acres. 1,200 cases of Zin.,
light dry and sweet late-harvest.

Lyeth Vineyard
Cloverdale, *Sonoma*. Founded 1981.
30,000 cases.
New winery with ambitions for Bordeaux-style reds and
whites. The vineyard is now in separate hands, but still
supplies the winery. The wines are settling down after
early clumsiness.

Lytton Springs Winery
Healdsburg, *Sonoma*. Founded 1977.
Owner: Richard Sherwin. Wine maker: Bura W. Walters.
Visits. 15,000 cases. 50 acres at Valley Vista, Russian River,
Sonoma. Wines: Chard., Sauv.Bl., Merlot, Zin.
Old vines, formerly the source of a well-regarded Ridge
(q.v.) wine, now make one of Sonoma's biggest (and most
expensive) Zinfandels. I have found it metallic, fierce and
hot, but many love such things.

Markham Winery
St. Helena, *Napa*. Founded 1978.
Owners: Sanraku. Wine maker: Robert Foley Jr. Visits. 20,000
cases. 250 acres in Napa Valley. Wines: Chard., Sauv.Bl.,
Muscat Bl., Merlot.
Production based on 3 vineyards, near Calistoga, Yount-
ville and Napa, gives a good range of wines.

Mark West Vineyards
Forestville, *Sonoma*. Founded 1976.
Owners and wine makers: Bob and Joan Ellis. Visits. 22,000
cases. 62 acres in Russian River Valley in Sonoma County.
Wines: Chard., Gewürz., J.R., P.N. (red and white).
Relatively cool vineyard producing white wines with
good fruity acidity (the Gewürztraminer is notable) plus a
sparkling Blanc de Noirs.

Louis M. Martini
St. Helena, *Napa*. Founded 1922.
President Louis P. Martini. Wine makers: Louis P. and
Michael R. Martini. Visits. 235,000 cases. 800 acres in Napa
and Sonoma counties. Wines: Cab.Sauv., P.N., Merlot, Zin.,
Barbera, Chard., J.R., Folle Blanche, Gewürz., Moscato
Ambile and Sem.

Three generations of Martinis have their name on the
short list of California's great individual wine makers.
Martini Cabernets of the 1960s rank alongside Beaulieu in
quality, but in a different style which, as Bob Thompson
has noted, appeals strongly to Englishmen weaned on
claret. Martini continues to go less for guts than good
manners in his wine. His Special Selection Cabernets are
best, but all are well-balanced. Pinot Noir (from Carneros)
is only modestly fruity, but again hauntingly well-
finished. Barbera and Zinfandel are true to type. Of white
the best is dry and spicy Gewürztraminer. Chardonnays
from Carneros and Russian River are the latest additions.

Martini & Prati Wines
Santa Rosa, *Sonoma*. Founded 1951.
Wine maker: Frank Vanucci. Visits. 20,000 cases. 62 acres.

Paul Masson Vineyards
Saratoga, *Santa Clara*. Founded 1852.
Owners: Vintners International (since 1987). Visits 6 m. cases.
4,500 acres in Monterey, San Benito and Santa Clara counties.
A wide range of table, dessert and sparkling wines.
The famous old firm was sold by Seagram in 1987. Known
recently for jugs rather than fine wines. Vintners are
reversing this trend and reducing production.

Mastantuono
Paso Robles, *San Luis Obispo*. Founded 1977.
President and wine maker: Pasquale Mastran. Visits.
15,000 cases. 15 acres. Wines: Zin., Fumé Bl., White Zin.,
Mus. Canelli, Cab.Sauv.
The most concentrated of Zinfandels, from Templeton
Vineyards, planted in 1925.

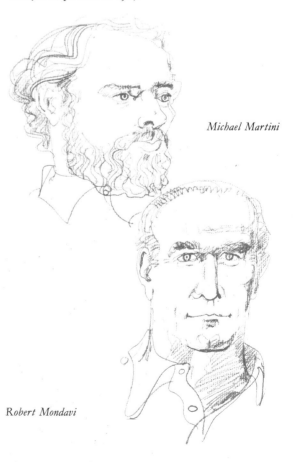

Michael Martini

Robert Mondavi

Mantanzas Creek Winery

Santa Rosa, *Sonoma*. Founded 1977.
Owner: Sandra P. MacIver. Wine maker: Bill Parker and
Susan Reed. Visits by appt. 30,000 cases. 50 acres in Bennett
Valley.

Expectations fulfilled: the first wine maker (to 1984) was
Merry Edwards, now at Merry Vintners (q.v.). Both Bill
Park and Susan Reed work to produce a style of wine that
combines traditional French cellar practices with the most
modern wine making methods. The Chardonnay made a
splendid London début, the Gewürztraminer is winey and
substantial and the Pinot Blanc a good Chardonnay-like
example of this variety.

Mayacamas Vineyards

Miles up in the hills above Napa, *Napa*.
Founded 1889. Refounded 1941.
Owners: Bob and Nonie Travers. Wine maker: Robert
Travers. Visits by appt. 5,000 cases. 50 acres in Napa. Wines:
Chard., Cab.Sauv., Sauv.Bl., P.N., Zin.

Mayacamas is the name of the mountains between Napa
and Sonoma. If it were the Indian word for 'white man's
strongest medicine' it would not be far wrong. The
Travers' predecessors, the Taylors, planted Chardonnay
and Cabernet in the 1940s in a spectacular natural
amphitheatre 1,000 feet up. The sun, the fogs, the winds,
the cold and the rocks of the hills conspire to concentrate
grape flavour into something you can chew. The hot
autumn of 1978 made the Chardonnay almost treacly.
Travers' Cabernets are awe-inspiring in colour and bite
for the first 5 years at least. Late-harvest Zinfandel he
makes from bought grapes when they are tasty enough.

McDowell Valley Vineyards

Hopland, *Mendocino*. Founded 1978.
Owners: Richard and Karen Keehn. Wine maker: John
Buchsenstein. Visits 100,000 cases. 600 acres in McDowell
Valley, Mendocino. Wines: Chard., Fumé Bl., Cab.Sauv., Zin.,
Syrah.

Ambitious, indeed visionary, venture to re-establish this
forgotten little vineyard valley in S. Mendocino with a
futuristic winery, using solar energy, deep cellars and
nocturnal harvesting. Syrah and Zinfandel are especially
good. To watch.

McLester

Inglewood, *Los Angeles*. Founded 1979.
Wine maker: Cecil McLester. 3,000 cases. Wines: Fumé Bl.,
Merlot, Cab.Sauv.

Meridian Vineyards

San Luis Obispo. Founded 1988. Wine maker: Charles Ortman.
700 acres, 30,000 cases. Wines: Chard., Cab.Sauv., Syrah.
The former Estrella River Winery, concentrating on
Chardonnay, first vintage 1988.

Merry Vintners

Santa Rosa, *Sonoma*. Founded 1984.
Wine maker Merry Edwards (ex-Mount Eden and Matan-
zas Creek) set up this winery with her family to make two
Chardonnays, a solid, classic one and a lighter 'food'
version for restaurants. Pinot Noir introduced in '86, and
there is the occasional Late Harvest Sauvignon Blanc.

Milano Winery

Hopland, *Mendocino*. Founded 1977.
Wine maker: Jim Milone. Visits. 10,000 cases. Wines: Chard.,
Sauv.Bl., Ch.Bl., Cab.Sauv., Zin., P.N., Gewürz.
Range of Chardonnays including, in 1985, an ice wine.

Mill Creek Vineyards

Healdsburg, *Sonoma*. Founded 1976.
President: Chas. W. Kreck. Wine maker: James Kreck. Visits.
15,000 cases. 65 acres in Russian River Valley, Sonoma.
Wines: Chard., Cab.Sauv., Sauv.Bl., Merlot, Gewürz.
Soft and agreeable rather than competition wines, but the
Chardonnay is underrated.

Mirassou Vineyards

San Jose, *Santa Clara*. Founded 1854.
Owners: The Mirassou family. Wine maker: Tom Stulz. Visits.
350,000 cases. 1,100 acres in Monterey and Santa Clara. A
wide range of table and sparkling wines.
The fifth generation of Mirassous run an enterprising
company with panache. Being squeezed out of increasingly urban San Jose, most of their vines are now in the
Salinas Valley, Monterey, where they pioneered field-
crushing. Demand and problems with the Salinas climate
have meant more grapes bought in from elsewhere in the
State. Their wines were more exciting 15 years ago.

Robert Mondavi Winery

Oakville, *Napa*. Founded 1966.
Principal: Robert Mondavi. Wine maker: Tim Mondavi.
Visits. 1.5 m. cases plus. 1,100 acres, with 300 more under
development. Cab.Sauv., P.N., Chard., Ch.Bl., Fumé Bl., J.R.
Mondavi's energy and his enquiring mind took less than
10 years to produce the most important development in
the Napa Valley since Prohibition. He fits the standard
definition of a genius better than anyone I know. His aim
is top quality on an industrial scale. Inspiration and
perspiration have taken him there.

The winery is (in the local jargon) state-of-the-art. The
art includes not only advanced analysis and every shiny
gadget but a personal knowlege of every French barrel
maker worth a hoop. Each vintage is like a frontier with
the Mondavi family cheering each other on to reach it –
and something new always develops.

Their best wine is their Cabernet Sauvignon Reserve; a
gentle titan you can drink after dinner with relish but
would do well to keep for 20 years. Their regular Cabernet
is a model of balance between berries and barrels. Each
vintage their Pinot Noir grow more velvety satisfying.
Among whites they are best known for Fumé Blanc,
Sauvignon and Semillon with the body and structure (and
barrel-age) of first-class Chardonnay. Their Chardonnay
(notably the Reserve) can be compared with the best. The
'78 had incredible richness and nerve. The Riesling is
rather sweet, but crisp and refreshing and will age well.
Late-harvest, botrytis-rotten Riesling is golden treacle.
Red and white table wines keep up the good work. Only
the Chenin Blanc disappoints me. Opus One, founded in
1979, is a Mondavi/Baron Philippe de Rothschild joint
venture using Napa grapes (the Opus One vineyard,
across the highway from the Mondavi winery, is now
bearing). A high-priced, Pauillac-inspired blend of Cabernet Franc, Cabernet Sauvignon and (sometimes) Merlot.

Robert Mondavi-Woodbridge is the label for useful
table wines from a second winery.

Chateau Montelena

Calistoga, Napa. Founded 1882.
Wine maker: Bo Barrett. Visits: 28,000 cases. 100 acres. Wines:
Chard., Cab.Sauv., Zin., J.R.

Monterey Peninsula Winery
Monterey, *Monterey*. Founded 1974.
Owners: Deryck Nuckton and Roy Thomas. Visits. 12,000 cases. Wines: mainly Zin. and Cab.Sauv. Chard., P.B., Merlot, Barbera. Second brand: Monterey Cellars.
Red wine specialist, using grapes from Amador, San Luis Obispo and Monterey counties to make many different one-vineyard Zinfandels and Cabernets, generally dense and heady, probably at their best quite young. Also Chardonnay in the same robust spirit.

The Monterey Vineyard
Gonzales, *Monterey*. Founded 1973.
Owner: The Seagram Classics Wine Co. Visits. 1,100 acres. 500,000 cases. Wines: Zin., Gewürz., Chard., Sauv.Bl., Fumé Bl.
Grapes from Monterey and other Central Coast counties go into a wide range of table wines. Strong-flavoured Monterey grapes have had most success in white varietals, especially Riesling, Sauvignon Blanc, Gewürztraminer and Sylvaner. Late harvesting produces 'Thanksgiving' Riesling (wonderful at 5 years) and 'December' Zinfandel, a splendid concentrated dry red. Classic wines are the mainstream, 'Limited Release' the top label.

Monteviña Wines
Plymouth, *Amador*. Founded 1973.
Owners: Sutter Home. Visits. 50,000 cases. 250 acres. Wines: Zin., Barbera, Sauv.Bl. and Chard (after 1988).
Zinfandels, red or white, and equally strong Sauvignon Blanc, from the Shenandoah Valley AVA, a revitalized area in the Sierra foothills.

Monticello Cellars
Big Ranch Road, *Napa*. Founded 1970.
Managing Partner: Jay Corley. Wine maker: Alan Phillips. 25,000 cases. 250 acres. Wines: Cab.Sauv., Chard., Sauv.Bl., P.N., Sem., Gewürz.
Well-considered Napa winery, which released its first wines in 1981, making a range of varietals. Best whites include consistently good Sauvignon Blanc, Semillon and Gewürztraminer. Two good Cabernets are made – Jefferson and Corley Reserve – and Pinot Noir shows promise.

Mont St. John Cellars
Napa, *Napa*. Founded 1979.
Owner: Louis Bartolucci. Wine maker: Andrea Bartolucci. Visits. 20,000 cases. 160 acres. Wines: various table wines.

J. W. Morris Wineries
Healdsburg, *Sonoma*. Founded 1975 in Concord, Alameda.
Owners: Ken and Tricia Toth. Wine maker: Dean Cox. 30,000–75,000 cases. 120 acres in La Reina, Monterey; St. Amant, Amador County. Wines: Chard., Sauv.Bl., Petite Sirah, and Zin.
At first charmingly known as 'J. W. Morris Port Works'. Vintage and Founder's Ruby are specialities. Changed hands and location in 1982, and table wines increased in importance. Other label is Black Mountain Vineyard for estate wines.

Mountain View Winery
Mountain View, *Santa Clara*. Founded 1980.
Owner and wine maker: Patrick Ferguson. Visits by appt. 150,000 cases. Wines: Chard., Sauv.Bl., P.N., Zin.

Mount Eden Vineyards
Saratoga, *Santa Clara*. Founded 1975.
Wine maker: Jeffrey Patterson. Visits by appt. 4,000 cases. 22 acres of vineyard in the Santa Cruz Mountains. Wines: Chard., P.N., Cab.Sauv.
Merry Edwards set the style of these wines on land that belonged to Martin Ray (q.v.), and since her departure the tradition has been maintained. The Chardonnay is a rich soft, spicy wine (in German terms, Pfalz-style). Pinot Noir deep and rich. Cabernet is tannic and gutsy.

Mount Palomar Winery
Temecula, *Riverside*. Founded 1975.
Owner: John Poole. Wine maker: Joseph Cherpin. Visits. 13,000 cases. 125 acres.

Mt. Veeder Winery
Mt. Veeder, *Napa*. Founded 1973, vineyard since 1965.
Owner: Franciscan Vineyards. Wine maker: Peter Franus. Visits by appt. 5,000 cases. 26 acres on Mt. Veeder. Wines: Cab.Sauv., Chard.
Rocky vineyard known for concentrated, earthy, gummy, tannic Cabernets. Chardonnay was added in 1985.

Chateau Napa-Beaucanon
Napa. Founded 1986.
Owners: Lebegue. Wine maker: Jean-Marie Maurezer. 20,000 cases. 190 acres.
French venture using Napa grapes for Cabernet, Chardonnay, Merlot etc.

Napa Creek Winery
St. Helena, *Napa*. Founded 1980.
Owner: Jack Schulze. Wine maker: Gordon Madley. 12,000 cases. Wines: Chard., J.R., Gewürz., Cab.Sauv., Merlot.

Navarro Vineyards
Philo, *Mendocino*. Founded 1975.
Principal and wine maker: Edward T. Bennett. Visits. 12,000 cases. 50 acres of vineyards in Anderson Valley and Mendocino of Chard., Gewürz., Wh.Ries., Cab.Sauv., P.N.
A grower taking advantage of a relatively foggy area to make sound, fresh wines, notably Chardonnay and Gewürztraminer.

Newton Vineyards
St. Helena, *Napa*. Founded 1979.
Partners: Peter and Sue Hua Newton. Wine maker: John Kongsgaard. 12,000 cases. 105 acres. Wines: Sauv.Bl., Cab.Sauv., Merlot, Chard.
Rich, enjoyable Chardonnay from bought-in grapes. The winery's own vineyards above St. Helena produce highly-rated Cabernet, Merlot and Sauvignon Blanc.

Nichelini Vineyard
St. Helena, *Napa*. Founded 1890.
Owner and wine maker: Jo-Ann Nichelini Meyer. 5,000 cases. 50 acres. Wines: Chenin Bl., Sauv.Vert, Cab.Sauv., Napa Gamay, Petite Sirah, Zin.

Niebaum Coppola Estate
Rutherford, *Napa*. Founded 1978.
Wine maker: Stephen Beresini. Visits. 3,500 cases. 110 acres.

Gustave Niebaum Collection
Napa. Owners: Heublein.
Top-range, single-vineyard Napa Cabernets and Chardonnays from the owners of Inglenook.

A. Nonini Winery

Fresno, *Fresno*. Founded 1936.
Wine makers: Reno and Tom Nonini. Visits. 30,000 cases. 200 acres. Wines: Chab.Bl., Golden Chasselas, White Zin., Barbera, Gren., Zin.

Obester Winery

Half Moon Bay, *San Mateo*. Founded 1977.
Wine maker: Paul and Sandy Obester. Visits. 8,000 cases.
In 1989 the Obesters bought a vineyard and winery in Mendocino's Anderson Valley. They also own Gmnello Winery.

Olson Vineyards

Redwood Valley, *Mendocino*. Founded 1982.
Owners: Donald and Nancy Olson. Visits. 7,000 cases (14,000 planned). 34 acres. Wines: Chard., Fumé Bl., Gam. Blush, Cab.Sauv., Pet.Sir., Zin.

Opus One

see Robert Mondavi Winery.

Orleans Hill Vinicultural Association

Woodland, *Yolo*. Founded 1980.
President/wine maker: Jim Lapsley. Visits (Sat.). 22,000 cases.

Pacheco Ranch Winery (alias RMS Cellars)

Ignacio, *Marin*. Founded 1979.
Owners: Rowland family. 1,000 cases. 15 acres.

Page Mill Winery

Santa Cruz Mountain, *Santa Clara*. Founded 1976.
Owner: Richard Stark. 2,500 cases of Chard., Cab.Sauv., Zin., Sauv.Bl., P.N.

Papagni Vineyards

Madera, *Madera*. Founded 1920, winery 1975.
President: Angelo Papagni. Wine master: John Daddino.
130,000 cases plus. Vineyards are the Clovis and Bonita ranches, Madera. Wines: Zin., Chard., Barbera, Charbono and many others.
A grape grower turned wine maker with such success that he has made critics reassess the qualities of the San Joaquin Valley. First with light Alicante Bouschet red and sweet Moscat d'Angelo; then with crisp and concentrated Chardonnay aged 6 months in French oak.

Parducci Wine Cellars

Ukiah, *Mendocino*. Founded 1933.
Principal: John A. Parducci. Wine maker: Tom Monostori.
Visits. 350,000 cases plus. 400 acres planted mainly in Cab.Sauv. and other other reds.
The first Mendocino winery, now run by the fourth generation, consistent in offering hearty big-scale reds (Cabernet Sauvignon, Petite Sirah, Zinfandel, Carignane and others). Their whites have been led by a fine Sauvignon Blanc and by sweetish French Colombard and Chenin Blanc. The unoaked Chardonnay is worth looking for. Grapes come from the family's home, Talmage and Largo ranches and growers in Mendocino and Lake counties.

Parson's Creek Winery

Near Ukiah, *Mendocino*. Founded 1979.
Wine maker: Jesse Tidewell. Up to 25,000 cases. Wines: Chard., Brut, Cab.Sauv. Grapes from Ukiah, Anderson and Alexander valleys.
A Canadian group has bought this winery and a 150-acre vineyard is being developed in Alexander Valley.

Pastori Winery

Geyserville, *Sonoma*. Founded 1975.
Wine maker: Frank Pastori. Visits. 10,000 cases. 60 acres.

Robert Pecota Winery

Calistoga, *Napa*. Founded 1978.
Owners: Robert and Susan Pecota. Visits by appt. 18,000 cases. 40 acres in Napa Valley. Wines: Cab., Sauv.Bl., Gam.Beauj., Chard.
A new vineyard is now bearing, the results being good Cabernet Sauvignon and an oak-aged Sauvignon Blanc. A Gamay from Napa grapes is made by *maceration carbonique*.

Pedrizzetti Winery

Morgan Hill, *Santa Clara*. Founded 1919.
Owners: the Pedrizzetti family. Wine maker: Allen Kreutzer.
Visits. 100,000 cases. Wines: a wide range of varietals.

What the jargon means

References to California wine in current literature, on labels and from winery tour guides are full of racy jargon. Some of the less self-explanatory terms are:

Botrytized (pronounced with the accent on the first syllable). Grapes or wine infected, naturally or artifically, with *botrytis cinerea*, the 'noble rot' of Sauternes: hence normally very sweet.

Brix. The American measure of sugar content in grapes, also known as Balling, approximately equal to double the potential alcohol of the wine if all the sugar is fermented. 19.3 Brix is equivalent to 10% alcohol by volume.

Cold stabilization. A near-universal winery practice for preventing the formation of (harmless) tartaric acid crystals in the bottle. The offending tartaric acid is removed by storing wine near freezing point for about 15 days.

Crush. A California term for the vintage; also the quantity of grapes crushed, measured in tons an acre.

Field-grafting. A method much used recently for converting established vines from one variety to another – usually red to white. The old vine top is cut off near the ground and a bud of the new variety grafted on.

Free-run juice. The juice that flows from the crushed grapes 'freely' before pressing. By implication, superior. Normally mixed with pressed juice.

Gas chromatograph. An expensive gadget for analysing a compound (e.g. wine) into its chemical constituents.

Gondola. A massive hopper for carrying grapes from vineyard to crusher, behind a tractor or on a truck.

Jug wines. Originally, wines collected from the winery in a jug for immediate use – therefore of ordinary quality. Now standard wines sold in large bottles.

Ovals. Barrels of any size with oval, rather than round, ends, kept permanently in one place and not moved around the cellar – the German rather than the French tradition.

Polish filtration. Nothing to do with Poland; a final filtration through a very fine-pored filter to 'polish' the wine to gleaming brilliance.

Pomace. The solid matter – skins, pips and stems – left after pressing.

Skin contact. Alas not that, but a reference to leaving the juice mixed with the skins before separating them. All red wines must have maximum skin contact. Some white wines gain good flavours from a few hours 'maceration' with their skins before fermentation. For the 'cleanest', most neutral wine, a wine maker would avoid any skin contact.

J. Pedroncelli Winery
Geyserville, *Sonoma*. Founded 1904.
Owners: John and James Pedroncelli. Wine maker: John Pedroncelli. Visits. 125,000 cases. 135 acres in Dry Creek Valley. Wines: many generic and varietal table wines.
An old reliable for local country jug wines, now making Zinfandel, Gewürztraminer, Chardonnay and Cabernet Sauvignon to a higher and stylish standard, and at very reasonable prices.

Robert Pepi Winery
Napa. Founded 1981.
Owners: the Pepi family. Founded 1981. 70 acres.
Specialist in Sauvignon Blanc which has added a very fine Chardonnay and Vine Hill Ranch Cabernet.

Pesenti Winery
Templeton, *San Luis Obispo*. Founded 1934.
Wine maker: Frank Nerelli. Visits. 33,000 cases. 65 acres.
Wines: Gray R., J.R., Gewürz., Zin. Rosé, Cab.Sauv. Rosé, White Zin., Cab.Bl., Muscat Carnelli, Cab.Sauv., Zin.

Joseph Phelps Vineyards
St. Helena, *Napa*. Founded 1972.
Owner: Joseph Phelps. Wine maker: Craig Williams. 65,000 cases. 340 acres in Napa Valley. Wines: Chard., Sauv.Bl., Cab.Sauv., Zin., Syrah., J.R.
An ex-builder with an unerring sense of style built his beautiful redwood barn in the choppy foothills east of St. Helena near the Heitz place. His achievement is like a scaled-down Robert Mondavi's; all his many wines are good and several are among the best. My favourites are Riesling, distinctly Germanic (whether dry or late-harvest) and beautiful with bottle-age; Syrah – real Rhône Syrah; Cabernets – far from obvious but inspriing confidence. The Insignia label is for a strongly tannic Cabernet/Merlot blend on Bordeaux lines not qualifying as 'varietal' by the rules. Phelps Chardonnay is also restrained at first, but secretly rich. The late-harvest Gewürztraminer ages beautifully.

R. H. Phillips Vineyard
Esparto, *Yolo*. Founded 1983.
Owners: the Giguiere family. Wine maker: Clark Smith. Visits by appt. 175,000 cases. 250 acres. Wines: Ch.Bl., Colombard, Sauv.Bl., Zin., etc.
Although many wines are made, the emphasis is on whites with Semillon as a 'target' variety. The intention is to double the size of the vineyards and become an estate winery.

Pine Ridge Winery
Yountville, *Napa*. Founded 1978.
Principal and wine maker: R. Gary Andrus. Visits. 41,200 cases. 147 acres. Wines: Cab.Sauv., Chard., Ch.Bl., Merlot.
Another winery revived to make Chardonnay of Carneros and Stag's Leap grapes, Cabernet from Rutherford. Also mild, fresh, off-dry Chenin Blanc.

Piper-Sonoma
Windsor, *Sonoma*. Founded 1980.
Owners: Piper Heidsieck. Wine maker: Chris Markell. Consultant: Michel Lacroix. Visits. 120,000 cases. Wines: Brut, Blanc de Noirs and Tête de Cuvée.
A Champo-California venture, now wholly owned by the French, making fine *méthode champenoise* wines from Pinot Noir and Chardonnay in various combinations.

Pommeraie Vineyards
Sebastopol, *Sonoma*. Founded 1979.
Partners: Curtis A. Yount and Judith A. Johnson. 2,000 cases.

Prager Winery & Port Works
St. Helena, *Napa*. Founded 1980.
Wine maker: James Prager. Visits by appt. 3,400 cases.

Preston Vineyards
Healdsburgs, *Sonoma*. Founded 1975.
Owner: Louis D. Preston. Wine maker: Tom Farella. 25,000 cases. 125 acres in Dry Creek Valley, Sonoma. Wines: Sauv.Bl., Zin., Gam., Ch.Bl.
One of Sonoma's best Sauvignons of the leaves-and-all school and a similarly vivid, not heavy, Zinfandel, Gamay, Cabernet and a Sauvignon-Chenin Blanc blend have been added.

Quady Winery
Madera, *Madera*. Founded 1977.
Principal and wine maker: Andrew Quady. Visits. 15,000 cases. Wines: vintage port, Essensia, Muscat dessert wine.
Quady uses Zinfandel from Amador County but has planted the classic Portuguese varieties, which produced their first crop in '82, under the name of Frank's Vineyard. Essencia is from Orange Muscat; Elysium is a red version from Muscat Hamburg grapes.

Quail Ridge
Napa, *Napa*. Founded 1978.
Owners: Heublein Inc. Wine maker: Elaine Wellesley. Vists by appt. 15,000 cases and increasing. Chard., Cab.Sauv., Sauv.Bl., Merlot.
Napa Chardonnay is barrel fermented, the Cabernet aged in new oak. Good if expensive wines.

Quivira
Sonoma. Founded 1986.
Owners: Henry and Holly Wendt. 90 acres. 12,000 cases.
Fine Sauvignon and Zinfandel from Dry Creek Valley, with Rhône-inspired wines to come.

A. Rafanelli Winery
Dry Creek Valley, *Sonoma*. Founded 1974.
Wine maker: Dave Rafanelli. Visits by appt. 60 acres. 6,000 cases plus of Zin. and Cabernet.
Outstanding Zinfandel and good Cabernet.

Rancho de Philo
Alta Loma, *San Bernadino*. Founded 1975.
Wine maker: Philo Biane. A few hundred cases. 20 acres.
Wine: 'Triple' Cream Sherry, 16 years old, made as a retirement pursuit by the ex-President of Brookside (q.v.).

Rancho Sisquoc Winery
Santa Maria, *Santa Barbara*. Founded 1972, winery 1978.
Wine maker: Harold Pfeiffer. Visits. 4,000 cases. 211 acres in Santa Maria Valley. (Part of the 38,000-acre James Flood Ranch.)

Ravenswood
San Francisco, *San Francisco*. Founded 1976.
Owner and wine maker: Joel Peterson. Visits by appt. 15,000 cases. Wines: Zin., Cab.Sauv.

Raymond Vineyards
St. Helena, *Napa*. Founded 1974.
Principal: Roy Raymond Sr. Visits. 110,000 cases. 90 acres of

Chard., Cab.Sauv., Ch.Bl., Ries.

An expanding family winery in experienced hands makes high-quality, typical oaky Napa Chardonnay and Cabernet in the same vein.

Ridge Vineyards

Cupertino, *Santa Clara*. Founded 1959.
Owner: Otsuka Co. (since 1987). Wine maker: Paul Draper. Visits. 40,000 cases. 50 acres. Vineyards near the winery plus grapes bought elsewhere (see below). Wines: Cab.Sauv., Zin., Pet.Sir.

One of California's accepted first-growths, isolated on a mountain-top south of San Francisco in an atmospheric old stone building that is cooled by a natural spring. The adjacent vineyard produces Montebello Cabernet but Cabernet and Petite Sirah are also bought at York Creek, Napa, and Zinfandel from Geyserville, Sonoma, Paso Robles and San Luis Obsipo.

All the wines have a reputation for darkness, intensity and needing long ageing. The York Creek Cabernet is heavier than the elegant, lingering Montebello. The Zinfandel from Geyserville can smell of honey, a beautiful wine. Ten years is a good age to allow for Montebello to reach maturity.

Ritchie Creek

St. Helena, *Napa*. Founded 1974.
Owner and wine maker: Richard Minor. 1,000 cases from 10 acres of vineyard in Spring Mountains. Wines: Cab.Sauv., Chard., Viognier.

River Road Vineyards

Forestville, *Sonoma*. Founded 1977.
Wine maker: Gary Mills. 10,000 cases. Wines: Chard., Sauv.Bl., White Zin., Cab.Sauv.

River Run Vintners

Watsonville, *Santa Cruz*. First harvest 1979.
Owner: Christine Arneson. Wine maker: J. Pawloski. 2,500 cases. 4 acres. Wines: Chard., W.R., Cab.Sauv., Zin., L.H. Zin.

J. Rochioli Vineyards

Healdsburg, *Sonoma*. Founded 1979.
Owners: Joe and Tom Rochioli. Visits. 4,500 cases. 130 acres owned, 25 acres leased. Wines: Chard., Sauv.Bl., P.N.

Roederer Estate

Mendocino.
Owners: The Roederer family. Wine maker: Michel Salgues. 50,000 cases, rising to 90,000. Wines: *Méthode champenoise*.

A large-scale venture owned by the Champagne house with 450 acres in the Anderson Valley. The first vintage, released in 1988, is impressive.

Rombauer Vineyards

St. Helena, *Napa*. Founded 1982.
Co-owners: Joan and Koerner Rombauer. Wine maker: Bob Levy. Visits by appt. 15,000 cases. Wines: Chard., Cab.Sauv., Merlot.

Well-made, classic Chardonnay and Cabernet. To watch. Merlot from 1986.

Rosenblum Cellars Winery

Emeryville, *Alameda*. Founded 1978.
Wine maker: Kent Rosenblum. Visits by appt. 5,000 cases. Wines: J.R., White Zin., Zin., Nouveau, Cab.Sauv., Sparkling Gewürz.

Roudon-Smith Vineyards

Santa Cruz, *Santa Cruz*. Founded 1972.
Owners: Bob and Annamaria Roudon, Jim and June Smith. Wine maker: Bob Roudon. Visits. 12 acres owned. 10,000 cases. Grapes from Santa Cruz, Monterey, Sonoma and Mendocino.

A 2-family affair, children and all, with outstanding stylish Chardonnay, balanced between firm and smooth like a good Meursault. The Cabernet matches it well in style; the Zinfandel is more burly.

Round Hill Cellars

St. Helena, *Napa*. Founded 1978.
President: Charles Abela. Wine maker: Jim Yerkes. Visits. 300,000 cases. Grapes from Napa, Sonoma and North Coast.

Not all new Napa wineries aim at Montrachet. Round Hill supplies a wider market with good-value versions of distinct variety-plus-region character, notably Napa Gewürztraminer and Fumé Blanc; Sonoma Cabernet. Rutherford Ranch is the label for the top wines.

Rutherford Hill Winery

St. Helena, *Napa*. Founded 1976.
Partners: Bill Jaeger and Chuck Carpy. Wine maker: Jerry Luper. Visits. 150,000 cases. The partners own some 800 acres in the valley. Wines: Chard., Gewürz., Merlot., Cab.Sauv., Sauv.Bl.

Compare the partners with Freemark Abbey. Here they use their nicknames and relax. The winery was built for Souverain but sold to the present owners in 1976. Now the idea is true fruity varietals with a light touch for restaurant-drinking and the better class of picnic – which in California is saying a lot. Largest production is of Chardonnay, Merlot and Cabernet Sauvignon.

Rutherford Vintners

Rutherford, *Napa*. Founded 1976.
Owners: Bernard and Evelyn Skoda. Wine maker: Bernard Skoda. Visits. 12,000 cases. 30 acres in Napa Valley. Wines: Cab.Sauv., J.R., P.N., Chard., Merlot.

The former manager of Louis M. Martini (q.v.) aims for delicacy and succeeds in balancing his wines without excess of alcohol or oak. His Chardonnay comes from Alexander Valley, Sonoma. Chateau Rutherford is a reserve Cabernet.

St. Andrews Winery

Napa, *Napa*. Founded 1980.
President: Imre Viskelety. Wine maker: Daryl Eklund. Visits by appt. 63 acres of Chard. Wines: Chard., Sauv.Bl., Cab.Sauv.

Chardonnay specialists, producing a barrel-fermented Vineyard Chardonnay and a stainless steel-fermented Winery Chardonnay from their own vineyard, as well as Sauvignon Blanc and Cabernet from bought-in grapes. Steady excellence.

St. Clement Vineyards

St. Helena, *Napa*. Founded 1975.
Owners: Sapporo USA. Wine maker: Dennis Johns. No visits. 10,000 cases. 20 acres. Wines: Cab.Sauv., Chard., Sauv.Bl., Merlot.

A small and specialized producer who sold to Sapporo in 1987; a great success with critics at the outset, though I found early Chardonnays too alcoholic for their fruit. The balance is apparently better now. The Sauvignon is well spoken of.

St. Francis Winery
Kenwood, *Sonoma*. Founded 1979.
Wine maker: Tom Mackey. Visits. 34,000 cases (nearly all estate wine) from 90 acres of Chard., J.R., Gewürz., Merlot, Cab.Sauv. and Muscat Canelli.
Merlot is doing well, and Chardonnay and Cabernet also bring in praise.

Saintsbury
Napa, *Napa*. Founded 1982.
Partners: Richard Ward and David Graves. Visits by appt.
Approaching 32,000 cases. Wines: Chard., P.N.
Burgundian inspiration here – Chardonnay and Pinot Noir are the only wines. Many consider them the leaders in their genre in America.

San Antonio Winery
Los Angeles. Founded 1917.
Owners: the Riboli family. Wine maker: Jon Alexander.
Visits. 400,000 cases. Wines: Chard., Cab.Sauv., Ch.Bl., J.R., White Zin.

Sanford Wines
Buellton, *Santa Barbara*. Founded 1981.
Co-owners: Richard and Thekla Sanford. Wine maker: Bruno D'Alfonso. Visits by appt. 10 acres. 30,000 cases. Wines: Chard., Sauv.Bl., P.N.
A winery in the Santa Ynez Valley founded by a former partner in nearby Sanford & Benedict. Sanford has earned a name for gentle, characterful, Pinot Noir, plus Chardonnay and Sauvignon Blanc.

San Martin Winery
San Martin, *Santa Clara*. Founded 1908.
Owners: New World Wines. Wine maker: Ronald Niino.
240,000 cases (some sold in bulk). Grapes from Monterey, Santa Barbara, Mendocino and San Luis Obispo. Many table wines.
An inventive, technically excellent and bargain-priced winery shaking off a scruffy image to emerge as the leader in 'soft' (i.e. about German-strength) white wines made to taste of the grape. Riesling, Sauvignon Blanc and Chardonnay do so. Petite Sirah, Zinfandel and late-harvest wines are also good buys.

Santa Barbara Winery
Santa Barbara, *Santa Barbara*. Founded 1962.
Owner: Pierre Lafond. Wine maker: Bruce McGuire. Visits.
28,000 cases. 75 acres.
Wines: Chard., Sauv.Bl, P.N., J.R., Zin.

Santa Cruz Mountain Vineyard
Santa Cruz, *Santa Cruz*. Founded 1974.
Principal and wine maker: Ken D. Burnap. 2,500 cases from 14 acres of vineyards in Santa Cruz Mountains of P.N., Cab.Sauv.
A locally respected specialist in powerful Pinot Noir, sometimes suffering from too much alcohol.

Santa Ynez Valley Winery
Santa Barbara, *Santa Barbara*. Founded 1976.
Owner: Doug Scott. Wine maker: Michael Brown. Visits.
20,000 cases. Grapes from 110 acres in Santa Ynez Valley, Santa Barbara, planted in Sauv.Bl., Chard., Ries., Gewürz., Cab.Sauv., Merlot.
A white wine specialist celebrated from birth for marvellously confident and vital Sauvignon Blanc.

Santino Wines
Plymouth, *Amador*. Founded 1979.
President: Nancy Santino. Wine maker: Scott Harvey. Visits.
30,000 cases. Wines: Zin. (red and white), Cab.Sauv., Sauv.Bl., Ries.
Emerging as the best winery of the area; hefty Zinfandels include a sweetish near-white one rather like a South German *Weissherbst*. Also late-harvest Riesling.

Sarah's Vineyard
Gilroy, *Santa Clara*. Founded 1978.
Wine maker: Marilyn Otteman. 2,000 cases. 7 acres.
Sarah's Chardonnay has a high reputation. Merlot and Rhône-variety blends are recent ideas.

V. Sattui Winery
St. Helena, *Napa*. Founded 1885, refounded 1975 (by the same family). Owner and wine maker: Daryl Sattui. Visits. 27,000 cases, all sold at the winery.
Wines: J.R., Cab.Sauv., Chard., Sauv.Bl., Gamay Rouge, White Zin.
Good Cabernet and Riesling draw the customers. There is also a picnic ground and a deli at the winery.

Sausal Winery
Healdsburg, *Sonoma*. Founded 1973.
Principal and wine maker: Dave Demostene. 14,000 plus cases.
125 acres in Alexander Valley, Sonoma. Wines: Zin., P.N., Chard., Cab., Sauv.Bl.
A former supplier of grapes and bulk wines launched (1979) with above-average Zinfandel and others.

Scharffenberger Cellars
Ukiah, *Mendocino*. Founded 1981.
Owners: Pommery. Visits by appt. 25,000 cases. Wines: Brut, Blanc de Blanc.
Champagne-owned pioneers of Mendocino sparklers, with grapes from Anderson Valley and other areas.

Schramsberg Vineyards
Calistoga, *Napa*. Founded 1862 by Jacob Schram, 1965 by Jack Davies.
Owners: Jack and Jamie Davies. Wine maker: Gregory Fowler. Visits by appt. 50,000 cases. 40 acres in Napa Valley.
Wine: bottle-fermented sparkling wines.
Robert Louis Stevenson drank 'bottled poetry' at Schram's ornate white, verandahed house. So have I, many times, under the Davies regime. Jack has visited just about every sparkling-wine cellar on earth and learned something in all of them. He practises his mystery in shiny steel, in old coolie-driven rock tunnels, and in his forest-clearing vineyard. His Blanc de Blancs is California's subtlest and driest, most age-worthy 'champagne', the Blanc de Noirs is outstanding, juicier and more generous, deserving 2–10 years' ageing, the Cuvée de Pinot a dry 'partridge-eye' pink and the Crémant a sweet, subtly Muscat, less fizzy party wine. A prestige cuvée is planned. Also a joint venture in northern Portugal.

Schug Cellars
Calistoga, *Napa*. Founded 1981 by Walter Schug and Jerry Seps. 8,000 cases. Wines: Pinot Noir, Chard.
A young enterprise by the brilliant wine maker of Joseph Phelps (q.v.) using rock cellars cut in 1880 for the Jacob Grimm Winery. Emphasis is on single-vineyard Chardonnay and Pinot Noir, mostly from Carneros grapes. Seps also owns Storybook Mountain.

Schramsberg, high in the hills near Calistoga,
where Robert Louis Stevenson drank 'bottled
poetry' with Jacob Schram, and Jack Davies
now makes splended sparkling wine

Sebastiani Vineyards

Sonoma, *Sonoma*. Founded 1904.
Owners: The Sebastiani family. Visits. 3.8 m. cases. 300 acres
in Sonoma Valley. Many wines.
A name intimately connected with the historic little city of
Sonoma (which even has a turn-of-the-century Sebastiani
Theatre). Sebastiani moved from being a bulk producer to
high quality with smooth speed. Today their Cabernets
are remarkable, their Barbera and Gewürztramer robust
and appetizing. Former president Sam Sebastiani left in
1986 to found his own winery.

Seghesio Winery

Healdsburg, *Sonoma*. Founded 1902.
President: Eugene Seghesio 85,000 plus cases. 350 acres.
Wines: Zin., Cab.Sauv., Colombard, Ch.Bl., Zin. (white), P.N.
A long-established concern that only began to bottle its
own wines in 1980, which offer notable value.

Sequoia Grove Vineyards

Napa, *Napa*. Founded 1980.
Wine maker: James Allen. Visits. 16,000 plus cases. 24 acres.
Wines: Estate Chard., Cab.Sauv.

Shafer Vineyards

Napa, *Napa*. Founded 1979.
Partners: John and Elizabeth Shafer. Wine maker: Doug
Shafer. Visits by appt. 12,000 cases. 150 acres. Wines: Chard.,
Cab.Sauv., Merlot from 40 acres at Stag's Leap, Napa.
Producer of immaculate Napa Cabernet and Merlot and
Carneros Chardonnay.

Charles F. Shaw Vineyard and Winery

St. Helena, *Napa*. Founded in 1979.
Owner: Charles F. Shaw Jr. Wine maker: Richard Forman.
Visits by appt. 40,000 cases. 47 acres in Napa County. Wines:
Gam., Chard., Cab.Sauv., Sauv.Bl.
The Shaws live in their vineyard and for their Gamay.
With carbonic maceration, then oak ageing, they aim to
produce Napa's equivalent of a Beaujolais Cru – a Fleurie
or Chénas, a 2- or 3-year wine. Chardonnay and Fumé
Blanc have been added recently.

Shenandoah Vineyards

Plymouth, *Amador*. Founded 1977.
Wine maker: Leon Sobon. Visits. 60,000 cases. 32 acres.
Wines: Vintage Port, Zin. Port, Orange Muscat, Black
Muscat, Zin., Cab.Sauv., Sauv.Bl., White Zin.

Sherrill Cellars

Woodside, *Santa Clara*. Founded 1973.
Wine maker: Jan Sherrill. Visits. 2,500 cases from Central
Coast; also called Skyline.
Wines: Chard., Sauv.Bl., Gamay Bl., Cab.Sauv., Petite Sirah,
Zin.

Sierra Vista Winery

Placerville, *El Dorado County*. Founded 1977.
Wine maker: John MacCready. Visits by appt. 6,000 cases
from 28.5 acres owned and 8.5 acres leased. Wines: Chard.,
Fumé Bl., White Zin., Cab.Sauv., Zin., Syrah.
Rhône blends plus Syrah have joined steady Cabernet,
Zinfandel and other wines.

Silver Oak Cellars
Oakville, *Napa*. Founded 1972.
Partners: Justin Meyer and Raymond Duncan. Wine maker: J. Meyer. Visits. 21 acres. 25,000 cases of Cab.Sauv. from Alexander Valley, Sonoma, grapes.

Three kinds of Cabernet Sauvignon: one, labelled Bonny's Vineyard, is aged 3 years in wood and 2 in bottle before release. Appreciated for forthright style. The Napa and Alexander Valley wines are softer (and less expensive).

Silverado Vineyards
Napa, *Napa*. Founded 1981.
Owner: Lillian Disney. Wine maker: John Stuart, 75,000 cases. 335 acres. Wines: Chard., Sauv.Bl., Cab.Sauv., Merlot.

Silverado's Chardonnay, Sauvignon Blanc and Cabernet Sauvignon are all ripe and sophisticated and share a growing reputation. Only estate grapes are used. 1986 saw the inauguration of reserve bottlings of Chardonnay and Cabernet Sauvignon.

Simi Winery
Healdsburg, *Sonoma*. Founded 1876.
Owner: Moët-Hennessy. Chairman: Michael Dixon. President: Zelma Long. Wine maker: Paul Hobbs. Visits 130,000 cases. 294 acres in Alexander Valley and Mendocino County. Wines: Chard., Ch.Bl., Zin., Cab.Sauv., Cab.Rosé, Sauv.Bl.

Simi 1935 Zinfandel is one of the very few antique California wines to have survived in any quantity. It is marvellous. The impressive old stone winery is now directed by Zelma Long, Mondavi-trained and one of California's most respected wine traders. Her aim is unemphatic harmony, polish and total professionalism. Subtle Alexander Valley Cabernet and splended Sauvignon Blanc plus oak-aged Zinfandel. Simi's barrel-fermented and -aged Chardonnays are regularly among the very best in California. It's Cabernet Rosé is irresistible.

Sky Vineyards
Mayacamas Mountains, *Sonoma*. Founded 1979.
Wine maker: Lore Olds. 1,600 cases. 12 acres.
Wine: Zin.

Smith-Madrone
St. Helena, *Napa*. Founded 1977.
Owner and wine maker: Stuart Smith. Visits by appt. 6,000 cases from 40 acres on Spring Mountain, Napa. Wines: J.R., P.N., Cab.Sauv.

Vineyards at 1,700 feet and total hard-working dedication are making remarkable wines in a simple cellar. Sweet, lemony Riesling; Cabernet, 31 months in new barrels and still fruity. Stew Smith even has a few of the rare Viognier vines from the Rhône. There will be no more Pinot Noir after the '85.

Sonoma-Cutrer Vineyards
Windsor, *Sonoma*. Founded 1981.
President: Brice Jones. Wine maker: William Bonetti. 75,000 cases plus. 600 acres. Wines: *Méthode champenoise* and Chard.

California's outstanding all-Chardonnay specialist, with a range of excellent wines from named vineyards: Les Pierres, Cutrer, Russian River Ranches. Aiming high with a sophisticated late-disgorged blanc de blancs, a 100% Chardonnay answer to Champagne. So far, Les Pierres is the best.

Sotoyome Winery
Healdsburg, *Sonoma*. Founded 1973.
Owners: John and Susan Mitchell. Visits by appt. 3,000 cases.
10 acres. Wines: Pet.Sir., Sir, Pale Sir.

Spottswoode Vineyard and Winery
St. Helena, *Napa*. Founded 1982.
Owners: Mary Novak. Wine maker: Tony Soter. 3,500 cases.
40 acres. Wines: Cab.Sauv., Sauv.Bl.

Spring Mountain Vineyards
St. Helena, *Napa*. Founded 1968 (since 1976 on present site).
President: Michael Robbins. Wine maker: Greg Vita. Visits by
appt. 25,000 cases. 44 acres in Spring Mountain and near the
town of Napa. Wines: Cab.Sauv., Chard., Sauv.Bl.

Spring Mountain Road climbs the hills west of St. Helena
to several splendid vineyards. Robbins' Victorian house
and faintly French-looking winery ('Falcon Crest' of a
T.V. serial) stand on the first slopes. Robbins aim is
elegance and finesse.

Stag's Leap Wine Cellars
Napa, *Napa*. Founded 1972.
Owners: Warren and Barbara Winiarski. Wine maker: Robert
Broman. Visits by appt. 40,000 cases plus. 44 acres in Napa
Valley. Wines: Cab. Sauv., Chard., J.R., Merlot, Pet.Sir.,
Sauv.Bl.

Winiarski is a professor of Greek turned wine maker,
whose Cabernets have startled the French with their
resemblance to great Bordeaux. My notes are full of
'harmony, elegance, feminine, finesse'. Compared with
Bordeaux they age relatively soon, offering, at 8 years,
consistent sweetness from lips to throat. 'Cask 23' is a
riper reserve Cabernet. Stag's Leap Merlot and Chardonnay get equally good reviews, although my favourite
remains the Cabernet. These standards have been maintained for recent vintages.

Stags' Leap Winery
Napa, *Napa*. Founded 1972.
President: Carl Doumani. 17,000 cases (planned 25,000) from
110 acres. Wines: Pet.Sir., Burg., Chen.Bl., Cab.Sauv., Merlot,
Chard.

The town of Sonoma, briefly the capital of California, is the
most historic and best preserved of the wine centres. At its
Franciscan Mission, priests planted the first grapes in the region

Stirling Vineyard crowns a knoll in the Napa Valley

P. and M. Staiger
Boulder Creek, *Santa Cruz*. Founded 1973.
Wine maker: Paul Staiger. Visits by appt. 400 cases. 5 acres.
Wines: Chard., Cab.Sauv., P.N.

Steltzner Vineyard
Napa, *Napa*. Founded 1983.
Owner and wine maker: Richard Steltzner. Visits by appt.
7,500 cases. 78 acres. Wines: Cab.Sauv., Sauv.Bl., late-harvest
Gewürz. (when possible).

Robert Stemmler Winery
Healdsburg, *Sonoma*. Founded 1977.
Co-owner: Trumbull Kelly. Principal and wine maker: Robert
Stemmler. Visits. 12,000 cases. 4 acres in Dry Creek Valley,
Sonoma. Wine: P.N. from bought-in Russian River Valley
grapes.

Sterling Vineyards
Calistoga, *Napa*. Founded 1969.
Owner: The Seagram Classics Wine Co. President: Thomas
Ferrell. Wine maker: Bill Dyer. Visits. 150,000 cases. 1,100
acres in Napa Valley. Wines: Cab.Sauv., Merlot, Chard.,
Sauv.Bl., P.N.

The long white building like a Greek monastery hugs the
top of a lump in the valley floor big enough to need cable
cars to get up it. British money built it in the 1960s; Coca-
Cola bought it in 1978, and Seagrams took over in '83. Ric
Forman, now with his own winery, designed the Sterling
style of original, serious wines. The Sterling speciality

used to be an austere Cabernet with a daring level of volatile acidity, but recent vintages have been more conventional. The stress now is on single-vineyard wines. The strong, dry Sauvignon Blanc can come as a relief after some of the more tropical-fruit flavours of the valley. Chardonnay follows the same lines. Three Palms is a Merlot-based blend.

Stevenot Winery
Murphys, *Calaveras*. Founded 1978.
Principal: Barden Stevenot. Wine maker: Steve Millier. Visits. 50,000 cases. 27 acres of estate vineyard. Wines: Ch.Bl., Zin., Fumé Bl., Muscat Canelli, Chard., Cab.Sauv.
Ambitious winery well-launched with Chenin Blanc and Zinfandel, followed up by Cabernet and Chardonnay.

Stonegate
Calistoga, *Napa*. Founded 1973.
Owners: James and Barbara Spaulding. Wine maker: David Spaulding. Visits by appt. 15,000 cases. 65 acres in Napa Valley plus grapes from another 100 plus acres. Wines: Cab.Sauv., Merlot, Chard., Sauv.Bl.
Estate wines much improved recently, especially the Chardonnays and Sauvignon Blanc.

Stony Hill Vineyard
St. Helena, *Napa*. Founded 1951.
President: Eleanor W. McCrea. Wine maker: Michael Chelini. Visits by appt. 4,000 cases. 42 acres in Napa Valley. Wines: Chard., J.R., Gewürz.
Fred McCrea was the first of the flood of men from busy offices who realized that the Napa Valley offered something better. He planted white grapes in the 1940s and made 25 vintages of his own understated style of wine. Neither the variety nor the maturation grabs your attention; the point seems to be boundless vigour and depth without an obvious handle. At a 1980 tasting of all the Chardonnay vintages of the 1960s, the '62 was best, in fact fabulous, but not markedly older than the '69. 1980s vintages have perhaps been heavier and riper. Eleanor McCrea has inherited her late husband's total integrity of purpose. A second label, SHV, uses non-estate grapes.

Storybook Mountain Vineyards
Calistoga, *Napa*. Founded 1979.
Owners: Dr. J. Bernard Seps. Visits by appt. 6,000 cases. 36 acres. Wine: Zinfandel.

Stratford
Napa. Founded 1982. 20,000 cases. Wines: Chard., Sauv.Bl., Cab.Sauv., Merlot.

Rodney Strong Vineyards
Sonoma. Owner: Rodney Strong. 375,000 cases.
Single-vineyard Chardonnays and Cabernets are the mainstay.

Stuermer Winery
Lower Lake, *Lake*. Founded 1977.
Wine maker: Dr. Daniel Stuermer. Visits by appt. 8,500 cases.
Founded as the Lower Lake Winery. Apart from the Stuermer Cabernet Sauvignon, most wines go under the name of Arcadin.

Sullivan Vineyards Winery
Rutherford, *Napa*. Founded 1972.
Wine maker: James Sullivan. Visits by appt. 4,500 cases.
Wines: Cab.Sauv., Merlot, Zin., Ch.Bl.

Summerhill Vineyards
Gilroy, *Santa Clara*. Refounded 1982.
Wine maker: Gary Hada. Visits. Approaching 30,000 cases.

Sunrise Winery
Cupertino, *Santa Clara*. Founded 1976.
Owners: Ronald and Rolayne Stortz. Weekend visits. 2,500 cases. 3 acres.

Sutter Home Winery
St. Helena, *Napa*. Founded 1874, refounded 1946.
President: Louis 'Bob' Trinchero. Wine maker: Steve Bertolucci. Visits 3 m. cases. 2,200 acres. Wines: Zin.
A family operation (named after another, pre-Prohibition family) that shows the virtue of specialization – oddly rare in California. 85% of the wine used to be Zinfandel of the gutsy kind from Amador County grapes, balanced in flesh and spirit to be worth laying down for 10 years or more. Then Trinchero pioneered white Zinfandel, and the winery has grown enormously since.

Joseph Swan Vineyards
Forestville, *Sonoma*. Founded 1969.
Wine maker: Rod Berglund. 1,200 cases. 10 acres in Russian River Valley, Sonoma. Wines: Zin., Chard., P.N., Cab.Sauv.
The late Joseph Swan's Zinfandel has always been a waiting-list wine for those whose cigar-scarred palates are looking for a perceptible flavour. His son-in-law carries on.

The 'bear flag' of the short-lived California Republic flies over the winery tower of Spring Mountain, built in 1979 in the style of the last century. Behind the façade is a rock tunnel; cellars dug for Tiburcio Parrot 100 years ago

Philip Togni Vineyard

St. Helena, Napa. Founded: 1983.
Owner and wine maker: Philip Togni. Visits by appt. 1,000
cases increasing to maximum 2,000. 10 acres on Spring
Mountain. Wines: Sauv.Bl., Cab.Sauv.

Topolos (Russian River Vineyard)

Forestville, *Sonoma*. Refounded 1980.
Wine makers: Jerry and Michael Topolos. Visits. 8,000 cases.
110 acres. Wines: Zin., Pet.Sir., Alicante Bouchet, Chard.,
Sauv.Bl., Cab.Bl.

Torres Vineyards

Sebastopol, *Sonoma*. Founded 1982.
Wine maker: Miguel Torres. 21 acres. First low key vintage
appeared in 1990.

Trefethen Vineyards

Napa, *Napa*. Founded 1886, refounded 1973.
Owners: The Trefethen family. President: Gene Trefethen.
Wine maker: David Whitehouse Jr. Visits. 70,000 cases. 600
acres in Napa Valley. Wines: J.R., Chard., P.N., Cab.Sauv.,
red and white 'Eshcol'.

The Trefethens bought the former 'Eshcol' vineyards, in
mid-valley near Napa, in 1968, leased their grand old
wooden barn to Moët-Hennessy for their first vintage of
Domaine Chandon (for which they grew many of the
grapes), then started using their best grapes to make their
own wine. The whole line is highly polished and
professional (and good value). Chardonnay attracted
most notice at first, but the clean mid-weight Cabernet,
the dry Riesling with no lush or melony touches and a
Pinot Noir that shows the nervous nature of this
thoroughbred make a classy stable. Late-released
'Library' wines show remarkable ageing potential. The
'83 Chardonnay was a noble wine in 1990. Blended
'Eshcol' table wines are some of the best value in the state.
Eshcol was the valley where the monster grape cluster
grew (Numbers XIII v. 23). So is this.

Trentadue Winery & Vineyards
Geyserville, *Sonoma*. Founded 1969.
Wine makers: Leo and Evelyn Trentadue. Visits 25,000 cases.
145 acres.

Tudal Winery
St. Helena, *Napa*. Founded 1979.
Wine maker: Arnold Tudal. 2,500 cases. 7 acres.
Wines: Cab.Sauv., Chard.

Tulocay Winery
Napa, *Napa*. Owners and wine makers: W. C. and Barbara
Cadman. Founded 1975. Visits by appt. 2,400 cases. Wines:
Cab.Sauv., P.N., Chard., all from Napa Valley grapes.
A small operation making full-flavoured reds designed for
laying down.

Tyland Vineyards
Ukiah, *Mendocino*. Founded 1979.
Owners: Dick and Judy Tijsseling. Weekend visits. 12,000
cases. Shares 300 acres with Tijsseling Vineyards. Wines:
Chard. Sauv.Bl., Cab.Sauv., White Zin., Zin. Also uses the
name Mendocino Estates.

Valley of the Moon
Glen Ellen, *Sanoma*. Founded 1939.
Wine maker: Harry Parducci Jr. Visits. 30,000 cases. 200 acres.
Wines: Chard., Sauv.Bl., Sem., Cab.Sauv., P.N., Zin.

Vega Vineyards Winery
Buellton, *Santa Barbara*. Founded 1979.
Wine maker: Bill Mosby. Visits 10,000 cases. 45 acres in the
Santa Ynez Valley. Wines: Chard. Gewürz., Pineau, P.N., J.R.

Ventana Vineyards Winery
Soledad, *Monterey*. Founded 1978.
Owners: J. Douglas and Shirley Meador. 42,000 cases. (60,000
planned). 400 acres on the west side of Salinas Valley. Many
wines including a *méthode champenoise* Pinot Noir.
A grower who also supplies half a dozen wineries with
grapes for named-vineyard wines, especially Chardonnay.
Ventana's own range has good Chardonnay, Pinot Blanc,
Riesling, Chenin Blanc, a 'botrytis' Sauvignon Blanc and
as many reds.

Vichon Winery
Oakville, *Napa*. Founded 1980.
Owner: Robert Mondavi family. Wine maker: Michael Weis.
Visits. 50,000 cases all from purchased grapes. Wines: Chard.,
Cab.Sauv., Sem.
Winery in the foothills above Oakville showing a distinct
sense of style and restraint with moderately oaky, nicely
racy Chardonnay (first, 1980) and Chevrignon, an elegant,
dry, well-balanced half-and-half blend of Sauvignon
Blanc and Semillon. Cabernet Sauvignon is well-balanced
and promising. Merlot and a Stag's Leap District
Cabernet are now on the list.

Villa Mt. Eden
Oakville, *Napa*. Founded 1881, refounded 1970.
Owners: Stimpson Lane. Wine maker: Michael McGrath.
Visits. 24,000 cases. 87 acres in Oakville, Napa. Wines:
Cab.Sauv., Chard., Chen.Bl.
A historic vineyard replanted has rapidly made a name for
beautifully made dry wines, first Gewürztraminer, now
abandoned, then one of the best Chenin Blancs, since
1975. Chardonnay, in three varieties, and Cabernet of
intensity but balance.

Walker Wines
Felton, *Santa Cruz Mountains*. Founded 1979.
Wine maker: Russ Walker. Visits by appt. 1,000 cases.

Weibel Champagne Vineyards
Mission San Jose, *Alameda/Mendocino*. Founded 1945.
President: Fred E. Weibel. Wine maker: Rick Casqueiro.
Visits. 750,000 cases. 450 acres in Mendocino. Many wines,
including sparkling wines.
The speciality is sparkling wine, mostly sold under other
merchants' labels. North-coast varietals have been intro-
duced at a winery at Ukiah, Mendocino.

Wente Bros.
Livermore, *Alameda*. Founded 1883.
Owners: The Wente family (Eric, President; Philip and Jean).
Wine maker: William Joslin. Visits. 300,000 cases. 2,300 acres
in Livermore Valley and Arroyo Seco, Monterey County;
produce most varieties of table wine.
One of the greater wine dynasties of America. The
founder, Carl, started with Charles Krug in the Napa
Valley and moved to the stony Livermore Valley because
land was cheaper. His sons Herman (wine maker and
marketer, d.1961), Ernest (grape grower, d.1981) and
Ernest's son Karl (d.1977) are greatly respected names.
Karl was a bold innovator, the first in California to build
steel fermenting tanks outdoors and a pioneer of Monterey vineyards. The fourth generation bought 600 more
potential vineyard acres (old Cresta Blanca and ranching
land) in Livermore and planted in 1982-83. They have also
built a sparkling winery at Greenfield, Monterey.
White wines made their name. In the early 1960s their
Sauvignon Blanc was my favourite; bold, sappy, old
Bordeaux style. Now it and Chardonnay are even better,
and Cabernet and Zinfandel complete an extremely sound
range. Sparkling wines are the latest venture.

William Wheeler Winery
Healdsburg, *Sonoma*. Founded 1979.
Owners: Domaines Paribas. Visits. 19,000 cases. 32 acres.
Wines: Sauv.Bl., White Zin., Cab.Sauv., Chard.

Whitbread/Bollinger/Antinori
see Atlas Peak.

Whitehall Lane Winery
St. Helena, *Napa*. Founded 1980.
Owner: Hideaki Ando. Wine maker: Arthur Finkelstein.
Visits. 20,000 cases. 22 acres. Wines: P.N., Chard., Merlot,
Cab.Sauv., Ch.Bl.
Success here with Pinot Noir of fresh and lively character.

White Oak Vineyards
Healdsburg, *Sonoma*. Founded 1980.
Owner: Bill Myers. 11,000 cases. 6 acres. Wines: Chard.,
Cab.Sauv., Zin., Sauv.Bl., Ch.Bl.
Private Reserve Chardonnay is rich and ripe, the Chenin
and Sauvignon also win praise.

Wild Home Winery
Paso Robles, *San Luis Obispo*. Founded 1983.
15,000 cases. 38 acres. Wines: P.N., Cab. Sauv., Merlot, Chard.
Another Pinot Noir specialist producing impressive
results.

Winters Winery

Winters, *Solano*. Founded 1980.
Wine maker: David Storm. 7,000 cases. 21 acres. Wines: Sauv.Bl., Pet.Sir., P.N., Zin., Barbera.

Woodbury Winery

San Rafael, *Marin*. Founded 1977.
Owner and wine maker: Russell T. Woodbury. Visits by appt. 2,000 cases. Grapes from the Alexander Valley.
Woodbury uses Zinfandel, Petite Sirah, Pinot Noir and Cabernet from old vines with pot-still brandy to make port for ageing.

Woodside Vineyards

Woodside, *Santa Clara*. Founded 1960.
Owners: Robert and Polly Mullen. Wine maker: Frank Churchill. Visits by appt. 1,000 cases. 5 acres. Wines: Chard., Cab.Sauv., Zin.

York Mountain Winery

Templeton, *San Luis Obispo*. Founded 1882.
Wine maker: Steve Goldman. Visits. 5,000 cases.

Zaca Mesa Winery

Los Olivos, *Santa Barbara*. Vineyards planted 1978.
Owner: John Chrisman. Wine maker: Ken Brown. Visits. 60,000 cases. 240 acres near winery, 650 acres in Santa Maria Valley planted in Sauv. Blanc., Chard., Ries., Cab.Sauv., P.N., Zin.

With Firestone (q.v.) one of the first to plant in the Santa Ynez Valley. Pioneer vineyards on the 1,500-foot flat-topped 'mesa' (former cow country) are phylloxera-free and ungrafted. Chardonnay and Riesling were the first two successes. They were followed by Sauvignon Blanc, and the Pinot Noir became impressive after 5 years. 'Cool' as the region is, a warm summer can produce blowsy and overstrong wines.

ZD Wines

Napa, *Napa*. Founded 1969.
Partners: Norman de Leuze and Gino Zepponi. Wine maker: Robert De Leuze. Visits by appt. 18,000 cases. 3.5 acres of Cab.Sauv., with grapes bought in Napa, Sonoma, Santa Barbara and San Luis Obispo for Chard. and P.N.
Pinot Noir and Chardonnay are the focus; the philosophy is to find the right grapes in any part of California.

Classification

The American wine trade has begun to see the advantages of some system of classification to help consumers through the jungle of California wine names. The first publicized attempt was made in 1982 by Ronald Kapon of the magazine *Liquor Store*, in association with *Les Amis du Vin* magazine, by asking 39 of the nation's leading retailers and restaurateurs to classify the best Cabernets of California in a fashion, and to a number, modelled on the 1855 classification of Bordeaux. No doubt later models of a classification, if the idea persists, will modify this arbitrary limit on numbers. It should also be remembered that the short track record of most of these wines bears no resemblance to the tightknit group of Médoc châteaux over a century of trading. Nonetheless the list has some historic value.

The 'first growths' were Beaulieu Private Reserve, Chappellet, Chateau Montelena, Heitz Martha's Vineyard, Mayacamas, Robert Mondavi Reserve, Stag's Leap Wine Cellars and Sterling Reserve.

The 'second-growths' were Burgess, Burgess 'Vintage Selection', Caymus, Clos du Val, Diamond Creek 'Red Rock Terrace' Diamond Creek 'Volcanic Hill', Jordan, Robert Mondavi, Joseph Phelps 'Insignia', Ridge 'Montebello', Ridge 'York Creek', Spring Mountain, Trefethen, Villa Mt. Eden.

When James Laube published his *California's Great Cabernets* in 1989 he too made a choice: his top wines were: Beaulieu Private Reserve, Beringer Private Reserve, Caymus Special Selection, Chateau Montelena, Diamond Creek Gravelly Meadow, Diamond Creek Volcanic Hill, Dunn Howell Mountain, Heitz Martha's Vineyard, Inglenook Reserve Cask, Mayacamas Vineyards, Robert Mondavi Reserve, Opus One, Joseph Phelps Eisele Vineyard, Joseph Phelps Insignia, Ridge Monte Bello, Stag's Leap Wine Cellars Cask 23.

An old water pump marks the Oakville Vineyards of Villa Mt. Eden

THE PACIFIC NORTHWEST

If, in the early 1970s, America was waking up to superlative quality from Napa and Sonoma, by the end of the decade the *avant-garde* were heralding the Pacific Northwest as the coming wine region, with strong hints that the new area would make something closer to the European model: wines less overbearing than the Calfornia champions. Much of this potential has been fulfilled, although the true taste of the Northwest has yet to emerge from a welter of grapes, wineries and valleys.

It was apparently a visit to Washington in 1967 by André Tchelistcheff, the dean of the Napa Valley, that gave the tentative wine makers of the northwest the confidence to start operating on a commercial scale. He tasted a Gewürztraminer, a variety that had not up to then performed well in California, and recognized the potential of more northerly growing conditions for grapes that tend to overripen in a warm climate. In fact the previous year David Lett, a California-trained wine maker, had shown his conviction by planting Pinot Noir, another problem grape in California, in the Willamette Valley south of Portland, Oregon.

Twenty five years has been ample time to justify their hopes. In fact it took only nine. In 1979, Lett's 1975 Pinot Noir was placed second in a competitive blind tasting in Paris organized by Robert Drouhin of Beaune: Drouhin's own 1959 Chambolle-Musigny won first place. The Oregon climate, as uncertain as that of Burgundy, seems ideal for this most temperamental grape.

But why the great leap over hundreds of miles of northern California to grow grapes so much farther north than Mendocino County, which already has cool and foggy areas? The answer seems to lie in the configuration of the coastal hills. North of Mendocino the barrier to ocean fog and rain clouds dies away in more broken terrain. Not until north of the Oregon border does the Coast Range reassert itself as a rain catcher, sheltering in the south the Umpqua, then farther north the Willamette Valley. The rainfall is a reasonable 40 inches, and the latitude just that of Bordeaux.

In complete contrast the vineyards of Washington have been planted two ranges back from the ocean, east of the much higher Cascade Mountains, in an area with a mere ten inches in a wet year – the Columbia River Basin and in particular the Yakima Valley. Its first vines were the American Concord, grown for jelly-making. But its deep sandy soil, long summer daylight and hot sunshine have proved ideal for wine grapes. The indications are that the latitude – 100 miles farther north than the Willamette Valley – and the continental extremes of temperature (very cold in winter and surprisingly chilly even on a summer night) are most suited for white grapes. They ripen well while keeping remarkably high acidity, with consequent intensity and length of flavour. A bonus has been a top dressing of free fertilizer: ash from the eruption of Mount St. Helens.

Thus the Pacific Northwest is not one area but two, very distinct in conditions and style, with over 16,000 acres of vines and over 100 wineries. What is confusing at present is that Oregon, which has the smaller number of vineyards, a mere quarter of the total, has much the same number of wineries. Many Oregon wines therefore contain Washington-grown grapes. Happily, though, Oregon has state wine laws that should put California to shame. The label must say where the grapes were grown. What is more, the old 'generic' terms (Chablis, Burgundy, etc.) are banned. And 'varietal' wines must contain 90 per cent of the grape variety named, with the sensible exception of Cabernet Sauvignon, where other Bordeaux varieties may make up 25 per cent of the blend.

Three regional designations are permitted on Oregon labels: Willamette Valley (AVA: nine counties from Portland 100 miles south to Eugene); Umpqua Valley (AVA: Douglas county, centred on Roseburg, another 50 miles south); and Rogue Valley (Jackson and Josephine counties, centred on Grant's Pass, 50 miles south again).

Washington's vineyards are concentrated in the Yakima Valley, but its established wineries are centred around Seattle. The three AVAs are Columbia Valley, Yakima Valley and Walla Walla Valley, south of the State line. Up to now the grapes have been transported the 150 miles over the Cascades to Seattle, but several companies have now built wineries near the vineyards, between the ridges of such unvinous-sounding ranges as the Rattlesnake and the Horse Heaven hills. Watch out for such names as Ahtanum Ridge and Wahluke Slope.

Washington has many young wineries producing promising wines. For the first time the state now has more *vinifera* wineries than Oregon. The proportion of grapes trucked to Oregon wineries that have no significant plantings accounts for the discrepancy, in a number of instances, between the annual production figures and the acreages. Neighbouring Idaho has six wineries on the latitude of central Oregon (but without its rain).

OREGON WINERIES

Adelsheim Vineyard
Newberg, OR 97132. Willamette Valley.
Owners: David and Virginia Adelsheim. Wine maker: David Adelsheim. 14,000 cases. 25 acres Chard, P.N., J.R., Sauv. Blanc. The winery first crushed in 1978, using mainly Washington grapes. Chardonnay, Sauvignon and Riesling are well made. Pinot Gris is a recent success and Chardonnay is impressive.

Alpine
Monroe, OR 97456. Upper Willamette Valley. Visits. Owners: Daniel and Christine Jepson. Wine maker: Daniel Jepson. 5,000 cases, 20 acres, Chard., Cab.Sauv., Gewürz., P.N., J.R. Estate-grown grapes make consistently fine, elegant Chardonnay, crisp Riesling and promising Pinot Noir.

Amity Vineyards
Amity, OR 97101. Willamette Valley.
Owners: Myron and Ione Redford, Janis Checchia. Wine maker: Myron Redford. 10,000 cases, 100 acres, mainly Chard., Gewürz., P.N., J.R.
An established winery, best so far for Pinot Noir, blended from Oregon and Washington grapes, both barrel-aged and 'Nouveau'.

Domaine Drouhin
Owner: Robert Drouhin.
A statement of faith in Oregon by the leading Beaune grower/négociant, whose oenologist daughter Véronique is in charge of 100 acres of vines in the Dundee Hills, not far from David Lett. No bottled results yet: one to watch.

Elk Cove Vineyards
Gaston, OR 97119. Willamette Valley.
Owners and wine makers: Joe and Pat Campbell. Visits. 12,000 cases. 45 acres Chard., Gewürz., P.N., J.R.
Individual vineyard bottlings to highlight importance of 'terroir' give increasingly good Pinot Noir, occasional botrytis Rieslings and barrel-fermented Chardonnays.

The Eyrie Vineyards
Dundee, OR 97128. Willamette Valley.
Owners: David and Diana Lett. Visits by appt. 8,000 cases. 46 acres Chard., Muscat Ottonel, P.Gris, P.Meunier, P.N. The pioneer of Pinot Noir in Oregon, making wine of great finesse that continues to improve after others have faded. Lett sees Pinot Gris as a better source of cash flow than Chardonnay, needing less age and no oak. He also produces unique Pinot Meunier, and dry Muscat Ottonel, but studiously avoids Riesling.

Hillcrest Vineyard
Roseburg, OR 97470. Umpqua Valley.
Owner: Richard Sommer. Wine maker: Phillip Gale. Visits. 13,000 cases, 35 acres Cab.Sauv., Gewürz., P.N., J.R.
The first post-Prohibition winery in Oregon, founded in 1961. Sommer specializes in Riesling, particularly late-harvest wines with decided sweetness and some noble rot. Umpqua is marginally warmer than Willamette – enough to encourage Cabernet and round out Pinot Noir.

Knudsen-Erath Winery
Dundee, OR 97115. Willamette Valley.
Owners: C. Calvert Knudsen and Richard Erath. Wine maker: Richard Erath. Visits. 40,000 cases. 45 acres Chard., P.N., J.R.

Oregon's second biggest winery, founded 1972, best regarded for Pinot Noir and Riesling, which are notable value for money. Now making Oregon Brut sparkling wine. Richard Erath pioneered the planting of *Vitis vinifera* in Oregon.

Panther Creek
Owner: Ken Wright.
A Californian, well-versed in Pinot Noir, is doing promising things with Willamette Valley wines.

Ponzi Vineyards
Beaverton, OR 97007. Willamette Valley.
Owners: Richard and Nancy Ponzi. Wine maker: Richard Ponzi. 9,000 cases. 12 acres Chard., P.Gris, P.N., J.R.
A small family operation but highly regarded, especially for dry Riesling and Chardonnay, and a house blend, 'Oregon Harvest'. Rather blunt, solid Pinot Noir.

Rex Hill
Newberg, OR 97132.
Owner: Paul Hart and Jan Jacobsen. Wine maker: Lynn Penner Ash. Visits. 9,000 cases. 18 acres Chard., P.N.
Firmly committed to Pinot Noir with a range of single-vineyard wines (Dundee Hills, Medici etc) and Chardonnay.

Shafer
Forest Grove, OR 97116.
Owner and wine maker: Harvey Schafer. Visits by appt. 8,000 cases. 20 acres. P.N., Chard., Ries., Sauv., Blanc., Gewürz.
A firm belief that quality stems primarily from the vineyard motivates Shafer, whose Chardonnay and Riesling have been praised. Also specialist in very good Pinot Noir, which produces both red and rosé.

Sokol Blosser Winery
Dundee, OR 97115. Willamette Valley.
Owners: The Sokol and Blosser families. Wine maker: Robert McRitchie. 21,000 cases. 45 acres Chard., Merlot, P.N., J.R.
The largest Oregon winery with a wide range of products including Merlot, Sauvignon Blanc and Müller-Thurgau, as well as the more typical Willamette Valley grapes. Merlot and slightly sweet Riesling are all successes with the critics. Yarnhill County Chardonnay is particularly promising, as is late-harvest Riesling.

Tualatin Vineyard
Forest Grove, OR 97116. Willamette Valley.
Owners: Bill Malkmus and William Fuller. Wine maker: William Fuller. 20,000 cases, 85 acres Chard., Gewürz., P.N.
The third-largest Oregon winery and one of the most consistent in the northwest. They have switched from Washington to home-grown grapes. Riesling, dry Muscat and Gewürztraminer have been particular successes. Estate-bottled Pinot Noir has caught up with the whites recently. Bill Fuller did a stint with the Louis Martini winery in the Napa Valley. A very experienced wine maker and a great ambassador for Oregon wine.

Yamhill Valley
McMinnville, OR 97128.
Owner: Partnership managed by Denis Burger. Wine maker: Denis Burger. 10,000 cases. 100 acres Chard., P.N.
Established in 1983 and gained acclaim with their first Pinot Noir and are continuing to do so.

Laboratory analysis plays its part in developing the Northwest's wines

OTHER PRODUCERS

Adams Vineyard
Portland. Owner: Peter Adams. Wine maker: David Ramey. 4,000 cases. Est. 1985. Chard. and P.N., both good.

Arterberry
McMinnville. Wine maker Fred Anterberry, Jr. 10,000 cases. P.N., Chard. for *méthode champenosie*. Archetypal Oregon family winery in the heartland of Oregon's wine industry, the Red Hills of Dundee. Established in 1979, began by making *méthode champenoise*. Still wine production started in 1982.

Bethel Heights Vineyard
Salem. 4,000 cases. 51 acres. Est. 1984. Owners: the Casteel family. P.N., Chard., Chenin Blanc. In the Eola Hills, a distinctive new area in an old volcanic crater.

Broadley Vineyard
Est. 1976. Owners: The Broadley family. Wine maker: Craig Broadlet. 3,500 cases. 15 acres Chard., P.N. The winery is a converted brick factory and produces Burgundian-style Pinot Noir and Chablis-style Chardonnay.

Château Benoit
Carlton (Willamette). Owners: Fred and Mary Benoit. Wine maker: Gerard Rottiers from Chablis. 10,000 cases. 42 acres, Chard., M.-Thurgau, P.N., J.R.

They are particularly proud of their sparkling wine.

Ellendale Vineyards
Dallas (Willamette). Owners: Robert and Ella Mac Hudson. Wine maker: Robert Hudson. 5,000 cases. 13 acres. Variety of wines, from White P.N. to Merlot, Chard. to Cab.Franc. 75% of their production is fruit and berry wine.

Forgeron Vineyard
Elmira (Willamette). Owners: George and Linda Smith. Wine maker: George Smith. 10,000 cases. 20 acres, 14 bearing. Cab.Sauv., Chard., M.-Thurgau, P.Gris, P.N., J.R. particularly good. One to watch.

Garden Valley Winery
Roseburg. 6,000 cases. Wine maker Richard Mansfield trained at Geisenheim, as is evident in the wines, both red and white.

Girardet Cellars
Est. 1971. Owner and wine maker: Philippe Girardet. 18 acres Chard., J.R., P.N. A Swiss with a high reputation for his classic-style Riesling and Chardonnay.

Henry Winery
Umpqua. Owners: Scott and Sylvia Henry. Wine maker: Scott Henry who began his wine making career by

designing oenological equipment. 10,000 cases. 31 acres, Chard., Gewürz., P.N.

Hidden Springs Winery
Amity (Willamette). Owners: The Byard and Alexanderson families. Wine makers: Don Byard and Alvin Alexanderson. 3,500 cases. 20 acres, Chard., P.N., J.R.

Hinman Vineyards
Eugene (Willamette). Owners and wine makers: Doyle Hinman and David Smith. 35,000 cases. 25 acres. One of the largest and most advanced wineries in the state. Gewürz., P.N., J.R. and good Cabernet from Washington grapes.

Hood River Vineyards
Hood River (on the Columbia River east of Portland). Owners: Cliff and Eileen Blanchette. Wine maker: Cliff Blanchette. 4,000 cases. 12 acres, Chard., Gewürz., Zin., P.N., J.R.

Montinore
Forest Grove. Major new (1987) venture: 425 acres planted, 150 P.N. To watch with interest.

Oak Knoll Winery
Hillsboro (Willamette). Owners: Ron and Marjorie Vuylsteke and John R. Kobbe. Wine maker: Ron Vuylsteke. 32,000 cases. No vineyards. Principal wines: Chard., Gewürz., P.N., J.R.

Oregon Estates Winery
Eugene. Seltzer and Dilley families.
Wine maker: Mike Dilley.
Rogue River
Grants Pass. Est. 1984 with 4 acres.
Chard. and Cab. Await results.
Siskiyou Vineyards
Est. 1978. Owner: C.J. "Suzi" David.

Wine maker: Donna Devine. 6,000
cases. 12 acres Cab.Sauv., Zin., P.N.
The southernmost winery in Oregon.
Good Cabernet and Pinot Noir.
Valley View Vineyards
Jacksonville (Applegate Valley). 7,000
cases. 26 acres. Wine maker: John
Guerrero. Slow-maturing Cab., good

Merlot, Chardonnay from a warm
corner. Muscat.
Veritas Vineyard
Newberg (N. Willamette Valley). Est.
1984. 20 acres. 3,000 cases. Owner: John
Howieson. P.N., Chard.

MAJOR WASHINGTON WINERIES

Arbor Crest
Spokane. Owners: the Mielke family. Wine maker: Scott
Harris. Est. 1982. Visits. 45,000 cases. 90 acres Chard.,
Cab.Sauv., Sauv.Blanc., Merlot, J.R.
Good wine making and ample capital have made this
Washington's most prolific medal winner. Sauvignon
Blanc, Merlot, Cabernet Sauvignon all arrive with perfect
acids and sugars needing little or no correction.

Château Ste. Michelle
Woodinville, WA 98072. Owner: US Tobacco. Wine makers:
Peter Bachman and Cheryl Barber. Visits. 1m. cases. 3,000
acres Chard., Cab.Sauv., Sauv.Blanc., Gewürz., Chenin Sem.,
Merlot, P.N., J.R., port.
Much the biggest concern in the Northwest, and with its
top wines among the best. The large showpiece winery at
Woodinville, 15 miles northeast of Seattle, has been
outgrown and in 1983 the 26 million dollar River Ridge
facility, which is three times as big, was built on the
Columbia River near Paterson. They have also restored an
old winery, at Grandview in the Yakima Valley, which is
used for fermentation of red wines. Grapes are all planted
on their own rootstock and come from two areas of the
Columbia Basin: Cold Creek (proving very successful for
Cabernet and Merlot) and Grandview, where whites do
best. The wines cover the full spectrum, all notably well
made, the whites being especially successful in the local
market.
Ste. Michelle, by virtue of its size, its technical
professionalism and its marketing ability, stands as a
worthy flagship for the whole wine making industry in the
Northwest. Oregon would benefit from something similar itself.

Chinook
Prosser, Yakima Valley. Est. 1984. 2,000 cases. Wine maker:
Kay Simon. Chard., Sauv.Bl.
Small-scale operation aiming for top quality and
succeeding.

Columbia (formerly Associated Vintners)
Bellevue, WA 98004. Est. 1962. A private corporation with 25
stockholders. Wine maker: David Lake, MW. 85,000 cases, no
vineyards. Visits by appt.
One of the pioneers of the Northwest, originally (1962) a
group of professors at the University of Washington.
Since 1976 it has been a fully commercial operation using
Yakima Valley grapes and directed by a British Master of
Wine, who worked with David Lett in Oregon. Now
making a wide variety of excellent wines including
Gewürztraminer, Cabernet Sauvignon, Merlot, Semillon,
Chardonnay and Riesling. The policy is to buy in grapes,
at any rate until vineyards have established a track record.
They have contracts with some of the best grape growers,
particularly Otis Vineyards and Red Willow and Wyckoff
in the Yakima Valley.

Columbia Crest Winery
Patersen, WA 98072. Wine maker: Doug Gore. Chard.,
Cab.Sauv., Sauv.Blanc., Merlot.
90% of the winery is underground making humidity and
temperature control easier, and providing excellent
storage conditions. Doug Gore takes the quality of his
wines very seriously and makes a good cross-section of
varietal wines, the best of which are the Merlot, the
Cabernet Sauvignon, the Sauvignon Blanc and the
Chardonnay.

Covey Run
(formerly Quail Run) Zillah, Yakima Valley WA 98953. Est.
1982. Wine maker: Dave Crippen. 40,000 cases. 180 acres.
Chard., Cab.Sauv., Fumé Blanc, Merlot, J.R.
An attractive winery making popular wines. Also
produce 'Ice Wine' from berries harvested in January.
Very sweet and intense.

Hinzerling
Prosser, Yakima Valley. Wine maker: Mike Wallace. First
vintage 1976. Visits. 6,000 cases. 30 acres. Ries., Gewürz.,
Cab.Sauv.
A family affair capable of excellent wine (such as botrytis
Gewürztraminer), but not consistent.

The Hogue Cellars
Prosser, WA 99350. Owners: Hogue family. Mike Hogue is
president and general manager. Wine maker: Rob Griffin.
Visits. 60,000 cases. 250 acres. Chard., Sem., Chenin Blanc,
Ries., Cab.Sauv., Merlot.
Substantial and consistent family winery, worth follow-
ing for a wide range of wines, especially whites.

Kiona Vineyards and Winery
Benton City, WA 99320. Est. 1979. Owners: Jim Holmes and
John Williams. Wine maker: Jim Holmes. Visits. 10,000 cases.
30 acres Chard., Cab.Sauv., Chenin Blanc, Merlot, J.R.
Fermentation and lab. work takes place in the Holmes'
garage and storage in the Williams' garage.

F.W. Langguth
Mattawa. 60,000 cases. 265 acres. First vintage 1982. Wine
maker: Max Zellweger.
Big-scale German investment in a state-of-the-art winery
designed to produce clean Riesling. No oak here.

Latah Creek
Spokane, WA 99216. Est. 1982. Wine maker and owner: Mike
Conway. Visits. 15,000 cases. No vineyards.
Emphasis on light fruity white wines with crisp acidity;
Chenin Blanc a particular success.

Leonetti

Walla, Walla. WA 99362.
Est. 1977. Wine maker Gary Figgins.
Visits by appt. 1,700 cases.
3 acres Cab.Sauv. and Merlot.

Selected grapes and new oak make for expensive but very worthwhile Merlot and Cabernet.

Mount Baker

Deming, WA 98244. First vintage 1982.
Owner: Al Stratton. Wine maker: Kurt Larsen.
Visits. 12,000 cases. 25 acres.
Chard., Gewürz., M.-Thurgau,
Madeleine Angevine.

Cool location has led to stress on whites. Much research for Washington State University into oak and different grapes.

Neuharth

Sequim, WA 98382. First vintage 1979. Owners: Eugene and Maria Neuharth. Wine maker: Eugene Neuharth. Visits. 2,570 cases. Grapes from Sagemoor: Chard., Cab., Merlot.

Grape-growing limited to an experimental plot of 34 varieties.

Preston

Pasco, WA 99301, Yakima Valley. Est. 1976. Owners: Bill and Joann Preston. Wine maker: Tomas Sans Souci. 80,000 cases. 181 acres. 14 varieties including Chard., Cab. Sauv., Fumé Blanc, Merlot, J.R.

Wide range from a quality-conscious operation.

Quilceda Creek

Snohomish, WA 98290.
Est. 1978. Owners: Alex and Jeanette
Golitzin. Wine maker: Alex Golitzin. 1,000 cases. Cab.Sauv.

Alex Golitzin concentrates singlemindedly on making great Cabernet in the Médoc tradition, and he has already made the best in the Northwest.

Salishan

La Center, SW Washington. Est. 1971. Owner/winemaker:
Joan Wolverton. 2,000 cases. 12 acres. P.N., Ries., Chard.,
Cab.Sauv.

Snoqualmie Winery

Snoqualmie, WA 98065.
Owner: Robert Rohan. Wine maker: Michael Januik.
Visits. 80,000 cases. 280 acres.
Chard., Fumé Blanc, Cab.Sauv., Merlot.

Founded in 1983 by Joel Klein who had formerly worked for Château Ste. Michelle, where he helped to design the winery.

Station Hills Vineyard and Winery

Wapato, WA 98951. Owner: Partnership.
David and Susanne Staton, general partners.
Wine maker: Rob Stuart. Visits by appt.
40,000 cases. 16 acres.
Chard., Cab.Sauv., Sauv.Blanc, Merlot, J.R.

The Stantons have moved from growing apples to growing grapes in what are now high-tech vineyards.

MAJOR IDAHO WINERIES

Ste. Chapelle

Caldwell, ID 83605. Owners: the Symms family. Est. 1970.
130,000 cases. 260 acres Ries., Gewürz., P.N., plus
Washington State grapes.

Founder Bill Broich, an excellent if restless wine maker, left in 1985 having established a fine track record with Riesling, Chardonnay, Gewürztraminer and sparkling wines made from Riesling, Chardonnay and Pinot Noir.

Rose Creek Vineyards

Hagerman (100 miles east of Ste. Chapelle). Est. 1984. 2,500 cases. 35 acres. Owner/wine maker: Jamie Mertin.

Springcreek

Boise. Est. 1986. Plans for 80,000 cases. 160 acres. Chard. and Ries.

OTHER REGIONS OF THE USA

The experience of centuries has seemed to show that the true wine-vine, *Vitis vinifera*, cannot successfully be grown in the climate of most of North America. The problems are extremes of cold in the north and centre and of heat and humidity in the south. The cold simply kills the vines in winter. Humidity brings rampant mildew; the heat of southern summers, a general malfunction of the vine (instead of respiring at night and building up sugar the plant continues to grow; the sugar is used in excessive foilage and the grapes, despite months of broiling heat, are scarcely ripe). The south, moreover, is plagued with a bacterial malady of the vine called Pierce's disease, transmitted by leaf-hoppers.

Two regions, the northeast (led by New York State) and the southeast, have strong wine traditions of their own based on native grapes which are adapted to their local climate. The New York industry is seeing a great revival (*see* pages 483–484). In the south the grape is the Muscadine, or Scuppernong, a plant very unlike the classic wine-vine (its grapes are like clusters of marbles with tough skins that slip off the flesh). The powerful flavour of its sweet wine was once immensely popular in America in a famous brand called

Virginia Dare. Scuppernong still flourishes but bears no relation to the wines of the rest of the world.

But now almost every state of the Union outside these areas has hopeful wine makers – hopeful of seeing their industry, fledgling or a century old, as some of them are, establish itself as part of the American wine boom.

A number of long-established wineries have distinct local markets. These tend, however, to be a disincentive to experimenting with new grapes. When it has been assumed for so long that *Vitis vinifera* cannot be grown, it is a brave wine maker who does more than dip a toe in the water with an acre or two of experimental planting.

With modern knowledge more and more dippers are reporting success. There are certainly odd spots, and probably quite large areas, where the micro-climate makes *vinifera* a practicable proposition after all. Isle St. George in Lake Erie, for example, now has 50 acres of *vinifera* vines which have survived winters with temperatures down to −17°C – but only by dint of being buried, as the Russians bury their vines, under 16 inches of earth for the winter. There is also a new race of hybrid vines, crosses

between *vinifera* and American natives, which show the hardiness of the natives without their peculiar flavours. These French-American hybrids have established themselves as the mainstay of the northeastern wine industry and many believe that their wine, unexciting up to now, can be greatly improved. The problem is that their names at present have little consumer appeal.

The wine boom is being led from the metropolitan areas of America, which have latched on to the varietal names of California. Riesling, Chardonnay, Cabernet Sauvignon have become household words. Seyval Blanc, Chelois, De Chaunac and half a dozen other hybrids have a long way to go. At present, in fact, wine growers in the eastern and central states are looking three ways at once: at the old American varieties of *Vitis labrusca*, the exciting but risky *viniferas*, and the hybrids between the two.

New York State has the biggest and best-established wine industry, but there is really no reason to think that it has overwhelming natural advantages. What the other regions lack is a bold entrepreneur to interpret their increasing range of wines to the critical metropolitan public.

NEW YORK STATE

The wine industry in New York State, long-established around the Finger Lakes south of Lake Ontario, has up to now been considered a maverick backwater by most wine lovers. Basing its wine-making on varieties and chance hybrids of the native *Vitis labrusca*, its characteristic wines have the peculiar scented *labrusca* character known as 'foxi-ness'. Most also have high acidity, usually masked by considerable sweetness.

Over the last 40 years the non-foxy French-American hybrids have become accepted by all but the most conservative wineries. While their wine has not yet proved exciting by European California standards, it is usually acceptable and occasionally very good. There are now several companies in New York, as elsewhere in the east, who see it as the mainstream future for their industry. At present about a quarter of New York wine is 'hybrid'.

Since the mid-1950s, however, there has been a vocal minority, originally led by Dr. Konstantin Frank, dedicated to proving that *vinifera* vines can successfully be grown in the Finger Lake area. Their successes, at least with white wines, have convinced many (though the hard winter of 1980 was a serious setback to this faith). There are now, therefore,

three parallel and often interwoven wine cultures in New York. The notes on the wineries below show which way the different companies are inclined.

America's wine boom started to affect New York in the mid-1970s, but in the late '80s there were setbacks. First Seagram and then Coca-Cola decided that the industry could be expanded. Seagram bought Gold Seal, the most forward-looking of the big wineries – but sold it again in 1990. Coca-Cola bought Taylors and Great Western. In 1976 the State law was changed to encourage 'farm wineries', lowering the licence fee for firms producing less than 50,000 gallons (about 21,000 cases) a year and easing restrictions on their sales.

The result was the rapid start-up of exactly the sort of small, open-minded enterprises New York needed to improve its image. Some three dozen small wineries were born or reborn, mainly in the Finger Lakes but also in the Hudson River Valley above New York City – which has a long history of nearly being a wine region – and on Long Island, where the maritime climate is much kinder than upstate. Long Island is booming, with several wineries benefitting from a 1985-established AVA.

NEW YORK STATE WINERIES

Benmarl Wine Company

Marlboro, N.Y. 12542. Founded 1957. Owners: Mark and Dene Miller. 10,000 cases. 75 acres of Verdelet, Vignoles, Chelois, Chard., Cab.Sauv., Seyval Bl., Baco Noir.

The restoration of a historic vineyard site in the Hudson River Valley where the hybrid Dutchess was raised in the 19th century. The Millers run it as a cooperative of some 400 wine lovers, the Société des Vignerons, who help finance, pick and drink their range of varietal Seyval, Baco Noir and Chardonnay and blended Cuvée du Vigneron. Their wines are all highly regarded in New York. The Chardonnay can be excellent.

Bully Hill Wine & Champagne Co.

Hammondsport, N.Y. 14840. Founded 1958. Owner: Walter S. Taylor. Wine maker: Gregg Learned. Visits. 70,000 cases. 175 acres.

The only member of the Taylor family still making wine – on the original family property on Lake Keuka. Wines are both *labrusca* and hybrids, well thought of as some of the best of the old school, and 'Champagne'. Splendid labels.

Canandaigua Wine Company, Inc.

Candaigua, N.Y. 14424. Founded 1945. A public company. Wine maker: Dominic Carisetti. 18m. cases. No vineyards.

Producers of *labrusca* wines under the brand names Richards (Wild Irish Rose) and J. Roget. Reputedly the nation's third-largest wine producer.

Casa Larga Vineyards Inc.

Fairport, N.Y. 14450. Founded 1976. Owners: The Colaruotolo family. Wine makers: Andrew and John Colaruotolo. Visits. 7,000 cases. 12 acres of Chard., Gewürz., Cab.Sauv., J.R.

They graft Concord and Delaware to *vitis vinifera* varieties.

Glenora Wine Cellars, Inc.

Glenora-on-Seneca, Dundee, N.Y. 14837. Founded 1977. Owners: E. Beers, E. Pierce, H. Kimball, E. Dalrymple. Wine maker: Jim Gifford. Visits. 50,000 cases. 500 acres of Chard., Ries., Seyval Bl., Cayuga, Ravat Bl.

One of the best-regarded smaller wineries of the Finger Lakes, specializing in German-style whites. Early issues of Chardonnay are also successful, and Riesling very good.

Gold Seal Vineyards Inc.

Hammondsport, N.Y. 14840

Formerly one of New York's biggest and best wineries. It was bought in 1990 by Taylors, who have closed it down, but still produce the excellent Charles Fournier 'champagne' under the Gold Seal label.

Great Western, The Pleasant Valley Wine Company

Hammondsport, N.Y. 14840. Founded 1860. Owner: Vintners International. Vineyards of Diamond. Dutchess, Delaware, Aurora, Seyval Bl., Baco Noir, Isabella.

The best wines made at Pleasant Valley, the state's oldest winery, are 'Champagne' and hybrid varietals, particularly Baco Noir, Verdelet, Aurora, de Chaunac. Others are *labrusca* and hybrid generics. Great Western 'Champagne' with orange juice makes a tolerable Buck's Fizz. The sparkling wines are fermented in bottle but disgorged and clarified by the transfer process, as are many New York 'Champagnes'. Also solera-system sherry.

Heron Hill Vineyards, Inc.

Hammondsport, N.Y. 14840. Founded 1977. Owners: Corporation. John Ingle, Jr., chairman. Wine maker: Peter Johnstone. Visits. 8,000 cases. 50 acres of Chard., Ries., Aurora, Ravat, Seyval Bl.

One of the successful new generation of wineries inclining New York towards *vinifera* wines. All their wines are crisp and 'Germanic', showing the influence of a cool ripening season, but even the Chardonnay is true to character. Good Riesling.

Hudson Valley Wine Co.

Catawba Highland, N.Y. 12528. Founded 1907. Owner: Herbert Feinberg. Wine maker: Edward Gogol. Visits. 20,000 cases. 125 acres of Delaware, Iona, Concord, Chelois, Baco Noir.

Edward Gogol was hired in 1988, he has 30 years wine making experience in California. Producers of generic-labelled chablis, burgundy, 'Champagne', etc., and varietal dry red Chelois.

Long Island Vineyard

Cutchogue, Long Island, N.Y. Founded 1973. Owners: Alexander and Louisa Hargrave. 54 acres of Chard., Riesling, Gewürz., Sauv.Blanc., P.N., Cab.Sauv.

Canada

The last decade has seen Canada emerge as a producer of some very adequate table wines to replace her formerly very poor dessert wines. There is now a total of 14,000 acres under vine, with wineries concentrated predominantly in the two provinces of British Columbia and Ontario, though a number of wineries are also developing across the rest of the country.

British Columbia, which has some 20 wineries and more than 4,000 acres of vines, is on the latitude of the Rhine, but has a wet maritime climate. The principal grape is the 'Okanagan Riesling', of unknown parentage but possibly Hungaro-American. The reds (50% of the total production) are the hybrids De Chaunac and Maréchal Foch. The biggest winery is Calona, at Kelowna, owned by Nabisco and producing the German-style Schloss Laderheim. The best is probably Chateau St. Clair, at Peachland, with Pinots Blanc and Noir, Foch, Gewürztraminer and Chenin Blanc.

Ontario, which suffers bitter continental winters although the Niagara peninsula is on the latitude of Rome, produces mainly white grapes (red accounts for 20% of production). The principal grapes are Riesling, Chardonnay, Gamay and other *vinifera* varieties, along with Vidal, Seyval Blanc, De Chaunac, Foch, Baco Noir and other hybrids. Of its 24 wineries, the largest are Andres, Bright's and Chateau Gai. Most larger wineries produce a full line of products – still white and red table wines, as well as sparkling, dessert and apéritif wines. The best wines are made by Charal (making good Seyval Blanc at Blenheim), Chateau des Charmes (Riesling, Aligoté and Chardonnay at Niagara-on-the-lake), and the pioneering Inniskillin (Foch, Riesling, Chardonnay, Gewürztraminer at Niagara). Ontario's wineries produce consistently award-winning wines.

One of New York's great surprises. The Hargraves have ideal conditions for *vinifera* vines on the North Fork of Long Island, 70 miles east of New York city with the ocean close by on three sides. Their Chardonnay and Sauvignon Blanc can easily be confused with top-rank California or Oregon wines. Cabernet and Pinot Noir are aged for 3 and 2 years respectively in new American oak barrels without losing a fine flavour of ripe fruit. Not surprisingly, neighbours are planting too.

Monarch Wine Co. Inc.
Brooklyn, N.Y. 11232. Founded 1934.
Owners: Leo Star and Meyer H. Robinson. Own vineyards also purchase Concord, Catawba, De Chaunac, Delaware.
The producers of the famous Kosher wine, Manischewitz, principally from Concord grapes. Also of Pol d'Argent, Le Premier Cru and Chateau Laurent New York State 'Champagnes' and importers of low-price European wines.

Plane's Cayuga Vineyard
Ovid, N.Y. 14521. Founded 1981.
Owners: Bob and Mary Plane. Wine maker: Dale Longwell.
Visits. 7,500 cases. 50 acres of Chard., Ries., Cayuga, Ravat, Chancellor and Vignoles.

The Taylor Wine Company Ltd.
Hammondsport, N.Y. 14840. Founded 1880. Owner: Vintners International. Wine maker: Steven Coon. Visits. 15m. cases.
1,570 acres of Dutchess, Delaware, Aurora, Seyval Bl., Baco Noir, De Chaunac and Isabella.
Producers of Taylor and Lake County brands of 'Champagnes', sherries and generics. Taylor's were the company that introduced French-American hybrids to New York and even now few of their vines are *vinifera* varieties.

Vinifera Wine Cellars
Hammondsport, N.Y. 14840. Founded 1962.
Owners: Dr Konstantin D. Frank & Sons. Wine maker: Eric Fry. Visits by appt. 9,000 cases. 70 acre vineyard with 60

European varieties (mostly) experimental, of (principally) J.R., Pinot Chard., Gewürz., P.N., Cab.Sauv., Gamay Beaujolais, Fetjaska, Pinot Gris, Pedro Ximénes, Furmint and Saperavi. The enthusiast who, with Charles Fournier, proved that *vinifera* vines will grow in upper New York State. Since 1965 he has made good, fine and sometimes brilliant white wine, including selected late-harvest Riesling, but less successful reds.

Wagner Vineyards
Lodi, N.Y. 14860. Owner: Bill Wagner. Wine maker: John Herbert and Ann Raffeto. Visits. 22,000 cases. 135 acres of Cayuga, Ravat, Seyval, De Chaunac, Ries., Chard., Gewürz., P.N., Aurora and Vidal.
An attractive Finger Lakes winery. 85% of production is dry varietal table wines. Medal-winners. The Chardonnay, including the "barrel-fermented" style is excellent, as are the Gewürztraminer and the Aurora.

Hermann J. Weimer Vineyard
Dundee, N.Y. 14837. Founded 1979.
Owner: Hermann J. Weimer. 35 acres (24 Riesling, 11 Chardonnay).
The Bernkastel-born ex-wine maker of Bully Hill has had striking success with Riesling (including a sparkling version and late-harvest) and now Chardonnay fermented in new French barrels – a departure for New York. He credits Seneca Lake, the biggest and deepest of the Finger Lakes, for the favourable Dundee microclimate. He is trying Pinot Noir, but Gewürztraminer suffers from bud injury in the winter cold.

Widmer's Wine Cellars, Inc.
Naples, N.Y. 14512. Founded 1888.
President: C. Hetterich. Wine maker: James Makepeace.
Visits. 500,000 cases. 250 acres of Niagara, Delaware, Cayuga White, Elvira, Aurora, Foch.
Best known for wood-aged sherries, Lake Niagara sweetish *labrusca* wines and Widmer-brand hybrids, mostly with generic names.

OTHER NEW YORK STATE WINERIES

Cagnasso Winery
Marlboro, N.Y. 12542. Founded 1977. Owners: Jospeh Cagnasso and June Ramey. 2,500 cases. 10 acres (80% hybrids, 20% *labrusca*). A Hudson River winery aiming at 'Italian'-style full reds and smooth, very dry whites.
Cascade Mountain Vineyards
Amenia, N.Y. 12501. Owners: The Wetmore family. Founded 1973. Wine maker: William Wetmore. 6,000 cases. 15 acres of Leon Millot, Foch, Seyval and Vidal. Careful producers of crisp, dry whites and rosé and fresh young reds, described as 'Spring' wines. Also an aged Reserved Red.
Johnson Estate
Westfield, N.Y. 14787. Founded 1962. Owner: Frederick S. Johnson. Wine maker: William Gulvin. 10,000 cases. 125 acres of Seyval Bl., Aurora, Vidal, Chancellor, Chelois, Cascade and Ives. Good-quality estate-bottled wines, including a dry white Delaware. Their French-American hybrid whites are

among the best of their kind.
Patricia & Peter Lenz
Suffolk County, Long Island, N.Y. 11058. Wine maker: Gary Gallerens. 6,500 cases. 25 acres of Gewürz., Chard., P.N., Merlot and Cab.Sauv. Close to the pioneer Hargraves property (*see* Long Island Vineyard). Very good Merlot.
Merritt Estate Winery Inc.
Forestville, N.Y. 14062. Owners: The Merritt family. Wine maker: William Merritt. 7,000 cases. 100 acres of Seyval Bl., Aurora, Maréchal, Foch, Baco Noir. A family estate making popular wines ranging from dry to very sweet, including bottled Sangria and ready-spiced mulled wine for serving hot to cold skiers.
North Salem Vineyard, Inc.
North Salem, N.Y. 10560. Founded 1965. Owner and wine maker: Dr. George W. Naumburg. 3,500 cases. 18 acres of Seyval Bl., Foch, Chancellor, Chelois, De Chaunac. A Hudson River

winery aiming to make fresh, light whites and reds for drinking young.
Royal Kedem Winery
Milton, N.Y. 12547. Owners: The Herzog family. Wine maker: Ernest Herzog. 500,000 cases. 180 acres of Seyval Bl., Aurora, De Chaunac. Chard., Sauv. Blanc., Cab.Sauv.
Walker Valley Vineyards
Walker Valley, N.Y. 12588. Founded 1978. Owner and wine maker: Gary Dross. 4,000 cases. 10 acres (55% white hybrids, 20% red hybrids, 15% Riesling, 10% Chard). A winery on a restored dairy farm.
Woodbury Vineyards
Dunkirk, N.Y. 14048. Founded 1979. Owners: The Woodbury family. Wine maker: Andrew Dabrowski. 15,000 cases. 28 acres of Chard., J.R., De Chaunac, Seyval Bl. and Niagara. An old farming family of the district who were the first (in 1970) to plant *vinifera* vines in Chautauqua County, on a gravel ridge overlooking Lake Erie.

NEW ENGLAND

Wine-making in New England is still on a small experimental scale, with opinions divided, as they are farther south, about the relative merits of hybrid and *vinifera* vines. *Vinifera* varieties will grow, at least right down by the coast where the ocean moderates the winters. Islands offer the best chance.

Martha's Vineyard, off the Massachusetts coast, now very properly has 37 acres of *vinifera* vines, at Chicama Vineyards, which grows Chardonnay, Riesling, Cabernet, Merlot and Pinot Noir.

The state of Rhode Island, deeply invaded by ocean inlets, has half a dozen small vineyards; the biggest, Sakonnet, growing both hybrid and *vinifera* vines. Prudence Island Vineyards, on that island in Narangansett Bay, has 16 acres of *vinifera* vines, the best being Chardonnay and Gewürztraminer.

Connecticut's first winery, Haight Vineyards at Litchfield, west of Hartford, managed to grow both *vinifera* (Chardonnay and Riesling) and the hybrid Maréchal Foch. Seven wineries have followed.

But there are also those who believe that the regional character of the northeast should be asserted by developing the best of the hybrids alone. The Hopkins Vineyard in New Preston, Connecticut, make attactive reds from hybrids.

New Hampshire's White Mountain vineyards seems to have dropped off the map, or perhaps gone underground, but fruit farmers as far afield as Vermont and Maine have been trying the odd patch.

East Coast vine varieties

Aurora (Seibel 5279). Early-ripening, pinky gold hybrid popular in the Finger Lakes for still and sparkling white wine, slightly peppery in taste.

Baco Noir (Baco No.1). One of the better red French hybrids for short-season regions. Dark colour, good sugar and high acid, makes slightly jammy wine capable of maturing.

Cascade (Seibel 13053). Very early, rather pale French hybrid, best for very light red or rosé.

Catawba. Famous old American variety still much grown for sparkling wine. Definitely foxy.

Cayuga. A recent white French hybrid with slightly lemony character.

Chambourcin (Joannès-Seyve 26205). A mid-season red bred in the Rhône valley, apparently very promising for quality.

Chancellor (Seibel 7053). A dark red French hybrid from the Rhône valley. Rich dark wine but disease-prone in humid areas.

Chelois (Seibel 10878). One of the best red French hybrids, healthy and widely grown for 'burgundy-style' wine.

Colobel (Seibel 8357). Intensely red-juiced blending grape.

Concord. The dark purple, powerfully foxy American grape used for jelly and sweet wines. Still the most planted.

Cynthiana (alias **Norton**, alias **Virginia Seedling**). American red grape used in the midwest for heavy foxy wines.

De Chaunac (Seibel 9549). Very hardy French red popular in Ontario and elsewhere for well-balanced wine.

Delaware. Old American pink grape, only slightly foxy, one of the standards for eastern 'Champagne'.

Dutchess. Similar to Delaware; even less foxy but also less healthy; bred in Dutchess County near the Hudson.

Elvira. A second-rate foxy old American white, dying out.

Isabella. Very foxy dark red old American variety.

Ives. Concord-style old American red, now rare.

Léon Millot (Kuhlmann 1922). Good-quality, Alsace-bred early red hybrid, similar to Maréchal Foch.

Maréchal Foch (or **Foch**) **(Kuhlmann 1882)**. One of the best red hybrids for the north; well-balanced fruity wine with moderate acid. It has Gamay genes.

Moore's Diamond. An old American white, not too foxy for moderately dry wine.

Niagara. Very foxy American white used for sweet wines.

Ravat 51. (alias **Vignoles**). A hybrid of Chardonnay being tried in the east, especially for 'Champagne'.

Ravat Noir. A French Pinot hybrid being grown experimentally.

Rayon d'Or (Seibel 4986). Healthy white French hybrid for warmer areas; well-balanced wine.

Rougeon (Seibel 5898). A red hybrid from the Rhône being tested by some growers.

Seibel (*see* the names given to the numbered crosses of this prolific Rhône-valley breeder).

Seyval Blanc (Seyve-Villard 5276). Bland but productive and healthy white hybrid rapidly becoming the most popular as a 'varietal'.

Seyve-Villard. The French breeder of Seyval Blanc and the crosses known as Villard.

Verdelet (Seibel 9110). Hardy white hybrid for the north, including Canada. Also a table grape.

Vidal Blanc (Vidal 256). Good-quality white hybrid for warmer areas. Has Trebbiano genes.

Villard Blanc (Seyve-Villard 12375). Well-established healthy heavy cropper; the Seyval Blanc of warmer areas.

Villard Noir (Seyve-Villard 18315). Red equivalent of the last; for warm areas.

THE MID-ATLANTIC

There is a growing feeling that the mid-Atlantic states of Virginia and Maryland, southern Pennsylvania and perhaps a belt stretching inland into West Virginia, Kentucky and Tennesee may have a promising future in wine-growing. It is a well-publicized fact that Thomas Jefferson had no luck, but modern vines, sprays and know-how have started to change the situation.

In the 1940s Philip Wagner made history at Boordy Vineyards, near Ryderwood in Maryland, by planting the first French-American hybrids in America. These vines had been bred by the French to bring phylloxera-resistance to France, but ironically it was to be America that appreciated their virtues of hardiness and vigour. Boordy Vineyards continues to produce hybrid wines, although it has been overtaken in ambition by others who are showing that *vinifera* is a possibility. The leader in these experiments has been Hamilton Mowbray of Montbray Wine Cellars at Westminster, northwest of Baltimore, who planted Chardonnay and Riesling in 1966 and Cabernet Sauvignon in 1972, and has been delighted with the results. A run of exceptionally cold winters unfortunately did some damage. Late-September Atlantic storms, coinciding with hurricanes, are another threat. But early October is usually fine and dry and Mowbray compares his Cabernet to Bordeaux petits châteaux, his Riesling to Alsace and his Chardonnay, aged one year in American oak, to a delicate white burgundy. Although there are only a few acres of *vinifera* vines in Maryland, the reception of the wine in Washington, D.C., is encouraging more planting. Even Mowbray, however, hedges his bets with hybrids. He has made a 'varietal' Seyve-Villard (alias Seyval Blanc) since 1966 in two styles, one young and fruity 'like a Loire wine' and the other oak-aged.

The Virginians are still wary of *vinifera*. Archie Smith of Meredyth Vineyards at Middleburg, who has been one of the leaders, was initially entirely sceptical and planted only hybrids, but has started to come round to Riesling and Chardonnay. Although they take more maintenance, are less reliable and produce smaller crops, he is encouraged by results, especially with Riesling. Much depends on the effectiveness of antirot treatments. Fungus infections develop immunity to one chemical and must be sprayed with another. Can the chemists produce enough alternatives? Barboursville Vineyards, Montdomaine cellars at Monticello and Prince Michael are also having success with Chardonnay and Riesling. The Virginia wine industry now has 40 wineries with 1,300 acres.

Foreign investors have more confidence. It made a great stir in 1976 when Zonin, a big wine company from the Veneto in Italy, bought 700 acres at Barboursville and started to plant *vinifera* vines (though the vineyard has only reached 48 acres so far). Since then a German investor, Dr. Gerhard Guth, has planted 25 acres which are said to be producing reasonable 'but light' wines. More Virginia wineries, Shenandoah, Farfelu and others, have *vinifera* trials going. The two deciding factors are going to be the health of the vines and the prices the public will pay.

Meanwhile the southeast corner of Pennsylvania apparently has much in common with Maryland. Soils and climates are very variable; there are certainly good vineyard sites among them. Frank Mazza, who abandoned *vinifera* trials at the other end of Pennsylvania on Lake Erie when 18 acres were wiped out, is happy with his south Pennsylvania Chardonnay and Riesling. He seems to be even happier with his white hybrids, which do exceptionally well in this climate.

John Crouch of Allegro Vineyards has 12 acres of Chardonnay and Cabernet Sauvignon. Richard Naylor, at York near the Maryland border, is happy with Riesling and Cabernet Sauvignon but more at ease with Vidal, Seyval, de Chaunac, Chambourcin and a host of other hybrids.

Everybody believes there is room for both schools. It is a toss-up between natural conditions and customers' reactions which comes out on top.

THE MIDWEST

Lake Michigan provides the heat storage to make life bearable for vines in parts of the northern midwest bordering the lake. Michigan is the state with most vineyards and wineries, the majority grouped not far from Chicago at the lake's southeast corner. Tabor Hill, Bronte, St. Julian and Warner are the biggest companies, the first at Hartford and the second two at Paw Paw, concentrate on hybrid vines. Bronte, in 1953, was the first company to produce a hybrid 'varietal', its red Baco.

Chateau Grand Travers is much farther north on the lakeshore, where the big bay called Grand

Traverse produces a tolerable winter microclimate which has encouraged successful planting of Riesling, Chardonnay, Merlot and Chenin Blanc.

Michigan's most surprising vineyard, however, is at Buchanan, near the lake and the Indiana border in the south. At Tabor Hill a small acreage of Riesling and Chardonnay is now more than 15 years old and steadily producing good-quality wine. Production is supplemented by grapes grown at Sagemoor Farms in Washington State and transported in refrigerated trucks – and also, as in all the eastern and widwestern wineries, by such hybrids as Vidal and Seyval Blanc and Baco Noir which carry no risk.

Wineries of the other states of the northern midwest are in Indiana, Illinois, Wisconsin and even Minnesota. Ohio's Lake Erie shore has promising *vinifera* vineyards.

The states of Missouri and Arkansas would seem improbable places to plant vines, but both have long-established vineyards. Missouri, indeed, enjoyed the distinction of having the first official appellation granted to a viticultural area in the United States, in 1980 when the Bureau of Alcohol, Tobacco and Firearms declared Augusta, just west of St. Louis, a designated region. Its first vines were planted in hills above the Missouri in the 1830s.

It is far too cold here for *vinifera* vines. Lucian Dressel, of Mount Pleasant Vineyards at Augusta, the leading wine maker of the region, makes his best white wines of the hybrids Seyval and Vidal Blanc and Riesling and his red of Villard Noir, which makes a lively, fruity wine. Dressel feels that Missouri wines can improve. At the moment the whites are better; compared with Finger Lakes hybrids they are less fruity and more full-bodied and can benefit from bottle-age.

Arkansas to the south has one unexpected outcrop of *vinifera* growing in the peculiar microclimate of a mountain plateau called Altus, settled in the 1870s by immigrants from Switzerland, Austria and Bavaria who understood mountains.

According to Al Wiederkehr, whose Swiss family founded its winery in 1880, thermal inversion currents produce a very tolerable climate in which Riesling, Chardonnay, Sauvignon Blanc, Muscat Ottonel, Cabernet, Pinot Noir and Gamay are all more or less at home. The majority of his considerable acreage – 400 acres – is planted in these grapes, although he is not burning his boats with hybrids.

And even the Mississippi Delta has its patch of Chardonnay and Cabernet, pioneers among the Scuppernongs and Muscadines.

THE SOUTHWEST

Much of the Southwest is too humid, and subject, like the deep south, to Pierce's disease, to make this a viable region for growing vines. Nevertheless, over the past two decades there has been a serious move towards establishing a modern wine industry of some quality. Prospects are positive for *vinifera* vines in certain parts of the area.

The State University of West Texas planted the biggest vineyards of the region, some 700 acres, in conditions akin to those of California's Central Valley; and it is still mainly in Texas that wineries are flourishing. Unlike in California, however, the vineyards are widely spread out across the vast state, whose total area is larger than France. There are around 450 growers and 25 wineries. Many grapes are also bought in from California and Washington State.

The cool dry climate of the high plateau area near Lubbock was the site of some of the first successful vineyards. Attention was drawn to the area by the premium wines from the Llano Estacado ('Staked Plains') ranch, where the McPherson family and their partners pioneered *vinifera* vines. Using California-style techniques, they grow Cabernet, Sauvignon Blanc, Chenin Blanc, Riesling, Gewürztraminer and Chardonnay. Many of their wines are

aged in wood and are able to hold their own against some of their Californian competitiors. Other promising Texan wineries include Pheasant Ridge in Lubbock, owned by the Cox family; Fall Creek Vineyards, 80 miles north of Austin; and Sanchez Creek in Weatherford, North Texas, where Ron Wetherington makes prize-winning, age-worthy *vinifera* wines. Ste Genevieve, at Fort Stockton, has planted a large acreage of Sauvignon Blanc and Chenin Blanc with French money and technical help.

Meanwhile several small wineries are successfully growing hybrids in the more difficult areas. In the 'dry' county of Springtown, the slightly eccentric La Buena Vida winery, led by young wine maker Steve Smith, stubbornly holds out against the *vinifera* vogue, specializing in hybrids to make passable still and sparkling wines and surprisingly rich, port-style dessert wines.

While most of the serious action is occurring in Texas, wineries are also springing up in other areas; New Mexico now has around 30 wineries – as many as Texas. Wine makers experimenting in such parts include Robert Webb of the R. W. Webb Winery in Arizona, and Michael and Patrick Johnson of La Chiripada Winery in New Mexico who produce drinkable regional wines.

AUSTRALIA

Australian wine swept into favour around the world in the mid 1980s with a suddenness that surprised almost everyone. The world was unprepared for such intensely fruity Chardonnays and Cabernet, lavishly seasoned with oak, at prices far below those for such wines in France or California. But then the world had resolutely ignored the quality of Australian wine for generations.

Until the revelation of the last few years it used to come as a real surprise to visitors to discover how important wine is in the country's life; how knowledgeable and critical many Australians are; how many wineries, wine regions and 'styles' (the favourite Australian wine word) this country, with a total population only a quarter of that of California, can profitably support. Extraordinarily little of the buzz of Australian winemanship penetrated overseas largely because her best wines are made in vast variety but in small quantities, and partly because lack of any kind of central direction made Australian labels a pathless jungle.

By the early '80s open-minded critics overseas were acknowledging that Australia's best wines are excellent: different in flavour from California's

but not a jot inferior, and presenting a far wider range of 'styles'. In Australia Shiraz (the Petite Syrah of the Rhône), Semillon and Rhine Riesling have been excellently grown for decades. First-class Chardonnay and Cabernet joined them in the '70s. Blends of Cabernet with Shiraz and Chardonnay with Semillon extend the range. California's very best wines are practically limited to Chardonnay, Cabernet and its blends with Merlot, and arguably a very small amount of Riesling and Sauvignon Blanc. In both cases Pinot Noir is on the threshold of success, but Australia, with new vineyards in cooler southern areas, probably has the edge.

The whirlwind of change and innovation is no less strong in Australia than in California, but the establishment through which it blows is far older. Until recently an astonishing number of wineries still belonged to the families that founded them over a century ago. They still have powerful traditions. Although nearly all have now changed hands, and most of their turnover today is in bulk wines sold in 'cask', or 'bag-in-box', they continue to make small high-quality lots from their best grapes. Medium-sized and little

Chatteau Tahbilk, Victoria, was established in 1860

boutique wineries have proliferated in direct competition with these established classics, adding to the alarming number of good wines there are to choose from.

Australia long ago lost any inhibitions (if she ever had any) about blending wines from different grapes and different regions – even as much as 1,000 miles apart. In these circumstances it takes a dedicated amateur to keep track of the new 'releases'. Labels carry the names of grapes, growers, makers, districts, vineyards, vintage dates and 'bin numbers' (a strange way of indicating a 'style' to the initiated). The facts (we assume) are all in good faith. But they often seem to have been compiled precisely to frighten away the honest, simple drinker.

It helps if we understand the traditions underlying the confusion. Until the recent boom, Australia's four main wine-growing states had only half a dozen quality areas of any importance. New South Wales had the (then almost moribund) Hunter River Valley, north of Sydney, Victoria had Rutherglen and its neighbourhood in the northeast, Great Western in the west (and the lonely Chateau Tahbilk in the middle). South Australia, throughout this century much the greatest producer, had the Barossa Valley,

Southern Vales and Clare, all grouped round Adelaide, and Coonawarra in the remote south. Western Australia had the Swan Valley at Perth.

In addition the Murray River, flowing between the three eastern states, irrigated large areas for low-quality wine, most of which was distilled.

Each of these areas had four grapes at most which it grew well for fine wines. And each was dominated by at most four or five considerable producers – a manageable number of permutations, even given the bin-number habit.

Once these producers began to cross regional lines, to buy grapes, vineyards, or their competitors, the pattern was blurred. Now new vineyards have been developed in a score of districts which are either entirely new to the vine but promise cooler growing conditions, or which (like many parts of Victoria) flourished as vineyards a century ago. It is still just possible to group these developments into rough geographical zones (*see* pages   –   ) – but certainly not yet to give each zone a regional character. Southeastern Australia from Adelaide to Sydney is starting to look on the map like one great wine area. Soon, it seems, the same will be true of the southwest. This does not stop your Australian enthusiast from trying to follow the 'quality of the fruit' through the maze of wine-makers' foibles.

Until Australia begins to develop a national appellation system the only means of selection will be through the maker's name. The following pages start with a list of the wine regions and their principal wineries. The listing that follows is of the wineries, with as much information as possible about the sources of their wines. With the accompanying tasting notes and commentaries a picture begins to emerge – one of the world's most exciting wine countries in early maturity.

THE REGIONS

NEW SOUTH WALES

Canberra Region of small new wineries centred around the Australian Capital Territory (ACT), many of them at relatively high altitude.
Wineries include: Lark Hill.
Hunter Valley Australia's oldest wine region. The Lower Hunter, around Pokolbin, some 100 miles north of Sydney, is long-established as a producer of serious Shiraz and Semillon which age superbly. Cloud cover mitigates the extreme summer heat but rain often dampens the vintage. Chardonnay and Cabernet have proved equally successful in the past ten to 15 years. The Upper Hunter, developed since the 1960s, is principally a white wine area, producing less ageable wines.
Wineries include: Allandale, Allanmere, Arrowfield, Brokenwood, Chateau Francois, Drayton's Bellevue, Evans Family, Hollydene Estate, Hungerford Hill, Lake's Folly, Lindemans, McWilliams, Marsh Estate, Petersons, Murray Robson, Rosemount, Rothbury Estate, Saxonvale, Simon Whitlam, Tulloch, Tyrrells, Wyndham Estate.
Mudgee Small, long-established area 100 miles west of the Hunter Valley and 1,200 feet higher, with a sunnier but later season. Mudgee's full-flavoured wines are controlled by a self-imposed appellation system. Chardonnay is often the best wine.
Wineries include: Botobolar, Craigmoor, Huntington Estate, Miramar, Montrose.
Murrumbidgee Irrigation Area Also known as Riverina, this richly fertile, flat, fruit-growing land lies around Griffith, 300 miles west of Sydney. Almost any vine seems to flourish if irrigated, giving quantity if not always quality.
Wineries include: De Bortoli, McWilliams.
Other areas A number of wineries in New South Wales lie outside the recognized wine regions in the south-east and north of the state. The most promising of these is Cassegrain.

VICTORIA

Central Victoria Most diffuse region, around the old gold-mining towns of Bendigo and Ballarat, 100 miles north by west of Melbourne. No big or long-established wineries, but excellent wines from Balgownie and others.

Wineries include: Balgownie, Chateau Le Amon, Delatite, Giaconda, Heathcote Winery, Hickinbotham, Wantirna, Yellowglen.
Geelong Small new area just west of Melbourne's Port Philip Bay. Cool conditions from maritime influence.
Wineries include: Bannockburn, Idyll Vineyard, Mount Anakie.
Goulburn Valley Important old but small area on the Hume Highway, 100 miles north of Melbourne. Excellent wines from Chateau Tahbilk and others.
Wineries include: Chateau Tahbilk, Mitchelton, Tisdall.
Great Western West-central area, some 140 miles west of Melbourne, including the famous old sparkling winery of Seppelts and ambitious new ventures.
Wineries include: Best's Wines, Mount Langhi Ghiran, Seppelts.
Macedon Small hilly region, northwest of Melbourne, with a handful of wineries.
Wineries include: Virgin Hills.
Mornington Peninsula Cool maritime-influenced region on the peninsula south-east of Melbourne.
Wineries include: Dromana Estate, Elgee Park.
Murray Valley Long-established, mainly irrigated area along the Murray River. Echuca, 150 miles north of Melbourne, makes fine table wines; further down-river to the west is dessert wine country, making outstanding sherries.
Wineries include: Lindemans, Mildara.
Northeast Victoria Illustrious area, between Milawa and Rutherglen on the New South Wales border, famous for superb dessert wines, especially Muscats, and heavy Shiraz. Milawa is now also a centre for fine white wine, led by Brown Brothers.
Winemakers include: All Saints, Baileys, Brown Brothers, Campbells, Chambers Rosewood, Morris, St Leonards, Stanton & Killeen.
Pyrenees Hilly region around the town of Avoca, 120 miles northwest of Melbourne. A handful of new wineries are showing increasing promise.
Wineries include: Chateau Remy, Taltarni.
Yarra Valley Old vine-growing region, 30 miles east of Melbourne, now increasingly fashionable and producing some of the best 'cool-climate' wines

from boutique wineries. Outstanding Chardonnay and Pinot Noir.
Wineries include: Coldstream Hills, Diamond Valley Vineyards, Domaine Chandon, Lillydale Vineyards, Mount Mary, Oakridge Estate, St Huberts, Seville Estate, Tarrawarra, Yarra Burn, Yarra Yering, Yeringberg.

SOUTH AUSTRALIA

Adelaide Hills Australia's most successful up-and-coming 'cool-climate' region, around the Mount Lofty Ranges to the southeast of Adelaide. Remarkable Riesling and Chardonnay are produced.
Wineries include: Henschke, Mountadam, Petaluma.
Adelaide Plains Formerly important vine-growing area, including Penfolds' Magill vineyard, now largely swallowed by the city suburbs.
Wineries include: Anglesey, Barossa Valley Estates, Penfolds, Tolley's Pedare, Woodley Wines.
Barossa Valley Oldest and most important region, 35 miles northeast of Adelaide, settled by Germans in the 1840s. Good all-round producer and home to many of Australia's largest wineries. The finest wines come from the Barossa Ranges to the east. Reds can be stern and tannic.
Wineries include: Basedows, Wolf Blass, Grant Burge, Leo Buring, Kaiser Stuhl, Krondorf, Peter Lehmann, Orlando, Penfolds, Rockford, Saltram, Seppelt, Tollana, Yalumba.
Clare Smaller area 40 miles north of Barossa with almost as long a history. 1,300-foot hills give it a cooler season in which Rhine Riesling does especially well, though Shiraz and Cabernet can also be fine.
Wineries include: Jim Barry, Jeffrey Grosset, Mitchell Cellars, Pike's Polish Hill River Estate, Quelltaler, Sevenhill, Stanley Wine Company, Taylors, Tim Knappstein, Watervale Cellars.
Coonawarra Remote area 250 miles southeast of Adelaide on an eccentric flat carpet of red earth over limestone with a high water table. Its latitude makes it relatively cool; its soil is absurdly fertile. The result is some of the best, most claret-like Cabernet, middle-weight Shiraz and excellent Rhine Riesling.

Wineries include: Bowen Estate, Brand's Laira, Chateau Reynella, Hollick, Katnook Estate, Leconfield, Lindemand, Mildara, Penfolds, Petaluma, Redman, Rosemount, Rouge Homme, Wynns.

Langhorne Creek Tiny historic area 47 miles southeast of Adelaide on rich alluvial soil.
Wineries include: Bleasdale, Temple Breuer.

Padthaway Northwards extension of Coonawarra, with a similar climate and soil. There is only one tiny winery, but Thomas Hardy, Lindemans, Seppelt and Wynns all have vines here.

Riverland The course of the Murray River northeast of Adelaide is dotted from Mildura to Morgan with bulk-producing irrigated vineyards. Large co-ops such as Berri and Renmano traditionally made fortified wines and brandy here, and now make good-value table wines too.
Wineries include: Angoves, Berri-Renmano.

Southern Vales Warm region immediately south of Adelaide, incorporating McLaren Vale. The many small wineries started here during the 1980s have raised more than a few eyebrows with some very interesting Rieslings and Chardonnays.
Wineries include: Andrew Garrett, Coriole, D'Arenberg, Thomas Fernhill Estate, Geoff Merrill, Richard Hamilton, Thomas Hardy, Kay Brothers Amery,

Marienberg, A Norman & Sons, Pirramimma, Ryecroft, Seaview, Wirra Wirra, Woodstock.

WESTERN AUSTRALIA

Lower Great Southern Area Sprawling region of diverse topography and soil, also known as Mount Barker/Frankland River. A growing number of wineries are attracted to the cool, slow ripening conditions here.
Wineries include: Alkoomi, Forest Hill, Goundrey Wines, Plantagenet.

Margaret River Western Australia's top-quality wine region (with prices to match), 200 miles south of Perth on a promontory with markedly oceanic climate. The area has proved its worth in the 1980s with sensational Cabernet and Chardonnay, good Semillon and Sauvignon, and even (unusually for Australia) with Zinfandel.
Wineries include: Ashbrook Estate, Cape Clairault, Cape Mentelle, Chateau Xanadu, Cullens, Leeuwin Estate, Moss Wood, Pierro, Redgate, Vasse Felix, Wrights.

Southwest Coastal Plain Long coastal plain between Perth and the Margaret River region, all maritime-influenced, but too spread-out to have any other distinguishing feature.
Wineries include: Capel Vale, Paul Conti, Peel Estate.

Swan Valley Traditional vine-growing area on the eastern outskirts of Perth. Long experience of its hot climate has

brought mastery of light, full-bodied white burgundy style, skillful light dry Verdelhos, very good Cabernets and some noble dessert wines.
Wineries include: Bassendean, Jane Brook Estate, Evans & Tate, Houghton, Olive Farm Wines, Sandalford, Westfield.

QUEENSLAND

Minor wine-producing state. Most vines are grown in the Granite Belt region just across the border with New South Wales, though a few maverick wineries slug it out with the best in the north.
Wineries include: Robinsons Family Vineyard.

TASMANIA

Following the search for a cooler climate to its logical conclusion, a number of new wineries have sprung up in Tasmania, near Launceston in the north of the island and Hobart in the south. Given the cool conditions, Champagne houses began to show an interest in the 1980s, Louis Roederer setting up a joint venture with Heemskerk.
Wineries include: Heemskerk, Moorilla Estate, Piper's Brook, St Matthias.

NORTHERN TERRITORY

Proud possessor of a single winery, Chateau Hornsby, at Alice Springs, obstinately irrigating in the fierce heat and producing passable wines too.

Principal grape varieties

Shiraz (alias Hermitage) Makes big, dark and tasty reds varying from deep, raisiny and tannic with salty mineral flavours (e.g. south of Adelaide and in northeast Victoria) to smooth, soft and relatively delicate in the Hunter Valley. With barrel-age (e.g. Grange Hermitage) it can become as glorious a wine here as in the Rhône valley. Also makes excellent port and blends superbly with Cabernet Sauvignon.
Cabernet Sauvignon Makes less well-balanced wine than Shiraz, tending to harshness and hollowness, and is improved by blending. Exceptions only in Coonawarra and parts of Victoria until Max Lake reintroduced it and small barrels to the Hunter Valley in the 1960s. Now it is widely successful, though still not at its best in South Australia except in the cooler Coonawarra area.
Chardonnay Recently introduced but sweeping the board almost everywhere. Works well both as rich, creamy wines or more restrained, austere ones.
Semillon At its best, in the Hunter

Valley (as 'Hunter Riesling'), is a total triumph: a light, dry, soft wine, Chablis-green when young and lively, ageing superbly for up to 20 years. Also good as 'Clare Riesling' in South Australia.
Rhine Riesling Modern methods have largely improved this superbly adaptable German grape – but sometimes filleted it too. The best today are excitingly flowery, just off-dry, satisfyingly acid and well worth several years' ageing.

Secondary grape varieties

Chenin Blanc Is used mainly as a blending grape.
Cinsaut (alias Oeillade) Common in the Barossa Valley, for blending and for ports.
Crouchen A rather ordinary grape known in Clare and Barossa as Clare Riesling.
Doradillo Bulk white grape of the irrigation areas, used for distilling, sherry and 'cask' wines.
Durif A Shiraz-like grape used occasionally in northeast Victoria for interesting dark wine.
Frontignac The brown Muscat used in

northeast Victoria for superbly luscious dessert and 'liqueur' wines.
Lexia (alias Gordo Blanco) A white Muscat used in the irrigation areas and Swan Valley to make a good light wine.
Marsanne Occasionally used in Victoria for long-lived big whites, and Swan Valley for blending.
Mataro Minor blending red, especially in the Barossa Valley.
Merlot A recent success in rounding out harsh Cabernets.
Muscadelle Used to good effect for rich sweet or dry wines in South Australia and northeast Victoria.
Pinot Noir A blending grape in the past, now coming into its own.
Riesling Rhine (German) Riesling is always so-called. Riesling alone means either Semillon or Crouchen.
Trebbiano Sometimes called White Hermitage or Ugni Blanc. Chiefly used for blending.
Verdelho An essential component of Australia's 'white burgundy' style of full, soft but agreeable wine.
Zinfandel Tried with some success in Margaret River, Western Australia.

AUSTRALIAN PRODUCERS

Alkoomi
Wingeballup Road, Frankland, *WA*. Est. 1971. 12,000 cases. Owners: Mervyn and Judith Lange. Vineyards: about 40 acres of Cab.Sauv., Rhine Ries., Shiraz, Malbec, Sauv.Bl., some Merlot and Sem. Wines: Cab., Malbec, Shiraz, Rhine Ries.
The pace-setter for the new Frankland area, best in dense, full-flavoured Cabernet and clean tannic Shiraz. Riesling is light and sweetish in the finish.

All Saints
All Saints Road, Wahgunyah, *Victoria*. Owners: The Sutherland family. 60,000 cases. Vineyards: 350 acres of mixed varieties.
Traditional old family winery in north-east Victoria, producing a full range of table, fortified and sparkling wines.

Allandale
Pokolbin, *NSW*. Est. 1978. 10,000 cases. Visits. Wine maker: Bill Sneddon. Vineyards: 15 acres of P.N., Sem. and Chard.
A new departure for the Hunter; a small winery set up largely to process small lots of grapes from named specialist growers. Chardonnays can be outstanding, others variable.

Allanmere
Lovedale Road, Allandale, *NSW*. Est. 1985. 3,000 cases. Wine maker: Newton Potter. Vineyards: 12 acres of Cab.Sauv. and Shiraz.
Small family-owned winery, making smooth reds from home-grown grapes and whites from bought-in grapes. The latter include Chardonnay, Semillon and a blend called 'Trinity'.

Anglesey
Heaslip'Road, Angle Vale, *SA*. Est. 1969. 8,000 cases. Owner: John Minnett and co-owners. Wine maker: Lindsay Stanley. Vineyards: 45 acres at Angle Vale.
Producer of inexpensive varietals and blended wines, including a successful pair of 'QVS' red (Cabernet/Shiraz/Malbec) and white (Semillon/Chenin Blanc) blends. Other wines include straight Cabernet, Chardonnay, Semillon, Sauvignon and Chenin, as well as blended Cabernet/Merlot, Cabernet/Malbec and Cabernet/Shiraz.

Angoves
Bookmark Ave., Renmark, *SA*. Founded 1886. Approx. 750,000 cases. Owners: The Angove family. Vineyards: 1,185 acres, including Rhine Ries., Sauv.Bl., Sylvaner, Traminer, Chard., Cab.Sauv., Shiraz, P.N.
A conservative old family company in the Riverland irrigated area. Tregrehan claret and Bookmark Riesling have long been well-known good-value lines. In the '80s new-look whites changed the firm's image: all simple, fruity, lightweight, well made and cheap.

Arrowfield
Jerry's Plains, Upper Hunter District, *NSW*. Est. 1969. 10,000 cases. Owners: W. R. Carpenter Ltd. Vineyards: 260 acres of Sem., Cab., Rhine Ries., Shiraz, Gewürz, and Chard.
The firm has now established a name for very good value. Best are a light spicy Cabernet Sauvignon and a big California-style Chardonnay, one of eight whites.

Ashbrook Estate
Willyabrup, Margaret River, *WA*. Est. 1975. Visits. Owners: the Devitt family. Wine maker: Tony Devitt. Vineyards: 30 acres of Chard., Sem., Cab.Sauv. and Verdelho, with small quantities of Ries., Sauv.Bl., Merlot and Cab.Franc.
Remote family-run winery in the middle of a red gum forest. Excellent and much sought-after white wines are produced, including Gold Label Rhine Riesling, well-made Semillon, crisp Sauvignon Blanc and rich Chardonnay. The oak-aged Cabernet is improving.

Bailey's
Glenrowan, *Victoria*. Est. 1870. 30,000 cases. Owners: Fielder Gillespie Davis. Wine maker: Steve Goodwin. Consultant: Harry Tinson. Vineyards: 110 acres of Muscat, Tokay, Shiraz, Cab.Sauv., some whites.
The famous makers of heroic Bundarra Hermitage, a caricature Aussie wine with a black and red label like a danger signal. A thickly fruity wine which ages 20 years to improbable subtlety. Even better (and amazing value) are their dessert Muscats and Tokays, profoundly fruity, intensely sweet and velvety. The best are labelled HJT.

Balgownie
Hermitage Road, Maiden Gulley, *Victoria*. Est. 1969. 15,000 cases. Visits. Owner: Mildara Wines. Vineyards: 35 acres of Cab.Sauv., Shiraz, P.N., Rhine Ries. and Chard.
Established by Stuart Anderson, who sold the winery to Mildara (q.v.) in 1986. This modest ex-pharmacist studied French methods and built one of the best names in Australia for Cabernet Sauvignon built like Château Latour. In 1982 the '74 was ready, the '76 still very tannic. In 1986 the '84 still had at least six years to go. The Hermitage is variable, at its best as aromatic as Christmas cake. Chardonnay and Pinot Noir are developing well. The Premier Cuvee range consists of Mildara wines blended at Balgownie.

Bannockburn Vineyards
Midland Highway, Bannockburn, *Victoria*. Est. 1974. 8,000 cases. Owner: Stuart Hooper. Wine maker: Gary Farr. Vineyards: 45 acres.
Traditional winery concentrating on Pinot Noir. Other wines are Chardonnay and Cabernet Sauvignon.

Jim Barry
Main North Road, Clare, *SA*. Est. 1968. 25,000 cases. Owner: Jim Barry. Wine maker: Mark Barry. Vineyards: 260 acres of Clare vines.
One of the largest wineries in Clare, producing a wide range of wines. Whites include Chardonnay, Sauvignon and both dry and sweet Rieslings. Among the reds are Cabernet, a Cabernet/Merlot blend, port and a remarkable Shiraz-based wine called Armagh.

Barossa Valley Estates
Angle Vale, Adelaide, *SA*. Owner: Berri-Renmano. Extensive range of varietals.
Owned by the giant Berri-Renmano cooperatives, this winery produces and exports good-value wines under the Barossa Valley Estates and more up-market Lauriston labels. Among the best of the BVE wines are Semillon/Chenin Blanc and Shiraz/Cabernet.

Basedows Wines

Barossa Valley, *SA*. Est. 1896. About 40,000 cases. Owners: a public company. Wine maker: Douglas Lehmann.

A small but sometimes excellent Barossa winery, well known for its dessert wines, plus claret, various ports and other fortified wines. In the late 1970s its Shiraz reached real heights of richness and complexity. Recently the Chardonnay and Semillon ('White Burgundy') have been doing well. The vineyards were sold in 1982, and grapes are now bought locally.

Bassendean Estate

147 West Road, Bassendean, Perth, *WA*. Est. 1951. 3,500 cases. Visits. Owners: Laurie and Moira Nicoletto. Vineyards: 5 acres, mainly Shiraz.

A conservative producer of typical soft and full-flavoured Swan Valley 'burgundies' which occasionally surprise (and delight) show judges with their elegance.

Berri Estate and Renmano

Berri, *SA*. Est. 1916. Berri 3m. cases; Renmano 1.5m. Visits. The huge Riverland coops, merged as Consolidated Cooperatives, have a rising profile. Berri's Rhine Riesling was always creditable; now their Cabernet blends with oak age are winning medals. Renmano blends Ruby Cabernet with Cabernet Sauvignon to achieve a sweetly fruity wine, and offers clean Sauvignon Blanc and Rieslings. The best wines are sold under the Chairman's Selection label.

Best's Wines

Great Western, *Victoria*. Est. 1920. 15,000 cases. Visits. Owners: The Thomson family. Vineyards: 125 acres. Wines include Shiraz, P. Meunier, Rhine Ries., Chard., Chasselas., Gewürz. and Mataro.

A famous old name in Victoria, conservative and highly picturesque in its original stone buildings. Great Western Hermitage No.0 is their best-known wine: not over-weight but tannic enough for balance. Pinot Meunier is also very long-lived. Recent Chardonnay is matured in wood and promises well. Carbonated sparkling wine from Irvine's White (alias Ondenc) is their best-seller.

Wolf Blass

Stuart Highway, Nuriootpa, Barossa Valley, *SA*. Est. 1969. 0.5m. cases. Owner: Wolf Blass Wines Ltd.

A winery built round the tasting, blending and marketing talents of a German whom nobody would describe as modest or quiet spoken. Blass blends popular ready-to-drink wines of strong varietal character, ignoring regions but making full use of new oak. His labels include Eaglehawk ('Bilyara'), Yellow Label, Grey Label and Black Label on an ascending price scale – none of them a bargain. Yellow Label Rhine Riesling is a huge seller. Blass's empire expanded during the late 1980s with the acquisition of Quelltaler and Tim Knappstein (q.v.), and the launching of a joint venture with Corbans in New Zealand. No company in Australia has a better record of medals in shows.

Bleasdale Vineyards

Langhorne Creek, *SA*. Est 1860. 30,000 cases. Visits. Owners: The Potts family. Vineyards: 100 acres. Wines: an astonishing variety.

The fifth generation of the pioneering Potts family operates this working slice of Australian history (it still has the huge old red-gum beam press). In this arid area the vineyards are irrigated by flooding through sluices from the Bremer River. The wines are cheap and very drinkable. A 15-year-old sweet Verdelho was excellent.

Botobolar

Botobolar Lane, Mudgee, *NSW*. Est. 1970. 6,000 cases (half red). Visits. Owners: Gil and Vincie Wahlquist. Vineyards: 66 acres. Wines: Cab.Sauv., Gewürz., Mataro, Shiraz, Crouchen, Chard., Rhine Ries., Trebbiano, Sem.

An engagingly personal winery run on ecological principles. Some products (e.g. Cabernet) are wholly successful, others (e.g. white Crouchen) a matter of taste and one or two (e.g. Budgee Budgee, a sweet white of Muscat and Shiraz) decidedly eccentric.

Bowen Estate

Coonawarra, *SA*. Est. 1972. 3,750 cases. Visits. Owners: Doug and Joy Bowen. Vineyards: 60 acres, Cab.Sauv. and Shiraz with some Rhine Ries., Chard., Merlot and Cab.Franc.

An ex-Lindeman's wine maker, Doug Bowen offers a near-model Coonawarra Cabernet which can age well. Riesling and Shiraz are also good examples of the area. He built a handsome new winery in 1982.

Brand's Laira

Coonawarra, *SA*. Est. 1966. 14,000 cases. Visits. Owners: The Brand family. Vineyards: 41 acres of Shiraz, Cab.Sauv., Malbec, Merlot, Chard., Cab.Franc and Rhine Ries.

Eric Brand started what has become like a modest Médoc Château, at first with fairly primitive methods. But his grapes are excellent, and from 1972 I have followed his Cabernets as some of Coonawarra's richest and best, needing 10 years to reach their peak. The Shiraz is very good but not so interesting; to my taste the blend of the two is better. Laira rosé is light and pretty.

Brokenwood

McDonald's Road, Pokolbin, Hunter Valley, *NSW*. Est. 1970. 15,000 cases. Visits. Owners: a partnership, including, until 1984, wine author James Halliday. Wine maker: Iain Riggs. Vineyards: 40 acres, mainly Cab. and Herm., with some Malbec, Merlot, Chard. and P.N.

An apparently amateurish operation to start with, but its partners have good palates. They pick early for 'cleanness' of structure, sometimes adding a big Coonawarra Cabernet for richness. The results are not typical of the Hunter Valley but have their own considerable harmony. Barrel-fermented Semillon and Chardonnay are produced from bought-in grapes.

Jane Brook Estate

Toodyay Road, Swan Valley, *WA*. Est. 1955. 5,000 cases plus bulk wines. Vineyards: 26 acres of Shiraz, Cab.Sauv., Sauv.Bl., Tokay, Sem., Chard., Verdelho.

A good Cabernet is countered by variable whites. Good when on form.

Brown Brothers

Milawa, *Victoria*. Est. 1889. 200,000 cases. Visits. Owners: The Brown family. Vineyards: 390 acres at Milawa, Mystic Park, Hurdle Creek and Whitlands. Also grapes on contract from 333 acres in King Valley.

Perhaps the closest approximation in Australia to the phenomenon of Robert Mondavi in California. In this case the third generation has furnished four able brothers to expand their father's remarkable work. New ideas are everywhere and growth almost alarming. New hill-top vineyards are providing excellent white grapes. The range is very wide: dry white Muscat, Late Harvest Rhine Riesling, Chardonnay, Pinot Noir, Merlot, Cabernet and old Shiraz have all given me great pleasure. Perhaps most of all the traditional Liqueur Muscat of the area.

Grant Burge
Jacob Creek, Barossa Valley, *SA*. 10,000 cases. Owner: Grant Burge. Vineyards: 350 acres of mixed varieties.
Grant Burge, a leading member of the consortium that runs Ryecroft (q.v.), makes a range of varietals including Chardonnay and wood-matured Semillon at this promising new winery.

Leo Buring
Para Road, Tanunda, Barossa Valley, *SA*. Est. 1945. Owner: Penfolds. Vineyards: 89 acres of Cab., Chard. and Rhine Ries. in the Barossa, and vines in the Hunter Valley.
This traditional Barossa winery, bought by Lindemans in 1962 and now owned by Penfolds, produces a wide range of wines at all quality levels, from the best-selling Liebfrauwine and uninspiring varietals to fine Bin and Reserve Bin wines, labelled (somewhat like the Lindemans wines) by bin numbers. Among the best are the Coonawarra Rhine Riesling DWQ19 and the Watervale Rhine Riesling DWC14. Cabernet is also good.

Campbells
Murray Valley Highway, Rutherglen, *Victoria*. Est. 1870. 30,000 cases. Visit. Owners: The Campbell family. Wine maker: Colin. Grape grower: Malcolm. Vineyards: 120 acres. Wines: Muscat, Tokay, Rhine Ries., Shiraz, Malbec, P.X.
Traditionally a producer of luscious dessert wines and Shiraz, since 1980 active in dry whites and a modern clean-cut Cabernet/Malbec blend. But Muscat, Tokay and port are still their backbone.

Cape Clairault
Willyabrup, Margaret River, *WA*. Est. 1976. 2,000 cases. Visits. Owners: Ian and Ani Lewis. Wine maker: Ian Lewis. Vineyards: 18 acres of Cab.Sauv., Sauv.Bl., Sem., Ries., Cab.Franc., Merlot.
Small winery which has won many medals. Wines include excellent Cabernet Sauvignon (blended with Cabernet Franc and Merlot), as well as a Classic Dry White blend, Sauvignon Blanc, wood-matured Semillon/Sauvignon and Riesling.

Cape Mentelle
Wallcliffe Road, Margaret River, *WA*. Est. 1976. 15,000 cases and expanding. Visits. Founder and director: David Hohnen. Owner: Veuve Cliquot-Ponsardin. Vineyards: 100 acres, mainly of Cab.Sauv. and Sem., with some Merlot, Shiraz, Zin., Cab.Franc., Sauv.Bl. and Chenin Bl.
David Hohnen was trained in California and worked on a vintage at Clos. Du Val. This shows in his very fruity and big-flavoured wines, including a massive Cabernet and a rare example of Australian Zinfandel. Twice winner of Australia's prestigious Jimmy Watson trophy, Hohnen also established the remarkable Cloudy Bay in New Zealand. He sold both wineries to Veuve Cliquot in 1990.

Cassegrain
Fernbank Road, Port Macquarie, *NSW*. Est. 1985. 45,000 cases and expanding. Wine maker: John Cassegrain. Vineyards: 420 acres; some grapes bought in from the Hunter. A new winery expanding very rapidly. Current wines include Chardonnay, Semillon, Gewürztraminer and Cabernet Sauvignon.

Capel Vale
Capel, nr. Bunbury, *WA*. Est 1973. Visits. Owners: Peter and Elizabeth Pratten. Wine maker: Alan Johnson. Vineyards: 24 acres of Shiraz, Cab.Sauv., Chard., Rhine Ries and Gewürz.
Very successful winery. Most wines, including 'Baudin' (a blend of Cabernet Sauvignon, Shiraz, Merlot and Cabernet Franc), are made from bought-in grapes. Chardonnays are home grown.

Chambers Rosewood
Rutherglen, *Victoria*. Est. 1860. Visits. Owners: The Chambers family. Vineyards: 110 acres at Rosewood. Many varieties. Wines: many.
Bill Chambers is a veteran wine maker, respected most of all for his old Liqueur Muscat and Tokay. As always in Rutherglen the rich dry reds are better than the whites.

Chateau Francois
Broke Road, Pokolbin, *NSW*. Est. 1969. 1,200 cases. No visits. Owner: Dr. Don Francois.
A very small vineyard of Semillon, Chardonnay, Shiraz, Pinot Noir. A weekend wine maker who does well in shows, especially with a Pinot Noir/Shiraz blend.

Chateau Hornsby
Petrick Road, Alice Springs, *Northern Territory*. Est. 1976. Visits. Owners: Denis and Miranda Hornsby. Vineyards: 7 acres of Cab.Sauv., Shiraz, Sem. and Rhine Ries.
Maverick winery, with heavily-irrigated vines, in the searing heat of the outback. Reds are full and clean-flavoured.

Chateau Le Amon
Calder Highway, Bendigo, *Victoria*. Est. 1973. 5,000 cases. Visits. Owners: Philip and Alma Leamon. Vineyards: 10 acres of Cab.Sauv., Shiraz, Sem. and Rhine Ries.
One of Victoria's successful small wineries, best known for powerful and deep Cabernet. Their 'dry red Beaujolais style' is good and a forthcoming Bordeaux-blend red is awaited with interest. Semillon and Riesling are blended.

Chateau Remy
Avoca, Pyrenees, *Victoria*. Est. 1960. 40,000 cases. Owners: Rémy Martin. Wine maker: Vincent Gere. Vineyards: 250 acres of Chard., Trebbiano, Shiraz and Cab.
The Trebbiano (Ugni Blanc in Cognac) was intended for brandy-making, but a change of direction in 1969 led to plantings of Chardonnay for sparkling wine. A French winemaker, a new building and new vineyards have produced reliable *méthode champenoise* wines, including a vintage sparkler, rosé and Cuvee Speciale Brut. Other wines include Cabernet-based Blue Pyrenees Estate and lighter Kindilan Nouveau.

Chateau Reynella
Southern Vales, *SA*. Est. 1838. 45,000 cases. Owner: Thomas Hardy & Sons.
A famous old name, particularly for ports and red wines, with a historic cellar and vineyard just south of Adelaide. Bought by Thomas Hardy in 1982, and now the headquarters of the huge company. The winery continues to make good wines – of which Cabernet and Rhine Riesling are the best – from bought-in Coonawarra grapes.

Chateau Tahbilk

Tahbilk, *Victoria*. Est. 1860. 40,000 cases. Visits. Owners: The Purbrick family. Vineyards: 300 acres of Rhine Ries., Cab.Sauv., Chard., Shiraz, Marsanne and a little Sem., Sauv.Bl. and Ch.Bl.

Victoria's most historic and attractive winery and one of Australia's best. The old farm with massive trees stands by the Goulburn River in lovely country, its barns and cellars like a film set of early Australia. English-born Eric Purbrick has ceded the wine-making to his Roseworthy-trained grandson Alister. Dry white Marsanne, starting life light but ageing to subtle roundness, is the main production. Riesling is crisp but full of flavour and also ages well. Special Bin reds (either Cabernet or Shiraz) are selected for maturing in 4,500-litre casks and only released at 6–7 years. A '64 Cabernet was perfection when tasted in 1982.

Chateau Xanadu

Wallcliffe Road, Margaret River, *WA*. Est. 1976. 7,000 cases. Owners: Drs. Lagan and Sheridan. Wine makers: John Smith and Conor Lagan. Vineyards: 50 acres of Sem., Chard., Cab.Sauv., P.N. and Cab.Franc.

Improving Margaret River winery (whose name was inspired by Coleridge's poem), producing fine Semillon and Chardonnay.

Coldstream Hills

Maddens Lane, Coldstream, Yarra Valley, *Victoria*. Est. 1985. 10,000 cases. (30,000 planned.) Owners: a public company. Wine maker: James Halliday. Vineyards: 37 acres, mainly of Chard. and P.N., with some Cab.Sauv., Cab.Franc and Merlot.

Promising new Yarra winery founded by the country's leading wine critic, James Halliday, and now a public company in which Thomas Hardy (q.v.) has a share. Under the Lilydale label, Halliday makes some of Australia's best Pinot Noir and Chardonnay, as well as an excellent red blend of Cabernet Sauvignon, Merlot and Cabernet Franc. Wines made from bought-in grapes are sold under the Four Vineyards label.

Paul Conti

Wanneroo Road, Wanneroo, *WA*. Est. 1948. 9,300 cases. Visits. Wine maker: Paul Conti. Vineyards: 42 acres of Cab.Sauv., Shiraz, Merlot, Grenache, P.N., Chard., Muscat, Ch.Bl.

A (stylistically) leading Swan Valley producer, with two well-placed vineyards at Marginiup and Yanchep. Elegant Hermitage and clean, balanced Chardonnay.

Coriole

Chaffeys Road, McLaren Vale, *SA*. Est. 1918. 11,200 cases. Visits. Owners: The Lloyd family. Vineyards: 53 acres of Cab.Sauv., Shiraz, Ch.Bl., Rhine Ries., Grenache and P.N.

Shiraz and blended Cabernet/Shiraz are the specialities of this good, small estate. Both have spicy ripeness.

Craigmoor

Mudgee, *NSW*. Est. 1858. 20,000 cases. Visits. Owners: Wyndham Estate. Vineyards: 140 acres of Chard., Sem., Shiraz., Cab.

The oldest-established Mudgee vineyard, long owned by the Roth family; a pioneer of a dry blend of Semillon and Chardonnay. The range of wines is wide, formerly made with a fairly heavy hand; recently more 'elegant'. Now part of the large Wyndham Estate group.

Cullen's

Caves Road, Cowaramup, Margaret River, *WA*. Est. 1971. 7,800 cases. Visits. Owners: Dr. Kevin and Diana Cullen. Wine makers: Diana and Vanya Cullen. Vineyards: 73 acres, mainly of Cab.Sauv., with Rhine Ries, Sauv.Bl., Chard. and some Merlot, P.N., Ch.Bl.

Cabernet, both straight and blended with Merlot and Malbec, have made their reputation. It is dense, tannic and so far more accessible in the blend. Oak-fermented Sauvignon Blanc has been a success and a 'Fumé Cabernet' (rosé) another. Also Rhine Riesling Auslese in very small quantities. The oak-aged wines carry a distinctive acorn and oakleaf label.

D'Arenberg

McLaren Vale, *SA*. Est. 1928. 42,000 cases. Visits. Owners: The Osborn family. Vineyards: 150 acres of Shiraz. Cab.Sauv., Gren., Palomino, Doradillo, Rhine Ries. and P.X.

D'Arry Osborn is an experienced wine maker with old-fashioned tastes; his best standard red is 'burgundy' (75% Grenache, 25% Shiraz) with a rustic spiciness that grows on you (and ages well). Hearty Cabernet, soft, juicy but dry white Palomino and soft sweet vintage port are equally characteristic.

De Bortoli Wines

De Bortoli Road, Bilbul, *NSW*. Est. 1928. Owners: the De Bortoli family. Wine maker: Darren Bortoli. 500,000 cases. Range of 60 wines.

Most of the production is everyday wines, but remarkable botrytis Semillon and sweet Rieslings and Gewürztraminers are also made, as well as a Jean-Pierre *méthode champenoise* wine.

Delatite

Stoney's Road, Mansfield, *Victoria*. Est. 1982. 14,000 cases. Owners: Robert and Vivienne Ritchie. Wine maker: Rosalind Ritchie. Vineyards: 60 acres of mixed varieties; some fruit bought in.

Successful family winery producing remarkable white wines and improving reds. Rhine Riesling and Gewürztraminer are among the best. Other wines include Pinot Noir, Cabernet/Merlot, Malbec, Sauvignon and a new sparkling wine.

Diamond Valley

Kinglake Road, St Andrews, Yarra Valley, *Victoria*. Est. 1976. 4,000 cases. Owners: David and Cathy Lance. Vineyards: 8 acres of Chard., Rhine Ries., P.N. and Cab.Sauv.

David Lance, formerly at St Huberts (q.v.) makes outstanding Pinot Noir, as well as Chardonnay, Riesling and Cabernet. A second range, Blue Label, is made from bought-in fruit.

Domaine Chandon

Maddens Lane, Coldstream, Yarra Valley, *Victoria*. Est. 1985. Owners: Louis Vuitton Moët Hennessy (France). Visits. Wine maker: Dr Tony Jordan. Vineyards: 50 acres of Chard. and P.N., with a little P. Meunier.

Exciting new investment established with the foreign expertise of Moët and the local knowledge of Tony Jordan, one of Australia's foremost wine consultants. Wines are made from both home-grown and bought-in fruit. The first commercial *méthode champenoise* sparkler was released in 1989, and the future looks highly promising.

Dromana Estate
Dromana, Mornington Peninsula, *Victoria*. 1,500 cases. Owner: Gary Crittenden. Vineyards: 10 acres of mixed varieties.

A leading estate in the up-and-coming Mornington Peninsula. Glorious Cabernet, Pinot Noir and Chardonnay are made. Other good wines, made from bought-in grapes, are sold under the Schinus Molle label.

Elgee Park
Merricks North, Mornington Peninsula, *Victoria*. 1,000 cases. Wine maker: Tod Dexter. Vineyards: 10 acres of Cab.Sauv., Cab.Franc, Merlot and Chard.

Oldest winery in the region, producing very good Cabernet, Chardonnay and Riesling.

Evans Family
Pokolbin, Hunter Valley, *N.S.W.* Est. 1980. 2,200 cases. Owners: Len Evans' family. Vineyards: 20 acres of Chard., P.N. and a little Gamay.

Writer and wine maker Len Evans produces 1,500 cases of well-received Chardonnay, 500 cases of Pinot Noir and 200 cases of Gamay at his small family vineyard. The wines, made at Rothbury (q.v.), are mostly exported.

Evans & Tate
Gnangara Road, Swan Valley, Redbrook Vineyard, Willyabrup, Margaret River, *WA*. Est. 1972. Owners: John and Toni Tate. Vineyards: 50 acres at Redbrook (Margaret River) and 10 acres at Gnangara. Shiraz, Cab.Sauv., Merlot, Cab.Franc, Chard., Sauv.Bl., Sem.

The old and new of Western Australia are combined in a winery that grows grapes in Swan Valley and the Margaret River, making and barrel-ageing wine at Gnangara. Shiraz from Gnangara is softer and fuller than the reds from Redbrook but a house style has emerged, using new oak and aiming for moderation in ripeness.

Thomas Fernhill Estate
Ingoldby Road, McLaren Flat, *SA*. Est. 1975. 5,000 cases. Owners: Wayne and Patricia Thomas. Vineyards: 1.5 acres of Cab.Sauv. (most grapes bought locally).

Rich mouth-filling Shiraz is the most impressive wine so far from an unusual little operation intending to use the cream of the local crop. Rhine Riesling has also been a critical success.

Forest Hill
Mt. Barker, *WA*. Est. 1965. 750 cases. Owners: Holmes à Court family. Vineyards: 50 acres of Rhine Ries., Cab.Sauv., Gewürz., Chard. and Sauv.Bl.

The first vineyard in the Mount Barker area, established by the state government for research and recently bought from the Pearse family by Robert Holmes à Court. It still makes some of the region's best wines, notably very intense-flavoured Cabernet Sauvignon and Riesling, both oak-aged and showing every sign of developing well in bottle. The wines are made at Plantagenet (q.v.).

Andrew Garrett
Kangarilla Road, McLaren Vale, *SA*. 60,000 cases. Owners: Suntory Aust. Pty. Ltd. Vineyards: 500 acres in McLaren Vale, Clare and Padthaway; some fruit bought in.

Highly successful and influential new winery, recently taken over by an Australian subsidiary of the Japanese Suntory corporation, making a bestselling range of varietals. Whites – a Chardonnay and a Sauvignon/Semillon blend – are best; reds include Cabernet/Merlot

and Shiraz. A popular Pinot Noir-based *méthode champenoise* wine is also made.

Giaconda
McClay Road, Beechworth, *Victoria*. 350 cases. Wine maker: Rick Kinzbrunner.

Small, fashionable winery in central Victoria producing successful Chardonnay, Pinot Noir and other wines.

Goundrey
Langton, Mount Barker, *WA*. Est. 1970. 5,000 cases. Owner: a public company. Visits. Wine maker: Rodney Hooper. Vineyards: 210 acres of Cab.Sauv., Rhine Ries., Chard., Shiraz, Sauv.Bl., P.N. and Cab.Franc.

Expanding winery with new investment, run part-time until 1983. The main Windy Hill varietal range includes a good Riesling, Chardonnay, Sauvignon Blanc, Shiraz and Cabernet. Blended wines, port and less good varietals are sold under the cheaper Denmark cellars label.

Jeffrey Grosset
Auburn, Clare, *SA*. Est. 1981. Owners: Catherine and Jeffrey Grosset. Vineyards: 12 acres (not yet producing); Clare grapes bought in.

One of Clare's most consistent high-quality wineries, producing elegant Cabernet, Riesling and Chardonnay from bought-in grapes.

Richard Hamilton
Main South Road, Willunga, Southern Vales, *SA*. Est. 1972. Owner: Dr. Richard Hamilton. 10,000 cases. 40 acres in Willunga, including Cab.Sauv., Ch.Bl., Chard., Sem., Sauv.Bl. and 80 acres in Coonawarra with Cab.Sauv., Cab.Fr. and Chard.

White-wine specialist with some interesting wood-aged Riesling, 'Fumé-Blanc' and Chardonnay.

Thomas Hardy
Willunga Road, McLaren Vale, *SA*. Est. 1857. Owners: The Hardy family. Vineyards: Keppoch – 284 acres of Rhine Ries., 217 of Shiraz, 82 Cab., 17 P.N., 42 Chard., 42 Gewürz., 6 Malbec; McLaren Vale – 12 acres. Bought grapes account for two thirds of production.

An Adelaide family dynasty in its fifth generation and still growing. Its origins were in McLaren Vale, where it still makes some of Australia's best fortified wines. In the 1970s plantings were largely moved south to the cooler Keppoch area. Table wines have traditionally been skilful blends (e.g. St Thomas Burgundy and the gutsy Nottage Hill Claret). In the 1970s with Brian Croser as consultant some outstanding wines emerged, especially reds labelled Eileen Hardy. Old Castle (Barossa) Riesling is their most famous white; Siegersdorf a rather finer and drier blend of Barossa and Keppoch grapes; Keppoch Riesling drier still. Eden Moselle is sweet. Bird Series wines are consistent and good value.

Hardy's owns Houghton in Western Australia, Chateau Reynella in Southern Vales and the Stanley Wine Company.

Heathcote Winery
High Street, Heathcote, *Victoria*. 5,000 cases. Owners: Doris and Kenneth Tudhope. Wine maker: Elain Tudhope. Vineyards: 40 acres of mixed varieties.

A technically-accomplished producer of varietals, which include a successful Chardonnay, Pinot Noir and Gewürztraminer.

Heemskerk

Pipers Brook, Launceston, *Tasmania*. Est. 1966. 8,000 cases.
Owner: Fesq, Haselgrove, Wiltshire & Co. Pty. Ltd. and
Louis Roederer of France. Vineyards: about 75 acres, with
more to plant. Largely Cab.Sauv., with Gewürz., Chard.,
P.N., and Rhine Ries.

In a remote and lovely spot on red soil within sight of the
island's north coast. Cabernet so far has been a shade
green but very promising. A collaboration with Louis
Roederer of Champagne, which now owns half of the
company, has resulted in the recent release of a sparkling
wine, and a new 125-acre vineyard in West Tamar.

Henschke

Keyneton, Mount Lofty Ranges, *SA*. Est. 1850s. 35,000 cases.
Owners: The Henschke family. Vineyards: 217 acres at
Keyneton and Eden Valley of Shiraz, Rhine Ries. plus Chard.,
Cab.Sauv., White Frontignac, Sem.

A fifth-generation family firm (Stephen is wine maker)
with two famous brands of Shiraz: Hill of Grace (deep
austere wine from ancient vines) and Mount Edelstone
(easier, more elegant red). Other wines include a crisp, dry
and delicate Rhine Riesling. Fashion has swung back to
their staunch conservative approach.

Hickinbotham Winemakers

Ferguson Street, Williamstown, *Victoria*. Est. 1981. 5,000
cases. Owner: The Hickinbotham family. Vineyards: 7 acres;
most grapes are bought in.

A family of innovative winemakers closely associated
with many of the most significant developments in
Australian wine production, but scarred by the death of
Bordeaux-trained Stephen Hickinbotham in an air crash.
Wines are produced from all over Victoria and from
Tasmania, with new vineyards planted in the Mornington
Peninsula.

Hollick

Racecourse Road, Coonawarra, *SA*. Est. 1982. 11,000 cases.
Owners: Ian and Wendy Hollick. Visits. Wine maker: Pat
Tocaciu. Vineyards: 65 acres of Cab.Sauv., Cab.Franc, Merlot,
P.N., Shiraz, Rhine Ries. and Chard.

Small Coonawarra producer making a successful range of
varietals: Cabernet, Pinot Noir and Shiraz for the reds;
Chardonnay and Riesling for the whites. Hollick's
Cabernet is a winner of the important Jimmy Watson
Trophy.

Hollydene Estate

Hollydene, Upper Hunter Valley, *NSW*. Owner: Wyndham
Estate. Vineyards: 225 acres of mixed varieties.

Another winery in Wyndham's Hunter/Mudgee empire.
Its range of good varietals, vinified for early drinking,
includes Chardonnay, Cabernet, Shiraz and
Semillon/Chardonnay.

Houghton

Dale Road, Swan Valley, *WA*. Est. 1859. about 270,000 cases.
Owner: Thomas Hardy and Sons. Vineyards: 587 acres, large
blocks at Houghton in the Swan Valley and Moondah Brook
north of Perth, and a smaller property in the Frankland River
area near Mt. Barker far to the south. Mostly Ch.Bl.,
Verdelho, Shiraz, Gren., Cab.Sauv., Malbec, Rhine Ries.,
Muscadelle.

The most famous name in Western Australia. For 50
vintages it was made by the legendary Jack Mann. From
1950–1976 Emu Wines owned the company. Now under

Hardy's its lustre has revived. White Burgundy is a little
lighter and more polished, Cabernet excellent and the
whole range honest and good value.

Hungerford Hill

Pokolbin, *NSW*. Est. 1967. About 10,000 cases. Owners:
Hooper Bailie Ltd. Wine maker: Adrian Sheridan. Vineyards:
100 acres in the Hunter Valley of Chard., Shiraz and Sem.,
Gewürz., Cab., Malbec and P.N.; 170 acres at Coonawarra of
Rhine Ries., Cab.Sauv., P.N. and Chard.

Two widely separated vineyards, some of whose best
wines are blended together. After early problems they are
concentrating on Hunter Chardonnay and Coonawarra
Cabernet and Riesling. Best wines have included Hunter
and Coonawarra Chards. 'Collection Series' is the top
level. Also some Coonawara Chardonnay 'Champagne'.

Huntington Estate

Cassilis Road, Mudgee, *NSW*. Est. 1968. 24,000 cases.
Owners: Bob and Wendy Roberts. Vineyards: 101 acres of
Shiraz, Cab.Sauv., Chard., Sem., P.N., Merlot and Sauv.Bl.

Cabernets from this little family estate have been some of
Mudgee's best, particularly those with a proportion of
Merlot. The Shiraz is bigger and plainer. It also leads
Mudgee in Chardonnay and Semillon.

Idyll Vineyard

Ballan Road, Moorabool, Geelong, *Victoria*. Est. 1966.
Owners: Daryl and Nini Sefton. Vineyards: 50 acres, mainly of
Shiraz, Cab.Sauv. and Gewürz.

The establishment of this winery in 1966 heralded the
rebirth of Geelong's vineyards, wiped out by phylloxera
in the late 19th century. Idyll's red wines range from an
elegant oaky chunky Cabernet/Shiraz blend to Shiraz-
based rosés. A good Gewürztraminer is also made.

Kaiser Stuhl

Sturt Highway, Nuriootpa, Barossa Valley, *SA*. Owners:
Penfolds. Vineyards: 1,500 acres of Barossa vines.

Now owned by Penfolds, this old Barossa winery has a 25-
year reputation for outstanding Rhine Riesling and very
good Shiraz and Cabernet. Individual (Green, Gold and
Purple Ribbon) Rieslings are some of Australia's best, at
moderate prices. Red Ribbon Shiraz is also worthwhile.

Katnook Estate

Coonawarra, *SA*. Wines since 1979. 12,000 cases. Owners:
Coonawarra Machinery Ltd. Vineyards: 1,200 acres of Chard.,
Cab.Sauv., Rhine Ries., Gewürz., Sauv.Bl., Shiraz, Merlot,
P.N., Cab.Fr., Malbec.

The small lots of fine wine released by this big grape-ranch
have been supervised by Australia's most advanced and
fashionable consultants, Brian Croser and Tony Jordan.
They include very intense and powerful Chardonnay,
Riesling along similar lines, lighter Gewürztraminer and
some rather jammy Cabernet (1980) – all wines that speak
more of beautiful ripe grapes than subtlety in the cellar.
The Sauvignon Blanc has been very good, and the
Riddoch Estate Cabernet/Shiraz has had great success in
Australia.

Kay Brothers Amery

Amery Vineyards, McLaren Vale, *SA*. Est. 1890. 15,500 cases.
Owners: The Kay family. Vineyards: 17 acres of Shiraz, Rhine
Ries., Cab.Sauv., Gewürz., P.N.

An old firm making sound wines, including Sauvignon
Blanc and typically full McLaren Vale Shiraz.

Tim Knappstein
Pioneer Avenue, Clare, *SA*. Est. 1976, as Enterprise Wines. 35,000 cases. Owner: Wolf Blass. Wine maker: Tim Knappstein. Vineyards: 115 acres of Clare vines, plus a vineyard at Lenswood in the Adelaide Hills.

Tim Knappstein made remarkable wines at Stanley Wine Company and has continued to excel at the winery he founded in 1976. The firm is now owned by Wolf Blass (q.v.), though Knappstein remains in charge. His excellent range of wines includes flowery Rhine Riesling, Fumé Blanc (Sauvignon/Semillon), densely fruity Cabernet Sauvignon, Cabernet/Merlot, Chardonnay, Gewürztraminer and a new Pinot Noir from his vineyard at Lenswood.

Krondorf
Krondorf Road, Barossa Valley, *SA*. Est. 1960s. 150,000 cases. Owners: Mildara. Vineyards: 60 acres at Lyndoch in the Barossa.

This old Barossa winery, originally called Falkenberg, was renamed in the 1970s and revamped in the early 1980s by Grant Burge and Ian Wilson. Now owned by Mildara (q.v.), its two ranges include a Barossa Rhine Riesling, a nice light Chardonnay, and several reds, of which the Barossa Cabernet is the best.

Lake's Folly
Pokolbin, *NSW*. Est. 1963. 6,000 cases. Owners: The Lake family. Wine maker: Stephen. Vineyards: 35 acres of Cab.Sauv., Chard., Shiraz, some Malbec.

At first the hobby, then the passion of a distinguished surgeon from Sydney, Max Lake. He started the first new Hunter winery in 40 years, ignoring tradition to prove that Cabernet can be the same splendid thing under Hunter skies as elsewhere. Then he did the same with Chardonnay, making vibrantly lively wines. Both can be among Australia's best. Max's son Stephen now makes the wines.

Lark Hill
Gundaroo Road, Bungendore, *NSW*. 2,000 cases. Owners: The Carpenter family. Wine maker: Sue Carpenter. Vineyards: 15 acres, some not yet producing.

The highest, and one of the best, wineries in the Canberra region. Wines include Chardonnay, Cabernet/Merlot and Riesling.

Leconfield
Penola-Naracoorte Road, Coonawarra, *SA*. Est. 1974. 7,000 cases. Owner: Dr. Richard Hamilton. Vineyards: 80 acres.

The retirement hobby of a professional wine maker, Syd Hamilton, bought in 1981 by his nephew, who also owns Willunga. Big-scale Cabernets and dry Rhine Riesling aged in oak have been the outcome so far.

Leeuwin Estate
Gnarawary Road, Margaret River, *WA*. Est. 1974. 30,000 cases. Vineyards: about 220 acres of Cab.Sauv., Rhine Ries., Chard., plus some P.N., Malbec, Sauv.Bl., and Gewürz.

A substantial very modern winery built with advice from Robert Mondavi in the green hills and woods of the Margaret River (the ocean only a jog away). The first Chardonnays were sensational if expensive, with aromas, liveliness, richness and grip to outdo anything in Australia and most in California. Rieslings have varied from excitingly steely to melon-rich, with an excellent Auslese. Gewürztraminer is light, dry and long. Pinot Noir succeeded well in '82. Cabernets are rich but not overripe. Leeuwin's founder, Denis Morgan, recently put the winery on the market, so its future looks a little uncertain.

Peter Lehmann Wines
Tanunda, Barossa Valley, *SA*. Est. 1980. 100,000 cases. Owners: Masterson Barossa Vignerons Proprietary Ltd. All grapes bought from the Barossa and Eden valleys.

Peter Lehmann is one of the great showmen of the Barossa, and one of its soundest winemakers. Two brand names – Peter Lehmann and Masterson – appear on a wide range of wines. The Semillon 'Sauternes' is among Australia's top sweet whites. Pinot Noir is winning medals; Cabernet and Shiraz can excel.

Lillydale Vineyards
Seville, Yarra Valley, *Victoria*. Est. 1976. 10,000 cases. Owners: Alex White and Martin Grinbergs. Vineyards: 25 acres of Yarra vines.

One of the largest Yarra wineries, whose co-founders were formerly at St Huberts (q.v.). Some of the region's best Chardonnay, Gewürztraminer and Riesling is made here. Other wines include Cabernet and Pinot Noir.

Lindeman's
Nyrang Road, Lidcombe, *NSW*. Founded 1870 as Ben Ean, bought by Lindeman's in 1912. Owners: Penfolds. Vineyards: Corowa, NSW. Watervale and Clare, SA. Lower Hunter, NSW: Karadoc, Victoria: 271 acres in Sunraysia district for cask wines. Coonawarra and Padthaway, SA.

Until recently the third-largest wine company in Australia, Lindeman's was taken over by Penfolds in 1990. In addition to the grapes they grow, Lindeman's buy vast quantities, particularly in the Barossa and Hunter valleys and Coonawarra. They are Australia's master blenders with some 400 different labels and a major share of the 'cask' market. Yet they maintain excellent individual wines from their own estates. These include: Rhine

Max Lake (right) and Len Evans: two champions of the Hunter.

Rieslings, both Lindeman's Watervale and Leo Buring's more austere Barossa. Also Rouge Homme Coonawarra and Padthaway Auslese. Semillon: Ben Ean Hunter Valley whites (and reds) are superb with bottle age. So is Porphyry 'Sauternes'. Cabernet: best from Rouge Homme, Coonawarra (q.v.). Chardonnay and Pinot Noir: very good from Padthaway. Dessert wines: excellent Corowa Muscats and Macquarie port. Matthew Lang is a range of selected wines from Karadoc.

McWilliams

Bulwara and Pyrmont Ridge Roads, Pyrmont, Sydney, *NSW*.
Est. 1877. 2.3m. cases. Visits. Owners: The McWilliam family.
Vineyards: in the Hunter Valley (Mount Pleasant) and near
Griffith in the Riverina irrigated area (where they have 3
wineries: Hanwood, Yenda and Beelbangera).

A single-minded and conservative family business with a large and loyal following, entirely in New South Wales. Their flagships are Mt. Pleasant Elizabeth Riesling and Philip-Hermitage, both of which have honourable histories and maintain high standards. Wines from Griffith are lighter commercial stuff, but always well made.

Marienberg

Coromandel Valley, McLaren Vale, *SA*. Est. 1966. 12,000
cases. Owners: The Pridham family. Wine maker: Ursula.
Vineyards: 40 acres of Rhine Ries., Shiraz, Cab.Sauv.,
Gewürz., Sem.

Australia's best-known woman wine maker has a fairly uninhibited way with oak. Her Shiraz is perhaps her best wine. The Riesling is hard to recognize except in the late-picked examples. Individual and not expensive.

Geoff Merrill

Pimpala Road, Reynella, *SA*. Est. 1983. 12,000 cases. Owner:
Geoff Merrill. Visits. Vineyards: 54 acres, almost all recently
planted.

Formerly chief wine maker at Thomas Hardy (q.v.), Merrill makes wines here almost entirely from outside grapes. The best wines are Geoff Merrill Cabernet Sauvignon and Chardonnay. A second label, Mount Hurtle, includes Cabernet and Sauvignon Blanc, both made from McLaren Vale grapes. A winery to watch.

Mildara Wines

Merbein, nr. Mildura, *Victoria*. Est. 1888. 550,000 cases.
Owners: The Hazelgrove family, Grants Glenfiddick and
Sanraku Corporation (Japan). Wine makers: Jack Schultz and
Tony Murphy. Vineyards: Coonawarra, Mildura and 59 acres
at Eden Valley. Main plantings are of Cab.Sauv., Rhine Ries.,
Chard., Traminer and Shiraz.

An old company that expanded during the 1980s, acquiring Yellowglen and Balgownie in Victoria, Krondorf in South Australia, and Morton Estate in New Zealand. Famous for some of Australia's better sherries from Mildura on the Murray River, and equally good Coonawarra table wines – the best of these are their Cabernets, outstanding since '79. Overall wine quality transformed since '78 following management changes at Coonawarra. Mildara's red and white Jamieson's Run blends have done well recently.

Miramar

Henry Lawson Drive, Mudgee, *NSW*. Est. 1974. 12,500 cases.
Owners: Iain MacRae and 3 partners. Vineyards: 60 acres of
Shiraz, Cab.Sauv., Sem., Rhine Ries., Chard., etc.

One of the most competent wineries in Mudgee, bringing out powerful characteristics in each variety, especially

Chardonnay, a Chardonnay/Semillon blend, Cabernet and Shiraz. Also a clean rosé and 'vintage port'.

Mitchell Cellars

Hughes Park Road, Seven Hill, Clare Valley, *SA*. Est. 1975.
12,000 cases. Owners: Andrew and Jane Mitchell.
Vineyards: 65 acres of Rhine Ries., Shiraz, Cab.Sauv.,
Merlot, Sem.

Wines include Rhine Riesling, wood-aged Semillon, Peppertree Shiraz and Cabernet. All are among Clare's best.

Mitchelton

Mitchellstown, Nagambie, *Victoria*. Est. 1969. 100,000 cases.
Owners: the Valmorbida family. Wine maker: Don Lewis.
Vineyards: Cab.Sauv., Rhine Ries., Chard., Marsanne,
Sem. Grapes also come from Coonawarra.

An extraordinary edifice like a 1970's monastery on the banks of the lovely Goulburn River. A lookout tower, aviary and restaurant were built to attract tourists. But the wines are another matter. The Mitchelton label is used for estate wines: excellent Marsanne, aged in cask, and distinctly aromatic for this grape, wood-matured Semillon, well-made Riesling and slightly dull Cabernet. 'Winemakers' Selection' is used for Coonawarra or blended wines; a fine velvety Coonawarra/Nagambie Cabernet and more highly flavoured Rieslings, some with noble rot. Thomas Mitchell is the second-quality label, e.g. Trebbiano 'chablis'. A very good range at modest prices.

Montrose

Henry Lawson Drive, Mudgee, *NSW*. Est. 1974. 20,000 cases.
Owners: Wyndham Estate. Vineyards: 280 acres of Chard.,
Cab.Sauv., Rhine Ries., Shiraz, Gewürz., P.N., Sem.,
Traminer and a few Italian varieties – Sangiovese, Nebbiolo
and Barbera.

An expanding Mudgee winery, now part of the Wyndham Estate group, with an Italian tilt towards light, sweetish, rather earthy reds and big sweet Chardonnay. Outside expertise helped bring about a quality leap in the mid-80s.

Moorilla Estate

Main Road, Berriedale, Hobart, *Tasmania*. Est. 1958. 700 cases.
Owners: Claudio Alcorso. Vineyards: 26 acres in the Derwent
Valley and 12 at Bream Creek to the east.

One of the first bold souls to look for quality in Tasmania, and in a cool corner at that. Frost, birds and underripeness are persistent problems. Riesling does best to give Moselle-like flavours. Cabernet, though made with love and care, tends to distinct greenness. Moorilla is now concentrating on Pinot Noir from the Derwent Valley vineyard which, in the past, has been superb. A distinctive cloth label reveals the owner's textile background.

Morris Wines

Mia Mia Vineyard, Rutherglen, *Victoria*. Est. 1859. 55,000
cases. Owners: Orlando Wines. Wine maker: Mick Morris.
Vineyards: 200 acres of Muscat, Tokay, Sem., Chard., Durif,
Shiraz, Cab.Sauv. here and at Balldale in *NSW*.

Morris's Liqueur Muscat is Australia's secret weapon: an aromatic silky treacle that draws gasps from sceptics. The old tin winery building is a treasure-house of ancient casks of Muscats and Tokays, so concentrated by evaporation that they need freshening with young wine before bottling. The dark red Cabernet and Durif are impressive but hard wines; Semillon and Chardonnay surprisingly good since Orlando's came under the same ownership.

Moss Wood

Metricup Road, Willyabrup, Margaret River, *WA*. Est. 1969. 3,000 cases. Owner: Keith Mugford. Vineyards: 21 acres of Cab., Sem., P.N. and Chard.

The winery that put the Margaret River among Australia's top-quality areas. Moss Wood Cabernet seems to define the style of the region: sweetly clean, faintly grassy, intensely deep and compact – almost thick, in fact, but without the clumsiness that implies. Definitely for very long ageing. Good Chardonnay and Pinot Noir are now also produced.

Mount Anakie

Staughton Vale Road, Anakie, *Victoria*. Est. 1968. 4,000 cases. Owners: Otto and Bronwyn Zambelli. 55 acres of Geelong vines.

Previously owned by the Hickinbothams (q.v.), this small winery now produces a range of wines including Dolcetto.

Mount Langhi Ghiran

Buangor, Ararat, *Victoria*. 6,500 cases. Owners: Ian Menzies and Trevor Mast. Vineyards: 52 acres of mixed varieties.

The bulk of this winery's production is divided between a rich, peppery Rhône-like Shiraz and a good Cabernet blend. Riesling and Pinot Noir are also produced.

Mount Mary

Coldstream West Road, Lilydale, Yarra Valley, *Victoria*. Est. 1971. 3,000 cases. Owners: Dr John and Marli Middleton. Vineyards: 20 acres of Cab., Cab.Franc, Merlot, Chard., P.N. and some Malbec.

A near-fanatical doctor's pastime which has become very serious indeed. His 'Cabernets' blend (Cab.Sauv. 50%, Cab.Franc and Merlot 22.5% each and Malbec 5%) is like a classic Bordeaux; mid-weight, complex and intensely fruity without any 'burn'. Mount Mary Chardonnays are strong, rich and golden; new-oak fermented and, like the Cabernets, ageing easily up to ten years.

Mountadam

Eden Valley, Adelaide Hills, *SA*. Est. 1972. 15,000 cases. Owner: Adam Wynn. Vineyards: 70 acres, mainly of Chard., with some Cab.Sauv., P.N. and Ries.

Adam Wynn, whose family founded the Coonawarra-based firm now owned by Penfolds, trained in Bordeaux and established this high-altitude winery with the help of his father David. The grapes grown here go into the Mountadam range of varietals. A second label, called David Wynn, includes Chardonnay, Cabernet, Shiraz and Riesling, all made from bought-in Eden Valley grapes.

A. Norman & Sons

Grants Gully Road, Clarendon, *SA*. Est. 1851. 150,000 cases. Owners: The Norman family. Vineyards: 106 acres at Angle Vale of Gewürz. and 69 acres at Marion of P.N., Ch.Bl., Cab.Sauv., Shiraz, Rhine Ries., Chard., Sauv.Bl., Merlot.

Still family-run after 140 years, and still fertile in good ideas. In 1973 the Normans produced South Australia's first Gewürztraminer. This, their Chenin Blanc and Pinot Noir are all original and well made. Norman's Conquest (*sic*) is a good-value sparkler.

Oakridge Estate

Seville, Yarra Valley, *Victoria*. Est. 1982. 3,000 cases. Owners: Jim and Irene Zitzlaff. Wine maker: Michael Zitzlaff. Vineyards: 20 acres, some not yet producing.

High-quality family winery which makes small quantities of two red wines: an excellent Cabernet Sauvignon and a Cabernet/Shiraz/Merlot blend.

Olive Farm

Great Eastern Highway, South Guildford, Perth, *WA*. Est. 1829. 6,500 cases. Owners: V. & J. Yurisich & Son. Vineyards: 35 acres of various vines.

Possibly the oldest winery in uninterrupted use and family ownership in Australia. Bargain well-made flagon wine is most of the business, but bottles of considerable quality – especially the Cabernet – are produced too. Prices are very modest.

Orlando

Rowland Flat, Barossa, *SA*. Est. 1847 by Johann Gramp. 5.5m. cases. Owner: Orlando Wines. Vineyards: about 600 acres spread over Barossa and in Eden and surrounding hills. Also at Ramco Riverland, where the Chard. is of particular importance, and at Steingarten in the Eastern Barossa Ranges. Large quantities of fruit are bought in.

One of the biggest and most technically advanced firms, recently bought back from its former owners, Reckitt and Colman, by management with the help of Pernod-Ricard (France), Crédit Agricole (France) and Magnum (New Zealand). Orlando, in turn, owns Morris (q.v.) in Victoria and has recently bought the Wyndham Group of Hunter and Mudgee wineries. Their best wines are white, especially Rhine Rieslings, of which their rare Steingarten has often been Australia's best in the steely style. Spätleses and Ausleses are exceptionally well made. Their leading red is Jacob's Creek Claret, a well-mannered beautifully packaged middleweight, Australia's biggest-selling bottled dry red. Its white sister wine is a remarkably good value Rhine Riesling. RF Cabernet and Chardonnay are good-value medium-price varietals; St Hilary Chardonnay, St Hugo Cabernet and St Helga Riesling all a step up in quality and price. Malbecs are also big and age-worthy. Eden Valley Gewürztraminer is softly spicy. Orlando's sparkling wine is called Carrington.

Peel Estate

Fletcher Road, Baldivis, nr. Mandurah, *WA*. Est. 1974. 5,000 cases. Owners: Will and Helen Nairn and an English syndicate. Vineyard: 37 acres of Cab.Sauv., Chard., Ch.Bl., Shiraz, Merlot, Verdelho and Zin.

Strong California influence shows in this blossoming estate. Chenin Blanc aged in oak is modelled on the lovely Chappellet Napa wine, California's best. Zinfandel is clean and aromatic, Shiraz with 15 months in French and American oak seems to be a wine for long ageing.

Penfolds

Nuriootpa Winery, Barossa Valley, *SA*. Est. 1844. Visits. Owner: Adelaide Steamships. Vineyards: about 5,000 acres in total, Magill, Clare, Coonawarra and at Morgan, SA. All varieties are both grown and bought in.

Penfolds was founded by a doctor and run by his descendants until 1962. The present owners took over in 1976. It remains the most esteemed red-wine company in Australia, above all for its brilliant Grange Hermitage, the one true first-growth of the southern hemisphere, and more recently for its Magill Estate Shiraz and Clare Estate Merlot blend. Grange, although Shiraz, tastes more like Bordeaux than Rhône wine. St. Henri claret, Private Bin reds, Bin 707 Cabernet, Bin 389 Cabernet Shiraz, Bin 128 Coonawarra Claret are all among the best of their class. The house style, using American oak, is almost as important as the origin of the grapes. Estate names in

South Australia are Kalimna, Auldana, Koonunga Hill and Modbury; in New South Wales, Dalwood in the Hunter Valley (for cheaper lines) and Minchinbury and Rooty Hill (for sparkling wines). White wines have never been Penfold's strong point: Pinot Riesling from the Hunter Valley is perhaps best. 'Ports' are excellent: Magill a bargain and Grandfather a legend.

Penfolds now owns a number of other wineries, including Kaiser Stuhl, Wynns, Tollana and Seaview in South Australia, and Tulloch in New South Wales.

Petaluma

Piccadilly, Adelaide, *SA*. Est. 1976. 35,000 cases plus 30,000 *méthode champenoise*. Owners: Len Evans, Colin Ryan, Denis Horgan, Brian Croser and Bollinger. Vineyards: 150 acres in the Adelaide Hills, 100 acres in Coonawarra and 49 acres in Clare.

The name to conjure with in small new luxury wineries. Petaluma makes Australia's most prestigious sparkling wine, Croser, and an excellent second label called Bridgewater Mill, both using the *méthode champenoise* under the guidance of Bollinger, which has owned a part-share in the firm since 1985. Brian Croser started the idea of buying small batches of the best grapes to process either at the College at Riverina, where he was senior lecturer, or in borrowed facilities. His first wine was a notable late-picked Rhine Riesling. In 1977 he made Australia's most impressive Chardonnay to date with grapes from Cowra, New South Wales. With partners he established a winery and small vineyard at Piccadilly near Adelaide. Both Chardonnay (now from Coonawarra) and Riesling (from Clare) have memorable impact, concentrated aromas and sheer class. The Adelaide Hills vineyards supply Chardonnay and Pinot Noir for the immaculate sparkling wine, known simply as 'Croser'.

Petersons

Mount View, Hunter Valley, *NSW*. Est. 1971. 6,000 cases. Owners: The Peterson family. Wine maker: Gary Reed. Vineyards: 40 acres of Chard., Sem., Cab.Sauv., Shiraz and P.N.

Acccomplished, trophy-winning small winery whose first releases were in 1981. Wines include an exceptional Chardonnay, a good Semillon, Cabernet, Shiraz and Pinot Noir.

Pierro

Willyabrup, Margaret River, *WA*. Est. 1980. 3,000 cases. Owner: Dr. Michael Peterkin. Visits. Vineyards: 15 acres of Chard., P.N., Sauv.Bl. and other varieties.

High-quality (and high-price) winery producing small quantities of well-received Chardonnay, Pinot Noir and Sauvignon Blanc.

Pike's Polish Hill River

Sevenhill, Clare, *SA*. Est. 1984. 6,000 cases. Owners: The Pike family. Vineyards: 30 acres at Polish Hill River, with half the grapes bought in.

Neil and Andrew Pike, who run this winery part-time when not working at Mitchell Cellars (q.v.) and Penfolds (q.v.) respectively, make good Riesling, Cabernet, Chardonnay, Shiraz and Sauvignon.

Max Schubert, creator of Grange Hermitage, the 'first-growth' of the southern hemisphere.

Pipers Brook
Bridport, *Tasmania*. Est. 1972. 3,900 cases. Owners: 17
shareholders. Wine maker: Dr. Andrew Pirie (the largest
shareholder). Vineyards: 30 acres (with 35 more planned) of
Cab., Chard., Pinot, Rhine Ries., Gewürz., Merlot, Cab.Franc.
The bold enterprise of an eclectic mind in search of ideal
conditions: cool but not too cool. Dr. Pirie stresses that
vines work most efficiently where evaporation is not too
high – 'when the grass stays green'. His hill-top vineyard
within sight of the island's north coast (and reach of sea
winds) has already made superb dry Riesling and austere
Chardonnay, very characteristic Pinot Noir and Cabernet
with lively and intense flavours promising great things.

Pirramimma
Johnston Road, McLaren Vale, *SA*. Est. 1892. 10,000 cases.
Owners: The Johnston family. Wine maker: Geoff Johnston.
Vineyard: 136 acres of Cab.Sauv., Shiraz, Mataro, Rhine Ries.,
Palomino, Chard. and other lesser varieties.
Long-established but recently much improved estate, still
making bulk wine but scoring high points for clean black-
berryish Cabernet, aromatic Riesling, a soft light Shiraz
and a bigger oak-aged one. Also gutsy vintage ports.

Plantagenet Wines
Mount Barker, *WA*. Est. 1968. 7,500 cases. Owners: one-third
owned by UK interests. Wine maker: John Wade. Vineyards:
70 acres at Mt. Barker, mainly Rhine Ries., with Cab.Sauv.,
Shiraz, Sauv.Bl., Merlot, some Chard.
The senior winery at Mount Barker. Their triumph to
date is exceptional Rhine Riesling of powerful Spätlese
style with a beautifully long dry finish. Cabernet and
Shiraz are less distinguished but could hardly be more.
Chardonnay and Chenin Blanc have been good recently.

Quelltaler
Clare-Watervale, Clare Valley, *SA*. Est. 1865 by the Sobels
family. 90,000 cases. Owners: Wolf Blass Wines Ltd.
Vineyards: 360 acres of Cab.Sauv., Rhine Ries., Shiraz, Sem.
A famous old name for reliable basic hock and claret,
bought in 1987 by Wolf Blass of the Barossa. Wood-aged
Semillon from old vines is perhaps the best wine.

Redgate
Boodjidup Road, Margaret River, *WA*. Est. 1977. 5,000 cases.
Owners: The Ullinger family. Vineyards: 40 acres of
Cab.Sauv., Cab.Franc, P.N., Ries., Sem. and Sauv.Bl.
Margaret River winery adopting a traditional wine-
making approach. Cabernet Sauvignon and Semillon are
both good, Riesling is made in late-harvest and dry
versions.

Redman
Naracoorte Road, Coonawarra, *SA*. Est. 1966. 22,000 cases.
Owners: The Redman family. Wine maker: Bruce Redman.
Vineyards: 80 acres, mainly of Shiraz, with some Cab.Sauv.
and a little Merlot.
Founded by the Redmans of Rouge Homme (q.v.) after
Lindeman's took over the company in 1965, this winery
produces just two red wines from Coonawarra vines. The
bulk of production is taken up with Shiraz-based Redman
Claret, the rest with Cabernet Sauvignon.

Robinsons Family Winery
Lyra Church Road, Ballandean, *Queensland*. Est. 1969. 5,000
cases. Owner and wine maker: John Robinson. Vineyards: 44
acres of Cab., Chard., P.N., Malbec, Gewürz., Shiraz.
A great rarity in Queensland, but only just north of the

New South Wales border. Very well made, if inevitably
stout red wines. Oak-age gives them surprising structure.
Whites have been less convincing.

Murray Robson Wines
Pokolbin, Hunter Valley, *NSW*. Est. 1988. 10,000 cases.
Owner: Murray Robson and partners. Vineyards: 125 acres
leased; some grapes bought in.
This new operation, set up by Murray Robson after he left
Briar Ridge (formerly Robson Vineyard), has no
vineyards or winery of its own; vines are leased and wines
vinified elsewhere. Robson's first wines, including Cabernet, Shiraz, Chardonnay, Sauvignon and Semillon, have
all done well in Australia.

Rockford
Krondorf Road, Tanunda, Barossa Valley, *SA*. Owners: the
O'Callaghan family. Vineyards: some Rhine Ries.; most grapes
bought in.
Small Barossa producer making a wide range of indivi-
dual wines.

Rosemount Estate
Denman, Upper Hunter District, *NSW*. Est. 1969. Wine
maker: Philip Shaw. Vineyards: about 1,000 acres in the Upper
Hunter and Coonawarra.
Rosemount has blended confidence and quality to
produce some of the most popular Australian premium
wines in export markets. Chardonnay, notably the Show
Reserve label and Roxburgh Vineyard bottlings, led the
way, but Fumé Blanc and late-harvest Rhine Rieslings are,
in different ways, excellent. Roxburgh Cabernet is big and
giving, the Coonawarra reds more oaky and vibrant.

Rothbury Estate
Broke Road, Pokolbin, Lower Hunter Valley, *NSW*. Est.
1969. Visits. 140,000 cases. Owners: a public company. Wine
maker: Peter Hall. Vineyards: 540 acres in the Lower Hunter
Valley, Upper Hunter and Cowra of Chard., Sem., P.N.,
Shiraz and Cab.Sauv. Also 30 acres of Sauv.Bl. at
Marlborough in New Zealand.
Long-lived Semillon in the true old Hunter style made the
reputation of this impressive winery; Syrah backed it up.
Production is now concentrated on barrel-fermented and
matured Chardonnay. Shiraz and Cabernet Sauvignon are
the two main red wines. Top wines, including spicy, high-
flavoured Chardonnays, bear the 'Reserve' label. Rothbury exports large quantities of its wine, as well as selling
by mail order to the Rothbury Estate Society.

Rouge Homme
Naracoorte Road, Coonawarra, *SA*. Est. 1908. Owners:
Penfolds. Wine maker: Greg Clayfield. Vineyards: 320 acres of
Cab.Sauv., Shiraz, P.N., Chard., Rhine Ries. and Sauv.Bl.
Old family winery of consistent quality bought by
Lindeman's in 1965 and now owned by Penfolds. Quality
remains high. The best wines here are the firm, rich
Coonawarra Cabernets, though the Shiraz/Cabernet
blend can also be good. Whites include a variable
Chardonnay and Estate Dry White, a blend of Sauvignon
and Riesling.

Ryecroft
Ingoldby Road, McLaren Flat, *SA*. Est. 1988; vineyards
replanted 1981. 20,000 cases. Owners: a consortium. Wine
maker: Nick Holmes. Vineyards: 124 acres of Cab.Sauv.,
Merlot, Malbec, Chard.
One of the oldest wineries in McLaren Vale, Ryecroft has

changed hands several times over the last 30 years. At present it produces agreeable Cabernet and Chardonnay.

St. Huberts
Maroondah Highway, Coldstream, Yarra Valley, *Victoria*. Est. 1968. 15,000 cases. Owner: a syndicate. Wine maker: Brian Fletcher. Vineyards: 55 acres of Cab., Shiraz, Rhine Ries., P.N., Chard. and Trebbiano.

For long a rather shambolic winery with some excellent wines and others disappointing. Riesling is their best wine; the 1977 at 5 years old was one of Australia's most vital and lovely. Recent late-harvest Rieslings have been notable, and the Cabernet can be good. A sparkling wine is on its way.

St. Leonard's Winery
Wahgunyah, *Victoria*. Est. 1866. 10,000 cases. 101 acres. Owner: Brown Brothers and Syndicate.

An old northeast Victoria winery name revived in the 1970s for a replanted vineyard in collaboration with Brown Bros. of Milawa (q.v.), who make the wines. Semillon, Orange Muscat, Chardonnay, Cabernet and Shiraz are all successful – the whites particularly so.

St Matthias Vineyard
West Tamar, *Tasmania*. 2,500 cases. Owners: Laurie and Adelle Wing. Vineyards: 20 acres of mixed varieties.

Up-and-coming winery in Australia's most up-and-coming cool-climate region. Well-situated vines on the banks of the River Tamar are vinified by Heemskerk (q.v.) into Chardonnay, Riesling, Pinot Noir and Cabernet/Merlot.

Saltram
Angaston Road, Barossa Valley, *SA*. Est. 1859. Owner: Seagrams. Vineyards: 70 acres of Chard., Rhine Ries., Cab., Shiraz, but great majority of grapes bought in.

A winery with a complicated history. It was bought from the original Salter family in 1972 by Dalgety's the graziers. In 1978 Seagrams took charge. For 20 years the wines were made by Peter Lehmann, whose Mamre Brook (Barossa) Cabernet became a classic. Metala Cabernet/Shiraz also survives his moving on. Brian Croser (*see* Petaluma) was subsequently consulted and a good-value Mamre Brook Chardonnay is one of the principal attractions. Pinnacle is the label for the best wines.

Sandalford
Caversham, Swan Valley, *WA*. Est. 1840. 50,000 cases. Visits. Owner: Caldbeck McGregor UK. Wine maker: Christian Morlaes. Vineyards: 350 acres, mainly Rhine Ries., Verdelho, Cab.Sauv. and Chard. in Margaret River, and 70 acres of Cab., Ch.Bl., Pedro Ximénez and Sem. at Caversham.

An atmospheric old property on the Swan River near Perth, next door to Houghton (q.v.). The Margaret River vines, including Verdelho, Cabernet, Riesling, Semillon and Shiraz, are best. Caversham wines include Cabernet, Zinfandel, Chenin/Verdelho and Semillon/Chardonnay. Sandalera is a delectable old 'madeira-style' dessert wine of Pedro Ximénez, aged for 7 years in small casks.

Saxonvale
Fordwich, Broke Road, Hunter Valley, *NSW*. Founded 1971. 50,000 cases. Owner: Wyndham Estate. Wine maker: Alasdair Sutherland. Vineyards: in Fordwich and Pokolbin, mostly Chard., Cab., Sem., Traminer and Shiraz.

An energetic young company with the technology to make a wide range well. Chardonnay and Semillon are their two best wines.

Seaview
Chaffey's Road, McLaren Vale, *SA*. Owners: Penfolds. Wine maker: Robin Moody.

Seaview, owned by Penfolds since 1985, makes Australia's bestselling range of wines – and a very creditable quality they are too. The best of the still table wines include the Cabernet Sauvignon, Cabernet/Shiraz and Shiraz, but it is Seaview's *méthode champenoise* sparkling wines, such as the Pinot Noir/Chardonnay, that score highest on a quality/price rating. They are among Australia's best sparkling wines.

Seppelt
Seppeltsfield via Tanunda, Barossa, *SA*. Est. 1851. Visits. Owners: the South Australian Brewing Company. Vineyards: Great Western, Victoria, of Ondenc, Rhine Ries., Chasselas, P.N., Chard., Shiraz and Cab.Sauv.; 417 acres at Keppoch, SA, of Rhine Ries., Sylv., Chard., Frontignan Bl., Cab.Sauv., Shiraz and P.N.; Seppeltsfield, Barossa Valley, SA; 296 acres at Drumborg, Victoria, of Rhine Ries., Ondenc, Muscadelle, Sylv., Gewürz., Chard., P.N., Chasselas and Cab.Sauv.; 306 acres at Barooga, NSW, near Rutherglen, of Chard., Ondenc, P.N., Muscat and Trebbiano; 395 acres at Qualco, SA, near Renmark, of Shiraz, Muscadelle, Rhine Ries., Doradillo, Cab.Sauv. and Ch.Bl.; Partalunga in the Adelaide hills, SA, planted with Rhine Ries., Chard., Sauv.Bl. and Cab.Sauv.

This vast acreage only supplies one third of Seppelt's needs for a kaleidoscope of wines. They dominate the sparkling market with Great Western 'Champagne'. Whites and reds range from such standards as Arawatta Riesling, Moyston Claret, Chalambar Burgundy and the Queen Adelaide range to Reserve bins and their top wines: Gold Label (Cabernet, Shiraz and Rhine Riesling) and Black Label and single-vineyard wines. 'District varietals' are new show-winning releases. One of Australia's most impressive companies and apparently on top form, winning innumerable prizes. Their Barossa H.Q. has vast stocks of fine old dessert wines, including some of Australia's best sherries and their legendary Para Liqueur port.

Sevenhill
Clare Valley, *SA*. Est. 1851. 8,000 cases. 130 acres. Wines: Rhine Ries., Tokay, Shiraz, Cab.Sauv., Merlot and Malbec.

An old Jesuit holding with its church and winery, principally making altar wine for many other Jesuit churches throughout Australia. They make a very good vintage port, and some long-lived reds, especially Shiraz/Cabernet.

Seville Estate
Linwood Road, Seville, *Victoria*. Est. 1962. 1,500 cases. 10 acres. Owners: Dr. Peter McMahon and family.

A tiny, exceptionally beautiful estate ranked as one of Australia's best. Cabernet is gently juicy like Pomerol, Chardonnay also low key but deep flavoured, Shiraz at 4 years spicy and almost honeyed – all taste (and are) luxuriously handmade. Most extraordinary are Riesling Beerenausleses, comparable with California's luscious best.

Stanley Wine Company
Dominic Street, Clare, *SA*. Est 1894. 100,000 cases and 6m. wine casks. Owner: Thomas Hardy & Sons. Vineyards: 600 acres in Clare.

The leading winery of the Clare district. It buys most of its grapes and bottles under the Stanley Leasingham label. Winemakers Selection is the top range: among the best are Bin 49 Cabernet, Bin 56 Cabernet/Malbec and two Rhine Rieslings (Bin 5 – sweetish; and Bin 7 – dry). Bestsellers include Bin 14 Chablis and Bin 68 Cabernet/Shiraz. 'Sauternes' is a speciality.

Stanton & Killeen
Rutherglen, *Victoria*. Est. 1875. 8,000 cases. Visits. Owners: The Stanton and Killeen families. Wine maker: Chris Killeen. 50 acres of Cab.Sauv., Shiraz, Muscat.

A small old family winery revitalized since 1970. Its Moodemere reds, both Cabernet and Shiraz, are now among the best in northeast Victoria. Dessert Muscats, Tokays and ports are luscious in the regional tradition, but light and elegant.

Taltarni
Moonambel, nr. Stawell, *Victoria*. Est. 1972. 40,000 cases. Owners: Red Earth Nominees Pty. Ltd. (John Goelet). Wine makers: Dominique Portet and Greg Gallagher. Vineyards: 290 acres, shallow gravel over clay, of Rhine Ries., Chard., Sauv.Bl., Ch.Bl., Cab.Sauv., P.N., Merlot, Malbec, Shiraz.

The brother winery to Clos du Val in the Napa Valley: extremely modern and well equipped without extravagance. Taltarni needs time to rival Clos du Val, but already its reds are imposing. 1977 and 1979 Special Reserve Cabernets were demonstrations of intent: enormous dark wines including pressings, built to last 20 years. More Merlot and Cabernet Franc have been added to recent vintages, bringing extra subtlety. Shiraz is made much lighter. Whites are less sure-footed.

Tarrawarra Vineyards
Healesville Road, Yarra Glen, Yarra Valley, *Victoria*. 6,500 cases. Owners: Marc and Eva Besen. Wine maker: David Wollan. Vineyard: 18 acres of Chard. and P.N.

Sophisticated new multi-million-dollar winery in Australia's trendiest wine region. The only release so far has been a good, but expensive, Chardonnay.

Taylors Wines
Auburn, Clare Valley, *SA*. Est. 1969. 200,000 cases. Owners: Taylor family. Vineyards: 750 acres of Cab.Sauv., Shiraz, P.N., Chard., and Rhine Ries.

Taylors began with reds, and makes pleasantly soft Cabernet. Whites were added in the mid-80s: the early-maturing, full Rhine Riesling is their best.

Temple Bruer
Milang Road, Angas Plains, *SA*. 4,000 cases. Owners: Barbara and David Bruer. Vineyards: 20 acres of Cab.Sauv., Cab.Franc, Shiraz, Merlot and Malbec; Ries. bought in.

Promising producer of mainly red wines – a straightforward Cabernet Sauvignon and more interesting Cabernet/Merlot and Shiraz/Malbec. A botrytized Riesling is also made from bought-in grapes.

Tisdall
Cornelia Creek Road, Echuca, *Victoria*. Est. 1979. About 40,000 cases (Rosbercon); 20,000 cases (Mt. Helen); plus bulk wines. Owner: Dr. Peter Tisdall. Wine maker: Jeff Clarke. 2 vineyards: Rosbercon (Echuca) – 80 acres of Colombard, Ch.Bl., Rhine Ries., Sem., Merlot, Cab.Sauv., Shiraz; Mt. Helen in Strathbogie Ranges, central Victoria – 110 acres of Cab.Sauv., Merlot, Rhine Ries., Chard., Sauv.Bl., Gewürz.

A substantial company making good commercial wines from Echuca (Murray Valley) grapes. Merlot is the best.

In the same winery John Ellis vinifies a different class of wine from young vineyards planted in the cool Strathbogie hills in central Victoria.

Tollana
Nuriootpa, Barossa Valley, *SA*. Est. 1888 as Tolley, Scott & Tolley. Owners: Penfolds. Wine maker: John Duval. Vineyards: Woodbury Estate, Eden Valley, 346 acres Rhine Ries., Cab.Sauv., Gewürz., Shiraz; Qualco, near Waikerie, 998 acres (500 for distilling wine).

An old Barossa brandy company taken over in 1961, was jerked into prominence in the late 1960s by the young Wolf Blass (q.v.), who made some splendid wines and said outrageous things about them. Since then Tollana has become a reliable name for very fruity and well-balanced Rhine Riesling, good Eden Valley Shiraz, Cabernet/Shiraz blended and Gewürztraminer.

Tolley's Pedare
30 Barracks Road, Hope Valley, nr. Adelaide, *SA*. Est. 1892. 260,000 cases. Visits. Owners: The Tolley family. Wine maker: Chris Tolley. Vineyards: 247 acres in the Barossa Valley; 247 acres at Qualco, Murray River.

One of Australia's largest family-owned wineries long based on bulk wines but changing gear since the mid-1980s. The name Pedare is now used for their premium wines, of which a crisp, cold-fermented Rhine Riesling, delicately spicy Gewürztraminer, Late Harvest Muscat, good Shiraz, Semillon, rosé and excellent ports are most remarkable. A name to watch.

Tulloch
De Beyers Road, Pokolbin, Hunter Valley, *NSW*. Est. 1893. 40,000 cases. Owners: Penfolds. Wine maker: Pat Auld. Vineyards: 65 acres in Pokolbin of Sem., Chard., Shiraz, Cab.Sauv. and P.N.

Now owned by Penfolds, but still managed by a member of the Tulloch family, this winery produces Hunter Riesling, Pokolbin dry red, and the premium Private Bin range which is doing well with Chardonnay, Semillon, a Semillon/Verdelho blend, and notably Hermitage and Cabernet. Glen Elgin is another name used for top wines.

Tyrrells
Broke Road, Pokolbin, Hunter Valley, *NSW*. Est. 1858. 360,000 cases. Owners: the Tyrrell family. Vineyard: 380 acres in the Hunter Valley and Upper Hunter.

Murray Tyrrell has been one of the main architects of the Hunter Valley revival of the 1970s, building on a traditional Semillon and Shiraz base but startling Australia with his well-calculated, not overstressed Chardonnays. His 'Bin 47' really led the way for Chardonnay in Australia. Pinot Noir has been much more variable (with '81 and '83 very good). 'Old Winery' is a premium commercial range of good character. 'Pinot Riesling' is a 50/50 Chardonnay/Semillon blend. Bestselling Long Flat Red and Long Flat White are serious (!) everyday wines. (The names are those of vineyards.)

Vasse Felix
Cowaramup, Margaret River, *WA*. Est. 1967. 8,000 cases. Owner: Holmes à Court family. Wine maker: David Gregg. Vineyard: 20 acres, Rhine Ries., Cab.Sauv., Shiraz, Malbec and Gewürz., with most fruit bought in.

The pioneer winery of Margaret River, and still level with the best, especially for very dark, firm and undoubtedly long-lived Cabernet. Late-picked Riesling and Gewürztraminer have both been very successful.

Virgin Hills

Lauriston West, *Victoria*. Est. 1968. 1,000 cases. Owner: Marcel Gilbert. Wine maker: Mark Sheppard. Vineyards: 40 acres of Cab.Sauv., Malbec, Shiraz, Cab.Fr., Merlot.
Virgin Hills makes just one wine, a Cabernet-based blend which has impressive power and concentration. Tom Lazar, the founder (now retired), believes he has made the best Australian wine ever. Certainly the very low yields give great power and fruit: they need time to show their true potential.

Wantirna Estate

Wantirna South, *Victoria*. Est. 1963. 1,000 cases. Owners: Reg and Tina Egan. Vineyards: 10 acres of Cab., Chard., P.N., Merlot, Rhine Ries.
A tiny estate in the suburbs of Melbourne, producing a Pinot Noir some consider Australia's best yet, a most gentlemanly Cabernet/Merlot blend and tiny quantities of other well-made wines. There is a waiting list for the mailing list.

Watervale Cellars

Watervale, Clare, *SA*. Est. 1977. 3,000 cases. Owners: Robert and Elizabeth Crabtree. Visits. Vineyards: 30 acres of mixed varieties, with half the grapes bought in from Clare and Watervale.
Consistently good Clare producer of Riesling, Shiraz/Cabernet and barrel-fermented Semillon.

Wendouree

Clare, *SA*. Est. 1895. 2,000 cases. Owner: The Liberman family. Wine maker: Tony Brady. 25 acres of Shiraz, Cab.Sauv., Malbec, Rhine Ries.
The late owner, Roly Birks, was one of the great conservative Aussie wine makers who made massive reds, largely used for blending by other wineries. The style is maintained by the new owner, especially in his Cabernet/Malbec/Shiraz; deep, dark, oak-scented. The Clare Riesling is also a fat, full-bodied wine. 'Vintage ports' are splendidly vigorous. Wendourie Pressings is a speciality made from the pressed wine of various grapes.

Westfield

Baskerville, Swan Valley, *WA*. Est. 1922. 3,000 cases. Owner: John and Mary Kosovich. Vineyard: 18 acres of Cab.Sauv., Shiraz, Chard., Merlot, Rhine Ries., Verdelho, Sem., Ch.Bl.
A Swan Valley miniature, notable for exceptional Semillon, good Cabernet and Verdelho.

Simon Whitlam

Broke, Hunter Valley, *NSW*. Est. 1982. 4,000 cases. Owners: David Clarke, Andrew Simon and Nicholas Whitlam. Vineyards: 20 acres of Chard., Sem., Cab.Sauv. and P.N.
Small but very high-quality producer of exciting Chardonnay and Cabernet, whose wines are made at Arrowfield (q.v.).

Wirra Wirra

McMurtrie Road, McLaren Vale, *SA*. Est. 1894, re-est. Est. 1969. 20,000 cases. Owners: Greg and Roger Trott. Vineyards: 82 acres of Cab.Sauv., Shiraz, Grenache, Rhine Ries., P.N., Merlot, Chard., Sauv.Bl.
The resurrection (in 1969) of a fine old bluestone winery to make ligher and more graceful wines than the usual macho McLaren Vale style. Rieslings are most remarkable. 'Church Block' is a Cabernet/Merlot/Shiraz blend. Pinot Noirs can be very good.

Woodley Wines

Glen Osmond (Adelaide), *SA*. Est. 1856. 350,000 cases. Owners: Seppelt.
A historic winery, with cellars in a former silver mine, bought by Seppelt in 1985. The elegant Queen Adelaide label is used for indifferent bought-in Barossa Riesling and McLaren Vale Cabernet/Shiraz claret.

Woodstock

Douglas Gully Road, McLaren Flat, *SA*. Est. 1974. 30,000 cases. Owners: the Collett family. Visits. Wine maker: Scott Collett. 60 acres of Cab.Sauv., Shiraz, Chard., Ries., Grenache.
Woodstock began producing wines in 1982. It now makes a wide range of varietals, including Cabernet, Shiraz and Chardonnay, as well as an excellent sweet Noble Dessert Wine.

Wrights

Cowaramup, Margaret River, *WA*. Est. 1974. 2,500 cases. Owners: Henry and Maureen Wright. Vineyards: 30 acres of Cab.Sauv., Rhine Ries., Shiraz, Sem. and Chard.
An unpretentious but quietly impressive winery. Dense, slightly earthy Cabernet, strongly flavoured Hermitage, broadly fruity, almost white-burgundy Riesling are clear expressions of Margaret River's exceptionally tasty grapes.

Wyndham Estate

Dalwood, Branxton, *NSW*. Est. 1928. 300,000 cases. Owners: Orlando Wines. Manager: Brian McGuigan. Wine maker: John Reynolds. Vineyards: large vineyards in the Hunter and Mudgee. Many varieties are bought in.
Wyndham Estate is the flagship winery of the large Hunter- and Mudgee-based Wyndham Group, now owned by Orlando (q.v.). Other wineries in the group include Hollydene, Richmond Grove, Saxonvale and Hunter Estate in the Hunter, and Craigmoor, Amberton and Montrose in Mudgee. Wyndham label wines include Bin 888 Cabernet/Merlot, Bin 444 Cabernet, Bin 555 Hermitage and Bin 222 Chardonnay, as well as an Auslese Riesling. Wines are vinified for immediate appeal.

Wynns

Memorial Drive, Coonawarra, *SA*. Est. 1918. 483,000 cases. Owners: Penfolds. Vineyards: Coonawarra – 1,186 acres of Cab.Sauv., Shiraz, Rhine Ries., Chard., P.N.; 'High Eden' (Barossa) – 524 acres of Rhine Ries.; Padthaway.
Wynn's most famous wines are Coonawarra Cabernet and Hermitage and a blend of the two; the Cabernet particularly successful. The Coonawarra Chardonnay is a good example of the drink-young style. Their bulk wines (and their rather good 'Samuel' port) come from Murrumbidgee grapes processed at another winery at Yenda.

Yalumba and Hill-Smith Estate

Eden Valley Road, Angaston, Barossa Valley, *SA*. Est. 1863. 415,000 cases. Visits. Owners: The Hill-Smith family. Vineyards: in the Barossa area, largely up at Pewsey Vale; near Walkerie on the Murray River. Almost all the grapes come from their own vineyards. Main varieties: Rhine Ries., Cab.Sauv., Chard., Gewürz., Merlot, Shiraz, Sauv.Bl.
The sixth generation of the Hill-Smith family is active in this distinctively upper-crust winery with an air of the turf about it. Their finest wines in the past were 'ports', but since the planting of higher and cooler land in the 1960s, their Pewsey Vale Rhine Rieslings have been very good and hugely popular. The drier Carte d'Or Riesling is one

of the best-value whites in Australia today. Wood-matured Semillon is good. Heggies Vineyard in the Barossa Hills makes very fine late-harvest Rieslings. Sparkling wines are also successful, especially *méthode champenoise* Yalumba D and good-value transfer method Angas Brut.

Reds in the past have been rather tough and dull, like many in Barossa. Galway Claret is a reliable mid-weight, but latterly the Signature series of reds has included some very good Cabernet/Shiraz and Cabernet/Malbec blends. Stocks of fine barrel-aged reds are now the biggest in Australia. Galway Pipe tawny is perhaps their best port, followed by a very rich Vintage.

Yarra Burn
Settlement Road, Yarra Junction, *Victoria*. 10,000 cases. Owners: David and Christine Fyffe. Vineyards: 24 acres of Yarra vines; half the grapes are bought in.
Somewhat variable boutique winery producing Chardonnay, Pinot Noir and Cabernet, as well as sparkling wine.

Yarra Yering
Briarty Road, Coldstream, Yarra Valley, *Victoria*. Est. 1969. 3,000 cases. Owner: Dr. Bailey Carrodus. Vineyards: 40 acres, Cab.Sauv., Shiraz, P.N., Malbec, Merlot, Sem. and Chard.
An individualist who initiated the wine revival of the Yarra Valley, with a well-tended vineyard producing small yields of high-quality fruit. Carrodus is not keen on varietal labelling: a Bordeaux-type blend is called Dry Red No.1, a Rhône-type, Dry Red No.2. Both are widely admired for harmonious composition. Pinot Noir he makes straight, and recent vintages have been highly praised.

Yellowglen
White's Road, Smythesdale, nr. Ballarat, *Victoria*. Est. 1971. 130,000 cases. 30 acres. Visits. Owners: Mildara. Wine maker: Jeffrey Wilkinson.
Yellowglen is determined to make Australia's best sparkling wine. Four *méthode champenoise* wines are made. The best is the Cuvée Victoria, made from Chardonnay, Pinot Noir and Pinor Meunier. A sparkling liqueur is also made. Nearly all the grapes are bought in.

Yeringberg
Coldstream, Yarra Valley, *Victoria*. Est. 1862. 800 cases in total of Cab., Chard., Pinot and Marsanne. Visits by appt. Owner: Guillaume de Pury. Vineyards: 5 acres of Cab., Merlot, Malbec, P.N., Chard. and Marsanne.
The remnant of a wonderful old country estate near Melbourne, rather tentatively making some excellent wines. Pinot Noir, Chardonnay, Cabernet and Merlot are delicate and charming. The potential of the old estate shows, though production is tiny.

NEW ZEALAND

While almost every Australian settler, it seems, planted vines for wine, the new New Zealanders did much less to exploit the temperate climate and fertile soils of their islands. No real wine industry, beyond isolated missions and private estates, existed until Dalmatian Kauri-gum workers and Lebanese immigrants started to provide for their own needs in the Auckland area early in the 20th century. Their products were crude, from poor vines unsuited to the warm humidity of Auckland. Phylloxera forced them to plant hybrids. Most of the wine was fortified and probably deserved its unflattering title of 'Dally plonk'. Nor did the small and strait-laced Anglo-Saxon community, frequently muttering about Prohibition, provide an encouraging market-place.

Matters began to change quite briskly on a local basis in the late 1960s, as New Zealanders developed both a tentative export market to Australia and Great Britain – and also a taste for wine themselves. In 1960 almost half of the total 958 acres of vines was in the Auckland area, and most of the rest in Hawke's Bay on the central east coast of the North Island. The '60s saw a trebling of the Auckland acreage and the development of Waikato, 40 miles south. They saw the Hawke's Bay vineyards double in size and an important new area spring up at Poverty Bay near Gisborne, north of Hawke's Bay.

Results were encouraging, even if the first mass plantings were decidedly unambitious. The market was most interested in cheap fortified wines – made all the cheaper by the illegal addition of water. For table wines Müller-Thurgau was widely considered to be as high a mark as New Zealand could profitably reach. Early planters mistakenly took German advice that their climate was closer to that of Germany than of France.

Experiments with Sauvignon Blanc and soon with Chardonnay in the '70s proved that the climate of the principal fruit-growing region, the east coast of North Island, was not so much German as central French. It was these east-coast areas that flourished in the 1970s, quintupling their acreage while Auckland's slightly shrank. But the '70s also saw the vine move to the South Island: by 1980 Marlborough, at its northern tip, had nearly 2,000 acres and experimental planting had moved as far south as Canterbury.

New Zealand's true potential as a producer of fine wine burst upon the world in the mid-1980s. To be precise, on a day in February 1985 when the wine critics, buyers and journalists of Britain attended a tasting (an annual event) at New Zealand House in London. Those who were present are not likely to forget the excitement of that morning, as it became clear that a dozen different wineries had produced white wines of a racy vitality and tingling fruitiness that are only met with on rare occasions anywhere.

The best of the Sauvignon Blancs were the most memorable wines, almost giving an extra dimension to this essentially second-league variety. The verdict was unanimous: New Zealand had jumped straight into the first division of the world's white wine producers.

Subsequent tastings confirmed the fact, adding Chardonnays of extremely sound quality, a few Rieslings, Chenin Blancs and Gewürztraminers of top quality by any standards, and some very promising red wines. Any shortcomings in the early quality of the reds should be put down more to inexperience than to the quality of the grapes.

New Zealand's natural gift is what the wine makers of Australia and California are constantly striving for: the growing conditions that give slowly ripened, highly aromatic fruit. It is still too soon to judge just how good her eventual best wines will be, but the signs so far indicate that they will have the strength, structure and delicacy of wines from (for example) the Loire, Alsace, possibly the Médoc, possibly Champagne – with a freshness and vigour that seem to be New Zealand's own.

THE REGIONS

THE NORTH ISLAND

Auckland Until the 1970s the largest New Zealand wine region, but its almost subtropical climate, with considerable cloud cover and frequent autumn rain, was never suited to the vine. It is now eclipsed as a grape-growing region (both in terms of quantity and quality) by Gisborne, Hawke's Bay and Marlborough to the south, though many important wine companies are still based here.

Wineries include: Babich Wines, Collard Brothers, Cooks McWilliams, Coopers Creek, Corbans, Delegat's, De Redcliffe Estates, Goldwater Estate, Kumeu River, Lincoln, Matua Valley Wines, Montana, Nobilo Vintners, St Nesbit,

Selaks, Stonyridge Vineyard, Villa Maria.

Gisborne Still the largest grape-growing region, though Marlborough is catching up fast. This fertile area on the east coast of the North Island is well-suited to white grape varieties, but suffers from autumn rains which force the harvest forward, and also from active phylloxera, which is causing almost total replanting. Wineries are few, as most grapes are sent for blending to the major producers in Auckland.
Wineries include: Matawhero Wines, The Millton Vineyard.

Hawke's Bay The North Island's top quality region, situated on the east coast south of Gisborne, in the rain shadow of the island's volcanic mountain centre. Its sunshine and its glorious mixture of soils – silt, shingle and clay – provide enormous potential for red and white grapes, and the number of wineries here is increasing.
Wineries include: Brookfields Vineyard, Esk Valley, Mission Vineyards, Ngatawara Wines, C J Pask, Te Mata Estate, Vidal Wine Producers.

Northland This rainy, humid region in the extreme north was the site of New Zealand's first vineyard, but it is ill-suited to grape-growing. There are only a handful of small wineries.
Wineries include: The Antipodean.

Waikato A small, rainy region, spreading eastwards from Waikato, about 45 miles south of Auckland, to the Bay of Plenty. There are scarcely 300 acres of vines here and major wineries, such as Morton Estate, source their grapes from Hawke's Bay, Gisborne or elsewhere.
Wineries include: Cooks McWilliams, Morton Estate.

Wairarapa Up-and-coming region at the southern end of the North Island, just north of Wellington. The good soil, low rainfall and autumn sunshine prompted the planting of vines in 1979 at Martinborough Vineyard. Pinot Noir and Chardonnay show promise.
Wineries include: Martinborough Vineyard.

THE SOUTH ISLAND

Canterbury One of several fledgling wine regions in the South Island, around Christchurch on the mid-east coast. Its coldish climate and low rainfall have lured an increasing number of small wineries here during the 1980s and resulted in some impressive Riesling and Pinot Noir.

Wineries include: Giesen, St Helena.

Marlborough/Blenheim Sunny, stony-soiled Marlborough, at the northeastern tip of the South Island, has proved the making of New Zealand's wine industry. Since it was pioneered by Montana in 1973, it has produced some of the world's best Sauvignon Blanc, and has now overtaken Hawke's Bay as the country's second-largest wine region. Its excellent soil, low rainfall (irrigation is essential, at least for young vines) and cool autumns, combined with its position in New Zealand's sunniest spot, are ideal for growing well-favoured fruit: Sauvignon, Chardonnay and Riesling have all proved very successful. Wind is the only serious problem. The crowds are forming: from Australian giants such as Thomas Hardy to the Champagne house of Deutz.
Wineries include: Cellier Le Brun, Cloudy Bay, Corbans Wines, Hunters Wines, Montana.

Nelson Very small, somewhat inaccessible region to the west of Marlborough, which shares some of that region's beneficial conditions, but suffers from autumn rainfall. Few wineries yet.
Wineries include: Weingut Seifried.

NEW ZEALAND PRODUCERS

The Antipodean
Glenfield, Auckland, North Island. Est. 1985. 350 cases. Owners: James and Petar Vuletic. Vineyards: 5 acres of Cab.Sauv., Merlot and Malbec.
Small, high-profile winery producing tiny quantities of one wine, an improving Bordeaux-style blend of Cabernet, Merlot and Malbec, aged in small oak barriques.

Babich Wines
Babich Road, Henderson, Auckland. Est. 1916. Owners: The Babich family. Wine maker: Joe Babich. Vineyards: 70 acres of sloping loam-on-clay. Sauv.Blanc, Merlot, Cab.Sauv., P.N., Chard., Palomino, Pinotage.
A well-established, thoroughly modernized winery making firm and fruity whites and wood-aged reds. Their Pinot Noir and Cabernet are less successful than their whites. Single-vineyard Irongate Chardonnay, oak-fermented, has won acclaim.

Brookfields Vineyard
Meeanee, Hawke's Bay. 5,000 cases. Owner: Peter Robertson. Vineyards: 7 acres of Chard. and Sauv.Bl.; most grapes bought in.
Owner Peter Robertson stresses varietal character and small volumes. New Nevers oak is bought each year for the Cabernet and Chardonnay. Other wines include a Sauvignon and a good Cabernet blend.

Cellier Le Brun
Renwick, Marlborough. Est. 1980. Owner: Daniel Le Brun. Vineyards: 50 acres of Chard., P.N. and Pinot Meunier on stony soil.
Daniel Le Brun's family were champagne makers in Epernay and here, with his wife Adele, he is making 10,000 cases of *méthode champenoise* to the classic formula, plus 5,000 cases of still Chardonnay. Early results from the modern winery are encouraging.

Cloudy Bay
Jacksons Road, Blenheim, Marlborough, South Island. Est. 1985. 22,000 cases. Owner: Veuve Clicquot Ponsardin S.A. (since 1990). Wine maker: Kevin Judd. Vineyards: 100 acres of Sauv.Bl., Sem., Cab.Sauv. and Merlot.
Founded in 1985 by the Australian entreprenuer David Hohnen, whose Western Australian winery Cape Mentelle had already received great acclaim, Cloudy Bay rapidly became the spearhead of New Zealand's assault on the international wine market in the late 1980s. Its pungent, nettle-sharp Sauvignon Blanc, made from vines grown in Marlborough's stony soil and near-ideal climate for white wines, is regarded by some as the finest expression of this grape's varietal character to be found anywhere, and frequently sells out all around the world within weeks of its release. It does not come cheap though, and neither do its two siblings, an excellent oaky Chardonnay and a relatively lean Cabernet/Merlot blend.

Collard Brothers
303 Lincoln Road, Henderson, Auckland. Est. 1910. Owners: Lionel, Bruce and Geoffrey Collard. Vineyards: 10 acres of the rolling Sutton Baron estate (Ries., Cab.Franc, Gewürz., Cab.Sauv., Merlot). 40-acre Rothesay vineyard, at Waimauku, 14 miles northwest, Chard., Sauv.Blanc, Cab.Franc, Cab.Sauv.
A small family company now moving towards French rather than German styles. They buy Chardonnay from Hawke's Bay and Tolaga to supplement their own

Rothesay grapes. Estate-grown Riesling and Gewürztraminer makes fruity, Germanic wines, while reds follow Bordeaux philosophy with new oak and a Cabernet-Merlot blend.

Cooks McWilliams
PO Box 26-019 Epsom, Auckland. Est. 1969.
Merged with McWilliams in 1984. Owner: Corbans Wines.
Wine maker: Kerry Hitchcock. Three wineries at
Te Kauwhata and Napier. Vineyards: 20 acres at
Te Kauwhata, Sauv.Blanc, 215 at Hawke's Bay,
Cab.Sauv., Cab.Franc, Merlot, Sauv.Blanc, Chard.,
Gewürz. Grapes are also bought in Gisborne
and Hawke's Bay.

The merger of Cooks and McWilliams in 1984 has left both names on the letterhead, and both labels are used, though since the takeover of Cooks McWilliams by Corbans in 1987 the McWilliams range has gradually been wound down. Cooks is an ultra-modern concern, active in exports. The top of their range is oak-aged Chardonnay of great charm, a light but vividly fruity Cabernet, firm and lively Gewürztraminer with some sweetness and appley sweet Chenin Blanc not unlike a Coteaux du Layon wine. Sauvignon Blanc 1989 from Hawke's Bay was long and tingling.

Coopers Creek
Main Road, Huapai, Auckland, North Island. Est. 1980.
17,000 cases. Owner: Andrew Hendry. Wine maker: Kim
Crawford. Vineyards: 17 acres at Hawke's Bay of Chard. and
P.N.; 10 acres at Huapai of Cab.Sauv. and Merlot; most grapes
bought in.

Successful small winery making high-quality varietals and popular blends. Coopers' best wines are its two Hawke's Bay Chardonnays, the finer of the two called 'Swamp Road'. Other good wines include Fumé Blanc, Coopers Dry White (a blend of Chardonnay, Semillon and Chenin Blanc) and Cabernet/Merlot.

Corbans Wines
426–448 Great North Road, Henderson, Auckland. Est. 1902.
750,000 cases, plus wine casks. Visits. Owners: Magnum
Corporation. Vineyards: 500 acres in Hawke's Bay and Te
Kauwhata. 200 acres in Marlborough. Two-thirds of grapes
bought in.

Founded by a Lebanese family in the early 20th century and, since the takeover of Cooks McWilliams (q.v.) in 1987, the country's second-biggest wine company after Montana (q.v.). Corbans produces five ranges of wine: the straight Corbans range, Stoneleigh, Liebestraum, Velluto Rosso and Robard & Butler. The finest is the Stoneleigh range, made from Corbans' excellent vineyard in the South Island, which includes Sauvignon, very good Rhine Riesling, oaky Chardonnay and Cabernet.

Delegat's
Hepburn Road, Henderson, Auckland. Est. 1947. Visits.
Owners: The Delegat family and the Wilson Group. Wine
maker: Brent Marris. Vineyards: contract growers exclusively
in the Gisborne and Hawke's Bay region. Chard., Sauv.Blanc,
Gewürz., Cab.Sauv.

Good whites from Gisborne and Hawke's Bay grapes include very fine and aromatic Chardonnay, Pinot Gris and a notable sweet Müller-Thurgau Auslese. Huapai Cabernet, though immature, seems big and 'wild', with real potential. Delegat's superior range, called Proprietors Reserve, includes a particularly rich and smooth Hawke's Bay Cabernet ('87).

De Redcliffe Estates
Mangatawhiri Valley, Auckland. Est. 1976. 19,000 cases.
Owner: Chris Canning. Vineyards: 40 acres of gravel-based
land with Cab.Sauv., Merlot, Chard. and Semillon, plus similar
area under contract with P.N., Sauv.Blanc and Chard.

All wines are wood-aged; the Chardonnay undergoes barrel fermentation too. Experiments with clonal selection and blending are under way with the aim of adding more substance to the light, elegant wines.

Esk Valley
Bay View, Napier, Hawke's Bay, North Island. Est. 1933 (as
Glenvale). Owners: Villa Maria.

This old family winery, previously called Glenvale, was taken over by Villa Maria (q.v.) in 1987. Its Hawke's Bay grapes go into a wide range of wines, including Cabernet, Chardonnay, particularly crisp and fruity Chenin Blanc, and a delicately oaky Cabernet/Merlot blend. Like other wineries in the Villa Maria group, it uses the 'Private Bin' and 'Reserve' labels.

Giesen
Burnham, Christchurch, South Island. Est. 1984. 1,000 cases.
Owners: Marcel, Alex and Theo Giesen. Wine maker: Marcel
Giesen. Vineyards: 53 acres of mixed varieties.

Small new winery founded by three German brothers in 1984. Whites, including a *méthode champenoise* sparkling wine, dominate production.

Goldwater Estate
Putiki Bay, Waiheke Island, Nr Auckland. Est. 1978. 1,500
cases. Owners: Kim and Jeanette Goldwater. Vineyard: 5
acres, Cab.Sauv., Cab.Franc, Merlot and Sauv.Blanc. 10 more
acres to be planted, mostly with Merlot.

Two wines – a Bordeaux-blend red and a wood-aged Sauvignon Blanc – in tiny quantities from a beautiful island vineyard which benefits from a warm, dry microclimate.

Hunters Wines
Rapaura Road, Blenheim (Marlborough district). Est. 1982.
25,000 cases. Visits. Owner: Jane Hunter. Vineyards: 40 acres
of Chard., Sauv.Blanc, Ries., Müller-Thurgau, Gewürz., Pinot
Gris, Cab.Sauv.; most grapes bought in.

Expanding family winery producing some of the South Island's best wines. The varietal range includes good barrel-fermented Chardonnay, Sauvignon Blanc and Rhine Riesling, with Cabernet and Pinot Noir recently added. Red and white blends are sold under the Spring Creek Estate label.

Kumeu River Wines
PO Box 24, Main Road, Kumeu, Auckland. Est. 1944 as San
Marino Wines. 17,000 cases. Owners: The Brajkovich family.
Vineyards: 46 acres of Chard., Cab.Sauv., Sauv., Cab.Franc,
Merlot, P.N.

A small Yugoslav family winery north of Auckland beginning to make firm, balanced Cabernet. The Kumeu River whites – a Chardonnay and a Sauvignon – are rich and stylish. Experience in St-Emilion (at Ch. Magdelaine) encouraged winemaker Michael Brajkovich to blend Merlot with Cabernets for his top red. Other wines (especially excellent concentrated Sauvignon Blanc) are sold under the Brajkovich and San Marino labels.

Lincoln
130 Lincoln Road, Henderson, Auckland, North Island. Est.
1937. Owners: Peter and John Fredatovich. Vineyards: 60

acres in Auckland; grapes bought in from Gisborne, Hawke's Bay and Marlborough.

Large family-owned winery producing a wide range of wines. Varietals include Chardonnay, Cabernet Sauvignon (a well-made, cedary and attractive '88), Gewürztraminer, Müller-Thurgau and a *macération carbonique* Gamay wine called Gamay Beaujolais. Blended red and white wines are sold under the Brigham Creek label.

Martinborough Vineyard

Martinborough, Wairarapa, North Island. 5,000 cases. Owners: the Schultz and Milne families. Wine maker: Larry McKenna. Vineyards: 25 acres of Wairarapa vines; grapes bought in.

Martinborough pioneered Wairarapa as a grape-growing region in the early 1980s, convinced of its suitability for Pinot Noir and Chardonnay. Other wineries followed, and it now produces some of New Zealand's most promising Pinot Noir, as well as Chardonnay, Sauvignon, Riesling and Gewürztraminer.

Matawhero Wines

Riverpoint Road, Gisborne. Est. 1976. 8,000 cases. Owners: The Irwin family. Vineyards: 100 acres of river loam, Gewürz., Ch.Bl., Chard., Müller-Thurgau, Sauv.Blanc.

A small-scale family operation whose hand-made wines have attracted much critical attention. Their Gewürztraminer is notably dry, aromatic and lingering. A blend of Gewürz and Müller-Thurgau is a huge improvement on Müller-Thurgau alone.

Matua Valley Wines

Waikoukou Road, Waimauku, Kumeu, Auckland. Est. 1974. 67,000 cases. Visits and restaurant. Owners: Ross and Bill Spence. Vineyards: 50 acres in Hawke's Bay of Cab.Sauv. and 110 acres in Auckland of Cab.Sauv., Sauv.Blanc, P.N. Müller-Thurgau, Chard., Gewürz.

A California-style winery just north of Auckland. Ross Spence is an uninhibited winemaker looking for original tastes. His best wines are Chardonnays from the Judd Estate vineyards at Gisborne and Egan Estate at Hawke's Bay. Also convincing 'Fume Blanc', Cabernet, and a fresh, slightly astringent but juicy Merlot.

The Millton Vineyard

Manutuke, Gisborne, North Island. Est. 1984. 6,000 cases. Owners: James and Annie Millton. Vineyards: 50 acres of Gisborne vines.

Successful organic winery to the west of Gisborne, producing an interesting range of styles including a fine botrytized Riesling. Among Millton's other wines are dry Riesling, Chardonnay, Sauvignon/Semillon, and a Chenin Blanc of golden luscious character that could come from Anjou.

Mission Vineyards

Church Road, Greenmeadows, Taradale, Hawke's Bay. Est. 1851. 35,000 cases. Visits. Owners: The Catholic Society of Mary. Vineyards: 110 acres of varied soils on flat land plus 25 under contract. Cab.Sauv., Sem., Sauv.Bl., Merlot, Gewürz., Müller-Thurgau, P. Gris, Chasselas, Chard., P.N., Dr. Hogg Muscat.

A historic and beautiful spot at the foot of grassy hills, seemingly old-fashioned but making remarkable white wines, including outstanding Sauvignon Blanc (some blended with Semillon), good Chardonnay and a subtle half-sweet Tokay d'Alsace (Pinot Gris). Reds are not yet up to this level.

Maori harvester

Montana Wines

PO Box 18–293, Glen Innes, Auckland 6. Est. 1961. Owners: A public company. No visits. Vineyards: 2,000 acres, mainly at Marlborough, also at Gisborne, plus a similar area under contract. Müller-Thurgau, Chard., Ries., Gewürz., Sauv.Bl., Dr. Hogg Muscat, Cab.Sauv., Pinotage, P.N.

New Zealand's biggest wine company, started by the Dalmatian Ivan Yukich, was extremely successful in expanding through the 1970s, when it pioneered the new Marlborough region. Most of its best varietal wines come from this region. During the 1980s it expanded further, taking over Penfolds (NZ) in 1986, and now has four wineries at Auckland, Gisborne, Marlborough and Hawke's Bay. Other proprietary names include Blenheimer, Ormond, Fairhall River and Lindauer sparkling. 50% of the whites are semi-sweet. Montana whites have 40% of the total white wine market. The Marlborough wines include a very dry Sauvignon Blanc, slightly spicy Riesling with good acidity, an excellent Chardonnay, a Gewürztraminer and a rather pale but firm Cabernet, with a Médoc-like 'cut'.

Morton Estate

Kati Kati, Bay of Plenty. Established 1979. 42,000 cases. Owner: the Australian firm Mildara (q.v.). Wine maker: John Hancock. Vineyards: 260 acres, mostly in Hawke's Bay.

This winery has benefited from the considerable talents of John Hancock, one of NZ's best wine makers, and its future looks solid under the new ownership of Mildara, which bought the firm in 1988. All of its wines, including excellent Chardonnay, Sauvignon, Fumé Blanc and Cabernet, are top-class. 'Reserve' wines are barrel fermented, all Chardonnay and most Sauvignon is oak-aged. Also Cabernet and Cabernet-based blends. Black Label wines make up a superior range. There is also a *méthode champenoise* wine, made from Pinot Noir and Chardonnay.

Ngatarawa Wines

Hastings, Hawke's Bay district. Est. 1980. Owners: Alwyn Corban and the Glazebrook family. Vineyards: 27 acres of sandy loam over gravel, 7 miles west of Hastings. Char., Sauv.Blanc., Ries., Cab.Sauv. and Merlot.

Ripe grapes, long periods on the skins and oak for fermentation give character to Alwyn Corban's wines. The Sauvignon has been well received internationally and a Cabernet 'port' has created interest. 'Stables Red' is a good-value blend. In good years he makes a Bordeaux-style blend called Glazebrook.

Nobilo Vintners
Station Road, Huapai Valley, Auckland. Est. 1943. 125,000 cases. Visits. Owners: A family-run private company. Wine maker: Nick Nobilo. Vineyards: 212 acres on rolling land of mixed clay and volcanic ash: 90 acres Cab.Sauv., 52 Pinotage, 29 P.N., 16 Merlot and 16 Malbec.

The Nobilos came from the Dalmatian island of Korcula. After problems with corporate shareholders the family have reconstituted their business and their vineyard to concentrate on red varieties that ripen well in the warm damp Auckland climate. White grapes are brought from Gisborne. Nick Nobilo is a passionate traditional wine maker looking for distinction and delicacy, not obvious 'varietal' tastes. His whites are light and refreshing but age well. Pinot Noir made by *macération carbonique*, then aged 2 years in French oak, is light but full of character. 'Concept One' includes Pinotage in a blend with Cabernet, best drunk fairly young.

CJ Pask
Korokipo Road, Hastings, Hawke's Bay, North Island. 6,000 cases. Owner: Chris Pask. Vineyards: 80 acres of Hawke's Bay vines.

Small, high-quality winery, producing successful Cabernet Sauvignon and Pinot Noir as well as Chardonnay, Sauvignon Blanc and red and white blends.

St Helena
Coutts Island, Belfast, Christchurch, South Island. Est. 1981. Owners: The Mundy family. Wine maker: Mark Rattray. Vineyards: 63 acres, mainly of P.N., with some Chard., Rhine Ries., P. Bl. and other white varieties.

Promising producer of Pinot Noir based in Canterbury, one of the South Island's fledgling wine regions. St Helena's white wines, including Chardonnay and Pinot Blanc, have also shown promise.

St Nesbit
Hingaia Road, Papakura, Auckland, North Island. Est. 1981. 1,000 cases. Owner: Anthony Molloy QC. Vineyards: 7 acres of Auckland vines, with more planned.

Growing boutique winery with only one wine, a well-made barrique-aged blend of Cabernet Sauvignon, Merlot and Cabernet Franc. The '87 was well-made and delicate with a fine scent, if a little hollow and lacking richness.

Selaks Wines
Old North Road, Kumeu, Auckland. Est. 1934. 29,000 cases. Owners: The Selak family. Vineyards: 153 acres of mixed varieties at Auckland, Gisborne and Marlborough.

An old concern founded by a Yugoslav pioneer family, now well equipped and modern in approach, with much wood fermenting of white wines. Selaks produces a wide, popular range of wines, and exports to Australia and the UK.

Stonyridge Vineyard
Ostend, Waiheke Island, Nr Auckland, North Island. Est. 1982. Owners: Stephen and Jane White. Vineyards: 5 acres of red varieties.

The second winery to be founded on Waiheke Island after Goldwater Estate (q.v.) makes small quantities of two red wines – Airfield Cabernet Sauvignon and a very good Cabernet blend called Larose.

Te Mata Estate
PO Box 335, Havelock North, Hawke's Bay. Est. 1896. 20,000 cases. Visits by appt. Owners: John Buck and Michael Morris. Vineyards: 62 acres on north slopes with limestone and shingle subsoil, newly planted with Cab.Sauv., Cab.Franc, Merlot, Chard., Sauv.Bl., Müller-Thurgau and Gewürz.

The oldest winery in New Zealand, recently restored and making one of the country's best Cabernet/Merlot blends; a very fine wine. This and Chardonnay are wood-aged. Müller-Thurgau and Fumé Blanc are medium-dry, Furmint sweet with high acidity. The owners see the conditions as similar to Sonoma, California, and aim to make long-lived wines with plenty of acid backbone.

Vidal Wine Producers
St. Aubyn's Street East, Hastings, Hawke's Bay. Est. 1905. Visits and restaurant. Owners: George Fistonich and Grant Adams. Wine maker: Kate Marris. Wines include: Chard., Cab.Sauv., Sauv., Sauv.Bl., Gewürz., P.N., Merlot.

An atmospheric yet technically advanced winery, now part of the Villa Maria group, offering very aromatic Gewürztraminer, restrained Chardonnay, a burgundy that tastes like claret, and a Cabernet with beautifully sweet and lively flavours, from a grower with old vines on shingle at Takaupau to the south. The '87 Cabernet/Merlot Reserve was full of sweet flavour. Most novel and exciting, a 100% Cabernet Sauvignon 'red blend' sparkling wine, fresh, yeasty, dry and deep – daring to imitate Krug. All this plus a barrel-lined restaurant with excellent food. Vidal's two ranges are sold under the Private Bin and superior Reserve labels.

Villa Maria
PO Box 43046, 5 Kirkbride Road, Mangere, Auckland. Est. 1961. Owners: George Fistonich and Grant Adams. Wine maker: Kym Milne. Vineyards: 12 acres of light volcanic soil at Mangere south of Auckland with Sauv.Bl., Cab.Sauv., P.N., Gewürz., and Chard. Most grapes grown on contract in Gisborne and Hawke's Bay.

A modern winery making full-flavoured, if not very aromatic, whites and light reds, aged briefly in oak. Gewürztraminer has done well in international shows, and the whole range is well thought of in Australia. The barrique-fermented Chardonnay is particularly good and the Private Bin Cabernet ('88) promising. Vidal Wines at Hawke's Bay also belongs to the partners here and, like Vidal, Villa Maria sells its wines under the Private Bin and superior Reserve labels.

Weingut Seifried
Upper Moutere, Nelson, South Island. Est. 1973. Owners: Hermann and Agnes Seifried. Vineyards: 60 acres of producing vines at Upper Moutere; 20 acres of new Chard. and Sauv.Bl. at Ruby Bay.

The largest winery in the South Island's promising Nelson region, and still expanding. Hermann Seifried's main wine is Rhine Riesling, made in dry and late-harvest styles. Good Chardonnay, Sauvignon Blanc, Gewürztraminer and Pinot Noir are also produced.

SOUTH AFRICA

South Africa entered the new-world fine-wine league in the mid-1970s – a decade later than California and Australia. She has not so far caught up with them, partly for self-imposed reasons. Government has purposely limited both the supply of good grapevines and the land to grow them on. Nonetheless there are those who argue that the natural conditions of the Cape for the vine are as good as any on earth. The essential grape varieties are now at last planted and coming into bearing. It is presumably a matter of a very few years before we see wines as excellent as Australia's bearing the bizarre Dutch names of the lovely estates of Stellenbosch and Franschhoek.

The natural advantages of the Coastal Region of the Cape are impressive. Ideal slopes can be found facing every point of the compass. There is an eight-month growth period; never any frost, never any hail, no autumn rain, very few of the diseases that plague other vineyards. The soil is so fertile that the normal ration of fertilizer is one tenth that needed by Europe's long-worked vineyards.

An important quality factor is the wide range of temperatures: cool nights between hot days, the Cape pattern, reduce night-time respiration from the vine leaves. The plant, unable to consume sugars accumulated during the day, stores more of them.

None of these conditions is a guarantee of good wine, but taken together, with intelligent handling, they encourage optimism.

What has been lacking in Cape history has been a demand for fine table wines. The one historically famous wine was the dessert Muscat of Constantia (which in Napoleon's time fetched prices as high as any wine in the world). Britain, the principal export market, has been more interested in Cape sherry than Cape claret. South Africans were the world's thirstiest brandy drinkers. It is only with gradual liberalization (non-white prohibition ended in 1962; grocers could sell wine from 1979) and legislation aimed at quality control (Wines of Origin were implemented in 1973) that conditions have been created for a healthy domestic table-wine market: the essential spring-board for exports.

Another problem has been the apparently benevolent presence of the KWV, an organization founded by the government in 1918 to protect grape farmers from low wine prices by fixing a minimum price and distilling the surplus. The KWV has been a bastion of protection and conservatism: the very thing a new wine industry can do without. Licences to plant vines are only granted to established growers, and licences can only be transferred with difficulty. At the same time the State has enforced crippling quarantine regulations on new vines, effectively holding up for over a decade the importation of the finest varieties. With such millstones round its neck even California would still be where it was in the 1950s.

The evidence that very fine wine is on the way is recent, but it is convincing. At present the finest wines of the Cape are its sherries and fortified wines in the manner of port, its rare naturally sweet dessert wines affected by noble rot, and a few of its estate reds made of Cabernet Sauvignon, formerly blended with Cinsaut but increasingly with the noble varieties Merlot and Cabernet Franc. There are also beginnings of great promise with the newly planted noble white varieties. And underpinning the whole industry, of inestimable value, there is South Africa's fortunate inheritance of the Steen, or Chenin Blanc, as its everyday white grape. It is a lucky country that will never go short of good cheap white wine.

South Africa in round figures
South Africa is the tenth largest wine producer, with 2.5% of total world production from 247,000 acres of vines. 92% of the grapes are white. Domestic wine consumption is 9.72 litres per head a year (USA 8.4 litres).

Wine production has risen from 44m. cases in 1960 to around 80 million, with over half the crop distilled. One third of the crop sold as wine is fortified.

There are 70 cooperatives producing 75% of the crop. The balance is produced by the 5,000 individual wine farmers and estates, the producer-wholesalers and the KWV.

The Nederburg auction
The key social and commercial event in the Cape wine calendar is the Nederburg auction, held at vintage time in March since 1975. In 1975 six participants entered 12,500 cases of 15 different wines. In 1981 there were 84 wines – 2,500 people attended the auction, including buyers from Europe and the Americas. The auction has helped to make the name of Nederburg Edelkeur, which regularly sets price records (*see* page 517).

REGIONS OF ORIGINS

Acreages are area under vine in 1980.

Benede-Orange The most northerly demarcated Region of Origin. Irrigated vineyards along the Orange River producing mainly wine for distilling.

Boberg An appellation for fortified wines grown in the Paarl and Tulbagh districts (qq.v.).

Bonnievale *See* Robertson

Breede River Valley The appellation for fortified wines grown in the Worcester, Robertson and Swellendam districts (qq.v.), east of the Drakenstein Mountains.

Coastal Region An appellation that may be given to wines made from grapes from Stellenbosch, Durbanville, Paarl, Constantia and Tulbagh Wine of Origin districts (qq.v.).

Constantia Once the world's most famous Muscat wine, from the Cape. Now the southernmost and coolest Region of Origin, producing quality wines. 1,025 acres.

Durbanville A small Wine of Origin district just north of Cape Town. 3,300 acres.

Eilandia *See* Robertson

Goree *See* Robertson

Klein (Little) Karoo The easternmost Wine of Origin district. Very little rainfall and all irrigated vineyards. Good only for dessert wine and brandy. 9,400 acres.

Olifantsrivier Northerly Wine of Origin district, with a warm dry climate. Mostly wine for distilling from irrigated vineyards. 17,300 acres.

Overberg Southern coastal Wine of Origin district. Contains Walker Bay ward, with some of the coolest vineyards. 3,700 acres.

Paarl South Africa's wine capital, 50 miles northeast of Cape Town. Its surrounding region is among the best in the country, particularly for white wine and sherry. Most of its wine is made by cooperatives. 54,000 acres.

Piquetberg A small western Wine of Origin district north of Tulbagh, towards the Olifants River. A warm dry climate gives mainly dessert wine and wine for distilling. 4,800 acres.

Riverside *See* Robertson

Robertson A small Wine of Origin district to the east of the Cape, and inland. Irrigated vineyards along the Kogmanskloof and Breede rivers provide some high-quality white and red table wines as well as fine fortified wines. Contains Eilandia, Goree, Riverside, Bonnievale and Vinkrivier wards. 21,700 acres.

Stellenbosch The beautiful old Cape Dutch town and its demarcated region 30 miles east of Cape Town, extending south to the ocean at False Bay. Most of South Africa's best estates, especially for

red wine, are in the mountain foothills of the region. 39,200 acres.

Swartland A warm Wine of Origin district around Malmesbury and Riebeek-Wes, between Tulbagh and the west coast. Most growers supply cooperatives. 40,700 acres.

Swellendam The easternmost Wine of Origin district of the Breede River. Mainly distilling wine. 1,360 acres.

Tulbagh A demarcated district sheltered in the hills north of Paarl, best known for the white wines of its 3 famous estates, Montpellier, Theuniskraal and Twee Jongegezellen. *See also* Boberg. 10,800 acres.

Walker Bay Extreme southerly demarcated region near Hermanus, SE of Stellenbosch. So far only one producer has tried its alleged ideally cool, slow-ripening microclimate.

Worcester Demarcated wine region round the Breede and Hex river valleys, east of Paarl. North of Worcester, up to Tulbagh, rainfall is high enough for good table wines, southeast to Swellendam irrigation is necessary. Many cooperative cellars make mainly dry white and dessert wines. 45,900 acres.

The traditional Cape Dutch architecture adds distinction to many of the estates

MAJOR PRODUCERS

Allesverloren
Riebeek West, *Swartland*. Founded 1974. Owner and wine maker: Fanie Malan. 395 acres. Wines: Cab.Sauv., port., Swartland Rood, T.B.
A specialist in port and recently full dry reds. A warm dry site gives very ripe, soft, sometimes rather raisin-flavoured Cabernet.

Alto
Stellenbosch. Founded 1920. Owners: Pieter du Toit and Distillers Corporation. 247 acres. Wines: Cab.Sauv., Rouge.
A superbly sited vineyard running straight up a mountainside near the sea for a mile and a half (in which it rises nearly 1,000 feet). The estate only makes red wine. The Cabernet has been a good but typically sturdy traditional Cape wine; Alto Rouge is a lighter, though still solid, blend. Both need considerable ageing.

Backsberg
Simondium, *Paarl*. Founded 1969. Owners: Michael and Sydney Back. Visits. 395 acres. Wines: Cab.Sauv., Chard., Ch.Bl., P'age, Sauv.Bl., Shiraz, Special Late Harvest, Steen.
Sydney Back was one of the pioneers of the return to high-density planting in the Cape. He is justified by very good red and, particularly, white wines. Local critics rate the Chardonnay, Sauvignon Blanc and Chenin Blanc some of the best yet produced in the Cape.

The Bergkelder
Stellenbosch. Member of the Oude Meester Group. Chief Executive: Dr. Julius Laszlo. Wine maker: Hoffie Hoffman. Wines: Fleur du Cap, Grünberger, J.C. Leroux sparkling wine and Stellenryck ranges, plus many estate wines bottled by The Bergkelder.
The second largest Stellenbosch merchant, buying wines from 17 top estates and making some very good wines from grapes bought in Stellenbosch and Paarl. The firm is a pioneer in improving Cape wines. Cabernet Sauvignon, Sauvignon Blanc, and *méthode champenoise* Pinot Noir show real promise.

Blaauwklippen
Stellenbosch. Founded 1972. Owner: Graham Boonzaier. Wine maker: Walter Finlayson. Visits: 18,000 cases. 295 acres. Wines: Cab.Sauv., Zin, P.N., Shiraz, Rh.Ries., Sauv.Bl., several blends.
One of the pioneers of lighter, fruity reds. Also known for delicate dry and rich semi-sweet whites. Overall quality is consistent and improving.

Bon Courage
Robertson. Founded 1984. Owner: André Bruwer. Visits. 12,000 cases. 370 acres. Wines: Bouquet Bl., C.Ries., Rh.Ries., Sauv.Bl., Blanc Fumé (wood mat.), Blanc de Noir, Cab.Sauv., Spec. Late Harv., Gewürz., Muscadel, Noble Late Harv.
A high average standard with full-bodied, richly-flavoured dry whites, semi-sweet whites and fortified wines have earned André Bruwer several estate Winemaker of the Year awards in young wine shows.

Le Bonheur
Muldersvlei, *Stellenbosch*. Founded 1973. Owners: Distillers Corp. & Michael Woodhead. 5,000 cases. 173 acres. Wines: Cab.Sauv., Blanc Fumé.
On the generally north-facing slopes of the Klapmutskop, these vineyards have been given the benefit of Wood-head's soil science background and are expected to produce some of the Cape's top whites. The Sauvignon Blanc is mouth-filling, with striking style.

Boplass
New winery at Calitzdorp. Early success with Tinta Barocia port-style wine.

Boschendal
Groot Drakenstein, *Paarl*. Founded 1977. Owner: RFF (Pty) Ltd. Wine maker: Achim von Arnim. Visits. 617 acres. Wines: red varietals plus many blends (inc. *Méthode Champ.*).
A large estate producing a wide range, chiefly blended whites, from shaded vineyards stretching for 8 miles along the side of Simonsberg. Reputation is slightly ahead of quality at this stage. Young vineyards of top varieties are coming into production.

Buitenverwachting
Constantia. Founded 1985. Owners: Buitenverwachting Farm Trust. Wine maker: Jean Daneel. Visits. 10,000 cases. 250 acres. Wines: Rh.Ries., Buiten Bl., L'Arrivé, Blanc Fumé, Sauv.Bl., Pinot Gris.
Once-famous property now completely replanted with top varieties, making wines from a combination of own and bought grapes. First efforts promising, especially Riesling. Even better wines are expected as vineyards mature.

Clos Cabrière
Franschhoek, *Paarl*. Founded 1984. Owners: Von Arnim family. Wine maker: Pieter Ferreira. Visits. 2,200 cases. 30 acres. Wines: Pierre Jourdan.
With Pinot Noir, Chardonnay and Pinot Blanc in the vineyard and a *méthode champenoise* cellar, this is a bold attempt at Champagne-quality sparkling wine. First vintages are very highly rated.

Cape Independent Winemaker's Guild
Loose grouping of ambitious wine makers, encouraging developments of vineyard and cellar techniques and raising standard of quality. Annual auction of scrutinised young wines sold under common Guild label is well attended and brings high prices.

Delaire Vineyards
New 90-acre estate at Helshoogte, Stellenbosch.

Delheim
Simonsberg, *Stellenbosch*. Founded 1941. Owners: The Hoheisen family. Chief Executive: Spatz Sperling. Wine maker: Kevin Arnold. Visits. 60,000 cases. 309 acres. Wines: Cab.Sauv., Gewürz. Heerenwyn (100% Steen), Noble Late Harvest, P'age, P.N., port, Grande Reserve (Cab.blend). Rh.Ries., Sauv.Bl., Shiraz, sparkling, various semi-sweet whites.
With the produce of vineyards 3 miles apart and bought-in grapes from neighbours, Delheim is able to produce a wide range. Striking advances in quality have been made recently. Some of the best whites in the Cape are being made, and the reds are leading the industry. Grande Reserve has massive structure and exciting palate and finish.

Eikendal
Helderberg, *Stellenbosch*. Founded 1984. Owners: Eikendal

Vineyards (Pty) Ltd. Wine maker: Josef Krammer. Visits. 10,000 cases. 210 acres. Wines: Blanc de Blanc, Spec. Late Harv., Cab.Sauv., Duc du Berry range.

First efforts with dry and semi-sweet whites and reds only moderate. Young vineyards of Cabernet Sauvignon are expected to improve the standard.

Fairview
Suider Paari, *Paarl*. Founded 1974. Owner: Cyril Back. Wine maker: Charles Back. Visits. 300 acres. Wines: Cab.Sauv., Shiraz, P'age, P.N., Ch.Bl., Sauv.Bl., B., blended reds and whites.

An estate with a reputation for very powerful and full-bodied reds, especially Shiraz, and unusual broad dry whites.

Gilbey's
Stellenbosch. Founded 1950. Owned by IDV (UK) and the Rembrandt South African Corporation. Wine maker: Dr. Arnold Schickerling. 240 acres at Kleine Zalze and 540 acres in Devon Valley. Wines: Bertrams, Valley, Festival ranges, Director's Reserve Zinfandel.

Two farms supplemented by grapes bought from Stellenbosch growers make a wide spectrum of wines. The Bertrams range has highly regarded reds. Valley and Festival are lower-priced wines for the mass market.

Glen Carlou
Promising new winery at Klapmuts, Paarl. Good early Chardonnay and Merlot.

Douglas Green
Milnerton, *Cape Town*. Founded 1942. Part of the Rennie's group. Wines: Douglas Green range, Côte de Rosé, Côte de Blanc, Fransteter, St. Augustine, St. Raphael, Valais Rouge.

A wholesaler without production facilities, buying wines from the KWV, private cellars and coops. Standards are a little uneven, but wines such as Douglas Green Cabernet Sauvignon are of good quality.

Goede Hoop
Bottclary, *Stellenbosch*. Founded 1976. Owner: Johan Besbier. 247 acres. Wines: Vintage Red (mostly Shiraz).

The majority of vines on these dry, stony slopes are grown without trellising, which helps to produce a medium-bodied, fruity blended red. Always reliable, seldom surprising.

Groot Constantia
Constantia, *Cape Town*. Founded 1685. Refounded 1975. Owners: Groot Constantia Control Board. Wine maker: Pieter du Toit. Visits. 30,000 cases. 284 acres. Wines: Cab.Sauv., Ch.Bl., Heerenrood (blend of Shiraz, Cab.Sauv. and port varieties). P'age, Sauv.Bl., Shiraz, Gewürz., W.Ries. and blended reds, whites and rosé.

The most famous estate of the Cape; source of the legendary Constantia Muscat of the early 19th century. All the vineyards have been replanted and clean fresh reds are now being made. Weisser Riesling has had several vintages that have matured into full and wholesome wines. Overall standard is a little disappointing.

Hamilton Russell Vineyards
Hemel-en-Aarde Valley, *Walker Bay*, Overberg. Founded 1974. Owner: Tim Hamilton Russell. Wine maker: Peter Finlayson. Visits. 12,000 cases. 138 acres. Wines: Chard., Sauv.Bl., P.N., Grand Cru Noir (Cab.Sauv./Merlot blend).

The southernmost estate in Africa, in a coastal valley behind Hermanus, averaging 2°C cooler than Stellenbosch. Concentration on Burgundy style, with small crops and new small wood, has already paid dividends. One of the few Cape Chardonnays to have firmness and real depth of flavour. Clear varietal character in all wines.

Hartenberg
Koelenhof, *Stellenbosch*. Founded 1958. Owner: Kenneth McKenzie. Wine maker: Danie Truter. Visits. 6,000 cases. 320 acres. Wines: Chatillon, L'Estreux, W.R., Blanc de Noir, Zin., Shiraz, Cab.Sauv.

Previously known as Montagne, this property has not produced the quality expected for many years. Good, solid wine with imposing price tags.

Haute Provence
New Franschaek estate with interesting Sauvignon Blanc.

Jacobsdal
Kuils River, *Stellenbosch*. Founded 1976. Owner: Cornelis Dumas. 296 acres. Wines: Pinotage.

Medium-bodied red with gentle fruit and long finish. One of the Cape's best examples of Pinotage.

Kanonkop
Muldersvlei, *Stellenbosch*. Founded 1973. Owner: Jannie Krige. Wine maker: Beyers Truter. Visits. 12,000 cases. 320 acres. Wines: Cab.Sauv., P'age., Paul Sauer Fleur, Rh.Ries., Sauv.Bl., blended white and red.

An outstanding estate specializing in classic-style reds. Cabernet is superbly fruity, well balanced and has a clean, slightly astringent finish. One of the Cape's first Bordeaux-style blends, Paul Sauer Fleur, is 40% Cabernet Sauvignon, 40% Cabernet Franc and 20% Merlot.

Klein Constantia
Constantia. Founded 1986. Owner: Doug Jooste. Wine maker: Ross Gower. Visits. 10,000 cases. 173 acres. Wines: Sauv.Bl., Rh.Ries., Shiraz, Cab.Sauv.

This newly replanted historic property made news with a trophy-winning Sauvignon Blanc from the maiden harvest. Vineyards are planted high on cool slopes, and may bring fame back to Constantia.

Koopmanskloof
Bottelary, *Stellenbosch*. Founded 1970. Owner: Stevie Smit. 1,482 acres. Wines: Rh.Ries., Blanc de Marbonne.

Low yields give intense fruit flavour to two of the Cape's lesser-known quality whites.

Laborie
Suider Paarl, *Paarl*. Founded 1972. Owner: KWV. Wine maker: Willier Hacker. Visits. 10,000 cases. 69 acres. Wines: Laborie (red); Blanc de Noirs (transfer-method sparkling); Ries.

A very attractive estate on the northeast slopes of the Paarl Mountain, owned by the KWV and used as a guesthouse. The rather standard wines are pretty rather than exciting sparkling wine mostly from Pinotage, a full-blooded blended red and a rounded off-dry white based on Rhine Riesling.

Landskroon
Suider Paarl, *Paarl*. Founded 1974. Owners: Paul and Hugo de Villiers. Wine maker: Paul de Villiers jnr. Visits. 543 acres on the southwest slopes of Paarl Mountain. Wines: Cab.Sauv., Cab.Franc, Shiraz, P'age., P.N., T.B., Cin., Bouquet Rouge, blended white, port.

The eighth generation of a Huguenot family who have made wine at the Cape for 3 centuries. Recently the first estate to make significant quantities of Cabernet Franc. The 2 Cabernets are not blended but sold separately. All the reds are ripe and robust in the style that spells Paarl to Cape connoisseurs.

Lemberg
Tulbagh. Founded 1984. Owners: Jan and Janey Muller. Wine maker: Janey Muller. Visits. 1,500 cases. 12 acres. Wines: Harslevelü, Sauv.Bl.

Tiny property in a warm area producing richly flavoured hand-made whites. Strong following.

L'Omarins
Franschock, *Paarl.* Owners: the Rupert family.

A new estate that has produced good Sauvignon Blanc and now has a stylish Cabernet.

Meerendal
Durbanville. Founded 1969. Owner: Kosie Starke. 309 acres. Wines: Shiraz, P'age.

Full-bodied reds with firmness and structure. Characteristically deep in colour, they reward long ageing. Marketed by the Bergkelder.

Meerlust
Faure, *Stellenbosch.* Owner: Nico Myburgh (whose family bought Meerlust in 1776). Wine maker: Georgio della Cia. 25,000 cases. 570 acres. Wines: Cab.Sauv., P.N., Rubicon (Cab.Sauv., Cab.Franc/Merlot blend).

One of the oldest farms in the Cape: a beautiful white manor house where vines have been grown for 290 years. Now a red-wine estate, which under Nico Myburgh's guidance has broken away from the hearty style of Cape reds and is producing a blend aimed squarely at the Médoc. Myburgh started planting Cabernet Sauvignon in the 1960s. Merlot, Cabernet Franc and Pinot Noir have been added. Myburgh's Bordeaux-style Rubicon blend is a courageous break with the prevailing 'varietal' orthodoxy. It is softer and rounder than the straight Cabernet which may well keep better. A very interesting delicately fruity Pinot Noir is made. Chardonnay is in the pipeline.

Middelsvlei
A Bergkelder Stellenbosch estate with good Pinotage and now producing Cabernet.

Montpellier
Tulbagh. Founded in 1970. Principal: De Wet Theron. Wine maker: Jan Theron. Visits. 35,000 cases. 370 acres. Wines: Ch.Bl., W.R., C.Ries., Gewürz., sparkling.

Like its neighbour Twee Jongegezellen, a specialist in white wines, for which the relatively warm Tulbagh has a surprising reputation. The Montpellier dry wines have tended to flatness for lack of acidity. 'Special Late Harvest' and sweet Tuinwingerd Rhine Riesling are better balanced.

Nederburg
Paarl. Founded 1936. Owner: Nederburg Wines (Pty) Ltd. Part of the Stellenbosch Farmers' Winery. Visits. 1,850 acres. Wines: wide range including the famous Edelkeur sweet wines.

The Cape's largest quality cellar, and scene of the now famous annual wine auction in March. Nederburg grows grapes in Paarl and buys from throughout the Coastal Region. The standard of the wines is high and improving.

Some old Cabernets, notably '66, '68, '74, '76, have matured well.

Baronne, a Cabernet-based blend, is oak-aged for 15 months and can be impressive. Paarl Riesling is reliable and the sparkling wine (Charmat process) clean and good value. Brözel's speciality is the lusciously rich, raisiny Edelkeur – an outstanding dessert wine by any standards, made of Steen and sometimes Riesling infected with noble rot. Edelkeur is intensely sweet at first and deserves several years ageing. Recently Brözel has won several international awards for Cabernet Sauvignon and Gewürztraminer.

Neethlingshof
Vlottenburg, *Stellenbosch.* Founded 1974. Owner: Hans-Joachim Schreiber. Wine maker: Günter Brözel. Visits. 25,000 cases. 690 acres. Wines: Blanc de Noir, Col., Ries., Cuvée Bl., Gewürz, W.R., B., Cab.Sauv., Lord Neethling Rouge.

After purchase in 1985 by H.J. Schreiber, a German banker, the vineyards have been extensively replanted and buildings carefully restored. The objective is to make premium wines and early efforts are pleasing.

L'Ormarins
Groot Drakenstein, *Paarl.* Founded 1969. Owner: Anthony Rupert. Wine maker: Nico Vermeulen. 333 acres. Wines: Ries., Rh.Ries., Sauv.Bl., Pinot Gris.

Extensive newly planted vineyards, high on contoured

Günter Brözel, cellar master at Neethlingshof.

slopes. This mountainside farm has been planted with all the classic varieties, with heavy emphasis on whites, in a determined effort to produce outstanding wines. The first results have recognizable varietal flavour and are fresh and readily drinkable.

Overgaauw

Stellenbosch Kloof, *Stellenbosch*. Founded 1906, on a farm owned by the family since 1783. Owners: David and Braam (son) van Velden. Visits. 10,000 cases. 160 acres. Wines: Cab.Sauv., Chard., Merlot, Tria Corda, Overtinto, Sylvaner, Sauv.Bl.

One of the first Cape growers of Merlot in vineyards on south slopes in the Stellenbosch Kloof Overgaauw, is at present producing a blend of Cabernet Sauvignon, Merlot called Tria Corda. The Chardonnay is good, the Cabernet is very good.

Rozendel

A boutique winery in Jonkershoek, Stellenbosch, with a good Cabernet, Merlot blend.

Rust-en-Vrede

Helderberg, *Stellenbosch*. Founded 1979. Owner and wine maker: Jannie Engelbrecht. Vists. 8,000 cases. Wines: Cab.Sauv., Shiraz, Pinot Noir, Tinta Barocca.

North-facing mountainside vineyards, just below Alto, producing ambitious reds which already win medals. Both Cabernet and Shiraz are given long, slow fermentation, producing deep, tannic wines that are designed to last for years. Early efforts look very promising. Pinot Noir and Merlot will soon be added.

Schoongezicht Rustenberg

Simonsberg, *Stellenbosch*. Founded 1913. Owner: Pam Barlow. Wine maker: Etienne le Riche. Visits. 15,000 cases. 198 acres. Wines: Cab Sauv., P.N., W.Ries., rosé, blended red and white.

Perhaps the most beautiful estate in the Cape; low white Dutch buildings shaded by enormous trees. A long-established and highly regarded producer of red wines with extensive vineyards on south-facing mountain slopes. Rustenberg is a light wine worth maturing. Cabernet Sauvignon has established itself among the best of the Cape. Pinot Noir has had a promising beginning. White wines (sold as Schoongezicht) are agreeable.

Simonsig

Koelenhof, *Stellenbosch*. Founded 1968. Owner: Frans Malan. Wine maker: Johann Malan. Visits. 100,000 cases. Wines: B., Cab.Sauv., Ch.Bol, Col., Gewürz., K., P'age, Ries., Shiraz., W.Ries. plus Noble Late Harvest, Kaapse Vonkel (100% Ch.Bl.) *méthode champenoise* sparkling, Vin Fumé blended white and other red, white and rosé blends.

With both northeast- and southeast-facing vineyards on gentle slopes, Simonsig has tended to concentrate on white wines. After early emphasis on varietals, Frans Malan and his 3 sons have a runaway success with a blended white (Vin Fumé) matured in wood. This innovative family were the first in the Cape to make a true *méthode champenoise* wine.

Spier

Lynedoch, *Stellenbosch*. Founded 1969. Owner: Niel Joubert. Chief Executive: Chris Joubert. Wine maker: B.W. Myburgh. Visits. 60,000 cases. 680 acres. Wines: P'age., Ries., Sauv.Bl., sp. wines, Col., Steen, several blended reds, whites, rosé.

A big estate with a wide variety of microclimates, producing a range of medium-quality wines, mostly white. Dry and semi-sweet Colombard and Chenin Blanc have a great deal of flavour. The Pinotage is consistently one of the Cape's better wines from this grape.

Stellenbosch Farmers' Wineries

Stellenbosch. Founded 1935. Owner: Cape Wine and Distillers Ltd. Production Director: Duimpie Bailey. Visits. Wines: Zonnebloem, Kellerprinz, Autumn Harvest, Virginia, Taskelder ranges, Château Libertas, Lanhzerac Rosé, La Gratitude, Capenheimer, other blends. Monis dessert wines.

The Cape's largest cellar presses some grapes, but buys large volumes of wine from private and coop cellars, blending to produce dry and semi-sweet products in all price ranges. Nederburg (q.v.) is their most prestigious product. Zonnebloem reds also have a well-founded reputation going back many years; Shiraz and Cabernet are both big wines with good colour, texture and length, fit to mature for a decade.

Thelema

A promising new winery in Banghoek, Stellenbosch, producing Cabernet, Chardonnay and Sauvignon Blanc.

Theuniskraal

Tullagh. Founded 1962. Partners: Rennie and Kobus Jordaan. 45,000 cases. 395 acres. Wines: Gewürz., Late Harvest, Ries., Sem., Steen.

An estate specializing in dry whites but no longer the leader it was. Cape tasters rate the Riesling (Cape and Rhine Riesling), as fragrant, fresh and well balanced. The Gewürztztraminer is full, rich, spicy and slightly sweet.

Twee Jongegezellen

Tulbagh. Founded 1950, on a farm in the Krone family for 200 years. Principal: N.C. Krone. Wine maker: Nicky Krone (son). 617 acres. Wines: Gewürz., Rh.Ries., Sauv.Bl., Schanderl, TJ 39, Ries., Steen, red and white blends.

Twee Jongegezellen ('TJ') was one of the pioneers of quality white wines in the Cape. The Krones experiment ceaselessly with everything from clonal selection to pruning techniques. Today, most of the grapes are harvested at night, giving the wines new vitality and grape character. Wines include Schanderl, a white blend based on a red clone of Frontignac isolated and bred in the estate's nurseries. This unlikely starting point leads to a wine of intense, fruity and altogether novel character. TJ 39, another blend, is full bodied, with a muscat style, but dry. Their latest experiment is a sparkling wine.

Uiterwyk

Stellenbosch Kloof, *Stellenbosch*. Founded 1946. Owner: Danie de Waal. Wine maker: Chris de Waal. Visits. 3,000 cases of estate-bottled wine. 295 acres. Wines: Cab.Sauv., P'age, Col., C.Ries.

A beautiful estate bottling a small quantity of its best wines in a traditional cellar. The Cabernet Sauvignon is a good example of a traditional cape red.

Uitkyk

Muldersvlei, *Stellenbosch*. Founded 1973. Owner: Distillers Corp. Wine maker: Dr. Harvey Illing. Potentially 100,000 cases. 400 acres. Wines: Carlonet Cab.Sauv., Carlsheim (Sauv.B./Ch.Bl. blend). Ries.

A large estate on the mountain slopes above a dignified 1788 mansion. The great expectations that followed the planting of vineyards high on the exposed mountainside have yet to be fully realized. Enigmatic microclimates have forced replanting of Cabernet on lower slopes and some whites to be cautiously moved higher. Carlsheim has developed complexity with increase in the quantity of Sauvignon in the blend and the age of vines. One of Cape's top reds, Carlonet, is also showing signs of further advances.

Union Wine

Wellington, *Paarl*. Founded 1964. Part of the Picardi Group. Wine maker: Johan Schreuder. 750,000 cases. 237 acres. Wines: Bellingham and Culemborg ranges.

A merchant buying grapes in the Paarl Valley and wines throughout the Cape to swell production from the vineyards they own. Bellingham is full, soft and easy to drink. 2% is exported.

Van Loveren

Robertson. Founded 1983. Owners: Nico and Wynand Retief. Wine maker: Wynand Retief. Visits. 15,000 cases. 265 acres. Wines: Harslevlü, Fernao Pires, Rh. Ries., Sauv.Bl., Col., Pinot Gris.

Full-bodied white wines with original stamp. Within a few years, the estate has become a feature of moderate-priced winelists. Quality is solid rather than outstanding.

Vergenoegd

Faure, *Stellenbosch*. Founded 1969. Owners: Jac and Brand Faure. Visits. 3,000 cases, 319 acres. Wines: Cin., Cab.Sauv., P'age., Shiraz, T.B., Sherry.

Vineyards are on level ground separated from False Bay by sand dunes and marshes. The sea lowers the temperature, though humidity is high except for the first 3 months of the growing season, when a southeast wind sweeps across the farm almost daily. Vines are grown on low trellises and produce intense, almost tarry red wines. The Cabernet can be too soft; Shiraz from old vines has been excellently deep and firm. Selected wines are bottled at the property, with most of the production going to the KWV.

Villiera

Koelenhof, *Paarl*. Founded 1975. Owners: Grier family. Wine maker: Jeff Grier. Visits. 20,000 cases. 235 acres. Wines: Cab.Sauv., Rh.Ries., Sauv.Bl., Cru Monro (Cab.Sauv./Mer.) Opperette, Gavotte, Garonne, Sonnet, Tradition.

Major advances in quality have shown since the Grier purchase in 1983. Tradition has rapidly become South Africa's top-selling *méthode champenoise*. Sauvignon, Riesling and Cabernet are stylish and age well.

Vriesenhof

Stellenbosch. Founded 1981. Owner: Jan Boland Coetzee. Visits. 3,000 cases. 27 acres. Wine: Cab.Sauv.

Jan Boland, previously in charge of Kanonkop, made the first wine from his small established vineyard of Cabernet in 1981. Highly rated Cabernet and Chardonnay and Cabernet Merlot blend.

Warwick

A new Stellenbosch estate producing Cabernet and very good Médoc-style blend.

Welgemeend

Klapmuts, *Paarl*. Founded 1974. Owner: Billy Hofmeyr. 3,000 cases. 30 acres. Wines: Welgemeend, Amade, Douelle, Cab.Sauv.

A tiny estate by South African standards, but an influential pioneer of red wines made in the style and by the methods of Bordeaux. Hofmeyr (a land surveyor, wine writer and now farmer) has demonstrated the merits of picking early, blending the 2 Cabernets with Merlot, Malbec and Petit Verdot, and maturing for up to 18 months in small, new oak barrels. His wines are rarely more than 12% alcohol and sometimes as low as 10.5% but with good tannin and clean-cut flavours. Amade is an early maturing blend of Pinotage, Grenache and Shiraz. Douelle is a Cab.Sauv., Malbec blend.

Weltevrede

Bonnievale, *Robertson*. Founded 1976. Owner: Lourens Jonker. Wine maker: B.J. Myburgh. Visits. 395 acres. Wines: Cape Ries., Sauv.Bl., Bl.Fumé, Rh.Ries., Col., Gewürz., Red Muscadel, Muscat de Hambourg.

Fresh, clean-style whites with great consistency. One of the first Cape cellars to wood-mature white wine.

De Wetshof

Robertson. Founded 1974. Owner: J.J. de Wet. Wine maker: Danie de Wet. 153 acres. Wines: Chard., Sauv.Bl., Rh.Ries.

Danie de Wet was trained in Germany and brought back boundless enthusiasm for white wines of styles not then found in South Africa. His experimental work with Rhine Riesling, Sauvignon Blanc and Chardonnay, and with his noble-rot sweet wine, Edeloes, has shaken old ideas about the Robertson area, and about South African whites in general. One of the most influential estates in the Cape.

Zandvliet

Ashton, *Roberston*. Founded 1975. Owner: Paul de Wet. Wine maker: Paul de Wet, jnr. 556 acres. Wine: Shiraz, P.N.

A considerable reputation based on a light but vigorous and tasty Shiraz. A Pinot Noir was introduced in 1983.

Zevenwacht

Kuils River, *Stellenbosch*. Founded 1973. Owners: consortium headed by Gilbert Colyn. Wine maker: Neil Ellis. Visits. 875 acres. Wines: Sauv.Bl., Gewürz., Rh.Ries., Blanc de Blanc, Bouquet Bl., Cab.Sauv., Shiraz, P'age, blended reds and whites.

Large-scale venture with wines only available through shareholders and restaurants. The Cabernet Sauvignon is impressive.

KWV (Kooperative Wijnbouwers Vereniging)

Paarl. Founded 1918.

The State cooperative to which all grape-farmers are obliged to belong (it has 6,000 members). It was founded to protect them from low prices but has long since had a policing function over the whole industry. It fixes an annual minimum price for 'good wine' and another for 'distilling wine' and declares an annual percentage surplus, determined by the size of the crop and the state of the market. All growers must deliver this percentage (often about one third) to the cooperative – the object being to prevent an oversupply. The KWV is not allowed to resell wine in South Africa except to other wineries.

The KWV has 5 wineries at Paarl (its magnificent HQ), Stellenbosch, Worcester, Rotherston and Montagu and 1 estate, Laborie at Paarl. 60 local cooperatives collect and crush grapes for it. Its principal products are brandies, sherries and port-style tawnies and rubies.

Its best sherries (the Cavendish Cape range) are of very high quality, comparable to their Spanish models. Tawnies and 'vintage character' are also very successful. Table wines (not available in South Africa, at least under these names) include the very reliable and good-value KWV Chenin Blanc, a pleasantly *spritzig* Riesling, a slightly sweet Weisser Riesling and a very sweet Special Late Harvest Steen. The best-known red is a blend called Roodeberg, of Pinotage, Shiraz, Cinsaut and Tinta Barocca.

CHILE

Chile has the potential for wines of really outstanding quality; as good as California's. The fruit of her vineyards is some of the finest in the world. The fact has been accepted by authorities for generations, yet the truly great wines of Chile are only now starting to be made. The missing element has been the marketplace. Chile's domestic market is relatively unsophisticated, lacking the means to buy and compare the best European and Californian wines. Her principal export markets are in Latin America. North America, another important market, tends to appreciate the low price rather than the exciting quality of Chilean imports. However frequent, and however true, the travellers' tales of exceptional old bottles of Cabernet, the signal for a quality wine industry had to come from Chile herself. It came in the late '80s, when a technological surge, aided by investment from Spain and France, moved Chile onto a new plateau of quality.

Wine has been made in Chile since missionaries introduced it in the mid-sixteenth century. Their grape, the País (the equivalent of California's Mission grape), is still widely grown for peasant wine and brandy. The quality wine industry started in 1851, when a number of landowners and entrepreneurs introduced the grapes and methods of Bordeaux. They chose the moment just before the twin scourges of phylloxera and oidium appeared in Bordeaux. Their stock was absolutely clean and has never been affected: isolation by the Andes and the Pacific means that Chile still has an entirely prephylloxera vineyard: a viticulturist's paradise.

Unfortunately both grape grower and wine maker have been hampered by politics for much of this century. The next state of experimentation – of enterprises willing to take the expensive steps towards great wine – has now begun with a number of wineries investing in modern stainless steel machinery and buying oak barrels from France and America.

Chile is divided into six viticultural regions with a total of 272,000 acres of wine grapes, just over half requiring irrigation. Only one region, the central valley zone, is of interest for top-quality wine. With 92,000 acres it produces almost half the national total, using irrigation to achieve an average crop of 60 hectolitres a hectare. It starts in the north on the Aconcagua River near the capital, Santiago, and runs south through the Metropolitan region, the former provinces of Santiago, Valparaiso, O'Higgins, Colchagua, Curicó and Talca; a distance of some 160 miles. The rivers Maipo, Cachapoal, Tinguiririca, Lontué and Maule, fed by Andean glaciers, carved the valleys and furnish the irrigation for all Chile's best vineyards. Further north the vineyards produce grapes for table wines and fortified wines.

Rainfall is low everywhere, increasing in the south, where conditions are marginally cooler, but summer rain is unknown. In the dry atmosphere rot is rare and the ungrafted vines are extraordinarily healthy. The Maipo valley has the finest reputation, but there is evidence that the cooler conditions and higher rainfall of the Maule and Lontué valleys in Talca can produce more lively and delicate wines and planting is in progress there.

Cabernet Sauvignon is much the most successful red grape, supported by Merlot and Malbec. Pinot Noir took longer to master but is now producing interesting wines. Riesling used to be considered the best white grape, but is now much outnumbered by the Sauvignon and Semillon of Bordeaux. Chardonnay is becoming less rare. New techniques introduced by among others, Miguel Torres of Spain, have radically improved the whites.

There are five official categories of wine, based on age. First category is at least four years old with an aristocratic name: 'Don . . .' or 'Dona'. The age declines to the fourth group, 'Gran Vino'. Fifth-category is carafe wine.

CHILE PRODUCERS

José Canepa

Camino Lo Sierra 1500, Maipù. founded 1930. Family owned. Visits by appt. 1,500 acres. Production: 500,000 cases.

A very modern winery – one of the largest and most modern in Latin America – with reliable and sometimes excellent wines. Vineyards are in Isla de Maipo, Curicó and Lontué in Talca province to the south. High-tech methods have produced some of Chile's best Sauvignon Blanc, Chardonnay and Semillon, and Bordeaux techniques make extremely sound Cabernet and Merlot.

Concha y Toro

Fernando Lazcano 1220, Puente Alto. Founded 1883. Public company. 3,700 acres. Production: 3.3m. cases. Visits.

The biggest and best-known Chilean bodega, with spacious and beautiful estates, and modern technology, based at Pirque, south of Santiago (and much visited by tourists). Their best-known brands are Marqués de Casa Concha and Casillero del Diablo; principal wines are Cabernet Sauvignon, Chilean Burgundy, rosé, Riesling and Sauvignon Blanc. 300 acres of new white varieties

(Chardonnay, Riesling, Chenin Blanc and Gewürztraminer) have been planted with California stock, plus a further 120 acres in the south of the region. The firm also owns vinification plants at San Miguel, Maipú, Buira, Cachapoal, La Gloria, Las Palmeras, El Estero, Pedehue, and Lontué.

Viña Errázuriz-Panquehue
Bandera 206, Santiago. Founded 1870. Owners: The Chadwick family. 414 acres.
The vines, planted by an ancestor of the present owners, once covered around 2,500 acres, and formed the largest privately owned vineyard in the world. The winery is in the Aconcagua Valley and is the northernmost of the large wineries. Around 44 acres grow Cabernet Sauvignon, while 370 acres of Sauvignon Blanc, Semillon and Chardonnay are grown further south in the Mataquito Valley.

Consiño Macul
Quilin con Canal San Carlos, Santiago. Founded 1882. Family owned. 660 acres, 300,000 cases, no grapes bought. Visits by appt.
A serenely beautiful old family estate on the outskirts of Santiago, criss-crossed with tall avenues of English oak against the vast backdrop of the Andes. Two thirds of the wines are red: light Don Luis and dark, substantial Don Matias and Antiguas Reservas Cabernets (aged 3 years in cask, 2 in bottle). The very dry rather 'green' whites are Semillon, Palacio Cousiño, Doña Isidora Riesling/Semillon and a little Chardonnay. The estate grows Merlot and Petit Verdot as well as Cabernet.

After passing through an unhappy patch in the mid-1970s it is once again the 'first-growth' of Chile and has now bought stainless steel equipment and new oak barrels.

Viña Manquehue
Vicuña Mackenna 2289, Santiago. Founded 1927. Family company. 600 acres. Visits by appt.
Run by the founder's son, José Rabat Comella, on the edge of Santiago, with vineyards on the Manquehue hill. José Rabat is the label of their better wines: Premium, Alcalde Jufré and Reservado Rabat; Cabernet, Sauvignon Blanc, Chardonnay and Semillon, mainly sold in South America. They also produce carbonated sparkling wine, and a sweet sherry-type wine.

Viñedos Ortiz SA – Viña Linderos
Liberatador Bernard O'Higgins Av. 1370, Santiago. Founded 1865. Owner: The Ortiz family. 200 acres of Cab.Sauv., Sauv.Blanc., Sem., Chard., Ries.
Founded by Linderos, a pioneer in introducing vines and vinification methods from Europe. The vineyards are close to the Andes and are irrigated by water from the Maipo river. Wines have been shipped abroad since 1884.

Viña San Pedro
Molina, VI Region. Founded 1865. Private company. 2,700 acres in Talca province, 60% Sauv.Bl., 40% Cab., 2.1m. cases. No visits.
A well-known old company whose Gato Blanco is one of Chile's most popular better-than-average whites. Gato Negro is a similar, rather plain red. Brands are Castillo de Molina, Llava de Oro and Las Encinas. A further 900 acres has recently been planted with Riesling, Chardonnay and Merlot.

Santa Carolina
Rodrigo de Araya 1431, Santiago. Founded 1875. Private company. 432 acres. Visits by appt.
One of the biggest and most popular bodegas in Chile with vineyards near Rapel, Lontué and in the Maipo Valley. They also purchase grapes from a further 2,200 acres. Their Cabernet (with Merlot and Cot), Semillon, Sauvignon and a little Chardonnay are very reasonably priced. Recently they have invested heavily in stainless steel and French oak barrels, there are also plans for a new vineyard near Linares, 500km. south of Santiago, where the climate is said to be like that in Napa.

Santa Rita
Buin. Founded 1880. Private company. 560 acres. Visits by appt.
One of the best-respected old family firms. New machinery has been installed and they are using oak barrels bought entirely in from France and America. Their most famous brand is '120', so-called because Bernardo O'Higgins (the liberator of Chile) and 120 men hid in the Santa Rita cellars after the battle of Rancagua. Other brands are Casa Real (the best), Real Audiencia and Gran Libertador. Exports are over 100,000 cases a year. Since the mid-'80s the wines have won prizes in international competitions in Yugoslavia, England, the USA and in particular at the 1986 Gault-Millau Olympiad in Paris, where its 1984 'Medelle Real 120' came top amongst the Cabernets. Santa Rita is the top exporter to the UK with 30,000 cases a year.

Tarapacá Ex Zavala
Rojas Magallanes con Canal San Carlos, La Florida, Santiago. Founded 1874. Private company. 173 acres. 112,000 cases a year. Visits.
One of the smaller bodegas and, apart from Cousiño Macul, the only one to grow all its own grapes. Brands are: Embajador, Canciller, Gran Canciller Cosecha, Borgoña, Chablis, Gran Tarapaca and Gran Reserva. Exports are mainly within South America.

Miguel Torres (Chile) Ltda.
Panamericana Sur, No.195, Curicó. Established 1978. Family owned. 370 acres of Cab.Sauv., Sauv.Blanc., Ries., Gewürz., Chard.
Miguel Torres Jr. of the famous Catalan family bought the small bodegas of Viña Maquehua in 1978. Since then complete replanting and modernization (Spanish stainless steel and American oak) has resulted in the first white wine to be made by cold fermentation. Torres was the first to introduce these new style Chilean wines. Their more delicate Cabernets pointed the way for many others. The main markets are Spain and the UK. 1990 marked the release of the Riserva Cabernet.

Undurraga
Camino Melipilla, Santiago. Founded 1885. Private company. 480 acres (P.N., Pinot Blanc, Cab., Ries., Sem.). 560,000 cases. Visits.
A famous family-owned firm in the central Maipo valley, maintaining an air of gracious colonialism with its (iron-roofed) old country house in lavish gardens. Traditional oak-aged wines are labelled Viejo Roble (old oak) but modern fresh wines are also made, among them 'champagnes', and each year Don Pedro Undurraga is reducing the amount of time the white wines spend in cask. Undurraga is now alone in using the once-common Chilean *caramayola*, a 70-centilitre flagon like the German

Bocksbeutel. Chileans rate their wines reliable and good value. One third is exported.

Viña Los Vascos Ltda.
Cañtén Valley west of San Fernando. Re-established 1975. Owners: Eyzaguirre family and Ch. Lafite Rothschild. 449 acres, Cab. Sauv., Sauv. Blanc., Chard.

The Eyzaguirre family, of Basque descent, arrived in 1755. Wine makers since 1772, they returned to the Cañetén Valley in 1975. Today three-quarters of the vineyard dates from the early 1940s with the rest having been replanted within the last five years. Modernization of the winery has been under the guidance of California-based Chilean oenologist Don Sergio Traverso. In 1988 Château Lafite-Rothschild bought 50 per cent of the company. New stainless steel fermenters and new French oak barrels have been brought in, and the old stone winery has been converted into a bottle maturation and reception area. Their Los Vascos wines are made solely for export. 1990 saw the first Rothschild-inspired vintage; another landmark for Chile.

ARGENTINA

Argentina's wine industry has reached a level of quality the world cannot ignore. Bordeaux's Vinexpo found this out when Argentina won a clutch of medals in 1989. Argentina could re-establish itself as one of the world's most important sources of good everyday wines. Its wine industry has 750,000 acres of wine grapes. It is a century old, yet modern – far more modern than Chile's – with massive industrial wineries the rule. So far there has been little place for the pursuit of excellence, but a massive turnover of agreeable wines in a style that owes more to Italy than France or even (with the exception of sherry types) Spain.

The centre of the industry is the province of Mendoza, in the rain shadow of the Andes on the same latitude as (and only 150 miles away from) Santiago in Chile. Mendoza alone has two and a half times as many wine vines as Chile and half of all those in South America. The whole area is irrigated and immensely productive; its basic workhorse grapes the old native Criolla and Malbec for red wine and the Palomino and Torrontes for white.

The strong Italian influence is evident: Barbera, Lambrusco, Nebbiolo, Sangiovese and Bonarda give character to the standard blends. The French red grapes planted recently, Cabernets Sauvignon and Franc, Merlot, Syrah and Pinot Noir, have so far scarcely improved on the best reds from the well-established Malbec. The tradition is to age red wines in old oak for years.

The superior white grapes are Semillon, Sylvaner (which is called 'Riesling'), Ugni Blanc, Chenin Blanc (usually called 'Pinot Blanc') and Chardonnay. Unblended one-variety wines are the exception. Some very good Chardonnay has been made recently. Oxidized sherry-style wines made of Palomino, Pedro Ximénez and Torrontes are popular. Sparkling wine has been remarkably perfected by Proviar, a subsidiary of Moët & Chandon.

The province of San Juan, north of Mendoza and hotter and drier, has 150,000 acres of irrigated vines, 90 per cent white for sherries, for export as concentrate or for distilling.

Neuquen and Rio Negro, south of Mendoza, have a climate more akin to that of Europe, though still deprived of rain by the Andean barrier. 44,000 acres here are planted with Malbec, Barbera and increasingly white grapes, since their acid balance makes them the crispest in Argentina. In the long run this may well be the best quality region.

ARGENTINA PRODUCERS

Bianchi
San Rafael, Mendoza. Founded 1927. A Seagram subsidiary with 250 acres. Their best wine is Cabernet Particular. Don Valentin is a good standard. Bianchi Borgogna (Barbera and Malbec) is the country's top-selling 'fine red'.
Humberto Canale
Rio Negro. Promising Semillon. Mendoza. Large growers of Cabernet, Merlot and Lambrusco. Bordeaux medals for Cabernet and Semillon.
Crillon
Godoy Cruz, Mendoza. Founded 1927. A Seagram subsidiary. No vineyards. Specialists in sparkling Crillon and Monitor.

Esmeralda
Cordoba. Large growers of Cabernet, Malbec, Sauvignon, Sylvaner, etc. St. Felician Cabernet is their best brand.
Flichman
5500 Mendoza. Good Merlot and Syrah and white and red 'Caballero de la Cepa'.
Angel Furlotti
Maipú, Mendoza. An important bodega with 2,500 acres, known for a blend of Cabernet, Merlot and Lambrusco.
Giol
Paraguay 4902, 1414 Buenos Aires. The huge cooperative of Maipu province. Canciller is the premium brand.

Goyenechea
Alsina 1970, 1090 Buenos Aires. A family-owned estate of 740 acres. Aberdeen Angus is their heavy-duty label; Marqués del Nevado more modern.
Bodegas Lopez
Godoy Cruz 2000, Buenos Aires. An old company with 2,500 acres, famous for its consistent Chateau Montchenot (exported as Don Federico). Merlot and Malbec are reckoned the best of their wood-aged reds. Cabernet Chateau Vieux is exported as Casona Lopez.
Bodegas Luigi Bosca
Small concern in Mendoza with a name for Malbec and Sauvignon Blanc.

Bodegas Nacari
Coop in La Rioja province. It has won medals in Bordeaux for its Torrontés white.

Norton
Suarez 2857, 1284 Buenos Aires. An old-established company with 1,250 acres, best known for oak-aged Perdriel Cabernet but also making some fresh whites of Riesling, Chardonnay, ect.

Orfila
San Martin, Mendoza. A family estate of 680 acres: Sauvignon, Chardonnay and Cabernet. Cautivo is their top label.

Peñaflor
Av. J.B. Justo 1015, Buenos Aires. The country's biggest wine company, with 4 modern bodegas and a huge range of wines, including the popular Andean brand, designed for export. Standards are creditable. Trapiche wines (esp. Medella) are excellent. Also good are Andean vineyards and Fond de Cave Chardonnay and Cabernet.

Proviar
Florida 378, 4°, 1351 Buenos Aires. They work under the supervision of Moët & Chandon, producing Champaña (Baron B is the top quality), a smooth light Castell Chandon white of Sauvignon, Semillon and Ugni Blanc, Valmont of Malbec and Cabernet Sauvignon and Valtour of Pinot Noir.

Roblevina
Southern Mendoza. Their Cabernet took top honours at Bordeaux Vinexpo '89.

Bodegas La Rural
Maipù 5501, Mendoza. A bodega with 620 acres, still wood-ageing reds lavishly but making Riesling and Gewürztraminer with a lighter touch. 'San Filipe' is their brand name.

Santa Ana
Guaymallen, Mendoza. A small family property of 95 acres largely planted with Barbera and Bonarda, but also good Syrah Val Semina and promising Sauvignon Blanc.

San Telmo
A large modern concern making good varietal wines in the California manner. The Malbec is especially good.

Suter
San Rafael, Mendoza. A Seagram subsidiary with 2,400 acres. Their Etiqueta Maron 'Pinot Blanc' is the brand leader in 'fine whites'.

Michel Torino, Bodega La Rosa
Cordoba 366, Salta 4400. An 870-acre property, 75% white Torrontes for a heavily fruity white 'Don David'. Cabernet is potent but well made.

Pascual Toso
San Jose, Mendoza. A small family concern best known for one of Argentina's best Cabernets.

Weinert
Parana 720, 1017 Buenos Aires. A modern winery without vineyards. Fresh and fruity wines, especially a Chardonnay without ageing in wood, and tough, old-fashioned reds.

Brazil

The immense domestic market of South America's largest country has led some of the biggest names in drinks – Cinzano, Domecq, Heublein, Martini & Rossi, Moët & Chandon and National Distillers – to invest in Brazil.

The 175,000 acres of vineyards are concentrated in the southernmost states of Rio Grande do Sul and to a lesser extent Santa Catarina, the Região do Vale do São Francisco, the Região de Viamão, the Regão de Pinheiro Machado and the Região de Santana do Livramento. Southern Rio Grande do Sul, between Uruguay and the Atlantic, lies on the latitude of Mendoza in Argentina. But here a warm wet oceanic climate makes grape-growing far more problematical. Until recently American and hybrid non-*vinifera* vines dominated.

In 1969 a subsidiary of the American Heublein Corporation, Dreher, introduced Cabernet. Barbera and other Italian varieties were already showing that *vinifera* could cope in well-chosen sites. One of the most promising is Bage, 700 feet up, 125 miles from the Atlantic and near the Uruguay border, chosen on the advice of the University of California and equated with California Region III.

Most of Brazil's vines are 300 miles farther north around Caxias do Sul, Garibaldi and Bento Gonçalves, towns founded by Italians a century ago. The biggest company, Vinicola Riograndense, produces Granja União wines at Caxias, and Dreher, the pioneer with quality vines, is at Bento Gonçalves.

Mexico

Mexico is the oldest producer of wine in the Americas, with winery buildings going back to the sixteenth century. Only recently, though, has the Mexican market demanded anything better than peasant wine and brandy (which still uses 90 per cent of the wine grapes grown). Progress towards quality has come in four main areas: Baja California, which benefits from cold Pacific currents, and dotted along the high mountain chain of the Sierra Madre, San Juan del Rio (100 miles north of the capital); Aguascalientes (250 miles north); and Saltillo, Parras and Torreon, 500 miles north, to the west of Monterey. Of these, Parras is the oldest and Baja California and Aguascalientes the most advanced. The noble grape varieties are newcomers, but investments by international companies are encouraging.

Mexico producers

Marqués de Aguayo SA
Ramos Arizpe No. 195, Hacienda el Rosario, Parras, Coahuila. The oldest winery in the Americas, founded in 1593, it now makes only brandy.

Cia. Vinicola de Aguascalientes
Av. Copilco No. 164, Col. Oxtopulco C.U., Mexico 20. Mexico's biggest wine company. The main product of its 15,000 acres is brandy. San Marcos is the table-wine brand, Champ d'Or the sparkling wine. The company also owns the Alamo brand and Cia-Vin. de Vergel at Gomez Palacio in Durango province, with its Tinto Noblejo, Bianco Verdizo, Tinto Viña Santiago, etc.

Industrias Vinicolas Domecq
Av. Mexico No. 91, Mexico 21. Largely brandy, but also the highly regarded Los Reyes table wines from Guadalupe.

Formex-Ybarra
Valle de Guadalupe, Mpio. de Ensenada, Baja California. 800 acres in Baja California produce the well-known Terrasola table wine..

Casa Madero
Bodegas de San Lorenzo, Parras, Coahuila. A historic and beautiful bodega founded in 1626, the second oldest in the Americas. 1,000 acres, brand name San Lorenzo.

Cavas de San Juan
San Juan del Rio, Queraturo. Mexico's southernmost and highest winery at 6,100 feet. 625 acres include Cabernet, Chardonnay and Pinot Noir Hidalgo, and (sparkling) Carte Blanche.

Bodegas de Santo Tomas
Av. Miramar No. 666, Ensenada, B.C. Owned by Elias Pando. Fame arrived with Dmitri Tchelistcheff, son of the renowned André of Beaulieu Vintners, who brought noble vines from the Napa Valley. Most of the vines are still such compromise varieties as Chenin Blanc, Carignan, Grenache, but plantings of Chardonnay, Cabernet and Pinot Noir have had some success.

Productos de Uva de Aguascalientes
PO Box 350, Aguascalientes, Ags. The Cetto family's main winery, producing Valle Redondo wines from 300 acres. They also own modern vineyards at Tecate, Tijuana, producing Calfia and F. Chauvenet brands.

ENGLAND

The fact that England and Wales are at the farthest northern limit of the zone where grapes will ripen has not discouraged some 1,000 landowners, farmers and gardeners from planting vineyards of from half an acre up to 200 acres. The revival of English wine-growing (it was probably introduced by the Romans, and was widespread in the Middle Ages) started slowly in the 1950s and accelerated rapidly in the 1970s. The excellent summer of 1976 encouraged many to think that wine-growing could be more than a hobby and part-time job. In spite of a succession of dismal harvests in the late '70s, with vintage rain a regular occurrence, the little industry has consolidated its position, helped by a run of extremely successful harvests in the late '80s. There are now about 400 vineyards covering almost 2,000 acres scattered across southern England and Wales, with concentrations in the traditional fruit-growing areas of Kent and Sussex, Essex and Suffolk, along the south coast through Hampshire as far as Devon and north through Berkshire, Wiltshire and Somerset as far as Worcester. In 1989 nearly 3.5 million bottles were produced: this was a large as well as a high-quality vintage.

It is too early to say that any regional styles have emerged. English wine is and presumably always will be a light, refreshing, slightly tart summer drink. The qualities it achieves best are floweriness, delicate fruitiness and a crisp clean freshness. Its acidity should be noticeable and matched with fragrant, fruity flowers, whether dry or semi-sweet. A little *spritz* is often a good idea. Recently, wine makers have successfully started to produce bottle-fermented sparkling wines and more complex, barrel-aged wines. More complex flavours are evolving as the vines age and the wine makers grow more skilful. It is apparent that good English wines can benefit from bottle-age – indeed that they need

it, particularly in vintages of high acidity.

In the cool climate with uncertain summers and autumns, early ripening and resistance to rot are two of the major factors governing the choice of grapes. The official EEC recommendations for Britain are Müller-Thurgau, Pinot Meunier (sometimes called Wrotham Pinot) and Auxerrois – which is successful in Luxembourg. Growers have concentrated on white grapes, above all Müller-Thurgau and the non-recommended French-American hybrid Seyval Blanc, whose wine is reliable, if neutral in character. Müller-Thurgau is less fashionable of late, with Seyval Blanc and classic French varieties more in favour. English growers are increasingly taking advantage of the new German aromatic crossings to give character and lift to their wine. Huxelrebe, Reichensteiner, Madeleine Angevine, Bacchus and Schönburger all have marked characters. Too marked, some feel, to produce very agreeable wine without a less aromatic element in the blend.

The industry's regulatory body, founded in 1967, is the English Vineyard Association. Since 1978 it has been empowered to grant a 'Seal of Quality' to wines submitted for its analysis and tasting.

Under EEC regulations a limit has been imposed on production levels (3.33 million bottles) and planted area (1,235 acres). England is some way off reaching its production limit but with acreage nearing 2,000, an official Vineyard Register is required. This is being drawn up by the Wine Standards Board, the body appointed by the Ministry of Agriculture to implement EEC wine laws in the UK. The classification of English wine is also subject to EEC regulations and subsequently no English wine may be classed as 'Quality Wine' but must be labelled 'Table Wine' – a situation which growers feel, with reason, to be unfair to the best of their products.

ENGLAND PRODUCERS

Adgestone Vineyard
Nr Sandown, Isle of Wight. Owners and wine makers: The Barlows. Visits. 28 acres.
Est. 1968, first vintage in 1970. This was one of the first commercial vineyards in the U.K. The vines are planted on well-sheltered, south-facing, chalky slopes which benefit from the Island's good climate. The grape varieties are exclusively Müller-Thurgau, Seyval Blanc and Reichensteiner. Light, fragrant, dryish wines which age exceedingly well.

Astley Vineyards
Nr Stourport on Severn, Worcester. Owners: The Baches.

Visits by appt. 4.5 acres.
Planting began in 1979 near a site with strong historical viticultural connections. Wines are made at the Three Choirs winery and have regularly been awarded the E.V.A. Seal of Quality. The wine is exported to West Germany. Good Kerner.

Beaulieu Abbey Vineyard
Lymington, Hampshire. Owner: Montagu Ventures Ltd. Visits by appt. 4.6 acres.
Planting by Lt. Col Robert and Mrs Margaret Gore-Browne in 1958, and the estate passed in 1974 to Mrs Gore-Brown's godson, Ralph Montagu. The grapes are

mainly Müller-Thurgau and are grown on an old monastic site where Cistercian monks made wine 700 years ago. Both the Gore-Brownes and the Montagus have been champions of English wine.

Barton Manor
East Cowes, Isle of Wight. Owners: The Goddard family. Wine maker: Anthony Goddard. Visits. 1989: 2,600 cases. 10.5 acres.

Planting began in 1976 and a further five acres are planned. The wines are aromatic, medium-dry, using a blend of grapes including Seyval-Blanc, Müller-Thurgau, and now Gewürztraminer grown under plastic tunnels. Consistently good, prize-winning wines.

Biddenden Vineyards
Nr Tenterden, Kent. Owners: Biddenden Vineyards Ltd. Wine maker: Richard Barnes. Visits. 20 acres.

One of the best-known and most successful vineyards in the South East, also making wine for other vineyards. Planting began 1969 and the first vintage was in 1974. Crisp, medium-dry white of Müller-Thurgau and Ortega, plus a Pinot Noir rosé. 1986 Gore-Browne trophy winner.

Carden Park
Malpas, Cheshire. Owner: John Broome. 9 acres.

This is England's (and possibly the world's?) most northerly vineyard, planted in an area of Cheshire with a micro-climate giving (say the owners) weather conditions similar to the Loire Valley. It was planted in 1978 and the first vintage produced in 1990. The grape variety is exclusively Seyval Blanc. The wine is made at Lamberhurst.

Carr Taylor Vineyards
Hastings, East Sussex. Owners: The Carr Taylors. Wine maker: David Carr Taylor. Visits. 21 acres.

Planting began 1974, first production 1976. These are among the best-known English wines. Varieties include Gutenborner, Huxelrebe, Kerner and Pinot Noir and a Kerner/Reichensteiner *méthode champenoise* which won the 1988 Gore-Brown trophy.

Chiltern Valley Wines
Hambledon, Oxfordshire. Owners: The Ealand family. Wine maker: David Ealand. Visits by appt. 1989: approx. 350 cases. 3 acres.

Small, very modern winery buying-in local grapes from several small vineyards and also using its own. They make four white wines, using Bacchus, Madeleine Angevine and Reichensteiner grapes grown on high, chalky, flinty slopes. Impressive, prize-winning quality.

Dembies Lane Estate
Ranmore Common, Surrey.

A major venture with 220 acres of mostly German varieties. Yet to crop; results awaited with interest.

Fonthill
Salisbury, Wiltshire. Owners: Michael Craig-McFeeley and John Edginton. Visits by appt. 9.5 acres.

The wines are made at Lamberhurst. They have been granted the E.V.A. Seal of Quality and won medals.

Hambledon
Mill Down, Hambledon, Hampshire.
Visits by appt. 15.5 acres.

Planting was started in 1951 by the former owner Major-General Sir Guy Salisbury-Jones who was in the forefront of the revival of viticulture in England. The south-facing, chalky site is planted with Auxerrois, Chardonnay, Pinot Meunier and Seyval Blanc.

Headcorn Vineyard
Headcorn, Kent. Owners: Headcorn Flowers Ltd. Visits. 14 acres.

Planting began in 1982 and recently an additional four acres were added. A winery is planned and wines are made at Tenterden Vineyards at present. Both their Wealden White and Huxelrebe have been awarded the E.V.A. Seal of Quality.

High Weald
East Sussex. Owner and wine maker: Christopher Lindler.

A well-equipped winery, without vineyards, which makes good wines under its own label and for several small growers.

Lamberhurst Vineyards
Nr Tunbridge Wells, Kent. Owner: K. McAlpine. 55 acres. Visits.

Planting began 1972, and this has long been the largest and most professional vineyard and winery in the country. It was also one of the first to make English wine on a truly commercial scale. Its own vineyards, including those at Horam, plus those for which it makes wine, amount to 125 acres. They use mainly Müller-Thurgau, Seyval Blanc, Reichensteiner and Schönburger grape varieties. Recently they have started *méthode champenoise*. A long list of prizes.

Moorlynch Vineyard
Nr Bridgwater, Somerset. Owners: The Rees family. Wine maker: Tom Rees. Visits. 11 acres.

Planting began in 1981, production in 1983. This vineyard, in an idyllic setting (the winery is in one of the 18th-century stone barns), has rapidly achieved success and the wines have been granted the E.V.A. Seal of Quality.

New Hall
Purleigh, Essex. Owners: The Greenwood family. Wine maker: S. W. Greenwood. Visit. 87 acres.

Started in 1969, this is one of the oldest, largest and best-situated sites in the country. The Greenwoods have invested much careful time and management, and produce award-winning whites and experimental reds.

Nutbourne Manor
Nr Pulborough, W. Sussex. Wine maker: David Shaw. Visits. 20 acres.

The first vintage was in 1984 and immediately won the E.V.A. Seal of Quality. Wines are made at High Weald Winery and include an elegant and tasty Schönburger, Bacchus and Huxelrebe. For sale in 1990.

Pulham
Nr Norwich, Norfolk. Owner: Pulham Vineyards Ltd. Wine maker: Peter Cook. Visit. 12.6 acres.

Planting began 1973 using mainly Müller-Thurgau grapes. They achieved early success with their Magdalen Rivaner which won the Gore-Browne Trophy in 1977. Other grape varieties include Auxerrois and Bacchus.

Rock Lodge Vineyard
Nr Haywards Heath, W. Sussex. Owners: the Cowderoy

family. Wine maker: David Cowderoy. Visits. by appt. 3 acres (10–20 planned).

Planting started in 1961. David Cowderoy was trained in winemaking in Australia. Grape varieties are mainly Müller-Thurgau and Reichensteiner and the aim is dry wines. *Méthode champenoise* 'Imperial' is the latest innovation.

Shawsgate Vineyard

Framlingham, Suffolk. Owner: I. S. Hutcheson. Wine maker: R. A. Hemphill. Visits. 17 acres.

Planting began in 1973 and the vineyard was purchased by the present owner in 1985, since when it has seen much new investment. Grapes include Chardonnay, Bacchus and Müller-Thurgau and the aim is a dry, full style. The Shawsgate 1986 was granted the E.V.A. Seal of Quality.

Tenterden Vineyards

Tenterden, Kent. Owner: Tenterden Vineyards Ltd. Wine maker: Stephen Skelton. Visits. 16 acres.

Started by Stephen and Linda Skelton in 1977 after two years working in a vineyard and winery in Germany. Award-winning wines from dry to sweet including Müller-Thurgau, Seyval Blanc and Gutenborner. Their recent oak-aged wines have been well-received. Many other grape varieites plus some experimental plots.

Three Choirs Vineyard

Nr Newent, Gloucestershire. Owners: Three Choirs Vineyard Ltd. Wine maker: Tom Day. Visits. 34 acres.

Vines were planted between 1974 and 1988. A well-equipped winery which also makes wines for neighbouring vineyards. Successful wines include a late harvest Huxelrebe.

Wellow Vineyard

Nr Romsey, Hampshire. Owner: The Vining family. Vists. 80 acres (100 planned for 1992).

Planting began 1985 and the first vintage was in 1987. This ambitious, very commercial venture is England's third-largest vineyard. 12 grape varieties including Chardonnay and predominantly Müller-Thurgau and Bacchus. A good late harvest Huxelrebe.

Westbury Vineyard

Nr Reading, Berkshire. Owner: Bernard Theobald. Wine maker: Helen Tarry. Visits. 12.5 acres.

Planting began 1978. Bernard Theobald is a highly individual, keen champion of English wine and has grown 11 grape varieties in commercial quantities since 1978. He has made England's first real red Pinot Noir. His Müller-Thurgau-Seyval 1982 was awarded a gold medal.

Wickham Vineyard

Shedfield, Hampshire. Owners: The Charnley family. Wine maker: John Charnley. Visits by appt. 9.5 acres.

Planting began in 1984 and the first production was in 1987. A winery is planned, to be housed in an 18th-century barn. One of only 7 wines to be awarded 3 stars in a 'Wine' magazine tasting in March 1989.

Wootton Vineyard

Wells, Somerset. Owners and wine makers: Major and Mrs Gillespie. Visits. 6 acres.

Planted in 1971, the first vintage was in 1973, since when they have been making consistently good, fresh and fruity wines. Principal grape varieties include Müller-Thurgau, Seyval Blanc, Auxerrois and Schonburger.

Wine is becoming part of rural England

Enjoying Wine

It is the inquisitive who enjoy wine most. The essence of the game is variety; you could taste a different wine every day of your life and yet not learn it all. Each wine evolves with time. There will always be new wines to taste, and new combinations of wine with food to try. There will always be more to learn about yourself, your palate and its reactions, too.

No single attitude or set of rules can apply to a commodity that can be either a simple foodstuff as basic as bread and cheese, or one of the most recherché of luxuries, or anywhere in between. There are enamel-mug wines and Baccarat-crystal wines, and there is no point in pretending that one is the other.

This chapter is concerned with choosing, buying, storing, serving and appreciating wine that is above the ordinaire or jug level. Once a wine has a named origin (as opposed to being an anonymous blend) it reflects a particular soil, climate, culture and tradition. For better or worse it has some character.

The mastery of wine consists in recognizing, bringing out and making the most of that character. I cannot improve on André Simon's definition of a connoisseur: 'One who knows good wine from bad, and appreciates the distinctive merits of different wines.' Thank heaven all white wines are not Moselles, however fresh, flowery and fragrant, or all reds great thumping Cabernets.

It is a crucial (but also a common) misunderstanding of the nature and variety of wine to say that a Barolo, for example, is better than a Rioja, or a Napa Cabernet than a Pauillac. The secret is to learn to understand and enjoy each of them for what it is.

There is only one essential I would press on you, if you are going to spend more than a bare minimum and buy wines above the jug level: make a conscious act of tasting. Become aware of the messages your nose and mouth are sending you – not just about wine, but about all food and drink. Seek out new tastes and think about them.

By far the greater part of all fine wine, and even – perhaps especially – of the best, is thrown away by being used as a mere drink. A great bottle of wine is certainly wasted if nobody talks about it, or at least tries to pinpoint in his own consciousness the wonderful will-o'-the-wisp of fragrance and flavour.

BUYING WINE

To buy wine and get exactly what you expect is the exception rather than the rule. Wine is a moving target; a kaleidoscope of vintners and vintages that never stands still. If this bothers you, there is a solution – stick to a brand. But you will be sacrificing the great fascination of wine; its infinite variety. Not to mention the fun of the chase: the satisfaction of finding a winner (and the chagrin of backing a dud).

There are few cardinal rules in such an open field, where one day you may be buying from the corner store, the next by mail-order and the third direct from the producer. But the first rule is absolute. Always buy ahead of your needs; never drink the bottle you have just bought. There are very good reasons for this rule. To start with you need time to think. If you go shopping knowing that you must bring home some wine, the chances are that what you buy will be unsuitable and you will probably pay more than you really want to.

Nobody can take in all the offerings of a well-stocked store at a glance. Do your wine buying when you are in the mood and have time to browse, to compare prices, to make calculations, to use reference books. By far the best place to do this is at home, by comparing the price lists of alternative suppliers. Avoid traders who have no list and rely on you to fall for this week's 'special'.

Your wine needs time to rest. Although many modern white and light-red wines are so stable that you could play skittles with them and do them no harm, all mature red wines need a settling period of at least several days after being moved. Your chances of serving a wine at its best are far greater if you can prepare it calmly at home.

Given time you can make an order that qualifies for a discount. Buying by the case is cheaper than buying by the bottle. Assuming you have a cupboard with a lock, and a reasonable resistance to temptation, you will use no more wine, and pay less.

An investment in pleasure

An investment in future pleasure is often one of the most profitable of all. Inflation aside, when you come to drink the wine, now better than when you bought it, the expenditure will be a thing of the past; the pleasure will seem a gift from the gods.

In fact, very little money is needed to convert you from a bottle-by-bottle buyer to the proud possessor of a 'cellar'. Calculate what you spend on wine in three months, or two months, or at a pinch only one month – and spend it all at once in a planned spree. Lock the wine away. Then continue to buy the same quantity as before but use it to replenish your stock, instead of for instant drinking. All you have done is to borrow three, two or one month's wine money and the interest on that is your

only extra expenditure. Your reward is wine you have chosen carefully and kept well, ready when you want it, not when you can get to the shops.

Make an effort to be clear headed about what you really need. Do not spend more than you can comfortably afford. Think twice before buying unknown wines as part of a package. Do not buy a quantity of wine you have never tasted and may not like. Consider whether home delivery is really practicable: will there be someone at home to answer the door? Can you easily lift the 40 or 50 pounds that a case of wine weighs?

One of the wiliest ways of broadening your buying scope is to join with a small group of like-minded people to form a syndicate. A syndicate can save money by buying bigger lots of everyday wine. It can spread risks. It can also bring within reach extraordinary bottles at prices that would make you, on your own, feel guilty for months. Three or four friends who have never tasted Château Lafite or Romanée-Conti will enjoy them more if they buy and open them together, sharing their opinions (and their guilt). While there may be laws that prevent an unlicensed citizen from selling wine, even to a friend, there is nothing to stop them sharing its cost.

The wine trade

The structure of the wine trade has changed radically in recent years from a fairly rigid pattern of brokers, shippers, agents, wholesalers and retailers to an intricate but fluid mixture of ingredients, some old and some new. It is not surprising that such a pleasant vocation has more volunteers than the army. The great growth areas have been in 'experts', writers and consultants, and in ingenious methods of selling with or without a shop.

In America the period has seen wine change from a minority – even a faintly suspect minority – interest to a national pastime. The wine trade has recruited regiments of specialists at every level. Locally the retailers are the most prominent; nationally the marketing men. But what remains sovereign (and to the foreigner most bizarre) is the changing legislation from state to state. Scarcely two are alike. New York, California, Texas, Florida and a few more states are relatively free to benefit from all the rich possibilities; the rest are more or less inhibited by local legislation. Even individual counties can stick their oar in and say what you may and may not drink. Seen from across the Atlantic it looks as though the Constitution is in mortal peril.

In Britain the changes started in the 1960s with the ponderous tread of the brewers, fearful that a growing taste for wine would erode their sales of beer, buying scores of traditional local wine shops and replacing them with chains tied to national brand-marketing ideas.

Whatever the merits of the old merchants (and many of them were excellent) the new shops were generally dismal, and the rising generation of vocational wine merchants – as opposed to accountants – wanted nothing to do with them. They found it easy to reinvent the old individualistic wine trade for the new generation of better travelled and more knowledgeable (if less wealthy) wine lovers. Some of them specialized in particular areas or styles of wine. Gerald Asher in London was the first, shipping the 'lesser' wines of France – names like Touraine and Roussillon, which today are considered almost classic. The old trade, weaned on Bordeaux and burgundy, had never heard of them and the brewers (most of them) preferred a simple life with tank trucks of a Spanish blend. Today there is a specialist for almost every area of the wine-growing world and it must be said that the brewers now employ some of the best.

Other wine merchants offer the old virtues of personal service, delivery to your door and credit (at a price). Personal service consists largely of word-of-mouth recommendations based on a regular customer's known tastes and resources. A very few firms, including some of the oldest and one or two of the youngest, are prepared to become as involved as family solicitors, keeping track of what a customer has in his cellar and reminding him to drink it when it has reached its best. Such firms are skilful at offering the best wines of a new vintage early, while they are still in their makers' cellars and long before they are even bottled, at 'opening' prices that rarely fail to rise once the wines come on the general market.

At the opposite extreme, making wine available and tempting to every shopper, are the supermarkets, offering at first a rather simple and limited range, sometimes under their own brand names, and now a remarkable collection including fine wines and esoteric discoveries. These are nearly always the cheapest places to buy single bottles, which are usually good value for money, if rarely memorable. In their early days of selling wine most supermarkets left a lot to be desired, particularly by way of explanation and description, but more recently helpful labels and even in some cases trained staff have appeared and the range has widened.

Learn while you drink

Mail-order wine merchants prosper on the proposition that the calm customer, reference book and calculator to hand, is likely to aim true and be satisfied. Wine clubs and societies, often offering a great deal of information about the wines they sell, and usually setting up periodic tastings for members, feed the urge to learn while you drink.

Discount stores doing cash-and-carry business appeal to bargain hunters. Magazines can be highly persuasive about their mixed case of the month. There has even been a wine investment programme linked to a life insurance policy. All in all, the efforts of marketing men make a subject which is already confusing a great deal more so.

In the last few years auctions have come to epitomize both the scholarship and the showmanship of wine. Michael Broadbent at Christie's, followed by Colin Fenton and then Patrick Grubb and David Molyneaux-Berry at Sotheby's, have become wine's ringmasters and at the same time the repositories of esoteric vinous knowledge. Auctions are now regularly used in the United States, Germany, South Africa and many countries besides Britain to sell and publicize at the same time. But the London auction houses have another role, simply to turn over private cellars, surplus stocks and awkward small amounts of wine that complicate a wine merchant's life. There is a steady flow of mature wine, young wine and sometimes good but unfashionable wine at absurdly low prices. Anyone can buy, but the real bargains are often in lots larger than an individual may want. It is common practice to form syndicates to buy and divide such lots.

Speculating in blue chips

The auction houses established a flourishing market in old wines whose value had been unknown before. In their wake a new class of, so to speak, second-hand wine merchants has sprung up. Their business can be compared with antiquarian booksellers, finding rare wines on behalf of collectors – for collectors there certainly are today, as there never were in the spacious days when a gentleman filled his cellars with first-growth claret as a matter of course.

Those who buy such blue-chip wines in quantity these days are more likely to be engaged in the less gentlemanly game of speculation. Wine is a commodity susceptible to buying cheap and selling dear – but happily with no certainty of success. In 1974, overconfident speculators in wine lost millions.

The more expensive the wine the greater the chance of its appreciation. But other factors come into it, too: the vintage and its reputation (which will shift, not always predictably, as time goes on); the general financial climate; the popularity of the château or grower in question; perhaps most of all the proven ability of the wine to age. It is the classed growths of Bordeaux and vintage port that are known or presumed to have the longest potential life span; therefore the biggest spread of opportunity for reselling at a profit. Modern burgundies and German wines are considered relatively poor risks, with or without justification. The very best Italian and Spanish wines, and such rarities as Tokay Essence, have a certain following. Some fine California wines undoubtedly will have a considerable following, once they have proved their ability to age.

CHOOSING WINE

One of the many advantages of living in wine-making country is the way it simplifies your choice. You drink the local wine, preferably made by friends. You tend to suit your diet to it; if the wine is delicate you will go easy on the seasoning; if it is strapping you will make meals of garlic and peppers. All bets are off in California, where your friends may make anything from a fragile Chenin Blanc to a galumphing Zinfandel, but most wine regions arrived at a balanced food and wine regime years ago.

In a country or region with no such traditions things are more complicated. In Britain, or the eastern United States, where the shops offer every wine there is, it is hardest of all to know where to start. Our wonderful variety makes a wonderfully difficult choice.

The realistic starting point, of course, is the price. The poorer you are the easier your choice will be. Together with the price goes the company and the occasion. If your companions are as interested in wine as you are you will want to seize the opportunity of discussing a good bottle with them. If they are indifferent, no matter how much you love them, remember that the wine itself is an occasion; it does not have to be fascinating too – unless to save you from death by boredom.

A moment in the limelight
In short, before you choose a wine, decide whether it is going to have even a moment in the limelight – and who, besides yourself, will be drinking it. Test yourself with your reaction to the behaviour of Voltaire, who habitually gave his guests Beaujolais while he drank the finest burgundies himself.

Whether you give priority to the food or the wine is the next question. Ideally they should share the stage as harmonious equals – no more rivals than a hero and heroine. In a restaurant the menu and the wine list should be offered to you at the same time.

In practice the proposition is probably either 'what shall we drink with the lamb tonight?' or 'what shall we eat with this bottle of Pomerol? You need, in fact, a two-way frame of reference; a mental image of the flavours of both food and wine so that you can match them.

It is surprising how often I am asked 'You don't have to drink red wine with meat and white wine with fish, do you?', usually with a sort of indignation that implies that this simple piece of lore is a savage attack on liberty and the constitution. Of course you don't have to. You may please yourself. But if you want to please yourself you could do worse than follow such sensible guidelines, based on sound reasons and centuries of practice.

The reasons are both chemical and aesthetic. The appetizing, refreshing quality of white wine is provided by acids that enhance the flavour of fish, while the saltiness of fish in turn emphasizes the fruity grape flavours of the wine. By contrast, the 'edge' of a red wine is not acidity but tannin, which reacts disastrously with the salt, which makes it bitter, and the fishy oils, which leave a lasting metallic tang in your mouth.

Of course there are exceptions. Certain fish (and, best of all, lampreys) are cooked in red wine to make a dish that goes excellently with a full-flavoured red – not Beaujolais but St-Emilion. Some people like cool, light-red wine with fresh poached salmon.

But on the aesthetic side the association of white wine with pale fish, and for that matter pale meat, is no accident either. Each foodstuff has its appropriate colour. The eye tells the brain what kind of flavour to expect. And the eye finds it natural to associate pale drink with pale food.

Some of the traditional associations have even simpler reasons. We drink dry white wine with goat cheese, for example, because the cheese's salty dryness makes us thirsty. Some associations are simply negative: we do not drink red wine with sweets because sugar, like salt, makes tannin taste bitter.

Strong, savoury, protein-rich meat and game dishes are the natural partners of vigorous red wines; their tannin finds a match, and so does their colour. But light grapey reds ask for a less strenuous marriage with poultry or veal or pale lamb.

What the French so evocatively call 'la cuisine douce', such rich things of gentle savour as foie gras, sweetbreads, quenelles and cream cheeses, has a similar affinity for sweet, or at least fat and unctuous, white wines.

Clearly there are broad classes of wine that are more or less interchangeable. They can be matched with similar classes of dishes to achieve satisfactory harmonies, if not perfect ones. There are other dimensions of taste that have to be taken into account, too.

Intensity is one: a powerful flavour, however appropriate, will annihilate a bland or timid one. Unfortunately this is the effect many strong cheeses have, even on splendid full-scale red wines. Style is another: there are hearty rustic tastes and pronounced urbane ones; garlic, if you like, and truffles. The wine and the food should belong to the same culture. Peasant and aristocrat rarely show one another off to advantage; neither will bread and cheese and great claret.

The total context of the meal is important. Is it leisurely or hurried? Fine wine deserves time. Is the day hot or cold? Even air conditioning fails to make big red wines a good idea in tropical heat.

There are a few dishes that destroy the flavour of wine entirely. The commonest is salad dressed with vinegar. Surprisingly, even some of France's best restaurants serve violently acetic salads. Vinegar is best avoided altogether;

A dinner with old friends to drink exceptional wines in their prime is the ultimate pleasure that wine offers. The dinner on this menu never (alas) took place, but is composed of wines and notes from several dinners at about the same period.

The scene is a London club. There are 12 guests. The food is simple and rich. The talk is unashamedly centred on the wines, with suitable excursions into reminiscence, poetry, flirtation and the rest.

I always scribble my tasting notes on the menu card. Remember that they were written in the heat of the moment, not the cool of a morning tasting — but this is what their makers made the wines for.

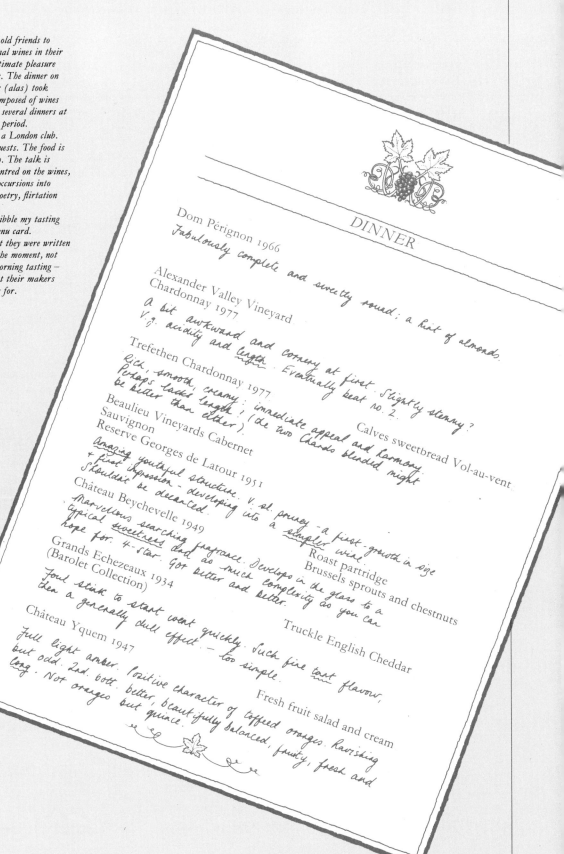

DINNER

Dom Pérignon 1966
Fabulously complete and sweetly round; a hint of almonds.

Alexander Valley Vineyard
Chardonnay 1977
A bit awkward and corseny at first. Slightly stemmy?
V.g. acidity and length. Eventually beat no. 2.

Calves sweetbread Vol-au-vent

Trefethen Chardonnay 1977
Rich, smooth, creamy; immediate appeal and harmony.
Perhaps lacks length; (de two Chards blended might
be better than either).

Beaulieu Vineyards Cabernet
Sauvignon
Reserve Georges de Latour 1951
Amazing youthful structure. V. sl. porney - a first-growth in size
+ first impression - developing into a simpler wine.
Shouldn't be decanted.

Château Beychevelle 1949
Marvellous searching fragrance. Develops in the glass to a
typical sweetness dad as much complexity as you can
hope for. 4-star. Got better and better.

Roast partridge
Brussels sprouts and chestnuts

Grands Echezeaux 1934
(Barolet Collection)
Foul stink to start went quickly. Such fine tart flavour,
then a generally dull effect. — too simple.

Truckle English Cheddar

Château Yquem 1947
Full light amber. Positive character of toffeed oranges. Ravishing
but odd. 2nd. bott. better, beautifully balanced, fruity, fresh and
long. Not oranges but quince.

Fresh fruit salad and cream

lemon juice makes a better salad dressing in any case. Salad dressings with vinegar include the red 'cocktail sauce' of American restaurants, too.

Chocolate is another flavour that dominates and spoils the taste of any wine. In my view, most desserts are better served without wine; creamy highly perfumed concoctions fight wine rather than complement it. So do syrupy, fruity ones. Citrus fruit is particularly guilty. Where a very rich gâteau is on the menu I sometimes drink a glass of madeira or even brandy with it. On the other hand raspberries and strawberries, and particularly wild strawberries, are a wonderful match for fine red wine. In Bordeaux they pour claret rather than cream over them.

There are times when no single wine will fill the bill. It happens in a restaurant where everyone is eating something different: one shellfish, another game, a third a dish with a creamy sauce. The cop-out answer is a neutral wine that will offend nobody. Liebfraumilch, 'blush' wines and Portuguese rosés have made fortunes by offering themselves as the safe bet. A more swashbuckling (if less digestible) choice is champagne. My suggestion is to start with a bottle of white wine that will match almost any hors d'oeuvre, and then (if it is a party of four or more) continue with both white and red. There is no good reason not to have both on the table at the same time.

The structure of a more formal meal with a succession of wines is the great opportunity of gastronomy. To achieve a graduated harmony of successive flavours it is worth taking pains. The ground rules are simple: follow lighter and more delicate with heavier and more pungent – both in wine and food. The fresh and hungry palate is susceptible to the subtlest flavours. Feeding fatigues it. It needs more powerful stimuli as the meal proceeds.

Occasionally the best way to bring out the singularity of a wine is to serve it concurrently with another which is similar but distinct; either slightly younger or from a neighbouring property.

Wine divided into ten basic styles

I have risked a rather arbitrary division of the infinite variety of wine into ten categories, and associated each category with a selection of dishes, as a guide to where to start to look, whether your starting point is the wine or the food.

No such generalization can be defended in every particular, but it is true to say that certain criteria of flavour, age and quality can be applied across the board. Some wines could appear equally in two different categories, but for the sake of clarity I have put them firmly where, in my judgement, they most often belong.

Dry white wines of neutral, simply 'winey' flavour

Among the cheapest wines, generally useful but too plain to be exciting, or to be particularly pleasant as apéritifs without the addition of extra flavour (such as blackcurrant or grenadine syrup).

These wines are better with simple food, especially with strong-flavoured or highly seasoned dishes, e.g. hors d'oeuvres (antipasto), aïoli or fish stew, mussels, herrings and mackerel (which need a rather acid wine to cut their oil), salade niçoise, red mullet, grilled sardines, terrines and sausages, curry or Chinese food (both of these are better for a little sweetness in the wine, e.g. Yugoslav Riesling). All should be served very well chilled (about 46°F/8°C).

Examples are: most branded 'jug' whites; Entre-Deux-Mers, Gaillac, Muscadet (Gros Plant du Pays Nantais or Aligoté for more acidity); southern French whites; many Swiss whites; most standard Italian whites (including Soave, Verdicchio, Orvieto Secco, Frascati, Pinot Bianco, Trebbiano, Sardinian and Sicilian wines); most standard Spanish and Portuguese whites; central and east European 'Welsch' Rieslings (i.e. Hungarian, Yugoslav, Bulgarian, etc.); California jugs ('Chablis') and many Chenin Blancs; South African 'Grands Crus'.

Light, fresh, grapey white wine with fruity and sometimes flowery aromas

This is the category of wine which has grown most in recent years, at the expense of the dry whites. Modern techniques, especially cold fermentation, capture whatever flavour the grape has (some have much more than others) and add as little as possible. The very aromatic German-style grapes are nearly always in this or the sweet white wine category.

All these wines make good apéritifs or refreshing between-meal or evening drinks, most of all in summer. Those with relatively high acidity are good with many first courses, but are dominated by seriously savoury dishes and lack the substance to be satisfying throughout a meal. Suitable dishes include: poached trout, crab salad, cold chicken. They need slightly less chilling than the previous category.

Wines include: German Tafelwein, Qualitätswein, most Kabinetts and some Spätleses; light French Sauvignons from the Dordogne and Touraine; Savoie whites (Crépy, Apremont); Portuguese vinho verde; certain California Chenin blancs and French Colombards; Australian 'moselles'; New Zealand and English Müller-Thurgaus and Seyval Blancs; Austrian Grüner Veltliners.

White wines with body and character, aromatic from certain grapes or with the bouquet of maturity

The fine French dry whites all come into this category. High flavour often makes them taste rich even when they are fully dry.

Without food, these wines can be too assertive; they are best matched with a savoury dish which is also rich in flavour and pale in colour, e.g. oysters, clams, lobsters and prawns, smoked fish, frogs' legs, snails, onion or leek tart, ballotines, prosciutto, salmon, turbot and other rich fish in butter, hollandaise or other rich sauces, scallops, poultry, sweetbreads, hard Swiss cheeses. Wines should only be lightly chilled (50°-55°F/10°-13°C).

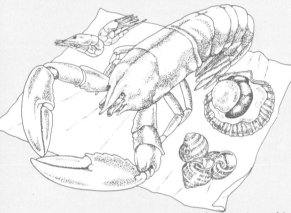

Examples are: all good mature Chardonnays (e.g. white burgundies after two or more years depending on their quality); their equivalents from California and Australia; Alsace Riesling, Gewürztraminer and Pinot Gris; Sancerre and Pouilly Fumé and Savennières from the Loire; fine white Graves; mature white Rhône wines (e.g. Hermitage Blanc) and young Condrieu; exceptional Italian whites (the best examples of Frascati, Soave Classico, Pinot Grigio, Cortese di Gavi, Montecarlo, Pomino, Traminer, etc.); best-quality mature Rioja and Penedès whites from Spain, manzanilla sherry or montilla fino; Hungarian Szürkebarát, Kéknelyü and Furmint; Austrian Rotgipfler, and Ruländer from either Austria or Baden; Australian Sémillons and dry Barossa and Coonawarra Rieslings with three or four years in bottle; California Johannisberg Riesling.

Sweet white wines

Varying from delicately fruity and lightly sweet to overwhelmingly luscious, these wines are to be sipped slowly by themselves and are rarely improved by food.

Very rich and highly flavoured desserts, however delicious, tend to fight sweet wines. Chocolate and coffee ones are fatal. If you want anything at all, the best choice is a dessert such as French apple or raspberry tart, crème brûlée, plain sponge cake or such fruit as peaches or apples. Sweet white wines are usually drunk after meals, but in France often as apéritifs, too. They are normally served very well chilled.

The finest natural sweet wines are produced by the action of 'noble rot'. These include Sauternes and Barsac and the best qualities of Ste-Croix-du-Mont and Monbazillac, which are the most potent, Vouvray and Anjou whites of certain years, late-gathered wines of Alsace and Austria, and the rare and expensive very late-harvested wines of Germany, Beerenausleses and Trockenbeerenausleses (which have recently been imitated with real success in California). German wines offer every gradation between the light flowery whites and the intensely sweet ones with the same delicately acid flavour. None of them is really a mealtime wine.

Sweet Muscats are found in most wine countries; the best 'natural' (not fortified) ones are made in the south of France at Beaumes de Venise and at Asti in northern Italy, where the very low-strength base wine for Spumante is delicious. Heavier brown Muscats are made in Languedoc and Roussillon, several parts of Italy (especially Sicily), on the east coast of Spain, at Setúbal in Portugal, in Greece and Russia and (perhaps the best) in northeast Victoria, Australia.

Rosé wines

Rosés are usually workhorse, compromise wines of adequate quality, made by fermenting the juice of red grapes very briefly with the skins, then separating it and making it like white wine. The great exception is pink champagne, which is made by adding still red wine to normal white champagne. Few things are more delicious. Rosés divide broadly into two camps: the light, pale purply pink, usually faintly sweet Loire style, and the drier, more orange-pink, stronger and more sunburnt Provençal variety. Portuguese carbonated fizzy rosés fit into the first category. Tavel from the Rhône and most rosés from Spain and Italy are stronger and drier. Some of Italy's best are called Chiaretto and are really very light reds. A third group that can be classed as rosé are *vins gris*, red-grape white wines merely shaded with colour, more grey than pink, and a fourth, *pelure d'oignon* ('onion skin'), which are very pale orange-brown. Both are usually made very dry; the *gris* more fruity and the onion skin more alcoholic. California 'blush' wines are a modern interpretation of the same tradition. *Vin gris* has recently become popular in California as a way of using surplus red grapes, often Pinot Noir or even Cabernet, to make white wine.

Rosés are best in summer with salads and on picnics, and the Provençal style with oily and garlicky or even oriental dishes. They have possibilities with such hors d'oeuvres as artichokes, crudités, salami or taramasalata. Pink wines need to be served really cold; colder than most whites. If this is difficult to arrange on a picnic choose a light red wine instead.

Grapey young reds with individuality, not intended to mature

Beaujolais is the archetype of a light red wine made to be drunk young while it is still lively with fresh grape flavour. Beaujolais-Villages is a better, stronger and tastier selection. Simple young Bordeaux, burgundy and Rhône reds, Cabernet from Anjou and Mondeuse from Savoie should have the same appeal. Similar wines are now made in the Midi (Corbières, Minervois, Roussillon, St-Chinian) by the Beaujolais technique of carbonic maceration but of grapes with less distinct flavour.

Italy's Valpolicella and Bardolino, Barbera and Dolcetto and even Chianti can be freshly fruity if they are caught young enough – which is not often. Fizzy red Lambrusco is a sort of caricature of the style. Spain provides few examples, although Valdepeñas has possibilities and no doubt will be made fresher in the future. Portugal's red vinho verde is an extreme example not to everyone's taste. California, Australia, South Africa and South America have been slow to master this style of wine. Light Zinfandels and Gamays from California sometimes achieve it.

In its liveliness and vigour this is perhaps the safest and best all-round class of red wine for mealtimes; appetizing with anything from pâté to fruit and often better than a more 'serious' or older wine with strong cheese, in mouthfuls rather than sips. For the same reason it is the easiest red wine to drink without food. It is always best served cool.

Ideal dishes include: pâtés and terrines (including those made from vegetables), quiches, salads, hamburgers, liver, ham, grilled meats, many cheeses, raspberries, plums, peaches or nectarines.

Plain everyday or 'jug' reds

These are unpretentious and anonymous blended wines with little body or flavour. French ordinaires in particular are often mere refreshment; dry, thin and frankly watery. Whether you prefer them or the usually softer and stronger Italian or Spanish style is a matter of taste. California's 'jug' reds have more body and are often rather sweet.

Most inexpensive imports from southern, central and eastern Europe, North Africa, Argentina, Chile, South Africa and Australia are in the classes that follow.

Like the 'neutral' cheap whites these are essentially wines for mealtimes, a healthy and stimulating accompaniment to almost any homely food. They are always best served rather cool. As drinks on their own they are improved by being iced in summer (as Sangria, with orange juice added) and 'mulled' on the stove with sugar and spices in winter.

The term 'table wine' has been adopted by the EEC as denoting the lowest category of quality; wines without a specific origin (i.e. this group). The commissioners in their wisdom have ignored its English meaning, which is any wine you drink at table, including the best. They have also bracketed all wines that do not conform to national laws of appellation regardless of the reason. This produces total absurdity, for example, in Italy, where several of the country's finest wines are nontraditional, therefore outside the DOC system, therefore vino da tavola, therefore officially relegated to jug-wine status.

Mature reds of light to medium strength and body

This category includes most of the world's finest red wines, epitomized by claret (red Bordeaux) and most of the typical wines of Burgundy and the Rhône, although some of the greatest fall into the next class, depending on the ripeness of the vintage. These wines need more care in serving than any others since they often throw a deposit in maturing.

They are wines for meat and game dishes with the best ingredients and moderate seasoning. Lamb, beef, veal (also sweetbreads and tongue), chicken, duck, partridge, grouse, pheasant are all ideal, although very gamey birds may need wines from the next category. Only mild cheeses should be served with these relatively delicate wines. They need to be served at a temperature of between 60° F and 65°F (15° and 18°C) to bring out their flavour.

Wines in this category (apart from French) include the best of Rioja and Penedès from Spain; Chianti Riservas, Tuscans such as Torgiano, Sassicaia and Tignanello, Carmignano, Venegazzú; Portuguese garrafeiras from Dão, Douro and Bairrada; top California, Oregon and Washington Cabernets and Pinot Noirs with the exception of a few mentioned in the next category; Coonawarra, Western Australian and some Hunter Valley reds (but above all Penfold's Grange Hermitage); top South African estates; Chilean Cabernet; Château Musar from the Lebanon and Cabernet from New Zealand.

Exceptionally concentrated, full-flavoured and powerful reds, usually but not always needing to mature

In Europe this category depends more on the vintage than the producer. Wines that achieve this status fairly regularly include Château Pétrus in Pomerol, Chambertin and Corton in Burgundy, Hermitage and Châteauneuf-du-Pape (Côte Rôtie is more often in the previous category), exceptional Roussillons (not for maturing); Barolo and Barbaresco, Brunello di Montalcino, Recioto and Recioto Amarone from Valpolicella; Spanish Vega Sicilia (and on a humbler level Priorato); Portuguese Barca Velha; Yugoslav Posip and Postup; Bulgarian Cabernet. Occasional vintages such as 1961 in Bordeaux and 1971 in Burgundy produce many such wines.

California, Australia and South Africa find it hard not to make such big reds. Most of their best wines are carefully restrained in ripeness, but in California many wines are made with maximum extract to be larger than life. Australia makes many such wines, especially in Victoria and the Southern Vales in South Australia.

Well-hung game and strong cheeses are the obvious candidates for these wines, although those in the appropriate price bracket are also excellent with barbecues and on picnics, when someone else is driving.

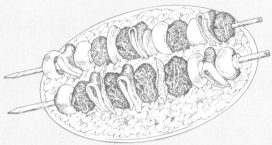

Fortified wines

Wines whose natural strength is augmented with added alcohol, either during the fermentation to preserve the natural sweetness (as in port) or after they have fermented to dryness, as a preservative (as in sherry). Since the role of these wines is largely determined by their sweetness, which is at their makers' discretion, all that can usefully be said is that dry versions (whether of port, sherry, madeira or their regional equivalents) are intended as apéritifs, while sweet ones are used either before or after meals according to local taste and custom. The French, for example, prefer sweet apéritifs, the Italians bitter ones and the British, who divide everything along class lines, some sweet and some dry. In all cases smaller glasses are needed because the alcoholic strength is higher than that of table wine.

They also have their uses with certain foods. Dry sherry is always drunk in Spain with tapas, which are infinitely various savoury snacks. It is one of the best wines for smoked eel. Old oloroso sherry, whether dry or with added sweetness, is very good with cake, nuts and raisins. Port, both vintage and tawny, is often drunk with cheese. Madeira has a cake especially designed for it.

Other wines in this category include Spanish Malaga and Tarragona, Sicilian Marsala, Cypriot Commandaria, French Vins Doux Naturels (e.g. Banyuls), Hungarian Tokay and a host of wines, usually with borrowed names, in the New World.

STORING WINE

The greatest revolution in the history of wine was the discovery that if air could be excluded from wine its life span was increased enormously. And, even better, that it could take on an undreamed-of range of flavours and a different, less grapey and infinitely more subtle and interesting smell.

The invention that made airtight storage possible was the cork, which came into use some time in the seventeenth century. It is possible that the ancient Greeks knew the secret, but all through the Middle Ages and up to the seventeenth century the premium was on new wine, not old. The latest vintage often sold for twice as much as the remnants of the previous one, which stood a good chance of having become vinegar. The only exceptions were the class of high-strength and possibly sweet wines generally known as sack, products of hot sunshine in the eastern Mediterranean, southern Spain and later the Canary Islands. Their constitution allowed them to age in barrels in contact with air and take on the nuttiness and warmth of flavour we associate with sherry.

Ageing in bottles under cork is a totally different process. Instead of oxidizing, or taking in oxygen, the wine is in a state of 'reduction' – in other words what little oxygen it contains (absorbed in the cellars, while being 'racked' from one cask to another, and in being bottled) is being used up (reduced) by the life processes within it. So long as it lives – and wine is a living substance with a remarkable life span – it is the battleground of bacteria, the playground of pigments, tannins, enzymes . . . a host of jostling wildlife preying on each other. No air gets through a good cork as long as it is kept wet, in contact with the wine, so that there is no risk of the vinegar process starting.

Whether the reduction process is beneficial, and for how long, is the determining factor in deciding when a bottled wine will be at its best.

Which wines to store

The great majority of wines are made with the intention of being ready to drink as soon as possible. This is true of all bulk wines, most white wines except very sweet and particularly full-bodied ones, nearly all rosés and the whole class of red wines that can be compared with Beaujolais – whose character and charm lie in a direct flavour of the grape. Reduction spoils their simple fruitiness. The only table wines that benefit from storage are a minority of sweet or very concentrated, intensely flavoury whites and those reds specifically made, by long vatting with their skins and pips, to take up pigments and tannins as preservatives – which include, of course, all the world's best.

Precisely how much of these elements combines with

Purpose-built private cellars are rare today, but they exist, in some cases with a degree of sophisticated planning undreamt of in the past. The cellar illustrated here is based on that of Tawfiq Khoury, a wine collector in San Diego, California. It has a total capacity of 40,000 bottles, with allowance for storage of every bottle size up to 8-bottle

Imperials. It is air conditioned to 52°F (11°C) and is also used as a tasting room for small private parties, a wine book library and a museum of rare old bottles and glasses.

All the shelves have a slope of one sixteenth of an inch to the back to keep any sediment at the bottom of the bottle.

The whole cellar is air conditioned to a constant 52°F (11°C) – perfect serving temperature for white wine and maturing temperature for reds. It is chilly for mere human beings: they have to wear an extra sweater.

A roll-top desk for keeping accounts and writing notes. Records of the stock are kept in a card-index system. The volume and complexity actually justifies a small computer.

The centre stacks are arranged in shelves in diamond pattern. One side is one bottle deep, holding 16 bottles, the other two deep, holding 32 bottles.

There is space for unopened cases on the floor

Random storing
The best way to make use of a limited number of pigeonholes in a storage rack is to put new acquisitions into whatever holes are empty, regardless of order – even if it means scattering a dozen bottles in random ones and twos. All that is needed is a clear grid reference system and an entry in your cellar book or card index for each pigeonhole you have used. This is the only way to avoid wasting space.

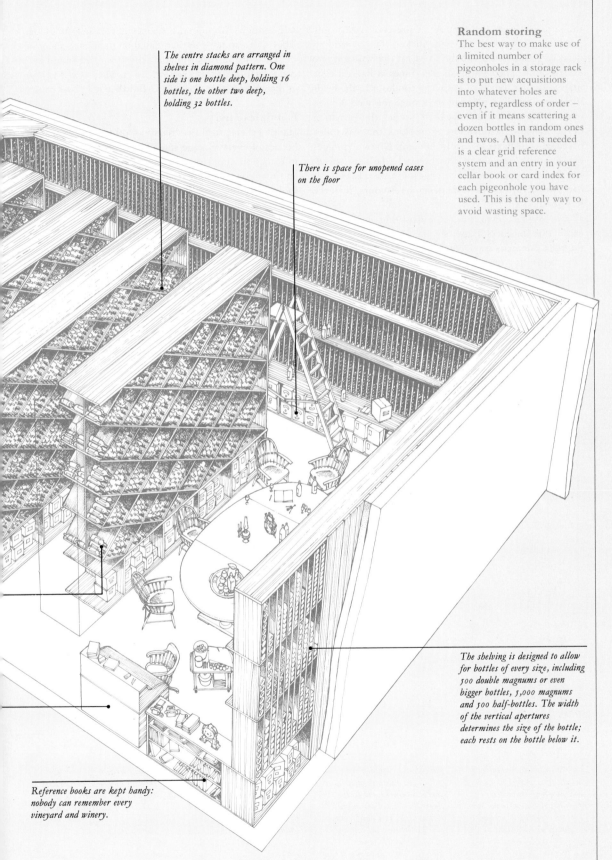

The shelving is designed to allow for bottles of every size, including 500 double magnums or even bigger bottles, 5,000 magnums and 500 half-bottles. The width of the vertical apertures determines the size of the bottle; each rests on the bottle below it.

Reference books are kept handy: nobody can remember every vineyard and winery.

the juice and how well they act as preservatives is only partly in the hands of the wine maker. The overriding decisive factor is the vintage. And no two vintages are exactly alike. The analysis of the grapes at harvest time may be similar, but each crop has stood out in the fields through a hundred different days since the vine flowers opened. The number and size of the grapes, the formation of the bunches, the thickness of the skins, the yeasts they gathered will always be subtly different. No two vintages develop in the same way or at precisely the same speed. But the better wines of each vintage will always last longer and mature further, to more delicious flavours, than the less good.

Thus laying down wines for maturing is always an exploratory business. Experts will give their opinion that the 1983 Bordeaux need from 5 to 15 years to reach their best, depending on their quality. Such a margin will be safe enough, although it is scarcely a very helpful guide. They will also tell you that, based on their assessment of the style of the 1985 vintage, which has less tannin and concentration (it was a record-size crop), its wines will be at their best before the 1983s. (But they may be wrong.)

Is it time to try?
Happily there are always plenty of other people opening bottles of every vintage and adding to a general pool of information about it, transmitted through wine books and magazines and catalogues. You will never have to look very far for an indication of whether it is time to try the wine you are storing. You can even tell a certain amount about the maturity of red wine without opening the bottle by holding its neck up to a strong light: the depth and quality of colour are quite readable through the glass.

Cellar log book

The Wine Society Cellar Book

DISTRICT *Burgundy* NAME *Volnay, Cuvée General Muteau (Hospices)* VINTAGE *1962*

RECEIVED				OPENED		
Source	Cost	Date	Qty	Date	Qty	Remarks
Berry Bros. (bottled by)	15/-	4·66	12	9·66	1	Dark, firm, great depth + future.
				4·68	2	With R.A.C., D.D. Still dark, round, lovely texture. A big volnay. Keep
				10·69	1	Marvellous balance, depth. Delicious "
				9·70	2	Developing well - sweetness with fine 'strike". With B.J. (Roast grouse)
				7·72	1	Colour still deep, full, firm, fragrant. Ideal. With M.B.
				11·72	3	With Ralphs. A dream - but one bottle poor, sl. corky.

The reason for methodically entering tasting notes in a cellar book is to keep an orderly biography of each wine you buy. It would be wrong to pretend I am always as methodical as this specimen page implies. Most of my tasting notes are muddled in pocket notebooks and on the sheets provided at organized tastings. But this page reminds me of what the wine cost and from whom it came. What it first tasted like and how it has developed. Who it was shared with and even with what food. Everyone can devise his own cellar book. In practice, I find there is no need for so many columns as above. The identity of the wine, the bottler, the price and date of acquisition can all go to the top, leaving more room for notes below.

The more difficult decision, assuming you intend to lay down some wine, is how much of which vintages to buy. It is probably a mistake to plunge too heavily for one vintage – you never know whether the next one will be better. It is more sensible to buy regularly as good vintages turn up, which in Bordeaux in recent years has been about two years out of three, in Burgundy one out of three, in the Rhône valley (well worth putting in your cellar) two out of three and in California, for the sort of reds we are talking about, the same.

Since there is rarely enough space (and never enough money) it is worth making a calculation of how much dinner-party wine you are likely to use, which in turn depends on how many of your friends share your passion. Let us suppose that you give an average of one dinner party a month for eight people, and each time use four bottles of mature wine (in addition to such current items

as young white wines and possibly champagne). Your annual consumption will be about 48 bottles. Perhaps you use another bottle a week on family occasions (or alone). That makes about eight dozens a year.

The theoretically ideal stock is arrived at by multiplying the annual consumption by the number of years it stays in the cellar. Since this number varies from perhaps two, for fine white wines, to ten or more for the best reds, a finer calculation is needed. Let us say that two of the eight dozens are two-year wines, four a five-year wines and two are ten-year wines. The total is $2 \times 2 + 4 \times 5 + 2 \times 10 = 44$ cases.

Besides table wines two other kinds of wine are worth laying down: champagne and vintage port. Champagne is a relatively short-term proposition. Vintage champagne almost invariably gains a noticeable extra depth of flavour over two or three years. Lovers of old champagne will

Storage systems

The commonest form of permanent wine rack is made of wooden bars joined with galvanized metal strips in a modular system which can be any shape or size. The wooden cases of the grander château wines are ideal storage. A new idea is a modular spiral system building up into a flight of steps.

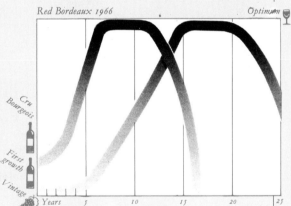

Maturity comparisons

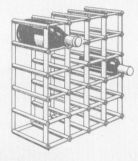

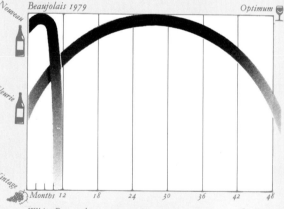

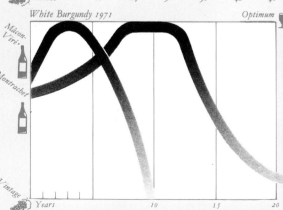

Every bottle proceeds at its own pace towards maturity with almost incredible differences between the fastest and the slowest, between even similar types from the same regions, varieties and seasons.

It is interesting to plot the life span of a range of wines in a graphic form. In these diagrams I have assumed a notional (and unmeasurable) 'optimum' for each wine; the time when all its potential is realized. The better the wine the longer this 'plateau

of perfection' is likely to be. The 'drinkability' of each wine up to the optimum is the vertical dimension of each diagram. For clarity it assumes that all wines are equally 'perfect' at some stage of their lives. The horizontal scale shows time measure from the vintage in years (or months, as indicated).

want to keep it far longer, up to 10 or even 20 years, until its colour deepens and its bubbles quieten. In Britain it is worth keeping non-vintage champagne for a year or two as well, but I have found that in America it is usually mature (sometimes overmature) by the time it reaches the customer.

Vintage port is an entirely different matter. The way the wine goes through almost its whole life cycle in the bottle is explained in the section on port. It needs cellaring longer than any other wine – except the almost unobtainable vintage madeira. All good vintages need 20 years or more to reach their hour of glory.

The practical arrangements for storing wine are a challenge to most householders. The ideal underground cellar is even more remote than its ideal contents. But the storage conditions that make an underground cellar ideal are relatively easy to reproduce upstairs (at least in temperate climates) if the space is available.

The conditions required are darkness, freedom from vibration, fairly high humidity and a reasonably even temperature. Darkness is needed because ultraviolet light penetrates even green glass bottles and hastens ageing prematurely. Vibration is presumed to be bad (on what evidence I am not sure; it would have to be pretty violent to keep any normal sediment in suspension). Humidity helps the corks to stay airtight; but much more important

is that the wine remains in contact with the corks inside the bottle. It is essential to store all wine horizontally, even if you only expect to keep it for a month or two. Excess humidity is a serious nuisance: it rapidly rots cardboard boxes and soon makes labels unreadable. My own answer to the label problem is to give each one a squirt of scentless hair lacquer before storing it away.

Temperature and time

Temperature is the most worrisome of these conditions. The ideal is anything between a steady 45°F and 65°F(7° and 18°C). A 50°F (10°C) cellar is best of all, because the white wines in it are permanently at or near the perfect drinking temperature. It is probable that wines in a cold cellar mature more slowly and keep longer than wines in a relatively warm one, but the excellent Mirabelle restaurant in London kept all its red wines – even the very old ones – permanently at serving temperature, about 65°F (18°C), and I have heard no complaints of premature ageing.

Chemists point out that chemical reaction rates double with each 10 degrees Centigrade (18 degrees Fahrenheit) increase in temperature. If the maturing of wine were simply a chemical reaction this would mean that a wine stored in a cellar at 68°F (19°C) would mature twice as fast

Bottle size, shape and capacity

The diagram below gives the contents of the usual standard-sized bottles and gives a conversion chart from fluid ounces to litres and vice versa.

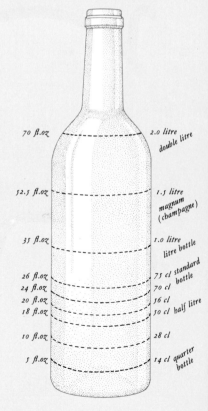

Bordeaux / Vintage Port / German wine bottle / Champagne / Beaujolais / Cubitainer

Sherry

Franconian

70 fl.oz	2.0 litre double litre
52.5 fl.oz	1.5 litre magnum (champagne)
35 fl.oz	1.0 litre litre bottle
26 fl.oz	75 cl standard bottle
24 fl.oz	70 cl
20 fl.oz	56 cl
18 fl.oz	50 cl half litre
10 fl.oz	28 cl
5 fl.oz	14 cl quarter bottle

Each European wine region has a long-established traditional bottle shape which helps to preserve an identity in the public mind. In most cases the New World wines based on the same grape varieties are also sold in the appropriately shaped bottles to help identify the style of their wineries.

Colour of glass is as important as shape. All Rhine wines are bottled in brown glass,

all Moselles in green. White Bordeaux is in clear glass, red Bordeaux is in green.

For table wines whose origin is not important the 'cubitainer' or 'bag-in-box' is a useful invention. The wine is in a plastic foil bag in a cardboard box. As it is drawn off through a tap the bag collapses, protecting the wine from harmful contact with air.

as one in a 50°F (10°C) cellar. But it is not so simple; wine is alive. Its ageing is not just chemical but a whole life process.

One should not exaggerate the effects of fluctuation, either. My own (underground) cellar moves gradually from a winter temperature of about 48°F (8°C) to a summer one of over 60°F (15°C) without the wine suffering in any detectable way. The most common difficulty arises in finding a steadily cool place in a house or apartment heated to 70°F (21°C) or more in winter, when the outside temperature can range from 60°F (15°C) plus to well below freezing. The answer must be in insulating a small room or large cupboard near an outside wall. In practice fine wines are successfully stored in blocked-up fireplaces, in cupboards under the stairs, in the bottoms of wardrobes . . . ingenuity can always find somewhere satisfactory.

The same applies to racks and 'bins'. A bin is a large open shelf (or space on the floor) where a quantity of one wine is laid bottle on bottle. In the days when households bought very few wines, but bought them a barrel at a time, the bin was ideal. For collections of relatively small quantities of many different wines racks are essential. They can either be divided into single-bottle apertures (one or two bottles deep) or into a diamond pattern of apertures large enough to take several bottles – a half-dozen or a dozen depending on the quantities you usually buy. I find it convenient to have both single-bottle and dozen-bottle racks.

A much more complex problem, as a collection grows, is keeping track of the bottles. It is difficult not to waste space if you deplete your stock in blocks. Where space is limited you want to be able to use every slot as it becomes vacant. This is the advantage of the random storage system. But its efficaciousness depends entirely on dedicated book-keeping. If this is not your line you are likely to mislay bottles just when you want them.

Very fine wines – most classed-growth Bordeaux, for instance – are shipped in wooden packing cases, which are perfect storage while the wine matures. If you do buy such wines by the complete case there is no point in unpacking it until you have reason to think the wine will be nearing maturity.

If possible make allowance in your storage arrangements for bigger-than-normal bottles. The 75-centilitre (26-fluid ounce) bottle has been accepted by generations as the most convenient regular size – although whether it was originally conceived as being a portion for one person or two is hard to say. But bigger bottles keep wine even better. Length of life, speed of maturity and level of ultimate quality are all in direct proportion to bottle size. Half-bottles are occasionally convenient, particularly for such powerful and expensive sweet wines as great Sauternes, where a little goes a long way. Otherwise, bottles are better, and magnums better still. Double magnums begin to be difficult to handle (and how often can you assemble enough like-minded friends to do justice to one?). The counsel of perfection is to lay down 6 magnums to every 12 bottles of each wine on which you pin really high hopes.

The reference section of this book gives typical examples of the potential life span of each class of wine. It is not necessarily only expensive wines that are worth laying down. Many Australian reds, for example, will evolve from a muscle-bound youth into a most satisfying maturity. One of my greatest successes was a barrel of a three-year-old Chilean Cabernet which I bottled in my amateurish way in my own cellar. It reached its quite delectable peak ten years later.

Experiment, therefore, with powerful, deep-coloured and tannic reds from whatever source. Be much more circumspect with white wines. Most of those that have proved that cellaring improves them beyond a year or two are expensive already: the better white burgundies, the best Chardonnays, Sauternes of the best châteaux and outstanding German Ausleses – which probably provide the best value for money today.

The neglected areas to add to these are Anjou and Vouvray from the Loire, top-quality Alsace wines, and what was once considered the longest lived of all white wines, the rare white Hermitage of the Rhône.

Red Bordeaux comes in several sizes. The bigger the bottle the longer the wine keeps, the slower it matures and the better it will become.

half bottle · whole bottle · magnum · double magnum · marie-jeanne · imperiale

Champagne is the only other wine with the same range of bottle sizes – but in this case for celebratory reasons.

quarter bottle · half bottle · bottle · magnum · jeroboam · rehoboam · methuselah

GLASSES

Each wine region has its own ideas about the perfect wineglass. Most are based on sound gastronomic principles that make them just as suitable for the wines of other regions, too. Perhaps the most graceful and universally appropriate is the shape used in Bordeaux. A few are flamboyantly folkloric – amusing to use in their context but as subtle as a dirndl at a dinner party. The traditional *römer* of the Rhine, for instance, has a thick trunk of a stem in brown glass ornamented with ridges and excrescences. It dates from the days when Rhine wine was preferred old and oxidized, the colour of the glass, and presumably when Rhinelanders wanted something pretty substantial to thump the table with. The Mosel, by contrast, serves its wine in a pretty shallow-bowled glass with a diamond-cut pattern that seems designed to stress the wine's lightness and grace. Alsace glasses have very tall green stems which reflect a faint green hue into the wine. Glasses like these are pleasant facets of a visit to the wine region, adding to the sense of place and occasion, but you do not need them at home.

The International Standards Organization has pre-empted further discussion by producing specifications for the perfect wine-tasting glass. Its narrowing-at-the-top shape is designed as a funnel to maximize the smell of the wine for the taster's nose. For ordinary table use this feature can be less pronounced. In all other respects it has the characteristics that any good glass should have: it is clear, unornamented, of rather thin glass with a stem long enough for an easy grip and an adequate capacity.

Capacity is important. A table wineglass should never be filled more than half full. A size which is filled to only one third by a normal portion (about 4 fl.oz/11 cl or an eighth of a bottle) is best of all. Anything larger is merely ostentatious.

Displaying the bubbles

Sparkling wines are best served in a slightly smaller but relatively taller glass filled to about three quarters of its capacity, giving the bubbles a good way to climb – one of the prettiest sights wine has to offer. They should never

Types of glasses

The champagne 'flute' allows the bubbles in the wine a long, rapid, attractive rise. Any similar shape will suit sparkling wines – but not the flat 'dish' glass.

A taller version of the 'dock' glass and the sherry copita, this is the basis of the international tasting glass. The narrow top funnels the scent of the wine.

A 'tulip' glass, suitable for champagne and any white wine and reds. The in-turned rim concentrates the bouquet.

The Paris goblet, staple of restaurants the world over, is ideal for claret or burgundy.

A sherry copita, traditional in Jerez. It also makes an excellent tasting glass.

For port, sherry or madeira the 'dock' glass is ideal.

under any circumstances be served in the shallow 'coupes' sometimes used by ignorant caterers.

Dessert wines, being stronger, are served in smaller portions in smaller glasses, usually filled to between a half and two thirds of their capacity. Their scents are more pungent than table wines; to plunge your nose into a wide bowl of port fumes would be almost overpowering.

When several wines are being served at the same meal it saves confusion if each has a slightly differeng glass. In any case guests should be told that the order of pouring is from left to right (i.e. the first wine is poured into the left-hand glass and so on in order). I imagine this tradition is for the practical reason that a right-handed drinker is less likely to knock over this first glass in reaching for his second. As a further precaution against confusion (if two or more similar wines are being poured) it is a simple matter to slip a little rubber band around the stem of one of the glasses.

Wineglasses should be as clean as you can possibly make them – which is unfortunately beyond the capacity of any dishwasher. Detergents inevitably leave a coating on the glass which may or may not have a taste or smell, but is always detectable to the touch, and even affects the fizz of champagne. There is only one way of achieving a perfectly clean, polished, brilliant glass. After washing with soap or detergent to remove grease it should be thoroughly rinsed in clean hot water, then not drained but filled with hot water and only emptied immediately before it is dried. Practice shows that a clean linen or cotton cloth polishes a warm wet glass perfectly (and very quickly) whereas it leaves smears and fluff on a cold one.

The best place to keep glasses is in a closed cupboard, standing right way up. On an open shelf they collect dust. Upside down on a shelf they pick up odours of wood or paint. An alternative to a closed cupboard is a rack where they hang upside down, but dust on the outside of a glass is no better than dust on the inside.

You can argue that there is only one perfect wineglass, equally ideal for all table wines but there is also a case for enjoying the traditional, sometimes fanciful, shapes adopted by different regions to promote the identity of their products.

Here a range of the most distinctive glasses is displayed with a carousel, which is a traditional German way of offering wines for tasting. At cafés in the Rheinpfalz or the Black Forest you can order as many as a dozen different 'open' house wines which will be brought in a sort of dumbwaiter with numbered holes. All the guests can then taste and discuss all the wines, while keeping them in order for reference.

The traditional white-wine glass of Alsace has a green stem to reflect colour into the bowl.

The traditional Rhine-wine or hock glass. The thick brown stem is designed to reflect colour into the wine.

The Trier glass, intended for Mosel. The engraving catches the light, making the green-gold wine look even more appetizing.

Anjou's traditional white-wine glass, with long stem and in-turned bowl.

SERVING WINE

The no-nonsense approach to serving wine takes up very little space or time. The cork is out before discussion starts. There are times, and wine, for this can-of-beans attack which it would be pretentious to deny. But here I put the case for taking trouble to make the most of every bottle. On the basis that anticipation is a part of every great pleasure I argue that you should enjoy reading the label, be aroused by handling the bottle, relish removing the capsule, feel stirred by plunging in the corkscrew.

Sensuous enjoyment is the entire purpose of wine. The art of appreciating it is to maximize the pleasure of every manoeuvre, from choosing to swallowing. The art of serving wine is to make sure that it reaches the drinker with all its qualities at their peak.

No single factor is as important to success or failure as temperature. The characteristic scent and flavour of wine consists of infinitely subtle volatile compounds of different molecular weights, progressively heavier from 'light' white wines to 'heavy' reds. It is the temperature that controls their volatility – the point at which they vaporize and come to meet your sense of smell.

Each grape variety seems to behave differently in this respect. The Riesling scent is highly volatile: a Moselle sends out its flowery message even when it is too cold to drink with pleasure. Champagne's powerful fragrance of grapes and yeasts can hardly be suppressed by cold (although I have known people who seem to try). The Sauvignon Blanc is almost as redolent as the Riesling; the Chardonnay much less so – less so, in fact, than the Gamay; Beaujolais is highly volatile at low temperatures. The Pinot Noir vaporizes its ethereal sapidity even in a

cool Burgundian cellar, whereas the Cabernets of Bordeaux hold back their aromas, particularly when they are young. In a Bordeaux *chai* it tends to be the oak you smell more than the wine. California and other warm-climate Cabernets are often more forthcoming.

Are aromas everything?

It will be seen that these observations tally more or less with the generally accepted norms of serving temperatures shown opposite. Not that aromas are everything. We expect white wines to be refreshingly cool; we expect red wines to awaken our palates with other qualities of vigour and completeness. It is fascinating to test how much your appreciation is affected by temperature. Taste, for instance, a good mature Meursault and a Volnay of the same quality (they are the white and red wines of the same vineyards, made of grapes with much in common) at precisely the same fairly cool temperature and with your eyes shut. You will find they are almost interchangeable.

It is time to forget the misleading word 'chambré' to describe the right temperature for red wines. Whatever the temperature of dining-rooms in the days when it was coined (and it must have varied from frigid to a fire-and-candle-heated fug) the chances of arriving at the right temperature by simply standing the bottle in the room where it is to be drunk are slight. An American dining-room at 70°F (21°C) plus is much too warm for wine. At that temperature the alcohol becomes unpleasantly heady. Mine, at 60°F (15°C), is good for burgundy but too cold for Bordeaux.

Everybody has, in his refrigerator, a cold place at a

Cooling vessels
Failing the ideal arrangement of storing white wine permanently at the perfect drinking temperature – that of a cool cellar – the most efficient way to chill it rapidly is by immersing the entire bottle in ice-cold water. A refrigerator takes up to 10 times as long as an ice-bath to achieve the same effect. Ice-cubes or crushed ice alone are inefficient. Ice must be mixed with cold water for rapid conduction of heat from the bottle. The perfect ice bucket is deep enough to immerse the whole bottle, neck and all: otherwise you have to put the bottle in upside down to start with to cool the neck. On the right is another idea: a sort of open-ended Thermos flask which keeps an

already chilled bottle cool by maintaining a wall of cold air around it.

Decorative antique champagne bucket

Ice buckets

Insulated plastic cylinder

The wineometer

Nothing makes or mars any wine so much as its temperature. The thermometer illustrated was specially designed for wine. It has the obvious disadvantage that it can only be used once the bottle is open. (Another kind clips around the outside of the bottle.) Experience soon makes any such gadget unnecessary. Here it serves to show the ideal temperatures for each category of wine. It is wrong, however, to be too dogmatic. Some people enjoy red wines several degrees warmer than the refreshing temperature I suggest for them here, and some like their white wines considerably colder than the moderate chill I advocate for the best appreciation of scent and flavour.

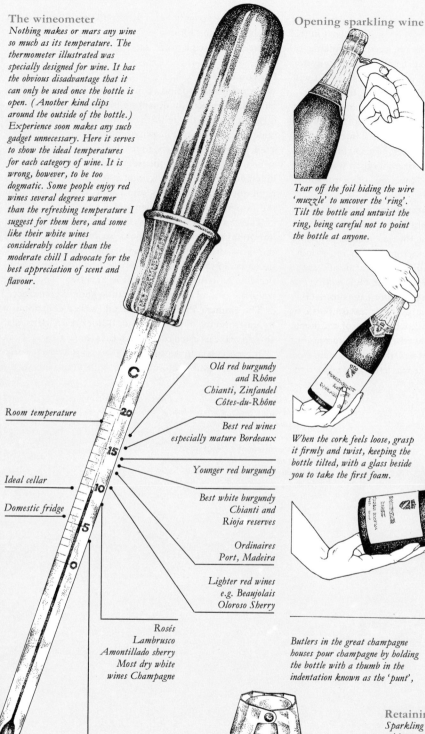

Room temperature

C

20

15

Ideal cellar

10

Domestic fridge

5

0

Old red burgundy and Rhône Chianti, Zinfandel Côtes-du-Rhône

Best red wines especially mature Bordeaux

Younger red burgundy

Best white burgundy Chianti and Rioja reserves

Ordinaires Port, Madeira

Lighter red wines e.g. Beaujolais Oloroso Sherry

Rosés Lambrusco Amontillado sherry Most dry white wines Champagne

Most sweet white wines Sparkling wines

Opening sparkling wine

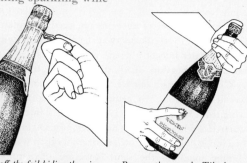

Tear off the foil hiding the wire 'muzzle' to uncover the 'ring'. Tilt the bottle and untwist the ring, being careful not to point the bottle at anyone.

Remove the muzzle. Tilt the bottle, holding the cork down firmly with your thumb. Ease the cork sideways and upwards with the other thumb.

When the cork feels loose, grasp it firmly and twist, keeping the bottle tilted, with a glass beside you to take the first foam.

Specially made pliers are sometimes used when a champagne cork is very stiff, or when opening a number of bottles.

Butlers in the great champagne houses pour champagne by holding the bottle with a thumb in the indentation known as the 'punt',

and their fingers supporting the weight. With practice this becomes the most comfortable and stylish way to do it.

Retaining the sparkle

Sparkling wines should be spur-of-the-moment celebratory drinks. When opening expensive bottles, it is a good idea to have a stopper that will keep the fizz intact if the celebration should be short-lived. The two models illustrated will keep partly filled bottles of méthode champenoise wines in good bubble for at least 24 hours.

constant temperature that can be used for cooling white wine. Nobody I have met has a 63°F (16°C) oven. On the other hand since an ice bucket is a perfectly acceptable (in fact by far the most efficient) way of chilling wine, why not a warm-water bucket for red? Water at 70°F (21°C) will raise the temperature of a bottle from 55°F to 65°F (15°–18°C) in about eight minutes, which is the same time as it would take to lower the temperature of a bottle of white wine from 65°F to 55°F (18°–13°C) in a bucket of icy water. (Ice without water is much less efficient in cooling.) In a fridge, incidentally, where air rather than water is the cooling medium, the same lowering of temperature would take about one hour.

Bold spirits who have accustomed themselves to microwave ovens will no doubt have experimented with them on red wine. I am told that the time it takes to warm a bottle from 55°F to 65°F is something under 20 seconds.

Bear in mind that the prevailing temperature affects the wine not only before it is poured out but while it is in your glass as well. Serve white wine on a hot day considerably colder than you want to drink it. Never leave a bottle or glass in the sun; improvise shade with a parasol, the menu, a book, under your chair . . . anywhere. At one sumptuous outdoor buffet in South Africa the white wine was admirably cold but the red wine was left on the table in the sun. Not only was it ruined beyond recognition but I nearly burnt my tongue on it. There are circumstances where the red wine needs an ice bucket too.

Do you decant?

Wine lovers seem to find a consensus on most things to do with their subject, but decanting is a divisive issue. There is one school of thought, the traditional, that holds that wine needs to 'breathe' for anything from a few minutes to a few hours, or even days, to reach its best. Its opponents, armed with scientific evidence, proclaim that it makes no difference or (a third view) that it is deleterious. Each is right about certain wines, and about its own taste. But they are mistaken to be dogmatic.

There are three reasons for decanting. The most important is to clean the wine of sediment. A secondary one is the attraction of the plump, glittering, glowing-red decanter on the table. The third is to allow the wine to breathe. Nobody argues with the first two. The debate revolves around when the operation should take place.

The eminent Professor Peynaud, whose contribution to gastronomy in general and Bordeaux in particular should make us listen carefully, writes (in *Le Goût du Vin*), 'If it is necessary to decant [at all], one should always do it at the last possible moment, just before moving to the

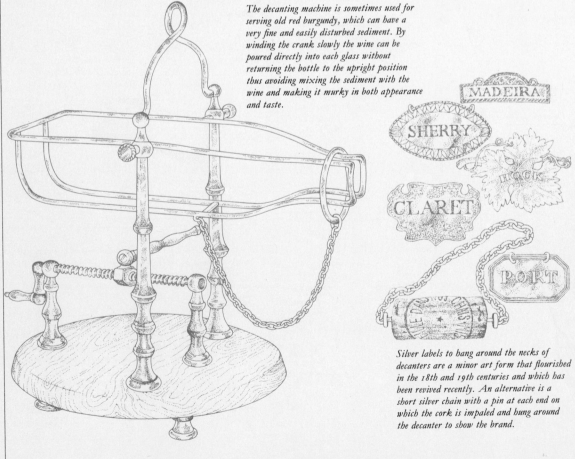

The decanting machine is sometimes used for serving old red burgundy, which can have a very fine and easily disturbed sediment. By winding the crank slowly the wine can be poured directly into each glass without returning the bottle to the upright position thus avoiding mixing the sediment with the wine and making it murky in both appearance and taste.

Silver labels to hang around the necks of decanters are a minor art form that flourished in the 18th and 19th centuries and which has been revived recently. An alternative is a short silver chain with a pin at each end on which the cork is impaled and hung around the decanter to show the brand.

table or just before serving [the wine]; never in advance.' The only justification Peynaud sees for aeration, or letting the wine breathe, is to rid it of certain superficial faults that sometimes arise, such as the smell of slight refermentation in the bottle. Otherwise, he says, decanting in advance does nothing but harm; it softens the wine and dulls the brilliance of its carefully acquired bouquet.

Scientifically minded Americans have come to much the same conclusions, although their consensus seems to be that decanting makes no difference that can in any way be reliably detected.

My own experience is that almost all wines change perceptibly in a decanter, but whether that change is for the better or worse depends partly on the wine and partly on personal taste.

There are wine lovers who prefer their wine softened and dulled; vintage port in particular is often decanted early to soothe its fiery temper: its full 'attack' is too much for them. They equate mellowness with quality. The Spanish equate the taste of oak (as in Rioja) with quality. Who can say they are wrong about their own taste?

The English have always had strong ideas about how their wines should taste. A hundred years ago they added Rhône or Spanish wine to claret; it was altogether too faint for them without it. There are surely some people who preferred the burgundies of the days before the strict application of the appellation laws to the authentic straight-from-the-grower burgundy we drink today. The Californians, too, have their own taste. They love direct, strong flavoured wines that often seem as though the transition from fruit juice was never fully completed. It is not surprising that ideas about decanting differ.

There are certain wines that seem to curl up when you open the bottle like woodlice when you turn over a log. The deeply tannic Barolo of Piedmont shows nothing but its carapace for an hour or sometimes several. If you drink it during that time you will have nothing to remember but an assault on your tongue and cheeks. But in due course hints of a bouquet start to emerge, growing stronger until eventually you are enveloped in raspberries and violets and truffles and autumn leaves.

The standard French restaurant practice is not to decant burgundy. If it is true that the Pinot Noir is more volatile than the Cabernet the practice makes sense: the contact with the air when pouring from bottle to carafe wakes the Bordeaux up; the burgundy does not need it.

Those who believe in decanting would give several hours' airing to a young wine, one or two to a mature wine (these terms being relative to the expected maturing time), and treat an old wine as an invalid who should be kept out of draughts. Yet strange to say it is an often repeated experience of those who have tasted very old and very great wines (Château Lafite 1803 was a case in point) that they can add layer upon layer of bouquet and flavour hour after hour – even, in some cases, tasting better than ever the following day. I regularly finish the bottles the

Decanting

There is much debate about whether and when to decant wine; whether 'breathing' is a good thing or not. Modern 'scientific' opinion tends to be against it. Certainly its effects are hard to predict, but if a rule of thumb is called for I suggest that:

Vigorous young ('young' in this context relates to the vintage – a great vintage is young at 10 years, a poor one up to 4 or 5) red Bordeaux, Cabernets, Rhône reds, Barolo and Barbaresco, heavy Zinfandels, Australian Shiraz, Portuguese reds and other similar tannic wines: decant at least 1 hour before drinking, and experiment with periods of up to 6 hours.

'Young' red burgundy, Pinot Noirs and Spanish wines: decant just before serving.

Fully mature wines of all kinds: decant just before serving. *But* do not finish the decanter precipitately unless the wine is obviously fading. If it seems to hold back, give it as long as it needs.

The best way to prepare red wine for decanting is to stand it upright for several days in advance. The corkscrew being used here is the Screwpull, which draws the cork up into itself with almost infallible ease.

Pour the wine in one continuous movement, holding the bottle neck over a light so that you can keep watch on the sediment. As soon as it approaches the neck, stop pouring.

If the bottle has not been prepared it may be necessary to decant it from a 'cradle'. I avoid doing this because it is difficult to watch the sediment.

Opening vintage port

Bottles of vintage port older than about 20 years often present a special problem: the cork becomes soft and crumbly and disintegrates in the grip of a corkscrew.

Spongy corks are almost impossible to remove. The answer is to cut the top off the bottle, which can be done in either of 2 ways shown below.

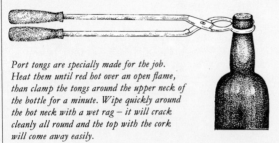

Port tongs are specially made for the job. Heat them until red hot over an open flame, than clamp the tongs around the upper neck of the bottle for a minute. Wipe quickly around the hot neck with a wet rag – it will crack cleanly all round and the top with the cork will come away easily.

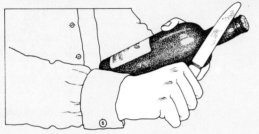

An equally effective and more spectacular way of opening an old bottle of port is to grasp it firmly in one hand and take a heavy carving knife in the other. Run the back of the knife blade

up the neck of the bottle to give a really sharp blow to the 'collar'. The neck will crack cleanly. Practise before making your début at a dinner party. Confidence is all.

If a port cork crumbles into the bottle it is possible to filter the wine through a clean muslin-lined glass or plastic funnel, or to use one of the handsome old-fashioned silver funnels which has a built-in strainer.

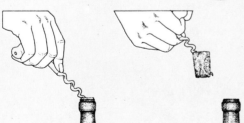

If a cork shows signs of weakness, or breaks in half when you pull it, the situation can sometimes be retrieved by

inserting the corkscrew into the remainder of the cork diagonally, and pushing towards the opposite side of the neck.

evening after opening them. The only general rule I have found is that the better the wine, taking both origin and vintage into account, the more it benefits from prolonged contact with the air. Sometimes a wine that is a distinct disappointment on opening changes its nature entirely. A bottle of Château Pontet-Canet 1961 (in 1982) had a poor, hard, loose-fitting cork and, on first tasting, a miserable timid smell and very little flavour at all (although the colour was good). Twenty-four hours later it seemed to have recharged its batteries; it opened up into the full-blooded, high-flavoured wine I had expected. The moral must be to experiment and keep an open mind.

The pros and cons of decanting are much more long winded than the process itself. The aim is simply to pour the wine, but not its sediment, into another receptacle (which can be a decanter, plain or fancy, or another bottle, well rinsed).

If there is enough advance warning take the bottle gently from its rack at least two days before you need it and stand it upright. Two days (or one at a pinch) should be long enough for the sediment to slide to the bottom. If you must decant from a bottle that has been horizontal until the last minute you need a basket or cradle to hold the bottle as near its original position as possible but with the wine just below cork level.

Cut the capsule right away. Remove the cork gently with a counter-pressure corkscrew. Then, holding the decanter in the left hand, pour in the wine in one smooth movement until you see the sediment advancing as a dark arrow towards the neck of the bottle. When it reaches the shoulder, stop pouring.

It makes it easier to see where the sediment is if you hold the neck of the bottle over a candle-flame or a torch, or (I find best) a sheet of white paper or a napkin with a fairly strong light on it. Vintage port bottles are made of very dark glass (and moreover are usually dirty), which makes it harder to see the sediment. If the port has been lying in one place for years its sediment is so thick and coherent that you can hardly go wrong. If it has been moved recently it can be troublesome, and may even need filtering. Clean damp muslin is the best material; I have found that coffee filter papers can give wine a detectable taste.

The French way with burgundy

Serving burgundy, if you follow the French practice and do not decant it, presents more of a problem. Restaurants often serve it from a cradle; the worst possible system because each time the bottle is tipped to pour and then tipped back the sediment is stirred into the remaining wine. The Burgundian answer to this is the splendid engine that tips the bottle continuously, as in the motion of decanting, but straight into the guests' glasses. Without such a machine I decant burgundies at the last minute – but only when they have sediment. Unless they are very old they are often clear to the last drop.

CORKS AND CORKSCREWS

The first corks must have been like stoppers, driven only halfway home. There is no known illustration of a corkscrew until 100 years after corks came into use.

Although screw-caps and crown closures now offer cheaper and simpler ways of keeping the wine in and the air out, cork remains the way fine wine is sealed.

What makes cork so ideal as a wine plug? Certainly its lightness, its cleanness, and the simple fact that it is available in vast quantities. It is almost impermeable. It is smooth, yet it stays put in the neck of the bottle. It is unaffected by temperature. It very rarely rots. It is extremely hard to burn. Most important of all it is uniquely elastic, returning, after compression, to almost exactly its original form. Corking machines are based on this simple principle: you can squeeze a cork enough to slip it easily into the neck of a bottle and it will immediately spring out to fill the neck without a cranny to spare.

As for its life span, it very slowly goes brittle and crumbly, over a period of between 20 and 50 years. Immaculately run cellars (some of the great Bordeaux châteaux, for example) recork their stocks of old vintages approximately every 25 years, and one or two send experts to recork the château's old wines in customers' cellars. But many corks stay sound for half a century.

The only thing that occasionally goes wrong with a cork is a musty smell that develops unaccountably. Corks are carefully sterilized in manufacture, but sometimes one or two of the many cells that make up the cork (there are 20 to 30 in a square millimetre) are infected with fungus. When these cells are in contact with wine the wine picks up the smell and becomes 'corky' or 'corked'. The problem is rare (one champagne house calculates the risk at 1.3:1,000) but when it happens it is instantly noticeable —and naturally disappointing. There is nothing to be done but to open another bottle.

Good-quality corks produce no other problems. Poor

Producing cork

Cork is the thick outer bark of the cork oak, *Quercus suber*, a slow-growing evergreen tree which has evolved this spongy substance for protection and insulation, particularly against fire. The world supply of cork is concentrated in the western Mediterranean area and the neighbouring-Atlantic coasts. Portugal, above all, furnishes half of the total, and almost all of the top-grade cork for use with wine.

The bark is cut into sheets from mature trees every 9 or 10 years between the months of June and August. (Each tree has a productive life of 165 years.) The sheets are stacked to dry for 3 months, then boiled in vats with fungicides. After several more months' storage in a dark, cold cellar, the corks are cut as plugs from the thickness of the bark.

The longest (up to 57 mm) and best-quality corks are graded for the best wine. Dust and scraps from the process are agglomerated to make cheap corks. For specialized use by champagne makers extra large corks are made of 3 layers glued together. A normal wine cork is 24 mm in diameter, compressed into an 18 mm neck. For champagne a 31 mm cork is compressed into a 17.5 mm neck, with the upper third protruding in the characteristic bulging mushroom shape.

Champagne corks (below) before and after bottling. Note the layers, with the best-quality cork at the base, in contact with the wine.

Brands on corks (below) indicate authenticity of the wine, showing producer and vintage, but phrases such as 'mise en bouteille dans nos chais' or 'caves' mean nothing. The shorter corks are for white wine.

cork-producing areas

ones do. Many Italian wine bottles have very hard, small, low-grade corks in necks that are narrower than the norm. They make it extremely tough going for the corkscrew, which sometimes pushes the cork in instead of pulling it out. If you have wiped the top of the cork clean with a damp cloth before starting to open the bottle, no harm is done. A gadget made of three parallel lengths of thick wire with a wooden handle is made for fishing for lost corks. It is reasonably effective, but a simpler answer is to leave the cork in and pour the wine out, holding the cork down with a knife or a skewer until it floats clear of the neck.

The quality of the corkscrew is most important. Enormous ingenuity has been expended on the engineering of corkscrews. The simple screw-with-a-handle has

long since been improved on by designs that use counter-pressure against the bottle. The straight pull is strictly for the young and fit: it can take the equivalent of lifting 80 pounds to get a cork out.

Various dodges are used to provide leverage, but the most important factor of all is the blade – the screw – that pierces and grips the cork. At all costs avoid narrow gimlets on the one hand and open spirals of bent wire on the other. The gimlet will merely pull out the centre of a well-installed cork; the bent wire will simply straighten if it meets with resistance. A good corkscrew blade is a spiral open enough to leave a distinct chimney up the middle, and made like a flattened blade with a sharp point and two cutting edges on its horizontal sides. The points of corkscrew design are illustrated below.

Types of corkscrew

Endless ingenuity has been applied to the mechanical problem of grasping a cork in a bottle and pulling it out without exertion. A straight pull with the bottle between your knees is neither dignified nor necessary; all you need is some sort of leverage against the rim of the bottle. Out of a catalogue of thousands of devices, these are some of the most popular and effective in current use.

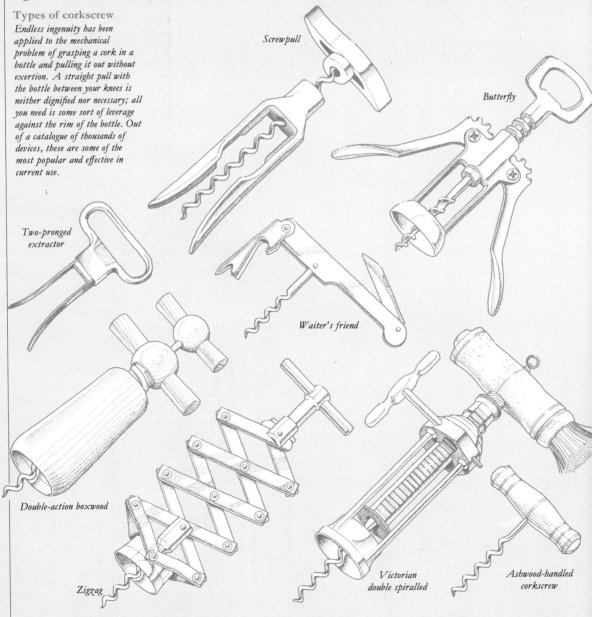

Screwpull

Butterfly

Two-pronged extractor

Waiter's friend

Double-action boxwood

Zigzag

Victorian double spiralled

Ashwood-handled corkscrew

TASTING WINE

There are wine tastings on every level of earnestness and levity, but to taste wine thoroughly, to be in a position to give a considered opinion, demands wholehearted concentration. A wine taster, properly speaking, is one who has gone through a professional apprenticeship and learned to do much more than simply enjoy what he tastes. He is trained to examine every wine methodically and analytically until it becomes second nature. Although I am by no means a qualified professional taster I often find myself, ridiculously, putting a glass of tap water through its paces as though I were judging it for condition and value. If I do not actually hold it up to the light I certainly sniff it and hold it in my mouth for a moment while I see how it measures up to some notional yardstick of a good glass of water. Then naturally I spit it out.

Whether or not you have any desire to train your palate (it has its disadvantages too; it makes you less tolerant of faulty or boring wines) it makes no sense to pay the premium for wines of character and then simply swallow them. It is one of the commonest misunderstandings about wine that if it is 'better' it will automatically give more pleasure. To appreciate degrees of quality you need conscious, deliberate awareness. You need to know what sort of quality you are looking for. And you need a method to set about finding it.

Pierre Poupon, one of the most eloquent of Burgundians, has written: 'When you taste don't look at the bottle, nor the label, nor your surroundings, but look directly inwards to yourself, to observe sensations at their birth and develop impressions to remember.' He even suggests shutting your eyes to concentrate on the messages of your nose and mouth.

Before dinner parties become like prayer meetings let me say that there is a time and place for this sort of concentration. But if you apply it at appropriate moments it will provide you with points of reference for a more sociable approach.

What, to start with, are you tasting for? A very basic wine tasting for beginners might consist of five wines to show the enormous variety that exists: a dry white and a sweet one; a light young red and a fine mature one, and a glass of sherry or port. The point here is that the wines have nothing in common at all. Another very effective elementary tasting is to compare typical examples of the half-dozen grape varieties that have very marked and easily recognized characters.

Most tastings are intended to compare wines with an important common factor, either of origin, age or grape variety. A tasting of Rieslings from a dozen different countries is an excellent way of learning to identify the common strand, the Riesling taste, and judge its relative success in widely different soils and climates. A variant of this, more closely focused, would be to take Rieslings of the same category of quality (Kabinett or Spätlese) from the four principal wine regions of Germany.

Vertical and horizontal tastings

Tastings of the same wine from different vintages are known in the jargon as 'vertical'; those of different wines (of the same type) in a single vintage are known as 'horizontal'.

Professional tastings concerned with buying are nearly always horizontal. The important thing here is that they should be comparing like with like. It is of no professional interest to compare Bordeaux with burgundy, or even Chablis with Meursault; if the Chablis is a good Meursault it is a bad (because untypical) Chablis. A Médoc that tasted like a Napa Valley wine would be a poor Médoc – although it might be hard to convice a Napa grower that the converse was true.

Most of us, of course, drink most of our wine with meals. We judge it, therefore, partly by how well it goes with the sort of food we like. Professional and competitive tasters always judge wine either by itself or in company with other wines, which gives them a different, and clearer, point of view. It is clearest of all when you are hungry and not tired; the end of the morning is the time most professionals prefer.

The ideal conditions, in fact, are rather unattractively clinical; a clean well-lit place without the suggestive power of atmosphere, without the pervasive smell of wine barrels, without the distraction of friendly chatter – and above all without the chunks of cheese, the grilled sausages and home-made bread that have sold most of the world's second-rate wine since time immemorial.

Whether you should know what you are tasting, or taste 'blind' and find out afterwards, is a topic for endless debate. The power of suggestion is strong. It is very difficult to be entirely honest with yourself if you have seen the label; your impressions are likely to reflect, consciously or otherwise, what you think you should find rather than simply what your senses tell you – like a child's picture of both sides of a house at once.

If I am given the choice I like to taste everything blind first. It is the surest method of summoning up concentration, forcing you to ask yourself the right questions, to be analytical and clear minded. I write a note of my opinion, then ask what the wine is or look at the label. If I have guessed it right I am delighted; I know that my mental image of the wine (or memory, if I have tasted it before) was pretty close to reality. If (which is much more frequent) I guess wrong, or simply do not know, this is my chance to get to know the wine, to taste it again carefully and try to understand why that grape, in that vineyard, in that year, produced that result. This is the time to share impressions with other tasters.

It is always interesting to find out how much common ground there is between several people tasting the same wine. So little is measurable, and nothing is reproducible, about the senses of smell and taste. Language serves them only lamely, leaning on simile and metaphor for almost everything illuminating that can be said.

The convenient answer, normally used at competitive tastings, is the law of averages. Ask a group of tasters to quantify their enjoyment, and reduce their judgement to scores, and the wine with the highest average score must be the 'best'. The disadvantage of averaging is that it hides the points of disagreement, the high and low scores given to the same wine by different tasters who appreciate or dislike its individual style, or one of whom, indeed, is a better judge than another. At a well-conducted tasting the chairman will therefore consider an appeal against an averaged score and encourage a verbal consensus as well, especially where gold medals hang on the result.

This is as close to a final judgement on wine quality as

fallible beings can get. But at best it represents the rating by one group of one bottle among the wines they tasted that day. It takes no account of other wines that were not tasted on the same occasion. All one can say about medal winners is that they are good of their sort.

For competitive tastings, taster against taster, 'blindness' is the whole point of the exercise. The individual (or team) with the widest experience and the best memory for tastes should win. For competitive tastings, wine against wine, it is the only fair method. But it can nonetheless produce misleading results. It tends to favour impact at the expense of less obvious but ultimately more important qualities. When California Cabernets are matched against red Bordeaux of similar age the Californians almost always dominate. They are like tennis players who win by serving ace after ace.

The grand tour

The act of tasting has been anatomized by many specialists. To me there are five aspects of wine that convey information and help me gauge its quality, origin, age, the grape varieties involved, and how long it will keep (and whether it will improve). They constitute the grand tour of its pleasures, the uplift excepted. To take them in order they are its appearance, smell, the first impression the wine makes in your mouth, its total flavour as you hold it there, and the taste it leaves behind.

I take each of these into account, note each separately (writing a note is not only an aide-mémoire, it forces you to make up your mind) and then draw a general conclusion. Tasting is a demanding discipline, quite distinct from the mere act of drinking. It sometimes has to be a quick and private little ceremony at a party where wine is not an accepted priority. Yet to contract the habit and apply a method of one kind or another is the only way to get full value out of your wine.

There is more to appearance than simply colour. Fine wine is brilliantly clear. Decanting should make sure that even old wine with sediment has the clarity of a jewel, capturing and reflecting light with an intensity that is a pleasure in itself.

Wine is more or less viscous, at one extreme forming heavy, slow-moving 'legs' on the walls of the glass, at the other instantly finding its own level like water. The more dense it is the more flavour-giving 'extract' and/or sugar it contains – which of course is neither good nor bad in itself; it must be appropriate to the kind of wine. On the other hand a deposit of crystals in white wine is (if anything) an indication of good quality; it is certainly not under any circumstances a fault.

'Colour [I quote Professor Peynaud] is like a wine's face. From it you can tell age, and something of character.' That is, you can if you have certain other information about the wine, which the smell will soon provide.

The best way to see its colour clearly is to hold the glass against a white surface – a piece of paper will do – and to

Tasting wine

The secret of getting the maximum pleasure out of wine is to remember that we smell tastes: it is our noses and the nerves high in the brain behind the nasal cavity that distinguish nuances of flavour – not our tongues, lips or palates. The mouth detects what is sweet, sour, salt, bitter, burning, smooth, oily, astringent. But the colour and character of a flavour lie in its volatile compounds, which need the nose to apprehend them. Thus the procedure for tasting wine pivots around the moment of inhalation: the crucial first sniff.

To taste, first look carefully at the precise colour, clarity and visual texture of the wine.

Swirl wine to volatize its aroma while you concentrate; then sniff. First impressions are crucial.

Take a generous sip, a third of a mouthful, and 'chew' it so that reaches all parts of your mouth.

The final judgement comes when the volatile compounds rise into the upper nasal cavity.

tip it slightly away from yourself so that you are looking through the rim of the liquid. Shallow silver tasting-cups are used in dark cellars, where it is hard for light to penetrate the depth of wine in a glass.

White wines grow darker as they age; reds go through a slow fading process from purplish through red to a brickish reddy brown (which can be seen even through the green glass of the bottle by looking at the neck against a light). In young wines the colour in the glass is almost uniform from edge to edge (making allowance, that is, for greater density where you are looking through more wine). In older wines the rim is usually decidedly paler. A browning rim is a sure sign of maturity in red wines.

Sheer redness is an indicator of quality rather than a virtue in its own right. The famous 1961 Bordeaux vintage can often be recognized across the room by its extraordinary glowing darkness – even in maturity a colour of pregnancy and promise. A Priorato from Spain might well manage to be even darker still, without being fit to be on the same table.

Burgundy rarely has the same deep tints, and never precisely the same hue as Bordeaux. Chianti is rarely deep red because of the proportion of white grapes in it. Rioja is also generally rather pale, but because it has been aged for so long in cask. Beaujolais is light coloured in a different way; more the translucent purple of grape juice. In general hot-country wines of good grape varieties, the Cabernets, for example, of Australia, California and South Africa, have more intensity of colour than their cool-country equivalents. Vintage port is deep purple-red, ruby port a much lighter, more watery colour, and tawny port, aged in wood for many years, anything from the brown red of old claret to a clear light amber when it is very old – the most extreme example of a red wine fading.

White wine has scarcely less variety than red. Chablis has a green light in its pale gold which is uncommon in other white burgundies. Moselles also have a touch of green, with less of the gold, while Rhine wines tend to a straw colour, deepening almost to orange in old sweet examples. Sherry is coloured by oxidation; young finos only very slightly, old olorosos to a mahogany brown. When great sweet Sauternes ages, it goes through all the tints of gold to arrive at a deep golden brown.

Hold your nose

You have only to hold your nose while you sip to realize that it is the organ that does most of the serious work of tasting. Unfortunately our sense of smell is our least cooperative, least stable faculty. While taste, like hearing and sight, is constantly awake, the sense of smell rapidly wearies. If you sniff more than half a dozen times in rapid succession at the same glass (or the same rose) its message becomes dimmed. Your nose needs a different stimulus.

For this reason wine tasters place a great deal of faith in their first impression. They swirl the wine once or twice to wet the sides of the glass and volatilize as much of the

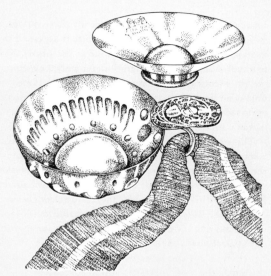

Silver tasting-cups are common in parts of France – particularly Burgundy – where wine is kept in dark cellars. It is easier to judge the colour of red wine in a shallow layer over the brightly reflecting silver than in a glass, where it is in a greater mass. The 'tastevin' worn on a ribbon around the neck has become the ceremonial symbol of Burgundy. The plainer version was made for Château Lafite Rothschild in Bordeaux.

The glass narrows at the top to concentrate aromas.

Swirl the wine to wet the sides of the glass; if it is viscous or sugary, it forms 'legs' as it slides down the glass.

Only a small amount of wine is needed when tasting.

An ideal tasting glass, to the specifications of the International Standards Organization, is about 6 inches (152 mm) high and would hold 7 fl. oz (215 ml). For tasting purposes it is usually only filled to about one fifth of capacity. The tall funnel shape is designed to capture the aroma, or bouquet, for the taster's nose. It needs a long enough stem to keep the hand away from the bowl. (Professional tasters often hold their glass by its foot.) The thinner the glass, within reason, the better. Wine is tasted more vividly from thin glass.

smell as possible. Then they exclude all other thoughts and sniff. The nerves of smell have instant access to the memory (their immediate neighbour in the brain). The first sniff should trigger recognition; possibly the memory of the identical wine tasted before. If the smell is unfamiliar it will at least give this piece of negative information, and suggest where in the memory-bank partially similar smells are to be found.

The smell will be the first warning sign if there is something wrong with the wine: a slight taint of vinegar, the burning sensation of too much sulphur, a mouldy smell from an unsound cork or an unclean barrel. Nowadays obvious faults like these are relatively rare. Most wines have a more or less agreeable but simple compound smell of grapes and fermentation, and in some cases barrel-wood; the smell we recognize as 'winey'. The better the wine, the more distinctive and characteristic this smell, the more it attracts you to sniff again.

At this stage certain grape varieties declare themselves. The 'classics' all set a recognizable stamp on the smell of their wine. Age transmutes it from the primary smell tasters call the 'aroma' to a more complex, less definable and more rewarding smell. This scent of maturity is known, by analogy with the mixed scents of a posy of flowers, as the 'bouquet'.

The essence of a fine bouquet is that you cannot put your finger on it. It seems to shift, perhaps from cedarwood to wax to honey to wildflowers to mushrooms. Mature Riesling can smell like lemons and petrol, Gewürztraminer like grapefruit, Chardonnay like butter – or rather, they can fleetingly remind you of these among many other things.

By the time the glass reaches your lips, then, you have already had answers, or at least clues, to most of the questions about wine: its overall quality, its age, perhaps its grape (and by deduction possibly its origin).

If all is well the taste will confirm the smell like the orchestra repeating the theme introduced by a soloist, adding the body of sound, the tonal colours that were missing. Only at this stage can you judge the balance of sweetness and acidity, the strength of the alcohol and whether it is counterpoised by the intensity of fruity flavours, and the quantity and quality of tannin.

Each wine has an appropriate combination of these elements; its quality is judged on whether they harmonize in a way that is both pleasant in itself and typical of its class. In fact, typical comes before pleasant. A young red wine may be disagreeably tannic and astringent; the taster's job is to judge it for the latent fruitiness that in time will combine with the tannins.

Different parts of your mouth pick up different facets of flavour. It is the tip of your tongue that recognizes sweetness, so sweetness is the first taste you become aware of. Acidity and saltiness are perceived by taste buds along the sides of your tongue and palate, bitterness by the soft back part of your tongue.

The tastes switch off in the same order: sugar after a mere two seconds or so; salt and acid after rather longer. Bitterness, which you notice last, lingers – a quality the Italians appreciate; many of their red wines (Valpolicella is an example) have a slightly bitter aftertaste.

Science can measure many (not all) of the chemical constituents that provide these sensations. It has identified more than 400 in wine up to now. But our perception of them is entirely personal. A few tasters, like a few musicians, may have 'perfect pitch', but most people probably have slight blind spots. Someone who takes three spoonfuls of sugar in coffee must have a high threshold of perception for sweetness. If you need to

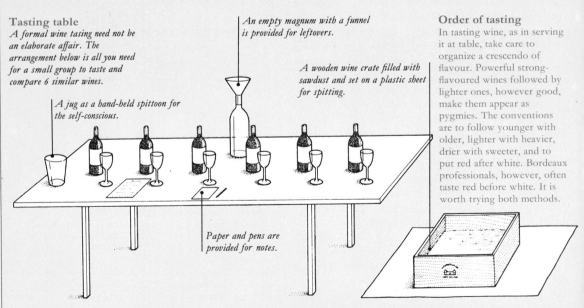

Tasting table
A formal wine tasing need not be an elaborate affair. The arrangement below is all you need for a small group to taste and compare 6 similar wines.

A jug as a hand-held spittoon for the self-conscious.

An empty magnum with a funnel is provided for leftovers.

A wooden wine crate filled with sawdust and set on a plastic sheet for spitting.

Paper and pens are provided for notes.

Order of tasting
In tasting wine, as in serving it at table, take care to organize a crescendo of flavour. Powerful strong-flavoured wines followed by lighter ones, however good, make them appear as pygmies. The conventions are to follow younger with older, lighter with heavier, drier with sweeter, and to put red after white. Bordeaux professionals, however, often taste red before white. It is worth trying both methods.

smother your food with salt you will hardly pick up the subtle touches of saltiness in wine.

Sweet, sour, salt and bitter in any case hardly start to express the variety of sensations that evolve in your mouth between sipping and swallowing. The moment of maximum flavour is when the wine reaches the soft palate and you start to swallow. Its vapour mounts directly to the olfactory nerves through the channels that link mouth and nose. At a serious tasting, where it is essential to spit the wine out to keep a clear head, this moment can be maximized by holding a small quantity in the very back of the mouth and breathing in through it between slightly parted lips. The grimace and the gurgling are a small price to pay for the redoubled concentration of flavour.

Red wines contain more or less tannin, the substance that turns hide to leather. Very tannic wine is so astringent (like walnut or broad-bean skins) that your mouth can begin to feel leathery and further tasting can be difficult. Tannin varies in taste and quality, too, from fully ripe, agreeable astringence, or the mouth-drying astringence of oak, to unripe green harshness.

Acids vary from harsh to delicately stimulating – not just in their concentration, or their power (measured in pH), but in their flavours. Of the wine acids malic is green-appley, citric is fresh and lemony, tartaric is harsh. Acetic is vinegary, lactic is mild, and succinic is a chemical cousin of glutamic acid. We owe much of the lipsmacking, appetizing taste of wine to tiny traces of succinic acid generated as a by-product of fermentation.

As for the alcohol itself, in low concentrations it merely has a faintly sweet taste, but at about 11 per cent by volume begins to give the mouth the characteristic feeling of winey warmth known as 'vinosity'. (German wines at eight or nine per cent lack this feeling.)

Add the ability of your tongue to differentiate between (more or less) fluid or viscous, to pronounce that one liquid feels like satin, another like velvet, and the permutations begin to be impressive. Finally, add the all-important element of persistence – the length of the final flavour. Really great wines have more to offer at the beginning, in the beauty of the bouquet, and at the end, in the way they haunt your breath for minutes after they have gone. Logical in all things, French scholars have even invented a unit of persistence; one second of flavour after swallowing is known as a 'caudalie'. According to one theory the hierarchy of the wines of Burgundy is in direct proportion to their caudalie-count.

A tasting scorecard produced by Michael Broadbent and myself in 1975 – but never a great success, because it tried to embody both descriptive and qualitative terms, and a scoring system. Many scorecard systems have been elaborated, most notably in California, where the Davis campus is the world headquarters of what it pleases them to call organoleptic evaluation. The high priests of the discipline have a long list of proscribed descriptive words which should be avoided because they are not sufficiently accurate, or are positively misleading. Unfortunately it includes most of my vinous vocabulary. The virtues of this card are that it helps you to analyse a wine methodically, reminding you of each aspect to think about in turn.

Name of Wine	Ch. Giscours	Vintage	1966	
District/type	Margaux	Date purchased	1969	
Merchant/bottler	J. Morgan Furze / C.B.	Price	£2.00 ?	DATE OF TASTING 15·1·82

SIGHT	Score (Maximum 4)	4	Comments
CLARITY: cloudy, bitty, dull, clear, brilliant DEPTH OF COLOUR: watery, pale, medium, deep, dark COLOUR: (White wines) green tinge, pale yellow, yellow, gold, brown (Red wines) purple/red, red, red/brown VISCOSITY: slight sparkle, watery, normal, heavy, oily			Col. still deep & strong with sl. whitening at edge.

SMELL	Score (Maximum 4)	3	Starts earthy / mineral: stones, wood – hessian?
GENERAL APPEAL: neutral, clean, attractive, outstanding, off (e.g. yeasty, acetic, oxidized, woody, etc) FRUIT AROMA: none, slight, positive, identifiable (e.g. Riesling) BOUQUET: none, pleasant, complex, powerful			Develops to sweetness, growing more high-pitched, near violets but with undercurrent of ripe fruit.

TASTE	Score (Maximum 9)	7	Still, powerful and warm;
SWEETNESS: (White wines) bone dry, dry, medium dry, medium sweet, very sweet TANNIN: (Red wines) astringent, hard, dry, soft ACIDITY: flat, refreshing, marked, tart BODY: very light and thin, light, medium, full bodied, heavy LENGTH: short, acceptable, extended, lingering BALANCE: unbalanced, good, very well balanced, perfect			excellently crisp & clear (typical Margaux). Essentially dry, a shade astringent. Long firm finish. V.V.G.

OVERALL QUALITY	Score (Maximum 3)	2½	HOW TO USE THIS CHART
			Wine appeals to three senses: sight, smell and taste. This card is a guide to analysing its appeal and an *aide-mémoire* on each wine you taste. Tick one word for each factor in the left-hand column and any of the descriptive terms that fit your impressions. Then award points according to the pleasure the wine gives you.
Coarse, poor, acceptable, fine, outstanding			

SCORING	Total Score (out of 20)	16½

INDEX

Properties and wines entitled Château are indexed under their names

A

Aargau 415
Abad, Tomás 393
Abate Nero 316
Abbazia dell'Annunziata 302
Abbazia di Novacella 314
Abbazia di Rosazzo 324
Abbé-Gorsse-de-Gorsse, Ch. L' 55
Abboccato 298
Abeille, Vignoble 203
Aberdeen Angus 522
Abruzzi 352-3
Abtey 271
Abymes 157
Acacia 447
Accademia Torregiorgi 303
Accomasso 303
Achia-Clauss 432
Ackerman-Laurance 168
Acros Bodegas los 372
Adami, Adriano 321
Adams Vineyard 480
Adanti, Fratelli 345
Adega Cooperativa de Moncao 400
Adega Regional de Colares 400
Adelaide Hills 491
Adelaide Plains 491
Adelberg 271
Adelmann, Graf, Brüssele 285
Adelsheim Vineyard 479
Adeneuer, J.J. 254
Adgestone Vineyard 524
Adissan, Caves Coopératives 219
Adler, Schwarzer 290-1
Adrailhou 231
Aeolos 433
Affaltrach, Schlosskellerei 286
Agassac, Ch. d' 68
AGE Bodegas Unidas 376
Agenais 233
Agiogitiko 432
Agione, Cave Coopérative 220
Agioritiko 433
Aglianico dei Colli Lucani 361
Aglianico del Taburno 353
Aglianico del Vulture 361
L'Agly Coop. 211
Agnes, Giacomo 311
Agos, Señori 378
Agos y Cia, Lopez 378
Agramont 373
Agricola Castellana Sociedad Cooperativa La Seca 373
Agricola de Gandesa, Cooperativa 383
Agricola di Cinqueterre, Cooperative 308
Aguascalientes, Cia. Vinicola de 523
Ahera, Dom. d' 434
Ahern Winery 447
Ahlren Vineyard 447
Ahr 237-8, 253-4
Ahrtaler Landwein 288
Aigle 412
Aigle Blanc 172
Aiguilloux, Ch. 212
Aïn Bessem Bouira 436
Aïn Merane 436

Aïn Souala 436
Aiola 341
L'Aixertell 384
Ajaccio 220
Al-Jazir 436
Alais, Dom. 170
Alameda 442
Alavesas, Bodegas 378
Albachiara 308
Albana di Romagna 294, 327
Albariño de Fefiñanes 372
Albariño de Palacio 372
Alberobello, Cantina Sociale Cooperativa 359
Albert, Jean 225
Albertini Frères 220
Albig 270
Albola, Castello d' 335
Alcamo 362
Aldeno, La Vinicola Sociale 316
Alder Fels 447
Aleatico di Gradoli 349
Aleatico di Puglia 356
Alella 368, 380
Alella Vinicola, Bodegas Cooperativa 383
Alellasol 383
Alentejo 398
Aleria, Cave Cooperative 220
Alexander Valley 440, 442
Alexander Valley Vineyards 447
Alezio 356
D'Alfonso del Sordo, Cantina 359
Algarve 398
Alger 436
Aliança 397
Aliança, Caves, Vinicola de Sangalhos 399
Alicante 368, 385
Alice Bel Colle, Vecchia Cantina Sociale di 303
Alighieri, Serègo 321
Aligoté 147, 430
Alkoomi 493
All Saints 493
Allandale 493
Allanmere 493
Allegrini 320
Allegro Vineyards 487
Allendorf, Fritz 261
Allesverloren 515
Allobrogie 234
Allora, V. Giacalone 364
Almadén Vineyards 447
Almansa 368, 385
Aloque 385
Aloxe-Corton 107, 119
Alphandery, Mme H. Gratiot 88
Alpine 479
Alsace 187-92
Alsace, Anne d' 190
Alsace Willm 192
Alsheim 269
Alta Aella 383
Alta Vineyard Cellar 447
La Rioja Alta 378
Altare, Elio 299
Altenbamberg 265
Altenkirch, Friedrich 261
Altesino 335
Alto 515
Alto Adige 313-17
Altrheingauer Landwein 288
Alvear 387
Alves, Adegas Camilo 399
Alzey 270
Weingut der Stadt 273

Ama, Fratello di 335
Amabile 298
Amadieu, Piere 197
Amador 442
Amador Foothill Winery 447
Amalia, Tenuta 330
Amance, Marcel 138
Amarante 397
Amarine, Dom. de l' 219
Amaro 298
Amarone 320
Ambra, Fattoria 341
D'Ambra Vini d'Ischia 355
American Viticultural Areas (AVAs) 440
Amiel, Mas 210
Aminteion 432
Amiot, Pierre & Fils, Do. 127
Amiral de Beychevelle 58
Amontillado 389-90
Amorosa 341
Amoroso 390
Amour, Ch. d' 162
Amouries, Dom. des 212
Amouroux, A. 202
Ampeau & Fils, Robert 127
Ampurdán 380
Ampurdán, Caves del 381, 383
Ampurdán-Costa Brava 368
Añada 390
Anatolia 434
Ancienne, Vinicole l' 208
Ancienne Cuvée Carnot 129
Andalucia 386
Anderson, S., Vineyard 447
Anderson Valley 442
Anderson Wine Cellars 447
Andlau-Barr Coop. 192
André, Pierre 127, 141
André Quancard André 51
André Roches, Mme. Vve. 222
Andrés 484
Andrieux, Albert 201
Andron-Blanquet, Ch. 66
Aney, Ch. 68
Anforio 311
Anfossi, Luigi 308
Los Angeles Diplomatico 393
Angelica 444
D'Angelo, Fratelli 361
L'Angélus, Ch. 86
Angerville, Dom. Marquis d' 127
Anges, Dom. des 197
Anglefort 157
Anglesey 493
Angliviel de la Beaumelle, Jean-Pierre 52, 79
Angludet, Ch. d' 55
Angoris 325
Angoves 493
Anheuser, August E. 266
Anheuser, Paul 266
Anheuser & Fehrs 266
Añina 390
Anjou 159
Anjou Coteaux de la Loire 159
Anjou Gamay 159
Anjou Mousseux 159
Anjou Pétillant 159
Anjou-Saumur 165-9

Anjou-Villages 159, 165-6
Anjoux & Cie 153
Anne de Joyeuses 214
Annereaux, Ch. des 98
Anseillan, Ch. 65
Anselme, Père 202
Anselmi 320
Anteo 311
Antica Podere Conti della Cremosina 300
Antichi Vigneti de Cantalupo 299
Antinori, Marchesi L. & P. 331, 335-6, 338-9, 345
The Antipodean 509
Antonelli 345
Antoniolo 299
Anzillotti Solazzi 348
Apelia 433
Apianum 354
Apollo 433
Apremont 157
Aprilia 349
Apulia 355-9
Aquila Rossa 383
Aquileia 323
Aragón 370-1
Arbignieu 157
Arbois Coop. 156
Arbor Crest 481
Arborea 365
Arcadin 474
Archambeau, Ch. d' 103
Archanes 433
Arche, Ch. d' 68, 79
Arche-Lafaurie, Ch. d' 79
Archembault, Pierre 173
Arcins, Ch. d' 68
Ardouin, Jean & Fils 66
D'Arenberg 496
Arengo 295
Arfeuille, Bernard d' 89, 96
Arfeuille, Maison d' 91
Arganza, Bodegas Palacio de 372-3
Arganza, Palacio de 371
Argens d' 231
Argentina 522-3
Argiano 335
Arini, Vito Curatolo 364
Arlay, Ch. d' 155
Arles 217
Arlot, Dom. de l' 127
Armand, Dom. du Comte 127
Armino 385
Arnaud-Jouan, Ch. 101
Arnauld, Ch. d' 68
Arnoults, Jacques 113
Arnoux & Fils 197-8
Arqueria, Ch. d' 198
De Arqueso, Manuel 391
Arricaud, Ch. 76
L'Arrosée, Ch. 86
Arrowfield 493
Arrowood 447
Arroyo Grande Valley 442
Arroyo Seco 442
Arroyo-Sonoma Winery *see* Bandiera Winery
Arrufiat 227
Arterberry 480
Artesa 380
Artiges-Arnaud 61
Artimino 341
Artois, Dom. d' 171
Arve-et-Lac 412
Arve-et-Rhône 412
Arvedi d'Emilei 321
Arvier, Co-Enfer 306
Arzenton, Mario 325

Ascagnano, Castello di 345
Aschrott, Geheimrat 258
Asciutto 298
Ashbrook Estate 493
Asprinio 361
Asprino 361
Assémat, Dom. 198
Assmannshausen 257
Associacão dos Produtores-Engarrafadores de Vinho Verde (APEVV) 397
Associated Vintners *see* Columbia 481
Asti, Duca d' 300
Asti Spumante 294, 298
Astley Vineyards 524
Astoria Vini 321
At-Amour, Ch. de 153
Atlas Peak Vineyards 447
Attems, Conti 325
Attica 432
Au Bon Climat 447
Aubert Frères, Maison 166
Auckland 508-9
Audas, Gautier 162
Aude, Vins de Pays 232-3
Audebert, Marcel et Hubert 170
Audebert & Fils 170
Audiffred, H. 129
Audoy, Cécile 65-6
Audy, Georges 94
Audy, Jean 94
Audy, Maison 91
Auflangen 270
Augusta, Isola 326
Aujas, Ernest 152
Auldana 502
Aumelas, Vicomté d' 231-2
Aupècle, Soc. 217
Auque, Jacques 225
Aurora 486
Aurora, Cooperativa Agricola 364
Ausbruch 421
Auslese 236-7, 240, 421
Ausone, Ch. 83-4
Auvernier, Ch. d' 415
Auxerrois 223, 227, 524
Luxembourg 268
Auxerrois, SICA du Vignoble 133
Auxey-Duresses 124
Aveleda, Quinta 400
Avelsbach 243
"L'Avenir" 213
Avery's 141
Avignonesi 335
Avril, Paul 203
Axarquia 386
Ayala 184
Aydie, Ch. d' 227
Ayl 243
Ayuso Roig, Fermin 385
Ayze 157
Aze Coop. 148
Azelia 303
Azienda 298
Azillanet, Caves Coopératives d' 216

B

Bâbeascà 429
Babić 429
Babich Wines 509
Bacarles 387
Bacchereto, Fattoria di 341
Bacchus 524
Bach, Masia 381
Bachelet, Dom. Denis 127
Bachelet-Ramonet Père & Fils, Dom. 127
Bachtobel, Schlossgut 415

Bacile di Castiglione, Barone 359
Backsberg 515
Baco Noir 486
Bacquey, Jeanne 57
Bacquey, Mme 57
Bad Dürkheim 275
Bad Kreuznach 265
Bad Münster 265
Baden 239, 286-91
Badette, Ch. 90
Badia a Coltibuono 335
Badis, Markgräflich 289
Badische Bergstrasse/ Kraichgau Bereich 286, 288
Badischer Winzerkeller 286
Badischer Winzerkeller eG 289
Badisches Frankenland Bereiches 286, 288
Badoglio Rota, Duchi 325
Badoux, Henri 414
Badstube 245
Bages Coop. 211
Baggiolino 341
Bagni 364
Bagnis, Jean & Fils 206
Bagnol, Dom. du 207
Bahans 52
Bahans-Haut-Brion 73
Bahl, Roger 192
Bailey's 493
Baillo, Paul 210
Bailly, Caves de 133
Bailly Père et Fils 175
Bailly-Reverdy, Bernard & Fils 174
Baiocchi, Cantine 341
Bairrada 397-8
Baixas Coop. 211
Balac, Ch. 68
Balande, Mas 210
Balaton, Lake 425
Balatonboglár 425
Balatonfüred-Csopak 425
Balbach, Bürgermeister Anton, Erben 271
Balbaina 390
Baldès, M. 224
Baldinelli Vineyards 447
Balestard La Tonnelle, Ch. 86
Balfour 391
Balgera, Franco 311
Balgownie 493
Balland-Chepuis, Dom. Jospeh 174
Ballard Canyon Vineyard 447
Balliencourt dit Courcol, E. de 95
Balmes Dauphinoises 234
Balverne Winery and Vineyards 447-8
Baly, Marcel 78
Banat 427
Bandiera Winery 448
Bandol 205
Bandol, Vins de 208
Banfi, Villa 296, 299, 335, 342
Bannockburn Vineyards 493
Banti, Erik 341
Banti, Jacopo 341
Banyula-dela-Aspres 211
Banyula "L'Etoile" Coop. 211
Baptiste, Cuvée Jean 140
Baracco 303
Barale, Fratelli 303
Barancourt 184
Barattieri, Conte Otto 330
Barbacarlo 309
Barbadillo, Antonio 391
Barbaresco 295
Barbaresco, Produttori del 299
Barbarin, Michel 57
Barbarossa di Bertinoro 327

La Barbatella, Cascina 303
Barbe, Ch. (Côtes de Bourg) 100
Barbé, Ch. (Premières Côtes de Blaye) 100
Barbe Blanche, Ch. de 92
Barbera 309, 327, 444
Barbera d'Alba 295
Barbera d'Asti 295
Barbera del Monferrato 295
Barberani-Vallesanta 345
Barberesco 294
Barbi, Fattoria dei 335
Barbier, René 381
Barboursville Vineyards 487
Barca Velha 397, 399
Barceló, Hijos de Antonio 387
Barco de Valdeorras Coop. 373
El Barco 373
Barde, Ch. 100
Barde-Haut, Ch. 90
Bardolino 318
Bardolino Recioto 318
Barengo 295
Barennes, Xavier 57
Baret, Ch. 76
Barge, G. et P. 195
Bargetto's Santa Cruz Winery 448
Barjac, Guy de 195
La Barjasse 195
Barletta, Cantina Sociale di 359
Barolet, Arthur 143
Barolo 294-6
Barolo, Marchesi di 299
Barolo Chinato 296
Barolo e di Fontafredda, Tenimenti di 301
Baron, Heredeos de Manuel 393
Baronne, Ch. la 212
Barossa Valley 490, 491
Barossa Valley Estates 493
Barquero, Bodegas Perez 387
Barrail, Ch. du 103
Barraud, Ch. 92
Barreau-Bader, Mme 94
Barréjat, Dom. 227
Barrel storage and fermentation 38-9
Barrère, Alfred 228
Barreyers, Ch. 68
Barros Almeida 400, 406
Barry, Jim 493
Barsac 46, 77
Barsönyös-Csaszar 426
Bart, Dom. 127-8
Barthes, Jean 215
Bartholomew, Frank 449, 460
Barton & Guestier 51
Barton family 58
Barton Manor 525
Bas-Médoc 46, 70-2
Bas-Rhin 187-8
Basedows Wines 494
Baseland 415
Basilicata 361
Basit-St-Martin family 79
Bass, Wolf 494
Bassendean Estate 494
Basses Mourettes 119
Les Basses Moutottes 119
Bassot, Thomas 128
Bastide Neuve, Dom. de la 207
Basting-Gimbel, Weingut 261
Bastor-Lamontagne, Ch. 82
Batailley, Ch. 61
Bâtard-Montrachet 125
Batasiolo 300
La Battistina 303

Battistotti, Riccardo 316
Baudry, Ch. 53
Bauget-Jouette 185
Le Bault de la Morinière, Comte Jean 128
Baumann, Friedrich 273
Baumard, Dom. des 166
Baumard, Jean 166
Bava 303
Bayard, Ch. (Gouze) 92
Bayard, Ch. (Laporte) 92
Bayerischer Bodensee-Landwein 288
Beau-Rivage, Ch. 101
Beau Séjour Bécot, Ch. 85
Beau Site, Ch. 66
Beau-Site-Haut-Vignoble, Ch. 67
Beau-Site Ch. 101
Beau Vallon Coop. 150
Beaucastel, Ch. de 202
Beaudet, Paul 153
Beaujeau, Dom. 166
Beaujolais 147, 149-54
Beaujolais en primeur 150
Beaujolais nouveau 150
Beaujolais supérieur 150
Beaujolais-villages 150-1
Beaulieu, Ch. de 207
Beaulieu Abbey Vineyard 524-5
Beaulieu Vineyard 448, 477
Beaumes-de-Venise 199
Beaumet Chaurey 185
Beaumont, Ch. 68
Beaumont, Ch. de 100
Beaune 120, 122
Beauregard, Ch. 59, 93-4
Beauregard, Ch. de 212
Beauregardes, Les 112
Beaurenard, Dom. de 202
Beauroy 112, 113
Beauséjour, Ch. 67, 85, 92
Bebina 432
Beblenheim, Caves de 192
Bécade, Ch. La 57
Beck, Gaston 189
Becker, Caves J. 189
Becker, J. B. 261
Becker family 223
Bécot, Michel & Fils 85
Bécot family 88
Beerenauslese 236, 237, 240, 421
Bégadan Coop. 72
Beira Alta 397
Beiras 397
Bel-Air, Cave Cooperative de 151, 152
Bel-Air, Ch. (Pomerol) 97
Bel-Air, Ch. (Puisseguin-St-Emilion) 92
Bel-Air, Ch. (Ste-Croix-du-mont) 102
Bel-Air, Ch. de (Lalande-de-Pomerol) 98
Bel-Air Lagrave, Ch. 57
Bel-Air-Marquis d'Aligre, Ch. 55
Bel-Orme-Tronquoy-de-Lalande, Ch. 68
Belair, Ch. (Premières Côtes de Blaye) 100
Belair, Ch. (St. Emilion) 85
Belesta Coop. 211
Belgrave, Ch. 67
Belicard, Pierre 153
Belin, Jules 139
Belingant, Ch. 222
Bell Canyon Cellars 449
Belland, Dom. Adrien 128
Belle Rose 64
Belle Rose, Ch. 65
Bellefont-Belcier, Ch. 90
Bellefont-Belcier-Guillier, Ch. 90
Bellegarde, Cave Coopérative de 219
Bellegrave, Ch. 90
Bellei, Francesco 330
Bellendorf 315

Bellerive, Ch. 71
Bellerose Vineyard 448
Bellet 206
Bellet, Ch. de 207
Bellevue, Ch. (Lower Medoc) 71
Bellevue, Ch. (Pomerol) 97
Bellevue, Ch. (Premières Côtes de Blaye) 100
Bellevue, Ch. (St-Emilion) 86
Bellevue, Ch. (St-Georges-d'Orques) 218
Bellevue-La-Forêt, Ch. 229
Bellevue-Laffout, Ch. 57
Bellicard d'Avignon 198
Bellisle-Mondotte, Ch. 90
Bellissen, Soc. Mesnard 215
Bellocq, Vinicole de 227
Belvedere, Fattoria 346
Belvedere Wince Co. 448
Ben Lomond Mountain 442
Benavente 371
Benede-Orange 514
Benettini, Conte Picedi 308
Beni M'Tir 436
Beni Sadden 436
Benincasa, Domenico 346
Benito 391
Benmarl Wine Co. 484
Bennwihr Coop. 192
Benoist, Philippe de 174
Benoit, Ch. 480
Bénovie 232
Bentzel-Sturmfeder-Horneck, Gräf 286
Bera-Cascina Palazzo 303
Bérange 199
Bérard & Fils 205
Berardenga-Fattoria di Felsina 337
Berbeito 408
Berberana, Bodegas 376
Berceo 378
Berceo, Gonzalo de 378
Berdiot 112
Bereich Bernkastel 244
Bereichs 238, 240
Bergaglio, Nicola 303
Bergat, Ch. 86
Berger, M. 170
Bergerac 221-3
The Bergkeller 515
Bergkloster 271
Bergstrasse Gebietswinzergenos-senschaft 279
Bergweiler-Prüm Erben see Pauly-Bergweiler, Dr.
Berici 318
Berin, Fabio 325
Beringer Vineyards 447-8
Berjal, Pierre 87
Berliquet, Ch. 86
Berlucci, Fratelli 311
Berlucci, Guido 310
Bern 415
Bernard, Dom. Georges 198
Bernard, François 57
Bernard, Oliver 73
Bernard family 67
Bernard-Massard, Caves 268
Bernarda, Rocca 326
Bernarde, Dom. la 206
La Bernardine 195, 205
Bernardins, Dom. des 198
Bernède, Jean 225
Bernkastel 242
Bernkastel-Kues 245
Beronia, Bodegas 392
Berri Estate 494
Berry Bros. & Rudd 131
Bersano (Antica Podere Conti della Cremosina) 300
Bertagna, Dom. 128
Bertani 320

Bertelli, A. 303
Berthault family 57
Berthelot, Paul 185
Bertier, Mme Dominique de 214
Bertinau, Ch. 93
Les Bertins, Ch. 71
Bertola 393
Bertran, José Lopez y Cia 383
Bertranon, Ch. 102
Besancenot-Mathouillet, Dom. 128
Besombes, Albert "Moc-Baril" 166
Bessac, Caves 202
Bessan 212
Besserat de Bellefon 178
Bessières, Henri 225
Bestimmate Anbaugebiete 238
Best's Wines 494
Bethel Heights Vineyard 480
Bethmann, P. de 75
Betz, C. 262
Bex 412
Beyaz 434
Beychevelle, Ch. 58
Beyer, Léon 189
Bezirkskellerei "Markgräflerland", Coop. 291
Biac, Ch. du 101
Bianchello del Metauro 347
Bianchi 348, 522
Bianco 298
Bianco & Figlio 303-4
Bianco Alcamo 362
Bianco d'Arquata 345
Bianco Capena 349
Bianco dei Colli Maceratesi 347
Bianco di Custoza 318
Bianco dell'Empolese 332
Bianco di Pitigliano 332
Bianco di Scandiano 327
Bianco della Valdinievole 332
Bianco della Vall d'Arbia 334
Bianco Vergine Valdichiana 332
Biarnès, M. Roger 82
Bibbiani 341
Bichat 303
Bichot, Maison Albert 128
Biddenden Vineyards 525
Bidon, Alain 150
Biel/Bienne, Lake 410-12
El Bierzo 371
Biesbrouck, Danielle 225
Biferno 354
Biffar, Josef 278
Bigaroux, Ch. 90
Bigi, Luigi & Figlio 345
Bigorre 233
Bigotière, Ch. de la 163
Bikavér 426
Bilbainas, Bodegas 376
Bilbao, Bodegas Ramon 378
Billard-Gonnet, Dom. 128
Billards, Dom. des 153
Billiard 185
Bindella, Rudolf 341
Bingen 269-70
Biondi Santi – Il Greppo 337
Biquette, Ch. 92
Birot, Ch. 101
Bischöflichen Weingüter Trier 247
Bischofskreuz Grosslage 276-8
Bisci, Fratelli 348
Bisol, Desiderio & Figli 321
Bissera, Tenuta 330-31

Bissey-sous-Cruchaud Coop. 148
Bisson, Enoteca 308
Biston-Brillette, Ch. 57
Bize & Fils, Simon 128
Bize-Leroy, Mme. Lalou 120-1, 136
Bizolières, Ch. de la 168
Bizot, Christian 181
Blaauwklippen 515
Black Mountain Vineyard 466
Blagny 124
Blaignan, Ch. 71
Blanc, Dom. du Mas 210
Blanc, Gérard 215
Blanc de Blances champagne 179
Blanc de Noirs champagne 179
Blanchard, Giles 114
Blanchet, Bernard 175
Blanchot 112⁸
Blanck, Dom. Paul & Fils 189
Blandy Brothers 408
Blankenhorn, Fritz 289
Blanquette de Limoux 214
Blanzac, Ch. 99
Blatnice 427
Blázques, Hijos de Agustin 391
Bleasdale Vineyards 494
Bleda, Bodegas 385
Blenheim (New Zealand) 509
Bloud, M. 226
Bloy, Ch. du 222
Blue Label 496
Bobadilla 391
Boberg 514
Boca 296
Bocksbeutels 280
Bodenheim 270
Bodensee Bereich 287
Bodet, Ch. 99
Boeckel, E. 189
Boeger Winery 448
Boetia 432
Boffa, Alfero 304
Boffa, Carlo and Figli 304
Bogazkere 434
Bogdanuşă 429
Bogle Vineyards Winery 448
Bohemia 427
Boidron, Jean Noel 87
Boiga, Podere 308
Boillot, Dom. Henri 128
Boillot, Jean-Marc 128
Boillot, Pierre 128
Boillot & Fils, Dom. Lucien 128
Bois Bruley, Dom. du 162
Bois de Candale 197
Bois de Dames, Dom. du 199
Bois de la Gard, Ch. 203
Bois de la Salle, Cave Cooperative du 153
Bois d'Oingt Coop. 150
Boissel-Rhodes 226
Boissenot, Professor 62
Boisset, Jean Claude 128
Boisson, Théphile & Fils 205
Boivin, Jacques 167
Boizel 184
Bolgheri 332
Bolla 320
Bollinger 180-1
Bollinger, J. 178
Bolognani 316
Boltère 204
Bon Courage 515
Bon Dieu des Vignes, Ch. 76
Bon-Pasteur, Ch. Le 94
Bonarda 309
Bonarda Piemontese 296
Bonde, Ch. 93
Le Bonheur 515

Boniface, Pierre 157
Bonneau, Ch. 68, 92
Bonneau, Etab. Marcel 91
Bonneau du Martray, Dom. 128-9
Bonnel, Christian 214
Bonnes Mares 115-6
Bonnet 184
Bonnet, Ch. (Entre-Deux-Mers) 102
Bonnet, Ch. (St-Emilion) 90
Bonnet, Jean Baptiste 215
Bonnevialle, J.M. 218
Bonnezeaux 159, 163, 165
Bonnievale 514
Bonny Doon Vineyard 448
Boordy Vineyards 487
Boplass 515
Boratto, Vittorio 304
Borba 398
Bordeaux 45-105
Bordeaux Supérieur 46
Bordelaise, La 52
Borderie, Jean 223
Borderie, Maurice 95
La Borderie, Ch. 222
Borges, H.M. Sucrs. 408
Borges & Irmão SARL 399
Borges E. Irmão 403
Borgo Canale 359
Borgogno, Giacomo & Figli 304
Borgogno, Serio & Battista 304
Borie family 58-9, 61
Borie-Manoux 51
Bornos, Palacio de 373
Bosca 304
Bosca, Bodegas Luigi 522
Boscaini, Paolo & Figli 321
Boscary, J. 217
Bosch-Guell, Bodegas 383
Boschendal 515
Bosco Eliceo 327
Il Bosco, Tenuta 311
Le Boscq, Ch. 66
Boseredon, Comte de 222
Le Bosq, Ch. 71
Bosquet des Papes 205
Bosquets, Dom. de 199
Bossi-Marchese Gondi, Fattoria di 341
Botinière, Dom. de la 164
Botobolar 494
Botrys 432
Botta, Felice 359
Botte, Donato 361
Botte, Giuseppe 361
Bottero, Robert 217
Botticino 309
Le Botti d'Oro 311
Böuard de Laforest 86
Bouchacourt 153
Bouchaine 448
Bouchard, Paul 128
Bouchard, Romain 198
Bouchard Aîné 133
Bouchard Aîné & Fils 129
Bouchard Père & Fils 129
Bouché Père & Fils 185
Boucher, Aimé 170
Bouches-du-Rhône 219
Bouchoc, Ch. 102
Bouchot-Lodot 128
Boudigand, Ch. 222
Boudon, Marie-Christine 56
Bougas, Solar das 400
Bougrier 170
Bougros 112-3
Bouilh, Ch. du 103
Le Bouis, Ch. 212
Bouillault, Léon & Fils 162
La Boulou Coop. 211
Bouloumié, André 225
Bouquignan, Ch. de 212
Bour family 198
Bourbonnais 234
Bourboulenc 201, 216

La Bourdelière 165
Bourdieu, Ch. 100
Le Bourdieu, Ch. 68
Bourdy, Caves Jean 155
Bourée, Pierre, Fils 129
Bourgneuf-Vayron, Ch. 94
Bourgogne 110, 147
Bourgogne Aligoté 107, 111
Bourgogne Aligoté de Bouzeron 144
Bourgogne Côte Chalonnaise 144
Bourgogne Grand Ordinaire 107, 111, 147
Bourgogne Ordinaire 111
Bourgogne Passe-tout-grains 107, 110
Bourgone Réserve Pierre André 127
Bourgueil 159, 163, 169
Bourgueneuf, Ch. de 97
Bourisset, Propriété 153
Bournac, Ch. 71
Bournazel, Comtesse Pierre de 81
Boursault, Ch. de 185
Bouscaut, Ch. 73
Bousquet, Ch. du 100
Boutari, J. & Son 432
Bouteilley, Ch. de 101
Bouvet-Ladubay 166, 168
Bovio, Gianfranco 304
Bowen Estate 494
Boyd-Cantenac, Ch. 53
Boyer, Pierre 55
Bozner Leiten 313
Brachetto d'Acqui 296
Braga 397
Braida-Giacomo Bologna 300
Braillon, Jean-Charles 153
Brajkovich 510
Bramaterra 296
Branaire-Ducru, Ch. 58
La Brancaia 341
Branchereau, Claude 166
Brand 188
The Brander Vineyard 448
Brandluft 189
Brand's Laira 494
Brandy 11
Brane-Cantenac, Ch. 53
Bratislava 426
Braubeberg 245
Bravo, J.B. and M.J. 79
Brauneberg 245
Breckinridge 459
Brédit, Marc 170
Breede River Valley 514
Breganze 318
Brema, Antiche Cantine 304
Bremm, Eduard 252
Brenner'sches Weingut 273
Brenot, Albert 131
Brentano, Baron von 258
Brethous, Ch. 101
Bretzenheim 265
Breuer, G. 262
Le Breuil, Ch. (du) 68
Brezza 304
Briante, Ch. de 151
Bricco 296
Bricco del Drago 296
Bricco dell'Uccellone 296
Bricco Manzoni 296
Bricco Mondalino, Poderi 304
Bricout, A. & Co. 185
Bridane, Ch. La 59
Bridge port 404
Briesgau Bereich 288
Brigaldara 322
Brigatti, Luciano 304
Brigham Creek 511
Bright's 484
Brillette, Ch. 57
Brindisi 356
Bringuier 212
Bristol sherry 390
Brix 467
Brixner 314

Brno 426
Broadley Vineyard 480
Brochet, François-Jean 96
Brocol 225
Brokenwood 494
Brolio Barone Ricasoli 337
Bronte 487
Brook, Jane, Estate 494
Brooksfields Vineyard 509
Brotte, Jean-Pierre 202
Brouilly 151
Broustet, Ch. 79
Brovia, Fratelli 304
Brown Brothers 494-5
Brown sherry 390
Bruc, Louis de 162
Bruce, David, Winery 448
Bruck, Lionel J. 129
Brugnano 341
Brugne, Jean 153
Brûlesécaille, Ch. 100
Le Brul 316
Brumont, Alain 227
Brun, Edouard & Co. 185
Brun, Georges 152
Brun, René 185
Bruna, Riccardo 308
Bründlmayer, Weingut 419
Brunel family 203
Brunel, Dom. 198
Brunello di Montalcino 294, 332
Brunet, Georges 207
Brunier family 204
Le Brun, Cellier 509
Brunori 348
Bruone, Maurice 152
Brusse, J. 206
Brusset, Dom. 198
Brut 179
Bryczek, Dom. Georges 129
Bual 407-8
Bucci, Fratelli 348
Bucelas 398
Bucy, Joseph de 133
Buehler Vineyards 449
Buena Vista Winery and Vineyards 449
La Buena Vida 488
Buffardel Frères 201
Bugey 157
Buhl, Reichsrat von 276
Buitenverwachting 515
Bujanda, Bodegas Martinez 378
Bullay 247
Bull's Blood 426
Bully Hill Wine & Champagne Co. 484
Bunan brothers 207
Bundner Herrschaft 415
Buonamico, Fattoria del 337
Bur, Vve. Paul 185
Burc, Charles 225
Burc & Fils 225
Burdon, John William 391
Burg Grosslage 281
Burg Layen 266
Burg Licheneck 288
Burg Neuenfels 287
Burg Rheinfels 254
Burg Rodenstein Grosselage 271
Burg Zähringen 288
Burge, Grant 495
Burgenland 417-18
Burgenlandischer Winzerverband Coop. 423
Bürgerspital zum Heiligen Geist 280, 281
Burgess Cellars 449, 477
Burgundy 106-48
  Californian 444
Burgweg 255, 264, 281
Buring, Leo 495, 500
Bürklin-Wolf, Dr. 276-7
Burle, Edmond 199
Burlotto, G.B. 304
Burmester, J.W. & Co. 400, 406

Burquet, Dom. Alain 129
Burtin 185
Les Busquières 203
Busso, Piero 304
Buttafuoco 309
Buxy Coop. 148
Buzbag 434
Buzet 226
Buzzetto di Quiliano 307
Buzzinelli, Fratelli 325
Bynum, David, Winery 449
Byzantis 432

C
C.A.Y.D. 394
Ca' Bianca 304
Ca' Bolano 325
Ca' del Bosco 311
Ca' del Bosco Franciacorta 357
Ca' Bruzzo 322
Ca' del Frati 311
Ca' del Monte 322
Ca'Roma 304
Ca' Ronesca 326
Ca' Vescovo 326
Caballero, Luis 391, 393
Cabanes, Ch. 77
La Cabanne, Ch. 94
Cabernet d'Anjou 159, 165
Cabernet de Saumur 159-60
Cabernet di Pramaggiore 318
Cabernet Franc 50, 425, 522
Cabernet Sauvignon 50, 225, 227, 425, 430, 432, 444, 482, 492, 522
La Cabestanyenca Coop. 211
Cabet, Cuvée 140
Cabreros 371
Cabrieres 217
Cabrieres, Dom. de 205
Cacc'e Mmitte di Lucera 356
Cacchi, Luigi & Figli, & Villa Cerna 338
Cacchiano, Castello di 337
Cáceres, Bodegas Marqués de 378
Caché Cellars 449
CACIB (Cooperativa Agricola Calabro Ionica Bianchese) 360
Cadaujac 73
Cadenasso Winery 449
Cadet-Bon, Ch. 90
Cadet-Piola, Ch. 86
Cadet-Pontet, Ch. 90
Cafaggio, Villa 341
Cafol, Ch. 99
Caggiolo 341
Cagnina di Romagna 327
Cagnosso Winery 485
Cahors 223-5
Caillavet, Ch. de 101
Cailleau, Pascal 168
Caillou, Ch. 79
Caillou Blanc 59
Le Caillou, Ch. 222
Le Caillou, Ch. 97
Cailloux, Dom. les 205
Cain Cellars 449
Cairanne 197, 199
Cairanne Coop. 200
Caix, Ch. 224
Cakebread Cellars 449
Calabria 359-60
Caladroy, Dom. de 210
Calamin 412
Calatayud 371
La Calbane 330
Calcinaia, Villa 341
La Caldalora 316
Caldaro 313
Calderón, Casa de 385
Caldor 51
Cálem, A.A. & Filho Lda. 403

Calendal, Mas 207
Calenzana, Cave
  Cooperative 220
Calera Wine Co. 449
California 438-77
Calissano, Luigi & Figli
  304
Calistoga 442
Calistoga Cellars 453
Calkarasi 434
Callaway Vineyard and
  Winery 450
Calliga, Ch. 432
Calo, Michele & Figli 359
Calon, Ch. 92
Calon-Ségur, Ch. 65
Calona 484
Calovi, Remo 316
Calvaire, Ch. 90
Le Calvane 341
Calveras 442
Calvet & Compagnia 51
Le Calvez, Mme.
  Jacqueline 216
Calvimont, Ch. de 103
Camarone 330
Camarsac, Ch. 102
Cambas, Andrew P. 432
Camborio 394
Camélon, Dom. de 101
Camensac, Ch. 67
Camera, Bodegas Delgado
  385
Camigliano 341
Campania 353-5
Campbells 495
Camperos 79
Campidano di Terralba 365
Campo de Borja 368, 371
Campo Fiorin 318
Campo La Daimieleña,
  Cooperativa del 386
Campo Viejo, Bodegas 376
Campogiovanni 341
Camus Père & Fils, Dom.
  129
Canada 484
Canandaigua Wine
  Company, Inc. 484
Canard-Duchêne 178
Canberra 491
Canciller 522
Candiale 341
Candida dei Colli Apuani
  332
Candido, Francesco 359
Cane 308
Canel, Adamo & Figli 322
Canelli, Castello di 301
Canelli-Suchet 158
Canepa, José 520
Canet, Ch. 102
Canevel 322
Cannonau di Sardegna
  365-6
Canon, Ch. 85, 99
Canon-de-Brem, Ch. 99
Canon-Fronsac 98-9
Canon-La-Gaffelière, Ch.
  86
Cansetto dei Mandorli 330
Cantalupo 353
Cantanghel, Maso 316
Cantegril, Ch. 79, 82
Cantegril-Verda, Dom. 200
Canteloup, Ch. 67
Cantemerle, Ch. 67
Cantenac, Ch. 90
Cantenac-Brown, Ch. 53
Canter 51
Canteranne, Ch. 90
Canterbury (New Zealand)
  509
Canterrane, Dom. de 210
Cantina Sociale di Canelli
  304
Cantina Sociale di Santa
  Maria della Versa 311
Cantina Viticoltori Trento
  314-15
Cantine Fratta, Antica 310
Canuet, Ch. 55

Cap de Fouste, Ch. 210-11
Cap-de-Mourlin, Ch. 86
Cap Léon Veyrin, Ch. 57
Cap Leucate 213
Capaccia, Podere 341
Capannelle 341
Caparone 450
Caparra & Siciliani 360
Caparzo, Tenuta 337
Capbern-Gasqueton, Ch.
  66
Capbern-Gasqueton,
  Philippe 55, 65
Capdemourlin, Jacques 86
Capdemourlin, Mme.
  Françoise 88
Cape Clairault 495
Cape Independent
  Winemaker's Guild 515
Cape Mentelle 495
Capel Vale 495
Capellini, Forlini 308
Capet-Guillier, Ch. 90
Capezzana, Tenuta di 337
Capitans, Ch. des 152
Capitel San Rocco 318
Capitelles Cassagnes,
  Cellier des 211
Capri 353
Capriano del Colle 309
Caprili 341
Çara Smokvica 429
Caraguihes, Ch. de 212
Caralt, Conde de 383
Caramany Coop. 211
Caramino 296
Carbonell y Cia 387
Carbonere 304
Carboneyre, Ch. 90
Carbonnieux, Ch. 73
Carcannieux, Ch. 71
Carcavelos 398
Cardaillan, Ch. de 81
Carden Park 525
Cardeto 346
Cardinal 322
Cardinal Richard 164
Cardinal Villemaurine, Ch.
  90
La Cardonne, Ch. 71
Carema 296
Carey, J., Cellars 450
Carignan 205, 210, 212,
  214, 220, 434, 444
Carignano del Sulcis 366
Carillon & Fils, Louis 129
Cariñena 370-1
Cariñeno 368
Carles, Ch. de 99
Carletti della Giovampaola
  339
Carmel 435
Carmel Valley 442
Carmenet 450
Les Carmes Haut-Brion,
  Ch. 76
Carmignani G. "Fuso"
  341
Carmignano 294, 332
Carmolüe, Jean-Louis 66
Carnelian 444
Carneros 442
Carneros, Dom. 454
Carneros Creek Winery
  450
Carnevale, Giorgio 304
Carone, Villa 351
Caronne-Ste-Gemme, Ch.
  68
Carpenè Malvolti 320
Carpineto 341
Carr Taylor Vineyards 525
Carras 432
Carras, Dom. 433
Carrascal 390
Les Carrelles, Ch. 100
Carrère, Edmond 88
Carretta, Tenuta 304
Les Carrierès 119
Carrión, Bodegas Miguel
  385
Carruades de Lafite 62, 65

Carso 323
Carta Nevada 383
Carte d'Or 164
Carte Noir 207, 218
Carteau-Côtes-Daugay, Ch.
  90
Carteau Matras, Ch. 90
du Cartillon, Ch. 68
Cartoixa Scala Dei 382
Carvalho, Ribeiro and
  Ferreira 399
Casa de Douro 401
Casa Larga Vineyards Inc.
  484
Casacanditella, Vinicola
  353
Casale del Giglio 351
Casalinho, Caves do 400
Le Casalte, Fattoria 341
Casavecchia di Nittardi 341
Cascade 486
Cascade Mountain
  Vineyards 485
Cascastel 213
Cascina du Feipu 308
Case Basse 337
La Case Bianche 322
Casenuove, Fattoria 341
Casetta dei Frati 330
Casilda Cream 394
Caslot-Galbrun 170
Caslot-Jamet 170
Casole 346
Casona Lopez 522
Cassan 232
Cassat, Ch. 92
Cassat, Pierre 88
Cassayre-Forni Cellars 451
Cassegrain 491, 495
Cassemichère, Ch. de la
  162
Cassignol 212
Cassis 205
Casteja, Emile 51, 61, 64,
  86
Castéja, Mme. 67
Castéja, Philippe 86
Castéja, Pierre 81
Castéja-Borie family 66
Castel, Pierre 51
Castel Frères 51
Castel Oualou, Dom. de
  198
Le castelas, Dom. 224
Castelgiocondo 337
Castelgreve 337
La Castellada 326
De Castellane 184
Castellare di Castellina 337
Castellari Bergaglio 304
Casteller 313
Castell'in Villa 337
La Castellina 311
Castello, Tenuta 311
Castellucci 348
Castelluccio 329
Castelluccio, Duchi di 353
de Castelnau 185
Castelvero, Antica Contea
  di 304
Castéra, Ch. du 71
Castiglion del Bosco 341
Castillo de Perelada 383
Castillo de Perelada 383
Castlét, Cascina 304
Castries 217
Catalan 233
Catalans, Les Vignerons
  211
Catalonia 380-84
Catawba 486
Caudrina-Dogliotti 300
Causses, Dom. des 198
Causses & Veyran, Caves
  Coopératives 218
Caux 232
Cauze, Ch. du 90
Cava 368, 381
Cava Emery 432
Cavacchioli 329
Cavalchina-Piona 322

Cavalieri di Benedetti,
  Fattoria dei 348
Cavalleri 311
Cavalotto, Fratelli 304
Cave Coopérative Vinicole
  152
Càvit 314-15
Caymus Vineyards 451,
  477
Cayrou, Ch. de 224
Cayuga 486
Cazalis, Jean-Pierre 223
de Cazanove, Charles 185
Cazebonne, Ch. 76
Cazes, Jean-Michel 53, 64,
  66
Cazès Frères 210
Cecilia di Baone 322
Les Cèdres 196, 205
Cellatica 309
Cenalsa, Bodegas 373
Cenatiempo, F. & C. 351
Cennatoio 341
Cépage 74
Cephalonia 432
Cerasuolo 362
Cerasuolo di Vittoria 362
Ceratti, Umberto 360
Cerdon 157
Ceretto 300
Cerro, Fattoria del 341
Certan de May, Ch. 94
Cerveteri 349
  Coop. 351
Cervignano Coop 323
Cervino, Casal 352
Cesanese del Piglio 350
Cesanese del Piglio,
  Cantina Sociale 352
Cesanese di Affile 349-50
Cesanese di Olevano
  Romano 350
Cesare, Pio 300
Cesari 330
Cessenon 232
Cevisur, Bodegas 385
Chablis 107, 112-14
  Californian 444
La Chablisienne Coop. 114
Les Chaboissières 165
Chaboud, J.F. 195
Chai 74
  maître de 74
Le Chai des Bordes 51
Les Chaillots 119
Chainier, Pierre 170
Chaintré, Ch. de 166
Chaintré Coop. 148
Chaize, Ch. de 151
Chalk Hill 442, 451
Chalone 442
Chalone Vineyard 451
Chambers Rosewood 495
Chambert, Ch. de 224
Chambert-Marbuzet, Ch.
  66
Chambertin 115
Chambertin Clos de Bèze
  115
Chambolle-Musigny 107,
  115-16
Chambolle-Musigny, Ch.
  de 129
Chambourcin 486
Chamboureau, Ch. de 168
Chambovet & Fils 198
Chamfort, Louis 200
Chamirey, Ch. 146
Chamirey, Ch. de 145
Chamisal Vineyard 451
Champagne 177-86
  Californian 444
  Société Generale de 185
Champagnon, Dom. 152
Champclos, Caves de 153
Champet, Emile 195
Chanay 157
Chancellor 486
Chandesais, Emile 145

Chandon, Dom. 454, 496
Chandon de Briailles,
  Dom. 129
Chanfreau, Jean 57
Chanfreau family 57
Chanoine Frères 185
Chanson Père & Fils 129
Chantalouette, Ch. 96
Chante Cigale, Dom. 202
Chante-Flûte 147
Chante-Perdrix 195
Chante-Perdrix, Dom. 205
Chantebled 436
Chantegrive, Ch. de 76,
  103
Chanton, Oscar AG 412
Chanut Frères 153
Chanvières, Cave des 175
Chanzy, Daniel 145
Chanzy-Daniel, Dom. 145
Chapelle-Chambertin 115
La Chapelle-Lescours, Ch.
  90
Chapelle-Madelaine, Ch. 90
La Chapelle 196
Chapelot 112
Chapoutier, M. 195
Chappellet 450-1, 477
Chappellet, Donn 450-1
Chapuis, Maurice 130
Charal 484
Charavin, Maurice 198
Charbaut & Fils, A. 184
Charbono 444
Chardonnay 327, 430, 444,
  492, 522
Chardonnay Coop. 148
Chardonne 412
Charlemagne 119
Charmail, Ch. 68
Charmes, Ch. des 484
Charmes-Chambertin 115
Charnay-Les-Mâcon Coop.
  148
Charrère, Antoine et Fils
  306
Charron, Ch. 100
Chartron & Trebuchet 130
Charvet, Fernand 152
Chassagne-Montrachet
  107, 124, 125
Chasse-Spleen, Ch. 57
Chasselas 188
Chasseloir, Ch. de 162
Château-Chalon 154
  Coop. 156
Châteaumeillant 159
Châteauneuf-de-Gadagne
  197
Châteauneuf-du-Pape 193,
  201-5
Châteauneuf-du-Pape,
  Caves Reflets de 204
Chatel 383
Chatelain, Jean-Claude 175
Chateldon 383
Le Chatelet, Ch. 87
Chatenay, Samuel 415
Chatenoy, Dom. de 176
Châtillon en Diois 201
Chatn, Jean 206
Chaume de Talvat 112
Les Chaumes, Ch. 100
De Chaunac 484, 486
Chautagne 157
  Coop. 157
Chauvenet 141
Chauvenet, F. 130
Chauvin, Ch. 87
Chave, J.L. 195
Chaves, Bodegas 373
Chavet, Georges 176
Le Chay, Ch. 92
Chayne, Ch. du 222
Chef de culture 74
Cheilly-Les-Maranges 126
Chelois 486
Chemical regulators and
  sprays 16
Chénas 151-2
Chénas, Cave du Ch. de
  152-3

Chénas, Ch. de 152
Chéné, Jean-Pierre 166
Chêne-Vieux, Ch. 92
Chenin Blanc 214, 444, 492, 522
Chenonceau, Ch. de 170
Cheravin, Robert 200
Cherchi, Giovanni 367
Chéreau-Carré 162, 164
Cheret-Pitres, Ch. 76
Cheron, Denis 198, 199
Cheste 385
Cheval Blanc, Ch. 84
Cheval Quancard 51
Chevalier, Dom. de 73-4
Chevalier d'Ars-Arcins, Ch. 70
Chevalier de Malle 81
Chevalier Fils 153
Le Chevalier de Stérimbourg 196
Cheverny 159
Chevillard, R. 133
Chevillon, Georges and Michel 130
Chevillon, Robert 130
Chevillot 130
Chevre, Ch., Winery 451
Cheysson, Dom. Emile 152
Chianti 316, 331-3
Californian 444
Chianti Classico 333
Chianti Colli Aretini 333
Chianti Colli Fiorentini 333
Chianti Colli Pisane 333
Chianti Colli Senesi 333
Chianti Geografico, Agricoltori del 338
Chianti Montalbano 333
Chianti Putto 333
Chianti Rufina 333
Le Chiantigiane 329, 341
La Chiara 304
Chiaretto 298
Chiarli-1860 329
Chiarlo, Michele (Duca d'Asti) 300
Chicama Vineyards 486
Chicane, Ch. 76
Chichet, Mas 210
Chiddo Vini 359
Le Chiesa di Santa Restituta 341
Chigé, Jean 228
Chigi Saracini 341
Chignin 157
Chignin-Bergeron 157
Chiles Valley 442
Chiltern Valley Wines 525
Chinchon-La-Bataille, Ch. 99
Chinon 159, 163, 169
Chinook 481
Chionetti, Quinto & Figlio 304
La Chiripada Winery 488
Chiroubles 152
La Chiusa, Tenuta 341
Chivite, Bodegas Julián 372
Choppin, Mlle. Françoise-Guigne 139
Chorey-Les-Beaune 122
Christian Brothers Winery 452
Christoffel, Jos. Jr. 247
Churchills 406
Chusclan 199
Chusclan Coop. 200
Ciacca Piccolomini d'Aragona 341
Cienega Valley 442
Cigales 371
Cigalière 203
Cigliuti, Fratelli 304
Cilento 353
Cilli Altotiberini 344
Cilurzo & Piconi 452
Cinqueterre 307
Cinsaut 201, 205, 220, 434, 492

Cintra 406
Cinzano, Francesco 300
Ciró 359
Cisa Asinara dei Marchesi di Gresy, Tenute 300
Cissac, Ch. 68
Citran Ch. 68
CIV (Emiglia-Romagna) 329
Civrac, Ch. de 100
Clair, Bruno 130
Clair-Dau, Dom. 130
de Clairefont, Ch. 54
Clairette 201, 214, 219
Clairette de Die 201
Coop. 201
La Clairette d'Aspiran 219
Clape, Auguste 195
La Clape 216-7
Clare 490-91
Clare, Ch. la 71
Claret 54
Clarettes, Ch. 207
Clarifying 35
Clarke, Ch. 57
Clarksburg 442
Classico 298
Clastron, Dom. de 207
Clauzel, Bertrand 56
Clauzet, Ch. 67
Clavelin, Hubert 156
Clavien, Gérald 412
Clavien, Michel 413
Clear Lake 442
Clemens, Villa 352
Cléray, Ch. du 164
Clerc-Milon, Ch. 61
Clerget, Dom. Y. 130
Clerget, Georges 130
Clerget, Raoul 130
Clerico 300
Cles, Barone de 316
Clevner of Klevner 188
Climate 14-15
Climens, Ch. 78
Clinet, Ch. 94
Clinia, Villa 341
Clocher, Ch. du 94
Cloquet, Ch. 97
Clos de l'Abbaye 166
Clos de l'Aiglerie 166
Clos de l'Arlot 127
Clos du Batuts 224
Clos Baudoin 172
Clos des Belles Mères 167
Clos de la Bergerie 167
Clos Bernarde 206
Clos la Bernarde 206
Clos du Bois 452
Le Clos du Bourg 171
Clos Cabrière 515
Clos Capitoro 220
Clos du Chapeau 127
Clos du Chêne Marchand 174
Clos du Chêne Vert 171
Clos de la Dioterie 171
Le Clos du Zahnacker 192
Clos de l'Echo 170
Clos des Epeneaux, Dom. du 132
Clos d'Ervocs 174
Clos des Forêts St Georges 127
Clos Fourtet 85
Clos Gaensbroennel 192
Clos de Galon 172
Clos de Gamot 224
Clos de la Gaucherie 170
Clos Haut-Peyraguey, Ch. 78
Clos des Jacobins, Ch. 88
Clos des Lambrays 115
Les Clos 112
Clos des Lutinières 172
Clos Maison Rouge 99
Clos du Marquis 59
Clos Mazeyres 97
Clos des Menuts 90
Clos Mireille 206
Clos du Monastère 76
Clos des Mulonnières 166

Clos Nicrosi 220
Clos de l'Olive 170
Clos des Ontinières 166
Clos de L'Oratoire 88
Clos des Orfeuilles 164
Clos des Papes 203
Clos du Papillon 166
Clos du Paradis Terrestre 166
Clos Pegase 452
Clos de la Poussie 174
Clos des Quarterons 172
Clos de la Reine Blanche 174
Clos René 96
Clos Renon, Ch. du 77
Clos de la Roche 115
Clos du Roi, Dom. du 203
Clos du Roy 82, 94, 174
Clos St-Denis 115
Clos St-Marc 129
Clos St-Michel, Dom. du 203
Clos St-Urbain 192
Clos de Ste-Catherine 166
Clos Ste-Magdelaine 208
Clos de Tart 115
Clos du Val Wine Co. 452, 477
Clos de Vougeot 116
Closel, Dom. du 166
Closerie du Grand-Poujeaux, Ch. La 57
Clotte, Ch. de 99
La Clotte, Ch. 87
Clouds, Les 145
Cloudy Bay 509
Cloverdale 442
La Clusière, Ch. 87
Cocci Grifoni 348
Coche-Dury, Jean-François 130
Cockburn 403
Cocumont, Cave Coopérative Intercommunale de 229
Codax, Martin 373
Codornio 383
Coffinet, Fernand 130
Coing de St-Fiacre, Ch. du 162
Col d'Orcia 300, 338
Colacicchi, Cantina 351
Colares 398
Colas Nouet, Ch. 93
De Colbert 217
Cold stabilization 37, 467
Coldstream Hills 496
Cole Ranch 442
Collage 74
Collard Brothers 509-10
Collavini 325
Colle dei Bardellini 308
Colle del Calvario 309, 311
Colle dei Cipressi 322
Colle Manora 304
Colle Picchioni 350-51
Colle del Sole-Polidori 346
Collefiorito 352
Collery 185
Collet, Jean 114
Collezione di Càvit 315
Colli Albani 349-50
Cantina Sociale 351
Colli Amerini 344
Cantina 344
Colli Berici 318
Cantina dei 322
Colli Bolognesi 327
Colli Bolognesi – Monte San Pietro-Castelli Medioevali 328
Colli di Bolzano 313
Colli di Catone 351
Colli del Cavaliere, Cantina Sociale 351
Colli Euganei 318-19
Colli Euganei, Cantina Sociale Cooperative dei 322
Colli Lanuvini 350
Colli di Luni 307

Colli al Matrichese-Poderi Emilio Constanti 338
Colli Mattani 344
Colli Morenici Mantovani del Garda 309
Colli Orientali del Friuli 323-4
Colli di Parma 328
Colli Perugini 344
Colli Piacentini 303, 328
Colli Tortonesi 296
Colli del Trasimeno 344
Colli di Tuscolo 352
Colline Lucchesi 333
Le Colline (Monsecco) 300
Collines de la Moure 232
Collines Rhodaniennes 231
Collio 324
Collio e dell'Isonzo, Cantina Produttori del 326
Collio Goriziano 324
Collioure 211
Collonge, Paul 152
Colobel 486
Colognole 341
Il Colombaio 312
Colombier Monpelou, Ch. 65
La Colombiera 308
Colombini 330
La Colonica 341
Colonnara 348
Colosi, Cantina 364
Colterenzio, Catina Sociale 316
Coltiva-Gruppo Italiano Vini 329
Colué 304
Columbia 481
Columbia Crest Winery 481
Columbia Valley 482
Combastet 217
Comelli, G.B. 326
Comigne, Ch. de 212
Cominciioli 311
La Commanderie, Ch. (Lalande-de-Pomerol) 98
La Commanderie, Ch. (Pomerol) 97
Commanderie, Cuvee de la 60
Commanderie de Peyrassol 206
Commanderie du Bontemps de Médoc et des Graves 60
Compagnie Française des Grands Vins 185
Comptoir des Vins du Maroc 436
Comptoir Vinicole de Champagne 185
Conca de Barberá 381
Concannon Vineyard 453
Concha y Toro 520-1
Concord 486
Condado, Bodegas Cooperativa Vinicola del 387
Condado de Huelva 368
Condamine, Cave de la 219
Condamine Bertrand, Ch. de la 218
Condomois 233
Condorcet, Dom. 204
Condrieu 194
Conegliano 318
Congress Springs Vineyards 453
Coninck, J. de 52
Conn Creek 453
Conne, Jean-Michel 414
Connecticut 486
Connesson family 207
Connétable Talbot 59
Conqueror 394
La Conseillante, Ch. 94
Consejos Reguladores 368, 390

Consentino Wine Co. 453
Consortium Vinicole de Bordeaux et de Gironde 51
Consorzio Romagnolo Vini Tipici 329
Consorzio Vitivinicolo Perugia (Co. Vi. P.) 346
Constant, Dom. 222
Constantia 513-4
Conterno, Aldo 300
Conterno, Giacoma 300
Conterno-Fantino 304
Contessa Matile 311
Conti, Pul 496
Conti Royale 454
Conti Sertoli Salis 311
Contini, Attilio 367
Contra Costa 442
Contratto, Giuseppe 300
Contucci 341
Conventi, Borgo 326
Cook, R. & J. 453
Cooks McWilliams 500, 510
Coonawarra 490-91, 500
Coopers Creek 510
Coos, Fratelli 326
Copa Remondo 379
Copertino 356
Cantina Sociale di 359
Coppo 300
Coppola, Niccolò 359
Coquilles, Ch. 76
Cora 304
Corbans Wines 510
Corbett Canyon Vineyards 453
"La Corbiere Bizanetoise", Cave Coopérative 213
Corbières 209, 212-13
Vins de Pays 233
Corbin, Ch. 87, 92
Corbin-Michotte, Ch. 87
Cordambles, Blanchard de 128
Cordier 66
Cordier, Etab. 51, 58, 59, 88, 174
Ch. Clos des Jacobins 88
Cordier, Jean 67
Cordier, Robert & Fils 176
Cordier family 78
Cordonnier, François 57
Cori 350
Coria, Giuseppe 363
Coriole 496
Cormeil-Figeac, Ch. 90
Cormerais Cheneau, Ch. de la 165
Cornacchia, Barone 353
Cornaiano, Catina Sociale 316
Cornaleto 311
Cornarea 300, 304
Cornas 194
Corneilla, Ch. de 210
Cornell 316
Il Corno, Fattoria 342
Coron Père & Fils 130
Corovin (Consorzio Romagnolo Vini Tipici) 329
Corral 378
Corral, Bodegas 378
Corre, Antonine 88
Les Correziens 91
Corsica 220
Cortese, Giuseppe 304
Cortese dell'Alto Monferrato 296
Cortese di Gavi 297
Corvo 362
Cos d'Estournel, Ch. 65
Cos Labory, Ch. 65-6
Cossart Gordon 408
Costa Brava 380
Costaripa 311
Costers del Segre 368, 380
Costieres de Nimes 219
Les Costos Roussos 216
Cot 227

Cotat, Francis & Paul 174
Côte d'Ambonnay 186
Côte de Beaune 122
Côte de Beaune-Villages 119, 126
Côte des Blancs 186
Côte Blonde 193
Côte de Bréchain 112
Côte de Brouilly 152
Côte Brune 193
Côte Chalonnaise 144-6
Côte de Cuissy 112
Côte d'Epernay 186
Côte de Fontenay 112
Côte de Jouan 112
La Cote 412
Côte de Léchet 112
Côte de Nuits-Villages 118
Côte d'Or 107, 114-43
Côte des Près-Girots 112
Côte Puyblanquet, Ch. 90
Côte Roannaise 160
Côte Rôtie 193-4
Côte de Savant 112
Côte de Vertus 186
Coteaux d'Aix-en-Provence 205-6
Coteaux d'Ancenis 159
Coteaux de l'Ardèche 231
Coteaux de l'Aubance 159
Coteaux des Baux-en-Provence 206
Coteaux de Bessiles 232
Coteaux du Briel 164
Coteaux de la Cabrerisse 232-3
Les Coteaux de Cabrières, Cave Coopérative 217
Coteaux de Carthage 435
Les Coteaux des Castellas, Cave Coopérative 217
Les Couteaux de Cebazan 218
Coteaux Cévenols 231
Coteaux de Cèze 231
Coteaux Champenois 179
Coteaux Charitois 234
Coteaux du Cher et de l'Arnon 234
Coteaux de la Cité de Carcassonne 233
Coteaux Coiffy 234
Coteaux du Creissan 218
Coteaux d'Enserune 232
Coteaux des Fenouillèdes 233
Coteaux Flaviens 231
Coteaux de Fontcaude 232
Coteaux du Giennois 160
Coteaux de Glanes 234
Coteaux du Grésivaudan 234
Coteaux du Haut Minervois 216
Coteaux de Languedoc 216-18
Coteaux du Languedoc 209
Coteaux de Laurens 232
Coteaux du Layon Chaume 160
Coteaux du Layon 160, 163, 165
Coteaux du Lézignanais 233
Coteaux du Libron 232
Coteaux du Littoral Audois 232
Coteaux du Loir 160
Coteaux de la Loire 161
Coteaux de Mascara 436
Les Coteaux de Minervois, Caves Coopératives 215
Coteaux de Miramont 233
Les Coteaux de Montferrand, Caves Coopératives 217
Coteaux de Murviel 232
Coteaux de Narbonne 233
Coteaux de Peyriac 233
Coteaux du Pont du Gard 231

Les Coteaux de Pouzola Minervois, Caves Coopératives 215
Coteaux du Quercy 234
Les Coteaux du Rieu Berlou 218
Coteaux de St-Drezery, Cave Coopérative de les 218
Coteaux du Salagou 232
Coteaux du Salavès 231
Coteaux de Saumur 160
Les Coteaux de St-Christol, Cave Coopérative 218
Les Coteaux de St-Gely-du-Fesc 217
Coteaux de Termènes 233
Coteaux et Terrassès de Montauban 234
Coteaux de Tlemcen 436
Coteaux des Travers, Dom. des 200
Coteaux d'Utique 435
Les Coteaux de Valflaunes 217
Coteaux Varois 208, 231
Coteaux du Vendômois 161
Coteaux de Verargues 217
Coteaux du Zaccar 436
Côtes d'Auvergne 159
Côtes Bernateau, Ch. 90
Côte de Blaye 46
Côtes-de-Bordeaux-St-Macaire 103
Côte de Bourg 46, 99-100
Côtes du Brian 232
Côtes du Brulhois 233
Côtes Brun et Blonde 196
Côtes de Buzet, Caves Reunis 226
Côtes Castillon 46
Côtes de Castillon 99
Côtes Catalanes 233
Côtes du Ceressou 232
Côtes de Duras 228
Côtes du Forez 159-60, 176
Côtes de Francs 46, 99
Côtes du Fronton 229
Les Côtes du Fronton, Cave Coopératives 229
Côtes du Gascogne 233
Côtes du Jura Coop. 156
Côtes de Lastours 233
Côtes de la Malepère 233
Côtes du Marmandais 229
Côtes du Marmandais, Société Coopérative Vinicole des 229
Côtes de Meliton 433
Côtes de Montravel 222
Côtes de la Mouleyre, Ch. 90
Les Côtes d'Olt 224
Côtes de Pérignan 233
Côtes de Prouille 233
Côtes de Provence 205
Côtes du Rhône Patriciens 204
Côtes du Rhône-Villages 199
Côtes du Tarn 234
Côtes de Thau 232
Côtes de Thongue 232
Côtes de Vaubarousse 112
Côtes Vermeilles 233
Côtes du Vidourle 231
Cotnari 429
El Coto, Bodegas 378
Coucy, Ch. 92
Coufran, Ch. 68
Couhins Inra Ch. 74
Couhins-Lurton, Ch. 74
Coulbois, Gérard 175
Coulée de Serrant 167
La Coulée de Serrant 165
Coullac, Ch. 102
Coulon, Paul 202
Couly, Dom. Rêne 170
Couly-Dutheil 170
Cour de Pierre, Les

Vignobles de la 168
Cour Pavillon, La 52
Courbon, Ch. de 76
Coteaux du Quercy 234
Courbu 227
Courcel, Dom. de 131
Cournoise 201
Coursodon, Pierre 195
Court-Les-Mûtes, Ch. 222
Courtakis, D. 433
Courteillac, Ch. 102
La Courtoise Coop. 200
Coustolle, Ch. 99
Coutelin-Merville, Ch. 66
Coutet, Ch. 78
Coutras 103
Couvent d'Alzipratu 220
Couvent-des-Jacobins, Ch. 87
Couvent des Templiers, Ch. 90
Covey Run 481
Coy, Dom. de 82
Crabitey, Ch. 76
Craigmoor 496
Cream sherry 390
La Crema 463
Crémant 132, 179
Crémant de Bourgogne 132-3, 147
Crémant de Limoux 214
Crémant de Loire 160
Crémat, Ch. de 206
Crepy 103
Cresta Blanca 453
Crete 432
Crianza de Castilla la Vieja, Bodegas de 373
Crillon 522
Criots-Bâtard-Montrachet 125
Croatia 428-9
Crochet, Lucien 174
Le Crock, Ch. 66
Croft & Co. 403-4
Croft Jerez 391
Croix, Dom. de la 165, 206
Croix de Bertinat, Ch. 90
La Croix, Ch. 94
La Croix du Casse, Ch. 97
La Croix de Gay, Ch. 95
La Croix de Millorit, Ch. 100
La Croix St André, Ch. 98
Croix-St-Georges, Ch. 94
La Croix-Toulifaut 94
La Croix St André, Ch. 98
Croix-St-Marc 79
Cruet 157, 158
Crus Bourgeois 47-8
Les Crus Cazedarnais 218
Les Crus de Montouliers" 215
Les Crus Faugères, Caves Coopératives 218
Crustacés 164, 189
Cruzeau, Ch. de 76
Crystal 189
CS del Cilento 355
Cubzac 103
Cucamonga 442
Cucugnan 233

Cudia 365
La Cuesta 391
Cugat, Ch. de 102
Culbertson, John, Winery 453
Cullen's 496
Cully 412
Cune Lanceros 376
Curbastro, Ricci 312
Curé-Bon-La-Madeleine, Ch. 87
Curebourse, Dom. de 53
Cusona, Fattoria di 338
Cuvaison Vineyard 453
Cuve 74
Cuvée les Amours 190
Cuvée Cabanon 217
Cuvée de Chasseur 207
Cuvée des Comtes d'Equisheim 189
Cuvée des Ecaillers 189
Cuvée des Monticaud 200
Cuvée le Président 436
Cuvée de Prestige 179
Cuvée St-Eloi 192
Cuvées des Felibres 203
Cuvelier & Fils 66
Cuvelier family 59
Cuvillo y Cia 393
CVBG (Consortium Vinicole de Bordeaux et de Gironde) 51
Cviček 428
CVNE (Compañía Vinícola del Norte de España) 376
Cynthiana 486
Cypress Lane 463

D
Dageneau, Didier 175
Dagueneau, Serge 175
Daheuiller, Claude 166
Dahlem, Dr., Erben 273
Dahra 436
Dalem, Ch. 99
Dalmatia 428-9
Dalwood 502
Dambach-La-Ville Coop. 192
Dame, Mas de la 206
La Dame Blanche, Ch. 68
Dame Noir 223
La Dame de Montrose 66
Damoy, Dom. Pierre 131
Daniel, John, Society 453
Danieli, Marina 326
Dão 397
Daphnes 432
Dar Bel Amri 436
Dard, Maurice 128
Dardagny 412
Darnat, Dom. 131, 133
Darricarrère, Jacques 57
Darroze, M. 152
Dassault, Ch. 87
Daubhaus 255
Daudet-Corcelle, Dom. 131
Daumas Gassac, Mas de 218
La Dauphine, Ch. de 99
Dauvissat, René and Vincent 113
Dauzac, Ch. 54
David & Foillard 153
Dayrem-Valentin, Ch. 55
Daysse, Dom. de la 199
De Bortoli Wines 496
De Schepper-de-Moor family 55
De Smet, Jean-Pierre 127
De Vita, Fratelli 364
Dealul Mare 429
Debró 426
Deer Park Winery 453
Defond, Marcel 185
Dehlinger Winery 453
Deidesheim 276
Deidesheim, Winzerverein 279

Deinhard, Dr. 277
Deinhard, Gutsverwaltung 247
Deinhard, Weingut des Hauses see Wegeler-Deinhard
Deinhard & Co. 239, 257
Dejean, Michèle 78
Del produttore all'origine 298
Delachanal, Ch. 152
Delaforce 404
Delaforce Sons & Co. 404
Delagrange-Bachelet, Dom. 131
Delaire Vineyards 515
Delalex, Claude 158
Delamotte Père & Fils 185
Delaporte, Vincent 175
Delarze, Henri 414
Delas Frères 195
Delatite 496
Delaware grape 486
Delbeck, Pascal 84
Delbez 217
Delclaud, Daniel 218
Delea, Angelo 416
Delegat's 510
Deletang Père et Fils 170
Delfour, Colette 225
Delgado Zuleta SA 393
Delgoulet, Marc 224
Delheim 515
Deligny, Jean 114
Della Staffa 311
Delmas, Jean-Bernard 73
DeLoach Vineyards 453
Delon, G. 59
Delon, Michel 58
Delorme, Jean-François 145
Delorme-Meulien, Caves 133
Delphi 432
Delvin Wine Cellars 454
Dembies Lane Estate 525
Demoiselles, Ch. des 99
DeMoor Winery 453
Demont, Jean Ernest 152
Demoulin, François 200
Denay, Hubert 170
Denmark Cellars 497
Denominaciones de Origen 368
Denominazione di Origine (DOC) 293
Denominazione di Origine Garantita (DOCG) 294
Derain, Michel 145
Dervieux-Thaise, Albert 195, 197
Descaves, Mme Jean 51
Deschamps, Louis 128
Desmeure Père & Fils 195
Desmirail, Ch. 54
Desmoulins, A and Co. 185
Despagne family 87
Despujol, François 96
Despujols, Jean 81
Dessilani, Luigi & Figlio 304
Desvignes, Louis 152
Deutelsberg 255
Deutsch-Ordens-Schlosskellerei 421
Deutscher Sekt 257
Deutscher Sekt bA 257
Deutscher Tafelwein 236
Deutsches Weintor, Gebiets-Winzergenossenschaft 278
Deutz 178, 453-4
Devoy, Dom. du 198
Deybach, Eugène 192
Deydier, Jean 203
Dézaley 174
Dezat, André 174
Dezat, Pierre & Alain 175
Dezize-Les-Maranges 126
Diabetiker geeignet 237

Diabetiker-wein 240
Diamond Creek 441
Diamond Creek Vineyards 454, 477
Diamond Valley 496
Diefenhardt, Weingut 262
Diel auf Burg Layen 266
Dienheim 270
Dievole 342
Diez de Morales, Celstino 391
Diez-Merito 391
Diffonty, Félicien 203
Diffonty, Remy 205
Dikman 434
Dillon, Ch. 68
Dillon, Dom. Clarence 73, 74, 75, 76
Dimiat 430
Dingač 429
Dinstlgut Loiben, Winzergenossenschaft 423
les Dionnières 195
Dissertori-Plattenhof, Anton 316
Distante Vini 359
Doat, Robert 150
Dr. Fischer, Weingut 247
Doctor vineyard 251, 252
Dr. Pest, Cuvée 143
Doisy-Daëne, Ch. 79
Doisy-Daëne-St-Martin, Ch. 79
Doisy-Dubroca, Ch. 81
Doisy-Védrines, Ch. 81
Dolce 298
Dolceacqua 307, 308
Dolcetto d'Acqui 296
Dolcetto d'Alba 296
Dolcetto d'Asti 296
Dolcetto di Diano d'Alba 297
Dolcetto di Dogliani 297
Dolcetto delle Langhe Monregalesi 297
Dolcetto di Ovada 297
Dôle 412
Dolle, Peter 422
Doluca, Villa 434
Dom Pérignon 181
Dombilck Grosselage 271
Domecq, Bodegas 376
Domecq, Industrias Vinicolas 523
Domecq, Pedro 391
Domergue family 95
Dominio de la Plana 378
Dominique, Ch. La 87
Dominode 140
Domklausenhof, Weingut 248
Doms, Ch. de 76
Don Alfonzo Bianco 354
Dona, Mas de la 210
Donati 316
Donati, Estb. 158
Donatien-Bahuaud & Cie 162
Donatsch, Familie 416
Donauland 418
Donauland-Carnuntum 419
Donna Maria Vineyards see Chalk Hill
Donnafugata 363
Donnaz, Caves Cooperative 306
Dönnhof, Hermann 266
Donnici 359
Dopff & Irion 189
Dopff "Au Moulin" 189
Doradillo 492
Doré, Noël 185
Dorgali, Cantina Sociale di 367
Doria 311
Dorices, Dom. des 162
Dorigati, Fratelli 316
Dorigo, Girolamo 326
Dorin 412
Dorsheim 266

Doudet-Naudin, Maison 131
Douhairet, Mlle. Armande 139
Doukkala 436
Douro 395, 397, 401-2
Dourthe family 57
Dourthe-Kressmann 67
Dousson, Robert 67
Dow's Port 405
Les Doyennes 165
Doz y Cia 393
Drăgăsani 429
Drago, Cascine 304
Drapier, Charles 128
Drathen, Ewald Theod 247
Dri, Giovanni 326
Driant, Emile 185
Driant, Robert 185
Drivinal, Union Vinicole 192
Droin, Jean-Paul 113
Dromana Estate 497
Drôme 199
Drouard, Joseph 163
Drouhin, Dom. 479
Drouhin, Maison Joseph 113, 131
Drouhin, Robert 131, 148
Dry Creek Valley 440, 442
Dry Creek Vineyard 454
Dry Sack 393
Dubini-Locatelli 346
Duboeuf, Georges 148, 153
Dubois, Michel 185
Dubois, Robert, & Fils 131
Dubois-Challon, Mme. J. 83, 85
Dubos 51
Duboseq, H. & Fils 66
Dubos, Philippe 51
Dubost, Yvon 95
Dubourdieu, Pierre 79
Dubreuil-Fontaine, P. Père & Fils, Dom. 131
Ducellier, Jean-Michel 67
Duchroth 264
Duckhorn Vineyards 454
Duclot 51
Ducru-Beaucaillou, Ch. 58
Ducs, Le Cellier des 163
Dueil 185
Le Due Terre 326
Duff Gordon 391
Dufouleur Frères 131
Dugast, R.E. 163
Duhart-Milon-Rothschild, Ch. 61
Duhr, Franz, Nachf. 251
Dujac, Dom. 131-2
Dulac, Ch. 58
Dulce apagado 390
Dulce de almibar 390
Dulce pasta 390
Dulong, J.M. 51
Dulong Frères & Fils 51
Dulos, Mme 56
Dumazet, Pierre 195
Dumeaux & Fils 225
Dunn Vineyards 454, 477
Dünweg, Otto 252
Dupin, Raymond 61
Duplessis, Ch. 57
Duplessis-Fabre, Ch. 57
Dupraz, Pierre 414
Duraf 492
Durand Laplaigne, Ch. 92
Durantou, Mme. G. 95
Duras 225
Duras, Société Coopérative Agricole de 228
Durban 213
Durban, Dom. 198
Durbanville 514
Duret, Cuvee 140
Durfort-Vivens, Ch. 54
Durieu de Lacarelle 150
Durney Vineyard 454
Durou & Fils 224

Durrbach, Eloi 207
Dutchess 486
Dutertre Père & Fils 170
Dutraive, Philippe 151
Dutruch Grand Poujeaux, Ch. 57
Duval-Leroy 185
Duxoup Wine Works 454

E
East India sherry 390
East Side Winery 454
Echarderie, Ch. de la 167
Echézeaux 116
Echu, Dom. de l' 163
Edelbeerenauslese 236
Edelfäule 241
Edmeades Inc. 454-5
Edna Valley 442
Edna Valley Vineyard 455
Eger 426
Eglantière, Dom. de l' 113
Eglise, Dom. de l' 97
L'Eglise-Clinet, Ch. 95
L'Eglise, Ch. 95
Egretier 217
Eguisheim Coop. 192
Eichberg 188
Eikendal 515-16
Eilandia 514
Einaudi, Luigi 301
Einzellage 236-7, 241
Einzellagen 238
Eisacktaler 314
Eisacktaler Kellereignossenschaft 317
Eisenberg 418
Eiswein 236, 237, 241, 421
Eitelsbach 243
El Dorado 442
Elba 333
Elbling 268
Elfenhof, Weingut 419
Elgee Park 497
Eliceo, Bosco 327
Eliniaux, Roland 185
Elk Cove Vineyards 479
Ellendale Vineyards 480
Elne Coop 211
Eltville 256, 258
Elvira 486
Elzenbaum, von 316
Embrès & Castelmaure 213
Emerald Riesling 444
Emilia-Romagna 327-31
Emir 434
Encépagement 74
Las Encinas 521
Enclave des Papes 201
Enclave des Papes, Union des Vignerons de l' 201
Enclos de Moncabon 54
L' Enclos, Ch. 95
Endrizzi, Fratelli 316
Engel, Dom. René 132
England 524-6
Englemann, Karl Fr. 262
Engrais 74
Enkirch 246
Eno-Friulia-Puiatti 325
Enocarboj, Cantina Sociale 364-5
Enotria 352
Cooperativa 352
Produttori Agricoli Associati 360
Entre-Deux-Mers 46, 101-2
Epesses 412
Epiré, Ch. d' 166
Episcopio-Pasquale Vuilleumier, Cantine 355
Equipe 5 317
Equipe Trentina Spumanti 317
Eral 379
Erbach 256
Erbaluce di Caluso 297
Erden 246
Eredi, Rudolf Carli 317
Eredi Virginia Ferrero 304

Erntebringer 255
Errázuiriz-Panquehue, Viña 521
Erste Österreiche Weingüter-Kooperation 421
L'Escadre, Ch. 100
Eschenauer, Louis 51, 52
Escherndorfer Lump 281
Eser, August 262
Esk Valley 510
Esmeralda 522
Esparrou, Ch. de l' 210
L'Espiègle 196
Espinglet, Ch. de l' 101
Est! Est!! Est!!! di Montefiascone 350
L'Estable 217
Estager, Barnard 66
Estager, Jean-Pierre 94
Estancia 458
Esterhazy'sche Schlossekelerei 419
Estola 385
Estrella River Winery see Meridian Vineyards
Etang des Colombes, Ch. 212
Etko/Haggipavlu 434
Etna 359
L'Etoile Coop. 156
Etschataler 314
Euboea 432
Euganean hills 318
Eugénie, Dom. 224
L'Evangile, Ch. 95
Evans & Tate 497
Evans Family 497
Evensen Vineyards & Winery 455
Eventail de Vignerons Producteurs 154
Ewig Leben Grosslage 281
Extra fino sherry 390
Eymery, Pierre 222
Eyrie Vineyards 479
Ezerjó 424

F
Faber Sektkellerie Faber 257
Fabre, Vignoble 203
Fabrini, Attilio 348
Le Fagé, Ch. 222
La Fagnouse, Ch. 90
Fagon, Cuvée 140
Fairview 516
Faiveley, François 132
Faiveley, Guy 132
Faiveley, Maison J. 132
Falchini-Il Casale, Ricardo 338
Falerio dei Colli Ascolani 347
Falerno 350
Falerno del Massico 353
Falernum 350
Falesco 352
Faleyrens, Ch. de 90
Falfas, Ch. 100
Fall Creek Vineyards 488
Faller, Théo 189-90
Fanetti 352
Fanti, Giuseppe 316
Fantinel 326
Fantroussière, Dom. de 207
Far Niente Winery 455
Fara 297
Fara Novarese, Cantina Sociale di 304
Farchione, Guardiani 353
Farfelu 487
Fargues, Ch. de 82
Farnet, Dom. 206
Farnet, Gabriel 206
Farneta, Tenuta di 342
Faro 362
Faros 429
Fassati 342
Fattoria Casalino 325

Fattoria Paradiso 329
Faucompret, Mme. Suzanne de 215
Faugères 216, 217
Faugeres, Ch. 99
Faurie-de-Souchard, Ch. 87
Favin, André 56
Favonio Attilio Simonini 359
Favorita 297
Faxi-Battaglia "Titulus" 348
Fay, Sando 311
Fayat, Clément 87
Fayau, Ch. 101
Faye 154
Fayolle, Jules & ses Fils 195
Féchy 412
Fécos 214
Fedrigotti-Foianeghe, Conti Bossi 315
Feiler-Artinger, Weingut 422
Feilluns Coop. 211
Feine 238
Feinste Auslese 238
Feipel-Staar 268
Felines Minervois 216
Felluga, Livio 325
Felluga-Russiz, Marco, Superiore 325
Fenals, Dom. les 212
Fenestra Winery 455
Fenton Acres Winery see Rochioli, J. 455
Féraud, Dom. des 206
Ferbos, Ch. de 103
Feriani, Ch. 435
Fernandez, Bodegas Alejandro 372
Fernandez, Jean-Michel 85
Fernandez, Manuel 391
Fernhill, Thomas, Estate 497
Feronia, Cantina Sociale Cooperativa 352
Ferrand, Ch. 90, 97
Ferrande, Ch. 76
Ferrando, Luigi 301
Ferrari (Alto Adige) 315
Ferrari (Veneto) 322
Ferrari-Carano 455
Ferraton & Fils, Dom. 195
Ferraud, Pierre 153
Ferre, Bodegas José L. 381
Ferreira, A.A. 399, 404
Ferrer, Gloria 455
Ferret, Christian 215
Ferrière, Ch. 54
Ferris, Bodegas Jésus 392
Ferro-Lazzarini, Villa dal 322
Ferrucci, Stephano 330
Ferservadou 225
Fert, Marcel 157
Ferté, Jacques de la 113
Fesles, Ch. de 167
Fetzer Vineyards 455-6
Feuerberg Grosslage 275
Feuerheerd Bros. & Co. 400, 406
Fèvre, William 113
Février, Marie-France 87
Feytit, Etab. Jean-René 91
Feytit-Clinet, Ch. 95
Fiano di Avellino 353-4
Fichard 158
Fici, Fratelli 365
Ficklin Vineyards 456
Fiddletown 442
Fiefs Vendéens 159, 234
La Fiefs-de-Lagrange 58
Field Stone Winery 456
Field-grafting 467
Fieuzal, Ch. de 74
Figeac, Ch. 85
Figeat, Paul 175
Filhot, Ch. 81
Le Filigare 342
Filippi 113

Filliatreau, Paul 167
Filsinger Vineyards & Winery 456
Filtration 40
Filzen 243
Finca Raimat, Bodegas 380
Fines Roches, Ch. des 203
Finger Lakes 483
Fini 330
Fining 39
Finkenauer, Carl 266
Fino sherry 389, 390
Fino viejo (vijissimo) 390
Fino-amontillado 390
La Fiole du Pape 202
Fiorano 350, 351
Fiore, Umberto 304
Fiorina, Franco 304-5
La Fiorita 346
Firestone Vineyard 456-7
Fischer, J., Erben 262
Fisher Vineyards 457
Fitou 212, 213
Fitz-Ritter, K. 277
Fiumi Petrangeli, Conti 346
Five Roses 356
Fixin 115
Flagey-Echézeaux 116
Flambeau d'Alsace 190
Fleur d'Alsace 190
La Fleur Gazin, Ch. 95
La Fleur Milon, Ch. 65
La Fleur-Pétrus, Ch. 95
Fleurance, B. & Fils 163
Fleurie 152
Fleurie, Ch. de 152
La Fleur, Ch. 90
Fleurot-Larose, Dom. 132
Flichman 522
Flonheim 270
Flora 444
Flora Springs Wine Co. 457
Floridène, Clos 76
Florimond-La-Brède, Dom. de 100
Florio 300, 363
Fognano-Talosa, Fattoria di 342
Foillard, M. 152
Fojanini, Fondazione 311
Folie a Deux 457
Folonari 311-12
Folonari, Ambrogio 294
Fombrauge, Ch. 90
Foncheureau, Ch. 102
Fongrave, Dom. de 102
Fonpiqueyre, Ch. 68
Fonplégade, Ch. 87
Fonquernie, L. 79
Fonrazade, Ch. 90
Fonréaud, Ch. 57
Fonroque, Ch. 87
Fonsalette, Ch. 204
Fonscolombe, Ch. de 206
Fonseca, J.M. da, Internacional 399
Fonseca, José-Maria da 398, 399
Fonseca Guimaraens 404
Font du Loup, Ch. de la 205
Font du Roi, Dom. de la 203
Font Gelado 197
Fontana Candida 351
Fontana di Papa 351
Fontanachiara 312
Fontanafredda (Tenimenti di Barolo e di Fontafredda) 301
Fontanarossa 365
Fonterutoli, Castello di 338
La Fontesole 219
Fontesteau, Ch. 69
Fonthill 525
Fontlade, Dom. de 208
Fontmuret, Ch. 92
Fontodi 338
Fontsainte, Dom. de 212

Foppiano, L., Wine Co. 458
Foradori 316
Foreau, A. 171
Forgeron Vineyard 480
Forli, Cantina Sociale di 330
Forman Winery 458
Formentini, Conti 326
Formex-Ybarra 523
Forner family 67
Forrester & Co. 404
Forset Hill 497
Forst 275
Forst, M. 59
Fort Médoc 70
Fort Vauban, Ch. 69
Forteto della Luja 304
Fortia, Ch. 203
Fortino Winery 458
Les Forts de Latour 60, 65
De Forville 304
Foschi, Crala 331
Foss Marai 322
La Fosse Tigné 165
Fossi 342
Foucault, J.-L. & B. 167
Fouloir-égrappoir 74
Four Vineyards 496
Fourcas-Dupré, Ch. 57
Fourcas-Hosten, Ch. 57
Fourchaume 111, 112
Le Fournas, Ch. 69
Les Fourneaux 112
Fourney, Ch. 90
Fournier, Eric 85
Fournier & Co. 185
Fournier family 79
Les Fournières 119
La Fourquerie, Ch. 99
Fourques Coop. 211
Fraccaroli, Fratelli 322
Fraisse, Dom. du 217
Fraisse Les Corbières 213
Franc Bigaroux, Ch. 90
Franc-Grâce-Dieu, Ch. 90
Franc-Mallet, Ch. 97
Franc-Mayne, Ch. 87
Français-Monier family 199
France, Ch. de 76
France Champagne 185
La France, Ch. 71, 102
Franche-Comté 234
Franciacorta 357
Franciscan Vineyards 458
Franco, Nino 322
Franco-Españolas, Bodegas 378
Francois, Ch. 495
Franche-Comté 234
Frangy 158
Franken 239, 280-3
Franken Gabietswinzergenossenschaft eG 283
Frankensteiner Hof Weingut Espenschied 262
Fränkischer Landwein 288
Frank's Vineyard 468
Franzia 458
Franzia Brothers Winery 458
Frascati 349, 350
Frascati, Cantina Produttori 351
Frattina, Villa 326
Frecciarossa 312
Free-run juice 467
Freemark Abbey Winery 458
Freiberger, H. 280
Freiherr von Schorlemer, Clemens 251
Freiherr von Schorlemer, Hermann 251
Freisa d'Asti 297
Freisa di Chieri 297
French Colombard 444
Frescobaldi, Marchesi de' 338
Freslier, André 171

Fresno 442
Freymond-Schneider family 88
Frick Winery 458
Friedrich-Wilhelm-Gymnasium, Siftung Staatliches 247-8
Friexedas Bove, J. 382
Freixenet 383-4
Fritz Cellars 458
Friuli-Venezia Giulia 323-7
Friuliani-La Delizia, Viticoltori 326
Frizzante 298
Frog's Leap Wine Cellars 458
Fronin, Mme. 79
Fronsac 98-9
Fronsac, Ch. de 99
Frontignan, Muscat de 219
Frontignac 492
Fruška Gora 427
Fuchsberg 257
Fugazza 331
Fumé Blanc 444
Furlotti, Angel 522
Furmint 424
Fürst Rudolf 283
Fürsteneck 288
Fürstlich Castell'sches Domänenamt 281

G
Gabbiano, Castello di 342
Gabiano 297
Gabiano, Castello di 305
Gaby, Ch. du 99
La Gaffelière, Ch. 86
Gagnard-Delagrange, Dom. 132
Gai, Ch. 484
Gaia & Rey 301
Gaierhof 315
Gaillac 225-6
Gaillac et du Pays Cordais 226
Gaillard, Ch. 90, 171
Gaillat, Dom. de 76
Gairoird, Ch. de 208
Gaja 301
Gaja, Angelo 301
Galán, Bodegas 385
Gales & Cie, Caves 268
Galestro 333
Galicia 371-2
La Galissonnière 164
Gallais-Bellevue, Ch. 71
La Gallais 248
Les Galluches 172
Gallo, Ernest and Julio 458, 548, 549
Gallo, Silvano 326
Gallo, Stelio 325
Gallura, Cantina Sociale 367
Gamay 225, 430, 434, 444
Gambellara, Cantina Sociale di 322
Gamberella 319
Gamza 430
Gan, Eden 458
Gan-Jurançon, Cave Coopérative de 228
Gancia, Fratelli 308
Garamache, Ch. 208
Garcia de Velasco, Francisco 197
Garcia Poveda, H.L. 385
Gard 199
Vin de Pays 231
Garda 308
La Garde 195
La Garde, Ch. 76
Garden Valley Winery 480
Le Gardéra, Ch. 101
Gardet & Co. 185
Gardie Coop. 214
Du Gardin 145
Gardine, Ch. de la 203
Gardinier, Xavier 67
Garlon, Jean 150
Garmes, Dom. des 175

Garofoli 348
Garrafeira 396
Garrett, Andrew 497
Les Garrigues 380
Les Garrigues, Dom. 198
Garriques, Dom. des 224
Garvey 392
Gastaldi 305
Gatinais, Comte de la 363-4
Gatti 305
Gattinara 297
Gau-Odernheim 270
Gaubert, Ch. 90
Gaudin, Ch. 65
Gaudrelle, Ch. de 171
Gauer Estate Vineyard 458
Gaujal, B. 218
Gaujal, C. 218
Gaunoux, Dom. F. 132
Gaunoux, Dom. Michel 132
Gauthier, P. 59
Gauthier, Rémy 128
Gavi 297
Gavi di Gavi 297
Gavotte, Dom. de la 199
Gavoty, Bernard 206
Le Gay, Ch. 95, 102
Gayon, Professor Ulysse 89
Gazin, Ch. 76, 95
Gazin, Ch. du 99
La Gazzella 306
Gebeitsinzergenossenschaft Rhg. eG 261
Gebhardt, Ernst 281
Gedeonseck 254
Geelong 491
Geisenheim 257
Gelin, Dom. Pierre 133
Gelz Zilliken, Forstmeister 248
Gemeinde 241
Genestière, Dom. de la 198
Geneva 409, 412, 414-15
Genouilly Coop. 148
Gentaz-Dervieux 197
Gentile, Dominique 220
Gentils, Lucien 185
Gentils, René 185
Geoffrey, Claude 151
Geoffrey, Dom. Alain 113
Gérant 74
Gerardin, François 222
Geraud, Ch. de 222
Gerbay, Ch. 99
Gerheinden 238
Germain, Dom. Jacques 133
Germain, François 133
Germain, Georges 151
Germain, H. & Fils 185
Germain, Jean 133
Geuyze, Ch. de 226
Gevrey-Chambertin 115
Gewürztraminer 188, 268, 430, 444
Geymüller, Domäiße Baron 419
Geyser Peak Winery 459
Geyserville 442
Gharb 436
Ghemme 297
Giacobazzi 329
Giaconda 497
Giacosa 305
Giacosa, Bruno 301
Giesen 510
Giesler 184
Gigondas 197
Coop. 200-1
Gilbert, Jean-Paul 176
Gilbey's 516
Gilby de Loudenne 52
Giles, Bodegas M. 394
Gilet Bayard, Ch. 92
Gilette, Ch. 82
Gillardi 305
Gillieres, Ch. des 163
Giloux, Patrick 150
Ginestet, Maison 52

La Ginestra, Cooperativa 365
Gioia del Colle 356
La Gioiosa 322
Giol 522
Giovanett-Castelfelder, Alphons 316
Gipfel 242
Girard, Michel 175
Girard-Madoux, J.-F. 157
Girard-Vollot & Fils, Dom. 133
Girard Winery 459
Girardet Cellars 480
Girardi in Cariano, Villa 322
Girasole 322
Giraud, Alain 87
Giraud, Dom. 87, 94
Giraud, Robert 89
Girault-Artois, Dom. 171
Girò di Cagliari 366
Gisborne 508, 509
Giscours, Ch. 54
Gisselbrecht, Maison Louis 190
Gisselbrecht, Willy & Fils 190
La Gitana 394
Gitton Père & Fils 174
Giulio, Lucio di 353
Giumarra Vineyards 459
La Giustiniana 305
Givry 144
GIVSO 229
Glana, Ch. du 59
Glantenay, Soc. des Doms. Bernard & Louis 133
Gleichenstein, Freiherr von 289
Glen Carlou 516
Glen Elgin 505
Glen Ellen Vineyards & Winery 549
Glenora Wine Cellars, Inc. 484
Glicine, Cantina del 305
Gloria, Ch. 47, 59
Gmnello Winery 467
Gobet 153
Gobillard, Paul 185
Goélane, Ch. de 102
Goffre-Viaud, Pierre 57
Gojer-Glogglehof, Anton 316
Gold Seal Vineyards Inc. 483, 484
Golden Chasselas 444
Golden Roy, Société Vinicole 185
Goldgrape Bereich Nierstein 271
Goldwater Estate 510
Gombaude-Guillot, Ch. 95
La Gombaude, Ch. 53
Gonçalves, Bento 523
Gondola 467
Gontet, Ch. 92
Gontier, Ch. 100
Gonzales y Dubosc 384
Gonzalez Byass 392
Gonzalez y Dubose 392
Gordon, Alexander 393
Gordon, Luis G. 393
Gordon & Rivero 393
La Gordonne, Ch. 208
Goree 514
Gorges & Côtes de Millau 234
Gorges de l'Herault 232
Gorgo 322
Gorizia 323
Gosset 184
Gotteshilfe 271
Gotto d'Oro 351
Gouachon, Dom. Elmerich 133
Goubard, Michel 145
Goud de Beaupuis, Dom. 133
Gouges, Dom. Henri 133
Goujon, Ch. 93

Goulaine, Marquis de 163-4
Goulard, Alexandre 114
Goulburn Valley 491
Gould Campbell 405
Goulet, Georges 184
Goundrey 497
Gourgazaud, Soc. 215
Gouron, René & Fils 171
Le Goutail 197
Govet, Philippe 152
Goyenechea 522
Graach 245-6
Grabner-Schierer 419
La Grâce Dieu, Ch. 90
La Grâce-Dieu-Les-Menuts, Ch. 90
Gracia Hermanos 387
Gradazione alcoolica 298
Gradignan 73
Gradnik 326
Gradoli, Cantina Sociale Cooperativa 352
Graf Eberhard Kuenburg-Schloss Sallegg 316
Graf Hardegg, Schlossweingut 419
Graf zu Hoensbroech 252
Grafenstück 274
Graham, W. & J. & Co. 404
Gran Barquero 387
Gran Cru Vineyards 549
Gran Toc 384
Grand Abord, Ch. du 76
Grand Barrail Lamarzelle Figeac, Ch. 87
Grand'Boise, Ch. 206
Grand Campdumy, Dom. du 206
Grand Caumont, Ch. du 212
Grand Chemarin 174
Grand Corbin, Ch. 87
Grand-Corbin-Despagne, Ch. 87
Grand Duroc Milon 64
Grand Duroc Milon, Ch. 65
Grand Enclos du Chateau de Cerons 103
Grand Fief de la Cormeraie 164
Grand-Jour, Ch. 100
Grand Listrac Coop. 57
Grand Mayne, Ch. 87
Grand Montmirail, Dom. du 198, 199
Grand Moueys, Ch. du 101
Grand Moulin, Ch. 69
Grand Moulin, Dom. du 170
Grand-Moulinet, Ch. 97
Grand-Pontet, Ch. 88
Grand Poujeaux 56
Grand-Puch, Ch. du 102
Grand-Puy-Ducasse, Ch. 61
Grand-Puy-Lacoste, Ch. 61
Grand-Renouil, Ch. 99
Grand Tinel, Dom. du 205
Grand Travers, Ch. 487-8
Grand Vaucroz, Dom. du 203
Grand-Village-Capbern, Ch. 66
Grand vin 74
Grand Vin Sec de Doisy-Daëne 79
Grandchamp, Bernard 84
Grande Lauzade, Dom. de la 208
Grande Rue 116
La Grande Gardiole, Ch. 205
Les Grandes Lolières 119
Grandis, Ch. 69
Le Grand Pompée 196
Grands Echézeaux 116
Grands Quaterons, Cuvée des 163
Grands Vins de Fleurie,

Cave Coopérative des 152
Grands Vins de Julienas, Cave Coopérative des 152
Grange des Aires, Dom. de la 217
Grange-Neuve, Ch. de 97
La Grange Neuve de Figeac 85
Grangeneuve, Dom. de 198-9
Grans-Fassian 252
La Grappe, Caves Coopératives 216
Grasso, Elio 305
Gratallops, Cooperativa de 383
Grate-Cap, Ch. 97
Gratien, Meyer & Seydoux, Etab. 168-9
Gratien Epernay, Alfred 184-5
Grattamacco 338
Graubünden 409, 415
Grava, Ch. du 101
Grave, Ch. la (Trigant de Boisset) 95
Grave del Friuli 323, 324
La Grave, Ch. de 100
La Grave, Dom. 76
Gravelines, Ch. 101
Graves 46, 49-50, 72-7
Graves de Vayre 103
Gravet, Ch. 90
La Gravière, Ch. 98
Gravina 356
Gravner, Francesco 325
Gray, Giorgio 315
Gray Riesling 444
Gréa, Ch. 156
Great Western 490, 491
Great Western, Pleasant Valley Wine Company 483, 484
Grechetto 344
Greco 344
Greco di Tufo 354
Green, Douglas 516
Green Hungarian 444
Green and Red Vineyard 460
Green Valley 442
Greenfield 442
Greenwood Ridge Vineyards 460
Gregoletto 322
Il Greppo 337
Il Greppone Mazzi 342
Gresco di Bianco 359-60
Grésigny 145
Gressier Grand-Poujeaux, Ch. 57
Greysac, Ch. 71
Grgich Hills Cellar 460
Gribelin, Gérard 74
Griffin Vineyards 461
Griffith 500
Grifo de Boldrino 346
Grignan, Comté de 231
Grignano, Fattoria di 342
Grignolino 444
Grignolino d'Asti 297
Grignolino del Monferrato Casalese 297-8
Grill 218
Grillet, Ch. 195
Grimond, Ch. 101
Griñon, Marqués de 385
Griotte-Chambertin 115
Gripa, Bernard 196
Grippat, Jean-Louis 196
Gris, Ch. 136
Gris de Boulaouane 436
Gris de Tunisie 435
Grivot, Etienne 133
Grivot, Jean 133
Grk 429
Groffier, Dom. Robert 133

Grognuz Frères 414
Grolet, Ch. 100
Groot Constantia 516
Groppello 357
Gros, Dom. Jean 134
Gros Moulin, Ch. 100
Gros Plant du Pays Nantais 160, 161, 162, 163
Grosjean, Delfino 306
Grosset, Jeffrey 497
Grosset-Château 167
Grosslagen 236-7, 238, 241
Grossot, Jean-Pierre 114
Groth Vineyards & Winery 460
Grover Gulch Winery 460
Gruaud-Larose, Ch. 58
Grumello 357
Grunhaus, Maximin 249
Grupo Sindical de Colonizacion No. 795 386
Gruy family 206
Guadet-St-Julien, Ch. 88
La Guardiense 355
Guarnieri, Carla 342
Guche Pigeon 174
Guelfi, Filomusi 353
Guenoc Valley 442
Guérets, Les 119
Guerneville 442
Guerrieri-Rizzardi 320
Guerrouane 436
Guettes 140
Gueyrot, Ch. 90
Guglielmi, Enzo 308
Guglielmi, Michele 308
Guglielmo, Emilio, Winery 460
Guibeau, Ch. 92
Guibon, Ch. 102
Guichard, La Baronne 96
Guichebourg, Comte de 155
Guigal, E. et M. 196
Guilbaud Frères 164
Guillemet, Pierre 53, 55
Guillemin La Gaffeliere, Ch. 90
Guillermier brothers 90
Guimaraens Vinhos 404
Guinaudie, Edward 88
Guindon, Jacques 164
Guinot, Ch. 90
Guionne, Ch. de 208
Guiraud, Ch. 78
Le Dauphin Ch. Guiraud 78
Guirouilh, Alexis 228
La Guita 394
Guitres 103
Güldenmorgen 270
Gunderloch, Weingut 271
Gundlach-Bundschu Winery 460
Guntersblum 270
Guntrum, Louis 239, 271
La Gurgue, Ch. 55
Gurpegui, Bodegas 378
Gutes Domtal 270
Gutrin, Michel 142
Gutsverwaltung Deinhard see Wegeler deinhard
Guttenberg 278
Guttenberg Liebfrauenberg 276
Gutturnio dei Colli Piacentini 328
Guy, F. & Peyre, S. 218
Guy, Rogr 185
Guyon, Dom. Antonin 134
Guyot, Jean Claude 175
Gyöngyös-Visonta 426

H
Haag, Fritz 248
Haart, Johann 252
Hacienda Wine Cellars 460
Haderburg 316
Haight Vineyards 486
Haimer, Gunter 422

Hajos 425
Hallgarten 256
Hallgarten, Arthur 239
Haloze hills 428
Hambledon 525
Hamilton, Richard 497
Hamilton Russell Vineyards 516
Hamm, Emile & Fils 185
Hammel 414
Hammel, Emil & Cie 278
Hammelburg, Winzergrenossenschaft 283
Hammelburger Burg 281
Hammerstein 254
Hanappier 51
Handley Cellars 460
Hanteillan, Ch. 69
Hanzell Vineyards 460
Haraszthy, Agoston 449, 460
Harbor Winery 460
Les Hardières 166
Hardy, Thomas 497
Harris port 405
Hárslevelü 424
Hartenberg 516
Harvesting 33
Harvey's of Bristol 392
Hasenklever, F. 129
Hasensprung 256
Hattenheim 256
Hauner, Carlo 363
Hauses Deinhard, Weingut des see Wegeler-Deinhard
Haut-Bages Libéral, Ch. 61
Haut-Bages Monpelou, Ch. 65
Haut-Bages-Averous 64
Haut-Bailly, Ch. 74
Haut-Batailley, Ch. 61, 64
Haut Bernon, Ch. 92
Haut-Beychevelle-Gloria, Ch. 59
Haut-Bommes, Ch. 82
Haut Breton Larigaudière, Ch. 55
Haut-Brignon, Ch. 101
Haut-Brion, Ch. 47, 73
Haut Brisson, Ch. 90
Haut-Canteloup, Ch. 71
Haut-Chaigneau, Ch. 98
Haut-Corbin, Ch. 88
Haut Franquet, Ch. 57
Haut Garin, Ch. 71
Haut-Lavallade, Ch. 90
Le Haut-Lieu 171
Haut Macô, Ch. 100
Haut-Maillet, Ch. 97
Haut-Marbuzet, Ch. 66
Haut-Médoc 46, 49-50, 56-7, 67-9
Haut-Montravel 222
Haut-Padarnac, Ch. 65
Haut Péchармant, Dom. de 222
Haut-Plantey, Ch. 90
Haut-Poitou 172
vin du 160
Haut Pontet, Ch. 90
Haut-Rhin 187
Haut-Sarpe, Ch. 88
Haut Savoie 157
Haut Ségottes, Ch. 90
Haute Faucherie, Ch. 92
Haute Perche, Dom. de 167
Haute Provence 516
Haute Vallée d'Aude 232
Haute Vallée de l'Orb 232
Hauterive, Ch. 71
Hautes Mourettes 232
Hautes Noelles, Dom. des 165
Hautevie en Pays d'Aude 232
La Hautière, Dom. 165
Hauts-Conseillants, Ch. Les 98
Hauts de Badens 232
Les Hauts de Pontet 64

Hawke's Bay 508, 509
Haywood Winery 460
Headcord Vineyard 525
Healdsburg 442
Heathcote Winery 497
Heating must 38
Les Heaumes, Ch. 100
Hecker Pass 442
Hecker Pass Winery 460
Heddesdorff, Freiherr von 248
Heemskerk 498
Heeter, Thomas 82
Heidsieck, Charles 178
Heidsieck Monopole 178
Heiligenthal 280
Heim 190
Heinrich Seip. 272
Heiss, Franz 422
Heitlinger, Albert 289
Heitz, Joe 460, 477
Heitz Wine Cellars 460
Hemus 431
Henkell & Co. 257
Henriot 179
Henriques & Henriques 408
Henry Winery 480
Henschke 498
Hérail, M. 226
Hérault 231-2
Hercules 432, 433
Herencia 379
Hermann J. Weimer Vineyard 485
Dom Hermano 400
Hermanos, Diez 400
Hermanos, Fernandez Cervera 373
Hermanoz, Diez Lda. 406
Hermitage 193, 194
L' Hermitage, Ch. 90
Hermitage la Garenne, Ch. 92
Hernandez, A. 52
Heron Hill Vineyards, Inc. 484
Herpfer, Christoph Hs. 281-2
Herrenberg 254, 281
Herrenberg, Weingut 251
Herrengarten 270
Herres, Peter 257
Herrlich 276, 278
Herrnhofer 315
Hess Collection Winery 461
Hessel, Dominique 57
Hessische Bergstrasse 237, 238, 279-80
Hessische Forschungsanstalt für Wein-, Obst- und Gartenbau 262
Heublein 399
Heuchelberg 284
Heulz, André 218
Heyl zu Herrnsheim, Freiherr 271-2
Hickinbotham Winemakers 498
Hidalgo, Emilio M. 393-4
Hidalgo y Cia, Vinicola 394
Hidden Springs Winery 480
High Weald 525
Hill, Cavas 384
Hill, William, Winery 461
Hill-Smith Estate 506-7
Hillcrest Vineyard 479
Hinman Vineyards 480
Hinzerling 481
Hirondelle 434
Hirtzberger, Franz 420
Hnos., Bodegas, Perez Pascuas 373
Hochheim 255
Hochmess 275
Hock 255
Hoen, Baron de 192

Hoen, Caves de 192
Höfer Schlossmühle, Dr.
 Josef 267
Hofkammer-Kellerei,
 Württembergische 285
Hofrat 281
Hofstätter, J. 315
Hofstück 276
Hogue Cellars 481
Hohenberg 288
Hohenlohe-Öhringen,
 Fürst zu 286
Hold, Sepp 420
Höllenpfad 274
Hollydene Estate 498
Holt Frères & Fils 54, 76
Homme Mort, l' 112
Honegger, Ruedi 416
Honigberg 281
Honigsäckel 275
Hood River Vineyards 480
Hop Kiln Winery 461
Hopkins Vineyard 486
Horeau, Louis 86
Horeau-Beylot, Maison 91
Hormes, Ch. des 69
Hornberg, Burg 286
Hornsby, Ch. 495
Hortevie, Ch. 59
Hosbag 434
Hospices de Beaune 136-7
Hospices de Nuits-St-
 Georges 140
Hospitalet, Ch. l' 95
Houghton 498
Houissant, Ch. 66
Hourbanon, Ch. 71
Hours, Charles 228
Hourtin-Ducasse, Ch. 69
Houssier, Claude 176
Hövel, Weingut von 248
Howell Mountain 442
Huber-Pacherhof, Josepf
 316
Huc, Mlle. 212
Hudelot, Alain 134
Hudelot-Noëllat, Dom.
 134
Hudson River Valley 483
Hudson Valley Wine Co.
 484
Hue, Philippe 217
Huelva 386
Huet, Gaston 171
Hugel 187
Hugel & Fils 190
Humberto Canale 522
Humboldt 442
Humbrecht, L. and O. 192
Hungerford Hill 498
Hunt, Roope 404
Hunter Valley 490, 491
Hunters Wines 510
Huntingdon Estate 498
Hupfeld Erben 262
Husch Vineyards 461
Hustopeče 427
Huxelrebe 524
Hyvernière, l' 164

I
Idaho 482
Idyll Vineyard 498
Igé Coop. 148
Igler, Hans 423
L'Ile de Beauté 220, 234
Ile Margaux, Dom. de l' 55
Illats 82
Illuminati, Dino 353
Imbottigliato nel'origine
 298
Immich-Batterieberg, Carl
 Aug. 252
Impernal 224
Indicacão de Provenencia
 Regulamentada (IPR) 395
Industrias Vinicolas del
 Oeste 385
Infantes de Orleans-
 Borbon, Bodegas de los
 394
Inferno 357

Infuhr, Karl 423
Ingelheim 270
Ingersheim et Environs
 Coop. 192
Inglenook (Napa Valley)
 461, 477
Inglenook (Navalle) 461
Inniskillin 484
Institut Agricole Régional
 306
Instituto Agrario
 Provinciale San Michele
 all'Adige 315
Internacionales, Bodegas
 392
La Invencible Coop. 386
Invierno 394
Ippolito, Vincenzo 360
Ipsheimer Burgberg 281
Iron Horse Vineyard 461
Irouléguy et du Pays
 Basque, des Vins d' 227
Irsch 243
Irun, Marqués de 393
Isabella 486
Ischia 354
Isembourg, Ch. d' 189
Isera, Catina Sociale di 316
Isle St. George 483
Isole e Olena 338
Isonzo 323, 324
Isore 172
d'Issan, Ch. 54
Istria 428, 429
Ivaldi, Domenico 305
Ivernal, Bernard 185
Ives 486
Izmir 434

J
Jabiol family 86, 87
Jaboulet Ainé, Paul 196,
 205
Jaboulet-Isnard 196
Jaboulet-Vercherre 134
Jacobo, Don 378
Jacobsdal 516
Jacquemont Père & Fils
 153
Jacquère 157
Jacques, Ch. des 153
Jacques Blanc, Ch. 90
Jacqueson, Paul & Hanri
 145
Jacquesson & Fils 185
Jacquinot & Fils 185
Jade 464
Jadot, Dom. Louis 130
Jadot, Louis 148
Jadot, Maison Louis 134,
 138
Jaffelin, Maison 134
Jaffre, André 151
Jamart & Co. 185
Jambon, Etienne 150
Jamek, Josef 420
Jamet, Joseph 197
Jamet, Pierre et Fils 171
Janicot, Dom. de 226
Jannière, Ch. de la 164
Janodet, Dom. Jacky 153
Janoueix, Joseph 88
Janoueix, Maison
 François-Bernard 91
Janoueix, Maison Joseph
 91
Jardin & Co. 185
Jardin de la France 162,
 234
Jasmin, Robert 196
Jasnières 160
Jau, Ch. de 210
Jauberie, Dom. de la
 222-3
Jaubert and Noury 210
Jaubertes, Ch. des 76
Jauffret, Jean-Paul 51
Jausserand, Jean Pierre 79
Javernand, Ch. 152
Javry, Paul 113
Jayer, Henri 134
Jean, Etab. Pierre 91

Jean, Michel 89
Jean-Gervais, Ch. 76
Jean-Voisin, Ch. 90
Jeandet, Henri 158
Jeanete, Dom. de la 208
Jekel Vineyards 461
Jems 400
Jerez Cortado Hidalgo 394
Jerez de la Frontera 388,
 389
Jerez quinado 390
Jerez Superior 390
Jermann 325
Jerusalem vineyard 428
Joguet, Charles 171
Johannisberg 257
Johannisberg (Bereich) 255
Johannisberg Riesling
 444-5
Johannishof, Weingut 262
Johnson Estate 485
Johnson-Turnball 462
Johnson's of Alexander
 Valley 461
Johnston, Nathaniel 52
Joinand-Borde, Mme. 87
Joliot, Dom. Jean & Fils
 134
Joliver, Pascal 175
Joly, Mme. A. 167
Jolys, Ch. 228
La Joncarde, Ch. 100
Jordan Vineyard and
 Winery 462, 477
Josephshof, Weingut 248
Joubert, Claude &
 Michelle 150
Jouennes d'Herville,
 Marquis de 146
Jouffre family 224
Jouffron, René & Fils 205
Jougla, Dom. des 218
Jourdan, Ch. 101
Jousseaume, J.B. 217
Jouves, Jacques 225
Jubiläums-Cuvée 271
Jubiläumsrube 271
Jug wines 467
Juge, Ch. du (Dupleich)
 101
Juge, Ch. du (Médeville)
 101
Juge, Marcel 196
Jugla, Bernard
 Ch. Pédesclaux 64
Juillot, Dom. Michel 145
Julien, Marcel 215
Juliénas 152
Juliénas, Ch. 152
Juliusspital-Weingut 280,
 282
Les Jumelles 196
Jumilla 368, 385
Junayme, Ch. 99
Jura 154-6
 Vins de Pays 234
Jurade de St-Emilion 83
Jurançon 228
Jurancon Noir 223
Le Jurat, Ch. 90
Jussas, Ch. de 100
Justa, Ch. 101
Juvé y Camps 384
Juvinière, Dom. de la 134

K
Kabinett 236, 237, 241, 421
Kadarka 424-5
Kaï-Nielsen, Wum 51
Kaiser Stuhl 498
Kaiserpfalz 271
Kaiserstuhl Bereich 287-8
Kalimera 355
Kalimna 502
Kalin Cellars 462
Kallstadter Annaberg 275
Kalterersee 313
Kamptal-Donauland 418
Kanitz, Graf von 259
Kanonkop 516
Kante, Edy 326
Kanzem 243

Kapellenberg 281
Karelas & Son 433
Karim, Dom. 435
Karly Wines 462
Karp-Schreiber, Christian
 248
Karst, Johannes & Söhne
 278
Karthäuserhof,
 Gutsverwaltung 248
Kasel 243
Katnook Estate 498
Kattus, Johann 420
Kavalkidere 434
Kay Brothers Amery 498
Kecskemet 425
Keenan, Robert, Winery
 462
Kefraga 435
Kehlburg 315
Keim, Alfred 215
Kékfrankos 425
Kéknyelü 424
Kellereignossenschaft
 Girlan 316
Kellereignossenschaft
 Shreckbichl 316
Kendall-Jackson Vineyard
 462
Kendermann, Hermann
 239
Kennedy, Kathryn,
 Winery 462
Kentucky 487
Kenwood 442
Kenwood Vineyards 462
Kenworthy Vineyards 462
Keo 434
Kern 442
Kern, Dr. 278
Kesseler, August 259
Kesselstatt, Reichsgarf von
 248
Kesten 245
Kettmeir 315, 321
Khalokhorio 434
Khedri 256
Kientzheim-Kaysersberg
 Coop. 192
Kies-Kieren 248
Kinheim 246
Kiona Vineyards and
 Winery 481
Kirchberg 281
Kirchenweinberg 284
Kirigin Cellars 462
Kirmisi 434
Kirschroth 264
Kirwan, Ch. 54
Kistler Vineyards 462
Kitterlé 188
La Kiuva 306
Klein Constantia 516
Klein (Little) Karoo 514
Klipfel, Dom. 190
Kloster Eberbach 256
Kloster Erbach 258
Kloster Heilsbruck 278
Kloster Liebfrauenberg
 276, 278
Klosterkellerie Muri-Gries
 317
Klosterneuburg, Kelleramt
 Chorherrensift 420-1
Klüsserath 244
Knappstein, Tim 499
Knight's Valley 442
Knipser Johannishof 277
Knudsen-Erath Winery
 479
Knyphausen, Freiherr zu
 259
Kobnert 275
Koch, Bürgermeister Carl,
 Erben 273
Kocher-Jagst-Tauber
 Bereich 284
Kocherberg 284
Koehler, Anne 190
Koehler-Ruprecht,
 Weingut 278
Koehler-Weidmann,

Weingut 272
Kolbenhofer 313
Königin Victoriaberg 259
Königsberg 242
Königsgarten 276, 278
Konocti Cellars Winery
 462
Konz 243
Koonunga Hill 502
Kooperative Wijnbouwers
 Vereniging (KWV) 519
Koopmanskloof 516
Kopke, C.N. & Co. 404
Kornell, Hans, Champagne
 Cellars 462-3
Kosmet 427-8
Kosovo 427-8
Köster-Wolf, Weingut 273
Kotsiphali 432
Kouros 433
Köwerich 244
Krajina 427
Kraški Teran 428
Krems,
 Winzergenossenschaft
 423
Kressman, Jean 76
Kreuznach 264
Kreydenweiss, Dom. Marc
 190
Krier Frères, Caves 268
Kriter Brut de Brut 140
Kritt 190
Krondorf 499
Krone, Weingut 259
Kronenberg 264
Krotenbrunnen 269, 270
Kröv 246
Kröver Nacktarsch 242
Krug 179
Krug, Charles, Winery 462
Kruger, Louis 185
Kruger-Rumpf, Weingut
 267
Kuehn 190
Kuentz-Bas 190
Kühn, Heinrich 262
Kumeu River Wines 510
Kunstler, Franz 259
Kupferberg, Christian
 Adalbert 257
Kurfürstenhof, Weingut
 see Heinrich Seip.
Kurfürstenstück 271
Kurfürstlay 245

L
Labastida, Cooperative
 Vinicola de 379
Labégorce, Ch. 55
Labégorce-Zédé, Ch. 55-6
Labeve, Pierre 200
Laborde, Ch. 98
Laborie 516
Labouré-Gontard 133
Labouré-Roi, Maison 134
Labouré-Roi 153
Labruyère, Roger 224, 225
Laburyère, Propriété 153
Lac, Ch. du 462
Lacave & Cia 394
Lacoste, Mme. 93
Lacoste-Boné 61
Lacoste-Loubat, Mme. 95
Lacrima di Morro d'Alba 347
Lacrimarosa d'Irpinia 354
Lacryma Christi del
 Vesuvio 354
Lacuesta Hnos Lda.,
 Martinez 378
Ladoix-Serrigny 118-19,
 119
Ladoucette, Baron Patrick
 de 175
Lafarge, Dom. Michel
 134-5
Lafaurie, Ch. 101
Lafaurie-Peyraguey, Ch. 78
Laffourcade, A. 167
Lafite-Rothschild, Ch. 59,
 62-3

Lafitte, Ch. 101
Lafleur, Ch. 95
Lafleur du Roy, Ch. 95
Lafões 397
Lafon, Ch. 57
Lafon, Dom. des Comtes 135
Lafon, René 135
Lafon-Rochet, Ch. 66
Lafond, Claude 176
Lafüe, Ch. 102
Lagar de Cervera 373, 378
Lagariavini 315
Lagariavini-I Vini del Concilio 316
Lageder, Alois 315
Lagenbach & Co. 239
Lago di Caldaro 313
Lagos, B.M. 394
Lagrange, Ch. 58, 95
Lagrasse, Cave Coopérative 213
Lagrave, Ch. 102
Lagrein 313
Lagrezette, Ch. 224
Lagüe, Ch. 99
La Lagune, Ch. 67
Lagunilla, Bodegas 378
Lahntal 254
Lake (California) 442
Lake's Folly 499
Lakespring Winery 463
Lalande-Borie 58
Lalande-Borie, Ch. 59
Lalande-de-Pomerol 98
Lalanne, Jacques 167
Lalannette-Pardiac, Ch. 103
Laleure Piot, Dom. 135
Lalibarde, Ch. 100
Lalou, Rene 182
Lamarche, Dom. Henri 135
Lamarque, Ch. 69, 102
Lamberhurst Vineyards 525
Lambert Bridge 463
Lambert des Granges, Marquis de 79
Lamberti 320
Lamblin & Fils 113
Lambrusc Grasparossa di Castelvetro 328
Lambruschi, Ottaviano 308
Lambrusco 328
Lambrusco di Sorbara 328
Lambrusco Mantovano 357
Lambrusco Reggiano 328
Lambrusco Salamino di Santa Croce 328
Lamé-Delille-Boucard 171
Lametina 360
Lamezia 360
Lamezia Lento, Cantina 360
Lamm-Jung, Weingut 262-3
Lamole 337
Lamole di Lamole 342
Lamothe, Ch. (Côtes de Bourg) 100
Lamothe, Ch. (Premières Côtes) 101
Lamothe, Ch. (Sauternes) 81
Lamothe-de-Bergeron, Ch. 69
Lamothe-Cissac, Ch. 69
Lamsac Coop. 211
Lamy, Dom. 135
Lamy, Hubert 135
Lamy, Jean & Fils 135
Lamy, René 135
Lan, Bodegas 378-9
Lançon 204
Landat, Ch. 69
Landé, Maurice 87
Lander 379
Landernberg,

Sclosskellerei Freiherr von 252
Les Landes et Verjuts 112
Landgräflich Hessisches Weingut 258
Landiras, Ch. de 76
Landmark Vineyards 463
Landon, Pierre & Joseph 164
La Landonne 196
Landskroon 516-17
Landwein 236, 241, 288
Landwein der Mosel 288
Landwein der Saar 288
Lanes, Ch. des 212
Lanessan, Ch. 69
Lang, Hans 263
Lang, Matthew 500
Langehof, Weingut 263
Langenbach, Fürstlich Hohenlohe 286
Langenlonsheim 265
Langguth, F.W. 481
Langhorne Creek 492
Langieu 157
Langlois-Château 169
Langoa-Barton, Ch. 58
Laniote, Ch. 88
Lanson 179
Lapalu, Claude 66
Lapelletrie, Ch. 90
Lapeyre, Ch. 90
Laplace, Jean-Louis 140
Larcis-Ducasse, Ch. 88
Large, André 151
Lark Hill 499
Larmande, Ch. 88
Laroche, Dom. 113
Laroque, Ch. 90
Larose-Trintaudon, Ch. 69
Laroze, Ch. 88
Larrivaux, Ch. 69
Larrivet-Haut-Brion, Ch. 76
Larroze, Ch. 226
Larsen, Merete 67
Lartigue, Ch. 67, 99
Lartigue de Brochon, Ch. 69
Lascombes, Ch. 54
Laskiriesling 429
Lassègue, Ch. 90
Lasserre, Pierre 96
Lastours, Ch. de 212
Latah Creek 481
Latisana 323, 324
Latium 349-52
Latour, Ch. 59-60
Latour, Louis 148
Latour, Maison Louis 135
Latour à Pomerol, Ch. 95-6
Latricières-Chambertin 115
Laubenheim 266
Lauber, Hans Jörg 416
Laudon-Rival family 206
Laudun 244
Lauerburg, J. 248
Laugauzère, M. 229
Laugel, Maison Michel 190
Laujac, Ch. 71
Launay, Ch. 102
Launay, Paul and Yves de 145
Lauréat 164
Laurel Glen Vineyards 463
Laurens 217
Laurensanne, Ch. 100
Laurent-Perrier 179, 181
Laurets, Ch. des 92
Laurette, Ch. 102
Laurier, Dom. 454
Lauriol 217
Laval family 95
Lavalière, Ch. 71
Lavau, Héritieres René 435
Lavaux 412
Lavigne, Honoré 128
Laville-Haut-Brion, Ch. 74
Lavis-Sorni-Salorno,

Cantina 316
Lazy Creek 463
Leacock 408
Leányka 424, 426
Lebèbvre, Jean Bernard 88
Lebègue, Maison 91
Lebègue & Compagnie 52
Lebreton, Jean-Yves 167
Lebuge, Maison 91
Leclerc, Dom. René 135
Leclerc, Philippe 135
Leconfield 499
Leconte 162
Leeuwin Estate 499
Leeward Winery 463
Leflaive, Dom. 135
Leflaive, Oliver, Frères 135
Legland, Bernard 114
Legrange de Lescure, Ch. 90
Legras, R. & L. 185
Lehmann, Peter, Wines 499
Leitgemeinde 238
Leiwen 245
Lemberg 517
Lemoine, J. 185
Lencquesaing, Mme. de 64
Lenoble, Damery 185
Lenz, Patricia & Pater 485
Léognan 73
Léon 371
Léon, Ch. 101
Léon, Jean 382
Léon Millot 486
Leone de Castris 358
Leonetti 482
Léoville-Barton, Ch. 58
Léoville Las Cases, Ch. 58
Léoville-Poyferre, Ch. 59
Lepitre, Abel 185
Leporati, Ermenegildo 305
Lequin-Roussot, Dom. 135
Lérida 380
Leroy, Maison 136
Lescombes, Mathieu 225
Lescours, Ch. 90
Lescure, Chantal 134
Lesquen, Vicomte & Vicomtesse de 86
Lesquerde Coop. 211
Lessini Durello 319
Lessona 368
Lestage, Ch. 57
Lestage Simon, Ch. 69
Lestage-Darquier-Grand Poujeaux, Ch. 57
Lestruelle, Ch. 71
Letrari 316
Lett, David 478
Lettere 354
Leu, Ch. de, Winery 451
Levante 385
Leverano 356
Lexia 492
Leydier, Jacques 198
Lhaskovetz 430
Liasora 322
Liatico 432
Libery School 451
Libes-Cavaille 218
Librandi 360
Lichine, Alexis 53
Lichine, Sacha 55
Lichine classification 49-50, 73
Licht-Bergweiler, P., Erben 252
Liebfraumilch 241, 269, 271, 282
Liebrauenmorgen 271
Liechtenstein, Prinz 421
Lieser 245
Lieujean, Ch. 69
Lièven, G.F.A. Dom., Ch. de Bellevue 152
Lignac, Robert 88
Lignères, Yves 217
Ligneris family 89
Lignier, Dom. Georges & Fils 136

Lignier, Hubert 136
Liguria 307-8
Lilliano (Antella) 342
Lilliano (Castellina) 342
Lillydale Vineyards 499
Lima 397
Lincoln (New Zealand) 510-11
Lindelberg 284
Lindeman's 499-500
Linderos, Viña 521
Lingenfelder, K. & H. 277
Liot, Ch. 82
Lippolis 359
Liquoroso 298
Lirac 203
Lisini 342
Lison-Pramaggiore 319
Listel 219
Listrac 56-7
Littoral Orb-Hérault 232
Live Oaks Winery 463
Livermore Valley 442
Livermore Valley Cellars 464
Liversan, Ch. 69
Livon, Dorino 326
Livran, Ch. 71
Lizzano 356-7
Ljutomer 428
Llamas, Anne 88
Llano Estacado 488
Los Lanos, Bodegas 385
Llava de Oro 521
Lleida 380
Llords and Elwood Winery 464
Loché, Ch. de 130
Locorotondo 357
Coop. 358
Lodali, Eredi 305
Lodi 442
Loeb, Sigmund 239
Loel 434
Loewen, Carl 253
Logado 433
Logis du Vivier 152
Lognac, Ch. 76
Lohr, J., Winery 464
Loin de l'Oeil 225
Loire 158-61, 163
Vins de Pays 234
Loire, Les Caves de la 168
Lombardo, Fratelli 198, 365
Lombardy 308-12
Lomblot, Société 435
Lones, Dom. des 198-9
Long Island 483
Long Island Vineyard 484-5
Long-Depaquit 113
Longariva 316
Longen 244
Longo, Giambattista 360
Longuich 244
Longval, Dom. de 198
Loosen-Erben, Benedict 253
Lopez, Bodegas 522
López, Bodegas Peñalba 372
Lopez de Heredia, R., Viña Tondonia 377
Lorch 257
Lorchhausen 257
Lorentz, André 190
Lorentz, Gustave 190
Lorettoberg 287
Loron, Jean, Ch. de 152
Loron & Fils 153
Lörsch 244
Los Angeles 442
Loubens, Ch. 102
Loudenne, Ch. 71
Loupiac 102
Louvière, Ch. la 76-7
Löwenstein, Fürst 259
Lower Lake Winery see Stuermer Winery
Lubéron 203

Lucas, Ch. 92
The Lucas Winery 464
Lucciano-Spallatti, Tenuta di 342
Ludon-Pomiés-Agassac, Ch. 69
Lugana 357
Luganese 416
Lugny Coop. 148
Lugny-St-Georges, Cave de 133
Luins 412
Lunel, Muscat de 219
Lungarotti, Dr. Giorgio 345, 346
Lupé-Cholet 136
Lupi 308
Lur Saluces, Comte Alexandre de 78, 81
Lurton, André 74, 85
Lurton, Lucien
Brane-Cantenac 53
Ch. Bouscaut 73
Ch. Climens 78
Ch. Desmirail 54
Ch. Doisy-Dubroca 81
Ch. Duplessis 57
Ch. Durfort-Vivens 54
Clos Fourtet 85
Lussac 89
Lussac, Ch. de 92
Lussac-St-Emilion 92
Lusseaud, Pierre 164
Lustau, Emilio 392-3
Lutry 412
Luxembourg 268
de Luze 52
Luze, Baron Geoffrey de 56
Luzzano, Castello di 312
Lycée Viticole 136
Lyeth Vineyard 464
Lynch-Bages, Ch. 64
Lynch-Moussas, Ch. 64
Lyonnat, Ch. du 92
Lytton Springs Winery 464

M
Mabileau, Jean-Claude 171
Maccario, Mario 308
MacCarthy, Ch. 66
MacCarthy-Moula, Ch. 66
McCrea, Fred 474
McDowell Valley 442
McDowell Valley Vineyards 465
Macedon 491
Machard de Gramont, Dom. 156, 158
Macharnudo 390
Machuraz 157
MacKenzie & Co. 404
McLester 465
Mâcon 146-8
Mâcon Blanc 147
Mâcon-Clessé 148
Mâcon Rouge 147
Mâcon Superieur 147
Mâcon-Villages 147
Mâcon-Viré 148
Macquin St-Georges, Ch. 93
Macrobrunn 256
Macul, Consiño 521
Maculan 320
McWilliams see Cooks McWilliams
La Madeleine, Ch. 88
Madeleine Angevine 524
Madera 442
Maderia 11, 407-8
Maderia Wine Co. 408
Madero, Casa 523
Madiran 227
Madonna della Vittoria 317
Madonna Isabella, Cascina 312
Maga, Lino 312
Magallonera, Bodegas la 373
Magaña, Bodegas 373

Magdelaine, Ch. 86
Magence, Ch. 77
Magenta, Dom. du Duc de 134, 138
Magnien, Dom. Henri 138
Magnin, Louis 158
Magon 435
Magredo, Borgo 326
Magrez, Bernard 52
Mähler-Besse family 52, 223
Maillard, Ch. 101
Mailly Grand Cru 185
Maimbray, Ch. de 175
Maindreieck Bereich 280, 281
Maine 486
Mainfray, Sylvain 167
Mainviereck Bereich 280
Maipo Valley 520
Mairano 312
Maire, Henri 156
Maison Blanche, Ch. 97
Maison des Chiroubles, Cave Cooperative 152
Maison Neuve, Ch. 93
Maître, Paul 171
Les Maitres Vignerons de la Presqu'ile de St-Tropez 207
Maizilly Père & Fils 138
Malabaila di Canale 305
Málaga 368, 386
Malandes, Dom. de 114
Malandes, Dom. des 113
Malartic-Lagravière, Ch. 74
Malaspina 331
Malbec 51, 227, 445
Malby, Dom. 199
Malescasse, Ch. 69
Malescot-St-Exupéry, Ch. 54
Malestroit de Bruc, Comte de 164
Malet-Roquefort, Comte Léo de 86, 89
Malga-Dayné 306
Maligny, Ch. de 113
Malle, Ch. de 81
Malle, M. de 81
Malleret, Ch. de 69
Malmaison, Ch. 57
Maltroye, Ch. de la 138
Malvasia 407-8, 432
Malvasia Bianca 445
Malvasia delle Lipari 362
Malvasia di Bosa 366
Malvasia di Cagliari 366
Malvasia di Casorzo d'Asti 298
Malvasia di Castelnuovo Don Bosco 298
Malves Bagnoles 216
Malvoise de Corse 220
Malvoisie 216
Mancey Coop. 148
La Mancha 368, 384
Manchuela 368, 385
Mandelhohe 276
Mandement 412
Manderville, Paul 215
Mandilari 432
Mandourelle, Ch. de 212
Mandrolisai 366
Manicle 157
Manissy, Ch. de 199
Mannaberg 288
Männle, Andreas 290
Manoncourt, Thierry de 85
Manquehue, Viña 521
Mansard Baillet 185
Mansengs 227
Mansy, Ch. 99
Mantanzas Creek Winery 465
Mantellassi 342
Mantiko 433
Mantinia 432
Mantlerhof, Weingut 421
Mantonico 360

Manuel, René 134
Manus, Régis 150
Manzanilla 390
Manzano, Fattoria di 342
La Marana Ruisgnani 220
Maranges 126
Marascal Côtes-du-Rhône 202
Marasciuolo, Gennaro 359
Marbuzet, Ch. de 65, 66
Marc, Mme 95
Marcarini 302
Marcarini-Cogno 302
Marcato 322
Marchand, Dom. Jean-Philippe 138
Marchand, Pascal 132
Marche, Associazione Cantine Cooperative 349
Marches de Bretagne 234
Il Marchese 352
The Marches 347-9
Marchetti 348
Marchio depositato 298
Marco 433
Maréchal Foch 484, 486
Maréchaudes 119
Marenco 305
Marestel 158
Marfil 383
Margaret River 492
Margaride, Casa Agricola Herd. de D. Luis 400
Margaux 46, 53-6
Margaux, Ch. 53
Maribor 428
Marienberg 281, 500
Mariengarten 275
Marienhof, Just 422
Marignan 158
Marin 158, 442
Marin, Giovanni 326
Maring-Noviland 245
Marino 350
Coop. 351
Marino Grandi Vini Siciliani 365
Marionnet, Henri 171
Maris, Jacques 216
Mark West Vineyards 464
Markgraf Babenberg 281
Markgräflerland Bereich 287
Markham Winery 464
Markopoulo Coop. 433
Marksburg 254
Marlborough (New Zealand) 509
Marly, Jacques 74
Marmilla, Cantina Sociale 367
Marmorelle 352
Marne Valley 186
Les Marnes 174
Marque nationale 268
Marquis d'Alesme-Becker, Ch. 55
Marquis de Mons, Ch. 90
Marquis de Terme, Ch. 55
Le Marquisat 153
Marsac-Séguineau, Ch. 56
Marsala 361, 362-3
Marsannay-la-Côte 114
Marsanne 194, 492
Marshall, Dom. Tim 138
Marshall, Tim 133
Martel, G.H. & Co. 185
Martha's Vineyard 486
Marthenot, Dom. 143
Martigné-Briand 165
Martillac 57
Martin, Georges 114
Martin, Henri 59
Martin-Jarry 164
Martina 357
Martina Franca 357
Martinborough Vineyard 511

Martine, Dom. de la 224
Martinens, Ch. 56
Martinez, Bodegas Faustino 377

Martinez Gassiot & Co. Ltd. 400, 406
Martinez Lacuesta Hnos 378
Marting, Ch. de 68
Martini, Conti 315, 317
Martini, Karl & Söhn 317
Martini, Louis M. 464
Martini & Prati Wines 464
Martini & Rossi 302
Martino, Armando 361
Martinolles, Dom. de 214
Martinon, Ch. 102
Martinsthal 255
Martouret, Ch. de 102
Maryland 487
La Marzelle, Ch. 88
Mascarello, Bartolo 302
Mascarello, Giuseppe, & Figlio 302
Mascaró, Cavas 384
Maschio 322
Masi 321
Maso Poli 315
Il Maso 322
Massé Père & Fils 185
Le Masse di San Leolino 342
Masseria di Majo Norante-Ramitello 354
Massimi Berucci 352
Masson, Jacques 89
Masson, Paul, Vineyards 464
Masson-Blondelet, J.-M. 175
Mastantuono 464
Mastroberardino 355
Mastroianni 342
Mataro 492
Matawhero Wines 511
Mateagudo 393
Mateus Rosé 395, 397, 398, 399
Mathelin, Raymond & Fils 150
Matheus-Lehnert, J. 253
Matilde, Contessa 331
Matilde, Villa 355
Matino 357
Mátraalya 426
Matras, Ch. 88
Matravidek 426
Matrot, Dom. Joseph and Pierre 138
Matta, Etienne 206
Matteucci, Guarini 331
Matua Valley Wines 511
Mau, Jean-François 52
Maucaillou, Ch. 57
Maufoux, Pierre 138, 142
Maufoux, Prosper 138
Maume, Dom. 138
Maures 231
Maurin, M. 198
Mauro, Paola di 351
Maury, Les Vignerons de 211
Mausse, Ch. 99
Mauvais, Ch. 57
Mauvezin, Ch. 88
Mauzac 214, 225
Mavro of Paros 432
Mavro Romeiko 432
Mavrodaphne 432
Mavron 433
Mavroudi 432
Mavrud 430
Max, Louis 130
Maximin Grünhaus 251
Mayacamas Vineyards 465, 477
Maye, Simon 413
Mayer, Franz 421
Meyer-Nakel 254
Mayne, Ch. du 82
Mayne d'Anice, Ch. 76
Mayne-Binet, Ch. 103
Mayne-Lévêque, Ch. 76
Mayne-Vieil, Ch. 99

Mayol de Lupé, Comtesses 136
Mazaga, Bodegas 387
Mazard, Bernard 214
Mazeau, H. 57
Mazerat, Ch. 90
Mazeris, Ch. 99
Mazeris-Bellevue, Ch. 99
Mazeyres, Ch. 97
Mazis-Chambertin 115
Mazoyères-Chambertin 115
Mazouna 436
Mazziotti, Italo 352
Mazzolino, Tenuta 311
Mazzucchelli, Villa 312
Méaume, Ch. 103
Mecvini 348
Meddersheim 264
Medina, José 394
Medoc 47, 52-72
Medoc Coop. 65
Médoc Noir 425
Meerendal 517
Meerlust 517
Meerspinne 276
Meffre, Etab. Gabriel 199
Meffre family 59, 200
Megia, Luis 385
Mehring 244
Meia Encosta 399
Meier, Anton 416
La Meirana 305
Les Meix 119
La Mejanelle 217
Meknes 436
Melini 338
Melissa 360
Mellot, A. 174
Melnik 430
Meloni Vini 367
Le Menaudat, Ch. 100
Mendoce, Ch. 100
Mendocino 440, 442
Mendoza 522
Mendrisiotto 416
Meneret-Capdemourlin family 88
Ménétou-Salon 160, 176
Ménota, Ch. de 82
Montecompatri-Colonna 351
Mentone, Ch. de 208
Méntrida 368
Mentzelopoulos family 53
Méo-Camuzet, Dom. 138
Méo-Camuzet family 134
Meraner Hugel 315
Meranese di Collina 314
Merced 443
Mercier 181
Mercier, L. & Fils 158
Mercredière, Ch. de la 162
Mercurey 144
Mercy Dieu, Dom. de la 174
Merdot & Co. 185
Meredyth Vineyards 487
Meridian Vineyards 465
Merlançon, Dom. de 208
Merlaut, Jean 52
Merlot 50-1, 223, 225, 328, 430, 434, 445, 492, 522
Merlot di Pramaggiore 319
Merlot (Lombardy) 309
Merlot (Veneto) 319
Mermillo, Jean 226
Mermoud, Luc 414
Mérode, Dom. Prince Florent de 138
Merotto 322
Merrill, Geoff 500
Merritt Island 443
Merritt Estate Winery Inc. 485
Merry Vintners 465
Mertesdorf 251
Meslin, Georges 88
Messias 397
Messias, Vinhos 400
Messinò, Ferdinando 360
Messo in bottiglia nel'origine 298

Mestre Père & Fils 138
Mestres Sagues, Antonio 384
Mestrezat SA 52
Métaireau, Gilbert 164
Métaireau, Louis 164
Metodo tradizionale 298
Metsovo 432
Mettenheim 269
Metternich, Fürst von 257
Metternich'sche Weingüter 421
Meunier-Lapha, Maison 176
Meurgey, Georges 128
Meursalt 124
Meursault 123-4
Meursault, Ch. de 138-9
Meyer 190
Meyer, Jos. & Fils 190
Meyerhof, Weingut 251
Meyney, Ch. 66
Le Meynieu, Ch. 69
Meyre, Alain 57
Les Meysonniers 195
Meyzonnier, Jacques 214
Mezesfeher 424
Mezzocorona, Cantina 317
Mialhe, William-Alain 56
Miali 359
Michaud, Alain 151
Michel, Dom. 454
Michel, Emile 185
Michel, Louis, & Fils 113
Michel, Robert 196
Michel Montaigne, Ch. de 223
Michelin, Noël 207
Michelot, Dom. Alain 139
Michi, Fattoria 342
Michigan 487-8
Middelvlei 517
Midi 209-19
Miele, Bernard 113
Milano Winery 465
Mildara Wines 500
Milhade, Maison Jean 91
Mill Creek Vineyards 465
Mille-Secousses, Ch. 100
Milliérioux, Paul 175
Millésime 74
Millet, Ch. 77
Million Rousseau, Michel 158
Milon, Ch. 90
The Milton Vineyard 511
Milz Laurentiushof 253
Minchinbury 502
Minervois 209, 214-16
Minervois, Laure 215
Minervois, Peyriac 215
Minheim 245
Minho 395, 396-7
Minis 429
Minuty, Ch. 206
Miolane, René 150
Miquel 218
Mirabella 365
Mirafiori 301
Miraflores 390
Miramar 500
Mirassou Vineyards 465
Mireval, Muscat de, Cave de Rabelais 219
Mirleau, Dom. de 166
Miscianello Tomarecchio 342
Missery, Maison P. 139
Mission 445
La Mission-Haut-Brion, Ch. 75
Mission Vineyard 511
Mississippi Delta 488
Missouri 488
Mitchell, Thomas 500
Mitchell Cellars 500
Mitchelton 500
Mittelhaardt 274, 275
Mittelhaardt-Deutsche Weinstrasse 274

Mittelheim 256
Mittelmosel 244, 244-6
Mittelrhein 238, 253-4
Mittnacht 190
Moccagatta 305
Mocenni 342
Modbury 502
Modesto 443
Modot, Dom. 143
Moët & Chandon 181
Moillard, Maison 139
Moines, Ch. des 92, 98
Moingeon-Gueneau Frères 133
Moio, Michele 355
Moldavia 429
Mole, Ch. de 92
Molin, André 133
Molina, Castillo de 521
Molinelli, Giancarlo 331
Molise 354
Mollet de Perelada, Cooperativa de 383
Mollex, Georges 158
Mommessin 153
Mommessin, Dom. 139
La Monacesca 348
Monarch Wine Co. Inc. 485
Monassier, Armand 145
Monbadon, Ch. 99
Monbazillac 222
Monbazillac, Ch. de 223
Monbouché, René 223
Monbousquet, Ch. 91
Moncada-Monte Giove, Conte 352
Monção 397
Moncet, Ch. 98
Monconseil Gazin, Ch. 100
Moncontour, Ch. 171
Moncucchetto 305
Mondavi, Robert 462-3, 465
  Opus One 465, 477
  Robert Mondavi Winery 465, 477
  Robert Mondavi Woodbridge 465
Monfalletto-Cordero Montezemolo 302
Monforte 296
Mongeard-Mugneret 139
Monica di Cagliari 366
Monica di Sardegna 366
Moniga del Garda 310
Monistrol, Marqués de 382
Monmousseau, J.M. 171
Monnet, Dom. René 152
Monnier, Dom. Jean & Fils 139
Monnier, Dom. René 139
Monopole 74
Monopole Clos des Ducs 127
Monrozier, Dom. 153
Monsanto 338
Monsecco 300
Monsignore, Tenuta del 331
Monsupello 312
Le Mont 171
Mont Baudile 232
Mont Bouquet 231
Mont-Caume 231
Mont de Milieu 112, 113
Mont d'Or, Dom. du 413
Mont-Redon, Dom. de 203
Mont-sur Rolle 412
Mont Tauch, Cave Coopérative 213
Montagliari 342
Montagne, Jacques 150, 151
Montagne de Reims 186
Montagne family 75
Montagne-St-Emilion 92-3
Montagnieu 157
Montagny 144
Montaguillon, Ch. 92
Montalba-Le-Château 211
Montalivet, Ch. 77

Montalto, Cella di 312
Montalto, Fratelli 365
Montana Wines 511
La Montanella 322
Montaud, Ch. 208
Montbray Wine Cellars 487
Montbrun, Ch. 56
Montdomaine 487
Monte, Castel del 356
Monte Antico 333
Monte Cristo, Bodegas 387
Monte Firidolfi 337
Monte Rossa 311
Monte Schiavo 348
Monte Vertine 338
Montebello 185
Montecarlo 333
Montecorno 322
Montée de Tonnerre 112
Montefalco 345
Montefiascone, Cantina di 352
Montegiachi, Tenuta 338
Montegrossi, Castello di 337
Montelaria, Ch., Winery 451
Montelena, Ch. 465, 477
Montelio 312
La Montelliana, Cantina, e dei Colli Asolani 322
Montello e Colli Asolani Piave
Montellori, Fattoria 342
Montemaggio 342
Montenidoli 342
Montepulciano 347
Montepulciano, Vecchia Cantina di 342-3
Montepulcino d'Abruzzo 352
Monterey 439, 443
Monterey Peninsula Winery 466
The Monterey Vineyard 466
Monterminod 158
Monterminod, Ch. de 158
Monternot 150
Monterosso Val d'Arda 328
Monterrey 371
Monterrey Coop. 373
Montescudaio 333
Montesecco, Fattoria di 348-9
Montesodi 338
Montestruc 234
Monteviña Wines 466
Montgilet, Dom. de 167
Monthélie 123
Monthelie-Douhairet, Dom. 139
Monthil, Ch. 72
Monthoux 158
Monti, Elio 353
Monticello Cellars 466
Montilla-Moriles 368, 386
Montille, Dom. Hubert de 139
Montinore 480
Montjoie, Dom. de 212
Montlabert, Ch. 91
Montlouis 160, 169
Montlouis Mousseux 160
Montmains 112
Montmains Butteaux 112
Montmains-Fôret 112
Montmélian 157, 158
Montner Coop. 211
Montori, Camillo 353
Montoro, Castello di 346
Montpellier 517
Montpeyroux 217
Montrachet 123
Montravel 222
Montresor 322
Montrose 500
Montrose, Ch. 66
Monts de la Grage 232

Monts du Tessalah 436
Monts Luisants 140
Montseret, Cave Coopérative 213
Montuni del Reno 328
Montvillers 185
Montys 164
Mony, Ch. 101
Monzel 245
Monzingen 264
Moorilla Estate 500
Moorlynch Vineyard 525
Moor's Diamond 486
Mor 426
Morange, Dom. de 102
Morat, Lake 410, 412
Moravia 426, 427
Moreau, Claude 171
Moreau, Michel and François 95
Moreau, Ph. 153
Moreau family 96
Moreau, J. &, Fils 114
Morel, G, Fils 185
Morellino di Scansano 333
Morey, Albert & Fils 139
Morey St-Denis 115
Morgan 404
Morgeot 138
Morgex et de la Salle, Le Cave du Vin Blanc de 306
Morgon 152
Morin, Ch. 66
Morines, Dom. des 163
Mornag, Ch. 435
Mornington Peninsula 491
Moro 331
Moroder 349
Morot, Albert 139
La Morra 296
Morris, J.W., Wineries 466
Morris Wines 500
Morton Estate 511
Mosbacher, George 278
Moscadello di Montalcino 334
Moscat Ottonel 430
Moscatel (sherry) 390
Moscato 445
Moscato d'Asti Spumante 298
Moscato di Cagliari 366
Moscato di Noto 363
Moscato di Sardegna 366
Moscato di Scanzo 357
Moscato di Siracusa 363
Moscato di Sorso-Sennori 366
Moscato di Trani 357
Moscato (Sicily) 363
Mosel 238
Mosel-Saar-Ruwer 237, 238, 242-53
Moselland eG Winzergenossenschaft 249
Moselor 242
Moser, Lenz 421
Moss Wood 501
Mossi 331
Möt Ziflon 298
Mothe, Ch. La 69
Motte, Dom. de 167
Mottron, Vins 167
Mouchet, Ch. 92
Moueix, Armand 52, 87, 91, 96
Moueix, Ch. 99
Moueix, Christian 95, 453
Moueix, Jean-François 51
Moueix, Jean-Pierre 86, 87, 88, 91, 93, 95, 96
Le Moulin 210
Moulin, Ch. du 92
Moulin, Dom. du 152
Moulin d'Arvigny 68
Moulin Bellegrave, Ch. 91
Moulin du Cadet, Ch. 88
Moulin des Carruades 65
Moulin des Costes 207
Moulin de Duhart 61
Moulin de la Gravelle 164

Moulin des Laurets, Ch. 92
Moulin de la Rose, Ch. 59
Moulin Rouge, Ch. 99
Moulin Rouge, Ch. du 69
Moulin-à-Vent 152-3
Moulin-à-Vent, Ch. 98
Moulin-à-Vent, Ch. du 153
Moulin à Vent, Ch. 57
Moulin-de-Calon, Ch. 66
Moulin-Pey-Labrie, Ch. 99
Moulin-Riche, Ch. 59
La Mouline 196
Moulinet, Ch. 96
Moulins Listrac, Ch. 92
Moulis 56-7
Moulis & Listrac 46
Moulis, Ch. 57
Mount Anakie 501
Mt. Badacsonyi 425
Mount Baker 482
Mount Eden Vineyards 466
Mount Hurtle 500
Mount Langhi Ghiran 501
Mount Mary 501
Mount Palomar Winery 466
Mount Pleasant Vineyards 488
Mount Veeder 443
Mt. Veeder Winery 466
Mountadam 501
Mountain View Winery 466
Moureau, Mme. & Fils 216
Mourvedre 201, 205, 212
Mousset, Société Louis 203
Mousset family 203
Moussière, Dom. la 174
Mouton-d'Armailcq 64
Mouton-Baronne-Philippe, Ch. 64
Mouton-Rothschild, Ch. 60-1
Moutonne 112
Moutottes, Les 119
Mouvèdre 210
Moyer, Dominique 171
Mudgee 491
Muerza, Bodegas 379
Muga, Bodegas 377
Mugneret, Bernard 140
Mugneret, Dom. Georges 139
Mugneret-Gibourg 140
Mugneret-Gouachon, Dom. 140
Mugnier, Fréderick 129
Mugnier, Henri 133
La Muiraghina 312
Mule Blanche 196
Mülheim 245
De Muller 382
Müller, Egon 250
Müller, Matheus 257
Müller, Rudolf 239
Müller, Rudolf, GmbH & Co. 249
Müller, Weingut 283
Müller-Catoir, Weingut 277
Müller-Dr. Becker, Weingut 273
Müller-Schartzhof, Egon 249
Müller-Thurgau 524
Müller-Thurgau (Lombardy) 309
Multier, Paul 196
Mumm 182
Mumm, Dom. 454
Mumm, G.H. von 259-60
Münster Sarmsheim 266
Murana, Salvatore 365
Murcia 385
Muré 190-1
Murfatlar 429
Murray River 490, 491
Murrieta, Marqués de 374, 377

Murrumbidgee 491
Musar, Ch. 435
Muscadelle 51, 492
Muscadet 160-5
Muscadet de Sèvre et Maine 160
Muscadet des Coteaux de la Loire 160
Muscadine 482
Muscardin 201
Muscat 189, 219, 432, 434, 445
Muscat of Alexandria 433
Muscat de Kelibia 435
Muscat of Lemnos 432
Muscat of Rion 432
Muscat of Samos 432
Musigny 116
Muskat Ottonel 425
Muskotály 425-6
Mussy, Dom. André 140
Mustilli 355
Myrat, Ch. de 81

N
Nackenheim 270
Nägler, Dr. Heinrich 263
Nágyburgundi 425
Nahe 237-8, 264-9
Nahe-Winzer eG 269
Nahegauer Landwein 288
Naigeon, J.-P. 140, 143
Naigeon-Chauveau, Maison 140
Nairac, Ch. 82
Naitana, Gian Vittorio 367
Nalys, Société du Domaine de 203
Naoussa 432
  Coop. 433
Napa 443
Napa-Beaucanon, Ch. 466
Napa Cellars see DeMoor Winery
Napa Creek Winery 466
Napa Valley 439-40, 443
Napolean amontillado 394
Napolitano, Fratelli 361
Naquad 435
Narbusto 309
Narby, Frank 78
Nardò 357
Narince 434
Nascari, Bodegas 522
Nascig 326
Nasco di Cagliari 366
Navajas, Bodegas 379
Navarra 368, 370
Navarra, Vinicola 373
Navarro, Ch. de 82
Navarro Vineyards 466
Néac 98
Nebbiolo 298, 445
Nebbiolo d'Alba 298
Nebbiolo del Piemonte 298
Nebbiolo delle Langhe 298
Nebbiolo di Carema, Produttori 302
Neckerauer, K. 278-9
Nederburg 513, 517
Neef 247
Neethlingshof 517
Négociant 74
Négrit, Ch. 93
Negroni, Bruno 331
Neipperg, Comtes de 86
Neipperg, Graf von 285
Neive, Castello di 302
Nelson 509
Nema Wine Producers Cooperative 433
Nemea 432-3
Nemes Kadar 425
Nenin, Ch. 96
Nera 312
Neri, Casanova dei 341
Nero 298
Nerthe, Dom. de la 203
Nervers, Ch. de 151
Nervesa, Abazia di 322
Nervi, Luigi & Italo 302

Nestuby, Dom. de 208
Neuchâtel, Lake 410, 412, 415
Neuharth 482
Neumagen-Dhron 245
Neuquen 522
Neusiedlersee 418
De Neuville 167, 169
Nevado, Marqués del 522
Neveu, Freiherr von 290
Neveu, Roger 175
New England 486
New Hall 525
New Hampshire 486
New South Wales 490-1
New York State 482-5
Newton Vineyards 466
Neyret-Gachet family 195
Neyroud, Alain 414
Neyroud, Jean & Fils 158
Ngatarawa Wines 511-12
Niagara 486
Nichelini Vineyard 466
Nicò, Fattoria 353
Nicodemo, Aloisio 360
Nicolas 141
Nicolay, Peter 249
Nicoreşti 429
Niebaum, Gustave, Collection 466
Niebaum Coppola Estate 466
Niederhausen 265
Niederösterreich 417-8
Nielluccio 220
Niepoort & Co. Ltd. 400, 406
Nierstein 269-70
Nierstein Bereich 269
Nikolai, Heinz 263
Nikolaihof-Geyerhof, Weingut 422
Nino Negri 311
Nipozzano, Castello di 338
Nitra 427
Nobilo Vintners 512
La Noë, Ch. 164
Noël-Bouton, E. and X. 145
Noellat, Dom. 136
La Noëlle, Cave Coopérative 165
Non admis 268
Nonini, A., Winery 467
Nony, Jean-Pierre 87
Nordheim, Winzergrenossenschaft 283
Norheim 265
Norman, A. & Sons 501
North Coast (California) 443
North Salem Vineyard, Inc. 485
Northern Territory 492
Northland 509
Norton 486, 523
Nosiola 314
Nostrano 416
Notton, Ch. 53
Nouvelles, Ch. de 212
Noval, Quinta do 404
Nozet, Ch. du 175
Nozzole 311
Nuestro Padre Jesus del Perdon Coop. 386
Nugnes, Fratelli 359
Nuits-St-Georges 118
Numero 2 66
Nuova Cappelletta 305
Il Nuraghe, Cantina Sociale 367
Nuragus di Cagliari 366
Nussbaumer 416
Nutbourne Manor 525

O
Oak Knoll Winery 480
Oakridge Estate 501
Oakridge Vineyards *see* East Side Winery
Oakville 442

Oberemmel 243
Oberemmeler Abteilhof 248
Obermosel 242
Obester Winery 467
Obrist 414
Ochoa, Bodegas 373
Ockenheim 270
Ockfen 243
Oddero, Fratelli 305
Odenwälder Winzergenossenschaft 279
Odernheim 264
Odoardi, Giovanni Battista 360
Odobeşti 429
Oenologue 74
Oestrich 256
Oetinger, Robert von 263
Ogier, A. & Fils 199
Ogliastra, Cantina Sociale 367
Ohler, Kommerzienrat P.A. 273
Ohnacker, Weingut 273
Oinoexagogiki, J. & G. Calligas 432
Oiselinière, Ch. de l' 164
Oisly et Thesée, La Confrérie des Vignerons de 172
Okanagan Riesling 484
Olarra, Bodegas 375, 377
Olasz 424
Olaszrizling 426
Old Castile 371
Old World port 404
Olifantsrivier 514
Oliva, Tenuta di 312
Olive Farm 501
Olivier, Ch. 75
Olivier family 198
Ollieux, Ch. des 212
Ollon 412
Ollwiller, Ch. 192
Oloroso 389-90
Olson Vineyards 467
Oltrepò Pavese 308-10
L'Omarins (Franschck) 517
L'Omarins (Groot Drakenstein) 517-18
Ondenc 225
Ondet-Raynaud, Béatrice 87
O'Neale, Rafael 394
Opere Trevigiane 322
Opol 430
Oppenheim 270
Optimum 316
Opus One 465, 477
Oran 436
Ordensgut 276
Ordonnance sur les Denrées Alimentaires (ODA) 409
Oregon 478-81
Oregon Estates Winery 481
Oreste Lini & Figli 331
Orfila 523
De Orgnac-L'Aven Coop 201
Orlandi 322
Orlando 501
Orléannais (vin de l') 160
Orleans Hill Viniculural Association 467
Orme aux Loups 174
Les-Ormes-de-Pez, Ch. 66
Les Ormes Sorbet, Ch. 72
Ormières, Jean-Pierre 215
Ormož 428
Ornellaia 338-9
Orsar, Caves SA 413
Orsat, Jacques-Alphonse & Philippe frères 413
Orschwiller Coop. 192
Orsolani 305
Orta Nova 357

Ortenau Bereich 288
Ortiz, Viñedos SA 521
Ortola, Yvon 218
Orvieto 344-5
Osann 245
Osborne 394
Ostertag, Dom. 191
Ostuni 357
Ostuni, Ottavianello di 357
Los Oteros 371
Otis Vineyards 481
Otoño 394
Ott, Doms. 207
Oudinot 185
L'Oustau-Vieil, Ch. 102
Ovals 467
Overberg 514
Overgaauw 518

P
Paarl 514
Pabiot, Didier 175
Pacheco Pass 442
Pacheco Ranch Winery 467
Pacherenc 227
Pacquet, François 153
Padirac, Vicomte de 66
El Padre 393
Padthaway 492, 500
Paez, Luis 394
Pagadebit di Romagna 328
Page Mill Winery 467
Pagès, Patrice 57
Pagliarese 343
I Paglieri Roagna 305
Pagnana, Fattoria 343
Pagnon, Jean 150
Paicines 442
Paillard, Bruno 185
Paillard, E.M. 185
País 520
Palace Hotel do Buçaco 399
Palacio, Bodegas 379
Palacio de Brejoeira 400
Palacios, Bodegas José 379
Palais Cardinal La Fuie, Ch. 91
Les Palais, Ch. 212
Palette 206
Palette, Ch. de 101
Pallavincini, Principe 352
Pallhuber, Maximilian 268
Les Pallierondes 198
Palma 390
Palmer, Ch. 55
Palo Cortado 390
Palomino y Vergara 393
Palomo, H. 59
Pamid 431
Pampelonne, Ch. de 207
Panet, Ch. 91
Panigon, Ch. de 72
Panis, Guy 215
Panisseau, Ch. de 223
Pannier, Remy 167
Pannonian Plain 425
Pantellaria, Agricoltori Associati di 363
Panther Creek 479
Panzano 337
Papagni Vineyards 467
Pape-Clément, Ch. 75
Paquette, Jean 206
Paradiesgarten 264
Paradiso, Fattoria 329
Paraza, Ch. de 214
Parc, Dom. du 218
Pardaillan, Ch. 100
Parducci Wine Cellars 467
Parent, Dom. 140
Paret, Ch. 99
Parigot-Richard 133
Paris, Dom. de 208
Park, Dom. du 224
Parnac, Ch. de 224
Parri 343
Parriere, Dom. de la 140
Parrina 334
La Parrina 343
Parsac, Ch. 93
Parsac-St-Emilion 93

Parson's Creek Winery 467
Partico dei Leoni 315
Parusso, Armando 305
Pascal SA 199
Pascaud, Pierre 79
Pascual SA 199
Pasini, Volpe 325
Pasini Produttori 312
Pask, C.J. 512
Paso Robles 442
Pasolini, M. 312
Pasolini Dall'Onda 331
Pasolini Dall'Onda-Enoagricola 343
Pasqua, Fratelli 322
Pasquero-Elia, Secondo 305
Pasquier-Desvignes 153
Passe-tout-grains 147
Passito 298
Passito di Pantelleria 363
Passito Le Muraglie 306
Passot, Georges and Alain 152
Pastori Winery 467
Pastoso 299
Pata de gallina 390
Patâche d'Aux, Ch. 72
La Patache, Ch. 97
Paternina, Bodegas Federico 377
Paternoster 361
Patissier 153
Pato, Luis 397, 400
Patras 432
Patriarche, Père 140
Patriarche Père & Fils 140
Patrimonio 220
Patris, Ch. 91
Pattono, Villa 302
Pauillac 59-65
Paul-Etienne Père & Fils 196
La Paulands 119
Paulinshof, Weingut 253
Paulliac 46
Pauly, Jacques 78
Pauly, Otto 249
Pauly-Bergweiler, Dr. 249
Paveil de Luze, Ch. 56
Pavelot, Jean-Marc 140
Pavie, Ch. 86
Pavie-Decesse, Ch. 88
Pavie-Macquin, Ch. 88
Paviglia, Dom. de 220
Pavillon, Ch. du 99, 102
Pavillon Blanc 53
Pavillon-Cadet, Ch. 88
Pavillon Rouge 53
Pavy, Gaston 171
Paxarete 390
Paymartin, Ch. 59
Pays Charentais 234
Pays d'Oc 234
Paziols 213
Pazz, Al 331
Pech d'André, Dom. du 216
Pech Latt, Ch. de 212
Pech-Redon, Dom. de 217
Péchot, Mas 210
Péconnet, Ch. 101
Pecorari, Francesco 326
Pecota, Robert, Winery 467
Pecs 425
Pédasclaux, Ch. 64
Pedrizzetti Winery 467
Pedroncelli, J. Winery 468
Pedrotti, Fratelli 317
Peel Estate 501
Pegaso 311
Pegasus, Ch. 433
Pein, Antoine 150
Pelaquié, Dom. 199
Pelegrin, François 67
Pelissero, Luigi 305
Pellaro 360
Pellegrino, Carlo 363
Pelleire, André 152
Pellerin 153
Peñafiel 397
Peñaflor 523

Penedès 368, 380
Penfolds 501-2
Pennsylvania 487
Pentro 354
Pepe, Emidio 352
Pepi, Robert, Winery 468
Pepin, Christian 167
Peppoli 343
Perabo, Fritz 263
Peraldi, Comte 220
Perazzi, Luigi 305
Perda Rubia 367
Perdrix, Les 140
Per'e Palummo 354
Pereira D'Oliveira Vinhos 408
Perenne, Ch. 100
Peresse 213
Peret 219
La Pertica, Cascina 312
Perla de Tirnave 429
Perlage 311
Perll, August 254
Perlwein 241
Pernand-Vergelesses 119
Pernaud, Ch. 82
Perrachon, M.J. 152
Perrazzo Vini d'Ischia 355
Perret, Jean-Claude 157
Perrichon, M. 153
Perrier, J. & Fils 158
Perrier, Joseph 182
Perrier-Jouët 182
Perrière, Dom de la 140
Perrin family 200, 202
Perrin, Antony 73
Perrodo, M. 55
Perron, Ch. 98
Perroud, Gilles 150
Perroy 412
Pertinace, I Vignaioli Elvio 305
Pesce, Cascina 303
Pesenti Winery 468
Pesos, Quinta dos 398
Pessac 73
Pessac-Leognan 46, 72-3
Pesson, Robert 175
Petaluma 502
Petersberg 254
Petersons 502
Petit, Désiré & Fils 156
Petit, Pierre 218
Petit Campdumy, Dom. du 206
Petit Crau 231
Petit Duc Côtes-du-Rhône 202
La Petit Eglise 95
Petit-Faurie-de-Soutard, Ch. 88
Petit-Refuge, Ch. 92
Petit Verdot 51
Petit-Village, Ch. 96
Petite Sirah 445
Les Petites Lolières 119
Petits Châteaux 47-8
Petriat, Jean Louis 58
Petriolo, Fattoria di 343
Petrucco, Lina & Paolo 326
Pétrus, Ch. 93, 97
Peychaud, Ch. 100
Peynaud, Professor Emile 9, 53, 75, 81, 82, 85, 89, 218, 373
Peyrabon, Ch. 69
Peyrat, Ch. 101
Peyrat, Ch. du 101
Peyraud, Lucien 207
Peyreau, Ch. 91
Peyrebon, Ch. 102
Peyredoulle, Ch. 100
Peyrelebade, Ch. 57
Peyrelongue, Ch. du 91
Peyros, Ch. de 227
Peza 432
    Coop. 433
de Pez, Ch. 67
Pézenas 232
Pezilla-La-Rivière 211
Pezinok 427

Pfaffengrund 276
Pfaffenheim-
  Gueberschwihr Coop.
  192
Pfälzer Landwein 288
Pfarrgarten 264
Pfarrkirche, Weingut der
  249
Pfeffingen, Weingut 277
Pheasant Ridge 488
Phélan-Ségur, Ch. 67
Phelps, Joseph, Vineyards
  468, 477
Philipponat 185
Phillips, R.H., Vineyard
  468
Piacentini 327
Piada, Ch. 82
Piat 148, 153-4
Piat d'Or 154
Piave 318
Piazzo, Armado 305
Pibran, Ch. 65
Pic, Albert 114
Pic St-Loup 217
Picamelot 133
Picard, Lucien 174
Les Picasses 172
Piceno, Consorzio Agrario
  Ascoli 349
Picenum 349
Pichelèbre, Ch. 99
Pichon, Ch. 69
Pichon-Longueville,
  Comtesse de Lalande, Ch.
  64
Pichon-Longueville au
  Baron de Pichon-
  Longueville, Ch. 64
Le Pici 343
Picòl Ross 328
Picolit 324
Picpoul de Pinet 218
Pied d'Aloup 112
Piedmont 294-306
Piedmont, Max-G. 253
Piemontese, Vinacola 305
Pierbone, Ch. 69
Pierlot, Jules 185
Pieropan 322
Pierrat, Dom. Martin 218
Pierre, Marcel 185
De Pierrefeu-du-Var 208
Pierrère, Ch. la 99
Pierreux, Ch. de 151
Pierro 502
Pierron, Ch. 226
Piesport 245
Pietrafitta 343
Pietraserena 343
Pieva del Vescova 346
Pighin, Fratelli 326
Pigna, Villa 348
Pike's Polish Hill River
  502
Pilgerpfad 271
Pilote de Villeneuve Les
  Corbières, Cave
  Coopérative 213
Pindefleurs, Ch. 91
Pine Ridge Winery 468
Pinet 218
Pinet, Cave Coopérative de
  218
Pinget, Gérard 414
Pingossière, Dom. de la
  164
Pinnacle 504
The Pinnacles 442
Pinon, J.B. 171-2
Pinord, Bodegas 383
Pinot (Lombardy) 310
Pinot (Piedmont) 298
Pinot Bianco 319, 328
Pinot Blanc 188, 268, 445
Pinot Grigio 319, 329
Pinot Gris 188, 268
Pinot Meunier 524
Pinot Nero 319
Pinot Noir 188, 430, 445,
  478, 492, 522
Pinot St. George 445

Pinson, Louis 114
Pinte, Dom. de la 156
Pipeau, Ch. 91
Piper Heidsieck 182
Piper-Sonoma 468
Piper's Brook 503
Pipet, Raymond 176
Pipoul 201
Pique-Caillou, Ch. 77
Piquetberg 514
Pires, João and Filhos 399
Piron, Ch. 77
Piron, Pierre 152
Pirramimma 503
Pisoni, Fratelli 317
Pistouley, Hubert 88
Pitigliano, Cantina
  Cooperativa 343
Pitray, Ch. de 99
Pittaro, Vigneti 326
Pitters, William 52
Pivot, Jean-Claude 150
Placer 442-3
Plageoles, Robert 226
Plaisance, Ch. 93
Planes, Dom. des 207
Plane's Cayuga Vineyard
  485
Planezes Coop. 211
Plantagenet Wines 503
Plantey, Ch. 65
Plantey de la Croix, Ch. 69
Plauto 311
Plavac 429
Plettenberg, Reichsgraf
  von 268
Plince, Ch. 96
Plot, Dom. du 201
Ployez-Jacquemart 185
Plozner 326
Pnte (Cantina Sociale
  Cooperative di Ponte di
  Piave) 322
Poças Junior, Porto, Lda.
  405
Pocé, Ch. de 170
Podere Lo Locco 342
Poderi Boscarelli 337
Poggetto 311
Poggi, Fratelli 343
Poggio, Castello del 305
Poggio, Tenuta di 343
Poggio al Sole 343
Poggio Romita 343
Poggio Rosso 343
Il Poggiolino 343
Il Poggiolo 343
Il Poggiolo, Fattoria 343
Poggione, Tenuta Il 339
Poilly 172-3, 175
Pouilly-Fuissé 147-8
Pouilly-sur-Loire, Cave
  Coopérative 175
Pouilly-Vinzelles 147-8
La Pointe, Ch. 96
Poiron, Henri 164
Pojer & Sandri 315
Pokalwein 241
Pol Roger 182-3
Poli, Giovanni 317
Poli, Maso 317
Pölich 244
Poligny, Caveau des
  Jacobins 156
Poliziano 339
Pollino 360
  Cantina Sociale Vini di
  360
Pomace 467
Pomerol 46, 49-50, 93-8
Pomeys, Ch. 57
Pomino 334
Pommard 122
Pommard, Ch. de 140
Pommeraie Vineyards 468
Pommery & Greno 183
Pomples, Dom. des 206
Poncet, Ch. 101
Ponche 429
Poncié, Soc. Civile du Ch.
  de 152
Poniatowski, Prince 172

Ponnelle, Bruno 140
Ponnelle, Maison Pierre
  140
Pons-Mure, Mme. 198
Ponsot, Dom. Jean-Marie
  140
Pontac, M. 81
Pontac-Lynch, Ch. 56
Pontet, Ch. 72
Pontet-Canet, Ch. 64
Pontifs, Dom. des 204
Pontoise-Cabarrus, Ch. 69
Ponzi Vineyards 479
Pope Valley see Napa
Popp, Ernst 283
Poppiano, Castello di 343
Porret, A. 415
Port 11, 401-6
Port (California) 445
Porta Rossa, Cantina della
  305
Portalegre 398
Porte-greffe 74
Portel 213
Portets 73
Portets, Ch. de 77
Portico di Leoni 317
Porzina, Villa 351
Pošip 429
Postup 429
Potel, Gérard 141
Potensac, Ch. 72
Potter Valley 443
Pouget, Ch. 55
Pouilly Fumé 160, 163, 173
Pouilly sur Loire 160
Poujeaux, Ch. 57
Poulachon, M.P. 152
Poulet Père & Fils 141
Poulvère, Ch. 223
Pouroquet family 88
Pourret, Ch. 91
Pousse d'Or, Dom. de la
  141
Poveda, Bodegas Salvador
  385
Pra, Graziano 322
Prà di Pradis 326
Pradel 208
Pradère, M. 59
Pradets 204
Pradikatswein 421
Pradis, Dom. du 198
Praeclarus 317
Prager, Franz 421
Prager Winery & Port
  Works 468
Pramaggiore 319
Prato, Baroni a 317
Prats, Bruno 65
Predicato 334
Predicato del Muschio 334
Predicato del Selvante 334
Predicato di Biturica 334
Predicato di Cardisco 334
Preignac, Ch. de 91
Premières Côtes de Blaye
  100-1
Premières Côtes de
  Bordeaux 46, 100-1
Premiovini 311
Les Pres, Ch. 152
Pressac, Ch. de 91
Pressing 34-5, 38
Preston 482
Preston Vineyards 468
Preticato 294
Preuses 112
Prieur, Dom. Jacques 141
Prieur, Martin 141
Prieur, Paul & Fils 174
Prieuré, Ch. du 203
Prieuré de Jocelyn, Dom.
  du 127
Prieuré-Lichine, Ch. 55
Le Prieuré, Ch. 89
Primavera 394
Primitivo di Manduria 357
Prince Michael 487
Princic, Doro 326
Principauté d'Orange 231

Prion, Etienne 87
Priorato 368, 380-1
Prissé Coop. 148
Privilegio 394
Privilegio Rey Sancho 376
Probstberg 244
Proby, Baron de 155
Prosecco di Conegliano-
  Valdobbiadene 319
Prošek 429
Protheau, Dom. Maurice
  & Fils 145
Protheau, François 145
Provence 205-8
  Vins de Pays 231
Proviar 522-3
Provins Valais 413
Prudence Hill Vineyards
  486
Prudence Island Vineyards
  486
Prüm, J.J. 249
Prüm Erben, S.A. 249
Pruning methods 16
Prunotto, Alfredo 302
Puffeney, Jacques 156
Le Pupille, Fattoria 343
Pupillin Coop. 156
La Purisima Coop. 386
Puy, Ch. du 93
Puy Castéra, Ch. 69
Puy-Blanquet, Ch. 91
Puyblanquet Carille, Ch.
  91
Puyfromage, Ch. 99
Puygeraud, Ch. 99
Puyguilhem, Ch. 99
Puymiran, Ch. 102
Py, Dom. du 152
Pyrenees (Australia) 491
Pyuj 428

Q
Quady Winery 468
Quail Ridge 468
Qualitätswein 237, 421
Qualitätswein bestimmter
  Anbaugebiete (QbA) 236
Qualitatswein mit Prädikat
  (QmP) 236, 241
Quancard, Joel 51
Quancard, M. 51
Quarante 218
Quarles Harris & Co. Lda.
  405
Quarts de Chaume 160,
  163, 165
Quatrourze 218
Queen Adelaide 506
Queensland 492
Quelltaler 503
Quénard family 157-8
Quentin, Ch. 91
La Querce, Fattoria 339
Querceto, Castello di 343
Querciabella, Fattoria 343
Querciavalle 343
La Querciolana 346
Queribus, Ch. de 213
Querre, Maison Daniel 91
Querre, Maison Michel 91
Les Queyrats, Ch. 77
Quié, Mme. L. and J.M.
  61
Quié, Mme. Paul & J.M.
  54
Quilceda Creek 482
Quilhanet, Ch. de 213
Quillardet, Charles 141
Quincy 160, 176
Quinsac, Ch. de 102
Quinta do Cotto 403
Quintarelli, Giuseppe 321

Quiot, Dom. Pierre 204
Quitot St-Pierre 204
Quivira 468

R
R 79
Rabasse-Charavin, Dom.
  199
Rabastens Coop. 226
Rabaud-Promis, Ch. 78-9
Rabelais 436
Rabezzana, Renato 305
Rabiega, Dom. Christianna
  208
Rača 427
Radda, Contessa di 338
Radikon 326
Raffaelli, Luigi 317
Raffault, Jean Maurice 172
Raffault, Olga 172
Le Rafou-Tillières 164-5
Raggi, Villa I 331
La Ragose 321
Ragot, Dom. 145
Rahoul, Ch. 77
Raifault, Ch. 172
Raïmat 380, 382
Raimond Père & Fils 68
Rainera Pérez Martin,
  Hijos de 394
Rajnairizling 425
Ralle, Eugène 185
Rallo, Nuova 363
Ramage La Batisse, Ch. 69
Ramandolo Classico 324
Rame, Ch. la 102
Rametz, Castel 317
Ramonet, Ch. 102
Ramonet-Prudhon 141
Ramonteu, Henri 228
Ramos-Pinto, Adriano,
  Vinhos 405
Rampolla, Castello dei 339
Ramu, Claude 414
Ranch de Philo 468
Ranch Sisquoc Winery 468
Rancoule, Guy 215
Rancoure, Mas 210
Randersacker,
  Winzergrenossenschaft
  283
Rapet Père & Fils 141
Rapitalà 362-4
Raposeira, Caves de 400
Rappenhof, Weingut 272
Rapsani 432
Rasiguères Coop. 211
Raspail, Dom. de 199
Rasteau 199
  Coop. 201
Ratti, Renato (Abbazia
  dell'Annunziata) 302
Ratzenberger, J. 254
Rauenthal 255-6
Rausan-Ségla, Ch. 55
Rauzan-Gassies, Ch. 55
Ravat 51 486
Ravat Noir 486
Ravello 354
Raveneau, François 114
Ravensburg 281
Ravenswood 468
Raya 390
Rayas, Ch. 204
Raymond, Ch. 102
Raymond, Jean 66
Raymond, Marc et fils 413
Raymond, Yves 57
Raymond-Lafon, Ch. 82
Raymond Vineyards 468-9
Raynaud, Noël 95
Rayne-Vigneau, Ch. 79
Rayon d'Or 486
Razgad 430
Re, Tenuta dei 305
Real Companhia Vinicola
  do Norte de Portugal
  399, 405
Rebholz, Weingut
  Ökonomierat 277-8
Rebstöckel 276

Rechsteiner 322
Recioto della Valpolicella 320
Recioto di Soave 319
Récolte 74
Recouly 217
Red Cap 130
Red Willow 481
De Redcliffe Estates 510
Redde, Michel & Fils 175
Redgate 503
Redman 503
Redondo 398
Redwood Valley 443
Regaleali 363
Regaleali-Conte Tasca d'Almerita 364
Regalo 433
Regensburger Landwein 288
Região Demarcada (RD) 395
Regione su Concali, Cantina Sociale 367
Regis de Gatimel, Comte de 200
Regisseur 74
Regnard, A., & Fils 114
Regnie 153
Reguengos de Monsaraz 398
Reh, Franz & Söhn 239, 249
Rehblach 270
Reichensteiner 524
Reichsgraf & Marquis zu Hoensbroech 289-90
Reil 246
La Reine Pédauque 134, 141
Rel Tesoro, Herederos del Marqués de 394
Remey, Castell del 381
Remoissenet Père & Fils 141
Rémon, Michel 114
Remoriquet, Henri & Fils 141
Remstal-Stuttgart Bereich 284
Rémy, Ch. 495
Renarde, Dom. de la 145
Renault 436
Rencine, Castello de 343
Rendement 74
Renmano 494
Renou, René 167
Réserve de Carvaillons 199
Réserve de la Comtesse 64
Respide, Ch. 77
Ress, Balthasar 260
Retout, Ch. du 70
Retsina 432
Retz 234
Reuschberg 280
Reutenauer, Luc 224
Reverchon, Edmund 249
Reverchon, J. & Fils 156
Reverdy, Jean & Fils 174
Reverend, Dom. du 213
Rex Hill 479
Rey, Ch. de 211
Rey de Oro 394
Reynal 383
Reynaud family 204
Reynella, Ch. 495
Reynier, Ch. 102
Reynon, Ch. 101
Reysson, Ch. 70
Rhein 237-8
Rheinart, Adolf, Erben 251
Rheinburgen-Landwein 288
Rheingau 237-8, 255-64
Rheingrafenstein 271
Rheinhessen 169-74, 238
Rheinischer Landwein 288
Rheinpfalz 238, 274-9
Rheinterrasse 269
Rhode Island 486

Rhodes 432
Rhône 193-201
Université du Vin 204
Vins de Pays 231
Rias Baixas 368, 372
Ribatejo 398
Ribaute, Ch. de 213
Ribeauvillé et Environs Coop. 224
Ribeiro 368, 372
Coop. 373
Ribera de Burgos 371
Ribera del Duero 368, 371
Ribereau-Gayon, Jean 89
Ribereau-Gayon, Pascal 89
Ribero del Duero Coop. 372
Riccadonna 302
Riccard, Claude 73
Riccine 339
Richeaume, Dom. 208
Richebourg 116
Richebourg, Ch. de 163
Richelieu, Ch. 99
Richon-le-Zion 435
Richou, Dom. 168
Richter, Max Ferd. 251
Richter-Boltendahl, Weingut 263
Ridge Vineyards 469, 477
Ridgecrest 459
Riedel, Jakob 263
Rieder, Christopher 207
Ries, K. 262
Riesling 188-9, 236, 268, 310, 430, 492
Rieussec, Ch. 79
Riffault, Pierre & Etienne 175
Riforma Agraria, Cantina Sociale della 367
Rigal, Mme. 87
Rigal & Fils 224
Rigault, Léon 128
Righetti, Luigi 322
Rigord family 206
Rimauresq, Dom. de 208
Rinaldi, Francesco & Figli 305
Rincione 365
Rincione Bianco 362
Rio Negro 522
Riogranense, Vinicola 523
Rioja 368, 374-9
Rioja Alavesa 375
Rioja Alta 375
Rioja Baja 370, 375
Rioja Vega 379
Riojanas, Bodegas 378
Rion, Dom. Bernard Père & Fils 141
Rion, Dom. Daniel 141
Rion, Patrice 141
Ripaille 158
Ripaille, Ch. de 158
Ripasso 318
Ripeau, Ch. 89
Riscal, Herederos Marques de 378
Riscal, Marqués de 371, 374
Riscalsa 378
Riserva (riserva speciale) 299
Ritchie Creek 469
Rittersberg 288
Riunite 329
Riuniti, Produttori 367
La Riva 394
La Rivalèrie, Ch. 100
Rivaner 268
Rivaz 412
Rivella, Ezio 335, 341-2
Rivenich 244
River Road Vineyards 469
River Run Vintners 469
Rivera 358
Riverland 492
Riverside 443, 514
Riverside Farm 458
Riviera del Garda Bresciano 310

Riviera Ligure di Pontente 307-8
Rivière, Maison Pierre 91
La Riviere, Ch. 99
De Rivoyre & Diprovin 52
Rizzardi, Guerrieri 318
Rizzi 305
Rizzi, Fratelli 331
Rkatziteli (Rkatsiteli) 430, 445
Roaix 199
Robbia, Luca della 341
Robert 436
Robert, Bodegas 383
Robertson 514
Robertson Bros. 405
Robin, Emile 152
Robin, Francis 89
Robin, Mlle. Marie 95
Robinsons Family Winery 503
Roblevina 523
Robola 433
Robson, Murray, Wines 503
Roc, Caves du 225
Roc de Boissac, Ch. 92
Roc de Lussac 89
Roc de Puisseguin 89, 92
Rocca -Cascina Rabajà, Bruno 305
Rocca di Castagnoli 339
Rocca di Fabri 346
Rocca delle Macie 339
Rocche Costamagna 305
Rocche di Manzoni 303
Roche 305
Roche, Ch. de la 167
Roche, Ch. La 101
Rochefort-sur-Loire 165
Rochegude 199
La Roche aux Moines 165
Rochemorin, Ch. de 77
Rocher, Ch. du 91
Rochettes, Dom. des 168
Rochiolo, J., Vineyards 469
Rock Lodge Vineyard 525-6
Rockfold 503
Rodano 343
Rodet, Antonin 146
Rodhain, François 86
Rodil 394
Roduit, Eloi et Gérard 413
Roeder, Myron 51
Roederer, Louis 183
Roederer, Théophile 185
Roederer Estate 469
Roero-Arneis del Roero 298
Roger, Jean-Max 175
Le Rognet et Corton 119
Le Rognet-Corton 119
Rogue River 481-2
Rohrbacher, Jean 185
Roiax 199
Le Roi Dagobert 192
Rol, Ch. de 91
Roland, Ch. 65
Rolet Père et Fils 156
Rolland, Ch. de 82
Rolland, Michel 94
Rollet, Marcel 152
Romagna, Cagnina di 327
Romagnoli, Cantine 331
Romain, Etab. Bernard Camp 208
Romane Machotte 197
Romanée-Conti 116, 120-1
Romanée-Conti, Dom. de la 141
Romanée-St-Vivant 116
La Romanée 116, 129
Romani, Castelli 349
Romarin, Dom. 199
Romasson, Ch. 207
Romate, Sanchez 394
Rombauer Vineyards 469
Romefort, Ch. 70
Romeira 399

Romer du Hayot, Ch. 82
Romerhof, Weingut 421
Römerlay 242
Rómulo 383
Roncada 326
Roncade, Castello di 321-2
Ronchi, Umani 348
Ronchi di Cialla 326
Ronco, Cantina Sociale 331
Rohco del Gnemiz 326
Ronziere, André 151
Rooty Hill 502
Ropiteau Frères 141-2
Roque Sestieres 213
Roquebrun, Les Vins de 218
Roquebrune, Dom. de 211
Roques, Ch. de 92
Roquemieu-Lacoste, Ch. 82
Rosa del Golfo 358
Rosato 299
Rosato del Salento 357
Rosazza, Torre 325
La Rose-Capbern, Ch. 66
La-Rose-Cotes-Rol, Ch. 91
Rose Creek Vineyards 482
Rosé d'Anjou 159, 165
Rosé de Loire 160
Rosé de Riceys 186
Rose Maréchal, Ch. de la 70
La Rose Pauillac, Coop. 65
La Rose Pourret, Ch. 91
Roseewein 241
Rosemount Estate 503
Rosenblum Cellars Winery 469
Rosenbühl 274-5
Rosengarten 264
Rosette 222
Rosewein 241
Rossese di Dolceacqua 307-8
Rossi, Georges 152
Rossignol, Dom. Philippe 142
Rosso 299
Rosso, Gigi 305
Rosso d'Arquata 345
Rosso Bartella 357
Rosso Canosa 357
Rosso di Cercatoia 334
Rosso di Cerignola 357
Rosso Cònero 347
Rosso Le Muraglie 306
Rosso di Montalcino 334
Rosso di Montepulciano 334
Rosso Piceno 347
Rosso della Quercia 353
Rosso dei Vigneti de Brunello 332
Rosstal 281
Rostaing, René 197
Rotaliana, Cantine Cooperativa 317
Rothbury Estate 503
Rothschild, Baron Eric de 62-3
Rothschild, Baron Philippe de 60-1, 64, 465, 477
Rothschild, Dom. Barons de 95
Rothschild family
Ch. Duhart-Milon-Rothschild 61
Ch. Lafite-Rothschild 59, 62-3
Rothschilde, Baron Edmond de 57
Rott 279
Rottensteiner, Hans 317
Rottensteiner, Heinrich 317
Rotwein 242
Roty, Joseph 142
Roubaud, Ch. 207
Roucas de St Pierre, Dom. du 198
Rouché 299
Rouchet 299
Les Roucoules 196
Roudier, Ch. 92

Roudil, Gabriel, Les Fils de 199
Roudon-Smith Vineyards 469
Rouet, Dom. du Ch. du 208
Rouge Homme 500, 503
Rougeon 486
Rouget, Ch. 96
Rouget, Emmanuel 134
Rougier, René 207
Roulot, Dom. Guy 142
Roumi 436
Roumier, Alain 142
Roumier, Dom. G. 142
Roumier, Jean-Marie 142
Roumieu, Ch. 82
Roumieu-Lacoste, Ch. 82
Round Hill Cellars 469
Rous, Dom. du Mas 211
Rousillon, Vins de Pays 233
Roussanne 194, 201
Rousseau, Charles 142
Rousseau, Dom. Armand 142
Rousseau, Dom. Louis 199
Rousset, Ch. 100
Rousset-Les-Vignes 199
Roussette de Bugey 157
Roussette du Savoy 157
Roussières, Dom. des 170
Roussillon 209-11
Rouvière, Mas de la 207
Roux, Charles 200
Roux, Hilarion, Les Fils de 199
Roux Père & Fils, Dom. 142
Rovira, Pedro 383
Royal Kedem Winery 485
Royal Oporto 399
Royal Oporto Wine Co. 405
Le Roy de Boiseaumarié, Baron 203
Rozendel 518
Rozes Lda. 400, 406
Rozier, Ch. 91
Ruat-Petit-Poujeaux, Ch. 57
Rubesco 344-5
Rubini 326
Rubino di Cantavenna 298-9
Ruby Cabernet 445
Ruchè 299
Ruchè de Castagnole Monferrato 299
La Ruchè Foncière, Dom. 220
Ruchottes-Chambertin 115
Rüdesheim (Nahe) 264
Rüdesheim (Rheingau) 257
Rueda 368, 371
Ruffino, I.L. 340
Ruinart Père & Fils 183
Ruiz, Bodegas 385
Ruiz, Felix, y Ruiz 394
Ruiz-Mateos, Zoila 393
Rully 144
Rümmelsheim 266
Ruppertsberger, Winzerverein 279
La Rural, Bodegas 523
Russian River Valley 440, 443
Russian River Vineyard *see* Topolos
Russin 412
Russiz, Villa 326
Russolo 322
Rust-en-Vrede 518
Rutherford 443
Rutherford, Ch. 469
Rutherford & Miles 408
Rutherford Estate 461
Rutherford Hill Cellars 469
Rutherford Hill Winery 469
Rutherford Ranch 469
Rutherford Vintners 469

Rutherglen 490
Ruwer 237-8, 242-3, 247-53
Ryecroft 503-4
Ryman, Henry 222

S
S.A.M.E. 185
Saar 237-8, 242-3, 247-53
Saar-Ruwer 242
Saarburg 243
Sables du Golfe du Lion, Vins des 219, 232
Sablet 199
Sablière, Ch. La 91, 102
Sabon, Jospeh, Les Fils de 204
Sabon, Noël 202
Sacceda 379
Sachsen, Villa 272-3
Sacotte 185
Sacramento 443
Sacy 185
Sadoux, Pierre-Jean 222
Sadova 429
Saget, Guy 175
Sagrantino di Montefalco 345
Sahel 436
Saier, Dom. 146
St. Alban 270
St-Amans, Prieuré de 213
St-Amour 153
St-André, Ch. 204
St-André-Corbin, Ch. 92
St-André de Figuière, Dom. de 207
St. Andreas Hospital Fonds Weingut der Stadt Offenburg 290
St. Andrews Winery 469
St-Antoine, Caves 224
St-Antoine, Dom. de 208
St-Aubin 123
St-Auréol, Ch. 213
St-Benezey, Dom. de 219
St-Bonnet, Ch. 72
St-Chinian 216, 218
St-Christol 218
St-Christophe, Ch. 91
St. Clair, Ch. 484
St. Clement Vineyards 469
St-Cyr en Bourg, Vignerons de Saumur à 169
St-Didier, Ch. de 224
St-Drezery 218
St-Emilion 46, 47, 49-50, 83-93
Coop. 89
St-Estèphe 46, 65-7
St-Estèphe, Ch. 67
St-Estève, Ch. 199
St-Exupery, de 217
St-Exupéry, Comtesse de 223
St-Felix de Lodez, Caves Coopératives 218
St. Francis Winery 470
St-Galderic 210
St. Gallen 415
St-Gayan, Dom. 200
St Gens, Dom. de 198
St. George, Dom. 454
St-Georges, Ch. 93
St-Georges (Côte-Pavie), Ch. 89
St-Georges-d'Orques 218
St-Georges-d'Orques, Caves Coopératives de 218
St-Georges-St-Emilion 93
St-Gervais 199
St. Helena 443, 512
St-Hubert 190
St Huberts 504
St Irminenhof, Weingut 248
St. Jean, Ch. 452
St-Jean, Dom. 208

St-Jean-de-Bebian, Prieuré de 218
St-Jean-de-la-Blaquière 218
St-Jean-de-Minervois 216
St. Johannishof, Weingut 251
St-Joseph 194-5
St. Julian 487
St-Julien, Prieuré 200
St-Julien 46, 57-9
St Lambert du Lettay 166
St. Leonard's Winery 504
St-Louis La Perdrix, Mas 219
St-Luc, Dom. 211
St Magdalener 314
St-Marceaux see Lepitre, Abel 1134
St Martin 113
St. Martin, Caves 268
St-Martin 213
St-Martin, Ch. 208
St. Martinus, Winzergenossenschaft 423
St. Matthias Vineyard 504
St-Maurice-sur-Eygues 199
St Maurice-L'Ardoise, Ch. 200
St-Micel 185
St-Michel, Dom. 142
St. Michel, Kellereignossenschaft 317
St. Nesbit 512
St-Nicolas de Bourgueil 160, 169
St Nikolaus Hospital 253
St Pantéléon-Les-Vignes 199
St-Paul, Ch. de 70
St-Péray 194
St-Pey, Ch. de 91
St-Pierre 204
St-Pierre, Ch. 77
St-Pierre-Sefivin, Caves 204
St-Pierre (-Sevaistre), Ch. 59
St-Pourçain 176
St-Pourçain-sur-Sioule 160
St. Remy, Caves 268
St Roch, Les Vignerons de 213
St-Roch les Vignes 207
St-Roch, Ch. 200
St. Rochuskapelle 270-71
St-Romain 124
St Saphorin 412
Saint Sardos 234
St-Saturnin 218
St-Saturnin, Cave Coopérative de 218
St Ursula Weinkellerei 239
St-Véran 147-8
St-Vincent, Ch. 219
St-Yzans Coop. 72
Saintout, P. 59
Saintsbury 470
Sais 436
Sakonnet 486
Sala, Castello della 345
Salabue, Castello di 305
Salaparuta, Duca di (Corva) 362, 364
Salas Acosta, Bodegas Miguel 387
Salceda 379
Šaldorf 427
Sales, Ch. de 96
Salice Salentino 357
Salinas Valley 443
Salins, François de 128
Salins du Midi, Dom. Viticoles des (Listel) 219
Salishan 487
La Salle de Poujeaux 57
Salm-Dalberg, Prinz zu 268
Salon 184
Saltram 504
Salzberg 284

Sambuca di Siciliana, Cantina Sociale 365
Sammontana, Fattoria di 343
Samori 331
Samos Nectar 433
Samos Union of Cooperatives 433
Sampigny-Les-Maranges 126
Samugheo, Cantina Sociale di 367
San Antonio Winery 470
San Benito 443
San Bernardino 443
San Cipriano 326
San Colombano 310
San Colombano al Lambro 310
San Cosma 343
San Diago 443
San Fabiano Calcinaia 343
San Felice 340
San Filipe 523
San Filippo dei Comunali 343
San Francesco, Fattoria 360
San Francisco 443
San Giovanni, Villa 325
San Giusto a Rentennano 340
San Grato 311
San Guido-Sassicaia, Tenuta 340
San Isidro, Cooperativa de 386
San Joaquin 443
San José de Ahuaron, Cooperativa Viticola 373
San Juan 522
San Juan, Cavas de 523
San Leonardo 314
San Leonardo, Tenuta 317
San Leonino, Fattoria 343
San Lucas 443
San Luis Obispo 443
San Marco 443
San Marino 510
San Martin Winery 470
San Matteo 351
San Michele, Cantina Sociale 317
San Michele, Castel 313
San Pasqual Valley 443
San Patrignano 331
San Pedro, Viña 521
San Pietro, Le Vigne di 322
San Pietro, Tenuta 305
San Polo in Rosso, Castello di 340
San Rocco 317
San Roque Coop. 373
San Severo 358
San Telmo 523
San Tommaso, Cantine Sociale Cooperativa 352
San Valero Coop. 373
San Vito in Fior di Selva 343
Sancerre 160, 163, 173-4, 175
Sancerre, Caves Coopérative des Vins de 174
Sancerre, Ch. de 175
Sanchez de Alva, Bodegas 394
De Sanctis 352
Sandalford 504
Sandeman & Co. 405
Sandeman Hermanos y Cía 393
Sanders, Jean 74
Sandrone, Luciano 303
Sanford Wines 470
Sangiovese dei Colli Pesaresi 347
Sangiovese di Romagna 329
Sangue di Giuda 310

Sanperetto 322
Sansonnet, Ch. 89
Sant'Angelo Vico L'Abate 337
Sant'Anna, Tenuta 322
Sant'Anna di Isola Capo Rizzuto 360
Sant'Antioco, Cantina Sociale 367
Sant' Elmo 319
Sant' Osvaldo 323
Santa Ana 523
Santa Barbara 443
Santa Barbara Winery 470
Santa Carolina 521
Santa Caterina 326
Santa Clara 443
Santa Clara Valley 443
Santa Croce 355
Santa Cruz Mountain Vineyard 470
Santa Cruz Mountains 443
Santa Lucia 359
Santa Maddalena 314
Santa Margherita 321
Santa Margherita, Vinicola 315
Santa Maria Valley 443
Santa Mavra of Levkas 432
Santa Rita 521
Coop. 386
Santa Sofia 322
Santa Valeria 343
Santa Ynez Valley 443
Santa Ynez Valley Winery 470
Santar, Conde de 397
Santenay 123-4
Santi 323
Santiago Ruiz, Vinos 373
Santino Wines 470
Santo Stefano, I Vignaioli di 300, 305
Santo Tomas, Bodegas de 523
Santorini 432
Sanz, Bodegas 373
São João 397
São João, Caves 400
São Luis, Quinta 404
Saporta, Marquis de 206
Saracco 305
Sarah's Vineyard 470
Saransot-Dupré, Ch. 57
Sardinia 365-7
Sardinian Gold 367
Sardus Pater 367
Sarget de Gruaud-Larose 58
Sarrat 227
Sarrau 154
Sarraute, Dom. 79
Sarria, Bodegas de 372
Sartène 220
Sartori 323
Le Sartre, Ch. 73, 77
Saso Rosso 346
Sassella 310
Sassicaia 332, 334
Sasso, Francesco 361
Satigny 412
Satoraljaujhely 426
Sattlerhof, Weingut 422-3
Sattui, V., Winery 470
Saturnia, Cooperativa Agricoltori (Draceno) 365
Sau, Dom. de 211
Saule, Dom. Ch. de la 146
Saumur 160, 163, 165, 168-9
Saumur-Champigny 160, 163, 165
Saumur Moussex 160-61
Saurejeau, Marcel 164
Sausal Winery 470
Saussignac 222
Sauternes 46, 54, 77-82
Sauveroy, Dom. du 168
Sauvignon Blanc 51, 430, 445
Sauvion & Fils 164
Sauzet, Dom. Etienne 142

Sava valley 428
Des Savarines, Dom. 225
Saviano 1760 355
Savigny-Les-Beaune 120
Savoie 157-8
Vins de Pays 234
Savoye, René 152
Savuto 360
Savuto, Cantina Sociale Vini del 360
Saxonvale 504
Scala Dei, Cellers de 382
Scali Caracciolo 353
Scamperle 323
Scarello & Figli 305
Scarpa 323
Scarpa, Antica Casa Vinicola 303
Scarsa Olivi, Cascina 305
Scavino, Paolo 303
SCEA de Quattre et Treilles 225
Sceriman, Villa 323
Schaefer, Karl 279
Schaeffer, Jean Nicholas 164-5
Schaffhausen 415
Schales, Weingut 273
Schalkstein 284
Scharffenberger Cellars 470
Scharzberg 242
Schaumwein 242
Schenk 414
Schenk, Bodegas 385
Schenkenböhl 275
Schiava 313
Schiele, Baron de 190
Schild 281
Schillerwein 242
Schinus Molle 497
Schiopetto, Mario 325
Schioppettino 324
Schisteil 218
Schlangengraben, Weingut 251
Schlatter, Hans 416
Schlink, Günther 268
Schloss Böchingen 257
Schloss Groenesteyn 258
Schloss Johannisberg 256-9
Schloss Lieser 251
Schloss Lüdwigshöhe 276
Schloss Ortenberg des Ortenaukreises 290
Schloss Reichenstein 254
Schloss Reinhartshausen 260
Schloss Rodeck 288
Schloss Saaleck-Städt, Weingut Hammelburg 283
Schloss Saarfels 257
Schloss Saarstein 253
Schloss Salem 290
Schloss Sallegg 317
Schloss Schönborn, Domanenweingut 260
Schloss Schönburg 254
Schloss Schwanburg 317
Schloss Stahlech 254
Schloss Staufenberg 289
Schloss Vollrads 260-1
Schlossberg 188, 279, 281
Schlossböckelheim 264
Schlosskapelle 264
Schlosstück 281
Schlossweingut Graf Hardegg 423
Schlotter, Valentin 263
Schlumberger, Dom. 191
Schlumberger, Hartmut 290
Schlumberger, Robert 421-2
Schmitt, Gustav Adolf 272
Schmitz, Hubert 253
Schneider, George Albrecht 273-4
Schneider, Jakob 268
Schneider, Ludwig,

GmbH 279
Schneider Michel, Nachf. 251
Schnepfenflug an der Weinstrasse 275
Schnepfenflug von Zellertal 274
Schoenenberg 188
Scholl & Hillebrand 239
Scholtz Hermanos 387
Schonburger 524
Schönleber-Blümlein, Weingut 263
Schoongezicht Rustenberg 518
Schoonmaker, Frank 140
Schoppenwein 242
Schozachtal 284
Schramsberg Vineyards 470
Schröder & Schÿler 52
Schroder and Schyler 53
Schubert, C. von 251
Schuch, Geschwister 272
Schug Cellars 470
Schultz-Werner, Oberst 274
Schumann-Nägler, Weingut 263
Schuster, Eduard 279
Schutterlindenberg 288
Schwäbischer Landwein 288
Schwarz, Franz 423
Schwarzenbach, Hermann 416
Schwarzerde 274
Schweich 244
Schweinhardt, Bürgmeister Willi, Nachf. 268
Schÿler, Jean-Henri 52
Sciacarello 220
Scintillant 165
La Scolca 297, 303
Scrimaglio 305-6
Scuppernong 482-3
SDVF (Societe de Distribution des Vins Fins) 52
Seagull Liebfraumilch 271
Seaview 504
Sebaste, Cantine 306
Sebastian, Don 376
Sebastian, Jacob, Nachf. 254
Sebastiani Vineyards 471
Secco 299
Seeheim 279
Segarcea 429
Seghesio Winery 471
Segonzac, Ch. 100
Ségriès, Ch. de 200, 204
Séguin-Manuel, Maison 142
Ségur, Ch. 70
Ségur, Ch. de 79
Ségura, Jean 217
Séguret 199
Seibel 486
Seifried, Weingut 512
Seigneurie de Gicon 200
Sekt 242, 257
Sektkellerei Spicka 257
Selaks Wines 512
Selbach-Oster 253
Selbach-Weins 253
Selezione Vigna Elisa 337
Sella 303
Sella & Mosca 365, 367
Selle, Ch. de 207
Seltz, Albert & Fils 191
La Selva, Coopérative 352
La Selva, Villa 343
Selvapiana 340
Selvole, Fattoria di 343
Semeillan-Mazeau, Ch. 57
Semeli 433
Semeli, Ch. 433
Sémillon 51, 222, 227, 434, 445, 492, 522
Semisecco 299

Senailhac, Ch. 102
Senard, Dom. Daniel 142
Sénéclauze, M. Ph. 55
Sénéjac, Ch. 70
Senilhac, Ch. 70
Sennece-Les-Mâcon 148
Señorial 379
Señorio del Condestable, Bodegas 385
Seppelt 504
Sequoia Grove Vineyards 471
Serbia 427-8
Sercial 407-8
Serenelli 349
Sergant, Ch. 98
Sérine 193
Serra, Vinos Jaime 383
Serralunga 296
La Serre, Ch. 89
Serre de Coiran 231
Serres, Bodegas Carlos 379
Serrig 243
Serrigny, Dom. de 142
Serristori, Conte 340
Serros, Bodegas Carlos 379
Servin, Marcel 114
Sestignan, Ch. 72
Setriolo 343
Settesoli 363
Settesoli, Cantina Sociale 364
Setúbal 398
Sevenhill 504
Seville Estate 504
Sèvre et Maine 161
Seynat-Dulos, J.P. 56
Seyssel 157-8
Seysses, Jacques 131
Seyval Blanc 486, 524
Seyve-Villard 486
Sfurzat (Sfursat) (Sforzato) 310
Shadow Creek 453
Shafer 472
Shafer Vineyards 471
Shaw, Charles F., Vineyard and Winery 471
Shawsgate Vineyard 526
Shenandoah 442, 487
Shenandoah Vineyards 471
Sherrill Cellars 471
Sherry 11, 368, 386, 388-94
Californian 445
Shiraz 492
Shumen 430
SHV 474
Siaurac, Ch. 98
SICA de Figari 220
Sichel, Peter 52, 55
Sichel Söhne, H. 239
Sichel, Maison 52
Sichère, Mme. L.D. 55
Sicily 361-5
Sick-Dreyer, Dom. 191-2
Sidaine family 66
Sidi Larbi 436
Sidi Rais 435
Sidi Salem 435
Siegel, Walter S. 239
Siegendorf, Klosterkeller 422
Sierra Foothills 443
Sierra Vista Winery 471
Sieur d'Arques 214
Sigalas Rabaud, Ch. 79
Sigognac, Ch. 72
Sigolsheim et Environs Coop. 192
Siklos 425
Silva & Cosens Ltd. 405
Silval, Quinta do 405
Silver Oak Cellars 472
Silverado Trail 443
Silverado Vineyards 472
Simi Winery 472
Simmern, Freiherrlich Langwerth von 260
Simmonet, Jean-Claude 114
Simmonet-Febvre 133
Simon, Bert 251

Simon, Ch. 82
Simone, Ch. 206-7
Simone, Villa 351
Simonnet-Febvre & Fils 114
Simonsig 518
Le Sincette 312
Sincomar 436
Single, Dom. du 224
Siran, Ch. 56
Les Sires de Vergy, Cuvée 140
Sirius 52
Siskiyou Vineyards 481
Sitère, Dom. de 227
Sitia 432
Sitsa 432
Sizzano 299
Sky Vineyards 472
Slavonia 428-9
Slovakia 426-7
Slovenia 427-8
Slovin of Ljubljana 428
Smederevka 430
Smith Woodhouse & Co. 405
Smith-Haut-Lafitte, Ch. 76
Smith-Madrone 472
Snoqualmie Winery 482
Soave 319
Soave, Cantina Sociale di 321
Soc. Viticole Beaujolais Coop. 150-51
Sociando-Mallet, Ch. 70
Société de Distribution des Vins Fins 52
Société des Vins Tardi 435-6
Société Générale de Champagne 185
Sodap Coop. 434
Soeurs Hospitalières, Cuvée des 140
Sogrape-Vinos de Portugal SARL 399
Sohlbach, Georg 263
Soiana 343
Soil 13
Sokol Blosser Winery 479
Solano-Green Valley 443
Soleil, Ch. 92
Solemacher, Freiherr von 251
Solera system 387
Le Soliel Nantais 164
Solimar 382
Solis, Bodegas Felix 385
Solitude, Dom. de la 204
Sologny 148
Solopaca 354
Soloperto, Giovanni 359
Somló 426
Sommerach, Winzergrenossenschaft 283
Somontano 368, 371
Sonnenborn 264
Sonnenglanz 188
Sonoma 440, 442-3
Sonoma-Cutrer Vineyards 472
Soos, Aymard de 215
Sopraceneri 416
Soprano, Pianpolvere 305
Sopron 426
Sorbaiano 343
Sori 296
Soria, Bodegas Joaquin 373
Sorni 314
Sorrel, Dom. 196
Sotò, José de 394
Sotoyome Winery 473
Sottoceneri 416
Soudars, Ch. 70
Soulez, Pierre & Yves 168
Soullaillou, Dom. 224
Soutard, Ch. 89
Southam's 400
Southern Vales 490, 492

Souverain, Ch. (Cellars) 451
Souzão 445
Soye, Jean 55
Spagnolli, Enrico 317
Spagnolli, Giuseppe 317
Spalletti-Tenuta di Savignano 329
Spanish Arch 394
Spanna 299
Sparr, Pierre & ses Fils 192
Spätlese 236-7, 242, 421
Spay, Paul 153
Specogna 326
Spessa, Castello di 326-7
Spiegelberg 270
La Spinetta-Rivetti, Cascina 303
La Spinosa 306
Spitaleri 218
Spottswoode Vineyard and Winery 473
Spring Creek Estate 510
Spring Mountain 443
Spring Mountain Vineyards 473, 477
Springcreek 482
Spritz 40
Spumante 299
Squillace 360
Squinzano 358
Staatliche Lehr-und Versuchsanstalt für Wein-und Obstbau Weinsberg 285
Staatliche Weinbaudomän Kloster Marienthal Ahr 254
Staatlichen Weinbaudomänen, Verwaltung der 268
Staatlichen Weinbaudomänen (Trier) 251
Staatlicher Hofkeller 280, 282
Staatliches Weinbauinstitut Freiburg Blankenhornsberg 289
Staatliches Weinbauinstitute (Baden) 289
Staatswein Meersburg 289
Staatsweingut Bergstrasse 280
Staatsweingut der Landes-Lehr-und Versuchsanstalt 272
Staatsweingut Weinbaulehranstalt (Nahe) 267-8
Staatsweingüter Kloster Erbach 258
Stabilimento 299
Stade Frankfurt am Main, Weingut der 262
Stadt Bensheim, Weingut der 280
Stag's Leap 443
Stag's Leap Wine Cellars 473, 477
Stags' Leap Winery 473
Staiger, P. and M. 473
Stanislaus 443
Stanley Wine Co. 504-5
Stanton & Killeen 505
Starkenburg 279
Starkenburger Landwein 288
Station Hills Vineyard and Winery 482
Stauch, Hartmut 279
Staufenberg 284
Ste-Affrique family 57
Ste-Anne, Dom. 200
Ste Antonin Rodet 141
Ste. Chapelle 482

Ste-Croix-du-Mont 102
Ste-Foy-Bordeaux 103
Ste. Genevieve 488
Ste. Michelle, Ch. 481
Stefaneşti 429
Steiermark 417, 419
Steige 281
Steigerwald Bereich 280-81
Steinberg 256
Steinmächer 255
Steinwein 280
Stellenbosch 514
Stellenbosch Farmers' Wineries 518
Steltzner Vineyard 473
Stemmler, Robert, Winery 473
Sterling Vineyards 473-4, 477
Stevenot Winery 474
Stift Schotlen, Weingut Nussdorf 422
Stiftkellerei Neustift 314
Stiftsberg 288
Stigler, Rudolf 290
Stodden, Jean 254
Stonegate 474
Stony Hill Vineyard 474
Stonyridge Vineyard 512
La Stoppa 329
Storybook Mountain Vineyards 474
Stratford 474
Stravecchio 299
Stromberg 284
Strong, Rodney, Vineyards 474
Strub, J. & H.A. 272
Struzziero, Giovanni 355
Stubenberg, Gräfi, Schlossweingut, Schloss Welkersdorf 422
Stucky, Werner 417
Studert-Prüm Maximinhof 253
Stuermer Winery 474
Sturm & Söhn 264
Styria 419
Suau, Ch. 82, 101
Suavia, Viticola 323
Subida di Monte 327
Subotiča 427
Südbadischer Landwein 288
Südliche Weinstrasse Bereich 274, 276
Südtirol see Alto Adige
Suduiraut, Ch. 79
Suhindol 430
Suisun Valley 443
Sullivan Vineyards Winery 474
Sultanye 434
Summerhill Vineyards 474
Summit 458
Sunrise Winery 474
Superiore 299
Superiore di Cartizze 319
Suremain, Hugues de 146
Suremain, Robert de 142
Suter 523
Sutter Home Winery 474
La Suvera 343
Svevo, Cantina Sociale 359
Swan, Joseph Vineyards 474
Swan, Malcolm 197
Swan Valley 490, 492
Swartland 514
Swellendam 514
Sybillenstein 271
Sylvaner 189, 445, 522
Syrah 193, 201, 205, 210, 212, 225, 445, 522
Szeged 425
Szekszárd 425
Szilváni 425
Szürkebarat 424

T
Tabor Hill 487-8
La Tâche 116, 121

Tafelwein 236-7, 242
Tafelwein Landwein 421
Tagliolo, Castello di 306
Tahbilk, Ch. 490, 496
Taichat 211
Tailhas, Ch. du 96
Taillan, Ch. du 70
Taille 74
Taillefer, Ch. 96
Taittinger 184
Talbot, Ch. 59
Talence 73
Talenti-Pian di Conte 343
Tallavignes, J.A. 216
Taltarni 505
Taluau, Joel 172
Tamborini, Eredi Carlo SA 417
Tamianka 430
Tanesse, Ch. 101
Tannat 227
Tannet 223
Tarapacá Ex Zavala 521
Tarczal, de 317
Tarerach Coop. 211
Targé, Ch. de 168
Targovishte 430
Tarik 436
Tarin 185
Tarragona 368, 380-81
Tarrawarra Vineyards 505
Tartegnin 412
Tasmania 492
Tassarolo, Castello di 303
Tassin, Bernard 185
Tasta, Ch. du 101
Tastes, Ch. de 102
Tattà 349
Tauberberg 285
Tauberklinge 288
Taughrite 436
Taurasi 354
Taurino, Cosimo 358
Tautavel "Les Maîtres Vignerons" 211
Tavel 203
  Coop. 201
Tayac, Ch. 56, 100
Taylor Fladgate & Yeatman 406
Taylors Wines 505
The Taylor Wine Company Ltd. 483, 485
Tchelistcheff, André 339, 448, 455, 478
Te Mata Estate 512
Técou Coop. 226
Tedeschi, Fratelli 321
Teiller, Jean 176
Teissier 217
Teixera, Perez 387
Tekel 434
de Telmont, J & Co. 185
Temecula 443
Tempier, Dom. 207
Temple Bruer 505
Templeton 443
Teneterden Vineyard 526
Tennesee 487
Terizzo 308
Terlan, Kellereignossenschaft 317
Terlaner 314
Terlano, Cantina Sociale 317
Termeno, Cantina Sociale 317
Teroldego 313
Teroldego Rotaliano 314
Terra Alta 368, 381
Terrabianca 343
Terrano di Carso 323
Terras Altas 399
Terrats Coop. 211
Le Terrazze 349
Le Terrazze di Roncosambacchio-Giovanetti 349
Terre da Vino 306
Terre del Barolo 303

Terre di Ginestra 365
Terre Ferme, Dom. 205
Terre Rosse (Vallania) 330
du Tertre, Ch. 55
Terrefort-Quancard, Ch. de 103
Terres-Blanche 207
Terret Noir 201
Terrey-Gros-Caillou, Ch. 59
Terrey-Gros-Caillou, Ch. du 70
Terroir de Cerbère 211
Terroirs Landais 234
Terry, Fernando A. de 394
Tertre-Daugay, Ch. 89
Teruzzi & Puthod-Ponte a Rondolino 340
Tesch, Erbhof 269
Tesseron, Guy 64, 66
Tessin 416-17
Testut, Dom. Phillipe 114
Testuz, Jean & Pierre 414
Tête, Louis 154
Teufelstor 281
Texas 488
Teynac, Ch. 59
Teyssier, Ch. 92
Teysson, Ch. 98
Thalabert, Dom. de 196
Thallern, Freigut 422
Thanisch, Dr. H. 251-2
Thau, Ch. de 100
Thaulero, Casal 352
Thébaud, Gabriel 165
Theil, F. and P. 57
Thelin, Jean de 215
Thénac, Ch. 223
Thénard, Société Divile du Dom. 146
Théo, Jacques 54
Thermenregion 419
Théron, J.-P. 57
Thessaly 432
Theulet et Marsalet, Dom. 223
Theuniskraal 518
Thévenin, Roland 142
Thévenin-Monthelie, Dom. René & Fils 142
Thévenot, Maurice 142
Thévenot Brun & Fils 142-3
Thézac-Pérricard 234
Thibar, Ch. 435
Thienpont, Luc 55
Thiergarten, Weingut 252
Thieuley, Ch. 102
Thill Frères 268
Thivin, Ch. 152
Thomas-Moillard, Dom. 139
Thompson Seedless 445
Thorin 148, 154
Thouarsais (vin de) 161
Three Choirs Vineyard 526
Thüngersheim, Winzergenossenschaft 283
Thurgau 415
Tia Antina 393
Ticinesi, Vinattieri 417
Ticino 416-17
Tiefenbrunner, J. 315
Tierra de Barros 384
Tiglio, Borgo del 327
Tignanello 334
Tigné 103
Tigny, Baron Gaël de 166
Tijou, Pierre Yves 168
Tili 346
Tillmanns, H., Erban 264
Timberlay, Ch. 103
Timok 427
Tio Pepe 392
Tiregand, Ch. 223
Tirnave 429
Tisdall 505
Tissier, Roger and Jean-Luc 151
Tissot, Jacques 156
Tobias, Oskar 253

Tocai di Lison 319
Tocai di San Martino della Battaglia 310
Togni, Philip, Vineyard 475
Tokajhegyaljai 426
Tokáji 426
Tokay 424, 426-7
Tokay Aszú 424
Tokay Aszú Essencia 424
Tokay d'Alsace 188
Tokay Essence 424
Tokay Szamorodni 424
Toledo 384
Tollana 505
Tolley's Pedare 505
Tollo, Cantina Sociale di 353
Tollot-Beau & Fils, Dom. 143
Tollot-Voarick, Dom. 143
Tolosan, Comté 234
Tommasi 321
Tonneau 74
Topolos 475
La Toppe au Vert 119
Torbato di Alghero 367
Du Torgan 233
Torgiano 294, 344-5
Toro 358, 371
Torok, Ladislaus 422
Torraccia, Dom. de 220
La Torraccia 349
Torre a Cona 343
Torre a Decima 343
Torre di Giano 345
Torre Ercolana 351
Torre Quarto 358-9
Torre Sveva 311
Torrebianco, Tenuta di 358
Torrepalino, Cantina Sociale 365
Torres, Miguel (Chile) Ltda. 521
Torres, Viñedos 380, 382-3
Torres Family 382
Torres Vineyards 475
Torresella, Cantine 321
Tortochot, Dom. 143
La Tosa 331
Toso, Michel, Bodega La Rosa 523
Toso, Pascual 523
Touchais, Les Vignobles 168
Touchais, Les Vins 168
La Touche, Ch. 165
Toumilon, Ch. 77
Tour, Dom. de la 208
La Tour l'Aspic, 64-5
Tour du Bief, Dom. de la 153
La Tour Blanche, Ch. 79
La Tour-Blanche, Ch. 72
Tour de By, Ch. 72
Tour Campanets, Dom. de la 208
La Tour Carnet, Ch. 67
Tour des Combes, Ch. 91
Tour d'Elyssas, Dom. de la 200
La Tour Figeac, Ch. 89
Tour de Grenet, Ch. 92
Tour de Gillet, Ch. 92
Tour Guillotin, Ch. 92
La Tour-Haut-Brion, Ch. 76
La Tour du Haut-Caussan, Ch. 72
Tour du Haut Moulin, Ch. 70
La Tour Léognan, Ch. 77
Tour-Léognan, Ch. 73
Tour de Lirac, Dom. de la 200
Tour de Marbuzet, Ch. 66-7
La Tour Martillac, Ch. 76
La Tour du Mirail, Ch. 70
La Tour-de-Mons, Ch. 56

La Tour Pibran, Ch. 65
La Tour-du-Pin-Figeac, Ch. 89
La Tour Prignac, Ch. 72
La Tour-Puymiraud, Ch. 102
Tour du Roc, Ch. 70
La Tour du Roc Milon, Ch. 65
Tour de Ségur, Ch. 92
La Tour St-Bonnet, Ch. 72
La Tour St-Joseph, Ch. 70
Tour-St-Pierre, Ch. 91
La Tour-des-Termes, Ch. 67
Tour du Vatican, Ch. 69
Touraine 161, 169-72
Touraine-Amboise 161
Touraine-Azay-Le-Rideau 161
Touraine-Mesland 161
Touraine Pétillant & Mousseux 161
Tourbillon 203
Tourelles, Ch. des 72
Tournefeuille, Ch. 98
La Tournelle des Moines 85
Tournelles, Dom. de 435
Tours, Ch. des 92
Tours de Malle, Ch. 81
Tourteau-Chollet, Ch. 77
Tourteran, Ch. 70
Tout-Vent, Dom. de 203
Toutigeac, Ch. de 102
Touzinat, Ch. 91
Traben-Trarbach 246
Tracy, Ch. de 175
Traenheim et Environs Coop. 192
Traisen 265
Trakya 434
Tramanal 323
Tramin, Kellereignossenschaft 317
Tramini 425
Trangosi, Yves 52
Trapaud, Ch. 91
Trapet, Dom. Louis 143
Trapet, Jean 143
Trappenberg 276, 278
Trás-os-Montes 397
Trasimeno, Cantina Sociale del 346
Travaglini 306
Travignoli 343
Tre Castelli 306
Tre Monti 331
Trebbiano 220, 492
Trebbiano d'Abruzzo 352
Trebbiano di Romagna 329
Trebbiano Val Trebbia 329
Trefethen Vineyards 475, 477
Treille, Dom. de la 127
Trelano 314
Tremblay, Gérard 114
Trenel Fils 154
Trentadue Winery & Vineyards 476
Trentino 313-17
Très Cañas 393
Très Cantous, Dom. des 226
Tresserre 211
Treuil de Nailhac, Ch. 222
Trevallon, Dom. de 207
Triacca, Fratelli 312
Trier 243
Trignon, Ch. du 200
Trimbach, F.E. 192
Trimoulet, Ch. 89, 91
Trinchero, Renato 306
Trinquevedel, Ch. de 200
Trintegnant, Dom. Jean 205
Trione, Harry 459
Trittenheim 245
Trocken 242
Trockenbeerenauslese (TBA) 236-7, 242, 421

Troesmes 112
Les Trois Couronnes 203
Les Trois Domaines 436
Troitzsch, Weingut 264
Tronconero 312
Tronquoy-Lalande, Ch. 67
Troplong-Mondot, Ch. 89
Trotanoy, Ch. 96
Trotignan, Jean-Paul 172
Trottevieille, Ch. 86
Tsantali, E. 433
Tualatin Vineyard 479
Tudal Winery 476
Tudernum, Cantina Sociale 346
Les Tuileries, Ch. 100
Tuke, Holdsworth 404
Tulare 443
Tulbagh 514
Tulloch 505
Tulocay Winery 476
Tuniberg Bereich 288
Tunisie, Union des Cooperatives Viticles de 435
Le Tuquet, Ch. 77
Turckheim Coop. 192
Turmeliere, Ch. de la 162
Turmhoff, Schloss 315
Turpenay, Dom. de 170
La Turque Côte Brune 196
Tursan 227
Tuscany 331-44
Tustal, Ch. de 102
Twee Jongegezellens 518
Tyland Vineyards 476
Tyrrells 505

U
Uberti 312
Uchaux 197
Udinese, Vinicola 327
Ugni Blanc 220, 430, 522
Ugo, Fattoria dell' 343
Uhlheim, Schlosskellerei 422
Uiterwyk 518
Uitkyk 518-19
Ukiah Valley 443
Umbria 344-6
Umpqua Valley 482
Umstadt 279
Undhof, Weingut, Fritz Saloman 422
Undurraga 521-2
Unger Moorhof, Alexander 423
UNIDOR (Union des Coopératives Vinicole de la Dordogne) 223
Union Agraria Coopérativa 383
Union Champagne 185
Union des Producteurs Plaimont, Caves Coopératives 227
Union of Ioannina Cooperatives 433
Union Vinicole Coopérative (Gaillac) 226
Union Wine 519
Unterbadischer Landwein 288
Upper Loire 172-5
Urfé 234
Utiel-Requena 368, 385
Utrero 379
Uva de Aguascalientes, Productos de 523
Uzège 231
Uzzano, Castello di 340

V
Vaccarèse 201
Vacheron, Dom. 174
Vacqueyras 197, 199
Vaeni 433
Vaille 217
Vaillons 112-3
Vaisinerie, Ch. 92

Val d'Agly 233
Val d'Arbia 334
Val de Cesse 233
Val di Cornia 334
Val de Dagne 233
Val di Maggio-Arnaldo Caprai 345
Val de Montferrand 232
Val di Nevola, Cantina Sociale 348-9
Val d'Or, Ch. 91
Val d'Orbieu 233
Val des Rois, Dom. du 198
Val di Sugga 340
Valais 409-13
Valat, André 200
Valbiferno, Cantina Cooperativa 354
Valcalepio 310
Valdadige 314
Valdeorras 368, 371
Valdepeñas 368, 384-5
Valdespino 394
Valdo 320, 323
Valdobbiadene 319
Valdobbiadene, Cantina Sociale di 323
Valea Călugărească 429
Valençay 161
Valencia 368, 385
Valenti, Luigi 312
Valentin 185
Valentini, Edoardo 353
Valette 154
Valfieri 302
Valgella 310
Valière, M. J.-C. 225
Vallana, Antonio & Figlio 306
Vallania 330
Vallarom 317
Valle 327
Valle d'Aosta 306
Valle Isarco 314
Valle d'Isarco, Cantina Sociale 317
Vallée de la Loire, Compagnie de la 168
Vallée du Paradis 233
Vallée du Rhône, Société des Vins Fins de la 204
Vallejo, Hijos de Francisco 387
Valley of the Moon 476
Valley View Vineyards 481
Vallone, Africole 358
Vallonières, Ch. des 204
Valmur 112
Les Valozières 119
Valpolicella 320
Valréas 198-9
Valrone, Ch. 100
Valsangiacomo fu Vittore, Fratelli 417
Valtellina 308, 310
Valtellina Superiore 310
Valtellinese, Enologica 312
Van Loveren 519
Vandelle Père & Fils 156
Vannier, André 114
Vannières, Ch. 207
Varela 394
Varenne, Ch. de la 165
Vargellas 406
Varichon & Clerc 157-8
Varietals 443
Varna 430
Varoilles, Dom. des 143
Los Vascos Ltda., Viña 522
Vaselli, Conti 346
Vasse Felix 505
Vatan, André 174
Vau de Vey 112
Vau Ligneau 112
Vaucelles, Comte Henri de 81
Vaucluse 199
Vaucoupin 112
Vaud 409, 411-12, 414

Vaudésir 112
Vaudieu, Ch. de 205
Vaudon, Pierre 185
Vaugelas, Ch. de 213
Vaulorent 112-13
Vaunage 231
Vaupulent 112
Vauroux, Dom. de 114
Vayron, Charles and Xavier 94
Vazart, Lucien 185
Vazzoler, Redi 327
Vecchie Terre di Montefili 340
Vecchio 299
Vecchio Samperi-De Bartoli 364
Vedrenne, Maison René 91
Vega Sicilia 371-2
Vega Vineyards Winery 476
Veiga França 408
Veldenz 245
Le Velette, Tenuta 346
Velhas, Caves 399
Velhas, Caves, Companhia Portuguesa de Vinhos de Marca 399
Velké Pavlovice 427
Velletri 351
Vendage Tardive 187
Vendemmia 299
Vendetti, Pasquale 355
Venegazzù della Casa 320
Venegazzù-Conte Loredan-Gasparini 321
Veneri, Ruggero 346
Veneto 318-23
Venica 327
De Venoge 185
Ventana Vineyards Winery 476
Vente des Vins Fins, Cave Coopérative de 158
Ventoux 203
Ventura 443
Venturini, Massimo 323
Venturini & Baldini 331
Verano 394
Verband Deutscher Prädikats- und Qualitätsweingüter (VdP) 242
Verband Neiderösterreichischen Gebietswinzergenos-senschaften 422
Verband Ostschweizer Landwirtschaftliche Genossenschaften (VOLG) 416
Vercelli, Andrea 308
Vercesi, Pietro 312
Vercots, Les 119
Verda, Antoine 200
Verdea 432
Verdelet 486
Verdelho 407-8, 492
Verdicchio, Cantina Cooperativa tra Produttori del 349
Verdicchio dei Castelli di Jesi 347
Verdicchio di Matelica 347
Verdier, Henri 168
Verdignan, Ch. 70
Verduno, Castello di 306
Verduzzo 324
Vereinigte Winzergenossenschaft Hallgarten Rhg. eG 261
Vereinigten Hospitien, Guterverwaltung der 252
Les Vergennes 119
Vergenoegd 519
Verger, Jean 151
Verger, Robert 151
Verhaegue, Charles 225
Veritas Vineyard 481
Vermentino 220, 308
Vermentino, Cantino Sociale del 367

Vermentino di Gallura 367
Vermentino di Sardegna 367
Vermont 486
Vernaccia, Cantina Sociale della 367
Vernaccia di Oristano 367
Vernaccia di San Gimignano 334
Vernaccia di Serrapetrona 347
Vernaux, Noëmie 140
Vernay, Georges 196
Vernous, Ch. 72
Vernus, André 151
Verona 318
Verquière, Dom. de 200
Verrazzano, Castello di 344
Vertzani 432
Verzé 148
Vesuvio 354
Vetrice, Villa 344
Veuve Ambal 133
Veuve Amiot, Maison 168
Veuve Clicquot-Ponsardin 184
Veuve Joubert, Mme. 152
Vevey, Alberto 306
Vi Novell 380
VI.TA-Viticoltori del Tappino 354
Viaillère 195
Viale, Pippo 308
La Viarte 327
Vic-Bilh-Madiran 227
Vicchiomaggio 340
Vicente, Suso y Pérez 373
Vichon Winery 476
Victoria 490-91
Vidal, Bernard 217
Vidal, Dominique 222
Vidal Blanc 486
Vidal-Fleury, J. 196
Vidal-Gaillard 217
Vidal Wine Producers 512
La Vidaubannaise 208
Videau, Ch. 101
Vidigueira 398
Vieil-Armand Coop. 192
Vieille Eglise, Dom. de la 152
La Vieille Ferme 200
La Vieille France, Ch. 77
Vieilles Vignes 143
Vienna 417
Vienot, Dom. Charles 143
Vietti 303
Vieux-Château Beaujus 72
Vieux Château Certan 96
Vieux-Château Chauvin 91
Vieux-Château Landon 72
Vieux-Château-St-André (Corbin) 92
Vieux Chênes, Ch. des 92
Vieux Rivalion, Ch. 91
Vieux Robin, Ch. 72
Vieux Sarpe, Ch. 91
Vieux Télégraphe, Dom. du 204
Le Vieux Moulin 52
Vigna al Monte 358
Vigna Niccolò da Uzzano 340
Vignals, Dom. des 224
Vignamaggio 340
Les Vignards 190
Vignau, August 227
Vignavecchia 344
Vigne dal Léon 327
La Vigne Blanche 148
Vignelaure, Ch. 206-7
Le Vigneron Savoyard Cave Coopérative 157
La Vigneronne 216
Vignerons de Buxy, Caves des 146
Les Vignerons de Cucugnan 213
Les Vignerons Provençaux 208
Vigneti Carlo Micara 352
Vigneti Le Monde 326

Vignole 344
Vignoles 486
Vigouroux, Georges 225
Vilányi 425
Vilariño-Cambados, Bodegas 373
VILE (Planta de Elaboracion y Embotellado de Vinos SA) 371-2
Villa Maria 512
Villa Mt. Eden 476-7
Villagrande, Barone di 365
Villaine, A. and P. de 146
Villaine, M. Aubert de 120-1
Villalier 216
Villamagna 348
Villamont, Henri de 143
Villanova, Tenuta 327
Villard, Mme. 54
Villard Blanc 486
Villard Noir 486
Villare 432
Villars, Ch. 99
Villars, Mme. B. 57, 61
Villeclare, Ch. de 211
Villegeorge, Ch. 70
Villemajou, Dom. de 213
Villemaurine, Ch. 89
Villenave-d'Ornon 73
Villeneuve 412
Villeneuve, Dom. de 217
Villette 412
Villiera 519
Vin de Bugey 157
Vin de Bugey Blanc 157
Vin de Corse 220
Vin doux naturel 11, 210
Vin Jaune 154-5
Vin de paille 154-5
Vin Santo 299, 319
Vin d'une nuit 197
Vin-Union Genève 415
Viña Lanciano 378
Viñas Tesos 378
Vinattieri 344
Vincent, Ch. 99
Vine Classé 268
Vinet, André, SA 165
Vinho maduro 395, 397
Vinho verde 368, 395-7
Vinhos de Moncao 400
Vinhos Messias, SARL 404
Vini Tipici 293
Vini Velletri, Consorzio Produttori 352
La Vinicola Iberica 383
Vinifera Wine Cellars 485
Vinification d'Aigne, Caves Coopératives 216
Vinimar 349
Vinmoselles S.C. 268
Vino cotto 299
Vino da arrosto 299
Vino da pasto 299
Vino da taglio 299
Vino da tavola 299, 316
Vino de color 390
Vino de pasto 390
Vino Nobile di Montepulciano 294, 335
Vino novello 299
Vino Santo (Greece) 432
Vinos Blancos 374-5
Vinos Blancos de Castilla 373
Vinos generosos 368
Vinos Rosados 375
Vinos tintos 375
Vinòt 299, 301
Les Vins Breban 208
Vins de Pays 230-4
Vins Rosés, Cave Coop. des Grands 143
Vins de Thouarsais 166
Vinsobres 199
Vinto Santo 335
Vinval 385-6
Vinzel 412
Vinzelles Coop. 148

Viognier 193-4
La Violette, Ch. 96
Vipava 428
Viré, Cave de 133
Viré Coop. 148
Virgen de la Viñas Coop. 386
Virgin Hills 506
Virginia 487
Virginia Dare 483
Virginia Seedling 486
Virieu-Le-Grand 157
Virou, Ch. 100
Visan 199, 386
Visconti 311
Vistarenni 344
Viticcio 344
Viticulteur 74
Vitivinicola, Cantina Cooperativa 346
Vitteau Alberti 133
Vivaldi 317
Voarick, Dom. Michel 143
Vocoret, Robert 114
Voerzio, Gianni 306
Voerzio, Roberto 303
Voge, Alain 196
Vogelsgärtchen 270
Vogtei Rötteln 287
Vogüé, Dom. Comte Georges de 143
Vojvodina 427
Völker, Berhard 283
Volla 355
Vollrads, Schloss 256
Volnay 122-3
Volpaia, Castello di 340
Volpi, Cantine 306
Volxem, Bernd van 252
Vosgros 112
Vosne-Romanée 116, 118
Vougeot 116
Voulte Gasparet, Ch. la 213
Vouvray 161, 163, 169
Vouvray Pétillant 170
Vouvray Pétillant Mousseux 161
Voyat, Ezio 306
Vrai Canon Bouché, Ch. 99
Vrancea 429
Vray-Canon-Boyer, Ch. 99
Vray-Croix-de-Gay, Ch. 96
Vriesenhof 519
Vrillon, Jean 172
Vugava 429
Vuillier, Albert 79
Vulture, Consorzio Vitacoltori Assciati del 361
Vulture, Società Cooperativa Vinicola del 361

W
Wachau 418
Wachau, Winzergenossenschaft 423
Wagner Vineyards 485
Wagner-Weritz, Weingut 264
Waikato 509
Wairarapa 509
Walch, W. 317
Waldrach 243
Walker Bay 514
Walker Valley Vineyards 485
Walker Wines 476
Walla Walla Valley 482
Walluf 255
Wantirna Estate 506
Waris, Jean 185
Warner 487
Warre & Co. 406
Warwick (South Africa) 519
Washington 478, 481-2
Watervale Cellars 506

Wawern 243
Webb, R.W., Winery 488
Wegeler-Deinhard 252, 278
Wegeler-Deinhard, Gutsverwaltung 261
Wehlen 246
Wehrheim, Eugen 273
Weibel Champagne Vineyards 476
Weil, Robert 261
Weiler, Heinrich 254
Weinbach, Dom. 190
Weinert 523
Weins-Prüm, Dr. F. 253
Weinzergenossenschaft Rheingräfenberg eG 269
Weisbaden 255
Weissherbst 242
Welgemeend 519
Wellow Vineyard 526
Weltevrede 519
Wendouree 506
Wente Bros. 476
Werner, Domdechant 261
Westbury Vineyard 526
Westfield 506
Westhalten et Environs Coop. 192
De Wetshof 519
Weydert, M 95
Wheeler, William, Winery 476
Whitbread/ Bollinger/ Antinori see Atlas Peak
White Mountain 486
White Oak Vineyards 476
Whitehall Lane Winery 476

Whitlam, Simon 506
Wibelsberg 189
Wickham Vineyard 526
Widmer's Wine Cellars, Inc. 485
Wiese & Krohn 400
Wiese & Krohn Sucrs. 406
Wild Geese 394
Wild Home Winery 476
Wild Horse Valley 443
Wilde, Mme. Françoise de 89
Willamette Valley 482
Williams & Humbert 393
Willow Creek 443
Wiltingen 243
Winery Lake 443
Winkel 256-7
Winters Winery 477
Wintrich 245
Winzenheim 265
Winzergenossenschaft Gumpoldskirchen Coop. 423
Wirra Wirra 506
Wirsching, Hans 282
Wisdom & Warter Ltd. 394
Wisdom sherry 394
Wolf, J.L., Erben 279
Wolfberger 192
Wolff-Metternich, Gräflich 291
Wolfsmagen Grosslagen 279
Wolkersdorf, Winzergenossenschaft 423

Wonnegau 269-70
Woodbury Vineyards 485
Woodbury Winery 477
Woodley Wines 506
Woodside Vineyards 477
Woodstock 506
Wootton Vineyard 526
Worcester (South Africa) 514
Worms 270
Wrights 506
Wrotham Pinot 524
Wunnenstein 284
Würtembergisch Unterland 284
Württemberg 239, 281-2, 283-6
Würzburg 281
Würzburger Stein 280
Wyckoff 481
Wyndham Estate 506
Wynn, David 501
Wynns 506

X
Xanadu, Ch. 496
Xhellah 436
Xynisteri 433

Y
Y (Ygrec) 78
Yakima Valley 482
Yakut 434
Yalumba 506-7
Yamhill Valley 479
Yarden Winery 435
Yarra Burn 507
Yarra Valley 491
Yarra Yering 507

Yeasts 36
Yecla 368, 385
Yellowglen 507
Yerasa 434
Yeringberg 507
Yolo 443
Yon-Figeac, Ch. 89
York Mountain 443
York Mountain Winery 477
Yountville 443
Yquem, Ch. d' 78, 80-1
Yuntero 386
Yvon Mau 52
Yvorne 412

Z
Zaca Mesa Winery 477
Zaccagnani, Ciccio 353
Zaccagnini, Fratelli 349
Zaer 436
Zagarolo 351
Zakinthos 432
Zandotti-Tenimento San Paolo, Conte 351
Zandvliet 519
Zanella, Maurizio 310
Zaragoza 371
Zardetto 323
ZD Wines 477
Zecca, Conti 359
Zédé, Dom. 56
Zelicourt, Général Jacques de 152
Zell 247
Zeller Schwarze Katz 242
Zellerbach, James D. 460
Zeltingen 246

Zemmour 436
Zenato 323
Zeni, Roberto 315
Zennata 436
Zentrale Badischer Winzerkeller (ZBW) 286
Zentralkellerei Rhein. Winzer. eG 274
Zerbina, Fattoria 330
Zerioli 331
Zerkhoun 436
Zevenwacht 519
Zichron-Jacob 435
Ziltener, André Père & Fils 143
Zimmerman, R. 422
Zimmermann-Graef G. bH & Co. 239
Zind-Humbrecht, Dom. 192
Zinfandel 445, 492
Zitsa 433
Znojmo 427
Don Zoilo 391
Zonin 321, 487
Zoopiyi 434
Zotzenberg 189
Zuc di Volpe 325
Zufferey, Maurice 413
Zuger, Jean-Claude 55
Zuger, Robert 54
Zuleta 393
Zuleta, Delgado 394
Župa 427
Župsko Crno 427
Zurich 415
Zweigelt 425
Zwierlein, Freiherr von 264

ACKNOWLEDGMENTS

Listed below are the names of the many people whose assistance has been invaluable in writing this book, whether their contribution was written, spoken or in their printed work, and to whom I offer my special thanks. First among these I count my tireless colleagues at Mitchell Beazley.

John Adams, Miranda Alexander, Richard Allen, Roddy Alvarado, Dr. Hans Ambrosi, Burton Anderson, Colin Anderson M.W., Marquis d'Angerville, Marchese Dot. Piero Antinori, Gerald Asher, Rafael Balào, David Balls, the late Martin Bamford M.W., Jean Barbet, Mr & Mrs Graham Barrett, Antony Barton, Lillian Barton, the late Professor Dr. Becker, Diana Beevers, Christine Behey Molines, Katie Benjce, Professor Harold Berg, Jean-Claude Berrouet, Alexis Bespaloff, the late Tim Bleach, Jean-Eugène Borie, Professor Roger Boulton, Gerald D. Boyd, Gordon Brown, Ross Brown, Brigitte Brugnon, Donn Chappelet, Tim Clarke, Michael Cliffe M.W., Bruce Coleman, Deeta Colvin, Professor James E. Cook, David Cossart, Alain de Courseulles, Henry Damant, Jean Demolombe, Professor A. Dinsmoor Webb, Beltran Domecq, Sarah Drake, Georges Duboeuf, Jean-Henri Dubernet, Hubrecht Duijker, Terry Dunleavy, Diana Durant, Evelyn Ellis, The English Vineyards Association, Jorge Erasodis, Len Evans, Charles Eve M.W., Pat Eve, Food and Wine from France, Derrick Foster, Geoffrey Francom, Fromm and Sichell Inc., Diane Furness, Janet Furze, André Gagey, Rosemary George M.W., the late Anthony Goldthorpe, Claudie Gomme, Richard Goodman, Dick Graff, Marie Christine Machard de Grammont, James Halliday, Robert Hardy, Peter Hasslacher, John Hawes, Serge Hochar, Denis Horgan, Russel Hone, the late Dr, G. Horney,

Stephanie Horner, Jean Hugel, V. Ishpekov, Gérard Jaboulet, Fiona Jamieson, Ian Jamieson M.W., Alan Johnson-Hill, Andrew Jones, A.N. Kasimatis, Tawfiq Khoury, Mark Kliewer, Graham Knox, Matt Kramer, Professor Ralph E. Kunkee, Anthony Lacey, Tony Laithwaite, Daniel Lawson, Scott Levy, John Lipitch, Nina Lobanov, Catherine Manac'h, Tim Marshall, Sarah Matthews, Pierre Maufoux, Richard Mayson, Malcolm McIntyre, Jean Miailhe, Dr. Franz Werner Michel, Dr. Eric Minaric, Janel Minore, Robert Mondavi, Christian Moueix, Alain Mozés, Mario B. Neves, Professor Ann Noble, Barbara Onderka, Richard O'Quinn, John Parkinson, David Peppercorn M.W., Mr J. Petridus, Professor Emile Peynaud, Andrew Pirie, the late Dr. Desiderius Pongracz, Michel Pons, Pierre Poupon, Bruno Prats, Q.E.D. Publishing, Jean Quénard, Alain and Sheila Querre, David Rayment, Jan and Maite Read, Mrs. Belle Rhodes, Dr. Bernard Rhodes, M. Jean Riére, Bertrand de Rivoyre, Geoffrey Roberts, Michael Rothwell, Eric de Rothschild, André Roux, Hamilton Russell, David Rutherford, Henry Ryman, Brian St. Pierre, Jean-Pierre Saboye, Raymond le Sauvage, Mark Savage, Walter Schug, Debbie Scott, Peter Sichel, Joanna Simon, Professor Vernon L. Singleton, Cornelia Smith-Bauer, Kerry Brady Stewart, Sue Style, Serena Sutcliffe M.W., Michael Symington, Michel Tesseron, David Thomas, M. Thomas, Bob and Harolyn Thompson, Helen Thompson, Miguel and Marimar Torres, Dip. Ing. Traxler, John and Janel Trefethen, Ugurlu Tunali, Michael Vaughan, Michel Villedey, Peter Vinding-Diers, Richard Vine, Jeremy Watson, Tony Willis, Grant Willoughby, James Earl Wilson, Wines from Spain, Robin Yapp.
Illustrators: Russell Barnett, Lindsay Blow, Bob Chapman, Edwina Keene, Aziz Khan, James Robins, John Woodcock.